Fodor's 2011 FLORIDA

D0832095

Fodor's Travel Publications New York, Toronto, London, Sydney, Auckland
www.fodors.com

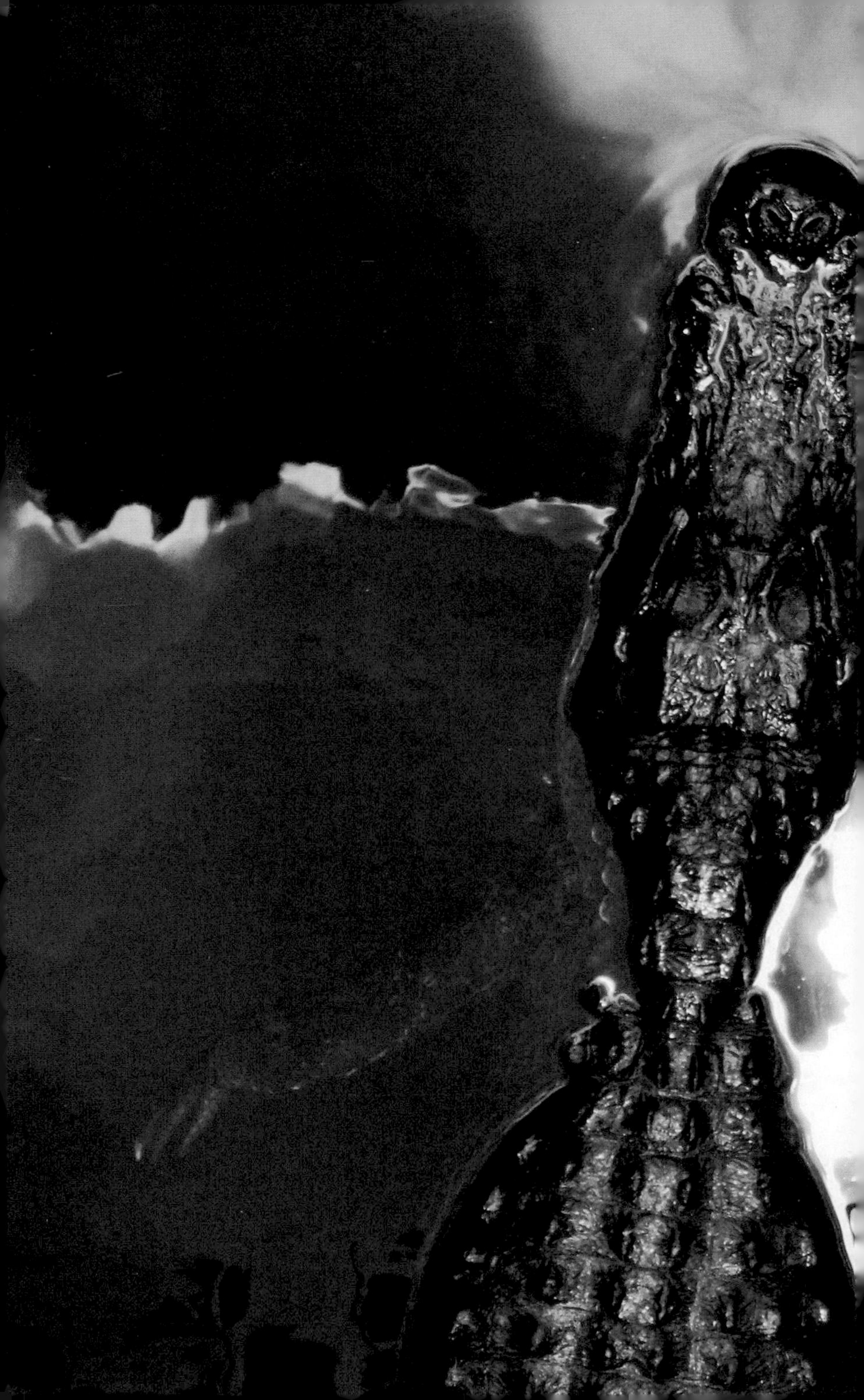

Be a Fodor's Correspondent

Share your trip with Fodor's.

Our latest guidebook to Florida—now in full color—owes its success to travelers like you. Throughout, you'll find photographs submitted by members of Fodors.com to our "Show Us Your... Florida" photo contest. We gratefully acknowledge the contest's sponsor, Visit Florida, whose support made the inclusion of these photos possible. Facing this page is a photograph of an alligator taken by Tim Souter from the boardwalk of the Anhinga Trail in Everglades National Park. On page 365 you'll find our grand prize–winning photograph, taken by Elizabeth Shevloff of her granddaughter, who thought that the sand was so white at Longboat Key that she mistook it for snow and went to work making angels. We've also included "Word of Mouth" quotes from travelers who shared their experiences with others on our forums.

We are especially proud of this color edition. No other guide to Florida is as up to date or has as much practical planning information, along with hundreds of color photographs and illustrated maps. If you're inspired and can plan a better trip because of this guide, we've done our job.

We invite you to join the travel conversation: Your opinion matters to us and to your fellow travelers. Come to Fodors.com to plan your trip, share an experience, ask a question, submit a photograph, post a review, or write a trip report. Tell our editors about your trip. They want to know what went well and how we can make this guide even better. Share your opinions at our feedback center at fodors.com/feedback, or email us at editors@fodors.com with the subject line "Florida Editor." You might find your comments published in a future Fodor's guide. We look forward to hearing from you.

Happy Traveling!

Tim Jarrell, Publisher

FODOR'S FLORIDA 2011

Editor: Debbie Harmsen, *lead project editor*; Salwa Jabado, Jess Moss

Editorial Contributors: Carolyn Galgano (Orlando hotel and restaurant editor), Laura Kidder (Orlando parks and sights editor), Jacinta O'Halloran
Writers: Elise Allen, Nathan Benjamin, Sam Benjamin, John Blodgett, Michael de Zayas, Jennifer Edwards, Teri Evans, Rona Gindin, Jennifer Greenhill-Taylor, Joseph Reed Hayes, Lynne Helm, Jennie Hess, Susan MacCallum-Whitcomb, Gary McKechnie, Dorianne Perrucci, Mary Thurwachter, Christina Tourigny, Chelle Koster Walton

Production Editor: Carrie Parker
Maps & Illustrations: David Lindroth; Mark Stroud, *cartographers;* Bob Blake, Rebecca Baer, *map editors;* William Wu, *information graphics*
Design: Fabrizio La Rocca, *creative director*; Guido Caroti, Siobhan O'Hare, *art directors*; Tina Malaney, Nora Rosansky, Chie Ushio, Jessica Walsh, Ann McBride, *designers*; Melanie Marin, *senior picture editor*
Cover Photo: (pink flamingos, Everglades) aceshot1/Shutterstock
Production Manager: Amanda Bullock

COPYRIGHT

Copyright © 2011 by Fodor's Travel, a division of Random House, Inc.

Fodor's is a registered trademark of Random House, Inc.

All rights reserved. Published in the United States by Fodor's Travel, a division of Random House, Inc., and simultaneously in Canada by Random House of Canada, Limited, Toronto. Distributed by Random House, Inc., New York.

No maps, illustrations, or other portions of this book may be reproduced in any form without written permission from the publisher.

ISBN 978-1-4000-0460-7

ISSN 0193-9556

SPECIAL SALES

This book is available at special discounts for bulk purchases for sales promotions or premiums. Special editions, including personalized covers, excerpts of existing books, and corporate imprints, can be created in large quantities for special needs. For more information, write to Special Markets/Premium Sales, 1745 Broadway, MD 6-2, New York, New York 10019, or e-mail specialmarkets@randomhouse.com.

AN IMPORTANT TIP & AN INVITATION

Although all prices, opening times, and other details in this book are based on information supplied to us at press time, changes occur all the time in the travel world, and Fodor's cannot accept responsibility for facts that become outdated or for inadvertent errors or omissions. So **always confirm information when it matters,** especially if you're making a detour to visit a specific place. Your experiences—positive and negative—matter to us. If we have missed or misstated something, **please write to us.** We follow up on all suggestions. Contact the Florida editor at editors@fodors.com or c/o Fodor's at 1745 Broadway, New York, NY 10019.

PRINTED IN CHINA

10 9 8 7 6 5 4 3 2 1

CONTENTS

Fodor's Features

MAPS

ABOUT THIS BOOK

Our Ratings

Sometimes you find terrific travel experiences and sometimes they just find you. But usually the burden is on you to select the right combination of experiences. That's where our ratings come in.

As travelers we've all discovered a place so wonderful that its worthiness is obvious. And sometimes that place is so experiential that superlatives don't do it justice: you just have to be there to know. These sights, properties, and experiences get our highest rating, **Fodor's Choice,** indicated by orange stars throughout this book.

Black stars highlight sights and properties we deem **Highly Recommended,** places that our writers, editors, and readers praise again and again for consistency and excellence.

By default, there's another category: Any place we include in this book is by definition worth your time, unless we say otherwise. And we will.

Disagree with any of our choices? Care to nominate a place or suggest that we rate one more highly? Visit our feedback center at www.fodors.com/feedback.

Budget Well

Hotel and restaurant price categories from ¢ to $$$$ are defined in the opening pages of each chapter. For attractions, we always give standard adult admission fees; reductions are usually available for children, students, and senior citizens. Want to pay with plastic? **AE, D, DC, MC, V** following restaurant and hotel listings indicate whether American Express, Discover, Diners Club, MasterCard, and Visa are accepted.

Restaurants

Unless we state otherwise, restaurants are open for lunch and dinner daily. We mention dress only when there's a specific requirement and reservations only when they're essential or not accepted—it's always best to book ahead.

Hotels

Hotels have private bath, phone, TV, and air-conditioning and operate on the European Plan (aka EP, meaning without meals), unless we specify that they use the Continental Plan (CP, with a continental breakfast), Breakfast Plan (BP, with a full breakfast), or Modified American Plan (MAP, with breakfast and dinner), or are all-inclusive (including all meals and most activities). We always list facilities but not whether you'll be charged an extra fee to use them, so always ask.

Listings

- ★ Fodor's Choice
- ★ Highly recommended
- ✉ Physical address
- ✣ Directions or Map coordinates
- 📫 Mailing address
- ☎ Telephone
- 📠 Fax
- 🌐 On the Web
- ✉ E-mail
- 🎟 Admission fee
- ⏲ Open/closed times
- Ⓜ Metro stations
- 💳 Credit cards

Hotels & Restaurants

- 🏨 Hotel
- 🛏 Number of rooms
- 👍 Facilities
- 🍽 Meal plans
- ✕ Restaurant
- ✍ Reservations
- 👔 Dress code
- 🚬 Smoking
- 🍷 BYOB

Outdoors

- ⛳ Golf
- ⛺ Camping

Other

- 👶 Family-friendly
- ⇨ See also
- ✉ Branch address
- ☞ Take note

1

Experience Florida

WHAT'S NEW

Each year more than 84 million visitors, representing all age groups and interests, flock to Florida. Its sun, sand, and sea are obvious draws, yet these account for only part of the narrow state's broad appeal. Theme-park enthusiasts come for first-class rides and attractions, while nature lovers find the outdoor options (ranging from snorkeling and fishing to boating and bird-watching) irresistible. Moreover, spring breakers, seniors, and sophisticated sybarites alike are lured by a diverse arts-and-entertainment scene. With such activities in play, the entire state exudes a vacationland vibe that keeps people coming back. For those returning, there's always something new under the sun.

World of Magic

In spring 2010, the ribbon was cut at the eagerly anticipated "Wizarding World of Harry Potter," a magical 20-acre attraction inside Universal's Islands of Adventure that is inspired by J. K. Rowling's best-selling books and films. Along with the requisite themed rides (including an intense twin Dragon Challenge coaster and more family-friendly Flight of the Hippogriff), the Wizarding World has been designed to conjure up charming locales, such as Hogwarts Castle, which are usually off-limits to mere Muggles. The shops and restaurants of Hogsmeade are being meticulously replicated, too, creating ample opportunities for bewitching merchandising. If you have ever wanted to sip Butterbeer or stock up on Quidditch equipment, here's your chance.

New Heights

Plans for the Great Orlando Wheel (the supersized Ferris wheel that was hyped as being Orlando's answer to the London Eye) are on hold. Nevertheless, the area does offer several other new alternatives for anyone who wants to get high. Downtown Disney has added a tethered balloon that allows 30 guests at a time to soar 400 feet in the air for a bird's-eye view of Walt Disney World; and Florida Eco-Safaris at Forever Florida has introduced a two-hour tree-top zipline experience. Want more? The Central Florida Zoo & Botanical Gardens is now site of the ZOOm Air Adventures Park. It's an arboreal obstacle course of sorts that consists of ziplines, suspended bridges, rope swings, and other gizmos ideal for Tarzan wannabes.

Rays on Display

In the summer of 2009, SeaWorld opened Manta, a marine exhibit–roller coaster that gives riders a headfirst, facedown glimpse at hundreds of real rays; then sends them swooping high above their habitat at over 55 MPH. Nonriders, meanwhile, can gape at shark rays, leopard rays, and more through Manta's floor-to-ceiling window. If you want to touch one, the Florida Aquarium in Tampa has a new tour that involves hand-feeding stingrays. Eager to get close to a different kind of ray? Head for the Charlotte Sports Park in Port Charlotte. Major League Baseball's Tampa Bay Rays moved spring training to this newly renovated stadium, and with an eighth the number of seats of its home field, fans can get closer to the action.

Must-See Museums

Tampa's Riverwalk premiered the History Center in early 2009 and the Tampa Museum of Art (home to five gleaming galleries and a sculpture garden) in early 2010. Just so kiddies don't feel neglected, the Glazer Children's Museum promises 175 interactive exhibits designed specifically for them when it's finished late in 2010. Down in Naples yet another new children's museum, C'MON, at this

writing was set to begin welcoming guests in fall 2010. While waiting for these to open, families can always visit two innovative spots that debuted in late 2008: the Charles and Linda Williams Children's Museum at Daytona Beach's Museum of Arts and Sciences, and the Kenan-Flagler Family Discovery Gallery at the Frost Art Museum in Miami.

Wreck Diving

Little wonder the Keys are a prime destination for divers: their aquarium clear waters are brimming with sea life. But coral and colorful fish are just the beginning. In the summer of 2009, the USNS *Vandenberg*, a 523-foot decommissioned Navy warship was intentionally sunk to create the world's second-largest artificial reef. She wasn't the first big ship to be scuttled in the Keys (the USS *Spiegel Grove* went down in 2002), and scores more were wrecked here over the centuries (including a Spanish galleon sunk off Islamorada in 1733). Nine such vessels now make up the Florida Keys National Marine Sanctuary's Shipwreck Trail. For diveworthy sites elsewhere in the state, click on "Underwater Archeology" at 🌐 *www.flheritage.com*.

The Suite Life

Believing the good times would last forever, Florida's upper-end hoteliers optimistically embarked on a mega building and renovation spree a few years back. Some pictured minimalist decor, others opulence galore. What none could foresee, unfortunately, was the looming recession. Since late 2008, Miami alone has seen iconic hotels (like the Eden Roc and Fontainebleau) get extreme makeovers, and new lodgings (including the Viceroy and Epic) make their debut. Needless to say, demand for luxury digs has taken a nosedive during the same period. The upside is that managers, eager to fill empty beds, are offering dazzling deals. Along with reduced rates, look for room upgrades, restaurant credits, and other valuable in-house perks.

Airport Facelifts

Millions have been spent over the past couple of years improving airports from Orlando to Okaloosa, Tampa to Tallahassee. For instance, the airport in Jacksonville (Florida's largest city) recently got a new concourse; and in Miami work is underway on a ground-transportation hub that will make going MIA at the MIA much less likely. But the biggest news is the spring 2010 opening of a $330-million airport in Panama City, the first built anywhere in the United States since 9/11. Because it sits on a 1,400-acre site, the Northwest Florida Beaches International Airport will be able to handle larger planes than the one it replaces. That translates into more traffic—which means more convenient flight schedules and more competitive airfares.

WHAT'S WHERE

Universal Orlando's Dueling Dragons Coaster.

The following numbers refer to chapters.

2 Panhandle. Southern gentility and redneck rambunctiousness make the Panhandle a colorful place—but it's the green Gulf waters and sugar-white sand that keep devotees coming back for more.

3 Northeast Florida. Though time rewinds in historic St. Augustine, it's on fast-forward in Daytona Beach and the Space Coast, where horse-drawn carriages are replaced by race cars and rocket ships.

4 Orlando and Environs. It's theme parks that draw most visitors to the area, yet downtown Orlando, Kissimmee, and Winter Park have enough sites, shops, and restaurants to make them destinations in their own right.

5 Walt Disney World. The granddaddy of attractions, Disney is four theme parks in one—Magic Kingdom, Animal Kingdom, Epcot, and Hollywood Studios. Plus it has a pair of water parks and Downtown Disney (an entertainment zone featuring Cirque du Soleil).

6 Universal Orlando. The movies are brought to life at Universal Studios while Islands of Adventure delivers gravity-defying rides and special-effects surprises—not to mention the new Wizarding World of Harry Potter. Nearby Wet 'n Wild is full of watery adventures.

7 SeaWorld Orlando. Marine mammals perform in SeaWorld's meticulously choreographed shows, and thrill seekers find their adrenaline rush on coasters. Sister park Discovery Cove offers a day-long, swim-with-the-dolphins escape. At Aquatica water park, one slide even dips into a dolphin habitat.

8 Tampa Bay Area. Tampa's Busch Gardens and Ybor City are only part of the area's appeal. Culture vultures flock to St. Petersburg and Sarasota for concerts and museums; while eco-adventurers veer north to the Nature Coast.

9 Lower Gulf Coast. Blessed with beaches, this was the last bit of coast to be settled. But as Naples's manicured golf greens and Fort Myers's mansions-cum-museums prove, it is far from uncivilized.

10 Palm Beach and the Treasure Coast. This area scores points for diversity. Palm Beach and environs are famous for their golden sand and glitzy residents, whereas the Treasure Coast has unspoiled natural delights.

11 Fort Lauderdale and Broward County. The "Suds and Sun Capital of the Universe" has grown up. The beaches that first attracted college kids are now complemented by luxe lodgings and upscale entertainment options.

12 Miami and Miami Beach. Greater Miami is hot—and we're not just talking about the weather. Art-deco buildings and balmy beaches set the scene. Vacations here are as much about lifestyle as locale, so prepare for power shopping, club hopping, and decadent dining.

13 The Everglades. Covering more than 1.5 million acres, the fabled "River of Grass" is the state's greatest natural treasure. Biscayne National Park (95% of which is underwater) runs a close second. It's the largest marine park in the United States.

14 Florida Keys. This slender necklace of landfalls, strung together by a 110-mi highway, marks the southern edge of the continental United States. It's nirvana for anglers, divers, literature lovers, and Jimmy Buffett wannabes.

Lifeguard Tower, South Beach, Miami.

Everglades tour boat.

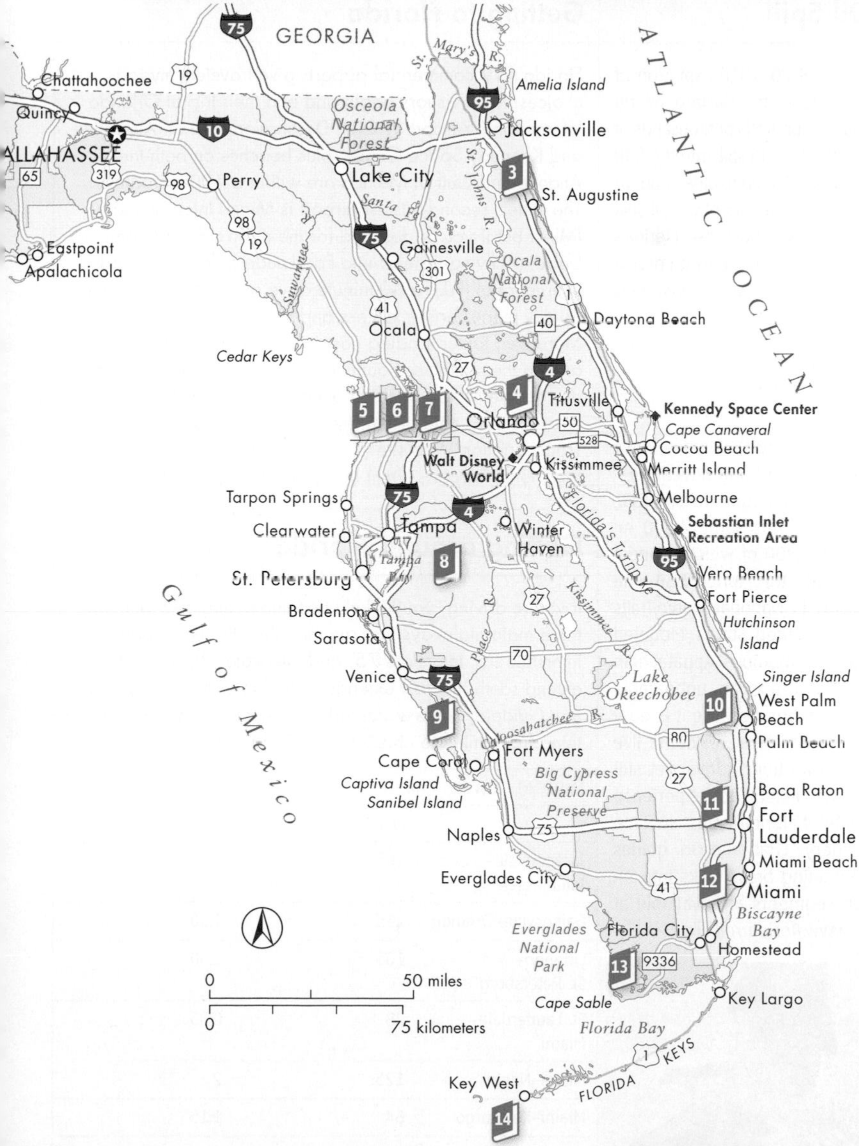

GEORGIA
ATLANTIC OCEAN
Gulf of Mexico
75
19
10
95
Chattahoochee
Quincy
ALLAHASSEE
65
319
98
Perry
Eastpoint
Apalachicola
Osceola National Forest
Amelia Island
Jacksonville
St. Mary's R.
St. Johns R.
Lake City
Santa Fe R.
3
St. Augustine
Gainesville
301
Ocala National Forest
1
Suwannee
41
Ocala
40
Daytona Beach
Cedar Keys
27
4
5
6
7
Titusville
Orlando
50
528
Kennedy Space Center
Cape Canaveral
Cocoa Beach
Merritt Island
Walt Disney World
Kissimmee
Melbourne
Tarpon Springs
Clearwater
Tampa
Tampa Bay
8
Winter Haven
Florida's Turnpike
Sebastian Inlet Recreation Area
St. Petersburg
Vero Beach
Fort Pierce
Kissimmee R.
Bradenton
Sarasota
Peace R.
Hutchinson Island
70
Venice
Lake Okeechobee
Singer Island
West Palm Beach
Palm Beach
9
10
80
Caloosahatchee R.
Fort Myers
Cape Coral
Captiva Island
Sanibel Island
Big Cypress National Preserve
Boca Raton
11
Fort Lauderdale
Naples
Miami Beach
Everglades City
12
Miami
Biscayne Bay
Everglades National Park
Florida City
Homestead
9336
13
0
50 miles
0
75 kilometers
Cape Sable
Key Largo
Florida Bay
FLORIDA KEYS
Key West
14

FLORIDA PLANNER

Oil Spill

The April 20, 2010 explosion of the Deepwater Horizon oil rig caused hundreds of thousands of gallons of oil to spill into the Gulf of Mexico. For up to date information on the impact of the oil spill on Florida's coast, see Florida's Department of Environmental Protection Web site: 🌐 *www.dep.state.fl.us/deepwaterhorizon.*

Trail Mix

For a change of pace, lose yourself—and find adventure—by hitting a nature trail. All told, the state has some 4,500 mi worth, 1,800 of which connect to create the Florida Trail, one of only 11 National Scenic Trails in the United States. Modeled on the ambitious Appalachian Trail, it offers an unbeatable combination because it is easy to access (most residents live within an hour's drive) yet still allows hikers to experience some of Florida's most sublime scenery. Grab-and-Go guides containing brass-tacks info on top segments are available at 🌐 *www.floridatrail.org.*

Getting to Florida

Florida's 19 commercial airports give travelers myriad choices. Most visitors begin and end their trip at Orlando International Airport (MCO). Destinations like St. Augustine and Kennedy Space Center, plus beaches on both the Atlantic and Gulf of Mexico are within a 100-mi radius. The state's second-busiest airport is Miami International (MIA). But if you're destined for the north side of Miami-Dade, try flying instead into Fort Lauderdale–Hollywood International (FLL), a 40-minute drive away. Its smaller size usually means easier access and shorter security lines. Moreover, lower landing costs attract budget carriers—among them jetBlue, Southwest, Spirit, and WestJet—that don't serve MIA. Checking out alternate airports elsewhere can also save time or money. The state's Department of Transportation Web site (🌐 *www.dot.state.fl.us/aviation/commercialairports.shtm*) has a handy airport map.

Getting around Florida

If you're driving, you'll likely become acquainted with the three main highways that run into, then through Florida: Interstate 95, Interstate 75, and Interstate 10. The first two extend south; the last extends west. The state's Transportation Guide at 🌐 *www.stateofflorida.com*, contains everything from mileage charts to details on turnpike tolls.

TYPICAL TRAVEL TIMES

	MILES	HOURS
Jacksonville–Tallahassee	165	2:50
Gainesville–Orlando	115	1:50
Orlando–St. Petersburg	105	1:50
Ft. Lauderdale–Miami	28	0:35
Miami–Naples	125	2
Miami–Key Largo	64	1:15
Key Largo–Key West	98	2

WHEN TO GO

Although Florida is a year-round vacation venue, it divides the calendar into regional tourism seasons. Holidays and school breaks are major factors. However, the clincher is weather, with the best months being designated as peak periods.

High season in southern Florida starts with the run-up to Christmas and continues through Easter. Snowbirds migrate down then to escape frosty weather back home, and festival-goers flock in because major events are held this time of year to avoid summer's searing heat and high humidity. Winter is also *the* time to visit the Everglades as temperatures, mosquito activity, and water levels are all lower (making wildlife easier to spot).

Northern Florida, conversely, receives the greatest influx from Memorial Day to Labor Day. Costs are highest then, but so are temperatures. (In winter, when the mercury dips into the 40s, you'd get a chilly reception on Panhandle beaches.) Specific areas, like Panama City Beach or Daytona Beach, attract throngs—and thongs—during spring break, too. In the latter, also expect revved-up revelers during Speed Weeks (late January and February) and Bike Week (early March).

Thanks to its theme parks, Central Florida is a magnet for children, meaning the largest crowds gather, logically enough, whenever class lets out. Line-ups at attractions do shrink after they return to school, though this area's hopping all year, with large numbers of international families and kid-free adults coming in the off-season. Spring and fall shoulder seasons are the optimal time to visit, both weatherwise and pricewise.

Climate

Florida is rightly called the Sunshine State—areas like Tampa Bay report 361 days of sunshine a year! But it could also be dubbed the Humid State. From June through September, 90% humidity levels aren't uncommon, nor are accompanying thunderstorms. In fact, more than half of the state's rain falls during these months. Florida's two-sided coastline also makes it a target for tropical storms. Hurricane season officially begins June 1 and ends November 30.

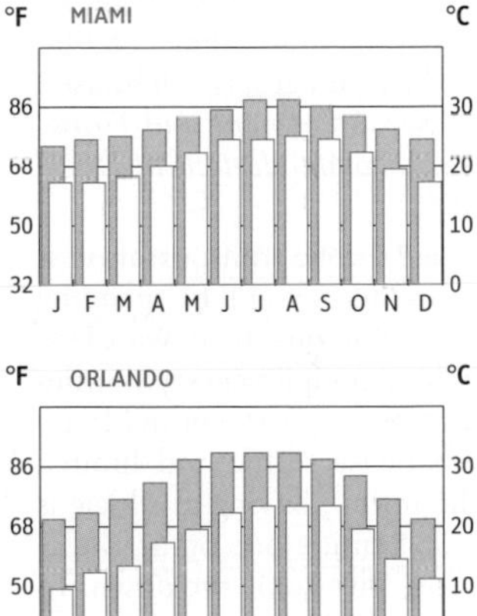

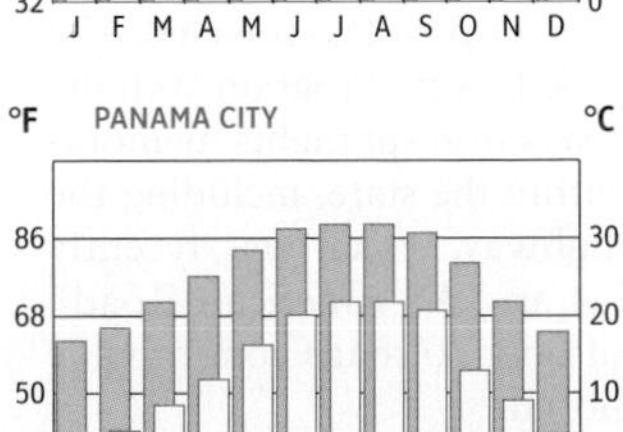

FAQS

I'm not crazy about spending seven nights in hotels. Any affordable alternatives? If you want to pretend you're lucky enough to live here, try a vacation rental. Aside from providing privacy, rentals let you set your own schedule and do your own cooking. The caveat is you may have to rent in weekly—not nightly—increments. Several companies specialize in the Orlando area, Magical Memories (☎ *866/535–7851* 🌐 *www.magicalmemories.com*) being one reliable bet. But in terms of coverage, geographically and pricewise, HomeAway (☎ *512/493–0382* 🌐 *www.homeaway.com*) wins, listing more than 18,000 Floridian condos, cottages, beach houses, and villas. ⇨ *See Apartment and House Rentals under Accommodations in Travel Smart Florida.*

Will I need a car? Public transportation is limited here. So unless you'll be spending your whole vacation on-site at Walt Disney World (where complimentary shuttles are available to resort guests) or in Miami Beach (where dense traffic and limited parking is the norm), having a vehicle is recommended. Renting one on arrival is wise, unless you drive your own down. To make car time less tedious, consider occasionally taking the road less traveled. The National Scenic Byways Program Web site (🌐 *www.byways.org*) spotlights memorable routes within the state, including the Overseas Highway, which was recently designated as an "All American Road" and is one of only 30 roads countrywide to be so honored.

How do I pick between Orlando's parks and Tampa's Busch Gardens? That's a tough call, especially if you haven't yet seen newer attractions like Aquatica at SeaWorld or Jungala at Busch Gardens. The good news is you don't have to choose, because the Busch Gardens Shuttle Express (☎ *800/221–1339* 🌐 *www.mearstransportation.com*) offers same-day round-trip service between designated locations in Orlando and the Tampa venue for only $10. The trip is free when you buy a six-park Orlando Flex Ticket Plus (good for 14 days unlimited entry to Universal, Islands of Adventure, SeaWorld, Aquatica, Wet 'n Wild, and Busch Gardens) or any Busch Gardens combination ticket.

Is Miami OK for families? Absolutely. Despite all the attention paid to G-strings, it retains areas with genuine G-rated appeal. Beyond the beaches, attractions like the interactive Children's Museum and the Museum of Science draw kids in droves. Want to go wild? Bypass the nightclubs and head instead to the MetroZoo or Seaquarium. If you dream of being named "best parent ever," sign your offspring up for a junior zookeeper program at the former or a dolphin swim at the latter.

Will the Deepwater Horizon oil spill affect my vacation? Deepwater Horizon, an offshore oil drilling platform owned by Transocean Ltd and under contract to BP, exploded on April 20, 2010. The rig leaked approximately 20,000 barrels per day into the Gulf of Mexico near Louisiana. At this writing, the oil had come ashore on Pensacola Beach and has affected 125 mi of Louisiana shoreline. For up to date information about the oil spill's impact on Florida, see Florida's Department of Environmental Protection Web site: 🌐 *www.dep.state.fl.us/deepwaterhorizon* as well as their Twitter feed: 🌐 *twitter.com/FLDEPalert*. Florida's state tourism board also posts updates and links to local communities at 🌐 *www.visitflorida.com/florida_travel_advisory*.

SOAKING IN THE SUN: FLORIDA'S BEST BEACHES

by Mary Thurwachter

Long before the world's most famous mouse took up residence here, Florida reeled in hordes of visitors who wanted to bask in the sun and splash in the surf. The 447-mi peninsula lays claim to 1,100 mi of flip-flop–friendly beaches, each with its own distinct character. Some shores are blessed with snow-white sand, some with an abundance of shells. Others have golden sand perfect for sandcastle-building or sea-turtle nesting. Ready to join the sun-and-sand set? Here's a roundup of Florida's best beaches in seven categories.

BEACH PLANNING

CHOOSING YOUR BEACH

When planning a beach trip to Florida, the first thing to decide is whether you want to be on the ocean or on the gulf.

Florida's ocean-side beaches are blessed with golden sands—some even packed hard enough to drive on—and clear turquoise-blue waters. Come here if you want to surf, dive, or watch the sunrise. On the downside, ocean-side beaches have to contend at times with the twin menaces of jellyfish and sea lice, which can sting and cause a rash.

Florida's gulf-coast beaches have white sandy shores; the best can be found in the Panhandle, where the water is emerald green. Come here if you want to collect seashells or watch a sunset. On the downside, gulf-side beaches seasonally endure red-tide algae that can make it difficult to breathe and cause itchy eyes. Jellyfish also are here, particularly in the late summer and fall.

The next thing to consider is when you're going, as beaches are not warm year-round. If you're going in the winter, choose a South Florida destination.

SAFETY TIPS

If you plan to swim, note the water's condition. Rip currents, caused when the tide rushes out through a narrow break in the water, can overpower even the strongest swimmer. If you do get caught in one, resist the urge to swim straight to shore—you'll tire before you make it. Instead, swim parallel to the shoreline until you are outside the current's pull, then head to the shore.

■TIP→ See our chapter beach spotlights for more regional information.

Seeing the stars at Lummus Park.

CELEBRITY SIGHTINGS

Chosen for their close proximity to top-notch hotels—the places that fluff pillows for stars—these beaches are palm-tree-adorned slices of paradise. The sand is soft enough to comfortably walk barefoot, and the water is warm and inviting. Tanning butlers, private cabanas, and trendy nightclubs are never far away—nor are paparazzi!

❶ **Lummus Park (South Beach),** Ocean Drive between 5th and 15th streets, Miami Beach. It's no accident that the park opens at 5 AM, when bars close and revelers totter over to watch the sun rise. Later in the day stars such as Lindsay Lohan, Jennifer Lopez, and Will Smith come out to freshen tans, frolic in the surf, play volleyball, or rollerblade on the boardwalk. Topless sunbathers are not uncommon.

❷ **Ponte Vedra Beach,** near Ponte Vedra Inn & Club, Northeast Florida

❸ **Lantana Beach,** near the Ritz-Carlton Palm Beach (in Manalapan), Palm Beach and the Treasure Coast

❹ **St. Pete Beach,** near the Don CeSar, Tampa Bay area

❺ **Islamorada Beach,** near The Moorings and Cheeca Lodge, the Florida Keys

❻ **Vanderbilt Beach,** near the Ritz-Carlton, Naples, the Lower Gulf Coast

❼ **Seagrove Beach,** near Seaside, in the Panhandle

Kids play at Clearwater Beach.

FAMILIES

To be considered for this category, beaches had to have picnic areas, showers, lifeguards, and sand suitable for building great sandcastles. Also, beachgoers to these slices of sand wear bathing (not birthday) suits. Having a playground area and being a site for annual festivals or events were not required but were worth bonus points.

❶ **Clearwater Beach,** Tampa Bay area. This gem for families features gorgeous white sand, attentive lifeguards, shallow waters that are clear and warm, a pier, and plenty of showers and restrooms. Bring some cash for renting certain amenities, like a beach umbrella or cabana, or for taking a whirl in the waves aboard a watercraft. Kids will want a pail and shovel, especially if you're coming during the Clearwater Fun 'n Sun Festival in April and May, where sandcastle-building contests are part of the festivities.

❷ **Delray Beach,** Palm Beach and the Treasure Coast

❸ **Hollywood Beach,** Hollywood, Fort Lauderdale and Broward County

❹ **Siesta Beach,** near Sarasota, Tampa Bay area

❺ **Harry Harris Park,** Tavenier (mile marker 92.5), the Florida Keys

❻ **Anastasia State Park,** St. Augustine, Northeast Florida

❼ **Fort Myers Beach,** the Lower Gulf Coast

Fido gets his paws wet at a Florida beach.

ANIMALS

Most beaches do not allow dogs. These Fido-friendly spots do, giving a pup a chance to dig up a seashell, chase a sand crab, fetch a Frisbee, and maybe even bodysurf. Most provide fresh water so our four-legged pals can quench their thirst and have sand soft enough for an easy-on-the-paws hike along the shore.

❶ **Jupiter Beach,** Jupiter, Palm Beach County. At this well-maintained 2.5-mi patch from Juno Beach north to Carlin Park boarded crosswalks framed by sea grapes lead you to the shoreline, and doggie bags are provided at each entrance. Dogs need to be leashed unless they respond well to your commands, in which case they can take a mad dash into the surf for a refreshing untethered swim.

❷ **St. Joe Beach,** Port St. Joe, north of Apalachicola, the Panhandle

❸ **Dog Beach,** Key West, adjacent to Louie's Backyard Restaurant near the southernmost point, the Florida Keys

❹ **Smyrna Dunes Park,** New Smyrna Beach, Northeast Florida

❺ **Rickenbacker Causeway and Beach,** Key Biscayne, Miami & Miami Beach

❻ **Abercrombie Park,** on Park Street at 38th Ave. N., St. Petersburg, the Tampa Bay Area

❼ **Flagler Beach,** north and south of 10th Street (but not at the 10th Street pier), Flagler Beach, Northeast Florida

Gathering in a handful of shells on the beach.

SEASHELLS

These pretty beaches were picked for their abundance of seashells and how easy it was to find them. In other words, these are places you won't have to dig deep to find a gift from the sea—from whelks to olives to conchs.

❶ **Bowman's Beach,** on Sanibel Island, the Lower Gulf Coast. While most beaches in Sanibel and Captiva are worthy hunting grounds for shell devotees, Bowman's, the most remote, tops them all. Guests reach this wide sandy beach by traipsing from the parking area through beach grass, pines, wetland, and a picnic area cooled by the shade of pine trees and sea grapes. The likelihood of leaving with a bag full of gorgeous shells is high. You might even score one of the island's most coveted shells, the junonia. Time spent here is worth enduring "the Sanibel Stoop," the nickname islanders have given the hunched-over position shell seekers assume.

❷ **Holmes Beach,** Anna Maria Island, the Lower Gulf Coast

❸ **St. Joe State Park,** on Cape San Blas, the Panhandle

❹ **Sombrero Beach,** Marathon, the Florida Keys

❺ **Vero Beach,** Palm Beach & the Treasure Coast

❻ **Turtle Beach,** Siesta Key, Tampa Bay area

❼ **Jacksonville Beach,** Northeast Florida

Enjoying a sunset at Caladesi Island State Park.

SOLITUDE & ROMANCE

We looked for shorelines that were uncrowded but beautiful, places you could walk a few hundred steps and find a strech of sand all to yourself or with your main squeeze. These selections are not public beaches where the masses come to drink in the sun; here the water laps gently against a silent shore.

❶ **Caladesi Island State Park,** a mile west of Dunedin, Tampa Bay Area. For a getting-away-from-it-all beach, this island retreat more than fits the bill: you can't even get to it by car but must take a boat. With crystal-clear waters and tiny waves, it's a good spot for swimming and fishing. You can paddle a kayak through the mangroves, hike on the nature trail, search for seashells, or just unwind with a romantic picnic on the white-sand shore.

❷ **Lovers Key State Park,** on County Rd. 865 between Fort Myers Beach and Bonita Beach in Lee County, the Lower Gulf Coast

❸ **Bahia Honda State Park,** Bahia Honda Key (mile marker 37), the Florida Keys

❹ **John U. Lloyd Beach Recreation Area,** Dania Beach, Fort Lauderdale and Broward County

❺ **St. George Island State Park,** St. George Island, the Panhandle

❻ **Blowing Rocks Preserve,** Jupiter, Palm Beach and the Treasure Coast

❼ **Canaveral National Seashore,** Titusville, Northeast Florida

Diving at John Pennekamp Coral Reef State Park.

Playing volleyball at Panama City Beach.

DIVING IN

Water clarity and warmth were key factors here, but we also looked for beaches that offer interesting things to eyeball underwater. Strap on a mask and snorkel and you'll definitely see something eye-catching, from colorful coral reefs and schools of fish, to the remains of shipwrecks in their watery graves.

❶ **John Pennekamp Coral Reef State Park,** mile marker 102.5, Key Largo, the Florida Keys. With shallow water reefs, submerged sculptures, and 55 kinds of coral, Pennekamp has been hailed as the Diving Capital of the World. The country's first underwater park showcases an eight-and-a-half-foot bronze sculpture "Christ of the Deep." Those who don't want to dive in can see the coral reefs—and some of the nearly 600 varieties of fish who live there—on a glass-bottom boat tour. A visitor center sports a 30,000-gallon aquarium and nature theater.

❷ **Bahia Honda State Park,** Bahia Honda Key (mile marker 37), the Florida Keys

❸ **Fort Lauderdale Beach,** Fort Lauderdale and Broward County

❹ **Fort Walton Beach,** the Panhandle

❺ **St. Andrew's State Recreational Area,** Panama City, the Panhandle

❻ **Egmont Key,** Tampa Bay, southwest of Fort DeSoto Beach, the Tampa Bay Area

❼ **Vero Beach,** Palm Beach and the Treasure Coast

PARTYING

Girls just wanna have fun, and that urge often takes them where the boys are. The ones they find at these beaches are tolerant of rowdiness and are never too far from bars, bands, and food. These beaches attract spring-breakers more than families with young children.

❶ **Panama City Beach,** the Panhandle. Seventeen miles of snowy-white sand and sparkling emerald-green water are enough to attract any beach lover, but at the Spring Break Capital of the World collegiate party animals find a special lure. MTV's televised concerts during spring break add fuel to the already hot word-of-mouth fire. When they're not drinking and dancing, free spirits looking for a legal high can tether themselves to a parachute and a speed boat for a bit of parasailing, and party girls can get a pedicure or scour the shops at Pier Park.

❷ **Cocoa Beach,** Northeast Florida

❸ **Lummus Beach (South Beach),** Miami Beach

❹ **Smathers Beach in Key West,** the Florida Keys

❺ **Lynn Hall Memorial Park,** Fort Myers Beach, the Lower Gulf Coast

❻ **Riviera Beach Municipal Beach,** on Singer Island, Palm Beach and the Treasure Coast

❼ **Fort Lauderdale Beach,** Fort Lauderdale and Broward County

QUINTESSENTIAL FLORIDA

H2O

Spanish explorer Ponce de León didn't find the Fountain of Youth when he swung through Florida in 1513. But if he'd lingered longer, he could have located 7,800 lakes, 1,700 rivers and creeks, and an estimated 350 springs. Over the centuries these have attracted American Indians, immigrants, opportunists, and, of course, countless outdoor adventurers. Boaters come for inland waterways and a 1,200-mi coast, and anglers are lured by 700 species of fish. (Florida claims 700 world-record catches, too, so concocting elaborate fish tales may not be necessary.) Snorkelers and divers curious to see what lies beneath can get face time with the marine life that thrives on the world's third-largest coral reef or bone up on maritime history in underwater archaeological preserves. Back on dry land, all those beaches are pretty impressive, too.

Theme Parks

Children tend to think of Florida as a playland that's liberally sprinkled with pixie dust. And who can blame them? Orlando's theme parks are among the most popular (and most publicized) attractions on earth. Walt Disney World opened the first of its four Floridian parks in 1971. Competitors like SeaWorld and Universal followed suit, transforming a swampy cattle-and-citrus town into Fun Central. Today, dozens of smaller Orlando venues—from water parks like Aquatica and Wet 'n Wild to a Christian one called Holy Land Experience—vie for visitors' dollars; and Busch Gardens in Tampa (85 mi southwest) scrambles for a piece of the pie with its own roundup of rides. Some locals love them. Others lament the dawn of the Disney Era. All, however, recognize that theme parks are now a fact of life.

Florida is synonymous with sunshine, and visitors routinely come to revel in it. However, the people who actually live here—a diverse group that includes Mouseketeers, millionaires, surfers, and rocket scientists—know that the state's appeal rests on more than those reliable rays.

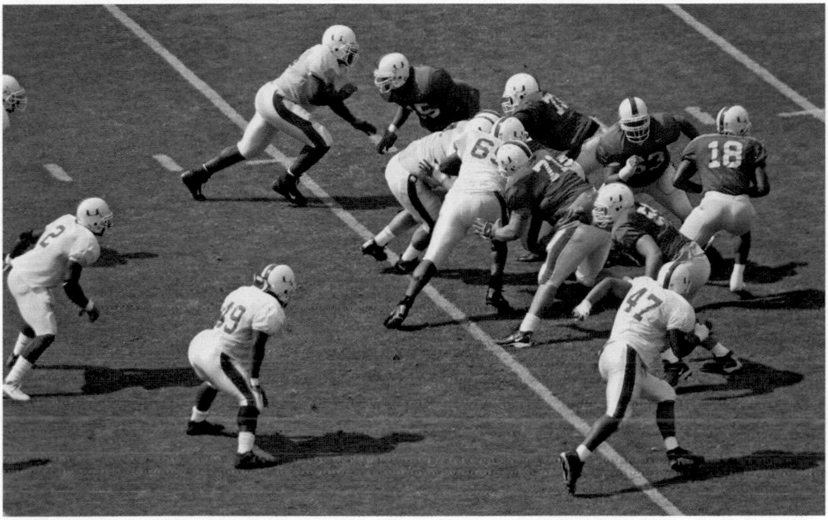

Superlative Sports

Panthers and Dolphins and Rays, oh my! Florida is teeming with teams—and residents take the games they play *very* seriously. Baseball fans regularly work themselves into a fever pitch: after all, the state has a pair of Major League franchises and hosts another 15 in spring when the Grapefruit League goes to bat (*see "Spring Training, Florida-Style" In-Focus feature in Chapter 8*). Those with a preference for pigskin might cheer for NFL teams in Jacksonville, Miami, and Tampa. But the state is also home to top-rated college teams, and two (the Gators and 'Noles) have especially fervent followings. Basketball lovers, meanwhile, feel the "Heat" in Miami or the "Magic" in Orlando, and hockey addicts stick around to watch the Florida Panthers and Tampa Bay Lightning. The Professional Golfers Association (PGA) is headquartered here as well.

Fabulous Food

Geography and gastronomy go hand in hand in Florida. Seafood, for instance, is a staple almost everywhere. Yet locals will point out that the way it is prepared changes considerably as you maneuver around the state. Northern restaurants show their regional roots with Cajun classics and Dixieland dishes. (It seems that virtually any fish can be crusted with pecans and served with greens!) In Southern Florida, menus typically highlight Floribbean cuisine, which marries Floridian, Caribbean, and Latin flavors. (Think mahimahi with mango salsa.) Inland, expect catfish, gator tails, and frogs' legs, all of which are best enjoyed at a Cracker-style fish camp with a side order of hush puppies. In keeping with the regional emphasis, assorted seafoods—along with peanuts, sweet corn, watermelons, and citrus fruits—all merit their own down-home festivals.

FLORIDA TOP ATTRACTIONS

A

B

Walt Disney World

(A) Like one of Snow White's dwarfs, Orlando was sleepy until Uncle Walt arrived 40 years ago. Today the city is booming—and so is Walt Disney World, which has grown into a 47-square-mi complex with four separate parks, scores of hotels, and satellite attractions like Blizzard Beach and Downtown Disney. Thanks to innovative rides and dazzling animatronics, these feature prominently in every child's holiday fantasy. Adults, however, don't have to channel their inner eight-year-old to have fun, because Walt Disney World also has grown-up amenities including championship golf courses, sublime hotels and spas, and fine restaurants that rank among North America's best.

South Beach

(B) You can't miss the distinctive forms, vibrant colors, and extravagant flourishes of SoBe's architectural gems. The world's largest concentration of art deco edifices is right here; and the Art Deco District, with more than 800 buildings, has earned a spot on the National Register of Historic Places (⇨ *see "A Stroll Down Deco Lane" In-Focus feature in Chapter 12*). The 'hood also has enough beautiful people to qualify for the Register of Hippest Places. The glitterati, along with assorted vacationing hedonists, are drawn by übertrendy shops and a surfeit of celeb-studded clubs. Divine eateries are the icing—umm, better make that the ganache—on South Beach's proverbial cake.

The Florida Keys

(C) These 800-plus islands are at once a unique landmass and a mass of contradictions. Long years of geographic isolation not only allowed tropical flora and fauna to flourish here, they enabled locals to nurture a quirky one-of-a-kind culture. Unfortunately, increased traffic on the Overseas Highway linking the Upper,

Middle, and Lower Keys to the mainland has threatened both. So the Keys now have a split personality. On one hand, they are a reef-rimmed paradise occupied by free spirits; on the other, a relatively mainstream realm composed of traffic jams, shopping malls, and trailer parks. Avoiding the latter can be tricky. But the charm of the former is ample reward.

Kennedy Space Center

(D) Though there are enough wide-open expanses to justify the area's moniker, it was NASA that put the "space" in Space Coast—and this is its star attraction. Space memorabilia and aeronautic antiques, ranging from Redstone rockets to the *Apollo XIV* command module, turn an outing here into a trip back in time for anyone who lived through the space race. Yet for contemporary kids its interactive bells and whistles open up a brave new world. (⇨ *See "Soaring High" In-Focus feature in Chapter 3.*) More down-to-earth types can also visit the Merritt Island National Wildlife Refuge (originally created as a buffer for the space program) and Canaveral National Seashore.

Tampa

(E) As a vibrant city with exceptional beaches, Tampa is perfect for indecisive folks who want to enjoy surf and sand without sacrificing urban experiences. Families will love Busch Gardens, a major zoo and theme park. Football and hockey fans will relish the chance to see the Buccaneers and Lightning play. Baseball is big, too: the Rays are based here, and the Yankees descend annually for spring training. (⇨ *See "Spring Training, Florida-Style" In-Focus feature in Chapter 8.*) When you need a break from the city, St. Pete Beach (famous for surreally beautiful strands) and St. Petersburg (home to the world's most comprehensive collection of Dalí's surrealist paintings) are a short drive away.

F

G

Go Fish

(F) Each October, Destin proves it is the "World's Luckiest Fishing Village" by inviting anglers young and old to compete in the monthlong Destin Fishing Rodeo. However, if you'd prefer to throw fish rather than catch them, head to Pensacola in late April for the Interstate Mullet Toss. (Participants line up to throw dead fish across the Florida–Alabama state line). Epicures will be relieved to hear that Pensacola also stages a September Seafood Festival. As if fish fried, broiled, battered, or grilled weren't appealing enough, gourmet options are added to the menu.

Hang 10

(G) Cocoa Beach, on the northeast coast, is Surf City for Floridians. Baby boomers may remember it as the place where Major Nelson dreamed of Jeannie. The community is better known today as the hometown of surfing's biggest celeb, Kelly Slater. He has won a record-breaking nine world championships, and totally tubular types can learn to emulate him at the Ron Jon Surf School. It offers group classes as well as semiprivate and one-on-one lessons for any level of expertise. Loaner equipment is included, but you can also purchase your own nearby at the massive Ron Jon Surf Shop.

Act Goofy

(H) If you have time for only one megapark, choose the original, Walt Disney World's Magic Kingdom. Approached with an open mind (and a couple of well-behaved kids), it really can feel like the "happiest place on Earth." Start by waving to Mickey on Main Street USA; then fly with Dumbo, take a spin in the Mad Hatter's Teacups, and catch the nighttime fireworks display over Cinderella's Castle. As an FYI, flume lovers can also have a blast on Splash Mountain. Just be forewarned—ride it more than once and

you'll spend the rest of your trip humming Brer Rabbit's theme song.

Enjoy the High Life

(I) If money could talk, you'd hardly be able to hear above the din in Palm Beach. The upper crust started calling it home, during winter at least, in the early 1900s. And today it remains a ritzy, glitzy enclave for both old money and the nouveau riche (a coterie led by The Donald himself, who owns the landmark Mar-a-Lago Club). Simply put, Palm Beach is the sort of place where shopping is a full-time pursuit and residents don't just wear Polo—they play it. Oooh and ahhh to your heart's content; then, for more conspicuous consumption, continue south on the aptly named Gold Coast.

Float Your Boat

(J) Mariners should set their compass for Fort Lauderdale (aka the Venice of America), where vessels from around the world moor along some two dozen finger isles between the beach and the mainland. Sailors can cruise Broward County's 300 mi of inland waterways by water taxi and tour boat, or bob around the Atlantic in a chartered yacht. Mariners should set their compass for Fort Lauderdale (aka the Venice of America), where vessels from around the world moor along some two dozen finger isles between the beach and the mainland. Sailors can cruise Broward County's 300 mi of inland waterways by water taxi and tour boat, or bob around the Atlantic in a chartered yacht. If you're in a buying mood, come in late October for the annual Fort Lauderdale International Boat Show. Billed as the world's largest, it has $3 billion worth of boats in every conceivable size, shape, and price range.

Live La Vida Local

(K) On the streets of Miami's Little Havana, just west of downtown, salsa tunes blare and the smell of spicy chorizo fills the air. (You can get a good whiff of tobacco, too, thanks to the cigar makers who still hand-roll their products here.) For nearly 50 years, the neighborhood's undisputed heart has been Calle Ocho, the commercial thoroughfare that hosts Carnaval Miami (*www.carnavalmiami.com*) each March. The festival's 10 frenetic days culminate in the world's longest conga line. Ambience- and amenity-wise, it is as close as you'll get to Cuba without running afoul of the federal government. (⇨ *See "Caribbean Infusion" In-Focus feature in Chapter 12.*)

Join the Papa-Papa-razzi

(L) Who's Your Papa? Ask that question around Key West and the answer will invariably be "Ernest Hemingway." The author lived and worked here for 11 years, during which time he penned *For Whom the Bell Tolls* and *A Farewell to Arms*. Today touring his former digs (Ernest Hemingway Home and Museum) and toasting his memory at Sloppy Joe's Bar on Duval Street is almost mandatory. To fully understand the Importance of Being Ernest, though, come in late July for Hemingway Days. Events include a fishing tournament and look-alike contest featuring Papa impersonators.

Feel Swamped

(M) No trip to southern Florida is complete without seeing the Everglades. At its heart is a river—50 mi wide but merely 6 inches deep—flowing from Lake Okeechobee into Florida Bay. For an up-close look, speed demons can board an airboat that careens through the marshy waters. Purists, alternately, may placidly canoe or kayak within the boundaries of Everglades National Park. Just remember to keep your hands in the boat. The

critters that call this unique ecosystem home (alligators, Florida panthers, and cottonmouth snakes for starters) can add real bite to your visit!

Be Beachy-Keen

(N) Ready to do something slightly more vigorous than applying SPF 45 and rolling over? Trade beach-bumming for beach-combing in Sanibel, the "Shell Capital of the World." Conchs, cockles, clams, coquinas—they're all here (the bounty is due to this barrier island's unusual east-west orientation). Of course, if you'd rather construct sand castles than do the Sanibel Stoop, you need only cross the 3-mi causeway to Fort Myers Beach. It has the finest building material and, every November, professional and amateur aficionados prove it during the American Sand Sculpting Championship. (⇨ *See "Shell-Bent on Sanibel Island" In-Focus feature in Chapter 9.*)

Clown Around

(O) Sarasota, once winter headquarters for Ringling Bros. and Barnum & Bailey, is proud of its circus heritage. Several troupes are still based here, including Royal Hanneford, Walker Brothers, and Circus Sarasota. Visitors who can't get enough of sawdust and sequins can see an impressive collection of vintage costumes, props, and parade wagons at the Ringling Circus Museum. The adjacent Tibbals Learning Center houses a mind-boggling ¾-inch-scale miniature circus with almost a million pieces. Sarasota even has a Circus Ring of Fame with bronze plaques honoring big-top bigwigs.

IF YOU LIKE

Animal Encounters

Florida is home to one supersized mouse and makes an ideal habitat for party animals. Yet there are other types of wildlife here, too. In terms of biodiversity, the state ranks third in the country with approximately 1,200 different kinds of critters.

■ **Birds.** Poised on two major migratory routes, Florida draws about 500 species of birds—and the 2,000-mi Great Florida Birding Trail helps you track them down. Through detailed guides and highway signs, it identifies sites where you may spy anything from bald eagles and burrowing owls to pink flamingos.

■ **Manatees.** They're nicknamed sea cows and resemble walruses. But Florida's official marine mammals are most closely related to elephants, which may account for their slow pace and hefty frames. In winter, scan the water for a telltale glassy patch (called a "footprint"), indicating that a manatee swims below.

■ **Sea Turtles.** Ready for a late-night rendezvous with the massive leatherbacks and loggerheads that lumber onto Floridian beaches to lay their eggs between May and October? Archie Carr National Wildlife Refuge, the world's second-largest sea-turtle-nesting site, organizes free turtle watches in June and July.

■ **Alligators.** Florida has more than 1.5 million resident alligators. You can witness them doing tricks at places like Gatorland, but gator spotting in swamps or roadside waterways is itself a favorite pastime. Eating the official state reptile in deep-fried-nugget form is popular, too. Mmm . . . tastes like chicken.

Life in the Fast Lane

The Sunshine State has been satisfying visitors' need for speed ever since Henry Ford and his snowbird buddies started using Ormond Beach as a test track. Today roller coasters, stock cars, supersonic jets, and spaceships add momentum to your vacation.

■ **Tampa.** If you think the pursuit of happiness is a high-speed activity, head for Busch Gardens, Florida's premier roller-coaster location. SheiKra is one of the world's tallest dive coasters, Kumba features one of the world's largest vertical loops, and Montu (a gut-churning inverted coaster) delivers a G-force of 3.85.

■ **Daytona Beach.** Daytona 500, NASCAR's most prestigious event, pulls in legions of devotees each February. But any time of year you can slip into a driving suit, then into the driver's seat of a Winston Cup–style stock car courtesy of the Richard Petty Driving Experience at Daytona International Speedway.

■ **Pensacola.** The National Museum of Naval Aviation displays 150-plus military aircraft and has motion-based simulators that let you "fly" an F/A-18. Better yet, the U.S. Navy Precision Flight Team (familiar to most of us as the Blue Angels) is based here, so you may get to observe them in action at 700 mph.

■ **Kennedy Space Center.** Whether you admire Buzz Aldrin or Buzz Lightyear, this spot has the right stuff. See a shuttle launch, gawk at rockets, or take your own giant leap with the Astronaut Training Experience. The daylong program consists of realistic training exercises culminating in a simulated mission.

Something Old, Something New

You don't have to look far for "New Florida." It's evident in skyscrapers and sprawling suburbs, in malls, multiplexes, and the ubiquitous condo complexes that obscure parts of the coast. Yet it is easy enough to find reminders of the state's rich past.

- **St. Augustine.** Fortify yourself at Castillo de San Marcos. Built by the Spanish to defend *La Florida*, this formidable 17th-century structure is America's oldest masonry fort. Even kids whose interest in architecture stops at Cinderella's Castle will be impressed by its turrets, moat, and double drawbridge.
- **Apalachicola.** A booming cotton-and-lumber industry turned this Panhandle town into a bustling port in the 19th century. Now it's part of the Forgotten Coast. Hundreds of preserved buildings, ranging from antebellum warehouses to gracious Victorian-style homes, give it a time-warped appeal.
- **Coral Gables.** You can soak up 1920s architecture in Miami Beach. But in nearby Coral Gables you can soak *in* it at the Venetian Pool, a vintage municipal lagoon fashioned from a quarry. Back in the day, it attracted Johnny Weissmuller, Esther Williams, and other legendary swimmers.
- **Cross Creek.** The backwoods scrub immortalized by Marjorie Kinnan Rawlings in the *Dirty Thirties* hasn't changed much. Nor has the Cracker-style house where the Pulitzer prizewinner wrote *The Yearling*. You can tour it from October through July and visit the surrounding farm and grove year-round.

Hitting the Greens

With more courses than any other state and weather that allows for year-round play, Florida is a dream destination for golfers. Ready to go fore it? The tourism board's new dedicated golf site (🌐 *www.golf.visitflorida.com*) will point you in the right direction.

- **The Breakers.** Floridian's fascination with golf began in 1896 when the state's first course opened at this Palm Beach resort. (Rockefellers, Vanderbilts, and Astors are all listed in the guest book.) Today, the original 70-par Ocean Course offers spectacular Atlantic views and challenging shots on 140 acres.
- **PGA Village.** Owned and operated by the PGA, this St. Lucie venue boasts three championship courses designed by Tom Fazio and Pete Dye, plus a 35-acre Golf Learning and Performance Center that can turn weekend duffers into scratch players. A free museum of golf memorabilia is also on-site.
- **Doral Golf Resort and Spa.** The Blue Monster understandably grabs the spotlight here: the par-72 course has been a stop on the PGA tour for more than 40 years. But the Miami resort has four other championship courses (including the new Jim McLean Signature Course) as well as McLean's own golf school.
- **Ginn Reunion Resort.** This spot near Orlando just keeps upping its game. Not content with having courses laid out by Tom Watson, Arnold Palmer, and Jack Nicklaus, it recently added the Annika Academy, a golf school named for LPGA phenom Annika Sörenstam and overseen by her coach, Henri Reis.

GREAT ITINERARIES

Since Florida is a long, lean peninsula anchored to the mainland by a "panhandle," the distances between destinations may surprise you. Panama City, for example, is closer to New Orleans than to Orlando; and Tallahassee, though only 8 mi from the Georgia border, is a whopping 465 mi from Miami Beach. Key West, similarly, is 494 mi from Jacksonville, yet only 90 mi from Cuba. When plotting your dream trip, study a map to determine how easy it will be to connect the dots—or simply follow one of these tried-and-true itineraries. If you have two or more weeks to drive through the state, you can do them all.

3 to 4 Days: Orlando

Anyone can easily spend a week doing the attractions. (Remember, Walt Disney World alone is roughly the size of San Francisco!) But unless you're a die-hard ride hound, a few days will let you sample them and still enjoy some of Orlando's other amenities. The hard part is deciding where to start. The Magic Kingdom has the greatest concentration of classic sites, and Epcot proves this really is a small world. Film buffs can get reel at Disney's Hollywood Studios or Universal Studios, and thrill seekers can get their hearts pumping at Islands of Adventure. As for wildlife encounters, you can do like Dolittle at Disney's Animal Kingdom or SeaWorld. On top of all that, there's a sufficient number of water parks—including both old favorites such as Wet 'n Wild and newer entries like Aquatica—to make you forget you're inland. In the city itself, art connoisseurs can survey the collection of modern paintings at the Orlando Museum of Art; and flower fans can check out Orlando blooms in the 50-acre Harry P. Leu Gardens. Boaters can take advantage of the area's numerous lakes, and golfers can link up on courses designed by the sport's biggest stars.

2 to 3 Days: Panhandle

Let's be honest: people come to Florida's Panhandle primarily for those white-sand beaches. Some of the best in the country are along this coastline, affectionately known as the Redneck Riviera. But it's possible to work on a tan and still work in some sightseeing. At Gulf Islands National Seashore, for instance, you can soak up the sun, cast a fishing net, take a hike, tour centuries-old forts, and have time left for a trip into historic Pensacola. Similarly, after beach time around Apalachicola Bay you can stop for oysters at a local raw bar (90% of Florida's haul comes from here); head north through the canopied roads around Apalachicola National Forest; then get a true taste of the Old South in moss-draped Tallahassee. Yet another day could be devoted to glorious Grayton Beach, where diving and kayaking can be followed up with a relaxing drive along Route 30A to cute, nostalgia-inducing communities like WaterColor and Seaside. When planning your trip, bear in mind that the Panhandle not only has its own time zone but its own tourism season—summer, and that's prime time for beach going.

2 to 3 Days: Space Coast

If you need proof that Florida was the first part of the United States to be settled, look no further than St. Augustine. It was founded by the Spanish in 1565, and visiting Castillo de San Marcos (its colonial-era fortress) or strolling the streets of the Old City that grew up around it allows you to experience life in the past lane. Taking in the stellar sites at the 700,000-acre Kennedy Space Center has just the opposite effect. Although it may seem centuries removed, the nation's oldest

continuously inhabited city is less than two hours by car from our launch pad to the moon. Between them, you can hear the call of the wild at Merritt Island National Wildlife Refuge, catch a wave like local surfing legend Kelly Slater, or blissfully hit the beach at Canaveral National Seashore (the 24-mi preserve remains undeveloped. So you lounge in the shelter of dunes, not the shadow of high-rises). Racier options also await—just reset your GPS for Daytona Beach. Its International Speedway, which has hosted NASCAR's Daytona 500 every February since 1959, is a must-see for stock-car enthusiasts, and there's plenty to do here year-round even if it's not a race day.

2 to 3 Days: Gold Coast and Treasure Coast

The opulent mansions of Palm Beach's Ocean Boulevard give you a glimpse of how the richer half lives. For exclusive boutique shopping, art gallery browsing, and glittery sightseeing, sybarites should wander down "The Avenue" (that's Worth Avenue to non–Palm Beachers). The sporty set will find dozens of places to tee up (hardly surprising given that the PGA is based here), along with tennis courts, polo clubs, even a croquet center. Those who'd like to see more of the Gold Coast can continue traveling south through Boca Raton to Fort Lauderdale (justifiably known as the "Yachting Capital of the World"). But to balance the highbrow with the low-key, turn northward for a tour of the Treasure Coast. Notable for its outdoor opportunities and Old Florida ambience, this region was named for the booty spilled by a fleet of Spanish galleons shipwrecked here in 1715, and for centuries treasure kept washing ashore south of Sebastian Inlet. These days you're more likely to discover manatees and golden surfing opportunities. You can also look for the sea turtles that lay their own little treasures in the sands from May through August.

2 to 3 Days: Miami Area

Greater Miami lays claim to the country's most celebrated strand—South Beach—and lingering on it tops most tourist itineraries. (The Ocean Drive section, lined with edgy clubs, boutiques and eateries, is where the see-and-be-seen crowd gathers.) Once you've checked out the candy-colored art-deco architecture, park yourself to ogle the parade of stylish people, or join them by browsing Lincoln Road Mall. Later, merengue over to Calle Ocho, the epicenter of Miami's

Cuban community. Elsewhere in the area, Coconut Grove, Coral Gables, and the Miami Design District (an 18-block area crammed with showrooms and galleries) warrant a visit as well. Since Miami is the sole U.S. city with two national parks and a national preserve in its backyard, it is also a convenient base for eco-excursions. You can take a day trip to the Everglades; get a spectacular view of the reefs from a glass-bottom boat in Biscayne National Park; then spot some rare wood storks in Big Cypress Swamp, which is best explored via Alligator Alley (Interstate 75).

2 to 3 Days: Florida Keys

Some dream of "sailing away to Key Largo," others of "wasting away again in Margaritaville." In any case, almost everybody equates the Florida Keys with relaxation. And—assuming you survive the traffic—they live up to their reputation, thanks to off-beat attractions and that fabled come-as-you-are, do-as-you-please vibe. Key West, alternately known as the Conch Republic, is a good place to get initiated. The Old Town has a funky, laid-back feel. So take a leisurely walk; pay your respects to Ernest Hemingway; then (if you haven't imbibed too much at one of the renowned watering holes) rent a moped to tour the rest of the island. Clear waters and abundant marine life make underwater activities another must. After scoping out the parrot fish, you can head back into town and join local Parrottheads in a Jimmy Buffett sing-along. When retracing your route to the mainland, plan a last pit stop at Bahia Honda State Park (it has ranger-led activities plus the Keys' best beach) or John Pennekamp Coral Reef State Park, which offers unparalleled snorkeling and scuba-diving opportunities for beginners and veterans alike.

TIPS

Now that one-way airfares are commonplace, vacationers visiting multiple destinations can fly into and out of different airports. Rent a car in between, picking it up at your point of arrival and leaving it at your point of departure. If you do this itinerary as an entire vacation, your best bet is to fly into and out of Orlando and rent a car from there.

Inquire about scheduled activities when visiting national and state parks or preserves. Many of them run free or low-cost ranger-led programs that run the gamut from walks and talks to campfires and canoe trips.

2 to 3 Days: Tampa Bay Area

Whether you bypassed Orlando's theme parks or simply want to add another one to your list, Busch Gardens is a logical starting point. With hair-raising rides and more than 2,700 animals, it appeals to adrenaline junkies and 'fraidy cats alike. Later you can catch a pro-sporting event (Tampa has Major League Baseball, football, and hockey teams) or catch an act in the Spanish-inflected Ybor City entertainment district. If you're more interested in catching some rays, try Caladesi Island State Park to the west of the city or Fort DeSoto Park at the mouth of Tampa Bay. From here, good day trips focused on cultural pursuits include visiting the museums in St. Petersburg and the thriving arts scene of Sarasota. Nature lovers may proceed north to Crystal River, where you can see—or even snorkel with—the gigantic but gentle manatees that congregate in the warm water November through March.

2

The Panhandle

WORD OF MOUTH

"The Beaches of South Walton is very family-oriented and has less crowded beaches. You'll find terrific restaurants that can seat your whole family."

—beachtrekker

WELCOME TO THE PANHANDLE

Pensacola beach.

TOP REASONS TO GO

★ **Snowy White Beaches:** Most of the Panhandle's Gulf Coast shoreline is relatively unobstructed by high-rise condos and hotels, and the white-powder sand is alluring.

★ **Lots of History:** Spanish, American Indian, and, later, French and English influences shaped the direction of this region and are well represented in architecture, historic sites, and museums.

★ **Slower Pace:** The Panhandle is sometimes referred to as "LA," or Lower Alabama. Southern through and through, the pace here is as slow as molasses—a fact Tallahassee plays up by claiming to be "Florida with a Southern accent."

★ **Capital Sites:** As the state capital (chosen because it was midway between the two earlier Spanish headquarters of St. Augustine and Pensacola), Tallahassee remains intriguing thanks to its history, historical museums, universities, and quiet country charm.

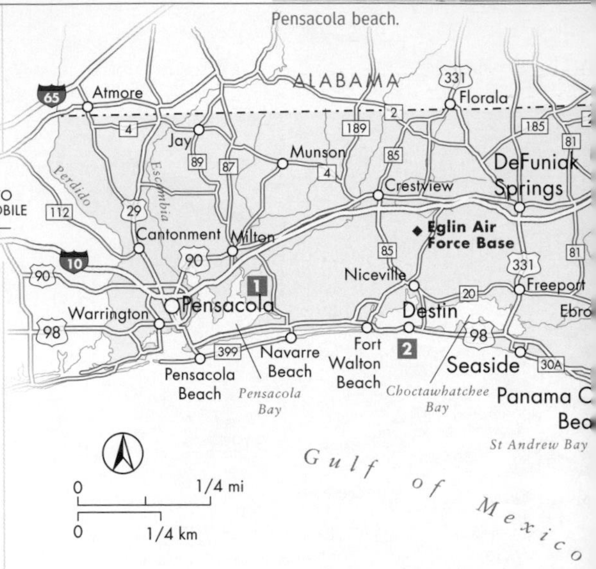

1 Around Pensacola Bay. By preserving architecture from early Spanish settlements, the city earns points for retaining the influence of these early explorers. The downtown district is compact and unique, plus there's the city's Naval Air Museum and its nearby beaches.

Pensacola.

2 The Emerald Coast. The Eglin Air Force Base and adjoining nature reserve span thousands of square miles of Gulf Coast land, and they don't plan to surrender it anytime soon. Miles of shoreline between Pensacola and Destin is nearly void of development, and farther east even the urban areas like Panama City Beach, Seaside, and Apalachicola have beaches that are well preserved and inviting.

Tallahassee, Supreme Court Building.

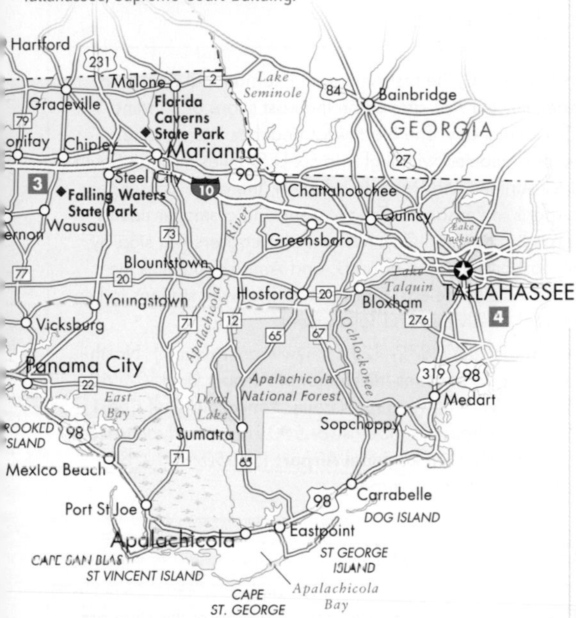

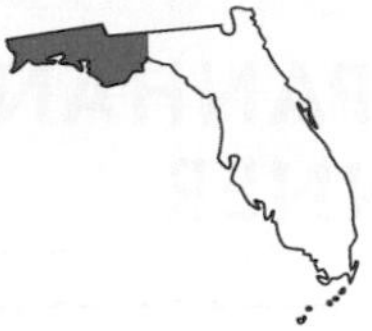

GETTING ORIENTED

The Panhandle is a large area, and the lack of sufficient air service can make it tough to access. However, two major east–west routes will introduce you to some fantastic back roads and waterfront drives. From Tallahassee, U.S. 90 is an early byway that roughly parallels its modern cousin, Interstate 10, but goes through small Old Florida towns like Marianna, Chipley, and DeFuniak Springs on its way to Pensacola. From Pensacola, U.S. 98 generally skirts along the Gulf of Mexico through seaside towns and communities like Fort Walton Beach, Destin, Panama City Beach, Seaside, and Apalachicola.

3 Inland Towns. The shoreline gets most tourist business, so the areas north are lightly trafficked, giving this region great appeal and access to Old Florida's small towns, quiet roads, rolling hills, and deep forests.

4 Tallahassee. In the state capital you can see the old and new capitols, visit the state's historical museum, attend an FSU football game, watch the famous FAMU Marching 100, and go for a country ride down canopied roads.

Pensacola Seville Historical District.

THE PANHANDLE PLANNER

When to Go

Peak season is Memorial Day to Labor Day, with another spike during spring break. Inland, especially in Tallahassee, high season is during the fall (football) and March to April. Vendors, attractions, and other activities will be in full swing in the summer. There's a "secret season" that falls around October and November. Things quiet down as students go back to school, but restaurants and attractions keep normal hours and the weather is moderate.

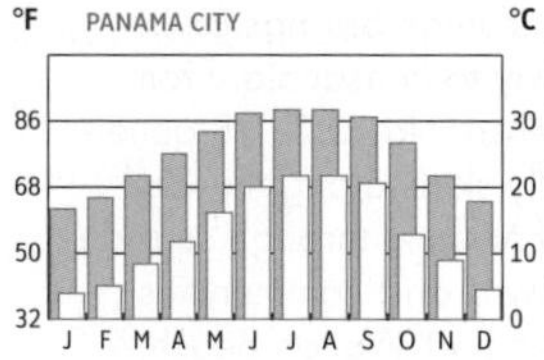

Crab cakes.

Getting Here

In May 2010, the first American international airport to open since 1995 arrived on the east shore of Panama City's West Bay. The Northwest Beaches International Airport debuted with flights to six U.S. cities through Southwest Airlines and Delta. In addition, there are passenger airports in Pensacola, Tallahassee, and a smaller county airport in Panama City. Many major carriers will stop by at least one of these airports, and Amtrak connects the Panhandle to the east and west coasts, with stations in Pensacola, Crestview, and Tallahassee.

Amtrak (☎ *800/872–7245* 🌐 *www.amtrak.com*). **Northwest Florida Beaches International Airport** (☎ *850/763–6751* 🌐 *www.newpcairport.com*). **Pensacola Gulf Coast Regional Airport** (☎ *850/436–5005* 🌐 *www.flypensacola.com*). **Tallahassee Regional Airport** (☎ *850/891–7800* 🌐 *www.talgov.com/airport*).

Getting Around

The main east–west arteries across the top of the state are Interstate 10 and U.S. 90. Interstate 10 can be monotonous, but U.S. 90 piques your interest by routing you along the main streets of several county seats. U.S. 98 snakes eastward along the coast, splitting into 98 and 98A at Inlet Beach before rejoining at Panama City and continuing on to Port St. Joe and Apalachicola. The view of the gulf from U.S. 98 can be breathtaking, especially at sunset. If you need to get from one end of the Panhandle to the other in a timely manner, drive inland to Interstate 10, where the speed limit runs as high as 70 mph in places. Major north–south highways that weave through the Panhandle are (from east to west) U.S. 231, U.S. 331, Route 85, and U.S. 29. From U.S. 331, which runs over a causeway at the east end of Choctawhatchee Bay between Route 20 and U.S. 98, the panorama of barge traffic and cabin cruisers on the twinkling waters of the Intracoastal Waterway will get your attention.

2

About the Restaurants

An abundance of seafood is served at coastal restaurants: oysters, crab, shrimp, scallops, and a variety of fish. Of course, that's not all there is on the menu. This part of Florida still impresses diners with old-fashioned comfort foods such as meat loaf, fried chicken, beans and cornbread, okra, and fried green tomatoes. You'll also find small-town seafood shacks where you can dine "Florida Cracker"–style on deep-fried mullet, cheese grits, coleslaw, and hush puppies. Restaurants, like resorts, vary their operating tactics off-season, so call first if visiting during winter months.

About the Hotels

Many of the lodging selections here revolve around extended-stay options: resorts, condos, and time-shares that allow for a week or more in simple efficiencies, as well as fully furnished homes. There are also cabins, such as the ones that rest between the dunes at Grayton Beach. In any case, these are great for families and get-togethers, allowing you to do your own housekeeping and cooking and explore the area without tour guides. Local visitors bureaus often act as clearinghouses for these types of properties, and you can also search online for vacation rentals. On the coast, but especially inland, the choices seem geared more toward mom-and-pop motels in addition to the usual line of chain hotels.

During the summer and over holiday weekends, always reserve ahead for top properties.

Assume that hotels operate on the European Plan (EP, no meals), unless we specify that they use the Breakfast Plan (BP, with full breakfast), Continental Plan (CP, Continental breakfast), Full American Plan (FAP, all meals), or Modified American Plan (MAP, breakfast and dinner), or are all-inclusive (AI, all meals and most activities).

WHAT IT COSTS

	¢	$	$$	$$$	$$$$
Restaurants	under $10	$10–$15	$15–$20	$20–$30	over $30
Hotels	under $80	$80–$100	$100–$140	$140–$220	over $220

Restaurant prices are per person for a main course at dinner. Hotel prices are for a standard double room, excluding 6% sales tax (more in some counties) and 1%–4% tourist tax.

Top Festivals

SPRING

Springtime Tallahassee. Held in late March or early April, the capital city's major cultural event has handmade works, stages with entertainment, and a crowd-pleasing parade. ☎ *850/224–5012* 🌐 *www.springtimetallahassee.com.*

Pensacola Jazzfest. Gyrate to the sounds of America's indigenous musical form during this early April event downtown. ☎ *850/433–8382* 🌐 *www.Jazzpensacola.com.*

FALL

Destin Fishing Rodeo. Anglers young and old compete in offshore and inshore categories throughout October. ☎ *850/837–6734* 🌐 *www.destinfishingrodeo.org.*

Pensacola Seafood Festival. Fried, broiled, battered, grilled, or served gourmet—the fish options abound at this September event in downtown Pensacola. And while that's the main course, side dishes to this family-friendly festival are arts and crafts, cooking demonstrations, children's activities, and live entertainment. ☎ *850/433–6512* 🌐 *www.fiestaoffiveflags.org/seafoodfestival.*

WINTER

Florida Seafood Festival. Apalachicola celebrates the oyster harvest with oyster-shucking and -eating contests. ☎ *888/653–8011* 🌐 *www.floridaseafoodfestival.com.*

PANHANDLE BEACHES

Pensacola Beach has soft sand perfect for playing in.

Not every stretch of Florida coastline features great beaches; some have rough sands, others may find you contending with rocks, mud, and stingrays when you wade in. What's appealing about the Panhandle—especially the Emerald Coast—are beaches that are marked by soft, powdery sands and clear, clean water.

About 20 quiet beach communities are clustered along Route 30A, which breaks off U.S. 98 east of Sandestin and runs along the water for more than 17 mi before rejoining with U.S. 98. Here, sugar-white, quartz-crystal sands and emerald-green waters make for some of the finest stretches of sand and sea in the country. Known as the Beaches of South Walton, many of these beaches are little more than a wide spot in the road, and all are among the least known and least developed in the Gulf Coast area, even though Grayton Beach, near Route 283, is regularly ranked among the country's top 20 beaches.

WHEN TO GO

The Panhandle beaches are best visited in the summer months. In late summer and fall, jellyfish can be a problem. Florida's Gulf Coast beaches also have to occasionally endure annoying red-tide algae that can make breathing difficult and cause itchy eyes. For current status on red tide in the area, go to 🌐 *www.myfwc.com*, the home page for Florida's Fish and Wildlife Research Institute.

THE PANHANDLE'S BEST BEACHES

PENSACOLA BEACH

Here you get miles of perfect beach and a convenient location, fringed by a commercial district and just over the bridge from Pensacola itself. Even though it was smacked by Hurricane Ivan and some homes will never be rebuilt, it's part of the Gulf Island National Seashore, and the stretch around Santa Rosa Island to the west and Opal Beach to the east gives you plenty of room to roam, especially with the reopening of CR 399, which is pleasantly absent of development. Just east of Pensacola Beach, it's a lovely stretch of nothing but sand and some convenient pull-outs. All in all, the beaches here provide a nice balance that blends privacy and accessibility, as well as passive lounging and active beach recreation. The sand is white and soft, and water adventures include scuba diving (explore the sunken *USS Oriskany*), fishing (the Pensacola Fishing Pier is 1,471 feet long!), kayaking, sailing, wave runners, surfing, and swimming. The water temperatures are in the 80s in the summer and in the 60s in the winter. For shopping, there's the Quietwater Beach Boardwalk.

GRAYTON BEACH

This area will take you back to Old Florida, where there were no condos, no strip malls, and no beach concessions. Instead, there's a state park that has preserved the area and its sea oats and miles of walking trails for a laid-back time in the outdoors. The park has even added cabins (sans telephones and televisions), so you can experience Florida's Gulf Coast in its natural state. There are big dunes, camping, ample bird watching and wildlife viewing, and on-the-water activities like canoeing, fishing, sailing, and swimming. It may be too slow-paced for kids, but just right for adults who want to ditch the schedule and get into the rhythm of nature.

PANAMA CITY BEACH

If your visit to the Panhandle is based purely on beach access and activities, then this is where you want to be. Granted, Front Beach Road can get crowded, but parallel roads can move you up and down the coast fairly swiftly. Then again, once you check into your condo or hotel you may never need to hit the road. Instead, plant yourself by the pool, which is usually no more than a few feet away from the Gulf waters—reached by stepping over the softest and whitest sands in the state. Paradise. A popular family retreat most times, families tend to steer clear during spring break, when it gets a bit crazy, but arrive in droves in the summer. For a peaceful excursion, arrive in the winter. You won't be able to swim, but the views are still splendid.

By Gary McKechnie

Florida's thin, green, northwest corner snuggles up between the Gulf of Mexico and the Alabama and Georgia state lines. The Panhandle is sometimes called "the other Florida," since in addition to palm trees, what thrives here are the magnolias, live oaks, and loblolly pines common in the rest of the Deep South. As South Florida's season is winding down in May, action in the northwest is just picking up. Part of the area is even in a different time zone: the Apalachicola River marks the dividing line between eastern and central time.

Until World War II, when activity at the Panhandle air bases took off, this section of the state was little known and seldom visited. But by the mid-1950s, the 100-mi stretch along the coast between Pensacola and Panama City was dubbed the Miracle Strip because of a dramatic property value rise. In the 1940s this beachfront land sold for less than $100 an acre; today that same acre can fetch hundreds of thousands of dollars. To convey the richness of the region, with its white sands and sparkling green waters, swamps, bayous, and flora, public-relations pros ditched the Redneck Riviera moniker that locals had created and coined the phrase Emerald Coast.

Politicians, developers, and community advocates haggle continuously over waterfront development, but as pro-growth realities meet the realities of the recession, the Panhandle remains, for the time being, a land of superlatives: it has the biggest military installation in the Western Hemisphere (Eglin Air Force Base), many of Florida's most glorious white-sand beaches, and the most productive fishing waters in the world (off Destin). It has glitzy resorts, campgrounds where possums and deer invite themselves to lunch, and every kind of lodging in between. Students of the past can wander the many historic districts or visit archaeological digs, while nature lovers can hunt, canoe, bike, and hike. And

2

GREAT ITINERARIES

3 DAYS

Visit **Grayton Beach** and **Seaside** and take advantage of some of Florida's finest beaches. On Day 2 drive to the capital, **Tallahassee,** and soak up some of the state's past. On Day 3, make a trip to nearby **Edward Ball Wakulla Springs State Park,** where you'll find one of the world's deepest springs—perfect for sightseeing (the pontoon-boat tour is a must) and swimming.

5 DAYS

Start with **Tallahassee.** Check out the local sights, including the state capitol, the Tallahassee Historic Trail, and Alfred B. Maclay Gardens State Park. Take another day to head west on Interstate 10, visiting **Falling Waters State Park** in Chipley in the morning and then exploring the cool, dark caves of the **Florida Caverns State Park** in Marianna in the afternoon when things heat up. On Day 3, head south out of Tallahassee toward **Edward Ball Wakulla Springs State Park,** where you can explore the spectacular springs either with a mask and snorkel or from inside a glass-bottom boat. In the afternoon, head down to **St. Marks National Wildlife Refuge and Lighthouse** to hike, swim, or have a leisurely picnic. Eventually make your way to the coast and take U.S. 98 west toward Apalachicola, where you can spend a day wandering around the historic downtown area and the waterfront. Set aside Day 5 for exploring **St. George Island.**

most anything that happens on water happens here, including scuba diving and fishing, from deep-sea charter boats or the end of a pier.

EXPLORING THE PANHANDLE

There are sights in the Panhandle, but sightseeing is not the principal activity here. It's better known for its rich history, military presence, and ample fishing and diving, and for being a spot to simply relax.

A good place to start your trek through northwest Florida is the region's and state's westernmost city, Pensacola. After viewing its antebellum homes, historic landmarks, and museum exhibits, head east on coastal U.S. 98 to Fort Walton Beach, the Emerald Coast's largest city, and on to neighboring Destin, where sportfishing is king. Continuing along the coast, there are a dozen or so family-friendly communities collectively known as the Beaches of South Walton. This is where you'll find some of the Panhandle's newest, most luxurious developments, such as WaterColor and Seaside, where luxury meets modern seaside chic in smartly designed vacation homes and intimate inns. The next resort center along the coast is Panama City Beach, and to the far southeast is historic Apalachicola, the Panhandle's oyster-fishing capital. Just to the south, St. George Island, a 28-mi-long barrier island bordered by the gulf and Apalachicola Bay, has vacation homes on one end and a pristine state park on the other.

Inland, a number of towns lie along Interstate 10, which crosses the historic Suwannee River on its long eastward trek from Jacksonville to the state capital, Tallahassee. If you want a more scenic route, take U.S. 90. This less traveled, original, two-lane back road takes you directly through the cute communities of Quincy, Marianna, DeFuniak Springs, Crestview, and Milton.

AROUND PENSACOLA BAY

In the years since its founding, Pensacola has come under the control of five nations, earning this old Southern city its nickname, the City of Five Flags. Spanish conquistadors, under the command of Don Tristan de Luna, landed on the shores of Pensacola Bay in 1559, but discouraged by a succession of destructive tropical storms and dissension in the ranks, de Luna abandoned the settlement two years after its founding. In 1698 the Spanish again established a fort at the site, and during the early 18th century control jockeyed between the Spanish, the French, and the British. Finally, in 1821, Pensacola passed into U.S. hands, although during the Civil War it was governed by the Confederate States of America and flew yet another flag. Across the bay lies Pensacola Beach on Santa Rosa Island, an area that has almost fully recovered from the devastation caused by Hurricane Ivan in 2004.

PENSACOLA

59 mi east of Mobile, Alabama via I–10.

Historic Pensacola consists of three distinct districts—Seville, Palafox, and North Hill—though they are easy to explore as a unit. Stroll down streets mapped out by the British and renamed by the Spanish, such as Cervantes, Palafox, Intendencia, and Tarragona. An influx of restaurants and bars has brought new nightlife to the historic districts, but one-way streets can make navigation a bit tricky, especially when it's dark. In recent years, the biggest change in town came courtesy of Mother Nature. In late 2004, Hurricane Ivan blew through, downing many of the town's stately oak trees, severely damaging countless homes and commercial properties, washing out bay-front roadways and a stretch of Interstate 10, and scaring the heck out of residents. The Pensacola Bay area has made great strides rebuilding paradise after Ivan's hit-and-run, but to this day recovery efforts continue. One example of urban renewal is at the southern terminus of Palafox Street—the $2.9 million Plaza DeLuna, a 2-acre park with open grounds, interactive water fountains, and an amphitheater. A quiet place to sit and watch the bay, fish, or enjoy the city's Thursday-evening sunset celebration, the park occupies the former site of the Bayfront Auditorium, which was wrecked by Ivan and razed in July 2005.

GETTING HERE AND AROUND

Pensacola Regional Airport has dozens of daily flights and is served by AirTran, American Airlines (American Eagle), Continental, Delta, Northwest, and US Airways. From the Pensacola Regional Airport via Yellow Cab it costs about $14 to go downtown or about $32 to Pensacola Beach. In Pensacola and Pensacola Beach, Escambia County Area Transit provides regular citywide bus service ($1.75), downtown trolley routes, tours through the historic districts, and free summer trolley service to the beach from mid-May to Labor Day on Friday, Saturday, and Sunday evenings as well as Saturday afternoons.

ESSENTIALS

Transportation Contacts **Escambia County Area Transit** (*ECAT* ☎ *850/595-3228* 🌐 *www.goecat.com*). **Pensacola Regional Airport** (☎ *850/436-5005* 🌐 *www.flypensacola.com*). **Yellow Cab** (☎ *850/433-3333*).

Visitor Information **Pensacola Visitor Information Center** (✉ *1401 E. Gregory St.* ☎ *850/434-1234 or 800/874-1234* 🌐 *www.visitpensacola.com*).

EXPLORING

TOP ATTRACTIONS

Fodor's Choice ★ **Pensacola Naval Air Station.** Locals almost unanimously suggest this as *the* must-see attraction of Pensacola. As you drive near it, don't be alarmed if you're suddenly struck with the shakes—they're probably caused by the U.S. Navy's Blue Angels' aerobatic squadron buzzing overhead. This is their home base, and they practice maneuvers here on Tuesday and Wednesday mornings at 8:30 from March to November. The Naval Air Station's bleachers hold about 1,000 people and they fill up fast, so get here early. Then stay late—the pilots stick around after the show to shake hands and sign autographs. During the show, cover your ears as the six F/A 18s blast off in unison for 45 minutes of thrills and skill. Watching the Blue Angels practice their aerobatics is one of the best "free" shows in all of Florida (your tax dollars are already paying for these jets).

Within the Pensacola Naval Air Station, the 300,000-square-foot **National Museum of Naval Aviation** (☎ *850/452-3604*) has examples of more than 140 aircraft that played important roles in aviation history. Among them are the NC-4, which in 1919 became the first plane to cross the Atlantic; the famous World War II fighter the F-6 *Hellcat;* and the Skylab Command Module. Other attractions include an atomic bomb (it's defused, we promise), *Mercury* and *Apollo* capsules, and the restored Cubi Bar Café—a very cool former airmen's club transplanted here from the Philippines. Relive the morning's maneuvers in the 14-seat motion-based simulator as well as an IMAX theater playing *Fighter Pilot, The Magic of Flight,* and other educational films such as *Straight Up (helicopters)* and *Hurricane on the Bayou.* ✉ *1750 Radford Blvd.* ☎ *850/453-2389, 800/327-5002, 850/453-2024 IMAX theater* 🌐 *www.navalaviationmuseum.org* 🎟 *Free, IMAX film $8, two films for $13* ⏲ *Daily 9-5.*

Seville Square Historic District. Established in 1559, this area is the site of Pensacola's first permanent Spanish colonial settlement, which beat St. Augustine's by six years. Its center is Seville Square, a live-oak-shaded park bounded by Alcaniz, Adams, Zaragoza, and Government streets. Roam these brick streets past honeymoon cottages and homes set in an oak-filled parklike setting. Many of the buildings have been converted into restaurants, commercial offices, and shops that overlook broad Pensacola Bay and coastal road U.S. 98, which you'll use to access the Gulf Coast and beaches. Within the Seville Square Historic District is the **Historic Pensacola Village,** a complex of several museums and historic homes whose indoor and outdoor exhibits trace the area's history back 450 years. The **Museum of Industry** (✉ *200 E. Zaragoza St.*), in a late-19th-century warehouse, is home to permanent exhibits dedicated to the lumber, maritime, and shipping industries—once mainstays of Pensacola's economy. A reproduction of a 19th-century streetscape is displayed in the **Museum of Commerce** (✉ *201 E. Zaragoza St.*). Also in the village are the **Julee Cottage** (✉ *210 E. Zaragoza St.*), the "first home owned by a free woman of color," **1871 Dorr House** (✉ *311 S. Adams St.*), and French-Creole **Lavalle House** (✉ *205 E. Church St.*).

Strolling through the area gives you a good (and free) look at many architectural styles, but to enter some of the buildings you must purchase an all-inclusive ticket at the Village gift shop in the Tivoli High House—which was once in the city's red-light district but now is merely a calm reflection of a restored home. Opt for the guided tour (11 AM, 1 PM, and 2:30 PM), and you'll experience the history of Pensacola as you visit the 1805 Lavalle House, the 1871 Dorr House, Old Christ Church, and the 1890s Lear-Rocheblave House. Tours last approximately 90 minutes to two hours. For information on home and museum tours within the district, contact Historic Pensacola Village. *Tivoli High House* ✉ *205 E. Zaragoza St.* ☎ *850/595–5985* 🌐 *www.historicpensacola.org* 🎟 *$6 includes tour and Wentworth Museum* ⏲ *Mon.–Sat. 10–4.*

T. T. Wentworth, Jr. Florida State Museum. Even if you don't like museums this is worth a look. Housed in the elaborate, Renaissance revival–style former city hall, it has an interesting mix of exhibits illustrating life in the Florida Panhandle over the centuries. One presentation you'll want to see is the City of Five Flags, which provides a nice introduction to Pensacola's history. Mr. Wentworth was quite a collector (as well as a politician and salesman), and his eccentric collection includes a mummified cat (creepy) and the size 37 left shoe of Robert Wadlow, the world's tallest man (not creepy, but a really big shoe). A wide range of both permanent and traveling exhibits include a rare collection of dollhouses, Black Ink (a look at African-Americans' role in printing), Hoops to Hips (a review of the fashion history), Civil War exhibits, and a kid-sized interactive area with a ship and fort that kids can play in and pretend to be colonial Pensacolans. ✉ *330 S. Jefferson St.* ☎ *850/595–5990* 🌐 *www.historicpensacola.org* 🎟 *Free* ⏲ *Mon.–Sat. 10–4.*

WORTH NOTING

North Hill Preservation District. Pensacola's affluent families, many made rich in the turn-of-the-20th-century timber boom, built their homes in this area where British and Spanish fortresses once stood. Residents still occasionally unearth cannonballs in their gardens. North Hill occupies 50 blocks, with more than 500 homes in Queen Anne, neoclassical, Tudor revival, and Mediterranean styles. Take a drive through this community, but remember these are private residences. Places of general interest include the 1902 Spanish mission–style **Christ Episcopal Church**; **Lee Square,** where a 50-foot obelisk stands as a tribute to the Confederacy; and **Fort George,** an undeveloped parcel at the site of the largest of three forts built by the British in 1778.

Palafox Historic District. Palafox Street is the main stem of historic downtown Pensacola and the center of the Palafox Historic District. The commercial and government hub of Old Pensacola is now an active cultural and retail district. Note the opulent Spanish Renaissance–style **Saenger Theater,** Pensacola's 1925 movie palace, which now hosts performances by the local symphony and opera, and the **Bear Block,** a former wholesale grocery with wrought-iron balconies that are a legacy from Pensacola's Creole past. On Palafox between Government and Zaragoza streets is a **statue of Andrew Jackson** that commemorates the formal transfer of Florida from Spain to the United States in 1821. While in the area, stop by Veterans Memorial Park, just off Bayfront Parkway near 9th Avenue. The ¾-scale replica of the Vietnam Memorial in Washington, D.C., honors the more than 58,000 Americans who lost their lives in the Vietnam War.

TOP GUN

The National Museum of Naval Aviation is one of only two locations nationwide that feature "Top Gun," four real F-14 military flight-training simulators with all the actual controls. Experience mock air-to-air combat, practice carrier landings, or simply cruise over Las Vegas, Iraq, Miramar, California, and other simulated sites during a 20-minute joyride. The $25 experience includes "cockpit orientation training."

Pensacola Museum of Art. Pensacola's city jail once occupied the 1906 Spanish revival–style building that is now the secure home for the museum's permanent collection of paintings, sculptures, and works on paper by 20th- and 21st-century artists—and we do mean secure: you can still see the actual cells with their huge iron doors. Traveling exhibits have focused on photography (Wegman, Leibovitz, Ansel Adams), Dutch masters, regional artists, and the occasional art-world icon, such as Andy Warhol or Salvador Dalí. ✉ *407 S. Jefferson St.* ☎ *850/432–6247* 🌐 *www.pensacolamuseumofart.org* 🎫 *$5, free Tues.* 🕒 *Tues.–Fri. 10–5, weekends noon–5.*

SPORTS AND THE OUTDOORS

CANOEING AND KAYAKING

Adventures Unlimited (✉ *Rte. 87* ☎ *850/623–6197 or 800/239–6864* 🌐 *www.adventuresunlimited.com*), on Coldwater Creek, rents light watercraft as well as campsites and cabins along the Coldwater and Blackwater rivers in the Blackwater State Forest. Canoe season lasts roughly from March through mid-November, but it rents year-round. Canoe and kayak rentals for exploring the Blackwater River—the purest sand-bottom river in the nation—are available from **Blackwater Canoe Rental** (✉ *6974 Deaton Bridge Rd., Milton* ☎ *850/623–0235 or 800/967–6789* 🌐 *www.blackwatercanoe.com*), northeast of Pensacola off Interstate 10 Exit 31.

DIVING

It's called the "Mighty O," but it was formerly known as the **USS *Oriskany*** (☎ *850/455–7702* 🌐 *www.mbtdivers.com*). The retired aircraft carrier was sunk 24 mi off the Pensacola Pass in 2006, and now the superstructure is the world's largest artificial reef. The "island" is accessible just 67 feet down, and the flight deck can be reached at 137 feet.

FISHING

For a full- or half-day deep-sea charter, try the **Beach Marina** (✉ *655 Pensacola Beach Blvd.* ☎ *877/650–3474 or 850/932–0304* 🌐 *www.pensacolabeachmarina.net*), which represents several charter outfits. Bottom fishing is best for amberjack and grouper, offshore trolling trips are searching for tuna, wahoo, and sailfish, and inshore charters are out to hook redfish, cobia, and pompano. For a complete list of local fishing charters, visit 🌐 *www.visitpensacola.com.*

GOLF

There are several outstanding golf courses in and around Pensacola, with the fees listed *below* reflecting a wide range that changes with the season. **The Club at Hidden Creek** (✉ *3070 PGA Blvd., Navarre* ☎ *850/939–4604* 🌐 *www.hiddengolf.com*) is an 18-hole course in Santa Rosa County, 20 mi from Pensacola; greens fee $20/$53 (with cart). **Lost Key Golf Club** (✉ *625 Lost Key Dr., Perdido Key Beach* ☎ *850/492–1300* 🌐 *www.lostkey.com*), a public, par-71, 18-hole Arnold Palmer Signature Design Course, was the first golf course in the world to be certified as an Audubon International Silver Signature Sanctuary; greens fee $40/$84 (with cart). **The Moors Golf Club** (✉ *3220 Avalon Blvd., Milton* ☎ *850/994–2744* 🌐 *www.moors.com*) is a public, 18-hole, par-70, Scottish links–style course designed by John LaFoy; greens fee $42/$52. The **Perdido Bay Golf Club** (✉ *1 Doug Ford Dr., Pensacola* ☎ *850/492–1223* 🌐 *www.perdidobaygolf.com*) has a well-kept 18-hole course; greens fee $29/$45 (with cart).

NIGHTLIFE AND THE ARTS

NIGHTLIFE

Hub Stacey's (✉ *312 E. Government St.* ☎ *850/469–1001* 🌐 *www.hubstaceys.com*), on the corner by Seville Square, is the friendly neighborhood local pub with 55 types of bottled beer, sidewalk tables, and a good vibe. **McGuire's Irish Pub** (✉ *600 E. Gregory St.* ☎ *850/433–6789* 🌐 *www.mcguiresirishpub.com*) is a restaurant and microbrewery that welcomes those of Irish descent, or anyone else who enjoys cold home-brewed ales, beers, or lagers. Its 8,500-bottle wine cellar includes vintages ranging from $14–$20,000. If you want a quiet drink, steer clear on Friday and Saturday nights—or when Notre Dame games are televised. Country-music lovers head to **Mesquite Charlie's** (✉ *5901 N. W St.* ☎ *850/434–0498*), with all the Western trappings. **New York Nick's** (✉ *9–11 S. Palafox St.* ☎ *850/469–1984* 🌐 *www.newyorknicks.net*) is a sports bar, rock-and-roll club, shrine to Bruce Springsteen, and popular downtown bar and grill. It's an "A+" spot for all the best "B's" in life—beer, billiards, burgers, and the Boss.

In the heart of the Historic District, the **Seville Quarter** (✉ *130 E. Government St.* ☎ *850/434–6211* 🌐 *www.rosies.com*) is Pensacola's equivalent of New Orleans's French Quarter. In fact, you may think you've traveled to Louisiana when you enter any of its nine rooms, seven bars, and two courtyards that offer disco, Motown acts, blues bands, and rockabilly trios—you name it. College students pack the place on Thursday, tourists come on the weekend, and military men and women from six nearby bases are stationed here nearly all the time. A classic Pensacola nightspot.

2

THE ARTS

The restored 1925 **Saenger Theatre** (✉ *118 S. Palafox St.* ☎ *850/595–3880* 🌐 *www.pensacolasaenger.com*) presents touring Broadway shows and concerts by **Pensacola's Symphony Orchestra** (☎ *850/435–2533* 🌐 *www.pensacolasymphony.com*).

WHERE TO EAT

$$$ ECLECTIC ✕ **Dharma Blue.** Geographically speaking, this trendy spot is in downtown Pensacola (on leafy Seville Square), but its cuisine is all over the map. The menu roams from Asia (sushi and spring-roll appetizers) to Italy (pan-fried chicken) to Mexico (lime-roasted chicken quesadilla) to the American South (fried-green-tomato club sandwich)—and wanders around to other dishes like blackened mahimahi, grilled duck breast, and peach-barbecue-glazed pork tenderloin. For dinner try tomato-crusted grouper with caper-cream sauce, the fish of the day (blackened, grilled, or tempura-fried), or Guinness-marinated sirloin with chipotle aioli. Dine inside under a collection of Southern folk art, or outside under café umbrellas and droopy oaks. ✉ *300 S. Alcaniz St.* ☎ *850/433–1275* 🌐 *www.dharmablue.com* 💳 *AE, MC, V* ⏲ *No lunch Sun.*

$$$ SEAFOOD ✕ **Fish House.** Come one, come all, come hungry, and come at 11 AM to witness the calm before the lunch storm. By noon the Fish House is packed with Pensacola's professionals, power players, and poseurs, all waiting for tables and the fresh fish brought in on the docks steps away. The wide-ranging menu of fish dishes is the bait, and each can be served in a variety of ways: ginger-crusted, grilled, blackened, pecan-crusted, or Pacific-grilled, which puts any dish over the top. The attentive service, bay front setting, and signature "Grits a Ya-Ya" dish (fresh gulf shrimp on a bed of smoked Gouda-cheese grits smothered with a portobello mushroom sauce) keeps diners in the net. Steaks, delicious homemade desserts, a sushi bar, more than 300 varieties of wine, and a full-service bar don't hurt the extraordinary popularity of this restaurant either. The hot-ticket table is one out on the deck at sunset. ✉ *600 South Barracks St.* ☎ *850/470–0003* 🌐 *www.fishhousepensacola.com* 💳 *AE, MC, V.*

$$ ECLECTIC ✕ **Global Grill.** When you have an appetite that begs for variety, consider this trendy yet friendly downtown Pensacola tapas restaurant. Come hungry and fill your eyes, plate, and belly from the selection of 48 different tapas, 11 entrées, and eight salads. Among the tapas are the high-demand quick-fried calamari with garlic-squash fries, the spicy seared tuna with five-pepper jelly, or the pork empanadas with cucumber cream. Wear an elastic waistband, because you may be tempted to try the 40-some others. To jazz things up, entrées have been added as well, with filet mignon, gulf shrimp, duck breast, grouper, salmon, and New York strip competing with the light appetizers. A perfect candidate to be franchised. ✉ *27 S. Palafox* ☎ *850/469–9966* 🌐 *www.dineglobalgrill.com* 💳 *AE, MC, V, D* ⏲ *Closed Sun. and Mon.*

$$$ IRISH ✕ **McGuire's Irish Pub.** Since 1977 this authentic Irish pub has promised its patrons "feasting, imbibery, and debauchery" seven nights a week. A sense of humor pervades the place, evidenced by the range of prices on hamburgers—$10–$100 depending on whether you want it topped with cheddar or served with caviar and champagne. Beer is brewed on the premises, and the wine cellar has more than 8,500 bottles. Menu items

Like an Old West town with a Victorian twist, historic Pensacola is eye candy for architecture buffs.

include corned beef and cabbage, great steaks, and a hickory-smoked prime rib. In an old firehouse, the pub is replete with antiques, moose heads, Tiffany-style lamps, and Erin-go-bragh memorabilia. As for the "richness" of the decor—on the walls and ceiling are nearly $800,000 in bills signed and dated by "Irishmen of all nationalities." ✉ *600 E. Gregory St.* ☎ *850/433–2849 or 850/433–6789* 🌐 *www.mcguiresirishpub.com* 💳 *AE, D, DC, MC, V.*

WHERE TO STAY

$$$ **Crowne Plaza–Pensacola Grand Hotel.** On the site of the restored historic Louisville & Nashville (L&N) railroad passenger depot, the Crowne Plaza has a rich heritage that remains: a 15-story glass tower, attached to the train depot by a glass atrium, guest rooms with all new furniture, and incredible views of historic Pensacola. Bi-level penthouse suites have whirlpool baths. **Pros:** great location near downtown; amenities perfect for business travelers. **Cons:** it's a box; there are more intimate choices closer to downtown. ✉ *200 E. Gregory St.* ☎ *850/433–3336 or 800/348–3336* 🌐 *www.pensacolagrandhotel.com* *200 rooms, 10 suites* *In-room: refrigerator, Wi-Fi. In-hotel: restaurant, bar, pool, gym* 💳 *AE, D, DC, MC, V.*

$$–$$$ ★ **New World Inn.** If you like your inns small, warm, and cozy, with the bay on one side and a short two-block walk to the downtown historic area on the other, then this is the inn for you. A complete room makeover was completed in 2007, with new bedding, carpeting, and wallpaper reflecting five periods of Pensacola's past: French and Spanish provincial, early American, antebellum, and Queen Anne. Several rooms have four-poster mahogany beds, and the rooms are large and

comfortable, but the old-style furnishings might benefit from a little new-world dusting. The lobby's collection of signed portraits of famous (and formerly famous) guests is a hoot. The cozy bar has a tapas menu, and a Continental breakfast is provided. **Pros:** perfect location downtown; unique boutique hotel. **Cons:** could use a spring cleaning atop the room renovations. ✉ *600 S. Palafox St.* ☎ *850/432–4111* 🌐 *www.newworldlanding.com* *14 rooms, 1 suite* *In-room: Wi-Fi. In-hotel: bar* *AE, MC, V* *CP.*

2

$$–$$$ **Residence Inn by Marriott.** In the downtown bay-front area this immaculately kept all-suites hotel is perfect for extended stays, whether for business or pleasure. The location is ideal for exploring Pensacola's historic streets on foot—rooms in the back have views of the bay—and families will especially appreciate the extra sleeper sofa, fully equipped kitchens, and free grocery delivery. Breakfast and evening social hour are complimentary. **Pros:** self-serve meal and dining options make a family retreat easier. **Cons:** ordinary hotel style. ✉ *601 E. Chase St.* ☎ *850/432–0202* 🌐 *www.marriott.com* *78 suites* *In-room: kitchen, refrigerator. In-hotel: tennis court, pool, gym, some pets allowed* *AE, D, DC, MC, V.*

PENSACOLA BEACH

5 mi south of Pensacola via U.S. 98 to Rte. 399 (Bob Sikes) Bridge.

After Hurricane Opal tore across this skinny barrier island in 1995 the damaged areas were redeveloped, sand was brought in to fill the eroded beachfront, and beach facilities and parking were added to what came to be known as the "Opal Day Use Area," named in honor of the hurricane responsible for the destruction. A local bartender even invented a potent but short-lived concoction called a "Raging Opal" to commemorate the storm.

It's doubtful, however, that any public parks or cocktails will be named after Hurricane Ivan, which devastated the area in 2004. The Category 4 storm wasn't an event that anyone around here cares to remember. The storm's tidal surge washed completely over the island in several places, and the obvious reminders of Ivan's visit—washed-out roads, devastated homes, uprooted lives, and erased sand dunes—are still visible and may well be for years to come.

Since the national media focused its attention on Pensacola Beach for not much longer than it took the storm to do its damage, the scope of the disaster might come as a surprise to many visitors: nearly half of the island's homes were destroyed; all of the island's hotels were closed for months (some never reopened); and the miles of sea-oat-covered, pristine dunes that protected the island from winter storms and gave the area its laid-back Florida look were leveled in hours. In short, Pensacola Beach was a city changed.

But locals here know the post-hurricane drill: dig in, dig out, and move on. Several hotels have reopened after complete renovations; homes and condos have been demolished or are being rebuilt; and city and state crews made significant progress in reconnecting roads to areas of the island rendered inaccessible by the storm. The biggest grand opening came when the main road that reaches historic Fort Pickens was cleared after several years of being buried under tons of sand. The other grand opening came in April 2009, when a lovely stretch of County Road 399 reopened to give travelers heading east a pristine seaside ride for the 15 blissfully undeveloped miles between Pensacola Beach and Navarre—one of the finest strands of sand in Florida.

EXPLORING

Fort Pickens. Constructed of more than 21 million locally made bricks, this fort dating back to 1834 once served as a prison for Apache chief Geronimo. A National Park Service plaque describes the complex as a "confusing jumble of fortifications," but the real attractions here are the beach, nature exhibits, a large campground, an excellent gift shop, and breathtaking views of Pensacola Bay and the lighthouse across the inlet. It's the perfect place for a picnic lunch and a bit of history, too. ✉ *At the western tip of the island, Ft. Pickens Rd.* ☎ *850/934–2635* *$8 per car* *Daily 7–sunset.*

SPORTS AND THE OUTDOORS

BEACH

At **Opal Beach Day Use Area** (✉ *Rte. 399, 5 mi east of Pensacola Beach*) there are barbecue areas, covered picnic facilities, and restrooms, along with a pristine coastline.

FISHING

The 1,471-foot-long **Pensacola Beach Gulf Pier** (✉ *41 Ft. Pickens Rd.* ☎ *850/934–7200* *www.fishpensacolabeachpier.com* *Observers $1.25, fishing $7.50*) touts itself as the longest pier on the Gulf of Mexico. This peerless pier hosts serious anglers who find everything they'll need here—from pole rentals to bait—to land that big one, but those looking to catch only a beautiful sunset are welcome, too. Check the pier's Web site for the latest reports on what's biting.

WHERE TO EAT

$$ SEAFOOD **Flounder's Chowder and Ale House.** The wide and peaceful gulf spreads out before you at this casual restaurant where, armed with a fruity libation, you're all set for a night of "floundering" at its best. Funkiness comes courtesy of an eclectic collection of objets d'art; tastiness is served in specialties such as seafood nachos and the shrimp-boat platter. Most signature dishes are charbroiled over a hardwood fire, and to cater to those who love the sea but not seafood, the extensive menu reveals more choices. Live entertainment is presented every night in season, with performances limited to weekends off-season. ✉ *800 Quietwater Beach Blvd.* ☎ *850/932–2003* *www.flounderschowderhouse.com* *AE, D, MC, V.*

THE EMERALD COAST

On U.S. 98, several towns, each with its own personality, are strung along the shoreline from Pensacola southeast to St. George Island. The side-by-side cities of Destin and Fort Walton Beach seemingly merge into one sprawling destination and continue to spread as more condominiums, resort developments, shopping centers, and restaurants crowd the skyline each year. The view changes drastically—and for the better—farther along the coast as you veer off 98 and enter Route 30A, the main coastal road that leads to a quiet stretch known as the Beaches of South Walton. Here building restrictions prohibit high-rise developments, and the majority of dwellings are privately owned homes, most of which are available to vacationers.

Continuing southeast on U.S. 98, you'll find Panama City Beach, whose "Miracle Strip," once crammed with carnival-like amusement parks, junk-food vendors, T-shirt shops, and go-kart tracks, has been nearly replaced by up-to-date shopping and entertainment complexes and new condos that have given the area a much-needed face-lift. Farther east, past the up-and-coming sleeper cities of Port St. Joe and Mexico Beach, you'll come to the quiet blue-collar town of Apalachicola, Florida's main oyster fishery. Watch oystermen ply their trade, using long-handled tongs to bring in their catch. Cross the Apalachicola Bay via the Bryant Patton Bridge to St. George Island. This unspoiled 28-mi-long barrier island offers some of America's most scenic beaches, including St. George Island State Park, which has the longest beachfront of any state park in Florida.

GETTING HERE AND AROUND

Northwest Florida Regional Airport in North Eglin on Highway 85 is served by American Airlines (American Eagle), Delta (Delta Connection), Continental (Continental Express), US Airways, and Northwest. From here you can take a number of car and cab services, including Checker Cab, to destinations such as Fort Walton Beach ($18) or Destin ($24).

ESSENTIALS

Transportation Contacts Northwest Florida Regional Airport (☎ *850/651–7160* 🌐 *www.flyvps.com*). **Checker Cab** (☎ *850/650–8294*).

Visitor Information Emerald Coast Convention and Visitors Bureau (☎ *850/651–7131 or 800/322–3319* 🌐 *www.destin-fwb.com*).

FORT WALTON BEACH

46 mi east of Pensacola via U.S. 98.

This coastal town dates from the Civil War but had to wait more than 75 years to come into its own. Patriots loyal to the Confederate cause organized Walton's Guard (named in honor of Colonel George Walton, onetime acting territorial governor of West Florida) and camped at a site on Santa Rosa Sound, later known as Camp Walton. In 1940 fewer than 90 people lived in Fort Walton Beach, but within a decade the city became a boomtown, thanks to New Deal money for roads and bridges and the development of Eglin Field during World War II. The military is now Fort Walton Beach's main source of income, but tourism runs a close second. Despite the inland sprawl of the town, independent merchants have created a cute little shopping district along U.S. 98.

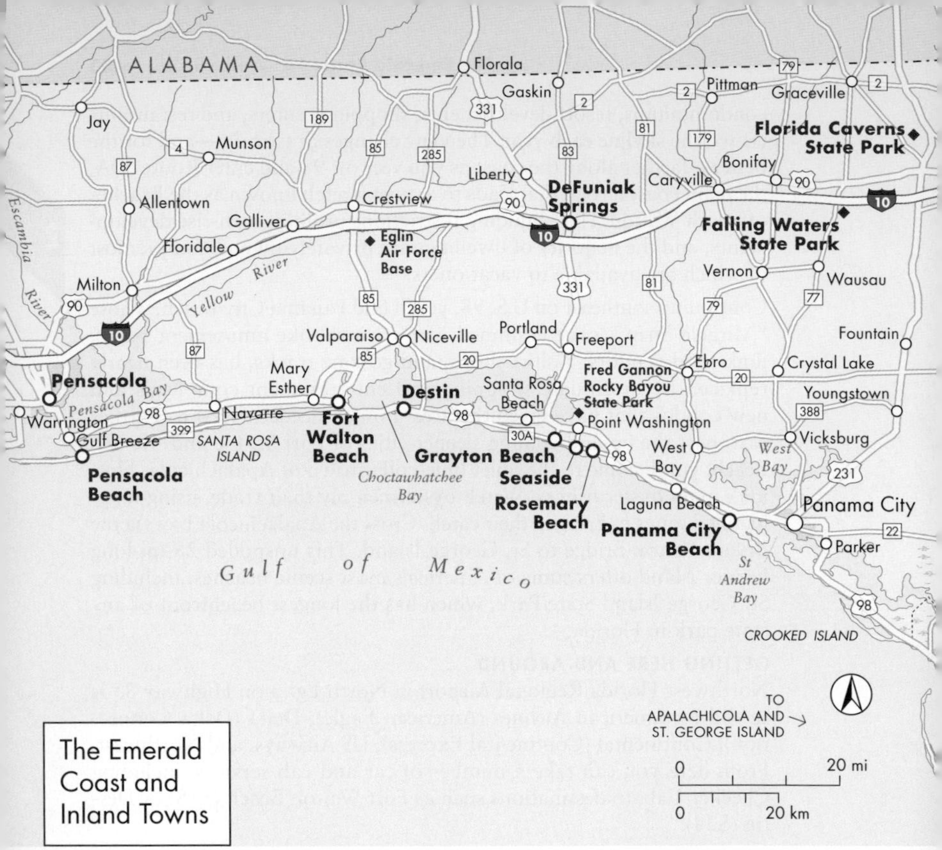
ALABAMA
Florala
Gaskin
Pittman
Graceville
Jay
Munson
Florida Caverns State Park
Bonifay
Liberty
DeFuniak Springs
Caryville
Allentown
Crestview
Galliver
Eglin Air Force Base
Falling Waters State Park
Floridale
Yellow River
Vernon
Wausau
Milton
Escambia River
Valparaiso
Niceville
Portland
Freeport
Fountain
Pensacola
Mary Esther
Destin
Santa Rosa Beach
Fred Gannon Rocky Bayou State Park
Ebro
Crystal Lake
Youngstown
Pensacola Bay
Warrington
Navarre
Fort Walton Beach
Point Washington
Gulf Breeze
SANTA ROSA ISLAND
Grayton Beach
Seaside
West Bay
Vicksburg
Pensacola Beach
Choctawhatchee Bay
Rosemary Beach
Laguna Beach
Panama City Beach
Panama City
Parker
Gulf of Mexico
St Andrew Bay
CROOKED ISLAND
TO APALACHICOLA AND ST. GEORGE ISLAND
0
20 mi
0
20 km
The Emerald Coast and Inland Towns

EXPLORING

★ **Air Force Armament Museum.** The collection at this museum just outside the Eglin Air Force Base's main gate contains more than 5,000 armaments (aka missiles, bombs, and aircraft) from World Wars I and II and the Korean and Vietnam wars. Included are uniforms, engines, weapons, aircraft, and flight simulators. You can't miss the museum—there's a squadron of aircraft including a B-17 Flying Fortress, an SR-71 Blackbird, a B-52, a B-25, and helicopters parked on the grounds in front. A continuously playing 32-minute movie, *Arming the Future*, features current weapons and Eglin's history and its role in their development. ✉ *100 Museum Drive (Rte. 85), Eglin Air Force Base* ☎ *850/651–1808* 🌐 *www.afarmamentmuseum.com* 🎫 *Free* ⏲ *Mon.–Sat. 9:30–4:30.*

Gulfarium. Opened in 1955, this is the oldest continuously operating marine park in Florida. In the style of several modest oceanographic attractions, it tosses in an assortment of sea life–themed shows and exhibits. Its main attraction is the Living Sea, a 60,000-gallon tank that simulates conditions on the ocean floor, and there are campy performances by trained porpoises, plus sea-lion shows and marine-life exhibits. Among other species here are otters, penguins, alligators, harbor seals, and sharks. The old-fashioned Dolphin Reef gift shop sells anything from conch shells to beach toys. There's also the Dolphin

Meet and Greet program, in which you sit on a ledge in a pool as spotted dolphins swim up to your lap. That experience lasts about 15–20 minutes and allows you to pet and feed the dolphin, while the upgraded option, Dolphin Encounter, actually has you in the water and playing (albeit all too briefly) with a dolphin. More expensive than the Meet and Greet, it does include park admission and lasts about 30 minutes. Visit the park's Web site for details on each program. ✉ *U.S. 98 E* ☎ *850/243–9046 or 800/247–8575* 🌐 *www.gulfarium.com* 🎫 *$18.75, dolphin 'Meet and Greet' $75, Dolphin Encounter $150* ⏲ *Daily 9–4, Feb. closed Mon.–Tue.*

SPORTS AND THE OUTDOORS

Eglin Air Force Base Reservation. With 810 mi of creeks and plenty of challenging, twisting wooded trails, this 1,045-square-mi base appeals to outdoors enthusiasts, who can hunt, fish, canoe, and swim here. For $10 you can buy a day pass to camp or hike or mountain bike on the Timberlake Trail, which is open from 7 AM to 4:30 PM, Monday through Thursday. Hours may change on Friday and Saturday, so call ahead. Permits can be obtained from the **Jackson Guard** (✉ *107 Rte. 85 N, Niceville* ☎ *850/882–4164* 🌐 *www.eglin.af.mil*).

John C. Beasley Wayside Park. Resting tranquilly atop the dunes is Fort Walton Beach's seaside playground on Okaloosa Island. Across the dunes, a boardwalk leads to the beach, where there are a dozen covered picnic tables, pavilions, changing rooms, and freshwater showers. Lifeguards are on duty in summer. ✉ *Okaloosa Island* ☎ *No phone.*

FISHING

Don't miss a chance to go out to the end of the ¼-mi-long **Okaloosa Island Pier** (☎ *850/244–1023* 🌐 *www.okaloosaislandpier.com*). It costs only a buck to walk the plank, $7 if you'd like to fish (you can buy bait and tackle, and rent poles).

GOLF

The **Fort Walton Beach Golf Club** (✉ *Rte. 189* ☎ *850/833–9528*) is a 36-hole municipal course whose links (Oaks and Pines) lie about 400 yards from each other. The two courses are considered by many to be among Florida's best public layouts; greens fee $32/$43 (with a shared cart). **Shalimar Pointe Country Club** (✉ *302 Country Club Dr., Shalimar* ☎ *850/651–1416* 🌐 *www.shalimarpointe.com*) has 18 holes with a pleasing mix of water and bunkers; greens fee $29/$45 (with cart).

NIGHTLIFE AND THE ARTS

NIGHTLIFE

The Boardwalk (✉ *1450 Miracle Strip Pkwy.*) is a massive dining and entertainment complex at the entrance to the Okaloosa Island Pier and includes several restaurants (Crab Trap Seafood and Oyster House, Floyd's Shrimp House, and Angler's) as well as an assortment of nightclubs. On the Boardwalk, **Howl at the Moon** (☎ *850/301–0111*), a Tuesday through Sunday–only dueling piano bar, waives the cover charge and offers furious sing-alongs that make this one of Fort Walton's most popular evening entertainment spots. The show starts at 8 PM, and rocks every night until 2. In Destin, **Nightown** (✉ *140 Palmetto St.* ☎ *850/837–7625* 🌐 *www.nightown.com*) is the largest dance club in northwest Florida. It provides two clubs under one roof, a mighty generous 14,000-square-foot lighted dance floor, a beach bar, live music, pool tables, plenty of drink specials and themed evenings—and it stays open seven nights a week until 4 AM.

WHERE TO EAT

$$ AMERICAN ✕ **Angler's.** Unless you sit in the water, you can't dine any closer to the gulf than at this casual beachside bar and grill next to the Gulfarium. Located at the entrance to Okaloosa Island Pier (and within a complex of other nightclubs and restaurants), Angler's houses the requisite sports bar with a million or more televisions (in the elevators and bathrooms even) broadcasting an equal number of sports events. Outside, a volleyball net tempts diners onto the sands. Snack on nachos and quesadillas or sample the fresh-catch dishes such as king crab and prawns or try Anglers Elizabeth, a fish fillet with shrimp, crabmeat, and hollandaise sauce. A perfect waterfront setting captures your image of a picturesque Gulf Coast eatery. ✉ *1030 Miracle Strip Pkwy. SE* ☎ *850/796–0260* 🌐 *www.anglersbeachside.com* ▬ *AE, D, MC, V.*

$$$ STEAK ★ ✕ **Pandora's Steakhouse and Lounge.** On the Emerald Coast the name Pandora's is synonymous with prime rib. Steaks are cooked over a wood-burning grill, and you can order your prime rib regular or extra-thick cut; fish aficionados should try the char-grilled yellowfin tuna or one of the daily specials. Cozy up in an alcove to enjoy your meal in peace or head to the lounge, where the mood turns a bit more gregarious with live entertainment Wednesday through Saturday. ✉ *1226 Santa Rosa Blvd.* ☎ *850/244–8669* 🌐 *www.pandorassteakhouse.com* ▬ *AE, D, DC, MC, V* ⏲ *Closed Mon.*

$$$ AMERICAN ✕ **Staff's.** Reputed to be Florida's oldest family-owned restaurant, this garage-turned-eatery for steaks and seafood dishes like Florida lobster and char-grilled amberjack has been attracting folks since 1913 folks. Also on the chock-full menu are items including seafood gumbo with okra, grouper, soft-shell crabs, scallops, and oysters. The grand finale is a trip to the delectable dessert bar; try a generous wedge of cherry cheesecake. Sip a Tropical Depression or a rum-laced Squall Line while you peruse a menu tucked into the centerfold of a tabloid-size newspaper filled with snippets of local history and family memorabilia, including cute bathing-beauty pix of the family's 1920 all-girl swim team. An even grander finale may be stopping in the quite authentic "Margaritaville-style" neighborhood lounge that features a pool table and a true Old Florida vibe. Don't miss it. ✉ *24 Miracle Strip Pkwy. SE* ☎ *850/243–3482* 🌐 *www.staffrestaurant.com* ▬ *AE, D, MC, V.*

WHERE TO STAY

$$ **Aunt Martha's Bed and Breakfast.** Although it was created in 2001, Aunt Martha's can transport you back half a century to when Florida was still a sleepy little state. Placed smack dab on the banks of Santa Rosa Sound and just a few steps from Staff's restaurant, its location is private and its atmosphere is neat as a pin. Five rooms feature floor-to-ceiling windows, a baby-grand piano is poised to be played, and a library is stocked for guests. In the morning, the pampering continues with an old-fashioned Southern breakfast. **Pros:** quiet sanctuary on the waterfront but with access to dining, shopping, and sites. **Cons:** not suited

for kids and families; primarily for romance and privacy. ✉ *315 Shell Ave. SE* ☎ *850/243–6702* 🌐 *www.auntmarthasbedandbreakfast.com* *5 rooms* *In-hotel: laundry service* 💳 *AE, D, MC, V.*

$$–$$$ **Ramada Plaza Beach Resort.** If your family loves the water, splash down at this beachside extravaganza. Activity here revolves around a 194,000-gallon pool (allegedly the area's largest) with a separate grotto pool and bar and spectacular swim-through waterfall that tumbles down from an island oasis; there's also a separate kiddie pool, a beachwear and beach-toy shop, as well as an 800-foot private beach. It's a popular spot for conventions, spring break, and families on a budget: there's no charge for additional guests under 18, and roll-away beds are only an extra $10 per night. For an extra-special evening, book an odd-numbered room between 1133 and 1143—the back door of each opens right into the pool. **Pros:** extravagant offerings for a family-friendly vacation—the pool may please the kids more than the gulf. **Cons:** may be too busy for romance travelers or seniors seeking peace and quiet. ✉ *1500 Miracle Strip Pkwy. SE* ☎ *850/243–9161 or 800/874–8962* 🌐 *www.ramadafwb.com* *309 rooms, 26 suites* *In-room: refrigerator. In-hotel: restaurant, bars, pools, gym, beachfront* 💳 *AE, D, DC, MC, V.*

DESTIN

8 mi east of Fort Walton Beach via U.S. 98.

Fort Walton Beach's "neighbor" lies on the other side of the strait that connects Choctawhatchee Bay with the Gulf of Mexico. Destin takes its name from its founder, Leonard A. Destin, a Connecticut sea captain who settled his family here sometime in the 1830s. For the next 100 years Destin remained a sleepy little fishing village until the strait, or East Pass, was bridged in 1935. Then recreational anglers discovered its white sands, blue-green waters, and abundance of some of the most sought-after sport fish in the world. More billfish are hauled in around Destin each year than from all other gulf-fishing ports combined, giving credence to its nickname, the World's Luckiest Fishing Village.

But you don't have to be the rod-and-reel type to love Destin. There's plenty to entertain the sand-pail set as well as senior citizens, and there are many nice restaurants, which you'll have an easier time finding if you remember that the main drag through town is referred to as both U.S. 98 and Emerald Coast Parkway. The name makes sense, but part of what makes the gulf look so emerald in these parts is the contrasting whiteness of the sand on the beach. Actually, it's not sand—it's pure, powder-soft Appalachian quartz that was dropped off by a glacier a few thousand years back. Since quartz doesn't compress (and crews clean and rake the beach each evening), your tootsies get the sole-satisfying benefit of soft, sugary "sand." Sand so pure it squeaks.

ESSENTIALS

Visitor Information Destin Chamber of Commerce (☎ *850/837–6241* 🌐 *www.destinchamber.com*).

Billfish, like the large blue marlin, are easy to find off Destin's coast and a favorite catch of sportfishers.

EXPLORING

Big Kahuna's Lost Paradise. The seasonal water park is the big draw here, with the Honolulu Half-pipe (a perpetual surfing wave), flume rides, steep and slippery slides, and assorted other methods of expending hydro-energy appealing to travelers who prefer freshwater thrills over the gulf (which is just across the street). This complex also has year-round family-friendly attractions: 54-hole miniature golf course, two go-kart tracks, an arcade, thrill rides for kids of all ages, and an amphitheater. ✉ *U.S. 98 E* ☎ *850/837–4061* 🌐 *www.bigkahunas.com* 🎟 *Grounds free, water park $37, miniature golf $6.39, go-karts $6.34, combination ticket (water park, golf, and two go-kart tickets) $56* ⏲ *Water park: early May–Memorial Day, weekends 10–5; Memorial Day–mid-Sept., daily 10–10.*

SPORTS AND THE OUTDOORS

FISHING

Destin has the largest charter-boat fishing fleet in the state. You can also pier-fish from the 3,000-foot-long Destin Catwalk and along the East Pass Bridge. **Adventure Charters** (✉ *East Pass Marina, 288 U.S. 98 E* ☎ *850/654–4070* 🌐 *www.destinfishingservice.com*) represents more than 90 charter services that offer deep-sea, bay-bottom, and light-tackle fishing excursions. **Destin Dockside** (✉ *East Pass Marina, 288 U.S. 98 E* ☎ *850/837–2622*) sells bait, tackle, and most anything else you'd need for a day of fishing. **Harbor Walk Marina** (✉ *66 Harbor Blvd., U.S. 98 E* ☎ *850/337–8250* 🌐 *www.harborwalk-destin.com*) is a rustic-looking waterfront complex where you can get bait, gas, tackle, food, and anything else you might need for a day of fishing. Party-fishing-boat excursions cost as little as $65, a cheaper alternative to chartering or renting your own boat.

GOLF

The **Indian Bayou Golf Club** (✉ *1 Country Club Dr. E, off Airport Rd., off U.S. 98* ☎ *850/837–6191* 🌐 *www.indianbayougolf.com*) has a 27-hole course; greens fee $55/$75 (with cart). The 18-hole **Kelly Plantation Golf Club** (✉ *307 Kelly Plantation Dr.* ☎ *850/650–7600* 🌐 *www.kellyplantationgolf.com*), designed by Fred Couples and Gene Bates, is a semiprivate course that runs along Choctawhatchee Bay; greens fee $59/139 (with cart). There's an 18-hole, semiprivate course at **Regatta Bay Golf and Country Club** (✉ *465 Regatta Bay Blvd.* ☎ *850/337–8080* 🌐 *www.regattabay.com*); greens fee $59/$129. For sheer number of holes, the **Sandestin Golf and Beach Resort** (✉ *9300 U.S. 98 W* ☎ *850/267–8211* 🌐 *www.sandestin.com*) tops the list, with 72. There are four courses, and peak fees are as follows (although prices change monthly): **Baytowne Golf Club at Sandestin,** greens fee: $85; **Burnt Pines Course,** greens fee: $135; **Links Course,** greens fee: $65; and the **Raven Golf Club,** greens fee: $125.

SCUBA DIVING

Although visibility here isn't on par with the reefs of the Atlantic Coast, local divers can explore artificial reefs, wrecks, and a limestone shelf. The views are about 50 feet and diving depths up to 90 feet. Take diving lessons, arrange excursions, and rent all the necessary equipment at **Emerald Coast Scuba** (✉ *502 Harbor Blvd.* ☎ *850/837–0955 or 800/222–0955* 🌐 *www.divedestin.com*). The specialty at **The Scuba Shop** (✉ *348 SW Miracle Strip Pkwy. No. 19* ☎ *850/243–1600* 🌐 *www.thescubashopfwb.com*) is wreck diving. It is closed on Tuesday and Wednesday.

SHOPPING

Don't call it a mall. **Destin Commons** (✉ *Mid-Bay Bridge and U.S. 98* ☎ *850/337–8700* 🌐 *www.destincommons.com*) is an "open-air lifestyle center." More than 70 high-end specialty shops are here, as well as a 14 screen theater, Hard Rock Cafe, a miniature train and a nautical theme park for kids. Encompassed with the community of Sandestin is the **Market at Sandestin** (✉ *9300 Emerald Coast Pkwy. W, Sandestin* ☎ *850/267–8092*) which has about two dozen upscale shops that peddle such goods as expensive chocolates and designer clothes in an elegant minimall in a courtyard setting. **Silver Sands Factory Stores** (✉ *10562 Emerald Coast Pkwy. W* ☎ *850/654–9771* 🌐 *www.silversandsoutlet.com*) is one of the Southeast's largest retail designer outlets. More than 100 shops sell top-name merchandise.

NIGHTLIFE

Folks come by boat and car to **AJ's Club Bimini** (✉ *116 U.S. 98 E* ☎ *850/837–1913* 🌐 *www.ajs-destin.com*), a supercasual bar and restaurant overlooking the marina. Nightly live music means young, lively crowds pack the dance floor. Affiliated with Pensacola's Dharma Blue, **Harbor Docks** (✉ *538 U.S. 98 E* ☎ *850/837–2506* 🌐 *www.harbordocks.com*) is another favorite with the local seafaring set. Here since 1979, the incredibly casual feel is marked by picnic tables and hibachi grills,

Destin's first sushi bar, and live music Thursday through Saturday. **Hog's Breath Saloon** (✉ *541 U.S. 98 E* ☎ *850/837–5991*) has a counterpart in Key West, but the feeling here is much the same as you'd find in Margaritaville. The festive atmosphere is enhanced by a solo performer during the week and more musicians showing up on the weekend to present good live music. The food—steaks, burgers, salads—isn't bad, either.

WHERE TO EAT

¢ SEAFOOD ✕ **Another Broken Egg Café.** Even though it moved to a new location in the Palm Shopping Center in late 2009, you can still find the café by following the line to this local-favorite breakfast and lunch retreat. This is the kind of restaurant you crave when you're on the road, where each morning starts with platters of pancakes, waffles, and French toast with special twists like blackberry grits and more than a dozen styles of omelet, including the "Hey Ricky," a Spanish omelet with avocado slices, green chilies, and onions. Crowded—and for a reason. ✉ *979 Hwy 98 (Harbor Blvd.)* ☎ *850/650–0499* ▭ *AE, D, MC, V* ⊙ *No dinner. Closed Mon.*

$$$ SEAFOOD ★ ✕ **Marina Café.** A harbor view, impeccable service, and sophisticated fare create one of the finest dining experiences on the Emerald Coast. The ocean motif is expressed in shades of aqua, green, and sand accented with marine tapestries and sea sculptures. The chef calls his creations contemporary Continental, offering diners a choice of thick USDA steaks, classic Creole, Mediterranean, or Pacific Rim dishes. One regional specialty is the popular pan-seared yellow-edge grouper with a blue-crab-meat crust. A special sushi menu is available, the wine list is extensive, and happy hour runs from 5 to 7. ✉ *404 U.S. 98 E* ☎ *850/837–7960* 🌐 *www.marinacafe.com* ▭ *AE, D, DC, MC, V* ⊙ *No lunch.*

WHERE TO STAY

$$–$$$ ★ **Bluewater Bay Resort.** A nice find that offers vacation rentals ranging from motel rooms to villas to patio homes, the resort is also popular for its 36 holes of championship golf (on courses designed by Jerry Pate and Tom Fazio). This upscale resort is 12 mi north of Destin via the Mid-Bay Bridge, on the shores of Choctawhatchee Bay. Tennis courts are privately owned, but you can use them for a special rate. **Pros:** variety is the spice here; many rooms have kitchens or kitchenettes for a self-sufficient stay. **Cons:** on the bay, not the gulf, so you'll have to drive to the seaside. ✉ *1940 Bluewater Blvd., Niceville* ☎ *850/897–3613 or 800/874–2128* 🌐 *www.bwbresort.com* *23 rooms, 22 suites* *In-hotel: restaurant, bar, golf course, tennis courts, pools* ▭ *AE, D, DC, MC, V.*

$$$–$$$$ Fodor's Choice ★ **Sandestin Golf and Beach Resort.** It's almost a city in itself and certainly its own little world with shopping, charter fishing, spas, salons, tennis, water sports, golf, and special events. Newlyweds, conventioneers, and families all find their fit in this 2,400-acre resort with accommodations spread across five areas: beachfront, beachside, village, bay side, and dockside. Each of the five neighborhood clusters offers a unique locale with villas, cottages, condominiums, boat slips, and an inn. All rooms have a view, either of the gulf, Choctawhatchee Bay, a golf course, a lagoon, or a natural wildlife preserve. This resort accommodates an assortment of tastes, from the simple to the extravagant (dial-up to

Continued on page 68

GONE FISHIN'

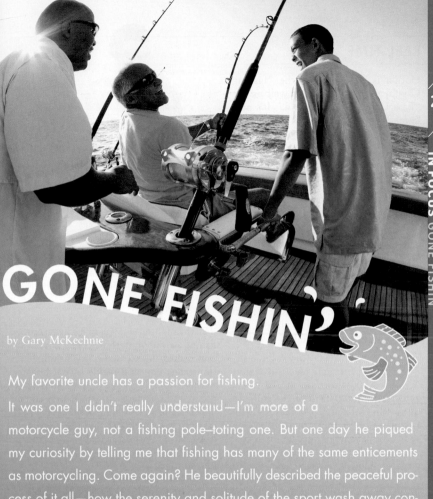

by Gary McKechnie

My favorite uncle has a passion for fishing. It was one I didn't really understand—I'm more of a motorcycle guy, not a fishing pole–toting one. But one day he piqued my curiosity by telling me that fishing has many of the same enticements as motorcycling. Come again? He beautifully described the peaceful process of it all—how the serenity and solitude of the sport wash away concerns about work and tune him into the wonder of nature, just like being on a bike (minus the helmet and curvy highways).

I took the bait, and early one morning a few weeks later, my Uncle Bud and I headed out in a boat to a secluded cove on the St. Johns River near DeLand. We'd brought our rods, line, bait, and tackle—plus hot chocolate and a few things to eat. We didn't need much else. We dropped in our lines and sat silently, watching the fog hover over the water. There was a peaceful stillness as we waited (and waited) for the fish to bite. There were turtles sunning themselves on logs and herons perched in the trees. We waited for hours for just a little nibble. I can't even recall now if we caught anything, but it didn't matter. My uncle was right: it was a relaxing way to spend a Florida morning.

REEL TIME

Florida is recognized as the "Fishing Capital of the World" as well as the "Bass Capital of the World." It's also home to some of the nation's most popular crappie tournaments.

Florida and fishing have a bond that goes back to thousands of years before Christ, when Paleo-Indians living along Florida's rivers and coasts were harvesting the waters just as readily as they were harvesting the land. Jump ahead to the 20th century and along came amateur anglers like Babe Ruth, Clark Gable, and Gary Cooper vacationing at central Florida fishing camps in pursuit of bream, bluegill, and largemouth bass, while Ernest Hemingway was scouring the waters off Key West in hopes of snagging marlin, tarpon, and snapper. Florida was, and is, a sportsman's paradise.

When he wasn't writing, Ernest Hemingway loved to fish in the Florida Keys. He's shown here in Key West in 1928.

A variety of fish and plentiful waterways—7,800 lakes and 1,700 rivers and creeks, not to mention the gulf and the ocean—are just two reasons why Florida is the nation's favorite fishing spot. And let's not forget the frost-free attributes: unlike their northern counterparts, Florida anglers have yet to drill through several feet of ice just to go fishing in the wintertime. Plus, a well-established infrastructure for fishing—numerous bait and tackle shops, boat rentals, sporting goods stores, public piers, and charters—makes it easy for experts and first-time fishermen to get started. For Floridians and the visitors hooked on the sport here, fishing in the Sunshine State is a sport of sheer ease and simplicity.

An afternoon on the waters of Charlotte County in southwest Florida.

CASTING WIDE

The same way Florida is home to rocket scientists and beach bums, it's home to a diverse variety of fishing methods. What kind will work for you depends on where you want to go and what you want to catch.

From the Panhandle south to the Everglades, fishing is as easy as finding a quiet spot on the bank or heading out on freshwater lakes, tranquil ponds, spring-fed rivers, and placid inlets and lagoons.

Perhaps the biggest catches are found offshore—in the Atlantic Ocean, Florida Straits, or the Gulf of Mexico. For saltwater fishing, you can join a charter, be it a private one for small groups or a large party one; head out along the long jetties or public piers that jut into the ocean; or toss your line from the shore into the surf (known as surf casting). Some attempt a tricky, yet effective form of fishing called net casting: tossing a circular net weighted around its perimeter; the flattened net hits the surface and drives fish into the center of the circle.

Surf casting on Juno Beach, about 20 mi north of Palm Beach.

FRESHWATER FISHING VS. SALTWATER FISHING

FRESH WATER

With about 8,000 lakes to choose from, it's hard to pick the leading contenders, but a handful rise to the top: Lake George, Lake Tarpon, Lake Weohyakapka, Lake Istokpoga, Lake Okeechobee, Crescent Lake, Lake Kissimmee, Lake George, and Lake Talquin. Florida's most popular freshwater game fish is the largemouth bass. Freshwater fishermen are also checking rivers and streams for other popular catches, such as spotted bass, white bass, Suwannee bass, striped bass, black crappie, bluegill, redear sunfish, and channel catfish.

SALT WATER

The seas are filled with some of the most challenging (and tasty) gamefish in America. From piers, jetties, private boats, and charter excursions, fishermen search for bonefish, tarpon, snook, redfish, grouper, permit, spotted sea trout, sailfish, cobia, bluefish, snapper, sea bass, dolphin (the short, squat fish, not Flipper), and sheepshead.

Tarpon

DID YOU KNOW?

The Florida Keys is the Sportfishing Capital of the World. Among the bounty brought in are all kinds of tuna—blackfin, skipjack, blue, or yellowfin.

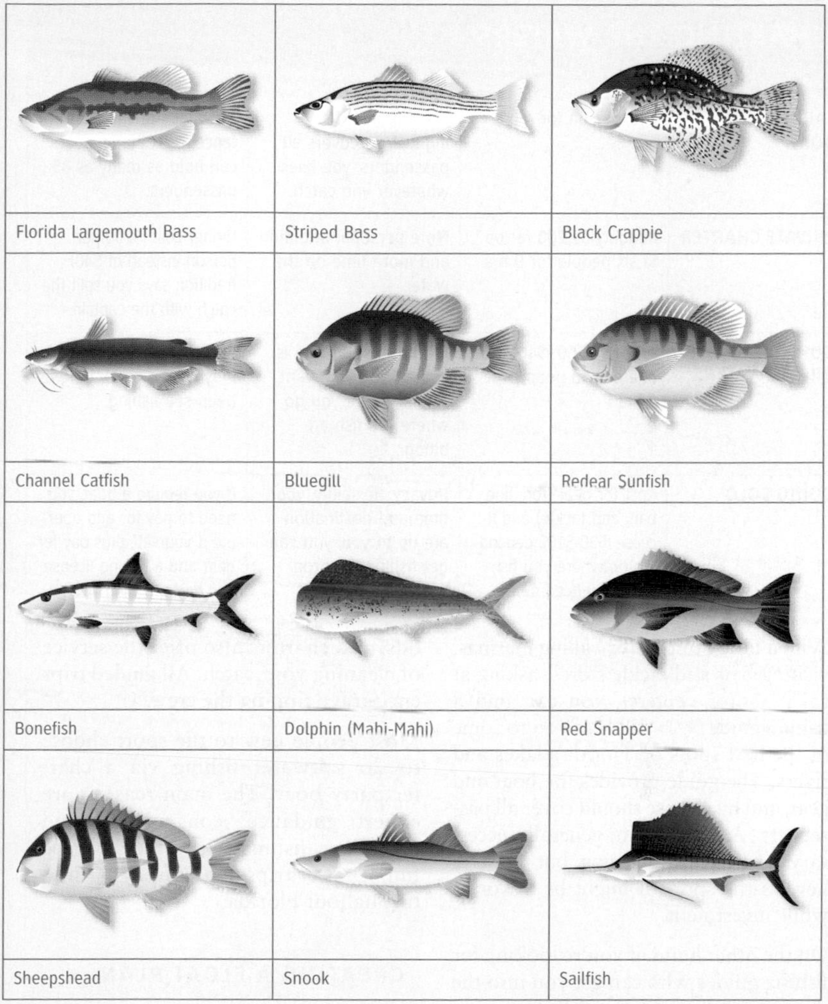
Florida Largemouth Bass
Striped Bass
Black Crappie
Channel Catfish
Bluegill
Redear Sunfish
Bonefish
Dolphin (Mahi-Mahi)
Red Snapper
Sheepshead
Snook
Sailfish

(top six) freshwater, (bottom six) saltwater

HERE'S THE CATCH

The type of fish you're after will depend on whether you fish in Florida's lake, streams, and rivers, or head out to sea. The Panhandle has an abundance of red snapper, while Lake Okeechobee is the place for bass fishing—although the largemouth bass is found throughout the state (they're easiest to catch in early spring, when they're in shallower waters). If you're looking for a good charter, Destin has the largest charter-boat fishing fleet in the nation. In the Florida Keys, you can fish by walking out in the very shallow water for hundreds of yards with the water only up to your knees; the fish you might reel in this way include bonefish, tarpon, and permit.

CHARTING THE WATERS

TYPE OF TRIP	COST	PROS	CONS
LARGE PARTY BOAT	$40/person for 4 hrs.	The captain's fishing license covers all passengers; you keep whatever you catch.	Not much privacy, assistance, or solitude: boats can hold as many as 35 passengers.
PRIVATE CHARTER	Roughly $1,200 for up to six people for 9 hrs.	More personal attention and more time on the water.	Higher cost ($200 per person instead of $40); tradition says you split the catch with the captain.
GUIDED TRIP FOR INLAND WATERS	Around $300–$400 for one or two people for 6 hrs.	Helpful if your time is limited and you want to make sure you go where the fish are biting.	Can be expensive and may not be as exciting as deep-sea fishing.
GOING SOLO	Cost for gear (rod, line, bait, and tackle) and license ($30-$100 depending on where you fish and if you need gear).	Privacy, flexibility, your time and destination are up to you; you can get fishing tips from your fellow anglers.	If you require a boat, you need to pay for and operate it yourself, plus pay for gear and a fishing license and find a fishing spot!

With a little hunting (by calling marinas, visiting bait and tackle stores, asking at town visitor centers), you can find a fishing guide who will lead you to some of the best spots on Florida's lakes and rivers. The guide provides the boat and gear, and his license should cover all passengers. A guide is not generally necessary for freshwater fishing, but if you're new to the sport, it might be a worthwhile investment.

On the other hand, if you're looking for fishing guides who can get you into the deep water for tarpon, redfish, snook, snapper, and dolphin, your best bet is to hang out at the marinas along the Florida coast and decide whether price or privacy is more important. If it's price, choose one of the larger party boats. If you'd prefer some privacy and the privilege of creating an exclusive passenger list, then sign up for a private charter. The average charter runs about nine hours, but some companies offer overnight and extended trips, too. Gear is provided in both charter-boat methods, and charters also offer the service of cleaning your catch. All guided trips encourage tipping the crew.

Most people new to the sport choose to do saltwater fishing via a charter party boat. The main reasons are expert guidance, convenience, and cost. Plus, fishing with others can be fun. Charter trips depart from marinas throughout Florida.

CREATING A FLOAT PLAN

If you're fishing in a boat on your own, let someone know where you're headed by providing a float plan, which should include where you're leaving from, a description of the boat you're on, how many are in the boat with you, what survival gear and radio equipment you have onboard, your cell phone number, and when you expect to return. If you don't return as expected, your friend can call the Coast Guard to search for you. Also be sure to have enough life jackets for everyone on board.

RULES AND REGULATIONS

To fish anywhere in (or off the coast of) Florida, you need a license, and there are separate licenses for freshwater fishing and saltwater fishing.

For non-residents, either type of fishing license cost $47 for the annual license, $30 for the 7-day one, or $17 for a 3-day license. Permits/tags are needed for catching snook ($2), crawfish/lobster ($2), and tarpon ($51.50). License and permit costs help generate funds for the Florida Fish and Wildlife Conservation Commission, which reinvests the fees into ensuring healthy habitats to sustain fish and wildlife populations, to improve access to fishing spots, and to help ensure public safety.

You can purchase your license and permits at county tax collectors' offices as well as wherever you buy your bait and tackle, such as Florida marinas, specialty stores, and sporting goods shops. You can also buy it online at 🌐 www.myfwc.com/license and have it mailed to you; a surcharge is added to online orders.

If you're on a charter, you don't need to get a license. The captain's fishing license covers all passengers. Also, some piers have their own saltwater fishing licenses that cover you when you're fishing off them for recreational purposes—if you're pier fishing, ask the personnel at the tackle shop if the pier is covered.

RESOURCES

For the latest regulations on gear, daily limits, minimum sizes and seasons for certain fish, and other fishing requirements, consult the extraordinary **Florida Fish and Wildlife Conservation Commission** (☎ 888/347–4356 🌐 www.myfwc.com).

WEB RESOURCES

Download the excellent, and free, Florida Fishing PDF at www.visitflorida.com/planning/guide. Other good sites:
www.floridafishinglakes.net
www.fishingcapital.com
www.floridasportsman.com

Wi-Fi depending on the unit you rent), but the gigantic suites at the Westwinds are a cut above the rest. Baytowne Wharf is the "downtown" of the complex and has art galleries, wine stores, and a "festival marketplace" of shops and restaurants, so once you get here, you won't need—or want—to leave. **Pros:** has everything you'd ever need in a resort—and more. **Cons:** lacks the personal touches of a modest retreat. ✉ *9300 Emerald Coast Pkwy. W* ☎ *850/267–8000 or 800/277–0800* 🌐 *www.sandestin.com* *175 rooms, 250 condos, 275 villas* *In-room: kitchen (some), refrigerator (some), Wi-Fi. In-hotel: 19 restaurants, bars, golf courses, spa, tennis courts, pools, gym, beachfront* 💳 *AE, D, DC, MC, V.*

WORD OF MOUTH

"The South Walton beaches along 30A are cooler than farther south that time of the year. Beautiful white sand, wonderful restaurants... a lot of things to do for all ages."

—Dana_M

GRAYTON BEACH

18 mi east of Destin via U.S. 98 on Route 30A.

The 26-mi stretch of coastline between Destin and Panama City Beach is referred to as the Beaches of South Walton. From the middle of this mostly residential stretch of the Panhandle you can see the monolithic condos of Destin and Panama City Beach in either direction, like massive bookends in the distance, flanking the area's low-slung, less imposing structures. A decidedly laid-back, refined mood prevails in these parts, where vacation homes go for millions and selecting a dinner spot is usually the day's most challenging decision. Accommodations consist primarily of private-home rentals, the majority of which are managed by local real estate firms. Also scattered along Route 30A are a growing number of boutiques selling everything from fine art to unique hand-painted furniture, to jewelry, gifts, and clothes.

Inland, pine forests and hardwoods surround the area's 14 dune lakes, giving anglers ample spots to drop a line and kayakers a peaceful refuge. Grayton Beach, the oldest community in this area, was founded in 1890. You can still see some of the old weathered-cypress homes scattered along narrow, crushed gravel streets. The secluded off-the-beaten-path town has been noticed with the addition of adjacent WaterColor, a high-end development of vacation homes with a stylish boutique hotel as its centerpiece. The architecture is tasteful, development is carefully regulated—no buildings taller than four stories are allowed—and bicycles and kayaks are the preferred methods of transportation. Stringent building restrictions, designed to protect the pristine beaches and dunes, ensure that Grayton maintains its small-town feel and look.

ESSENTIALS

Beaches of South Walton Visitor Information Center (☎ *850/267–1216 or 800/822–6877* 🌐 *www.beachesofsouthwalton.com*).

2

EXPLORING

Eden Gardens State Park. Scarlett O'Hara might be at home here on the lawn of an antebellum mansion amid an arcade of moss-draped live oaks in nearby Point Washington. Tours of the mansion are given every hour on the hour, and furnishings inside the spacious rooms date as far back as the 17th century. The surrounding grounds—the perfect setting for a picnic lunch—are beautiful year-round, but they're nothing short of spectacular in mid-March, when the azaleas and dogwoods are in full bloom. ✉ *Rte. 395, Point Washington* ☎ *850/231–4214* 🎫 *Gardens $3, mansion tours $3* ⏲ *Daily 8–sunset, mansion tours hourly Thurs.–Mon. 10–3.*

SPORTS AND THE OUTDOORS

Fodor's Choice ★

Grayton Beach State Park. If you want to see what Florida looked like when only Indians lived here, come to Grayton Beach State Park. One of the most scenic spots along the Gulf Coast, this 2,220-acre park is composed primarily of untouched Florida woodlands within the Coastal Lowlands region. It also has salt marshes, rolling dunes covered with sea oats, crystal-white sand, and contrasting blue-green waters. The park has facilities for swimming, fishing, snorkeling, and camping, and there's an elevated boardwalk that winds over the dunes to the beach, as well as walking trails around the marsh and into the piney woods. Notice that the "bushes" you see are actually the tops of full-size slash pines and Southern magnolias, an effect created by the frequent shifting of the dunes. Even if you are just passing by, the beach here is worth the stop. Thirty fully equipped cabins are available for rent, and in 2009 a campground loop with 24 new sites (with sewer, electric, and water) was added to give even more visitors a chance to see Old Florida (⇨ *Where to Stay*). ✉ *357 Main Park Rd., off Rte. 30A* ☎ *850/231–4210* 🌐 *www.floridastateparks.org/graytonbeach* 🎫 *$5 per vehicle, up to 8 people* ⏲ *Daily 8–sunset.*

SHOPPING

Grayton Beach House of Art (✉ *26 Logan La.* ☎ *850/231–9997* 🌐 *www.house-of-art.com*) specializes in the works of a handful of self-taught folk artists, who reveal an eclectic mix of styles and subjects, from roosters and frogs to dancers and dogs. The **Shops of Grayton** (✉ *Rte. 283 [Grayton Rd.], 2 mi south of U.S. 98* ☎ *No phone*) is a colorful complex of eight Cracker-style cottages selling gifts, artwork, and antiques.

WHERE TO EAT

$$$$
ECLECTIC
Fodor's Choice ★

✕ **Fish Out of Water.** Time your appetite to arrive at sunset and you'll witness the best of both worlds: sea oats lumbering on gold-dusted dunes outside and a stylish interior that sets new standards of sophistication for the entire Panhandle. Colorful, handblown glass accent lighting that "grows" out of the hardwood floors, plush taupe banquettes, oversize handmade lamp shades, and a sleek bar area that screams New York (complete with a cloud-white curtain wall) create an atmosphere worthy of the inventive cuisine. Influences range from Asian (Thai-style grouper with lobster-coconut broth) to Southern (Low Country shrimp and scallops with creamy grits) to classic Continental (porcini-crusted osso buco), but all are convincingly wrought and carefully presented.

If you saw the Truman Show, you may recognize several places in Seaside, where the movie was filmed.

The extensive wine list keeps pace with the menu offerings. ✉ *34 Goldenrod Circle, 2nd fl. of WaterColor Inn* ☎ *850/534–5008* 🌐 *www.watercolorinn.com* ▭ *AE, D, DC, MC, V* ⏲ *No lunch.*

$$ SEAFOOD ★ ✕ **Picolo Restaurant and Red Bar.** You could spend weeks here just taking in all the funky-junky, eclectic toy-chest memorabilia—from Marilyn Monroe posters to flags to dolls—dangling from the ceiling and tacked to every available square inch of wall. The contemporary menu is small, although it includes what you'd expect to find in the Panhandle: crab cakes, shrimp, crawfish, etc. It also serves breakfast. In season, it can seat hundreds of people a day, so expect a wait. Blues and jazz musicians play nightly in the Red Bar. You can't make up a place like this. ✉ *70 Hotz Ave.* ☎ *850/231–1008* 🌐 *www.theredbar.com* ▭ *No credit cards.*

WHERE TO STAY

$$ ★ **Cabins at Grayton Beach State Park.** Back-to-nature enthusiasts and families love to retreat to stylish accommodations set among the sand pines and scrub oaks of this pristine state park. The two-bedroom duplexes (each named after a different species of tree found in the park) sleep up to six and have tin roofs, white trim, and tropical wooden-window louvers, and the beach is a leisurely five-minute walk away via a private boardwalk. Modern conveniences include central heat and air-conditioning and full-size kitchens complete with pots and pans. Gas fireplaces, barbecue grills, and screen porches add a homey touch. How homey? There is no daily maid service, you'll need to bring your own sheets and towels, and there are no room phones or televisions. Regardless, they're often booked solid as much as 11 months in advance, so call to check for cancellations. In 2009 the property added a campground

loop with 24 new sites (with sewer, electric, and water). **Pros:** rare and welcome preservation of Old Florida; pure peace and quiet; what a gulf vacation is meant to be. **Cons:** if you're accustomed to abundant amenities, you won't find them here. ✉ *357 Main Park Rd.* ☎ *800/326–3521 for reservations* 🌐 *www.reserveamerica.com* *30 cabins* *In-room: no phone, kitchen, no TV* ▭ *AE, MC, V.*

$$$$ Fodor's Choice ★ **WaterColor Inn and Resort.** Nature meets seaside chic at this boutique property, the crown jewel of the area's latest—and largest—planned communities. Rooms are done in seashell tones with sea-blue comforters and accents; stylish armoires and desks look as natural and unfinished as driftwood. Dune-level bungalows have private courtyards with outdoor showers, whereas upper rooms have huge balconies and walk-in showers with windows overlooking the gulf so you can see the sea while you scrub—delightful! Standard rooms come with a king-size bed and a queen sleeper sofa, but consider one of the three rotunda rooms for something larger and more spectacular. Included in your room rate is one hour of canoeing, one hour of tennis, and breakfast. An extra $35 will afford you a complete beach setup—two chairs, umbrella, and towels. **Pros:** perhaps the ultimate vacation experience on the gulf; upscale and fancy. **Cons:** upscale and fancy; you may feel like it caters exclusively to Ivy Leaguers and CEOs, which might make it hard to relax. ✉ *34 Goldenrod Circle* ☎ *850/534–5000* 🌐 *www.watercolorresort.com* *60 rooms* *In-room: safe, refrigerator, Wi-Fi. In-hotel: restaurant, pool, beachfront, Internet terminal* ▭ *AE, D, DC, MC, V* *CP.*

SEASIDE AND ROSEMARY BEACH

2 mi east of Grayton Beach on Route 30A.

Seaside is a thriving planned community with old-fashioned Victorian architecture, brick streets, restaurants, retail stores—and a surfeit of art galleries. The brainchild of Robert Davis, Seaside was designed to promote a neighborly, old-fashioned lifestyle, and there's much to be said for an attractive, billboard-free village where you can park your car and walk everywhere you need to go. Pastel-color homes with white-picket fences, front-porch rockers, and captain's walks are set along redbrick streets, and all are within walking distance of the town center and its unusual cafés and shops. The community is so reminiscent of a storybook town that producers chose it for the set of the 1998 film *The Truman Show*, starring Jim Carrey.

The community has come into its own in the last few years, achieving a comfortable, lived-in look and feel that had escaped it since its founding in the late 1970s: some of the once-shiny tin roofs are starting to rust around the edges, and the foliage has completely matured, creating pockets of privacy and shade. There are also more signs of a real neighborhood with bars, record shops, and bookstores added to the mix. Still, while Seaside's popularity continues to soar, it retains a suspicious sense of *Twilight Zone* perfection that can weird out some visitors. Summer months can be crowded with the retired-CEO and prep-school-student-and-parent sets, so if you're seeking a little solitude, you might prefer visiting during the off-season—between Labor Day and Memorial Day.

About a dozen miles east down Route 30A is **Rosemary Beach**, a fledgling development that is a variation on the theme pioneered by Seaside's founders. Incidentally, between Seaside and Rosemary Beach a few other "New Urbanism"–style planned neighborhoods are trying to carve out a niche as they deal with the new reality of an enduring recession. Of these artificially realistic towns, though, Rosemary Beach seems to have a head start with a few restaurants and shops. Despite the attempts at jump-starting growth, the focus here is still on preserving the local environment (the landscape is made up completely of indigenous plants) and maintaining its small-town appeal. You can already see a nascent sense of community sprouting at the Town Green, a perfect patch of manicured lawn fronting the beach, where locals gather with their wineglasses to toast the sunset.

SPORTS AND THE OUTDOORS

OUTFITTERS A few miles from Seaside in Seagrove Beach, **Butterfly Bike & Kayak** (✉ *3657 E. Rte. 30A* ☎ *850/231–2826* 🌐 *www.butterflybikerentals.com*) rents bikes, kayaks, scooters, and golf carts and has free delivery and pickup. Consult the **Cabana Man** (☎ *850/231–5046*) for beach chairs, umbrellas, rafts, kayaks, and anything else you might need for a day at the beach. If there's no answer, just head to the beach and you'll find him (or his assistants) there.

SHOPPING

Seaside's central square and open-air market, along Route 30A, offer a number of unusual and whimsical boutiques carrying clothing, jewelry, and arts and crafts. n the heart of Seaside, there's a collection of small shops and artists' galleries in an area called Ruskin Place that has everything from toys and pottery to fine works of art.

NIGHTLIFE

Down the road at Rosemary Beach, **Courtyard Wine & Cheese** (✉ *66 Main St., Rosemary Beach* ☎ *850/231–1219* 🌐 *www.courtyardwineandcheese.com*) is a sophisticated wine bar (with free Wi-Fi) that opens onto a Tuscan-style courtyard and stocks 150 wines, fine cheeses, and artwork, too. It's closed Monday.

WHERE TO EAT

$$$$ CONTINENTAL ✕ **Bud & Alley's**. This down-to-earth beachside bistro (named for a pet cat and dog) has been a local favorite since 1986. Tucked in the dunes by the gulf, the rooftop Tarpon Club bar makes a great perch for a sunset toast (guess the exact moment the sun will disappear and win a drink). Daily salad specials are tangy introductions to such entrées as grilled black grouper, seared diver scallops with creamy grits, a marinated pork chop with sweet-potato hash browns, and a taco bar. ✉ *2236 E. Rte. 30A, Seaside* ☎ *850/231–5900* 🌐 *www.budandalleys.com* 💳 *MC, V* ⏲ *No lunch*.

$$$$ CONTINENTAL ★ ✕ **Café Thirty-A**. About a mile and half east of Seaside in a beautiful Florida-style home with high ceilings and a wide veranda, this restaurant has an elegant look—bolstered by white linen tablecloths—and impeccable service. The menu changes nightly and includes such entrées as wood-oven-roasted wild king salmon, sesame-crusted rare yellowfin tuna, and grilled Hawaiian butterfish. Even if you're not a Southerner,

you should try the appetizer of grilled Georgia quail with creamy grits and sage fritters. With nearly 20 creative varieties, the martini menu alone is worth the trip. ✉ *3899 E. Rte. 30A, Seagrove Beach* ☎ *850/231–2166* 🌐 *www.cafethirtya.com* ▭ *AE, D, DC, MC, V* ⏲ *No lunch.*

$$$ SEAFOOD ✕ **The Great Southern Cafe.** Jim Shirley, founder of Pensacola's very popular Fish House, brought Grits a Ya Ya here as well, putting this restaurant right on the town square in Seaside. Breakfast is served from 8 to 11, before the menu segues to regional fare, including gulf shrimp, Apalachicola oysters, and fresh vegetables such as collards, okra, black-eyed peas, fried green tomatoes, and sweet potatoes. Oysters and po'boys stuffed with shrimp bring a little of N'awlins to the beach. Beer and wine and a full liquor bar are here to boot. ✉ *83 Central Sq.* ☎ *850/231–7327* 🌐 *www.thegreatsoutherncafe.com* ▭ *AE, MC, V.*

WHERE TO STAY

$$$$ ★ **Seaside Cottage Rental Agency.** When residents aren't using their homes, they rent out their pricey one- to six-bedroom, porticoed, faux-Victorian cottages furnished with fully equipped kitchens, TV/VCR/DVDs, and vacuum cleaners—a perfect option for a family vacation or a large group. **Pros:** gulf breezes blowing off the water; unspoiled sugar-white beaches are a short stroll away. **Cons:** not much here for those who just want the basic comforts of a full-service hotel. ✉ *Rte. 30A, Box 4730 32459* ☎ *850/231–2222 or 866/976-6198* 🌐 *www.cottagerentalagency.com* *275 units* *In-room: a/c, kitchen, refrigerator, DVD (some), Wi-Fi (some). In-hotel: tennis courts, pools, bicycles* ▭ *AE, D, MC, V.*

PANAMA CITY BEACH

21 mi southeast of Seaside off U.S. 98.

In the early 2000s, a dizzying number of high-rises built along the Miracle Strip—about two dozen in total—led to the formation of a new moniker for this stretch of the Panhandle: the "Construction Coast." But the vast majority of the new buildings have been condominiums, not hotels, many (but certainly not all) of the older mom-and-pop motels that once gave this town its beach-resort flavor have fallen victim to the wrecking ball, and the recession has eased the threat of overdevelopment. Still, the spate of invasive growth did turn the main thoroughfare, Front Beach Road, into a dense mass of traffic that peaks in spring and between June and August when college students descend en masse from neighboring states. The bright side of the changing landscape is that many of the attractions that gave parts of this area a seedy reputation (i.e., strip joints and dive bars) were driven out and replaced by new retailers and the occasional franchise "family" restaurant or chain store.

The one constant in this sea of change, however, is the area's natural beauty that, in some areas at least, manages to excuse its gross overcommercialization. The shoreline in town is 17 mi long, so even when a mile is packed with partying students, there are 16 more where you can toss a beach blanket and find the old motels that managed to survive. What's more, the beaches along the Miracle Strip, with their powder-soft sand and translucent emerald waters, are some of the finest in the state; in one sense, anyway, it's easy to understand why so many condos are being built here.

Cabanas, umbrellas, sailboats, Wave Runners, and floats are available from any of dozens of vendors along the beach. For an aerial view, for about $30 you can strap yourself beneath a parachute and go parasailing as you're towed aloft behind a speedboat a few hundred yards offshore. And St. Andrews State Park, on the southeast end of the beaches, is treasured by locals and visitors alike. The area's incredible white sands, navigable waterways, and plentiful marine life that attracted Spanish conquistadors today draw invaders of the vacationing kind—namely families, the vast majority of whom hail from nearby Georgia and Alabama. **■TIP→ When coming here, be sure to set your sights for Panama City Beach. Panama City is its beachless inland cousin.**

GETTING HERE AND AROUND

The new Northwest Beaches International Airport opened in May 2010 on the east shore of Panama City's West Bay, with routes operated by Delta and Southwest. From the airport to the beach area, depending on the location of your hotel, it's about $15–$27 by taxi. Try Yellow Cab or Checker Cab.

When navigating Panama City Beach by car, don't limit yourself to Front Beach Road—the stop-and-go traffic will drive you nuts. You can avoid the congestion by following parallel roads like Back Beach Road and U.S. 98. Also, anywhere along this long stretch of beachfront, look for "sunrise" signs that indicate an access point to the beach—they're a treasure to find, especially when you happen across one in the midst of a quiet residential neighborhood and know that a private and quiet beach experience is just a few feet away. The Baytown Trolley serves Bay County, including downtown Panama City and the beaches ($1.25, $3 for an all-day pass).

ESSENTIALS

Transportation Contacts Baytown Trolley (*850/769–0557 www.baytowntrolley.org*). **Checker Cab** (*850/784–1115*). **Northwest Florida Beaches International Airport** (*850/763–6751 www.newpcairport.com*). **Yellow Cab** (*850/763–4691*).

Visitor Information Panama City Beach Convention and Visitors Bureau (*850/233–5070 or 800/722–3224 www.visitpanamacitybeach.com*).

EXPLORING

Gulf World Marine Park. It's certainly no SeaWorld, but with a tropical garden, tropical-bird theater, plus alligator and otter exhibits, the park is still a winner with the kids. The stingray petting pool and the shark-feeding and scuba demonstrations are big crowd pleasers, and the old favorites—performing sea lions, otters, and bottle-nosed dolphins—still hold their own. If you're really nautically minded, consider some of the specialty programs, including the Trainer for a Day program, which allows you to go behind the scenes to assist in food preparation and training sessions and make an on-stage appearance in the Dolphin Show. The $199, six-hour program includes a souvenir photo, lunch,

Get up close and personal with intriguing seashells on undeveloped Shell Island.

and a trainer T-shirt. In Swim with a Dolphin, you'll spend some time being pulled around the dolphin habitat, receive a dolphin kiss, and get a dolphin "handshake." Priced at $150, the session lasts between 75 and 90 minutes. Park admission is included with both programs. ✉ *15412 Front Beach Rd.* ☎ *850/234–5271* 🌐 *www.gulfworldmarinepark.com* 🎫 *$24* ⏲ *Late May–early Sept., daily 9–7:30; call for hrs at other times of year.*

Shipwreck Island Waterpark. Once part of the now-defunct Miracle Strip Amusement Park operation, this 6-acre water park has everything from speedy slides and tubes to the slow-moving Lazy River. Oddly enough, admission is based on height: 50 inches, $32; between 35 and 50 inches, $27; under 35 inches, free. Wear flats. ✉ *12201 Middle Beach Dr.* ☎ *850/234–0368* 🌐 *www.shipwreckisland.com* 🎫 *$32* ⏲ *Mid-Apr.–May, weekends 10:30–5; June–early Sept., daily 10:30–5.*

Fodor's Choice ★ **St. Andrews State Park.** At the southeastern tip of Panama City Beach, all at once the hotels and condos and traffic stops and there suddenly appears a pristine 1,260-acre park that includes beaches, pinewoods, and marshes. Complete camping facilities are here and a snack bar, too, as well as places to swim, pier-fish, and hike on clearly marked nature trails. Board a ferry to **Shell Island**—a 700-acre barrier island in the Gulf of Mexico with some of the best shelling between here and southwest Florida's Sanibel Island. A rock jetty creates a calm, shallow play area that is perfect for young children. Come to this spectacular park for a peek at what the entire beach area looked like before developers sank their claws into it. ✉ *4607 State Park La.* ☎ *850/233–5140* 🌐 *www.floridastateparks.org* 🎫 *$8 per vehicle, up to 8 people* ⏲ *Daily 8–5.*

SPORTS AND THE OUTDOORS

CANOEING

Rentals for a trip down Econofina Creek, known as Florida's most beautiful canoe trail, are supplied by **Econofina Creek Canoe Livery** (✉ *Strickland Rd., north of Rte. 20, Youngstown* ☎ *850/722–9032* 🌐 *www.canoeeconfinacreek.net*). Single kayaks are $35, double kayaks and canoes rent for $45. No checks or credit cards.

DIVING

Snorkeling and scuba diving are extremely popular in the clear waters here. If you have the proper certification, you can dive among dozens of ships sunk by the city to create artificial reefs. The **Panama City Dive Center** (✉ *4823 Thomas Dr., Panama City Beach* ☎ *850/235–3390* 🌐 *www.pcdivecenter.com*) offers instruction, rentals, and charters.

SHOPPING

Occupying a huge swath of land that had once been an amusement park is **Pier Park** (✉ *16230 Front Beach Rd.* ☎ *850/236–9974* 🌐 *www.discoverpierpark.com),* a very active and diverse 900,000-square-foot entertainment/shopping/dining complex that creates the downtown that Panama City Beach lacked. Anchor stores including Dillard's, JCPenney, and Target keep things active during the day, and clubs like Jimmy Buffett's Margaritaville and the 16-screen Grand Theatre keep things hopping after dark. Other stores like Ron Jon Surf Shop and a Fresh Market offer even more reason to see this vibrant and enjoyable complex.

NIGHTLIFE

Boatyard (✉ *5325 North Lagoon Dr.* ☎ *850/249–9273* 🌐 *www.boatyardclub.com*) is a multilevel, indoor-outdoor waterfront nightclub and restaurant that presents a regular lineup of bands, ranging from blues to steel drums to classic rock and beyond (DJs round out the entertainment roster).

Courtesy of spring break, Panama City Beach features one of the nation's most famous clubs, the hedonistic **Club La Vela** (✉ *8813 Thomas Dr.* ☎ *850/234–4866* 🌐 *www.clublavela.com*). While springtime finds it transformed into a whirlpool of libido, a full slate of concerts by acts that have included Aerosmith, Creed, and Ludacris, international DJs, 48 bar stations, swimming pools, a tropical waterfall, and dance halls with names like Thunderdome, Underground, Night Gallery, Rock Arena, and the Pussykat Lounge all guarantee a full-tilt party in the Panhandle.

Pineapple Willy's (✉ *9875 S. Thomas Dr.* ☎ *850/235–0928* 🌐 *www.pwillys.com*) is an eatery and bar geared to families and tourists—as well as sports fans. The signature rum drink, the Pineapple Willy, was the inspiration for its full slate of tropical drinks and the hangout's tiki attitude.

WHERE TO EAT

$$ SEAFOOD ✕ **Billy's Steamed Seafood Restaurant, Oyster Bar, and Crab House.** Join the throng of locals who really know their seafood, then roll up your sleeves and dig into some of the gulf's finest blue crabs and shrimp seasoned to perfection with Billy's special recipe. Homemade gumbo, crawfish, shrimp, crab claws, fish tacos, whole lobsters, and the day's catch as

well as sandwiches and burgers round out the menu. It's no-frills dining, but you may get a kick out of hanging out with some real Florida folks who consider table manners optional. ✉ *3000 Thomas Dr.* ☎ *850/235–2349* 🌐 *www.billysoysterbar.com* 💳 *AE, D, MC, V.*

$$$ AMERICAN ✕ **Boars Head**. An exterior that looks like an oversize thatch-roof cottage sets the mood for dining in this ersatz-rustic restaurant and tavern. Inside you'll find the dark woods and dim lighting of steak restaurants of the 1970s, which is understandable considering that Boar's Head opened in 1978. From opening day, prime rib has been the number-one people pleaser—with blackened seafood and broiled shrimp with crabmeat stuffing always a close second. Its motto: "Good food, simply prepared." ✉ *17290 Front Beach Rd.* ☎ *850/234–6628* 🌐 *www.boarsheadrestaurant.com* 💳 *AE, D, DC, MC, V* ⊗ *No lunch.*

$$$ SEAFOOD ✕ **Boatyard**. The same folks who operate Schooners on the beach side opened this larger, more stylish establishment overlooking a marina on the Grand Lagoon. For dinner, choose from the five-spice seared tuna, spicy bowtie pasta with shrimp and tasso, or the aptly named Fried Shrimp You Can't Live Without. The coconut-and-plantain-crusted grouper is a knockout, as is the pan-roasted catch with bacon, mushrooms, and grits (this is definitely the South). There are a kids' menu, an extensive wine list, a full bar, and flat-screen televisions, and the upstairs deck area is a great place to get away from the beach for a long, lazy lunch or romantic sunset dinner. Be aware that Boatyard kicks into high gear at sundown, transforming into one of the hottest nightspots in town. ✉ *5325 N. Lagoon Dr.* ☎ *850/249–9273* 🌐 *www.boatyardclub.com* 💳 *AE, D, DC, MC, V.*

$$ SEAFOOD ✕ **Schooners**. Thanks to a clientele that's mostly local, this beachfront spot—which is really tucked away down a small avenue—bills itself as the "last local beach club," and more boldly, "the best place on Earth." It's actually a perfect place for a casual family lunch or early dinner: kids can have burgers and play on the beach while Mom and Dad enjoy grown-up drinks and more substantial fare such as homemade gumbo, steak, or simply prepared seafood like crab-stuffed shrimp, gulf-fresh grouper, and grilled tuna steaks. One sign of Schooner's casual atmosphere is the ceremonial firing of the cannon when the sun disappears into the gulf, a crowd favorite that fires up an all-around good vibe. Late-night folks pile in for live music and dancing. ✉ *5121 Gulf Dr.* ☎ *850/235–3555* 🌐 *www.schooners.com* 💳 *AE, D, MC, V.*

WHERE TO STAY

$$$–$$$$ Fodor's Choice ★ **Bay Point Golf Resort & Spa**. Across the Grand Lagoon from St. Andrews State Park, this expansive property exudes sheer elegance. The tropical-chic feel starts in the light-filled lobby, with its polished marble floors, glowing chandeliers, potted palms, and colorful floral paintings. Quiet guest rooms continue the theme with light-wood furnishings and armoires, floral-print fabrics, and private balconies or patios overlooking the lush grounds and peaceful bay. Rooms on the upper floors of the main building have expansive views of the bay and the gulf beyond, and villas are a mere tee-shot away from the hotel. A meandering boardwalk (which doubles as a jogging trail) leads to a private beach with an open-air bar and water sports. The 12,000-square-foot spa offers massages, facials, manicures, pedicures, and waxing. **Pros:** quiet and away from the madness of Panama City Beach; complete range of services and activities. **Cons:** may be too expansive and generic for those seeking a small, intimate resort. ✉ *4200 Marriott Dr.* ☎ *850/236–6000 or 800/874–7105* 🌐 *www.marriottbaypoint.com* *316 rooms, 78 suites* *In-room: refrigerator (some), Wi-Fi. In-hotel: 5 restaurants, bars, golf courses, pools, gym* *AE, D, DC, MC, V.*

$$–$$$ ★ **Edgewater Beach Resort.** You can sleep at least four and as many as eight in the luxurious one-, two-, and three-bedroom apartments in beachside towers and golf course villas. Rooms are elegantly furnished with wicker and rattan, and the resort centerpiece is a Polynesian-style lagoon pool with waterfalls, reflecting ponds, footbridges, and more than 20,000 species of tropical plants. With plenty of swimming and sporting options, this is a good beachfront option for longer stays or family vacations. **Pros:** variety of lodging options; 110 acres of beautiful beachfront property. **Cons:** overwhelming for those looking for a quiet getaway. ✉ *11212 Front Beach Rd.* ☎ *850/235–4044 or 800/874–8686* 🌐 *www.edgewaterbeachresort.com* *520 apartments* *In-room: kitchen, refrigerator. In-hotel: 2 restaurants, bars, golf course, tennis courts, spa, beachfront, Internet terminal* *D, DC, MC, V.*

$$–$$$ **Legacy by the Sea.** Nearly every room at this 14-story, pastel-peach hotel has a private balcony with commanding gulf views. Rooms are designed with families in mind, from the fully equipped kitchens to the two televisions and waterproof sofa cushions to the door that conveniently separates the bedroom area from the rest of the unit. There's a gulf-front pool and hot-tub area (with a kiddie pool), and freebies include Continental breakfast, daily newspaper, local calls, and an airport shuttle. A variety of water-sports options, including parasailing and Jet-Skiing, is offered by on-site concessionaires. The hotel's closed-circuit cable channel, airing nothing but live security-camera feeds (inside the elevator, around the pool, in the common areas), makes keeping an eye on the kids a breeze—and keeping an eye on unsuspecting adults a hoot. Note that prices vary wildly depending on the season and the type of room you reserve. **Pros:** shopping, dining, and attractions are within walking distance; all the amenities a family (or college kids) need. **Cons:** in the heart of a crowded and congested district; can be difficult to access in peak seasons. ✉ *15325 Front Beach Rd.* ☎ *850/249–8601 or 888/886–8917* 🌐 *www.legacybythesea.com* *278 rooms, 78 suites* *In-room: kitchen. In-hotel: pool, Wi-Fi hotspot* *AE, D, DC, MC, V* *CP.*

APALACHICOLA

65 mi southeast of Panama City Beach off U.S. 98.

It feels like a long haul between Panama City Beach and here. Add an odd name and a town's below-the-radar reputation to that long drive and you may be tempted to skip Apalachicola. But you shouldn't. It's a weirdly fascinating town that, for some reason, has a growing cosmopolitan veneer. And that makes it worth a visit.

Twenty percent of the state's shrimp and 10% of the country's oysters come from Apalachicola Bay.

Meaning "land of the friendly people" in the language of its original American Indian inhabitants, Apalachicola—known in these parts as simply Apalach—lies on the Panhandle's southernmost bulge. European settlers began arriving in 1821, and by 1847 the southern terminus of the Apalachicola River steamboat route was a bustling port town. Although the town is now known as the Oyster Capital of the World, oystering became king only after the local cotton industry flagged—the city's extra-wide streets, built to accommodate bales of cotton awaiting transport, are a remnant of that trade—and the sponge industry moved down the coast after depleting local sponge colonies. But the newest industry here is tourism, and visitors have begun discovering the Forgotten Coast, as the area is known, flocking to its intimate hotels and B&Bs, dining at excellent restaurants, and browsing in unique shops selling everything from handmade furniture to brass fixtures recovered from nearby shipwrecks. If you like oysters or want to go back in time to the Old South of Gothic churches and spooky graveyards, Apalachicola is a good place to start.

ESSENTIALS

Visitor Information Apalachicola Bay Chamber of Commerce (☎ *850/653–9419* 🌐 *www.apalachicolabay.org*).

EXPLORING

Drive by the **Raney House,** circa 1850, and **Trinity Episcopal Church,** built from prefabricated parts in 1838. The town is at a developmental turning point, pulled in one direction by well-intentioned locals who want to preserve Apalachicola's port-town roots and in the other by long-time business owners who fear preservation will inhibit commercial growth. For now, however, the city exudes a refreshing authenticity—think Key West in the early 1960s—that many others in the Sunshine State lost long ago, one that might be lost to Panama City Beach–style overdevelopment unless local government institutes an official historic-preservation committee.

SHOPPING

The best way to shop in Apalachicola is just to stroll around the tiny downtown area. There are always new stores joining old favorites and somewhere along the way you'll find something that'll pique your interest. The **Tin Shed** (✉ *170 Water St.* ☎ *850/653–3635*) has an impressive collection of antiques and knickknacks, from brass luggage tags to 1940s nautical charts to sponge-diver wet suits to hand-glazed tiles and architectural elements salvaged from demolished buildings. It's closed Sunday. The **Grady Market** (✉ *76 Water St.* ☎ *850/653–4099* 🌐 *www.gradymarket.com*), on the 1st floor of the Consulate Inn, is a collection of more than a dozen boutiques, including several antiques dealers and the gallery of Richard Bickel, known for his stunning black-and-white photographs of local residents.

WHERE TO EAT

$$ CONTINENTAL ✕ **Apalachicola Seafood Grill.** Where will you find the world's largest fish sandwich? Right here in downtown Apalachicola. Here since 1908, it's where the locals go for lunch and dinner, noshing on blue-crab cakes, seafood gumbo, fresh grouper, shrimp, and hamburgers. The decor is iconic diner, with a giant flamingo on the ceiling for that added Florida charm. ✉ *100 Market St.* ☎ *850/653–9510* ▭ *AE, D, MC, V* ⊙ *No dinner Sun.*

$$ SEAFOOD ✕ **Boss Oyster.** "Shut up and shuck." That's the advice from this rustic Old Florida restaurant—and it should know, since many consider this the top oyster restaurant in Florida's oyster capital. Located at the Apalachicola River Inn, this is where you can eat your oysters fried, Rockefeller-style, on the half shell, or Greek, Mexican, English, with garlic, with shrimp, with crab, with hot peppers, with—oh, just eat 'em with gusto at this laid-back eatery overlooking the Apalachicola River. In addition to oysters, it lays down jumbo gulf shrimp, blue crabs, bay scallops, and fresh gulf grouper. Eat alfresco at picnic tables or inside in the busy, rustic dining room, but don't let the modest surroundings fool you—oysters aren't cheap here or anywhere in Apalach. The menu also includes such staples as steak and pizza. ✉ *125 Water St.* ☎ *850/653–9364* 🌐 *www.apalachicolariverinn.com/boss.html* ▭ *AE, D, DC, MC, V.*

$$ CONTINENTAL ★ ✕ **Magnolia Grill.** Chef-owner Eddie Cass has earned local and regional acclaim from major food critics who have discovered the culinary pearl in this oyster town. In addition to meat dishes such as char-grilled pork tenderloin served with raspberry-bordelaise sauce, Eddie pays tribute to local seafood with a broiled seafood feast that includes three of the freshest market fish served with locally harvested shrimp, scallops, and Apalachicola Bay oysters. Dinners here tend to be leisurely events (this is the South, after all), and the stellar desserts—anything chocolate will wow you—deserve an hour of their own. The restaurant is small, so

reservations are recommended. ✉ *99 11th St.* ☎ *850/653–8000* 🌐 *www.chefeddiesmagnoliagrill.com* ▭ *MC, V* ⏲ *Closed Sun. No lunch.*

$$ AMERICAN ✕ **Owl Café.** Located in a behemoth clapboard building on a prime corner in downtown Apalachicola, this old-fashioned, charming lunch and dinner spot pleases modern palates, both in the white-linen elegance of the dining room and in the colorful garden terrace. The food is an artful blend of old and new as well: the chicken wrap seems as much at home on the lunch menu as the crab quesadillas. Dinner seafood specials are carefully prepared and include lump-crab cakes, Atlantic salmon, and authentic jambalaya. Fine wines for adults and special menu selections for children along with a cluttered gift shop make this a family-friendly place. At night, the mood shifts to a casual lounge setting with a full liquor bar—and if the liquor bar lacks enough choices there's a 3,000-bottle wine cellar featuring 250 selections from around the world. ✉ *15 Ave. D* ☎ *850/653–9888* 🌐 *www.owlcafeflorida.com* ▭ *AE, MC, V* ⏲ *No dinner Sun.*

$$$ LATIN AMERICAN ★ ✕ **Tamara's Aka Floridita.** Mixing Florida flavors with South American flair, Tamara, a native Venezuelan, opened this colorful bistro more than a decade ago. Now owned by her daughter and son-in-law, the restaurant has new digs in a 1920s-era building, complete with stamped-tin ceiling and original brick walls. For starters, try the creamy black-bean soup or the pleasantly spicy oyster stew; for dinner choose from seafood paella, prosciutto-wrapped salmon with mango-cilantro sauce, or margarita chicken and scallops with a tequila-lime glaze. All entrées come with black beans and rice, fresh vegetables, and focaccia bread, but if you still have room for dessert, try the fried-banana split or the *tres leches* (cake soaked in three types of milk), a South American favorite. The chef, who keeps watch over the dining room from an open kitchen, is happy to accommodate most any whim. ✉ *71 Market St.* ☎ *850/653–4111* 🌐 *www.tamarascafe.com* ▭ *AE, D, MC, V.*

WHERE TO STAY

$$$–$$$$ **The Consulate.** These four elegant suites, on the 2nd story of the former offices of the French consul, range in size from 650 to 1,650 square feet and combine a 19th-century feel with 21st-century luxury. Antique architectural details add more than a hint of charm, and custom-built kitchens and full-size washers and dryers make living easy. The two front units share an expansive balcony, where you can take in the constant parade of fishing vessels headed out the Intracoastal Waterway. The homelike amenities make this a popular spot for families, larger groups, and even wedding parties, and discounts are given for stays longer than two nights. The Grady Market, a locally owned art and clothing boutique, occupies the building's 1st floor. **Pros:** large rooms; more character than you'd find in a chain hotel. **Cons:** a bit pricey, especially for Apalachicola. ✉ *76 Water St.* ☎ *850/653–1515 or 877/239–1159* 🌐 *www.consulatesuites.com* *4 suites* *In-room: kitchen, DVD. In-hotel: laundry facilities, Wi-Fi hotspot* ▭ *AE, MC, V.*

$$–$$$ **Coombs Inn.** A combination of neighboring homes and a carriage house, this is an entire complex created with a Victorian flair. Seventeen fireplaces and an ornate oak staircase with lead-glass windows on the landing lend authenticity to this restored 1905 mansion. Of

the 23 rooms in the collection, no two guest rooms are alike, but all are appointed with Victorian-era settees and four-poster or sleigh king beds. A full breakfast is served in the dining room, an afternoon social includes tea and cookies, and occasionally the inn offers weekday specials. You can stay in the villa or a renovated carriage house. Popular for weddings and receptions, these may be the most elegant homes in Apalachicola. Free tours are offered in the afternoon if the accommodations are not in use. **Pros:** clean and comfortable; on-site, friendly owner who's happy to assist with travel tips and suggestions. **Cons:** be prepared to meet and greet other guests at the inn; if you favor complete privacy, a hotel may suit you better. ✉ *80 6th St.* ☎ *850/653–9199* 🌐 *www.coombshouseinn.com* *23 rooms* *In-room: Wi-Fi. In-hotel: bicycles, Wi-Fi hotspot* ▭ *D, MC, V* *CP.*

$$–$$$ **Gibson Inn.** One of a few inns on the National Register of Historic Places still operating as a full-service facility, this turn-of-the-20th-century hostelry in the heart of downtown is easily identified by its wraparound porches, intricate fretwork, and captain's watch. Large rooms are furnished with period pieces like four-poster beds, antique armoires, and pedestal lavatories. Extremely popular for weddings and special events, the inn equally impresses overnight visitors with its cleanliness, style, service, and rocking-chair-rich wraparound porch. For an authentic Apalachicola experience, enjoy waking up here and starting the day with breakfast on the veranda. **Pros:** smack dab in the center of town; peaceful veranda. **Cons:** may get a little busy when weddings are taking place in the main lobby. ✉ *51 Ave. C* ☎ *850/653–2191* 🌐 *www.gibsoninn.com* *28 rooms, 2 suites* *In-room: Wi-Fi. In-hotel: restaurant, bar, Wi-Fi hotspot, some pets allowed* ▭ *AE, MC, V.*

ST. GEORGE ISLAND

8 mi southeast of Apalachicola via the Bryant Patton Bridge off U.S. 98.

Cross the long, long bridge leading east out of Apalachicola and then look to your right for another lengthy span that will take you south to pristine St. George Island. Sitting 5 mi out into the Gulf of Mexico, the island is bordered by both Apalachicola Bay and the gulf, offering vacationers the best of both to create a nostalgic seaside retreat. The rich bay is an angler's dream, whereas the snowy-white beaches and clear gulf waters satisfy even the most finicky beachgoer. Indulge in bicycling, hiking, canoeing, and snorkeling, or find a secluded spot for reading, gathering shells, or bird-watching. Accommodations mostly take the form of privately owned, fully furnished condos and single-family homes.

THE OUTDOORS

Fodor's Choice ★ **St. George Island State Park.** This is Old Florida at its undisturbed best. On the east end of the island are 9 mi of undeveloped beaches and dunes—the longest beachfront of any state park in Florida. Sandy coves, salt marshes, oak forests, and pines provide shelter for many birds, including bald eagles and ospreys. Spotless restrooms and plentiful parking make a day at this park a joy. ✉ *1900 E. Gulf Beach Drive* ☎ *850/927–*

2111 ⊕ www.floridastateparks.org/stgeorgeisland ✉ $6 per vehicle, up to 8 people ⊙ Daily 8–sunset.

WHERE TO EAT

¢ PIZZA ✕ **BJs.** In any other locale you might think twice before dining at a restaurant that advertises "kegs-to-go" on the menu, but this is an island, so establishments tend to wear several hats (some even sell live bait). Fear not. This simple beach shack serves solid, if predictable, sandwiches (grilled chicken, turkey club, BLT), salads (Caesar, tuna, fried chicken), and appetizers (buffalo wings, cheese sticks, onion rings), but the pizza is definitely worth stopping for. Pies range from white pizza with chicken and bacon to shrimp-and-mozzarella to build-your-own personal pie (choose from 15 toppings). Beer and wine are available, and there are pool tables to pass the time while you wait for your order. ✉ *105 W. Gulf Beach Dr.* ☎ *850/927–2805* *Reservations not accepted* ▭ *MC, V.*

WORD OF MOUTH

"St. George Island for a day at the beach is great. Great fresh seafood!"

—MollyinFL

$$$ SEAFOOD ✕ **Blue Parrot.** You'll feel like you're sneaking in the back door as you climb the side stairs leading to an outdoor deck overlooking the gulf (this is Apalach's only restaurant on the beach). Or if you can, grab a table indoors. During special-event weekends, the place is packed, and service may be a little slow. The food is hard to beat if you're not looking for anything fancy. Baskets of shrimp, oysters, and crab cakes—fried or char-grilled and served with fries—are more than one person can handle. Daily specials are listed on the blackboard. ✉ *68 W. Gorrie Dr.* ☎ *850/927–2987* ▭ *AE, D, MC, V.*

INLAND TOWNS

Farther inland, where the northern reaches of the Panhandle butt up against the back porches of Alabama and Georgia, you'll find a part of Florida that goes a long way toward explaining why the state song is "Swannee River" (and why its parenthetical title is "Old Folks at Home"). Stephen Foster's musical genius notwithstanding, the inland Panhandle area is definitely more Dixie than Sunshine State, with few lodging options other than the chain motels that flank the Interstate 10 exits and a decidedly slower pace of life than you'll find on the tourist-heavy Gulf Coast. But the area's natural attractions—hills and farmland, untouched small towns, pristine state parks—make for great day trips from the coast should the sky turn gray or the skin red. Explore underground caverns where eons-old rock formations create bizarre scenes, visit one of Florida's up-and-coming wineries, or poke around small-town America in DeFuniak Springs. Altogether, the inland area of the Panhandle is one of the state's most satisfyingly soothing regions.

DEFUNIAK SPRINGS

28 mi east of Crestview on U.S. 90 off I–10.

This scenic spot has a rather unusual claim to fame: at its center lies a nearly perfectly symmetrical spring-fed lake, one of only two such naturally circular bodies of water in the world (the other is in Switzerland). A sidewalk encircles the lake, which is dotted by pine and shade trees, creating a very pleasing atmosphere for a long-distance mosey. In 1848 the Knox Hill Academy was founded here, and for more than half a century it was the only institution of higher learning in northwestern Florida. In 1885 the town was chosen as the location for the New York Chautauqua educational society's winter assembly. The Chautauqua programs were discontinued in 1922, but DeFuniak Springs attempts to revive them, in spirit at least, by sponsoring a countywide Chautauqua Festival in April. Christmas is a particularly festive time, when the sprawling Victorian houses surrounding the lake are decorated to the nines. There's not a tremendous amount to see here, but if you have the good sense to travel U.S. 90 to discover Old Florida, at least take the time to travel Circle Drive to see its beautiful Victorian homes. Also take a little time to walk around the small downtown area and drop in its bookstores, cafés, and small shops.

EXPLORING

Walton-DeFuniak Public Library. By all accounts, this 16-by-24-foot building is Florida's oldest library continuously operating in its original structure. Opened in 1887, the original space has been added to over the years. The library now contains nearly 30,000 volumes, including some rare books, many older than the structure itself. The collection also includes antique musical instruments and impressive European armor. ✉ *3 Circle Dr.* ☎ *850/892–3624* ⏲ *Mon. and Wed.–Sat. 9–5, Tues. 9–8.*

Chautauqua Winery. Open since 1989, this winery and its vintages have slowly won respect from oenophiles wary of what was once considered to be an oxymoron at best: "Florida wine." The winery has won honors in national and international competitions, with wines that vary from dry, barrel-fermented wines to Southern favorites like sweet muscadine and blueberry wines. Fourteen vats ranging in size from 1,500 to 6,000 gallons generate a total of 70,000 gallons of wine. Take a free tour to see how ancient art blends with modern technology; then retreat to the tastefully decorated tasting room and gift shop. ✉ *I–10 and U.S. 331* ☎ *850/892–5887* 🌐 *www.chautauquawinery.com.*

TAKE A TOUR

Some of the finest examples of Victorian architecture in the state can be seen while you are walking or motoring around Circle Drive, the road that wraps around Circle Lake. The circumference is marked with beautiful Victorian specimens like the Walton-DeFuniak Public Library, the Dream Cottage, and the Pansy Cottage. Most of the other notable structures are private residences, but you can still admire them from the street.

WHERE TO STAY

¢–$ **Hotel DeFuniak.** You can't miss this Depression-era two-story redbrick structure on a quiet corner a few blocks from peaceful Lake DeFuniak—just look for the two-tone 1937 Buick permanently moored out front. Each room has a different theme decor, from Asian to art deco to French country, and contains a combination of period antiques and reproductions. At the hotel restaurant, **Bogey's** (*850/951–2233*), the dinner menu centers around fresh gulf seafood, yet also includes chicken, steak, and veal. It's an unusual find in a small town, and one of the nicer places to stay in this part of the Panhandle. **Pros:** applause for the owners who created a sweet little retreat in the heart of downtown. **Cons:** DeFuniak can be eerily empty and quiet at night. *400 E. Nelson Ave. 850/892–4383 or 877/333–8642 www.hoteldefuniak.com 7 rooms, 4 suites In-hotel: restaurant, Wi-Fi hotspot AE, D, MC, V CP.*

FALLING WATERS STATE PARK

35 mi east of DeFuniak Springs via U.S. 90 and Rte. 77.

This site of a Civil War–era whiskey distillery and, later, an exotic plant nursery—some imported species still thrive in the wild—is best known for also being the site of one of Florida's most notable geological features—the Falling Waters Sink. The 100-foot-deep cylindrical pit provides the background for a waterfall, and there's an observation deck for viewing this natural phenomenon. The water free-falls 67 feet to the bottom of the sink, but where it goes after that is a mystery. *Rte. 77A, Chipley 850/638–6130 www.floridastateparks.org/fallingwaters $5 per vehicle, up to 8 people Daily 8–sunset.*

FLORIDA CAVERNS STATE PARK

13 mi northeast of Falling Waters off U.S. 90 on Rte. 166.

Marianna is a cute and pristine community, and a short drive from the center of town you can see what's behind, or—more accurately—what's beneath it all. Take a ranger-led cave tour to see stalactites, stalagmites, soda straws, columns, rim stones, flowstones, and "waterfalls" of solid rock at these underground caverns where the temperature hovers at an oh-so-pleasant 68°F year-round. Some of the caverns are off-limits to the public or open for scientific study only with a permit, but you'll still see enough to fill a half-day or more—and you'll be amazed that caverns of this magnitude exist anywhere in the Sunshine State. Don't forsake the quiet, preserved, and peaceful woodlands, which encompass 10 distinct communities including upland glade, hardwood forests, and floodplains, forests, and swamps. There are also hiking trails, campsites, and areas for swimming, horseback riding, and canoeing on the Chipola River. *3345 Caverns Rd. (off U.S. 90 on Rte. 166), Marianna 850/482–1228, 800/326–3521 for camping reservations www.floridastateparks.org/floridacaverns Park $5 per vehicle, up to 8 people; caverns $8 Daily 8–sunset; cavern tours Thurs.–Mon. 9–4.*

TALLAHASSEE

61 mi southeast of Florida Caverns on I–10.

Tallahassee maintains a tranquility quite different from the sun-and-surf coastal towns. Tallahassee is Florida with a Southern accent. The only Southern capital spared in the Civil War, Tallahassee has preserved its past. So along with Florida State University, the perennial Seminoles football champions, and FAMU's fabled "Marching 100" band, the city has more than a touch of the Old South. Vestiges of the city's colorful past are found throughout. For example, in the capitol complex, the turn-of-the-20th-century Old Capitol building is strikingly paired with the New Capitol skyscraper. The canopies of ancient oaks and spring bowers of azaleas line many streets; among the best "canopy roads" are St. Augustine, Miccosukee, Meridian, Old Bainbridge, and Centerville, all dotted with country stores and antebellum plantation houses. If you visit between March and April, you'll find flowers in bloom, the legislature in session, and the Springtime Tallahassee festival in full swing.

GETTING HERE AND AROUND

Just 14 mi south of the Georgia border, Tallahassee is midway between Jacksonville and Pensacola and is nearer to Atlanta than Miami. Tallahassee Regional Airport is served by American Airlines, Continental, Delta, Northwest, and US Airways (US Airways Express). From the airport to downtown is around $20 via City Taxi or Yellow Cab.

ESSENTIALS

Transportation Contacts City Taxi (☎ *850/562–4222*). **Tallahassee Regional Airport** (☎ *850/891–7800* 🌐 *www.talgov.com/airport*). **Yellow Cab** (☎ *850/575–1022*).

Visitor Information Tallahassee Area Convention and Visitors Bureau (☎ *850/606–2305 or 800/628–2866* 🌐 *www.visittallahassee.com*).

EXPLORING

DOWNTOWN

Downtown Tallahassee Historic Trail. A route originally mapped and documented by an eager Eagle Scout as part of a merit-badge project, this trail has become a Tallahassee sightseeing staple. The starting point is the New Capitol, where you can pick up maps and descriptive brochures at the visitor center. You'll walk through the Park Avenue and Calhoun Street historic districts, which will take you back to territorial days and the era of postwar reconstruction. The trail is dotted with landmark churches and cemeteries, along with outstanding examples of Greek revival, Italianate, and prairie-style architecture. Some houses are open to the public. The **Brokaw-McDougall House** (✉ *329 N. Meridian St.* 🎫 *Free* ⏲ *Weekdays 9–3*) is a superb example of the Greek revival and Italianate styles. The **Meginnis-Monroe House** (✉ *125 N. Gadsden St.* 🎫 *Free* ⏲ *Tues.–Sat. 10–5, Sun. 2–5*) served as a field hospital during the Civil War and is now an art gallery.

Museum of Florida History. If you thought Florida was founded by Walt Disney, stop here. The displays explain Florida's past by highlighting

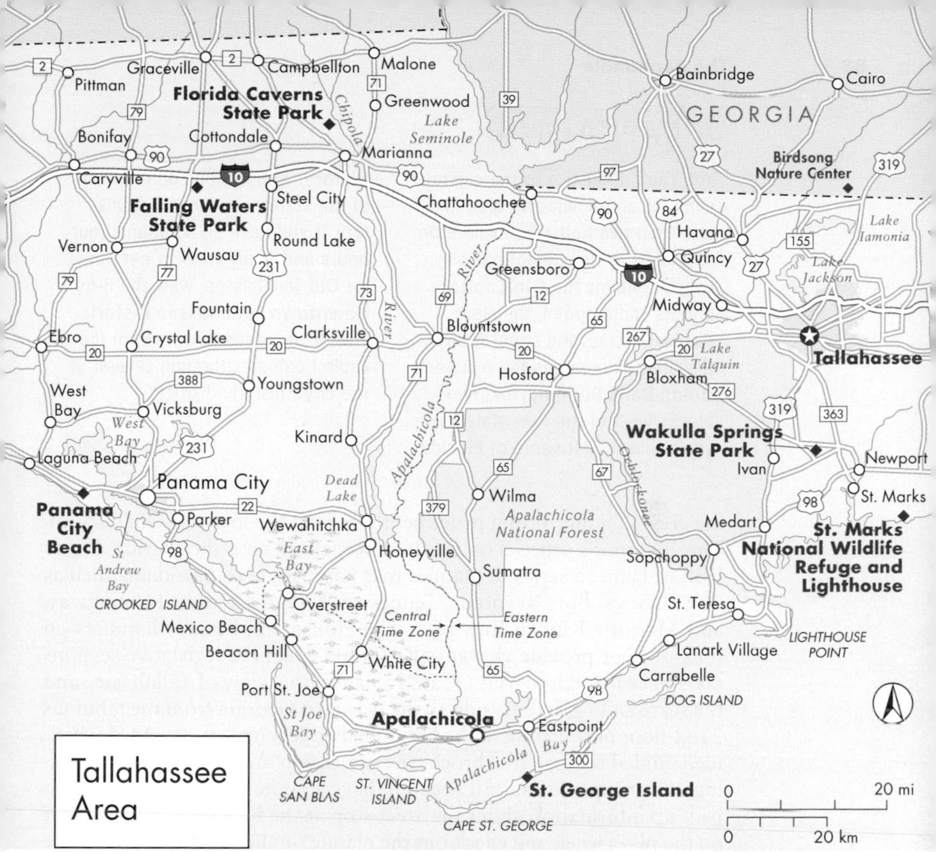

the unique geological and historical events that have shaped the state. Exhibits include a mammoth armadillo grazing in a savanna, the remains of a giant mastodon found in nearby Wakulla Springs, and a dugout canoe that once carried American Indians into Florida's backwaters. Florida's history also includes settlements by the Spanish, British, French, and Confederates who fought for possession of the state. Gold bars, weapons, flags, maps, furniture, steamboats, and other artifacts underscore the fact that although most Americans date the nation to 1776, Florida's residents had been building settlements hundreds of years earlier. If this intrigues you, one floor up is the **Florida State Archives and Library,** where there's a treasure trove of government records, manuscripts, photographs, genealogical records, and other materials. FYI: It was in these archives that researchers found footage of a young Jim Morrison appearing in a promotional film for Florida's universities. ✉ *500 S. Bronough St.* ☏ *850/245–6400, 850/245–6600 library, 850/245-6700 archives* 🌐 *www.museumoffloridahistory.com* 🎟 *Free* ⏲ *Weekdays 9–4:30, Sat. 10–4:30, Sun. noon–4:30.*

★ **New Capitol**. In the 1960s, when there was talk of relocating the capital to a more central location like Orlando, Panhandle legislators got to work and approved the construction of a 22-story modern skyscraper that would anchor the capital right where it was. It's perfectly placed at

A CAPITAL TOUR

You can't do justice to the capitol complex and downtown area in less than two hours. To explore on foot, start at the capitol complex, which contains the **Old Capitol** and its counterpoint, the **New Capitol.** Across the street from the older structure is the restored **Union Bank Building,** and two blocks west of the new statehouse you'll find the **Museum of Florida History,** with exhibits on many eras of the state's history and prehistory. If you have an additional four hours and really want to get a feel for Old Tallahassee, walk the 8-mi **Downtown Tallahassee Historic Trail** as it wends its way from the capitol complex through several of the city's historic districts.

the crest of a hill, sitting prominently behind the low-rise Old Capitol. The governor's office is on the 1st floor, along with the Florida Artists Hall of Fame, a series of plaques that pay tribute to Floridians such as Ray Charles, Burt Reynolds, Tennessee Williams, Ernest Hemingway, and Marjorie Kinnan Rawlings. The House and Senate chambers on the 5th floor provide viewer galleries for when the legislative sessions take place (March to May). Catch a panoramic view of Tallahassee and the surrounding countryside all the way into Georgia from the fabulous 22nd-floor observation deck. Although budget cuts have stopped scheduled guided tours, a free brochure can get you around; if you're traveling in a group you can call ahead to have a guide usher you around. To pick up information about the area, stop at the Florida Visitors Center on the plaza level, and check out the plaque on the north wall facing the elevators. It's dedicated to Senator Lee Wissenborn ". . . whose valiant effort to move the Capitol to Orlando was the prime motivation for the construction of this building." ✉ *400 S. Monroe St.* ☎ *850/488–6167* 🌐 *www.myfloridacapitol.com* 🎟 *Free* ⏲ *Visitor center weekdays 8–5.*

★ **Old Capitol.** The centerpiece of the capitol complex, this 1842 structure has been added to and subtracted from several times. Having been restored, the jaunty red-and-white-striped awnings and combination gas-electric lights make it look much as it did in 1902. Inside, it houses a must-see museum of Florida's political history as well as the old Supreme Court chambers and Senate Gallery—a very interesting peek into the past. ✉ *S. Monroe St. at Apalachee Pkwy.* ☎ *850/487–1902* 🎟 *Free* ⏲ *Self-guided tours weekdays 9–4:30, Sat. 10–4:30, Sun. noon–4:30; call ahead for guided tours.*

DID YOU KNOW?

Several Tarzan movies as well as such flicks as *Creature from the Black Lagoon* (with Richard Carlson, Julie Adams, and Richard Denning), *Coastlines* (with Josh Brolin), *Airport* (with Jack Lemmon), *Ulee's Gold* (with Peter Fonda), *Something Wild* (with Melanie Griffith, Jeff Daniels, and Ray Liotta) were filmed in the Tallahassee area.

Union Bank Building. Chartered in 1833, this is Florida's oldest bank building. Since it closed in 1843, it has played many roles, from ballet school to bakery. It has been restored to what is thought to be its original appearance and currently houses Florida A&M's Black Archives Extension, which depicts black history in Florida. Call ahead for directions and for hours, which are subject to change. ✉ *Calhoun St. at Apalachee Pkwy.* ☎ *850/561–2603* *Free* ⏲ *Weekdays 9–4.*

AWAY FROM DOWNTOWN

Alfred B. Maclay Gardens State Park. Starting in December, the grounds at this 1,200-acre estate are afire with azaleas, dogwood, Oriental magnolias, spring bulbs of tulips and irises, banana shrubs, honeysuckle, silverbell trees, pansies, and camellias. Allow half a day to wander past the reflecting pool into the tiny walled garden and around the lakes and woodlands. The Maclay residence (open January through April only) is furnished as it was in the 1920s; picnic areas, gardens, and swimming and boating facilities are open to the public. ✉ *3540 Thomasville Rd.* ☎ *850/487–4556* 🌐 *www.floridastateparks.org/maclaygardens* *$6 per vehicle, up to 8 people; extra $4 per person for garden admission Jan.–Apr. (blooming season); free rest of year* ⏲ *Daily 8–sunset.*

Fodor's Choice ★ **Edward Ball Wakulla Springs State Park.** Known for having one of the deepest springs in the world, this very picturesque and highly recommended park remains relatively untouched, retaining the wild and exotic look it had in the 1930s, when the films *Tarzan* and *Creature from the Black Lagoon* were shot here. Even if they weren't, you'd want to come here and see what Florida really looks like. Beyond the lodge is the spring where glass-bottom boats set off deep into the lush, jungle-lined waterways to catch glimpses of alligators, snakes, nesting limpkins, and other waterfowl. It costs $50 to rent a pontoon boat and go it alone—it may be worth it since an underground river flows into a pool so clear you can see the bottom more than 100 feet below. The park is 15 mi south of Tallahassee on Route 61. If you can't pull yourself away from this idyllic spot, spend the night in the 1930s Spanish Mediterranean–style lodge. ✉ *550 Wakulla Park Dr., Wakulla Springs* ☎ *850/926–0700* 🌐 *www.floridastateparks.org/wakullasprings* *$6 per vehicle, up to 8 people; boat tour $8* ⏲ *Daily 8–sunset; boat tours offered 9:30–4:30.*

Tallahassee Museum. Not exactly a museum, this is really an expansive, bucolic park that showcases a peaceful and intriguing look at Old Florida, located about 20 minutes from downtown. The theme and presentation here is of a working 1880s pioneer farm that offers daily hands-on activities for children, such as soap-making and blacksmithing. A boardwalk meanders through the 52 acres of natural habitat that make up the zoo, which has such varied animals as panthers, bobcats, white-tailed deer, bald eagles, red wolves, hawks, owls, otters, and black bears—many of which were brought here injured or orphaned. Also on-site are nature trails, a one-room schoolhouse dating from 1897, and an 1840s Southern plantation manor, where you can usually find someone cooking on weekends. It's peaceful, pleasing, and educational. ✉ *3945 Museum Dr.* ☎ *850/575–8684* 🌐 *www.tallahasseemuseum.org* *$9* ⏲ *Mon.–Sat. 9–5, Sun. 12:30–5.*

St. Marks National Wildlife Refuge and Lighthouse. As its name suggests, this attraction is of both natural and historical interest. Natural salt

DID YOU KNOW?

There are many types of speleothems (cave formations). The two you hear spelunkers say the most are probably stalactites and stalagmites. Formed from dripping water, stalactites (shown here at Florida Caverns State Park) are carrot-shaped formations that hang down from a cave ceiling. Formations that go the other direction—from the ground up, due to mineral deposits—are called stalagmites.

marshes, tidal flats, and freshwater pools used by early natives set the stage for the once-powerful Fort San Marcos de Apalache that was built nearby in 1639. Stones salvaged from the fort were used in the lighthouse, which is still in operation. In winter the 100,000-acre-plus refuge on the shores of Apalachee Bay is the resting place for thousands of migratory birds of more than 300 species, but the alligators seem to like it year-round (keep your camera ready and you're bound to get a photo op). The visitor center has information on more than 75 mi of marked trails. Hardwood swamps and pine woodlands also provide habitat for wood ducks, black bears, otters, raccoons, deer, armadillos, coyotes, feral hogs, fox squirrels, gopher tortoises, and woodpeckers. Twenty-five miles south of Tallahassee, the refuge can be reached via Route 363. ✉ *1255 Lighthouse Rd., St. Marks* ☎ *850/925–6121* 🌐 *saintmarks.fws.gov* 🎫 *$5 per vehicle* ⏲ *Refuge daily sunrise–sunset; visitor center weekdays 8–4, weekends 10–5.*

NIGHTLIFE AND THE ARTS

NIGHTLIFE

There are endless options for after-dark entertainment for Tallahassee's government and university populations. When you're in town, be sure to check the college newspapers for the latest developments. For decades, **The Moon** (✉ *1105 E. Lafayette St.* ☎ *850/878–6900, 850/222–6666 event line* 🌐 *www.moonevents.com*) has been one of the capital city's most active nightclubs, capable of changing its music to suit the tastes of the new students attending FSU. Live bands and DJs have kept this club going since 1985 and will likely sustain its collegiate appeal for years to come. **Floyd's Music Store** (✉ *666-1 W. Tennessee St.* ☎ *850/222–3506* 🌐 *www.floydsmusicstore.com*) hosts local and touring acts, such as Daughtry and Kenney Chesney. Other performers, from dueling pianos to assorted DJs, round out the schedule.

THE ARTS

If you're too shy to crash a frat party, here's a more civilized evening out: **Florida State University** (☎ *850/645–7949 School of Music, 850/644–6500 School of Theatre* 🌐 *www.music.fsu.edu*) plays host to more than 400 concerts and recitals annually in year-round performances by its School of Music, and many productions by its School of Theatre. The **Tallahassee Little Theatre** (✉ *1861 Thomasville Rd.* ☎ *850/224–8474* 🌐 *www.tallahasseelittletheatre.org*) has a six-production season that runs from September through May. The season of the **Tallahassee Symphony Orchestra** (☎ *850/224–0461* 🌐 *www.tallahasseesymphony.org*) tends to run October through April; performances are usually held at a local Baptist church.

WHERE TO EAT

$$ ITALIAN ✕ **Andrew's 228.** Part of a smart complex in the heart of the political district, this two-story "urban Tuscan villa" (contradiction noted) is the latest of owner Andy Reiss's restaurant incarnations to occupy the same space (the last was Andrew's Second Act). Leaning toward

Guided tours are given daily at Florida's Old Capitol in Tallahassee. It sits in front of the 22-story New Capitol.

upscale, the menu includes a range of chicken, steak, pasta, and fish dishes such as grouper picatta, pesto salmon, wild-mushroom risotto, chicken marsala, and double-cut pork chops. If you're so inclined, try the specialty $6 martini. ✉ *228 S. Adams St.* ☎ *850/222–3444* 🌐 *www.andrewsdowntown.com* 💳 *AE, D, MC, V* ⏲ *No lunch. Closed Sun.*

$$$ STEAK ✕ **Chez Pierre.** You'll feel as if you've entered a great-aunt's old plantation home in this restored 1920s house set back from the road in historic Lafayette Park. Since 1976, its warm, cozy rooms, gleaming hardwood floors, and large French doors separating dining areas have created an intimate place to go for authentic French cuisine. There are also dining areas where you can savor a meal under a canopy of oak trees. You may think you're dining with Scarlett at Tara. Try the tournedos of beef or one of the special lamb dishes. The Sunday brunch is one of the most popular around. ✉ *1215 Thomasville Rd.* ☎ *850/222–0936* 🌐 *www.chezpierre.com* 💳 *AE, D, MC, V.*

¢ AMERICAN ✕ **Hopkins' Eatery.** Locals in the know flock here for superb salads, homemade soups, and sandwiches—expect a short wait at lunchtime—via simple counter service. Kids will like the traditional peanut butter–and-jelly sandwich (with bananas and sprouts, if they dare); adults might opt for a chunky chicken melt, smothered beef, or garden vegetarian sub. The spearmint iced tea is a must-have, as is a slice of freshly baked chocolate cake. A second location on North Monroe Street offers the same menu. ✉ *1415 Market St.* ☎ *850/668–0311* ✉ *1660-9 N. Monroe St.* ☎ *850/386–4258* 🌐 *www.hopkinseatery.com* 💳 *AE, D, DC, MC, V* ⏲ *Closed Sun. No dinner Sat.*

$ ASIAN **Rice-Bowl Oriental.** Bamboo woodwork and thatched-roof booths lend an air of authenticity to this Asian-hybrid spot tucked away in a Tallahassee strip mall. Chinese, Japanese, Thai, and Vietnamese favorites are all represented here, from General Tso's chicken to fresh sushi to green curry and rice-noodle dishes. The all-you-can-eat lunch buffet (Sunday to Friday, $6.95), complete with entrées, salads, soups, and fresh sushi, just might be one of the best deals in town. *3813 N. Monroe St. 850/514–3632 AE, D, MC, V.*

WHERE TO STAY

$$$–$$$$ ★ **Governors Inn.** Only a block from the capitol, this plushly restored historic warehouse is abuzz during the week with politicians, press, and lobbyists. It's a perfect location for business travelers, and, on weekends, tourists who want to visit downtown. Rooms are a rich blend of brass, mahogany, and classic prints. The Governor also extends free valet parking, a complimentary breakfast, and was seen in the HBO movie *Recount* about Florida's goofball handling of the 2000 election. Well placed, well run. **Pros:** a few steps from museums, restaurants, and the capitol; the rooms and lobby are warm and inviting. **Cons:** during session and football season, the district can get crowded and busy, and accessing the area may be a challenge. *209 S. Adams St. 850/681–6855 or 800/342–7717 www.thegovinn.com 29 rooms, 12 suites In-room: refrigerator (some), Wi-Fi. In-hotel: laundry service, Wi-Fi hotspot, parking (free) AE, D, DC, MC, V CP.*

¢ **Super 8.** The quiet courtyard with its own pool and the darkly welcoming cantina (where a complimentary Continental breakfast is served) convey the look of old Spain. Rooms are furnished in heavy Mediterranean style, and come with two double beds or one king. Time it right: rates double on FSU football home-game weekends. **Pros:** close to the capitol; great rates. **Cons:** it's a Super 8, so it lacks the character of higher-priced lodging. *2801 N. Monroe St. 850/386–8286 www.super8.com 108 rooms, 23 suites In-room: Wi-Fi. In-hotel: pool AE, D, MC, V CP.*

Northeast Florida

WORD OF MOUTH

"We were on Amelia Island Memorial Day a year ago. The days were lovely, perfectly sunny, not hot or humid, but evenings on the beach were BRRRRRR. . . . That was one of my favorite beach vacations, actually, because it wasn't sweltering."

—NewbE

WELCOME TO NORTHEAST FLORIDA

Ryan Newman & Matt Kenseth.

TOP REASONS TO GO

★ **Tee Time:** "Above par" describes the golf scene in these parts, from award-winning courses to THE PLAYERS Championship to the World Golf Hall of Fame.

★ **A Need for Speed:** Few things will get racing fans as revved up as Daytona USA, the official attraction of NASCAR, and tours of Daytona International Speedway, home of the Daytona 500 and Coke Zero 400.

★ **Northeast Florid-aaah:** Oceanfront destination spas like the Spa at the Ponte Vedra Inn & Club, the Shores Resort & Spa, and the Ritz-Carlton Spa, Amelia Island are amusement parks of a different kind.

★ **Seems Like Olde Times:** The nation's oldest city, St. Augustine, is a must-see for anyone interested in the founding of Florida.

★ **Good Natured:** A wealth of state and national parks means canoeing, fishing, sunbathing, hiking, bird-watching, and camping opportunities are all within a short drive.

1 Jacksonville. With a metro-area population of 1.3 million, Jacksonville has the social and cultural appeal of a big city (think museums, nightlife, shopping, and dining) but the down-to-earth charm of a small town (boiled peanuts, anyone?).

2 St. Augustine. You don't have to be a history buff to enjoy the Oldest City, the historic capital of this part of Florida. Founded in 1565, it's the oldest European settlement. Foodies, golfers, art lovers, and beach bums will find plenty to do here, too (namely, eat, play, shop, and loaf).

3 Daytona Beach and Inland Towns. The Daytona 500, Bike Week, and spring break put it on the map, but Daytona Beach has become a popular family vacation destination. Without beaches or theme parks, DeLand, Gainesville, Micanopy, and the Ocala National Forest aren't what most folks picture when they think of Florida, but they pay off big time in pristine, laid-back leisure activities.

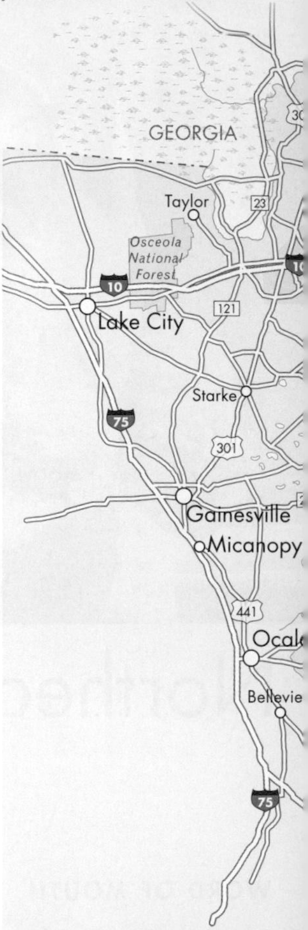

Homes in St. Augustine.

t. Augustine beach.

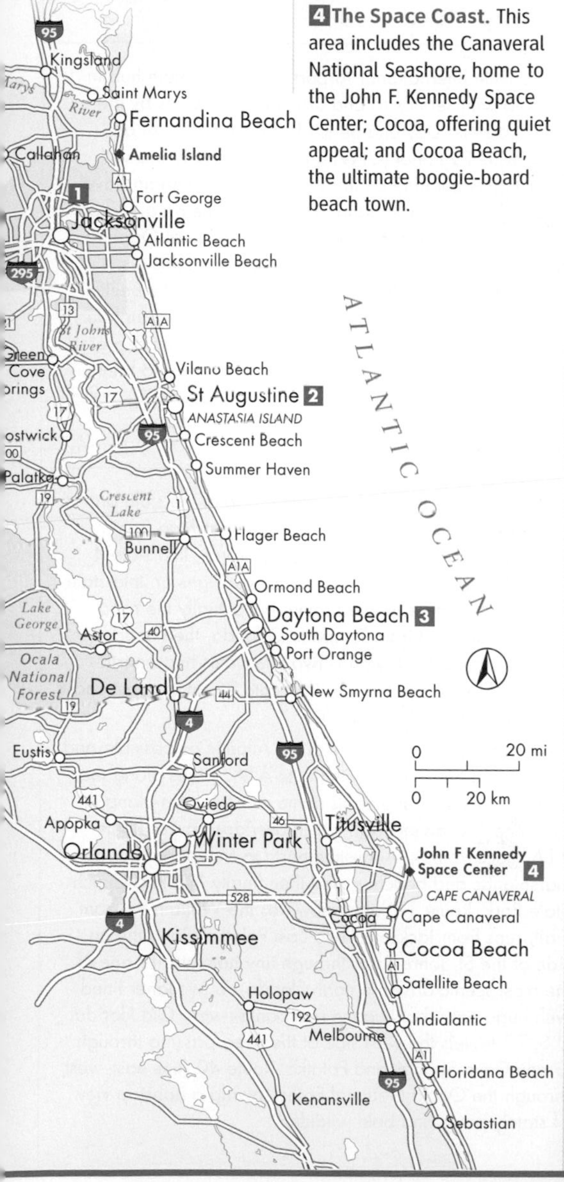

4 The Space Coast. This area includes the Canaveral National Seashore, home to the John F. Kennedy Space Center; Cocoa, offering quiet appeal; and Cocoa Beach, the ultimate boogie-board beach town.

GETTING ORIENTED

Northeast Florida has diverse, encompassing waterfront towns and inland cities like Fernandina Beach and Gainesville, as well as the area's "capital" of Jacksonville. About two hours south of Jacksonville on Interstate 95, Titusville, the entry point for the Kennedy Space Center, marks the northern perimeter of the Space Coast, which also includes Cocoa and Melbourne. If you take U.S. 1, it lengthens the trip, but the scenery makes up for the inconvenience. Route A1A (mostly called Atlantic Avenue south of St. Augustine) is the main road on all the barrier islands, and it's here that you find the best beaches.

Marineland,
St. Augustine.

NORTHEAST FLORIDA PLANNER

When to Go

It's not 90°F and sunny here every day. In winter the temperature can dip below freezing, and sudden thunderstorms happen almost daily in summer. For the most part, the weather is fair, averaging in the low 50s in Jacksonville and low 60s in Cocoa Beach in winter. Summer temperatures hover around 90, but the humidity makes it seem far hotter. April and May are good months to visit, since the ocean is beginning to warm up and the beaches aren't yet packed.

Tours

TourTime, Inc. (☎ *904/282-8500 or 800/822-4278* 🌐 *www.tourtimeinc.com*) offers custom group and individual motor-coach tours of Jacksonville, Amelia Island, and St. Augustine, as well as overnight trips to Silver Springs, Kennedy Space Center, Orlando, Okefenokee Swamp, and New Orleans. Prior arrangements are required.

St. Augustine.

Getting Here

Jacksonville International Airport (JAX) is the main hub in the area with service to and from all major cities by the major carriers. Daytona Beach International (DAB) and Gainesville Regional (GNV) are smaller operations with fewer flights but may be more convenient in certain travel situations. Although Orlando isn't part of the area, visitors to northeastern Florida often choose to arrive at Orlando International Airport (MCO) since cheaper flights are often available. Driving east from Orlando on the Beeline Expressway brings you to Cocoa Beach in about an hour; to reach Daytona from Orlando, take the Beeline Expressway to Interstate 95 and drive north for about two hours.

Getting Around

East–west traffic travels the northern part of the state on Interstate 10, a cross-country highway stretching from Santa Monica to Jacksonville. Farther south, Interstate 4 connects Florida's west and east coasts. Signs on Interstate 4 designate it an east–west route, but actually the road rambles northeast from Tampa to Orlando, then heads north–northeast to Daytona. Two interstates head north–south on Florida's peninsula: Interstate 95 on the east coast and Interstate 75 on the west.

If you want to drive as close to the Atlantic as possible and are not in a hurry, stick with Route A1A. It runs along the barrier islands, changing its name several times along the way. The Buccaneer Trail, which overlaps part of Route A1A, goes from St. Augustine north to Mayport, through marshlands and beaches, and then finally into Fort Clinch State Park. Route 13, also known as the William Bartram Trail, runs from Jacksonville to East Palatka along the east side of the St. Johns River through tiny hamlets. It's one of the most scenic drives in north Florida—a two-laner lined with huge oaks that hug the riverbanks—very Old Florida. U.S. 17 travels the west side of the river, passing through Green Cove Springs and Palatka. Route 40 runs east–west through the Ocala National Forest, giving a nonstop view of stately pines and bold wildlife.

About the Restaurants

The ocean, St. Johns River, and numerous lakes and smaller rivers are teeming with fish, and so, naturally, seafood dominates local menus. In coastal towns, catches are often from the restaurant's own fleet. Shrimp, snapper, flounder, and grouper are especially prevalent. Northeast Florida also boasts a variety of award-winning, fine-dining restaurants, ethnic eateries, and more barbecue joints than you can shake a hickory chip at.

About the Hotels

For the busy seasons—during summer in and around Jacksonville, and during summer and holiday weekends all over Florida—always reserve well ahead for the top properties. Jacksonville's beach hotels fill up quickly for PGA's THE PLAYERS Championship in mid-May. Daytona Beach presents similar lodging dilemmas during the Daytona 500 (mid-February), Bike Week (late February–early March), spring break (March), and the Coke Zero 400 (early July). St. Augustine stays busy all year because of its historic character. Fall is the slowest season; rates are low and availability is high, but it is also the prime time for hurricanes.

Assume that hotels operate on the European Plan (EP, no meals), unless we specify that they use the Breakfast Plan (BP, with full breakfast), Continental Plan (CP, Continental breakfast), Full American Plan (FAP, all meals), or Modified American Plan (MAP, breakfast and dinner), or are all-inclusive (AI, all meals and most activities).

WHAT IT COSTS

	¢	$	$$	$$$	$$$$
Restaurants	under $10	$10–$15	$15–$20	$20–$30	over $30
Hotels	under $80	$80–$100	$100–$140	$140–$220	over $220

Restaurant prices are per person for a main course at dinner. Hotel prices are for a standard double room, excluding 6% sales tax (more in some counties) and 1%–4% tourist tax.

Top Festivals

WINTER

Space Coast Birding and Wildlife Festival. Birders flock to Titusville for five days of field trips, seminars, and workshops by leading ornithologists each January event. ☎ *800/460–2664 or 321/268–5224* 🌐 *www.nbbd.com/fly.*

SPRING

Bike Week. More than 500,000 riders from across the country come to Daytona for 10 days of races, plus demo rides, parades, even coleslaw wrestling. ☎ *386/255–0981* 🌐 *www.officialbikeweek.com.*

Springing the Blues Festival. Nationally recognized performers and local talent entertain blues lovers during this free three-day affair at the Jacksonville Beach pavilion the first full weekend of April. 🌐 *www.springingtheblues.com.*

Rhythm and Ribs Festival. Champion barbecuers fire up the grill in April at this St. Augustine event. 🌐 *www.rhythmandribs.net.*

SUMMER

Florida International Festival. Gentleman, *stop* your engines. The London Symphony Orchestra is the star attraction at this biennial July event in Daytona Beach. ☎ *386/226–1927* 🌐 *www.fif-lso.org.*

3

NORTHEAST FLORIDA'S BEACHES

Northeastern Florida's primary draw is its beaches. Hugging the coast are long, slender barrier islands whose entire eastern sides make up a broad band of spectacular sand. Except in the most populated areas, development has been modest and beaches are lined with funky, appealing little towns.

These towns range from Jacksonville Beach to historic St. Augustine and Daytona Beach and on to the surfer's paradise of Cocoa Beach. Also in Northeast Florida are Amelia Island and Fernandina Beach, an idyllic playland amid Victorian buildings and natural surroundings. Here, wildlife viewing and water sports are key.

Separated from the mainland by the Intracoastal Waterway, Jacksonville's main beaches include the laid-back towns of Jacksonville Beach, Neptune Beach, Atlantic Beach, and Ponte Vedra Beach.

QUIETER BEACHES

Small and scenic, **Paradise Beach** is a 1,600-foot stretch of sand that's part of a 10-acre park north of Indialantic, about 20 mi south of Cocoa Beach on Route A1A. It has showers, restrooms, picnic tables, a refreshment stand, and lifeguards in summer. Meanwhile, **Satellite Beach,** about 15 mi south of Cocoa Beach on Route A1A, is popular for family vacations because of its lack of crowds.

NORTHEAST FLORIDA'S BEST BEACHES

AMELIA ISLAND/FERNANDINA BEACH

Far from the madness of some of the popular spring-break beaches, the shores of Amelia Island put you close to nature. Here, you can watch sea turtles carve out their nests, pound the beach on horseback or fish for tarpon, kingfish, and amberjack. Access the beach on Fletcher Avenue.

DAYTONA BEACH

The World's Most Famous Beach is fronted with a mixture of tall condos and apartments, hotels, low-rise motels, and flashy nightclubs. Although the hurricanes of 2004 and 2005 caused hundreds of millions of dollars in damage to the Daytona area, most commercial properties and many smaller family-owned properties have since reopened. Traffic can get backed up, as driving on the sand is allowed (be careful, because cars can, and do, get stuck). No-car zones are less frenetic and more family-friendly.

COCOA BEACH

As home to **Ron Jon Surf Shop** (the world's largest surf shop) and the **Cocoa Beach Surf Company** (the world's largest surf complex), and the birthplace of nine-time world surfing champion Kelly Slater, it's only fitting that Cocoa Beach be dubbed "Surfing Capital of the East Coast." Grommets looking to follow in his aqua shoes should head to the beach at 3rd Street North (renamed "Slater Way" in his honor), where he learned the basics, then head to the **East Coast Surfing Hall of Fame and Museum** (located inside the Cocoa Beach Surf Company on Atlantic Avenue) for inspiration. Stretching 800 feet over the Atlantic, the Cocoa Beach Pier is an everyday gathering spot as well as a beachside grandstand for space-shuttle launches. There are several souvenir shops, bars, and restaurants, and a bait-and-tackle shop. It costs $3 to park here, and another $1 for access to the fishing part of the pier.

JACKSONVILLE BEACHES

The northernmost of Jacksonville's beaches, Atlantic Beach is more subdued but a favorite with local surfers. Adjacent Neptune Beach is largely residential and draws bicyclists and in-line skaters who cruise up and down 1st Street. Just south is Jacksonville Beach, which has a decidedly more active shoreline, with volleyballs and Frisbees buzzing through the air and portable radios blaring everything from Kanye West to Van Halen. With multimillion-dollar homes stretching for miles, Ponte Vedra is the most difficult beach to access but makes for a lovely drive down Route A1A. Lifeguards are on duty on the more populated stretches of the beaches from 10–6 in summer.

Updated by Jennifer Edwards

Some of the oldest settlements in the state—indeed in all of the United States—are in northeastern Florida, although the region didn't get much attention until the Union army came through during the Civil War. The soldiers' rapturous accounts of the mild climate, pristine beaches, and lush vegetation captured the imagination of folks up North. First came the speculators and the curiosity seekers. Then the advent of the railroads brought more permanent settlers and the first wave of winter vacationers. Finally, the automobile transported the full rush of snowbirds—seasonal residents escaping from harsh Northern winters.

They still come to soak up sun on the beach, to tee up year-round, to bass-fish and bird-watch in forests and parks, and some snowbirds also party in the clubs and bars of Daytona Beach—a popular spring-break destination. They also soak in the region's living history. Tortuous, towering live oaks, plantations, and antebellum-style architecture recollect the Old South, and the mossy marshes of Silver Springs and the St. Johns River look as untouched and junglelike today as they did generations ago. St. Augustine is a showcase of early U.S. history, and Jacksonville is a young but sophisticated metropolis with its own unique history.

JACKSONVILLE

399 mi north of Miami, on I–95.

One of Florida's oldest cities and at 841 square mi the largest city in the continental United States, Jacksonville makes for an underrated vacation spot. It offers appealing downtown riverside areas, handsome residential neighborhoods, the region's only skyscrapers north of Daytona, a thriving arts scene, and, for football fans, the NFL's Jaguars and the NCAA Gator Bowl. Remnants of the Old South flavor the city, especially in the Riverside/Avondale historic district, where moss-draped oak trees frame prairie-style bungalows and Tudor-revival mansions and palm trees, Spanish bayonet, and azaleas populate the landscape.

EXPLORING JACKSONVILLE

Because Jacksonville was settled along both sides of the twisting St. Johns River, a number of attractions are on or near a riverbank. Both sides of the river, which is spanned by myriad bridges, have downtown areas and waterfront complexes of shops, restaurants, parks, and museums. Some attractions can be reached by water taxi or Skyway Express monorail system—scenic alternatives to driving back and forth across the bridges—but a car is generally necessary.

GETTING HERE AND AROUND

The main airport for the region is Jacksonville International Airport. It's served by AirTran, American, Continental, Delta, jetBlue, Northwest, Southwest, United, and US Airways. At the airport, free shuttles run from the terminal to all parking lots (except the garage) around the clock. Taxi service is available from a number of companies including Gator City Taxi and Yellow Cab–Jacksonville, with fares to downtown approximately $38–$43 and to the beaches and Amelia Island about $55. Shuttle service is available from Gator City Shuttle for approximately $32.50 for one to three people going downtown, $52.50 for one to three people going to the beaches and Amelia Island. Town Car service is available from Carey Jacksonville for approximately $76 to downtown and $85 to the beaches and Amelia Island (one to four people); reservations are required.

Connecting the north and south banks of the St. Johns River in Jacksonville, the S.S. Marine Taxi runs between several locations, including the Crowne Plaza Jacksonville Riverfront and the Jacksonville Landing. The one-way trip takes about five minutes. During football season the water taxi also makes trips to Jacksonville Municipal Stadium on game days and for special events like the Florida/Georgia game. The ferry runs Sunday through Thursday 11–9; Friday and Saturday 11–11 (except during rain or other bad weather), with special hours on game days and for special events. One-way fare is $3, special-event fare is $5. The Jacksonville Transportation Authority serves Jacksonville and the beaches via buses, shuttles, and trolley lines.

ESSENTIALS

Transportation Contacts Carey Jacksonville (☎ *904/992–2022*). **Gator City Shuttle** (☎ *904/741–6828*). **Gator City Taxi** (☎ *904/741–0008*). **Jacksonville International Airport** (*JAX* ☎ *904/741–4902* 🌐 *www.jia.aero*). **Jacksonville Transportation Authority** (*JTA* ☎ *904/630–3100* 🌐 *www.jtafla.com*). **S.S. Marine Taxi** (☎ *904/733–7782* 🌐 *www.jaxwatertaxi.com*). **Yellow Cab–Jacksonville** (☎ *904/355–8294*).

Visitor Information Jacksonville and the Beaches Convention and Visitors Bureau (✉ *550 Water St., Suite 1000, Jacksonville* ☎ *904/798–9111 or 800/733–2668* 🌐 *www.visitjacksonville.com*).

A GOOD TOUR

Numbers correspond to the Jacksonville map.

Start your morning at the riverfront campus of Jacksonville University, site of the **Alexander Brest Museum & Gallery** ❶. After browsing the collections, head south on University Boulevard and east on Arlington Expressway to **Kona Skatepark** ❷, where you can practice your sausage grinds or watch X-treme athletes riding the concrete wave. Next, head west on the Arlington Expressway over the Mathews Bridge onto State Street to Jefferson Street, then follow the signs for Riverside to get to the **Cummer Museum of Art & Gardens** ❸. After touring the museum and its grounds, head back on Riverside Avenue toward the Acosta Bridge and take the first exit, San Marco Boulevard. Two blocks north is the **Museum of Science & History** ❹. Walk a block south to the Automated Skyway Express station and take a monorail across the river to the **Jacksonville Landing** ❺, where you can shop and grab some lunch. Afterward, walk four blocks north to the **Museum of Contemporary Art Jacksonville** ❻. Head back to the Landing to recross the river, but for the return trip, catch a water taxi. On the road again, go back over the Acosta Bridge and stay on Broad Street to 1st Street, where you'll find the **Karpeles Manuscript Library Museum** ❼. Next, proceed west on State Street to Interstate 95 north, then take the Heckscher Drive exit east to Zoo Road for the **Jacksonville Zoo and Gardens** ❽. Finally, head back to Interstate 95 north and exit east at Dunn Avenue, which becomes Busch Road, and visit the **Anheuser-Busch Jacksonville Brewery** ❾.

TIMING

Jacksonville's sprawl dictates a generous amount of time for reaching and touring these sights. Allow at least two days, six hours a day (including driving time), budgeting at least an hour for each attraction, more for the zoo and art museums.

Numbers in the margin correspond to the Jacksonville map.

EXPLORING

TOP ATTRACTIONS

❸ **Cummer Museum of Art & Gardens.** The world-famous Wark Collection of early-18th-century Meissen porcelain is just one reason to visit this former riverfront estate, which includes 13 permanent galleries with more than 5,000 items spanning more than 8,000 years, and 3 acres of riverfront gardens reflecting northeast Florida's blooming seasons and indigenous varieties. Art Connections allows kids to experience art through hands-on, interactive exhibits. One of the museum's newest additions, the Thomas H. Jacobsen Gallery of American Art, focuses on works by American artists, including Max Weber, N.C. Wyeth, and Paul Manship. ✉ *829 Riverside Ave.* ☎ *904/356–6857* 🌐 *www.cummer.org* 🎟 *$10, free Tues. 4–9* ⏲ *Tues. 10–9, Wed.–Sat. 10–5, Sun. noon–5.*

❺ **Jacksonville Landing.** During the week, this riverfront festival marketplace caters to locals and tourists alike, with specialty shops, full-service restaurants—including a sushi bar, Italian bistro, and a steak house—and

Alexander Brest Museum and Gallery **1**
Anheuser-Busch Jacksonville Brewery **9**
Cummer Museum of Art & Gardens **3**
Jacksonville Landing **5**
Jacksonville Zoo and Gardens **8**
Karpeles Manuscript Library Museum **7**
Kona Skatepark **2**
Museum of Contemporary Art Jacksonville **6**
Museum of Science & History **4**

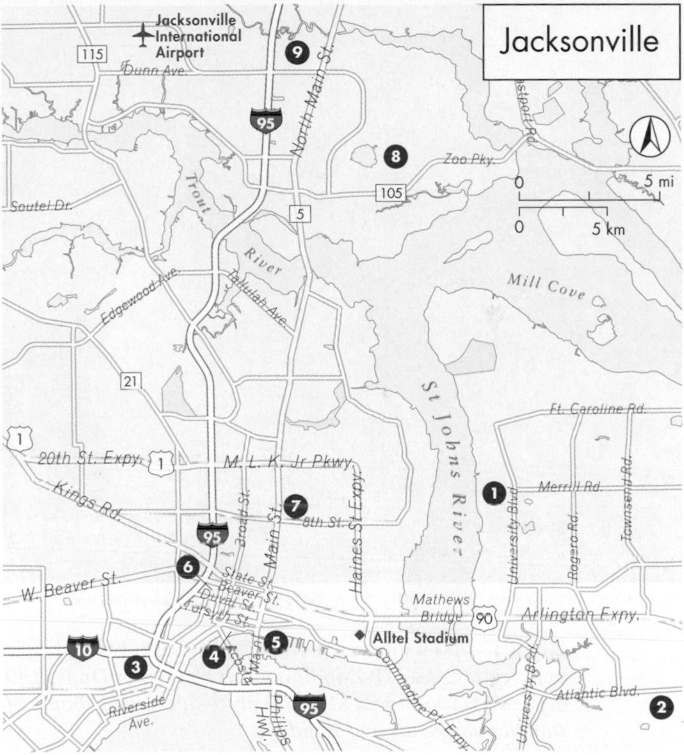

an internationally flavored food court. On weekends the Landing hosts more than 250 events each year, ranging from the good clean fun of the Lighted Boat Parade and Christmas Tree Lighting to the just plain obnoxious Florida/Georgia game after-party, as well as live music (usually of the local cover-band variety) in the courtyard. ✉ *2 Independent Dr.* ☎ *904/353–1188* 🌐 *www.jacksonvillelanding.com* 🎫 *Free* 🕐 *Mon.–Thurs. 10–8, Fri. and Sat. 10–9, Sun. noon–5:30; restaurant hrs vary.*

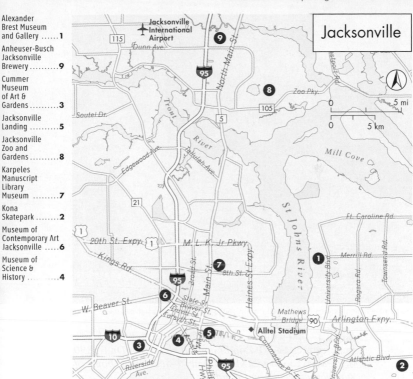

8 Fodor's Choice ★ **Jacksonville Zoo and Gardens.** Encompassing more than 120 acres on Jacksonville's north side, this midsize zoo is home to 1,000 unique plant species and 1,500 rare and exotic animals from barking tree frogs and Madagascar hissing cockroaches to dusky pygmy rattlesnakes and giant anteaters. Among the zoo's outstanding exhibits are its collection of rare waterfowl and the Serona Overlook, which showcases some of the world's most venomous snakes. The Florida Wetlands is a 2½-acre area with black bears, bald eagles, white-tailed deer, and other animals native to Florida. The African Veldt has alligators, elephants, and white rhinos, among other species of African birds and mammals; and the Range of the Jaguar, winner of the Association of Zoos and Aquarium's Exhibit of the Year, includes 4 acres of exotic big cats as well as 20 other species of animals. New additions include Play Park, complete with a splash park, forest play area, maze, and discovery building; and Stingray

Rainbox Lorikeet might pop by and say hello while you're touring the Jacksonville Zoo.

Bay, a 17,000-gallon pool where visitors can pet and feed the mysterious creatures. ✉ *370 Zoo Pkwy., off Heckscher Dr. E* ☎ *904/757–4463* 🌐 *www.jaxzoo.org* 🎫 *$13* ⏲ *Daily 9–5; extended hours offered during summer weekends and holidays.*

6 Fodor's Choice ★ **Museum of Contemporary Art Jacksonville.** In this loftlike downtown building, the former headquarters of the Western Union Telegraph Company, a permanent collection of 20th-century art shares space with traveling exhibitions. The museum encompasses five galleries and ArtExplorium, a highly interactive educational exhibit for kids, as well as a funky gift shop and Café Nola, open for lunch on weekdays and for dinner on Thursday and Friday. MOCA Jacksonville (previously known as the Jacksonville Museum of Modern Art) also hosts film series, lectures, and workshops throughout the year, and packs a big art-wallop into a relatively small 14,000 square feet. Sunday is free for families. ✉ *Hemming Plaza, 333 N. Laura St.* ☎ *904/366–6911* 🌐 *www.mocajacksonville.org* 🎫 *$8* ⏲ *Tues., Wed., Fri., and Sat. 10–4, Thurs. 10–8, Sun. noon–4; hrs subject to change.*

WORTH NOTING

1 **Alexander Brest Museum & Gallery.** Boehm and Royal Copenhagen porcelain and Steuben glass are among the collections at this Jacksonville University museum. Also on display are cloisonné pieces, pre-Columbian artifacts, and one of the finest collections of ivory anywhere from the early 17th to the late 19th century. ✉ *Jacksonville University, Phillips Fine Arts Bldg., 2800 University Blvd. N* ☎ *904/256–7371* 🌐 *arts.ju.edu* 🎫 *Free* ⏲ *Weekdays 9–4.*

9 **Anheuser-Busch Jacksonville Brewery Tour.** Beer lovers will appreciate this behind-the-scenes look at how barley, malt, rice, hops, and water form the "King of Beers." Guided tours take guests through the entire brewing and bottling process. Or you can hightail it through the self-guided tour and head straight to the free beer tastings (for those guests 21 years and older, that is). ✉ *111 Busch Dr.* ☎ *904/696–8373* 🌐 *www.budweisertours.com* 🎟 *Free* 🕒 *Mon.–Sat. 10–4; guided tours Mon.–Sat. 10–3 on the ½ hr.*

7 **Karpeles Manuscript Library Museum.** File this one under "hidden treasure," because the majority of folks who live in Jacksonville have never even heard of, let alone visited, Karpeles. That's too bad, because this museum, in a 1921 neoclassical building on the outskirts of downtown, has displayed some priceless documents, such as the original draft of the Bill of Rights, the Emancipation Proclamation signed by Abraham Lincoln, handwritten manuscripts of Edgar Allan Poe and Charles Dickens, and musical scores by Beethoven and Mozart. Manuscript exhibits change every three months or so and coincide with monthly art exhibits. Also on the premises is an antique-book library, with volumes dating from the late 1800s, and a children's museum. ✉ *101 W. 1st St.* ☎ *904/356–2992* 🌐 *www.rain.org/~karpeles/jax.html* 🎟 *Free* 🕒 *Tues.–Sat. 10–4, Sun. noon–4.*

2 **Kona Skatepark.** Built back in the '70s—before most of its patrons were even born—this extreme-sport outpost still has its original bowls, plus updates like an 80-foot-wide vertical ramp, two street courses, and one of the area's few snake runs (a high-speed downhill run with banked turns). Skateboard legend Tony Hawk digs the park's retro feel so much that he named it one of his five favorite U.S. skate parks. The park, which also caters to in-line skaters, rents boards, skates, and safety equipment (required of all skaters) and offers lessons. Rates are reduced on weekdays. And as proof that you're never too old to skate, skaters over 30 get half off every Wednesday night and those over 65 skate free every day. ✉ *8739 Kona Ave.* ☎ *904/725–8770* 🌐 *www.konaskatepark.com* 🎟 *$2.50–$10* 🕒 *Mon.–Thurs. 1–9, Fri. 1–10, Sat. 10–10, Sun. noon–9.*

4 **Museum of Science & History.** You won't find any mad scientists here, but you'll probably find lots of giggling ones. Targeted at the elementary- and middle-school set, MOSH aims to educate and entertain kids about science and history through a variety of interactive exhibits like the JEA Science Theatre, where they'll participate in live experiments related to electricity and electrical safety; the Florida Naturalist's Center, where they can explore northeast Florida wildlife (like American alligators, gopher turtles, and various native snakes and birds); and the Universe of Science, where they'll learn about properties of physical science through hands-on demonstrations. Other permanent exhibits include Atlantic Tails, an exploration of whales, dolphins, and manatees; Currents of Time, chronicling 12,000 years of northeast Florida history; and Prehistoric Park, featuring a life-size Allosaurus skeleton. The Alexander Brest Planetarium hosts daily shows on astronomy, and, on weekends, Cosmic Concerts, 3-D laser shows set to pop music. ✉ *1025 Museum Circle* ☎ *904/396–6674* 🌐 *www.themosh.org* 🎟 *$9 adult, planetarium*

$1 and Extreme Science Show $1 (in addition to admission), Cosmic Concerts $7–$9 ⏲ Weekdays 10–5, Sat. 10–6, Sun. 1–6.

SPORTS AND THE OUTDOORS

BASEBALL

The **Jacksonville Suns** (✉ *301 A. Phillip Randolph Blvd.* ☎ *904/358–2846*), the AA minor-league affiliate of the Florida Marlins, play at the $34 million Baseball Grounds of Jacksonville.

BOAT TOURS

River Cruises (☎ *904/306–2200* 🌐 *www.jaxrivercruises.com*) has relaxing lunch and dinner-dancing cruises and private sightseeing charters aboard the Annabelle Lee and Lady St. Johns paddleboats; schedules vary with the season.

FOOTBALL

Jacksonville Municipal Stadium (✉ *1 Stadium Pl.* ☎ *904/633–6100)* 🌐 *www.jaxevents.com*) is home to the NFL's **Jacksonville Jaguars** (☎ *904/633–6000, 904/633–2000 tickets*). Jacksonville kicks off each year with its own New Year's Day bowl game, the **Konica Minolta Gator Bowl** (☎ *904/798–1700* 🌐 *www.gatorbowl.com*), which usually hosts NCAA top-10 teams from the ACC, Big East, or Big 12 conferences, or Notre Dame. Billed as the "World's Largest Outdoor Cocktail Party," the **Florida vs. Georgia Football Classic** (☎ *904/630–3690*), or the Florida/Georgia Game, as it's better known, celebrates one of college football's most heated rivalries—between the Florida Gators and Georgia Bulldogs—every fall.

GOLF

Champions Club at Julington Creek (✉ *1111 Durbin Creek Blvd.* ☎ *904/287–4653*) is well maintained and reasonably priced; greens fee $23/$55, depending on whether you're a resident. The 6,891-yard course at **Cimarrone Golf Club** (✉ *2800 Cimarrone Blvd.* ☎ *904/287–2000* 🌐 *www.cimarronegolf.com/*) has a water or marsh feature on every hole; greens fee $50/$60 (discounts available online). The **Eagle Harbor Golf Club** (✉ *2217 Eagle Harbor Pkwy., Orange Park* ☎ *904/269–9300*) has an 18-hole, par-72 course designed by Clyde Johnston and has a driving range, club rentals, and discount packages; greens fee $41/$64. **Magnolia Point Golf and Country Club** (✉ *3670 Clubhouse Dr., Green Cove Springs* ☎ *904/284–3559*) boasts a "player-friendly" course with beautiful scenery and wildlife; greens fee $29/$65. **Panther Creek Golf Club** (✉ *11368 Panther Creek Pkwy.* ☎ *904/783–2600* ☎ *www.magnoliapointgolfclub.com*) is northeast Florida's premier public course; greens fee $36/$56. **Windsor Parke Golf Club** (✉ *13823 Sutton*

PLAY BALL!

Jacksonville became Major League Baseball's first spring-training location when the city hosted the Washington Statesmen in 1888. Spring training has since moved south, but the baseball tradition has continued. Some of the game's best players—Hank Aaron, Nolan Ryan, Tom Seaver, Randy Johnson, and Alex Rodriguez—have done a stint on Jacksonville's farm-league teams.

Park Rd. ☎ *904/223–4653* ☎ *www.windsorparke.com*) has 18 holes (par 72) on tree-lined fairways and amid natural marshlands; greens fee $39/$55.

SHOPPING

At **Five Points** (✉ *Intersection of Park, Margaret, and Lomax Sts., Riverside*) you'll find a small but funky shopping district of new and vintage-clothing boutiques, shoe stores, and antiques shops, as well as a handful of eateries and bars, not to mention some of the most colorful characters in the city. **The Shoppes of Avondale** (✉ *St. Johns Ave., between Talbot Ave. and Dancy St.*) highlight upscale clothing and accessories boutiques, art galleries, home-furnishings shops, a chocolatier, and trendy restaurants. **San Marco Square** (✉ *Intersection of San Marco and Atlantic Blvds.*) has dozens of interesting apparel, home, and jewelry stores and restaurants in 1920s Mediterranean-revival–style buildings. One of northeast Florida's newest shopping destinations, **St. Johns Town Center** (✉ *4663 River City Dr., Southside* ☎ *904/642–8339*) is an outdoor "lifestyle center" with shops not found anywhere else in northeast Florida, including Anthropologie, Apple, Lucky Brand Jeans, and Sephora, as well as the Cheesecake Factory, P.F. Changs, and Maggiano's Little Italy.

NIGHTLIFE AND THE ARTS

NIGHTLIFE

Inside the Ramada Inn Mandarin, the **Comedy Zone** (✉ *3130 Hartley Rd.* ☎ *904/292–4242* 🌐 *www.comedyzone.com*) is the area's premier comedy nightclub. Technically, **Eclipse** (✉ *4219 St. Johns Ave.* ☎ *904/387–3582*) is a dance club that serves up a mix of moods and music styles for the twentysomething set. Wine snobs, rejoice! At **The Grotto** (✉ *2012 San Marco Blvd.* ☎ *904/398–0726* 🌐 *www.grottowine.com*) you can enjoy more than 70 wines by the glass. **Harmonious Monks** (✉ *10550 Old St. Augustine Rd.* ☎ *904/880–3040*) claims to have "the world's most talented waitstaff." They certainly might be the most energetic, performing throughout the night and encouraging customers to dance on the bar.

Jack Rabbits (✉ *1528 Hendricks Ave.* ☎ *904/398–7496* 🌐 *www.jackrabbitsonline.com*) welcomes the latest and greatest indie bands and budding rock stars. The self-proclaimed "neighborhood lounge with a dash of dance club style," **Mark's** (✉ *315 E. Bay St.* ☎ *904/355–5099* 🌐 *www.marksjax.com*) attracts the beautiful people for theme nights like Indie Lounge Tuesdays. **Metro** (✉ *2929 Plum St.* ☎ *904/388–8719* 🌐 *www.metrojax.com*) is more than just a gay bar: it's like seven gay bars rolled into one, including a piano bar, dance club, lounge, and drag-show cabaret.

Fans of Christian music flock to the **Murray Hill Theatre** (✉ *932 Edgewood Ave. S* ☎ *904/388–7807* 🌐 *www.murrayhilltheatre.com*), a no-smoking, no-alcohol club. At 12,000 square feet, **Plush** (✉ *845 University Blvd. N* ☎ *904/743–1845* 🌐 *plushjax.com*) is certainly Jacksonville's largest

DID YOU KNOW?

The Jacksonville Jazz Festival takes place within a five-block area centered around Laura Street in the heart of downtown. Festival highlights include performances by renowned jazz musicians and jazz piano and youth jazz talent competitions.

nightclub; it's also the loudest. **Square One** (✉ *1974 San Marco Blvd.* ☎ *904/306–9004*) has an upscale singles' scene, with live music on weekends. Billing itself as the city's premier underground venue, **TSI** (✉ *333 E. Bay St.* ☎ *904/424–3531* 🌐 *www.clubtsi.com*) hosts local and national indie bands like Bonde do Role, VHS or Beta, The Death Set, and Black Kids. The **Twisted Martini** (✉ *Jacksonville Landing, 2 Independent Dr.* ☎ *904/353–8464* 🌐 *www.thetwistedmartini.com*) is a glitzy meat market complete with designer martinis, chichi bar food, and a VIP area with bottle service. It also offers live music, hosting stars like Colbie Caillat.

3

THE ARTS

Northeast Florida's major presenter of professional national and international touring attractions is the **FCCJ Artist Series** (✉ *501 W. State St.* ☎ *904/632–3373*). **The Florida Theatre** (✉ *128 E. Forsyth St.* ☎ *904/355–2787*) presents concerts, dance productions, and special events, as well as a classic-movie series. The **Jacksonville Symphony Orchestra** (☎ *904/354–5547*) performs at the Jacoby Music Hall in the Times-Union Center for the Performing Arts and gives outdoor concerts at downtown's Metro Park.

The riverfront **Metropolitan Park** (✉ *1410 Gator Bowl Blvd.* ☎ *904/630–0837*) is a 27-acre riverfront venue that hosts the city's major musical and cultural events, such as the Jacksonville Jazz Festival in April and Freedom, Fanfare and Fireworks on July Fourth. Each spring, the Jacksonville Jazz Festival (🌐 *www.jaxjazzfest.com*) centers around downtown's Laura Street. Dubbed "the Harlem of the South" in the 1920s, historic La Villa is the site of the **Ritz Theatre** (✉ *829 N. Davis St.* ☎ *904/632–5555*), which hosts musical and theatrical events of particular interest to the African-American community. One of the oldest continuously operating community theaters in the United States, **Theatre Jacksonville** (✉ *2032 San Marco Blvd.* ☎ *904/396–4425*) presents outstanding productions ranging from Shakespeare to programs for children.

WHERE TO EAT

$ ITALIAN ✕ **Al's Pizza**. Although it fits the criteria of a neighborhood pizza joint—cheap, casual, and frequented by locals—this funky-chic pizzeria looks more like a hangout for hipsters than Jacksonvillians low on dough (pardon the pun). The main draw is the pizza, particularly Al's gourmet white pie, but eggplant parmigiana, stuffed shells, and lasagna are also good. The Riverside location caters to its more upscale clientele with table service and a separate bar area. Service can be spotty. ✉ *1620 Margaret St., #201, Riverside* ☎ *904/388–8384* ✉ *14286 Beach Blvd., Intracoastal West* ☎ *904/223–0991* ✉ *8060 Philips Hwy., Southside* ☎ *904/731–4300* 🌐 *www.alspizza.com* ✍ *Reservations not accepted* 💳 *AE, D, MC, V.*

$ AMERICAN ★ ✕ **bb's**. Sleek yet cozy, this hip bistro is as popular with corporate muckety-mucks looking to close a deal as it is with young lovebirds seemingly on the verge of popping the question (though shouting the question might be more appropriate, considering how loud the dining room can get on weekends). The concrete floors and a stainless-steel wine bar provide an interesting backdrop for comfort-food-inspired entrées and daily specials that might include char-grilled beef tenderloin, prosciutto-wrapped pork chops, or mushroom triangoli ravioli. On the lighter side, grilled pizzas, sandwiches, and salads, especially warm goat-cheese salad, are favorites. Although a wait is practically guaranteed, you can pass the time sizing up the display of diet-destroying desserts. ✉ *1019 Hendricks Ave., Southbank* ☎ *904/306–0100* 🌐 *www.bbsrestaurant.com* 💳 *AE, D, MC, V* ⏲ *Closed Sun.*

¢ AMERICAN ✕ **Biscottis.** The local artwork on the redbrick walls is a mild distraction from the jovial crowds (from yuppies to soccer moms to metrosexuals) jockeying for tables in this midsize restaurant. Elbows almost touch, but no one seems to mind. The menu offers the unexpected: wild mushroom ravioli with a broth of corn, leek, and dried apricot; or curry-grilled swordfish with cucumber-fig bordelaise sauce. Be sure to sample from Biscottis' decadent dessert case (we hear the peanut butter ganache is illegal in three states). Brunch, a local favorite, is served until 3 on weekends. ✉ *3556 St. Johns Ave., Avondale* ☎ *904/387–2060* 🌐 *www.biscottis.net* ✍ *Reservations not accepted* 💳 *AE, MC, V.*

$$$ ECLECTIC ✕ **Bistro Aix.** When a Jacksonville restaurant can make Angelinos feel like they haven't left home, that's saying a lot. With its slick black-leather booths, 1940s brickwork, velvet drapes, and intricate marbled globes, Bistro Aix (pronounced "X") is just that place. Regulars can't get enough of the creamy onion soup, crispy calamari, and house-made potato chips with warm blue-cheese appetizers or entrées like oak-fired fish Aixoise, grilled salmon, and filet mignon. Adventurous diners can sample diverse dishes on a prix-fixe menu for $29. Aix's resident pastry chef ensures no sweet tooth leaves unsatisfied. For the most part, waitstaff are knowledgeable and pleasant, though some patrons find their demeanor snooty, except, of course, the ones from L.A. Call for preferred seating. ✉ *1440 San Marco Blvd., San Marco* ☎ *904/398–1949* 🌐 *www.bistrox.com* ✍ *Reservations not accepted* 💳 *AE, D, DC, MC, V* ⏲ *No lunch weekends.*

¢ SOUTHERN ★ ✕ **Clara's Tidbits.** Hearing locals speak of Tidbits' best-selling side dish is a little like listening to Homer Simpson talk about doughnuts ("Mmm, potato salad")—dreamy and lustful. Although not every item on the menu has such a hypnotic hold on its customers, the lunch-only restaurant has a devoted customer base, mostly San Marco and downtown worker bees, who generate buzz about chicken-supreme pitas, French dips, veggie surprise, and the Tidbit Special, seasoned chicken chunks and pasta on a bed of lettuce topped with avocado and cheddar. It's open fewer than 20 hours a week and there's almost always a line 10 deep. Don't be discouraged. It moves fast. ✉ *1076 Hendricks Ave., San Marco* ☎ *904/396–0528* 🌐 *www.tidbitsfood.com* ✍ *Reservations not accepted* ⏲ *Closed weekends. No dinner* 💳 *AE, MC, V.*

$–$$ SEAFOOD ✕ **Clark's Fish Camp.** It's out of the way and hard to find, but every mile and missed turn will be forgotten once you step inside this former bait shop overlooking Julington Creek. Clark's has one of the largest menus in town, with more than 160 appetizers and entrées, including the usual—shrimp, catfish, and oysters—and the unusual—ostrich, rattlesnake, and kangaroo. In keeping with the more bizarre entrées is the decor, best described as early American taxidermy: hundreds of stuffed birds and critters gaze upon you in the main dining room, and preserved lions, gazelles, baboons, even a rhino, keep a watchful eye in the bar. One person's kitschy may be another's creepy. Reservations accepted for parties of eight or more. ✉ *12903 Hood Landing Rd., Mandarin* ☎ *904/268–3474* 🌐 *www.clarksfishcamp.com* 💳 *AE, MC, V* ⏲ *No lunch weekdays.*

¢ AMERICAN ★ ✕ **European Street Café.** Wicker baskets and lofty shelves brimming with European confections and groceries like Toblerone and Nutella fill practically every inch of space not occupied by café tables. The menu is similarly overloaded, with nearly 100 deli sandwiches and salads. Notable are raspberry-almond chicken salad and the "Blue Max," with pastrami, corned beef, Swiss cheese, sauerkraut, hot mustard, and blue-cheese dressing. This quirky spot is favored by area professionals looking for a quick lunch, as well as the under-40 set doing 23-ounce curls with one of the restaurant's 20-plus beers on tap (plus more than 100 in bottles). The San Marco and Beach Boulevard locations offer live music Thursday and Saturday nights, respectively. ✉ *2753 Park St., Riverside* ☎ *904/384–9999* ✉ *1704 San Marco Blvd., Marco* ☎ *904/398–9500* ✉ *5500 Beach Blvd., Southside* ☎ *904/398–1717* ✍ *Reservations not accepted* 💳 *AE, D, MC, V.*

¢ AMERICAN ✕ **The Loop Pizza Grill.** Standing in line to place your order, you may think this Jacksonville-based chain is just another fast-food joint. But one look at the menu, chock-full of designer salads, specialty pizzas, and upscale sandwiches, not to mention the stylish dining room's upholstered booths, funky light fixtures, and tiled floors, and you'll realize you're in McDreamland. The big sellers here are the burgers (the Loop 'N Cheddar and Loop 'N Blue, in particular) and pizzas (both California-thin and Chicago-thick), but sandwiches like the portobello mushroom and Cajun chicken merit special mention. ✉ *2014 San Marco Blvd., San Marco* ☎ *904/399–5667* 🌐 *www.looppizzagrill.com* ✉ *9965 San Jose Blvd., Mandarin* ☎ *904/262–2210* ✉ *4000 St. Johns Ave., Suite 21, Avondale* ☎ *904/384–7301* ✉ *8221 Southside Blvd., Baymeadows* ☎ *904/645–7788* ✍ *Reservations not accepted* 💳 *AE, D, MC, V.*

$$$ ECLECTIC Fodor's Choice ★ ✕ **Matthew's.** Local foodies sing chef Matthew Medure's praises not only for his culinary creativity but also his dazzling presentation, which stands out quite strikingly against the very spare decor of stainless steel, polished bronze, and terrazzo flooring. The menu changes nightly, but might include lemon-roasted Amish chicken with honey-truffle spaghetti squash, or herb-roasted rack of lamb with mustard-pistachio crust. Complement your meal with one of 450 wines (topping out at more than $1,000 per bottle), then dive into one of the warm soufflés for dessert. ✉ *2107 Hendricks Ave., San Marco* ☎ *904/396–9922* 💳 *AE, D, DC, MC, V* ⏲ *Closed Sun. No lunch.*

$ BARBECUE ✕ **Sticky Fingers.** In the South, barbecue joints are a dime a dozen, yet this chain smokehouse manages to stand out year after year. Perhaps it's the atypical environment—meals are served on real dishes rather than paper plates, soft lighting replaces harsh fluorescents, and B.B. King plays in the background instead of Tim McGraw. Maybe it's because the staff go out of their way to make sure you're satisfied. Probably, it's the classic, Memphis-style smoked ribs, slow-cooked over aged hickory and available in five versions, including Memphis-style dry, Tennessee whiskey, and Carolina sweet. A full bar sweetens the deal. ✉ *8129 Point Meadows Way, Southside* ☎ *904/493–7427* 🌐 *www.stickyfingers.com* ✉ *13150 City Station Dr., Northside* ☎ *904/309–7427* 💳 *AE, D, MC, V.*

$ THAI ✕ **Taste of Thai.** Ravenous regulars dominate the tightly packed tables at this warm family-owned restaurant in a nondescript strip mall down the street from Memorial Medical Center (which would explain the many diners in scrubs). For more than 10 years, proprietress Aurathai Sellas, who might just be the most cheerful person in the entire restaurant business, has prepared the exotic dishes of her homeland, including *pla lad prig* (hot and spicy fish), *goog thod* (crispy shrimp), and chicken in peanut sauce, as well as pad thai. There may be fancier Thai restaurants in town, but none has the service and loyalty of this one. Reservations are accepted for parties of six or more. ✉ *4317 University Blvd. S, Southside* ☎ *904/737–9009* 🌐 *www.tasteofthaijax.com* 💳 *AE, D, MC, V* ⏲ *Closed Sun. No lunch Mon.*

WHERE TO STAY

$$$ **Crowne Plaza Jacksonville Riverfront.** A staple on Jacksonville's south bank for decades, the former Hilton Jacksonville Riverfront maintains its commanding presence but now as a Crowne Plaza property. Its location on the south side of the St. Johns River puts it within walking distance of restaurants, the Automated Skyway Express, and the water taxi; the swanky Ruth's Chris Steak House is one of the on-site restaurants. Guests wanting to live like a king can book the San Marco (aka the Elvis Room), a premier suite with Jacuzzi tub and two balconies that Presley called home during numerous trips to Jacksonville. **Pros:** newly renovated rooms; riverfront balconies; friendly staff. **Cons:** small bathrooms; loud air-conditioning units; no free parking. ✉ *1201 Riverplace Blvd.* ☎ *904/398–8800* 🌐 *www.cpjacksonville.com* *292 rooms, 30 suites* *In-room: refrigerator (some), Wi-Fi. In-hotel: 2 restaurants, room service, bars, pool, gym, laundry service, Wi-Fi hotspot, parking (paid)* 💳 *AE, D, MC, V.*

$$ **House on Cherry Street.** Guests of this early-20th-century Avondale inn rave about its gracious and fascinating hostess, owner Victoria Freeman, who bends over backward to make every stay memorable. Whether it's fresh flowers in every room or afternoon tea selected from her tea garden, Freeman believes it's all in the details. Guest rooms, full of pewter, Oriental rugs, antique canopy beds, and other remnants of a rich past, are often described as comfortable, roomy, and immaculately clean. The parks and gardens of the chic Avondale district are a walk away. **Pros:** riverfront location; warm hospitality; evening cocktail hour. **Cons:** only four rooms; no in-room phones; closed six months of the year. ✉ *1844 Cherry St.* ☎ *904/384–1999* 🌐 *www.houseoncherry.com* *4 rooms* *In-room: no phone, Wi-Fi. In-hotel: parking (free), no kids under 12* 💳 *AE, MC, V* *CP.*

$$$ **Hyatt Regency Jacksonville Riverfront.** In Jacksonville it doesn't get much more convenient than this downtown waterfront hotel. Perched on the north bank of the St. Johns River, the 19-story property is within walking distance of the Jacksonville Landing, Florida Theatre and Times-Union Center, corporate office towers, and the county courthouse. The former Adam's Mark Hotel now includes the Plaza III Steakhouse and rooms updated with Florida-style decor, triple-sheeted beds, pillow-top mattresses, and sliding-glass doors. Since northeast Florida's largest hotel encompasses 110,000 square feet of meeting space, chances are pretty good you'll share an elevator with someone wearing a name tag (if you're not wearing one yourself). **Pros:** riverfront location; newly renovated; rooftop pool and gym. **Cons:** not all rooms are riverfront; slow valet service; no minibars. ✉ *225 E. Coastline Dr.* ☎ *904/588–1234* 🌐 *www.jacksonville.hyatt.com* *966 rooms, 21 suites* *In-room: refrigerator (some), DVD (some), Internet. In-hotel: 3 restaurants, room service, bar, pool, gym, laundry facilities, laundry service, Wi-Fi hotspot, parking (paid), some pets allowed* *AE, D, DC, MC, V.*

$$$ ★ **The Inn at Oak Street.** Built in 1902 as a private residence, the three-story, 6,000-square-foot Frame Vernacular–style building was restored and reopened as a bed-and-breakfast popular for romantic weekends and girlfriend getaways. Rooms include the cozy and romantic Boudoir room, with a four-poster bed and an inlaid-tile fireplace, and the more modern St. John's Room, with cobalt-hue walls and a geometric bedspread. Each room has a private bath—some with whirlpool tubs and others with double-head showers—and second-story rooms offer balconies. Mornings start with a hearty breakfast in the dining room; evenings wind down with wine and refreshments in the parlor. **Pros:** meticulously clean; walking distance to restaurants; private bathrooms. **Cons:** hardwood floors can be noisy; not for families with small children; no pool. ✉ *2114 Oak St.* ☎ *904/379–5525* 🌐 *www.innatoakstreet.com* *6 rooms, 1 suite* *In-room: refrigerator, Internet. In-hotel: gym, Wi-Fi hotspot, parking (free), no kids under 12* *AE, D, MC, V* *BP.*

$$$ ★ **Omni Jacksonville Hotel.** The Omni cemented its reputation as Jacksonville's most luxurious and glamorous hotel with a multimillion-dollar makeover in 2005, and it's still crisp as a new dollar bill. Spacious guest rooms are decorated in downtown urban style (think neutral grays and creams, dark wood, stainless steel, and flat-screen TVs), and well-maintained. A splashy marble-floor lobby leads to the reception area, an upscale lounge—J Bar—and Juliette's Bistro, with cozy banquettes and tables that bask in the airiness of a lofty atrium. The Omni also has the distinction of maintaining its 400-employee workforce, despite the economic downturn, so its trademark service is still up to par. Bell service is exemplary; many porters have 10-plus years on the job, so they can, and will happily, help you find just about anything. **Pros:** downtown location; large rooms; rooftop pool. **Cons:** congested valet area; pricey on-site restaurant; chaotic when there's a show at the Times-Union Center across the street. ✉ *245 Water St.* ☎ *904/355–6664 or 800/843–6664* 🌐 *www.omnijacksonville.com* *342 rooms, 4 2-bedroom suites* *In-room: kitchen (some), Wi-Fi. In-hotel: restaurant, room service, bar,*

pool, gym, laundry service, Wi-Fi, parking (paid), some pets allowed ▭ *AE, D, DC, MC, V.*

$$$ **Riverdale Inn.** In the early 1900s, Jacksonville's wealthiest residents built mansions along Riverside Avenue, dubbed "The Row": the three-story Riverdale Inn is only one of two such homes remaining. Previous owners took great care in preserving the home's original details, including heart-of-pine floors, crown moldings, and original shingle façade. Despite its age—more than a century—the mansion feels pristine and squeaky-clean inside and out. Guest rooms, some with fireplaces, are individually decorated to evoke a turn-of-the-century feel. Some rooms have claw-foot tubs and shower combinations; others have only showers. The inn is within walking distance of numerous restaurants, the Cummer Museum of Art & Gardens, and Five Points. Or simply stumble downstairs to the Row Restaurant and Gum Bunch Pub. **Pros:** on-site restaurant and pub; close to area restaurants and shops; private bathrooms. **Cons:** small rooms; restaurant and pub can be noisy; limited parking. ✉ *1521 Riverside Ave.* ☎ *904/354–5080* 🌐 *www.riverdaleinn.com* *7 rooms, 3 suites* *In-room: refrigerator (some), DVD (some), Wi-Fi. In-hotel: restaurant, bar, parking (free), some pets allowed, no kids under 12* ▭ *AE, D, MC, V.*

JACKSONVILLE AREA

JACKSONVILLE BEACHES

20 mi east of Jacksonville, on U.S. 90 (Beach Boulevard).

Separated from the mainland by the Intracoastal Waterway, Jacksonville's main beaches run along the barrier island that includes the laid-back towns of Jacksonville Beach, Neptune Beach, Atlantic Beach, and Ponte Vedra Beach. The northernmost of Jacksonville's beaches, Atlantic Beach is quieter but a favorite with local surfers. Adjacent Neptune Beach is largely residential and draws bicyclists and in-line skaters who cruise up and down 1st Street. Just south is Jacksonville Beach, which has a decidedly more active shoreline, with volleyballs and Frisbees buzzing through the air and portable radios blasting everything from Kanye West to Van Halen. With multimillion-dollar homes stretching for miles, Ponte Vedra is the most difficult beach to access, but makes for a lovely drive down Route A1A. Lifeguards are on duty on the more populated stretches of the beaches from 10 to 6 in summer.

EXPLORING

Adventure Landing and Shipwreck Island Water Park. With go-karts, two miniature-golf courses, laser tag, batting cages, kiddie rides, and an arcade, Adventure Landing is more like an old-time boardwalk than a high-tech amusement park. But when the closest theme park is more than two hours away, you make do. The largest family-entertainment center in northeast Florida also encompasses Shipwreck Island Water Park, which features a lazy river for tubing, a 500,000-gallon wave pool, and three extreme slides—the Rage, HydroHalfpipe, and Eye of the Storm. ✉ *1944 Beach Blvd., Jacksonville Beach* ☎ *904/246–4386*

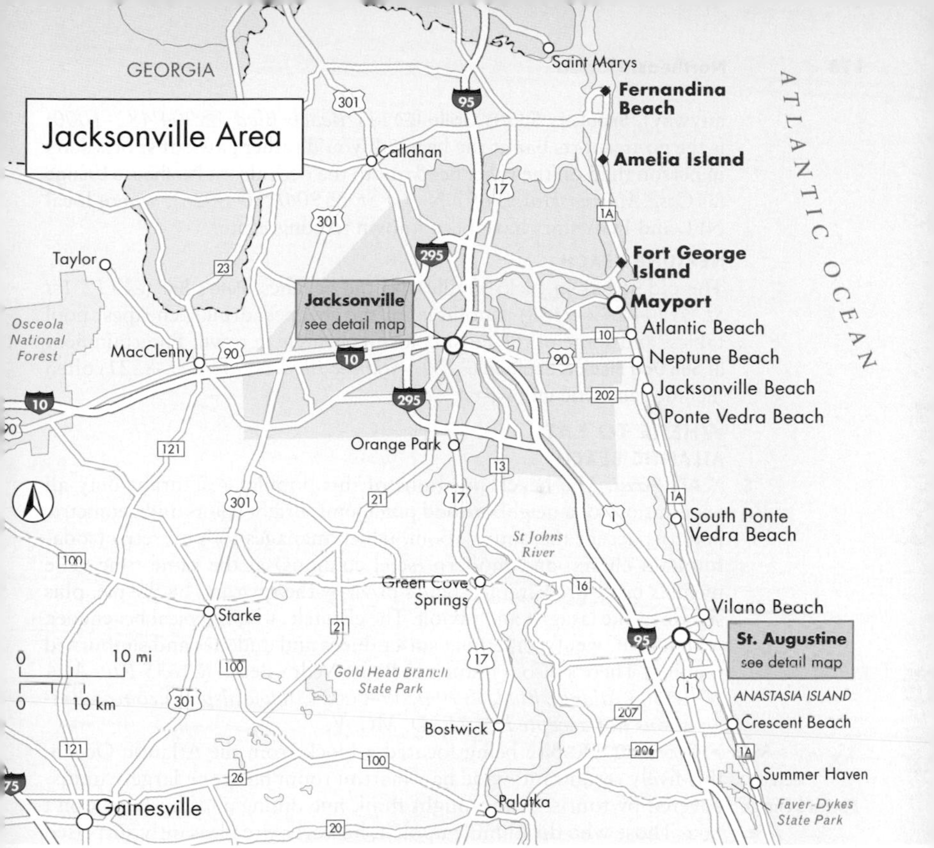

🌐 *www.adventurelanding.com* 🎫 *Adventure Landing free (fees for rides and games), Shipwreck Island $27.99* ⏲ *Adventure Landing: Mon.–Thurs. and Sun. 10* AM*–10* PM*, Fri. and Sat. 10* AM*–midnight. Shipwreck Island: call, hrs vary; Shipwreck Island closed late Sept.–late Mar.*

SPORTS AND THE OUTDOORS

BIKING

Champion Cycling (✉ *1303 N. 3rd St., Jacksonville Beach* ☎ *904/241–0900*) rents beach cruisers by the hour and by the day. **Ponte Vedra Bicycles** (✉ *250 Solana Rd., Ponte Vedra Beach* ☎ *904/273–0199*) includes free bike maps with your rental.

NIGHTLIFE

JACKSONVILLE BEACH

A groovy, low-key lounge during the week, **The Atlantic** (✉ *333 N. 1st St.* ☎ *904/249–3338*) becomes jam-packed with twentysomethings on weekends. **Fionn MacCool's** (✉ *333 N. 1st St., Suite 150* ☎ *904/242–9499*) is, first and foremost, an Irish pub, but its menu is nothing to shake a shillelagh at. Hoist a pint o' Guinness and sing along with Emerald Isle troubadours at **Lynch's Irish Pub** (✉ *514 N. 1st St.* ☎ *904/249–5181*). The beautiful people gather at the **Ocean Club** (✉ *401 N. 1st St.* ☎ *904/242–8884*) for dancing, flirting, and drinking, not necessarily in that order. With nearly 80 TVs and an impressive menu (by sports-bar standards anyway), **Sneakers Sports Grille** (✉ *111 Beach Blvd.* ☎ *904/482–1000*) is the go-to sports bar at the beach. If you'd rather gawk at sports stars in person than on the tube, head out to the oceanfront **Penthouse Lounge** (✉ *Casa Marina Hotel, 691 N. 1st St.* ☎ *904/270–0025*), where local NFL and PGA stars have been known to congregate.

NEPTUNE BEACH

The oldest bar in Jacksonville and the beaches, **Pete's Bar** (✉ *117 1st St.* ☎ *904/249–9158*) is notable for the cheapest drinks, cheapest pool tables, and some of the most colorful clientele in town. Entertainment at **Sun Dog Steak & Seafood** (✉ *207 Atlantic Blvd.* ☎ *904/241–8221*) often includes acoustic guitarists.

WHERE TO EAT

ATLANTIC BEACH

$ ITALIAN ✕ **Al's Pizza**. The beach locations of this popular restaurant defy all expectations of a neighborhood pizza joint. Bright colors and geometric patterns accent the dining room, which manages to look retro (soda-fountain chairs) and modern (steel columns) at the same time. The menu is fairly predictable; there's pizza by the slice and by the pie, plus standbys like lasagna and ravioli. The clientele, too, is typical beachgoer, with lots of twentysomething surfer dudes and dudettes and sunburned families. There's also a branch in Ponte Vedra Beach (✉ *635 Rte. A1A N*). ✉ *303 Atlantic Blvd.* ☎ *904/249–0002* 🌐 *www.alspizza.com* ✍ *Reservations not accepted* ▭ *AE, D, MC, V.*

$$$ ECLECTIC Fodor's Choice ★ ✕ **Ocean 60**. Despite being located a block from the Atlantic Ocean, this lively restaurant–wine bar–martini room has gone largely undiscovered by tourists, who might think fine dining and flip-flops don't mix. Those who do stumble upon it, however, are pleasantly surprised to find that a casual aura befits Ocean 60's eclectic seasonal menu, with signature items like walnut-grilled salmon and Mayport prawns, Kona-coffee-grilled rack of lamb, and Buddha's Delight, vegetables sautéed with cellophane noodles and Thai coconut and Kaffir lime broth. Things are anything but laid-back on Friday and Saturday nights, however, when live music and potent cocktails attract the party crowd. ✉ *60 Ocean Blvd.* ☎ *904/247–0060* 🌐 *www.ocean60.com* ▭ *D, MC, V* ⊙ *Closed Sun.*

$$ AMERICAN ★ ✕ **Ragtime Tavern & Seafood Grill**. A New Orleans theme prevails at this loud place that attracts a lively crowd ranging in age from 21 to midlife crisis. Bayou bouillabaisse (lobster, shrimp, scallops, fish, crab, clams, and crawfish in a creole-court bouillon) and Ragtime shrimp (deep-fried fresh shrimp rolled in coconut) are the true specialties here, along with microbrews made on the premises. If you aren't into creole and Cajun, try a po'boy sandwich or fish sizzled on the grill. ✉ *207 Atlantic Blvd.* ☎ *904/241–7877* 🌐 *www.ragtimetavern.com* ✍ *Reservations not accepted* ▭ *AE, D, MC, V.*

$ SOUTHERN ✕ **Sticky Fingers**. Like its counterpart across the ditch (beach-speak for the Intracoastal Waterway), the Atlantic Beach location of this über-popular barbecue joint is known for its inviting atmosphere, perky staff, and spectacular service. Oh, yeah, and some people really seem to like the ribs, too. Slow cooked over aged hickory, the ribs come in five versions, including Memphis-style dry, Tennessee whiskey, and

Beaches make great places to drop a line and see if the fish are biting.

Carolina sweet. The hickory-smoked chicken wings are arguably the best wings in town. ✉ *363 Atlantic Blvd. #1* ☎ *904/241–7427* 🌐 *www.stickyfingers.com* ⚠ *Reservations not accepted* ▭ *AE, D, MC, V.*

JACKSONVILLE BEACH

¢ AMERICAN ✕ **European Street Café**. After more than 25 years of dominance in Jacksonville, the colorful and quirky family-owned eatery finally lands at the beach with the same ambitious menu of sandwiches, salads, and soups; overflowing gourmet-food section; mind-boggling beer list; and cookies big enough to knock someone unconscious. An impressive, hand-carved bar is a favorite hangout for thirsty locals who belly up for monthly beer tastings and daily happy hour 2–7 PM. The senior crowds prefer to sip their carafes of zinfandel in the bustling dining room. ✉ *992 Beach Blvd.* ☎ *904/249–3001* ⚠ *Reservations not accepted* ▭ *AE, D, MC, V.*

WHERE TO STAY

ATLANTIC BEACH

$$$ **One Ocean**. Atlantic Beach's only high-rise oceanfront hotel isn't just one of the newest resorts in Jacksonville and the beach area, it is also the area's most memorable. Open since mid-2008, One Ocean captures the serenity of the sea through a color palette of sea-foam green, sand, and sky blue, and reflective materials like glass and marble. The sophisticated yet relaxed atmosphere is similar to that of an art gallery, a theme that is carried through to the original photographs that hang in every room. Some guests may balk at the $25 resort fee above and beyond the room rate, but considering all it includes (Wi-Fi, mini-refrigerator and amenities cabinet stocked with your favorite soft drinks and snacks,

coffee delivery, and clothes-steaming service), it's not a bad deal. The resort is also pet- and kid-friendly, and it has the only oceanfront spa in northeast Florida. **Pros:** exceptional service; walking distance to restaurants and shops; all rooms have ocean view; 24-hour room service. **Cons:** tiny bathroom; no self-parking on property; resort fee. ✉ *1 Ocean Blvd.* ☎ *904/249–7402* 🌐 *www.oneoceanresort.com* *190 rooms, 3 suites* *In-room: safe, refrigerator, Wi-Fi. In-hotel: 3 restaurants, room service, bar, pool, gym, spa, beachfront, children's programs (ages 5–12), laundry service, parking (paid), some pets allowed* ▭ *AE, D, DC, MC, V.*

JACKSONVILLE BEACH

$$$ **Casa Marina Hotel.** Compared with nearby oceanfront inns, it's small. But Casa Marina's creature comforts and rich history—including a stint as military housing during World War II and host to Franklin Delano Roosevelt and Al Capone in its early days—make it a big hit with visitors and locals (especially of the wedding-party kind) looking for a peaceful retreat with character. Rooms are spacious, with comfy beds, and most have some view of the ocean. Unwind in the large courtyard behind the hotel with a drink from the bar, or take a stroll on the beach. Take note that Friday and Saturday nights can get a little noisy with the Penthouse Lounge (and all those drunken groomsmen) in operation. **Pros:** oceanfront location; comfortable beds; good alternative to chain hotels. **Cons:** no pool; inconsistent restaurant hours; room service only available on weekends. ✉ *691 1st St. N* ☎ *904/270–0025* 🌐 *www.casamarinahotel.com* *7 rooms, 16 suites* *In-room: refrigerator. In-hotel: 2 restaurants, room service, bars, beachfront, Wi-Fi hotspot, parking (free)* ▭ *AE, D, MC, V.*

NEPTUNE BEACH

$$ **Sea Horse Oceanfront Inn.** Lacking the hoity-toity decor and amenities of other beachfront properties, this bright-pink-and-aqua '50s throwback (you check in at the motel office, not a grand lobby) caters to budget-minded guests seeking an ultracasual, laid-back vibe. Rooms are modestly decorated and equipped, but feature an ocean view with a private balcony or patio. The kidney-shaped pool and lounge chairs are pretty standard issue but make for a refreshing respite from the hot Florida sun. The Lemon Bar is a hot spot for locals and hotel guests. **Pros:** beach access with private walk-over; popular bar on-site; walking distance to restaurants and shops. **Cons:** no-frills decor; no room service. ✉ *120 Atlantic Blvd.* ☎ *904/246–2175 or 800/881–2330* 🌐 *www.seahorseoceanfrontinn.com* *39 rooms, 1 suite* *In-room: kitchen, refrigerator, Wi-Fi. In-hotel: bar, pool, beachfront, Wi-Fi hotspot, parking (free)* ▭ *AE, D, MC, V.*

PONTE VEDRA BEACH

$$$$ Fodor's Choice ★ **The Lodge & Club.** This Mediterranean-revival oceanfront resort—with its white-stucco exterior and Spanish roof tiles—is luxury lodging at its best. Rooms are spacious and have cozy window seats, appealing artwork, and private balconies overlooking the Atlantic Ocean. Some units include a whirlpool tub and gas fireplace. Guests consistently praise staff for going the extra mile, whether it's accommodating special diets in the dining room or coordinating day trips and shopping excursions.

Relax in one of three pools or on the private beach. Guests at the Lodge have full access to sports, recreation, and spa facilities at sister property Ponte Vedra Inn & Club, less than 2 mi away. There's also turndown service and high tea. **Pros:** high-end accommodations; excellent service; private beach. **Cons:** non-valet parking—can be a hike to and from car; most recreation facilities are off-site at Ponte Vedra Inn & Club; $18 gratuity charge automatically added to bill nightly. ✉ *607 Ponte Vedra Blvd.* ☎ *904/273–9500 or 800/243–4304* 🌐 *www.pvresorts.com* *42 rooms, 24 suites* *In-room: safe, kitchen (some), refrigerator (some). In-hotel: 2 restaurants, room service, bars, pools, gym, beachfront, water sports, bicycles, children's programs (ages 4–12), laundry service, Wi-Fi hotspot, parking (free)* *AE, D, DC, MC, V.*

3

$$$$ **Fodor's Choice** ★ **Ponte Vedra Inn & Club.** Considered northeast Florida's premier resort for decades, this 1928 landmark continues to wow guests with its stellar service and sharp rooms and common areas. Accommodations are in a series of white-brick, Spanish-style buildings lining the beach; rooms are extra large, and most have ocean views. The main house holds the registration area and some common spaces, including a big living room with fireplace. The inn's renowned full-service spa attracts the rich and famous, including actors, supermodels, and former first ladies. **Pros:** accommodating, friendly staff; private beach; adults-only pool. **Cons:** charge for umbrellas and chaises on the beach; crowded pool; $18 gratuity charge automatically added to bill nightly. ✉ *200 Ponte Vedra Blvd.* ☎ *904/285–1111 or 800/234–7842* 🌐 *www.pvresorts.com* *205 rooms, 45 suites* *In-room: safe, kitchen (some), refrigerator (some), DVD, Wi-Fi. In-hotel: 4 restaurants, room service, bars, golf courses, tennis courts, pool, gym, spa, beachfront, bicycles, children's programs (ages 2–12), laundry service, parking (free)* *AE, D, DC, MC, V.*

$$$ **Sawgrass Golf Resort & Spa, a Marriott Resort.** One of the top golf resorts in the country and host hotel of the world-famous THE PLAYERS Championship, the Sawgrass Golf Resort & Spa has plenty to offer golfers, including playing privileges on the renowned TPC at Sawgrass Stadium Course. This is truly a full-service resort, whether you've come to laze about (the resort includes a 25,000-square-foot, full-service spa and allows guests access to the Cabana Beach Club, a private beach club nearby) or get active playing an Arnold Palmer–designed 18-hole mini-golf course, swimming in one of four pools or fishing in freshwater lakes and ponds. A $16-million room-renovation project in 2007 has given the resort a face more befitting its name. **Pros:** championship golf courses; readily available shuttle; efficient staff. **Cons:** beach not within walking distance; overrated food; no free parking. ✉ *1000 PGA Tour Blvd.* ☎ *904/285–7777 or 800/457–4653* 🌐 *www.sawgrassmarriott.com* *508 rooms, 24 suites, 80 villas* *In-room: kitchen (some), refrigerator, Wi-Fi. In-hotel: 8 restaurants, room service, bars, golf course, tennis court, pools, gym, spa, bicycles, children's programs (ages 5–12), laundry facilities, laundry service, parking (paid), some pets allowed* *AE, D, DC, MC, V.*

MAYPORT

20 mi northeast of downtown Jacksonville, on Rte. A1A/105.

Dating back more than 300 years, this is one of the oldest fishing communities in the United States. It has several excellent and very casual seafood restaurants and a large commercial shrimp-boat fleet. It's also home to the third-largest naval facility in the country, Naval Station Mayport.

GETTING HERE AND AROUND

The arrival of the **St. Johns River Ferry** (☎ *904/241–9969* 🌐 *www.stjohnsriverferry.com*) in 1948 represented a huge convenience to local residents, plus a fun activity to share with kids. The ferry (the Jean Ribault) continues to delight passengers young and old as they drive aboard the 153-foot vessel and embark on the 10-minute cruise across the river between Mayport and Fort George Island. Cost is $3 per motorcycle, $5 per car ($1 additional per axle), $1 for pedestrians. It departs daily; call for departure times.

EXPLORING

Fodor's Choice ★ **Kathryn Abbey Hanna Park** is a 450-acre oceanfront property just north of Atlantic Beach. It's filled with spectacular beaches, biking and hiking trails, wooded campsites, and a 60-acre freshwater lake, perfect for swimming, kayaking, and canoeing. The lake area also includes picnic tables, grills, and a quarter-acre water park with fountains and squirting hoses. Throughout the park there are restrooms, showers, and snack bars, open April through Labor Day, as well as lifeguards supervising all water activities during summer. Surfers in the know head to "the poles" for the best wave action in town. The park includes nearly 300 campsites and cabins with fees ranging from $20 to $34 per day. ✉ *500 Wonderwood Dr.* ☎ *904/249–4700* 🎫 *$3 per vehicle* ⏲ *Apr.–Oct., daily 8–8; Nov.–Mar., daily 8–6.*

FORT GEORGE ISLAND

25 mi northeast of Jacksonville, on Rte. A1A/105.

One of the oldest inhabited areas of Florida, Fort George Island is lush with foliage, natural vegetation, and wildlife. A 4-mi nature and bike trail meanders across the island, revealing shell mounds dating as far back as 5,000 years.

EXPLORING

Kingsley Plantation. Built in 1792 by Zephaniah Kingsley, an eccentric slave trader, this is the oldest remaining cotton plantation in the state. The ruins of 23 tabby (a concretelike mixture of sand and crushed shells) slave houses, a barn, and the modest Kingsley home are open to the public via self-guided tours and reachable by ferry or bridge. ✉ *Rte. A1A–Heckscher Dr., north of St. Johns River Ferry* ☎ *904/251–3537* 🌐 *www.nps.gov/timu/historyculture.kp.htm* 🎫 *Free* ⏲ *Daily 9–5; ranger talks daily at 2.*

Talbot Island State Parks. The Talbot Island State Parks, including Big and Little Talbot islands, have 17 mi of gorgeous beaches, sand dunes, and golden marshes that hum with birds and native waterfowl. Come to picnic, fish, swim, snorkel, or camp. Little Talbot Island, one of the few undeveloped barrier islands in Florida, has river otters, marsh rabbits, raccoons, alligators, and gopher tortoises. Canoe and kayak rentals are available, and the north area is considered the best surfing spot in northeast Florida. A 4-mi nature trail winds across Little Talbot, and there are several smaller trails on Big Talbot. ✉ *12157 Heckscher Dr.* ☎ *904/251–2320* 🌐 *www.floridastateparks.org/littletalbotisland* 🎫 *$5 per vehicle, up to 8 people; $4 per motorcycle, $2 for pedestrians and bicyclists* 🕒 *Daily 8–sundown.*

AMELIA ISLAND (FERNANDINA BEACH)

35 mi northeast of Jacksonville.

At the northeastern-most reach of Florida, Amelia Island has beautiful beaches with enormous sand dunes along its eastern flank, a state park with a Civil War fort, sophisticated restaurants, interesting shops, and accommodations that range from B&Bs to luxury resorts. The town of Fernandina Beach is on the island's northern end; a century ago casinos and brothels thrived here, but those are gone. Today there's little reminder of the town's wild days, though one event comes close: the Isle of Eight Flags Shrimp Festival, held during the first weekend of May in Fernandina.

ESSENTIALS

Visitor Information Amelia Island Tourist Development Council (✉ *102 Centre St., Fernandina Beach* ☎ *800/226–3542* 🌐 *www.ameliaisland.com*).

TAKE A TOUR

Amelia River Cruises and Charters (☎ *904/261–9972* 🌐 *www.ameliarivercruises.com*) takes guests on a narrated tour of Fernandina's historic waterfront, salt marshes, and Cumberland Sound.

EXPLORING

★ **Amelia Island Historic District.** In Fernandina Beach, this district has more than 50 blocks of buildings listed on the National Register of Historic Places; 450 ornate structures built before 1927 offer some of the nation's finest examples of Queen Anne, Victorian, and Italianate homes. Many date to the haven's mid-19th-century glory days. Pick up a self-guided-tour map at the chamber of commerce, in the old train depot—once a stopping point on the first cross-state railroad—and take your time exploring the quaint shops, restaurants, and boutiques that populate the district, especially along Centre Street.

★ **Fort Clinch State Park.** One of the country's best-preserved and most complete 19th-century brick forts, Fort Clinch was built to discourage further British intrusion after the War of 1812 and was occupied in 1863 by the Confederacy; a year later it was retaken by the North. During the Spanish-American War it was reactivated for a brief time, but no battles were ever fought on its grounds (which explains why it's so well preserved). Wander through restored buildings, including furnished barracks, a kitchen, and a repair shop. Living-history reenactments of Civil War garrison life are scheduled throughout the year. The 1,086-

WORD OF MOUTH

"On this particular day, the beach was strewn with starfish. They were everywhere. And they were still alive. I took a quick picture and then proceeded to run up and down the beach trying to save every one of them. I hope that I succeeded."
—photo by funinthetub, Fodors.com member

acre park surrounding the fort has camping, nature trails, carriage rides, a swimming beach, and surf and pier fishing. Nature buffs will enjoy the variety of flora and fauna, especially since Fort Clinch is the only state park in northeast Florida designated by the Florida Fish and Wildlife Conservation Commission as a viewing destination for the eastern brown pelican, green sea turtle, and loggerhead sea turtle. ✉ *2601 Atlantic Ave.* ☎ *904/277–7274* 🌐 *www.floridastateparks.org/fortclinch* 🎫 *$6 per vehicle, up to 8 people, $2 pedestrians, bicyclists* 🕒 *Daily 8–sundown.*

A BANNER BEACH

Fernandina Beach is also known as the "Isle of Eight Flags," a moniker derived from the fact that it is the only American site to have been under eight different flags (French, Spanish, British, Patriots, Green Cross of Florida, Mexican Revolutionary Flag, National Flag of the Confederacy, and United States). Every May the Isle of Eight Flags Shrimp Festival also celebrates another of Fernandina's claims to fame: birthplace of the modern shrimping industry.

3

SPORTS AND THE OUTDOORS

BEACH

Amelia Island's eastern shore includes **Main Beach**, a 13-mi stretch of white-sand beach edged with dunes, some 40 feet high. It's one of the few beaches in Florida where horseback riding is allowed.

HORSEBACK RIDING

Kelly Seahorse Ranch (✉ *7500 1st Coast Hwy., Amelia Island* ☎ *904/491–5166* 🌐 *kellyranchinc.com*), located within the Amelia Island State Park, takes guests on horseback rides on the beach.

KAYAKING

Kayak Amelia (✉ *13030 Heckscher Dr., Amelia Island* ☎ *904/251–0016* 🌐 *www.kayakamelia.com*) takes adventurous types on guided tours of salt marshes and Fort George River and also rents equipment for those looking to create their own adventures. Reservations required.

NIGHTLIFE

The oldest continuously operating bar in Florida, the **Palace Saloon** (✉ *117 Centre St.* ☎ *904/491–3332*) entertained the Rockefellers and Carnegies at the turn of the 20th century but now caters to common folk.

WHERE TO EAT

$$–$$$ SEAFOOD Fodor's Choice ★

✕ **Beech Street Grill.** Housed in an 1889 sea-captain's house, this highly regarded Fernandina Beach restaurant caters to locals who crave its comfort-food-inspired dishes like tenderloin meat loaf with spinach, ham, and provolone cheese with shiitake-mushroom gravy and chive whipped potatoes, as well as visiting foodies who have heard the quiet buzz about this cozy, coastal, two-story Victorian from afar. Hardwood floors and marble fireplaces aside, one of Beech Street's most treasured fixtures is pianist John "If-you-can-hum-it-I-can-play-it" Springer, who has been entertaining diners for decades. Delicious nightly fish specials and outstanding wine list. ✉ *801 Beech St.* ☎ *904/277–3662* 🌐 *www.beechstreetgrill.com* ✍ *Reservations essential* 💳 *AE, D, DC, MC, V* 🕒 *No lunch.*

$$$$ ECLECTIC Fodor's Choice ★ **Salt.** This Ritz-Carlton, Amelia Island restaurant continues to set the culinary standard in northeast Florida with inventive cuisine highlighting seasonal ingredients that might include peekytoe crab salad with watermelon and peanuts or Kurobuta pork chop and truffled potato gratin. The impressive wine list has more than 500 bottles (20 by the glass), service is nothing short of impeccable, and there's a view of the Atlantic Ocean from every table. For a unique dining experience, reserve A Seat in the Kitchen, a private dining room within the kitchen where you'll watch the chefs at work and enjoy a personalized five-course meal. Collared shirts are recommended. *The Ritz-Carlton, 4750 Amelia Island Pkwy. 904/277–1028 www.ritzcarlton.com Reservations essential AE, D, DC, MC, V Closed Mon. No lunch.*

$$$ SEAFOOD **Verandah Restaurant.** Although located on Amelia Island Plantation, this family-friendly restaurant is open to non-resort guests, many of whom drive from Jacksonville to dine here. The dining room has a casual vibe to it, with floral prints and roomy booths, but the menu is all business. Fresh seafood dishes are a highlight, including red snapper with pecan, crab meunière, pasta paella, and surf-and-turf, as is the "famous" Verandah salad, a meal in itself. And if you luck out and find she-crab soup on the menu (it's seasonal and not always available), order yourself the biggest bowl or bucket they have. *6800 1st Coast Hwy. 904/321–5050 www.aipfl.com/Restaurants/Verandah_Menu.htm AE, D, MC, V No lunch.*

WHERE TO STAY

$$ **Amelia Hotel at the Beach.** Across the street from the beach, this mid-size inn is not only convenient but an economical and family-friendly alternative to the luxury resorts and romantic and kid-unfriendly B&Bs that populate the area. The beach and several restaurants are within walking distance, particularly convenient for families. Parents will also appreciate the hotel-wide no-smoking policy and Continental breakfast served each morning in the lobby. Rooms are modestly furnished and have ocean views (provided you're not near-sighted) and pool views (considering the pool is practically in the parking lot, it's not much to look at). **Pros:** complimentary breakfast; free Wi-Fi; comfy beds. **Cons:** small pool; not all rooms have balconies; no on-site restaurant. *1997 S. Fletcher Ave. 904/206–5200 or 877/263–5428 www.ameliahotel.com 86 rooms In-room: kitchen (some), refrigerator, Wi-Fi. In-hotel: pool, gym, Wi-Fi hotspot, parking (free) AE, D, MC, V CP.*

$$$$ Fodor's Choice ★ **Amelia Island Plantation.** The first-rate golf, tennis, and spa facilities are big draws at this sprawling, family-oriented resort where accommodations include full-service hotel rooms as well as 1-, 2-, and 3-bedroom villas. All hotel rooms are oceanfront with private balconies or patios, though first-floor rooms have a better view of the marsh or golf course than the Atlantic. If the sound of waves crashing on the beach doesn't lull you to sleep, the pillow-top mattresses should do the trick. Villas are privately owned, so availability, amenities, and decor vary. With its ancient oaks, marshes, and lagoons, the resort is also a worthy destination for hiking, biking, and bird-watching. **Pros:** family-friendly; variety

of outdoor activities; shuttle service throughout property. **Cons:** far removed from facilities (golf course, shops, tennis courts); quality of villas inconsistent; a hike to some hotel rooms. ✉ *6800 1st Coast Hwy.* ☎ *904/261–6161 or 800/874–6878* 🌐 *www.aipfl.com* *249 rooms, 361 1-, 2-, and 3-bedroom villas* *In-room: safe, kitchen (some), refrigerator (some), DVD (some). In-hotel: 10 restaurants, room service, bars, golf courses, tennis courts, pools, gym, spa, beachfront, water sports, bicycles, children's programs (ages 3 and up), laundry facilities (some), laundry service, Wi-Fi hotspot, some pets allowed* *AE, D, MC, V.*

3

$$$$ ★ **Elizabeth Pointe Lodge.** Guests at this oceanfront inn, built to resemble an 1890s sea-captain's house, can't say enough about the impeccable personal service, beginning with its legendary gourmet breakfasts (dill scrambled eggs and French toast are among the crowd pleasers) and ending with social hour every evening with wine and hors d'oeuvres in the library. Oceanside units have great water views, albeit through disappointingly small windows. The Tradewinds Suite, with its ocean-view, private patio, and plantation-style shutters, is the most romantic. A chair-lined porch offers everyone a chance to rock in ocean breezes, and on cold nights guests can cluster around the living-room fireplace. An adjacent cottage has additional rooms and a suite. **Pros:** beachfront location; hospitable staff; 24-hour desk attendant; convenient to various indoor and outdoor recreation possibilities. **Cons:** pricey for a B&B; not all rooms are oceanfront ✉ *98 S. Fletcher Ave.* ☎ *904/277–4851 or 800/772–3359* 🌐 *www.elizabethpointelodge.com* *24 rooms, 1 2-bedroom cottage* *In-room: kitchen (some), DVD, Wi-Fi. In-hotel: beachfront, laundry facilities, Wi-Fi hotspot, parking (free)* *AE, D, MC, V* *BP.*

$$$ **Florida House Inn.** The rambling two-story clapboard main building, more than 150 years old, is definitely of another era, with creaking floors and small doors. But what the Florida House lacks in polish, it makes up for in character—and characters, like Laurel and Hardy, who reportedly bunked down at the inn. Rooms have handmade quilts and hooked rugs but also include such modern amenities as king-size beds and whirlpool tubs. Some even have fireplaces. The Frisky Mermaid Bar and Grille, a lively pub on the 1st floor of the main house, can be a blessing or a curse, depending on if you're trying to catch up on your social skills or catch up on your sleep (request a room in the south wing or in one of the carriage houses across the street if you're attempting the latter). **Pros:** proximity to Centre Street; free use of scooters; free Wi-Fi. **Cons:** bar can be noisy; loud air-conditioning. ✉ *22 S. 3rd St.* ☎ *904/261–3300 or 800/258–3301* 🌐 *www.floridahouseinn.com* *22 rooms, 1 suite, 1 carriage house* *In-room: DVD (some), Wi-Fi. In-hotel: restaurant, bar, bicycles, parking (free), some pets allowed* *AE, D, MC, V.*

$$$$ Fodor's Choice ★ **The Ritz-Carlton, Amelia Island.** Guests know what to expect from the Ritz-Carlton (namely, elegance, superb comfort, and excellent service), and the Amelia Island location is certainly no exception. All accommodations in the eight-story building have balconies and ocean views; suites and rooms are spacious and luxurious and are furnished with

heavy print draperies, plush carpet, framed prints, and beds so comfortable, you'll need a drag-out call instead of a wake-up call. Public areas are exquisitely maintained, and fine cuisine can be had at a choice of restaurants, including Salt. Room service is available 24/7. **Pros:** fine-dining restaurant; world-class spa; private beach access; accommodating staff. **Cons:** no self-parking; lack of nightlife; a drive to sites and restaurants. ✉ *4750 Amelia Island Pkwy.* ☎ *904/277–1100* 🌐 *www.ritzcarlton.com/ameliaisland* *444 rooms, 44 suites* *In-room: safe, Wi-Fi. In-hotel: 4 restaurants, room service, bars, golf course, tennis courts, pools, gym, spa, beachfront, bicycles, children's programs (ages 5–12), laundry service, Wi-Fi hotspot* *AE, D, DC, MC, V.*

ST. AUGUSTINE

35 mi south of Jacksonville, on U.S. 1.

Founded in 1565 by Spanish explorers, St. Augustine is the nation's oldest city and has a wealth of historic buildings and attractions. In addition to the historic sites on the mainland, the city has 43 mi of beaches on two barrier islands to the east, both reachable by causeways. Several times a year St. Augustine holds historic reenactments, such as December's Grand Christmas Illumination, which commemorates the town's British occupation.

The core of any visit is a tour of the historic district, a showcase for more than 60 historic sites and attractions, plus 144 blocks of houses listed on the National Register of Historic Places. You could probably spend several weeks exploring these treasures, but don't neglect other, generally newer, attractions found elsewhere in town.

ESSENTIALS

Visitor Information St. Augustine, Ponte Vedra, & The Beaches Visitors and Convention Bureau (✉ *500 San Sebastian View* ☎ *904/829–1711 or 800/653–2489* 🌐 *www.getaway4florida.com*) is open daily 8:30–5:30.

TAKE A TOUR

In St. Augustine, the Old Town Trolley Tour (☎ *904/829–3800* 🌐 *www.historictours.com/staugustine*) of St. Augustine conducts fully narrated tours covering more than 100 points of interest. As the nation's oldest continually operated carriage company, the St. Augustine Transfer Company (☎ *904/829–2391* 🌐 *www.staugustinetransfer.com*) offers historic and ghost tours via horse-drawn carriage, as well as the Spirits of St. Augustine Ghost Walk. Drivers specialize in either history or specters, so be sure to ask a few questions before hopping aboard if you have a particular interest.

Numbers in the margin correspond to the St. Augustine map.

EXPLORING

TOP ATTRACTIONS

5 **Castillo de San Marcos National Monument.** This massive structure is three
Fodor's Choice ★ centuries old, and it looks every century of it. The fort was constructed of coquina, a soft limestone made of broken shells and coral. Built by the Spanish to protect St. Augustine from British raids (English pirates

Built to protect Spain's St. Augustine, the Castillo de San Marcos still stands along the shore.

were handy with a torch), the fort was used as a prison during the Revolutionary and Civil wars. Park rangers provide an introductory narration, after which you're on your own to explore the moat, turrets, and 16-foot-thick walls. Garrison rooms depict the life of the era, and special cannon-firing demonstrations are held on weekends from Memorial Day to Labor Day. Children under 16 are admitted free and must be accompanied by an adult. Save the receipt, since admission is valid for seven days. ✉ *1 S. Castillo Dr.* ☎ *904/829–6506* 🌐 *www.nps.gov/casa* 🎫 *$6* ⏲ *Daily 8:45–5:15, last ticket sold at 4:45.*

13 **Cathedral Basilica of St. Augustine.** The cathedral has the country's oldest written parish records, dating from 1594. Restored in the mid-1960s, the current structure (1797) had extensive changes after an 1887 fire. If you're around for the holidays, be sure to stop in for the gorgeous Christmas Mass, held at midnight on Christmas Eve among banks of flickering candles and gilded walls. ✉ *40 Cathedral Pl.* ☎ *904/824–2806* 🌐 *www.thefirstparish.org* 🎫 *Donation welcome* ⏲ *Weekdays 9–4:30.*

9 **Flagler College.** Originally one of two posh hotels Henry Flagler built in 1887, this building—now a small liberal-arts college—is a riveting Spanish Renaissance Revival structure with towers, turrets, and arcades decorated by Louis Comfort Tiffany. The former Hotel Ponce de León is a National Historic Landmark, having hosted U.S. presidents Grover Cleveland, Theodore Roosevelt, and Warren Harding. Tours are offered daily through Flagler's Legacy Tours. ✉ *74 King St.* ☎ *904/829–6481, 904/823–3378 tour information* 🌐 *www.flagler.edu* 🎫 *Tours $7* ⏲ *Daily 10–3, tours begin on the hour.*

8 ★ **Lightner Museum.** In his quest to turn Florida into an American Riviera, Henry Flagler built two fancy hotels in 1888—the Ponce de León, which became Flagler College, and the Alcazar, which now houses this museum. The building showcases three floors of furnishings, costumes, and Victorian art glass, plus not-to-be-missed ornate antique music boxes (demonstrations daily at 11 and 2). The Lightner Antiques Mall perches on three levels of what was the hotel's indoor pool. ✉ *75 King St.* ☎ *904/824–2874* 🌐 *www.lightnermuseum.org* 🎫 *$10* 🕙 *Museum daily 9–5, last admission at 4.*

HOPE SPRINGS ETERNAL

Whether or not the St. Augustine's world-renowned Fountain of Youth has actual curative powers is debatable. But visitors to North America's first historical site (Ponce de León's expedition landed in the vicinity in 1513) who are brave enough to drink the foul-smelling water will get a dose of 42 minerals, including iron and—not surprising—sulfur.

15 **Mission of Nombre de Dios.** The site, north of the historic district, commemorates where America's first Christian mass was celebrated. A 208-foot-tall stainless-steel cross marks the spot where the mission's first cross was planted in 1565. Also on the property is the Shrine of Our Lady of La Leche, the first shrine devoted to Mary in the United States. The history is enthralling, but locals return often to bask in the beautiful peace that resides here. The landscape is exquisitely maintained and the mission is criss-crossed with walking paths. ✉ *27 Ocean Ave.* ☎ *904/824–2809 or 800/342–6529* 🌐 *www.missionandshrine.org* 🎫 *Donation requested* 🕙 *Weekdays 8–5, Sat. 9–5, Sun. 10–5.*

12 **Plaza de la Constitución.** The central area of the original settlement was laid out in 1598 by decree of King Philip II, and little has changed since. At its center is a monument to the Spanish constitution of 1812, and at the east end is a public market dating from Early American days. Just beyond is a statue of Juan Ponce de León, who "discovered" Florida in 1513. ✉ *St. George St. and Cathedral Pl.*

17 ★ **St. Augustine Alligator Farm Zoological Park.** Founded in 1893, the Alligator Farm is one of the oldest (and, at times, smelliest) zoological attractions in Florida and is credited with popularizing the alligator in the national consciousness and helping to fashion an image for the state. In addition to oddities like Maximo, a 15-foot, 1,250-pound saltwater crocodile, and a collection of rare albino alligators, the park is also home to Land of Crocodiles, the only place in the world to see all 23 species of living crocodilians. Reptiles are the main attraction, but there's also a wading-bird rookery, an exotic-birds and mammals exhibit, and nature trails. Educational presentations are held throughout the day, and kids will love the wild-animal shows, alligator wrestling and all. ✉ *999 Anastasia Blvd.* ☎ *904/824–3337* 🌐 *www.alligatorfarm.us* 🎫 *$21.95* 🕙 *Daily 9–5.*

OFF THE BEATEN PATH

Constructed in 1938, **Marineland's Dolphin Conservation Center**, 18 mi south of St. Augustine, is the world's first oceanarium. This National Register of Historic Places designee has come a long way from marine film studio to theme park to its current iteration as dolphin research,

A GOOD TOUR

A good place to start is the **St. Johns County Visitor Information Center** ❶ to pick up maps, brochures, and information. It's on San Marco Avenue between Castillo Drive and Orange Street. From there, cross Orange Street to reach the **City Gate** ❷, the entrance to the city's restored area. Walk south on St. George Street to the **Oldest Wooden Schoolhouse** ❸. Directly across from it is the **Colonial Spanish Quarter Museum** ❹. Go out Fort Alley and cross San Marco Avenue to the impressive **Castillo de San Marcos National Monument** ❺. Then head west on Cuna Street and turn left on Cordova Street. Walk south three blocks to Valencia Street and turn right. At the end of the block is the splendid **Flagler Memorial Presbyterian Church** ❻. Head one block south on Sevilla Street and turn left on King Street to find the **Government House Museum** ❼ and three more of Henry Flagler's legacies: the **Lightner Museum** ❽, **Flagler College** ❾, and the Casa Monica Hotel. Continue two blocks east on King Street and turn right onto St. George Street to reach the **Ximenez-Fatio House Museum** ❿. Afterward, head a few blocks south down Aviles Street to St. Francis Street for a look at a microcosm of the city's history, the **Oldest House** ⓫ (not to be confused with the Oldest Wooden Schoolhouse). Head back north to the Bridge of Lions, the **Plaza de la Constitución** (known colloquially, though not necessarily factually, as the Slave Market) ⓬, and the **Cathedral Basilica of St. Augustine** ⓭. You have to cross the Bridge of Lions to get to Anastasia Island and the historic **St. Augustine Lighthouse & Museum** ⓮, but it's worth the effort.

Several attractions are beyond this walk, including two of particular historic note: the **Mission of Nombre de Dios** ⓯, north of the visitor center, is the site of America's first Christian mass; and well north of the city's cluster of sights is the **Fountain of Youth National Archaeological Park** ⓰, marking the location of the famed spring.

TIMING

Allot eight hours for the tour, covering it in two days if possible. Though most sights keep the same hours (daytime only), a few are not open on Sunday. Weekday mornings generally have the smallest crowds.

education, and entertainment center. The formal dolphin shows are history, but visitors can have a far more memorable experience with interactive programs that allow them to swim with and feed the animals, become a dolphin trainer for a day, or create dolphin art (programs start at $75). Those who prefer not to get so up close and personal can watch the action in the dolphin habitats through 6-by-10-foot acrylic windows. The 1.3-million-gallon facility is home to 11 dolphins, including Lilly, a rare "blonde" dolphin, and Nellie, the oldest dolphin born in a marine park (she was born at Marineland in 1953). Reservations are required. ✉ *9600 Ocean Shore Blvd.* ☎ *904/471–1111 or 888/279–9194* 🌐 *www.marineland.net* 🎟 *General admission $8; call for program prices* ⏲ *Daily 8:30–4:30.*

Anastasia State Park **19**
Castillo de San Marcos National Monument **5**
Cathedral Basilica of St. Augustine .. **13**
City Gate **2**
Colonial Spanish Quarter Museum **4**
Flagler College **9**
Flagler Memorial Presbyterian Church **6**
Fountain of Youth National Archaeological Park **16**
Government House Museum .. **7**
Lightner Museum **8**
Mission of Nombre de Dios **15**
Oldest House .. **11**
Oldest Wooden Schoolhouse **3**
Plaza de la Constitución ... **12**
St. Augustine Alligator Farm Zoological Park **17**
St. Augustine Lighthouse & Museum **14**
St. Johns County Visitor Information Center **1**
World Golf Hall of Fame ... **18**
Ximenez-Fatio House Museum **10**

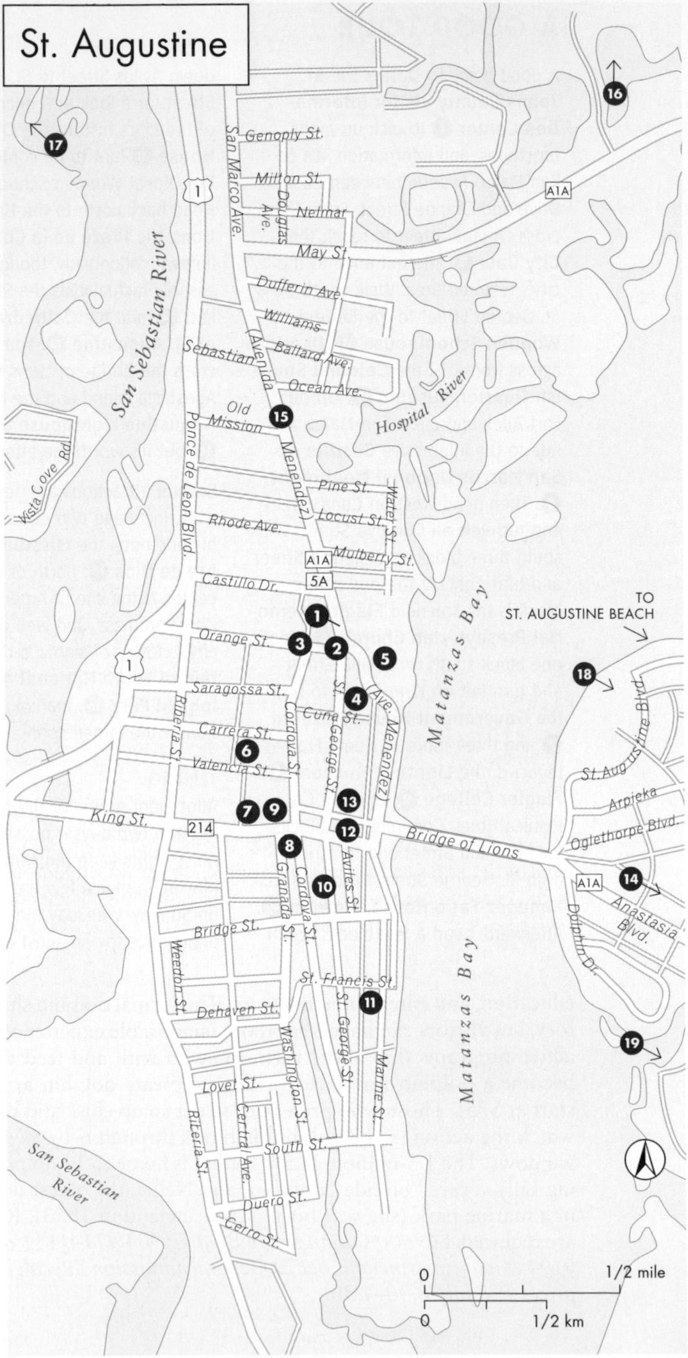

WORTH NOTING

19 **Anastasia State Park.** With 1,700 protected acres of bird sanctuary, this Anastasia Island park draws families that like to hike, bike, camp, swim, and play on the beach. Speaking of beaches: the ones here are the most secluded in the area. ✉ *1340 Rte. A1A S* ☎ *904/461–2033* 🌐 *www.floridastateparks.org/anastasia* 🎟 *$8 per vehicle, $2 for pedestrians or bicyclists* 🕒 *Daily 8–sundown.*

2 **City Gate.** Located at the northernmost end of the colorful shops and sites of St. George Street, the gate is a relic from the days when the Castillo's moat ran westward to the river, and the Cubo Defense Line (defensive wall) protected against approaches from the north. The old coquina gates set the tone for St. George Street, the historic lane filled with Old World balconies and quaint little shops. ✉ *St. George St. and Orange St.*

4 **Colonial Spanish Quarter Museum.** Wander through the narrow streets at your own pace in this living-history museum depicting the lives of Spanish soldiers and their families in 1740s St. Augustine. Along the way you may see a blacksmith building his shop (a historic reconstruction) or artisans busy at candle-dipping, spinning, weaving, or cabinetmaking. The buildings themselves are reconstructed and built on the original foundations. Kids will love the historical costumes and a recounting of history accessible even to the smaller ones. ✉ *29 St. George St.* ☎ *904/825–6830* 🌐 *www.historicstaugustine.com* 🎟 *$6.95, $4.25 children 6–17* 🕒 *Daily 9–5:30, last ticket sold at 4:45.*

6 **Flagler Memorial Presbyterian Church.** To look at a marvelous Venetian Renaissance–style structure, head to this church, built by Flagler in 1889. The dome towers more than 100 feet and is topped by a 20-foot Greek cross. ✉ *32 Sevilla St.* ☎ *904/829–6451* 🌐 *www.memorialpcusa.org* 🕒 *Weekdays 8:30–4:30.*

16 **Fountain of Youth National Archaeological Park.** Here's the thing about "North America's first historical site": you either love it or you hate it. Fans of the grade-A tourist trap appreciate the kitsch factor. They laugh at the cheesy costumes and educational displays. They chuckle at the tired planetarium show. They sip from the legendary Fountain of Youth, if only to mock Ponce de León and his followers for believing such foul-tasting water could hold magical powers. They wonder where in the world the peacocks that roam around the 15-acre park came from. If you don't appreciate kitsch, you'll only be disappointed in the dated exhibits and uninterested employees and wish you had spent your money on a roast-beef sandwich. ✉ *11 Magnolia Ave.* ☎ *904/829–3168 or 800/356–8222* 🌐 *www.fountainofyouthflorida.com* 🎟 *$8* 🕒 *Daily 9–5.*

7 **Government House Museum.** With a collection of more than 300 artifacts from archaeological digs and Spanish shipwrecks off the Florida coast, this museum reflects five centuries of history. ✉ *48 King St.* ☎ *904/825–5033* 🌐 *www.staugustinegovernment.com/visitors/govhouse.cfm* 🎟 *$2.50* 🕒 *Weekdays 9–4:30; weekends 10–4:30.*

11 **Oldest House.** Known as the Gonzalez-Alvarez House, the Oldest House (technically, the oldest surviving Spanish-colonial dwelling in Florida), is a National Historic Landmark. The current site dates from the early

NEWPORT OF THE SOUTH

Henry Morrison Flagler, who, with John D. Rockefeller, founded the Standard Oil Company, first visited the tiny town of St. Augustine in 1885 while honeymooning with his second wife. His choice proved to be very fortunate for the city. It was during this trip that Flagler decided to make St. Augustine "the Newport of the South": a winter resort for wealthy Northern industrialists. And to get his select clientele to Florida, he built the luxurious Florida East Coast Railway, which eventually would stretch from New York all the way to the Florida Keys.

To incorporate the city's Spanish heritage, Flagler chose Spanish Renaissance Revival as his architectural theme. He created the St. Augustine Golf Club and the St. Augustine Yacht Club so there would be leisure activities to enjoy in the warm climate. He also built the city's hospital, churches, the city hall, and winter residences. The most visible manifestations of Flagler's dream were the spectacular hotels with castlelike towers, turrets, and red-tile roofs. His most opulent hotel resort, the Ponce de León, is now a private four-year liberal-arts college that bears his name; another flagship resort, the Alcazar, has been turned into the Lightner Museum; the Casa Monica Hotel is again functioning as a luxury resort, more than a century after Flagler created it; and despite the wrath of multiple hurricanes, most of the railroad routes Flagler built and developed are still in use today.

1700s, but a structure has been on this site since the early 1600s. Much of the city's history is seen in the building's changes and additions, from the coquina blocks—which came into use to replace wood soon after the town burned in 1702—to the house's enlargement during the British occupation. Most visitors can't get over how small the house is. The Oldest House complex also encompasses the Museum of Florida's Military History, Manucy Museum, Page L. Edwards Gallery, a gift shop, and an ornamental garden. ✉ *14 St. Francis St.* ☎ *904/824–2872* 🌐 *www.staugustinehistoricalsociety.org* 🎫 *$8* 🕘 *Daily 9–5, tours every ½ hr.*

❸ **Oldest Wooden Schoolhouse.** In another instance of exaggerated advertising in the Old City, the Oldest Wooden Schoolhouse is actually thought to be merely one of the nation's oldest schoolhouses. Nevertheless, the tiny 18th-century building of cypress and cedar has a fascinating history—told by automated mannequins of a teacher and students—including having served as a guardhouse and sentry shelter during the Seminole Wars. ✉ *14 St. George St.* ☎ *888/653–7245* 🌐 *www.oldestwoodenschoolhouse.com* 🎫 *$3.50* 🕘 *Sun.–Thurs. 9–5, Fri. 9–6, Sat. 9–7.*

⓮ **St. Augustine Lighthouse & Museum.** Its beacon no longer guides ships to St. Augustine's shores, but the historic lighthouse continues to draw thousands of visitors each year. The 1874 structure replaced an earlier lighthouse built by the Spanish when the city was founded in 1565. The visitor center has an exhibit gallery and a store. With more than 200 steps from top to bottom, the winding staircase might be difficult

Get a bird's-eye view of St. Augustine from atop the historic city's 1874 lighthouse.

for some, but those who make the journey say getting a little winded is well worth the trip. ✉ *81 Lighthouse Ave.* ☎ *904/829–0745* 🌐 *www.staugustinelighthouse.com* 🎟 *$9* ⏲ *Aug.–June, daily 9–6; July, daily 9–7.*

1 **St. Johns County Visitor Information Center.** Start your day of sightseeing here, where you can pick up maps and other information on local attractions, and friendly hosts offer tips for getting around, dining, and accommodations. Even if you don't need maps, it's worth popping inside this beautiful building just to appreciate the cool, wonderfully maintained interior and to get a close-up look at the stone arches. ✉ *10 Castillo Dr.* ☎ *904/825–1000* 🎟 *Free* ⏲ *Daily 8:30–5:30.*

18 **World Golf Hall of Fame.** This stunning tribute to the game of golf is the centerpiece of **World Golf Village,** an extraordinary complex that includes 36 holes of golf, a golf academy, several accommodations options, a convention center, spa, and a variety of restaurants, including Murray Bros. Caddyshack. The Hall of Fame features an adjacent IMAX theater and houses a variety of exhibits combining historical artifacts and personal memorabilia with the latest in interactive technology. Stand up to the pressures of the TV camera and crowd noise as you try to sink a final putt, take a swing on the museum's simulator, or snap a photo as you walk across a replica of St. Andrews' Swilcan Burn Bridge. Once you're sufficiently inspired, see how you fare on the 18-hole natural-grass putting course. ✉ *1 World Golf Pl.* ☎ *904/940–4123* 🌐 *www.wgv.com* 🎟 *$20.50 (includes all-day admission to the museum, one IMAX film, and one round on the putting course)* ⏲ *Mon.–Sat. 10–6, Sun. noon–6.*

10 **Ximenez-Fatio House Museum.** Built as a merchant's house and store in 1798, the place became a tourist boardinghouse in the 1800s. It's been restored to look like it did during its inn days—romantic yet severe, with balconies that hearken back to Old Spain and sparely appointed rooms. Guided tours are available. ✉ *20 Aviles St.* ☎ *904/829–3575* 🌐 *www.ximenezfatiohouse.org* 🎫 *$5* 🕒 *Tues.–Sat. 11–4.*

OFF THE BEATEN PATH

Thousands of years of water flowing from the shore of the St. Johns River to the town of Palatka, 35 mi southwest of St. Augustine, created a 59-acre steep-head ravine. In 1933 the FDR's Works Progress Administration transformed the ravine into a spectacular garden by planting more than 95,000 azaleas, 11,000 palm trees, and 250,000 ornamental plants, creating **Ravine Gardens State Park.** A 1.8-mi paved road loops around the ravine giving visitors a view of the gardens, as well as brooks and rocky outcroppings, while stairs and trails allow access into the ravine. Picnic tables and grills and restrooms are available. Although any month is a good time to hike the shaded glens, for a truly stunning scene head here between late January and April when the 64 varieties of azaleas are in full bloom. ✉ *1600 Twig St.* ☎ *386/329–3721* 🌐 *www.floridastateparks.org/ravinegardens* 🎫 *$5 per vehicle, up to 8 people; $2 for pedestrians and bicyclists* 🕒 *Daily 8–sundown.*

SPORTS AND THE OUTDOORS

BEACHES

The very popular **St. Augustine Beach** (✉ *1200 Rte. A1A S* ☎ *No phone* 🎫 *Free*) is the closest beach to downtown. It's on the northern end of Anastasia Island, directly east of town. **Vilano Beach** (✉ *Coastal Hwy. at the Vilano Beach Causeway* ☎ *No phone* 🎫 *Free*), 2 mi north of St. Augustine, is slowly blossoming into a bustling community with a town center, cozy restaurants and outdoor cafés, condos, and hotels. The area is popular with fishermen, skim boarders, and bird-watchers since 125 species of birds call it home. This isn't a good place to take little ones swimming, though, as the beaches aren't developed and currents can be fierce.

FISHING

Tailin' Spots Charters (✉ *U.S. 1 and Rte. 207* ☎ *904/669–2775* 🌐 *www.tailinspots.com*) offers full- and half-day charters, in addition to overnight and extended-stay trips. **St. Augustine Deep Sea Fishing** (✉ *Cat's Paw Marina, 220 Nix Boat Yard Rd.* ☎ *904/829–8040* 🌐 *www.sealovefishing.com*) has half- or full-day fishing trips.

GOLF

The **Pine Course at the Grand Club** (✉ *400 Pine Lakes Pkwy., Palm Coast* ☎ *386/446–6330*), designed by Arnold Palmer and Ed Seay, is reasonably priced; greens fee $45/$65. As part of its complex, **World Golf Village** (✉ *21 World Golf Pl.* ☎ *904/940–4000*) has two 18-hole layouts named for and partially designed by golf legends Sam Snead, Gene Sarazen, Arnold Palmer, and Jack Nicklaus. The courses are the **Slammer & Squire** (☎ *904/940–6088*), greens fee $109/$139; and the **King & Bear** (☎ *904/940–6200*), greens fee $139/$169.

SHOPPING

Just north of St. Augustine, off Interstate 95, are the **St. Augustine Premium Outlets** (✉ *2700 Rte. 16* ☎ *904/825–1555*), with 85 designer and brand-name outlets. **Prime Outlets** (✉ *500 Belz Outlet Blvd.* ☎ *904/826–1311*) recently added to its 60 name-brand stores a 90,000-square-foot expansion featuring Gucci, Saks Fifth Avenue's OFF 5TH, and Michael Kors. Walk along car-free **St. George Street** (✉ *Between Cathedral Pl. and Orange St.*) to check out the art galleries and one-of-a-kind shops with candles, home accents, handmade jewelry, aromatherapy products, pottery, books, and clothing.

NIGHTLIFE

Live music haven **Café Eleven** (✉ *501 Rte. A1A Beach Blvd.* ☎ *904/460–9311*) specializes in catch-them-before-they-get-too-big bands. The rustic **Mill Top Tavern** (✉ *19 St. George St.* ☎ *904/829–2329*) is famous for its live, local music. If you're staying on Anastasia Island, the "World Famous" **Oasis Deck and Restaurant** (✉ *4000 Rte. A1A S, at Ocean Trace Rd.* ☎ *904/471–3424*) is your best bet for nightly entertainment, offering 24-ounce draft beers, beach access, and what many locals consider the best burgers in town. Something is always happening at **Scarlett O'Hara's** (✉ *70 Hypolita St.* ☎ *904/824–6535*)—some nights it's blues or jazz bands; on others it might be disco, Top 40, or karaoke. The veranda overlooking Matanzas Bay at **The Tini Martini Bar** (✉ *Casablanca Inn, 24 Ave. Menendez* ☎ *904/829–0928*) is the perfect place to enjoy a cocktail while people-watching and listening to live music.

WHERE TO EAT

$$$ ECLECTIC Fodor's Choice ★ ✕ **95 Cordova**. Tucked away on the 1st floor of the Casa Monica Hotel, this restaurant serves classic cuisine with an international flair. Sup in one of three dining rooms, including the main room with intricate Moroccan-style chandeliers, wrought-iron chairs, and heavy wood columns, or the Sultan's Room, a gold-dipped space accented with potted palms and a silk-draped ceiling. The exotic furnishings are inherently romantic but still lend an appropriate feel to dinner with friends or business associates. Innovative dishes with New World, Middle Eastern, and Asian flavors change seasonally and highlight local seafood and produce. The tasting menu offers diners six international courses paired with the restaurant's outstanding wines. ✉ *95 Cordova St.* ☎ *904/810–6810* 🌐 *www.casamonica.com/dining/dining.asp* 💳 *AE, D, MC, V.*

$$$$ FRENCH ✕ **Collage**. Foodies seeking a new dining experience in the Oldest City head to Collage for "artful global cuisine" in a warm and intimate setting. Tucked away on Hypolita Street in the historic district, the 48-seat restaurant highlights local seafood with four fresh-fish entrées each day and the signature dish, Florida bouillabaisse with littleneck clams, mussels, scallops, whitefish, and lobster. For dessert, the bougainvillea, an original dessert inspired by the colorful flowering plants that frame the building, is made of strawberries, ice cream, and cabernet-vanilla sauce

served in a leaf-shaped phyllo cup. ✉ *60 Hypolita St.* ☎ *904/829–0055* 🌐 *www.collagestaug.com* ▭ *AE, MC, V* ⊙ *No lunch.*

$$ SPANISH ★ ✕ **Columbia.** Arroz con pollo, fillet *salteado* (with a spicy sauce), and a fragrant seafood paella are the same time-honored Cuban and Spanish dishes served at this heir to the original Columbia that was founded in Tampa in 1905. Befitting its cuisine, the restaurant has a white-stucco exterior and an atrium dining room full of palm trees, hand-painted tiles, and decorative arches. The wait can be off-putting, especially during summer, when the tourists are out in full force, but a glass of homemade sangria or a refreshing mojito usually manages to take the edge off. ✉ *98 St. George St.* ☎ *904/824–3341* 🌐 *www.columbiarestaurant.com* ▭ *AE, D, DC, MC, V.*

$$ SEAFOOD ✕ **O.C. White's Seafood & Spirits.** Don't even go inside the General Worth house, circa 1791, since the best part about dining at this bay-front eatery is being on the water. Local favorites include coconut shrimp, blue-crab cakes, Caribbean jerk chicken, and Alaskan snow-crab clusters. Beef lovers may want to try the 20-ounce porterhouse or the 12-ounce New York strip. Ask for an upstairs table to admire the marina or one in the courtyard when the jasmine is in bloom. Reservations are not accepted on weekends. ✉ *118 Ave. Menendez* ☎ *904/824–0808* 🌐 *www.ocwhites.com* ▭ *AE, D, MC, V* ⊙ *No lunch weekdays.*

$ SOUTHERN Fodor's Choice ★ ✕ **Salt Water Cowboy's.** Rustic handmade twig furniture and 100-year-old hardwood floors are reminders that this spot, hidden in the salt marshes flanking the Intracoastal Waterway, began as a secluded fish camp (with more "fragrant" reminders at low tide). Award-winning Minorcan clam chowder, oyster stew, barbecued ribs, and crispy fried chicken are standard fare, along with blackened and broiled seafood, steamed oysters, and steak. For more adventuresome palates, the menu includes frogs' legs, alligator, and cooter (fried soft-shell turtle rolled in seasoned bread crumbs). ✉ *299 Dondanville Rd.* ☎ *904/471–2332* 🌐 *www.saltwatercowboys.com* ✍ *Reservations not accepted* ▭ *AE, D, DC, MC, V* ⊙ *No lunch.*

WHERE TO STAY

$$$$ Fodor's Choice ★ 🏨 **Casablanca Inn Bed & Breakfast on the Bay.** Breakfast comes with scenic views of the Matanzas Bay at this restored 1914 Mediterranean-revival stucco-and-stone house, just north of the historic Bridge of Lions. Rooms vary in size and shape; some have separate sitting rooms, some have views of the bay, and some have whirlpool tubs, but all are decorated with period and reproduction furniture and feature Sleep Number beds and flat-screen TVs. You can enjoy breakfast on the patio or in the sunny dining room. **Pros:** comfy beds; friendly staff; complimentary snacks and beverages. **Cons:** some rooms have no view; street noise in some rooms. ✉ *24 Ave. Menendez* ☎ *904/829–0928 or 800/826–2626* 🌐 *www.casablancainn.com* ⇨ *23 rooms, 13 suites* 🛎 *In-room: kitchen (some), DVD, Internet. In-hotel: bar, Wi-Fi hotspot, parking (free), some pets allowed, no kids under 8,* ▭ *AE, D, MC, V* 🍽 *BP.*

$$$ ★ 🏨 **Casa de Solana.** There's a reason you feel like you're stepping back in time when you enter this 1820s-era inn made of coquina and handmade bricks: it's on the oldest street in the oldest European-settled city in the

country. Innkeepers Jeffrey Sonia and Luis Castro's warm hospitality and attention to detail hearken back to days of yore. In addition to a hearty breakfast, visitors enjoy social hour every evening at 4:30 and homemade desserts at 6:30. Most rooms have a whirlpool tub, fireplace, and balcony; some have private entrances and their own ghost (steer clear of the Montejurra Room if you don't want to share space with a 150-year-old Spanish infantryman). Add-on services like breakfast delivered to your door, picnic baskets, and floral arrangements make the inn especially popular with those *en el amor*. **Pros:** excellent service; gourmet breakfast; location. **Cons:** some small rooms; parking three blocks away; "forced" socialization. ✉ *21 Aviles St.* ☎ *877/824–3555* 🌐 *www.casadesolana.com* *10 rooms* *In-room: DVD, Wi-Fi. In-hotel: Wi-Fi hotspot, parking (free), some pets allowed* ▭ *AE, D, DC, MC, V.*

3

$$$$ **Fodor's Choice** ★ **Casa Monica Hotel.** Hand-stenciled Moorish columns and arches, handcrafted chandeliers, and gilded iron tables decorate the lobby of this late-1800s Flagler-era masterpiece. A retreat for the nation's wealthiest until the Great Depression put it out of business, it has returned to its perch as St. Augustine's grande dame. The turrets, towers, and wrought-iron balconies offer a hint of what's inside. Rooms—dressed in blues, greens, and whites—include wrought-iron two- and four-poster beds and mahogany writing desks and nightstands. The downtown location is within walking distance of many attractions. Guests also have access to the Serenata Beach Club in Ponte Vedra (7 mi away), including three pools, private beach access, and beach-equipment rentals. **Pros:** location; architecture and decor; service. **Cons:** busy lobby; expensive parking; $14 daily resort fee; small rooms. ✉ *95 Cordova St.* ☎ *904/827–1888 or 800/648–1888* 🌐 *www.casamonica.com* *138 rooms, 14 suites* *In-room: safe, kitchen (some), refrigerator (some), Internet, Wi-Fi. In-hotel: restaurant, room service, bar, pool, gym, laundry service, Wi-Fi hotspot, parking (free)* ▭ *AE, D, DC, MC, V.*

$$$$ **Hilton St. Augustine Historic Bayfront.** Travelers who want to stay in the heart of historic St. Augustine but don't want to be surrounded by antiques and chintz will find this Spanish-colonial-inspired hotel (read: non-B&B) overlooking Matanzas Bay a comfortable and convenient alternative. Nineteen separate buildings make up the nontraditional Hilton property, most of which have water or city-attraction views. Given its location in the thick of the Oldest City, the hotel caters to the tourist throngs with services such as in-room refrigerators, coin laundry, and cell-phone rentals. The staff is knowledgeable about the local attractions and dining options and happy to offer suggestions. **Pros:** location; comfortable beds; great for families. **Cons:** 4 PM check-in; expensive parking; noise from the road. ✉ *32 Ave. Menendez* ☎ *904/829–2277 or 800/445–8667* 🌐 *www.hiltonhistoricstaugustine.com* *72 rooms* *In-room: refrigerator, Internet, Wi-Fi. In-hotel: restaurant, room service, bar, pool, gym, laundry facilities, laundry service, parking (paid)* ▭ *AE, D, MC, V.*

$$$ **Inn on Charlotte Bed & Breakfast.** Innkeeper Lynne Fairfield says guests comment that staying at her inn reminds them of visiting a friend or family member's home, assuming they offer gourmet breakfast every

morning, wine and finger foods every afternoon, and cozy rooms with whirlpool tubs. Some rooms feature a private balcony, perfect for sipping complimentary lemonade or wine and people-watching. The inn, situated on a quaint brick street, also hosts a variety of events throughout the year, such as cooking classes and book signings with local authors. If you want to bring kids under 21, you must rent the entire inn. **Pros:** location; gourmet breakfast; afternoon refreshments; excellent service. **Cons:** cancellation fee; weekend street noise. ✉ *52 Charlotte St.* ☎ *904/829–3819 or 800/355–5508* 🌐 *www.innoncharlotte.com* ⇨ *8 rooms* ♘ *In-room: Wi-Fi. In-hotel: parking (free), no kids under 21* ▭ *AE, D, MC, V.*

$$$ **Old City House Inn & Restaurant.** Touches of Paris, Venice, and India are just a few of the surprises within this small two-story inn's coquina walls, where innkeepers Ilse and James Philcox have decorated the rooms to reflect international cities or themes. Although it's downtown and near busy attractions, the property's tall brick walls and lush foliage offer ample privacy, though some rooms are noisier than others. Friday-night wine-and-cheese parties on the porch enable guests to get to know each other and swap ghost stories (legend has it that a Spanish soldier who accidentally shot himself still patrols the hallway). Each room has its own entrance, and a second-floor deck is perfect for taking in sunsets. **Pros:** location; romantic; on-site restaurant. **Cons:** thin walls; may have to share room with a ghost! ✉ *115 Cordova St.* ☎ *904/826–0113* 🌐 *www.oldcityhouse.com* ⇨ *7 rooms, 2 suites* ♘ *In-room: DVD (some). In-hotel: restaurant, bicycles, parking (free), no kids under 10* ▭ *AE, D, MC, V* 🍴 *BP.*

$$$ ★ **Renaissance Resort at World Golf Village.** If you want to be within walking distance of all World Golf Village has to offer, this full-service resort is an excellent choice. Rooms and suites surround a 10-story atrium, at the bottom of which is a restaurant set amid tropical foliage and streams. Guest rooms are stylish and elegant with colonial Asian decor and spa-inspired bathrooms. The hotel is adjacent to the World Golf Hall of Fame and borders championship golf courses. And if you don't know the difference between a bogey and a birdie, not to worry; the PGA TOUR Spa Laterra is but a free shuttle ride away. Guests also have access to a 24-hour fitness center and billiards room and privileges at the private oceanfront Serenata Beach Club. **Pros:** breakfast buffet; friendly staff; large bathrooms. **Cons:** small pool; no pets. ✉ *500 S. Legacy Trail* ☎ *904/940–8000 or 888/740–7020* 🌐 *www.worldgolfrenaissance.com* ⇨ *301 rooms, 28 suites* ♘ *In-room: safe, refrigerator, Wi-Fi. In-hotel: restaurant, room service, bar, golf course, tennis court, pool, gym, laundry facilities, laundry service, Wi-Fi hotspot, parking (free)* ▭ *AE, D, DC, MC, V.*

$$$ **St. Francis Inn Bed & Breakfast.** If the walls of this late-18th-century house in the historic district—and the oldest inn in the Oldest City—could talk, they would tell of slave uprisings, buried doubloons, and Confederate spies. The inn, a guesthouse since 1845, offers rooms, suites, a room in the former carriage house, and a five-room cottage. Furnishings are a mix of antiques and just plain old, the vibe is serene, the food fresh and gourmet (there's a chef on property), and a stay

includes thoughtful extras like free admission to the Anastasia Athletic Club, beach-house access, and nightly desserts. **Pros:** warm hospitality; family-friendly cottage; Southern breakfast buffet; short walk to historic district. **Cons:** small rooms; small pool; dated decor. ✉ *279 St. George St.* ☎ *904/824–6068 or 800/824–6062* 🌐 *www.stfrancisinn.com* *12 rooms, 4 suites, 1 2-bedroom cottage* *In-room: kitchen (some), refrigerator (some), DVD, Wi-Fi. In-hotel: pool, bicycles, Wi-Fi hotspot, parking (free), some pets allowed, no kids under 10 in main house,* *AE, D, DC, MC, V* *BP.*

3

DAYTONA BEACH AND INLAND TOWNS

The section of the coast around Daytona Beach offers considerable variety, from the unassuming bedroom community of Ormond Beach to the spring-break and auto-racing capital of Daytona Beach— and go just 75 mi to the south and you've got speeding rockets instead of speeding cars. (Down that way is the Canaveral National Seashore, nestled between New Smyrna Beach and Cocoa Beach. ⇨ *See The Space Coast section.)*

Inland, peaceful little towns are separated by miles of two-lane roads, running through dense forest and flat pastureland and skirting one lake after another. There's not much to see but cattle and the state's few hills. Gentle and rolling, they're hardly worth noting to people from true hill country, but they're significant enough in Florida for much of this area to be called the "hill and lake region."

DAYTONA BEACH

65 mi south of St. Augustine.

Best known for the Daytona 500, Daytona has been the center of automobile racing since cars were first raced along the beach here in 1902. February is the biggest month for race enthusiasts, and there are weekly events at the International Speedway *(⇨ see In-Focus feature "The Race Is on in Daytona")*. During race weeks, bike weeks, spring-break periods, and summer holidays, expect extremely heavy traffic. On the mainland, near the inland waterway, several blocks of Beach Street have been "street-scaped," and shops and restaurants open onto an inviting, broad brick sidewalk.

GETTING HERE AND AROUND

Delta, US Airways, and Airgate Aviation Inc. serve Daytona Beach International Airport. From the airport, Yellow Cab–Daytona Beach runs to beach hotels for about $18–$25. DOTS Transit Service has scheduled service connecting the Daytona Beach and Orlando International airports, the Sheraton Palm Coast area, DeLand (including its train station), New Smyrna Beach, and Sanford; fares are $35 one way and $65 round-trip between the Daytona and Orlando airports, $35 one way and $65 round-trip from the Orlando airport to DeLand.

Daytona Beach has an excellent bus network, Votran, which serves the beach area, airport, shopping malls, and major arteries, including service to DeLand and New Smyrna Beach and the Express Link to Orlando. Exact fare is required for Votran ($1.25) and JTA ($1–$1.50) if using cash.

HURRY UP AND WAIT

To snowbirds, a trip to Daytona Beach in mid-February might sound like a great idea. Just don't plan it for the weekend of the Daytona 500. Assuming you can even find a hotel room, it will probably cost you double the usual rate. If you plan on leaving your hotel room, you'll most likely get stuck in bumper-to-bumper traffic. And when you get to your destination, it might not be open. Of course, you could give in and go to the race, but you'll never get a ticket.

ESSENTIALS

Transportation Contacts Daytona Beach International Airport (*DAB ☎ 386/248–8069 ⊕ www.flydaytonafirst.com*). **DOTS Transit Service** (*☎ 386/257–5411 or 800/231–1965 ⊕ www.dots-daytonabeach.com*). **Votran** (*☎ 386/756–7496 ⊕ www.votran.com*). **Yellow Cab–Daytona Beach** (*☎ 386/255–5555*).

Visitor Information Daytona Beach Area Convention and Visitors Bureau (*✉ 126 E. Orange Ave., Daytona Beach ☎ 800/854–1234 ⊕ www.daytonabeach.com*).

EXPLORING

Museum of Arts & Sciences. One of the largest museums in Florida, this behemoth structure has a humanities section with displays of Chinese art, and glass, silver, gold, and porcelain examples of decorative arts. The museum also has the largest collection of Cuban art outside of Cuba, Florida American Indian items, pre-Columbian art, Indian and Persian miniature paintings, and an eye-popping complete skeleton of a giant sloth that is 13 feet long and 130,000 years old. Kids will love the Charles and Linda Williams Children's Museum, a 9,000-square-foot addition filled with interactive science experiments; a 2½-acre outdoor contemporary-sculpture garden, and a planetarium with laser-light shows. *✉ 352 S. Nova Rd. ☎ 386/255–0285 ⊕ www.moas.org ☞ $12.95 ⊙ Tues.–Sat. 9–5, Sun. 11–5.*

Southeast Museum of Photography. The largest photography museum in the Southeast and one of only 13 in the country, this internationally renowned museum at Daytona State College has exhibits focused on photojournalism, fashion, and new media. *✉ 1200 W. International Speedway Blvd., Bldg. 1200 ☎ 386/506–4475 ⊕ www.smponline.org ☞ Donation welcome ⊙ Call for hrs.*

OFF THE BEATEN PATH

Ponce Inlet. At the southern tip of the barrier island that includes Daytona Beach is this sleepy town with a small marina, a few bars, and casual seafood restaurants. Boardwalks traverse delicate dunes and provide easy access to the beach, although storms have caused serious erosion. Marking this prime spot is the bright-red, century-old **Ponce de León Inlet Light Station,** a National Historic Monument and museum, the tallest lighthouse in the state and the second-tallest in the country. Climb to the top of the 175-foot-tall lighthouse tower for a bird's-eye view of Ponce Inlet. *✉ 4931 S. Peninsula Dr., Ponce Inlet ☎ 386/761–1821 ⊕ www.ponceinlet.org ☞ $5 ⊙ Memorial Day–Labor Day, daily 10–9; after Labor Day, daily 10–6; last admission 1 hr prior to closing.*

If the action on Daytona Beach is too much for you, soar above it by parasailing.

Ponce Inlet's **The Manatee Scenic Boat Tours** (*386/761–2027 or 800/881–2628 www.manateecruise.com)* takes guests on narrated cruises of the Intracoastal Waterway. Kids will love looking for the boats' namesake, also known as "sea cows," and your guide might tell you how (sun-delirious?) sailors may have mistaken them for mermaids.

SPORTS AND THE OUTDOORS

Tomoka State Park. This scenic park is perfect for fishing, camping, hiking, canoeing, and bird-watching, with more than 160 species to see. It is the site of a Timucuan Indian settlement discovered in 1605 by Spanish explorer Alvaro Mexia. Wooded campsites, bicycle and walking paths, and guided canoe tours on the Tomoka and Halifax rivers are the main attractions. *2099 N. Beach St, 3 mi north of Ormond Beach 386/676–4050, 800/326–3521 (Reserve America) for camping reservations www.floridastateparks.org/tomoka $5 per vehicle, up to 8 people, $2 pedestrians, camping $24 per night Daily 8–sundown.*

BEACH

★ Billing itself as the World's Most Famous Beach, **Daytona Beach** permits you to drive your car right up to your beach site (from one hour after sunrise to one hour before sunset), spread out a blanket, and have all your belongings at hand (with the exception of alcohol, which is prohibited); this is especially convenient for beachgoers who are elderly or have disabilities. However, heavy traffic during summer and holidays makes it dangerous for children, and families should be extra careful or stay in the designated car-free zones. The speed limit is 10 MPH, and there's a $5 fee for beach driving every month but December and January. *To get your car on the beach, look for signs on Route A1A* *indicating beach access via beach ramps. Sand traps are not limited to the golf course, though—cars can get stuck.*

BOAT TOUR

In Daytona Beach, **A Tiny Cruise Line** (☎ *386/226–2343* 🌐 *www.visitdaytona.com/tinycruise*) leaves from the public marina and explores the Intracoastal Waterway.

FISHING

Finest Kind II Sport Fishing Charters (✉ *Inlet Harbor Marina, 133 Inlet Harbor Rd., Ponce Inlet* ☎ *386/527–0732* 🌐 *www.finestkind2fishing.com*) offers everything you could need and (hopefully) more with half-day, full-day, and night fishing excursions, as well as burial at sea! **Sea Spirit Fishing** (✉ *Inlet Harbor Marina, 133 Inlet Harbor Rd., Ponce Inlet* ☎ *386/763–4388* 🌐 *www.seaspiritfishing.com*) has 4- to 10-hour private and group charters.

GOLF

Indigo Lakes Golf Club (✉ *312 Indigo Dr.* ☎ *386/254–3607* 🌐 *www.indigolakesgolf.com*) has 18 holes of golf; greens fee $29. The public courses at **LPGA International Legends Course** (✉ *1000 Champions Dr., Daytona Beach* ☎ *386/523–2001* 🌐 *www.lpgainternational.com*) have 36 holes; greens fee $120/$130. **Pelican Bay South Country Club** (✉ *350 Pelican Bay Dr.* ☎ *386/788–6496* 🌐 *www.pelicanbaycc.com*) rents clubs and has a pro shop and a restaurant, in addition to two 18-hole courses; greens fee $35/$45. There's an 18-hole course at **Spruce Creek Golf & Country Club** (✉ *1900 Country Club Dr., Port Orange* ☎ *386/756–6114* 🌐 *www.sprucecreekgolf.com*), along with practice and driving ranges, rental clubs, a pro shop, and a restaurant; greens fee $39/$49.

WATER SPORTS

Catch air at **Daytona Beach Parasail** (✉ *Silver Beach Ramp, Silver Beach Ave. and Rte. A1A* ☎ *386/547–6067* 🌐 *www.daytonaparasailing.com*). Rent surfboards or boogie boards at **Salty Dog Surf Shop** (✉ *700 E. International Speedway Blvd.* ☎ *386/258–0457* 🌐 *www.saltydogsurfshop.com*) or **Maui Nix** (✉ *635 N. Atlantic Ave.* ☎ *386/253–1234* 🌐 *www.mauinix.com/store*).

SHOPPING

Daytona Flea and Farmers Market (✉ *2987 Bellevue Ave.* ☎ *386/253–3330*) is one of the largest in the South and draws residents from all over the state.

NIGHTLIFE AND THE ARTS

NIGHTLIFE

Ocean Walk (✉ *250 N. Atlantic Ave.* ☎ *386/258–9544*) is a lively, always-hopping cluster of shops, restaurants, and bars right on the ocean, including the **Mai Tai Bar** (☎ *386/947–2493*). Spring breakers congregate by the thousands at **The Oyster Pub** (✉ *555 Seabreeze Blvd.* ☎ *386/255–6348*). At **Razzle's Nightclub** (✉ *611 Seabreeze Blvd.* ☎ *386/257–6236*), DJs play high-energy dance music from 8 PM–3 AM.

THE ARTS

Jazz, big band, blues, and folk acts perform at the outdoor, oceanfront **Daytona Beach Bandshell** (✉ *250 N. Atlantic Ave.* ☎ *386/671–8250* 🌐 *www.daytonabandshell.com*). Internationally acclaimed orchestras and soloists appear as part of the **Daytona Beach Symphony Society** (✉ *140 S. Beach St., Suite 107* ☎ *386/253–2901* 🌐 *www.dbss.org*). The **Ocean Center at Ocean Walk Village** (✉ *101 N. Atlantic Ave.* ☎ *386/254–4500 or 800/858–6444* 🌐 *www.oceanwalkvillage.com*) hosts concerts, conventions, boat shows, and rodeos, and is home to the Daytona ThunderBirds indoor football team. **Peabody Auditorium** (✉ *600 Auditorium Blvd.* ☎ *386/671–3460* 🌐 *www.peabodyauditorium.org*) is used for concerts and programs year-round.

3

WHERE TO EAT

$ SEAFOOD **Aunt Catfish's on the River.** Don't be surprised if your server introduces herself as your cousin, though you've never seen her before in your life. You see, everybody's "cousin" at Aunt Catfish's (as in, "Can I get you another mason jar of sweet tea, Cousin?"). The silly Southern hospitality is only one of the draws at this wildly popular seafood restaurant. The main lure, of course, is the food: fried chicken, fried shrimp, fried catfish, and crab cakes. Hot cinnamon rolls and hush puppies come with every entrée and can be a meal in themselves. Bring your appetite and your patience—a wait is practically guaranteed. Sunday brunch lures empty stomachs with made-to-order eggs and French toast, and a chocolate fountain. Aunt Catfish's is on the west bank of the Intracoastal Waterway (off U.S. 1, before crossing the Port Orange Causeway), just south of Daytona. ✉ *4009 Halifax Dr., Port Orange* ☎ *386/767–4768* 🌐 *auntcatfishontheriver.com* *Reservations not accepted* 💳 *AE, MC, V.*

$ AMERICAN **Daytona Brickyard.** It's not just the locals who swear that the Brickyard's charbroiled sirloin burgers are the best they've ever tasted—devotees have been known to drive from Georgia just for lunch. Given its name and location in the heart of NASCAR country, the popular bar and grill is covered in racing memorabilia. Dang, even the floor and the tablecloths are black-and-white checkered. But don't mistake the racing theme to mean the place merely serves greasy bar food to Joe Sixpacks. It also feeds T-bone and New York strip steaks to doctors. ✉ *747 International Speedway Blvd.* ☎ *386/253–2270* 🌐 *www.daytonabrickyard.com* *Reservations not accepted* 💳 *AE, MC, V.*

$$$ STEAK ★ **Gene's Steak House.** Quiet and intimate, this family-operated restaurant and race-car-driver hangout has long upheld its reputation as the best place for steaks in the area (since 1948, to be exact) despite its nondescript exterior and somewhat out-of-the-way location west of town. Gene's has a decidedly old-school, supper-club vibe, with classics like escargot baked in puff pastry, French onion soup, and Gene's special-recipe Roquefort dressing. Signature entrées include cooked-to-order filet mignons, sirloins, and porterhouses. Seafood is also on the menu, and the wine list is one of the state's largest, with bottles ranging from $19 to $1,200. ✉ *3674 W. International Speedway Blvd.* ☎ *386/255–2059* 🌐 *www.genessteakhouse.com* 💳 *AE, D, MC, V* ⊗ *Closed Mon. No lunch.*

Continued on page 150

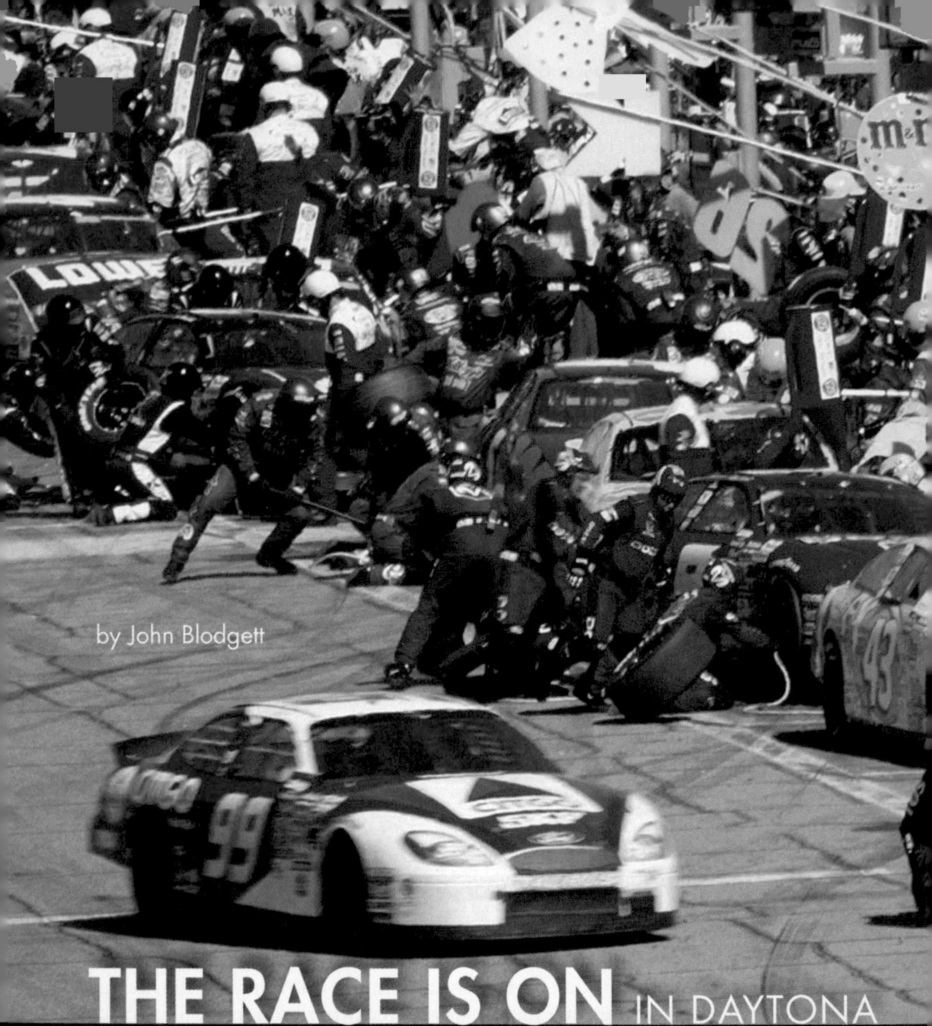

by John Blodgett

THE RACE IS ON IN DAYTONA

It's morning on race day. Check the weather—rain or shine? The race won't run if it's raining, but bring a poncho just in case, and pack some sunscreen, too (maybe even throw in a beach umbrella). Oh, and don't forget your binoculars and ear plugs. Fill your cooler with snacks and drinks—yes, it's allowed. Got your waterproof padded seat? Good. If you have a radio scanner, bring it to listen in on the pit crews; if you don't, you can rent one at the track for $50 ($30 for Sprint customers). This handheld device, in addition to its scanning capabilities, provides live video feeds, driver statistics, and auto replay.

You're here! Welcome to Daytona International Speedway—the storied race track that is home to one of America's most famous races, the Daytona 500. Hope you like crowds, because you'll be jostling with upward of 200,000 fellow race fanatics. The gate opens at 8 AM, and the 2010 race begins at 1 PM. The hours in between are one of the best times to seek autographs from your favorite racers in their garages near the Sprint FANZONE (drivers also can be approached throughout race weekend as they hang out at their respective souvenir haulers).

Watching the race is a sensory experience: 43 cars powered by 800 or more horsepower make

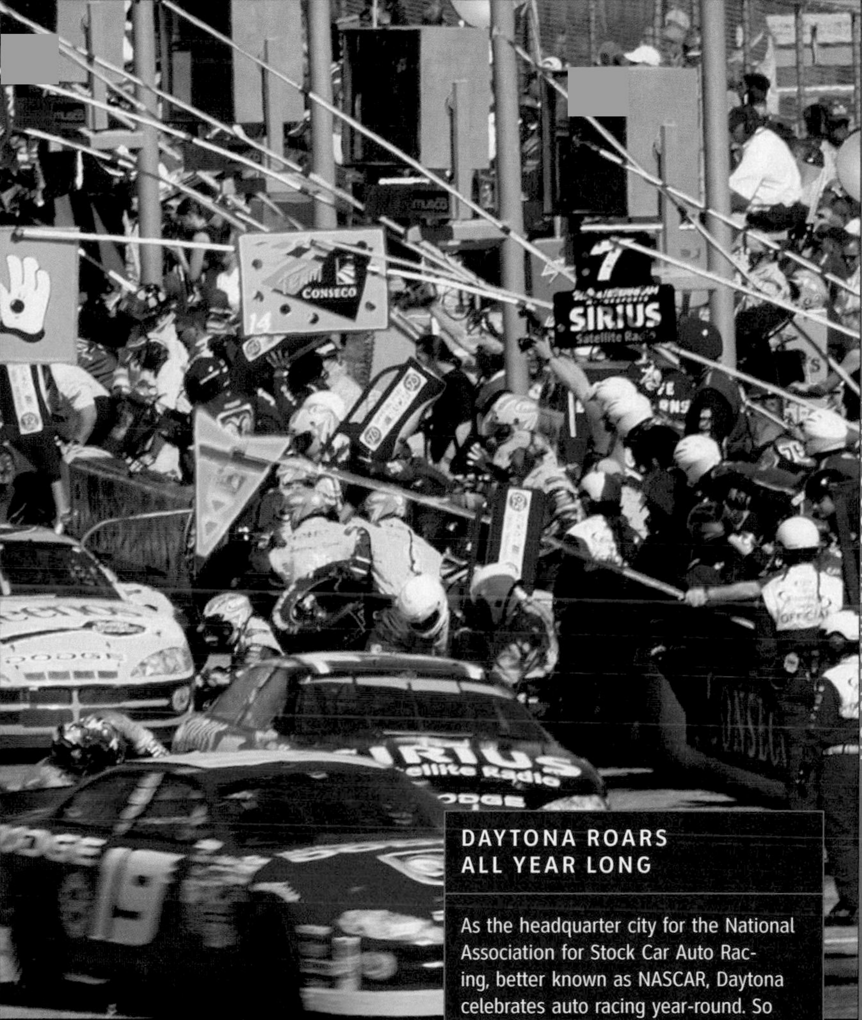

for a constant roar; there's the smell of hot rubber, fuel, and exhaust; and, if you happen to be down low by the track itself, you might be pelted by flecks of tire as the pack blasts by at speeds approaching 190 mph. Every so often, let your binoculars wander—you might just see a past champion or other celebrity.

A few hours later the adrenaline-packed race is finished and your ears will be ringing (unless you remembered plugs). Now it's time to cheer the victor and wait in line to go find your car. This is when you grab another beverage from your cooler and relive the race with the fans next to you.

DAYTONA ROARS ALL YEAR LONG

As the headquarter city for the National Association for Stock Car Auto Racing, better known as NASCAR, Daytona celebrates auto racing year-round. So while the Daytona 500 happens just one day out of 365, there's plenty for you to see and do every day at the speedway's 480-acre complex. You can go to other races, tour the facilities, spend several hours at an interactive visitor center that lets you feel what it's like behind the wheel, and even jump into a stock car yourself. Major races are held during nine weekends, and an assortment of other races take place throughout the year. On non-race days the Speedway is host to R&D of racing vehicles, car shows, and other events. For motorcycles, there's the Daytona Supercross by Honda in March.

THE LAPS ALONG THE WAY

The first official Daytona 500 was held on February 22, 1959, with 59 cars in front of 41,000 fans. It has been held each year in late February ever since. In the half century that followed, cash awards have grown from $68,000 to $18 million, with fewer drivers—43—but triple the fans—200,000. Every year the 500-mi (200-lap) race marks the beginning of NASCAR's premier Sprint Cup series and generally offers the greatest monetary reward. Winning the Daytona 500 has been equated with a Super Bowl victory, and much as in that sport, the final moments can be the most memorable and most important.

GETTING TICKETS

For tickets to the Daytona 500 or any other races held at the speedway, contact the Daytona Speedway ticket office (✉ 1801 W. International Speedway Blvd., Daytona Beach ☎ 800/PIT-SHOP [748–7467] 🌐 www.daytonainternationalspeedway.com). Single ticket prices to the Daytona 500 range from $55 to $185, primo seats go quickly, so the sooner you order the better. Grandstand seats typically sell out days or weeks in advance.

David Stremme #40
Ricky Rudd #21
Carl Edwards #99
David Gilliland #38
Dale Earnhardt, Jr. #88

NASCAR'S FINEST

David Pearson
"The Silver Fox"
105 NASCAR wins
retired in 1986.

Dale Earnhardt
"The Intimidator"
"Ironhead"
Killed during the 2001 Daytona 500.

Richard Petty
"King Richard,"
Most NASCAR wins (200) and Daytona victories (7).

Jeff Gordon
Youngest winner of the NASCAR Winston Cup (Sprint Cup) and the Daytona 500.

THE MUSEUM: GETTING INTO THE ACTION

Jeff Gordon's Daytona car.

Ryan Newman's Daytona Car.

The Daytona 500 Experience, the raceway's visitor center (formerly called Daytona USA) adjacent to the track, has flashy exhibits, including one on the history of auto racing with a rotating display of cars; an IMAX film about NASCAR; and The Walk of Fame, featuring the handprints, footprints, and signatures of famous NASCAR drivers—but that's just the beginning. The fun really revs up with the interactive stations that put you into the action. Test your tire-changing and fueling skills against a real pit crew in a 16-second pit stop experience, computer-design your own race car, and feel the thrill of a race from the driver's seat with motion simulators like Daytona Dream Laps (included in the cost of admission) and Acceleration Alley ($5 in addition to price of admission), a highly realistic head-to-head racing experience in an 80%-scale stock car at speeds reaching 200 mph.

As part of the museum admission, you can take a 30-minute, open-tram and narrated tour of the famous oval track, including the garage area and its daunting 31-degree banks. Tours run every hour on the half-hour until 5 AM. Track tours are not given during certain race days—see www.daytona500experience.com for specifics.

For more time on the track, sign up for a three-hour motorcoach tour as part of the Daytona 500 Experience VIP Hot Pass (🎫 $55 Thurs.–Sun. only; reservations required). ✉ 1801 W. International Speedway Blvd. (just across from the speedway) ☎ 386/681-6800 🌐 www.daytona500experience.com 🕓 May–Sept., daily 9–7; Oct.–Apr., daily 9–5; 🎫 $24 (extra costs for track tours, Richard Petty Driving Experience, and Acceleration Alley).

GET BEHIND THE WHEEL

Want more than a simulation? At the **Richard Petty Driving Experience** (☎ 800/BE-PETTY [237-3889]) you can ride shotgun—or for more dough, drive yourself—in a stock car on the Daytona International Speedway (ride-alongs are $135; call for other prices and to reserve a ride). You suit up, helmet and all, and slide into the car through the window, just like you're Jeff Gordon. Be sure to get a photo afterward so all your friends believe you when you tell them how you zoomed around at speeds in excess of 150 mph!

$$$ SEAFOOD Fodor's Choice ★ **Martini's Chophouse.** Local beautiful people seem to flock to this trendy South Daytona Beach eatery and lounge as much for the scene as they do for the food. The bar area, done in tangerine with splashes of lime green, is a modern meeting place for the after-work crowd, and the outdoor deck and bar attract a livelier bunch. Those who do deign to dine will appreciate the chef's use of homegrown herbs and creative sauces in dishes such as marinated skirt steak with chimichurri sauce and barbecue-grilled Chilean salmon with cucumber and melon relish, which can be enjoyed in the sleek dining room or in the garden, complete with a 20-foot lighted waterfall and fire pit. *1815 S. Ridgewood Ave, South Daytona Beach 386/763–1090 AE, D, MC, V Closed Sun. and Mon.*

WHERE TO STAY

$$$ ★ **Hilton Daytona Beach Oceanfront Resort.** Perched on the only traffic-free strip of beach in Daytona, this high-rise hotel is as popular with families as it is with couples. Every room has a great ocean view, and the Old Florida decor (nostalgic prints, rattan headboards, and sandy palettes) is warm and inviting. If beach bumming isn't your thing, check out the spacious sundecks and two pools or take a stroll down to the pier or boardwalk, both within walking distance. The hotel is also connected to the Ocean Walk Shoppes via covered walkways. **Pros:** spacious rooms; beach access. **Cons:** small pool; extra charges; spotty valet service. *100 N. Atlantic Ave. 386/254–8200 or 866/536–8477 www.daytonahilton.com 744 rooms, 52 suites In-room: Wi-Fi. In-hotel: 7 restaurants, room service, bars, pools, gym, beachfront, laundry facilities, laundry service, Wi-Fi hotspot AE, D, DC, MC, V.*

$$$ **Perry's Ocean Edge Resort.** Perhaps more than any other property in Daytona, Perry's has a die-hard fan base, many of whom started coming to the oceanfront resort as children, then returned with their children and their children's children. Parents and kids alike are kept happy with the free homemade doughnuts and coffee served in the lush solarium every morning, and the clean indoor pool surrounded by a 10,000-square-foot-atrium with a retractable roof. Two renovations, after significant hurricane damage, added fun new features like a pool tiki bar and spa (the largest in Daytona Beach) and spiffed up the decor. Most rooms have kitchens and great ocean views. Some suites come with a special kids' room, complete with bunk beds. **Pros:** spacious rooms; helpful staff; nice pools; family-friendly. **Cons:** small bathrooms; slow elevators; limited TV channels. *2209 S. Atlantic Ave. 386/255–0581 or 800/447–0002 www.perrysoceanedge.com 200 rooms In-room: safe, kitchen, Internet, Wi-Fi. In-hotel: restaurant, bar, pools, gym, beachfront, children's programs (ages 4–12), laundry facilities, parking (free) AE, D, DC, MC, V CP.*

$$$ Fodor's Choice ★ **The Shores Resort & Spa.** Rustic furniture and beds swathed in mosquito netting lend themselves to the Old Florida decor at this 11-story beachfront resort, but there's nothing primitive about the hotel's amenities, including a luxury four-poster bed and a 42-inch plasma TV in every room, the Indonesian-inspired spa Indulge, and Azure restaurant and bar overlooking the ocean. Rooms are spacious and have views of either the ocean or the Intracoastal Waterway. **Pros:** beachfront;

spa; friendly staff; 24-hour room service. **Cons:** expensive restaurant; crowded pool; not all rooms have balconies. ✉ *2637 S. Atlantic Ave., Daytona Beach Shores* ☎ *386/767–7350 or 866/934–7467* 🌐 *www.shoresresort.com* *212 rooms, 1 suite* *In-room: safe, refrigerator (some), DVD, Wi-Fi. In-hotel: restaurant, room service, bars, pool, gym, spa, beachfront, laundry service, Wi-Fi hotspot, parking (free), some pets allowed* *AE, D, DC, MC, V.*

$$–$$$ Fodor's Choice ★ **Wyndham Ocean Walk Resort.** Kids definitely won't be bored at this high-rise beachfront resort that boasts four swimming pools, a water-slide, lazy river, game room, indoor miniature-golf course, activities center, and the only traffic-free beach in Daytona Beach. Guests also appreciate the 1-, 2-, and 3-bedroom condominium-style units equipped with kitchens (dishware and utensils included), washers, and dryers, as well as the proximity to the shops and restaurants of Ocean Walk Village. Because the property doubles as a hotel and time-share resort, certain amenities such as room service and valet parking aren't offered. **Pros:** family-friendly; beachfront; great facilities; spacious accommodations. **Cons:** no room service; very slow elevators. ✉ *300 N. Atlantic Ave.* ☎ *386/323–4800 or 800/347–9851* 🌐 *www.oceanwalk.com* *200 1-, 2-, and 3-bedroom suites* *In-room: safe, kitchen, refrigerator, DVD (some). In-hotel: 2 restaurants, bars, golf course, pools, gym, spa, beachfront, water sports, children's programs (ages 5 and up), laundry facilities, Wi-Fi hotspot* *AE, D, DC, MC, V.*

DELAND

21 mi southwest of Daytona Beach on U.S. 17.

The quiet town is home to Stetson University, established in 1886 by hat magnate John Stetson. Several inviting state parks are nearby, and as for activities, there's great manatee-watching during winter, as well as skydiving for both spectators and participants.

EXPLORING

Gillespie Museum. One of the most historically and scientifically significant collections of gems and minerals in the world can be found on the Stetson University campus. ✉ *Stetson University, Michigan and Amelia Aves.* ☎ *386/822–7330* 🌐 *www.gillespiemuseum.stetson.edu* *$2* *Call for hrs.*

Museum of Florida Art. Located in the Cultural Arts Center across from Stetson University, this museum highlights Florida artists and works of art pertaining to Florida, as well as hosting national traveling exhibitions (past shows have featured the work of Ansel Adams, William Wegman, and the Audubon Society). ✉ *600 N. Woodland Blvd.* ☎ *386/734–4371* 🌐 *www.delandmuseum.com* *Donation welcome* *Tues.–Sat. 10–4, Sun. 1–4.*

SPORTS AND THE OUTDOORS

Blue Spring State Park. February is the top month for sighting sea cows at this designated manatee refuge, but they begin to head here in November, as soon as the water gets cold enough (below 68°F. Your best bet for spotting a manatee is to walk along the boardwalk.). The park, once a river port where paddle wheelers stopped to take on cargoes of oranges, also contains a historic homestead that is open to the public. Home to the largest spring on the St. Johns River, the park offers hiking, camping, and picnicking facilities. ✉ *2100 W. French Ave., Orange City* ☎ *386/775–3663* 🌐 *www.floridastateparks.org/bluespring* 🎫 *$6 per vehicle, up to 8 people, $2 for pedestrians and bicyclists* ⏲ *Daily 8–sundown.*

De León Springs State Park. Near the end of the 19th century, this park was promoted as a fountain of youth to winter guests. Today visitors are attracted to the year-round 72°F springs for swimming, fishing, canoeing, and kayaking. Nature trails draw hikers and outdoors enthusiasts. Explore an abandoned sugar mill at **Lake Woodruff National Wildlife Refuge**—accessible through De León Springs—which also has 18,000 acres of lakes, creeks, and marshes for scuba diving, canoeing, and hiking. ✉ *601 Ponce de León Blvd., 6 mi north of DeLand off U.S. 17, De León Springs* ☎ *386/985–4212* 🌐 *www.floridastateparks.org/deleonsprings* 🎫 *$6 per vehicle, up to 8 people, $2 for pedestrians and bicyclists* ⏲ *Daily 8–sundown.*

WHERE TO EAT

$ AMERICAN ✕ **Main Street Grill.** At first glance, this downtown restaurant looks like any nondescript, casual chain restaurant—with an uninspired menu to boot—but on closer inspection, the local favorite makes a name for itself with original twists on the expected like French onion–steak sandwich, chicken-cordon-bleu pasta, and Southern-fried shrimp. The extensive menu offers a variety of chicken, beef, and seafood entrées, as well as sandwiches and salads. Dine inside the historic brick building surrounded by colorful murals depicting downtown DeLand or outside on the patio by the manatee fountain. Regular diners praise the friendly and efficient waitstaff—and the cinnamon buns as big as your head. ✉ *100 E. New York Ave.* ☎ *386/740–9535* 🌐 *www.mainstreetgrilldeland.com* ✍ *Reservations not accepted* 💳 *AE, MC, V.*

$ AMERICAN ✕ **Original Holiday House.** Don't be surprised if Holiday House makes you miss your Nana, since the DeLand institution has been preparing old-fashioned comfort food just like Grandma used to make since 1959. The homey restaurant, located across from the Stetson University campus, is enormously popular with senior citizens, families, and college students who fill their bellies with turkey and dressing, roast beef, mashed potatoes, and plenty of veggies. Although the main draw is the buffet—salad only, salad and vegetables only, or the full buffet for $11.25—the menu also includes a short list of sandwiches and entrées. Unlike your Nana, Holiday House uses only organic vegetables, bans MSG from all foods, and offers sugarless desserts. ✉ *704 U.S. 17* ☎ *386/734–6319* ✍ *Reservations not accepted* 💳 *D, MC, V* ⏲ *Closed Mon.*

OCALA NATIONAL FOREST

Eastern entrance 40 mi west of Daytona Beach, northern entrance 52 mi south of Jacksonville.

This breathtaking 383,000-acre wilderness with lakes, springs, rivers, hiking trails, campgrounds, and historic sites has three major recreational

The Florida Trail goes through Ocala National Forest, taking hikers past hardwoods, pines, and prairies

areas (listed here from east to west): **Alexander Springs** (✉ *Off Rte. 40 via Rte. 445 S*) has a swimming lake and a campground; **Salt Springs** (*visitor center,* ✉ *14100 State Road 19*) has a natural saltwater spring where Atlantic blue crabs come to spawn each summer (and the area received a sidewalk and landscaping update in the latter half of 2009); and **Juniper Springs** (✉ *14100 Rte. 40 N*), which includes a stone waterwheel house, a campground, a natural-spring swimming pool, and hiking and canoe trails. About 30 campsites are sprinkled throughout the park and range from bare sites to sites with electric hookups, showers, and bathrooms. Credit cards are not accepted. ✉ *Visitor center, 17147 Rte. 40 E, Salt Springs* ☎ *352/625–2520* 🌐 *www.fs.fed.us/r8/florida* *Alexander Springs, Salt Springs, Juniper Springs: $4.*

SPORTS AND THE OUTDOORS

CANOEING

The 7-mi **Juniper Springs run** is a narrow, twisting, and winding canoe ride, which, although exhilarating, is not for the novice. Canoe rentals and guided tours are available through **Juniper Springs Canoe Rentals** (☎ *352/625–2808*) inside the park.

FISHING

Captain Tom's Custom Charters (☎ *352/236–0872*) allows you to charter fishing trips ranging from three hours to a full day and offers sightseeing cruises as well. Trips are by reservation only.

HORSEBACK RIDING

JNB Horse Haven Farm (✉ *Rte. 42 between Weirsdale and Altoona, Lady Lake* ☎ *352/821–4756 or 800/731–4756* 🌐 *www.jnbhorsehavenfarm.com*), located within the Ocala National Forest, offers nature trail rides for beginner, intermediate, and advanced riders, as well as group and private lessons.

MICANOPY

36 mi north of Ocala on U.S. 441, off I–75.

Though this was the state's oldest inland town, site of both a Timucuan Indian settlement and a Spanish mission, there are few traces left from before white settlement, which began in 1821. Micanopy (pronounced micka-no-pee) does still draw those interested in the past, however. The main street of this beautiful little town has quite a few antiques shops, and in fall roughly 200 antiques dealers descend on the town for the annual Harvest Fall Festival.

EXPLORING

★ **Paynes Prairie Preserve State Park.** The 20,000-acre wildlife preserve has ponds, lakes, trails, and a visitor center with a museum as well as a wintering area for many migratory birds where alligators, wild horses, and a herd of American bison also roam. There was once a vast lake here, but a century ago it drained so abruptly that thousands of beached fish died in the mud. The remains of a ferry stranded in the 1880s can still be seen. Swimming, boating, picnicking, and camping are permitted. ✉ *Off U.S. 441, 100 Savannah Blvd.* ☎ *352/466–3397* 🌐 *www.floridastateparks.org/paynesprairie* 🎟 *$6 per vehicle, up to 8 people, $4 for singles, $2 for pedestrians and bicyclists* ⏲ *Daily 8–sunset.*

OFF THE BEATEN PATH

Marjorie Kinnan Rawlings State Park. The presence of Rawlings, whose works include *The Yearling* and *Cross Creek,* permeates this National Historic Landmark home where the typewriter rusts on the ramshackle porch, the closet where she hid her booze during Prohibition yawns open, and clippings from her scrapbook reveal her legal battles and marital problems. Bring lunch, and picnic in the shade of one of Rawlings' citrus trees. Then visit her grave a few miles away at peaceful Island Grove. ✉ *18700 Rte. 325 S, Cross Creek* ☎ *352/466–3672* 🌐 *www.floridastateparks.org/marjoriekinnanrawlings* 🎟 *$3 per vehicle, up to 8 people; tours $3* ⏲ *Daily 9–5; tours Thurs.–Sun. at 10, 11, and hourly 1–4 Oct.–July.*

WHERE TO EAT AND STAY

¢ PIZZA ✕ **Blue Highway Pizzeria.** As proof that tasty pizza and friendly servers transcend all ages, income levels, and backgrounds, Blue Highway is as popular with locals and University of Florida students as it is with snowbirds and tourists. Pizza is, of course, the main attraction at the brightly colored building on the side of the highway, especially Frank's specialty pies like the Carne Combo with pepperoni, sausage, salami, and three kinds of cheese; and the Abruzzese with meatballs and sliced roasted garlic. But the menu also features sandwiches, calzones, panini, and salads with homemade dressings, and a nice selection of beer and wine. For a sinfully savory treat, try the formagadilla; it's kind of like a quesadilla, only it's made with a pungent mix of fontina and garlic. ✉ *204 U.S. 441 NE* ☎ *352/466–0062* 🌐 *www.bluehighwaypizza.com* ✍ *Reservations not accepted* 💳 *MC, V.*

$$$ **Herlong Mansion.** Spanish moss clings to the stately oak trees surrounding this restored mansion built in the 1800s. The imposing Greek Revival–style B&B has Corinthian columns and wide verandas perfect for relaxing in a rocker. Rooms and suites have period furniture, Oriental rugs, lead-glass windows, and claw-foot tubs; some rooms have whirlpools. A multicourse breakfast, which is included in the rate, is an event here. Emphasis is on personal attention without intrusion; guests appreciate the service without feeling rushed. **Pros:** large private bathrooms; gourmet breakfast; evening wine and cheese reception. **Cons:** no phones in rooms; no TVs in some rooms; some small and windowless rooms; 14-day cancellation policy. ✉ *402 NE Cholokka Blvd.* ☎ *352/466–3322 or 800/437–5664* 🌐 *www.herlong.com* *12 rooms, 2 cottages* *In-room: no phone, DVD (some), no TV (some), Wi-Fi. In-hotel: Wi-Fi hotspot, parking (free), no kids under 12* *AE, D, MC, V* *BP.*

GAINESVILLE

11 mi north of Micanopy on U.S. 441.

The University of Florida anchors this sprawling town. Visitors are mostly Gator football fans and parents of university students, so the styles and costs of accommodations are primarily aimed at budget-minded travelers rather than luxury-seeking vacationers. The surrounding area encompasses several state parks and interesting gardens and geological sites.

GETTING HERE AND AROUND

Gainesville Regional Airport is served by Delta and US Airways. From the airport, taxi fare to the center of Gainesville is about $20; some hotels provide free airport pickup.

ESSENTIALS

Transportation Contact Gainesville Regional Airport (*GNV* ☎ *352/373–0249* 🌐 *www.gra-gnv.com*).

Visitor Information Gainesville/Alachua County Visitors and Convention Bureau (✉ *30 E. University Ave., Gainesville* ☎ *352/374–5260 or 866/778–5002* 🌐 *www.visitgainesville.com*).

EXPLORING

Florida Museum of Natural History. Located on the campus of the University of Florida, the state's official museum of natural history and the largest natural-history museum in the Southeast has holdings of more than 20 million objects and specimens. In addition to active collections in anthropology, archaeology, botany, mammalogy, and ornithology, the museum features several interesting replicas, including a Maya palace, a typical Timucuan household, and a full-size model of a Florida cave and mangrove forest. The museum's newest permanent exhibit, the Butterfly Rainforest, houses 55 to 65 species of butterflies in a 6,400-square-foot, screened, free-flight vivarium. Butterfly releases take place Saturday and Sunday at 2, 3, and 4. ✉ *University of Florida Cultural Plaza, SW 34th St. at Hull Rd.* ☎ *352/846–2000* 🌐 *www.flmnh.ufl.edu* *Museum $6, Butterfly Rainforest $9.50* *Mon.–Sat. 10–5, Sun. 1–5.*

Samuel P. Harn Museum of Art. At 86,800 square feet, the Harn Museum is one of the largest university art museums in the Southeast. The museum has four main collections: Asian, with works dating back to the Neolithic Era; African, encompassing costumes, domestic wares, and personal adornments; Modern, featuring the works of Georgia O'Keeffe, William Morris Hunt, and George Bellows; and Contemporary, with original pieces by Willem de Kooning and Andy Warhol. ✉ *UF Cultural Plaza, SW 34th St. and Hull Rd.* ☎ *352/392–9826* 🌐 *www.harn.ufl.edu* 🎫 *Donations accepted* ⏲ *Tues.–Fri. 11–5, Sat. 10–5, Sun. 1–5.*

LATER, GATORS

Depending on what time of year you visit, Gainesville's population could be plus or minus 50,000. Home to one of the largest colleges in the country, the University of Florida, Gainesville takes on a different personality during the summer when the majority of students return home. During the fall and spring terms, the downtown streets are teeming with students on bikes, scooters, and foot, but in summer it's much more laid-back.

Devil's Millhopper Geological State Park. Scientists surmise that thousands of years ago an underground cavern collapsed and created this geological wonder that is designated as a National Natural Landmark. See the botanical wonderland of exotic subtropical ferns and trees growing in the 500-foot-wide, 120-foot-deep sinkhole. You pass a dozen small waterfalls as you head down 236 steps to the bottom. Pack your lunch and enjoy it in one of the park's picnic areas. And bring Spot, too; just keep him on a leash while he's at the park. Guided walks with the park ranger are offered Saturday mornings at 10. ✉ *4732 Millhopper Rd., off U.S. 441* ☎ *352/955–2008* 🌐 *www.floridastateparks.org/devilsmillhopper* 🎫 *$4 per vehicle, up to 8 people, $2 for pedestrians and bicyclists* ⏲ *Wed.–Sun. 9–5.*

NIGHTLIFE

1982 Bar (✉ *919 W. University Ave.* ☎ *352/371–9836*) features live music five nights a week and drinking games every night. Locals head to **Calico Jack's Oyster Bar** (✉ *3501 SW 2nd Ave.* ☎ *352/375–2337* 🌐 *www.calicojacks.net*) for seafood, beer, and live music. Get your caffeine and live-music fixes at **Common Grounds** (✉ *210 SW 2nd Ave.* ☎ *352/372–7320* 🌐 *www.commongroundslive.com*), which spotlights an eclectic mix of bands. Gainesville's oldest bar, **Lillian's Music Store** (✉ *112 SE 1st St.* ☎ *352/372–1010*), has rock and Top 40 music, bands, and karaoke. **Market Street Pub** (✉ *120 SW 1st Ave.* ☎ *352/377–2927*) brews its own beer and has live music on weekends and a DJ some weeknights. **The Swamp Restaurant** (✉ *1642 W. University Ave.* ☎ *352/377–9267* 🌐 *swamprestaurant.com*) attracts college students by the pitcher, especially on game day.

WHERE TO EAT

$ AMERICAN ✕ **Bistro 1245.** Get high-quality meals at bargain-basement prices at this trendy yet surprisingly down-to-earth restaurant that shares a roof with Leonardo's by the Slice. Some call the small dining room cramped, while others find the close quarters to be romantic. However you look at it, the menu is full of comfort foods with a twist, such as maple-roasted chicken breast, spicy shrimp pasta, seared-tuna club sandwich, and bison sirloin. In keeping with its unpretentious atmosphere, guests are invited to pick their own wine from the restaurant's wine rack. For a lighter meal and a lighter price, order from the lunch menu in the evening. ✉ *1245 W. University Ave.* ☎ *352/376–0000* 🌐 *www.leonardos706.com/bistro* ▭ *AE, D, MC, V.*

$$ LATIN AMERICAN ✕ **Emiliano's Café.** Linen tablecloths and art deco–style artwork create a casual, elegant feel at this Gainesville institution serving Pan-Latin cuisine for more than 20 years. Dine indoors or beneath the stars on the sidewalk café. Start with the Galician stew (a family recipe) or the black-bean soup, and then move on to one of the chef's signature dishes—Spanish saffron rice with shrimp, clams, mussels, fresh fish, chicken, artichoke hearts, peas, asparagus, and pimientos. Emiliano's also offers an extensive tapas menu with nearly 40 items to mix and match, and tempting desserts like the original chipotle brownie cake. Live jazz fills the air Monday and Wednesday nights. ✉ *7 SE 1st Ave.* ☎ *352/375–7381* 🌐 *www.emilianoscafe.com* ▭ *AE, D, MC, V.*

¢ ITALIAN ✕ **Leonardo's by the Slice.** It's ironic that the kitschy pizza joint with a '50s flair is surrounded by a white-picket fence, since most of its patrons and employees are far from conventional. College students, especially the pierced and tatted kind, flock to the Gainesville landmark not only because it's cheap but because it has the best pizza in town. Available in thick or thin varieties, by the pie and, of course, by the slice, Leonardo's pizza comes in a handful of varieties (like veggie, pepperoni, Greek, and spinach tomato). It also offers calzones, salads, and pasta such as baked ziti and spinach lasagna, with no entrée over $8. ✉ *1245 W. University Ave.* ☎ *352/378–2001* 🌐 *www.leonardos706.com* ✍ *Reservations not accepted* ▭ *AE, D, MC, V.*

$$–$$$ CONTINENTAL Fodor's Choice ★ ✕ **Paramount Grill.** This tiny, fine-dining restaurant may have single-handedly changed the perception of Gainesville from a college town fueled by pizza, chicken wings, and pitchers of beer to an up-and-coming culinary destination with imaginative menus driven by fresh Florida produce. What Paramount is lacking in size and glitzy decor it makes up for with its menu. Try one of the five house salads and such entrées as grilled duck breast over wild-mushroom ravioli or blackened salmon with black-bean crepes. If you miss lunch here, try the Sunday brunch. ✉ *12 SW 1st Ave.* ☎ *352/378–3398* 🌐 *www.paramountgrill.com* ▭ *AE, MC, V* ⊙ *No lunch Sat.*

WHERE TO STAY

$$$ 🏨 **Laurel Oak Inn.** Guests who stay at this 1885 Queen Anne–style dwelling say they're so comfortable and at ease they feel like they're staying in a home, not an inn. That's not far from the truth since the innkeepers live on the 3rd floor of the main house. The inn's Southern hospitality begins with a three-course gourmet breakfast and continues with complimentary beverages throughout the day and social hour in the evenings. The "bedchambers" come with thoughtful touches such as plush robes, house bath salts, and organic coffee. Rooms feature a fireplace or wood stove, most with thermo-massage tubs. Lush gardens and stately oak trees give the property a secluded feel, though

downtown Gainesville is just a short walk away. **Pros:** three-course breakfast; location; hospitable staff. **Cons:** processing fee for cancelations; not family-friendly; no pool. ✉ *221 SE 7th St.* ☎ *352/373–4535* 🌐 *www.laureloakinn.com* *5 rooms, 1 cottage* *In-room: Wi-Fi. In-hotel: parking (free), no kids under 16* *MC, V* *BP.*

$$$ **The Magnolia Plantation Bed and Breakfast Inn.** You'll be within minutes of historic downtown and the University of Florida, and owners Joe and Cindy Montalto will welcome you like old friends, whether you stay in the main house, built in 1885, or in one of six adorable cottages. The inn's unique French Second Empire architecture is one of only a handful of such examples in the Southeastern United States. All rooms have a gas fireplace and private baths. Though the inn is just minutes from downtown, it is surrounded by lush tropical gardens, fountains, and ponds across the nearly 2-acre property. A full breakfast is standard fare and is served in the formal dining room or delivered to your cottage. Children and pets are welcome with prior approval. **Pros:** friendly service; breakfast; nightly social hour. **Cons:** small rooms; seven-day cancellation policy; some uncomfortable beds. ✉ *309 SE 7th St.* ☎ *352/375–6653 or 800/201–2379* 🌐 *www.magnoliabnb.com* *5 rooms, 6 cottages* *In-room: kitchen (some), DVD (some), no TV (some). In-hotel: laundry facilities, parking (free), some pets allowed* *AE, D, MC, V* *CP.*

Fodor's Choice ★

$$$ **Sweetwater Branch Inn Bed & Breakfast.** You'll find such modern conveniences as hair dryers, Internet, and business services mixed with Southern charm and hospitality, all wrapped up in two grand Victorian homes surrounded by lush tropical gardens. Gleaming hardwood floors and antique furnishings lend a European flair to nicely appointed rooms. The Sweetwater is in historic downtown, adjacent to the University of Florida, and within walking distance of many of the area's better restaurants and entertainment venues. **Pros:** Southern-style breakfast; Jacuzzi suites. **Cons:** spotty service; frequent on-site weddings. ✉ *625 E. University Ave.* ☎ *352/373–6760 or 800/595–7760* 🌐 *www.sweetwaterinn.com* *7 rooms, 4 cottages, carriage house* *In-room: kitchen (some), refrigerator (some), DVD (some), Wi-Fi. In-hotel: parking (free)* *AE, MC, V* *CP.*

THE SPACE COAST

South of the Daytona Beach area along the coast is the Canaveral National Seashore, Merritt Island National Wildlife Refuge, and the John F. Kennedy Space Center. This area is also home to the laid-back town of Cocoa Beach, which attracts visitors on weekends year-round since it's the closest beach to Orlando, 50 mi to the east.

ESSENTIALS

Visitor Information **Space Coast Office of Tourism** (✉ *430 Brevard Ave., Suite 150, Cocoa Village* ☎ *321/433–4470* 🌐 *www.space-coast.com*).

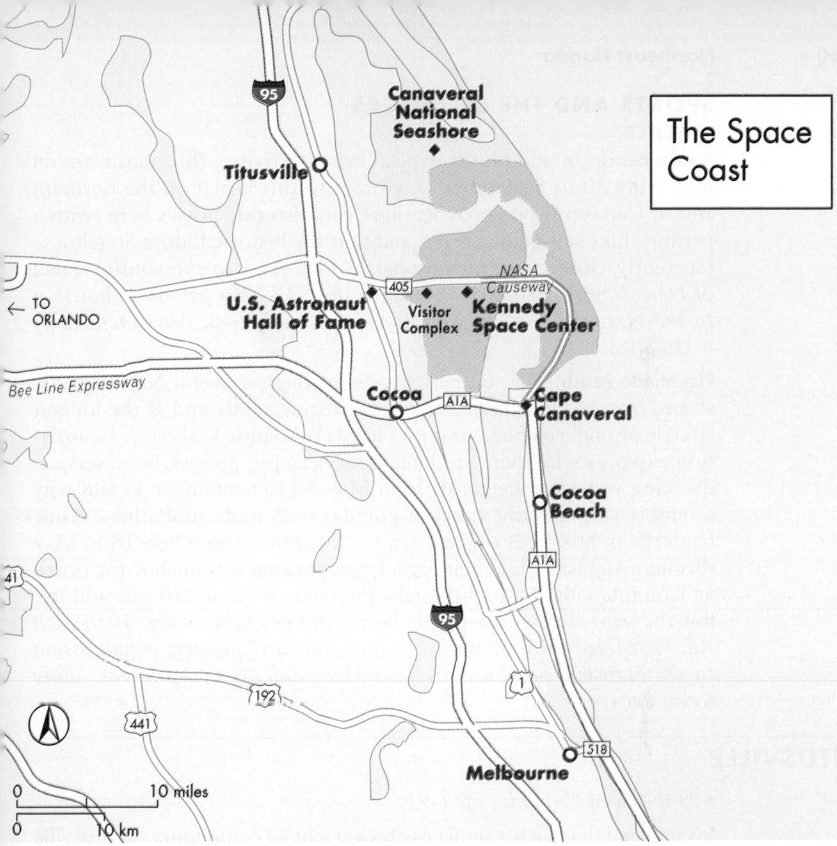

CANAVERAL NATIONAL SEASHORE

★ Miles of grassy, windswept dunes and a virtually empty beach await you at this remarkable 57,000-acre park on a barrier island with 24 mi of undeveloped coastline spanning from New Smyrna to Titusville. The unspoiled area of hilly sand dunes, grassy marshes, and seashell-sprinkled beaches is a large part of NASA's buffer zone and is home to more than 1,000 species of plants and 300 species of birds and other animals. Surf and lagoon fishing are available, and a hiking trail leads to the top of an American Indian shell midden at Turtle Mound. For an additional charge, visitors can take a pontoon-boat tour ($20) or participate in the turtle-watch interpretive program ($14). Reservations required. A visitor center is on Route A1A at Apollo Beach. Weekends are busy, and parts of the park are closed before, during, and after launches, so call ahead. ✉ *Visitor Information: 7611 S. Atlantic Ave., Titusville* ☎ *386/428–3384* 🌐 *www.nps.gov/cana* 🎫 *$3 per person* 🕐 *Nov.–Mar., daily 6–6; Apr.–Oct., daily 6* AM*–8* PM.

SPORTS AND THE OUTDOORS

BEACHES

Apollo Beach. In addition to typical beach activities (lifeguards are on duty May 30 to September 1), visitors to this beach on the northern end of Canaveral National Seashore can also ride horses here (with a permit), hike self-guided trails, and tour the historic Eldora Statehouse (currently closed for renovations). ✉ *Rte. A1A to the southern end of New Smyrna Beach* ☎ *386/428–3384* 🎫 *$3 per person (admission to the National Seashore)* ⏲ *Nov.–Mar., daily 6–6; Apr.–Oct., daily 6* AM–*8* PM.

Playalinda Beach. The southern access for the Canaveral National Seashore, remote Playalinda Beach has pristine sands and is the longest stretch of undeveloped coast on Florida's Atlantic seaboard. Its isolation explains why there are limited services (no phones, food service, drinking water, or lifeguards from May 30 to September 1) and why a remote strand of the beach is popular with nude sunbathers. Aside from them, hundreds of giant sea turtles come ashore here from May through August to lay their eggs. Eight parking lots anchor the beach at 1-mi intervals. To get here, take Interstate 95 Exit 220 east and follow the signs. Take bug repellent in case of horseflies. ✉ *Rte. 402/Beach Rd.* ☎ *321/867–4077* 🌐 *www.nps.gov/cana* 🎫 *$3 per person (admission to the National Seashore)* ⏲ *Nov.–Mar., daily 6–6; Apr.–Oct., daily 6* AM–*8* PM.

TITUSVILLE

67 mi east of Orlando, off I–95.

It's unusual that such a small, easily overlooked community of Titusville could accommodate what it does, namely the magnificent Merritt Island National Wildlife Refuge and the entrance to the Kennedy Space Center, the nerve center of the U.S. space program *(⇨ see In-Focus feature, "Soaring High at Kennedy Space Center")*.

EXPLORING

American Police Hall of Fame & Museum. You know police officers deserve your respect, and you'll be reminded why at this intriguing attraction. In addition to memorabilia like the Robocop costume and Blade Runner car from the films, informative displays offer insight into the dangers officers face every day: drugs, homicides, and criminals who can create knives from dental putty and guns from a bicycle spoke (really). Other historical exhibits include invitations to hangings, police patches, how you collect evidence at a crime scene, and a rotunda where more than 7,000 names are etched in marble to honor police officers who have died in the line of duty. The 24-lane shooting range provides rental guns (Tuesday to Friday noon–8, weekends noon–6). ✉ *6350 Horizon Dr.* ☎ *321/264–0911* 🌐 *www.aphf.org* 🎫 *$12* ⏲ *Daily 10–6.*

Valiant Air Command Warbird Museum & Tico Airshow. Although its exterior looks sort of squirrelly, what's inside here is certainly impressive. Aviation buffs won't want to miss memorabilia from World Wars I and II, Korea, and Vietnam, as well as extensive displays of vintage military flying gear and uniforms. There are posters that were used to identify

Japanese planes, plus there's a Huey helicopter and the cockpit of an F-106 that you can sit in. In the north hangar it looks like activity day at the senior center as a volunteer team of retirees busily restores old planes. It's an inspiring sight, and a good place to hear some war stories. The lobby gift shop sells real flight suits, old flight magazines, bomber jackets, books, and T-shirts. ✉ *6600 Tico Rd.* ☎ *321/268–1941* 🌐 *www.vacwarbirds.org* 🎫 *$18* ⏲ *Daily 9–5.*

WORD OF MOUTH

"We have been to KSC several times. Keep to the basic tour. The Astronaut Hall of Fame is also nice. My children's only complaint was that they showed pretty much the same film at each stop. I would recommend staying at the Hilton on Cocoa Beach; it is in a quieter area with a nice beach. There are lots of good restaurants in the area." —cbr

SPORTS AND THE OUTDOORS

Fodor's Choice ★ **Merritt Island National Wildlife Refuge.** Owned by the Florida Fish and Wildlife Service as well as National Aeronautics and Space Administration (NASA), this 140,000-acre refuge, which adjoins the Canaveral National Seashore, acts as a buffer around Kennedy Space Center while protecting 1,000 species of plants and 500 species of wildlife, including 15 considered federally threatened or endangered. It's an immense area dotted by brackish estuaries and marshes and patches of land consisting of coastal dunes, scrub oaks, pine forests and flatwoods, and palm and oak hammocks. You can borrow field guides and binoculars at the visitor center (4 mi east of Titusville) to track down falcons, ospreys, eagles, turkeys, doves, cuckoos, owls, and woodpeckers, as well as loggerhead turtles, alligators, and otters. A 20-minute video about refuge wildlife and accessibility—only 10,000 acres are developed—can help orient you. You might take a self-guided tour along the 7-mi **Black Point Wildlife Drive.** The dirt road takes you back in time, where there are no traces of encroaching malls or mankind and it's easy to visualize the tribes who made this their home 7,000 years ago. On the **Oak Hammock Foot Trail** you can see wintering migratory waterfowl and learn about the plants of a hammock community. If you exit the north end of the refuge, look for the **Manatee Observation Area** just north of the Haulover Canal (maps are at the visitor center). They usually show up in spring and fall. There are also fishing camps scattered throughout the area. Most of the refuge is closed 24 hours prior to a shuttle launch. ✉ *Rte. 402, across Titusville Causeway* ☎ *321/861–0667, 321/861–0668 visitor center* 🌐 *www.fws.gov/merrittisland* 🎫 *Free* ⏲ *Daily sunrise–sundown; visitor center weekdays 8–4:30, weekends 9–5 (Nov.–Mar.).*

WHERE TO EAT AND STAY

$ SEAFOOD ★ ✕ **Dixie Crossroads.** This sprawling restaurant is always crowded and festive, but it's not just the rustic setting that draws the throngs—it's the seafood. The specialty is the difficult-to-cook rock shrimp, which are served fried, broiled, or steamed. Diners with a hearty appetite can opt for the all-you-can-eat rock shrimp, small shrimp, tilapia, or catfish. You might have to wait (up to 90 minutes) for a table, but if you don't have time to wait, you can order takeout or eat in the bar area.

And a word to the wise: as tempting as those corn fritters dusted with powdered sugar are, don't fill up on them. ✉ *1475 Garden St., 2 mi east of I–95 Exit 220* ☎ *321/268–5000* 🌐 *www.dixiecrossroads.com* *Reservations not accepted* 💳 *AE, D, DC, MC, V.*

$$ **Hampton Inn Titusville.** Proximity to the Kennedy Space Center and reasonable rates make this four-story hotel a top pick for visitors wanting to see a launch in person (though rates do generally go up just before launches). Guests deem the rooms clean, comfortable, and quiet (when the sky isn't reverberating with the sound of rocket thrusters, that is) and larger than those in comparable hotels. The property also scores points for conveniences like 24/7 coffee and tea service in the lobby, complimentary hot breakfast, and microwaves and refrigerators in every room. **Pros:** free Internet; extra-comfy beds; convenient to I–95. **Cons:** thin walls; no restaurant on-site; no room service. ✉ *4760 Helen Hauser Blvd.* ☎ *321/383–9191* 🌐 *www.hamptoninn.com* *86 rooms, 4 suites* *In-room: refrigerator, Internet. In-hotel: pool, gym, laundry facilities, laundry service, Wi-Fi hotspot, parking (free)* *CP.*

COCOA

17 mi south of Titusville, on U.S. 1.

Not to be confused with the seaside community of Cocoa Beach, the small town of Cocoa sits smack-dab on mainland Florida and faces the Intracoastal Waterway, known locally as the Indian River. There's a planetarium and a museum, as well as a rustic fish camp along the St. Johns River, a few miles inland.

Folks in a rush to get to the beach tend to overlook Cocoa's Victorian-style village, but it's worth a stop and is perhaps Cocoa's most interesting feature. Within the cluster of restored turn-of-the-20th-century buildings and cobblestone walkways you can enjoy several restaurants, indoor and outdoor cafés, snack and ice-cream shops, and more than 50 specialty shops and art galleries. The area hosts music performances in the gazebo, arts-and-crafts shows, and other family-friendly events throughout the year. To get to Cocoa Village, head east on Route 520—named King Street in Cocoa—and when the streets get narrow and the road curves, make a right onto Brevard Avenue; follow the signs for the free municipal parking lot.

EXPLORING

BCC Planetarium & Observatory. Based at Brevard Community College, this planetarium and observatory has one of Florida's largest public-access telescopes. The 24-inch telescope allows visitors to view objects in the solar system and deep space. The on-campus planetarium has two theaters, one showing a changing roster of nature documentaries, the other hosting laser-light shows as well as changing planetarium shows. Science Quest Exhibit Hall has hands-on exhibits, including scales calibrated to other planets (Vegas-era Elvis would have weighed just 62 pounds on the moon). The International Hall of Space Explorers displays exhibits on space travel. Show schedules and opening hours may vary, so it's best to call ahead. ✉ *1519 Clearlake Rd., Bldg. 19* ☎ *321/433–7373* 🌐 *www.brevardcc.edu/planet* *Observatory and*

3

exhibits free; film or planetarium show $7; both shows $11; laser show $7, triple combination $16 ⏲ Call for schedule.

SPORTS AND THE OUTDOORS

AIRBOAT RIDES

Twister Airboat Rides. If you haven't seen the swampy, alligator-ridden waters of Florida, then you haven't really seen Florida. Guests on these rides go on a unique and thrilling wildlife tour where eagles and wading birds coexist with water moccasins and gators. The Coast Guard–certified deluxe airboats hit speeds of up to 45 mph and offer unparalleled opportunities to photograph native species. The basic tour lasts 30 minutes, but 60- and 90-minute ecotours are also available at an additional cost. Twister Airboat Rides is inside the Lone Cabbage Fish Camp, about 9 mi west of Cocoa's city limits, 4 mi west of Interstate 95. ✉ *8199 Rte. 520 at St. Johns River* ☎ *321/632–4199* 🌐 *www.twisterairboatrides.com* 🎫 *$22* ⏲ *Daily 10–5:30.*

SHOPPING

You could spend hours browsing in the more than 50 boutiques and shops of **Cocoa Village** (✉ *Rte. 520 and Brevard Ave.* ☎ *321/631–9075*) along Brevard Avenue and Harrison Street, which has the densest concentration of shops. Although most are of the gift and clothing variety, the village is also home to several antiques shops, art galleries, florists, bookstores, and even a tattoo parlor and a spa.

NIGHTLIFE AND THE ARTS

In 1918 the building that now holds the **Cocoa Village Playhouse** (✉ *300 Brevard Ave.* ☎ *321/636–5050*) was a Ford dealership that sold Model Ts. After that, it evolved into the Aladdin Theater, a vaudeville house, and then did a turn as a movie theater before being purchased by Brevard Community College. The September-through-June performance schedule has musicals starring local talent. The rest of the year the stage hosts touring professional productions, concerts, and, in summer, shows geared to children on vacation.

WHERE TO EAT

$$$ CAFÉ Fodor's Choice ★

✕ **Café Margaux**. Eclectic, creative, and international is the perfect way to describe the cuisine and the decor at this charming Cocoa Village spot. The menu blends French, Italian, and Asian influences with dishes like tenderloin of beef brochette, sesame-seared ahi with green tea and bamboo risotto, and braised veal scaloppine, and also features more exotic fare such as duck and ostrich. The themed dining rooms are elaborately decorated with dramatic but not necessarily coordinating window treatments, wallpaper, and artwork. ✉ *220 Brevard Ave.* ☎ *321/639–8343* 🌐 *www.margaux.com* 💳 *AE, D, MC, V* ⏲ *Closed Sun.*

$ ECLECTIC

✕ **Lone Cabbage Fish Camp**. The word "rustic" doesn't even begin to describe this down-home, no-nonsense restaurant (translation: you eat off paper plates with plastic forks) housed in a weathered, old, clapboard shack along with a bait shop and airboat-tour company. Set your calorie counter for plates of catfish, frogs' legs, turtle, and alligator (as well as burgers and hot dogs). Dine inside or on the outdoor deck overlooking the St. Johns River with live music every Sunday. Who knows, you might even see your dinner swimming by. ✉ *8199 Rte.*

520 at St. Johns River ☎ 321/632–4199 ⛵ Reservations not accepted ▭ AE, MC, V.

CAPE CANAVERAL

5 mi east of Cocoa via Rte. A1A.

The once-bustling commercial fishing area of Cape Canaveral is still home to a small shrimping fleet, charter boats, and party fishing boats, but its main business these days is as a cruise-ship port. Cocoa Beach itself isn't the spiffiest place around, but what is becoming quite clean and neat is the north end of the port where the Carnival, Disney, and Royal Caribbean cruise lines set sail, as well as Sun Cruz and Las Vegas Casino Lines. Port Canaveral is now Florida's second-busiest cruise port for multiday cruises, which makes this a great place to catch a glimpse of these giant ships even if you're not headed out to sea.

EXPLORING

The Cove at Port Canaveral. Whether you're at Port Canaveral for a cruise or are just passing through, this retail marketplace on the south side of the harbor has enough restaurants, entertainment venues, and shops to keep you occupied. Since most of the bars and eateries are located on the public waterfront area, you'll have a unique view of the cruise ships—and their colorful passengers. ✉ *Glen Cheek Dr. and Scallop Dr., Port Canaveral* 🎫 *Free* ⏲ *Hours vary by business.*

SPORTS AND THE OUTDOORS

Jetty Park. Come here for a wonderful taste of the real Florida. The 4½-acre beach and oceanfront campground has more than 150 campsites for tents and RVs, picnic pavilions, bike paths, and a 1,200-foot-long fishing pier that doubles as a perfect vantage point from which to watch a liftoff of the space shuttle. Lifeguards are on duty all year, and beach wheelchairs are available for rent. A jetty constructed of giant boulders adds to the landscape, and a walkway that crosses it provides access to a less-populated stretch of beach. Real and rustic, this is Florida without the theme-park varnish. ✉ *400 E. Jetty Rd., Port Canaveral* ☎ *321/783–7111* 🌐 *www.jettypark.org* 🎫 *$5 per car, $7 for RVs for fishing or beach; camping $18–$29 for basic, $22–$32 with water and electric, $25–$34 full hookup* ⏲ *Daily 7 AM–9 PM.*

WHERE TO STAY

$$$ 🏨 **Radisson Resort at the Port.** For cruise-ship passengers who can't wait to get under way, this splashy resort, done up in pink and turquoise, already feels like the Caribbean. Guest rooms have wicker furniture, hand-painted wallpaper, tropical-theme decor, and ceiling fans. The pool is lushly landscaped and features a cascading 95-foot mountain waterfall, tiki bar, and occasional appearances by the "Radisson parrots," about a dozen renegade birds who call the resort home (can you blame them?). This resort, directly across the bay from Port Canaveral, is not on the ocean, but it does provide complimentary transportation to the beach, Ron Jon Surf Shop, and the cruise-ship terminals at Port Canaveral. **Pros:** cruise-ship convenience; pool area; free shuttle. **Cons:** three-day cancellation policy; rooms around the pool can be noisy; loud air-conditioning in some rooms; no breakfast. ✉ *8701*

Astronaut Blvd. ☎ 321/784–0000 or 888/201–1718 ⊕ www.radisson.com/capecanaveralfl ⇨ 284 rooms, 72 suites ♨ In-room: kitchen (some), refrigerator (some), Internet, Wi-Fi. In-hotel: restaurant, bar, tennis court, pool, gym, laundry facilities, laundry service, Wi-Fi hotspot ▭ AE, D, MC, V.

$$$ **Residence Inn Cape Canaveral/Cocoa Beach.** Billing itself as the closest all-suites hotel to the Kennedy Space Center, this four-story Residence Inn, painted cheery yellow, is also convenient to other area attractions such as the Cocoa Beach Pier, the Brevard Zoo, and Cocoa Village, and is only an hour from the Magic Kingdom. Considerably larger than traditional hotel rooms, the one- and two-bedroom suites include a full kitchen—dishwasher and all—and separate living and sleeping areas. The morning buffet and nightly manager's reception are popular with guests who aren't hoping to remain incognito. **Pros:** helpful staff; free breakfast buffet; pet friendly. **Cons:** less than picturesque views; street noise in some rooms. ✉ *8959 Astronaut Blvd. ☎ 321/323–1100 or 800/331–3131 ⊕ www.marriott.com ⇨ 150 suites ♨ In-room: kitchen, Internet, Wi-Fi. In-hotel: pool, gym, laundry facilities, laundry service, Wi-Fi hotspot, parking (free), some pets allowed ▭ AE, D, MC, V ¶ BP.*

3

COCOA BEACH

5 mi south of Cape Canaveral.

After crossing a long and high bridge just east of Cocoa Village, you'll drop down upon a barrier island. A few miles farther and you'll reach the Atlantic Ocean and picture-perfect **Cocoa Beach** at Route A1A. This is one of the Space Coast's nicest beaches, with many wide stretches that are excellent for biking, jogging, power walking, or strolling. In some places there are dressing rooms, showers, playgrounds, picnic areas with grills, snack shops, and surf-side parking lots. Beach vendors offer necessities, and guards are on duty in summer. As the closest beach to Orlando, Cocoa Beach is popular with Central Floridians looking for a quick getaway or vacationers looking to extend their stay. The city is also considered the capital of Florida's surfing community.

ESSENTIALS

Visitor Information Cocoa Beach Convention and Visitors Bureau (✉ *8501 Astronaut Blvd., Suite 4, Cape Canaveral ☎ 321/454–2022 or 877/321–8474 ⊕ www.visitcocoabeach.com).*

SPORTS AND THE OUTDOORS

BEACHES

Alan Shepard Park. Named for the former astronaut, this 5-acre oceanfront park, aptly enough, provides excellent views of shuttle launches. Facilities include 10 picnic pavilions, shower and restroom facilities, and more than 300 parking spaces. Those spaces are in high-demand on launch days, but the park's a nice break any other day, too. Parking is $7 per day, $10 per day on weekends and holidays from early March through Labor Day. Shops and restaurants are within walking distance. ✉ *East end of Rte. 250 ☎ 321/868–3274.*

Continued on page 176

The astronauts prepare for the launch of Endeavour STS-118 on Pad 39-A.

SOARING HIGH AT THE KENNEDY SPACE CENTER

by John Blodgett

Ever since the National Aeronautics and Space Administration (NASA) was founded, in 1958, the United States has been working on missions that launch us heavenward. When these dreams are about to become reality, and it's time for blastoff, Kennedy Space Center in Cape Canaveral, Florida, is where the action is.

NASA FROM COAST TO COAST

The Vehicle Assembly Building houses the space shuttle before a launch.

You've heard the words: "Houston, the *Eagle* has landed." And *Apollo 13*'s "Houston, we have a problem." But have you wondered, "Why are they talking to Houston if they left from Florida?"

NASA actually has operations at centers scattered across the United States. Its major centers are in Florida, Texas, and California. NASA's Launch Operations Center, known as the Kennedy Space Center, in Cape Canaveral, Florida, is where the famous countdowns are heard as a mission prepares for launch. You could say this is like NASA's big airport for outbound flights.

Once a mission (with a crew inside) is airborne, Houston takes over. In addition to operating all manned space flights, the Lyndon B. Johnson Space Center in Houston, Texas, is home base for American astronauts. They train here in laboratories that simulate weightlessness and other space-related concepts.

Not to be left out, the West Coast also gets a piece of the space-action pie. At Moffet Field, in California's Silicon Valley, the Ames Research Center is research and development central for NASA technology. If a mission can't happen because the technology isn't there yet, it's the job of the Ames Research Center to figure it out. Also in California is the Dryden Flight Research Center, at Edwards Air Force Base in Southern California. The center is where a lot of smart people who know a lot of about aerodynamics get to test out their ideas; it's also where space shuttle orbiters land.

So, in a nutshell, you could say California is the brains of NASA's operations, Texas is its heart, and Florida is its wings.

NASA TIMELINE

OCT. 1958: NASA begins operating with 8,000 employees and $100 million. Ten days later, *Pioneer* I takes off.

MAY 1961: Alan B. Shepard, Jr., becomes the first person in space.

FEB. 1962: John Glenn is the first American to orbit the Earth.

JUNE 1965: Edward H. White II is the first American to walk in space.

DEC. 1968: Three astronauts orbit the moon aboard *Apollo 8*.

JULY 1969: *Apollo 11* brings man to the moon.

JULY 1976: *Viking 1* lands on Mars.

APRIL 1981: First space shuttle orbiter launches two astronauts into space.

JAN. 1986: Space shuttle *Challenger* explodes 73 seconds after launch; seven onboard astronauts die.

APRIL 1990: Hubble telescope launches.

JULY 1997: Mars Pathfinder lands on the red planet.

JULY 1999: Eileen Collins is the first woman to command a space shuttle mission.

FEB. 2002: Mars Odyssey begins mapping the red planet.

FEB. 1, 2003: Space shuttle *Columbia* explodes over Texas 15 minutes before scheduled landing; seven astronauts on board die.

JULY 2004: Cassini–Huygens spacecraft begins orbiting Saturn.

MARCH 2009: Shuttle *Discovery* launches for a two-week mission to the International Space Station.

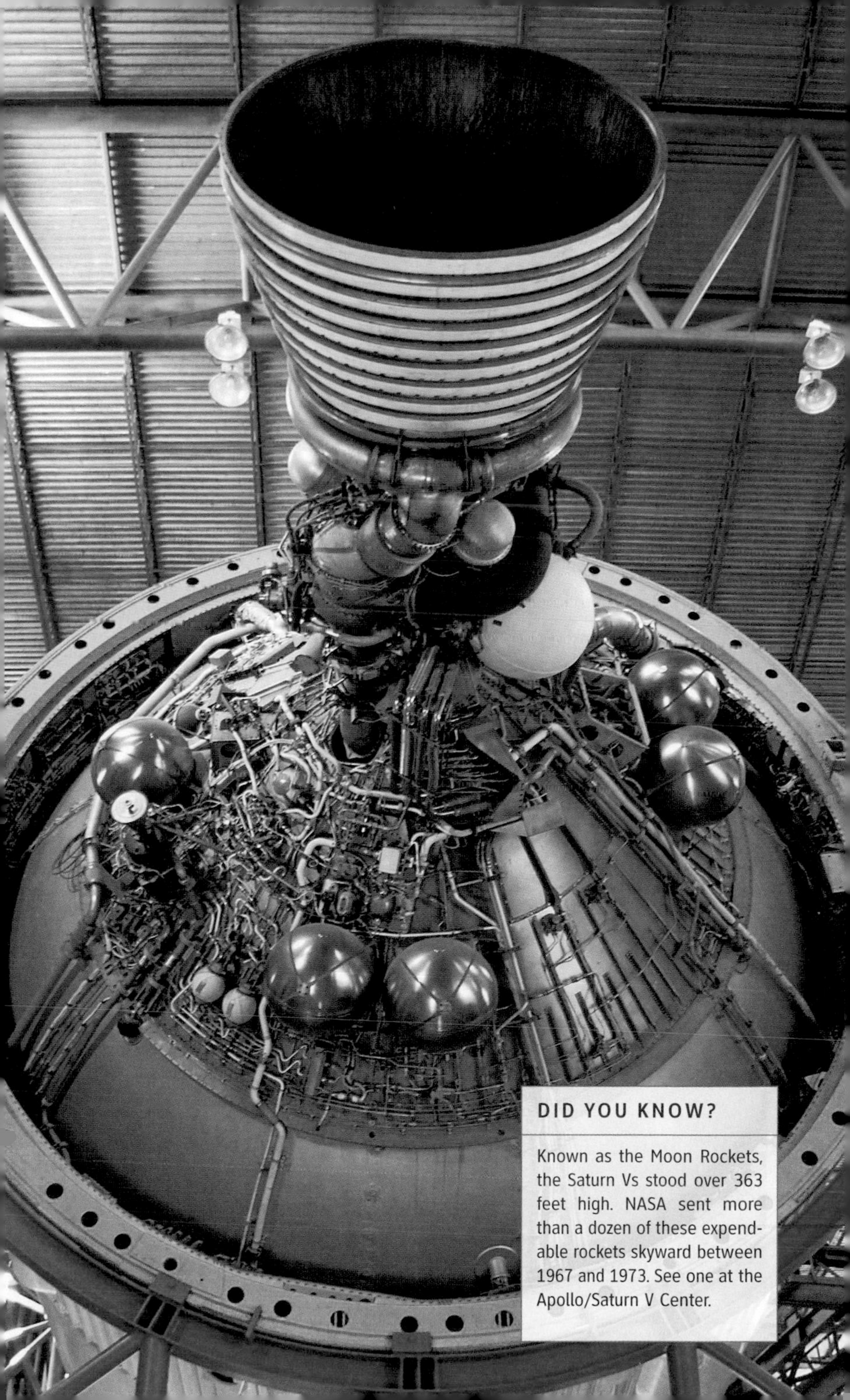

DID YOU KNOW?

Known as the Moon Rockets, the Saturn Vs stood over 363 feet high. NASA sent more than a dozen of these expendable rockets skyward between 1967 and 1973. See one at the Apollo/Saturn V Center.

THE KENNEDY SPACE CENTER

The 140,000-acre Kennedy Space Center is one of central Florida's most popular sights. The must-see attraction gives you a hands-on opportunity to learn about the past, present, and future of America's space program. View old rockets and other artifacts from space flight operations, talk with astronauts during Q&As, experience a simulated launch, and become part of the awed crowd on launch days as you watch the blastoff from a viewing site on the grounds or nearby.

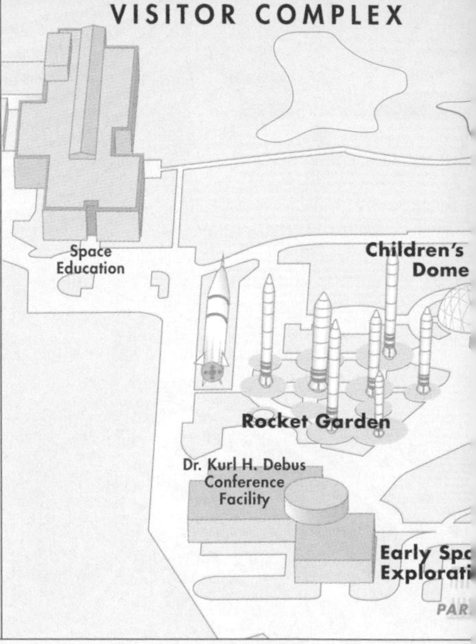
VISITOR COMPLEX
Space Education
Children's Dome
Rocket Garden
Dr. Kurl H. Debus Conference Facility

VISITOR COMPLEX

The Kennedy Space Center Visitor Complex is the starting place for your visit. It's home to several attractions and is also where you can board the bus for tours of the center beyond the visitor complex.

EXHIBITS

The **Early Space Exploration** display highlights the rudimentary yet influential Mercury and Gemini space programs; **Robot Scouts** is a walk-through exhibit of unmanned planetary probes; and the **Exploration Space: Explorers Wanted** exhibit immerses visitors in exploration beyond Earth. Don't miss the outdoor **Rocket Garden,** with walkways winding beside rockets, from early Atlas spacecraft to a Saturn IB. The most moving exhibit is the **Astronaut Memorial.** The 70,400-pound black-granite tribute to astronauts who lost their lives in the name of space exploration stands 42½ feet high by 50 feet wide.

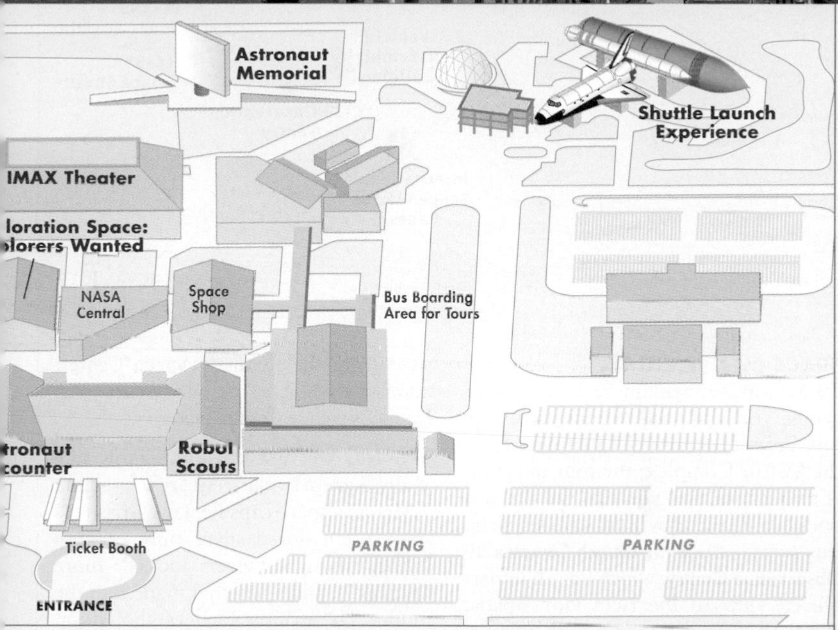
Astronaut Memorial
Shuttle Launch Experience
IMAX Theater
loration Space:
lorers Wanted
NASA Central
Space Shop
Bus Boarding Area for Tours
ronaut
counter
Robot Scouts
Ticket Booth
PARKING
PARKING
ENTRANCE

INTERACTIVE SHOWS AND RIDES

Astronaut Encounter Theater has two daily programs where NASA astronauts share their adventures in space travel and show a short film. More befitting Walt Disney World or Universal Studios (complete with the health warnings), the **Shuttle Launch Experience** is the center's newest and most spectacular attraction. Designed by a team of astronauts, NASA experts, and renowned attraction engineers, the 44,000-square-foot structure uses a sophisticated motion-based platform, special-effects seats, and high-fidelity visual and audio components to simulate the sensations experienced in an actual space-shuttle launch, including MaxQ, Solid Rocker Booster separation, main engine cutoff, and External Tank separation. The journey culminates with a breathtaking view of Earth from space. For those under 48 inches, the redeveloped **Children's Play Dome** enables kids to play among the next generation of spacecraft, climb a moon-rock wall, and crawl through rocket tunnels.

MOVIES

At the world's only back-to-back twin **IMAX Theater** the dream of space flight comes to life on a movie screen five stories tall with dramatic footage shot by NASA astronauts during missions. Realistic 3-D special effects will make you feel like you're in space with them. Films alternate throughout the year.

BEYOND THE VISITOR COMPLEX

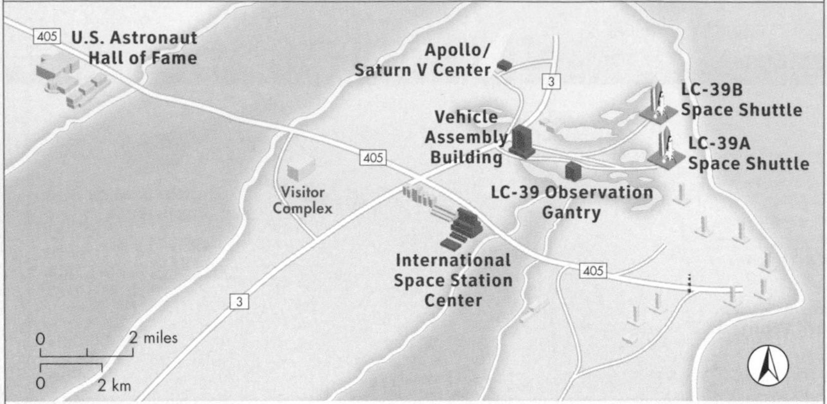

SPACE CENTER TOURS

To explore the remainder of the space center, you will need to take a tour by bus. Buses depart every 15 minutes from the Visitor Complex; the tour duration is two hours, but you can get off and back on again at will at various sites. Bus stops include the **Launch Complex 39 Observation Gantry,** which has an unparalleled view of the twin launchpads; the **Apollo/Saturn V Center,** with a don't-miss presentation at the Firing Room Theatre, where the launch of America's first lunar mission, 1968's *Apollo VIII*, is re-created with a ground-shaking, window-rattling liftoff; and the **International Space Station Center,** where NASA is building pieces of the space station. This bus tour is included with admission; two others are available for additional fees (*see Add-Ons*).

U.S. ASTRONAUT HALL OF FAME

The original Mercury 7 team and the later Gemini, Apollo, Skylab, and shuttle astronauts contributed to make the United States Astronaut Hall of Fame the world's premium archive of astronauts' personal stories. Authentic memorabilia and equipment from their collections tell the story of human space exploration. This stand-alone attraction is across the river from the Kennedy Space Center; admission to it is included with your Kennedy Space Center ticket.

You can see one-of-a-kind items like Wally Schirra's relatively archaic Sigma 7 Mercury space capsule, Gus Grissom's spacesuit (colored silver only because NASA thought silver looked more "spacey"), and a flag that made it to the moon. The exhibit First of the Moon focuses on crew selection for Apollo 11 and the Soviet Union's role in the space race. One of the more challenging activities at the hall of fame is a space-shuttle simulator that lets you try your hand at landing the craft—and afterward replays a side view of your rolling and pitching descent. Don't miss Astronaut Adventure, an area with interactive exhibits about space travel. There are also videos of historic moments.

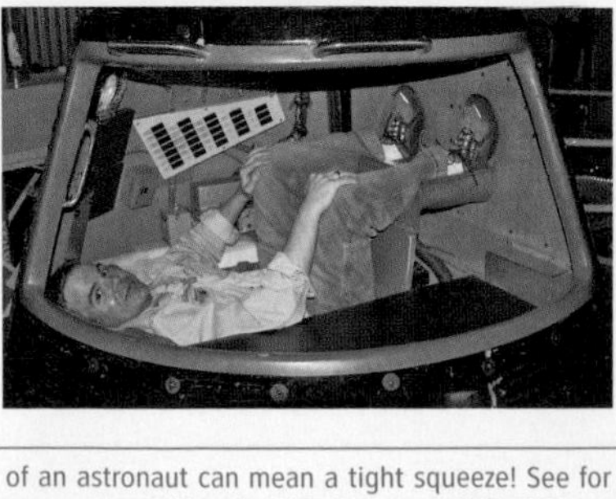

The life of an astronaut can mean a tight squeeze! See for yourself at the U.S. Astronaut Hall of Fame.

ADD-ONS

The following tours and programs are available for extra cost beyond admission and should be reserved in advance.

- **Discover KSC: Today and Tomorrow** ($21) brings visitors to sites seldom accessible to the public, such as the Vehicle Assembly Building, the shuttle landing strip, and the 6-million-pound crawler that transports the shuttle to its launch pad.
- See how far the space program has come on the **Cape Canaveral: Then and Now Tour** ($21). It puts you up close to the original launch pads, brings you to the Air Force Space and Missile Museum, and lets you watch the active unmanned rocket program.
- During **Lunch with an Astronaut** ($23), astronauts talk about their experiences and engage in Q&A (kids often ask "How do you eat/sleep/relieve yourself in space?").
- If you or one of your little ones wants to live the life of an astronaut, you can enroll in **Astronaut Training Experience** (ATX). The $145 cost includes astronaut gear, lunch, a VIP tour of the Kennedy Space Center, and a half day of hands-on learning. Held at the United States Astronaut Hall of Fame, this is an intense half-day experience where you can dangle from a springy harness for a simulated moonwalk, spin in ways you never thought possible in a multi-axis trainer, and either work Mission Control or helm a space shuttle (in a full-scale mock-up) during a simulated landing. Reserve your spot well in advance.

Cape Canaveral Then and Now Tour.

PLANNING YOUR TRIP

GETTING HERE

The Kennedy Space Center and the U.S. Astronaut Hall of Fame are near Titusville on Cape Canaveral, about a 45- to 60-minute drive from Orlando. From Orlando International Airport, take the north exit to 528 East (the Beeline Expressway) and drive east to the exit marked "407, Titusville, Kennedy Space Center." Take 407 until you reach Rte. 405 (Columbia Boulevard/NASA Parkway) and then turn right. After approximately 1 mi you will see the U.S. Astronaut Hall of Fame on your right. Continue another 5 mi until you reach the visitor complex, your starting point for all tours.

BUDGETING YOUR TIME

Plan to spend a full day at the center and hall of fame, or at the very least, several hours.

ADMISSION

Your $38 admission ticket grants you access for two days (within the span of one week) to Kennedy Space Center Visitor Complex and related tours as well as the U.S. Astronaut Hall of Fame, which is just across the causeway.

CONTACT INFORMATION

✉ Off Rte. 405

☎ 321/449-4444

🌐 www.kennedyspacecenter.com

🎫 $38

🕒 Daily 9 AM to 5:30 PM. (Call ahead for restrictions if you're visiting on a launch day.)

SHUTTLE COMPONENTS

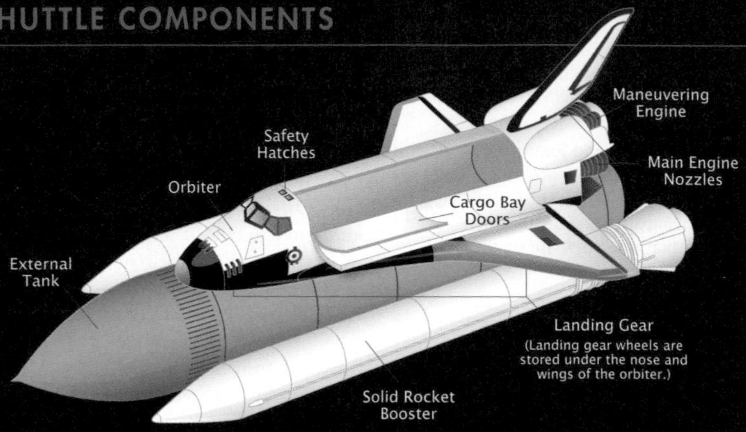
Maneuvering Engine
Safety Hatches
Main Engine Nozzles
Orbiter
Cargo Bay Doors
External Tank
Landing Gear
(Landing gear wheels are stored under the nose and wings of the orbiter.)
Solid Rocket Booster

ROCKET VS. SHUTTLE

When the space shuttle orbiter *Columbia* blasted off on April 12, 1981, NASA launched its Space Transportation System—a planned fleet of manned, reusable spacecraft that can transport crew, cargo, and experiments into space and return to Earth to land like an aircraft. The system is a radical departure from the days when manned lunar modules were thrust into space at the tip of a disposable rocket, to return to the planet by parachute and then be plucked from the ocean. (Shuttles are launched piggyback on a huge, single-use fuel tank; its two solid rocket boosters return via parachute.) Modern traditional rockets are used only to deploy instruments like unmanned probes into space.

EXTERNAL TANK—provides a platform for the shuttle and fuel for the two booster rockets that transport the shuttle into space. It separates from the shuttle within the first 10 minutes of the flight and falls into the ocean.

SOLID ROCKET BOOSTER—one of two rockets used to launch the shuttle into space. Each returns to Earth via parachute to be restored for use on a future mission.

ORBITER—another name for the space shuttle, which rides piggyback on the fuel tank until it can launch into space under its own rocket power. The crew is inside.

CARGO BAY DOORS—the two long doors on the back of the orbiter that open to allow payload to be deployed into space by means of a manipulating arm.

LANDING GEAR—the retractable wheels under the nose and wings of the orbiter, which allow it to land like a typical aircraft.

ENTRY HATCH—this door allows astronauts to enter the shuttle, and doubles as an escape hatch.

MANEUVERING ENGINES—a number of smaller orbiter engines, on the nose and in the tail section, which allow the craft to make fine positioning adjustments while in space.

MAIN ENGINE NOZZLES—the three engines at the rear of the orbiter that propel the craft to space.

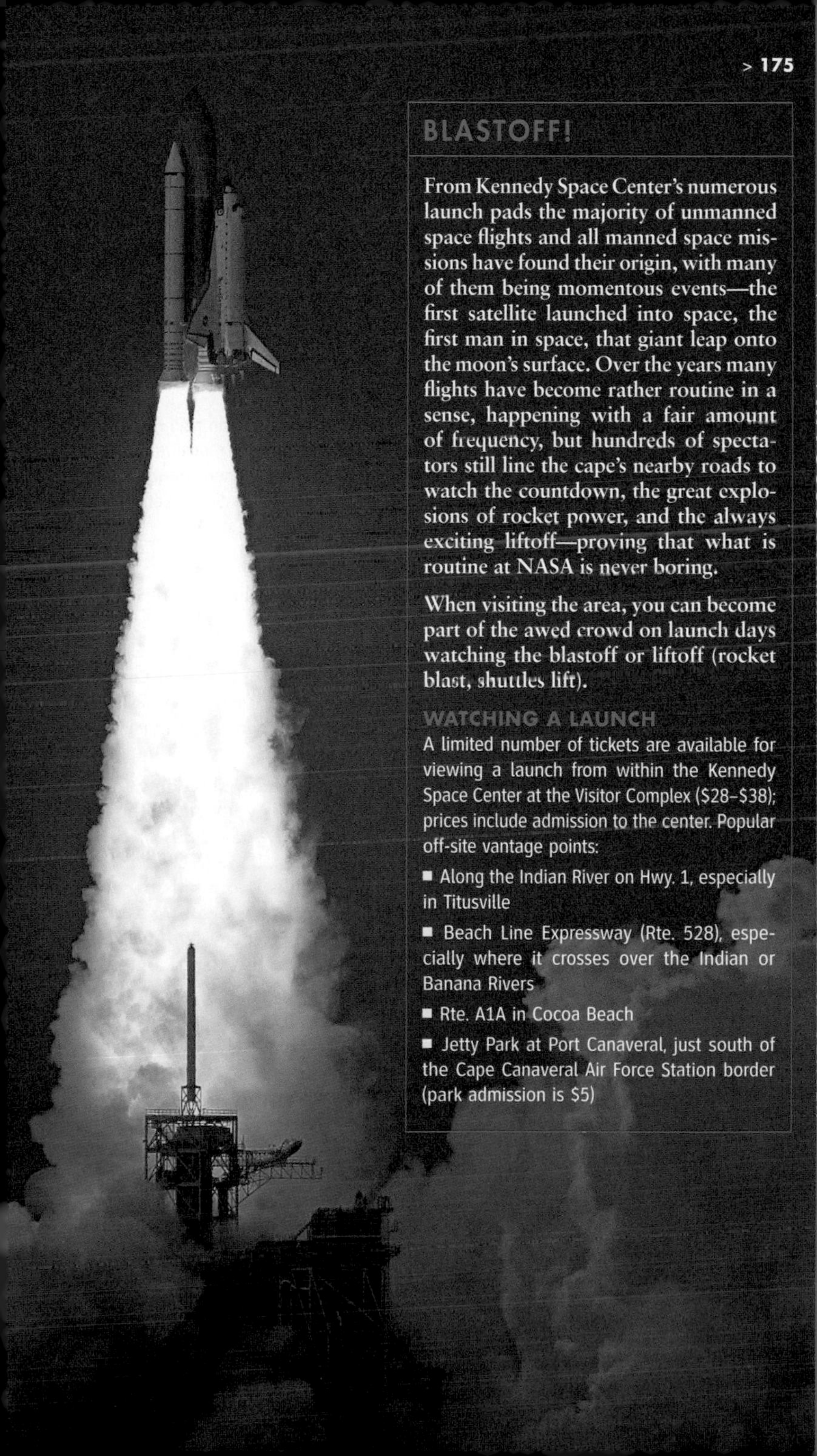

BLASTOFF!

From Kennedy Space Center's numerous launch pads the majority of unmanned space flights and all manned space missions have found their origin, with many of them being momentous events—the first satellite launched into space, the first man in space, that giant leap onto the moon's surface. Over the years many flights have become rather routine in a sense, happening with a fair amount of frequency, but hundreds of spectators still line the cape's nearby roads to watch the countdown, the great explosions of rocket power, and the always exciting liftoff—proving that what is routine at NASA is never boring.

When visiting the area, you can become part of the awed crowd on launch days watching the blastoff or liftoff (rocket blast, shuttles lift).

WATCHING A LAUNCH

A limited number of tickets are available for viewing a launch from within the Kennedy Space Center at the Visitor Complex ($28–$38); prices include admission to the center. Popular off-site vantage points:

- Along the Indian River on Hwy. 1, especially in Titusville
- Beach Line Expressway (Rte. 528), especially where it crosses over the Indian or Banana Rivers
- Rte. A1A in Cocoa Beach
- Jetty Park at Port Canaveral, just south of the Cape Canaveral Air Force Station border (park admission is $5)

Sidney Fischer Park. The 10-acre oceanfront has showers, playgrounds, changing areas, picnic areas with grills, snack shops, and plenty of well-maintained, inexpensive surf-side parking lots. Beach vendors carry necessities for sunning and swimming. The parking fee is $5 for cars and RVs. ✉ *2100 block of Rte. A1A* ☎ *321/868–3252.*

LIFE IMITATES ART

In the early 1960s, Cocoa Beach was a sleepy, little-known town. But in 1965 the sitcom *I Dream of Jeannie* premiered. The endearing show centered around an astronaut, played by Larry Hagman, and his "Jeannie" in a bottle, Barbara Eden, and was set in Cocoa Beach. Though the series was never shot in Florida, creator Sidney Sheldon paid homage to the town with local references to Cape Kennedy (now known as the Kennedy Space Center) and Bernard's Surf.

FISHING

The **Cocoa Beach Pier** (✉ *401 Meade Ave.* 🌐 *www.cocoabeachpier.com* ☎ *321/783–7549*) has a bait-and-tackle shop and a fishing area. Although most of the pier is free to walk on, there's a $1 charge to enter the fishing area at the end of the 800-foot-long boardwalk, and a $3.50 fishing fee. You can rent rods and reels here. ■ **TIP→** The pier is a great place to watch space-shuttle launches.

KAYAKING

Specializing in manatee encounters, **Adventure Kayak of Cocoa Beach** (☎ *321/480–8632* 🌐 *www.kayakcocoabeach.com*) takes guests on one- and two-person kayak tours of mangroves, channels, and islands.

SURFING

If you can't tell a tri-skeg stick from a hodaddy shredding the lip on a gnarly tube, then you may want to avail yourself of the **Ron Jon Surf School** (✉ *150 E. Columbia La.* ☎ *321/868–1980*) or the **Cocoa Beach Surf Company** (✉ *4001 N. Atlantic Ave.* ☎ *321/799–9930*). They teach grommets (dudes) and gidgets (chicks) from kids to seniors in groups and one-on-one. **Ron Jon Watersports** (✉ *4275 N. Atlantic Ave.* ☎ *321/799–8888*) and the **Cocoa Beach Surf Company** (✉ *4001 N. Atlantic Ave.* ☎ *321/799–9930*) rent surfboards, body boards, and wet suits, as well as umbrellas, chairs, and bikes.

SHOPPING

Cocoa Beach Surf Company (✉ *4001 N. Atlantic Ave.* ☎ *321/799–9930*) is the world's largest surf complex with three floors of boards, apparel, sunglasses, and anything else a surfer, wannabe-surfer, or souvenir-seeker could need. Also on-site are a 5,600-gallon fish and shark tank, the Shark Pit Bar & Grill, and the **East Coast Surfing Hall of Fame and Museum.**

Fodor's Choice ★ It's impossible to miss the **Ron Jon Surf Shop** (✉ *4151 N. Atlantic Ave., Rte. A1A* ☎ *321/799–8888* 🌐 *www.ronjonsurfshop.com*). With a giant surfboard and an aqua, teal, and pink art deco facade, Ron Jon takes up nearly two blocks along Route A1A. What started in 1963 as a small T-shirt and bathing-suit shop has evolved into a 52,000-square-foot superstore that's open every day 'round the clock. The shop has water-sports gear as well as chairs and umbrellas for rent and sells every kind of beachwear, surf wax, plus the requisite T-shirts and flip-flops. ■**TIP→** For up-to-the-minute surfing conditions, call the store and press 3 and then 7 for the Ron Jon Surf and Weather Report.

NIGHTLIFE

The **Cocoa Beach Pier** (✉ *401 Meade Ave.* ☎ *321/783–7549*) is for locals, beach bums, surfers, and people who don't mind the weather-worn wood and sandy, watery paths. The Mai Tiki Bar claims that "No Bar Goes This Far," which is true, considering it's at the end of the 800-foot pier. Come to the Boardwalk Friday night for the Boardwalk Bash, with live acoustic and rock-and-roll music, drop in Saturday for more live music, and come back Wednesday evening to catch the reggae band. For great live jazz, head to **Heidi's Jazz Club** (✉ *7 Orlando Ave. N* ☎ *321/783–4559*). Local and nationally known musicians (Boots Randolph and Mose Allison have taken the stage) play Tuesday through Sunday, with showcase acts appearing on weekends.

3

WHERE TO EAT

$$$ GERMAN ✕ **Heidelberg.** As the name suggests, the cuisine here is definitely German, from the sauerbraten served with potato dumplings and red cabbage to the beef Stroganoff and spaetzle to the classically prepared Wiener schnitzel. All the soups and desserts are homemade; try the Viennese-style apple strudel and the rum-zapped almond-cream tortes. Elegant interior touches include crisp linens and fresh flowers. There's live music Friday and Saturday evenings. You can also dine inside the jazz club, Heidi's, next door. ✉ *7 N. Orlando Ave., opposite City Hall* ☎ *321/783–6806* 🌐 *www.heidisjazzclub.com* ▭ *AE, MC, V* ⊗ *Closed Mon. Closed Tues. in summer. No lunch Sun.*

$ SEAFOOD ✕ **Oh Shucks Seafood Bar.** At the only open-air seafood bar on the beach, at the entrance of the Cocoa Beach Pier, the main item is oysters, served on the half shell. You can also grab a burger here, crab legs by the pound, or Oh Shucks' most popular item, coconut beer shrimp. Some diners complain that the prices don't jibe with the ultracasual atmosphere (e.g., plastic chairs), but they're also paying for the "ex-Pierience." There's live entertainment on Friday and Saturday. ✉ *401 Meade Ave., Cocoa Beach Pier* ☎ *321/783–7549* ▭ *AE, D, MC, V.*

WHERE TO STAY

$$ **Best Western Ocean Beach Hotel & Suites.** Folks who loved Cocoa Beach's Ocean Suite Hotel will love this Best Western property since it now encompasses the five-story, all-suites building that's particularly popular with families. Located just a half block from the Cocoa Beach Pier, the former Ocean Suite Hotel is in a great location, especially for shuttle launches. The newly renovated suites are still modest but feature two TVs, a separate living room, wet-bar area with sink, refrigerator, microwave, sofa bed, and a private balcony. ■**TIP→** Skip the standard motel rooms and stick with the suites in the "Tower." **Pros:** free Internet; complimentary breakfast. **Cons:** not all rooms have an ocean view; small bathrooms; noise from the pier. ✉ *5600 N. Ocean Beach Blvd.* ☎ *321/784–4343 or 800/367–1223* 🌐 *www.bestwesterncocoabeach.com* *50 suites* *In-room: refrigerator, Internet. In-hotel: 2 restaurants, pools, laundry facilities* ▭ *AE, D, MC, V* ¶◎¶ *CP.*

Popular with families, Cocoa Beach is an easy day trip for Orlando or Kennedy Space Center visitors.

$$ **Doubletree Hotel Cocoa Beach Oceanfront.** Proximity to the beach and comforts like microwaves and refrigerators—and Doubletree's famous chocolate-chip cookies—make this five-story hotel a favorite of vacationing families as well as Orlandoans on weekend getaways. Guest rooms are West Indies–inspired, with dark oak furniture, colorful tropical prints, and sunny yellow walls. Most rooms are oceanfront with private balconies, though all offer ocean views. **Pros:** private beach; refrigerator and microwave in every room; comfy beds. **Cons:** extra charge for beach-chair rental; loud air-conditioning in some rooms; slow elevators; no breakfast with standard room. ✉ *2080 N. Atlantic Ave.* ☎ *321/783–9222* 🌐 *www.cocoabeachdoubletree.com* *148 rooms, 12 suites* *In-room: refrigerator, Wi-Fi. In-hotel: restaurant, room service, bar, pool, gym, beachfront, laundry facilities, laundry service, parking (free)* *AE, D, DC, MC, V.*

$$$ ★ **Hilton Cocoa Beach Oceanfront.** You can't get any closer to the beach than this seven-story oceanfront hotel. Most rooms have ocean views, but for true drama get a room on the east end, facing the water. If sand isn't your thing, enjoy the ocean breeze and live music on the 10,000-square-foot deck surrounding "the largest pool on the Space Coast." The property also offers a variety of water-sport rentals and surf lessons. With purple, gold, and green soft goods, room decor is more Mardi Gras than beach resort, and yet rooms also feature Hilton Serenity Beds. **Pros:** beachfront; friendly staff; clean. **Cons:** small bathrooms; no balconies; room windows don't open; breakfast not included with standard rate. ✉ *1550 N. Atlantic Ave.* ☎ *321/799–0003* 🌐 *www.hiltoncocoabeach.com* *285 rooms, 11 suites* *In-room: refrigerator, Wi-Fi. In-hotel: 3 restaurants, room service, bar, pools, gym,*

beachfront, laundry facilities, laundry service, parking (free) ▭ *AE, D, DC, MC, V.*

$$$ ★ **Inn at Cocoa Beach.** One of the area's best, this charming oceanfront inn has spacious, individually decorated rooms with four-poster beds, upholstered chairs, and balconies or patios; most have ocean views. Deluxe rooms are much larger, with a king-size bed, sofa, and sitting area; most also have a dining table. Jacuzzi rooms are different sizes. Included in the rate are afternoon socials in the breezeway, evening wine and cheese, and a Continental breakfast. **Pros:** quiet; romantic; honor bar. **Cons:** no on-site restaurant; "forced" socializing. ✉ *4300 Ocean Beach Blvd.* ☎ *321/799–3460, 800/343–5307 outside Florida* 🌐 *www.theinnatcocoabeach.com* *50 rooms* *In-room: safe, DVD (some). In-hotel: pool, beachfront, Wi-Fi hotspot, parking (free)* ▭ *AE, D, MC, V* *CP.*

$$$$ Fodor's Choice ★ **The Resort on Cocoa Beach.** Even if the beach weren't in its backyard, this family-friendly, oceanfront property offers enough activities and amenities—from tennis and basketball courts to a game room and 50-seat movie theater—to keep everyone entertained. Organized activities begin at 9 and run through 2:30, with offerings including arts and crafts projects and scavenger hunts for kids and pool volleyball and bingo for adults. The two-bedroom, two-bathroom suites won't win any interior design awards, but they offer all of the comforts of home with a separate living room, dining area, and fully equipped kitchen, 42-inch plasma TV with DVD player, whirlpool tub, and washer and dryer. **Pros:** full kitchens; in-room washers and dryers; large balconies. **Cons:** check-in not until 4 and check out at 10; not all rooms are oceanfront; slow elevators. ✉ *1600 N. Atlantic Ave.* ☎ *321/783–4000* 🌐 *www.theresortoncocoabeach.com* *124 suites* *In-room: kitchen, DVD, Internet. In-hotel: restaurant, bars, tennis court, pools, gym, children's programs (ages 4–12), laundry facilities, Wi-Fi hotspot, parking (free)* ▭ *AE, D, MC, V.*

$–$$ **Wakulla Suites Resort.** This kitschy two-story motel in a converted 1970s apartment building is clean and comfortable, surrounded by tropical gardens, and just off the beach. Some rooms are a block away from the water, and a few are just a walk down the boardwalk. The bright rooms are fairly ordinary, decorated in tropical prints. Completely furnished suites, designed to sleep six, are great for families; each includes two bedrooms and a living room, dining area, and fully equipped kitchen. The throw-back property isn't for everyone, but those who dig it return year after year. **Pros:** kitchen; barbecue grills. **Cons:** lots of kid noise; a hike to the beach; seven-day cancelation policy. ✉ *3550 N. Atlantic Ave.* ☎ *321/783–2230 or 800/992–5852* 🌐 *www.wakullasuites.com* *117 suites* *In-room: kitchen, Internet, Wi-Fi. In-hotel: pool, laundry facilities, Wi-Fi hotspot, parking (free)* ▭ *AE, D, MC, V.*

MELBOURNE

20 mi south of Cocoa, on U.S. 95.

Despite its dependence on the high-tech space industry, this town is decidedly laid-back. The majority of the city is on the mainland, but a small portion trickles onto a barrier island, separated by the Indian River Lagoon and accessible by several inlets, including the Sebastian Inlet.

EXPLORING

Fodor's Choice ★ **Brevard Zoo.** At the only American Zoo and Aquarium Association–accredited zoo built by a community, stroll along the shaded boardwalks and get a close-up look at alligators, crocodiles, giant anteaters, marmosets, jaguars, eagles, river otters, kangaroos, exotic birds, and kookaburras. Alligator, crocodile, and river-otter feedings are held on alternate afternoons—although the alligators do not dine on the otters. Stop by Paws-On, an interactive learning playground where kids and adults can crawl into human-size gopher burrows, beehives, and spider webs; get cozy with several domestic animals in Animal Encounters; hand-feed a giraffe in Expedition Africa or a lorikeet in the Australian Free Flight Aviary; and step up to the Wetlands Outpost, an elevated pavilion that's a gateway to 22 acres of wetlands through which you can paddle kayaks and keep an eye open for the 4,000 species of wildlife that live in these waters and woods. ✉ *8225 N. Wickham Rd.* ☎ *321/254–9453* 🌐 *www.brevardzoo.org* 🎫 *$12.50 for general admission; $17 for admission, a train ride, and food for the lorikeets* ⏲ *Daily 9:30–5, last admission at 4:15.*

SPORTS AND THE OUTDOORS

BASEBALL

Even though they play in our nation's capital during the regular season, the **Washington Nationals** (✉ *5800 Stadium Pkwy., Viera* ☎ *321/633–4487* 🌐 *www.nationals.com*), formerly the Montreal Expos, use Melbourne's Space Coast Stadium for their spring-training site. For the rest of the season, the facility is home to the **Brevard County Manatees** (☎ *321/633–9200*), one of the Milwaukee Brewers' minor-league teams.

NIGHTLIFE AND THE ARTS

The **Maxwell C. King Center for the Performing Arts** (✉ *3865 N. Wickham Rd.* ☎ *321/242–2219 box office* 🌐 *www.kingcenter.com*) is one of the premier performance centers in Central Florida. Oddly enough, top-name performers often bypass Orlando to appear in this comfortable 2,000-seat hall. Call for a performance schedule.

Orlando and Environs

PLAN FOR THE PARKS, PICK YOUR HOTEL, EXPLORE ORLANDO

WORD OF MOUTH

"Get the Park Hopper Pass...to visit all the parks. Check out dining with Disney characters. My daughter loved the princess breakfast. Now that she's 13, she prefers Universal Studios. If you have time, spend a day there, too. One of the most memorable experiences was [swimming with the dolphins] at Discovery Cove."

—KendraM

WELCOME TO ORLANDO AND ENVIRONS

Shamu at SeaWorld.

TOP REASONS TO GO

★ **Magic and Fantasy:** Unleash your inner child, in the glow of Cinderella Castle, at WDW's Magic Kingdom. Fireworks transform the night skies—and you—at this park and at Epcot. And, over at Universal's Islands of Adventure we have just, two words: Harry Potter.

★ **The Planet and Beyond:** Visit Epcot's 11 countries, complete with perfect replicas of foreign monuments, unique crafts, and traditional cuisine. Then venture beyond the Earth with a trip to the Kennedy Space Center.

★ **Amazing Animals:** Safari through Africa in Disney's Animal Kingdom, get splashed by Shamu at SeaWorld, kiss a dolphin at Discovery Cove, and watch gators wrestle at Gatorland.

★ **Shopping Opps:** Hit the national chains at Orlando's upscale malls, or browse Winter Park's unique Park Avenue boutiques. Don't forget the mouse ears: Main Street U.S.A. and Downtown Disney are filled with the best classic souvenirs, and some quirkier items as well.

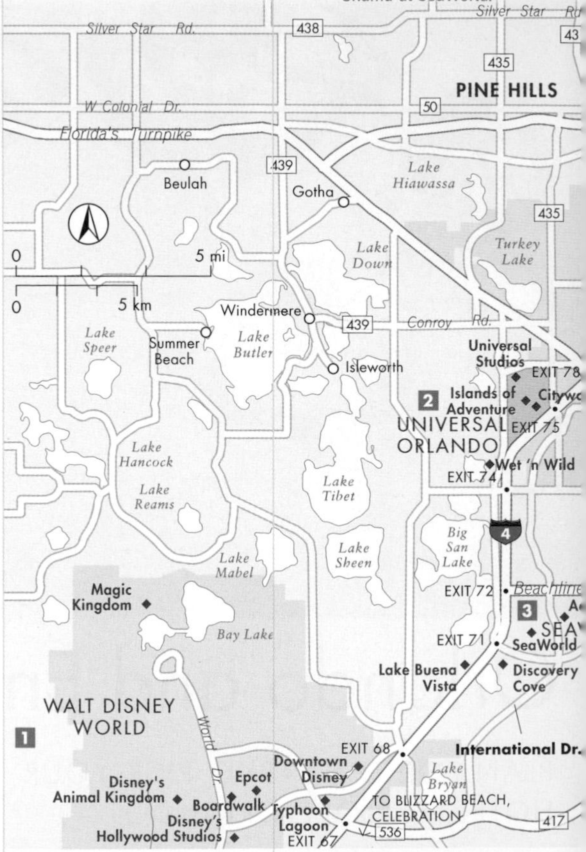

1 Walt Disney World. Walt Disney's original decree that his parks be ever-changing, along with some healthy competition from Universal Studios and SeaWorld, has kept the Disney Imagineers dreaming up new entertainment and installing higher-tech thrills and attractions.

2 Universal Orlando. While Disney creates a fantasy world for those who love fairy tales, Universal Orlando is geared to older kids, adults, and anyone who enjoys pop culture. Movie and TV fans love this place. Two other parks—Islands of Adventure (IOA) and Wet 'n Wild—add to the fun.

Nick Hotel.

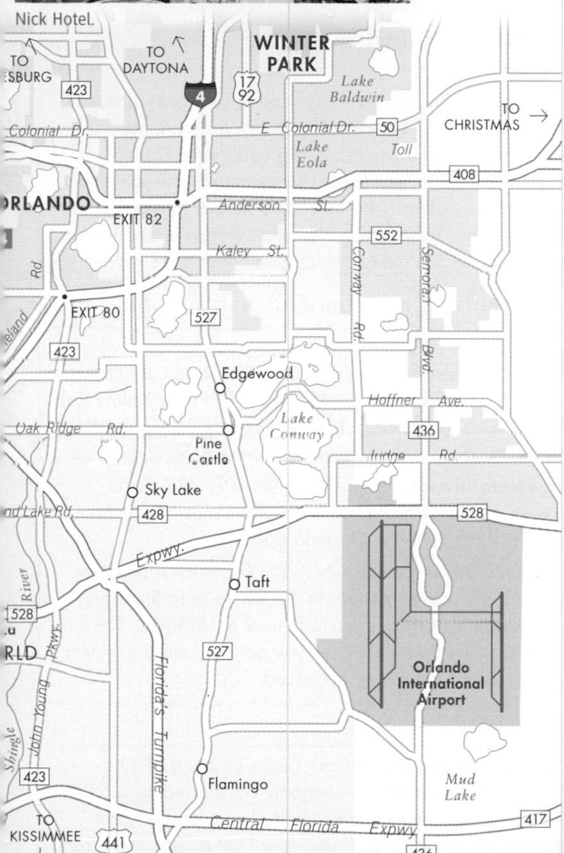

3 SeaWorld and Discovery Cove. Less glitzy than Walt Disney World or Universal, SeaWorld and Discovery Cove are worth a visit for a low-key, relaxing, ocean-themed experience. If you want to get more keyed up, pay a call on SeaWorld's Aquatica water park.

4 Orlando and Environs. Once you've exhausted the theme parks, or have been exhausted by them, turn your attention to a wealth of offerings, including museums, parks, and gardens, in Winter Park, Kissimmee, and elsewhere.

GETTING ORIENTED

Thanks to Disney World, Orlando is the gateway for many visitors to central Florida. The city sits about two hours east of Tampa (home to yet another theme park, Busch Gardens) and an hour southwest of Kennedy Space Center. Edging Orlando to the south is Kissimmee, with home-grown attractions like Gatorland. Looking for more laid-back local flavor? You'll find it just 20 miles northeast of Orlando in the charming Winter Park suburb.

Universal Orlando.

4

ORLANDO AND ENVIRONS PLANNER

Getting Here

All the major and most discount airlines fly into **Orlando International Airport** (*MCO ☎ 407/825-2001 🌐 www.orlandoairports.net*).

The **Beachline Expressway** (aka Beeline Expressway or Route 528), a toll road, gets you from the airport to area attractions. Depending on the location of your hotel, follow it west, and either exit at SeaWorld for the International Drive (I-Drive) area or stay on it to Interstate 4, and head west for Disney and U.S. 192–Kissimmee or east for Universal and downtown Orlando.

The **Central Florida Greenway (SR 417)** is a faster way from the airport to Disney than the Beachline, but tolls are heftier.

Magical Express

If you're staying at a Disney hotel, this free service will deliver your luggage from your home airport to your hotel (and back again) *and* shuttle you to and from your resort. ■ **TIP→** **You must book before departure (866/599-0951; www.disneysmagicalexpress.com); have your flight information handy.**

Getting Around

If you're spending your entire vacation on Disney property, you can use its fleet of buses, trams, boats, and monorail trains exclusively. If you're staying outside the Disney resort—or want to visit a non-Disney attraction—you'll need to use cabs, shuttles (your hotel may have a free one), and/or rental cars. Some hotels also offer shuttles to and from Universal and SeaWorld, which don't have transit systems.

CABS, SHUTTLES, AND PUBLIC TRANSPORTATION

Many non-Disney hotels offer free airport shuttles. If yours doesn't, cab fare from the airport to the Disney area runs $55–$75. Try **Star Taxi** (*☎ 407/857-9999*) or **Yellow Cab Co.** (*☎ 407/422-2222*). **Town & Country Transportation** (*☎ 407/828-3035*) charges $75 one-way for a town car.

The **Mears Transportation Group** (*☎ 407/423-5566 🌐 www.mearstransportation.com*) offers shuttle and charter services throughout the Orlando area.

The **I-Ride Trolley** (*☎ 407/248-9590 🌐 www.iridetrolley.com*) serves most attractions in the I-Drive area (including SeaWorld). It won't get you to Disney or Universal. The **LYNX** (*☎ 407/841-5969 🌐 www.golynx.com*) bus system provides service throughout Orlando.

CAR RENTAL

Rates vary seasonally and can begin as low as $30 a day/$149 a week for an economy car (excluding 6.5% rental car tax). If you're staying on Disney property but want to rent car for a day, you might get a better daily rate if you reserve for two or more days, then return the car early. (Just be sure there aren't any penalties for this.)

ROAD CONDITIONS AND SERVICE

Rush hours are weekdays 6–10 AM and 4–7 PM. Dial *511 for traffic advisories (www.fl511.com). Dial *347 (*FHP) for the Florida Highway Patrol. Most Florida highways are also patrolled by Road Rangers, a free roadside service. The **AAA Car Care Center** (*☎ 407/824-0976*) near the Magic Kingdom provides emergency services, including free towing even for non-AAA members on Disney property, weekdays 7–7, Saturday 7–4.

Transit Times and Costs

AIRPORT TO:	BY SHUTTLE	BY TAXI/CAR
Magic Kingdom	*30–45 min.; $33 round-trip (RT); $20 one way (OW)*	*35 min.; approx. $62 (taxi fare)*
Downtown Disney	*30–45 min.; $33 RT; $20 OW*	*25–30 min.; approx. $45*
Animal Kingdom/ Hollywood Studios	*30–45 min.; $33 RT; $20 OW*	*35 min.; approx. $55*
Universal	*30–40 min.; $33 RT; $20 OW*	*20 min.; approx. $40*
Kissimmee	*30–45 min.; $33 RT; $20 OW*	*30 min.; approx. $50*
I-Drive (Doubletree Castle)	*30–40 min.; $29 RT; $18 OW*	*20 min.; approx. $35*
Downtown Orlando	*30 min.; $28 RT; $17 OW*	*30 min.; approx. $35*

MAGIC KINGDOM TO:	BY SHUTTLE	BY TAXI/CAR
Downtown Disney	*N/A (use Disney transportation)*	*10–15 min.; approx. $25*
Animal Kingdom/ Hollywood Studios	*N/A (use Disney transportation)*	*15 min.; approx. $20*
Universal	*N/A*	*25 min.; approx. $35*
Kissimmee	*30 min.; $18 RT*	*25–30 min.; approx. $30*
I-Drive (Doubletree Castle)	*35 min.; $18 RT*	*30 min.; approx. $35*
Downtown Orlando	*N/A*	*40 min.; approx. $40*

UNIVERSAL TO:	BY SHUTTLE	BY TAXI/CAR
Magic Kingdom	*N/A*	*20 min.; approx. $20*
Downtown Disney	*N/A*	*20 min.; approx. $25*
Animal Kingdom/ Hollywood Studios	*N/A*	*30 min.; approx. $40*
Kissimmee	*30 min.; $18 RT*	*25 min.; approx. $45*
I-Drive (Doubletree Castle)	*25 min.; $18 RT*	*5–10 min.; approx. $10*
Downtown Orlando	*N/A*	*10 min.; approx. $25*

Orlando Routes

Beachline Expressway: Toll road from the airport to International Drive (I-Drive) and Disney (roughly $2). Also good for Universal, SeaWorld, and Space Coast.

Interstate 4: Main east–west highway between Tampa and Daytona; it follows a north–south track through Orlando. **■TIP→** **Think north when I-4 signs say east (toward Daytona, say), and south when they say west (toward Tampa).** Key exits are:

–Exit 64B: Magic Kingdom/U.S. 192; *heavy* peak-season traffic near this exit.

–Exit 65: Animal Kingdom, ESPN Wide World of Sports.

–Exit 67: Epcot/Downtown Disney, Typhoon Lagoon, Universal; less-congested exit.

–Exit 68: Downtown Disney, Typhoon Lagoon.

–Exits 71 and 72: SeaWorld.

–Exits 72, 74A, and 75A: I-Drive.

–Exits 74B and 75A: Universal Orlando Resort.

Semoran Blvd: main road to Winter Park. Heavily traveled but moves well; plenty of amenities.

Spacecoast Parkway or Irlo Bronson Memorial Highway (U.S. 192): Runs east–west to Kissimmee or Universal and downtown Orlando. Continues east to Space Coast. Crosses I–4 at Exits 64A and 64B.

ORLANDO AND ENVIRONS PLANNER

Area Contacts

Florida Tourist Board: ☎ *850/488–5607* ⊕ *www.visitflorida.com*

Kennedy Space Center: ☎ *321/449–4444* ⊕ *www.kennedyspacecenter.com*

Kissimmee/St. Cloud Visitors Bureau: ☎ *407/944–2400* ⊕ *www.floridakiss.com*

Orlando Visitors Bureau: ☎ *407/363–5872 or 800/972–3304* ⊕ *www.visitorlando.com*

Space Coast Office of Tourism: ☎ *321/433–4470* ⊕ *www.space-coast.com*

Tampa Bay and Company: ☎ *800/368–2672 or 813/223–1111* ⊕ *www.visittampabay.com*

Winter Park Welcome Center: ☎ *407/599–3399* ⊕ *www.cityofwinterpark.org*

WHEN TO GO

Spring is gorgeous: sunny and temperate. April and May can be nippy or warm. Summer is hot and humid—water parks are the best ways to keep cool. Crowds are thick and lines are long, but hours are extended. Late summer and fall comprise hurricane season, but late in September through November, days are beautiful and temperatures cooler.

Disney Packages

Cruises: Disney Cruise Line ships have activities and amenities to thrill family members of all ages. From Florida's Port Canaveral, you can sail to the Bahamas, Caribbean, or Panama Canal.

Fairy Tale Weddings & Honeymoons. Some 1,500 couples tie the knot at Disney World every year. At the Fairy Tale Wedding Pavilion and many other locations, the bride can ride in a Cinderella coach, have rings borne to the altar in a glass slipper, and spend time with Mickey and Minnie at the reception. Check out the interactive Web site, disneyweddings.disney.go.com.

Magic Your Way Vacations. These packages bundle hotel, parks admission, and an array of add-on options—dining plans, airfare, Park Hopper passes, spa treatments—that make it easy to customize your trip. They can also offer good value for money. Just do your homework so you'll know that, if you *aren't* interested in seeing Cirque du Soleil, it's best not to splurge on the Platinum Plan, which includes tickets to this show. You'll also be sure to determine how many park meals and snacks you'll truly need before investing in a dining plan.

Grand Gatherings. If you're planning a group trip, you must look into this service. It allows groups of eight or more to tailor entertainment and meals to their needs. Contact central reservations for information.

Universal Packages

Vacation Package. Universal offers its own plans and ever-changing roster of deals to help you maximize value. (When starting your research, check out the "Hot Deals" section of the Web site.) Basic packages include hotel and park admission, but can be expanded to include airfare; dining; rental cars; show tickets; spa treatments; admission to SeaWorld, Wet'n Wild, Aquatica, Busch Gardens, and Discovery Cove; and a VIP treatment that lets you skip many theme park lines. Note, though, that this last perk is free to guests at Universal hotels.

Parks Tickets

Per-day, per-person, at-the-gate admissions range from roughly $40–$50 at Aquatica or Wet 'n Wild to about $70–$80 at Universal, Disney, and SeaWorld. Discovery Cove runs between $189 without a dolphin swim to $299 with it, though prices vary seasonally. Combo ticket plans can save money, but be sure to weigh what they offer against your needs.

DISNEY

Magic Your Way: With this plan, the more days you stay, the greater your per-day savings. For instance, a one-day ticket costs $79 for anyone age 10 and up, whereas a five-day ticket costs $228 (or just under $46 per day). There are also add-ons:

Park Hopper: This lets you move from park to park within a single day and adds $52 to the price of a ticket, no matter how many days your ticket covers. The flexibility is fantastic—you can spend the day at Animal Kingdom, for example, then hit Magic Kingdom for fireworks.

Water Park Fun and More: With this $52-per-ticket add-on, you get admission to Typhoon Lagoon, Blizzard Beach, and other Disney attractions.

No Expiration: This add-on (prices vary) lets you use your ticket for more than one trip to Disney (e.g., use five days of a seven-day Magic Your Way ticket on one visit and two days on another).

UNIVERSAL, SEAWORLD, BUSCH GARDENS TAMPA

Universal Parks: A one-day Park to Park ticket is $109 (ages 10 and up); a seven-day version is nearly $170 (a better per-day value at just over $24 a day). Add the Express PLUS (prices vary) option to skirt ride lines; City-Walk Party Pass (roughly $12) for one-night venue access; CityWalk Party Pass and Movie (almost $21) for a free movie; and Length-of-Stay Wet 'n Wild pass (about $48).

SeaWorld and Busch Gardens Parks: There are various ticket plans for SeaWorld Orlando parks and Busch Gardens Tampa Bay, which are all run by one company.

Orlando FlexTicket: This gives you up to 14 consecutive days' unlimited entry to (but not parking at) Universal and SeaWorld parks and select CityWalk venues. It costs nearly $260 (ages 10 and up). The Flex Ticket Plus (nearly $300) includes admission to Busch Gardens and free shuttle service between it and various Orlando locations.

Parks Planning Contacts

DISNEY

Central Reservations: ☎ *407/932–7639 (407/W-DISNEY)*

Dining: ☎ *407/939–3463 (407/WDW-DINE)*

Fairytale Weddings & Honeymoons: ☎ *321/939–4610;* 🌐 *disneyweddings.disney.go.com*

Golf: ☎ *407/939–4653 (407/WDW-GOLF)*

Hotel: ☎ *407/939–7429*

Vacation Packages: ☎ *407/939–7675*

Tickets: ☎ *407/939–1289*

Web Site: 🌐 *disneyworld.disney.go.com*

SEAWORLD

Discovery Cove: ☎ *877/557–7404* 🌐 *www.discoverycove.com*

SeaWorld: ☎ *888/800–5447* 🌐 *www.seaworld.com/orlando*

UNIVERSAL

Main Number: ☎ *407/363–8000*

Dining: ☎ *407/224–3613; 407/224–4012 for character meals*

Hotel: ☎ *888/273–1311*

Vacation Packages: ☎ *877/801–9720*

Web Site: 🌐 *www.universalorlando.com*

4

Disney *Magic Your Way* Price Chart

TICKET OPTIONS

TICKET	1-DAY	2-DAY	3-DAY	4-DAY	5-DAY	6-DAY	7-DAY	10-DAY
BASE TICKET								
Ages 10-up	$79	$156	$219	$225	$228	$231	$234	$243
Ages 3-9	$68	$133	$187	$192	$195	$198	$201	$210
Base Ticket admits guest to one of the four major theme parks per day's use. Park choices are: Magic Kingdom, Epcot, Disney's Hollywood Studios, Disney's Animal Kingdom. 8- and 9-day tickets are also available.								
ADD: Park Hopper	$52	$52	$52	$52	$52	$52	$52	$52
Park Hopper option entitles guest to visit more than one theme park per day's use. Park choices are any combination of Magic Kingdom, Epcot, Disney's Hollywood Studios, Disney's Animal Kingdom.								
ADD: Water Parks Fun & More	$52 2 visits	$52 2 visits	$52 3 visits	$52 4 visits	$52 5 visits	$52 6 visits	$52 7 visits	$52 10 visits
Water Parks Fun & More option entitles guest to a specified number of visits to a choice of entertainment and recreation venues. Choices are Blizzard Beach, Typhoon Lagoon, DisneyQuest, Disney's Oak Trail golf course, and Wide World of Sports.								
ADD: No Expiration	n/a	$18	$24	$52	$73	$84	$115	$210
No expiration means that unused admissions on a ticket may be used any time in the future. Without this option, tickets expire 14 days after first use.								

MINOR PARKS AND ATTRACTIONS

TICKET	AGES 10-UP	AGES 3-9
Typhoon Lagoon or Blizzard Beach 1-Day 1-Park	$45	$39
DisneyQuest 1-Day	$41	$35
Disney's ESPN Wide World of Sports	$13.50	$10
Cirque du Soleil's *La Nouba*	$69–$120	$56–$97

*All prices are subject to Florida sales tax

Get wet on the 12-story Summit Plummet at Disney's Blizzard Beach.

Universal Orlando Ticket Price Chart

TICKET OPTIONS					
TICKET	**1-DAY**	**2-DAY**	**3-DAY**	**4-DAY**	**7-DAY**
BASE TICKET					
Ages 10-up	$79	$110	$125	$135	$160
Ages 3-9	$69	$97	$110	$118	$140
Base Ticket admits guest to one park per day, either Universal Studios or Islands of Adventure.					
ADD: Park-to-Park option	$30	$15	$15	$10	$10
Park-to-Park Ticket allows guest to go back and forth between Universal Studios and Islands of Adventure.					
ADD: Wet 'n Wild Length of Stay Ticket	$48	$48	$48	$48	$48
Wet 'n Wild Length of Stay Ticket gives guest admission to the water park for 14 consecutive days, beginning with the first day of use.					
ADD: CityWalk Party Pass	$12	$12	$12	$12	$12
CityWalk Party Pass and Movie	$21	$21	$21	$21	$21
CityWalk Party Pass gives guest one-night access to CityWalk clubs and venues (some of which require you to be at least 21). CityWalk Party Pass and Movie adds to that a free movie at the AMC Universal Cineplex 20.					
ADD: 1- and 2-Park Express PLUS Pass	$26 off-season, $56 peak season				
Gives guest access to much shorter lines at Universal Studios and Islands of Adventure rides. (Note that this pass is included in the room rate at Universal Resort hotels.)					
All prices are subject to Florida sales tax					

By Elise Allen, Joseph Reed Hayes, Rona Ginden, Jennifer Greenhill-Taylor

There's magic in Orlando, and we don't just mean the NBA team. The city and its environs teem with magical experiences, both natural and Imagineered. With endless joys and excitements for people of all ages, it's no wonder that more than 50 million people visit every year.

The most obvious source of Orlando's magic is Disney World. And with four theme parks, two water parks, 20 or so themed hotels, shopping districts, and countless dining options, you could spend a lengthy vacation entirely on Disney property and still not see it all.

Universal Studios and Islands of Adventure offer their own thrills, including the new Wizarding World of Harry Potter. There are also SeaWorld, Discovery Cove—where you can have the truly magical experience of swimming with the dolphins—and Busch Gardens Tampa. To take a break from the theme parks, you can visit Winter Park's Charles Hosmer Morse Museum for what may well be the world's largest collection of Tiffany glass; go hiking, swimming, or canoeing in Wekiwa Springs State Park; or head to Space Coast.

You could also just take it easy. Even in the midst of a whirlwind theme-park tour, you can laze by the pool, indulge in a spa treatment, play a round of golf, or leisurely shop an afternoon away.

The key to an ideal Orlando vacation is planning. Figure out well in advance who's going, what everyone wants to do on this trip, and what you'll save for the next. If your stay will center around theme parks, decide which parks to visit on which days, buy your ticket and hotel package, and make meal reservations—all long before leaving home.

When you're actually in Orlando, though, try to be flexible. Your plans form the backbone of your trip and you want it to be strong, but things will come up—moods will change, plans will alter. That's OK. For the most part, it's not difficult to change segments of your itinerary once you're on the ground. Planning is key to enjoying Orlando and all it offers, but so is taking a deep breath, allowing for the occasional detour, and going with the flow of your vacation.

EXPLORING

There's more to an Orlando experience than walking 10 mi a day in the theme parks. Travelers were flocking to central Florida's communities, lakes, streams, and golf courses decades before Disney arrived. In addition to myriad outdoor activities, Orlando and its environs offer plenty of noteworthy cultural sights.

ORLANDO

15 mi northeast of Walt Disney World; off I–4, take Exit 82C or 83B eastbound.

Downtown has high-rises; sports venues; interesting museums, restaurants, and nightspots; and numerous parks. A few steps away are delightful residential neighborhoods with brick-paved streets and live oaks dripping with Spanish moss.

EXPLORING

CENTRAL ORLANDO

Harry P. Leu Gardens. A few miles outside of downtown—on the former lakefront estate of a citrus entrepreneur—is this 50-acre garden. Among the highlights are a collection of historical blooms (many varieties of which were established before 1900), ancient oaks, a 50-foot floral clock, and one of the largest camellia collections in eastern North America (in bloom November–March). Mary Jane's Rose Garden is filled with more than 1,000 bushes. The simple 19th-century Leu House Museum, once the Leu family home, preserves the furnishings and appointments of a well-to-do Florida family. ✉ *1920 N. Forest Ave., Lake Ivanhoe* ☎ *407/246–2620* 🌐 *www.leugardens.org* 🎟 *$7; free first Mon. of every month* 🕒 *Garden daily 9–5; guided house tours daily on hr and ½ hr 10–3:30* ✥ *1:F1.*

Mennello Museum of American Folk Art. One of the few museums in the United States devoted to folk art has intimate galleries, some with lovely lakefront views. Look for the nation's most extensive permanent collection of Earl Cunningham paintings as well as works by many other self-taught artists. There's a wonderful video about Cunningham and his "curio shop" in St. Augustine. ✉ *900 E. Princeton St., Lake Ivanhoe* ☎ *407/246–4278* 🌐 *www.mennellomuseum.com* 🎟 *$4* 🕒 *Tues.–Sat. 10:30–4:30, Sun. noon–4:30* ✥ *1:F1.*

★ **Orlando Science Center.** With exhibits about the human body, mechanics, computers, math, nature, the solar system, and optics, there's something for every child's inner geek. The four-story internal atrium is home to live gators and turtles. The 300-seat Dr. Phillips CineDome, a movie theater with a giant eight-story screen, offers large-format IWERKS films and planetarium programs. The Crosby Observatory and Florida's largest publicly accessible refractor telescope are here, as are several smaller telescopes. ✉ *777 E. Princeton St., Lake Ivanhoe* ☎ *407/514–2000 or 888/672–4386* 🌐 *www.osc.org* 🎟 *$17; parking $5; tickets include all permanent and special exhibits, films, live science presentations, and planetarium shows* 🕒 *Thurs.–Tues. 10–5* ✥ *1:F1.*

INTERNATIONAL DRIVE

Fun Spot. Four go-kart tracks offer a variety of driving experiences for children and adults. Though drivers must be at least 10 years old and meet height requirements, parents can drive smaller children in two-seater cars on several of the tracks, including the Conquest Track. A dozen or so rides range from the dizzying Paratrooper to an old-fashioned Revolver Ferris Wheel. Inside the arcade, traditional games get as much attention as the high-tech ones. ✉ *5551 Del Verde Way, I–4 to Exit 75A, International Drive* ☎ *407/363–3867* 🌐 *www.funspot.tutengraphics.com* 🎟 *$14.95–$34.95 depending on package; arcade tokens 25¢ each or $25 for 120* ⏲ *Daily 10 AM–midnight* ✥ *1:D3.*

Ripley's Believe It or Not! Odditorium. A 10-foot-square section of the Berlin Wall. A pain-and-torture chamber. A Rolls-Royce constructed entirely of matchsticks. A 26-by-20-foot portrait of van Gogh made from 3,000 postcards. These and almost 200 other oddities (shrunken heads included) speak for themselves in this museum-cum-attraction. ✉ *8201 International Dr., International Drive* ☎ *407/351–5803 or 800/998–4418 Ext. 3* 🌐 *www.ripleysorlando.com* 🎟 *$18.95; free parking* ⏲ *Daily 9:30 AM–midnight; last admission at 11 PM* ✥ *1:D3.*

WonderWorks. The building seems to be sinking into the ground at a precarious angle and upside down. The upside-down theme continues only as far as the lobby. After that, it's a playground of 100 interactive experiences—some incorporating virtual reality, others educational, and still others pure entertainment. You can experience an earthquake or a hurricane, pilot a fighter jet using simulator controls, make giant bubbles in the Bubble Lab, play laser tag, design and ride your own roller coaster, and lie on a bed of real nails. ✉ *9067 International Dr., International Drive* ☎ *407/351–8800* 🌐 *www.wonderworksonline.com* 🎟 *$19.95; parking $2–$6* ⏲ *Daily 9 AM–midnight* ✥ *1:D4.*

SPORTS AND THE OUTDOORS

BALLOONING

Fodor's Choice ★ **Bob's Balloons.** Bob's offers one-hour rides over protected marshland and will even fly over Disney World if conditions are right. You meet in Lake Buena Vista at dawn, where a van takes you to the launch site. It takes about 15 minutes to get the balloon in the air, and then you're off on an adventure that definitely surpasses Peter Pan's Flight in the Magic Kingdom. There are seats in the basket, but you'll probably be too thrilled to sit down. ☎ *407/466–6380 or 877/824–4606* 🌐 *www.bobsballoons.com* 🎟 *$90–$175 per person* 💳 *D, MC, V.*

GOLF

★ **Champions Gate Golf Club.** There's a David Leadbetter Golf Academy as well as two distinct courses designed by Greg Norman. The 7,406-yard International has the feel of the best British Isles courses, whereas the 7,048-yard National course is designed in the style of the better domestic courses, with a number of par-3 holes with unusual bunkers. ✉ *1400 Masters Blvd., Champions Gate* ☎ *407/787–4653 Champions Gate, 407/787–3330 or 888/633–5323 Leadbetter Academy* 🌐 *www.championsgategolf.com* 🎟 *Greens fees $65–$187* ✥ *1:B6.*

Grand Cypress Golf Resort. The Grand Cypress Academy of Golf, a 21-acre facility, has lessons and clinics. The North and South courses have fairways constructed on different levels, giving them added definition. The New Course, designed by Jack Nicklaus, was inspired by the Old Course at St. Andrews and has deep bunkers, double greens, a snaking burn, and even an old stone bridge. ✉ *1 N. Jacaranda, Orlando* ☎ *407/239–1909 or 800/835–7377* 🌐 *www.grandcypress.com* *Greens fees $120–$250* ✣ *1:C5.*

MINIATURE GOLF

Fodor's Choice ★ **Hawaiian Rumble Adventure Golf.** Who can resist golfing around an erupting volcano? Hawaiian Rumble combines a tropical setting with waterfalls, tunnels, tiki gods, and flame-belching mountains. ✉ *8969 International Dr., International Drive* ☎ *407/351–7733* 🌐 *www.hawaiianrumbleorlando.com* *$9.95–$14.95* ⏲ *Sun.–Thurs. 9 AM–11:30 PM, Fri. and Sat. 9 AM–midnight* ✣ *1:D4.*

Pirate's Cove Adventure Golf. Two 18-hole courses wind around artificial mountains, through caves, and into lush foliage. The beginner's course is called Captain Kidd's Adventure; the more advanced course is Blackbeard's Challenge. ✉ *8501 International Dr., International Drive* ☎ *407/352–7378* 🌐 *www.piratescove.net* *$10.95–$16.50* ⏲ *Daily 9 AM–11:30 PM* ✣ *1:D3.*

SHOPPING

FACTORY OUTLETS

★ **Prime Outlets Orlando.** The massive complex houses Saks Fifth Avenue OFF 5TH, Neiman Marcus Last Call, Victoria's Secret Outlet, the only outlet store for Baccarat and Lalique crystal, and a Disney outlet. Searching for bargains works up an appetite, and there are plenty of places to eat here, either in the well-lit food court or in one of several sit-down restaurants. ✉ *5401 W. Oak Ridge Rd., International Drive* ☎ *407/352–9600* 🌐 *www.primeoutlets.com* ⏲ *Mon.–Sat. 10 AM–11 PM, Sun. 10–9* ✣ *1:D3.*

Orlando Premium Outlets. Smart shoppers have lunch on International Drive and take the I-Ride Trolley here. You'll find the Kleins (Anne and Calvin), Gap, Nike, Adidas, Timberland, Polo, Armani, Burberry, Tommy Hilfiger, Mikasa, and about 100 other stores. ✉ *8200 Vineland Rd., International Drive* ☎ *407/238–7787* 🌐 *www.premiumoutlets.com/orlando* ⏲ *Mon.–Sat. 10 AM–11 PM, Sun. 10–9* ✣ *1:D5.*

MALLS

Fodor's Choice ★ **Mall at Millenia.** Its high-end shops include Gucci, Dior, Burberry, Chanel, Jimmy Choo, Hugo Boss, Cartier, Tiffany, and Ferragamo. You'll also find Neiman Marcus, Bloomingdale's, Bang & Olufsen, Ikea, and an Apple store. ✉ *4200 S. Conroy Rd., South Orlando* ☎ *407/363–3555* 🌐 *www.mallatmillenia.com* ⏲ *Mon.–Sat. 10–9:30, Sun. 11–7* ✣ *1:E3.*

Pointe Orlando. This entertainment complex is within walking distance of five top hotels and the Orange County Convention Center. It's home to WonderWorks; an IMAX theater; and specialty shops such as Armani Exchange, Tommy Bahama, Chico's, and Victoria's Secret. Restaurants include the very high-end Capital Grille, the Oceanaire Seafood Room, Cuba Libre, Funky Monkey Wine Company, B.B. King's Blues

DID YOU KNOW?

Walt Disney World has 99 holes of golf on five championship courses as well as two miniature golf courses. Golfers who stay at a Disney property get free cab fare from the hotel to the course and back.

Club, and Taverna Opa. ✉ *9101 International Dr., International Drive* ☎ *407/248–2838* 🌐 *www.pointeorlando.com* ⏲ *Mon.–Sat. noon–10, Sun. noon–8; restaurant hrs vary* ✣ *1:D4.*

NIGHTLIFE

BARS

Antigua. The multi-block-long entertainment complex called Church Street is a restaurant and bar hot spot, with Antigua being a contender for flashiest of them all. The music in the multilevel, four-bar lounge is loud; the lighting is dramatic; and the waterfall (yes, you read that correctly) cascades 20 feet. No wonder the pretty people pack the place. ✉ *46 West Church St., Downtown Orlando* ☎ *407/649–4270* 🌐 *www.churchstreetbars.com* 🎟 *$5–$10* ⏲ *Wed.–Sat. 10 PM–2:45 AM* ✣ *1:F1.*

4

ICEBAR. Thanks to the miracle of refrigeration, this is Orlando's coolest bar—literally and figuratively. Fifty tons of pure ice is kept at a constant 27°F and has been cut and sculpted by world-class carvers into a cozy (or as cozy as ice can be) sanctuary of tables, sofas, chairs, and a bar. The staff loans you a thermal cape and gloves, and drinks are served in glasses made of crystal-clear ice. ✉ *Pointe Orlando, 8967 International Dr., International Drive* ☎ *407/426–7555* 🌐 *www.icebarorlando.com* ⏲ *Daily 11 AM–2 AM* ✣ *1:D4.*

Wally's. Some would say that one of Orlando's oldest bars (circa 1953) is a dive, but that doesn't matter to the students, bikers, lawyers, and barflies who land here to drink surrounded by the go-go-dancer wallpaper and '60s-era interior. ✉ *1001 N. Mills Ave., Downtown Orlando* ☎ *407/896–6975* ⏲ *Mon.–Sat. 7:30 AM–1 AM, Sun. noon–10* ✣ *1:F1.*

MUSIC CLUBS

★ **B.B. King's Blues Club.** The blues-musician-turned entrepreneur has clubs in Memphis, Nashville, Las Vegas, and West Palm Beach as well as Orlando. Like the others, the root of the club is music. There's a dance floors and two stages for live performances by the B.B. King All-Star Band or visiting musicians. The club doubles as a restaurant with catfish bites, po' boys, ribs, and other comfort foods. Oh, yeah, and there's a full bar. ✉ *Pointe Orlando, 9101 International Dr., International Drive* ☎ *407/370–4550* 🌐 *www.bbkingclubs.com* ⏲ *Daily 11 AM–2 AM* ✣ *1:D4.*

Firestone Live. Based in an old automotive repair shop, this multilevel, high-energy club draws international music acts. Something's always going on to make the crowd hop: DJ mixes, big band, jazz, hip-hop, rock. Often the dance floor is semicontrolled chaos. ✉ *578 N. Orange Ave., Downtown Orlando* ☎ *407/872–0066* 🌐 *www.firestonelive.net* ✣ *1:F1.*

Social. Beloved by locals, Social serves full dinners Wednesday through Saturday and offers up live music seven nights a week. You can sip trademark martinis while listening to anything from alternative rock to rockabilly to undiluted jazz. Hours and prices vary. ✉ *54 N. Orange Ave., Downtown Orlando* ☎ *407/246–1419* 🌐 *www.thesocial.org* ✣ *1:F1.*

KISSIMMEE

18 mi south of Orlando, 10 mi southeast of Walt Disney World (WDW).

Although Kissimmee is primarily known as the gateway to Disney (technically, the park is in both Osceola and Orange counties), its non-WDW attractions just might tickle your fancy. They range from throwbacks to old-time Florida or to dinner shows for you and 2,000 of your closest friends. With at least 100,000 acres of freshwater lakes, the Kissimmee area brings anglers and boaters to national fishing tournaments and speedboat races. A 50-mi-long series of lakes, the Kissimmee Waterway, connects Lake Tohopekaliga—a Native American name that means "Sleeping Tiger"; locals call it Lake Toho—with huge Lake Ocheechobee in south Florida, and, from there, to both the Atlantic Ocean and the Gulf of Mexico.

Gatorland. This campy attraction near the Orlando–Kissimmee border on U.S. 441 has endured since 1949 without much change. The Gator Gulley Splash Park is complete with giant "egrets" spilling water from their beaks, dueling water guns mounted atop giant gators, and other water-park splash areas. There's also a small petting zoo and an aviary. A free train ride takes you through an alligator breeding marsh and a natural swamp setting where you can spot gators, birds, and turtles. A three-story observation tower overlooks the marsh. For a glimpse of 37 giant rare and deadly crocodiles, check out the Jungle Crocs of the World exhibit. To see eager gators leaping out of the water to catch their food, come on cool days for the Gator Jumparoo Show (summer heat just puts them to sleep). There's also a Gator Wrestlin' Show. This is a real Florida experience, and you leave knowing the difference between a gator and a croc. ✉ *14501 S. Orange Blossom Trail, between Orlando and Kissimmee* ☎ *407/855–5496 or 800/393–5297* 🌐 *www.gatorland.com* *$22.99; discount coupons online* ⏲ *Daily 9–6* ✣ *1:E5.*

SPORTS AND THE OUTDOORS

FISHING

Lake Charters. This outfitter conducts trips from November to May on Lake Toho (January through April is high season, so reserve accordingly). It's possible to catch a 14-pound bass here. Rods and reels are included in the costs, and transportation is available. Half-day freshwater trips for one or two people cost $250; six-hour trips are $300, and full-day trips are $350. You can also buy your licenses ($17–$30) here. ✉ *1650 Justin Matthew Way, St. Cloud* ☎ *407/891–2275 or 877/326–3575* 🌐 *www.lakecharter.com.*

SHOPPING

Lake Buena Vista Factory Stores. Although it has scant curb appeal, it does have a good collection of standard outlet stores for Aeropostale, Bass, Eddie Bauer, Fossil, Gap, Izod, Liz Claiborne, Nike, Tommy Hilfiger, and Old Navy. ✉ *15657 S. Apopka Vineland Rd., Lake Buena Vista* ☎ *407/238–9301* 🌐 *www.lbvfs.com* ⏲ *Mon.–Sat. 10–9, Sun. 10–6* ✣ *1:D5.*

192 Flea Market Outlet. Its 400 booths are open daily. The all-new merchandise includes tons of items: toys, luggage, sunglasses, jewelry, clothes, beach towels, sneakers, electronics, and the obligatory T-shirts. ✉ *4301 W. Vine St., Hwy. 192, Kissimmee* ☎ *407/396–4555* 🌐 *www.192fleamarketprices.com* ⏲ *Daily 9–6* ⊕ *1:D6.*

NIGHTLIFE

Arabian Nights. This palatial arena has seating for more than 1,200. The 25-act dinner show is complete with about 60 horses, centers around the quest of an Arabian princess to find her true love, and includes a buffoonish genie, a chariot race, and an intricate dance on horseback. The kitchen serves such things as USDA Choice and certified Black Angus sirloin. ✉ *3081 Arabian Nights Blvd., Kissimmee* ☎ *407/239–9223, 800/553–6116, 800/533–3615 in Canada* 🌐 *www.arabian-nights.com* 🎟 *$63.99, including tax* ⏲ *Shows nightly, times vary* 💳 *AE, D, MC, V* ⊕ *1:C6.*

Capone's Dinner and Show. This show brings you back to gangland Chicago of the 1930s. The evening begins in an old-fashioned ice-cream parlor, but say the secret password, and you're ushered inside Al Capone's private Underworld Cabaret and Speakeasy. Dinner is an all-you can-eat American and Italian buffet that includes beer, alcoholic mixed drinks, and cocktails for kids. ✉ *4740 W. Irlo Bronson Memorial Hwy., Kissimmee* ☎ *407/397–2378* 🌐 *www.alcapones.com* 🎟 *$49.99* ⏲ *Daily 7:30* 💳 *AE, D, MC, V* ⊕ *1:D6.*

Medieval Times. In a huge, ersatz-medieval manor you'll see a tournament of sword fights, jousting matches, and other games on a good-versus-evil theme. No fewer than 30 charging horses and a cast of 75 knights, nobles, wizards, and maidens participate. That the show takes precedence over the meat-and-potatoes fare is obvious: everyone sits facing forward at long, narrow banquet tables. ✉ *4510 W. Irlo Bronson Memorial Hwy., Kissimmee* ☎ *407/396–1518 or 800/229–8300* 🌐 *www.medievaltimes.com* 🎟 *$59.95* ⏲ *Castle daily 9–4, village daily 4:30–8, performances usually daily at 8 but call ahead* 💳 *AE, D, MC, V* ⊕ *1:D6.*

BOK TOWER GARDENS

57 mi southwest of Orlando; 42 mi southwest of WDW.

Fodor's Choice ★ You'll see citrus groves as you ride south along U.S. 27 to the small town of Lake Wales and the **Bok Tower Gardens.** This appealing sanctuary of plants, flowers, trees, and wildlife has been something of a local secret for years. Shady paths meander through pine forests with silvery moats, mockingbirds and swans, blooming thickets, and hidden sundials. The majestic, 200-foot Bok Tower is constructed of coquina—from seashells—and pink, white, and gray marble. The tower houses a carillon with 57 bronze bells that ring out each day at 1 and 3 PM during 30-minute live recitals of early American folk songs, Appalachian tunes, Irish ballads, or Latin hymns. The landscape was designed in 1928 by Frederick Law Olmsted, Jr., son of the planner of New York's Central Park. The grounds include the 20-room, Mediterranean-style Pinewood Estate, built in 1930 and open for self-guided touring. ✉ *1151 Tower Blvd., Lake Wales* ☎ *863/676–1408* 🌐 *www.boktower.org* 🎟 *$10 adults, Pinewood Estate general tour $6. 50% off admission Sat. 8–9 AM; holiday tour prices higher* ⏲ *Daily 8–6* ⊕ *1:B6.*

WEKIWA SPRINGS STATE PARK

13 mi northwest of Orlando, 28 mi north of WDW.

Fodor's Choice ★ The river, springs, and surrounding 6,400-acre **Wekiwa Springs State Park** are well suited to camping, hiking, picnicking, swimming, canoeing, and fishing. The area is also full of Florida wildlife: otters, raccoons, alligators, bobcats, deer, turtles, and birds. You can rent canoes ($16 for two hours and $3.20 per hour after that) in the town of Apopka, near the park's southern entrance. ✉ *1800 Wekiva Circle, Apopka* ☎ *407/884–2008, 800/326–3521 for campsite bookings* 🌐 *www.floridastateparks.org* 🎟 *$2 per pedestrian or bicycle; $6 per vehicle* ⏲ *Daily 8–dusk* ✥ *1:E1.*

WINTER PARK

6 mi northeast of Orlando; 20 mi northeast of WDW.

This peaceful, upscale community may be just outside the hustle and bustle of Orlando, but it feels like a different country. The lovely, 8-square-mi village has brick-paved streets, boutique-lined Park Avenue, historic buildings, and well-maintained lakes and parkland. Even the town's bucolic nine-hole golf course is on the National Register of Historic Places.

Fodor's Choice ★ **Charles Hosmer Morse Museum of American Art.** The world's most comprehensive collection of work by Louis Comfort Tiffany—including immense stained-glass windows, lamps, watercolors, and desk sets—is in this museum. Many of the works were rescued from Tiffany's Long Island estate, Laurelton Hall, after a 1957 fire destroyed much of the property. Among the draws is the 1,082-square-foot Tiffany Chapel, originally built for the 1893 world's fair in Chicago. The museum also contains American decorative art and paintings from the mid-19th to the early-20th centuries. ✉ *445 N. Park Ave., Winter Park* ☎ *407/645–5311* 🌐 *www.morsemuseum.org* 🎟 *$3; Nov.–Apr., Fri. free 4–8* ⏲ *Tues.–Sat. 9:30–4, Sun. 1–4; Nov.–Apr., Fri. until 8* ✥ *1:F1.*

Cornell Fine Arts Museum. On the Rollins College campus, this museum houses Florida's oldest art collection (its first paintings acquired in 1896)—one with more than 6,000 works, from Italian Renaissance to 19th- and 20th-century American and European paintings. Special exhibitions feature everything from Native American artifacts to Soviet propaganda posters. ✉ *Rollins College, 1000 Holt Ave., Winter Park* ☎ *407/646–2526* 🌐 *www.rollins.edu/cfam* 🎟 *$5* ⏲ *Tues.–Fri. 10–4, weekends noon–5* ✥ *1:F1.*

Scenic Boat Tour. Head north from Park Avenue, and, at the end of Morse Avenue, you'll find the launching point for this tour, a Winter Park tradition since 1938. The one-hour cruise takes in 12 mi of waterways, including three lakes and oak- and cypress-shaded canals built in the 1800s as a transportation system for the logging industry. A well-schooled skipper shares stories about the moguls who built their mansions along the shore and points out wildlife. ✉ *312 E. Morse Blvd., Winter Park* ☎ *407/644–4056* 🌐 *www.scenicboattours.com* 🎟 *$10* ⏲ *Daily 10–4.*

WHERE TO EAT

You'll find the all-American-standby burger-and-fries combo everywhere in Orlando, yet the ambitious chefs behind Orlando's theme park and independent restaurants provide loads of better options—much better. Locally sourced foods, creative preparations, and clever international influences are all the rage here, giving even die-hard foodies surprisingly satisfying meals. Theme-park complexes have some of the best restaurants in town, although you may opt for a car rental to seek out the local treasures.

RESERVATIONS

All WDW restaurants and most restaurants elsewhere in greater Orlando take reservations. To book restaurant reservations within Walt Disney World, call ☎ *407/939–3463* (*WDW–DINE*) or book online at *www.disneyworld.com/dining*. Reservations are accepted 180 days in advance. For Universal Orlando reservations, call ☎ *407/224–9255* (theme parks and CityWalk) or ☎ *407/503–3463* (hotels). Learn about the complex's 50-plus restaurants at *www.universalorlando.com*; press the Dining tab.

MEAL PLANS

If you're staying at one of Disney's lodging facilities, you may find one of the Disney Dining Plan deals to be of great value. The options are tweaked annually, but each plan entitles you to a certain number of meals and snacks per day in restaurants of specific categories. To learn more, visit *www.disneyworld.com* and type Disney Dining Plans into the search box. Universal Orlando offers an all-you-can-eat-from-lunch-on deal for the walk-up eateries inside the two theme parks (but not the restaurants in CityWalk). Tickets can be purchased at the theme-park ticket office, at participating restaurants, or at *www.universalorlando.com/dining*.

PRICES

WHAT IT COSTS

	¢	$	$$	$$$	$$$$
AT DINNER	under $8	$8–$14	$15–$21	$22–$30	over $30

Prices are per person for a median main course, at dinner, excluding tip and tax of 6.5 %.

WALT DISNEY WORLD AREA

MAGIC KINGDOM

$$$$ AMERICAN

Cinderella's Royal Table. Cinderella and other Disney princesses appear at breakfast time at this eatery in the castle's old mead hall; you should book reservations up to 180 days in advance to be sure to see them. The Once Upon a Time Breakfast offers all-you-can-eat items such as scrambled eggs, sausages, bacon, French toast, and beverages. The Fairytale Lunch, a prix-fixe table-service meal, includes entrées like pan-seared salmon with herbed rice and pasta pomodoro. The prix-fixe dinner features selections such as roast lamb chops with herb pesto and

Map 1: Where to Explore, Eat, and Stay in the Orlando Area

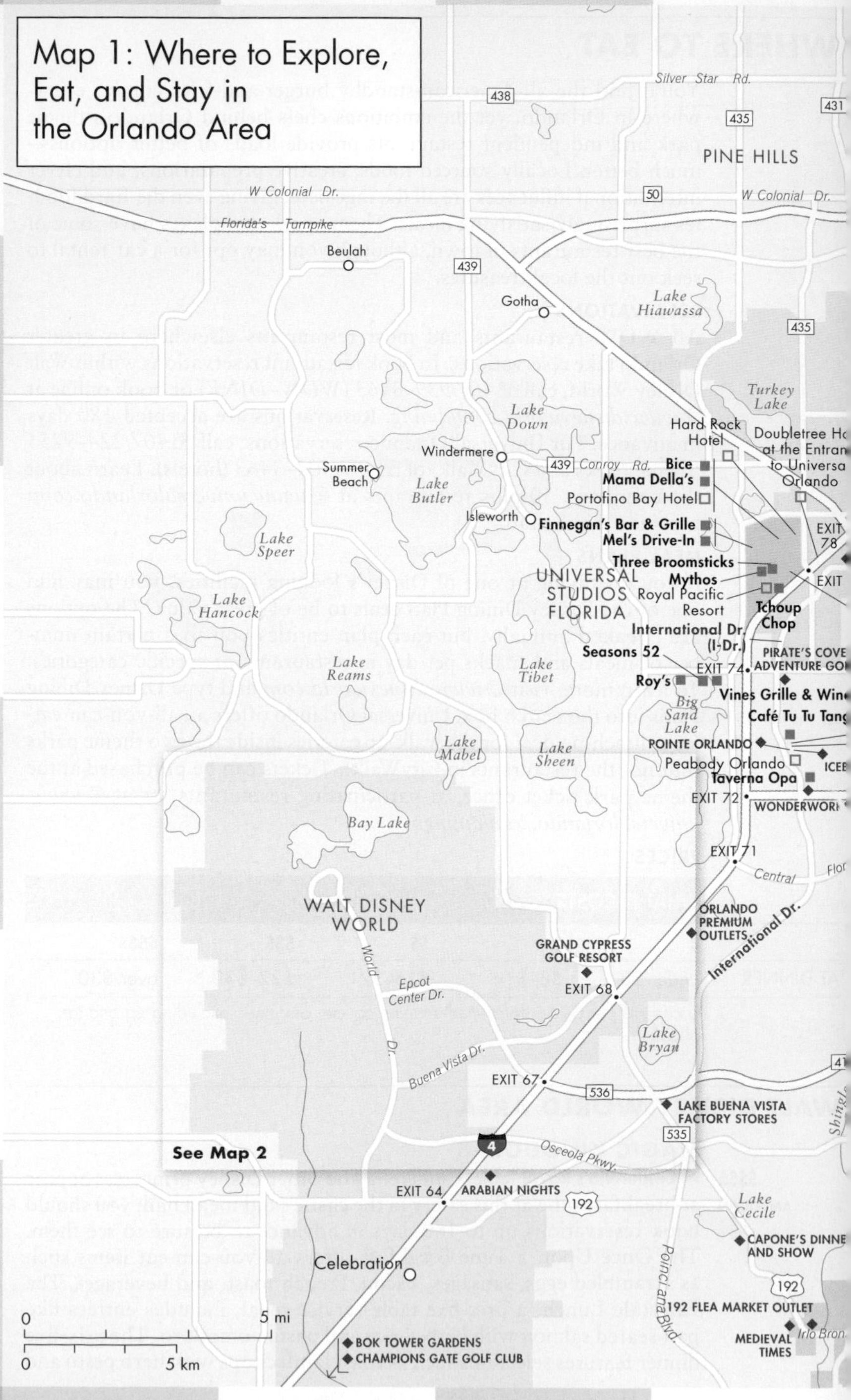
A
B
C
D
1
2
3
4
5
6
Silver Star Rd.
438
431
435
PINE HILLS
W Colonial Dr.
50
W Colonial Dr.
Florida's Turnpike
Beulah
439
Gotha
Lake Hiawassa
435
Turkey Lake
Lake Down
Hard Rock Hotel
Doubletree Ho
at the Entran
to Universa
Orlando
Windermere
439 Conroy Rd.
Summer Beach
Lake Butler
Bice
Mama Della's
Portofino Bay Hotel
Isleworth
Finnegan's Bar & Grille
Mel's Drive-In
EXIT 78
Lake Speer
Three Broomsticks
Mythos
UNIVERSAL STUDIOS FLORIDA
Royal Pacific Resort
EXIT
Lake Hancock
Tchoup Chop
International Dr. (I-Dr.)
Seasons 52
PIRATE'S COVE
ADVENTURE GO
Lake Reams
Lake Tibet
EXIT 74
Roy's
Big Sand Lake
Vines Grille & Win
Café Tu Tu Tang
Lake Mabel
Lake Sheen
POINTE ORLANDO
Peabody Orlando
ICEB
Taverna Opa
EXIT 72
WONDERWOR
Bay Lake
EXIT 71
Central
Flor
WALT DISNEY WORLD
World Dr.
ORLANDO PREMIUM OUTLETS
International Dr.
GRAND CYPRESS GOLF RESORT
Epcot Center Dr.
EXIT 68
Lake Bryan
Buena Vista Dr.
EXIT 67
536
LAKE BUENA VISTA FACTORY STORES
535
Shingle
4
Osceola Pkwy.
See Map 2
EXIT 64
ARABIAN NIGHTS
192
Lake Cecile
Poinciana Blvd.
CAPONE'S DINNE AND SHOW
Celebration
192
192 FLEA MARKET OUTLET
MEDIEVAL TIMES
Irlo Bron
0
5 mi
0
5 km
BOK TOWER GARDENS
CHAMPIONS GATE GOLF CLUB

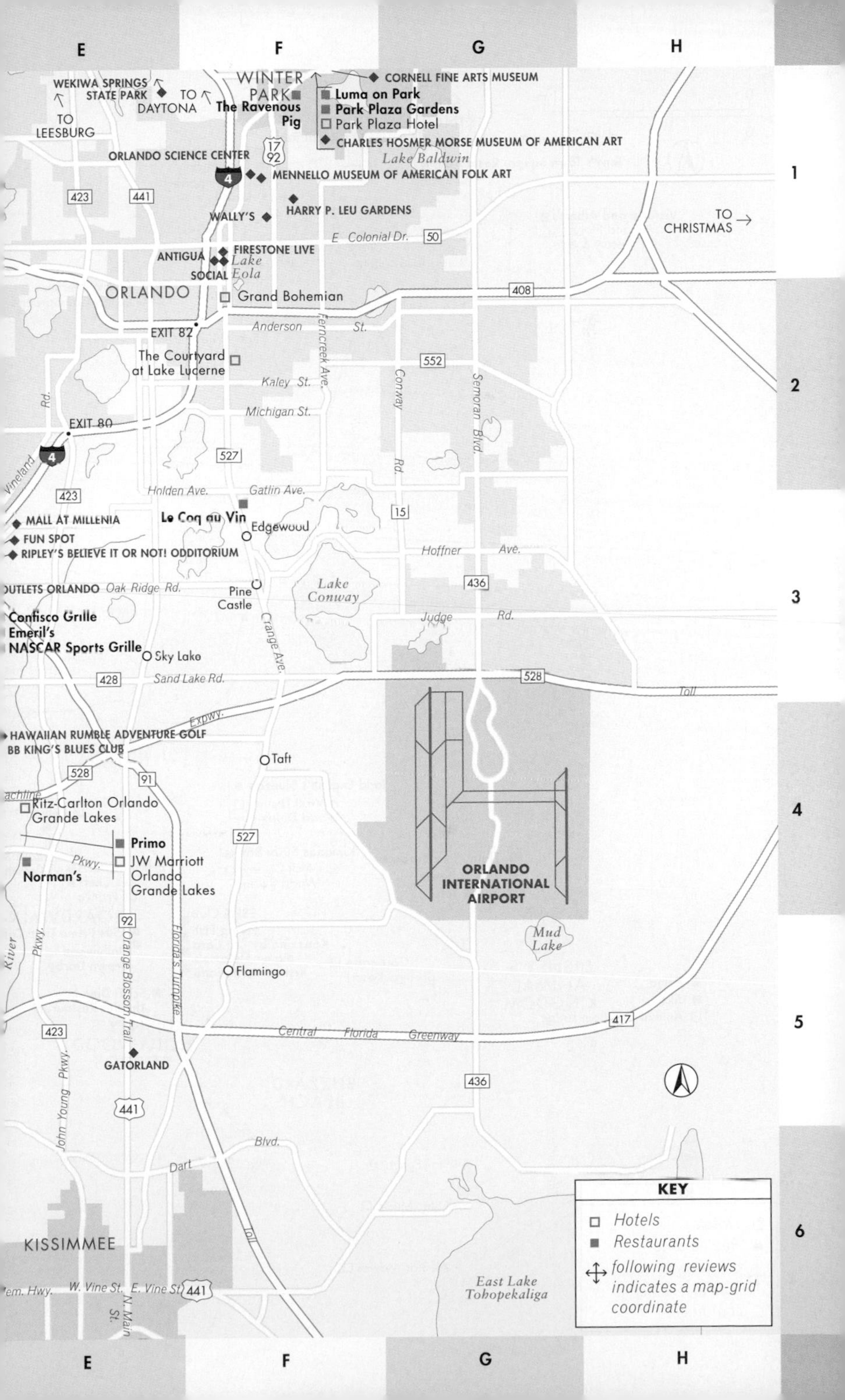

E
F
G
H
WEKIWA SPRINGS STATE PARK
TO LEESBURG
TO DAYTONA
WINTER PARK
The Ravenous Pig
CORNELL FINE ARTS MUSEUM
Luma on Park
Park Plaza Gardens
Park Plaza Hotel
CHARLES HOSMER MORSE MUSEUM OF AMERICAN ART
Lake Baldwin
ORLANDO SCIENCE CENTER
17 92
MENNELLO MUSEUM OF AMERICAN FOLK ART
4
423
441
HARRY P. LEU GARDENS
WALLY'S
TO CHRISTMAS
E Colonial Dr.
50
ANTIGUA
FIRESTONE LIVE
Lake Eola
SOCIAL
ORLANDO
Grand Bohemian
408
EXIT 82
Anderson St.
Ferncreek Ave.
The Courtyard at Lake Lucerne
552
Kaley St.
Conway Rd.
Semoran Blvd.
Michigan St.
Rd.
EXIT 80
Vineland
527
423
Holden Ave.
Gatlin Ave.
MALL AT MILLENIA
Le Coq au Vin
Edgewood
15
FUN SPOT
RIPLEY'S BELIEVE IT OR NOT! ODDITORIUM
Hoffner Ave.
OUTLETS ORLANDO
Oak Ridge Rd.
Pine Castle
Lake Conway
436
Confisco Grille
Emeril's
NASCAR Sports Grille
Judge Rd.
Orange Ave.
Sky Lake
428
Sand Lake Rd.
528
Toll
Expwy.
HAWAIIAN RUMBLE ADVENTURE GOLF
BB KING'S BLUES CLUB
Taft
528
91
Ritz-Carlton Orlando Grande Lakes
527
Primo
Pkwy.
JW Marriott Orlando Grande Lakes
Norman's
ORLANDO INTERNATIONAL AIRPORT
92
Orange Blossom Trail
Florida's Turnpike
Mud Lake
River
Pkwy.
Flamingo
417
423
Central Florida Greenway
GATORLAND
436
John Young Pkwy.
441
Blvd.
Dart
Toll
KISSIMMEE
em. Hwy.
W. Vine St.
E. Vine St.
441
N. Main St.
East Lake Tohopekaliga
KEY
Hotels
Restaurants
following reviews indicates a map-grid coordinate
1
2
3
4
5
6

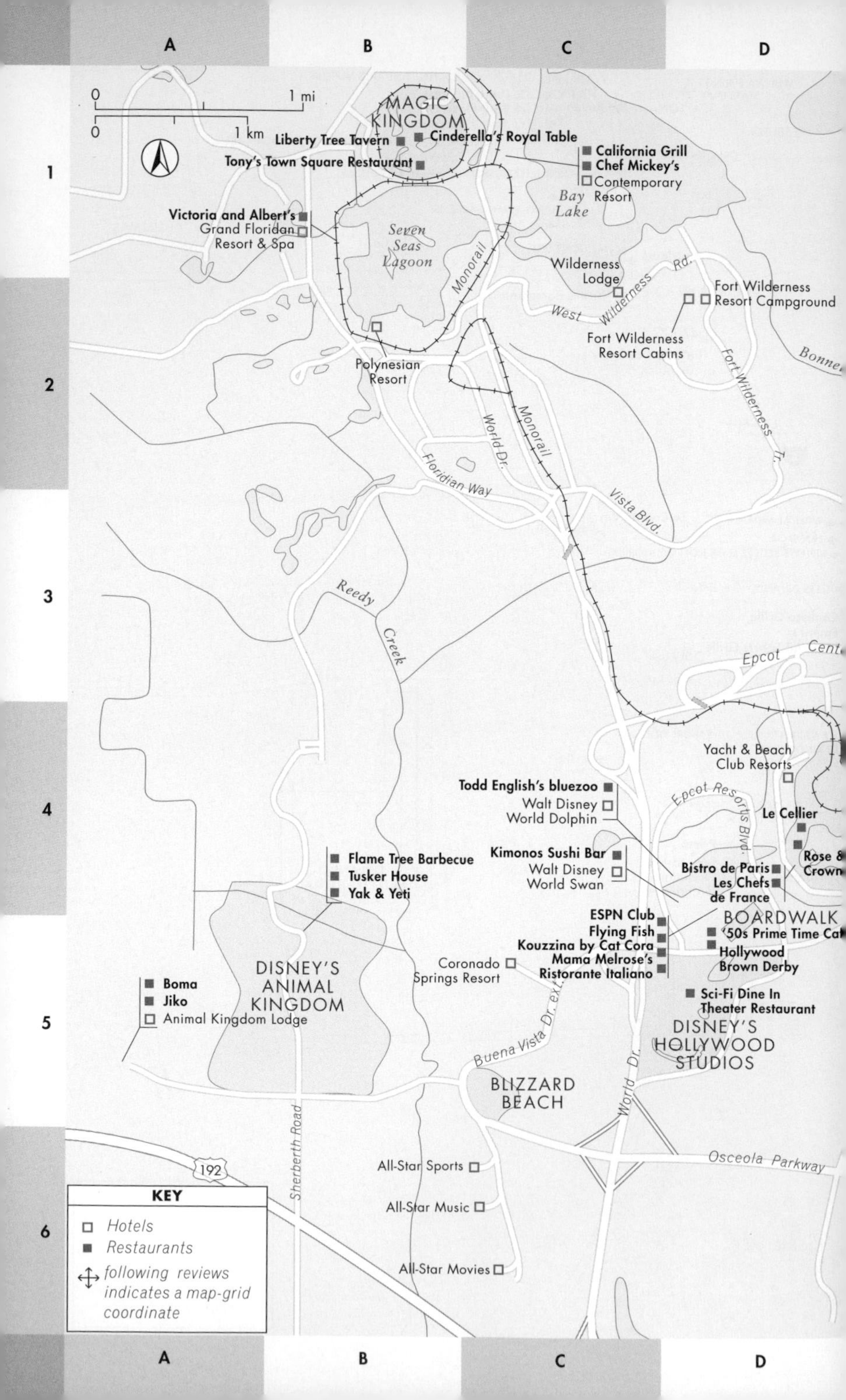

A
B
C
D
1
2
3
4
5
6
0
1 mi
0
1 km
MAGIC KINGDOM
Liberty Tree Tavern
Cinderella's Royal Table
Tony's Town Square Restaurant
California Grill
Chef Mickey's
Contemporary Resort
Bay Lake
Victoria and Albert's
Grand Floridian Resort & Spa
Seven Seas Lagoon
Monorail
Wilderness Lodge
West Wilderness Rd.
Fort Wilderness Resort Campground
Fort Wilderness Resort Cabins
Polynesian Resort
Fort Wilderness Tr.
World Dr.
Monorail
Floridian Way
Vista Blvd.
Reedy Creek
Epcot Cent
Yacht & Beach Club Resorts
Todd English's bluezoo
Walt Disney World Dolphin
Epcot Resorts Blvd.
Le Cellier
Flame Tree Barbecue
Tusker House
Yak & Yeti
Kimonos Sushi Bar
Walt Disney World Swan
Bistro de Paris
Les Chefs de France
Rose & Crown
ESPN Club
Flying Fish
Kouzzina by Cat Cora
Mama Melrose's Ristorante Italiano
BOARDWALK
'50s Prime Time Ca
Hollywood Brown Derby
Sci-Fi Dine In Theater Restaurant
Coronado Springs Resort
DISNEY'S ANIMAL KINGDOM
Boma
Jiko
Animal Kingdom Lodge
Buena Vista Dr. ext.
DISNEY'S HOLLYWOOD STUDIOS
BLIZZARD BEACH
World Dr.
Sherberth Road
192
Osceola Parkway
All-Star Sports
All-Star Music
All-Star Movies
KEY
Hotels
Restaurants
following reviews indicates a map-grid coordinate
A
B
C
D

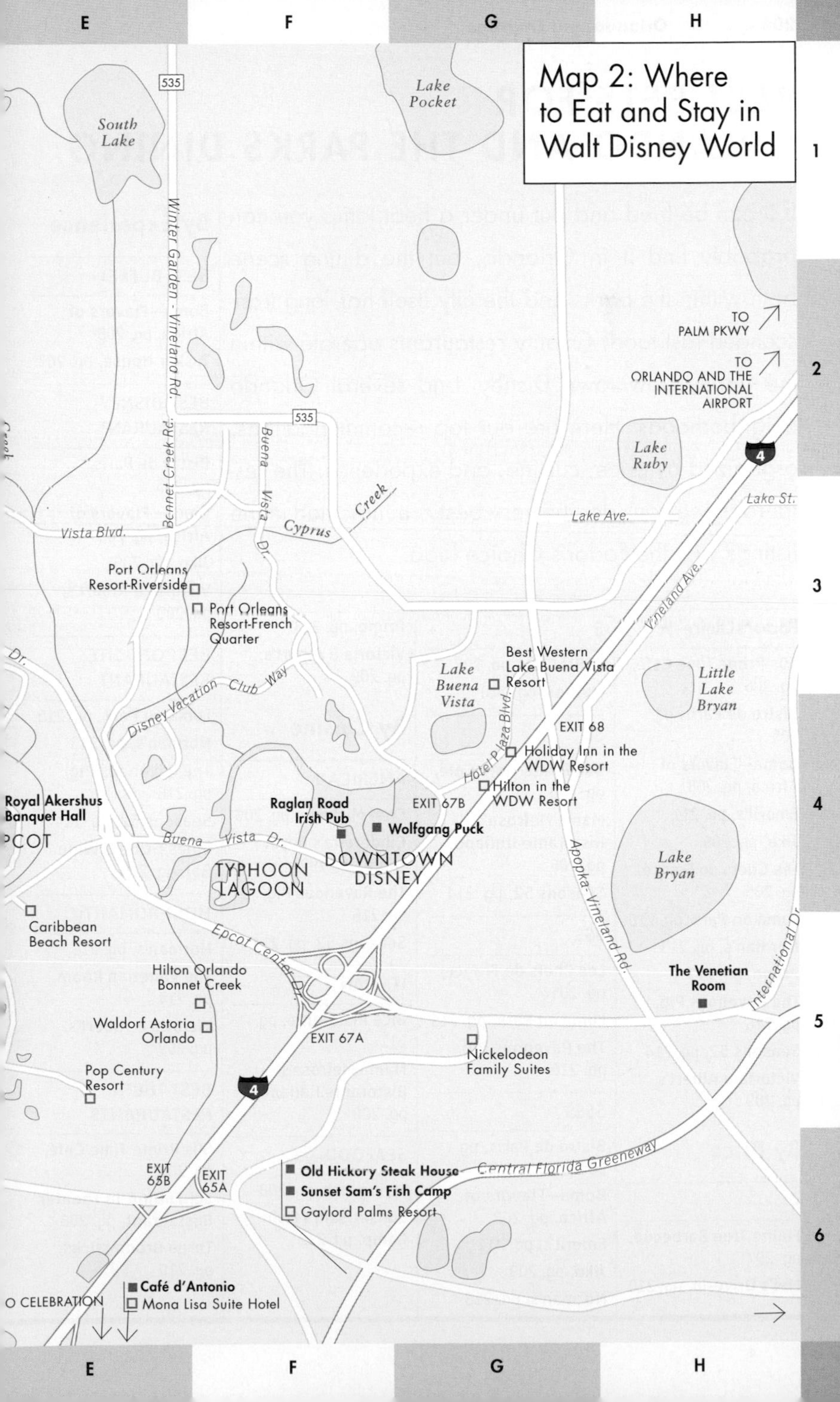

E
F
G
H
1
2
3
4
5
6
535
South Lake
Lake Pocket
Winter Garden - Vineland Rd.
TO PALM PKWY
TO ORLANDO AND THE INTERNATIONAL AIRPORT
Bonnet Creek Rd.
Buena Vista Dr.
Lake Ruby
4
Lake St.
Cyprus Creek
Lake Ave.
Vista Blvd.
Vineland Ave.
Port Orleans Resort-Riverside
Port Orleans Resort-French Quarter
Disney Vacation Club Way
Best Western Lake Buena Vista Resort
Lake Buena Vista
Little Lake Bryan
Hotel Plaza Blvd.
EXIT 68
Holiday Inn in the WDW Resort
Hilton in the WDW Resort
Royal Akershus Banquet Hall
Raglan Road Irish Pub
EXIT 67B
Wolfgang Puck
EPCOT
Buena Vista Dr.
DOWNTOWN DISNEY
TYPHOON LAGOON
Apopka-Vineland Rd.
Lake Bryan
Caribbean Beach Resort
Epcot Center Dr.
International Dr.
Hilton Orlando Bonnet Creek
The Venetian Room
Waldorf Astoria Orlando
EXIT 67A
Nickelodeon Family Suites
Pop Century Resort
Central Florida Greeneway
EXIT 65B
EXIT 65A
Old Hickory Steak House
Sunset Sam's Fish Camp
Gaylord Palms Resort
Café d'Antonio
Mona Lisa Suite Hotel
CELEBRATION

Map 2: Where to Eat and Stay in Walt Disney World

BEST BETS FOR ORLANDO AND THE PARKS DINING

If it can be fried and put under a heat lamp you can probably find it in Orlando, but the dining scene both within the parks and the city itself has long transcended fast food. Quality restaurants operate within the parks, Downtown Disney, and several Orlando neighborhoods. Here are our top recommendations, organized by price, cuisine, and experience. The restaurants we consider the very best are indicated in the listings with the Fodor's Choice logo.

Fodor's Choice ★

50s Prime Time Café, pg. 206
Bistro de Paris, pg. 205
Boma—Flavors of Africa, pg. 208
Emeril's, pg. 211
Jiko, pg. 209
Les Chefs de France, pg. 205
Luma on Park, pg. 215
Norman's, pg. 213
Primo, pg. 213
The Ravenous Pig, pg. 216
Seasons 52, pg. 214
Victoria & Albert's, pg. 209

By Price

¢

Flame Tree Barbecue, pg. 207
Mel's Drive-In, pg. 210

$

ESPN Club, pg. 208
Mythos, pg. 210

$$

50s Prime Time Café, pg. 206
Mama Melrose's Ristorante Italiano, pg. 206
Seasons 52, pg. 214

$$$

Les Chefs de France, pg. 205
Luma on Park, pg. 215
The Ravenous Pig, pg. 216

$$$$

Bistro de Paris, pg. 205
Boma—Flavors of Africa, pg. 208
Emeril's, pg. 211
Jiko, pg. 209
Norman's, pg. 213
Primo, pg. 213
Victoria & Albert's, pg. 209

By Cuisine

AMERICAN

Chef Mickey's, pg. 209
Cinderella's Royal Table, pg. 199
The Ravenous Pig, pg. 216
Seasons 52, pg. 214

ITALIAN

Bice Ristorante, pg. 211
Mama Melrose's Ristorante Italiano, pg. 206

SEAFOOD

Flying Fish, pg. 208
Sunset Sam's Fish Camp, pg. 212

By Experience

BEST BUFFET

Boma—Flavors of Africa, pg. 208
Tusker House, pg. 207

BEST DISNEY RESTAURANT

Bistro de Paris, pg. 205
Boma—Flavors of Africa, pg. 208
Jiko, pg. 209
Victoria & Albert's, pg. 209

BEST OFF-SITE RESTAURANT

Luma on Park, pg. 215
Norman's, pg. 213
The Ravenous Pig, pg. 216
Seasons 52, pg. 214
Vines Grille & Wine Bar, pg. 215

MOST ROMANTIC

Norman's, pg. 213
The Venetian Room, pg. 214
Victoria & Albert's, pg. 209

BEST THEME RESTAURANTS

50s Prime Time Café, pg. 206
Sci-Fi Dine-In Theater Restaurant, pg. 206
Three Broomsticks, pg. 210

roast prime rib of beef with cabernet sauce. When you arrive at the Cinderella Castle, a photographer snaps a shot of your group in the lobby. A package of photographs will be delivered to your table during your meal. ✉ *Cinderella Castle* ☎ *407/939–3463* ✍ *Reservations essential* ▭ *AE, D, DC, MC, V* ✥ *2:B1.*

$$$ AMERICAN ✕ **Liberty Tree Tavern.** This "tavern" is dry, but it's a prime spot on the parade route, so you can catch a good meal while you wait. Order colonial-period comfort food for lunch like hearty pot roast cooked with a cabernet wine–and-mushroom sauce, or turkey and dressing with mashed potatoes. The restaurant is decorated in lovely Williamsburg colors, with Early American–style antiques and lots of brightly polished brass. ✉ *Liberty Square* ☎ *407/824–6461* ▭ *AE, D, DC, MC, V* ✥ *2:B1.*

$$–$$$ ITALIAN ✕ **Tony's Town Square Restaurant.** Inspired by the animated classic *Lady and the Tramp,* Tony's offers everything from spaghetti with meatballs, to a New York strip steak, to a catch of the day served with pancetta-tossed orzo pasta. There's no wine list, but you can get the lemonade punch in a collector's mug. The most tempting desserts are the lemon walnut layer cake or the pistachio crème brûlée. ✉ *Main St., U.S.A., Liberty Sq.* ☎ *407/939–3463* ▭ *AE, D, DC, MC, V* ✥ *2:B1.*

EPCOT

$$$$ FRENCH Fodor's Choice ★ ✕ **Bistro de Paris.** The great secret in the France pavilion—and, indeed, in all of Epcot—is the Bistro de Paris, upstairs from Les Chefs de France. The sophisticated menu changes regularly and reflects the cutting edge of French cooking; representative dishes include pan-seared scallops, venison medallions with caramelized apple and cranberries, and rack of lamb with thyme, ratatouille and a thin onion tart. Come late, ask for a window seat, and plan to linger to watch the 9 PM Epcot light show. ✉ *France Pavilion, World Showcase* ☎ *407/939–3463* ▭ *AE, D, DC, MC, V* ⊙ *No lunch* ✥ *2:D4.*

$$$$ CANADIAN ✕ **Le Cellier Steakhouse.** This charming eatery with stone arches and dark-wood paneling has a good selection of wine and Canadian beer. Aged beef is king, although many steaks appear only on the dinner menu. The prix-fixe menu has choices ranging from salt-crusted prime rib to salmon prepared two ways. But you can also order à la carte. Desserts pay tribute to the land up north with crème brûlée made with maple sugar, and a Canadian Club chocolate cake. ✉ *Canada Pavilion* ☎ *407/939–3463* ▭ *AE, D, DC, MC, V* ✥ *2:D4.*

$$$ FRENCH Fodor's Choice ★ ✕ **Les Chefs de France.** What some consider the best restaurant at Disney was created by three of France's most famous chefs: Paul Bocuse, Gaston Lenôtre, and Roger Vergé. Classic escargots, a good starter, are prepared in a casserole with garlic butter; you might follow up with roasted breast of duck and leg confit, or grilled beef tenderloin with black pepper sauce. Make sure you finish with crepes *au chocolat.* The nearby Boulangerie Pâtisserie offers tarts, croissants, éclairs, napoleons, and more, to go. ✉ *France Pavilion* ☎ *407/939–3463* ▭ *AE, D, DC, MC, V* ✥ *2:D4.*

$$ BRITISH ✕ **Rose & Crown.** If you're an Anglophile, this is the place to soak up both the suds and British street culture. "Wenches" serve up traditional English fare—fish-and-chips, cottage pie (ground beef with onions, carrots,

4

and peas, topped with Duchess potatoes), and the ever-popular bangers and mash (sausage over mashed potatoes). Potato-and-leek soup or Scotch egg make good appetizers. Vegetarians will even find a tasty vegetarian shepherd's pie. The terrace has a splendid view of IllumiNations. ✉ *United Kingdom* ☎ *407/939–3463* ▭ *AE, D, DC, MC, V* ✣ *2:D4.*

$$$$ SCANDINAVIAN **✕ Royal Akershus Banquet Hall.** This Norwegian restaurant has become the site of character buffets at all three meals, with an array of Disney princesses. The ever-changing Norwegian menu at this restaurant is as extensive as you'll find on this side of the Atlantic. Appetizers are offered buffet style, and usually include herring, goat-milk cheese, peppered mackerel, and gravlax (cured salmon served with mustard sauce) or *fiskepudding* (a seafood mousse with herb dressing). For your main course, chosen à la carte, you might try traditional ground pork and beef *kjottkake* (dumplings), or mustard-glazed seared salmon. ✉ *Norway* ☎ *407/939–3463* ▭ *AE, D, DC, MC, V* ⌂ *Reservations essential* ✣ *2:E4.*

DISNEY'S HOLLYWOOD STUDIOS

$$ AMERICAN Fodor's Choice ★ **✕ 50's Prime Time Café.** Who says you can't go home again? If you grew up in middle America in the 1950s, just step inside. While *I Love Lucy* and *The Donna Reed Show* clips play on a television screen, you can feast on meat loaf, pot roast, or fried chicken, all served on a Formica tabletop. At $15, the meat loaf is one of the best inexpensive dinners in any local theme park. Enjoy it with a malted-milk shake or root-beer float (or a bottle of wine), and follow it up with a '50s Hula Hoop Boston Cream cupcake or s'mores. The place offers some fancier dishes, such as olive oil–poached salmon, which are good but out of character with the diner theme. ✉ *Hollywood Blvd.* ☎ *407/939–3463* ▭ *AE, D, DC, MC, V* ✣ *2:D5.*

$$$ AMERICAN **✕ Hollywood Brown Derby.** At this reproduction of the famous 1940s Hollywood restaurant, the walls are lined with movie-star caricatures. The specialty is the Cobb salad, which by legend was invented by Brown Derby founder Robert Cobb; the salad consists of finely chopped lettuce enlivened by loads of tomato, bacon, turkey, blue cheese, chopped egg, and avocado, all tossed table-side. Other menu choices include grilled salmon with spinach and warm bacon vinaigrette, and house-cured duck pastrami with vanilla–white balsamic–melon-pear salad. ✉ *Hollywood Blvd.* ☎ *407/939–3463* ▭ *AE, D, DC, MC, V* ✣ *2:D5.*

$$ ITALIAN **✕ Mama Melrose's Ristorante Italiano.** To replace the energy you've no doubt depleted by miles of theme-park walking, you can load up on carbs at this casual Italian restaurant that looks like an old warehouse. Good main courses include Italian sausage served atop rigatoni pasta with tomato-basil sauce, and grilled tuna with tomato risotto and olive-caper butter. The sangria, available by the carafe, flows generously. ✉ *Streets of America* ☎ *407/939–3463* ▭ *AE, D, DC, MC, V* ✣ *2:D4.*

$$–$$$ AMERICAN **✕ Sci-Fi Dine-In Theater Restaurant.** If you don't mind zombies leering at you while you eat, then head to this enclosed faux drive-in, where you can sit in a fake candy-color '50s convertible and watch trailers from classics like *Attack of the Fifty-Foot Woman* and *Teenagers from Outer Space*. The menu includes slow-roasted barbecue ribs, a beef-and-blue-

cheese salad, sautéed shrimp with bow-tie pasta, and a huge Reuben sandwich with fries or melon slices. The hot-fudge sundaes are delicious. ✉ *Echo Lake* ☎ *407/939–3463* ▭ *AE, D, DC, MC, V* ✥ *2:D5.*

DISNEY'S ANIMAL KINGDOM

¢–$ FAST FOOD ✕ **Flame Tree Barbecue.** This counter-service eatery is one of the relatively undiscovered gems of Disney's culinary offerings. There's nothing fancy here, but you can dig into ribs, barbecued chicken, and pulled pork and barbecued beef sandwiches with several sauce choices. The outdoor tables, set beneath intricately carved wood pavilions, make great spots for a picnic, and they're not usually crowded. ✉ *Discovery Island* ▭ *AE, D, DC, MC, V* ✥ *2:B5.*

$$$$ AMERICAN ✕ **Tusker House.** This restaurant offers all-buffet dining three meals a day, starting with a character breakfast (Donald's Safari Breakfast), and buffets for lunch and dinner without Donald and his crew. Tusker's offers fare like spice-rubbed rotisserie chicken, curry chicken, carved top sirloin roast, rotisserie pork loin, along with the kids' standards like mac and cheese and chicken drumsticks served with mashed potatoes. Prices change seasonally. ✉ *Harambe* ☎ *407/939–3463* ✍ *Reservations essential* ▭ *AE, D, DC, MC, V* ✥ *2:B5.*

$$ ASIAN ✕ **Yak & Yeti.** The location of this pan-Asian cuisine, sit-down eatery—the only full-service restaurant inside Disney's Animal Kingdom—certainly makes sense. It's just at the entrance to the Asia section, in a two-story, 250-seat building that is pleasantly faux-Asian, with cracked plaster walls, wood carvings, and tile mosaic tabletops. Standout entrées include the roast duckling with orange-wasabi, and the tempura shrimp with coconut-ginger rice and plum sauce. ✉ *Disney's Animal Kingdom* ☎ *407/939–3463* ▭ *AE, D, DC, MC, V* ✥ *2:B5.*

DOWNTOWN DISNEY

$$$ IRISH ✕ **Raglan Road Irish Pub.** Some would argue that the phrase "authentic Irish pub at Disney's Pleasure Island" is oxymoronic, particularly when that pub seats 600 people. But if Irish grub's your thing, Raglan's is on target: the shepherd's pie is higher quality than the usual version, prepared with beef and lamb and jazzed up with house spices. And you don't have to settle for plain fish-and-chips here (though you can for $17); there's also panfried lemon sole and chips. You can also get lots of hearty soups and plenty of Irish beer and whiskey. The entertainment alone makes this place worth the visit. A good, four-person Irish house band, Tuskar Rock, performs nightly, as does Danielle Fitzpatrick, herself an Irish import, who performs lively folk dances on stage each evening. ✉ *Pleasure Island* ☎ *407/938–0300* 🌐 *www.raglanroadirishpub.com* ▭ *AE, D, MC, V* ✥ *2:F4.*

$$$–$$$$ AMERICAN ✕ **Wolfgang Puck.** There are lots of choices here, from wood-oven pizza at the informal Puck Express to fine-dining meals in the upstairs formal Dining Room. There are also a sushi bar and an informal café; the café is quite literally a happy medium and may be the best bet for families hoping for a bit of elegance without the pressure of a formal dinner. At Express try the barbecue chicken, or spinach and mushroom pizza. At the café, midprice entrées like bacon-wrapped meat loaf, and pumpkin ravioli with brown butter sauce, fried sage, and port-wine

glaze are winners, and you can always try the pizza pie that made Puck famous: smoked salmon with dill cream, red onion, chili oil, and chives. The Dining Room always offers inspired entrées like lobster risotto with lemon preserve. ✉ *West Side* ☎ *407/938–9653* 🌐 *www.wolfgangpuckorlando.com* ▭ *AE, DC, MC, V* ✣ *2:F4.*

DISNEY'S BOARDWALK

$ AMERICAN ✕ **ESPN Club.** Not only can you watch sports on a big-screen TV here (the restaurant has 108 monitors), but you can also periodically see ESPN programs being taped in the club itself and be part of the audience of sports-radio talk shows. Food ranges from an outstanding half-pound burger, made with Angus chuck, to an excellent Reuben with plenty of corned beef, sauerkraut, and cheese. If you want an appetizer, try the Macho Nachos, crispy corn tortilla chips piled high with spicy chili, shredded cheddar cheese, sour cream, spicy salsa, and sliced jalapeños. This place is open quite late by Disney standards—until 2 AM on Friday and Saturday. ✉ *Disney's BoardWalk* ☎ *407/939–5100* ▭ *AE, D, DC, MC, V* ✣ *2:D4.*

$$$$ SEAFOOD ✕ **Flying Fish.** The murals along the upper portion of the walls pay tribute to Atlantic seaboard spots of the early 1900s. This is a place where you put on your "resort casual" duds to "dine," as opposed to putting on your flip-flops and shorts to "chow down." The chefs take the food so seriously that the entire culinary team takes day trips to local farms to learn their foodstuffs' origins. Flying Fish's best dishes include potato-wrapped red snapper, which is so popular it has been on the menu for several years, and oak-grilled Bay of Fundy salmon. ✉ *Disney's BoardWalk* ☎ *407/939–2359* ▭ *AE, D, DC, MC, V* ⊙ *No lunch* ✣ *2:D4.*

$$$ MEDITERRANEAN ✕ **Kouzzina by Cat Cora.** Celebrity-chef Cat Cora and Disney joined forces in 2009 to open an upbeat family-oriented Greek restaurant along the BoardWalk. From an exhibition *kouzzina* (the Greek word for kitchen), the culinary team puts out hearty portions of Cora's family favorites, including the familiar starter *spanakopita* (spinach pie) and an amazing side dish of brussels sprouts sautéed with lemon and capers. Entrées range from a sweet cinnamon-stewed chicken to a whole fish pan-roasted with braised greens, olives, fennel, and smoked chili. Be sure to get a refreshing, sweet, coffee frappé to go with your *loukoumades* (donuts with warm honey) or Greek cookies. ✉ *Disney's BoardWalk* ☎ *407/939–3463* ▭ *AE, D, DC, MC, V* ✣ *2:D4.*

WDW RESORTS

$$$$ AFRICAN Fodor's Choice ★ ✕ **Boma—Flavors of Africa.** Boma takes Western-style ingredients and prepares them with an African twist—then invites guests to walk through an African marketplace–style dining room to help themselves at the extraordinary buffet. Look for entrées such as roasted pork, chicken, beef, and fish served with tamarind and other robust sauces; intriguing salads; and some of the best hummus this side of the Atlantic. Don't pass up the soups, as the hearty chicken-corn porridge is excellent. The zebra dome dessert is chocolate mousse covered with white chocolate and striped with dark chocolate. All meals are prix fixe, and prices change seasonally. The South African wine list is outstanding. ✉ *Disney's Animal Kingdom Lodge* ☎ *407/939–3463* ✍ *Reservations essential* ▭ *AE, D, DC, MC, V* ⊙ *No lunch* ✣ *2:A5.*

$$–$$$ AMERICAN

✕ **California Grill.** The view of the surrounding Disney parks from this 15th-floor restaurant is as stunning as the food, especially at night, when you can watch the nightly Magic Kingdom fireworks from the dining room. The menu changes regularly, but choices might include seared bison with white-corn-and-mushroom "risotto," turnips, chestnuts, and pinot noir–juniper emulsion; or handmade cavatelli pasta with wild mushrooms, buttercup squash, winter kale, and truffle-mascarpone cream. ✉ *Contemporary Resort* ☎ *407/939–3463* ✍ *Reservations essential* ▭ *AE, D, DC, MC, V* ✣ *2:B2.*

$$$$ AMERICAN

✕ **Chef Mickey's.** This is the holy shrine for character meals, with Mickey, Minnie, and Goofy always around for breakfast and dinner—it's not a quiet spot to read the *Orlando Sentinel.* Folks come here for entertainment and comfort food. The breakfast buffet includes omelets cooked to order, mountains of pancakes, and even a breakfast pizza. The dinner buffet includes prime rib, baked ham, and changing specials like beef tips with mushrooms or tamarind-glazed salmon. ✉ *Contemporary Resort* ☎ *407/939–3463* ▭ *AE, D, DC, MC, V* ✣ *2:B2.*

$$$$ AFRICAN Fodor's Choice ★

✕ **Jiko.** The name of this restaurant means "the cooking place" in Swahili, and it is certainly that. The dining area surrounds two big, wood-burning ovens and a grill area where you can watch cooks in North African–style caps working on your meal. The menu here is more African inspired than purely African, but does include authentic entrées like Swahili curry shrimp from an East African recipe and short ribs with a Kenyan coffee-barbecue sauce. The menu changes periodically but typically includes entrées such as maize-crusted wreckfish with tomato-butter sauce, and chicken with goat cheese potatoes, preserved lemon, and harissa. ✉ *Disney's Animal Kingdom Lodge* ☎ *407/939–3463* ✍ *Reservations essential* ▭ *AE, D, DC, MC, V* ⊗ *No lunch* ✣ *2:A5.*

$ JAPANESE

✕ **Kimonos.** Knife-wielding sushi chefs prepare world-class sushi and sashimi but also other Japanese treats like soups and salads at this sleek hotel sushi bar, where dark teak dominates the décor, and servers wear kimonos. Popular rolls include the Dragon roll (giant shrimp, tuna, and avocado), Dancing Eel Roll (crab, avocado, and eel), and the Bagel Roll (smoked salmon, cream cheese, and scallion). Cocktails are a draw here, too, along with nightly karaoke. ✉ *Walt Disney World Swan* ☎ *407/934–3000* 🌐 *www.swandolphinrestaurants.com/kimonos* ▭ *AE, D, DC, MC, V* ⊗ *No lunch* ✣ *2:D4.*

$$$$ AMERICAN

✕ **Todd English's bluezoo.** Celebrity-chef Todd English oversees this cutting-edge seafood eatery, a sleek, modern restaurant that resembles an underwater dining hall, with blue walls and carpeting, aluminum fish suspended from the ceiling, and bubblelike lighting fixtures. The menu is creative and pricey, with entrées like the 2-pound Maine "Cantonese lobster," fried and tossed in a sticky soy glaze; and Florida grouper with black-truffle spaetzle, black radish, and black-truffle vinaigrette. ✉ *Walt Disney World Dolphin* ☎ *407/934–1111* 🌐 *www.thebluezoo.com* ▭ *AE, D, DC, MC, V* ⊗ *No lunch* ✣ *2:D4.*

$$$$ ONTINENTAL …rs Choice ★

✕ **Victoria & Albert's.** At this ultraposh award-winning Disney restaurant, two servers dressed in his-and-hers Victorian costumes anticipate your every need. There's also a sommelier to explain wine pairings. This is one of the plushest fine-dining experiences in Florida—a regal

4

meal in a tasteful Victorian-style room—a space so sophisticated that children under 10 aren't on the guest list. The six-course, prix-fixe menu ($125; wine is an additional $60) changes daily. Appetizers might include chorizo-crusted duck, or walnut oil–seared duck with hearts of palm and cheese fondue; entrées may be Florida black grouper with artichokes, fennel, leeks, and *jamón Ibérico* (Spanish ham), or Kurobuta pork tenderloin and belly with beets and sherry-bacon vinaigrette. For most of the year, there are two seatings, at 5:45 and 9. In July and August, however, there's generally just one seating at 6:30. Make your reservations at least 90 and up to 180 days in advance. ☒ *Grand Floridian Resort & Spa* ☎ *407/939–3862* *Reservations essential* *Jacket required* ▭ *AE, D, DC, MC, V* ⊙ *No lunch* ✣ *2:B1.*

UNIVERSAL ORLANDO AREA

UNIVERSAL STUDIOS

$$ IRISH ✕ **Finnegan's Bar & Grill.** Finnegan's offers classic Irish comfort food like shepherd's pie, Scotch eggs (eggs wrapped in sausage and bread crumbs and fried), corned beef and cabbage, bangers and mash (sausage and mashed potatoes), and fish-and-chips, plus Guinness, Harp, and Bass on tap. If shepherd's pie isn't your thing, there are also steaks, burgers, and a darn good chicken salad. Irish folk music, sometimes live, completes the theme. ☒ *New York* ☎ *407/363–8757* ▭ *AE, D, MC, V* ✣ *1:D3.*

¢–$ AMERICAN ✕ **Mel's Drive-In.** At the corner of Hollywood Boulevard and Vine is a flashy '50s eatery with a pink-and-white 1956 Ford Crown Victoria parked out in front. For burgers and fries, this is one of the best choices in the park, and it comes complete with a roving doo-wop group during peak seasons. You're on vacation—go ahead and have that extra-thick shake or the decadent chili-cheese fries. ☒ *Hollywood Blvd.* ☎ *407/363–8766* *Reservations not accepted* ▭ *AE, D, MC, V* ✣ *1:D3.*

ISLANDS OF ADVENTURE

$ AMERICAN ✕ **Confisco Grille.** You could walk right past this full-service restaurant without noticing it, but this is one of the better eateries inside the theme parks. The menu changes often, but typical entrées include a good beef fillet with mashed potatoes and sautéed spinach, baked cod with spinach and mashed potatoes, and Thai noodles with chicken, shrimp, tofu, and bean sprouts. Wine is available by the glass. ☒ *6000 Universal Blvd., Port of Entry* ☎ *407/224–4404* ▭ *AE, D, MC, V* ⊙ *No lunch* ✣ *1:D3.*

$ ECLECTIC ✕ **Mythos.** The name is Greek, but the dishes are eclectic. The menu, which changes frequently, usually includes mainstays like pistachio-crusted roast pork tenderloin and cedar-plank salmon with citrus butter. The building itself is enough to grab your attention. It looks like a giant rock formation from the outside and a huge cave (albeit one with plush upholstered seating) from the inside. Mythos also has a waterfront view of the big lagoon in the center of the theme park. (When it's slow in the park, Mythos is only open for lunch.) ☒ *6000 Universal Blvd., Lost Continent* ☎ *407/224–4534* ▭ *AE, D, MC, V* ✣ *1:D3.*

$–$$ BRITISH ✕ **Three Broomsticks.** Harry Potter fans can taste pumpkin juice and butterbeer, cauldron cakes and treacle fudge. The otherworldly goodies a sold along with traditional English fare such as fish-and-chips, shepherd's pie, and Cornish pasty at Three Broomsticks, part of Universal's new Wizarding World of Harry Potter attraction. Rickety staircases and gaslit chandeliers bring a bit of overcast Hogsmeade to sunny Orlando. ✉ *6000 Universal Blvd., Wizarding World of Harry Potter* ☎ *407/224–4534* ▭ *AE, D, MC, V* ✣ *1:D3.*

CITYWALK

$$$$ CREOLE Fodor's Choice ★

✕ Emeril's. The popular eatery is a culinary shrine to Emeril Lagasse, the famous Food Network chef who occasionally makes an appearance. And while the modernistic interior of 30-foot ceilings, blond woods, a second-story wine loft, and lots of galvanized steel looks nothing like the Old French Quarter, the hardwood floors and linen tablecloths create an environment befitting the stellar nature of the cuisine. Entrées may include andouille-crusted red snapper with toasted pecans and crispy shoestring potatoes; bone-in rib eye with Emeril's Worcestershire sauce; chili-glazed rotisserie duck with wild mushroom bread pudding; and double-cut pork chops with caramelized sweet potatoes. ✉ *6000 Universal Blvd.* ☎ *407/224–2424* 🌐 *www.emerils.com* ✍ *Reservations essential* ▭ *AE, D, MC, V* ✣ *1:D3.*

$ AMERICAN

✕ NASCAR Sports Grille. Filled with race-car simulator games and racing memorabilia, this eatery might not look like the place to grab a sublime meal, but that's not the case. This theme restaurant has a reputation as a good place for grub. Selections worth trying include the Southern-style pot roast and the slow-roasted baby back rib platter with sweet potatoes; the Talladega cheeseburger with a side of fries is a cut above the standard theme-park burger. ✉ *6000 Universal Blvd.* ☎ *407/224–7223* 🌐 *www.nascarsportsgrille.com* ▭ *AE, D, MC, V* ✣ *1:D3.*

4

UNIVERSAL HOTELS

$$$–$$$$ ITALIAN

✕ Bice Ristorante. Trendy, pricey Bice is the Orlando unit of an international upscale chain of Italian restaurants. Bice (pronounced "*BEACH*-ay") is an Italian nickname for Beatrice, as in Beatrice Ruggeri, who founded the original Milan location of this family restaurant in 1926. But the word "family" does not carry the connotation "mom and pop" here, where cream-colored starched linens set the stage for sophisticated cuisine. The restaurant retains its frescoed ceilings, marble floors, and picture windows overlooking great views of the artificial (but appealing) bay just outside. This restaurant is expensive (a simple spaghetti Bolognese with homemade pasta is $25), but some of the entrées that seem worth it include the osso buco with saffron risotto. ✉ *Loews Portofino Bay Hotel, 5601 Universal Blvd.* ☎ *407/503–1415* 🌐 *www.orlando.bicegroup.com* ▭ *AE, DC, MC, V* ⊙ *No lunch* ✣ *1:D3.*

$$$ ITALIAN

✕ Mama Della's Ristorante. "Mama" is always on hand (this is a coveted job for middle-aged actresses who do a good Italian accent), strolling among the tables, wearing an apron and making small talk. The food is no theme-park fantasy—it's excellent. The menu has Italian classics like chicken marsala, veal parmigiana, and spaghetti with meatballs and Bolognese sauce, and all of the pastas are made in-house. Outdoor seating on a patio offers viewing of the hotel's nightly Musica Della Notte (Music of the Night) opera show. ✉ *Loews Portofino Bay Hotel, 5601*

Universal Blvd. ☎ *407/503–3463* 🌐 *www.loewshotels.com* ▭ *AE, D, DC, MC, V* ⊙ *No lunch* ✣ *1:D3.*

$$$ HAWAIIAN ✕ **Tchoup Chop.** With its cathedral ceiling, the inside of this restaurant looks almost churchlike in a modern-glitzy kind of way, and the food at Emeril Lagasse's Pacific-influenced restaurant is certainly righteous. The decorators included lots of bamboo, bright glazed tile, an exposition kitchen and a long zero-edge pool with porcelain lily pads running the length of the dining room. The menu combines Lagasse's signature bold flavors with Polynesian fusion cooking. Entrées change seasonally, but representative dishes include mochi-seared sea scallops with butternut squash risotto and creamy Thai curry-lobster sauce, and smoked-sea-salt grilled fillet of beef tenderloin. ✉ *Royal Pacific Resort, 6300 Hollywood Way* ☎ *407/503–2467* 🌐 *www.emerils.com* ⌂ *Reservations essential* ▭ *AE, D, DC, MC, V* ✣ *1:D3.*

ORLANDO METRO AREA

KISSIMMEE

$$$$ STEAK ✕ **Old Hickory Steakhouse.** If paying $44 for a 10-ounce Angus center-cut tenderloin (and an extra $7 for a side of mashed potatoes) and eating it inside a rustic-looking faux-Everglades homestead seems a bit surreal, remember that this is not your average restaurant. The purposely shabby dining rooms are a playful movie-set kind of edifice designed for effect; be assured, the service is as polished as at any serious steak house. Dine on the deck under the soaring glass atrium, and you'll overlook the hotel's simulated Everglades wildlife. ✉ *Gaylord Palms Resort, 6000 W. Osceola Pkwy., I–4 Exit 65* ☎ *407/586–1600* 🌐 *www.gaylordpalms.com* ▭ *AE, DC, MC, V* ⊙ *No lunch* ✣ *2:F6.*

$$$$ SEAFOOD ✕ **Sunset Sam's Fish Camp.** Often restaurants with a great decor or an architectural gimmick don't bother to back it up with good food. But that's not the case with Sunset Sam's. The cuisine here, focused on great fish offerings, is on par with the grand look of the place, with its 60-foot sailboat floating in a giant indoor lagoon. Starters are big enough to be a meal, and include crispy coconut-fried shrimp and Blue Hill Bay mussels in curried coconut-lime broth. Entrées are pricey but not exorbitant, and include, seasonally, blackened swordfish, seared ahi tuna, and salmon with avocado-mango salsa. ✉ *Gaylord Palms Resort, 6000 W. Osceola Pkwy., I–4 Exit 65, Gaylord Palms Resort* ☎ *407/586–1101* 🌐 *www.gaylordpalms.com* ▭ *AE, D, DC, MC, V* ✣ *2:F6.*

CELEBRATION

$$ ITALIAN ✕ **Café d' Antonio.** As at the rest of the restaurants in the Disney-created community of Celebration there's an awning-covered terrace overlooking the lake.The wood-burning oven and grill are worked pretty hard here, and the mountains of hardwood used in the open kitchen flavor the best of the menu—the pizza, the grilled fish and chicken, the steaks and chops, and even the lasagna. Standouts include *pappardella al salmon* (wide, ribbon pasta with salmon, sweet peas, and a brandy-and-cheese sauce) and ravioli stuffed with lobster and ricotta cheese, tossed in tarragon cream with brandy and capers. ✉ *691 Front St.* ☎ *407/566–2233* 🌐 *www.antoniosonline.com* ▭ *AE, D, MC, V* ✣ *2:E6.*

INTERNATIONAL DRIVE

$$ ECLECTIC

Café Tu Tu Tango. The food here is served tapas-style—everything is appetizer-size but plentiful, and inexpensive. The eclectic menu is fitting for a restaurant on International Drive. If you want a compendium of cuisines at one go, try the black-bean soup with cilantro sour cream, the baby lamb chops with "gingerapple" glaze, the pan-seared shrimp and chicken pot stickers, or the chipotle chicken *ropa vieja*. The wine list includes more than 50 wines from several countries, both by the bottle and the glass. The restaurant is designed to resemble an artist's loft; artists paint at easels while diners sip drinks like Matisse Margaritas. *8625 International Dr.* *407/248–2222* *www.cafetututango.com* *Reservations not accepted* *AE, D, MC, V* *1:D4.*

$$$$ AMERICAN Fodor's Choice ★

Norman's. Celebrity-chef Norman Van Aken brings impressive credentials to the restaurant that bears his name, as you might expect from the headline eatery in the first and only Ritz-Carlton in Orlando. Van Aken's culinary roots go back to the Florida Keys, where he's credited with creating "Floribbean" cuisine, a blend that is part Key West and part Caribbean – although he now weaves in flavors from all continents. The Orlando operation is a formal, sleek restaurant with marble floors, starched tablecloths, waiters in black-tie, and a creative, if expensive, menu. The offerings change frequently, and are offered à la carte and in four-, five-, and seven-course tasting menus. In addition to ceviches tossed table-side, classics from Norman's include yucca-stuffed crispy shrimp with sour-orange sauce, pan-cooked yellowtail with citrus butter, and grilled pork "Havana" with "21st-century" mole and smoky plantain crema. *Ritz-Carlton Grande Lakes, 4000 Central Florida Pkwy.* *407/393–4333* *www.normans.com* *AE, D, DC, MC, V* *No lunch* *1:E4.*

$$$$ ITALIAN Fodor's Choice ★

Primo. James Beard award–winner Melissa Kelly cloned her Italian-organic Maine restaurant in an upscale Orlando hotel and brought her farm-to-table sensibilities with her. Here the daily dinner menu pays tribute to Sicily's lighter foods with produce grown in a hotel garden. Homemade cavatelli is tossed with wild mushrooms and spinach and topped with shaved truffles. Duck breast is glazed with chestnut honey and paired with house-made pancetta, apple compote, roasted turnips, and braised red cabbage. Desserts are just as special, with the likes of Meyer lemon–scented crème brûlée and a bowl of hot zeppole tossed in organic cinnamon and sugar. *JW Marriott Orlando, Grande Lakes* *4040 Central Florida Pkwy, South Orlando* 407/393–4444 *www.primorestaurant.com* *Reservations essential* *AE, D, DC, MC, V* *No lunch.* *TK*

$$ GREEK

Taverna Opa. This high-energy Greek restaurant bills itself as offering "fun with a capital F," possibly because the ouzo flows like a mountain stream, the Greek music almost reaches the level of a rock concert, and the roaming belly dancers actively encourage diners to take part in the mass Zorba dancing (which often happens on the tops of dining tables). The only thing missing is the Greek restaurant tradition of throwing dinner plates, made up in part by the throwing of torn-up paper napkins, which sometimes reaches near-blizzard level. The food, by the way, is also excellent. Standouts include traditional staples like *spanakopita* (phyllo pastry with spinach and feta cheese), *saganaki* (the traditional flaming cheese appetizer), and perhaps the most famous Greek entrée, *moussaka* (layers of roasted eggplant, potatoes, and ground meat, topped with béchamel sauce). ✉ *9101 International Dr., Pointe Orlando* ☎ *407/879–2481* 🌐 *www. tavernaoparestaurant.com* 💳 *AE, D, DC, MC, V* ✣ *1:D4.*

LAKE BUENA VISTA

$$$$ CONTINENTAL

✕ **The Venetian Room.** Inside the Caribe Royale All-Suite Hotel & Convention Center, one of Lake Buena Vista's many convention hotels, this place was definitely designed for execs on expense accounts. But the serene, luxurious, and romantic atmosphere makes it a great place for dinner with your significant other. The architecture alone is enough to lure you in. It's designed to look like Renaissance Venice: the entryway has a giant copper dome over the door and the dining room has dark-wood furniture, crystal chandeliers, and carpets that could grace a European palace. A good starter is the seared diver scallops with porcini asparagus risotto and pancetta crisp, although the ultrarich lobster bisque is hard to resist. You can follow that with a good filet mignon, or blood-orange duck l'orange and ruby Port wine–bing cherry reduction. ✉ *Caribe Royale All-Suite Hotel & Convention Center, 8101 World Center Dr., Lake Buena Vista Area* ☎ *407/238–8060* 🌐 *www. thevenetianroom.com* 💳 *AE, D, DC, MC, V* ⏲ *No lunch* ✣ *2:H5.*

SAND LAKE ROAD

$$$–$$$$ HAWAIIAN

✕ **Roy's.** Chef Roy Yamaguchi has more or less perfected his own cuisine type—Hawaiian fusion, replete with tropical fruit–based sauces and lots of imagination. The menu changes seasonally, but typical dishes include treats like Hawaiian-style butterfish with a sizzling Chinese vinaigrette or hibachi-style grilled Atlantic salmon with Japanese citrus sauce. If your tastes remain on the mainland, go for classics like garlic-honey-mustard beef short ribs or the "Cowboy" center-cut 16-ounce, bone-in rib eye. The crunchy, golden lobster pot stickers are one of the best appetizers in Orlando. ✉ *7760 W. Sand Lake Rd., Plaza Venezia, I–4 Exit 74A* ☎ *407/352–4844* 🌐 *www.roysrestaurant.com* 💳 *AE, D, DC, MC, V* ⏲ *No lunch* ✣ *1:D3.*

$$ AMERICAN

Fodor's Choice ★

✕ **Seasons 52.** Parts of the menu change every week at this innovative restaurant, which serves what's in season. Meals here tend to be healthful yet hearty and very flavorful. You might have the grilled rack of lamb with Dijon sauce, pork tenderloin skillet with polenta, or salmon cooked on a cedar plank and accompanied by grilled vegetable, or, if you prefer a light meal, go for what the menu calls "entrée salads," like the tamarind-glazed salmon salad with a cumin-lime vinaigrette. An impressive wine list with dozens of selections by the glass complements the long and colorful menu. Another health-conscious concept adopted at Seasons 52 is the "mini indulgence" dessert: classics like chocolate cake, butterscotch pudding, and rocky-road ice cream served in portions designed not to bust your daily calorie budget. Although the cuisine is haute, the prices are modest—not bad for a snazzy, urbane, dark-wood-walled bistro and wine bar. ✉ *7700 Sand Lake Rd., I–4 Exit 75A* ☎ *407/354–5212* ✉ *463 E. Altamonte Dr., I–4 Exit 92, Altamonte*

Springs ☎ *407/767–1252* 🌐 *www.seasons52.com* ▭ *AE, D, DC, MC, V* ✥ *1:D3.*

$$$$ AMERICAN ✕ **Vines Grille & Wine Bar.** Live jazz and blues music fills the night at the bar section of this suave restaurant, but the food and drink in the snazzy main dining room are headliners in their own right. The kitchen specializes in double-cut Kurobuta pork chops, essentially as thick as *Webster's New Collegiate Dictionary,* plus hardwood-and-charcoal cooked steaks, like the 22-ounce rib eye, and sublime fish dishes like crab-crusted black grouper. The wine list here is extensive, with offerings from Napa Valley, New Zealand, Australia, Chile, Italy, and France. The crowd tends to dress up, but suit jackets and ties are not required. ✉ *7533 W. Sand Lake Rd., I–4 Exit 74A* ☎ *407/351–1227* 🌐 *www.vinesgrille.com* ▭ *AE, D, DC, MC, V* ⊙ *No lunch* ✥ *1:D3.*

CENTRAL ORLANDO

$$$ FRENCH ✕ **Le Coq au Vin.** After decades under the care of chef-owner Louis Perrotte, local legend Le Coq au Vin has new owners—and a different menu. Guests can still treat themselves to rich French classics, but can also choose from a list of creative, Florida-influenced fare. The hideaway, owned by Sandy and Reimund Pitz, is in a small house in south Orlando, seating 100 people in three dining rooms. The menu changes seasonally, but the namesake dish is always available. ✉ *4800 S. Orange Ave., South Orlando* ☎ *407/851–6980* 🌐 *www.lecoqauvinrestaurant.com* ▭ *AE, DC, MC, V* ⊙ *Closed Mon.* ✥ *1:F3.*

WINTER PARK

$$$ AMERICAN Fodor's Choice ★ ✕ **Luma on Park.** Park Avenue was itself a tourist attraction decades before the advent of Walt Disney World. Although Luma on Park is a 21st-century place, serving what it calls "progressive American cuisine," it's also very much in line with Winter Park's 19th-century past. The chic contemporary setting includes terrazzo floors accented by plush carpets and seating areas in alcoves that create a cozy feel. A high point is the wine cellar, which holds 80 varieties of fine wine, all available by the half glass, glass, and bottle. The menu changes frequently and always includes pastas and salumi prepared from scratch. On recent visits standouts included two appetizers: roasted turnip-pear soup with Aleppo-pepper oil, and lacianato kale ravioli with toasted-garlic brodo. Notable entrées include Faroe Island ocean trout with quinoa, maitake mushrooms and tangerine broth, and Niman Ranch pork schnitzel with sage–brown-butter grits and honey-glazed cranberries. ✉ *250 S. Park Ave.* ☎ *407/599–4111* 🌐 *www.lumaonpark.com* ✍ *Reservations essential* ▭ *AE, MC, V* ✥ *1:F1.*

$$$ CONTINENTAL ✕ **Park Plaza Gardens.** Sitting at the sidewalk café and bar is like sitting on the main street of the quintessential American bustling town. But the locals know the real gem is hidden inside—an atrium with live ficus trees, a brick floor, and brick walls that give the place a Vieux Carré feel. Chef John Tan's menu is composed of traditional Continental fare with elements of American, French, and Asian flavors, like rack of lamb or tenderloin topped with Boursin cheese. One dish with the Florida touch is baked grouper with lemon jasmine rice and tomato-ginger coulis. Lunch offerings include glazed salmon and a good blue-cheese

burger. ✉ *319 Park Ave. S* ☎ *407/645–2475* 🌐 *www.parkplazagardens.com* 💳 *AE, D, MC, V* ⊕ *1:F1.*

$$$ AMERICAN Fodor's Choice ★ ✕ **The Ravenous Pig.** A trendy, vibrant gastropub in one of Orlando's most affluent enclaves, the Pig is arguably Orlando's most popular foodie destination. Run by husband-and-wife chefs James and Julie Petrakis, the restaurant dispenses delicacies such as roast suckling pig with rye gnocchi dumplings, and grilled cobia (a white-fleshed Florida fish) with collards and persimmon chutney. The menu changes daily but often includes less expensive pub fare like lobster tacos and homemade pretzels with a taleggio-porter fondue. A good dessert is the "Pig Tails," essentially a basket full of piping hot, pig tail–shaped doughnuts with a chocolate-espresso dipping sauce. ✉ *1234 N. Orange Ave.* ☎ *407/628–2333* 🌐 *www.theravenouspig.com* ✍ *Reservations essential* 💳 *AE, D, MC, V* ⏲ *Closed Sun. and Mon.* ⊕ *1:F1.*

WHERE TO STAY

With tens of thousands of lodging choices available in the Orlando area, from tents to deluxe villas, there is no lack of variety in price or amenities. Narrowing down the possibilities can be part of the fun.

More upscale hotels are opening, as visitors demand more luxurious surroundings, such as luxe linens, tasteful and refined decor, organic toiletries and more. But no matter what your budget or desires, lodging comes in such a wide range of prices, themes, and guest-room amenities, that you will have no problem finding something that fits your needs.

RESERVATIONS

You can book many accommodations—Disney-owned hotels and some non-Disney-owned hotels—through the **WDW Central Reservations Office** (☎ *407/934–7639* 🌐 *www.disneyworld.com*). People with disabilities can call **WDW Special Request Reservations** (☎ *407/939–7807*). When booking by phone, expect to chat with a robot first, then a real person. Packages can be arranged through the **Walt Disney Travel Co.** (☎ *407/934–7639* 🌐 *www.disneyworld.com*). Avoid checkout headaches by asking about the resort fee. Many hotels and resorts charge this fee, and few tell you until checkout, so be sure to ask about it.

PRICES

In the Orlando area, there's an inverse relationship between temperature and room rates. The hot and humid weather in late summer and fall brings low prices and possibly hurricanes. Conversely, the balmy days of late February, March, and April attract lots of visitors; hotel owners charge accordingly. Rates are often low from early January to mid-February, from late April to mid-June, and from mid-August to the third week in November.

WHAT IT COSTS					
	¢	$	$$	$$$	$$$$
FOR TWO PEOPLE	under $100	$100–$174	$175–$249	$250–$350	over $350

Price categories reflect the range between the least and most expensive standard double rooms in nonholiday high season, based on the European Plan (with no meals) unless otherwise noted. County and resort taxes (10%–12%) are extra.

WALT DISNEY WORLD

Disney-operated hotels are fantasies unto themselves. Each is designed according to a theme and each offers the same perks: free transportation from the airport and to the parks, the option to charge all your purchases to your room, special guest-only park-visiting times, and much more. If you stay on-site, you'll have better access to the parks and you'll be more immersed in the Disney experience.

MAGIC KINGDOM RESORT AREA

$$$–$$$$ **Contemporary Resort.** The first hotel to open here nearly 40 years ago, has been completely renovated several times to maintain a sleek, modern look. The monorail runs through the lobby, so it takes just minutes to get to the Magic Kingdom and Epcot. Upper floors of the main tower (where rooms are more expensive) offer great views of activities in and around the Magic Kingdom, including the nightly fireworks and the boat traffic on Bay Lake and the Seven Seas lagoon. **Pros:** easy access to Magic Kingdom; Chef Mickey's is here, the epicenter of the character-meal world; launching point for sunset Bay Lake cruises. **Cons:** a mix of conventioneers and vacationers (there's an on-site convention center) means that it is sometimes too frenzied for the former and too staid for the latter; among the most kid-intensive of the pricier Disney hotels. ☎ *407/824–1000* *1,013 rooms, 25 suites* *In-room: safe, refrigerator, Wi-Fi. In-hotel: 3 restaurants, room service, tennis courts, pools, gym, beachfront, children's programs (ages 4–12), laundry facilities, laundry service, Wi-Fi hotspot* *AE, D, DC, MC, V* ✥ *2:C1.*

$$$ **Fort Wilderness Resort Cabins.** This 700-acre campground is a resort in itself, with cabins and campsites. With its dozens of entertainment options, including biking, outdoor movies, and singing around the campfire—and the very popular Hoop-Dee-Doo Musical Review and Backyard BBQ character event—a family can have a truly memorable vacation in real Florida wilderness. The cabins, which resemble log mobile homes, can accommodate four grown-ups and two youngsters, and each cabin has a fully equipped kitchen, and daily housekeeping is provided. **Pros:** cabins don't constitute roughing it (they have air-conditioning); you can save a fortune by cooking, but you don't have to, thanks to the three-meals-a-day restaurant and nightly barbecue. **Cons:** shuttle to Disney theme parks is free but slow; coin-op laundry is pricey ($2 to wash, $2 to dry). ☎ *407/824–2900* *421 cabins* *In-room: kitchen, Internet. In-resort: restaurant, tennis courts, pools, bicycles, laundry facilities* *AE, D, DC, MC, V* ✥ *2:D2.*

BEST BETS FOR ORLANDO AND THE PARKS LODGING

With thousands of hotels to choose from, ask yourself first what your family truly wants to do in Orlando during your visit. This invariably leads to an on-property vs. off-property debate, and more questions. To assist you, here are our top recommendations by price (any property listed here has at least some rooms in the noted range) and experience. The very best properties—those that provide a particularly remarkable experience in their price range—are designated in the listings with the Fodor's Choice logo.

Fodor's Choice ★

All-Star Sports, Music & Movies Resorts, pg. 223
Animal Kingdom Lodge, pg. 223
Best Western Lake Buena Vista Resort, pg. 225
Coronado Springs Resort, pg. 221
Fort Wilderness Resort Campground, pg. 220
Grand Floridian Resort & Spa, pg. 220
Mona Lisa Suite Hotel, pg. 229
Nickelodeon Family Suites by Holiday Inn, pg. 231
Portofino Bay Hotel, pg. 227
Ritz-Carlton Orlando Grande Lakes, pg. 230
Royal Pacific Resort, pg. 227
Waldorf Astoria Orlando, pg. 231

By Price

¢

Best Western Lake Buena Vista Resort, pg. 225
Fort Wilderness Resort Campground, pg. 220

$

All-Star Sports, Music & Movies Resorts, pg. 223
Mona Lisa Suite Hotel, pg. 229
Pop Century Resort, pg. 223

$$

Coronado Springs Resort, pg. 221
Grand Bohemian, pg. 232
Nickelodeon Family Suites by Holiday Inn, pg. 231
Royal Pacific Resort, pg. 227
Walt Disney World Dolphin or Swan, pg. 224–225

$$$

Animal Kingdom Lodge, pg. 223
Fort Wilderness Resort Cabins, pg. 217
Portofino Bay Hotel, pg. 227
Ritz-Carlton Orlando Grande Lakes, pg. 230

$$$$

Grand Floridian Resort & Spa, pg. 220
Polynesian Resort, pg. 220
Waldorf Astoria Orlando, pg. 231

By Experience

MOST KID-FRIENDLY

All-Star Sports, Music & Movies Resorts, pg. 223
Nickelodeon Family Suites by Holiday Inn, pg. 231
Pop Century Resort, pg. 223

BEST POOLS

JW Marriott Orlando Grande Lakes, pg. 229
Portofino Bay Hotel, pg. 227
Ritz-Carlton Orlando Grande Lakes, pg. 230

MOST ROMANTIC

Park Plaza Hotel, pg. 232
Portofino Bay Hotel, pg. 227
Wilderness Lodge, pg. 220

WHERE SHOULD I STAY?

	VIBE	PROS	CONS
Disney	Thousands of rooms at every price; convenient to Disney parks; free transportation all over WDW complex.	Perks like early park entry and Magical Express, which lets you circumvent airport bag checks.	Without a rental car, you likely won't leave Disney. On-site buses, while free, can take a big bite of time out of your entertainment day.
Universal	On-site hotels offer luxury and convenience. There are less expensive options just outside the gates.	Central to Disney, Universal, SeaWorld, malls, and I-4; free water taxis to parks from on-site hotels.	On-site hotels are pricey; expect heavy rush-hour traffic during drives to and from other parks.
I-Drive	A hotel, convention-center, and activities bonanza. A trolley runs from one end to the other.	Outlet malls provide bargains galore; diners enjoy world-class restaurants; it's central to parks; many hotels offer free shuttles.	Transportation can be pricey, in cash and in time, as traffic is often heavy. Crime is up, especially after dark, though area hotels and businesses have increased security.
Kissimmee	It's Replete with mom 'n' pop motels and restaurants and places to buy saltwater taffy.	It's just outside Disney, very close to the Magic Kingdom. Lots of Old Florida charm.	Some motels here are a little seedy. Petty crime in which tourists are victims is rare—but not unheard of.
Lake Buena Vista	Many hotel and restaurant chains here. Adjacent to WDW, which is where almost every guest in your hotel is headed.	Really close to WDW; plenty of dining and shopping options; easy access to I-4.	Heavy peak-hour traffic. As in all neighborhoods near Disney, a gallon of gas will cost 10%–15% more than elsewhere.
Central Orlando	Parts of town have the modern high-rises you'd expect. Other areas have oak-tree-lined brick streets winding among small, cypress-ringed lakes.	Lots of locally owned restaurants and some quaint B&Bs. City buses serve the parks. There's good access to I-4.	You'll need to rent a car. And you will be part of the traffic headed to WDW. Expect the 25-mi drive to take at least 45 minutes.

4

¢ Fodor's Choice ★ **Fort Wilderness Resort Campground.** Bringing a tent or RV is one of the cheapest ways to stay on WDW property, especially considering that sites accommodate up to 10. Tent sites with water and electricity are real bargains. RV sites cost more but are equipped with electric, water, and sewage hookups as well as outdoor charcoal grills and picnic tables. The campground has 15 strategically located comfort stations where you can take a hot shower, as well as laundry facilities, restaurants, a general store—everything you need. Tents can be rented for $30 a night, and staff will even set them up for you, so it's easy to camp here with virtually no gear of your own. **Pros:** Disney's most economical lodging; pets allowed ($5 nightly fee per campsite, not per pet). **Cons:** amount of walking within the camp can be a bit much for some; shuttle rides to Disney parks take too long; the bugs can be irritating, especially around twilight, except in winter. ☎ *407/824–2742 or 407/934–7639* *799 campsites* *In-hotel: pools, hot tub, snack bar, laundry facilities, tennis* *AE, D, DC, MC, V* ✣ *2:D2.*

$$$$ Fodor's Choice ★ **Grand Floridian Resort & Spa.** On the shores of the Seven Seas Lagoon, this red-roofed Victorian is all delicate, white-painted gingerbread, rambling verandas, and brick chimneys. It's Disney's flagship resort, with everything from its best-appointed guest rooms to the high-quality hotel amenities. Although you won't look out of place walking through the lobby in flip-flops, afternoon high tea and a pianist playing nightly in the lobby are among the more genteel touches. **Pros:** on the monorail route; home to Victoria & Albert's, one of Disney's best restaurants; if you're a couple with no kids, this can be among the least noisy of the on-property Disney hotels. **Cons:** some say it's not ritzy enough to match the room rates; conference center and convention clientele lend to the stuffiness; Victoria & Albert's no longer seats kids younger than 10. ☎ *407/824–3000* *867 rooms, 90 suites* *In-room: safe, Internet. In-hotel: 6 restaurants, bars, room service, tennis courts, pools, gym, spa, beachfront, children's programs (ages 4–12), laundry facilities, laundry service, Wi-Fi hotspot* *AE, D, DC, MC, V* ✣ *2:B2.*

$$$$ **Polynesian Resort.** You may not think you're in Fiji, but it's not hard to pretend here, especially after downing a few of the tropical drinks available in the Great Ceremonial House—aka the lobby. In the three-story atrium lobby orchids bloom alongside coconut palms and banana trees, and water cascades from volcanic-rock fountains. At the evening luau, Polynesian dancers perform before a feast with Hawaiian-style roast pork. **Pros:** on the monorail; great aloha-spirit atmosphere. **Cons:** pricey; not good for those bothered by lots of loud children. ☎ *407/824–2000* *847 rooms, 5 suites* *In-room: safe, Internet. In-hotel: 4 restaurants, room service, bar, pools, gym, beachfront, children's programs (ages 4–12), laundry facilities, laundry service, Wi-Fi hotspot* *AE, D, DC, MC, V* ✣ *2:B2.*

$$$–$$$$ **Wilderness Lodge.** The architects outdid themselves with this seven-story hotel modeled after the majestic turn-of-the-20th-century lodges of the American Northwest. The hotel's showstopper is its Fire Rock Geyser, a faux Old Faithful that erupts with sometimes alarming regularity, near the large pool, which begins as an artificially heated hot spring in the lobby. **Pros:** high wow-factor architecture; boarding point

for romantic Bay Lake sunset cruises. **Cons:** ferry toots its horn at every docking; no direct shuttle to Magic Kingdom. ☎ *407/824–3200* *727 rooms, 31 suites* *In-room: safe, Internet. In-hotel: 3 restaurants, room service, pool, bicycles, children's programs (ages 4–12), laundry facilities, laundry service, Wi-Fi hotspot* *AE, D, DC, MC, V* ✣ *2:C2.*

EPCOT RESORT AREA

$$ **Caribbean Beach Resort.** Six palm-studded "villages," all awash in dizzying pastels and labeled with names straight from the Caribbean, each with its own pool, share 45-acre Barefoot Bay and its white-sand beach. Bridges connect to a 1-acre path-crossed play and picnic area called Parrot Cay. You can rent boats to explore the lake, or rent bikes to ride along the 1½-mi lakefront promenade. **Pros:** plenty of on-site outdoor activities, like volleyball, giving the place a lush summer-camp feel; convenient to Epcot, Disney's Hollywood Studios, and Downtown Disney. **Cons:** you don't truly feel swept away to a tropical island; the only swimmable waters are in the pools, not the lake; walks from your room to the beach or a restaurant can be up to 15 minutes. ☎ *407/934–3400* *2,112 rooms* *In-room: safe, Internet. In-hotel: restaurant, room service, pools, beachfront, bicycles, laundry facilities, laundry service, Wi-Fi hotspot* *AE, D, DC, MC, V* ✣ *2:E4.*

$$ Fodor's Choice ★ **Coronado Springs Resort.** Because of its 95,000-square-foot convention center and the adjacent 60,000-square-foot ballroom, and moderate price, this is Disney's most popular convention hotel. But since the meeting space is in its own wing, the resort is also popular with families who appreciate its casual Southwestern architecture, its lively, Mexican-style food court, and its elaborate swimming pool, which has a Mayan pyramid with a big slide. **Pros:** great pool with a play area–arcade for kids and a bar for adults; lots of outdoor activities. **Cons:** some accommodations are a half-mile from the restaurants; standard rooms are on the small side; kids may find the subdued atmosphere boring. ☎ *407/939–1000* *1,917 rooms* *In-room: safe, Internet. In-hotel: 2 restaurants, room service, bar, pools, gym, spa, bicycles, laundry service, Wi-Fi hotspot* *AE, D, DC, MC, V* ✣ *2:C5.*

$$$$ **Yacht and Beach Club Resorts.** These big Seven Seas Lagoon inns seem straight out of a Cape Cod summer, with their nautical decor and waterfront locale. The five-story Yacht Club has hardwood floors, a lobby full of gleaming brass and polished leather, an oyster-gray clapboard facade, and evergreen landscaping; there's even a lighthouse on its pier. Rooms have nautical-print bedspreads and wrought-iron headboards. At the Beach Club, a croquet lawn and cabana-dotted white-sand beach set the scene. Stormalong Bay, a 3-acre water park with slides and whirlpools, is part of this club. Both lodgings have "quiet pools," which are secluded and largely kid-free, albeit nondescript. **Pros:** location, location, location—it's easy to walk to Epcot and the BoardWalk, and Disney's Hollywood Studios is a fun, 20-minute ferry ride away. **Cons:** distances within the hotel—like, from your room to the front desk—can seem vast; high noise factor. ☎ *407/934–8000 Beach Club, 407/934–7000 Yacht Club* *1,213 rooms, 112 suites* *In-room: safe, Internet, Wi-Fi. In-hotel: 4 restaurants, room service, tennis courts, pools, gym,*

4

PARK-STAY PERKS

DISNEY PERKS

Extra Magic Hours. You get special early and late-night admission to certain Disney parks on specified days. Call ahead for details so you can plan your early- and late-visit strategies.

Free Parking. Parking is free for Disney hotel guests at Disney hotel and theme-park lots.

Magical Express. If you're staying at a Disney hotel, you don't need to rent a car, think about finding a shuttle or taxi, or worry about baggage handling, thanks to this free service.

At your hometown airport, you'll check your bags in and won't see them again till you get to your Disney hotel. At Orlando International Airport, you'll be met by a Disney rep who will lead you to a coach that takes you to your hotel. Your luggage will be delivered separately, and usually arrives in your room an hour or two after you do.

On departure, the process works in reverse (though only on some participating airlines, so check in advance). You get your boarding pass and check your bags at the hotel. At the airport you go directly to your gate, skipping check-in. You won't see your bags until you're in your hometown airport. Participating airlines include American, Continental, Delta, JetBlue, Northwest, Southwest, and United.

Charging Privileges. You can charge most meals and purchases throughout Disney to your hotel room.

Package Delivery. Anything you purchase at Disney—at a park, a hotel, or in Downtown Disney—can be delivered to the gift shop of your Disney hotel for free.

Priority Reservations. Disney hotel guests get priority reservations at Disney restaurants and choice tee times at Disney golf courses up to 30 days in advance.

Guaranteed Entry. Disney theme parks sometimes reach capacity, but on-site guests can enter even when others would be turned away.

UNIVERSAL PERKS

Head-of-the-Line Access. Your hotel key lets you go directly to the head of the line for most Universal Orlando attractions. Unlike Disney's Fastpass program, you don't need to use this at a specific time; it's always good.

Priority Seating. Many of Universal's restaurants offer priority seating to those staying at on-site hotels.

Charging Privileges. You can charge most meals and purchases throughout Universal to your hotel room.

Delivery Services. If you buy something in the theme parks, you can have it sent directly to your room, so you don't have to carry it around.

Free Loaners. Some on-site hotels have a "Did You Forget?" closet that offers everything from kid's strollers to dog leashes to computer accessories. There's no fee for using this service.

beachfront, bicycles, children's programs (ages 4–12), laundry service, Wi-Fi hotspot ▭ *AE, D, DC, MC, V* ✥ *2:D4.*

ANIMAL KINGDOM RESORT AREA

$ Fodor's Choice ★ **All-Star Sports, All-Star Music, and All-Star Movies Resorts.** Stay here if you want the quintessential Disney-with-your-kids experience, or if you're a couple that feels all that pitter-pattering of little feet is a reasonable tradeoff for a good deal on a room. (Hint: for a little peace, request a room away from pools and other common areas.) In the Sports resort, Goofy is the pitcher in the baseball-diamond pool; in the Music resort you'll walk by giant bongos; and in the Movies resort, huge characters like *Toy Story*'s Buzz Lightyear frame each building. Each room has two double beds, an armoire, and a desk. At 260 square feet, these are the smallest rooms in any Disney hotel, which helps keep the room rate down. The food courts sell standard fare, and you can have pizza delivered to your room. **Pros:** unbeatable price for a Disney property. **Cons:** no kids' clubs or programs, possibly because this is on the bottom tier of Disney hotels in terms of room rates; distances between rooms and on-site amenities can seem vast. ☎ *407/939–5000 Sports, 407/939–6000 Music, 407/939–7000 Movies* *1,700 rooms, 215 family suites at Music; 1,920 rooms at Movies and Sports* *In-room: safe, Internet. In-hotel: room service, bars, pools, laundry facilities, laundry service, Internet terminal* ▭ *AE, D, DC, MC, V* ✥ *2:C6.*

$$$–$$$$ Fodor's Choice ★ **Animal Kingdom Lodge.** Giraffes, zebras, and other wildlife roam three 11-acre savannas separated by the encircling arms of this grand hotel, designed to resemble a "kraal" or animal enclosure in Africa. Entering the vast atrium lobby is like entering a cathedral, with a roof formed of thatch rather than marble. A massive clay chimney structure dominates the right-hand side of the four-story lobby. Cultural ambassadors give talks about their African homelands, the animals, and the artwork on display; evenings include storytelling sessions around the fire circle on the Arusha Rock terrace. **Pros:** extraordinary wildlife and cultural experiences; Jiko and Boma restaurants in the main Lodge serve excellent African cuisine, and Sanaa, in Kidani Village, serves African food with an Indian influence. **Cons:** shuttle to parks other than Animal Kingdom can take more than an hour; guided savanna tours available only to guests on the concierge level, where the least expensive room is $100 a night higher than the least expensive rooms in other parts of the hotel. ☎ *407/934–7639* *972 rooms, 499 suites or villas* *In-room: safe, Internet. In-hotel: 3 restaurants, bar, pools, gym, spa, children's programs (ages 4–12), laundry facilities, laundry service, Wi-Fi hotspot* ▭ *AE, D, DC, MC, V* ✥ *2:A5.*

$ **Pop Century Resort.** Giant jukeboxes, 65-foot-tall bowling pins, an oversized Big Wheel and Rubik's Cube, and other pop-culture memorabilia are scattered throughout the grounds. Items from mood rings to eight-track tapes are incorporated into the architecture; wall-mounted shadow boxes display toys, fashions, and fads from each decade since the 1950s. Brightly colored rooms are functional for families, with two double beds or one king. **Pros:** great room rates; hotel provides a trip down memory lane. **Cons:** big crowds at the front desk; big crowds (and noise) in the food court; small rooms; lots of small kids around.

☎ 407/934–7639 ⇨ 2,880 rooms ☝ In-room: safe, Internet. In-hotel: room service, bar, pools, gym, laundry service, Wi-Fi hotspot ☰ AE, D, DC, MC, V ✣ 2:E5.

DOWNTOWN DISNEY RESORT AREA

$$ **Port Orleans Resort–French Quarter.** Ornate Big Easy–style row houses with wrought-iron–trimmed balconies cluster around squares planted with magnolias. Lamp-lighted sidewalks are named for French Quarter thoroughfares. Because this place is relatively quiet, it appeals more to couples than families with kids, although, like any WDW hotel, it is not devoid of youngsters. **Pros:** authentic, fun New Orleans–style atmosphere; lots of water- recreation options, including boat rentals; "standard view" rooms have a view of the parking lot, but in peak season they are $25 a night cheaper than the rooms with better views. **Cons:** even though there are fewer kids here, public areas can still be quite noisy; shuttle service is slow; food court is the only on-site dining option. *☎ 407/934–5000 ⇨ 1,008 rooms ☝ In-room: safe, Internet, refrigerator. In-hotel: pool, bicycles, laundry facilities, laundry service, Wi-Fi hotspot ☰ AE, D, DC, MC, V ✣ 2:E3.*

$$ **Port Orleans Resort–Riverside.** Buildings look like plantation-style mansions (in the Magnolia Bend section), and rustic bayou dwellings (in the Alligator Bayou section) and you can typically pick which section you want. The registration area looks like a steamboat interior, and the 3½-acre, old-fashioned swimming-hole complex called Ol' Man Island has a pool with slides, rope swings, and a nearby play area. **Pros:** carriage rides; river cruises; lots of recreation options for kids. **Cons:** shuttle can be slow; no shortage of extremely noisy youngsters, if that's a concern. *☎ 407/934–6000 ⇨ 2,048 rooms ☝ In-room: safe, Internet. In-hotel: restaurant, pools, gym, bicycles, laundry facilities, laundry service ☰ AE, D, DC, MC, V ✣ 2:E3.*

OTHER ON-SITE HOTELS

Although not operated by the Disney organization, the Swan and the Dolphin just outside Epcot, and the hotels along Hotel Plaza Boulevard near Downtown Disney call themselves "official" Walt Disney World hotels. While the Swan and Dolphin have the special privileges of on-site Disney hotels, such as free transportation to and from the parks and early park entry, the Downtown Disney resorts have their own systems to shuttle hotel guests to the parks.

EPCOT RESORT AREA

$$–$$$ **Walt Disney World Dolphin.** World-renowned architect Michael Graves designed the neighboring Dolphin and Swan hotels. Outside, a pair of 56-foot-tall sea creatures bookend this 25-story glass pyramid. The fabric-draped lobby resembles a giant sultan's tent. All rooms have either two queen beds or one king, with pillow-top mattresses, down comforters with crisp white duvet covers, and overstuffed pillows. These amenities make the beds here some of the kingdom's most comfortable. **Pros:** access to all facilities at the Walt Disney World Swan; easy walk or boat ride to BoardWalk; good on-site restaurants. **Cons:** self-parking is $10 a day; a $10 a day "resort fee" covers Wi-Fi and

Internet access, use of health club, and local phone calls; room-charge privileges stop at the front door, and don't extend to the Disney parks. ✉ *1500 Epcot Resorts Blvd., Lake Buena Vista* ☎ *407/934–4000 or 800/227–1500* 🌐 *www.swandolphin.com* *1,509 rooms, 112 suites* *In-room: safe, Internet. In-hotel: 9 restaurants, room service, bars, tennis courts, pools, gym, spa, beachfront, children's programs (ages 4–12), Wi-Fi hotspot* *AE, D, DC, MC, V* ✣ *2:C4.*

$$–$$$ **Walt Disney World Swan.** Facing the Dolphin across Crescent Lake, the Swan is a twin in many ways to its sister hotel, but with two 46-foot swans gracing the rooftop, so you can tell from a distance which hotel is which. The Grotto, a 3-acre water playground complete with waterslides, waterfalls, and all the trimmings, lies between and is shared by the Dolphin and Swan, and Disney's BoardWalk and the Fantasia Gardens miniature-golf complex are nearby. **Pros:** charge privileges and access to all facilities at the Dolphin (but not inside Disney World); easy walk to BoardWalk; free boats take you to the BoardWalk and Epcot; good on-site restaurants. **Cons:** like the Dolphin, the Swan levies a $10 per night resort fee, which includes in-room Internet access, health club privileges, and 60 minutes a day of free local phone calls. ✉ *1200 Epcot Resorts Blvd., Lake Buena Vista* ☎ *407/934–3000 or 800/248–7926* 🌐 *www.swandolphin.com* *756 rooms, 55 suites* *In-room: safe, Internet. In-hotel: 8 restaurants, room service, bars, tennis courts, pools, gym, spa, beachfront, children's programs (ages 4–12), Wi-Fi hotspot* *AE, D, DC, MC, V* ✣ *2:C4.*

DOWNTOWN DISNEY RESORT AREA

¢–$ Fodor's Choice ★ **Best Western Lake Buena Vista Resort.** A near-total face-lift during 2010 gave this Best Western resort, just minutes away from Downtown Disney, a real boost. Guest rooms received new carpeting, bedding, luxury linens, and crisp duvets; bathrooms were tiled in Italian ceramics. All rooms have private balconies with updated furnishings to watch the spectacular views of the nightly Disney fireworks. **Pros:** free Wi-Fi and parking, not to mention the price, make this one of the best bargains on Hotel Row; close to Downtown Disney. **Cons:** inconvenient to Universal and downtown Orlando. ✉ *2000 Hotel Plaza Blvd., Lake Buena Vista* ☎ *407/828–2424 or 800/937–8376* 🌐 *www.lakebuenavistaresorthotel.com* *325 rooms* *In-room: Wi-Fi. In-hotel: 3 restaurants, room service, pools, gym, laundry facilities, laundry service, Wi-Fi hotspot* *AE, D, DC, MC, V* ✣ *2:G3.*

$$–$$$ **Hilton in the WDW Resort.** Befitting the fantasy world most theme-park visitors seek, the entrance is behind a waterfall, leading into a starkly modern, newly renovated lobby. Although not huge, rooms are decorated in a restrained, neutral palette, with flat-screen TVs and work tables. Many on the upper floors have great views of Downtown Disney, just a short walk away. **Pros:** close to Downtown Disney; because this is an "official" Disney hotel (although not a Disney-operated one) you get the same early-entrance privileges to Disney Parks; free shuttle bus; kids' program. **Cons:** pricier than similar lodgings farther from Disney; Internet and Wi-Fi fee; inconvenient to Universal and downtown Orlando. ✉ *1751 Hotel Plaza Blvd., Lake Buena Vista* ☎ *407/827–4000, 800/782–4414 reservations* 🌐 *www.hilton.com* *814 rooms,*

27 suites ♿ *In-room: safe, Internet, Wi-Fi. In-hotel: 7 restaurants, room service, pools, gym, children's programs (ages 3–12), laundry facilities, laundry service, Wi-Fi hotspot* ▭ *AE, DC, MC* ✥ *2:G4.*

$ **Holiday Inn in the WDW Resort.** The very modern lobby, with its glass-roofed atrium, muted colors, contemporary furnishings and linen sheers over floor to ceiling windows, indicates the hotel's low-key elegance. Rooms reflect the same ambience, with crisp white linens, minimalist wood furniture and headboards, and flat-screen TVs. Within an easy and safe walking distance of Downtown Disney, the hotel also offers free transportation to and from Disney parks. **Pros:** walking distance to Downtown Disney; free transportation to all Disney parks; free Wi-Fi and wired Internet access. **Cons:** no free shuttle to Universal or Sea-World; not convenient to Orlando ✉ *1805 Hotel Plaza Blvd., Downtown Disney, Lake Buena Vista* ☎ *407/828–8888 or 1/800–423–0908* 🌐 *www.hiorlando.com* *323 rooms* ♿ *In-room: safe, Internet, Wi-Fi (free). In-hotel: restaurant, room service, bars, pool, gym, safe, laundry service, Wi-Fi hotspot, parking* ▭ *AE, D, DC, MC, V* ✥ *2:G4.*

UNIVERSAL ORLANDO AREA

Universal Orlando's on-site hotels were built in a little luxury enclave that has everything you need, so you never have to leave Universal property. In minutes you can walk from any hotel to CityWalk, Universal's dining and entertainment district, or take a ferry that cruises the adjacent artificial river.

¢–$ **Doubletree Hotel at the Entrance to Universal Orlando.** The name sounds awkward but it's very descriptive, and the conveniently located hotel is a hotbed of business-trippers and pleasure-seekers thanks to a location right at the Universal Orlando entrance. Don't worry about noisy conventioneers—the meeting and convention facilities are isolated from the guest towers. If you happen to stay here on business, though, note that the teleconferencing center lets you connect with points all over the world, but you have to pay for Internet access in the room. **Pros:** within walking distance of Universal and area shops and restaurants; free shuttle to Universal. **Cons:** on a fast-lane tourist strip; need a rental car to reach Disney, I-Drive, or downtown Orlando; daily fee for Wi-Fi in room. ✉ *5780 Major Blvd., I–4 Exit 75B* ☎ *407/351–1000* 🌐 *www.doubletreeorlando.com* *742 rooms, 15 suites* ♿ *In-room: safe, Wi-Fi. In-hotel: restaurant, room service, pool, gym, laundry facilities, laundry service, Wi-Fi hotspot* ▭ *AE, D, DC, MC* ✥ *1:D3.*

$$$–$$$$ **Hard Rock Hotel.** Inside the California mission–style building you'll find rock memorabilia from an Elvis jump suit to the slip Madonna wore in her "Like a Prayer" video, and a 2,500-plus-square-foot presidential suite aptly named the Graceland. Rooms have black-and-white photos of pop icons, 32-inch flat-panel TVs, and iHome docking stations. Kid-friendly suites have a small extra room for children, and, best of all, your hotel key card lets you bypass lines at Universal. **Pros:** shuttle, water taxi, or short walk to Universal and CityWalk; preferential treatment at Universal rides; charge privileges on your room extend to the two other on-property Universal hotels. **Cons:** rooms and meals are pricey; loud rock music in public areas may annoy some people; fee for gym and in-room Wi-Fi. ✉ *5800 Universal Blvd., Universal Studios Orlando* ☎ *407/503–7625 or 800/232–7827* 🌐 *www.universalorlando.com* *621 rooms, 29 suites* *In-room: safe, refrigerator, Internet, Wi-Fi. In-hotel: 3 restaurants, room service, bars, pool, gym, children's programs (ages 4–14), laundry service, Wi-Fi hotspot, some pets allowed* *AE, D, DC, MC, V* ✥ *1:D3.*

$$$ Fodor's Choice ★ **Portofino Bay Hotel.** The charm and romance of Portofino, Italy, destination of the rich and famous in Europe, are conjured up at this lovely luxury resort by Loews. Part of the fun is exploring this waterfront "village" from end to end; the charm is not knowing what you'll find around a corner or down some steps. The illusion is sustained by the details from cobblestone streets to variegated row houses lining the boat-dotted "bay," and inviting archways that lead to narrow stairways and piazzas. Three pools offer aquatic fun or peaceful sunning. **Pros:** Italian-villa atmosphere; large spa; short walk or ferry ride to CityWalk, Universal Studios, and Islands of Adventure; preferential treatment at Universal rides; you can charge meals and services (and use the pools) at the Hard Rock and the Royal Pacific Resort. **Cons:** rooms and meals are noticeably expensive; daily fee for in-room high-speed Internet or Wi-Fi, as well as for access to the fitness center. ✉ *5601 Universal Blvd., Universal StudiosOrlando* ☎ *407/503–1000 or 800/232–7827* 🌐 *www.universalorlando.com* *699 rooms, 51 suites* *In-room: safe, Internet, Wi-Fi. In-hotel: 3 restaurants, room service, bar, pools, gym, spa, children's programs (ages 4–14), laundry service, Wi-Fi hotspot, some pets allowed* *AE, D, DC, MC, V* ✥ *1:D3.*

$$–$$$ Fodor's Choice ★ **Royal Pacific Resort.** The entrance—a broad, covered footbridge high above a tropical stream—sets the tone for the Pacific Rim theme of this hotel, which is on 53 acres planted with lush shrubs, soaring bamboo, and palms. The focal point is a 12,000-square-foot, lagoon-style pool, which has a small beach and an interactive water-play area. All guest rooms have bright, tropical bed coverings, bamboo ceiling accents, and electronics that include iPod station clock radios and 32-inch flat-panel televisions. **Pros:** Emeril's restaurant (don't fail to eat there at least once); preferential treatment at Universal rides; serene, Zen garden vibe. **Cons:** rooms can feel cramped; $10-a-day fee for Internet access unwarranted given rates. ✉ *6300 Hollywood Way, Universal Orlando Orlando* ☎ *407/503–3000 or 800/232–7827* 🌐 *www.universalorlando.com* *1,000 rooms, 113 suites* *In-room: safe, Wi-Fi. In-hotel: 3 restaurants, room service, bars, pool, gym, children's programs (ages 4–14), laundry facilities, laundry service, Wi-Fi hotspot, some pets allowed* *AE, DC, MC, V* ✥ *1:D3.*

ORLANDO METRO AREA

KISSIMMEE

$$$–$$$$ **Gaylord Palms Resort.** Built in the style of a grand turn-of-the-20th-century Florida mansion, this resort is meant to awe. Inside its enormous atrium, covered by a 4-acre glass roof, are re-creations of Florida icons such as the Everglades, Key West, and old St. Augustine. A renovation scheduled to be completed in late 2010 brings new carpeting,

Fodor's Choice ★

Royal Pacific Resort.

All-Star Music Resort, Orlando

The Ritz-Carlton Orlando, Grande Lakes

Waldorf Astoria Orlando

Nickelodeon Family Suites

Coronado Springs Resort

wallpaper, upgraded bed linens, and bigger flat-screen TVs to the rooms, which carry on the Florida themes with colorful, tropical decorations. **Pros:** you could have a great vacation without ever leaving the grounds; free shuttle to Disney. **Cons:** rooms are pricey; not much within walking distance (although the hotel is so big, you can take quite a hike inside the building); shuttles to Universal and SeaWorld are available, but through an outside firm, at a price. ✉ *6000 Osceola Pkwy., I–4 Exit 65* ☎ *407/586–0000* 🌐 *www.gaylordpalms.com* *1,406 rooms, 86 suites* *In-room: safe, Internet. In-hotel: 5 restaurants, bars, pools, gym, spa, children's programs (ages 4–12), laundry service, Wi-Fi hotspot* ▭ *AE, D, DC, MC, V* ✣ *2:F6.*

4

CELEBRATION

$–$$ Fodor's Choice ★ **Mona Lisa Suite Hotel.** On the edge of the Disney-created community of Celebration, the hotel is a brief shuttle ride away from the restaurants, cafés, and shops in the village. Much like a European boutique hotel in style, the Mona Lisa is very human in scale, and crisply minimalist in decor. An oversized closeup detail from Leonardo da Vinci's Mona Lisa greets visitors at the entrance to the unpretentiously welcoming lobby, and hand-painted details from other art masterworks adorn the public areas. **Pros:** free shuttle to downtown Celebration and all of the theme parks; golf privileges at Celebration Golf; spa privileges at Celebration Day Spa; concierge service. **Cons:** busy U.S. 192 is close by; $12 a day resort fee; if you want to go anywhere besides Celebration and the parks, you'll need a car. ✉ *225 Celebration Pl., Celebration Celebration* ☎ *866/404–6662 or 407/964–7000* 🌐 *www.monalisasuitehotel.com* *240 suites, 93 1-bedroom, 147 2-bedroom* *In-room: safe, kitchen, Wi-Fi. In-hotel: 2 restaurants, room service, bar, pool, Wi-Fi hotspot, parking (paid)* ▭ *AE, D, DC, MC, V* ✣ *1:C6.*

INTERNATIONAL DRIVE

$$–$$$ **JW Marriott Orlando Grande Lakes.** With more than 70,000 square feet of meeting space, this hotel caters to a convention clientele. But because it's part of a lush resort that includes a European-style spa and a Greg Norman–designed golf course, it also appeals to those looking to relax. All room interiors were upgraded in 2010 to reflect the natural environment of Florida in colors and feel, using organic cottons, with a duvet cover that is changed between guests. The good news about this place is that you get Ritz-Carlton amenities at JW Marriott prices. **Pros:** pool is great for kids and adults; shares amenities with the Ritz, including a world-class, albeit expensive, health and beauty spa; shuttle service to SeaWorld and Universal. **Cons:** things are spread out on the grounds; you need a rental car to reach Disney and other area offerings. ✉ *4040 Central Florida Pkwy., International Drive, Orlando* ☎ *407/206–2300 or 800/576–5750* 🌐 *www.grandelakes.com* *1,000 rooms, 64 suites* *In-room: Wi-Fi. In-hotel: 5 restaurants, room service, bars, golf course, pool, gym, spa, laundry service, laundry facilities, Wi-Fi hotspot* ▭ *AE, D, DC, MC, V* ✣ *1:D4.*

$$–$$$ **Peabody Orlando.** The famed Peabody ducks have a bigger playground to waddle through, as the hotel's $450-million expansion opened in late 2010. The five coddled canards still exit their elevator at 11 AM and

march to a rousing Sousa tune along the lobby to the fountain in the atrium, where they entertain guests until just past teatime. Then they proceed back to the elevator, and are whisked away to their pricey penthouse aerie. Many more guests can join in the fun, as the luxury hotel doubled its number of guest rooms, added restaurants, an expanded spa, a new pool, a huge amount of meeting space, all housed in a new tower that dwarfs the original 27-story hotel. **Pros:** adjacent to convention center (business travelers take note); good spa; short walk to shops and restaurants. **Cons:** pricey; $15 optional daily hotel service fee includes Wi-Fi; on a congested section of I-Drive. ✉ *9801 International Dr., International Drive, Orlando* ☎ *407/352–4000 or 800/732–2639* 🌐 *www.peabodyorlando.com* *1,641 rooms, 193 suites, 5 penthouse suites* *In-room: safe, Internet, Wi-Fi, refrigerator (some). In-hotel: 13 restaurants, bars, room service, tennis courts, pool, gym, spa, Wi-Fi hotspot* ▭ *AE, D, DC, MC, V* ✢ *1:D3.*

$$$–$$$$ **Ritz-Carlton Orlando Grande Lakes.** Orlando's first and only Ritz is a particularly extravagant link in the luxury chain. Service is exemplary, from the fully attended porte-cochere entrance to the 18-hole golf course and 40-room spa. Rooms and suites have large balconies, elegant wood furnishings, down comforters, and decadent marble baths (with separate showers and tubs). An enclosed hallway connects the Ritz to the nearby JW Marriott Hotel, where you'll find more restaurants and a kid-friendly water park. **Pros:** truly luxurious; impeccable service; great spa; golf course. **Cons:** pricey; need a rental car to reach Disney and area shops and restaurants; $9.50 daily fee for Wi-Fi. ✉ *4012 Central Florida Pkwy., Orlando* ☎ *407/206–2400 or 800/576–5760* 🌐 *www.grandelakes.com* *584 rooms, 64 suites* *In-room: Wi-Fi. In-hotel: 6 restaurants, room service, bars, golf course, pool, gym, spa, children's programs (ages 5–12), laundry service, Wi-Fi hotspot* ▭ *AE, D, DC, MC, V* ✢ *1:E4.*

Fodor's Choice ★

LAKE BUENA VISTA AREA

$$$–$$$$ **Hilton Orlando Bonnet Creek.** Next door to the Waldorf Astoria hotel, and connected to it via a convention hall, the hotel is part of the Bonnet Creek resort area, right next to Disney World's own vast forest lands. The hotel is not quite as plush as the Waldorf, but it is an amenity-laden property just the same. It targets corporate-types, but also offers great appeal for families, with its 2-acre lagoon pool, resort pool, children's program, and, of course, transportation to Walt Disney World. Guests at the Hilton can use facilities at the Waldorf, including the Waldorf Astoria Spa by Guerlain and the Waldorf restaurants. **Pros:** wonderful setting for a hotel—Disney is just moments away, but the views southwest over the golf course and forest beyond give it a remote air; free Disney shuttle. **Cons:** nothing within walking distance; you will need to rent a car; $10 a day Internet-access fee. ✉ *14100 Bonnet Creek Resort Lane, Bonnet Creek, Orlando* ☎ *407/597–5500* 🌐 *www.hiltonbonnetcreek.com* *1,000 rooms, 36 suites* *In-room: safe, Internet, Wi-Fi. In-hotel: 4 restaurants, room service, bars, golf course, pools, gym, spa, children's programs (ages 4–12), laundry service, Wi-Fi hotspot* ▭ *AE, D, DC, MC, V* ✢ *2:F5.*

$$–$$$ Fodor's Choice ★ **Nickelodeon Family Suites by Holiday Inn.** The Nickelodeon theme extends everywhere, from the suites, where separate kids' rooms have bunk beds and SpongeBob wall murals, to the two giant water-park pools. Kids will look forward to wake-up calls from Nickelodeon stars, character breakfasts, live entertainment, mass slimings, and a 3-D movie theater. The accommodations are so thoroughly designed for kids, it is not the best place for those without youngsters. **Pros:** extremely kid-friendly; free Disney, Universal Orlando, and SeaWorld shuttles; massive discounts (up to 50% off standard rates) for active-duty military; you can save about $20 on a room a night with memberships like AAA and AARP; mini-golf course. **Cons:** not within walking distance of Disney or Downtown Disney; may be too frenetic for folks without kids. ✉ *14500 Continental Gateway, Orlando* ☎ *407/387–5437 or 866/462–6425* 🌐 *www.nickhotels.com* *777 suites* *In-room: safe, kitchen (some), refrigerator, Internet. In-hotel: 7 restaurants, room service, pools, gym, children's programs (ages 4–12), laundry facilities, laundry service, Wi-Fi hotspot* *AE, D, DC, MC, V* ✣ *2:G5.*

$$$–$$$$ Fodor's Choice ★ **Waldorf Astoria Orlando.** While it doesn't duplicate the famed Waldorf Astoria Hotel in New York, the Waldorf Astoria Orlando echoes the original with imagination and flair, from the clock under the dome in the center of the circular lobby to tiny, black-and-white accent tiles on the floors of the guest rooms. Original, specially commissioned art decorates the walls in guest rooms and public spaces. If you want a butler, one is available. If you want a massage, the Guerlain spa exudes relaxation the minute you walk in the door. If golf is your choice, a vast Rees Jones–designed course fills the view from the lobby, bar, or balcony rooms. The hotel connects to and shares a convention hall and meeting space with the Hilton Bonnet Creek. **Pros:** a lavish and luxurious hotel, spa, and golf resort, next to Disney. **Cons:** if you can bear to leave the cabana you'll need a car to see anything else in the area. ✉ *14200 Bonnet Creek Resort La., Orlando* ☎ *407/597–5500* 🌐 *www.waldorfastoriaorlando.com* *328 rooms, 169 suites* *In-room: safe, Internet. In-hotel: 5 restaurants, room service, bars, golf course, pool, gym, spa, children's programs (ages 4–12), laundry service, Wi-Fi hotspot* *AE, D, DC, MC, V* ✣ *2:F5.*

CENTRAL ORLANDO

$–$$ **The Courtyard at Lake Lucerne.** These four beautifully restored Victorian houses that surround a palm-lined courtyard were architectural treasures more than 50 years before Disney came to Orlando and have kept their own brand of magic even now, as they collectively make up one of the better historic inns you'll find in the southeast United States. Although it's almost under an expressway bridge, there's no traffic noise. You can sit on one of the porches and imagine yourself back in the time when citrus ruled and the few visitors arrived at the old railroad station on Church Street, six blocks away. **Pros:** serenity; great Victorian architecture; the azaleas in this neighborhood are alive with color in spring; short walk to Lake Eola and downtown restaurants. **Cons:** far from theme parks and I-Drive; walking in some parts of downtown can be a bit dicey. ✉ *211 N. Lucerne Circle E, Downtown Orlando, Orlando* ☎ *407/648–5188* 🌐 *www.orlandohistoricinn.*

com 15 *rooms,* 15 *suites* *In-room: Wi-Fi. In-hotel: Wi-Fi hotspot, laundry services* *MC, V* *CP* *1:F2.*

$$–$$$ **Grand Bohemian.** This European-style property is downtown Orlando's only luxury hotel, and is part of the locally owned Kessler chain. Opposite city hall, the Grand Bohemian showcases more than 100 pieces of art from the Kessler collection—including a rare Imperial Grand Bösendorfer piano, which sits in a posh ground-floor lounge. Rooms have dark-wood furnishings with brushed-silver accents. **Pros:** art gallery; quiet, adult-friendly atmosphere; great restaurant; sophisticated entertainment; short walk to Lake Eola and downtown restaurants and clubs. **Cons:** kids may find it boring; meals are relatively expensive. *325 S. Orange Ave., Downtown Orlando, Orlando* *407/313–9000 or 866/663–0024* *www.grandbohemianhotel.com* *249 rooms, 36 suites* *In-room: Wi-Fi. In-hotel: restaurant, room service, bar, pool, gym, parking (paid)* *AE, D, DC, MC, V* *1:F2.*

WINTER PARK

$$–$$$ **Park Plaza Hotel.** Small and intimate, this 1922 establishment feels almost like a private home. The best accommodations are front garden suites with a living room that opens onto a balcony usually abloom with impatiens and bougainvillea. **Pros:** romantic; great balconies overlooking Park Avenue; shops and restaurants adjacent; in-house restaurant is in a brick-walled courtyard; Amtrak station is about a block away. **Cons:** the railroad tracks are a lot closer than the station, and you can sometimes hear train noise at night; no small children allowed; small rooms; Disney is 60 minutes away. *307 Park Ave. S, Winter Park* *407/647–1072 or 800/228–7220* *www.parkplazahotel.com* *27 rooms* *In-room: Wi-Fi. In-hotel: restaurant, room service, parking (free), laundry service, Wi-Fi hotspot, no kids under 5* *AE, DC, MC, V* *1:F1.*

5

Walt Disney World

ENJOYING THE WHOLE WORLD

WORD OF MOUTH

"If I had one day only, I would spend it in the Magic Kingdom. Epcot is nice but if you like rides and have never been to Disney, it has to be MK. Nothing beats it."

–Nyetzy

Join, Ask, Share. www.fodors.com/community/

WELCOME TO WALT DISNEY WORLD

Magic Kingdom.

TOP REASONS TO GO

★ **Nostalgia:** Face it—Mickey and company are old friends. And you probably have childhood pictures of yourself in front of Cinderella Castle. Even if you don't, nobody does yesteryear better: head to Main Street, U.S.A. or Hollywood Boulevard and see.

★ **Memories in the Making:** Who doesn't want to snap photos of Sis on the Dumbo ride or of Junior after his Splash Mountain experience? The urge to pass that Disney nostalgia on to the next generation is strong.

★ **The Thrills:** For some this means roller-coasting to an Aerosmith sound track or simulating space flight; for others it's about cascading down a water-slide or going on safari.

★ **The Chills:** If the Pirates of the Caribbean cave doesn't give you goose bumps, try the Haunted Mansion or Twilight Zone Tower of Terror.

★ **The Spectacle:** The list is long: fireworks, laser-light displays, arcade games, parades. . . .

1 Magic Kingdom. Disney's emblematic park is home to Space Mountain and Pirates of the Caribbean.

2 Epcot. Future World's focus is science, technology, and hands-on experiences. In the World Showcase, you can tour 11 countries without getting jet lagged.

3 Disney's Hollywood Studios. Attractions at this re-creation of old-time Hollywood include Rock 'n' Roller Coaster and Twilight Zone Tower of Terror.

4 Animal Kingdom. Amid a wildlife preserve are an Asian-themed water ride, an African safari ride, and shows.

5 6 Water Parks. Blizzard Beach's best (worst?) ride is the 55-mph dead-drop from Summit Plummet. Water babies love Typhoon Lagoon's Ketchakiddie Creek.

7 Downtown Disney. It's a shopping, dining, entertainment hub in three parts: the Marketplace, Pleasure Island, and the West Side.

8 Disney's BoardWalk. At this lakeside district, you can dine, shop, or cut a rug in an old-style dance hall.

9 Celebration. Disney's utopian residential community near Kissimmee recalls the Magic Kingdom's Main Street, U.S.A., but without swarms of tourists.

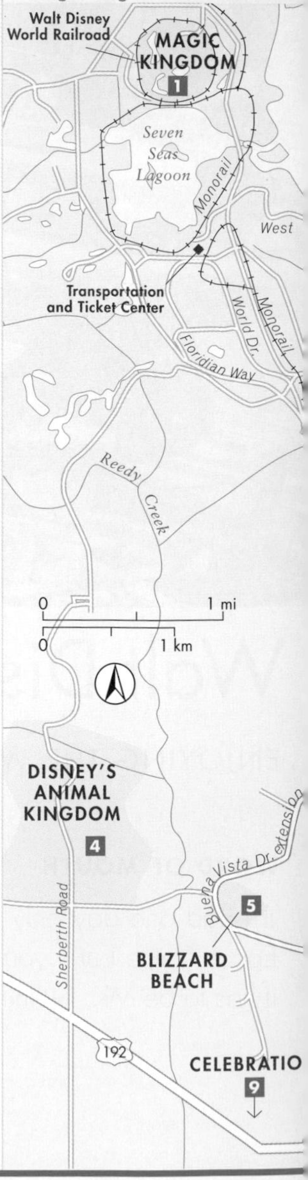

Magic Kingdom.

GETTING ORIENTED

Walt Disney World straddles Orange and Osceola counties to the west of Interstate 4. Four exits will get you to the parks and resort areas: 64B, 65, 67, and 68. To reach hotels along I-Drive use Exit 72, 74A, or 75A.

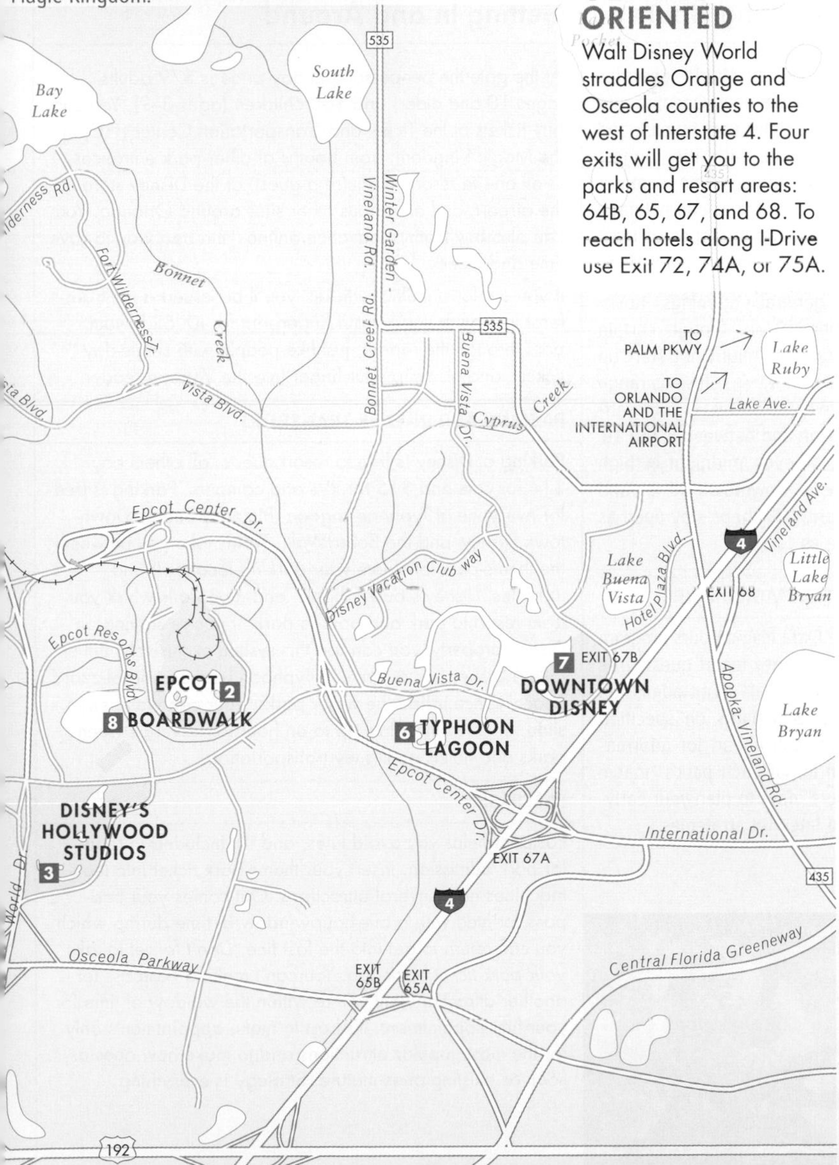

Bay Lake
South Lake
535
Wilderness Rd.
Fort Wilderness Tr.
Bonnet Creek
Vista Blvd.
Winter Garden - Vineland Rd.
Bonnet Creek Rd.
Buena Vista Dr.
Cypress Creek
TO PALM PKWY
TO ORLANDO AND THE INTERNATIONAL AIRPORT
Lake Ruby
Lake Ave.
435
Vineland Ave.
Epcot Center Dr.
Disney Vacation Club way
Lake Buena Vista
Hotel Plaza Blvd.
4
EXIT 68
Little Lake Bryan
Epcot Resorts Blvd.
7 EXIT 67B
EPCOT 2
DOWNTOWN DISNEY
8 BOARDWALK
Buena Vista Dr.
6 TYPHOON LAGOON
Apopka-Vineland Rd.
Lake Bryan
Epcot Center Dr.
DISNEY'S HOLLYWOOD STUDIOS
3
International Dr.
EXIT 67A
World Dr.
Osceola Parkway
EXIT 65B
EXIT 65A
Central Florida Greeneway
192

5

WALT DISNEY WORLD PLANNER

Operating Hours

Walt Disney World operates 365 days a year. Opening and closing times vary by park and by season, with the longest hours during prime summer months and year-end holidays. The parking lots open at least an hour before the parks do.

In general, openings hover around 9 AM, though certain attractions might not start up till 10 or 11 AM. Closings range between 5 and 8 PM in the off-season and between 8 and 10, 11, or even midnight in high season. Downtown Disney and BoardWalk shops stay open as late as 11 PM.

EXTRA MAGIC HOURS

The Extra Magic Hours program gives Disney resort guests free early and late-night admission to certain parks on specified days—call ahead for information about each park's "magic hours" days to plan your early- and late-visit strategies.

Shrek 4-D.

Getting In and Around

At the gate the per-person per-day price is $79 adults (ages 10 and older) and $68 children (ages 3–9). You can buy tickets at the Ticket and Transportation Center (TTC) in the Magic Kingdom, from booths at other park entrances, in all on-site resorts if you're a guest, at the Disney store in the airport, and at various other sites around Orlando. You can also buy them in advance online—the best way to save time and money.

If you opt for a multiday ticket, you'll be issued a nontransferable pass that uses your fingerprint for ID. Slide your pass through the reader, just like people with single-day tickets, and also slip your finger into the V-shape reader.

PARKING AND IN-PARK TRANSPORT

Parking at Disney is free to resort guests; all others pay $14 for cars and $15 for RVs and campers. Parking is free for everyone at Typhoon Lagoon, Blizzard Beach, Downtown Disney, and the BoardWalk. Trams take you between the theme-park lots (*note your parking location!*) and turnstiles. Disney's buses, boats, and monorails whisk you from resort to park and park to park. If you're staying on Disney property, you can use this system exclusively. Either take a Disney bus or drive to Typhoon Lagoon and Blizzard Beach. Once inside the water parks, your can walk, swim, slide, or chill out. Allow up to an hour for travel between parks and hotels on Disney transportation.

FASTPASS

Fastpass helps you avoid lines, and it's included in regular park admission. Insert your theme-park ticket into the machines near several attractions. Out comes your Fastpass, printed with a one-hour window of time during which you can return to get into the fast line. *Don't forget to take your park ticket back, too.* You can't make a Fastpass for another attraction until you're within the window of time for your first appointment. It's best to make appointments only for the most popular attractions and to make new ones as soon as existing ones mature. Strategy is everything.

Doing Disney Right

If you remember nothing else, keep in mind these essential strategies, tried and tested by generations of Disney fans.

- **Buy tickets before leaving home**. It saves money and gives you time to look into all the ticket options. It also offers an opportunity for you to consider vacation packages and meal plans. Before you can sing "M-I-C-K-E-Y" you'll be organized and ready for a fun, successful Disney trip.

- **Make dining reservations before leaving home.** If you don't, you might find yourself eating fast food (again) or leaving Disney for dinner. On-site restaurants, especially those featuring character appearances, book up fast.

- **Arrive at least 30 minutes before the parks open.** We know, it's your vacation and you want to sleep in. But you probably want to make the most of your time and money, too. Plan to be up by 7:30 am each day to get the most out of your park visits. After transit time, it'll take you 15-20 minutes to park, get to the gates, and pick up your park guide maps and *Times Guide*.

- **See top attractions in the morning.** And we mean *first thing.* Decide in advance on your can't-miss attractions, find their locations, and hotfoot it to them before 10 AM.

- **Use Fastpass.** Yes, use the Fastpass. It's worth saying twice. The system is free, easy, and it's your ticket to the top attractions with little or no waiting in line.

- **Use Baby Swap.** Disney has a theme-park "rider switch" policy that works like this: one parent waits with the baby or toddler while the other parent rides the attraction. When the ride ends, they switch places with minimal wait.

- **Build in rest time.** Who wants to become overly hot, tired, and grumpy? Start early and then leave the parks around 3 or 4 PM, thus avoiding the hottest and most crowded period. After a couple hours' rest at your hotel, head back for a nighttime spectacle or to ride a big-deal ride or two (lines often are shorter around closing time).

- **Create an itinerary, but leave room for spontaneity.** Decide which parks to see on each day, and know your priorities, but don't try to plot your trip hour by hour. If you're staying at a Disney resort, find out which parks have Extra Magic Hours on which days.

- **Eat at off hours.** To avoid the mealtime rush hours have a quick, light breakfast at 7 or 8 am, lunch at 11 am, and dinner at 5 or 6 pm.

Other Disney Services

If you don't mind shelling out $175–$315 an hour (with a six-hour minimum), you can take a customized **VIP Tour** with guides who help you park hop and get good seats at parades and shows. These tours don't help you skip lines, as at Universal, but they make navigating easy. Groups can have up to 10 people, and it pays to book up to three months ahead.

At character meals—breakfasts, lunches, or dinners—Mickey, Belle, or other characters sign autographs and pose for photos. Book through Disney's dining reservations line up to 180 days out; these hugging-and-feeding frenzies are wildly popular. They're also a good way to spend the morning on check-out day.

Disney Contacts

Dining Reservations: ☎ *407/939-3463*

Golf Reservations: ☎ *407/939-4653*

Guest Info: ☎ *407/824-4321*

VIP Tours: ☎ *407/560-4033*

WDW Travel Company: ☎ *407/939-1289*

Web: *www.disneyworld.com*

By Jennie Hess

Mickey Mouse. Tinker Bell. Cinderella. What would childhood be like without the magic of Disney? When kids (and let's be honest, adults, too) want to go to "the" theme park, they're heading to Disney. Here you're walking amid people from around the world and meeting characters like Snow White and Donald Duck while rides whirl nonstop and the irrepressible "It's a Small World" tune and lyrics run through your head. You can't help but believe dreams really do come true here.

The secret to enjoying Disney is to have a good plan and the flexibility to take detours when magical moments occur. You probably can persuade your children to rush to the big-deal rides early in the morning when timing matters most, but don't expect them to keep up that pace all day. Cushion your itinerary with extra time so they can pause when the spirit moves them. Let your motto be "quality over quantity." It's better to tour the parks in a relaxed fashion. Why disappoint your little ones by passing up the chance to hobnob with Princess Jasmine in your hurry to get to Pirates of the Caribbean—only to find a 30-minute wait at the ride entrance.

It's also important that your kids are involved in the vacation planning and are aware of the need for a park strategy. Let each family member choose one or two top rides or attractions for each park. Everything else should be icing on the cake. Run through the plan before you enter the park; if children know ahead of time that souvenirs are limited to one per person and that ice-cream snacks come after lunch, they're likely to be more patient than if they're clueless about your plans and dazzled by every merchandise cart they encounter.

DID YOU KNOW?

The quintessential Disney icon, the Cinderella Castle, was inspired by the palace built by the mad Bavarian king Ludwig II at Neuschwanstein. At 180 feet, it's 100 feet taller than Disneyland's Sleeping Beauty Castle.

THE MAGIC KINGDOM

ENTER A FAIRYTALE

The Magic Kingdom is the heart and soul of the Walt Disney World empire. It was the first Disney outpost in Florida when it opened in 1971, and it's the park that launched Disney's presence in France, Japan, and Hong Kong.

For a landmark that wields such worldwide influence, the 142-acre Magic Kingdom may seem small—indeed, Epcot is more than double the size of the Magic Kingdom, and Animal Kingdom is almost triple the size when including the park's expansive animal habitats. But looks can be deceiving. Packed into seven different "lands" are nearly 50 major crowd pleasers and that's not counting all the ancillary attractions: shops, eateries, live entertainment, character meet-and-greet spots, fireworks shows, and parades. Many rides are geared to the young, but the Magic Kingdom is anything but a kiddie park. The degree of detail, the greater vision, the surprisingly witty spiel of the guides, and the tongue-in-cheek signs that crop up in the oddest places—"Prince" and "Princess" restrooms in Fantasyland, for instance—all contribute to a delightful sense of discovery.

GETTING ORIENTED

The park is laid out on a north–south axis, with Cinderella Castle at the center and the various lands surrounding it in a broad circle.

As you pass underneath the railroad tracks, symbolically leaving behind the world of reality and entering a world of fantasy, you'll immediately notice the adorable buildings lining Town Square and Main Street, U.S.A., which runs due north and ends at the Hub (also called Central Plaza), in front of Cinderella Castle. If you're lost or have questions, cast members are available at almost every turn to help you.

TOP ATTRACTIONS

FOR AGES 7 AND UP

Big Thunder Mountain Railroad. An Old West–themed, classic coaster that's not too scary; it's just a really good, bumpy, swervy thrill.

Buzz Lightyear's Space Ranger Spin. A shoot-'em-up ride where space ranger wannabes compete for the highest score.

Mickey's PhilharMagic. The only 3-D film experience at Disney that features the main Disney characters and movie theme songs.

Space Mountain. The Magic Kingdom's scariest ride, recently renovated, zips you along the tracks in near-total darkness except for the stars.

Splash Mountain. A long, tame boat ride ends in a 52½-foot flume drop into a very wet briar patch.

Haunted Mansion. With its razzle-dazzle special effects, this classic is always a frightful hoot.

FOR AGES 6 AND UNDER

Goofy's Barnstormer. WDW's starter coaster for kids who may be tall enough to go on Big Thunder Mountain and Space Mountain but who aren't sure they can handle it.

Dumbo the Flying Elephant. The elephant ears get them every time—get in line very early or try later in the day.

The Magic Carpets of Aladdin. On this must-do for preschoolers you can make your carpet go up and down to avoid water spurts as mischievous camels spit at you.

The Many Adventures of Winnie the Pooh. Hang onto your honey pot as you get whisked along on a windy-day adventure with Pooh, Tigger, Eeyore, and friends.

Pirates of the Caribbean. Don't miss this waltz through pirate country, especially if you're a fan of the movies.

VISITING TIPS

- Try to come toward the end of the week, because most families hit the Magic Kingdom early in a visit.
- Ride a star attraction during a parade; lines ease considerably. (But be careful not to get stuck on the wrong side of the parade route when it starts, or you may never get across.)
- At City Hall, near the park's Town Square entrance, pick up a guide map and a *Times Guide*, which lists showtimes, character-greeting times, and hours for attractions and restaurants.
- Book character meals early. Main Street, U.S.A.'s **Crystal Palace Buffet** has breakfast, lunch, and dinner with Winnie the Pooh, Tigger, and friends. All three meals at the **Fairy Tale Dining** experience in Cinderella Castle are extremely popular—so much so that you should reserve your spot six months out. At a **Wonderland Tea Party** weekday afternoons in the Grand Floridian Resort, kids can interact with Alice and help decorate (and eat) cupcakes.

5

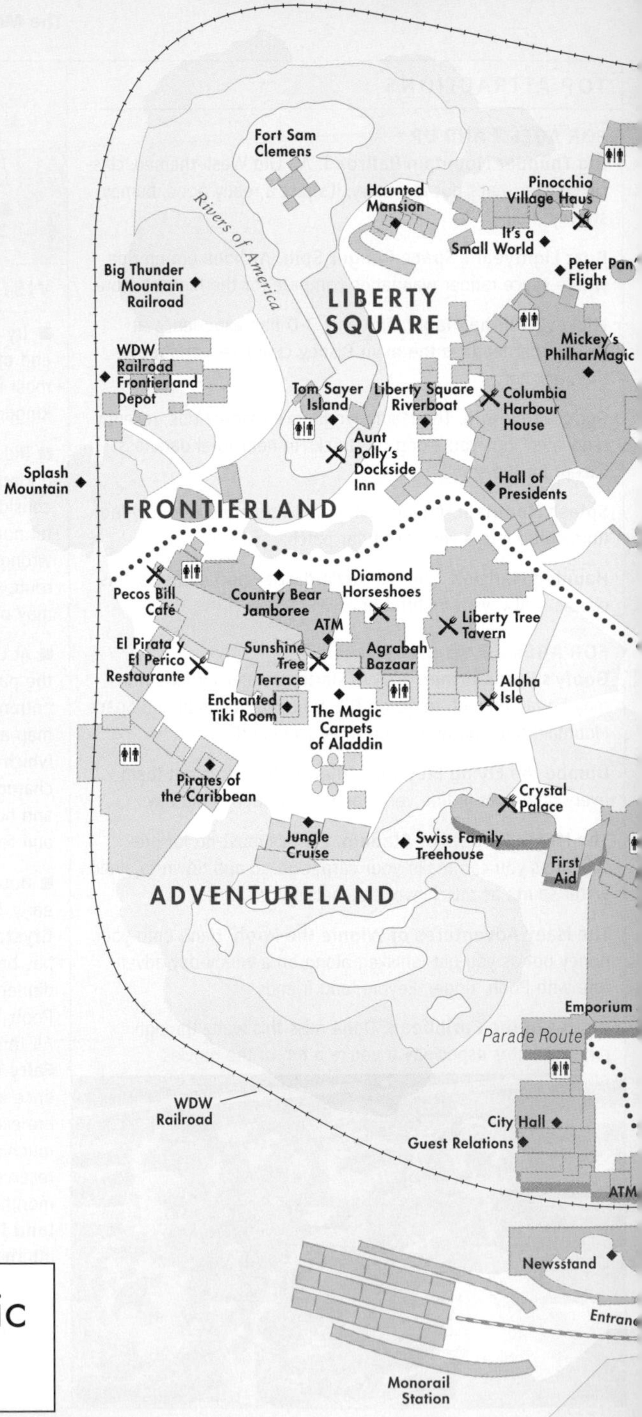

The Magic Kingdom

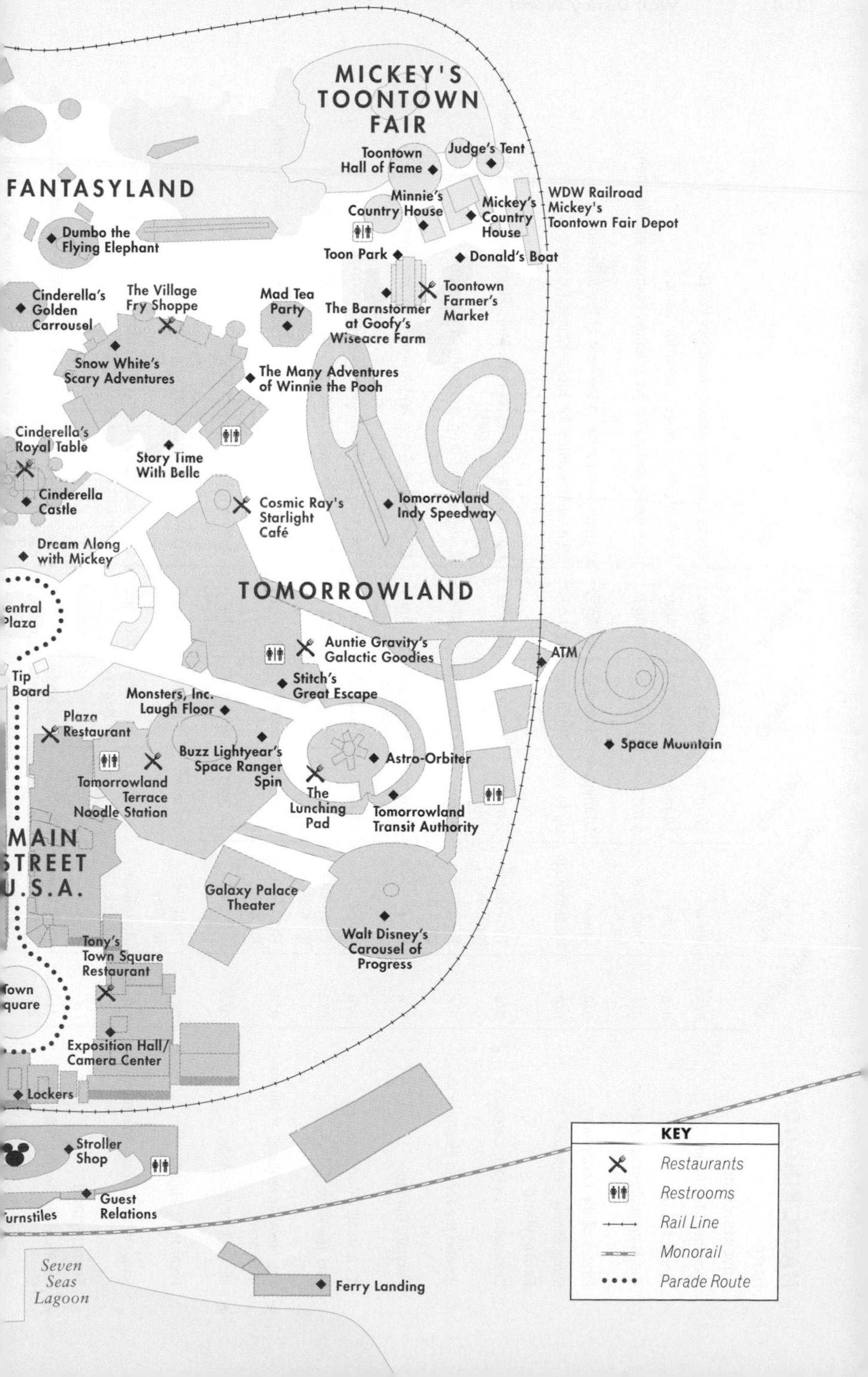

MICKEY'S TOONTOWN FAIR
Toontown Hall of Fame
Judge's Tent
FANTASYLAND
Minnie's Country House
Mickey's Country House
WDW Railroad Mickey's Toontown Fair Depot
Dumbo the Flying Elephant
Toon Park
Donald's Boat
Cinderella's Golden Carrousel
The Village Fry Shoppe
Mad Tea Party
The Barnstormer at Goofy's Wiseacre Farm
Toontown Farmer's Market
Snow White's Scary Adventures
The Many Adventures of Winnie the Pooh
Cinderella's Royal Table
Story Time With Belle
Cinderella Castle
Cosmic Ray's Starlight Café
Tomorrowland Indy Speedway
Dream Along with Mickey
TOMORROWLAND
entral Plaza
Auntie Gravity's Galactic Goodies
ATM
Tip Board
Stitch's Great Escape
Monsters, Inc. Laugh Floor
Plaza Restaurant
Space Mountain
Buzz Lightyear's Space Ranger Spin
Astro-Orbiter
Tomorrowland Terrace Noodle Station
The Lunching Pad
Tomorrowland Transit Authority
MAIN STREET U.S.A.
Galaxy Palace Theater
Walt Disney's Carousel of Progress
Tony's Town Square Restaurant
Town Square
Exposition Hall/ Camera Center
Lockers
Stroller Shop
Guest Relations
urnstiles
Seven Seas Lagoon
Ferry Landing
KEY
Restaurants
Restrooms
Rail Line
Monorail
Parade Route

MAGIC KINGDOM

NAME	Height Req.	Type of Entertainment	Duration	Crowds	Audience	Tips
Adventureland						
Enchanted Tiki Room	n/a	Show	12 mins.	Light	All Ages	Come when you need a refresher in a/c.
Jungle Cruise	n/a	Cruise	10 mins.	Heavy	All Ages	Use Fastpass or come during the parade.
The Magic Carpets of Aladdin	n/a	Thrill Ride for Kids	3 mins.	Heavy	All Ages	Visit while waiting for Frontierland Fastpass appointment.
Pirates of the Caribbean	n/a	Cruise	10 mins.	Moderate	All Ages	A good destination in the heat of the afternoon.
Swiss Family Treehouse	n/a	Walk-through	Up to you	Moderate	All Ages	Visit while waiting for Jungle Cruise Fastpass.
Fantasyland						
Cinderella's Golden Carrousel	n/a	Thrill Ride for Kids	2 mins.	Moderate to Heavy	Families	Come while waiting for Peter Pan's Flight Fastpass, during afternoon parade, or after dark.
Dumbo the Flying Elephant	n/a	Thrill Ride for Kids	2 mins.	Moderate to Heavy	Small Kids	Come at rope drop. No shade in afternoon.
Fairytale Garden	n/a	Show	25 mins.	Moderate to Heavy	All Ages	Check *Times Guide*, and arrive early for a bench.
it's a small world	n/a	Cruise	11 mins.	Moderate	All Ages	Tots may beg for a repeat ride; it's worth it.
Mad Tea Party	n/a	Thrill Ride for Kids	2 mins.	Moderate	Small Kids	Come in the early morning. Skip it if wait is 30 mins.
★ The Many Adventures of Winnie the Pooh	n/a	Thrill Ride for Kids	3½ mins.	Heavy	All Ages	Use Fastpass. Come early, late in the afternoon, or after dark.
★ Mickey's PhilharMagic	n/a	3-D Film	12 mins.	Heavy	All but Small Kids	Use Fastpass or arrive early or during a parade.
Peter Pan's Flight	n/a	Thrill Ride for Kids	2½ mins.	Heavy	All Ages	Try evening or early morning. Use Fastpass first.
Snow White's Scary Adventures	n/a	Thrill Ride for Kids	3 mins.	Moderate to Heavy	All Ages	Come very early, during the afternoon parade, or after dark. May scare toddlers and pre-schoolers.
Frontierland						
★ Big Thunder Mountain Railroad	At least 40"	Thrill Ride	4 mins.	Absolutely!	All but Small Kids	Use Fastpass. Most exciting at night when you can't anticipate the curves.
Country Bear Jamboree	n/a	Show	17 mins.	Heavy	All Ages	Visit before 11 am. Stand to the far left lining up for the front rows

★ Splash Mountain	At least 40″	Thrill Ride with Water	11 mins.	Yes!	All but Small Kids	Use Fastpass. Get in line by 9:45 am, or ride during meal or parade time. You may get wet.
Tom Sawyer Island	n/a	Playground	Up to you	Light	Kids and Tweens	Afternoon refresher. It's hard to keep track of toddlers here.
Liberty Square						
Hall of Presidents	n/a	Show/Film	25 mins.	Moderate	All but Small Kids	Come in the morning or during the parade.
★ Haunted Mansion	n/a	Thrill Ride	8 mins.	Moderate	All Ages	Nighttime adds extra fear factor.
Liberty Square Riverboat	n/a	Cruise	15 mins.	Light to Moderate	All Ages	Good for a break from the crowds.
Main Street U.S.A.						
Walt Disney World Railroad	n/a	Railroad	21 mins.	Moderate to Heavy	All Ages	Board with small children for an early start in Toontown or hop on midafternoon.
Mickey's Toontown Fair						
The Barnstormer at Goofy's Wiseacre Farm	At least 35″	Thrill Ride for Kids	1 min.	Moderate to Heavy	Small Kids	Come during evening if your child can wait.
Tomorrowland						
Astro-Orbiter	n/a	Thrill Ride for Kids	2 mins.	Moderate to Heavy	All Ages	Skip unless there's a short line.
★ Buzz Lightyear's Space Ranger Spin	n/a	Interactive Exp.	5 mins.	Heavy	All Ages	Come in the early morning and use Fastpass. Kids will want more than one ride.
Monster's Inc. Laugh Floor	n/a	Film	15 mins.	Moderate to Heavy	All Ages	Come when you're waiting for your Buzz Lightyear or Space Mountain Fastpass.
★ Space Mountain	At least 44″	Thrill Ride	2½ mins.	You Bet!	All but Small Kids	Use Fastpass, or come at the beginning or the end of day or during a parade.
Stitch's Great Escape	At least 40″	Simulator Exp.	20 mins.	Moderate to Heavy	All but Small Kids	Use Fastpass. Visit early after Space Mountain, Splash Mountain, Big Thunder Mountain, or during a parade.
Tomorrowland Indy Speedway	54″ to drive	Thrill Ride for Kids	5 mins.	Moderate	All but Small Kids	Come in the evening or during a parade; skip on a first-time visit; 32″ height requirement to ride shotgun.
Tomorrowland Transit Authority	n/a	Railroad	10 mins.	Light	All Ages	Come with young kids if you need a restful ride.
Walt Disney's Carousel of Progress	n/a	Show	20 mins.	Light to Moderate	All Ages	Skip on a first-time visit unless you're heavily into nostalgia.

★ = Fodor's Choice

EPCOT

TRAVEL THE GLOBE

EPCOT BY BOAT

Epcot is a big place at 305 acres; a local joke suggests that the acronym actually stands for "Every Person Comes Out Tired." But still, the most efficient way to get around is to walk.

To vary things, you can cruise across the lagoon in an air-conditioned, 65-foot water taxi; they depart every 12 minutes from two World Showcase Plaza docks at the border of Future World.

The boat closer to Mexico zips to a dock by the Germany pavilion; the one closer to Canada heads to Morocco. You may have to stand in line to board, however.

Nowhere but at Epcot can you explore and experience the native food, entertainment, culture, and arts and crafts of countries in Europe, Asia, North Africa, and the Americas. What's more, employees at the World Showcase pavilions actually hail from the countries the pavilions represent.

Epcot, or "Experimental Prototype Community of Tomorrow," was the original inspiration for Walt Disney World. Walt envisioned a future in which nations coexisted in peace and harmony, reaping the miraculous harvest of technological achievement. The Epcot of today is both more and less than his original dream. Less, because the World Showcase presents views of its countries that are, as an Epcot guide once put it, "as Americans perceive them"—highly idealized. But this is a minor quibble in the face of the major achievement: Epcot is that rare paradox—a successful educational theme park that excels at entertainment, too.

GETTING ORIENTED

Epcot is composed of two areas: Future World and the World Showcase. The inner core of Future World's pavilions has the Spaceship Earth geosphere and a plaza anchored by the computer-animated Fountain of Nations. Bracketing it are the crescent-shaped Innoventions East and West, with hands-on, high-tech exhibits, and immersion entertainment.

Six pavilions compose Future World's outer ring. Each of the three east pavilions has a ride and the occasional post-ride showcase; a visit rarely takes more than 30 minutes. The blockbuster exhibits on the west side contain rides and interactive displays; each exhibit requires at least 90 minutes.

World Showcase pavilions are on the promenade that circles the World Showcase Lagoon. Each houses shops, restaurants, and friendly foreign staffers; some have films or displays. Mexico and Norway offer tame rides. Entertainment is scheduled at every pavilion except Norway.

TOP ATTRACTIONS

Soarin'. Everyone's hands-down favorite: feel the sweet breeze as you "hang glide" over California landscapes.

The American Adventure. Many adults and older children love this patriotic look at American history; who can resist the Audio-Animatronics hosts, Ben Franklin and Mark Twain?

Honey, I Shrunk the Audience. You've gotta watch out when you're in the same room as clumsy inventor Wayne Szalinski.

IllumiNations. This amazing musical laser-fountains-and-fireworks show is Disney nighttime entertainment at its best.

Mission: SPACE. Blast off on a simulated ride to Mars, if you can handle the turbulence.

Test Track. Your car revs up to 60 mph on a hairpin turn in this wild ride on a General Motors proving ground.

MIND GAMES

Although several attractions provide high-octane kicks, Epcot's thrills are mostly for the mind. The park is best for school-age children and adults, but there's interactive entertainment for everyone at Innoventions. And most attractions provide some diversions for preschool children. At the 15 or so **Kidcot Fun Stops**, younger children can try their hands at crafts projects—like designing a mask and adding special touches at each pavilion along the way.

VISITING TIPS

■ Epcot is so vast and varied, you really need two days to explore. With just one day, you'll have to be highly selective.

■ Go early in the week, when others are at Magic Kingdom.

■ If you like a good festival, visit during the International Flower & Garden Festival (early to mid-March through May) or the International Food & Wine Festival (late September through mid-November).

5

Epcot

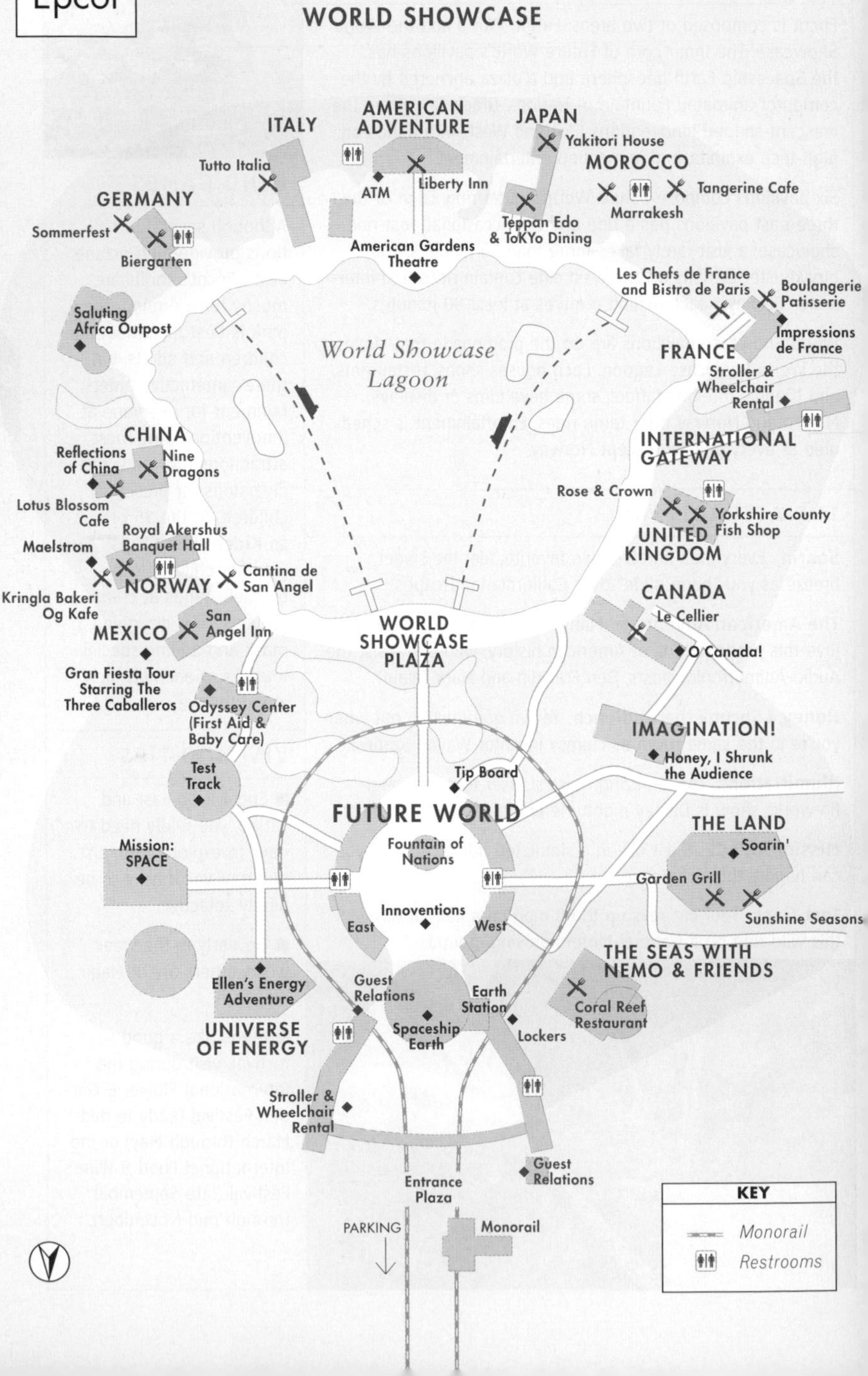
WORLD SHOWCASE
ITALY
AMERICAN ADVENTURE
JAPAN
Yakitori House
MOROCCO
Tutto Italia
ATM
Liberty Inn
Tangerine Cafe
Marrakesh
GERMANY
Sommerfest
Biergarten
Teppan Edo & ToKYo Dining
American Gardens Theatre
Les Chefs de France and Bistro de Paris
Boulangerie Patisserie
Saluting Africa Outpost
Impressions de France
World Showcase Lagoon
FRANCE
Stroller & Wheelchair Rental
CHINA
Reflections of China
Nine Dragons
INTERNATIONAL GATEWAY
Lotus Blossom Cafe
Rose & Crown
Yorkshire County Fish Shop
Royal Akershus Banquet Hall
Maelstrom
UNITED KINGDOM
Cantina de San Angel
NORWAY
Kringla Bakeri Og Kafe
CANADA
San Angel Inn
MEXICO
WORLD SHOWCASE PLAZA
Le Cellier
O Canada!
Gran Fiesta Tour Starring The Three Caballeros
Odyssey Center (First Aid & Baby Care)
IMAGINATION!
Honey, I Shrunk the Audience
Test Track
Tip Board
FUTURE WORLD
THE LAND
Soarin'
Fountain of Nations
Mission: SPACE
Garden Grill
Sunshine Seasons
Innoventions
East
West
THE SEAS WITH NEMO & FRIENDS
Ellen's Energy Adventure
Guest Relations
Earth Station
Coral Reef Restaurant
UNIVERSE OF ENERGY
Spaceship Earth
Lockers
Stroller & Wheelchair Rental
Guest Relations
Entrance Plaza
KEY
Monorail
Restrooms
PARKING
Monorail

DID YOU KNOW?

Walt Disney's original conception for the Epcot Center—as a sort of futuristic master-planned community—didn't quite pan out in the park but instead took form in the town of Celebration, near Kissimmee.

EPCOT

NAME	Height Req.	Type of Entertainment	Duration	Crowds	Audience	Tips
Future World						
The Circle of Life (The Land)	n/a	Film	20 mins.	Moderate to Heavy	All but Small Kids	Come early or for your toddler's afternoon nap.
Ellen's Energy Adventure (Universe of Energy)	n/a	Ride-Through	45 mins.	Moderate	All Ages	Best seats are to the far left and front of the theater.
Honey, I Shrunk the Audience (Imagination!)	n/a	3-D Film	14 mins.	Moderate to Heavy	All Ages	Come in the early morning or just before closing. Take off the 3-D glasses if little kids get scared.
Innoventions	n/a	Walk-Through	Up to you	Moderate to Heavy	All Ages	Come before 11 am or after 2 pm.
Journey into Imagination with Figment (Imagination!)	n/a	Ride-Through	8 mins.	Light	Small Kids	Ride while waiting for Honey, I Shrunk the Audience Fastpass. Warn toddlers about darkness at the end of the ride.
Living with the Land (The Land)	n/a	Cruise	14 mins.	Moderate	All but Small Kids	The line moves quickly, so come anytime.
★ Mission: SPACE	At least 44"	Thrill Ride	4 mins.	You Bet!	All but Small Kids	Come before 10 am or use Fastpass. Don't ride on a full stomach.
The Seas with Nemo & Friends	n/a	Ride- and Walk-Through	Up to you	Moderate to Heavy	Small Kids	Get Nemo fans here early in the morning.

★ Soarin' (The Land)	At least 40"	Simulator Ride	5 mins.	Heavy	All but Small Kids	Use Fastpass, or come early, or just before closing.
Spaceship Earth	n/a	Ride-Through	15 mins.	Moderate to Heavy	All Ages	Ride while waiting for Mission: SPACE Fastpass appointment or just before closing.
★ Test Track	At least 40"	Thrill Ride	5 mins.	Heavy	All but Small Kids	Come in morning with Fastpass. The ride can't function on wet tracks, so don't come after a downpour.
World Showcase						
★ The American Adventure Show	n/a	Show/Film	20 mins.	Heavy	All Ages	Arrive 10 mins. before the Voices of Liberty or the Spirit of America Fife & Drum Corps are slated to perform.
America Gardens Theatre	n/a	Live Show	Varies	Varies	Varies	Arrive an hour or so ahead of time for holiday and celebrity performances.
Gran Fiesta Tour Starring the Three Caballeros	n/a	Cruise	9 mins.	Moderate to Heavy	All Ages	Especially good if you have small children.
Impressions de France	n/a	Film	20 mins.	Moderate	All but Small Kids	Come after dinner.
Maelstrom	n/a	Thrill Ride for Kids with Water	10 mins.	Moderate to Heavy	All Ages	Use Fastpass for after lunch or dinner.
O Canada!	n/a	Film	14 mins.	Moderate to Heavy	All Ages	Come when World Showcase opens or in the evening. No strollers permitted.
Reflections of China	n/a	Film	14 mins.	Moderate	All Ages	Come anytime. No strollers permitted.

★ = Fodor's Choice

HOLLYWOOD STUDIOS

MAKE MOVIE MAGIC

Disney's Hollywood Studios were designed to be a trip back to Tinseltown's Golden Age, when Hedda Hopper, not tabloids, spread celebrity gossip and when the girl off the bus from Ohio could be the next Judy Garland.

The result is a theme park that blends movie-production capabilities and high-tech wonders with breathtaking rides and nostalgia. The park's old-time Hollywood ambience begins with a rosy-hued view of the movie-making business presented in a dreamy stage set from the 1930s and '40s, amid sleek Art Moderne buildings in pastel colors, funky diners, kitschy decorations, and sculptured gardens populated by roving actors playing, well, roving actors. There are also casting directors, gossip columnists, and other colorful characters.

Thanks to a rich library of film scores, the park is permeated with music, all familiar, all evoking the magic of the movies, and all constantly streaming from the camouflaged loudspeakers at a volume just right for humming along. The park icon, a 122-foot-high Sorcerer Mickey Hat that serves as a gift shop and Disney pin-trading station, towers over Hollywood Boulevard.

WELCOME TO THE 'HOODS

The park is divided into sightseeing clusters. **Hollywood Boulevard** is the main artery to the heart of the park and is where you find the glistening replica of Graumann's Chinese Theater.

Encircling it are **Sunset Boulevard**, the **Animation Courtyard, Pixar Place, Commissary Lane, the Streets of America area**, and **Echo Lake**.

The entire park is 135 acres and has just 20 major attractions (compared with Magic Kingdom's 40-plus). It's small enough to cover in a day and even repeat a favorite ride or two.

TOP ATTRACTIONS

FOR AGES 8 AND UP

The Twilight Zone Tower of Terror. The TV-classic theming of this free-fall "elevator" screamer is meticulous.

Indiana Jones Epic Stunt Spectacular! The show's Indy double and supporting cast re-enact *Raiders of the Lost Ark* scenes with panache.

Toy Story Midway Mania! 3-D glasses? Check. Spring-action shooter? Check. Ride and shoot your way through with Buzz, Woody, and others.

The Magic of Disney Animation. Take a behind-the-scenes look at the making of Disney films.

Rock 'n' Roller Coaster Starring Aerosmith. Blast off to rockin' tunes on a high-speed, hard-core coaster.

The American Idol Experience. If you don't get chosen to test your pipes, you can vote for your favorite Idol wannabe.

FOR AGES 7 AND UNDER

Block Party Bash. It's a high-energy, interactive parade where you can play along with the toys from *Toy Story* or shout it out with Mike and Sully of *Monsters, Inc.*

Honey I Shrunk the Kids Movie Set Adventure. Youngsters love to romp among the giant blades of grass and bugs at this imaginative playground.

MuppetVision 3-D. Children (and most adults) shriek with laughter during this 3-D movie involving Kermit, Miss Piggy, and other lovable Muppets.

Playhouse Disney—Live on Stage! The preschool crowd can't get enough of the characters here from Disney Channel shows like "Mickey Mouse Clubhouse" and "Little Einsteins."

Beauty and the Beast—Live on Stage. Watch the dinnerware spring to life in this stage show performed in an open-air theater.

VISITING TIPS

Visit early in the week, when most people are at Magic Kingdom and Animal Kingdom.

Check the tip board periodically for attractions with short wait times to visit between Fastpass appointments.

■ Be at the Fantasmic! amphitheater at least an hour before showtime if you didn't book the dinner package.

■ Need a burst of energy? On-the-run hunger pangs? Grab a slice at Pizza Planet Arcade at **Streets of America**. Alternatively, **Hollywood Scoops Ice Cream** on Sunset is the place to be on a hot day.

■ If you're planning on a fast-food lunch, eat before 11 AM or after 2:30 PM. There are quick-bite spots are all over the park and several stands along Sunset. Get a burger (meat or veggie) or chicken strips at **Rosie's All-American Cafe,** a slice of pizza from **Catalina Eddie's,** or a hunk of smoked bird at **Toluca Legs Turkey Co.**

5

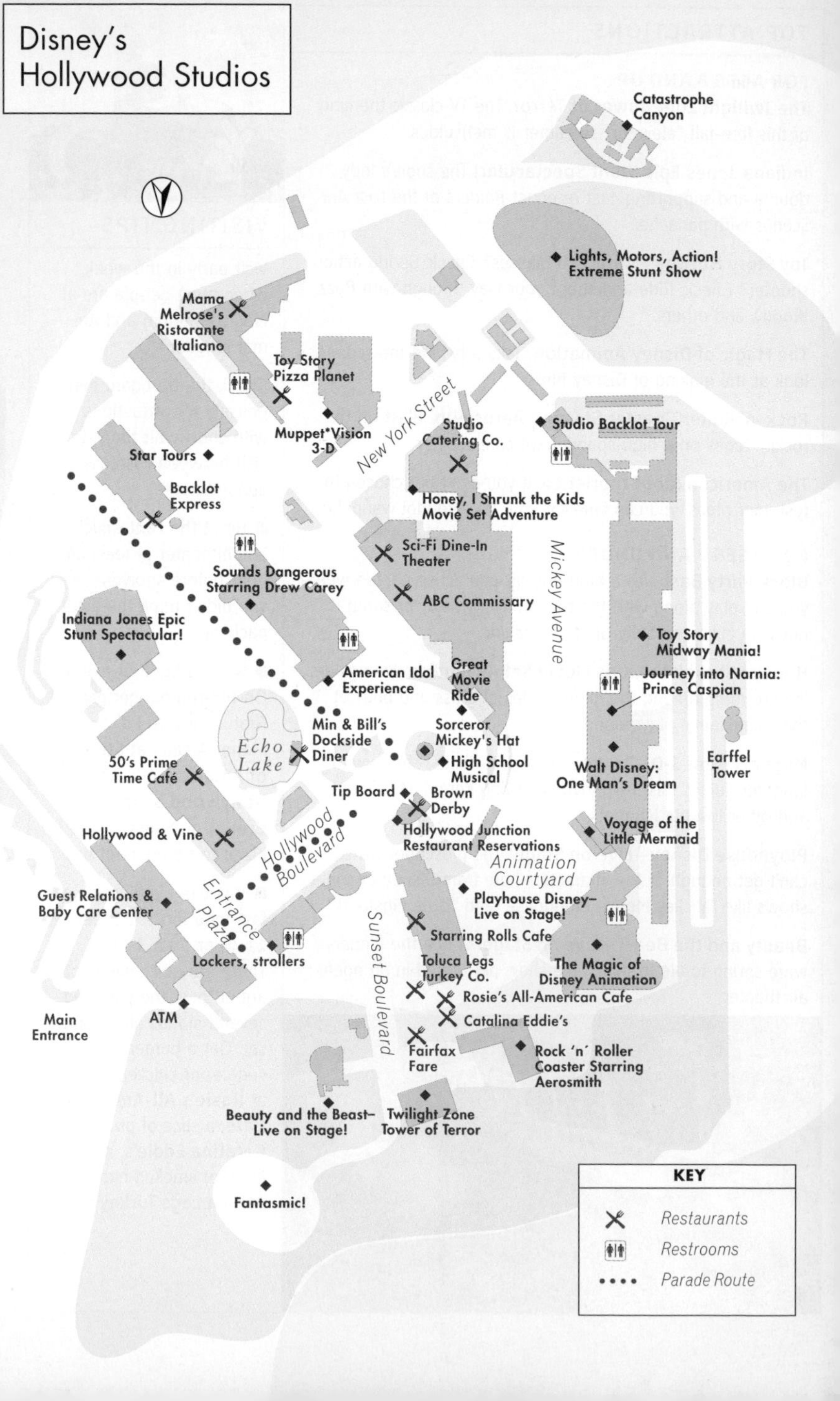
Disney's Hollywood Studios
Catastrophe Canyon
Lights, Motors, Action! Extreme Stunt Show
Mama Melrose's Ristorante Italiano
Toy Story Pizza Planet
Muppet*Vision 3-D
New York Street
Studio Catering Co.
Studio Backlot Tour
Star Tours
Backlot Express
Honey, I Shrunk the Kids Movie Set Adventure
Sci-Fi Dine-In Theater
Mickey Avenue
Sounds Dangerous Starring Drew Carey
ABC Commissary
Indiana Jones Epic Stunt Spectacular!
Toy Story Midway Mania!
American Idol Experience
Great Movie Ride
Journey into Narnia: Prince Caspian
Min & Bill's Dockside Diner
Echo Lake
Sorceror Mickey's Hat
High School Musical
Earffel Tower
50's Prime Time Café
Walt Disney: One Man's Dream
Tip Board
Brown Derby
Hollywood & Vine
Hollywood Boulevard
Hollywood Junction Restaurant Reservations
Voyage of the Little Mermaid
Animation Courtyard
Guest Relations & Baby Care Center
Entrance Plaza
Playhouse Disney–Live on Stage!
Sunset Boulevard
Starring Rolls Cafe
Lockers, strollers
Toluca Legs Turkey Co.
The Magic of Disney Animation
Rosie's All-American Cafe
Main Entrance
ATM
Catalina Eddie's
Fairfax Fare
Rock 'n' Roller Coaster Starring Aerosmith
Beauty and the Beast–Live on Stage!
Twilight Zone Tower of Terror
Fantasmic!
KEY
Restaurants
Restrooms
Parade Route

DID YOU KNOW?

MGM's film *The Wizard of Oz*, released in 1939, used the Technicolor process—making Dorothy's ruby-red slippers really stand out!

DISNEY'S HOLLYWOOD STUDIOS

NAME	Height Req.	Type of Entertainment	Duration	Crowds	Audience	Tips
Animation Courtyard						
Journey Into Narnia: Prince Caspian	n/a	Walk-Through/ Film	15 mins.	Light	All but Small Kids	Come while waiting for Fastpass appointment.
The Magic of Disney Animation	n/a	Tour	15+ mins.	Moderate	All Ages	Come in the morning or late afternoon. Toddlers may get bored.
Playhouse Disney— Live on Stage!	n/a	Show	22 mins.	Moderate to Heavy	Small Kids	Come first thing in the morning, when your child is most alert and lines are shorter.
Voyage of the Little Mermaid	n/a	Show	17 mins.	Heavy	All Ages	Come first thing in the morning. Otherwise, wait until after 5.
Walt Disney: One Man's Dream	n/a	Walk-Through/ Film	20+ mins.	Light to Moderate	All but Small Kids	See this attraction while waiting for a Fastpass appointment.
Echo Lake						
The American Idol Experience	n/a	Show	25 mins./ 45 mins.	Yes!	All but Small Kids	Check *Times Guide*, for showtimes. Arrive at least 30 minutes early for seats inside the theater.
Indiana Jones Epic Stunt Spectacular!	n/a	Show	30 mins.	Moderate to Heavy	All but Small Kids	Come at night, when the idol's eyes glow. Sit up front to feel the heat of a truck on fire.
Sounds Dangerous Starring Drew Carey	n/a	Show	12 mins.	Moderate	All but Small Kids	Arrive 15 minutes before show. You sit in total darkness.
Star Tours	At least 40"	Simulator Exp.	5 mins.	Moderate to Heavy	All but Small Kids	Come before closing, early morning, or get a Fastpass. Keep to the left in line for the best seats.
Hollywood Boulevard						
Great Movie Ride	n/a	Ride/Tour	22 mins.	Moderate	All but Small Kids	Come while waiting for Fastpass appointment. Lines out the door mean 25-min. wait—or longer.

Pixar Place						
Toy Story Midway Mania!	n/a	Interactive Ride	7 mins.	Heavy	All Ages	Come early; use Fastpass.
Streets of America						
Honey, I Shrunk the Kids Movie Set Adventure	n/a	Playground	Up to you	Moderate	Small Kids	Come after you've done several shows and your kids need to cut loose. Keep an eye on toddlers who can quickly get lost in the caves and slides.
Lights, Motors, Action! Extreme Stunt Show	n/a	Show	33 mins.	Heavy	All but Small Kids	For the best seats, line up for the show while others are lining up for the parade.
Muppet*Vision 3-D	n/a	3-D Film	25 mins.	Moderate to Heavy	All Ages	Arrive 10 mins. early. And don't worry—there are no bad seats.
Studio Backlot Tour	n/a	Tour	35 mins.	Moderate	All but Small Kids	People sitting on the left can get wet. Come early; it closes at dusk.
Sunset Boulevard						
Beauty and the Beast— Live on Stage!	n/a	Show	30 mins.	Moderate to Heavy	All Ages	Come 30 mins. before showtime for good seats. Performance days vary, so check ahead.
★ Rock 'n' Roller Coaster Starring Aerosmith	At least 48"	Thrill Ride	1 min., 22 secs.	Huge	All but Small Kids	Ride early, then use Fastpass for another go later.
★ Twilight Zone Tower of Terror	At least 40"	Thrill Ride	10 mins.	You Bet!	All but Small Kids	Use Fastpass. Come early or late evening.

★ = Fodor's Choice

ANIMAL KINGDOM

GO ON SAFARI

Disney's Animal Kingdom explores the stories of all animals—real, imaginary, and extinct. Enter through the Oasis, where you hear exotic background music and find yourself surrounded by gentle waterfalls and gardens alive with exotic birds, reptiles, and mammals.

At 403 acres and several times the size of the Magic Kingdom, Animal Kingdom is the largest in area of all Disney theme parks. Animal habitats take up much of that acreage. Creatures here thrive in careful re-creations of landscapes from Asia and Africa. Throughout the park, you'll also learn about conservation in a low-key way.

Amid all the nature are thrill rides, a 3-D show (housed in the "root system" of the iconic Tree of Life), two first-rate musicals, and character meet and greets. Cast members are as likely to hail from Kenya or South Africa as they are from Kentucky or South Carolina. It's all part of the charm.

GETTING ORIENTED

Animal Kingdom's hub is the Tree of Life, in the middle of Discovery Island. The park's lands, each with a distinct personality, radiate from Discovery Island.

To the southwest is Camp Minnie-Mickey, a character-greeting location and live-show area. North of the hub is Africa, where Kilimanjaro Safaris travel across extensive savanna. In the northeast corner is Rafiki's Planet Watch and conservation activities.

Asia, with thrills like Expedition Everest and Kali River Rapids, is east of the hub, and DinoLand U.S.A. brings T. rex and other prehistoric creatures to life in the park's southeast corner.

TOP ATTRACTIONS

DISCOVERY ISLAND

Tree of Life—It's Tough to Be a Bug! This clever and very funny 3-D movie starring Flik from the Disney film *A Bug's Life* is full of surprises, including "shocking" special effects. Some kids under 7 are scared of the loud noises.

AFRICA

Festival of the Lion King. Singers and dancers dressed in fantastic costumes representing many wild animals perform uplifting dance and acrobatics numbers and interact with children in the audience.

Kilimanjaro Safaris. You're guaranteed to see dozens of wild animals, including giraffes, zebras, hippos, rhinos, and elephants, living in authentic, re-created African habitats. If you're lucky, the lions and cheetahs will be stirring, too.

ASIA

Expedition Everest. The Animal Kingdom's cleverly themed roller coaster is a spine-tingling trip into the snowy Himalayas to find the abominable snowman. It's best reserved for brave riders 7 and up.

Kali River Rapids. You and seven fellow adventurers raft through rapids, waterfalls, and other features. Stow stuff in lockers, and wear ponchos—you're going to get wet.

DINOLAND, U.S.A.

DINOSAUR. Extremely lifelike giant dinosaurs jump out as your vehicle swoops and dips. We recommend it for fearless kids 8 and up.

Finding Nemo—The Musical. Don't miss a performance of this outstanding musical starring the most charming, colorful characters ever to swim their way into your heart.

VISITING TIPS

- Try to visit during the week. Pedestrian areas are compact, and the park can feel uncomfortably packed on weekends.
- Plan on a full day here. That way, while exploring Africa's Pangani Forest Exploration Trail, say, you can spend 10 minutes (rather than just two) watching vigilant meerkats stand sentry or tracking a mama gorilla as she cares for her infant.
- Arrive a half hour before the park opens as much to see the wild animals at their friskiest (morning is a good time to do the safari ride) as to get a jump on the crowds.
- For updates on line lengths, check the Tip Board, just after crossing the bridge into Discovery Island.
- Good places to rendezvous include the outdoor seating area of Tusker House restaurant in Africa, in front of DinoLand U.S.A.'s Boneyard, and at the entrance to Festival of the Lion King at Camp Minnie-Mickey.

DID YOU KNOW?

Hakuna matata, the name of a song in Disney's *The Lion King*, is Swahili for "No problems." Tim Rice wrote the song, and Elton John sings it. Animal Kingdom presents its Festival of the Lion King show at Camp Minnie-Mickey.

Disney's Animal Kingdom

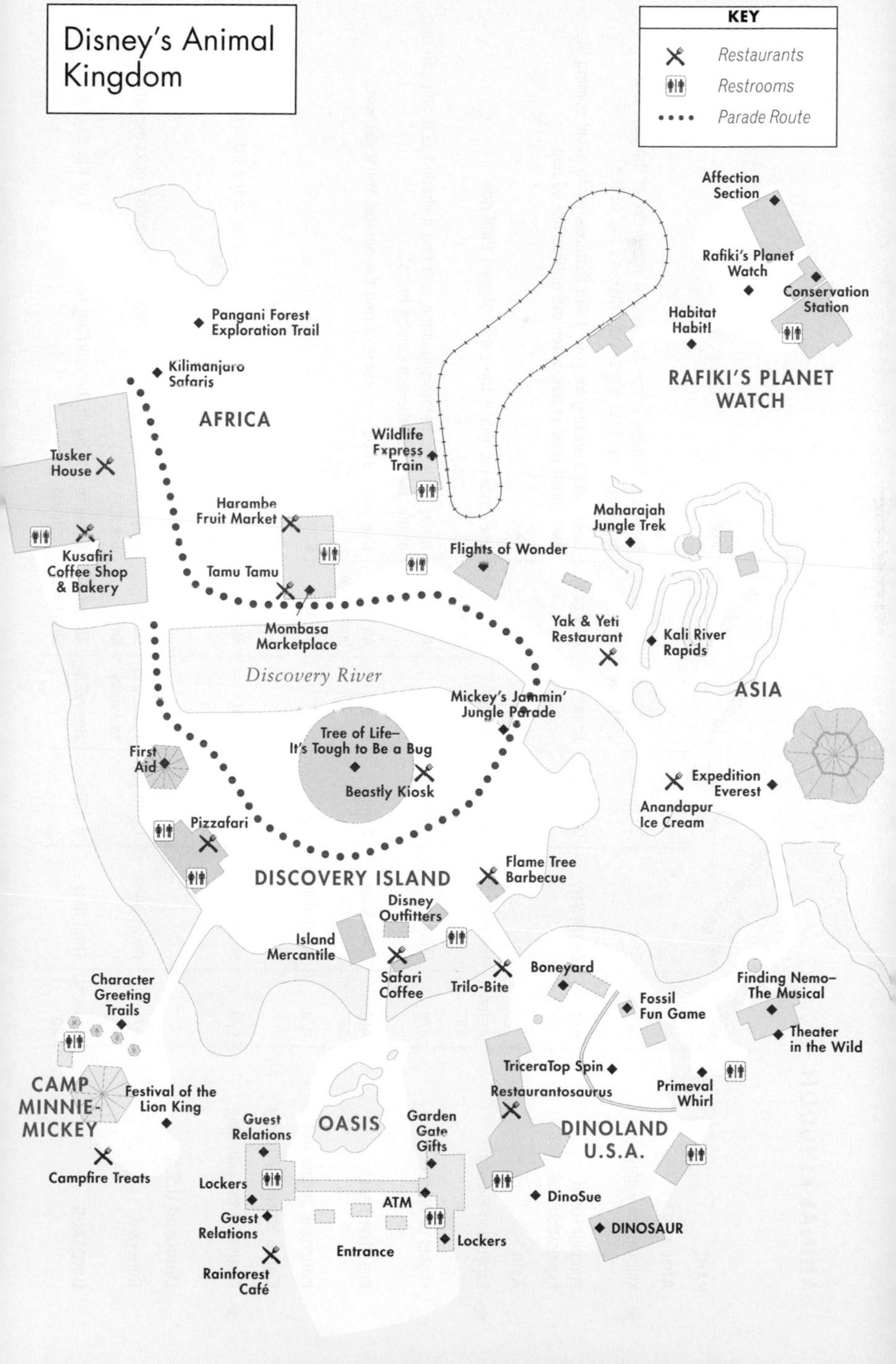

ANIMAL KINGDOM

NAME	Height Req.	Type of Entertainment	Duration	Crowds	Audience	Tips
Africa						
★ Kilimanjaro Safaris	n/a	Tour	20 mins.	Moderate to Heavy	All Ages	Do this first thing in the morning. If you arrive at the park late morning, save it for day's end, when it's not so hot.
Pangani Forest Exploration Trail	n/a	Zoo/Aviary	Up to you	Light	All Ages	Come while waiting for your safari Fastpass; try to avoid coming at the hottest time of day, when the gorillas like to nap.
Asia						
★ Expedition Everest	At least 44″	Thrill Ride	2½ mins.	Huge	All but Small Kids	Use Fastpass. This is the park's biggest thrill ride.
Flights of Wonder	n/a	Show	30 mins.	Light	All Ages	Arrive 15 mins. before showtime, and find a shaded seat beneath one of the awnings—the sun can be brutal.
Kali River Rapids	At least 38″	Thrill Ride	7 mins.	Heavy	All but Small Kids	Use your Fastpass or come during the parade. You'll get wet.
Maharajah Jungle Trek	n/a	Zoo/Aviary	Up to you	Light	All Ages	Come anytime.
Camp Minnie-Mickey						
★ Festival of the Lion King	n/a	Show	28 mins.	Light	All Ages	Arrive 40 mins. before showtime. Sit in one of the front rows to increase your kid's chance of being chosen.
DinoLand U.S.A.						
Boneyard	n/a	Playground	Up to you	Moderate to Heavy	Small Kids	Play here while waiting for DINOSAUR Fastpass, or come late in the day.
DINOSAUR	At least 40″	Thrill Ride	4 mins.	Heavy	All but Small Kids	Come first thing in the morning or at the end of the day, or use Fastpass.

★ Finding Nemo–The Musical	n/a	Show	30 mins.	Heavy	All Ages	Arrive 40 mins. before showtime. Take little kids here while big kids wait for Expedition Everest.
Fossil Fun Games	n/a	Arcade/Fair	Up to you	Light	All but Small Kids	Bring a pocketful of change and a stash of ones.
Primeval Whirl	At least 48"	Thrill Ride	2½ mins.	Heavy	All Ages	Kids may want to ride twice. Take your first spin early, then use Fastpass if the wait is more than 20 mins.
TriceraTop Spin	n/a	Thrill Ride for Kids	2 mins.	Heavy	Small Kids	Ride early while everyone else heads for the safari or while waiting for your Fastpass appointment for DINOSAUR.
Discovery Island						
★ Tree of Life—It's Tough to Be a Bug!	n/a	3-D Film	20 mins.	Moderate to Heavy	All but Small Kids	Do this after Kilimanjaro Safaris. Fastpass is available. Small children may be frightened.
Rafiki's Planet Watch						
Rafiki's Planet Watch	n/a	Walk-Through/ Zoo/Aviary	Up to you	Moderate	All Ages	Come in the late afternoon after you've hit all key attractions.
Wildlife Express Train	n/a	Train Ride	5 mins.	Moderate	All Ages	Head straight to Affection Section with little kids to come face-to-face with domesticated critters.

★ = Fodor's Choice

THE WATER PARKS

RIDE THE WAVES

SUPPLIES

Typhoon Lagoon: You can get inner tubes at Castaway Creek and inner tubes, rafts, or slide mats at many of the rides. Borrow snorkel gear at **Shark Reef** (your own isn't allowed) and life vests at **High 'N Dry.** Near the main entrance is **Singapore Sal's,** where you can pick up free life jackets, buy sundries, and rent (or buy) towels and lockers.

Blizzard Beach: Get free life vests or rent towels and lockers at **Snowless Joe's**. Inner tubes, rafts, and slide mats are provided at the rides. Buy beach gear or rent towels or lockers at **Beach Haus. Shade Shack** is the place for a new pair of sunglasses.

There's something about a water park that brings out the kid in us, and there's no denying that these are two of the world's best. What sets them apart? It's the same thing that differentiates all Disney parks—the detailed themes.

Whether you're cast away on a balmy island at Typhoon Lagoon or washed up on a ski resort–turned–seaside playground at Blizzard Beach, the landscaping and clever architecture will add to the fun of flume and raft rides, wave pools, and splash areas. Another plus: the vegetation has matured enough to create shade. The Disney water parks give you that lost-in-paradise feeling on top of all those high-speed wedgie-inducing waterslides. They're so popular that crowds often reach overflow capacity in summer.

Your children may like them so much that they'll clamor to visit more than once. If you're going to Disney for five days or more between April and October, add the Water Park Fun & More option to your Magic Your Way ticket. Of course, check the weather to make sure the temperatures are to your liking for running around in a swimsuit.

WHAT TO EXPECT

Most people agree that kids under 7 and older adults prefer Typhoon Lagoon. Bigger kids and teens like Blizzard Beach better because it has more slides and big-deal rides. Indeed, devoted waterslide enthusiasts generally prefer Blizzard Beach to other water parks.

TYPHOON LAGOON

You can speed down waterslides with names like Crush 'N' Gusher and Humunga Kowabunga or bump through rapids and falls at Mt. Mayday. You can also bob along in 5-foot waves in a surf pool the size of two football fields, or, for a mellow break, float in inner tubes along the 2,100-foot Castaway Creek. Go snorkeling in Shark Reef, rubberneck as fellow human cannonballs are ejected from the Storm Slides, or hunker down in a hammock or lounge chair and read a book. Ketchakiddie Creek for young children replicates adult rides on a smaller scale. It's Disney's version of a day at the beach—complete with friendly Disney lifeguards.

BLIZZARD BEACH

Disney Imagineers have gone all out here to create the paradox of a ski resort in the midst of a tropical lagoon. Lots of verbal puns and sight gags play with the snow-in-Florida motif. The centerpiece is Mt. Gushmore, with its 120-foot-high Summit Plummet. Attractions have names like Teamboat Springs, a white-water raft ride. Themed speed slides include Toboggan Racer, Slush Gusher, and Snow Stormers. Between Mt. Gushmore's base and its summit, swim-skiers can also ride a chairlift converted from ski-resort to beach-resort use—with multihued umbrellas and snow skis on their undersides.

VISITING TIPS

- In summer, come first thing in the morning (early birds can ride several times before the lines get long), late in the afternoon when park hours run later, or when the weather clears after a thunder-shower (rainstorms drive away crowds). Afternoons are also good in cooler weather, as the water is a bit warmer. To make a whole day of it, avoid weekends, when locals and visitors pack in.
- Women and girls should wear one-piece swimsuits unless they want to find their tops somewhere around their ears at the bottom of the waterslide.
- Invest in sunscreen and water shoes. Plan to slather sunscreen on several times throughout the day. An inexpensive pair of water shoes will save tootsies from hot sand and walkways and from grimy restroom floors.
- Arrive 30 minutes before opening so you can park, buy tickets, rent towels, and snag inner tubes before the crowds descend, and, trust us, it gets very crowded.

5

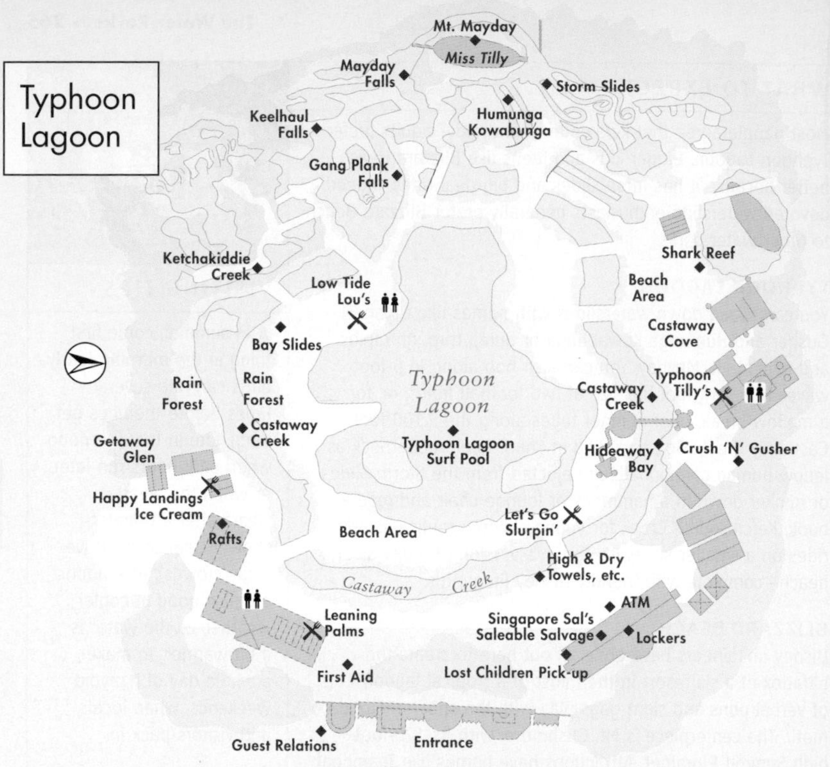
Typhoon Lagoon
Mt. Mayday
Miss Tilly
Mayday Falls
Storm Slides
Humunga Kowabunga
Keelhaul Falls
Gang Plank Falls
Shark Reef
Ketchakiddie Creek
Beach Area
Low Tide Lou's
Castaway Cove
Bay Slides
Typhoon Lagoon
Typhoon Tilly's
Rain Forest
Rain Forest
Castaway Creek
Castaway Creek
Getaway Glen
Typhoon Lagoon Surf Pool
Hideaway Bay
Crush 'N' Gusher
Happy Landings Ice Cream
Let's Go Slurpin'
Rafts
Beach Area
High & Dry Towels, etc.
Castaway Creek
ATM
Leaning Palms
Singapore Sal's Saleable Salvage
Lockers
First Aid
Lost Children Pick-up
Guest Relations
Entrance

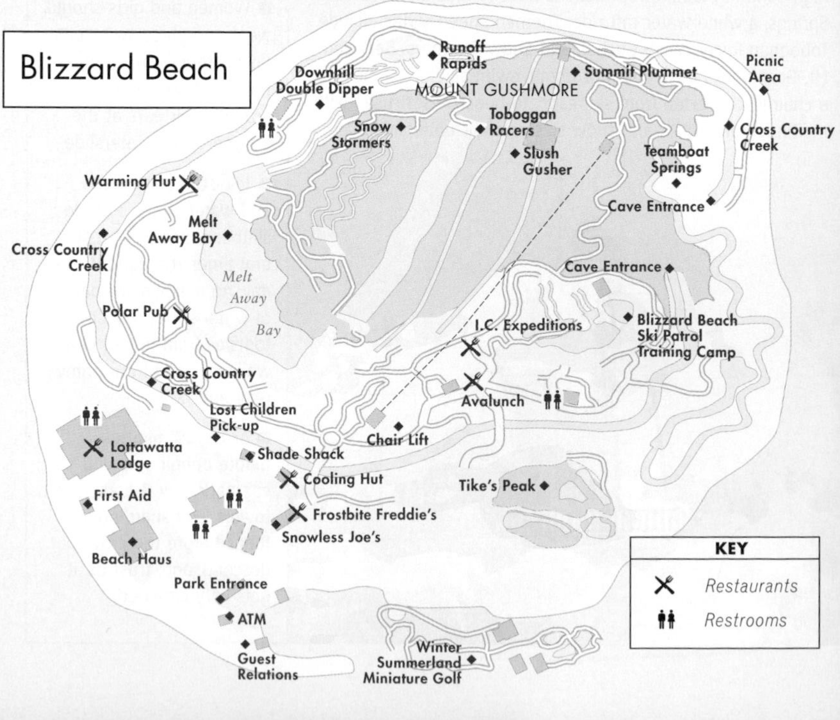
Blizzard Beach
Runoff Rapids
Downhill Double Dipper
Summit Plummet
Picnic Area
MOUNT GUSHMORE
Snow Stormers
Toboggan Racers
Cross Country Creek
Slush Gusher
Teamboat Springs
Warming Hut
Cave Entrance
Melt Away Bay
Cross Country Creek
Cave Entrance
Melt Away Bay
Polar Pub
I.C. Expeditions
Blizzard Beach Ski Patrol Training Camp
Cross Country Creek
Avalunch
Lost Children Pick-up
Lottawatta Lodge
Chair Lift
Shade Shack
Cooling Hut
Tike's Peak
First Aid
Frostbite Freddie's
Snowless Joe's
Beach Haus
KEY
Restaurants
Restrooms
Park Entrance
ATM
Guest Relations
Winter Summerland Miniature Golf

DID YOU KNOW?

One of Typhoon Lagoon's most popular attractions is the Crush 'n' Gusher, an exhilarating raft-ride that propels you through one of three slides, the Banana Blaster, Coconut Crusher, and Pineapple Plunger and ends with a heart-pounding drop into Hideaway Bay.

DISNEY'S WATER PARKS

NAME	HEIGHT REQ.	TYPE OF ENTERTAINMENT	DURATION	CROWDS	AUDIENCE	TIPS
TYPHOON LAGOON						
Bay Slides	Under 60"	Waterslide for Kids	Up to You	Light to Moderate	Small Kids	Parents: be prepared for your kids to ride again and again.
Castaway Creek	n/a	River/Stream Ride	Up to 20 mins.	Vary by Season	All Ages	Spend 20 mins. on a full, leisurely circuit or zoom along with the current.
★ Crush 'N' Gusher	At least 48"	Thrill Ride with Water	1 min.	Moderate to Heavy	All but Small Kids	Ride first thing in the morning to avoid long lines.
Gangplank Falls	n/a	Waterslide	1 min.	Vary by Season	All but Small Kids	It takes two people to carry the heavy inner tubes, and four or five to ride in them.
Humunga Kowabunga	At least 48"	Waterslide	4 secs.	Heavy	All but Small Kids	You can race friends or family as there are three slides here.
Keelhaul Falls	n/a	Waterslide	1 min.	Vary by Season	All but Small Kids	Ride before or after nearby Mayday Falls.
Ketchakiddie Creek	Under 48"	River/Stream Ride	Up to You	Light	Small Kids	Parents can take turns watching kiddies here and riding thrill slides elsewhere.
Mayday Falls	n/a	Waterslide	1 min.	Vary by Season	All but Small Kids	While you're in the neighborhood, ride Keelhaul Falls too.
Shark Reef	n/a	Pool Area; Aquarium	Up to You	Heavy	All but Small Kids	It's popular: come early or late, especially if you want to linger.
Storm Slides	n/a	Waterslide	15–20 secs.	Moderate to Heavy	All but Small Kids	Try each of the three slides for different twists.
★ Typhoon Lagoon Surf Pool	n/a	Wave Pool; Beach Area	Up to You	Heavy	All Ages	Time your bodysurfing to the waves, which come every 90 seconds.

BLIZZARD BEACH						
Chair Lift	At least 48" alone; 32" w/ an adult	Thrill Ride	2 mins.	Light to Moderate	All but Small Kids	Don't want to wait to get up Mt. Gushmore? Head for the single-rider line or just hike up.
Cross Country Creek	n/a	River/Stream Ride	25 mins.	Vary by Season	All Ages	This is the best way to get around the park!
Downhill Double Dipper	At least 48"	Waterslide	Under 10 secs.	Heavy	All but Small Kids	Ride early or face the postlunch crowds.
Melt-Away Bay	n/a	Wave Pool; Beach Area	Up to You	Vary by Season	All Ages	Arrive early to snag an umbrella (for shade) and an inner tube (for deeper waters).
Runoff Rapids	n/a	Waterslide	35 secs.	Light to Moderate	All but Small Kids	Be sure to try both slides.
Ski Patrol Training Camp	n/a	Waterslide; Thrill Ride with Water	Up to You	Light to Moderate	All but Small Kids	Hate lines? Come early or head to the zip-line drop or iceberg obstacle course.
★ **Slush Gusher**	At least 48"	Waterslide	15 secs.	You Bet!	All but Small Kids	Crowded days see 90-minute waits; come early.
Snow Stormers	n/a	Waterslide	20 secs.	Moderate to Heavy	All Ages	Hold on tight!
★ **Summit Plummet**	At least 48"	Waterslide	10 crazy secs.	Absolutely	All but Small Kids	Make your first stop! Summer afternoon waits can be two hours.
Teamboat Springs	n/a	River/Stream Ride	1½ mins.	Moderate	Families	There are no age or height requirements, tubes seat groups, and lines move fast.
★ **Tike's Peak**	48" and under	Pool Area	Up to You	Vary by Season	Small Kids	Adults must be accompanied by children no more than 48' tall!
Toboggan Racers	n/a	Waterslide/Game	10 secs.	Moderate to Heavy	All but Small Kids	It's more fun if you race.

★ = Fodor's Choice

OTHER DISNEY ACTIVITIES

EXPLORING THE REST OF THE WORLD

Try to budget in a few hours to explore Disney's "other" places. Several of them are no-admission-required charmers; one is a high-tech, high-cover-charge gaming wonderland.

DISNEY'S BOARDWALK

Disney's BoardWalk is within walking distance of Epcot and across Crescent Lake from Disney's Yacht and Beach Club Resorts and fronting a hotel of the same name. You'll be drawn to some good restaurants, souvenir shops, surreys, saltwater taffy vendors, and performers.

After sunset, the mood is festive. Bars include the Atlantic Dance Hall (Top 40 dance club), Big River Grille & Brewing Works (brewpub), the ESPN Club (sports bar), and Jellyrolls (piano bar). If you're here when Epcot is ready to close, you can watch the park fireworks from the bridge that connects BoardWalk to the Yacht and Beach Club Resorts.

DOWNTOWN DISNEY

East of Epcot and close to Interstate 4 (I–4) along a large lake, this shopping, dining, and entertainment complex has three areas: the Marketplace, Pleasure Island, and West Side. You can rent lockers, strollers, or wheelchairs, and there are two Guest Relations (aka Guest Services) centers.

In the **Marketplace,** the easternmost area, you can meander along winding sidewalks and explore hidden alcoves. Children love to splash in fountains that spring from the pavement and ride the miniature train and old-time carousel ($2). There are plenty of spots to grab a bite or sip a cappuccino along the lakefront. The Marketplace is open from 9:30 AM to 11 PM.

When it was a nightlife destination, the area known as **Pleasure Island** charged admission after dark for access to its bars, comedy clubs, and dance spots. But the nightclubs have closed and the place is undergoing a makeover to be completed in 2012. That said, Raglan Road Irish Pub and Restaurant still offers live Irish music six nights a week, and the upscale cigar bar, Fuego Cigars by Sosa, serves wine and spirits.

The main attractions in the hip **West Side** are the House of Blues Music Hall, Cirque du Soleil, and DisneyQuest virtual indoor theme park and arcade. You can also ride the Characters in Flight ($16 ages 10 and up; $10 ages 3–9) helium balloon that's tethered here, shop in boutiques, or dine in such restaurants as the Wolfgang Puck Café and Planet Hollywood.

SHOPPING

Though you can't turn a Disney corner without seeing a store or cart, certain areas within the parks and Downtown Disney offer the best shopping opportunities. And it really pays to know where these opportunities are: not only can you maximize your time, but you can also minimize your spending.

Downtown Disney. Why spend valuable touring time shopping in the theme parks when you can come here (for no entry fee) on your first or last day? The perfect place for one-stop souvenir shopping, Downtown Disney has dozens of stores, including the vast, hard-to-top World of Disney, the super-kid-friendly LEGO Imagination Center, and the über-hip Tren-D clothing and accessory shop.

Epcot World Showcase. Fine goods and trinkets from all over the world, some handcrafted, are sold at the pavilions representing individual countries here. Check out the Japanese and Chinese kimonos, Moroccan fezzes, French wines, Norwegian sweaters, and Mexican wood carvings. A United Kingdom shop even helps you research your family coat of arms, which you can buy as a paper printout or dressed up with paint or embroidery.

5

Main Street, U.S.A., Magic Kingdom. The Main Street buildings, with forced-perspective architecture and elaborately decorated facades, beckon, but don't waste precious touring time shopping in the morning. Come back later for custom-made watches, hand-blown crystal, cookware, princess dresses, mouse ears and, of course, fairy-tale-themed snow globes.

Discovery Island, Animal Kingdom. Although there are some great shops in Africa and Asia, many of the goods are concentrated in this hub. You'll find plush panda and leopard backpacks for kids, several types of safari hats, and even a "Green Corner" at Disney Outfitters, where earth-minded jewelry, "lucky" bamboo plants, and organic cotton T-shirts are hits.

Hollywood Boulevard, Hollywood Studios. If you're a size 0 or 2 like soap-opera diva Susan Lucci, you may want to take home the pink coat she wore on *All My Children* ($1,000 at Sid Cahuenga's One-of-a-Kind shop just inside the park). Or you can buy more affordable togs at the Boulevard's Keystone Clothiers (adults), L.A. Prop Cinema Storage (kids), and Mickey's of Hollywood (all in the family).

OUTDOOR ACTIVITIES AND SPORTS

GOLF

Where else would you find a sand trap shaped like the head of a well-known mouse? Disney has 72 holes of golf on four championship courses—all on the PGA Tour route—plus a 9-hole walking course. The original Palm and Magnolia 18-hole courses are southwest of the Magic Kingdom near the Grand Floridian and Polynesian resorts, as is the 9-hole Oak Trail walking course. The Lake Buena Vista 18-hole course is northwest of Downtown Disney. The newer, 18-hole Osprey Ridge is east of Fort Wilderness Resort.

Tee times are available daily from 6 until 6. You can book them up to 90 days in advance if you're staying at a WDW-owned hotel, 60 days ahead if you're staying elsewhere. One-on-one instruction from PGA-accredited professionals is available at the Palm, Magnolia, and Lake

TOP SOUVENIRS

If you're scratching your head trying to figure out what could be the most memorable souvenir, you've got options.

Make-Your-Own Mouse Ear Hat. For $12 and up, you can customize your ears—from fuzzy pink to shiny silver—at The Chapeau in the Magic Kingdom.

Indiana Jones Fedora. This brown crushable wool felt fedora (about $37) is a Halloween party favorite. Pick one up at Indiana Jones Adventure Outpost in Hollywood Studios.

Zulu Basket. Uniquely patterned telephone wire baskets at Mombassa Marketplace in the Animal Kingdom ($23–$52) are woven by South Africa's Zulu people.

Kimono. Kids' and adults' poly-rayon or silk kimonos, at China or Japan shops in Epcot ($33–$170), never go out of style.

Princess Dress. Many a little girl's treasure is her Cinderella, Aurora, Belle, or Ariel dress ($60) from Tinker Bell's Treasures, Magic Kingdom, or World of Disney, Downtown Disney Marketplace.

Double Light Saber. Let double the force be with you! At Tatooine Traders in Hollywood Studios, kids can build their own light saber ($19.99 single; $22.95 double) with customized crystals, hilts, and blades.

Mickey Computer Mouse. A wireless optical computer mouse styled after the Big Cheese's white-gloved hand is $30 at Mickey's of Hollywood in Hollywood Studio.

Plush Character Toy. Dumbo, Goofy, Nemo—you name the Disney character, and there's a plush toy—in one of many sizes and at just about any Disney park or Downtown Disney. Prices run about $10 to $50.

Buena Vista. Prices for private lessons vary: 45 minutes cost $75 for adults and $50 for youngsters 17 and under. For tee times and private lessons, call Walt Disney World Golf & Recreation Reservations at ☎ *407/939–1500.*

TENNIS

You can play tennis at six Disney hotels: BoardWalk (two hard courts), Fort Wilderness Resort (two hard courts), Old Key West Resort (three hard courts), Disney's Saratoga Springs Resort & Spa (two Hydro-grid clay courts), and Disney's Yacht Club Resort (one hard court). Courts are available without charge on a first-come, first-served basis for resort and non-resort guests. All have lights and most have lockers and racquets available to rent or borrow. Disney offers lessons at some of its tennis complexes.

6

Universal Orlando

THE STUDIOS, ISLANDS OF ADVENTURE, WET 'N WILD

WORD OF MOUTH

"You definitely should plan a day each for [Universal Studios and Islands of Adventure]. And it *is* worth it to get the front-of-line privileges . . . but [even with these] you still can spend a day at each park. If you finish one early, check out your hotel pool!"

—FL_Mom

WELCOME TO UNIVERSAL ORLANDO

Vineland Rd.
UNIVERSAL STUDIOS FLORIDA
1
Lake Marsha
Woodgreen Dr.
ISLANDS OF ADVENTURE
2
CITYWALK
3
Hollywood Way
Universal Blvd.
Parson Brown Dr.
Edgeworth Dr.
Adventure Way
4
EXITS 30A & 75A
International Dr.
Wallace Rd.
Sandy Lake
4
Spring Lake
Universal Blvd.
Sand Lake Rd.
EXITS 29 & 74

TOP REASONS TO GO

★ **More Than You Bargain For:** Universal Orlando is more than just a single Hollywood-themed amusement park; it's also Islands of Adventure theme park; the CityWalk entertainment complex; and the Hard Rock Hotel, Portofino Bay, and Royal Pacific resorts. Wet 'n Wild water park is also affiliated with Universal.

★ **Theme-Park Powerhouse:** Neither SeaWorld nor any of Disney's four theme parks can match the energy at Universal Studios and Islands of Adventure. Wild rides, clever shows, and an edgy attitude all push the envelope here.

★ **A New Experience:** If your Orlando vacations have been based primarily at Disney, Universal will help you expand your range. In time, it may even become your first stop.

★ **Party Central:** Throughout the year, Universal adds special events—Mardi Gras, Halloween Horror Nights, the Rock the Universe Christian-music celebration—to the calendar.

1 Universal Studios. It's a creative and quirky tribute to Hollywood past, present, and future. Overall, the collection of wild rides, quiet retreats, live shows, street characters, and clever movies (both 3-D and 4-D) are as entertaining as the motion pictures they celebrate.

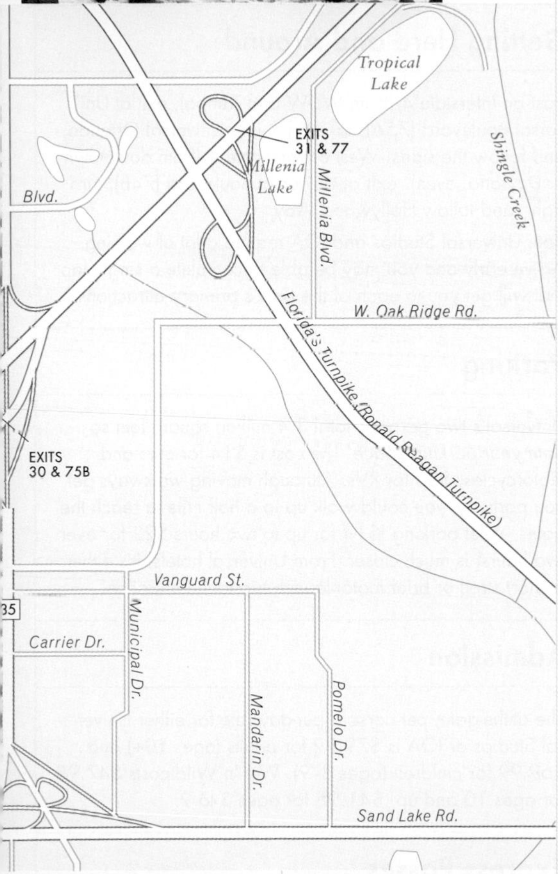
Tropical
Lake
EXITS
31 & 77
Millenia
Lake
Shingle Creek
Blvd.
Millenia Blvd.
Florida's Turnpike (Ronald Reagan Turnpike)
W. Oak Ridge Rd.
EXITS
30 & 75B
Vanguard St.
35
Carrier Dr.
Municipal Dr.
Mandarin Dr.
Pomelo Dr.
Sand Lake Rd.

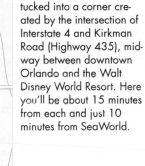

GETTING ORIENTED

Universal Orlando is tucked into a corner created by the intersection of Interstate 4 and Kirkman Road (Highway 435), midway between downtown Orlando and the Walt Disney World Resort. Here you'll be about 15 minutes from each and just 10 minutes from SeaWorld.

6

2 Islands of Adventure. IOA has the ability to break new ground—as it did in 2010 with the premiere of an entire land dedicated to Harry Potter. Add a variety of attractions that bring you face-to-face with Spider-Man, the Hulk, velociraptors, and the Cat in the Hat, and there's every reason to head to the islands.

3 CityWalk. Locals and visitors come to this sprawling entertainment and retail complex to watch movies, dine at theme restaurants, shop for everything from cigars to surf wear, and stay up late at nightclubs celebrating the French Quarter, Jamaica, and Latin America.

UNIVERSAL ORLANDO PLANNER

Operating Hours

Universal Studios and IOA are open 365 days a year, from 9 AM to 7 PM, with hours as late as 10 PM in summer and at holidays. Wet 'n Wild is also open 365 days a year, weather permitting, but with widely varying hours. Usually it's open from 10 AM to 5 PM, with summer hours from 9:30 AM until 9 PM. Call for exact hours during holiday periods.

CONTACTS

Universal Dining Reservations: ☎ *407/224–3613 general, 407/224–4012 IOA character meals*

Universal Main Number: ☎ *407/363–8000*

Universal Room Reservations: ☎ *888/273–1311*

Universal Vacation Packages: ☎ *877/801–9720*

Universal Web: 🌐 *www.universalorlando.com*

Wet 'n Wild Main Number: ☎ *407/351–1800 or 800/992–9453*

Wet 'n Wild Web: 🌐 *www.wetnwild.com*

Getting Here and Around

East on Interstate 4 (from WDW and Tampa), exit at Universal Boulevard (75A); take a left into Universal Orlando, and follow the signs. West on Interstate 4 (from downtown or Daytona, even), exit at Universal Boulevard (74B), turn right, and follow Hollywood Way.

Both Universal Studios and IOA require a lot of walking. Arrive early and you may be able to complete a single lap that will get you to each of the park's primary attractions.

Parking

Universal's two garages total 3.4 million square feet so *note your parking space.* The cost is $14 for cars and motorcycles, $20 for RVs. Although moving walkways get you partway, you could walk up to a half mile to reach the gates. Valet parking ($14 for up to two hours $22 for over two hours) is much closer. From Universal hotels, it's either a short stroll or brief motor-launch trip to the entrance.

Admission

The at-the-gate, per-person, per-day rate for either Universal Studios or IOA is $79.99 for adults (ages 10+) and $69.99 for children (ages 3–9). Wet 'n Wild costs $47.95 for ages 10 and up, $41.95 for ages 3 to 9.

Express Passes

At select attractions, watch for **Express Pass** kiosks, where you can get a ticket with a reserved time slot. After procuring one (you can only get one at a time), roam around, return at the appointed hour, and wait in line about 15 minutes—as opposed to as much as an hour. The **Express PLUS Pass** ($26 off-season or $53 in peak season) gets you to the front of each line without an appointment. If crowds are thin and lines are moving fast, skip this pass. Also, if you're a guest at Universal hotel, this perk is free; your room key card serves as the pass.

Universal and Wet 'n Wild Like a Pro

■ **Arrive early**—as early at 8 AM if the parks open at 9. Seriously. Better to share Universal or Wet 'n Wild with hundreds of people rather than thousands.

■ **Visit on a weekday.** Crowds are lighter, especially fall through spring, when kids are in school.

■ **Don't forget anything in your car.** Universal's parking areas are at least a half mile from park entrances and a round-trip will eat up valuable time. At Wet n' Wild, parking's closer, but who wants to towel off, get dressed. and walk across the street for a hairbrush?

■ **Consider valet parking.** It costs almost twice as much as regular parking, but it puts you much closer to Universal's park entrances and just steps from CityWalk.

■ **Look into the Express PLUS Pass.** It really is worth the extra cost to be able to jump to the front of ride lines during peak seasons (summer and holidays).

■ **Ride solo.** At Universal some rides have a Single Rider line that moves faster than regular lines.

■ **Take advantage of park concessions.** If you're in a hurry to reach the parks and don't feel you can stop for a bite, don't worry—there are plenty of dining options inside. At CityWalk there's a Starbucks, a Cinnabon, and other quick-bite eateries.

■ **Get expert advice.** The folks at Guest Services (aka Guest Relations) in both Universal and Wet 'n Wild have great insight. At Universal, reps will create a custom itinerary, free of charge.

■ **Check out Child Swap.** At certain Universal attractions, one parent can enter the attraction, take a spin, and then return to take care of the baby while the other parent rides without having to wait in line again.

Other Services

All-you-can-eat, daylong **meal deals** are good at three sit-down restaurants in Universal (Mel's Drive-In, Louie's Italian, International Food and Film Festival) and three in IOA (Circus McGurkus Café Stoopendous, Comic Strip Café, The Burger Digs). The cost is $20 a day for adults, $10 daily for kids; an extra $9 a day buys all-you-can-drink soda.

IOA's **character breakfasts** at Confisco's Grill feature Spider-Man, Scooby-Doo, Woody Woodpecker, Curious George, and Seuss characters. Reservations are a good idea.

For People with Disabilities

The *Studio Guide for Guests with Disabilities* (aka *Rider's Guide*) details special entrances and viewing areas, interpreters, Braille scripts, and assistance devices. In general, if you can transfer from your wheelchair unassisted or with the help of a friend, you can ride many attractions. Some rides have carts that accommodate manual wheelchairs, though not motorized wheelchairs or electric convenience vehicles (ECVs).

Assistive-listening devices are available for shows at Universal (Twister, Men in Black, Terminator, Beetlejuice, Animal Actors, A Day in the Park with Barney) and IOA (Cat in the Hat, Sindbad, Spider-Man).

By Gary McKechnie

For two decades or so Universal and Disney have been going head-to-head. While Disney creates a fantasy world for people—especially young children—who love fairy tales, Universal Orlando is geared to older kids, adults, and anyone who enjoys high-energy thrills and pop culture, and the movies.

Where Disney may roll out a new land or retrofit an old ride once a decade, Universal knows that guests expect something different each time they visit. And the park delivers. In recent years, Univeral Studios alone has replaced Alfred Hitchcock with Shrek, Hanna-Barbera with Jimmy Neutron, King Kong with The Mummy, Back to the Future with the virtual-reality Simpsons ride, and Earthquake with Disaster! In 2009, Hollywood Rip Ride Rockit—an interactive roller coaster—was introduced.

Things haven't been static at Islands of Adventure (IOA)—thanks to the opening of the Wizarding World of Harry Potter—or at the CityWalk shopping/nightlife complex. A well-intentioned but less-than-successful jazz club became a karaoke stage, a Motown restaurant became the Red Coconut Lounge, and a series of stores were switched out to give the complex a new look. In addition, Universal has given the Blue Man Group its very own theater.

A few miles away, on the tourist strip known as International Drive, is Wet 'n Wild—owned by Universal since 1998 and believed to America's first water park. Wet 'n Wild does with aquatics what Universal does with theatrics: provides over-the-top entertainment, albeit in the form of super waterslides and fantastic plunges. (To wit: Bomb Bay, which drops you 76 nearly-vertical feet down a slide and into the pool. Spooky, splashy fun.)

Despite the adrenaline-charging attractions at Wet n' Wild, it's not hard to chill out lazing about the park's beaches and pools. And, at Universal, you can slow down with some leisurely shopping at CityWalk; a concert at Hard Rock Live; and a languorous, elegant dinner at Emeril's.

DID YOU KNOW?

The Blue Man Group always consists of three performers. They communicate their messages through music, gestures, audio-visuals, special effects, and eye contact but no spoken words. Matt Goldman, Phil Stanton, and Chris Wink created the group.

UNIVERSAL STUDIOS

STEP INTO THE MOVIES

Universal Studios appeals primarily to those who like loud, fast, high-energy attractions—generally teens and adults. Covering 444 acres, it's a rambling montage of sets, shops, soundstages housing themed attractions, reproductions of New York and San Francisco, and some genuine moviemaking paraphernalia.

On a map, the park appears neatly divided into six areas positioned around a huge lagoon. There's Production Central, which covers the entire left side of the Plaza of the Stars; New York, with street performances at 70 Delancey; the bicoastal San Francisco/Amity; futuristic World Expo; Woody Woodpecker's KidZone; and Hollywood.

What's tricky is that—since it's designed like a series of movie sets—there's no straightforward way to tackle the park. You'll probably make some detours and do some backtracking. To save time and shoe leather, ask theme-park hosts for itinerary suggestions and time-saving tips.

TOURING TIPS

- A few things aren't allowed on park grounds, including alcohol and glass containers; hard-sided coolers; soft-sided coolers larger than 8.5 inches wide by 6 inches high by 6 inches deep; coolers, suitcases, and other bags with wheels.
- Upon entering, avoid the temptation to go left toward the towering soundstages, looping the park clockwise. Head right—bypassing shops, restaurants, and some crowds—to top attractions like The Simpsons Ride and Men in Black.
- Good rendezvous points include the Lucy Tribute near the entrance, Mel's Drive-In, and Beetlejuice's Graveyard Revue.

TOP ATTRACTIONS

FOR AGES 7 AND UP

Hollywood Rip Ride Rockit. On this coaster, added in 2009, you select the sound track.

Men in Black: Alien Attack. The "world's first ride-through video game" gives you a chance to plug away at an endless swarm of aliens.

Revenge of the Mummy. It's a jarring, rocketing indoor coaster that takes you past scary mummies and billowing balls of fire (really).

Shrek 4-D. The 3-D film with sensory effects picks up where the original film left off—and adds some creepy extras in the process.

The Simpsons Ride. It puts you in the heart of Springfield on a wild-and-crazy virtual-reality experience.

Terminator 2 3-D. This explosive stage show features robots, 3-D effects, and sensations that all add extra punch to the classic film series.

Twister . . . Ride It Out. OK. It's just a special-effects show—but what special effects! You experience a tornado without having to head to the root cellar.

Universal Horror Make-Up Show. This sometimes gross, often raunchy, but always entertaining demonstration merges the best of stand-up comedy with creepy effects.

FOR AGES 6 AND UNDER

Animal Actors on Location! It's a perfect family show starring a menagerie of animals whose unusually high IQs are surpassed only by their cuteness and cuddle-ability.

A Day in the Park with Barney. Small children love the big purple dinosaur and the chance to sing along.

Curious George Goes to Town. The celebrated simian visits the Man with the Yellow Hat in a small-scale water park.

WHERE TO SNACK

Keep things moving with lunch at a fast-food spot. Or slow things down at sit-down restaurant with priority seating, which gives you the first available seat after a reserved time.

- Full-service restaurants include **Finnegan's Bar and Grille** (Irish pub), and **Lombard's Seafood Grille** (seafood).

- Among the self-serve restaurants are **Classic Monsters Cafe** (seasonal, with pizzas, pasta, salads, rotisserie chicken); **Richter's Burger Co.** (burgers, salads); the **International Food and Film Bazaar** (pizza, gyros, stir-fried beef, and other multiculti dishes).

- Other choices include **Mel's Drive-In,** a Happy Days–era soda shop–burger joint; **Beverly Hills Boulangerie** for breakfast croissants and pastries; **Schwab's Pharmacy** for ice cream; **Louie's Italian Restaurant** (pizza, spaghetti, salads); and the **KidZone Pizza Company** for pizza, chicken tenders, and other kid-geared dishes.

Universal Studios

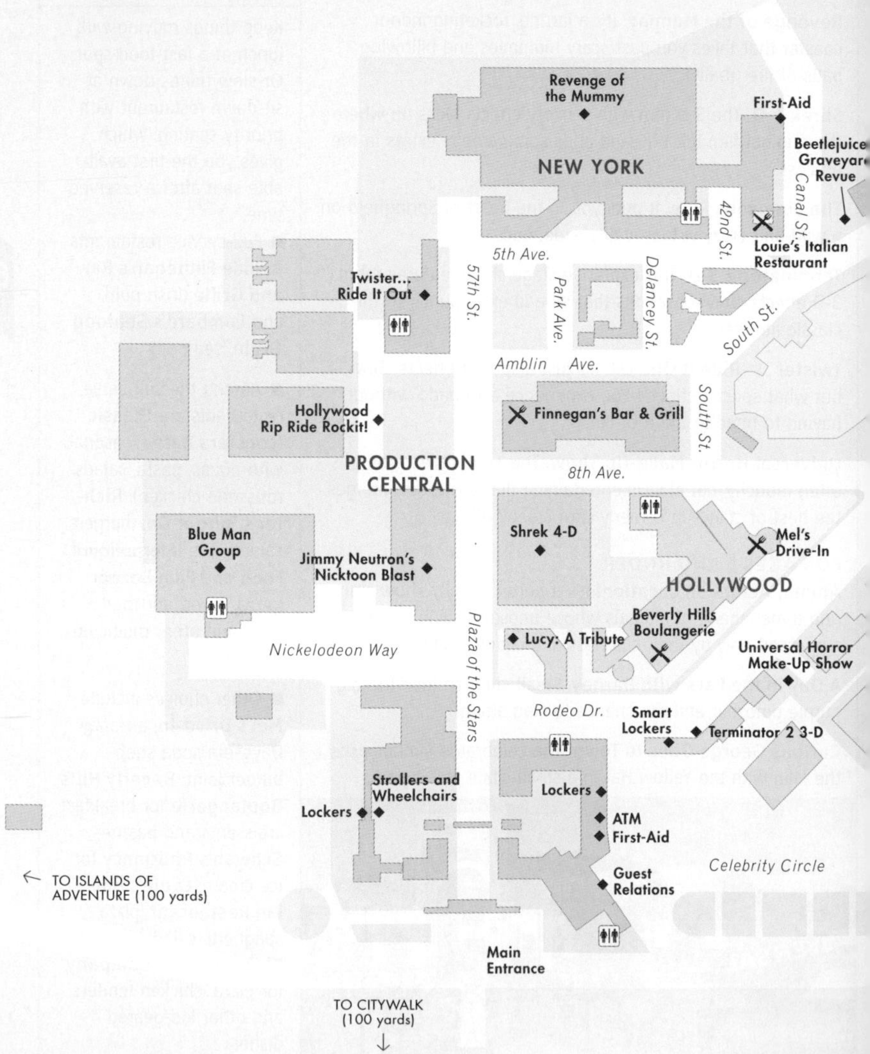

Revenge of the Mummy
First-Aid
Beetlejuice Graveyard Revue
NEW YORK
Canal St.
42nd St.
Louie's Italian Restaurant
5th Ave.
57th St.
Park Ave.
Delancey St.
South St.
Twister... Ride It Out
Amblin Ave.
Finnegan's Bar & Grill
South St.
Hollywood Rip Ride Rockit!
PRODUCTION CENTRAL
8th Ave.
Blue Man Group
Jimmy Neutron's Nicktoon Blast
Shrek 4-D
Mel's Drive-In
HOLLYWOOD
Beverly Hills Boulangerie
Plaza of the Stars
Nickelodeon Way
Lucy: A Tribute
Universal Horror Make-Up Show
Rodeo Dr.
Smart Lockers
Terminator 2 3-D
Strollers and Wheelchairs
Lockers
Lockers
ATM
First-Aid
Guest Relations
Celebrity Circle
TO ISLANDS OF ADVENTURE (100 yards)
Main Entrance
TO CITYWALK (100 yards)

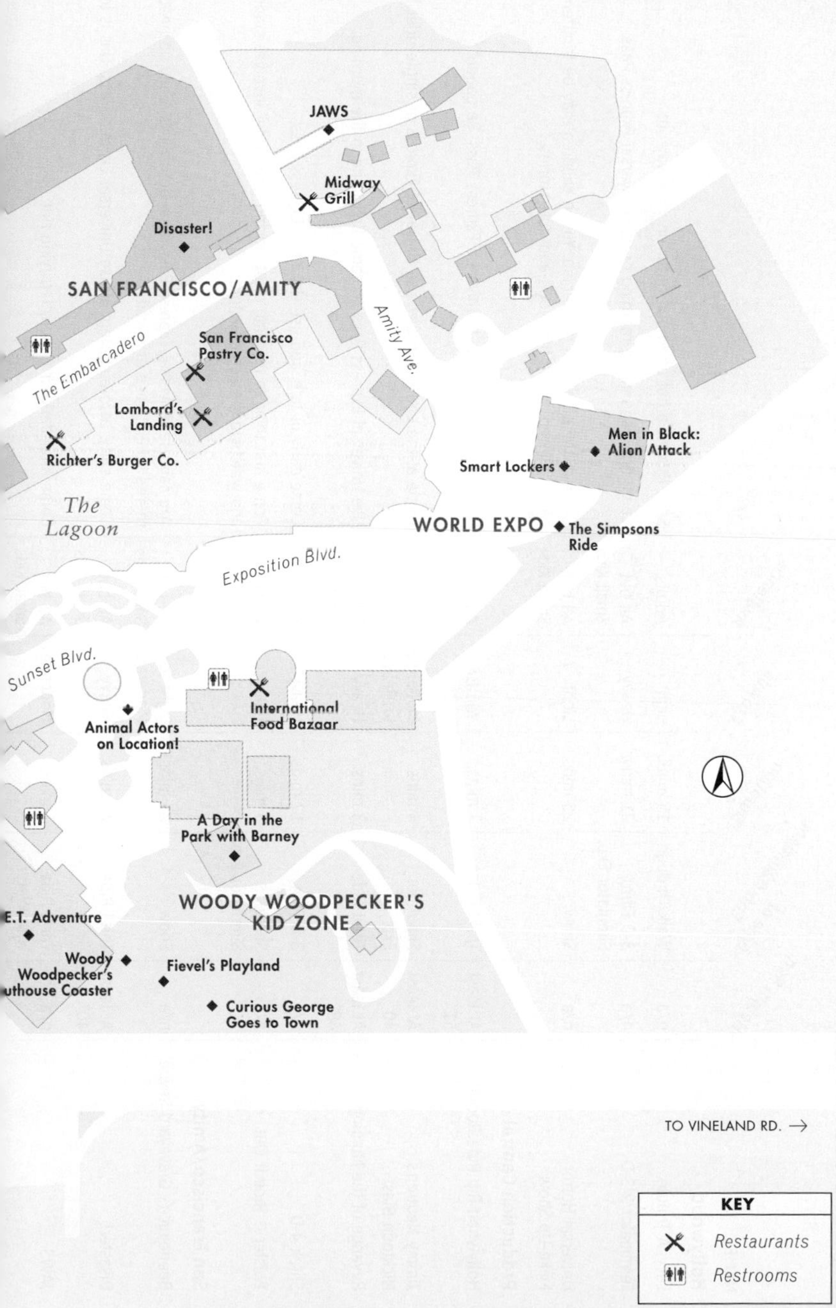
JAWS
Midway Grill
Disaster!
SAN FRANCISCO/AMITY
Amity Ave.
San Francisco Pastry Co.
The Embarcadero
Lombard's Landing
Richter's Burger Co.
Men in Black: Alien Attack
Smart Lockers
The Lagoon
WORLD EXPO
The Simpsons Ride
Exposition Blvd.
Sunset Blvd.
International Food Bazaar
Animal Actors on Location!
A Day in the Park with Barney
WOODY WOODPECKER'S KID ZONE
E.T. Adventure
Woody Woodpecker's
uthouse Coaster
Fievel's Playland
Curious George Goes to Town
TO VINELAND RD. →
KEY
Restaurants
Restrooms

UNIVERSAL STUDIOS

NAME	Height Req.	Type of Entertainment	Duration	Crowds	Audience	Tips
Hollywood						
Lucy: A Tribute	n/a	Walk-Through	15 mins.	Light	Adults	Save this for a hot afternoon or for on your way out.
Terminator 2 3-D	n/a	3-D Film/ Simulator Exp.	21 mins.	Heavy	All but Small Kids	Come first thing in the morning or use Universal Express Pass.
★ Universal Horror Make-Up Show	n/a	Show	25 mins.	Light	All but Small Kids	Come in the afternoon or evening. Young children may be frightened; older children eat up the blood-and-guts stories.
Production Central						
★ Hollywood Rip Ride Rockit!	At least 51″	Thrill Ride	2 mins.	You Bet!	All but Small Kids	Come early, late, or use a Universal Express Pass. Be patient.
Jimmy Neutron's Nicktoon Blast	At least 40″	Simulator Exp.	8 mins.	Moderate to Heavy	All Ages	Come at the end of the day; use Universal Express or single-rider line.
Revenge of the Mummy	At least 48″	Thrill Ride	3 mins.	Heavy	All but Small Kids	Use Universal Express Pass, or come first thing in the morning.
Shrek 4-D	n/a	3-D Film	12 mins.	Heavy	All Ages	Come early or late, and use Universal Express Pass.
Twister . . . Ride It Out	n/a	Show/ Simulator Exp.	3 mins.	Heavy	All but Small Kids	Come first thing in morning or at closing. This "ride" involves standing and watching the action unfold.
San Francisco/Amity						
Beetlejuice's Graveyard Revue	n/a	Show	25 mins.	Light to Moderate	All but Small Kids	You can use Universal Express Pass here, but there's really no need as there's little chance of a wait.
Disaster!	At least 40″	Thrill Ride	20 mins.	Heavy	All but Small Kids	Come early, before closing, or use Universal Express Pass. This is loud.
JAWS	n/a	Thrill Ride with Water	7 mins.	Moderate	All but Small Kids	Come after dark for a more terrifying ride.

Woody Woodpecker's KidZone						
A Day in the Park with Barney	n/a	Show	20 mins.	Light	Small Kids	Arrive 10–15 mins. early on crowded days for a good seat—up close and in the center.
Animal Actors on Location!	n/a	Show	20 mins.	Moderate to Heavy	All Ages	Stadium seating, but come early for a good seat.
Curious George Goes to Town	n/a	Playground with Water	Up to you	Moderate to Heavy	Small Kids	Come in late afternoon or early evening. Bring a towel.
E.T. Adventure	n/a	Thrill Ride for Kids	5 mins.	Moderate to Heavy	All Ages	Come early morning or use Universal Express Pass.
Fievel's Playland	n/a	Playground with Water	Up to you	Light to Moderate	Small Kids	Generally light crowds, but there are waits for the waterslide. On hot days come late.
Woody Woodpecker's Nuthouse Coaster	At least 36"	Thrill Ride for Kids	1½ mins.	Moderate to Heavy	Small Kids	Come at park closing, when most little ones have gone home.
World Expo						
Men in Black: Alien Attack	At least 42"	Thrill Ride	4½ mins.	Heavy	All but Small Kids	Solo riders can take a faster line, so split up. This ride spins.
★ The Simpsons Ride	40"	Thrill Ride/ Simulator Exp.	6 mins.	Heavy	All but Small Kids	Use Universal Express Pass.

★ = Fodor's Choice

ISLANDS OF ADVENTURE

EXPLORE NEW LANDS

When Islands of Adventure (IOA) opened in 1999, it took attractions to a new level—a practice that continues with The Wizarding World of Harry Potter, opened in 2010. From Marvel Super Hero Island and Toon Lagoon to Seuss Landing and the Lost Continent, most attractions are impressive—some even out-Disney Disney.

You pass through the turnstiles and into the Port of Entry plaza, a bazaar that brings together bits and pieces of architecture, landscaping, music, and wares from many lands—Dutch windmills, Indonesian pedicabs, African masks. Egyptian figurines adorn the massive archway inscribed with the notice THE ADVENTURE BEGINS. From here, themed islands—arranged around a large lagoon—are connected by walkways that make navigation easy.

When you've done the full circuit, you'll recall the fantastic range of sights, sounds, and experiences and realize there can be truth in advertising. This park really *is* an adventure.

TOURING TIPS

- Invest in a Universal Express Plus Pass for the right to head to the front of the line and see the park without a sense of urgency.
- Ask hosts about their favorite experiences—and their suggestions for saving time.
- If the park's open late, split the day in half. See part of it in the morning, head off-site to a restaurant for lunch, then head to your hotel for a swim or a nap (or both). Return in the cooler, less crowded evening.
- Take time to explore little-used sidewalks and quiet alcoves and other sanctuaries that help counter the manic energy of IOA.

TOP ATTRACTIONS

FOR AGES 7 AND UP

The Amazing Adventures of Spider-Man. Get ready to fight bad guys and marvel at the engineering and technological wizardry on this dazzling attraction.

Dudley Do-Right's Ripsaw Falls. Even if its namesake is a mystery to anyone born after the 1960s, everyone loves the super splashdown at the end of this log-flume ride dedicated to the exploits of the animated Canadian Mountie.

Eighth Voyage of Sindbad. Jumping, diving, punching—is it another Tom Cruise action film? No, it's a cool, live stunt show with a love story to boot.

Incredible Hulk Coaster. This super-scary coaster blasts you skyward before sending you on no less than seven inversions. It will be hard to walk straight after this one.

FOR AGES 6 AND UNDER

The Cat in the Hat. It's like entering a Dr. Seuss book: all you have to do is sit on a moving couch and see what it's like when the Cat in the Hat drops by to babysit.

Popeye and Bluto's Bilge-Rat Barges. This tumultuous (but safe) raft ride lets younger kids experience a big-deal ride that's not too scary—just wild and wet.

WHERE TO SNACK

The park's three Meal Deal (all you can eat) options are **Circus McGurkus Café Stoo-pendous** (chicken, pasta, pizza, burgers, salads) in Seuss Landing; **The Burger Digs** (hamburgers, chicken sandwiches, chicken fingers, milk shakes) in Jurassic Park; and the **Comic Strip Café** (Asian, Italian, American, and fish) in Toon Lagoon. Also in Toon Lagoon is **Blondie's Deli** (jumbo sandwiches).

Pizza Predattoria and the seasonal **Thunder Falls Terrace** (rotisserie chicken and ribs) are in Jurassic Park, and near the Port of Entry is **Confisco's Grill,** with its steaks, salads, sandwiches, soups, and pasta. This is where character breakfasts are held; there's also a neat little pub.

The ultimate dining experience is the Lost Continent's **Mythos Restaurant.** Although its Continental dishes change seasonally, the warm, gooey, chocolate-banana cake is a constant.

Islands of Adventure

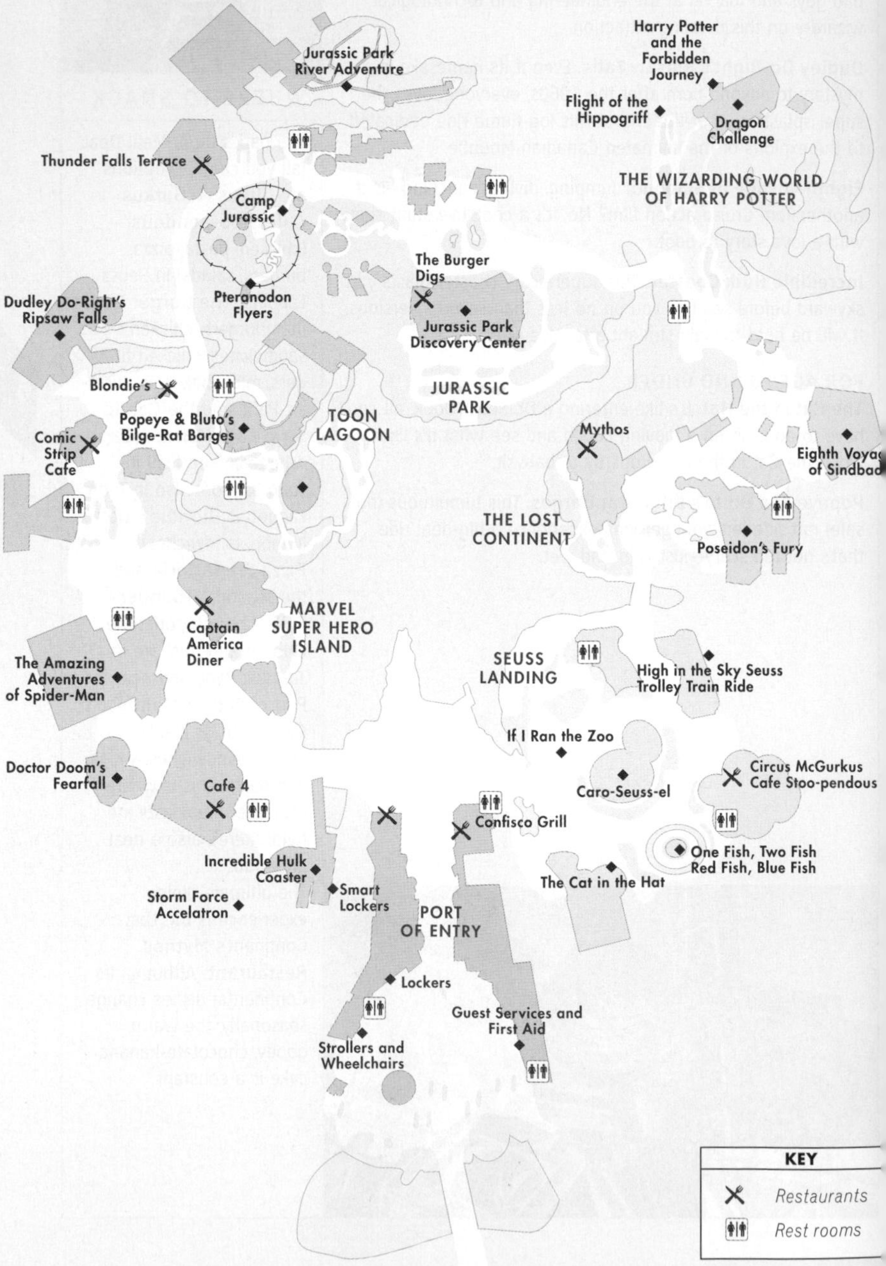

Jurassic Park River Adventure
Harry Potter and the Forbidden Journey
Flight of the Hippogriff
Dragon Challenge
THE WIZARDING WORLD OF HARRY POTTER
Thunder Falls Terrace
Camp Jurassic
Pteranodon Flyers
The Burger Digs
Jurassic Park Discovery Center
Dudley Do-Right's Ripsaw Falls
Blondie's
JURASSIC PARK
Popeye & Bluto's Bilge-Rat Barges
TOON LAGOON
Mythos
Comic Strip Cafe
Eighth Voyag
of Sindbad
THE LOST CONTINENT
Poseidon's Fury
Captain America Diner
MARVEL SUPER HERO ISLAND
SEUSS LANDING
High in the Sky Seuss Trolley Train Ride
The Amazing Adventures of Spider-Man
If I Ran the Zoo
Doctor Doom's Fearfall
Cafe 4
Caro-Seuss-el
Circus McGurkus Cafe Stoo-pendous
Confisco Grill
One Fish, Two Fish Red Fish, Blue Fish
Incredible Hulk Coaster
Smart Lockers
The Cat in the Hat
Storm Force Accelatron
PORT OF ENTRY
Lockers
Guest Services and First Aid
Strollers and Wheelchairs
KEY
Restaurants
Rest rooms

DID YOU KNOW?

The *Cat in the Hat* celebrated its 50th birthday in 2007. The birthday festivities included a nationwide literacy initiative by Random House Children's Books, the publisher of Dr. Suess's classic tales.

ISLANDS OF ADVENTURE

NAME	Height Req.	Type of Entertainment	Duration	Crowds	Audience	Tips
Jurassic Park						
Camp Jurassic	n/a	Playground	Up to you	Light to Moderate	All Ages	Come anytime.
Jurassic Park Discovery Center	n/a	Walk-Through	Up to you	Light	All but Small Kids	Come anytime.
Jurassic Park River Adventure	At least 42"	Thrill Ride with Water	6 mins.	Heavy	All but Small Kids	Use Universal Express Pass. Come early or late.
Pteranodon Flyers	At least 36"	Thrill Ride for Kids	2 mins.	Heavy	All Ages	Skip this on your first visit. 36" to 48" can ride but must do so with an adult.
Lost Continent						
Eighth Voyage of Sindbad	n/a	Show	25 mins.	Light	All but Small Kids	Stadium seating, but arrive at least 15 mins. early. Don't sit too far up front.
Poseidon's Fury	n/a	Simulator Exp.	20 mins.	Heavy	All but Small Kids	Come at the end of the day. Stay to the left for best spot. Get in first row each time.
Marvel Super Hero Island						
★ The Amazing Adventures of Spider-Man	At least 40"	Simulator Exp.	4½ mins.	Absolutely	All but Small Kids	Use Universal Express Pass, or come early or late in day. Don't miss the bad guys in the wanted posters.
Doctor Doom's Fearfall	At least 52"	Thrill Ride	1 min.	Light to Moderate	All but Small Kids	Use Universal Express Pass, or come later in the day. Regardless, come with an empty stomach.
Incredible Hulk Coaster	At least 54"	Thrill Ride	2¼ mins.	Yes!	All but Small Kids	Come here first. Effects are best in the morning. The front row is best.
Storm Force Accelatron	n/a	Thrill Ride	2 mins.	Light	All but Small Kids	Come whenever—except right after eating.

Seuss Landing						
Caro-Seuss-el	n/a	Thrill Ride for Kids	2 mins.	Moderate	All Ages	Use Universal Express Pass, or end your day here.
The Cat in the Hat	n/a	Thrill Ride for Kids	4½ mins.	Heavy	All Ages	Use Universal Express Pass here, or come early or at the end of the day.
High in the Sky Seuss Trolley Train Tour	At least 34″	Railroad	3 mins.	Heavy	All Ages	Kids love trains, so plan to get in line! 34″ to 48″ can ride but must do so with an adult.
If I Ran the Zoo	n/a	Playground with Water	Up to you	Heavy	Small Kids	Come toward the end of your visit.
One Fish, Two Fish, Red Fish, Blue Fish	n/a	Thrill Ride for Kids	2+ mins.	Heavy	Small Kids	Use Universal Express Pass, or come early or late in day. Skip it on your first visit.
Toon Lagoon						
Dudley Do-Right's Ripsaw Falls	At least 44″	Thrill Ride with Water	5½ mins.	Heavy	All but Small Kids	Ride the flume in late afternoon to cool down, or at day's end. There's no seat where you can stay dry.
Me Ship, The Olive	n/a	Playground	Up to you	Heavy	Small Kids	Come in the morning or at dinnertime.
Popeye and Bluto's Bilge-Rat Barges	At least 42 ″	Thrill Ride with Water	5 mins.	Heavy	All but Small Kids	Come early in the morning or before closing. You will get wet.
The Wizarding World of Harry Potter						
Dragon Challenge	At least 54″	Thrill Ride	3 mins.	Heavy	All but Small Kids	Use Universal Express Pass.
Flight of the Hippogriff	At least 36″	Thrill Ride for Kids	1 min.	Moderate	Small Kids	Keep an eye on the line, and come when there's an opening.
Harry Potter and the Forbidden Journey	At least 48″	Walk-Through/ Ride-Through/ Thrill Ride	50 mins.	Yes!	All but Small Kids	Come early and use Universal Express Pass. Note there's a maximum height restriction of 6'3″ and a weight restriction of 250 pounds and under.

★ = Fodor's Choice

WET 'N WILD

THE WATERY WILD SIDE

Since 1977 Wet 'n Wild has been a place to cool off and take a break from the theme parks. Even though the Atlantic Ocean is a mere 50 mi east of Orlando and the Gulf of Mexico is just 90 mi to the west, neither has the massive slides, tube rides, knee-ski lines, and gentle rapids.

Wet 'n Wild has plenty of competition thanks to Disney's Blizzard Beach and Typhoon Lagoon themed water parks and SeaWorld's flashy, splashy Aquatica. But Wet 'n Wild still has the advantage of its location: it's right on the International Drive tourist corridor and a short drive from Universal Orlando.

The park has also earned credit for decades of giving swimmers and aquatic thrill seekers what they're looking for—the most incredible plunges, dives, spins, and swirls they've ever experienced.

WHERE TO EAT

A day here involves nearly nonstop walking, climbing, plunging, and swimming, so eat a high-protein meal and plenty of snacks to keep your energy going. Although there isn't one large restaurant, there are plenty of snack stands and food kiosks scattered throughout the park.

Two standouts include **Manny's Pizza** (pizza, spaghetti, and subs) and the main eating establishment, **Surf Grill,** which serves hamburgers, hot dogs, chicken, BBQ beef sandwiches, along with more healthy choices such as veggie burgers, baked potatoes, and salads. Smaller kiosks feature cotton candy, ice cream, funnel cakes, and other 'carnival-style' selections.

VISITING TIPS

■ Want to save a bundle? Visit after 2 PM, and the admission price drops by half.

■ Note that inner tubes for Surf Lagoon (aka the Wave Pool) are $4 with a $2 deposit. How much are life jackets? Don't be silly—they're free.

■ To claim a prime beach spot, arrive 30 minutes before the park opens, or visit on a cloudy day. If it looks like rain all day, though, head elsewhere.

■ Men should wear a true bathing suit, and women should opt for a one-piece rather than a bikini. Cutoff shorts or any garment with rivets, metal buttons, or zippers aren't allowed.

■ Wading slippers are a good idea (put them in a locker, or plan to carry them when taking a plunge, though). The rough, hot sidewalks and sandpaperlike pool bottoms can do a number on your feet.

■ Stash money, keys, prescription glasses, and other valuables in a locker.

■ Be patient with the lines here. Just when you think you've arrived, you discover there's another level or two to go.

■ To bypass lines at seven popular rides, get an Express Pass. One-time (i.e., single-use) passes for those rides cost $15. Perpetual passes, which you can use again and again on the popular attractions, cost $25. There is a limited number of passes sold each day; all the more reason to get here early.

■ OK. So you arrived armed with a swimsuit and a towel. But what about sunscreen? You can buy it and other necessities or souvenirs at the Breakers Beach Shop near the park entrance. And if you did forget your towel, renting one here costs $2 with a $2 deposit. Rent a three pack, though, and you'll save $2.

TOP WET 'N WILD ATTRACTIONS

Bomb Bay. You drop through the floor of a cylinder and plummet down a nearly vertical slide—as they say, the first step is a doozy.
Storm. Nestled in an inner tube, you slip into a surreal spin around a massive basin that slowly but surely washes you . . . down the drain.
Disco H20. Why spin through a watery disco to a 1970s soundtrack? To experience the aquatic dance-hall sensation that makes this ride so popular.
Brain Wash. Lighting effects and surreal sounds accompany your five-story drop and spin around a 65-foot domed funnel.
Lazy River. This calming stream is a good antidote to all the adrenaline.
Surf Lagoon. If the beach is out of reach, take advantage of the sand and surf here.

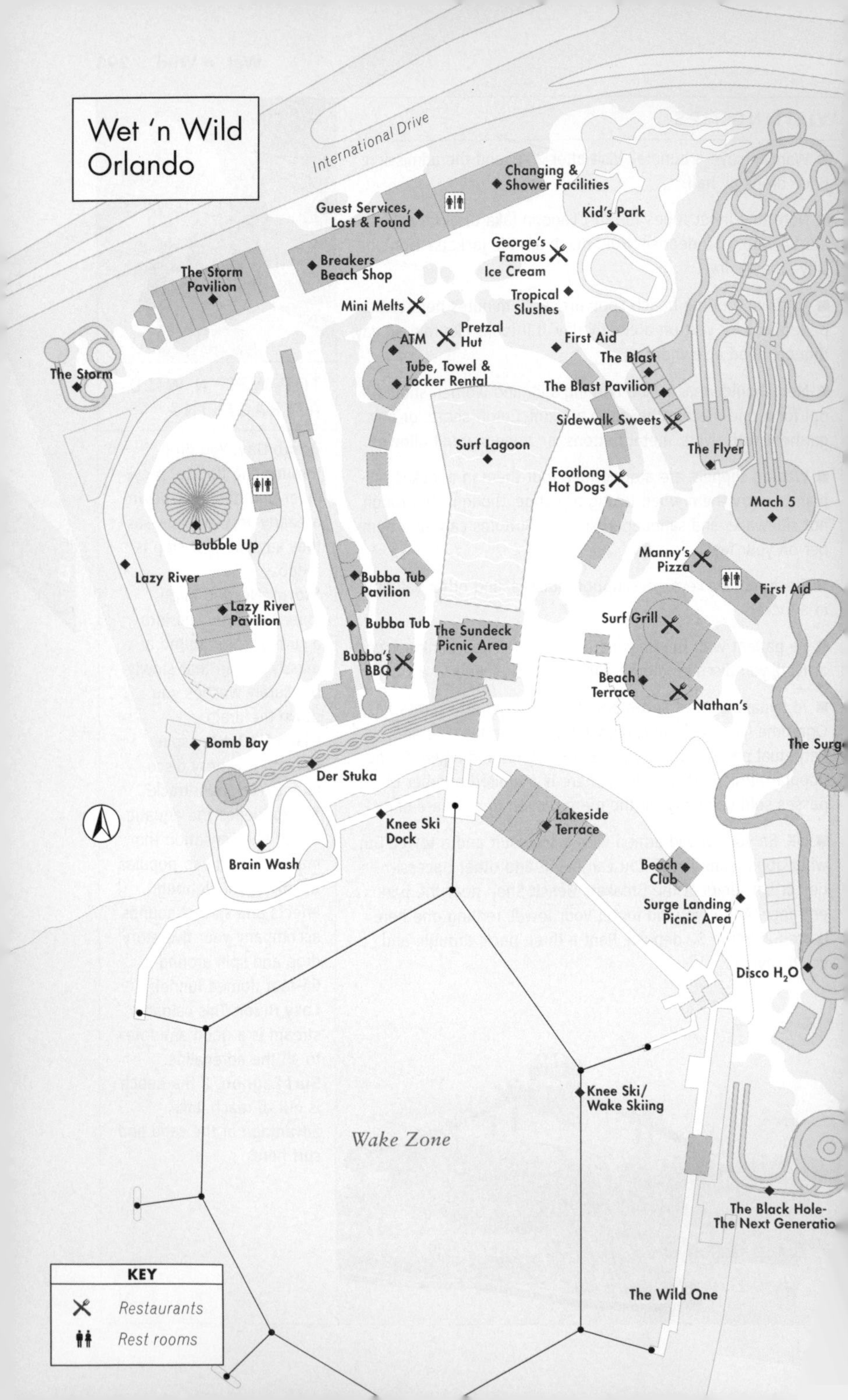
Wet 'n Wild Orlando
International Drive
Changing & Shower Facilities
Guest Services, Lost & Found
Kid's Park
George's Famous Ice Cream
The Storm Pavilion
Breakers Beach Shop
Tropical Slushes
Mini Melts
Pretzal Hut
ATM
First Aid
The Storm
Tube, Towel & Locker Rental
The Blast
The Blast Pavilion
Sidewalk Sweets
Surf Lagoon
The Flyer
Footlong Hot Dogs
Mach 5
Bubble Up
Manny's Pizza
Lazy River
Bubba Tub Pavilion
First Aid
Lazy River Pavilion
Surf Grill
Bubba Tub
The Sundeck Picnic Area
Bubba's BBQ
Beach Terrace
Nathan's
Bomb Bay
The Surge
Der Stuka
Knee Ski Dock
Lakeside Terrace
Brain Wash
Beach Club
Surge Landing Picnic Area
Disco H_2O
Knee Ski/ Wake Skiing
Wake Zone
The Black Hole- The Next Generatio
The Wild One
KEY
Restaurants
Rest rooms

[illegible] 'N WILD WATER PARKS

NAME	HEIGHT REQ.	TYPE OF	DURATION	CROWDS	AUDIENCE	TIPS
Black Hole: The Next Generation	36" with an adult, 48" without	Waterslide	1 min.	Heavy	All but Small Kids	Try it very early (or very late) or invest in an Express Pass.
The Blast	36" with an adult, 48" without	Waterslide	Under 1 min.	Heavy	Families	Keep an eye on the line and come when it looks short.
★ Bomb Bay	At least 48"	Waterslide	Under 1 min.	Heavy	All but Small Kids	Watch the line.
★ Brain Wash	At least 48"	Waterslide	1 min.	Heavy	Families	Try it very early (or very late) or invest in an Express Pass.
Bubba Tub	36" with an adult, 48" without	Waterslide	Under 1 min.	Moderate	Families	Early, late, or EXPRESS Pass.
Bubble Up	42"–64" only	Pool Area	Up to You	Light	Small Kids	Come when your kids are ready.
Der Stuka	At least 48"	Waterslide	1 min.	Moderate	All but Small Kids	Come early, late, or use an Express Pass.
★ Disco H20	36" with an adult, 48" without	Waterslide	1 min.	Heavy	Families	Come early, late, or use an Express Pass.
The Flyer	36" with an adult, 48" without	Waterslide	1 min.	Heavy	Families	Keep an eye on the line and head over when it's short.
Kids' Park	Under 48" to ride the rides	Pool Area	Up to You	Moderate to Heavy	Small Kids	Come when you need a break but the kids still have energy.
Knee Ski/ Wakeboard	At least 56"	Thrill Ride with Water	Over 1 min.	Vary by Season	Tweens and Teens	It sosts extra, but the pass is good all day.
Lazy River	n/a	Pool Area	Up to You	Moderate	All Ages	Come whenever you wish
Mach 5	n/a	Waterslide	1 min.	Moderate	All but Small Kids	Come early, late, or when the line looks short.
The Storm	At least 48"	Waterslide	1 min.	Moderate	All but Small Kids	Come early or late.
Surf Lagoon	Those under 48" must wear flotation devices	Beach Area	Up to You	Moderate to Heavy	All Ages	Come anytime.

★ = Fodor's Choice

OTHER UNIVERSAL ACTIVITIES

SHOPPING

If you just pass through the parks focused on the main rides, you may not notice that you're essentially walking through an outdoor mall. That said, there are a few key shopping areas.

TOP AREAS

Universal. The largest collection of stores is near the park gates around Production Central and Hollywood. Here the inventory ranges from silver-screen collectibles to the usual souvenirs and kitsch. The Universal Studios Store offers one-stop shopping.

Islands of Adventure. The largest concentration of stores is near the gates at the Port of Entry. And a central emporium—the Trading Company—carries nearly every coveted collectible from nearly every park shop.

CityWalk. This 30-acre entertainment and retail complex is at the hub of promenades that lead to Universal Studios and Islands of Adventure. Shops here sell fine jewelry, cool beachwear, fashionable clothing, and stylish accessories. Where are the best stores of them all? Near the entrance/exit of the complex.

Wet 'n Wild. You may not need a lot when you're hanging out wearing a bathing suit, but even Wet 'n Wild knows that you probably will need (or just want) something. One store—the Breakers Beach Shop—carries beachwear and other assorted gear.

NIGHTLIFE

Unlike at Disney, Universal has nightlife for adults who want to party. The epicenter is CityWalk, which has, among other things, an over-the-top discotheque, a theater for the popular Blue Man Group, and a huge hall where karaoke's king.

Clubs have individual cover charges, but it's far more economical to pay for the whole kit and much of the caboodle. Choose a Party Pass (a one-price-all-clubs admission) for $11.99; a Party Pass-and-a-Movie for $15 (plus tax); a Movie-and-a-Meal for $21.95; or a Party Pass-and-a-Meal for $21.

With 20 screens, there's certain to be a movie you'll like at AMC Universal cineplex. Meals (tax and gratuity included) are served at Jimmy Buffett's Margaritaville, the Hard Rock Cafe, NASCAR Sports Grille, and others. And after 6 PM the $14 parking fee drops to $3. However, it's a long haul from the garage to CityWalk—if you prefer, simply call a cab. They run at all hours.

CITYWALK

BARS AND CLUBS

Jimmy Buffett's Margaritaville. Buffett tunes fill the air at the restaurant here and at Volcano, Land Shark, and 12 Volt bars. There's a Pan Am Clipper suspended from the ceiling, music videos projected onto sails, limbo and hula-hoop contests, a huge margarita blender that erupts

TOP SOUVENIRS

Each park has an item or two that tells folks where you've been (and that you're a savvy shopper). Here are a few top picks.

Shop like Homer. At Apu Nahasapeemapetilon's Kwik-E-Mart, near the Simpsons Ride at Universal Studios, Marge wigs and Homer T-shirts or boxer shorts are natural choices.

Shop like an Egyptian In any number of stores you'll find an assortment of super-hero and film-themed souvenirs—from Spider-Man gear and Incredible Hulk fists to Egyptian hats and clothing from *The Mummy.* **Pair Up.** At Seuss Landing in IOA, Thing 1 and Thing 2 T-shirts are always a hit with couples and siblings. Or how about a couple of red-and-white-striped Cat in the Hat mugs?

Make Some Magic. Visit IOA's Wizarding World of Harry Potter and you may find you're one of the first to return home with a Nimbus 2000 broomstick.

Dry Off. Check out Wet 'n Wild's collection of beach towels—one of the few souvenirs you may actually use after you go home.

6

"when the volcano blows," live music nightly—everything that Parrotheads need to roost. ☎ *407/224-2692* 🌐 *www.margaritaville.com* 🎟 *$7 after 10* PM ⏲ *Daily 11:30* AM*–2* AM.

Bob Marley—A Tribute to Freedom. This club, modeled after the so-called King of Reggae's home in Kingston, Jamaica, is like a museum, with more than 100 photographs and paintings showing pivotal moments in Marley's life. Off the cozy bar is a patio where you can be jammin' to a (loud) live band that plays from 8 PM to 1:30 AM nightly. ☎ *407/224–2692* 🎟 *$7 after 8* PM ⏲ *Weekdays 4* PM*–2* AM*, weekends 2* PM*–2* AM.

the groove. Prepare for an under-30 crowd, lots of fog, swirling lights, and sweaty bodies. The '70s-style Green Room is filled with the kind of stuff you threw out when Duran Duran hit the charts. The Blue Room is sci-fi Jetson-y, and the Red Room is hot and romantic in a bordello sort of way. ☎ *407/224–2692* 🎟 *$7* ⏲ *Daily 9* PM*–2* AM.

Latin Quarter. A tribute to Latin music and dance, this place is spicy hot—salsa hot, even. Although there is a restaurant, most people come for the nightclub. It's a 21st-century version of Ricky Ricardo's Tropicana, with a design based on Aztec, Inca, and Maya architecture. There's even an Andes Mountain range, complete with waterfalls, around the dance floor. ☎ *407/224–2692* 🎟 *$7; price may vary for certain performances* ⏲ *Mon.–Thurs. 5* PM*–2* AM*, Fri. and Sat. noon–2* AM.

Pat O'Brien's. It's an exact reproduction of the legendary New Orleans bar, complete with flaming fountain and dueling pianists. The draw here is the Patio Bar, where a wealth of tables and chairs allow you to do nothing but enjoy your potent, rum-based Hurricanes. ☎ *407/224–2692* 🌐 *www.patobriens.com* 🎟 *$7 after 9* PM ⏲ *Patio Bar daily 4* PM*–2* AM*; piano bar daily 6* PM*–2* AM.

Red Coconut Club. The interior is part Vegas lounge, part Cuban club, and part Polynesian tiki bar—all circa the 1950s. There's a full bar, signature martinis, an extensive wine list, and VIP bottle service. Hang out in the Rat Pack–style lounge, on the balcony, or with the happening bar crowd. A DJ or live music pushes the energy with tunes ranging from Sinatra to rock. ☎ *407/224–2692* 🎫 *$7 after 9* PM ⏲ *Sun.–Wed. 8* PM*–2* AM*, Thurs.–Sat. 6* PM*–2* AM.

Rising Star. Here you and other hopeful (and hopeless) singers can let loose. Instead of singing to recorded music, you're accompanied by a band complete with backup singers—and all before an audience. Although the band's not here on Sunday and Monday, the backup singers are on hand every night. ☎ *407/224–2692* 🎫 *$7* ⏲ *Nightly 8* PM*–2* AM*, 21 and up; 18 and up on Thurs.*

SHOWS

Blue Man Group. The Sharp-Aquos Theatre is home to one act: the Blue Man Group, who present 90 minutes of surreal and silly routines—greatly appreciated by anyone who enjoys juvenile humor, which, as it turns out, happens to be most people. How many marshmallows can one Blue Man catch in his mouth? Many. Is it really art when a Blue Man spits paint onto a spinning canvas? Can someone really create music out of a spaghetti twist of PVC tubing? ☎ *407/BLUE–MAN (258–3626)* 🎫 *Adults advance purchase from $64, children 9 and under from $25 (add $10 when buying at the box office)* ⏲ *Daily showtimes vary, call for schedule.*

Hard Rock Café. The Hard Rock here is the largest on earth. This means more memorabilia than ever, including Beatles rarities such as cutouts from the *Sgt. Pepper* cover, John Lennon's famous "New York City" T-shirt, Paul's original lyrics for "Let It Be," and the doors from London's Abbey Road studios. At the Hard Rock Live concert hall, seats are hard and two-thirds don't face the stage, but there's a performance just about every night. Warning: you can't bring large purses or bags inside, and there are no lockers at CityWalk. ☎ *407/224–2692* 🌐 *www.hardrocklive.com* 🎫 *Cover prices vary* ⏲ *Daily from 11* AM*, with varying closing times, generally around midnight.*

RESORT BARS

There are several lounges within Universal's resort hotels, each themed and each a sanctuary where you can relax with a soothing libation.

Royal Pacific Resort. Jake's American Bar has a South Pacific look (it's themed as the retreat of an island-hopping airline pilot), English and Asian entrées, cocktails, a full liquor bar, and live background music. The **Orchid Court Lounge and Sushi Bar** is resplendent with orchids, hand-carved Balinese furniture, and South Seas martinis and drinks.

Portofino Bay. At the dockside **Thirsty Fish** bar, sunsets are accompanied by wine and live jazz. **Bar American** specializes in martinis and other cocktails, and grappa.

Hard Rock Hotel. The **Beach Club** is a pool–beach bar and grill where you can sip a tropical drink or cold beer. The evening's certainly more upscale at the **Velvet Lounge,** a hip retreat that's home to the monthly Velvet Sessions rock-and-roll cocktail party.

7

SeaWorld Orlando

SEAWORLD, DISCOVERY COVE, AQUATICA

WORD OF MOUTH

"SeaWorld has fewer rides but fewer lines. It also has animal shows. . . . the Shamu show is amazing, but Pets Ahoy is terrific."

—321go

"SeaWorld . . . is very manageable on a 100+ heat index day, with all the "splash" potential and air-conditioned areas . . ."

—rattravelers

SEAWORLD ORLANDO PLANNER

Operating Hours

SeaWorld opens daily at 9 AM and closes at 7 PM, with extended hours during the summer and holidays. Hours at Discovery Cove also vary seasonally, although it's generally open daily from 9 to 5:30. Aquatica is open at 9 AM, with closing times varying between 5 and 10 PM depending on the season. Allow a full day to see each attraction.

Contacts

Aquatica: ☎ *888/800–5447* 🌐 *www.aquaticabyseaworld.com*

Busch Gardens Tampa: ☎ *877/557–7404* 🌐 *www.buschgardens.com/bgt*

Discovery Cove: ☎ *877/557–7404* 🌐 *www.discoverycove.com*

SeaWorld: ☎ *888/800–5447* 🌐 *www.seaworld.com*

Beluga at SeaWorld.

Getting Here

West on Interstate 4 (toward Disney) take Exit 72; from the east, take Exit 71. Either way you'll be heading east on the Beachline Expressway (aka Route 528); the first right-hand exit leads you to International Drive. Turn left and you'll soon see the entrance to Aquatica on your left. Sea Harbor Drive—leading to SeaWorld's entrance—will be on your right. To reach Discovery Cove, head past Aquatica to the intersection of International Drive and the Central Florida Parkway. The park's entrance will be on your left.

PARKING

Parking costs $12 for a car, and $15 for an RV or camper. For $20 you can pull into a one of the six rows closest to the front gate. Parking is free at Discovery Cove.

Admission

SeaWorld, Discovery Cove, Aquatica, and Busch Gardens Tampa Bay fall under the SeaWorld Parks & Entertainment umbrella, and you can save by buying combo tickets. Regular one-day tickets to **SeaWorld** cost $74.95 (adults) and $64.95 (children ages 3–9), excluding tax. **Aquatica** admission is $41.95 (adults) and $35.95 (children 3–9).

Reserve **Discovery Cove** visits well in advance—attendance is limited to about 1,000 a day. Tickets (with a dolphin swim) start at $199 (off-season) but are generally around $289. Forgo the dolphin swim and save $100. Either fee includes access to all beach and snorkeling areas and the free-flight aviary; meals and snacks; use of a mask, snorkel, swim vest, towel, locker, and sunscreen; parking; and a pass for 14 days of unlimited admission to SeaWorld Orlando, Aquatica, or Busch Gardens Tampa.

QUICK QUEUE PASSES

SeaWorld's Quick Queue pass, which costs $14.95–$24.95 per person depending on the season, gets you to the front of the line at major attractions and shows. Neither Discovery Cove nor Aquatica has such a pass.

Smart SeaWorld

- **Avoid weekend and school-holiday visits.** These are the busiest times, so plan around them if you can.
- **Wear sneakers or water shoes**—no heels or slip-on sandals.
- **Pack dry clothes.** You can get wet just by being toward the front at the Shamu show or riding Journey to Atlantis. Alternatively, carry a rain poncho.
- **Budget for food for the animals.** Participating in animal feedings is a major part of the SeaWorld experience. A small carton of fish costs $5.
- **Pick up a map/show schedule inside the entrance.** Spend a few minutes planning so you can casually stroll from show to show and have time for learning, testing out thrill rides, *and* enjoying a leisurely meal.
- **Be open to learning.** SeaWorld's trainers and educators are always at the ready to share information about the park's wildlife.

Discovery Done Right

- **Make reservations well in advance.** Prized June dates, for instance, can sell out in March. If there aren't openings when you call, though, don't despair. Call back often to inquire about cancellations.
- **Think about your eyewear.** Park masks don't accommodate glasses, and there's a limited number of prescription masks (first-come, first-served). Consider wearing contacts as an alternative.
- **Don't bring your own wet suit or fins.** Every guest must wear a Discovery Cove–issued wet suit or vest—not a bad idea, as the water can be cold.
- **Leave belongings in your locker.** The plastic passes you're given are all you need to pick up your meals, soft drinks, and—if you're over 21—alcoholic drinks.
- **Be flexible when it comes to weather.** If weather is really bad (e.g., a daylong thunderstorm) on your reserved day, attempts will be made to reschedule for while you're in town. If that's not possible, you'll have to settle for a refund.
- **Have a dolphin relay a message.** The Special Occasion Package enlists the help of a bottlenose dolphin to deliver love notes, wedding proposals, birthday or anniversary greetings, and the like.

Aquatica Advice

- **Buy tickets in advance.** Tickets bought ahead of time online or at another park allow early entry to Aquatica, which, in turn, increases your chances of hitting all the big-deal flume and tube rides—possibly more than once.
- **Be open to animal encounters.** The Commerson's dolphins of Dolphin Plunge have scheduled feeding times, and you can see macaws perched on tree limbs and small mammals on display in Conservation Cabanas—usually attended to by knowledgeable educators.
- **Pack beach supplies.** You'll save a few bucks by having your own towels, lotion, water shoes, and snacks.
- **Take care of yourself.** Fight fatigue by eating a good breakfast, drinking plenty of water, and nibbling on high-energy snacks. Avoid sunburn by re-applying sunscreen often—even the waterproof stuff washes off.
- **Save your soles.** Water shoes protect your feet from hot sand and sidewalks and the rough surfaces in some pools.

By Gary McKechnie

SeaWorld and Discovery Cove offer a relatively low-key, ocean-themed experience and are designed for animal lovers and those who prefer the natural to the man-made. Aquatica, on the other hand, suits those who are looking for the action of waterslides, wave lagoons, and beaches.

At SeaWorld you can catch a series of high-energy shows involving dolphins, whales, sea lions, a huge walrus, and even cats and dogs. Plus you can ride three thrilling coasters: Kraken, considered one of the scariest rides in Florida; Journey to Atlantis, a splashy flume ride; and the park's newest coaster, Manta, which is designed to make you feel like you're sailing along with a giant manta ray.

If you had visited SeaWorld prior to 2010, you might recognize a slight, but important, difference on this trip at shows involving Shamu and his extended family. Trainers are more cautious about their interactions with the killer whales due to the tragic death of one of their colleagues in February 2010.

Discovery Cove is more of a laid-back oasis. In your wet suit or swim vest (provided) you can spend a magical day snorkeling among tropical fish; getting up close to tropical birds in an aviary; relaxing on the beach; and, for a short period and extra charge, interacting with dolphins. You'll pay roughly three times as much as for a ticket to SeaWorld, but your ticket includes 14 days of unlimited access to either SeaWorld or Aquatica or Tampa's Busch Gardens either before or after your visit to Discovery Cove.

There's no denying that SeaWorld's water park, Aquatica, was designed to compete with Disney's Blizzard Beach and Typhoon Lagoon and Universal's Wet 'n Wild. There's also no denying that it does so—admirably. It's aesthetically pleasing, with tropical, tiki-theme, and eye-popping color schemes. It's also universally appealing, with 36 waterslides of varying thrill levels, six rivers and lagoons, pint-size attractions for toddlers, and plenty of calm sandy stretches.

SeaWorld Orlando

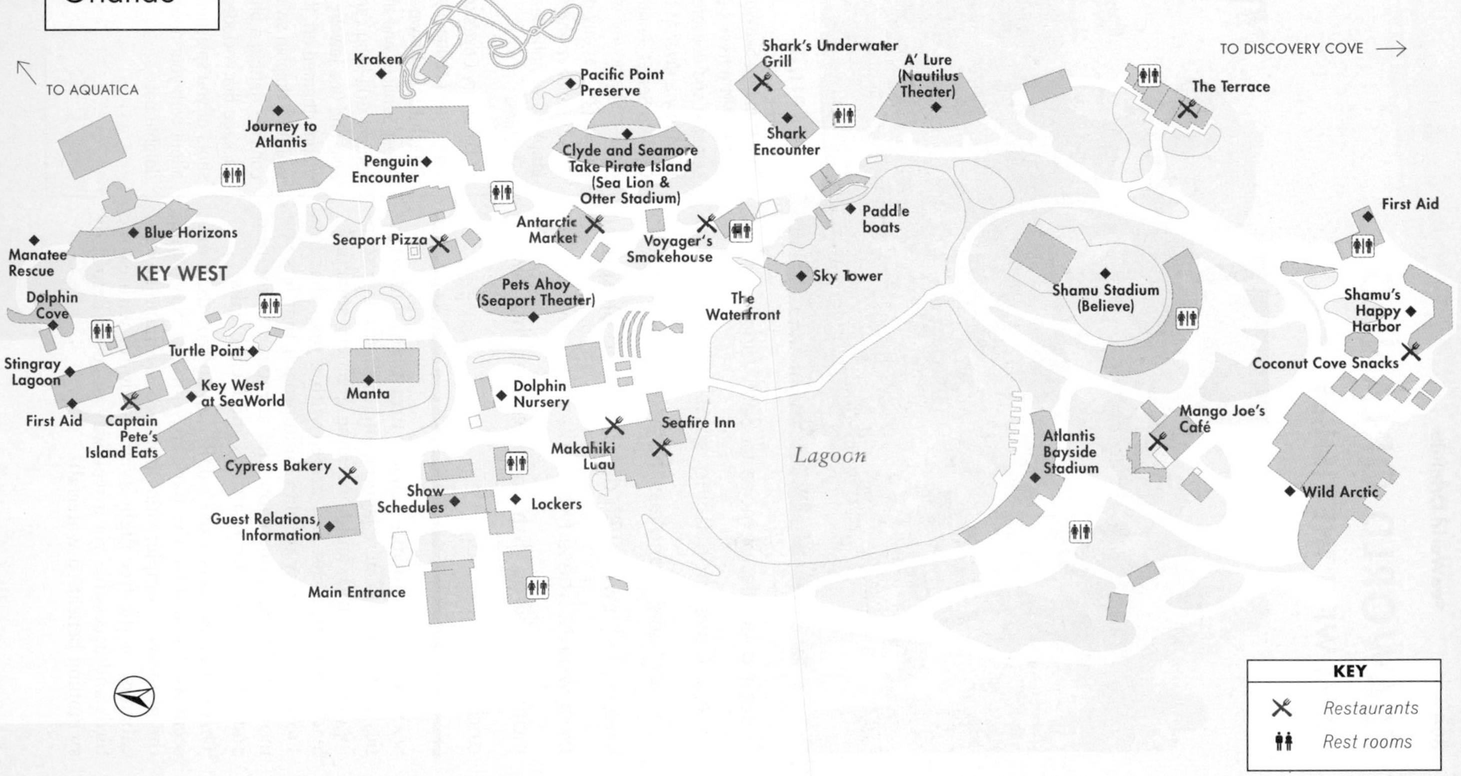

TO AQUATICA
TO DISCOVERY COVE
Kraken
Journey to Atlantis
Penguin Encounter
Pacific Point Preserve
Clyde and Seamore Take Pirate Island (Sea Lion & Otter Stadium)
Shark's Underwater Grill
Shark Encounter
A' Lure (Nautilus Theater)
The Terrace
Blue Horizons
Manatee Rescue
KEY WEST
Dolphin Cove
Stingray Lagoon
First Aid
Captain Pete's Island Eats
Turtle Point
Key West at SeaWorld
Seaport Pizza
Antarctic Market
Voyager's Smokehouse
Paddle boats
Sky Tower
The Waterfront
Pets Ahoy (Seaport Theater)
Manta
Dolphin Nursery
Cypress Bakery
Guest Relations, Information
Show Schedules
Lockers
Main Entrance
Makahiki Luau
Seafire Inn
Lagoon
Shamu Stadium (Believe)
Atlantis Bayside Stadium
Mango Joe's Café
First Aid
Shamu's Happy Harbor
Coconut Cove Snacks
Wild Arctic
KEY
Restaurants
Rest rooms

SEAWORLD ORLANDO

SWIM WITH THE FISHIES

There's a whole lot more to SeaWorld and Discovery Cove than being splashed by Shamu. You can see manatees face-to-snout, learn to love an eel, swim with dolphins, and be spat at by a walrus. These two parks celebrates all the mammals, birds, fish, and reptiles that live in and near the ocean.

SeaWorld's performance venues, attractions, and activities surround a 17-acre lagoon, and the artful landscaping, curving paths, and concealing greenery sometimes lead to wrong turns. But armed with a map that lists showtimes, it's easy to plan an approach that lets you move fluidly from one show and attraction to the next and still have time for rest stops and meal breaks.

Thanks to Discovery Cove's daily cap on crowds, it may seem as if you have the park to yourself. Navigating the grounds is simple; signs point to swimming areas, cabanas, or the free-flight aviary—aflutter with exotic birds and accessible via a walkway or (even better) by swimming beneath a waterfall.

SHOPPING

One standout SeaWorld souvenir is a fresh pearl selected and delivered to you by a diver at the Oyster's Secret. Another is a plush Shamu toy, which you can find at any gift store, including **Shamu's Emporium**, right near the turnstiles.

At Discovery Cove's top shop—the cabana-style **Beach Kiosk** between Guest Services and the Laguna Grill—you can also find fine jewelry and marine-themed art. If you do a dolphin swim, consider getting a photo package that includes shots of you splashing about with your newfound dolphin pal.

TOP SEAWORLD ATTRACTIONS

Manta. SeaWorld likes to claim this is two attractions in one: while waiting in line, you walk past 10 supercool aquariums filled with rays and fish. But the big thrill is the amazingly fast coaster at the front of the line.

Kraken. It takes you on a high-speed chase with a dragon. But who's chasing who? Fast and furious.

Pets Ahoy. Anyone who has ever loved a pet, or wanted one, has to see the talented cats, dogs, birds, and pig in this cute and clever show.

Journey to Atlantis. Although it seems a little dated, the Splash Mountain–esque ride still provides thrills—especially on its last, steep, wet drop.

Believe. The park's flagship attraction and mascot are irresistible. In a show four years in the making, you'll see several Shamus performing graceful aquabatics that are guaranteed to thrill.

Clyde and Seamore Take Pirate Island. Head for Sea Lion & Otter Stadium to watch this slapstick comedy routine starring an adorable team of water mammals and their trainers.

TOP DISCOVERY COVE ATTRACTIONS

Snorkeling Pools. The snorkeling pools may well be Discovery Cove's must underhyped attractions. It's a real thrill to float lazily and silently amid tropical fish, to swim beneath a waterfall into an elaborate aviary, and to dive down a few feet to peer at sharks and barracuda through the porthole of a wrecked ship. There's also on-site snorkeling instruction for novices.

Private Cabanas. Granted, admission to Discovery Cove isn't cheap, but if you can pony up a little more (about $175), you'll enjoy complete privacy, personalized service, and a well-stocked mini-refrigerator in these tropical waterfront sanctuaries.

HOW IT BEGAN

Hard to believe that four frat brothers intent on creating a restaurant would inadvertently build the foundation for one of the world's most popular theme parks. In the early 1960s, UCLA grads Milton Shedd, David DeMott, George Millay, and Ken Norris were ready to parlay their talent and ambition into an underwater restaurant, but as plans changed they ended up building San Diego's SeaWorld, which opened in early 1964.
Within the first year, the park welcomed more than 400,000 visitors. It took several more years before the second SeaWorld, in Ohio, opened. This was followed in 1973 by Orlando's SeaWorld, and, in 1988—under the then-new ownership of publishing firm Harcourt Brace Jovanovich—a fourth park in San Antonio.

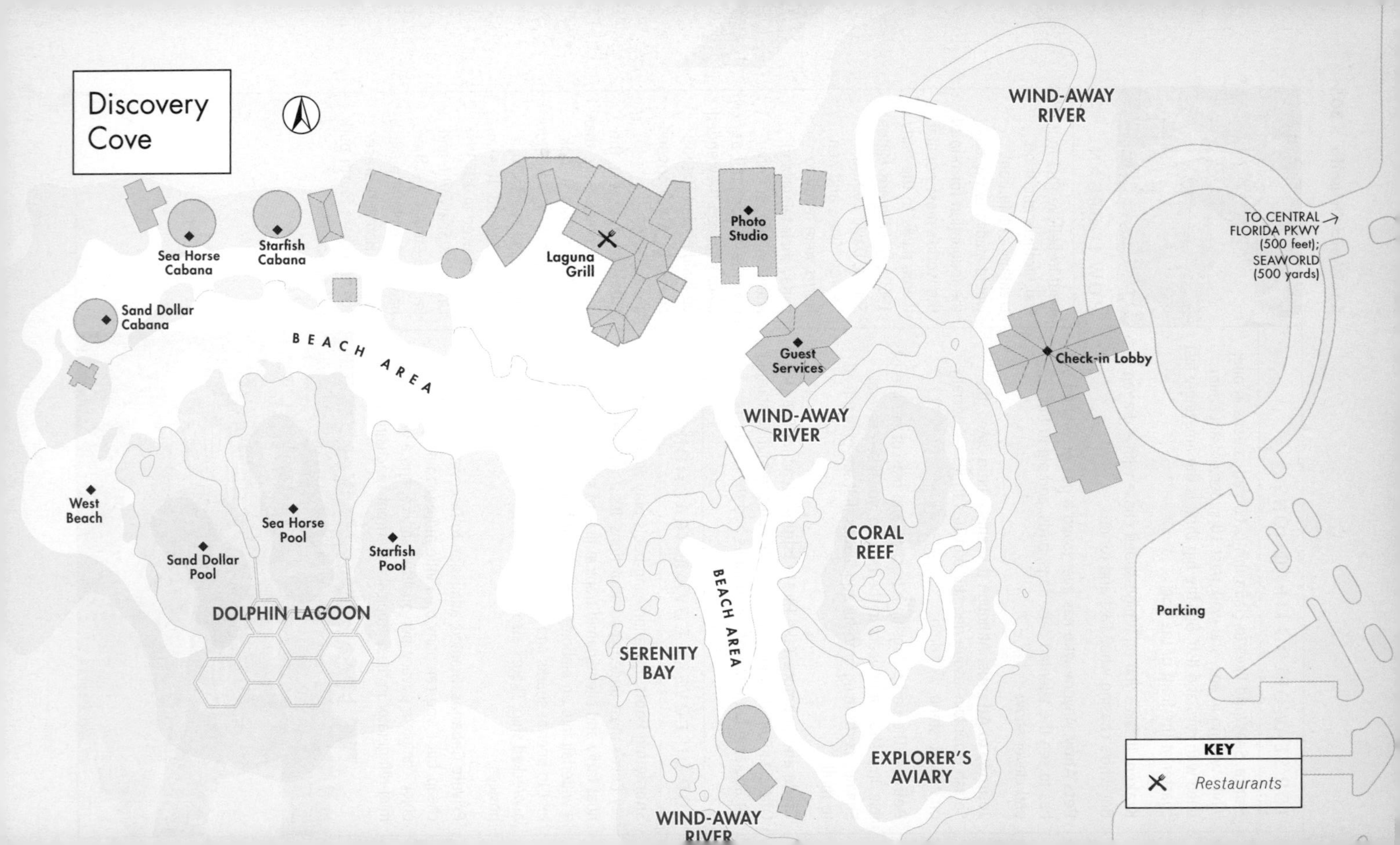
Discovery Cove
Sea Horse Cabana
Starfish Cabana
Sand Dollar Cabana
Laguna Grill
Photo Studio
WIND-AWAY RIVER
TO CENTRAL FLORIDA PKWY (500 feet); SEAWORLD (500 yards)
BEACH AREA
Guest Services
Check-in Lobby
WIND-AWAY RIVER
West Beach
Sea Horse Pool
Sand Dollar Pool
Starfish Pool
DOLPHIN LAGOON
CORAL REEF
BEACH AREA
SERENITY BAY
Parking
EXPLORER'S AVIARY
WIND-AWAY RIVER
KEY
Restaurants

DID YOU KNOW?

Commerson's dolphins (*Cephalorhynchus commersonii*) were named after Philibert Commerçon, an 18th-century scientist who saw them swimming in the Strait of Magellan in South America.

SEAWORLD ORLANDO AND DISCOVERY COVE

NAME	Height Req.	Type of Entertainment	Duration	Crowds	Audience	Tips
Sea World						
A'Lure, the Call of the Ocean	n/a	Show	20 mins.	Heavy	All Ages	Plenty of seats, but arrive 15 mins. early for a wide selection.
Blue Horizons	n/a	Show	20 mins.	Heavy	All Ages	Arrive 20 mins. before showtime.
Dolphin Nursery	n/a	Aquarium	Up to you	Light	All Ages	Come during a Shamu show so the kids can be up front.
Journey to Atlantis	At least 42"	Thrill Ride with Water	6 mins.	Heavy	All but Small Kids	You can make a beeline here first thing or come about an hour before closing. But the best time for this is at night.
Key West at SeaWorld	n/a	Walk-Through/ Aquarium	Up to you	Light to Moderate	All Ages	If too crowded, wander until crowds disperse.
★ Kraken	At least 54"	Thrill Ride	6 mins.	Heavy	All but Small Kids	Get to the park when it opens and head straight to Kraken; otherwise, hit it near closing time or during a Blue Horizons show.
Manatees Rescue	n/a	Aquarium	Up to you	Light to Moderate	All Ages	Come during a Shamu show but *not* right after a dolphin show.
★ Manta	At least 54"	Thrill Ride with Water	6 mins.	You Bet!	All but Small Kids	Come first thing or late in the day, or purchase a Quick Queue pass for front-of-ride access.
Pacific Point Preserve	n/a	Aquarium	Up to you	Light	All Ages	Come anytime.
Penguin Encounter	n/a	Aquarium	Up to you	Moderate to Heavy	All Ages	Come during dolphin and sea lion shows, and before you've gotten soaked at Journey to Atlantis, or you'll freeze.
Pets Ahoy	n/a	Show	15–20 mins.	Moderate to Heavy	All Ages	Gauge the crowds, and come here early if necessary.
★ Sea Lion & Otter Stadium	n/a	Show	40 mins.	Light	All Ages	Sit toward the center for the best view, and don't miss the beginning.

Shamu's Happy Harbor	n/a	Playground with Water	Up to you	Heavy	Small Kids	Don't come first thing in morning, or you'll never drag your child away. Bring a towel to dry them off.
★ Shamu Stadium (Believe)	n/a	Show	30 mins.	Moderate to Heavy	All Ages	Come 30 mins. early for early-afternoon shows. Don't miss close-up encounters.
Shark Encounter	n/a	Aquarium	Up to you	Light to Moderate	All Ages	Come during the sea lion show.
Sky Tower	n/a	Tour/ Thrill Ride	6 mins.	Light	All Ages	Come whenever there's no line. Note the extra $3 charge, though.
Stingray Lagoon	n/a	Aquarium	Up to you	Moderate to Heavy	All Ages	Walk by if it's crowded, but return before dusk.
Turtle Point	n/a	Zoo	Up to you	Light	All Ages	Come anytime.
Wild Arctic	At least 42"	Simulator Exp./ Aquarium	5+ mins.	Moderate to Heavy	All Ages	Come during a Shamu show. You can skip the ride if you just want to see the mammals.
Discovery Cove						
Beaches	n/a	Beach Area	Up to you	Light	All Ages	Arrive early and head to the far side for a private spot.
Coral Reef	n/a	Aquarium/ Pool Area	Up to you	Light to Moderate	All Ages	Monitor crowds and come when they're lightest. Popular with teens.
★ Dolphin Lagoon	n/a	Pool	45–60 mins.	n/a	All but Small Kids	Be mindful of your appointment time.
Explorer's Aviary	n/a	Aviary	Up to you	Light to Moderate	All Ages	Come early, when the birds are most active.
Wind-Away River	n/a	Aquarium	Up to you	Light to Moderate	All Ages	When it gets hot, slip into the water. Popular with teens.

★ = Fodor's Choice

AQUATICA

SPLASH IN TROPICAL SEAS

Aquatica, which opened in 2008, takes cues from SeaWorld and Discovery Cove in design and mood—marine-life motifs are everywhere. It also gives competitor water parks a run for their money with thrilling slides, broad beaches, calming rivers, and an area for small kids.

The park also takes its cues from the tropics. Right after you clear the parking lot, you'll see a tropical pastiche of buildings. Yup. That's definitely an island vibe you're detecting. Upon entering, you feel as if you've left central Florida for the Caribbean or Polynesia, even.

Go with it. Get into a groove, and relax and enjoy yourself. You might be drawn to the series of super-fast waterslides (some of which conclude by sending you into serene streams). Or you might feel the pull of the white-sand beaches beside the twin wave pools, where you can laze in the sun, venturing out every so often to try a ride or climb into an inner tube and float down a river.

Hey, it's your vacation. You're at Aquatica. Do what you like.

SHOPPING

Numerous small shops and kiosks sell beach towels, surf wear, and sunglasses—which rank high on the list of top souvenirs. You can also pick up more practical items such as sunscreen, water shoes, and flip-flops.

In addition, be on the lookout for handmade crafts and tropical- or tiki-themed souvenirs. **Adaptations** gets top-shop points for its beach apparel and surf wear from names like Roxy and Quicksilver.

FOOD FOR THOUGHT

Even though the waters are exhilarating, you'll be amazed at how much energy it takes to cover all the rides and attractions at Aquatica. You need to stay hydrated and well-nourished, which can be a costly proposition.

The park allows guests to bring in a small cooler of "serving-size" snacks, bottled water, and baby food in plastic containers. It's not so keen on "family-sized" servings (think sandwiches, pizza, and 2-liter bottles of soft drinks).

TOP AQUATICA ATTRACTIONS

Dolphin Plunge. Aquatica's commercials love to showcase this attraction, where you slip through a winding string of pitch-black tubes and then a stretch of clear tubes through the Commerson's dolphins' habitat.

Wave Pools. The lagoons here aren't too deep and are perfect for cooling off. About every 10 minutes a series of small waves move across them, enabling you to bob around like a cork.

Tassie's Twisters. After hopping into an inner tube and sloshing at a high speed through an enclosed tube, you're flung into a huge circular basin and spiraled into a drain and down a slide.

Taumata Racer. Eight colorful tubes are lined up and waiting for you. Following a countdown, you launch yourself into your chute, and following a twisting and turning ride, end up on a long and slippery slide into the splash-down pool.

WATER, WATER, EVERYWHERE

Since the days of the Roman baths, people have been on the lookout for new ways to enjoy water. For Americans, the big breakthrough came after World War II when a growing middle class with a little more money and a well-deserved desire to relax helped inspire the concept of a water park. The earliest parks included a few standard aquatic thrills: waterslides, tube slides, wave pools, and flowing rivers. Today there are well over 200 water parks in the United States (with Wisconsin claiming about 10% of the total). They range from a simple collection of slides and streams to incredible, over-the-top, exquisitely themed experiences like—Aquatica. For more information on water parks and where they're at, check out www.waterparks.com.

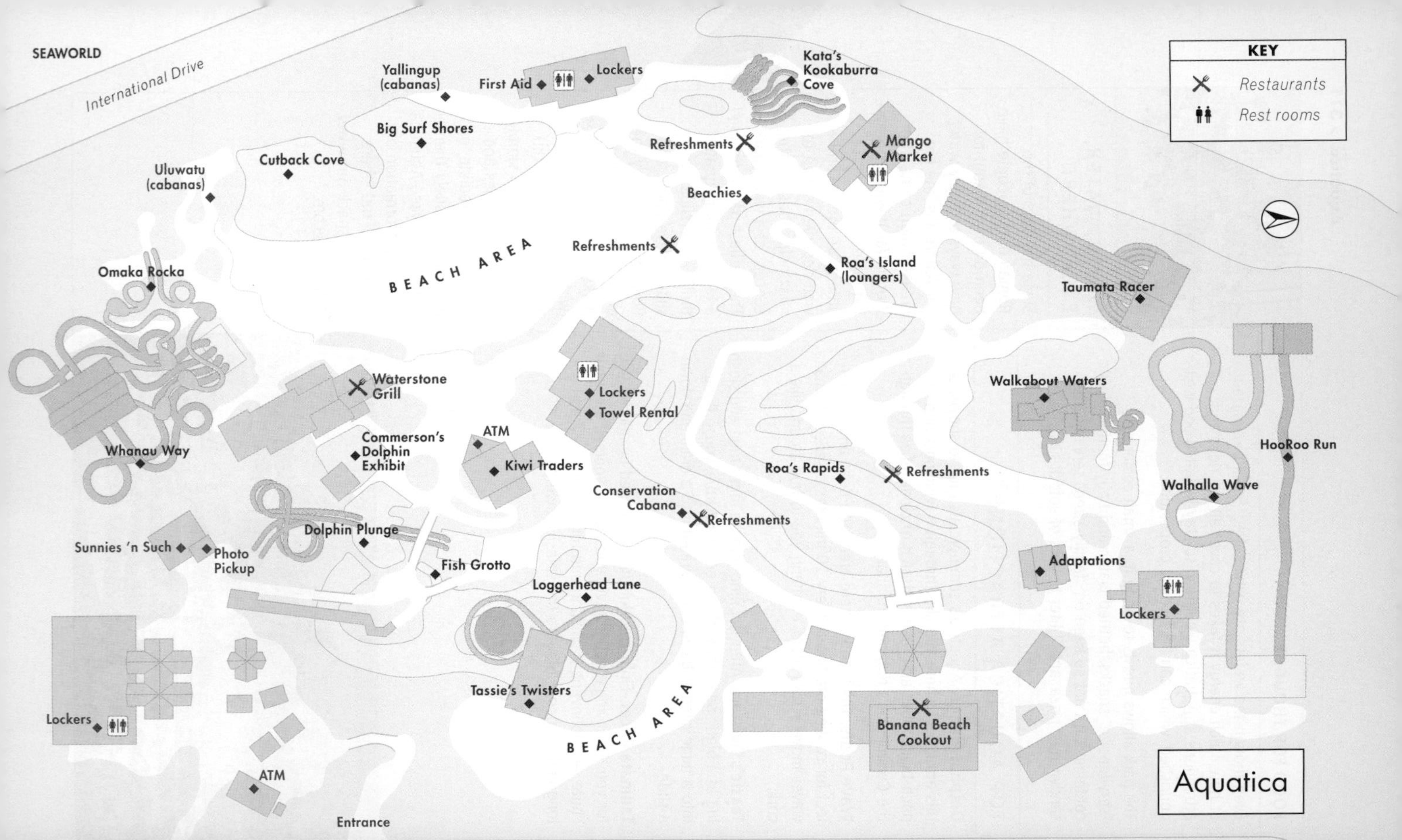
Aquatica
KEY
Restaurants
Rest rooms
SEAWORLD
International Drive
Yallingup (cabanas)
First Aid
Lockers
Kata's Kookaburra Cove
Big Surf Shores
Refreshments
Mango Market
Cutback Cove
Uluwatu (cabanas)
Beachies
Refreshments
BEACH AREA
Roa's Island (loungers)
Omaka Rocka
Taumata Racer
Waterstone Grill
Lockers
Towel Rental
Walkabout Waters
ATM
Commerson's Dolphin Exhibit
Whanau Way
Kiwi Traders
HooRoo Run
Roa's Rapids
Refreshments
Walhalla Wave
Conservation Cabana
Refreshments
Dolphin Plunge
Sunnies 'n Such
Photo Pickup
Fish Grotto
Adaptations
Loggerhead Lane
Lockers
Tassie's Twisters
BEACH AREA
Banana Beach Cookout
Lockers
ATM
Entrance

AQUATICA WATER PARK

	NAME	HEIGHT REQ.	TYPE OF ENTERTAINMENT	DURATION	CROWDS	AUDIENCE	TIPS
	Big Surf Shores and Cutback Cove	n/a	Wave Pool	Up to you	Vary by Season	Tweens and Up	Arrive early to stake your claim on the beach.
★	Dolphin Plunge	At least 48″	Waterslide	1 min.	Absolutely	Tweens and Up	Keep an eye on the line, and step up when it's light.
	HooRoo Run/Walhalla Wave	At least 42″	Waterslide	30 secs.	Heavy	All but Small Kids	Arrive early or later—or be patient.
	Kata's Kookaburra Cove	Under 48″	Playground with Water	Up to you	Moderate to Heavy	Small Kids	Adults must be accompanied by a child no more than 48 inches tall.
	Loggerhead Lane	At least 48″	River/Stream Ride	Up to you	Light	Tweens and Up	Try it during lunchtime.
	Omaka Rocka	At least 48″	Waterslide	Mere seconds	Heavy	All but Small Kids	Keep an eye on the line.
	Roa's Rapids	Under 51″ must wear life vest	River/Stream Ride	Up to you	Light	All Ages	Visit during lunchtime.
	Tassie's Twister	Under 48″ must wear life vest	Waterslide	1 min.	Heavy	Tweens and Up	Watch the line.
	Taumata Racer	At least 42″	Waterslide	30 secs.	Light to Moderate	All but Small Kids	Watch the line.
	Walkabout Waters	36″–42″ (main pool); over 42″ (large) slides. Under 48″ wear life vest on larger slides.	Playground with Water	Up to you	Heavy	All but Small Kids	Save it for when you need a break.
	Whanau Way	Under 48″ must wear life vest	Waterslide	1 min.	Heavy	All but Small Kids	Come during lunch or end of day.

★ = Fodor's Choice

DID YOU KNOW?

SeaWorld's over-the-top theatrical show, Blue Horizons, takes place above water and below. This extravaganza features the ever-popular bottlenose dolphins, exotic birds, and acrobatic performers, including aerialists and divers to showcase elements of both the sea and the sky.

The Tampa Bay Area

WORD OF MOUTH

"The north beach (at Fort DeSoto park) is huge. You can escape the crowds if you want—head to an area where there is nothing but beach, water, and scrubby trees."

—Malesherbes

WELCOME TO THE TAMPA BAY AREA

Ybor City.

TOP REASONS TO GO

★ **Art Gone Wild:** Whether you take the guided tour or chart your own course, experience the one-of-a-kind collection at the Salvador Dalí Museum in St. Petersburg.

★ **Cuban Roots:** You'll find great food and engaging shops in historic Ybor City, which is just east of downtown Tampa.

★ **Beachcomer Bonanza:** Caladesi Island State Park has some of the best shelling on the Gulf Coast, and its five-star sunsets are a great way to end the day.

★ **Culture Fix:** If you love the arts, there's no finer offering in the Bay Area than at the Florida State University Ringling Center for the Cultural Arts in Sarasota.

Ringling Museum of Art.

1 Tampa/St. Petersburg Area. State-of-the-art zoos and museums in the communities north and west of Tampa Bay promise to broaden your imagination, and some of Florida's best beaches tempt you with sparkling waters. The area includes Clearwater, Dunedin, and Tarpon Springs.

2 South of Tampa Bay: Sarasota County. Barrier islands lure travelers to another battery of white-sand beaches, but Sarasota's cultural treasures are the true draw for many of its visitors.

Home of John Ringling, Sarasota.

GETTING ORIENTED

On the east side of the bay, industry- and business-oriented Tampa also offers attractions such as Busch Gardens. To the west, St. Petersburg and Clearwater use beaches and barrier islands as calling cards. Moving to the south, Sarasota's arts scene is among the finest in Florida.

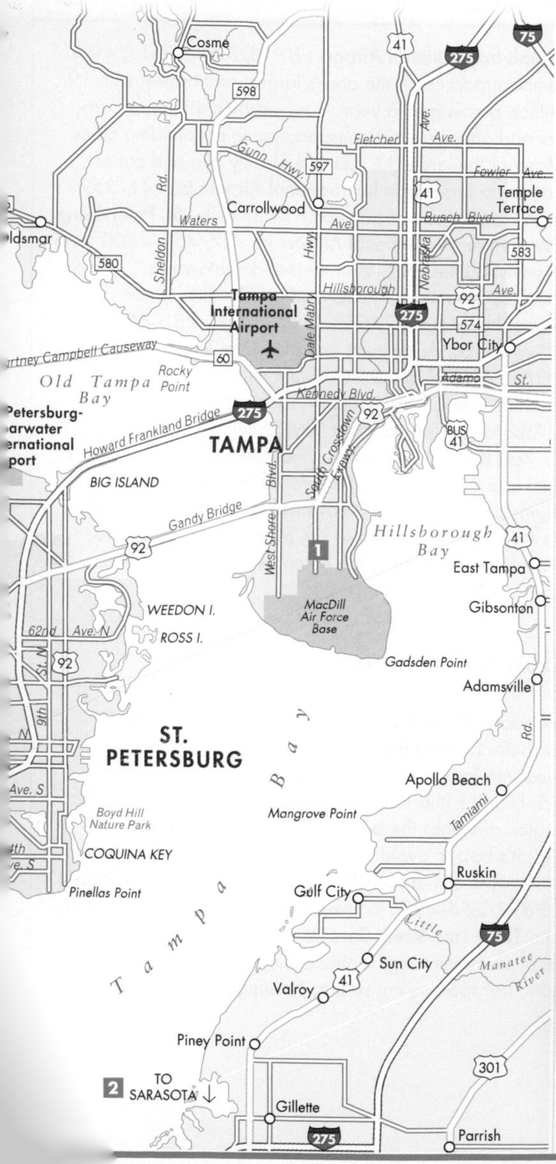

Busch Gardens.

TAMPA BAY AREA PLANNER

When to Go

Winter and spring are high season, and the level of activity is double what it is in the off-season. In summer there are huge afternoon thunderstorms, and temperatures hover around or above 90°F during the day. Luckily the mercury drops to the mid-70s at night, and beach towns have a consistent onshore breeze that starts just before sundown, which enabled civilization to survive here before air-conditioning arrived.

Visitor Information

Greater Tampa Chamber of Commerce (✉ *615 Channelside Dr., Box 420, Tampa* ☎ *813/228–7777 or 800/298–2672* 🌐 *www.tampachamber.com*).

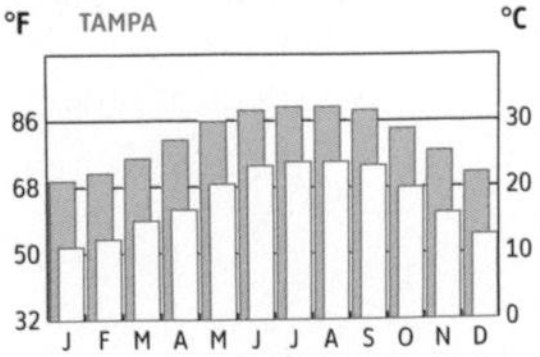

Getting Here

Tampa International Airport (☎ *813/870–8700* 🌐 *www.tampaairport.com*), the area's largest and busiest with 19 million passengers a year, is served by most major carriers and offers ground transportation to surrounding cities. Many of the large U.S. carriers also fly into and out of **Sarasota–Bradenton International Airport** (☎ *941/359–2777* 🌐 *www.srq-airport.com*). Meanwhile, **St. Petersburg–Clearwater International Airport** (☎ *727/453–7800* 🌐 *www.fly2pie.com*), 9 mi west of downtown St. Petersburg, is much smaller and has limited service. **SuperShuttle** (☎ *727/572–1111 or 800/282–6817* 🌐 *www.supershuttle.com*) and **Blue One Transportation** (☎ *813/282–7351* 🌐 *www.blueonetransportation.com*) provide Tampa International Airport service to and from Hillsborough (Tampa, Plant City), Pinellas (St. Petersburg, St. Pete Beach, Clearwater), and Polk (Lakeland) counties. Taxi fare from the airport within 10 mi (including downtown Tampa) is $15–$30. **Amtrak** (☎ *800/872–7245* 🌐 *www.amtrak.com*) trains run from the Northeast, the Midwest, and much of the South into Tampa; the station is at 601 N. Nebraska Avenue.

Getting Around

Interstates 75 and 275 span the Bay Area from north to south. Coming from Orlando, you're likely to drive west into Tampa on Interstate 4. Along with Interstate 75, U.S. 41 (the Tamiami Trail) stretches the length of the region and links the business districts of many communities; it's best to avoid it and all bridges during rush hours (7–9 AM and 4–6 PM). **Hillsborough Area Regional Transit** (☎ *813/254–4278* 🌐 *www.hartline.org*) serves the county, and **TECO Line Street Cars** (☎ *813/254–4278* 🌐 *www.tecolinestreetcar.org*) replicate the city's first electric streetcars, transporting cruise-ship passengers to Ybor City.

About the Restaurants

Fresh gulf seafood is plentiful—raw bars serving oysters, clams, and mussels are everywhere. Tampa's many Cuban and Spanish restaurants serve spicy paella with seafood and chicken, *boliche criollo* (sausage-stuffed eye-round roast) with black beans and rice, *ropa vieja* (shredded flank steak in tomato sauce), and other treats. Tarpon Springs adds classic Greek specialties. In Sarasota the emphasis is on ritzier dining, but many restaurants offer extra-cheap early-bird menus for those dining before 6 PM.

About the Hotels

Many convention hotels in the Tampa Bay Area double as family-friendly resorts—taking advantage of nearby beaches, marinas, spas, tennis courts, and golf links. However, unlike Orlando and some other parts of Florida, the area has been bustling for more than a century, and its accommodations often reflect a sense of its history. You'll find a turn-of-the-20th-century beachfront resort where Zelda and F. Scott Fitzgerald stayed, a massive all-wood building from the 1920s, plenty of art deco, and throwbacks to the Spanish-style villas of yore. But one thing they all have in common is a certain Gulf Coast charm.

Assume that hotels operate on the European Plan (EP, no meals), unless we specify that they use the Breakfast Plan (BP, with full breakfast), Continental Plan (CP, Continental breakfast), Full American Plan (FAP, all meals), or Modified American Plan (MAP, breakfast and dinner), or are all-inclusive (AI, all meals and most activities).

WHAT IT COSTS

	¢	$	$$	$$$	$$$$
Restaurants	under $10	$10–$15	$15–$20	$20–$30	over $30
Hotels	under $80	$80–$100	$100–$140	$140–$220	over $220

Restaurant prices are per person for a main course at dinner. Hotel prices are for a standard double room, excluding 6% sales tax (more in some counties) and 1%–4% tourist tax.

Boat Tours

Dolphin Landings Charter Boat Center (✉ *4737 Gulf Blvd., St. Pete Beach* ☎ *727/360–7411* 🌐 *www.dolphinlandings.com*) has daily four-hour cruises to unspoiled Egmont Key at the mouth of Tampa Bay. Aboard the glass-bottom boats of **St. Nicholas Boat Line** (✉ *693 Dodecanese Blvd., Tarpon Springs* ☎ *727/942–6425*), you take a sightseeing cruise of Tarpon Springs' historic sponge docks and see a diver at work. On **Captain Memo's Pirate Cruise** (✉ *Clearwater Beach Marina, Clearwater Beach* ☎ *727/446–2587* 🌐 *www.captainmemo.com*), crew members dressed as pirates take you on sightseeing and sunset cruises in a replica of a 19th-century sailing ship. The ***Starlite Princess*** (✉ *Clearwater Beach Marina, at the end of Rte. 60, Clearwater Beach* 🌐 *www.starlitecruises.com*), an old-fashioned paddle wheeler, and *Starlite Majesty*, a sleek yacht-style vessel, make sightseeing and dinner cruises.

8

TAMPA BAY BEACHES

Tampa Bay gets rave reviews for having some of the state's best beaches. The allure includes warm water from spring through fall, gentle waves (when there are any at all), good shelling, and usually smaller crowds than ocean-front beaches. These are great places to go for romantic walks, or enjoy spectacular sunsets.

Tampa Bay–area beaches include Madeira Beach (called Mad Beach by locals), where you can see dolphins at play, and North Redington Beach, once a vacation spot for Marilyn Monroe and Joe DiMaggio. In Sarasota County, beaches range from artsy Siesta Key to the mansion-fronted Casey Key. Farther south, Venice beaches are good for shelling, but they're most known for their wealth of sharks' teeth and fossils, washed up from the ancient shark burial grounds just offshore. To learn more, contact **Tampa Bay Beaches Chamber of Commerce** (✉ *6990 Gulf Blvd., St. Pete Beach* ☎ *800/944–1847* 🌐 *www.tampabaybeaches.com*) or **Sarasota Convention & Visitors Bureau** (✉ *701 N. Tamiami Trail (U.S. 41), Sarasota* ☎ *800/800–3906* 🌐 *www.sarasotafl.org*).

WHEN TO GO

Tampa Bay area beaches are very popular but also very crowded in the summer, when families flock here, as well as in the winter, when snowbirds land to escape the cold in their home states. Arguably, the best times to visit are early fall and late spring, when there are fewer people and milder temperatures. But do check on red tide, an occasionally appearing algae that can cause breathing difficulty and itchy eyes; it is most common September to November, but it can happen at any time of year (🌐 *research.myfwc.com*).

TAMPA BAY'S BEST BEACHES

BEACH AT SOUTH LIDO PARK

At the southern tip of Sarasota's island, at 2201 Ben Franklin Drive in Lido Key, South Lido Park has one of the best beaches in the region, but note that there are no lifeguards. The sugar-sand beach offers little for shell collectors, but try your luck at fishing, take a dip in the gulf, or picnic as the sun sets through the Australian pines into the water. Facilities include nature trails, canoe and kayak trails, restrooms, and picnic grounds.

CALADESI ISLAND STATE PARK

The beach at Caladesi, accessible by ferry from Honeymoon Island State Recreation Area, offers three reasons to visit: pure white beaches, beautiful sunsets and, by Florida standards, relative seclusion. Oh, we left out the fact that this is an excellent spot for bird watching.

CLEARWATER BEACH

You will find crowds on weekends and during spring break, which are a turn-off for some, but this sun-worshippers' shrine off State Road 60 is the west coast's best muscle beach. Expect to see tanned bods draped with minimal bikinis and Speedos, plenty of hot cars, and sunsets nearly as grand as at Caladesi.

PASS-A-GRILLE BEACH

Located where Tampa Bay meets the Gulf of Mexico in southern Pinellas County, this long-popular beach is wide and still dotted with small dunes and sea oats, two throwbacks that are rapidly vanishing in Florida. Pass-a-Grille (also called St. Pete Beach) tends to be crowded on weekends and during summer and spring break.

SIESTA BEACH

This 40-acre park at 948 Beach Road in Siesta Key, Sarasota, has nature trails, a concession stand, fields for soccer and softball, picnic facilities, a playground, restrooms, a fitness trail, and tennis and volleyball courts. This beach has fine, powdery, quartz sand that squeaks under your feet, very much like the sand along the state's northwestern coast. It has been ranked as one of the country's top beaches.

TURTLE BEACH

Only 14 acres, this beach-park at 8918 Midnight Pass Road in Siesta Key, Sarasota, is popular with families and is more secluded than most gulf beaches. It doesn't have the soft sand of Siesta Beach, but it does have boat ramps, a canoe and kayak launch, bay and gulf fishing, picnic facilities, restrooms, and a volleyball court.

Updated by Christina Tourigny

Planning and preserves have partially shielded pockets of the Tampa Bay Area from the overdevelopment that saturates much of the Atlantic coast. Tampa has Florida's third-busiest airport and a vibrant business community and is one of the state's largest metro areas. Even so, it is less fast-lane than Miami.

Whether you feel like long walks on white-sand beaches, testing your nerve on thrill rides, or wandering through upscale shopping districts, there's something to your liking in the diverse Bay Area. Bright, modern Tampa is the area's commercial center. It's a full-fledged city, with a modest high-rise skyline and highways jammed with traffic. Across the bay, St. Petersburg's compact downtown has interesting restaurants, shops, and museums on the southeast side of the Pinellas County peninsula. The county's western periphery is rimmed by barrier islands with beaches, quiet parks, and little, laid-back beach towns. To the north, communities such as Tarpon Springs, settled by Greek sponge divers, celebrate their ethnic heritage. To the south lie resort towns, including sophisticated Sarasota, which, like the Pinellas County beaches, fill up in winter with snowbirds escaping the cold.

TAMPA/ST. PETERSBURG AREA

The core of the northern bay comprises the cities of Tampa, St. Petersburg, and Clearwater. A semitropical climate and access to the gulf make Tampa an ideal port for the cruise and freight industries. The waters around Clearwater and St. Petersburg are often filled with pleasure and commercial craft, including boats with day and night trips featuring gambling in international waters.

It's fitting that an area with a thriving international port should als be populated by a wealth of nationalities. The center of the Cub community is the east Tampa enclave of Ybor City, whereas north Clearwater, in Dunedin, the heritage is Scottish. North of Dune Tarpon Springs has supported a large Greek population for decade is the largest producer of natural sponges in the world. Inland, to the east and north of Tampa, it's all suburban sprawl, freeways, shopping malls, and—the main draw—Busch Gardens.

TAMPA

84 mi southwest of Orlando via I–4.

Tampa, the west coast's business and commercial hub, has a sprinkling of high-rises and heavy traffic. A concentration of restaurants, nightlife, stores, and cultural events is amid the bustle.

GETTING HERE AND AROUND

Downtown Tampa's **Riverwalk**, on Ashley Drive at the Hillsborough River, connects waterside entities such as the Florida Aquarium, the Channelside shopping and entertainment complex, and Marriott Waterside. The landscaped park is 6 acres and extends along the Garrison cruise-ship channel and along the Hillsborough River downtown. The walkway is being expanded as waterside development continues.

ESSENTIALS

Visitor Information Tampa Bay & Company (✉ *401 E. Jackson St., Suite 2100, Tampa* ☎ *800/368–2672 or 813/223–1111* ⊕ *www.visittampabay.com*). **Ybor City Chamber Visitor Bureau** (✉ *1600 E. 8th Ave., Suite B104, Tampa* ☎ *813/241–8838* ⊕ *www.ybor.org*).

EXPLORING

TOP ATTRACTIONS

Numbers in the margin correspond to the Downtown Tampa map.

1 ★ **Florida Aquarium.** Although eels, sharks, and stingrays are the headliners, the Florida Aquarium is much more than a giant fishbowl. This architectural landmark features an 83-foot-high, multitier, glass dome, 250,000 square feet of air-conditioned exhibit space, and more than 20,000 aquatic plants, and animals representing species native to Florida and the rest of the world. Floor-to-ceiling interactive displays, behind-the-scenes tours, and in-water adventures allow kids to really get hands-on—and even get their feet wet. Adventurous types (certified divers age 15 and up) can dive with mild-mannered sharks and sea turtles, participate in shark-feeding programs (age 12 and up), or shallow-water swim with reef fish such as eels and grouper (age six and up). However, you don't have to get wet to have an interactive experience: boasting the most high-tech aquarium gallery in the country, the Ocean Commotion exhibit offers virtual dolphins and whales, multimedia displays and presentations, and even allows kids to upload video to become a part of the exhibit. The Coral Reef Gallery is a 500,000-gallon tank with viewing windows, an awesome 43-foot-wide panoramic opening, and a walk-through tunnel that gives the illusion of venturing into underwater depths. There you see a thicket of elkhorn coral teeming with tropical fish and a dark cave reveals sea life you would normally see only on night dives. If you have two hours, try *Bay Spirit*'s Wild Dolphin Ecotour, which takes up to 130 passengers onto Tampa's bay in a 72-foot catamaran for an up-close look at bottlenose dolphins and other wildlife. The outdoor Explore a Shore exhibit, which gives

Adventure Island 5
Busch Gardens 4
Florida Aquarium 1
Lowry Park Zoo 3
Museum of Science & Industry 6
Ybor City 2

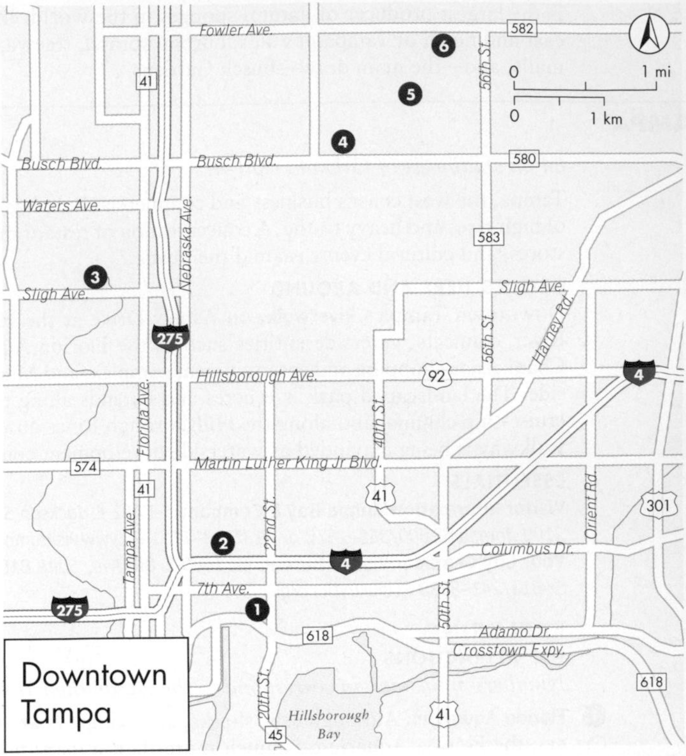

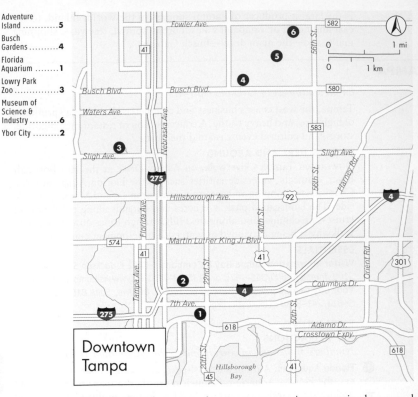

younger kids a chance to release some energy, is an aquatic playground with a waterslide, water-jet sprays, and a climbable replica pirate ship. Last but not least, two black-footed African penguins make twice daily appearances in the aquarium lobby. ✉ *701 Channelside Dr., Downtown, Tampa* ☎ *813/273–4000* 🌐 *www.flaquarium.org* 🎫 *Aquarium $19.95, Ecotour $21.95; Aquarium/Ecotour combo $35.95; parking $6* ⏲ *Daily 9:30–5.*

2 **Ybor City.** Tampa's lively Latin quarter is one of only four National Historic Landmark districts in Florida. It has antique-brick streets and wrought-iron balconies. Cubans brought their cigar-making industry to Ybor (pronounced *ee*-bore) City in 1886, and the smell of cigars—hand-rolled by Cuban immigrants—still wafts through the heart of this east Tampa area, along with the strong aroma of roasting coffee. These days the neighborhood is one of Tampa's hot spots, if at times a rowdy one, as empty cigar factories and historic social clubs have been transformed into trendy boutiques, art galleries, restaurants, and nightclubs.

Fodor's Choice ★

Step back into the past at **Centennial Park** (✉ *8th Ave. and 18th St.*) which re-creates a period streetscape and hosts the Fresh Market eve Saturday. The **Ybor City Museum State Park** provides a look at the h tory of the cigar industry. Admission includes a tour of La Casita, o the shotgun houses occupied by cigar workers and their families late 1890s. ✉ *1818 E. 9th Ave., between Nuccio Pkwy. and 22nd St., from 7th to 9th Ave., Tampa* ☎ *813/247–6323* 🌐 *www.ybormuseum.org* 🎟 *$4, walking tours $6* ⏲ *Daily 9–5; walking tours Sat. 10:30.*

3 **Lowry Park Zoo.** Natural-habitat exhibits such as the white tiger cubs and clouded leopards in Asia Gardens make the 56-acre Lowry Park Zoo one of the best small-scale animal parks in the country. Safari Africa is the home of Tamani, an elephant born in 2005, and residents of the nearby Ituri Forest include cheetahs and lovably plump pygmy hippos. The stars at Primate World range from cat-size red-ruffed lemurs to a colony of heavyweight Bornean orangutans that love to ham for the camera. For hands-on experiences, Lowry has more options than most large parks, including chances to ride a camel, feed a giraffe, or serve as a perch for energetic lorikeets. Majestic red-tailed hawks and other raptors are displayed in the Birds of Prey Center, and you can come face-to-face with American alligators, Florida panthers, black bears, and red wolves at the Florida Wildlife Center. Kookaburras and kangaroos populate the Wallaroo Station children's zoo, and gentle creatures of another kind star at the Manatee Aquatic Center. Speaking of manatees, they are among the occasional sights on the hour-long Hillsborough River Odyssey Ecotour, where you also may spot wild hawks and herons. There are also water-play areas, rides, shows, and restaurants. ✉ *1101 W. Sligh Ave., Central Tampa* ☎ *813/935–8552* 🌐 *www.lowryparkzoo.com* 🎟 *$20.95* ⏲ *Daily 9:30–5.*

4 **Busch Gardens.** *See the highlighted listing in this chapter.*

Fodor's Choice

8

WORTH NOTING

From spring until fall, rides named Tampa Typhoon, Gulf Scream, and 5 Key West Rapids promise heat relief at **Adventure Island**, a corporate cousin and neighbor of Busch Gardens. Tampa's most popular "wet" park features waterslides and artificial wave pools in a 30-acre package. One of the attraction's headliners, Riptide, challenges you to race three other riders on a sliding mat through twisting tubes and hairpin turns. Planners of this park also took the younger kids into account, with offerings such as Fabian's Funport, which has a scaled-down wave pool and interactive water gym. Along with a volleyball complex and a surf pool, there are cafés, snack bars, picnic and sunbathing areas, changing rooms, and, the newest addition, private cabanas. ✉ *1001 Malcolm McKinley Dr., less than 1 mi north of Busch Gardens, Central Tampa* ☎ *813/987–5660 or 888/800–5447* 🌐 *www.adventureisland.com* 🎟 *$44.95; parking $10* ⏲ *Mid-Mar.–late Oct., daily 10–5.*

6 The **Museum of Science & Industry** is a fun and stimulating scientific playground, though at times some exhibits aren't working properly. When it's hitting on all cylinders, you learn about Florida weather, anatomy, flight, and space by seeing *and* by doing. At the Gulf Coast Hurricane Exhibit, you can experience what a hurricane and its 74-mph winds feel like, though crowds sometimes mean a long wait. The BioWorks Butterfly Garden is a 6,400-square-foot engineered ecosystem project that demonstrates how wetlands can clean water plus serve as a home for butterflies. The 100-seat Saunders Planetarium—Tampa's

BUSCH GARDENS

ENTER AFRICA

Busch Gardens opened in Tampa on March 31, 1959 by the Anheuser-Busch company. It was originally designed as an admission-free animal attraction to accompany the plant, but it eventually was turned into a theme park, adding more exotic animals, tropical landscaping, and rides to entertain its guests.

Today the 335-acre park has nine distinct territories packed with roller coasters, rides, eateries, shops, and live entertainment. The park is best known for its incredible roller coasters and water rides, which draw thrill-seekers from around the globe. These rides tend to cater to those over the age of 10. With this in mind, Busch Gardens created the **Sesame Street Safari of Fun,** which is designed solely with children under 5 in mind. There's a lot packed into this area: junior thrill rides, play areas (some with water), and shows—all of which make it exciting for the kids.

GETTING ORIENTED

The park is set up on a north–south axis with Nairobi being the center of the surrounding areas.

Your first encounter at the park is the Moroccan market (grab a map here). There are several small eateries and souvenir shops in this area. If you head west from Morocco you'll get to the Bird Gardens, Sesame Street Safari of Fun, Stanleyville, and Jungala. Heading north you'll find Nairobi, Timbuktu, and the Congo. Heading east takes you to Egypt and the Serengeti Plain. If you get lost, there are team members available almost everywhere to help you.

TOP ATTRACTIONS

FOR AGES 7 AND UP

Sheikra. The newest roller coaster is 200 feet tall and has a 200-foot vertical descent, and isn't for the faint of heart.

Montu. This 150-foot tall inverted coaster reaches speeds of 60 mph, and has a zero-G roll and seven inversions.

Gwazi. The largest, fastest wooden dueling roller coaster in the world, boasting crossing speeds of 100 mph.

Kumba. Riders on this coaster experience weightlessness, cobra rolls, corkscrews, and inverted rolls.

Wild Surge. You're shot out of a mountain crater up a 40-foot structure and then bounced up and down, creating a freefall experience.

Rhino Rally. A Land Rover takes passengers on an off-road safari with up-close animal encounters and a raging river adventure. Sometimes the river adventure isn't working.

Cheetah Chase. It's a pint-size roller coaster with twists and turns throughout.

FOR AGES 6 AND UNDER

Air Grover. Take a ride on Grover's plane and soar through the Sahara on this junior coaster.

Rosita's Djembe Fly-Away. Rosita takes you on a swing ride that sends you above the African canopy.

Oscar's Swamp Stomp. Get wet stomping and splashing your way through this cool water area.

Bert and Ernie's Watering Hole. It's a water adventure filled with bubblers, geysers, jets, dumping buckets, and more.

Zoe-Petra & the Hippos of the Nile. A kid-size flume ride with Zoe's hippo friends that gives children a river glimpse of Africa.

VISITING TIPS

- The park is least crowded during the week, with weekends bringing in a lot of locals. Summer and the holidays also are crowded.
- Ride the thrill rides as early as possible. Think about purchasing a Quick Queue pass for $14.95, which grants you no-wait access. It's only good once per ride but insures you will hit all the big rides quickly.
- Bring extra quarters for all the locker rentals at each of the coasters.
- You can pick up a map at the entrance, which lists show times, meet-the-keeper times and special hours for attractions and restaurants.
- Vegetarians will enjoy **Zagora Café** veggie burgers or **The Colony House's** delicious vegetable platter. Your best food bet's the All Day Dining Deal, $29.95 per adult and $13.95 per child. It's accepted at most dining venues. If eating at the Colony House, you'll want to make your reservations immediately upon entering the park.

8

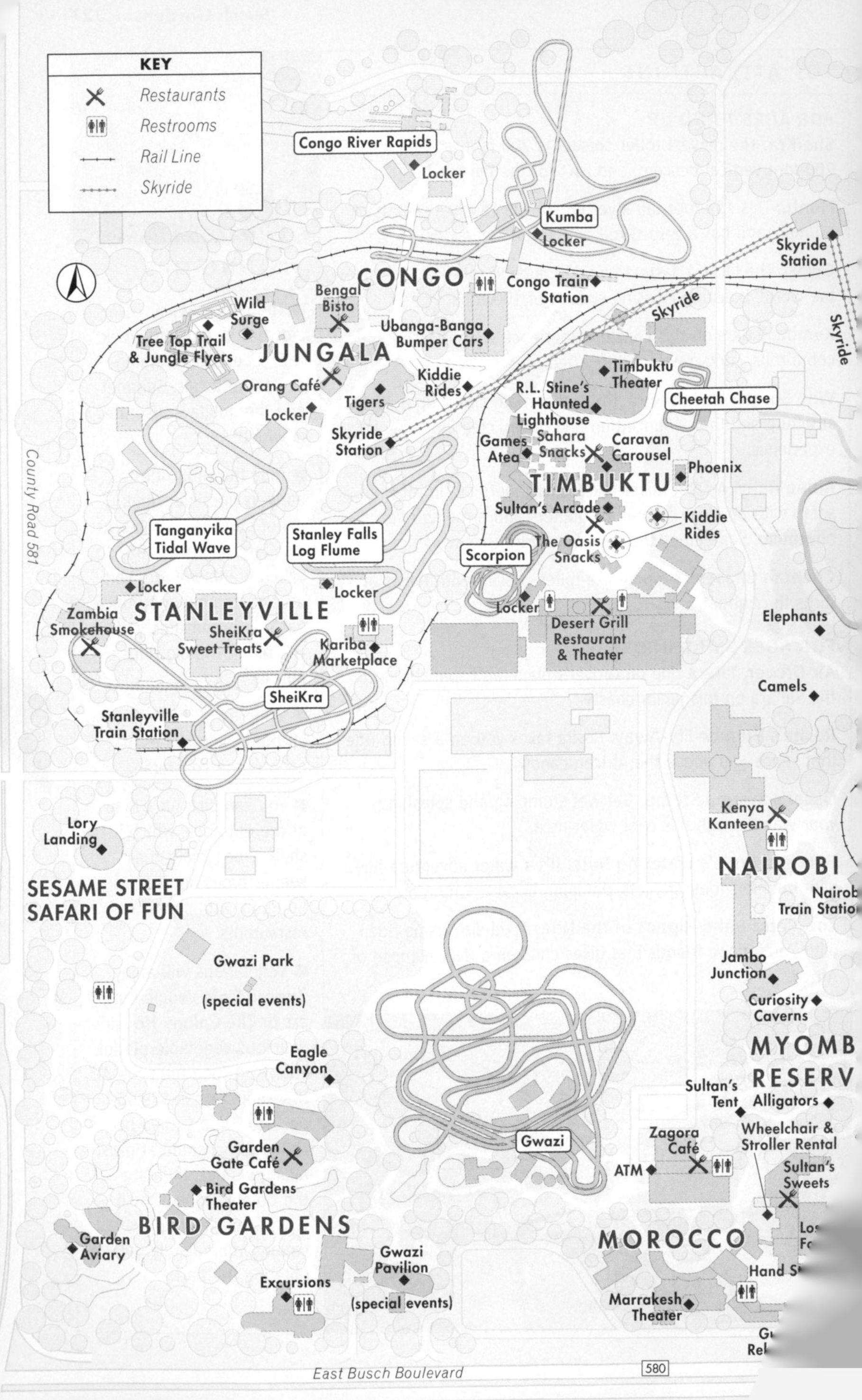
KEY
Restaurants
Restrooms
Rail Line
Skyride
Congo River Rapids
Locker
Kumba
Locker
Skyride Station
CONGO
Congo Train Station
Skyride
Skyride
Bengal Bisto
Wild Surge
Tree Top Trail & Jungle Flyers
JUNGALA
Ubanga-Banga Bumper Cars
Orang Café
Kiddie Rides
Tigers
Locker
Skyride Station
Timbuktu Theater
R.L. Stine's Haunted Lighthouse
Cheetah Chase
Games Atea
Sahara Snacks
Caravan Carousel
Phoenix
TIMBUKTU
Sultan's Arcade
Kiddie Rides
The Oasis Snacks
Scorpion
County Road 581
Tanganyika Tidal Wave
Stanley Falls Log Flume
Locker
Locker
Locker
Zambia Smokehouse
STANLEYVILLE
SheiKra Sweet Treats
Kariba Marketplace
Desert Grill Restaurant & Theater
Elephants
SheiKra
Camels
Stanleyville Train Station
Lory Landing
Kenya Kanteen
NAIROBI
SESAME STREET SAFARI OF FUN
Gwazi Park
(special events)
Jambo Junction
Curiosity Caverns
Eagle Canyon
Sultan's Tent
Alligators
Wheelchair & Stroller Rental
Garden Gate Café
Gwazi
Zagora Café
ATM
Sultan's Sweets
Bird Gardens Theater
BIRD GARDENS
MOROCCO
Garden Aviary
Gwazi Pavilion
(special events)
Excursions
Marrakesh Theater
East Busch Boulevard
580

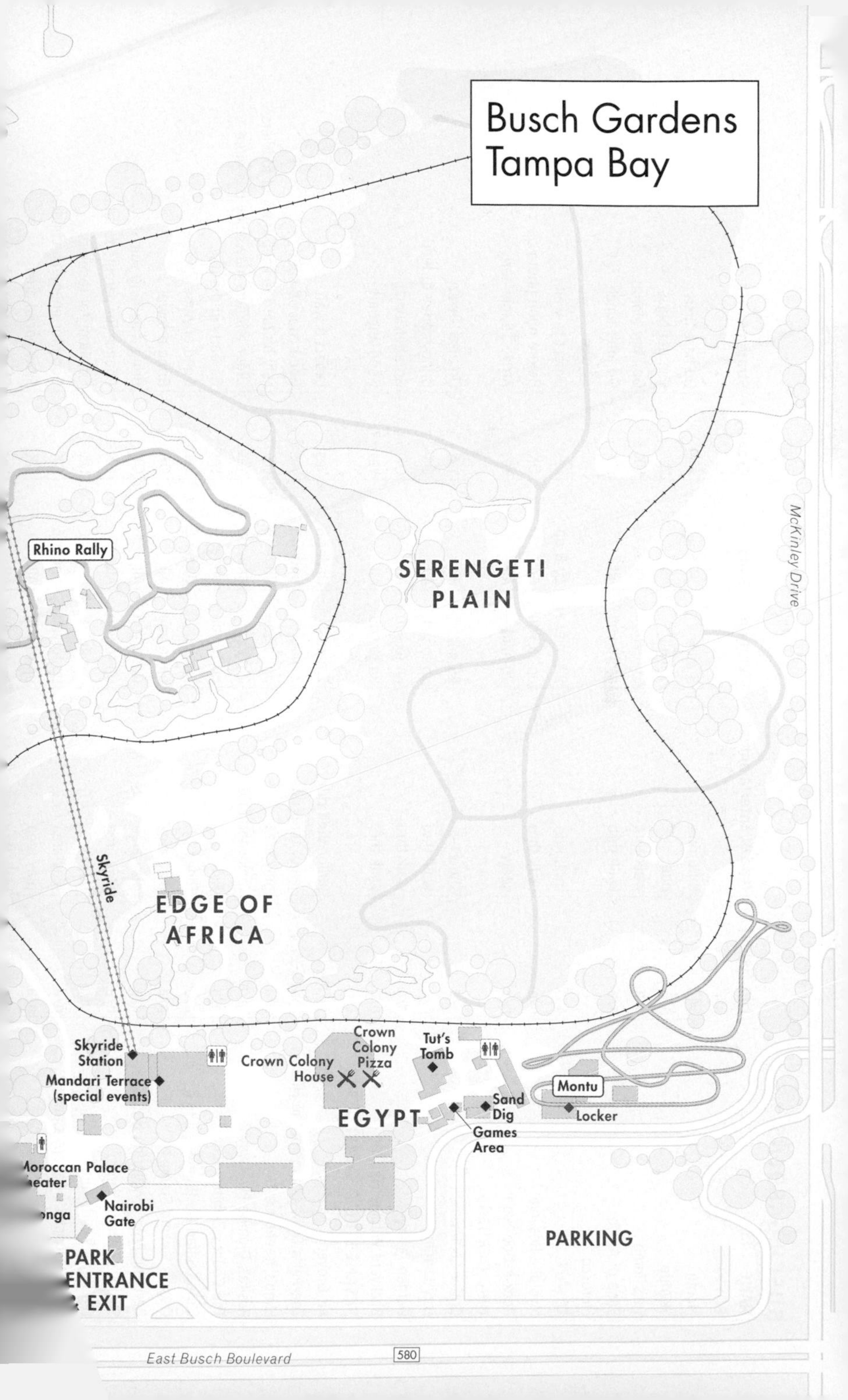
Busch Gardens Tampa Bay
Rhino Rally
SERENGETI PLAIN
McKinley Drive
Skyride
EDGE OF AFRICA
Skyride Station
Mandari Terrace (special events)
Crown Colony House
Crown Colony Pizza
Tut's Tomb
EGYPT
Sand Dig
Games Area
Montu
Locker
Moroccan Palace
eater
Nairobi Gate
nga
PARK
ENTRANCE
EXIT
PARKING
East Busch Boulevard
580

BUSCH GARDENS

NAME	Min. Height	Type of Entertainment	Duration	Suits	Crowds	Strategy
EGYPT						
Montu	54"	thrill ride	3 min.	14 & up	Yes!	Go here first
Skyride	n/a	ride	5 min.	All	Yes	Can get busy
Tut's Tomb	n/a	walk thru	10 min.	All	OK	Go after Montu
Edge of Africa	n/a	walk thru	up to you	All	OK	Go after lunch
Morocco						
GWAZI	48"	thrill ride	2.5 min.	10 & up	Yes!	Expect to wait
Myombe Reserve	n/a	walk thru	up to you	All	OK	Before noon photo op
Rock-A-Doo-Wop	n/a	show	20 min.	All	Yes	Arrive 15 min early
BIRD GARDENS						
Critter Castaway	n/a	show	25 min.	All	Yes	Do after Gwazi
Lory Landing	n/a	walk thru	up to you	All	OK	Bring money to feed
Garden Aviary	n/a	walk thru	up to you	All	OK	Go after lunch
Backyard Wildlife Habitat	n/a	walk thru	up to you	All	Yes	Good anytime
SESAME STREET SAFARI OF FUN						
Air Grover	n/a	junior thrill ride	2 min.	Under 6	Yes!	Expect a wait
Zoe-Petra & the Hippos of the Nile	n/a	junior thrill ride	3 min.	Under 6	Yes	Good cool off spot
Elmo's Treehouse Trek	n/a	play area	up to you	Under 6	OK	May be hard to keep track of toddlers.
Rosita's Djembe Fly-Away	n/a	junior thrill ride	2 min.	Under 6	Yes	Older toddlers may enjoy this more.
The Count's Zambezi Rally	n/a	Ride	up to you	Under 6	Yes	Go early in the day.
Elmo's Safari Go-Round	n/a	Ride	3 min.	Under 6	Yes	Good anytime
Oscar's Swamp Stomp	n/a	play area	up to you	All	OK	Bring a towel
Bert and Ernie's Watering Hole	n/a	play area	up to you	All	OK	Bring a bathing suit
Slimey's Sawara Sand	n/a	play area	up to you	All	OK	Chance for parents to relax
Big Bird's Whirly Birdy	n/a	ride	3 min.	Under 6	OK	Excellent for toddlers
[illegible]ie Monster's Canopy Crawl	n/a	play area	up to you	Under 6	OK	Good for energetic children
[illegible]om	n/a	play area	up to you	All	OK	Slow paced area
[illegible]h Me	n/a	walk thru	up to you	All	Yes	Photo/autograph op

	54"	thrill ride	2.5 min.	14 & up	Yes!	Use the lockers
...ne	46"	thrill ride	3 min.	10 & up	Yes	Lengthy lines
...ka Tidal Wave	48"	thrill ride	2 min.	10 & up	Yes	Bring a change of clothes or poncho
...UNGALA						
Jungle Flyers	48"	junior thrill ride	3 min.	6 to 13	Yes	Skip for other rides
Wild Surge	38"	thrill ride	2 min.	5 & up	Yes!	Gets crowded
Tree Top Trails	n/a	walk thru	up to you	All	Yes	Close-up views
Tiger Lodge	n/a	walk thru	up to you	All	Yes	Morning photo op
Orangutan Overlook	n/a	walk thru	up to you	All	Yes	Very entertaining
Jungala Stiltwalkers	n/a	show	15 min.	All	ok	Bring extra clothes or poncho
CONGO						
Congo River Rapids	42"	thrill ride	6 min.	10 & up	Yes!	Go early or before closing
Kumba	54"	thrill ride	3 min.	14 & up	Yes!	
Ubanga-Banga Bumper Cars	42"	ride	2 min.	8 & up	yes	Long wait times
Timbuktu						
Carousel Caravan	n/a	ride	3 min.	All	ok	Slow paced ride
Cheetah Chase	46"	junior thrill ride	2 min.	All	yes	Very popular
Pirate 4-D Movie	n/a	show	15 min.	All	ok	Arrive 15 min early
Phoenix	48"	thrill ride	2 min.	12 & up	yes	Go after Scorpion
Scorpion	42"	thrill ride	2 min.	14 & up	yes	Go during Dance to the Music show
Dance to the Music	n/a	Seasonal show	20 min.	All	yes	Arrive 15 min. before show
Lights, Camera, Action!	n/a	show		All		Good break from the sun
NAIROBI						
Rhino Rally	39"	vehicle ride	10 min.	10 & up	yes	This ride is rough and can get wet
Serengeti Express	n/a	vehicle ride	12-35 min.	All	no	Great way to relax and see the park
Curiosity Caverns	n/a	walk thru	up to you	All	no	Good to get out of the sun.
Elephant Habitat	n/a	walk thru	up to you	All	ok	Go during Meet the Keeper
Rhino Habitat	n/a	walk thru	up to you	All	yes	Earlier the better
Edge of Africa	n/a	walk thru	up to you	All	ok	Great break from the crowds

DID YOU KNOW?

One of six roller coasters at Busch Gardens, the steel, 60-foot-tall Scorpion twists and turns at speeds near 50 mph and then throws you into a 360-degree vertical loop. During the 1½-minute ride you'll experience a 3.5 G-force.

only planetarium—has afternoon and evening shows, one of them a trek through the universe. For adventurous spirits, there's a high-wire bicycle ride 30 feet above the floor. There's also an impressive IMAX theater, where films are projected on a hemispherical 82-foot dome. ✉ *4801 E. Fowler Ave., 1 mi north of Busch Gardens, Northeast Tampa* ☎ *813/987–6100 or 800/995–6674* 🌐 *www.mosi.org* 🎫 *$23.95* ⏲ *Weekdays 9–5, weekends 9–6.*

SPORTS AND THE OUTDOORS

BASEBALL

Locals and tourists flock each March to see the **New York Yankees** (✉ *George M. Steinbrenner Field, 1 Steinbrenner Dr., near corner of Dale Mabry Hwy. and Martin Luther King Jr. Blvd., off I–275 Exit 41B, Central Tampa* ☎ *813/879–2244 or 813/875–7753*) play about 17 spring-training games at 11,000-seat Steinbrenner Field. Call for tickets. From April through September, the stadium belongs to a Yankee farm team, the **Tampa Yankees,** who play 70 games against the likes of the Daytona Cubs and the Sarasota Red Sox.

FOOTBALL

Seeing the National Football League's **Tampa Bay Buccaneers** (✉ *Raymond James Stadium, 4201 N. Dale Mabry Hwy., Central Tampa* ☎ *813/879–2827* 🌐 *www.buccaneers.com*) play isn't easy without connections, since the entire stadium is booked by season-ticket holders years in advance. But tickets can be found in the classifieds of newspapers such as the *Tampa Tribune* and *St. Petersburg Times*. The Arena Football League **Tampa Bay Storm** (✉ *St. Pete Times Forum, 401 Channelside Dr., Downtown* ☎ *813/301–6900* 🌐 *www.tampabaystorm.com*) plays about 16 games in its March–June season. The Storm has a hot rivalry with the Orlando Predators.

8

GOLF

Babe Zaharias Golf Course (✉ *11412 Forest Hills Dr., Northeast Tampa* ☎ *813/631–4374*) is a challenging par-70, 18-hole public course with water hazards on eight holes; greens fee $26/$48. A pro is on hand to give lessons. **Bloomingdale Golfers Club** (✉ *4113 Great Golfers Pl., Southeast Tampa* ☎ *813/685–4105*) is an 18-hole, **par-72 course** with a two-tiered driving range, a 1-acre putting green, and a restaurant; greens fee $30/$80. **The Claw at USF** (✉ *13801 N. 46th St., North Tampa* ☎ *813/632–6893*) is named for its many dog-legged fairways. The 18-hole, par-71 course is on a preserve with moss-draped oaks and towering pines; greens fee $20/$45. **The Club at Eaglebrooke** (✉ *1300 Eaglebrooke Blvd., Lakeland* ☎ *863/701–0101*) is a par-72, 18-hole course about 30 mi east of Tampa; greens fee $55/$65. The public 18-hole 71-par course at **Tournament Players Club of Tampa Bay** (✉ *5300 W. Lutz Lake Fern Rd., Lutz* ☎ *813/949–0090*), 15 mi north of Tampa, was designed by Bobby Weed and Chi Chi Rodriguez; greens fee $99/$109. About 10 mi north of Tampa International Airport, **Westchase Golf Club** (✉ *11602 Westchase Golf Dr., Tampa* ☎ *813/854–2331*) has a wooded 72-par, 18-hole course with bridges and bulkheads; greens fee $49/$59. Golfers rotate from the back nine holes to the front nine.

SHOPPING

MALLS

Ybor City's destination within a destination is the dining and entertainment palace **Centro Ybor** (⊠ *1600 E. 8th Ave., Ybor City*). It has shops, trendy bars and restaurants, a 20-screen movie theater, and GameWorks, an interactive playground developed by Steven Spielberg. **Channelside** (⊠ *615 Channelside Dr., Downtown*) offers movie theaters, shops, restaurants, and clubs. The official Tampa Bay visitor center is also here. If you want to grab something at Neiman Marcus or Nordstrom on your way to the airport, the upscale **International Plaza** (⊠ *2223 N. West Shore Blvd., Airport Area*) has Betsey Johnson, J.Crew, L'Occitane, Louis Vuitton, Tiffany & Co., and many other shops. **Old Hyde Park Village** (⊠ *Swan Ave. near Bayshore Blvd., Hyde Park*) is a typical shopping district, just like the ones you find in every major American city. Williams-Sonoma and Brooks Brothers are mixed in with bistros and sidewalk cafés.

SPECIALTY SHOPS

For the mildly unusual to the downright bizarre, stop at **Squaresville** (⊠ *508 S. Howard Ave., near Downtown* ☎ *813/259–9944*), which stocks everything from Cuban clothing to Elvis posters to Bettie Page clocks. If you are shopping for hand-rolled cigars, head to Ybor City, where a few hand-rollers practice their craft in small shops. One of the more popular stops is the **King Corona Cigar Factory** (⊠ *1523 E. 7th Ave., Ybor City* ☎ *888/248–3812*).

NIGHTLIFE AND THE ARTS

NIGHTLIFE

Although there are more boarded storefronts than in the past, the biggest concentration of nightclubs, as well as the widest variety, is found along 7th Avenue in Ybor City. It becomes a little like Bourbon Street in New Orleans on weekend evenings. **Centro Cantina** (⊠ *1600 E. 8th Ave., Ybor City* ☎ *813/241–8588*) has a balcony overlooking the crowds on 7th Avenue. There's live music Thursday through Sunday nights, a large selection of margaritas, and more than 30 brands of tequila. Food is served until 2 AM.

At International Plaza, **Blue Martini Lounge** (⊠ *2323 N. West Shore Blvd., West Tampa* ☎ *813/873–2583*) has live entertainment nightly, except Monday, and a menu of killer martinis. International Plaza's **Bay Street** (⊠ *2223 N. West Shore Blvd., Airport Area*) has become one of Tampa's dining and imbibing hot spots. Considered something of a dive—but a lovable one—by a loyal and young local following that ranges from esteemed jurists to nose-ring-wearing night owls, the **Hub** (⊠ *719 N. Franklin St., Downtown* ☎ *813/229–1553*) is known for having one of Tampa's best martinis and one of its most eclectic jukeboxes.

Skippers Smokehouse (⊠ *910 Skipper Rd., Northeast Tampa* ☎ *813/971–0666* 🌐 *www.skipperssmokehouse.com*), a junkyard-style restaurant and oyster bar, has live reggae on Wednesday, rock on Thursday, and great smoked fish every night.

THE ARTS

On the Hillsborough River, the 345,000-square-foot **Tampa Bay Performing Arts Center** (✉ *1010 W. C. MacInnes Pl., Downtown* ☎ *813/229–7827* 🌐 *www.tbpac.org*) is the largest such complex south of the Kennedy Center in Washington, D.C. Among the facilities are the 2,500-seat Carol Morsani Hall, a 1,047-seat playhouse, the 200-seat Teco Theater, a 300-seat cabaret theater, and a 120-seat black-box theater. Opera, concerts, drama, and ballet performances are presented here. In a restored 1926 movie palace, the **Tampa Theatre** (✉ *711 N. Franklin St., Downtown* ☎ *813/274–8982* 🌐 *www.tampatheatre.org*) hosts films, concerts, and special events.

WHERE TO EAT

$$$$ STEAK Fodor's Choice ★

✕ **Bern's Steak House.** With the air of an exclusive club, this is one of Florida's finest steak houses. Rich mahogany paneling and ornate chandeliers define the legendary Bern's, where the chef ages his own beef, grows his own organic vegetables, roasts his own coffee, and maintains his own saltwater fish tanks. There's also a Cave Du Fromage, housing a discriminating selection of artisanal cheeses from around the world. Cuts of topmost beef are sold by weight and thickness. There's a 60-ounce strip steak that's big enough to feed your pride (of lions), but for most appetites the veal loin chop or 8-ounce chateaubriand is more than enough. The wine list includes approximately 7,000 selections (with 1,000 dessert wines). After dinner, tour the kitchen and wine cellar before having dessert upstairs in a cozy booth. The dessert room is a hit. For a real jolt, try the Turkish coffee with an order of Mississippi mud pie. Casual business attire is recommended. ✉ *1208 S. Howard Ave., Hyde Park* ☎ *813/251–2421* 🌐 *www.bernssteakhouse.com* *Reservations essential* 💳 *AE, D, MC, V.*

$$ ECLECTIC

✕ **Café Dufrain.** Dogs can tag along if you dine on the patio at pet-friendly Café Dufrain, a riverside eatery popular with an upscale crowd. Fido gets a little treat from the staff, while diners get a treat from the chef with the pan-seared sea bass served with polenta and wilted arugula or Dufrain's cioppino—a delightful dish with sea bass, lobster, shrimp, and spicy sausage. Seal the deal with the mango cheesecake. In mild weather, opt for the waterfront view of downtown Tampa. ✉ *707 Harbour Post Dr., Downtown* ☎ *813/275–9701* 🌐 *www.cafedufrain.com* 💳 *AE, D, MC, V.*

$$ SPANISH Fodor's Choice ★

✕ **Columbia.** Make a date for some of the best Latin cuisine in Tampa. A fixture since 1905, this magnificent structure with an old-world air, spacious dining rooms, and a sunny courtyard takes up an entire city block and seems to feed the entire city—locals as well as travelers—throughout the week, but especially on weekends. The paella, bursting with seafood, chicken, and pork, arguably is the best in Florida, and the 1905 salad—with ham, olives, cheese, and garlic—is legendary. The menu has Cuban classics such as *boliche criollo* (tender eye of round stuffed with chorizo sausage), *ropa vieja* (shredded beef with onions, peppers, and tomatoes), and *arroz con pollo* (chicken with yellow rice). Don't miss the flamenco dancing show every night but Sunday. ✉ *2117 E. 7th Ave., Ybor City* ☎ *813/248–4961* 🌐 *www.columbiarestaurant.com* 💳 *AE, D, DC, MC, V.*

8

$ MEXICAN ★ ✕ **Estela's.** Despite its nondescript storefront, Estela's is a favorite among those who enjoy authentic Central American cuisine and Mexico's best beers. Expect the usual entrées (enchiladas, fajitas, and chiles rellenos) mixed with delightful starters (chicken soup with avocado slices) and a palate-pleasing rib-eye steak with rice, beans, and guacamole. Warning: the place gets very crowded for weekday lunches. ✉ *209 E. Davis Blvd., Downtown* ☎ *813/251–0558* 🌐 *www.estelas.com* ▭ *MC, V.*

$ SOUTHERN ✕ **Kojak's House of Ribs.** Few barbecue joints can boast the staying power of this family-owned and -operated pit stop, which had its debut in 1978. In the last three decades, it has earned a following of sticky-fingered regulars who have turned it into one of the most popular barbecue stops in central Florida. It could pass for a century-old Cracker house complete with veranda, pillars supporting the overhanging roof, and brick steps. Day and night, three indoor dining rooms and an outdoor dining porch have a steady stream of hungry patrons digging into tender pork spareribs that are dry-rubbed and tanned overnight before visiting the smoker for a couple of hours. Then they're bathed in the sauce of your choice. Kojak's also has a nice selection of sandwiches, including sloppy chicken and country-style sausage. ✉ *2808 Gandy Blvd., South Tampa* ☎ *813/837–3774* 🌐 *www.kojaksbbq.com* ▭ *AE, D, MC, V* ⏲ *Closed Mon.*

¢ AMERICAN ✕ **Mel's Hot Dogs.** Talk about a tubular experience. Visitors as well as passersby usually are greeted by a red wiener-mobile (you have to see it to believe it), parked on the north side of the highway near Busch Gardens. Those lucky enough to venture inside find walls dotted with photos from fans and a hot-diggity menu that's heaven for tube-steak fans. You can order a traditional dog, but try something with a little more pizzazz, such as a bacon-cheddar Reuben-style bow-wow on a poppy-seed bun, or the Mighty Mel, a quarter-pounder decked out with relish, mustard, and pickles. To avoid lunch crowds, arrive before 11:30 or after 1:30. ✉ *4136 E. Busch Blvd., Central Tampa* ☎ *813/985–8000* 🌐 *www.melshotdogs.com* ▭ *No credit cards* ⏲ *Closed Sun.*

¢ CUBAN ★ ✕ **Papito's Cuban Café & Bar.** It's one of the best budget eateries in Tampa, and while the cafeteria-style line can be a bit slow, the tasty home cooking—roast pork, chicken and yellow rice, and more—is worth waiting for. If you prefer something a little more casual, just inside the front door you can order a pressed Cuban sandwich. Dine in with the locals or take out. ✉ *5305 Ehrlich Rd., North Tampa* ☎ *813/849–7675* ▭ *MC, V.*

$$$ ASIAN ✕ **Roy's.** Chef Roy Yamaguchi's Pan-Asian restaurant has fresh ingredients flown in every day from around the Pacific. Some menu items change daily, so call ahead if you don't want to be surprised. Regular dishes include roasted macadamia-nut-crusted mahimahi with lobster sauce and blackened ahi tuna with spicy soy-mustard sauce. Can't decide? Try the prix-fixe menu, usually around $35 for three courses. For dessert, choices include chocolate soufflé and fruit cobbler. ✉ *4342 Boy Scout Blvd., Airport Area* ☎ *813/873–7697* 🌐 *www.roysrestaurant.com* ▭ *AE, D, DC, MC, V.*

$$ SOUTHERN ✕ **Stumps Supper Club.** The menu is as lively as the entertainment at o of Tampa's more popular restaurant-nightclub combos. Southern vitt

are the house specialty—they're reminiscent of Sunday dinner at one of our aunts' houses. The Brunswick stew (chicken mingling with butter beans and veggies in tomato broth) is close to perfection. The meat loaf comes under creamy ham gravy, and the obligatory country-fried steak does not disappoint. Sides include corn bread, cheese grits, black-eyed peas, and collard greens. Decorated in flea-market chic, Stumps takes food quite seriously. Friday and Saturday nights after 9 you'll bump into Jimmy James & the Velvet Explosion, a six-piece band that relives Elvis, ABBA, Motown, and KC & the Sunshine Band. ✉ *615 Channelside Dr., Downtown* ☎ *813/226–2261* 🌐 *www.stumpssupperclub.com* 💳 *AE, D, DC, MC, V* ⏲ *No lunch weekdays.*

WHERE TO STAY

$$$ ★ **Don Vicente de Ybor Historic Inn.** Built as a home in 1895 by town founder Don Vicente de Ybor, this inn shows that the working-class cigar city had an elegant side, too. From the beige-stucco exterior to the white marble staircase in the main lobby, this boutique hotel is an architectural tour de force. Rooms have parquet floors, canopy beds, and private baths; most have wrought-iron balconies. Common areas have crystal chandeliers, Tiffany lamps, and Persian carpets. **Pros:** elegant rooms; rich in history; walking distance to nightlife. **Cons:** rowdy neighborhood on weekend nights. ✉ *1915 Republica de Cuba, Ybor City* ☎ *813/241–4545 or 866/206–4545* 🌐 *donvicenteinn.com* *13 rooms, 3 suites* *In-room: Internet, Wi-Fi. In-hotel: restaurant, bar, laundry service, Wi-Fi hotspot* 💳 *AE, D, DC, MC, V* *BP.*

$$–$$$ ★ **Hilton Garden Inn Tampa Ybor Historic District.** Although its modern architecture makes it seem out of place in this historic district, this chain hotel's location across from Centro Ybor is a plus. There is an on-site restaurant that serves breakfast, but be sure to take at least one day off to visit one of the nearby eateries for a traditional breakfast of *café cubano* or *café con leche* with a wedge of Cuban bread slathered with butter. **Pros:** good location for business travelers; reasonable rates. **Cons:** chain-hotel feel; far from downtown. ✉ *1700 E. 9th Ave., Ybor City* ☎ *813/769–9267* 🌐 *www.hiltongardeninn.com* *93 rooms, 2 suites* *In-room: refrigerator, Internet, Wi-Fi. In-hotel: restaurant, pool, laundry facilities, laundry service, Wi-Fi hotspot* 💳 *AE, D, DC, MC, V.*

$$$–$$$$ ★ **Saddlebrook Resort Tampa.** If you can't get enough golf and tennis, here's your fix. Saddlebrook is one of west Florida's top resorts, largely because it has so many things in one spot—36 holes of championship golf; the Arnold Palmer Golf Academy; 45 clay, grass, and artificial-surface tennis courts; a Harry Hopman tennis program; a full-service spa; a fitness center; and a kids' club. Varied accommodations include one- and two-bedroom suites, making it a good place for families. **Pros:** away from urban sprawl; great choice for the fitness minded. **Cons:** a bit isolated. ✉ *5700 Saddlebrook Way, Wesley Chapel* ☎ *813/973–1111 or 800/729–8383* 🌐 *www.saddlebrookresort.com* *540 rooms, 407 suites* *In-room: safe, kitchen (some), Internet, Wi-Fi. In-hotel: 4 restaurants, room service, bars, golf courses, tennis courts, pools, gym, spa, bicycles, children's programs (ages 4–12), laundry service, Wi-Fi hotspot* 💳 *AE, D, DC, MC, V* *MAP.*

8

$$$–$$$$ **Tampa Marriott Waterside Hotel & Marina.** Across from the Tampa Convention Center, this downtown hotel was built for conventioneers but is also convenient to tourist spots such as the Florida Aquarium and the Channelside and Hyde Park shopping districts. At least half the rooms and most of the suites overlook the concrete-walled channel to Tampa Bay, which has sparse boat traffic except on weekends; the bay itself is visible from the higher floors of the 27-story tower. The pillared lobby has real palm trees growing out of the gleaming tile floors, and the coffee bar overlooks the water. Il Terrazzo is the hotel's formal dining room. **Pros:** great downtown location; near shopping. **Cons:** gridlock during rush hour; area sketchy after dark; chain-hotel feel. ✉ *700 S. Florida Ave., Downtown* ☎ *888/268–1616* 🌐 *www.marriott.com* *681 rooms, 36 suites* *In-room: safe, kitchen (some), Internet, Wi-Fi. In-hotel: 3 restaurants, room service, bars, pool, gym, spa, laundry facilities, laundry service, Wi-Fi hotspot, parking (paid)* *AE, D, DC, MC, V.*

$$$–$$$$ **Westin Tampa Harbour Island.** Few folks think of the islands when visiting Tampa, but this 12-story hotel on a 177-acre man-made islet is a short drive from downtown Tampa. The rooms are decorated in whites and bright colors, and many have terrific views of the water or the downtown skyline. Service is attentive. There's a marina and a new fitness center with free weights and the latest exercise equipment. **Pros:** close to downtown; nice views; on the TECO streetcar line. **Cons:** a bit far from the action; chain-hotel feel. ✉ *725 S. Harbour Island Blvd., Harbour Island* ☎ *813/229–5000* 🌐 *www.starwoodhotels.com/westin* *299 rooms, 19 suites* *In-room: safe, refrigerator (some), Internet, Wi-Fi. In-hotel: restaurant, room service, bar, pool, laundry service, Wi-Fi hotspot, parking (paid), some pets allowed* *AE, DC, MC, V.*

ST. PETERSBURG

21 mi west of Tampa.

St. Petersburg and the Pinellas coast form the thumb of the hand that juts out of Florida's west coast and grasps Tampa Bay. There are two distinct parts of St. Petersburg: the at-times-snobbish downtown and cultural area, centered on the bay; and the more laid-back but pricey beach area, a string of barrier islands that faces the gulf and includes St. Pete Beach, Treasure Island, and Madeira Beach. Causeways link beach communities to the mainland peninsula.

GETTING HERE AND AROUND

U.S. 19 is St. Petersburg's major north–south artery; traffic can be heavy, and there are many lights, so use a different route when possible. One viable option is the Veterans Expressway/Suncoast Parkway, a toll road that runs from west Tampa to northern Hernando County. Interstate 275 heads west from Tampa across Tampa Bay to St. Petersburg, swings south, and crosses the bay again on its way to Terra Ceia, near Bradenton. Along this last leg—the Sunshine Skyway and its stunning suspension bridge—you'll get a bird's-eye view of bustling Tampa Bay. U.S. 92 yields a spectacular view of Tampa Bay, and Route 679 take you along two of St. Petersburg's most pristine islands, Cabbage ar

BayWalk **11**
Bayshore Boulevard Trail ..**7**
Clearwater Beach **21**
Clearwater Marine Aquarium **20**
Egmont Key **17**
Florida Holocaust Museum **9**
Fort De Soto Park **14**
Great Explorations ... **13**
Konger Tarpon Springs Aquarium **24**
Museum of Fine Arts **10**
Pass-A-Grille Beach **15**
St. Nicholas Cathedral **22**
Salvador Dalí Museum **12**
Sand Key Park **19**
Sponge Factory **23**
Suncoast Seabird Sanctuary **18**
Sunken Gardens **8**
Treasure Island **16**

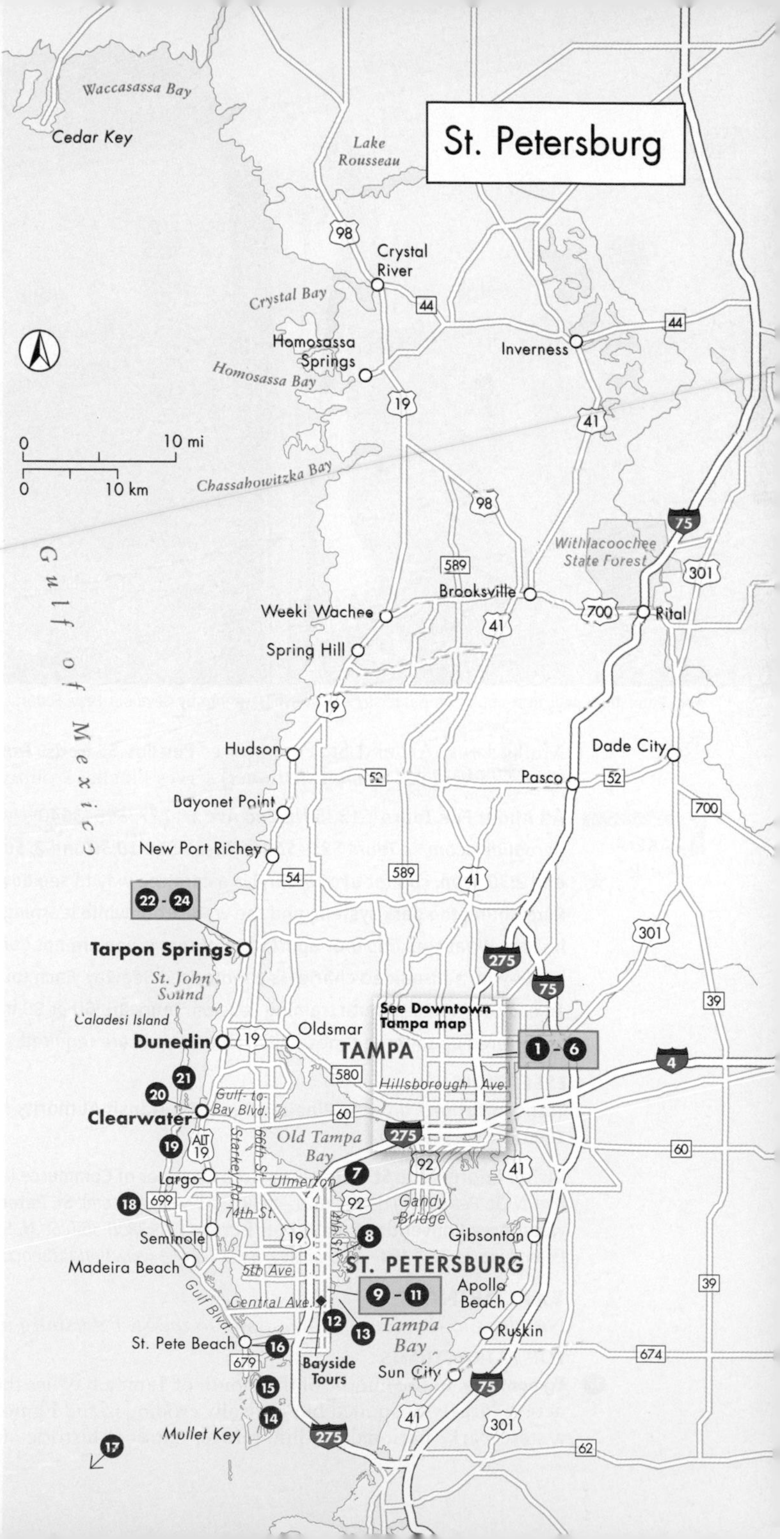

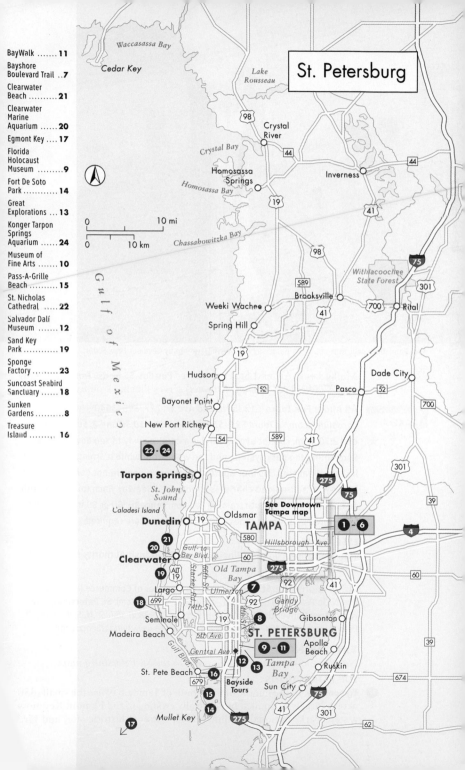

St. Petersburg
Waccasassa Bay
Cedar Key
Lake Rousseau
Crystal River
Crystal Bay
Homosassa Springs
Homosassa Bay
Inverness
Chassahowitzka Bay
Gulf of Mexico
0 10 mi
0 10 km
Withlacoochee State Forest
Brooksville
Rital
Weeki Wachee
Spring Hill
Hudson
Dade City
Pasco
Bayonet Point
New Port Richey
Tarpon Springs
St. John Sound
Caladesi Island
Dunedin
Oldsmar
See Downtown Tampa map
TAMPA
Hillsborough Ave.
Clearwater
Gulf-to-Bay Blvd.
Old Tampa Bay
Starkey Rd.
66th St.
Largo
Ulmerton
Gandy Bridge
74th St.
4th St.
Seminole
Madeira Beach
Gibsonton
ST. PETERSBURG
5th Ave.
Central Ave.
Gulf Blvd.
Apollo Beach
Tampa Bay
Ruskin
St. Pete Beach
Bayside Tours
Sun City
Mullet Key

A St. Petersburg pelican stares down passersby on the wharf; photo by Seymour Levy, Fodors.com member

Mullet keys. Around St. Petersburg, **Pinellas Suncoast Transit Authority** (☎ *727/540–1900* 🌐 *www.psta.net*) serves Pinellas County.

TAKE A TOUR

★ **All About Fun Tours** (✉ *335 NE 2nd Ave.* ☎ *727/896–3640* 🌐 *www.gyroglides.com* 🎫 *Tours $35–$50* ⏱ *Tues.–Sat. 10:30 and 2, Sun. 12:30 and 2:30, Mon. call for availability*) is a carefree way to see downtown St. Petersburg, the park system, and the waterfront while learning about local history. What sets this tour apart from others is you are not going by bus or boat—your self-guided chariot is a motorized Segway. Each tour starts with an easy 15- to 20-minute training session. Tours are 60 or 90 minutes and are offered up to three times daily. Reservations are required.

ESSENTIALS

Transportation Contacts Pinellas Suncoast Transit Authority (☎ *727/540–1900* 🌐 *www.psta.net*).

Visitor Information St. Petersburg Area Chamber of Commerce (✉ *100 2nd Ave. N, St. Petersburg* ☎ *727/821–4069* 🌐 *www.stpete.com*). **St. Petersburg/Clearwater Area Convention and Visitors Bureau** (✉ *13850 58th St. N, Suite 2200, St. Petersburg* ☎ *727/464–7200 or 877/352–3224* 🌐 *www.floridasbeach.com*).

EXPLORING

Numbers in the margin correspond to the St. Petersburg map.

TOP ATTRACTIONS

17 **Egmont Key.** In the middle of the mouth of Tampa Bay lies the small (350 acres), largely unspoiled but critically eroding island Egmont Key, now a state park, national wildlife refuge, national historic site, and bird

sanctuary. On the island are the ruins of Fort De Soto's sister fortification, Fort Dade, built during the Spanish-American War to protect Tampa Bay. The primary inhabitants of the less-than-2-mi-long island are the threatened gopher tortoise and box turtles. Shelling and nature-viewing are rewarding. The only way to get here is by boat. **Dolphin Landings Tours** (☎ *727/367–4488* 🌐 *www.dolphinlandings.com*) runs a four-hour shelling trip, a two-hour dolphin-sighting excursion, back-bay or party-boat fishing, and other outings.

12 Fodor's Choice ★ **Salvador Dalí Museum.** The Spanish surrealist certainly had a different way of viewing our world, as evidenced by exhibits at this museum, which holds the world's most comprehensive collection of his work. The mind-expanding paintings in this downtown headliner include *Eggs on a Plate Without a Plate*, *The Hallucinogenic Toreador,* and more than 90 other oils. You'll also discover more than 2,000 additional works including watercolors, drawings, sculptures, photographs, and objets d'art. Free hour-long tours are led by well-informed docents. How did the collection end up here? A rich industrialist and friend of Dalí's, Ohio magnate A. Reynolds Morse, was looking for a museum site after his huge collection began to overflow his mansion. The people of St. Petersburg vied admirably for the collection, and the museum was established here as a result. At press time, a new museum—twice the size of this facility—was scheduled to open just south of the Mahaffey Theater and Baker in January 2011. ✉ *1000 3rd St. S* ☎ *727/823–3767 or 800/442–3254* 🌐 *www.salvadordalimuseum.org* 🎫 *$15* ⏲ *Mon.–Wed. and Sat. 9:30–5:30, Thurs. 9:30–8, Fri. 9:30–6:30, Sun. noon–5:30.*

8 **Sunken Gardens.** This is 100-year-old botanical paradise. Check out photos of its colorful past in the gift shop. Explore the cascading waterfalls and koi ponds, and walk through the butterfly house and exotic gardens where more than 50,000 tropical plants and flowers thrive amid groves of some of the area's most spectacular palm trees. The on-site restaurant and hands-on kids' museum make this place a family favorite. ✉ *1825 4th St. N* ☎ *727/551–3102* 🌐 *www.sunkengardens.org* 🎫 *$8* ⏲ *Mon.–Sat. 10–4:30, Sun. noon–4:30.*

WORTH NOTING

7 **Bayshore Boulevard Trail.** If you like to get out and walk, talk, jog, bike, and inline skate with locals, you might want to take to this 8.6-mi trail in the downtown area and convenient to anywhere in the south Tampa area. It's a good spot for just standing still and taking it all in, too, with its spectacular views of downtown Tampa and the Hillsborough Bay area. Locals gather here when there's a launch at Cape Canaveral—views are superb. The trail is open from dawn to dusk daily. ✉ *Bayshore Blvd.* ☎ *727/549–6099.*

11 **BayWalk.** Downtown St. Petersburg gets an infusion of vibrancy from BayWalk, a shopping, dining, and entertainment mall in a square-block complex incorporating California mission–style design and courtyard areas lined with trendy eateries, bars, shops, and a 20-screen movie theater. It's best for adults to stroll the plaza and restaurants in the afternoon and early evening, since teenagers overtake BayWalk at night. ✉ *Bordered by 2nd St. N, 2nd Ave. N, 1st St. N, and 3rd Ave. N* ☎ *727/895–9277.*

> **WORD OF MOUTH**
>
> "My favorite beach is Ft. De Soto. it's just outside St. Pete Beach, but it's a county park and you can't stay there—which is part of its beauty. Aside from the old fort, there are no structures there, just dunes, sea oats, and beach (great shelling too)." —OO

9 **Florida Holocaust Museum.** The downtown Florida Holocaust Museum is one of the largest of its kind in the United States. It has the permanent History, Heritage, and Hope exhibit, an original boxcar, and an extensive collection of photographs, art, and artifacts. One compelling display includes portraits and biographies of Holocaust survivors. The museum, which also has a series of rotating exhibits, was conceived as a learning center for children, so many of the exhibits avoid overly graphic content; signs are posted outside galleries if the subject matter might be too intense for kids. ✉ *55 5th St. S* ☎ *727/820–0100* 🌐 *www.flholocaustmuseum.org* 🎫 *$12* ⏲ *Daily 10–5.*

14 **Fort De Soto Park.** Spread over five small islands, 1,136-acre Fort De Soto Park lies at the mouth of Tampa Bay. It has 7 mi of beaches, two fishing piers, a 4-mi hiking-skating trail, picnic and camping grounds, and a historic fort that kids of any age can explore. The fort for which it's named was built on the southern end of Mullet Key to protect sea lanes in the gulf during the Spanish-American War. Roam the fort or wander the beaches of any of the islands within the park. ✉ *3500 Pinellas Bayway S, Tierra Verde* ☎ *727/582–2267* 🎫 *Free* ⏲ *Beaches, daily sunrise–sunset; fishing and boat ramp, 24 hrs.*

13 **Great Explorations.** "Don't touch" are words never spoken here. The museum is hands-on through and through, with a Robot Lab, Climb Wall, Lie Detector, Fire House, Vet's Office, and other interactive play areas, including the new Tree House. Smart exhibits like the Tennis Ball Launcher, which uses compressed air to propel a ball through a series of tubes, and Sound Waves, where Styrofoam pellets in a clear tube show differences in sound frequencies, employ low-tech to teach kids (and parents) high-tech principles. ✉ *1925 4th St. N* ☎ *727/821–8992* 🌐 *www.greatexplorations.org* 🎫 *$9* ⏲ *Mon.–Sat. 10–4:30, Sun. noon–4:30.*

10 **Museum of Fine Arts.** One of the city's cornerstones, this museum is a gorgeous Mediterranean-revival structure that houses outstanding collections of European, American, pre-Columbian, and Asian art. Major works here by American artists range from Whistler to O'Keeffe to Rauschenberg and Lichtenstein, but the museum is known for its collection of French artists, including Fragonard, Cézanne, Monet, Rodin, Gauguin, and Renoir. There are also photography exhibits that draw from a permanent collection of more than 1,200 works. In 2008 the Hazel Hough Wing opened, more than doubling the museum's exhibit space. A new café offers visitors a lunch respite and a beautiful view of the bay. Docents give narrated gallery tours. ✉ *255 Beach Dr. NE* ☎ *727/896–2667* 🌐 *www.fine-arts.org* 🎫 *$14* ⏲ *Tues.–Sat. 10–5, Sun. 1–5.*

SPORTS AND THE OUTDOORS

BEACHES

15 **Pass-A-Grille Beach**, at the southern end of St. Pete Beach, has parking meters, a snack bar, restrooms, and showers. It and Clearwater Beach are two of the area's most popular saltwater swimming holes. ✉ *Off Gulf Blvd. (Rte. 699), St. Pete Beach.*

16 **Treasure Island** (✉ *11260 Gulf Blvd.*) is a free beach north of Pass-A-Grille with dressing rooms, metered parking, and a snack bar.

BASEBALL

Major League Baseball's **Tampa Bay Rays** (✉ *Tropicana Field, 1 Tropicana Dr., off I–175* ☎ *727/825–3137* 🌐 *tampabay.rays.mlb.com*) completed an improbable worst-to-first turnaround when they topped the American League Eastern Division in 2008. Tickets are available at the box office for most games, but you may have to rely on the classifieds sections of the *Tampa Tribune* and *St. Petersburg Times* for popular games.

SHOPPING

Designer boutiques, movie theaters, and trendy restaurants can be found at the downtown shopping plaza **Florida Craftsmen Galleries** (✉ *501 Central Ave.* ☎ *727/821–7391* 🌐 *www.floridacraftsmen.net*), which gives 125 local craftsmen a chance to exhibit glassware, jewelry, furniture, and more. **John's Pass Village and Boardwalk** (✉ *12901 Gulf Blvd., Madeira Beach* 🌐 *www.johnspass.com*) is a collection of shops and restaurants in an old-style fishing village, where you can pass the time watching pelicans cavorting and dive-bombing for food. A five-story structure on the bay front, the **Pier** (✉ *800 2nd Ave. NE* 🌐 *www.stpete pier.com*), near the Museum of Fine Arts, looks like an inverted pyramid. Inside are numerous shops and eating spots.

More than 150 art dealers sell their wares at **Art & Antiques** (✉ *Beach St. between 1st and 2nd Aves.*). One of the state's more notable bookstores is **Haslam's** (✉ *2025 Central Ave.* ☎ *727/822–8616* 🌐 *www.haslams.com*), a family-owned emporium that's been doing business just west of downtown St. Petersburg for more than 70 years. The store carries some 300,000 volumes, from cutting-edge best sellers to ancient tomes. If you value a good book or simply like to browse, you could easily spend an afternoon here.

NIGHTLIFE

Joyland Country Music Nightclub (✉ *5520 14th St.* ☎ *941/756–6060* 🌐 *www.joylandcountry.com*) is the local hotspot Wednesday to Saturday for live country music and dancing. At **Cha Cha Coconuts** (✉ *The Pier* ☎ *727/822–6655* 🌐 *www.chacha-coconuts.com*) crowds catch live contemporary music Friday through Sunday year-round. **Coliseum Ballroom** (✉ *535 4th Ave. N* ☎ *727/892–5202*) has ballroom dancing and group lessons on most Wednesday afternoons and Saturday nights.

At **Marchand's** (✉ *Vinoy Hotel, 501 5th Ave. NE* ☎ *727/894–1000* 🌐 *www.marchandsbarandgrill.com*), sophisticated locals and well-informed out-of-towners gather at the bar for after-dinner cocktails and dancing to top-notch jazz bands Friday and Saturday. It's the most genteel place in town for a nightcap. The **Rare Olive** (✉ *300 Central Ave.,* *corner of 3rd St.* ☎ *727/822–7273* 🌐 *www.rareolive.com*) adds a touch of class to an otherwise jeans-and-T-shirt nightlife scene.

WHERE TO EAT

$ SEAFOOD ✕ **Crabby Bill's.** Nothing fancy about the crab-man's place—just some of the area's tastiest seafood served family-style (picture long picnic-style tables) in a friendly atmosphere. The fried-grouper sandwich is tasty, but you can also order it grilled, broiled, or blackened. Crustaceans are the house specialty, meaning your choice of blue, soft-shell, king, and, from October to May, delicious though costly stone crabs, among others. There's also a good selection of other treats, including flounder, bay scallops, and farm-raised oysters. Diners usually dress in the official uniform of Florida beaches: shorts, T-shirts, and flip-flops. ✉ *5100 Gulf Blvd.* ☎ *727/360–8858* 🌐 *www.crabbybills.com* 💳 *D, MC, V.*

$ SEAFOOD ✕ **Hurricane Seafood Restaurant.** Sunsets and gulf views are the bait that hooks regulars as well as travelers who find their way to this somewhat hidden St. Pete Beach pit stop. Dating to 1977, it's mainly heralded as a watering hole where you can hoist a cold one while munching on one of the area's better grouper sandwiches. (Speaking of this sweet white fish, it's the real deal here, which—be warned—isn't always a guarantee in some restaurants.) There's also a range of seafood and steak entrées. The aforementioned sunsets are best seen from the rooftop sundeck. ✉ *807 Gulf Way, St. Pete Beach* ☎ *727/360–9558* 🌐 *www.thehurricane.com* 💳 *AE, D, MC, V.*

$$$$ ECLECTIC ★ ✕ **Marchand's Bar & Grill.** Opened in 1925, this wonderful eatery in the posh Renaissance Vinoy Resort has frescoed ceilings and a spectacular view of Tampa Bay. Upscale and special-occasion diners are drawn to Marchand's by an imaginative and ever-changing menu. A visit might offer a deliciously rare lamb duo (T-bone and double chop) with cheese and pesto-smashed spuds, halibut poached in vanilla-bean olive oil, or lump-crab-and-cheese ravioli with crunchy duck cracklings. The wine list is extensive, including a number of by-the-glass selections. There's live jazz Friday and Saturday nights. ✉ *Renaissance Vinoy Resort, 501 5th Ave. NE* ☎ *727/824–8072* 🌐 *www.marchandsbarandgrill.com* 💳 *AE, D, DC, MC, V.*

$$ SEAFOOD ✕ **PJ's Oyster Bar & Seafood Restaurant.** Follow the crowds to this back-alley eatery where 60 varieties of beer flow as freely as the rolls of paper towels mounted on wire hangers overhead. Seafood selections range from fried catfish and grouper to more elegant options such as blackened yellowfin tuna. The all-day menu includes sandwiches and pasta. Come after work weekdays or on weekends if you enjoy making new friends. ✉ *7500 Gulf Blvd.* ☎ *727/367–3309* 🌐 *www.pjsoysterbar.com* 💳 *AE, MC, V* ⊗ *No lunch.*

$$$ SEAFOOD ✕ **Salt Rock Grill.** This hot spot is where tourists and locals converge to enjoy a fun and lively beachside atmosphere. A band plays Saturday and Sunday nights during summer, and couples get close on the patio bar and beach. But the rock-solid (if slightly less than imaginative) menu is the best reason to come. Don't believe the Caribbean lobster is a "monster"—at 1¼ pounds it's on the small side, but it's twice cooked including a finish on the grill and quite tasty. The showstopper is the cioppino (shrimp, king crab, lobster, mussels, fish, and clams with a

Continued on page 350

SPRING TRAINING, FLORIDA-STYLE

by Jim Tunstall

Sunshine, railroads, and land bargains were Florida's first tourist magnets, but baseball had a hand in things, too. The Chicago Cubs led the charge when they opened spring training in Tampa in 1913—the same year the Cleveland Indians set up camp in Pensacola.

Over the next couple of decades, World War I and the Great Depression interrupted normal lives, but the Sunshine State became a great fit for the national pastime. Soon, big-league teams were flocking south to work off the winter rust.

At one point, the Florida "Grapefruit League" held a monopoly on spring training, but in 1947 Arizona's "Cactus League" started cutting into the action.

Today, roughly half of Major League Baseball's 30 teams arrive in Florida in February for six weeks of calisthenics, tryouts, and practice games. The clubs range from the Detroit Tigers, who have been in the same city (Lakeland) longer than any other team (since 1934), to the Tampa Bay Rays, who moved to a new spring home (Port Charlotte) in 2009.

The Los Angeles Dodgers play the Washington Nationals in Viera during a spring training game.

HERE COME THE FANS

Cardinals fans take advantage of spring training's easier access to players.

Florida's spring training teams play 25 or 30 home and away games, to the delight of 1.68 million annual ticker buyers. Diehards land as soon as the first troops—pitchers and catchers—come to practice around the third week of February. Intersquad games start in the fourth week, while the real training schedule begins by the end of February or first of March and lasts until the end of the month or early April. These games don't count in the regular season, but they give managers and fans a good idea of which players will be on the opening-day rosters, and who will be traded, sent to the teams' minor leagues, or told it's time to find a regular day job.

Spring training games provide a great excuse for local baseball fans to cut out of work early, while visitors from the North can leave ice, snow, and sleet behind. And who doesn't want a few chili dogs, brats, burgers, and brews on a March day?

Spring training's draw is more than just a change of venue with an early sample of concession-stand staples. There is also the ample choice of game sites. Teams are scattered around most of the major tourist areas of central and southern Florida, so those coming to watch the games can try a different destination each spring—or even make a road trip to several. Baseball fans also like that it's a melting pot—teams from more than a dozen cities are represented here.

Finally, you can't beat the price—tickets are usually cheaper than during the regular season—nor the access you have to baseball celebrities. In fact, the relaxed atmosphere of spring training makes most players more willing to sign your ball, glove, or whatever. You can get autographs during pregame workouts (practice sessions), which are free, as well as after the game.

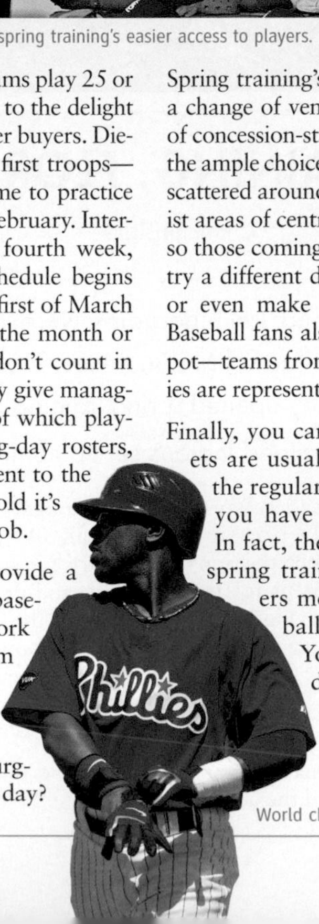

World champion Jimmy Rollins.

3 TIPS

- **Have a game plan.** Don't just show up. Most teams only have about 15 home games, and those involving the Yankees, Red Sox, and other popular clubs often are sold out weeks in advance. Consider buying tickets ahead of time, and if needed, make hotel room reservations at the same time.

- **Beat the crowds.** The best chance to do this is to go to a weekday game. You'll still encounter lots of fans, but weekday games generally aren't as stuffed as weekenders. Also, every team only has a few night games; if you want to attend one, book it by Christmas.

- **Pack a picnic.** Some stadiums let you bring coolers through the turnstiles. Many game attendees also gather for a tailgate party, grilling burgers and sipping a lemonade or beer while jawing with fellow fans (have a chair in tow).

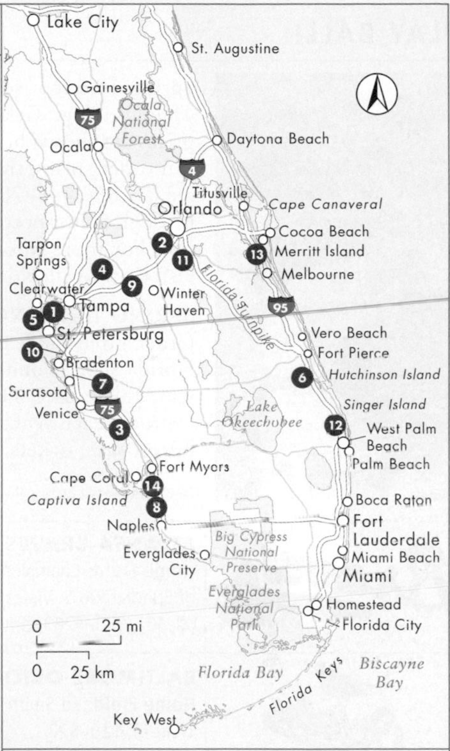

Atlanta Braves	2	New York Yankees	4
Baltimore Orioles	7	Philadelphia Phillies	1
Boston Red Sox	14	Pittsburgh Pirates	10
Detroit Tigers	9	St. Louis Cardinals/ Florida Marlins	12
Houston Astros	11	Tampa Bay Rays	3
Minnesota Twins	8	Toronto Blue Jays	5
New York Mets	6	Washington Nationals	13

(above) Hammond Stadium in Ft. Myers is where the Minnesota Twins practice.
(right) St. Louis Cardinals Chris Duncan is tagged out at Tradition Field in Port St. Lucie.

PLAY BALL!

Spring training schedules are determined around Thanksgiving. Ticket prices change each year; 2009 prices are shown here. For all of these teams, you also can order spring training tickets through Ticketmaster (☎ 866/448–7849 🌐 www.ticketmaster.com) or through the respective team's box office or team Web site. For more information about any of the teams, visit 🌐 www.floridagrapefruitleague.com.

SPRING TRAINING GUIDE

Order a free Guide to *Florida Spring Training* from the **Florida Sports Foundation** (✉ 2930 Kerry Forest Parkway, Tallahassee, FL ☎ 850/488–8347). Published in February each year, it's packed with information about teams, sites, tickets, and more.

New York Mets catcher Ramon Castro.

ATLANTA BRAVES

Home Field: Champion Stadium, Walt Disney World Wide World of Sports, 700 S. Victory Way, Kissimmee. **Tickets:** $15–$32
☎ 407/939–4263 🌐 www.braves.mlb.com

BALTIMORE ORIOLES

Home Field: Ed Smith Stadium, 1090 N. Euclid Ave., Sarasota. **Tickets:** $10–$22
☎ 954/776–1921 🌐 www.orioles.mlb.com

BOSTON RED SOX

Home Field: City of Palms Park, 2201 Edison Ave., Fort Myers. **Tickets:** $10–$26
☎ 239/334–4700, 877/733–7699 🌐 www.redsox.mlb.com

DETROIT TIGERS

Home Field: Joker Marchant Stadium, 2301 Lakeland Hills Blvd., Lakeland. **Tickets:** $12–$22
☎ 863/686–8075 🌐 www.tigers.mlb.com

FLORIDA MARLINS

Home Field: Roger Dean Stadium (shared with St. Louis Cardinals), 4751 Main St., Jupiter. **Tickets:** $14–$31
☎ 561/775–1818 🌐 www.marlins.mlb.com

HOUSTON ASTROS

Home Field: Osceola County Stadium, 631 Heritage Parkway, Kissimmee. **Tickets:** $10–$22
☎ 321/697–3200 🌐 www.astros.mlb.com

MINNESOTA TWINS
Home Field: Hammond Stadium, 14100 Six Mile Cypress Parkway, Fort Myers. **Tickets:** $12–$23
☎ 239/768-4270 🌐 www.twins.mlb.com

NEW YORK METS
Home Field: Tradition Field, 525 NW Peacock Blvd., Port St. Lucie. **Tickets:** $7–$22
☎ 772/871-2115 🌐 www.mets.mlb.com

NEW YORK YANKEES
Home Field: Steinbrenner Field, 1 Steinbrenner Dr., Tampa **Tickets:** $18–$33
☎ 813/879-2244 🌐 www.yankees.mlb.com

PHILADELPHIA PHILLIES
Home Field: Bright House Networks Field, 601 N. Old Coachman Rd., Clearwater. **Tickets:** $11–$30
☎ 727/467-4457 🌐 www.phillies.mlb.com

PITTSBURGH PIRATES
Home Field: McKechnie Field, 17th Avenue W. & 9th St., Bradenton. **Tickets:** $10–$18
☎ 941/748-4610 🌐 www.pirates.mlb.com

ST. LOUIS CARDINALS
Home Field: Roger Dean Stadium (shared with Florida Marlins), 4751 Main St., Jupiter. **Tickets:** $14–$27
☎ 561/775-1818 🌐 www.cardinals.mlb.com

TAMPA BAY RAYS
Home Field: Charlotte County Sports Park, 2300 El Jobean Rd., Port Charlotte. **Tickets:** $9–$23
☎ 727/825-3250 🌐 www.rays.mlb.com

TORONTO BLUE JAYS
Home Field: Dunedin Stadium, 373 Douglas Ave., Dunedin **Tickets:** $15–$22
☎ 727/733-0429 🌐 www.bluejays.mlb.com

WASHINGTON NATIONALS
Home Field: Space Coast Stadium, 5800 Stadium Parkway, Viera. **Tickets:** $9–$26
☎ 321/633-4487 🌐 www.nationals.mlb.com

sourdough crust). In fair weather, dine on the dock; otherwise ask for a table with a view of the water. ✉ *19325 Gulf Blvd.* ☎ *727/593–7625* 🌐 *www.saltrockgrill.com* 💳 *AE, MC, V.*

$ SEAFOOD Fodor's Choice ★ ✕ **Ted Peters Famous Smoked Fish.** Picture this: flip-flop-wearing anglers and beach-towel-clad bathers lolling on picnic benches, soaking up a beer, and devouring oak-smoked salmon, mullet, and mackerel. Everything comes to the table with heaped helpings of potato salad or coleslaw. If you're industrious enough to have hooked your own fish, the crew will smoke it for about $1.50 per pound. If not, there's always what many consider to be the best burger in the region. The popular smoked fish spread is available to go. There's also indoor seating at Ted's, which has been a south-side fixture for more than six decades. Closing time is 7:30 PM. ✉ *1350 Pasadena Ave. S, South Pasadena* ☎ *727/381–7931* ✍ *Reservations not accepted* 💳 *No credit cards* ⏲ *Closed Tues.*

$ AMERICAN ✕ **TooJay's.** Kippered salmon and roast brisket with potato pancakes are the mainstays at this kosher-style deli that's busy at breakfast, lunch, and dinner. Other selections include salmon cakes, shepherd's pie, and shrimp salad. Don't miss the éclair, a house specialty. The restaurant is nothing fancy, but it's bright and friendly, and management ensures you're waited on promptly. Everything on the menu is available for takeout. ✉ *141 2nd Ave. N, BayWalk* ☎ *727/823–3354* 🌐 *www.toojays.com* ✍ *Reservations not accepted* 💳 *AE, D, DC, MC, V.*

WHERE TO STAY

$$$–$$$$ Fodor's Choice ★ **Don CeSar Beach Resort.** You have to love the story—real or imagined—about Thomas Rowe's ghost. As legend has it, the man who built this Roaring Twenties–era hotel came back after death to meet his beloved. Some guests and staff swear they see the couple occasionally having a rendezvous in the garden (more romantic than spooky); others say Rowe appears in corridors and rooms. On a more documented level, the Don once was a favorite of F. Scott and Zelda Fitzgerald, Babe Ruth, and Clarence Darrow. Today the "Pink Palace," as it's called thanks to its paint job, is a gulf-coast landmark with remarkable architecture. Its exterior and public areas have turn-of-the-last-century elegance. Ditto for the rooms, and the staff is known for friendly old-world service. The hotel's fitness center and spa have recently undergone extensive renovations. The restaurant, Maritana Grille, specializes in Florida seafood and is lined with huge fish tanks. **Pros:** romantic destination; great beach; tasty dining options. **Cons:** quite pricey. ✉ *3400 Gulf Blvd., St. Pete Beach* ☎ *727/367–6952 or 800/282–1116* 🌐 *www.doncesar.com* *277 rooms, 40 suites, 70 condos* *In-room: safe (some), Internet, Wi-Fi. In-hotel: 3 restaurants, room service, bars, pools, gym, spa, beachfront, children's programs (ages 4–12), laundry service, Wi-Fi hotspot, parking (paid), some pets allowed* 💳 *AE, D, DC, MC, V.*

$$$–$$$$ Fodor's Choice ★ **Renaissance Vinoy Resort & Golf Club.** Built in 1925, making it the same vintage as the Don CeSar, the Vinoy is a luxury resort in a quiet, quaint neighborhood. Thoughtful renovations keep its yesteryear glamour and place on the National Register of Historic Places. Some of the units are cramped by today's standards, so ask for one of the spacious rooms for more comfort. Those on the bay side have better views of Tampa Bay.

A tiny bay-side beach several blocks away is good for strolling (but not swimming). Transportation is provided to better beaches 30 minutes away. Other offerings include access to a Ron Garl–designed golf course with a stunning clubhouse, an expansive marina, and pool attendants who deliver drinks. **Pros:** charming property; friendly service; close to downtown museums. **Cons:** pricey; not on the beach. ✉ *501 5th Ave. NE* ☎ *727/894–1000* 🌐 *www.vinoyrenaissanceresort.com* *345 rooms, 15 suites* *In-room: Internet. In-hotel: 5 restaurants, room service, bars, golf course, tennis courts, pools, gym, spa, laundry facilities, laundry service, Wi-Fi hotspot* *AE, D, DC, MC, V.*

$$$–$$$$ **TradeWinds Islands Resort.** The TradeWinds is very popular with foreign travelers who enjoy the indoor waterways complete with paddleboats. It's also one of the few pet-friendly resorts in the area, boasting a play area and a room-service menu for dogs and cats. Most rooms have a view of the beach, though you may have to crane your neck in some. The best views are from gulf-front suites with balconies or those overlooking the Intracoastal Waterway. All rooms are currently receiving furniture, lighting, and linen upgrades. There are on-site swimming lessons for children and adults. **Pros:** great beachfront location; close to restaurants. **Cons:** lots of conventions. ✉ *5500 Gulf Blvd., St. Pete Beach* ☎ *727/363–2212* 🌐 *www.justletgo.com* *584 rooms, 103 suites* *In-room: safe, kitchen, refrigerator, Internet, Wi-Fi. In-hotel: 11 restaurants, bars, tennis courts, pools, gym, spa, beachfront, children's programs (ages 4–15), laundry facilities, laundry service, Wi-Fi hotspot, parking (paid)* *AE, D, DC, MC, V.*

CLEARWATER

12 mi north of St. Petersburg via U.S. 19.

Residential areas are a buffer between the commercial areas that center on U.S. 19 and the beach, which is moderately quiet during winter but buzzing with life during spring break and summer. There's a quaint downtown area on the mainland, just east of the beach.

ESSENTIALS

Visitor Information Clearwater Regional Chamber of Commerce (✉ *1130 Cleveland St., Clearwater* ☎ *727/461–0011* 🌐 *www.clearwaterflorida.org*).

EXPLORING

Numbers in the margin correspond to the St. Petersburg map.

18 When pelicans and other birds become entangled in fishing lines, locals sometimes carry them to the nonprofit **Suncoast Seabird Sanctuary,** founded by Ralph Heath and dedicated to the rescue, repair, recuperation, and release of sick and injured birds. At times there are hundreds of land and sea birds in residence, including egrets, herons, gulls, terns, sandhill cranes, hawks, owls, and cormorants. ✉ *18328 Gulf Blvd., Indian Shores* ☎ *727/391–6211* 🌐 *www.seabirdsanctuary.com* *Donations* *Tours Wed. and Sun. at 2.*

19 South of Clearwater Beach, on Sand Key at Clearwater Pass, **Sand Key Park** has a lovely beach, plenty of green space, a playground, and a

Clearwater's Bait House lures in those heading to the pier to fish; photo by watland, Fodors.com member.

picnic area in an otherwise congested area. ✉ *1060 Gulf Blvd.* ☎ *727/588–4852.*

20 The **Clearwater Marine Aquarium** is a laid-back attraction offering an opportunity to participate in the work of saving and caring for endangered marine species. Many of the sea turtles, dolphins, and other animals living at the aquarium were brought here to be rehabilitated from an injury or saved from danger. The dolphin exhibit has an open-air arena giving the dolphins plenty of room to jump during their shows. The aquarium conducts tours of the bays and islands around Clearwater, including a daily cruise on a pontoon boat (you might just see a wild dolphin or two), and kayak tours of Clearwater Harbor and St. Joseph Sound. ✉ *249 Windward Passage* ☎ *727/441–1790* 🌐 *www.cmaquarium.org* *$13* 🕘 *Mon.–Thurs. 9–5, Fri. and Sat. 9–7, Sun. 10–5.*

SPORTS AND THE OUTDOORS

BEACHES

21 Fodor's Choice ★ Connected to downtown Clearwater by Memorial Causeway, **Clearwater Beach** (✉ *Western end of Rte. 60, 2 mi west of downtown Clearwater*) is on a narrow island between Clearwater Harbor and the gulf. It has a widespread reputation for beach volleyball. There are lifeguards here as well as a marina, concessions, showers, and restrooms. Around Pier 60 there's a big, modern playground. This is the site of a nightly sunset celebration complete with musicians and artisans. It's one of the area's nicest and busiest beaches, especially on weekends and during spring break, but it's also one of the costliest in terms of parking fees, which can reach $2 per hour.

BASEBALL

The **Philadelphia Phillies** (✉ *Bright House Networks Field, 601 N. Old Coachman Rd.* ☎ *727/441–8638*) get ready for the season with spring training here (late February to early April). The stadium also hosts the Phillies' farm team.

BIKING

The **Pinellas Trail** is a 35-mi paved route that spans Pinellas County. Once a railway, the trail runs adjacent to major thoroughfares, no more than 10 feet from the roadway, so you can access it from almost any point. The trail, also popular with in-line skaters, has spawned trailside businesses such as repair shops and health-food cafés. There are also many lovely rural areas to bike through and plenty of places to rent bikes. Be wary of traffic in downtown Clearwater and on the congested areas of the Pinellas Trail, which still needs more bridges for crossing over busy streets. To start riding from the route's south end, park at Trailhead Park (37th Street South at 8th Avenue South) in St. Petersburg. To ride south from the north end, park your car in downtown Tarpon Springs (East Tarpon Avenue at North Stafford Avenue). ☎ *727/464–8201*.

MINIATURE GOLF

The live alligators advertised on the roadside sign for **Congo River Golf** (✉ *20060 U.S. 19 N* ☎ *727/797–4222*) are not in the water traps but in a fenced-off lagoon. The reptiles do, however, add a Florida touch to this highly landscaped course tucked into a small parcel of land adjacent to Clearwater's busiest north–south thoroughfare. Admission is $9.50–$10.50. Closed mid-October through April, weekends only April, May, October.

8

WHERE TO EAT

$$$ AMERICAN ✕ **Bob Heilman's Beachcomber**. The Heilman family has fed hungry diners since 1920. Although it's very popular with tourists, you'll also rub shoulders with devoted locals. Despite the frequent crowds, the service is fast and friendly. The sautéed chicken is an American classic—arriving with mashed spuds, gravy, veggie du jour, and fresh baked bread. Or try the New Bedford sea scallops, broiled with lemon, capers, or pan-seared with roasted peppers. ✉ *447 Mandalay Ave., Clearwater Beach* ☎ *727/442–4144* 🌐 *www.heilmansbeachcomber.com* 💳 *AE, D, DC, MC, V.*

$ SEAFOOD ✕ **Frenchy's Rockaway Grill**. Quebec native Mike "Frenchy" Preston runs four eateries in the area, including the fabulous Rockaway Grill. Visitors and locals alike keep coming back for the grouper sandwiches that are moist and not battered into submission. (It's also real grouper, something that's not a given these days.) Frenchy also gets a big thumbs-up for his she-crab soup, and, on the march-to-a-different-drummer front, the cheddar-stuffed shrimp. In mild weather, eat on the deck, though the screaming yellow-and-turquoise paint job can be nearly as blinding as the sun. ✉ *7 Rockaway St.* ☎ *727/446–4844* 🌐 *www.frenchysonline.com* 💳 *AE, MC, V.*

WHERE TO STAY

$$$–$$$$ **Safety Harbor Resort & Spa**. Although it's not for everyone, those who enjoy old-school pampering love this hotel's 50,000-square-foot spa, which has the latest in therapies and treatments. Request a treatment room overlooking Tampa Bay—the sunsets can be gorgeous—and plan to spend a little downtime in the tranquility garden. Accommodations are continuously being upgraded, so expect to find high-end mattresses and luxurious linens. The pleasant hamlet of Safety Harbor is also a point of interest, with charming shops along the nearby main street. The resort was built over hot springs on Tampa Bay in 1926, but little of the original architecture remains. The springs still function, however, feeding into pools, the spa, and water coolers. **Pros:** charm to spare; good choice for pampering. **Cons:** far from attractions; staff can be chilly. ✉ *105 N. Bayshore Dr., Safety Harbor* ☎ *727/726–1161 or 888/237–8772* 🌐 *www.safetyharborspa.com* *175 rooms, 16 suites* *In-room: a/c, Internet, Wi-Fi. In-hotel: restaurant, tennis courts, pools, gym, spa, laundry facilities, laundry service, Wi-Fi hotspot* *AE, D, DC, MC, V.*

$$$–$$$$ ★ **Sheraton Sand Key Resort**. Expect something special—a modern property and one of the few uncluttered beaches in the area. The nine-story resort is set on 10 well-manicured acres, and many rooms have excellent gulf views; others keep an eye over an adjacent park. All rooms have balconies or patios, those on higher floors have beautiful views of the water. Considered one of the top convention hotels in the area, the resort has amenities—such as a beautiful private beach—that make it ideal for leisure travelers, too. **Pros:** private beach; great views; flat-screen TVs and Nintendo Wii in room. **Cons:** near crowded Clearwater Beach; views come with a high price tag. ✉ *1160 Gulf Blvd., Clearwater Beach* ☎ *727/595–1611* 🌐 *www.sheratonsandkey.com* *375 rooms, 15 suites* *In-room: Wi-Fi. In-hotel: 4 restaurants, room service, bars, tennis courts, pool, gym, beachfront, water sports, children's programs (ages 3–15), Wi-Fi hotspot* *AE, D, DC, MC, V.*

$$–$$$ **Wingate Inn—Clearwater/St. Pete**. The Wingate is a pleasant motel close to the attractions of northern Pinellas County. Rooms are clean, modern, and not cramped, but this is a chain. **Pros:** friendly staff; waffle station at breakfast. **Cons:** a bit far from the sites. ✉ *5000 Lake Blvd., Clearwater* ☎ *727/299–9800* 🌐 *www.wingateinnclearwater.com* *84 rooms* *In-room: refrigerator, Internet, Wi-Fi. In-hotel: pool, gym, laundry facilities, Wi-Fi hotspot* *AE, D, DC, MC, V.*

DUNEDIN

3 mi north of Clearwater.

If the sound of bagpipes and the sight of men in kilts appeals to you, you might catch an earful or a glimpse if your timing is right. Founded and named by two Scots in the 1880s, this town hosts the Highland Games in March and the Celtic Festival in November, both of which pay tribute to the town's heritage. Dunedin also has a nicely restored historic downtown—only about five blocks long—that has become a one-stop shopping area for antiques hunters and is also lined with gift shops and good nonchain eateries.

GETTING HERE AND AROUND

From Clearwater, take U.S. 19 to Route 580, then go west about 8 to 10 mi.

ESSENTIALS

Visitor Information **Greater Dunedin Chamber of Commerce** (✉ *301 Main St., Dunedin* ☎ *727/733–3197* 🌐 *www.dunedin-fl.com*).

SPORTS AND THE OUTDOORS

BEACHES

Caladesi Island State Park. Quiet, secluded, and still wild, this 3½-mi-long barrier island is one of the best shelling beaches on the Gulf Coast, second only to Sanibel. The park also has plenty of sights for birders—from common sandpipers to majestic blue herons to rare black skimmers—and miles of trails through scrub oaks, saw palmettos, and cacti (with tenants such as armadillos, rabbits, and raccoons). The landscape also features mangroves and dunes, and the gradual slope of the sea bottom makes this a good spot for novice swimmers and kids. You have to get to Caladesi Island by private boat (there's a 108-slip marina) or through its sister park, Honeymoon Island State Recreation Area, where you take the hourly ferry ride across to Caladesi. Ferry rides cost $9 per person. ✉ *Dunedin Causeway* ☎ *727/469–5942* 🎫 *$5 per car* ⏲ *Daily 8–sunset.*

BASEBALL

The **Toronto Blue Jays** (✉ *Knology Park, 373 Douglas Ave., north of Hwy. 580* ☎ *727/733–9302*) play about 18 spring-training games here in March.

8

WHERE TO EAT

$$$ CONTINENTAL ✕ **Bon Appétit.** Known for its creative fare, this waterfront restaurant has a menu that changes frequently, offering such entrées as broiled rack of lamb in herbed walnut crust and sautéed veal sweetbreads with mushrooms in brown butter. The roasted grouper in garlic and lemon butter gets well-deserved plaudits from many patrons. Bon Appétit has staying power, serving at the same location for more than three decades. It's a great place to catch a sunset over the Gulf of Mexico. There's a pianist Wednesday through Sunday evenings and a Sunday brunch. ✉ *148 Marina Plaza* ☎ *727/733–2151* 🌐 *www.bonappetitrestaurant.com* 💳 *AE, D, DC, MC, V.*

$$ MEXICAN ★ ✕ **Casa Tina.** Vegetarians can veg out here on roasted chiles rellenos (cheese-stuffed peppers), enchiladas with vegetables, and a cactus salad that won't prick your tongue but will tickle your taste buds with the tantalizing flavors of tender pieces of cactus, cilantro, tomatoes, onions, lime, and *queso fresco* (a mild white cheese). There also are tamales, tacos, and tortillas prepared dozens of ways. The place is often crowded, and service can be slow as a result, but there's a reason everyone's eating here. ✉ *369 Main St.* ☎ *727/734–9226* 💳 *AE, D, MC, V* ⏲ *Closed Mon.*

$$$ STEAK ✕ **Spoto's Italian Grille.** It's a simple formula: aged Angus beef expertly prepared and pasta cooked to perfection. This restaurant serves about every cut of beef you can imagine, from a huge porterhouse to a petit fillet to succulent prime rib. If red meat isn't what you're looking for,

there's also a variety of fresh fish entrées. ✉ *1280 Main St.* ☎ *727/734–0008* 🌐 *www.spotossteakjoint2.com* 💳 *AE, D, MC, V* ⏲ *No lunch.*

TARPON SPRINGS

10 mi north of Dunedin on Alternate U.S. 19.

Tucked into a little harbor at the mouth of the Anclote River, this slowly growing town was settled by Greek immigrants at the end of the 19th century. They came to practice their generations-old craft of sponge diving. Although bacterial and market forces seriously hurt the industry in the 1940s, sponging has had a modest return, mostly as a focal point for tourism. The docks along Dodecanese Boulevard, the main waterfront street, are filled with sweet old buildings with shops and eateries. Tarpon Springs' other key street is Tarpon Avenue, about a mile south of Dodecanese. This old central business district has become a hub for antiques hunters. The influence of Greek culture is omnipresent; the community's biggest celebration is the annual Greek Orthodox Epiphany celebration in January, in which teenage boys dive for a golden cross in Spring Bayou, a few blocks from Tarpon Avenue, during a ceremony followed by a street festival in the town's central business district.

ESSENTIALS

Visitor Information **Tarpon Springs Chamber of Commerce** (✉ *11 E. Orange St.* ☎ *727/937–6109* 🌐 *www.tarponsprings.org*).

EXPLORING

Numbers in the margin correspond to the St. Petersburg map.

22 **St. Nicholas Greek Orthodox Cathedral** is a replica of St. Sophia's in Istanbul and an excellent example of New Byzantine architecture. It's the home of a weeping icon that received national and international headlines in the 1970s. ✉ *36 N. Pinellas Ave.* ☎ *727/937–3540* 🎟 *Donation suggested* ⏲ *Daily 9–4.*

23 **The Sponge Factory** is a shop, museum, and cultural center that reveals more than you ever imagined about how a lowly sea creature created the industry that built this village. See a film about these much-sought-after creatures from the phylum *porifera* and how they helped the town prosper in the early 1900s. You'll come away converted to (and loaded up with) natural sponges. ✉ *510 Dodecanese Blvd., off U.S. 19* ☎ *727/938–5366* 🌐 *www.spongedocks.net* 🎟 *Free* ⏲ *Daily 10–6.*

24 Although it's not on par with larger tanks in Tampa and Clearwater, the **Konger Tarpon Springs Aquarium** is an entertaining destination. There are some good exhibits, including a 120,000-gallon shark tank complete with a coral reef. (Divers feed the sharks several times daily.) Also look for tropical fish exhibits and a tank where you can touch baby sharks and stingrays. ✉ *850 Dodecanese Blvd., off U.S. 19* ☎ *727/938–5378* 🌐 *www.tarponspringsaquarium.com* 🎟 *$6.75* ⏲ *Mon.–Sat. 10–5, Sun. noon–5.*

DID YOU KNOW?

Sponging began in Tarpon Springs 120 years ago. At one time it was the state's leading industry. Divers harvest the sponges and visitors can bid on some of them at the weekly auctions on the Sponge Docks.

WHERE TO STAY

$$$–$$$$ ★ **Innisbrook Resort & Golf Club**. A massive pool complex with a 15-foot waterslide and a sandy beach are part of the allure of this sprawling resort. But 72 holes of golf, including the challenging Copperhead course, are the real magnets. Bald eagles and herons are sometimes seen on the grounds, which are beautifully maintained. Guest suites are in 24 two- and three-story lodges tucked among the trees between golf courses. Some of the roomy suites have balconies or patios. Innisbrook has enough restaurants and lounges to make it self-contained, though there are other dining options in the area. **Pros:** great for serious golfers; varied dining options. **Cons:** far from attractions. ✉ *36750 U.S. 19 N, Palm Harbor* ☎ *727/942–2000 or 800/456–2000* 🌐 *www.innisbrookgolfresort.com* *620 suites* *In-room: a/c, kitchen (some), Internet, Wi-Fi. In-hotel: 4 restaurants, bars, golf courses, tennis courts, pools, gym, spa, bicycles, laundry facilities, laundry service, Wi-Fi hotspot* *AE, D, MC, V.*

SOUTH OF TAMPA BAY: SARASOTA COUNTY

Sarasota County anchors the southern end of Tampa Bay. A string of barrier islands borders it with 35 mi of gulf beaches, as well as two state parks, 22 municipal parks, and more than 30 golf courses, many open to the public. The city of Sarasota has a thriving cultural scene dating to circus magnate John Ringling, who chose this area for the winter home of his circus and his family.

BRADENTON

49 mi south of Tampa.

Named for early physician Joseph Braden, this Manatee River city has some 20 mi of beaches and is well situated for access to fishing, both fresh- and saltwater. It also has its share of golf courses and historic sites dating to the mid-1800s.

EXPLORING

Numbers in the margin correspond to the Sarasota County map.

1 **South Florida Museum & Parker Manatee Aquarium**. Snooty, the oldest manatee in captivity, is the headliner here. Programs about the endangered marine mammals run four times daily. View changing exhibits such as digital images of water and other natural resources in the East Gallery; glass cases and roll-out drawers on the 2nd floor allow you to look at exhibits normally out of public view. At the Bishop Planetarium (with a domed theater screen), programs presented range from black holes to Jimi Hendrix, Pink Floyd, and other rockers. ✉ *201 10th St. W* ☎ *941/746–4131* 🌐 *www.southfloridamuseum.org* *$15.95* *Jan.–Apr. and July, Mon.–Sat. 10–5, Sun. noon–5; May, June, and Aug.–Dec., Tues.–Sat. 10–5, Sun. noon–5.*

2 Fodor's Choice ★ **De Soto National Memorial**. One of the first Spanish explorers to land in North America, Hernando de Soto, came ashore with his men and 200 horses near what is now Bradenton in 1539; this federal park heralds that landing. During the height of tourist season, mid-December to

late April, park workers dress in period costumes at Camp Uzita, demonstrate the use of 16th-century weapons, and show how European explorers prepared and preserved food for their overland journeys. The season ends with a reenactment of the explorer's landing. The site also offers a film and short nature trail through the mangroves. ✉ *75th St. NW, Bradenton* ☎ *941/792–0458* 🌐 *www.nps.gov/deso* 🎟 *Free* 🕐 *Visitor center daily 9–5, grounds daily dawn–dusk.*

SARASOTA

30 mi south of Tampa and St. Petersburg.

Sarasota is a winter destination and in some cases permanent home to some of Florida's most affluent residents. Circus magnate John Ringling and his wife, Mable, started the city on the road to becoming one of the state's hotbeds for the arts. Today, cultural events are scheduled year-round, and there is a higher concentration of upscale shops, restaurants, and hotels than in much of the Tampa Bay Area. Across the water from Sarasota lie the barrier islands of **Siesta Key, Longboat Key,** and **Lido Key,** with myriad beaches, shops, hotels, condominiums, and houses.

GETTING HERE AND AROUND

Sarasota is accessible from Interstate 75 and Interstate 275, and U.S. 41. The town's public transit company is **Sarasota County Area Transit (SCAT)** (☎ *941/316–1234*). Fares for local bus service range from 75¢ to $3 (for an all-day pass); exact change is required.

ESSENTIALS

Transportation Contact Sarasota County Area Transit (SCAT) (☎ *941/316–1234*).

Visitor Information Sarasota Convention and Visitors Bureau (✉ *701 N. Tamiami Trail, Sarasota* ☎ *941/957–1877 or 800/522–9799* 🌐 *www.sarasotafl.org*).

EXPLORING

Numbers in the margin correspond to the Sarasota County map.

TOP ATTRACTIONS

3 Fodor's Choice ★ **Florida State University Ringling Center for the Cultural Arts.** Along Sarasota Bay, Ringling built a grand home that was patterned after the Palace of the Doges in Venice. This exquisite mansion of 32 rooms, 15 bathrooms, and a 61-foot Belvedere Tower was completed in 1925, and is a must-visit today. Its 8,000-square-foot terrace overlooks the dock where Ringling's wife, Mable, moored her gondola. The **John and Mable Ringling Museum of Art** is the state art museum of Florida and houses 500 years of art, including a world-renowned collection of Rubens paintings and tapestries. The **Ringling Circus Museum** displays circus memorabilia from its ancient roots to modern day. The Tibbals Learning Center, which opened in early 2006, focuses on the American circus and the collection of Howard Tibbals, master model builder, who spent 40 years building the world's largest miniature circus. This impressive to-scale replica of the circa 1920s and '30s Ringling Bros. and Barnum & Bailey Circus is authentic from the number of pancakes the circus cooks are flipping, to the exact likenesses and costumes of the performers (painstakingly re-created from photography and written accounts), to the correct names

DID YOU KNOW?

Sometimes called "sea cows," manatees are aquatic relatives of elephants. They can weigh more than 1,500 pounds and live 50-plus years. There are more than 3,000 in Florida's coastal waters.

of the animals marked on the miniature mess buckets. Tibbals's passion to re-create every exact detail continues in his on-site workshop, where kids can ask him questions and watch him carving animals and intricate wagons. ✉ *U.S. 41, ½ mi west of Sarasota-Bradenton Airport* ☎ *941/359–5700* 🌐 *www.ringling.org* 🎟 *$25* ⏲ *Daily 10–5.*

5 **Marie Selby Botanical Gardens.** A don't-miss attraction for plant and flower lovers—especially those attracted to orchids, which make up nearly a third of the 20,000 species here. You can stroll through the Tropical Display House, home of orchids and colorful bromeliads gathered from rain forests, and wander the garden pathway past plantings of bamboo, ancient banyans, and mangrove forests along Little Sarasota Bay. Although spring sees the best blooms, the greenhouses make this an attraction for all seasons. The added bonus is a spectacular view of downtown. There are rotating exhibits of botanical art and photography in a 1924 restored mansion. Enjoy lunch at the Selby Café. ✉ *811 S. Palm Ave.* ☎ *941/366–5731* 🌐 *www.selby.org* 🎟 *$17* ⏲ *Daily 10–5.*

WORTH NOTING

6 **Mote Marine Aquarium.** The 135,000-gallon shark tank here lets you view bull, sandbar, and other sharks from above and below the surface. Other tanks show off eels, rays, and other marine creatures native to the area. There's also a touch tank where you can get friendly with horseshoe crabs, conchs, and other creatures. Hugh and Buffett are the resident manatees and, though not as venerable as Snooty at the Parker Manatee Aquarium, they have lived here since 1996 as part of a research program. There's also a permanent sea-turtle exhibit. Many visitors take the 105-minute boat trip onto Sarasota Bay, conducted by **Sarasota Bay Explorers** (☎ *941/388–4200* 🌐 *www.sarasotabayexplorers.com*). The crew brings marine life on board, explains what it is, and throws it back to swim away. You are almost guaranteed to see bottlenose dolphins. Reservations are required. ✉ *1600 Ken Thompson Pkwy., City Island, Sarasota* ☎ *941/388–4441* 🌐 *www.mote.org* 🎟 *Aquarium $17, boat excursion $26, combined ticket $36* ⏲ *Aquarium daily 10–5; boat tours daily 11, 1:30, and 4.*

4 **Sarasota Jungle Gardens.** One of Florida's better throwback attractions, Sarasota Jungle Gardens fills 10 acres with native and exotic animals as well as tropical plants. The lush gardens date to 1936, and still have the small-world feel of yesterday's Florida. You'll find red-tailed hawks and great horned owls in the birds of prey show, American alligators and a variety of snakes in the reptile encounter, and bugs of many varieties in a show called Critters and Things. You can talk to trainers and get to know such plants as the rare Australian nut tree and the Peruvian apple cactus in the gardens. Also on-site are flocks of flamingos, reptiles, and a butterfly garden. ✉ *3701 Bay Shore Rd.* ☎ *941/355–1112* 🌐 *www.sarasotajunglegardens.com* 🎟 *$15* ⏲ *Daily 10–5.*

OFF THE BEATEN PATH

Solomon's Castle shows off Florida's wackier side. Namesake Howard Solomon got an itch in 1972 to build a castle. The 12,000-square-foot work in progress is constructed of thousands of offset aluminum printing plates. Inside, you'll find tons of odd sculptures, including a knight assembled from Volkswagen parts and an elephant made of oil drums.

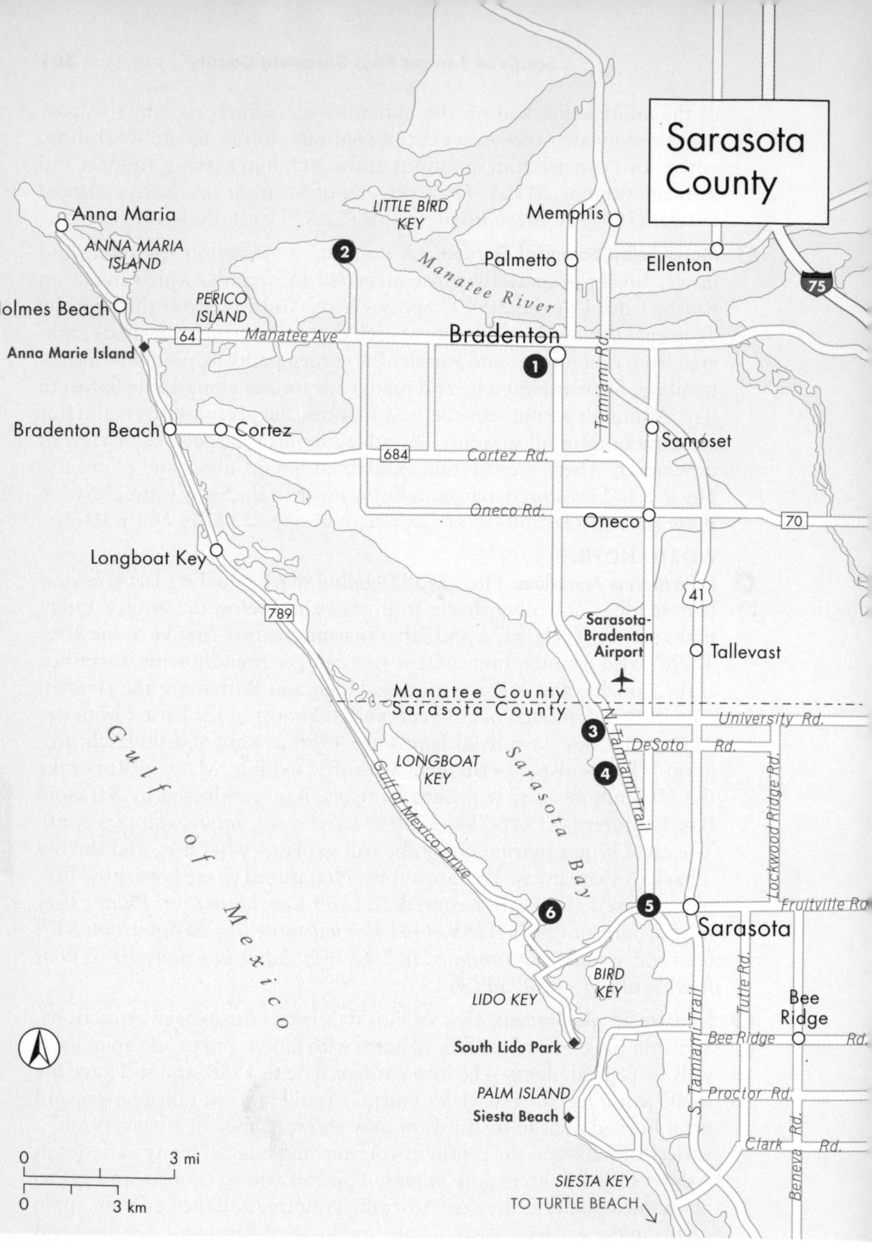

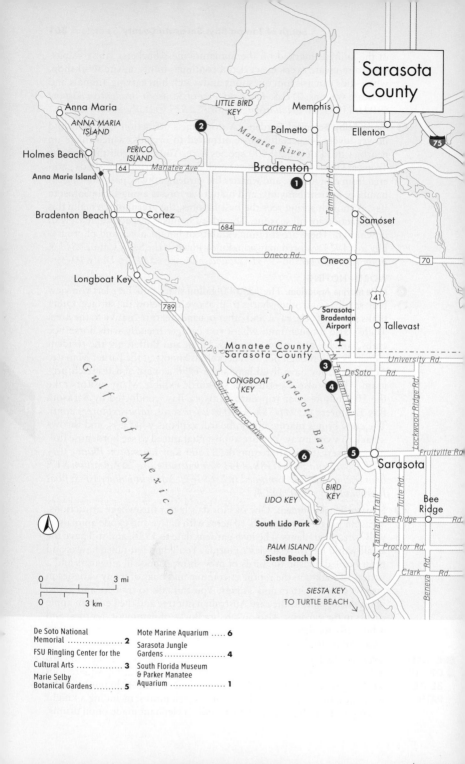

Sarasota County
Anna Maria
ANNA MARIA ISLAND
LITTLE BIRD KEY
Memphis
Palmetto
Ellenton
Manatee River
75
Holmes Beach
PERICO ISLAND
64
Manatee Ave
Bradenton
Anna Marie Island
Tamiami Rd.
Bradenton Beach
Cortez
Samoset
684
Cortez Rd.
Oneco Rd.
Oneco
70
Longboat Key
41
789
Sarasota-Bradenton Airport
Tallevast
Manatee County
Sarasota County
University Rd.
DeSoto Rd.
Gulf of Mexico
LONGBOAT KEY
Sarasota Bay
N. Tamiami Trail
Gulf of Mexico Drive
Lockwood Ridge Rd.
Fruitville Rd
Sarasota
BIRD KEY
LIDO KEY
Tutle Rd.
Bee Ridge
Bee Ridge Rd.
South Lido Park
S. Tamiami Trail
Proctor Rd.
PALM ISLAND
Siesta Beach
Clark Rd.
Beneva Rd.
SIESTA KEY
TO TURTLE BEACH
0 3 mi
0 3 km

De Soto National Memorial **2**
FSU Ringling Center for the Cultural Arts **3**
Marie Selby Botanical Gardens **5**
Mote Marine Aquarium **6**
Sarasota Jungle Gardens **4**
South Florida Museum & Parker Manatee Aquarium **1**

There's also a restaurant (open Friday and Saturday nights in season) that's a full-scale model of a Spanish galleon. The castle is 40 minutes east of Sarasota. ✉ *4533 Solomon Rd., Ona* ☎ *863/494–6077* 🌐 *www.solomonscastle.com* 🎟 *$10* ⏲ *Oct.–June, Tues.–Sun. 11–4.*

SPORTS AND THE OUTDOORS

BASEBALL

The Baltimore Orioles (✉ *Ed Smith Stadium, 1090 N. Euclid Ave.* ☎ *954/776–1921*) have spring training here in March.

GOLF

Bobby Jones Golf Course (✉ *1000 Circus Blvd.* ☎ *941/955–8097*) has 45 holes and a driving range; greens fee $36/$27. **Bobcat Trail Golf Club** (✉ *1350 Bobcat Trail, North Port* ☎ *941/429–0500*) is a semiprivate 18-hole course 35 mi from Sarasota; greens fee $49/$27. Semiprivate **Forest Lakes Golf Club** (✉ *2401 Beneva Rd.* ☎ *407/654–4653*) has a practice range and 18 holes; greens fee $45/$32. **Heron Creek Golf & Country Club** (✉ *5303 Heron Creek Blvd., North Port* ☎ *941/423–6955 or 800/877–1433*) has a semiprivate 27-hole course; greens fee $52/$37. There are 27 holes at the Ron Garl–designed **University Park Country Club** (✉ *7671 Park Blvd., University Park* ☎ *941/359–9999*). This club is private but does allow nonmembers limited play after 11 AM; greens fee $70/$50.

SHOPPING

The **Ringling Art Museum Store** (✉ *5401 Bay Shore Rd.* ☎ *941/359–5700* 🌐 *www.ringling.org*) is a fun place to pick up clown noses, ringmaster hats, and circus-themed T-shirts. **L. Boutique** (✉ *610 S. Pineapple Ave., Downtown* ☎ *941/906–1350* 🌐 *www.lboutiques.com*) features the trendiest fashions and most stylish handbags from top designers. **St. Armands Circle** (✉ *John Ringling Blvd. at Ave. of the Presidents*) is a cluster of oh-so-exclusive shops just east of Lido Beach.

8

THE ARTS

One of the best theaters in Sarasota, the $5 million **Asolo Repertory Theatre** (✉ *5555 N. Tamiami Trail* ☎ *941/351–8000* 🌐 *www.asolo.org*) stages productions November to June. The **Sarasota Opera** (✉ *The Edwards Theater, 61 N. Pineapple Ave.* ☎ *941/366–8450*) performs from February through March in a historic 1,033-seat downtown theater. Internationally known artists sing the principal roles, supported by a professional chorus of young apprentices. Performers at the **Sarasota Orchestra** (✉ *709 N. Tamiami Trail* ☎ *941/953–4252* 🌐 *www.fwcs.org*) include members of the Florida West Coast Symphony, Florida String Quartet, Florida Brass Quintet, Florida Wind Quintet, and New Artists Piano Quartet.

WHERE TO EAT

$$ ITALIAN

✕ **Café Baci.** A longtime favorite for its northern Italian cuisine, Café Baci attracts loyal locals as well as savvy travelers. Menu highlights include veal simmered with white wine, lemon, and capers; red snapper with tomatoes, black olives, rosemary, and white wine; and sautéed shrimp, scallops, fish, mussels, and clams bathed in a broth and served over risotto. The interior is not as enticing as the entrées, but resembles an English garden, with splashes of green and white and slightly outdated floral accents. ✉ *4001 S. Tamiami Trail* ☎ *941/921–4848* 🌐 *www.cafebaci.net* 💳 *AE, D, DC, MC, V.*

$$$$ STEAK/SEAFOOD Fodor's Choice ★ ✕ **Euphemia Haye.** Named for its original owner, this place has good food, a friendly staff, and intimate lighting, though the prices can cause credit cards of the unsuspecting to light up. Treats include lamb shank braised in a red-wine garlic sauce, crispy barbecued duckling in a sweet and spicy sauce, and a very tasty pistachio-crusted red snapper. The upstairs Haye Loft, once the home of the original owner's grandson, has been converted into a lounge and dessert room. ✉ *5540 Gulf of Mexico Dr., Longboat Key* ☎ *941/383–3633* 🌐 *www.euphemiahaye.com* ▭ *AE, D, MC, V.*

WORD OF MOUTH

"If you love a Florida environment with cultural activities nearby I would recommend the Sarasota area. Many towns like Bradenton, Venice, Nokomis, Anna Maria, Longboat Key or Siesta Key are close to Sarasota. There are good plays, music, opera, and ballet. There's a fantastic restaurant area around Main Street." —LN

$ AMERICAN ✕ **The Old Salty Dog.** A view of New Pass between Longboat and Lido keys and affordable eats make this a popular stop, especially for visitors to Mote Marine Aquarium. Its open-air dining area is comfortable even in summer, thanks to a pleasant breeze. Quarter-pound hot dogs, fish-and-chips, wings, and burgers set the menu's tone. Locals hang out at the bar, shaped from the hull of an old boat. ✉ *1601 Ken Thompson Pkwy., City Island* ☎ *941/388–4311* ✉ *5023 Ocean Blvd., Sarasota* ☎ *941/349–0158* 🌐 *www.theoldsaltydog.com* ✍ *Reservations not accepted* ▭ *MC, V.*

$$$$ AMERICAN ✕ **Ophelia's on the Bay.** The view is the first thing to lure you to this intimate waterfront spot. Daytime, you'll get glimpses of Little Sarasota Bay, its mangrove trees, and wildlife like ospreys and dolphins; at night, plan to sit outside (except in the buggier months of July and August) for a delightful view. The menu changes nightly, but entrées might include braised lamb osso buco with button mushrooms, plum tomatoes, and spuds; plump sea scallops (expect at least a half pound) accompanied by polenta and maple-glazed pancetta; and tuna (big-eye, yellowfin, and more), which owner Jane Ferro, who is also the grandniece of the restaurant's namesake, has flown in from Hawaii. ✉ *9105 Midnight Pass Rd., Siesta Key* ☎ *941/349–2212* 🌐 *www.opheliasonthebay.net* ▭ *AE, D, DC, MC, V* ⊙ *No lunch.*

$ AMERICAN ✕ **Yoder's.** Pies—key lime, egg custard, strawberry rhubarb, and others—are the main event at this family restaurant in the heart of Sarasota's Amish community, but don't miss enjoying at least one meal here. Entrées are served family style—feeding two to three people—and typically include meat loaf, liver and onions, turkey and dressing, and a wonderful goulash. Breakfasts include big stacks of pancakes. If you're in the mood for a sandwich, there are plenty to choose from, including belly-filling Manhattans (roast beef, turkey, or meatloaf on homemade bread and joined with mashed potatoes and gravy). The place gets crowded around noon and early evening. ✉ *3434 Bahia Vista* ☎ *941/955–7771* 🌐 *www.yodersrestaurant.com* ✍ *Reservations not accepted* ▭ *MC, V* ⊙ *Closed Sun.*

"When my granddaughter saw the beach for the first time at Longboat Key the sand was so white that she thought it was snow and wanted to make angels." —photo by Elizabeth Shevloff, Fodors.com member.

WHERE TO STAY

$$–$$$ **Best Western Midtown.** Here's a three-story motel that's comfortable and very affordable, especially from mid-April through early February. Set back from U.S. 41 and somewhat removed from traffic noise, it's within walking distance of a shopping center and several restaurants—including the popular Michael's on East—and is central to area attractions and downtown. Rooms have sitting areas. **Pros:** central location; good rates. **Cons:** chain-hotel feel; bland furnishings. ✉ *1425 S. Tamiami Trail* ☎ *941/955–9841 or 800/937–8376* 🌐 *www.bwmidtown.com* *100 rooms* *In-room: a/c, refrigerator (some), Internet. In-hotel: pool, laundry facilities* ▭ *AE, D, DC, MC, V* 🍴 *CP.*

$$$–$$$$ ★ **Colony Beach & Tennis Resort.** If tennis is your game, this is *the* place to stay—it's one of Florida's best racquet clubs, and tennis greats such as Björn Borg have made it their home court. Ten of its courts are clay hydrosurfaced (the other 11 are hard), and the pros are all USPTA–certified. It runs clinics and camps at all levels, and with the guaranteed match-making program, you can play with a pro when no one else is available. There are even rackets and lessons for children, plus excellent free kids' programs. The Colony dining room has a reputation for good food and wine. Suites sleep up to eight. Among the suites are a two-story penthouse and three private beach houses that open onto sand and sea. The exterior and interior of the lodging buildings are truly outdated; the bed linens could have come from Motel 6. **Pros:** a must for tennis fans; not far from trendy St. Armands shopping. **Cons:** pricey; not for those who don't love tennis; rooms lack polish of pricey resorts. ✉ *1620 Gulf of Mexico Dr., Longboat Key* ☎ *941/383–6464 or 800/426–5669* 🌐 *www.colonybeachresort.com* *235 suites* *In-*

room: safe, kitchen, Internet, Wi-Fi. In-hotel: 2 restaurants, bars, tennis courts, pool, gym, spa, beachfront, water sports, bicycles, children's programs (ages 3–17), laundry facilities, laundry service, Wi-Fi hotspot ▭ *AE, D, DC, MC, V.*

$$$$ **Longboat Key Club & Resort.** This beautifully landscaped property is one of the best places to play golf in the state, and among the top tennis resorts in the country. Water is the test on both golf courses, which have excellent pro shops. Hobie Cats, kayaks, and deep-sea charters are available. If you just want to chill, check out the hammocks between buildings 1 and 2. All rooms have balconies overlooking the golf course, beach, or private lagoon where manatees and dolphins are occasionally spotted. Golf and dining facilities are for guests only. **Pros:** upscale vibe; lovely grounds. **Cons:** service can feel snooty. ✉ *301 Gulf of Mexico Dr., Longboat Key* ☎ *941/383–8821, 800/237–8821, or 888/237–5545* 🌐 *www.longboatkeyclub.com* *23 rooms, 95 suites* *In-room: a/c, kitchen (some), refrigerator, Internet, Wi-Fi. In-hotel: 5 restaurants, room service, bars, golf course, tennis courts, pool, gym, spa, beachfront, water sports, bicycles, children's programs (ages 5–12), laundry facilities, Internet terminal, Wi-Fi hotspot* ▭ *AE, DC, MC, V.*

$$$$ ★ **Ritz-Carlton, Sarasota.** Developers like to say that this hotel is circus magnate John Ringling's realized dream, and it certainly has a style the impresario would have coveted. Fine artwork and fresh-cut flowers decorate marble-floored hallways. Rooms have marble bathrooms, and private balconies with views of the bay, the marina, or the downtown skyline. A private 18-hole Tom Fazio–designed golf course is 12 mi northeast of the property on the Braden River. A European-style spa and guest-and-members-only beach facility on Lido Key, about 4 mi away, make this city resort full-service. Vernona restaurant serves regional organic cuisine and overlooks yachts in the marina. **Pros:** Ritz-style glitz; lots of amenities. **Cons:** long distance to golf course; not on the beach. ✉ *1111 Ritz-Carlton Dr.* ☎ *941/309–2000 or 800/241–3333* 🌐 *www.ritzcarlton.com/resorts/Sarasota* *266 rooms, 30 suites* *In-room: safe, Wi-Fi. In-hotel: 2 restaurants, room service, bars, golf course, tennis courts, pool, gym, spa, children's programs (ages 5–12), laundry service, Wi-Fi hotspot, some pets allowed* ▭ *AE, D, DC, MC, V.*

The Lower Gulf Coast

WITH FORT MYERS, NAPLES, AND THE COASTAL ISLANDS

WORD OF MOUTH

"Fly into Ft. Myers, rent a car and take the short drive to Sanibel and (connected by bridge) Captiva. . . . There are great restaurants on both islands and shopping, as well. Paddle through the Ding Darling Sanctuary. Your Tween Waters beach is heavenly, and the Sanibel beaches are, too. Shelling is fun and very productive."

—ginnyfrye

Join, Ask, Share. www.fodors.com/community/

WELCOME TO THE LOWER GULF COAST

TOP REASONS TO GO

★ **Heavenly Beaches:** Whether you go to the beach to sun, swim, gather shells, or watch the sunset, the region's Gulf of Mexico beaches rank among the best.

★ **Edison and Ford Winter Estates:** A rare complex of two famous inventors' winter homes comes complete with botanical-research gardens, Edison's lab, and a museum.

★ **Island Hopping:** Rent a boat or jump aboard a charter for lunch, picnicking, beaching, or shelling on a subtropical island adrift from the mainland.

★ **Naples Shopping:** Flex your buying power in downtown Naples's charming shopping districts or in lush outdoor centers around town.

★ **Watch for Wildlife:** On the edge of Everglades National Park, the region protects vast tracts of fragile land and water where you can see alligators, manatees, dolphins, roseate spoonbills, and hundreds of other birds.

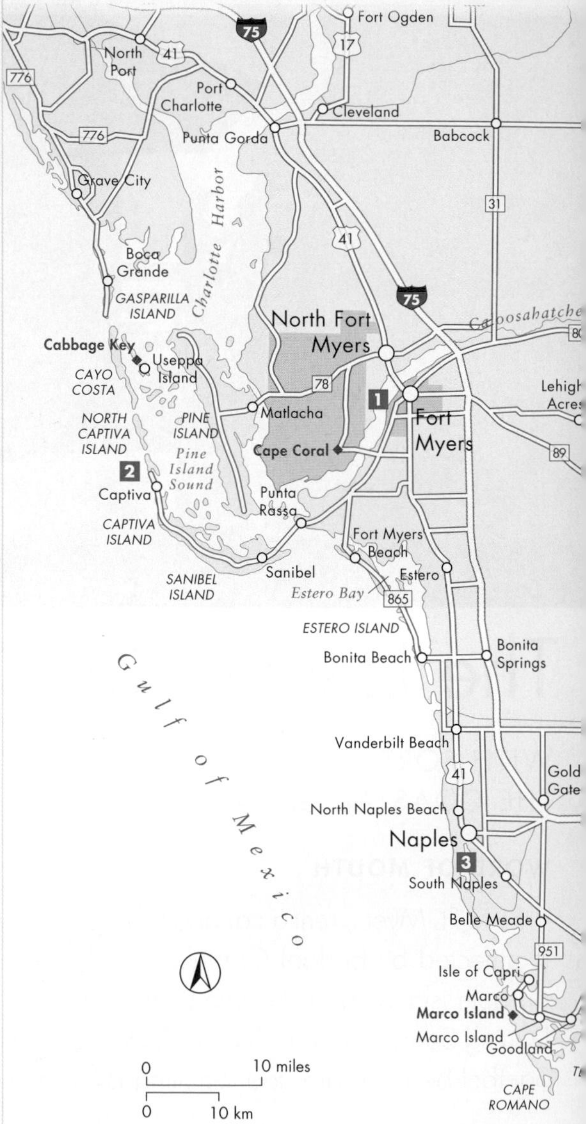

Fort Myers beach.

River
Alva
29
Falda
Corkscrew
Immokalee
29
Sunniland
Everglades Parkway (toll)
75
(Alligator Alley)
Miles City
Big Cypress National Preserve
Royal Palm Hammock
29
Copeland
41
Everglades City
THOUSAND ISLANDS
Everglades National Park
Chokoloskee

1 Fort Myers Area. Don't miss the Edison and Ford Winter Estates along royal-palm-lined McGregor Boulevard. For museums, theater, and art, the up-and-coming downtown River District rules.

2 The Coastal Islands. Shells and wildlife refuges bring nature-lovers to Sanibel and Captiva islands. Fort Myers Beach is known for its lively clubs and shrimp fleet. For true seclusion, head to the area's unbridged island beaches.

3 Naples Area. Some of the region's best shopping and dining take up residence in historic buildings trimmed with blossoms and street sculptures in Old Naples. Hit Marco Island for the boating lifestyle and funky-fish-village character.

Ding Darling Wildlife Refuge.

Naples Pier.

GETTING ORIENTED

The Lower Gulf Coast of Florida, as its name suggests, occupies a stretch of coastline along southernmost west Florida, bordered by the Gulf of Mexico. It lies south of Tampa and Sarasota, directly on the other side of the state from West Palm Beach and Fort Lauderdale. In between the two coasts stretch heartland agricultural areas and Everglades wilderness. The region encompasses the major resort towns of Fort Myers, Fort Myers Beach, Sanibel Island, Naples, and Marco Island, along with a medley of suburban communities and smaller islands.

LOWER GULF COAST PLANNER

When to Go

In winter this is one of the warmest areas of the United States, although occasionally temperatures drop below freezing in December or January. From February through April you may find it next to impossible to find a hotel room.

Numbers drop the rest of the year, but visitors within driving range, European tourists, and convention clientele still keep things busy. Temperatures and humidity soar, but discounted room rates make summer attractive. Summer, however, is rainy season, but most storms occur in the afternoon. Hurricane season runs from June through November.

Getting Here

Southwest Florida International Airport (RSW) (☎ *239/768–1000* 🌐 *www.flylcpa.com*) is the major airport for the region, with many airlines flying into and out of it. Delta Connection and a couple of private charters service **Naples Municipal Airport** (☎ *239/643–0733* 🌐 *www.flynaples.com*). Private pilots land at both RSW and Page Field in Fort Myers. North Captiva Island has a private airstrip.

Transportation companies include **Aaron Airport Transportation** (☎ *239/768–1898 or 800/998–1898*) and **Sanibel Island Taxi** (☎ *239/472–4160*).

Getting Around

If driving, U.S. 41 (the Tamiami Trail) also runs the length of the region. Sanibel Island is accessible from the mainland via the Sanibel Causeway (toll $6 round-trip). Captiva Island lies across a small pass from Sanibel's north end, accessible by bridge.

Be aware that the destination's popularity, especially during winter, means traffic congestion at peak times of day. Avoid driving when the locals are getting to and from work.

About the Restaurants

In this part of Florida fresh seafood reigns supreme. Succulent native stone-crab claws, a particularly tasty treat, in season from mid-October through mid-May, are usually served hot with drawn butter or chilled with tangy mustard sauce. Supplies are typically steady, since fishermen take only one of their claws, which regenerates in time for the next season. Other seafood specialties include fried-grouper sandwiches and Sanibel pink shrimp. In Naples's highly hailed restaurants, mingle with locals, winter visitors, and other travelers and catch up on the latest culinary trends.

About the Hotels

Lodging in Fort Myers, the islands, and Naples can be pricey, but there are affordable options even during the busy winter season. If these destinations are too rich for your pocket, consider visiting in the off-season, when rates drop drastically. Beachfront properties tend to be more expensive; to spend less, look for properties away from the water. In high season—Christmas through Easter—always reserve ahead for the top properties. Fall is the slowest season: rates are low and availability is high, but this is also the prime time for hurricanes. New resorts have been popping up around the region. Naples Bay Resort opened in February 2008 and Fort Myers's Hotel Indigo in March 2009. In Cape Coral, The Resort at Marina Village, the town's first luxury property, opened November 2009.

Assume that hotels operate on the European Plan (EP, no meals), unless we specify that they use the Breakfast Plan (BP, with full breakfast), Continental Plan (CP, Continental breakfast), Full American Plan (FAP, all meals), or Modified American Plan (MAP, breakfast and dinner), or are all-inclusive (AI, all meals and most activities).

WHAT IT COSTS

	¢	$	$$	$$$	$$$$
Restaurants	under $10	$10–$15	$15–$20	$20–$30	over $30
Hotels	under $80	$80–$100	$100–$140	$140–$220	over $220

Restaurant prices are per person for a main course at dinner. Hotel prices are for a standard double room, excluding 6% sales tax (more in some counties) and 1%–4% tourist tax.

Special Tours

To sight some manatees, hook up with **Manatee & River Tours** (✉ *16991 Rte. 31, Fort Myers* ☎ *239/693–1434* 🌐 *www.manateeandrivertours.com*). Near Marco Island, **Manatee Sightseeing Adventure** (☎ *239/642–8818 or 800/379–7440* 🌐 *www.seemanatees.com*) offers tours to sight these gentle creatures.

Captiva Cruises (✉ *McCarthy's Marina, Captiva* ☎ *239/472–5300* 🌐 *www.captivacruises.com*) runs shelling, nature, luncheon, beach, and sunset cruises to and around the out islands of Cabbage Key, Useppa Island, Cayo Costa, and Gasparilla Island. Excursions cost $25 to $45 each.

One of the best ways to see the J.N. "Ding" Darling National Wildlife Refuge is by taking a canoe or kayak tour with **Tarpon Bay Explorers** (✉ *900 Tarpon Bay Rd., Sanibel* ☎ *239/472–8900* 🌐 *www.tarponbayexplorers.com*). The knowledgeable naturalist guides can help you see so much more of what's there among the mangroves and under the water's surface.

Manatee Tour Boat.

9

LOWER GULF COAST BEACHES

Gorgeous, long, white-sand beaches fringe the Lower Gulf Coast and barrier islands. Known ultimately for their great shelling and kid-friendly waves, the beaches here range from the natural, undeveloped sands of Sanibel Island to the manicured parks of Naples.

Sanibel Island holds the highest reputation for seashells on the seashore in these parts due to the east-west torque at its south end. Shelling is best at low tide and after a storm has washed shells ashore. Remember, collecting live shells (ones with flesh inside) is illegal on Sanibel Island and in all state and national parks, so look only for uninhabited specimens. Local laws outside of Sanibel and the parks limit the taking of live shells to two per person per species per day.

All of the beaches charge for parking; some are resident-only designated and require a car sticker. (Many of the latter you can walk or ride a bike to if you're looking for quiet and seclusion. If you're really looking to escape, rent a boat and hit the bridgeless islands of Don Pedro, Cayo Costa, North Captiva, and Keewaydin.)

WORD OF MOUTH

"No franchise restaurants [on Sanibel] other than a Subway, a Dairy Queen and a 7/11 but there are lots of good restaurants that are sophisticated if that's your style or kid friendly if that's a better fit. We began going there years ago when our family really needed some down-time, a chance to talk to each other and rest. We're now on the next generation and the kids love to rent bikes, play volleyball on the beach and pick up shells. It is a real vacation."
—lukehead

THE LOWER GULF COAST'S BEST BEACHES

BAREFOOT BEACH PRESERVE

Although it's not easy to reach—the drive from Bonita Beach Road along Lely Barefoot Boulevard to this Collier County treasure takes you through a speed-bump-mined development—it's worth the inconvenience if you're looking for a natural encounter along with your beach play. Past the speed bumps, gopher tortoises crossing the road will slow you down. Beachgoers come for shells, canoeing, and to explore nature in gardens and exhibits off the beach.

BOWMAN'S BEACH

Long, wide Bowman's Beach, on Sanibel's northwest end, is the island's most secluded strand. Walk the length of the beach and leave humanity behind, finding some of the area's greatest concentrations of shells along the way. In fact, while most beaches in Sanibel and Captiva are worthy hunting grounds for shell devotees, Bowman's tops them all. This is because Bowman's is the hardest to reach, most spread-out, and least populated of the island's many beaches. You might even score one of the island's most coveted shells, the Junonia. The sunsets at the north end are spectacular.

DELNOR-WIGGINS PASS STATE PARK

Its placement across the pass from Barefoot Beach and a preserved bay backdrop make Delnor-Wiggins in North Naples popular with both fishermen and nature lovers. Rangers conduct birding and sea turtle programs at different times of year. Beach buffs adore its stretch of sand immune from the high-rise rash to the south. Picnic facilities and an observation tower attract families.

LOVERS KEY STATE PARK

Among Florida's most visited parks, this barrier island south of Fort Myers Beach, on Route 865, is a natural haven. Birds flock to its estuary, kayakers paddle through, and a gazebo on the beach hosts many a wedding. Lovers Key got is name because, for years, it was accessible only by boat, and only lovers ventured here for a little remote romance.

LOWDERMILK PARK

Looking for pure fun with your beach day, hold the nature lessons? That's what prettily landscaped Lowdermilk in Naples is all about. Families appreciate the grassy lawn, playground, volleyball nets, picnic facilities, shallow waters, duck pond, and food concession at this beach on Gulf Shore Boulevard at Banyan Boulevard.

TURNER BEACH

This patch of undulating sand on the southern tip of Captiva is a good spot for catching the setting sun. Due to the strong currents here it's much better for surfing than swimming.

Updated by Chelle Koster Walton

With its subtropical climate and beckoning family-friendly beaches, the Lower Gulf Coast, also referred to as the state's southwestern region, is a favorite vacation spot of Florida residents as well as visitors. Vacationers tend to spend most of their time outdoors—swimming, sunning, shelling, fishing, boating, and playing tennis or golf.

The region has several distinct travel destinations. Small and historic downtown Fort Myers rises inland along the Caloosahatchee River, and the rest of the town sprawls in all directions. It got its nickname, the City of Palms, from the hundreds of towering royal palms that inventor Thomas Edison planted between 1900 and 1917 along McGregor Boulevard, a historic residential street and site of his winter estate. Edison's idea caught on, and more than 2,000 royal palms now line 14-mi-long McGregor Boulevard. Museums and educational attractions are the draw here. Across the river, Cape Coral has evolved from a mostly residential community to a resort destination for water-sports enthusiasts.

Off the coast west of Fort Myers are more than 100 coastal islands in all shapes and sizes. Connected to the mainland by a 3-mi causeway, Sanibel is known for its superb shelling, fine fishing, beachfront resorts, and wildlife refuge. Here and on Captiva, to which it is connected by a short bridge, multimillion-dollar homes line both waterfronts. Just southwest of Fort Myers is Estero Island, home of busy Fort Myers Beach, and farther south, Lovers Key State Park and Bonita Beach.

Farther down the coast lies Naples, once a small fishing village and now a thriving and sophisticated town. It's a smaller, more understated version of Palm Beach, with fine restaurants, chichi shopping areas, and—locals will tell you—more golf holes per capita than anywhere else in the world. A half hour south basks Marco Island, best known for its beaches and fishing. See a maze of pristine miniature mangrove islands when you take a boat tour from the island's marinas into Ten Thousand Islands National Wildlife Refuge. Although high-rises line much of Marco's waterfront, the tiny fishing village of Goodland, an outpost of Old Florida, tries valiantly to stave off new development.

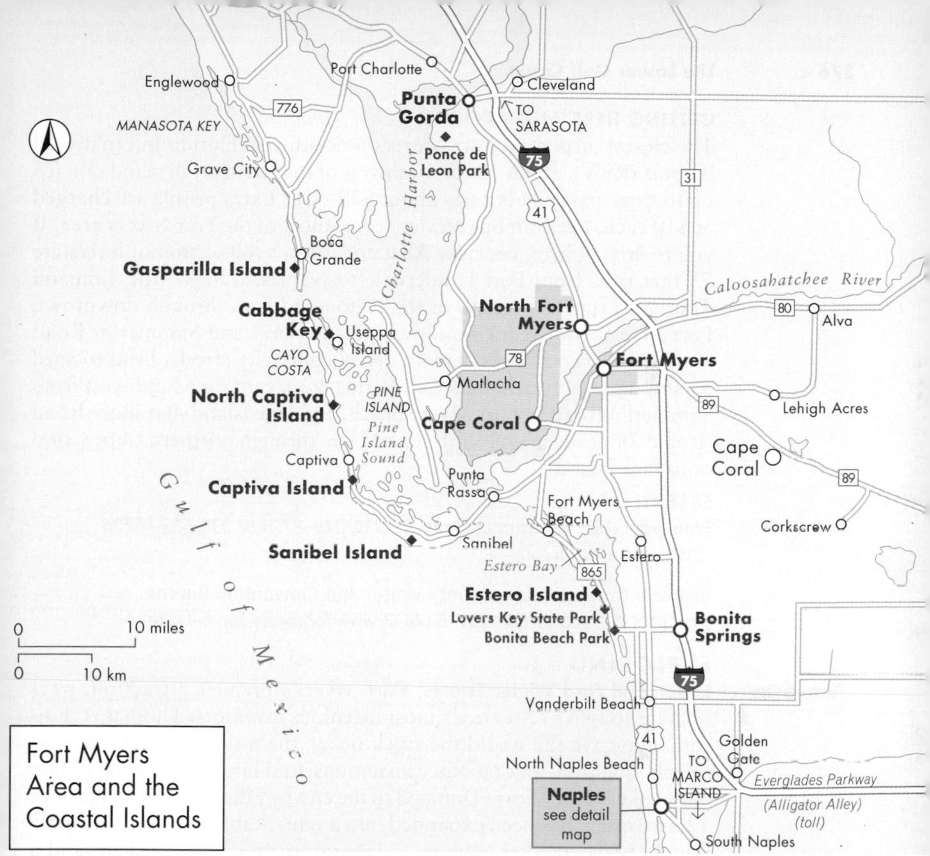

FORT MYERS AREA

In Fort Myers, old Southern mansions and their modern-day counterparts peek out from behind stately palms and blossomy foliage. Views over the broad Caloosahatchee River, which borders the city's small but businesslike cluster of office buildings downtown, soften the look of the area. These days, it's showing the effects of age and urban sprawl, but planners work at reviving what has been termed the River District. North of Fort Myers are small fishing communities and new retirement towns, including Boca Grande on Gasparilla Island; Englewood Beach on Manasota Key; Port Charlotte, north of the Peace River; and Punta Gorda, at the convergence of the Peace River and Charlotte Harbor.

FORT MYERS

90 mi southeast of Sarasota, 140 mi west of Palm Beach.

The city core lies inland along the banks of the Caloosahatchee River, a half hour from the nearest beach. The town is best known as the winter home of inventors Thomas A. Edison and Henry Ford.

GETTING HERE AND AROUND

The closest airport to Fort Meyers is Southwest Florida International Airport (RSW), about 12 mi southwest of town. An on-demand taxi for up to three passengers costs about $20–$30. Extra people are charged at $10 each. LeeTran bus service serves most of the Fort Myers area. If you're driving here, consider Alligator Alley, a toll section of Interstate 75 that runs from Fort Lauderdale to Naples. U.S. 41 (the Tamiami Trail) also runs the length of the region and goes through downtown Fort Myers. McGregor Boulevard (Route 867) and Summerlin Road (Route 869), Fort Myers's main north–south city streets, head toward Sanibel and Captiva islands. San Carlos Boulevard runs southwest from Summerlin Road to Fort Myers Beach, and Pine Island–Bayshore Road (Route 78) leads from North Fort Myers through northern Cape Coral onto Pine Island.

ESSENTIALS

Transportation Contact **LeeTran** (☎ *239/275–8726 or 239/533—8726* 🌐 *www.rideleetran.com*).

Visitor Information **Lee County Visitor and Convention Bureau** (☎ *239/338–3500 or 800/237–6444* 🌐 *www.fortmyers-sanibel.com*).

EXPLORING

Fodor's Choice ★ **Edison and Ford Winter Estates**, Fort Myers's premier attraction, pays homage to two of America's most ingenious inventors: Thomas A. Edison, who gave the world the stock ticker, the incandescent lamp, and the phonograph, among other inventions; and his friend and neighbor, automaker Henry Ford. Donated to the city by Edison's widow, his once 12-acre estate has been expanded into a remarkable 26 acres, with two homes, two caretaker cottages, a laboratory, botanical gardens, and a museum. The laboratory, newly renovated in 2009, contains the same gadgets and gizmos as when Edison last stepped foot into it. Visitors can see many of his inventions, along with historic photographs and memorabilia, in the museum. Edison traveled south from New Jersey and devoted much of his time here to inventing things (there are 1,093 patents to his name), experimenting with rubber for friend and frequent visitor Harvey Firestone, and planting hundreds of plant species collected around the world. Next door to Edison's two identical homes is Ford's "Mangoes," the more modest seasonal home of Edison's fellow inventor. It's said that the V-8 engine in essence was designed on the back porch. The property's oldest building, the Caretaker's House, dates to 1860. Research garden renovation is ongoing. Tours are guided or audio self-guided. One admission covers both homes; museum tickets and botanical-garden tickets are also available. ✉ *2350 McGregor Blvd.* ☎ *239/334–3614* 🌐 *www.efwefla.org* 🎫 *$20* ⏲ *Daily 9–5:30; tours at 11, 1, and 3.*

In a restored railroad depot, the **Southwest Florida Museum of History** showcases the area's history dating to 800 BC. Displays include prehistoric animals and Calusa artifacts, a reconstructed *chickee* hut, canoes, clothing and photos from Seminole settlements, historical vignettes, changing exhibits, and a replicated Florida Cracker house. A favorite attraction is the *Esperanza,* a private railcar from the 1930s that was

View 200 phonographs, an invention Thomas Edison patented in 1878, at his Fort Myers winter estate.

lovingly restored in 2008. ✉ *2031 Jackson St.* ☎ *239/321–7430* 🌐 *www.swflmuseumofhistory.com* 🎟 *$9.50* 🕘 *Tues.–Sat. 10–4.*

★ Kids can't wait to get their hands on the wonderful interactive exhibits at the **Imaginarium Hands-On Museum**, a lively museum-aquarium combo that explores the environment, physics, anatomy, weather, and other science and lifestyle topics. Check out the marine life in the aquariums, touch tanks, the living-reef tank, and the outdoor lagoon; visit a tarantula, python, hissing cockroach, juvenile alligator, and other live critters in the Animal Lab; dig for dinosaur bones; slap a hockey puck; watch a 3-D movie in the theater or a hands-on show; then prepare to get blown away in the Hurricane Experience. ✉ *2000 Cranford Ave.* ☎ *239/321–7420* 🌐 *www.imaginariumfortmyers.com* 🎟 *$12* 🕘 *Mon.–Sat. 10–5, Sun. noon–5.*

For a look at Florida's native animals and habitats, head to the **Calusa Nature Center & Planetarium**. Boardwalks lead through subtropical wetlands, a birds-of-prey aviary, and a butterfly house. There are snake, alligator, butterfly, and other live-animal demonstrations several times daily, and a new Insectarium with interactive displays will make you think before you swat at Florida's insect kingdom. A dome theater is planned for the near future. The 90-seat planetarium has astronomy shows daily and special laser shows. There's also a re-created Seminole Indian village. ✉ *3450 Ortiz Ave.* ☎ *239/275–3435* 🌐 *www.calusanature.org* 🎟 *$9* 🕘 *Mon.–Sat. 9–5, Sun. 11–5.*

★ At **Manatee Park** you may glimpse Florida's most famous marine mammal. When gulf waters are cold—usually from November to March—the gentle sea cows congregate in these waters, which are warmed by the outflow of a nearby power plant. Pause at any of the three observation decks and watch for bubbles. Hydrophones allow you to eavesdrop on their songs. Periodically one of the mammoth creatures—mature adults weigh hundreds of pounds—will surface. The park rents kayaks in winter and on summer weekends, and offers kayaking clinics and free guided walks. ✉ *1¼ mi east of I–75 Exit 141 at 10901 Rte. 80* ☎ *239/741–3028* 🌐 *www.leeparks.org* *Parking $1 per hr, $5 daily* ⏲ *Daily 8–sunset. Gates locked promptly at closing time. Visitor center daily 9–4.*

SPORTS AND THE OUTDOORS

BASEBALL

The region has become a popular outpost for spring training teams, with two already in Fort Myers. As of press time, the Chicago Cubs were considering a move here from their current spring training home in Mesa, Arizona.

The **Boston Red Sox** (✉ *2201 Edison Ave.* ☎ *239/334–4700* 🌐 *www.redsox.com*) train in Fort Myers every spring. The **Minnesota Twins** (✉ *Lee County Sports Complex, 14100 Six Mile Cypress Pkwy.* ☎ *239/768–4210* 🌐 *www.redsox.com*) play exhibition games in town during March and early April. From April through August, the Miracle (🌐 *www.miraclebaseball.com*), a Twins single-A affiliate, play home games at the Complex.

BIKING

The longest bike path in Fort Myers is along Summerlin Road. It passes commercial areas and close to Sanibel through dwindling wide-open spaces. Linear Park, which runs parallel to Six Mile Cypress Parkway, offers more natural, less congested views. The new Trailhead Park links it to Ten Mile Linear Park to the east for 30 mi of pathway. For a good selection of rentals, try the **Bike Route** (✉ *8595 College Pkwy. Suite B-1* ☎ *239/481–3376* 🌐 *thebikeroute.com*).

FISHING

Anglers head for the gulf, its bays, and estuaries for saltwater fishing—snapper, sheepshead, mackerel, and other species. The Caloosahatchee River, Orange River, canals, and small lakes offer freshwater alternatives.

GOLF

★ The driving range and 18-hole course at the **Eastwood Golf Club** (✉ *4600 Bruce Herd La.* ☎ *239/321–7485*) are affordable, especially if you don't mind playing at unfavorable times (midday in summer, for example). Many golfers enjoy the lack of development around the course, which poses challenges with its water hazards and doglegs. Fees include cart and tax; fees without cart included are available at certain times; greens fee $65/$28. The **Fort Myers Country Club** (✉ *3591 McGregor Blvd.* ☎ *239/321–7489*), with 18 holes, challenges golfers with its small greens. It's the town's oldest course. Lessons are available. Its clubhouse holds a lively restaurant and bar; greens fee $45/$30. Head to the **Shell Point Golf Club** (✉ *17401 On Par Blvd.* ☎ *239/433–9790*) for an 18-hole course and a driving range; greens fee $99/$49 (including cart).

SAILING

★ **Southwest Florida Yachts** (✉ *3444 Marinatown La. NW* ☎ *239/656–1339 or 800/262–7939* 🌐 *www.swfyachts.com*) charters sailboats and offers lessons.

SHOPPING

★ **Bell Tower Shops** (✉ *Cleveland Ave. and Daniels Pkwy.* ☎ *239/489–1221* 🌐 *www.thebelltowershops.com*), an open-air shopping center renovated in 2009, has about 40 stylish boutiques and specialty shops, a Saks Fifth Avenue, and 20 movie screens. **Edison Mall** (✉ *Colonial Blvd. at Cleveland Ave.* 🌐 *www.edison-mall-fl.com*) is the largest air-conditioned indoor mall in Fort Myers, with several major department stores and more than 150 specialty shops. Along its boardwalks, **Sanibel Tanger Factory Outlets** (✉ *McGregor Blvd. and Summerlin Rd.* ☎ *888/471–3939* 🌐 *www.tangeroutlet.com*) has outlets for Van Heusen, Maidenform, Coach, Liz Claiborne, and Samsonite, among others. Just east of Fort Myers, more than 900 vendors sell new and used goods at **Fleamasters Fleamarket** (✉ *1.7 mi west of I–75 Exit 138 on Rte. 82* ☎ *239/334–7001* 🌐 *www.fleamall.com*), Friday through Sunday 8–4.

NIGHTLIFE AND THE ARTS

THE ARTS

The **Barbara B. Mann Performing Arts Hall** (✉ *Edison State College, 13350 Edison Pkwy., off College Pkwy.* ☎ *239/481–4849* 🌐 *www.bbmannpah.com*) presents Broadway plays, concerts, musicals, and comedy shows.

★ The **Broadway Palm Dinner Theatre** (✉ *1380 Colonial Blvd.* ☎ *239/278–4422* 🌐 *www.broadwaypalm.com*) serves buffet dinners along with some of Broadway's best comedies and musicals. There's also a 90-seat black-box theater that hosts smaller scale productions.

★ In the restored circa-1920 Arcade Theatre downtown, **Florida Rep** (✉ *2267 1st St.* ☎ *239/332–4488 or 877/787–8053* 🌐 *www.floridarep.org*) stages professional entertainment from Neil Simon shows to musical revues mostly geared to a mature crowd.

NIGHTLIFE

Ichabod's Wicked Good Food & Drink (✉ *13851 S. Cleveland Ave.* ☎ *239/267–1611*) hosts live rock and other popular music Tuesday–Saturday night. **Laugh In Comedy Café** (✉ *College Plaza, 8595 College Pkwy.* ☎ *239/479–5233* 🌐 www.laughincomedycafe.com), south of downtown, has comedians Friday and Saturday. **Stevie Tomato's Sports Page** (✉ *11491 S. Cleveland Ave.* ☎ *239/939–7211*) has big-screen TVs and good munchies.

WHERE TO EAT

$$$ AMERICAN ★ ✕ **Bistro 41.** Shoppers and businesspeople meet here for some of the town's most dependable and inventive cuisine. Amid brightly painted, textured walls and a display kitchen, the menus roam from salmon BLT croissant and rotisserie chicken to pork chop mojo with roasted-corn–tomato salsa and cedar-plank salmon. To experience the kitchen at its imaginative best, check the night's specials, which often include daringly done seafood (crabmeat-crusted tripletail fish with caramelized plantains and passion-fruit beurre blanc, for instance) and usually cost

9

more than regular menu items (around $25). When weather permits, ask for a table on the patio. On Sunday there's a limited menu. ✉ *13499 S. Cleveland Ave.* ☎ *239/466–4141* 🌐 *www.bistro41.com* *Reservations essential* 💳 *AE, D, MC, V.*

$ MEXICAN ✕ **Chile Ranchero.** Latinos and gringos alike converge on this authentic little corner of Mexicana along busy Tamiami Trail. You can't beat the prices or the portions. The staff speaks Spanish and so does the menu, with English subtitles. Dishes appeal to American and Latin palates, with a range from tongue tacos and steak ranchero to seafood soup and excellent nachos con ceviche. ✉ *11751 S. Cleveland Ave., No. 18* ☎ *239/275–0505* 💳 *AE, D, MC, V.*

$$ ITALIAN ✕ **Cibo.** Its flavor-bursting Italian food and its propensity for fresh, quality ingredients keep it at the head of the class for local Italian restaurants. In contrast to the sophisticated black-and-white setting, the menu comes in colors from classic Caesar salad with shaved Grana Padano and spaghetti and meatballs to salmon piccata and New York strip with mascarpone polenta and baby broccolini. The lasagna Napoletana is typical of the standards set here—a generous square of pasta layered with fluffy ricotta, meat ragu, mozzarella, and the totally fresh-tasting, garlicky pomodoro sauce. ✉ *12901 McGregor Blvd.* ☎ *239/454–3700* 💳 *AE, MC, V* ⏲ *No lunch.*

$ ITALIAN ✕ **Il Pomodoro Cucina Italiana.** We say tomato or tomahtoe, but in Italy, they say pomodoro. But there's much more than the use of fresh tomatoes to recommend this place to the locals who find their way off the beaten culinary path. It starts with hot, crusty, garlic-glazed rolls, and Caesar salad with a flavorful dressing and drifts of Parmesan. From there you have your pick from combinations of classic Italian subs, pastas and sauces, pizzas, and proteins. The same menu applies lunch and dinner, but with different pricing. It ranges from standard veal parmigiana and lasagna to gnocchi pomodoro (gnocchi smothered in a thick marinara sauce) and chicken rollatini stuffed with fresh spinach and mozzarella and topped with a mushroom Marsala sauce. ✉ 9681 Gladiolus Dr. ☎ 239/985–0080 🌐 *www.ilpomodororestaurant.com* 💳 *AE, D, MC, V* ⏲ *Closed Sun. No lunch Sat.*

¢ AMERICAN ★ ✕ **Philly Junction.** From the bread (Amorosa rolls) to the corned beef, almost everything here comes from Philadelphia. Not only are the Philly cheesesteaks delicious and authentic, but the burgers and other sandwiches are excellent—and the prices are among the lowest around. Stay for an old-fashioned sundae, or join the Philly natives for pork roll and scrapple at breakfast. The strip-mall café occupies two rooms sided with natural wood board-and-bead paneling. Signs at every table humorously reveal "25 Ways to Tell You're from Philly." ✉ *4600 Summerlin Rd.* ☎ *239/936–6622* 💳 *MC, V* ⏲ *No dinner Sun.*

$$$ VIETNAMESE ✕ **Saigon Paris Bistro.** Irish omelet, Belgian waffles, crepes, table-side steak au poivre, Vietnamese sea bass, Waldorf chicken salad: this eatery's extensive menu clearly travels farther abroad than its name implies. And it does it with utmost taste and flavor, as its faithful local clientele will attest. The best deals are the lunchtime and early-bird meals. It also offers three-course Vietnamese or Parisian dinners for $30. Leave room for crepes à la Grand Marnier table-side or something from the

bakery, and a cup of fresh-roasted coffee (hence the second part of its name). The interior provides a soothing surprise in this busy part of town, with a water feature, fireplace, and classic columns. ✉ *12995 S. Cleveland. Ave., No. 118* ☎ *239/936–2233* 🌐 *www.frenchroastcafe.net* 💳 *AE, D, MC, V.*

$ SEAFOOD ✕ **Shrimp Shack.** Seafood lovers flock to this venue with its vivacious staff, bustle, and colorful, cartoonish wall murals. There's a wait for lunch in winter season and a brisk take-out business with drive-through. Southern-style deep frying prevails—whole-belly clams, grouper, shrimp, onion rings, hush puppies, and fried pork loins—though you can get certain selections broiled or blackened, and there's some New England flavor with seafood rolls. Create your own basket by selecting two or three fried, broiled, or blackened choices. This is your place if you like your seafood simple. ✉ *13361 Metro Pkwy.* ☎ *239/561–6817* 💳 *AE, D, DC, MC, V.*

$$$ SOUTHERN ★ ✕ **The Veranda.** Restaurants come and go quickly as downtown reinvents itself, but this one has endured since 1979. A favorite of business and government bigwigs, it serves imaginative Continental fare with a trace of a Southern accent. Notable are tournedos with smoky sour-mash-whiskey sauce, rack of lamb with rosemary-merlot sauce, herb-crusted honey-grilled salmon, and a grilled seafood sampler with saffron-cream fettuccine, all served with homemade honey-drizzled bread and muffins with pepper jelly. The restaurant is a combination of two turn-of the-20th-century homes, with a two-sided central brick fireplace, and sconces and antique oil paintings on its pale-yellow walls. Ask for an outdoor courtyard table when weather permits. ✉ *2122 2nd St.* ☎ *239/332–2065* 🌐 *www.verandarestaurant.com* 💳 *AE, MC, V* ⊗ *Closed Sun. No lunch Sat.*

WHERE TO STAY

$$$–$$$$ **Hilton Garden Inn.** This compact, prettily landscaped low-rise is near Fort Myers's cultural and commercial areas, and a business clientele favors it for its convenience. Rooms, done in florals and light-color wood, are spacious, with marble vanities in the bath, and have high-speed Internet access and free HBO. A huge aquarium in the lobby adds a nice Florida feel for vacationers. **Pros:** near performing-arts center; enjoyable restaurant; large rooms. **Cons:** chain feel; small pool; at busy intersection. ✉ *12600 University Dr.* ☎ *239/790–3500* 🌐 *www.fortmyers.gardeninn.com* *109 rooms, 17 suites* *In-room: refrigerator, Internet, Wi-Fi. In-hotel: restaurant, bar, pool, laundry facilities, laundry service, Internet terminal, Wi-Fi hotspot* 💳 *AE, DC, MC, V.*

$$$$ Fodor's Choice ★ **Sanibel Harbour Resort & Spa.** Vacationing families and businesspeople who want luxury without sky-high price tags flock to this high-rise resort complex. It is not on Sanibel proper but instead towers over the bay at the last mainland exit before the causeway. Choose from three lodging options—a concierge club–style inn, the hotel, and condos—all with sweeping views of island-studded San Carlos Bay. There's also tennis, the best resort spa in the Fort Myers area, restaurants (one of which is a buffet-dining yacht), the gorgeous circular windowed Charley's Bar, and a large free-form pool, among other facilities and activities. Rent a kayak, take a wildlife-viewing cruise, or go fishing. The beach

9

is small and bay-side, but transportation to Sanibel's beaches is free. **Pros:** luxury accommodations; full amenities; great views. **Cons:** daily-amenities fee added to rate; unspectacular beach. ✉ *17260 Harbour Pointe Dr., Fort Myers* ☎ *239/466–4000 or 800/767–7777* 🌐 *www.sanibel-resort.com* *283 rooms, 64 suites, 37 condominiums* *In-room: safe, Internet, Wi-Fi. In-hotel: 6 restaurants, room service, bars, tennis courts, pools, gym, spa, beachfront, children's programs (ages 5–12), Internet terminal, Wi-Fi hotspot* ▭ *AE, D, DC, MC, V.*

CAPE CORAL AND NORTH FORT MYERS

13 mi from downtown Fort Meyers.

GETTING HERE AND AROUND

Four bridges cross from Fort Myers to Cape Coral and North Fort Myers. Pine Island–Bayshore Road (Route 78) leads from North Fort Myers through northern Cape Coral onto Pine Island.

EXPLORING

Fodor's Choice ★ **Sun Splash Family Waterpark** is the place to cool off when summer swelters. It has a dozen wet and dry attractions, including seven thrill waterslides; the Lilypad Walk, where you step from one floating "lily pad" to another; an arcade; a family pool and Tot Spot; and a river-tube ride. In 2008 the park debuted three of its most daring slides to date, including the X-celerator. ✉ *400 Santa Barbara Blvd.* ☎ *239/574–0558* 🌐 *www.sunsplashwaterpark.com* *$17* *Mid-Mar.–Sept., call or visit the Web site for hrs.*

Shell Factory & Nature Park, once a shopping attraction and a survivor from Florida's roadside-attraction era, is an entertainment complex where you'll find restaurants, bumper boats, miniature golf, and a musical lighted fountain show (8 PM). Admission is $5 for each attraction, open from 11 to 7. The Nature Park ($10, 10–5) contains a petting zoo with camels, llamas, and goats; a walk-through aviary; an Eco-Lab with reptiles and small animals; a prairie-dog habitat; and a gator slough. Shell Factory also hosts annual events such as the Gumbo Fest in January and the Chili & Rib Fest in February. ✉ *2787 N. Tamiami Trail, North Fort Myers* ☎ *239/995–2141* 🌐 *www.shellfactory.com* *$5–$10 per attraction* *Mid-Mar.–Sept., call for hrs.*

SPORTS AND THE OUTDOORS

GOLF

Coral Oaks Golf Course (✉ *1800 NW 28th Ave.* ☎ *239/573–3100*) has an 18-hole layout and a practice range. Arthur Hill designed the championship par-72 course, which has lots of lakes, ponds, wildlife, and mammoth live oaks. After 2 PM you can save money by walking the course; greens fee $59/$69 (including cart).

WHERE TO EAT

¢ AMERICAN ✕ **Bert's Bar & Grill**. Looking to hang out with the locals on Pine Island? Here you'll find cheap eats, live entertainment, a pool table, and a water view to boot. Speaking of boots, you're likely to see some of the clientele wearing white rubber fishing boots, known here as Pine Island Reeboks. Order fried oysters, a burger, pizza, or a grouper Reuben melt from the

DID YOU KNOW?

Seven waterslides—sometimes called flumes and water chutes—are among the attractions at Sun Splash Family Waterpark in Cape Coral. The 14-acre attraction is southwest Florida's largest water park.

no-nonsense menu, and enjoy live music most days. ✉ *4271 Pine Island Rd., Matlacha* ☎ *239/282–3232* 🌐 *www.bertsbar.com* ▭ *D, MC, V.*

$$ AMERICAN ★ ✕ **Rumrunners.** Cape Coral's best casual cuisine is surprisingly affordable, considering the luxury condo development that rises around it and the size of the yachts that pull up to the docks. Caribbean in spirit, with lots of indoor and outdoor views of a mangrove-fringed waterway, it serves bistro specialties such as seafood potpie, pork marinated with rum and orange juice, bronzed salmon, and a warm chocolate bread pudding that is addictive. Bar staff is affable and welcoming. ✉ *5848 Cape Harbour Dr., at the Marina at Cape Harbour, off Chiquita Blvd.* ☎ *239/542–0200* 🌐 *www.capeharbourdining.com* ▭ *AE, D, MC, V.*

$ THAI ✕ **Siam Hut.** Lunch and dinner menus at this Cape Coral fixture let you design your own stir-fry, noodle, or fried-rice dish. Dinner specialties include fried crispy frogs' legs with garlic and black pepper, a sizzling shrimp platter, fried whole tilapia with curry sauce, salads, and pad thai (rice noodles, egg, ground peanuts, vegetables, and choice of protein). Get your food fiery hot or extra mild. Two traditional Thai tables allow you to sit on floor pillows (conveniently with backs), or you can opt for a more conventional table or booth. ✉ *4521 Del Prado Blvd.* ☎ *239/945–4247* ▭ *MC, V* ⊙ *Closed Sun. No lunch Sat.*

WHERE TO STAY

$$$$ **Resort at MarinaVillage.** Opened in November 2009 as Cape Coral's first luxury resort, this 19-story high-rise sits alongside a marina fringed with mangroves. Full-service with a variety of high-end accommodations, restaurants and a deli-market, retail stores, and a spa, it caters to families and water-sports enthusiasts. A free shuttle boat ferries guests the 45-minute distance to the beaches of Fort Myers Beach. Kayak and bike use is complimentary. Pets are allowed in some of the units, and there's a dog park nearby. **Pros:** full-service marina; new designer appointments; great kayaking. **Cons:** pricey; no beach; high-rise. ✉ *5951 Silver King Blvd.* ☎ *239/463–0559 or 888/372–9256* 🌐 *www.marinavillageresort.com* *83 studios, 83 1-bedroom condos, 48 2-bedroom condos, 16 3-bedroom condos* *In-room: safe, kitchen (some), refrigerator, Internet, Wi-Fi. In-hotel: 3 restaurants, room service, bars, pools, gym, spa, water sports, bicycles, children's programs (all ages), laundry facilities, Internet terminal, Wi-Fi hotspot, some pets allowed* ▭ *AE, D, DC, MC, V.*

$$–$$$ **Tarpon Lodge.** If you're looking for no-frills escape, this aptly named lodge, built in 1926 on a sweep of green lawn with magnificent views out to sea, may do the trick. Rooms are small and simple, and the sunny restaurant dishes up creative surprises. It's in the fishing village of Pineland, on the edge of Pine Island Sound, settled in the 16th century by Calusa Indians and near an archaeological site and trail. **Pros:** waterfront view; historic property; great restaurant. **Cons:** old digs; far from other restaurants; far from beach. ✉ *13771 Waterfront Dr., Pineland* ☎ *239/283–3999* 🌐 *www.tarponlodge.com* *21 rooms, 2 cottages* *In-room: a/c, no phone. In-hotel: restaurant, bar, pool, Wi-Fi hotspot* ▭ *AE, MC, V* *CP.*

THE COASTAL ISLANDS

A maze of islands in various stages of habitation fronts Fort Myers mainland, separated by the Intracoastal Waterway. Some are accessible via a causeway; to reach others, you need a boat. If you cut through bay waters, you have a good chance of being escorted by bottlenose dolphins. Mostly birds and other wild creatures inhabit some islands, which are given over to state parks. Traveler-pampering hotels on Sanibel, Captiva, and Fort Myers Beach give way to rustic cottages, old inns, and cabins on quiet Cabbage Key and Pine Island, which have no beaches because they lie between the barrier islands and mainland. Others are devoted to resorts. When exploring island beaches, keep one eye on the sand: shelling is a major pursuit in these parts.

GASPARILLA ISLAND (BOCA GRANDE)

43 mi northwest of Fort Meyers.

Before roads to the Lower Gulf Coast were even talked about, wealthy Northerners came by train to spend the winter at the **Gasparilla Inn,** completed in 1913 in Boca Grande on Gasparilla Island, named, legend has it, for a Spanish pirate who set up headquarters in these waters. Although condominiums and modern sprawl creep up on the rest of Gasparilla, much of the town of Boca Grande evokes another era. The mood is set by the Old Florida homes and tree-framed roadways. The island's calm is disrupted in the spring when anglers descend with a vengeance on Boca Grande Pass, considered among the best tarpon-fishing spots in the world.

GETTING HERE AND AROUND

Boca Grande is more than an hour's drive northwest of Fort Myers. Day-trippers can catch a charter boat or rent a boat, dock at Boca Grande Marina, and rent a bike or golf cart for a day of exploring and lunching. North of it stretches a long island, home to Don Pedro Island State Park and Palm Island Resort, both accessible only by boat, and the off-the-beaten-path but car-accessible island of Manasota Key and its fishing resort community of Englewood Beach.

9

EXPLORING

The island's beaches are its greatest prize and lie within **Gasparilla Island State Park and Boca Grande Lighthouse Museum** at the south end. The long, narrow beach ends at Boca Grande Pass, famous for its deep waters and tarpon fishing. The pretty, two-story, circa-1890 lighthouse once marked the pass for mariners. In recent years it has been restored as a museum that explores the island's fishing and railroad heritage. *Box 1150, Boca Grande 941/964–0060 www.floridastateparks.org/gasparillaisland $3 per vehicle; $2 suggested donation to lighthouse Park daily 8–sunset; lighthouse Nov.–May, Mon.–Sat. 10–4, Sun. noon–4; June, July, Sept., and Oct., Wed.–Sat. 10–4, Sun. noon–4.*

DID YOU KNOW?

Florida's Pine Island, about 30 minutes from Fort Myers, actively seeks to have its own charm and prohibits its high-rise development. Visitors can enjoy viewing its mangroves, colorful galleries, and seafood houses.

SPORTS AND THE OUTDOORS

CANOEING AND KAYAKING

Grande Tours (*12575 Placida Rd., Placida 941/697–8825 www.grandetours.com*) leads kayaking excursions along the creeks and open waters around Charlotte Harbor. The cost is $50 for two hours. Also available are kayaking lessons, fishing excursions, and rentals.

WHERE TO EAT AND STAY

$$ AMERICAN **The Loose Caboose.** Revered by many—including Katherine Hepburn in her time—for its homemade ice cream, this is also a good spot for solid, affordable fare, from burgers and a Thanksgiving wrap (turkey and cranberry sauce) to chicken potpie and crispy duck with orange-teriyaki sauce. Housed in the town's historic depot, it offers indoor and patio seating in an all-American setting. *433 W. 4th St. 941/964–0440 www.loosecaboose.biz* *D, MC, V* *No lunch mid-Apr. to mid-Nov.*

$$$$ ★ **Gasparilla Inn & Club.** Social-register members such as the Vanderbilts and DuPonts still winter at the gracious pale-yellow wooden hotel built by shipping industrialists in the early 1900s. Lodge rooms are not lavishly decorated by today's standards, but they received a face-lift in recent years to coordinate with the inn's feminine Victorian air. The cottage rooms spread around the inn in charming historic digs. The inn takes up much of the town of Boca Grande with its rich-blooded amenities—sprawling lawns, a golf course, croquet, and a beach club with a 10-room spa. In recent years the inn has gone from a mandatory meal plan in high season to more flexible packages customized to guests' desires. In summer (July through mid-Oct.), the inn proper closes and only the cottages are available for lodging. Gentlemen are required to wear a jacket in the main dining room during the winter season. **Pros:** historic property; nicely renovated. **Cons:** expensive rates; the quirks of a very old building. *500 Palm Ave., Boca Grande 941/964–2201 or 800/996–1913 www.gasparillainn.com 142 rooms In-room: Internet, Wi-Fi. In-hotel: 3 restaurants, golf course, tennis courts, pools, gym, spa, beachfront, Wi-Fi hotspot* *AE, D, MC, V.*

9

CABBAGE KEY

5 mi south of Boca Grande

Cabbage Key is the ultimate in island-hopping escape in these parts. Some say Jimmy Buffett was inspired to write *Cheeseburger in Paradise* after a visit to its popular restaurant.

GETTING HERE AND AROUND

You'll need to take a boat—from Bokeelia or Pineland, on Pine Island, or from Captiva Island—to get to this island, which sits at Mile Marker 60 on the Intracoastal Waterway. Local operators offer day trips and luncheon cruises.

WHERE TO STAY

$–$$ **Cabbage Key Inn.** Atop an ancient Calusa Indian shell mound and accessible only by boat, the friendly, somewhat quirky inn built by novelist and playwright Mary Roberts Rinehart in 1938 welcomes guests seeking quiet and isolation. It's surrounded by 100 acres of tropical vegetation, through which a natural trail runs. In addition to the inn rooms, there are guest cottages scattered throughout the property, some of which have kitchens and can accommodate up to eight guests. Rooms range from bare-bones to more modern and family-friendly. There's a full-service marina and a restaurant whose dining room is papered with thousands of dollar bills. One of the many perks of staying here is close access to the remote and pristine beach of Cayo Costa, a short boat trip from Cabbage Key. **Pros:** plenty of solitude; Old Florida character. **Cons:** two-night minimum stay; accessible only by boat; limited amenities, some rooms have no TV. *Box 200, Pineland 33945 239/283–2278 www.cabbagekey.com 6 rooms, 7 cottages In-room: no phone, kitchen (some), no TV (some). In-hotel: restaurant, bar MC, V.*

SANIBEL AND CAPTIVA ISLANDS

23 mi southwest of downtown Fort Meyers.

Sanibel Island is famous as one of the world's best shelling grounds, a function of the unusual east–west orientation of the island's south end. Just as the tide is going out and after storms, the pickings can be superb, and shell seekers performing the telltale "Sanibel stoop" patrol every beach carrying bags of conchs, whelks, cockles, and other bivalves and gastropods. (Remember, it's unlawful to pick up live shells.) Away from the beach, flowery vegetation decorates small shopping complexes, pleasant resorts and condo complexes, mom-and-pop motels, and casual restaurants. But much of the narrow road down the spine of the island is bordered by nature reserves that have made Sanibel as well known among bird-watchers as it is among seashell collectors.

Captiva Island, connected to the northern end of Sanibel by a bridge, is quirky and engaging. At the end of a twisty road lined with million-dollar mansions lies a delightful village of shops, eateries, and beaches.

GETTING HERE AND AROUND

Sanibel Island is approximately 23 mi southwest of downtown Fort Myers, and Captiva lies north of 12-mi-long Sanibel.If you're flying into Southwest Florida International Airport, an on-demand taxi for up to three passengers to Sanibel or Captiva costs about $56–$75; additional passengers are charged $10 each. Sanibel Island is accessible from the mainland via the Sanibel Causeway (toll $6 round-trip). Captiva Island lies across a small pass from Sanibel's north end, accessible by bridge.

ESSENTIALS

Visitor Information **Sanibel and Captiva Islands Chamber of Commerce** (*1159 Causeway Rd., Sanibel 239/472–1080 www.sanibel-captiva.org*).

EXPLORING

Fodor's Choice ★ To help you identify your Sanibel Island beach finds, stop at the **Bailey-Matthews Shell Museum**, where a shell-finder display identifies specimens from local waters in sizes ranging from tiny to huge. Thirty-five vignettes and exhibits explore shells in the environment, art, and history, including a life-size display of native Calusa and how they used shells for

Continued on page 392

SHELL-BENT ON SANIBEL ISLAND

by Chelle Koster Walton

Sanibel Island beachgoers are an unusual breed: they pray for storms; they muck around tidal pools rather than play in the waves; and instead of lifting their faces to the sun, they have their heads in the sand—almost literally—as they engage in the so-called "Sanibel Stoop."

Odd? Not when you consider that this is Florida's prime shelling location, thanks to the island's east-west bend (rather than the usual north-south orientation of most beaches along the coastline). The lay of the land means a treasure trove of shells—more than 400 species—wash up from the Caribbean.

These gifts from the sea draw collectors of all levels. Come winter, when the cold and storms kill the shellfish and push them ashore, a parade of stoopers forms on Sanibel's shores.

The reasons people shell are as varied as the shellers themselves. The hardcore compete and sell, whereas others collect simply for the fun of discovery, for displaying, for use in gardens, or for crafts. The typical Sanibel tourist who comes seeking shells is usually looking for souvenirs and gifts to take home.

WHERE TO SHELL

Shelling is good anywhere along Sanibel's gulf-front. Remote **Bowman's Beach** (*off Sanibel-Captiva Road at Bowman's Beach Rd.*) offers the least competition. Other public accesses include **Lighthouse Beach** (Periwinkle Way), **Tarpon Bay Beach** (Tarpon Bay Rd.), and **Turner Beach** (Sanibel-Captiva Rd.). If you want to ditch your car (and crowds), walk or bike using **resident access beaches** (along the Gulf drives). If you want to search with others and get a little guidance, you can join shelling cruises from Sanibel and Captiva islands to the un-bridged island of Cayo Costa. For information contact, **Captiva Cruises** (☎ 239/472-5300, 🌐 www.captivacruises.com) or **Adventures in Paradise** (☎ 239/472-8443, 🌐 www.adventureinparadiseinc.com).

Captiva Island
Captiva
Turner Beach
Wulfert
Bowman's Beach
SANIBEL ISLAND
Sanibel
Tarpon Bay Beach
Lighthou
Beach

Cockle

Conch

Junonia

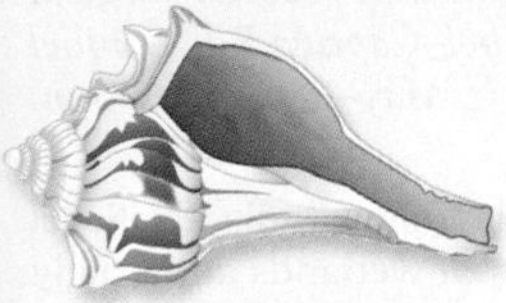

Lightning Whelk

Sand Dollar

Scallop

TYPES OF SHELLS

Cockles: The common Sanibel bivalve (hinged two-shelled mollusk), the heart cockle (named for its Valentine shape) is larger and more bowl-like than the scallop, which makes it a popular, colorful find for soap dishes, ashtrays, and catch-alls.

Conchs: Of the large family of conchs, fighting conchs are most commonly found on Sanibel. Contrary to its macho name, the fighting conch is one of the few vegetarian gastropods. While alive, the shell flames brilliant orange; it fades under tropical sunshine.

Junonias: These olive-shaped, spotted gastropods (single-shell mollusks) are Sanibel's signature, though somewhat rare, finds. People who hit upon one get their picture in the local paper. Resorts have been accused of planting them on their beaches for publicity.

Lightning Whelks: The lightning variety of whelk is "left-handed"—opening on the opposite side from most gastropods. Early islanders used them for tools. The animals lay their miniature shell eggs in papery egg-case chains on the beach.

Sand Dollars: Classified as an echinoderm not a mollusk, the thin sand dollar is brown and fuzzy while alive, studded with tiny tubes for breathing and moving. Unoccupied shells bleach to a beautiful white textured pattern, ideal for hanging on Christmas trees.

Scallops: No surprise that these pretty little bivalves have "scalloped" edges. They invented the word. Plentiful on Sanibel beaches, they come in a variety of colors and sizes.

SHELLING LIKE A PRO

Veteran shell-seekers go out before the sun rises so they can be the first on the beach after a storm or night of high tides. (Storms and cold fronts bring in the best catches.)

Most shellers use a bag to collect their finds. But once you're ready to pack shells for transport, wash them thoroughly to remove sand and debris. Then wrap fragile species such as sand dollars and sea urchins in tissue paper or cotton, then newspaper. Last, place your shells in a cardboard or plastic box. To display them, restore the shell's luster by brushing it with baby oil.

Sanibel shops sell books and supplies for identifying your finds and turning them into craft projects.

tools and vessels. Handle shell specimens and play games in the colorful kids' lab. A 6-foot globe at the center of the museum rotunda highlights shells from around the world. ✉ *3075 Sanibel–Captiva Rd., Sanibel* ☎ *239/395–2233 or 888/679–6450* 🌐 *www.shellmuseum.org* 🎟 *$7* ⏲ *Daily 10–5.*

In existence for 40 years and currently caring for more than 4,000 wildlife patients each year, the **Clinic for the Rehabilitation of Wildlife (C.R.O.W)** debuted its first-ever visitor center in 2009. The center offers a look inside the world of wildlife medicine through exhibits, videos, interactive displays, touch screens, and a critter cam that records surgical procedures and patients' progress. ✉ *3883 Sanibel–Captiva Rd., Sanibel* ☎ *239/472–3644* 🌐 *www.crowclinic.org* 🎟 *$5* ⏲ *May–Oct., Tues–Sun. 10–4; Nov.–Apr., Tues.–Sat. 10–4.*

Fodor's Choice ★ More than half of Sanibel is occupied by **J.N. "Ding" Darling National Wildlife Refuge**, the subtly beautiful 6,300 acres of wetlands and jungly mangrove forests named after a conservation-minded Pulitzer prize-winning political cartoonist. The masses of roseate spoonbills and ibis and the winter flock of white pelicans here make for a good show even if you're not a die-hard bird-watcher. Birders have counted some 230 species, including herons, ospreys, and the timid mangrove cuckoo. Raccoons, otters, alligators, and a lone American crocodile also can be spotted. The 4-mi Wildlife Drive is the main way to explore the preserve; drive, walk, or bicycle along it, or ride a specially designed open-air tram with an on-board naturalist. There are also a couple of short walking trails, including one to a Calusa shell mound. Or explore from the water via canoe or kayak (guided tours are available). The best time for bird-watching is in the early morning about an hour before or after low tide, and the observation tower along the road offers prime viewing. Interactive exhibits in the free visitor center, at the entrance to the refuge, demonstrate the refuge's various ecosystems and explain its status as a rest stop along a major bird-migration route. Because Wildlife Drive is closed to vehicular traffic on Friday, try to time your visit for another day. ✉ *1 Wildlife Dr., off Sanibel–Captiva Rd. at MM 2, Sanibel* ☎ *239/472–1100 for refuge, 239/472–8900 for tram tours* 🌐 *www.fws.gov/dingdarling* 🎟 *$5 per car, $1 for pedestrians and bicyclists, tram $13* ⏲ *Education Center Jan.–Apr., daily 9–5; May–Dec., daily 9–4; Wildlife Drive Sat.–Thurs. 7:30–½ hour before sunset.*

★ For a good look at snowy egrets, great blue herons, alligators, and other inhabitants of Florida's wetlands, follow the 4½ mi of walking trails at the 1,800-acre wetlands managed by the **Sanibel–Captiva Conservation Foundation**. See island research projects and nature displays, visit a butterfly house, and touch sea creatures. Guided walks are available on and off property; the beach walk is especially enjoyable and pleasantly educational. ✉ *3333 Sanibel–Captiva Rd., Sanibel* ☎ *239/472–2329* 🌐 *www.sccf.org* 🎟 *$3* ⏲ *Oct., Nov., and May, weekdays 8:30–4; Dec.–Apr., weekdays 8:30–4, Sat. 10–3; June–Sept., weekdays 8:30–3.*

★ The charming **Sanibel Historical Museum & Village** shows off buildings from the island's past—a general store, a one-room schoolhouse, a 192 post office, a garage housing a Model T Ford, a 1925 winter-vacatic cottage, and the 1913 Rutland House Museum, with old documents and photographs, artifacts, and period furnishings. ⊠ *950 Dunlop Rd., Sanibel* ☎ *239/472–4648* 🌐 *www.sanibelmuseum.org* *$5* ⏲ *Nov.–Apr., Wed.–Sat. 10–4; May–mid-Aug., Wed.–Sat. 10–1.*

SPORTS AND THE OUTDOORS

BEACHES

Red tide, an occasional natural beach occurrence that kills fish, also has negative effects on the human respiratory system. It causes scratchy throats, runny eyes and noses, and coughing. Although the effects are not long-term, it's a good idea to avoid the beach when red tide is in the vicinity (look for posted signs).

Alison Hagerup Beach Park (⊠ *Captiva Dr., Captiva* *Parking $2 per hr, $10 for 8 hr*), formerly Captiva Beach, is acclaimed as one of the nation's most romantic beaches for its fabulous sunsets—the best view on Sanibel and Captiva. The parking lot is small, so arrive early. Facilities are limited to portable restrooms, but stores and restaurants are nearby. Long, wide **Bowman's Beach** (⊠ *Bowman Beach Rd., Sanibel* ☎ *239/432–3700* *Parking $2 per hr*), on Sanibel's northwest end, is the island's most secluded strand. It was once known for its nudists (no longer legal), but is now known for its shell collecting and spectacular sunsets at the north end—try to spot the green flash said to occur just as the sun sinks below the horizon. Facilities include a playground, a fitness trail, and a canoe launch

The beach at **Gulfside Park Preserve** (⊠ *Algiers La. off Casa Ybel Rd., Sanibel* ☎ *239/472–3700* *Parking $2 per hr*) is quiet, safe from strong currents, and good for solitude, bird-watching, and shell-finding. There are restrooms, picnic tables, and long stretches to stroll, plus a loop trail to hike. At Sanibel's southern tip, the frequently photographed **Sanibel Lighthouse,** built in 1884, before the island was settled, guards **Lighthouse Beach** (⊠ *Periwinkle Way, Sanibel* ☎ *239/472–3700* *Parking $2 per hr*). Although the lighthouse is not open to the public, the area around it has been a wildlife refuge since 1950. A fishing pier, nature trail, and restrooms are available.

Tarpon Bay Beach (⊠ *Tarpon Bay Rd., off Sanibel–Captiva Rd., Sanibel* ☎ *239/472–3700* *Parking $2 per hr*) is centrally located and safer for swimming than beaches at the passes, where waters move swiftly. It is, however, one of the more populated beaches, lined with low-rise condos and resorts set back behind vegetation. You can walk for miles in either direction. **Turner Beach** (⊠ *Captiva Dr., Captiva* *Parking $2 per hr*) is *the* sunset-watching spot on the southern tip of Captiva. Strong currents through the pass make swimming tricky, and parking is limited. Surfers head here when winds whip up the waves.

BIKING

Everyone bikes around flat-as-a-pancake Sanibel and Captiva—on bikeways that edge the main highway in places, on the road through the wildlife refuge, and along side streets. Free maps are available at bicycle liveries. On Sanibel, rent by the hour or the day at **Billy's Bikes** (⊠ *1470 Periwinkle Way, Sanibel* ☎ *239/472–5248* 🌐 *www.billysrentals.com*), which also rents motorized scooters and leads Segway tours. On

9

Captiva, bikes are available at **Jim's Rentals** (✉ *11534 Andy Rosse La., Captiva* ☎ *239/472–1296* 🌐 *www.yolo-jims.com*).

CANOEING AND KAYAKING

★ One of the best ways to scout out the wildlife refuge is by paddle. Rent a canoe or kayak from the refuge's official concessionaire, **Tarpon Bay Explorers** (✉ *900 Tarpon Bay Rd., Sanibel* ☎ *239/472–8900* 🌐 *www.tarponbayexplorers.com*). Guided tours are also available.

FISHING

Local anglers head out to catch mackerel, pompano, grouper, snook, snapper, tarpon, and shark. To find a charter captain on Sanibel, ask around at **Sanibel Marina** (✉ *634 N. Yachtsman Dr., Sanibel* ☎ *239/472–2723*). On Captiva, the place to look for guides is **'Tween Waters Marina** (✉ *15951 Captiva Dr., Captiva* ☎ *239/472–5161* 🌐 *www.tween-waters.com/marina*).

GOLF

Rent clubs and take lessons as well as test your skills against the water hazards on the 18-hole course at the **Dunes Golf & Tennis Club** (✉ *949 Sandcastle Rd., Sanibel* ☎ *239/472–2535*); greens fee $110/$42.

TENNIS

At the **Dunes Golf & Tennis Club** (✉ *949 Sandcastle Rd., Sanibel* ☎ *239/472–3522*) there are seven clay courts and two pros who give lessons.

SHOPPING

Sanibel is known for its art galleries, shell shops, and one-of-a-kind boutiques; the several small open-air shopping complexes are inviting, with their tropical flowers and shady ficus trees. The largest cluster of complexes is **Periwinkle Place** (✉ *2075 Periwinkle Way, Sanibel* ☎ *239/769–2289* 🌐 *www.periwinkleplace.com*), with nearly 30 shops. At **She Sells Sea Shells** (✉ *1157 Periwinkle Way, Sanibel* ☎ *239/472–6991*), everything imaginable is made from shells, from mirrors to lamps to Christmas ornaments. The owner wrote the book on shell art, and you can buy it here.

Fodor's Choice ★ Expect the unexpected in wildlife art at artist-owned **Jungle Drums** (✉ *11532 Andy Rosse La., Captiva* ☎ *239/395–2266* 🌐 *www.jungledrumsgallery.com*), where fish, sea turtles, and other wildlife are depicted with utmost creativity and touches of whimsy. If you're looking for souvenirs above and beyond the usual, this is the place to find them.

WHERE TO EAT

$$$ AMERICAN ✕ **Bubble Room.** This lively, kitschy visitors' favorite is fun for families and nostalgic types with fat wallets. Servers wear scout uniforms and funny headgear. Electric trains circle overhead, glossies of Hollywood stars past and present line the walls, and glass tabletops showcase old-time toys. There's so much going on that you might not notice your food is not quite as happening, and somehow that's okay. After graz ing your basket of cheesy bubble bread and sweet, yeasty sticky bur go for aged prime rib or shrimp sautéed in spicy tequila garlic but The homemade triple-layer cakes, delivered in hefty wedges, are standing, and the gooey orange crunch cake is a signature favorit

prepared to wait for a table in season. ✉ *15001 Captiva Dr., Captiva* ☎ *239/472–5558* 🌐 *www.bubbleroomrestaurant.com* ✍ *Reservations not accepted* ▭ *AE, D, DC, MC, V.*

$$$ SEAFOOD ✕ **Green Flash.** Good food and sweeping views of quiet waters and a mangrove island keep boaters and others coming back to this casual indoor-outdoor restaurant. Seafood dominates, but there's a bit of everything on the menu, from barbecued shrimp and bacon to grilled swordfish to pork tenderloin wrapped in prosciutto and puff pastry. For lunch, try the Green Flash sandwich (smoked turkey and prosciutto or vegetables, both with cheese on grilled focaccia). On cool, sunny days, grab a table out back dockside. ✉ *15183 Captiva Dr., Captiva* ☎ *239/472–3337* 🌐 *www.greenflashcaptiva.com* ▭ *AE, D, DC, MC, V.*

¢ AMERICAN ✕ **Lazy Flamingo.** At two Sanibel locations, this is the friendly neighborhood hangout enjoyed by locals and visitors alike. The original in Santiva (between Sanibel and Captiva) has counter service only; the other is larger (but there's still often a wait) and provides table service. Both have a funky nautical look à la Key West and a popular following for their "Dead Parrot Wings" (Buffalo wings coated with tongue-scorching hot sauce), grouper sandwiches, burgers, and steamer pots. ✉ *6520C Pine Ave., Sanibel* ☎ *239/472–5353* ✉ *1036 Periwinkle Way, Sanibel* ☎ *239/472–6939* 🌐 *www.lazyflamingo.com* ✍ *Reservations not accepted* ▭ *AE, D, MC, V.*

$$ SEAFOOD ✕ **McT's Shrimphouse and Tavern.** At this informal Sanibel landmark, the menu predictably spotlights fresh seafood. The baked oysters make great starters. If you're a seafood fiend, go for the Sanibel steamer (pricey, but it can easily feed two) or all-you-can-eat shrimp and crab. Besides more than 15 shrimp entrées, ribs, steak, and chicken Romano are available. Few can resist the Sanibel mud pie, an enormous ice-cream concoction heavy on the Oreo crumbs. Stop in for a before- or after-dinner drink in the bar with the upside-down tree forest. ✉ *1523 Periwinkle Way, Sanibel* ☎ *239/472–3161* ✍ *Reservations not accepted* ▭ *AE, D, MC, V.*

¢ AMERICAN ✕ **Over Easy Café.** Locals head to this chicken-themed eatery mainly for breakfast and lunch, although it also serves dinner in season. Kick-start the day with the egg Reuben sandwich, veggie Benedict, or a custom omelet made with whole eggs, whites only, or egg substitute. The lunch menu includes a vast variety of salads, sandwiches, and burgers. Indoor dining is cheerful; outdoors, pet-friendly. ✉ *630-1 Tarpon Bay Rd., Sanibel* ☎ *239/472–2625* 🌐 *www.overeasycafesanibel.com* ✍ *Reservations not accepted* ▭ *AE, D, MC, V* ⏲ *No dinner May–mid-Nov.*

$$$ AMERICAN ★ ✕ **Traders Store & Café.** In the midst of a warehouse-size store, this bistro, accented with artifacts from exotic places, is a favorite of locals. The marvelous sesame-seared tuna lunch salad with Asian slaw and wasabi vinaigrette exemplifies the creative fare. For dinner, go for the barbecued baby back ribs, macadamia-crusted grouper, or any of the day's finely crafted specials. A local crooner entertains two nights a week. The bar serves light nibbles and happy-hour twofers. ✉ *1551 Periwinkle Way, Sanibel* ☎ *239/472–7242* ▭ *AE, D, MC, V.*

9

WHERE TO STAY

$$$$ **Casa Ybel Resort.** At this time-share resort, palm trees, quiet ponds, and gazebos set the mood on 23 acres of gulf-facing grounds. Inside the two-floor stilt buildings, the one- and two-bedroom apartments are roomy and contemporary, with full kitchens, wicker furniture, tasteful patterns, and big screened-in porches that look out to the beach. **Pros:** on the beach; good restaurants; lots of recreational opportunities. **Cons:** spa treatments in-room only or beachside; minimum stay requirement in some units. *2255 W. Gulf Dr., Sanibel 239/472–3145 or 800/276–4753 www.casaybelresort.com 40 1-bedroom units, 74 2-bedroom units In-room: a/c, safe, kitchen, DVD, Internet, Wi-Fi. In-hotel: 2 restaurants, bars, tennis courts, pool, beachfront, children's programs (ages 4–11), Wi-Fi hotspot AE, D, DC, MC, V.*

$$$$ **Sanibel's Seaside Inn.** Tucked among the tropical greenery, this beachfront inn is a pleasant alternative to the area's larger resorts. Suites are done up in charming cottage style with rattan furnishings and have full kitchens and flat-screen TVs. Rooms come with a handy wet-bar area equipped with a coffeemaker, toaster, microwave, and small fridge. Continental breakfast and bikes are complimentary. You may use amenities at Sundial Beach Resort and the Dunes Golf Club. **Pros:** intimate feel; lots of character; beautiful beachfront. **Cons:** No restaurant. *541 E. Gulf Dr., Sanibel 239/472–1400 or 888/295–4560 www.seasideinn.com 32 rooms, 6 cottages, 4 suites In-room:a/c, kitchen (some), refrigerator, Wi-Fi. In-hotel: pool, beachfront, bicycles, laundry facilities, Wi-Fi hotspot AE, D, DC, MC, V CP.*

$$$$ Fodor's Choice ★ **South Seas Island Resort.** After a top-to-bottom renovation, this 330-acre resort looks rejuvenated, with refurbished accommodations, 19 swimming pools, reinvented private restaurants and shops, a new family waterslide complex, and a remodeled 9-hole golf course with lush water features. Stylish low-rise accommodations are scattered all over the property but are concentrated at either end, near the marina and the small shopping complex. Dunes fringe a pristine 2½-mi beach, and mangroves edge the main road. Entry gates and water on three sides give the resort a delicious seclusion, but trolleys take you around the property and into the village. **Pros:** full range of amenities; exclusive feel; car-free transportation. **Cons:** high rates; a bit isolated; spread out. *5400 Plantation Rd., Captiva 239/472–5111 or 888/222–7848 www.southseas.com 106 rooms, 487 suites In-room: a/c, kitchen. In-hotel: 4 restaurants, room service, bars, golf course, tennis courts, pools, gym, spa, beachfront, water sports, bicycles, children's programs (ages 3–18) AE, D, DC, MC, V.*

$$$$ ★ **Sundial Beach & Golf Resort.** Sanibel's largest resort encompasses 400 privately owned one- and two-bedroom condos, most of which are in its rental program. It caters to groups in fall, families in winter. The latter hang around the main pool with its seashell slide, the shell-strewn beach, and the Eco-Center, where they can pet sea creatures and sign up for family activities and kids' camp. **Pros:** plenty of amenities; great beach. **Con**[illegible] conference crowds; packed pool area. *1451 Middle Gulf Dr., Sani*[illegible] *239/472–4151 or 866/565–5093 www.sundialresort.com* [illegible] *1-bedroom units, 136 2-bedroom units In-room: a/c, safe, kit*[illegible]

Internet, Wi-Fi. In-hotel: 2 restaurants, bars, tennis courts, pools, gym, beachfront, water sports, bicycles, children's programs (ages 4–12), Internet terminal, Wi-Fi hotspot ▭ *AE, D, DC, MC, V.*

$$$–$$$$ **'Tween Waters Inn.** Besides its great beach-to-bay location, this inn has historic value. In the 1930s, Pulitzer Prize–winning cartoonist and conservationist "Ding" Darling, namesake of Sanibel's refuge, stayed in its historic cottages, which are the most charming of the property's accommodations. Water-sports enthusiasts especially like the rentals and charters at the marina. The pool bar and Crow's Nest lounge, both of which serve food, are popular with locals and visitors alike. **Pros:** great views; lots of water-sports options; free Internet. **Cons:** beach is across the road; rooms are bland. ✉ *Captiva Dr., Captiva* ☎ *239/472–5161 or 800/223–5865* ⊕ *www.tween-waters.com* *32 rooms, 24 efficiencies, 40 suites, 4 2-bedroom suites, 2 3-bedroom suites, 19 cottages* *In-room: a/c, kitchen (some), Wi-Fi. In-hotel: restaurant, bar, tennis courts, pool, gym, spa, beachfront, bicycles, laundry facilities, Internet terminal, Wi-Fi hotspots* ▭ *AE, D, DC, MC, V* *CP.*

$$$–$$$$ **Waterside Inn.** Palm trees, sea-grape trees, pastel cottages, and white sand set the scene at this quiet beachside vacation spot. Rooms and efficiencies in the main building are modestly furnished, with bright cobalt-blue-and-white interiors, and have balconies or patios and at least a partial view of the gulf. Single-story cottages are named for fruits—apricot, kiwi, raspberry, and so on—and are painted appropriately on the outside. **Pros:** beachfront location; intimate feel; small pets allowed in most cottages. **Cons:** no restaurants within walking distance; office closes at night. ✉ *3033 W. Gulf Dr., Sanibel* ☎ *239/472–1345 or 800/741–6166* ⊕ *www.watersideinn.net* *4 rooms, 10 efficiencies, 13 cottages* *In-room: a/c, kitchen (some), refrigerator, Wi-Fi (some). In-hotel: pool, beachfront, bicycles, laundry facilities, Internet terminal, Wi-Fi hotspot, some pets allowed* ▭ *AE, D, MC, V.*

9

ESTERO ISLAND (FORT MYERS BEACH)

18 mi southwest of Fort Meyers.

Crammed with motels, hotels, and restaurants, this island is one of Fort Myers's more frenetic gulf playgrounds. Dolphins are frequently spotted in Estero Bay, part of the Intracoastal Waterway, and marinas provide a starting point for boating adventures, including sunset cruises, sightseeing cruises, and deep-sea fishing. At the southern tip, a bridge leads to Lovers Key State Park.

GETTING HERE AND AROUND

San Carlos Boulevard in Fort Myers leads to Fort Myers Beach's high bridge, Times Square, and Estero Boulevard, the island's main drag. Estereo Island is 18 mi southwest of Fort Myers.

EXPLORING

At the 17-acre **Lynn Hall Memorial Park**, in the commercial northern part of Estero Island, the shore slopes gradually into the usually tranquil and warm gulf waters, providing safe swimming for children. And since houses, condominiums, and hotels line most of the beach, you're never far from civilization. There are picnic tables, barbecue grills, playground equipment, and a free fishing pier. A bathhouse with restrooms, a pedestrian mall, and a number of restaurants are nearby. Parking is $2 per hour. ✉ *Estero Blvd.* ☎ *239/463–1116* ⏲ *Daily 7 AM–11 PM.*

OFF THE BEATEN PATH

Lovers Key State Park. Once a little-known secret, this out-of-the-way park encompassing 1,616 acres on four barrier islands and several uninhabited islets is gaining popularity among beachgoers and birders. Bike, hike, or walk the park's trails; go shelling on its 2½ mi of white-sand beach; take a boat tour; or rent a canoe, kayak, or bike. Trams run regularly from 9 to 5 to deliver you and your gear to South Beach. The ride is short but often dusty. North Beach is a five-minute walk from the concession area and parking lot. Watch for osprey, bald eagles, herons, ibis, pelicans, and roseate spoonbills, or sign up for a free excursion to learn fishing and cast-netting. There are also restrooms, picnic tables, a snack bar, and showers. On the bay side, playgrounds and another picnic area cater to families, plus there are boat ramps, kayak rentals, and a bait shop. ✉ *8700 Estero Blvd.* ☎ *239/463–4588* 🌐 *www.floridastateparks.org/loverskey* 🎫 *$4–$8 per vehicle, $2 for pedestrians and bicyclists* ⏲ *Daily 8–sunset.*

SPORTS AND THE OUTDOORS

BIKING

Fort Myers Beach has no designated trails, so most cyclists ride along the road. **Fun Rentals** (✉ *1901 Estero Blvd.* ☎ *239/463–8844* 🌐 *www.funrentals.org*) advertises bike-rental rates anywhere from two hours to a week. Rent bikes in Lovers Key State Park through **Nature Recreation Management** (✉ *8700 Estero Blvd., Fort Myers Beach* ☎ *239/765–7788* 🌐 *www.naturerecreationmanagement.com*). Fees are $18 for a half day, $25 for a full day.

CANOEING

Lovers Key State Park offers both kayak rentals and guided kayaking tours of its bird-filled estuary. **Nature Recreation Management** (✉ *8700 Estero Blvd., Fort Myers Beach* ☎ *239/765–7788* 🌐 *www.naturerecreationmanagement.com*) charges $45 for its guided tours on Monday, Wednesday, and Saturday. Rentals begin at $32 for a half day, $42 for a full day.

FISHING

Getaway Deep Sea Fishing (✉ *18400 San Carlos Blvd.* ☎ *800/641–3088 or 239/466–3600* 🌐 *www.getawaymarina.com*) can arrange everything from half-day party-boat charters to full-day excursions, fishing equipment included. Rates start at $55 for a half-day trip.

GOLF

The **Fort Myers Beach Golf Course** (✉ *4200 Bay Beach La., off Estero Blvd.* ☎ *239/463–2064* 🌐 *www.fmbgc.com*) has 18 holes and a practice range in the midst of a condo community but filled with birds; greens fee $50/$25.

WHERE TO EAT

$$$ SEAFOOD

✕ **Matanzas Inn.** Watch boats coming and going whether you sit insic or out at this rustic Old Florida–style restaurant right on the doc alongside the Intracoastal Waterway. When the weather coopera tables outdoors, under umbrellas, provide the best ambience. Insi rustic shack gives way to a more formal dining area in the back; there's a bar upstairs with sweeping views and live music nightly. You can't miss with shrimp from the local fleets—delicately cornmeal-breaded, stuffed, or done Alfredo with scallops. The Matanzas Steamer (market price), a house specialty, heaps on the fish and shellfish. This is true Fort Myers Beach style, meaning service can be a bit gruff—and slow. ✉ *416 Crescent St.* ☎ *239/463–3838* 🌐 *www.matanzasrestaurant.com* ✍ *Reservations not accepted* ▭ *AE, D, MC, V.*

$$ SEAFOOD ✕ **Parrot Key Caribbean Grill.** For something more contemporary than Fort Myers Beach's traditional shrimp and seafood houses, head to San Carlos Island on the east side of the high bridge where the shrimp boats dock. Parrot Key sits marina-side near the shrimp docks and exudes merriment with its Floribbean cuisine and island music. The all-day menu takes tropical cues with dishes such as habanero-pepper wings, chicken sandwich with kiwi-strawberry-mango-barbecue sauce, fillet topped with blue cheese, and fried oysters with creole mustard. There's live entertainment weekends from 7 to 10 PM. ✉ *2400 Main St.* ☎ *239/463–3257* 🌐 *www.myparrotkey.com* ✍ *Reservations not accepted* ▭ *AE, D, MC, V.*

¢ GREEK ✕ **The Plaka.** A casual long-timer and a favorite for a quick breakfast, lunch breaks, and sunset dinners, Plaka—Greek for "fun"—has typical Greek fare such as moussaka, pastitsio, gyros, and roast lamb, as well as burgers, sandwiches, fried seafood, and strip steak. Refurbished in 2007, the place lies along a row of casual sidewalk restaurants in a pedestrian mall near the beach. There's indoor dining, but grab a seat on the porch or under an umbrella on the patio. ✉ *1001 Estero Blvd.* ☎ *239/463–4707* ✍ *Reservations not accepted* ▭ *AE, D, MC, V.*

$$$ AMERICAN ✕ **The Sandy Butler.** Visitors to Fort Myers Beach can find fine dining—if they're willing to drive a few miles off the island. This huge complex is part market and part restaurant (it seats 150 diners next door), and a favorite haunt for Sanibel and Fort Myers foodies. Luncheon sandwiches dare beyond the norm: Caprese on a baguette and triple-decker vegetarian clubs, for instance. At dinner, there's everything from a stuffed Cornish hen ($23) to seared sesame ahi tuna ($24) to chateaubriand for two ($70). The trio of crèmes brûlées is a true treat—especially the cayenne-chocolate selection. ✉ *17650 San Carlos Blvd.* ☎ *239/482–6765* 🌐 *www.sandybutler.com* ▭ *AE, D, MC, V.*

WHERE TO STAY

$$$$ **DiamondHead.** This 12-story resort sits on the beach, and many of the suites, especially those on higher floors, have stunning views. Units are done in rich fall tones but show a little wear and tear. Each has a living room with queen-size sleeper sofa, a separate bedroom, and a kitchenette. The well-organized children's programs include everything from crafts to scavenger hunts to sand golf. **Pros:** on the beach; nice views; kitchen facilities. **Cons:** heavy foot and car traffic; tiny fitness center; not the best value on the beach. ✉ *2000 Estero Blvd.* ☎ *239/765–7654 or 888/765–5002* 🌐 *www.diamondheadfl.com* *124 suites* *In-room: a/c, kitchen, Internet, Wi-Fi. In-hotel: 2 restaurants, bar, pool, gym, beachfront, children's programs (ages 4–14), laundry facilities, Internet terminal, Wi-Fi hotspots* ▭ *AE, D, MC, V.*

9

$$$$ ★ **Lovers Key Resort.** Views can be stupendous from upper floors in this 14-story tower just north of Lovers Key State Park. The gulf seems to stretch forever, and dolphins and manatees in the estuary put on quite a show. Most of the plantation-style condominiums have spa bathtubs with a window view. All of the one- and two-bedroom units have full kitchens and handsome decor that continues the lobby theme of bamboo, palms, and pineapples. The lagoon-style waterfall pool sits bayside. Extended-stay rates offer discounts. **Pros:** excellent views; off the beaten path; spacious accommodations. **Cons:** no true beach; far from shopping; limited amenities. *8771 Estero Blvd. 239/765–1040 or 877/798–4879 www.loverskey.com 100 condominiums In-room: a/c, kitchen, Internet, Wi-Fi. In-hotel: restaurant, pool, gym, beachfront, laundry facilities, Internet terminal, Wi-Fi hotspots AE, D, DC, MC, V.*

$$$–$$$$ **Outrigger Beach Resort.** On a wide gulf beach, this casual resort has rooms and efficiencies with configurations to suit different guests' needs. The standard rooms offer your basic motel setup; efficiencies are roomier and work well for families. All open up to a shared porch or balcony. You'll also find a broad sundeck, tiki cabanas, sailboats, and a beachfront pool with a popular tiki bar. **Pros:** beautiful beach; water-sports rentals; family-friendly vibe. **Cons:** can be noisy; crowded pool area; old-school feel. *6200 Estero Blvd. 239/463–3131 www.outriggerfmb.com 76 rooms, 68 efficiencies In-room: a/c, safe, kitchen (some), refrigerator, Wi-Fi (some). In-hotel: 2 restaurants, bar, pool, beachfront, bicycles, Internet terminal AE, MC, V.*

NAPLES AREA

As you head south from Fort Myers on U.S. 41, you soon come to Estero and Bonita Springs, followed by the Naples and Marco Island areas, which are sandwiched between Big Cypress Swamp and the Gulf of Mexico. East of Naples the land is largely undeveloped and mostly wetlands, all the way to Fort Lauderdale. Naples itself is a major vacation destination that has sprouted pricey high-rise condominiums and golfing developments, plus a spate of restaurants and shops to match. A similar but not as thorough evolution has occurred on Marco Island, the largest of the Ten Thousand Islands.

ESTERO/BONITA SPRINGS

10 mi south of Fort Meyers via U.S. 41.

Towns below Fort Myers have started to flow seamlessly into one another since the opening of Florida Gulf Coast University in San Carlos Park and as a result of the growth of Estero and Bonita Springs, agricultural communities until the 90s. In recent years the area has become a shopping mecca of mega-outdoor malls mixing big-box stores, smaller chains, and restaurants. Bonita Beach, the closest beach to Interstate 75, has evolved from a fishing community into a strip of upscale homes and beach clubs built to provide access for residents of inland golf developments.

GETTING HERE AND AROUND

U.S. 41 (Tamiami Trail) runs right through the heart of these two adjacent communities. You can also reach them by exits 123 and 116 off Interstate 75.

EXPLORING

Opened in 1936 and one of the first attractions of its kind in the state, **Everglades Wonder Gardens** captures the beauty of untamed Florida. The old-fashioned, rather cramped zoological gardens have Florida panthers, black bears, crocodiles and alligators, tame Florida deer, flamingos, otters, and birds. There's also a funky natural-history museum. Tours, which include otter and alligator feedings, run continuously, the last starting at 4:15. The swinging bridge over the alligator pit is a real thrill. ✉ *27180 Old U.S. 41* ☎ *239/992–2591* *$15* ⏲ *Daily 9–5.*

★ Tour one of Florida's quirkier chapters from the past at **Koreshan State Historic Site.** Named for a religious cult that was active at the turn of the 20th century, Koreshan preserves a dozen structures where the group practiced arts, worshipped a male-female divinity, and created its own branch of science called cosmogony. The cult floundered when leader Cyrus Reed Teed died in 1908, and in 1961 the four remaining members deeded the property to the state. Rangers and volunteers lead tours and demonstrations, and the grounds are lovely for picnicking and camping. Canoeists paddle the Estero River, fringed by a forest of exotic vegetation the Koreshans planted. ✉ *3800 Corkscrew Rd. at U.S. 41 (Tamiami Trail), Estero* ☎ *239/992–0311* 🌐 *www.floridastateparks.org/koreshan* *$5 per vehicle with up to 8 passengers; $2 per bicyclist, pedestrian, or extra passenger* ⏲ *Daily 8* AM*–sunset.*

OFF THE BEATEN PATH

Fodor's Choice ★

Corkscrew Swamp Sanctuary. To get a feel for what this part of Florida was like before civil engineers began draining the swamps, drive 13 mi east of Bonita Springs (30 mi northeast of Naples) to these 11,000 acres of pine flatwood and cypress, grass-and-sedge "wet prairie," saw-grass marshland, and lakes and sloughs filled with water lettuce. Managed by the National Audubon Society, the sanctuary protects North America's largest remaining stand of ancient bald cypress, 600-year-old trees as tall as 130 feet, as well as endangered birds, such as wood storks, which often nest here. This is a favorite destination for serious birders and is the gateway to the Great Florida Birding South Trail. If you spend a couple of hours to take the 2¼-mi self-guided tour along the boardwalk, you'll spot ferns, orchids, and air plants, as well as wading birds and possibly alligators and river otters. A nature center educates you about this precious, unusual habitat with a dramatic re-creation of the preserve and its creatures in the Swamp Theater. ✉ *375 Sanctuary Rd. W, 16 mi east of I–75 on Rte. 846* ☎ *239/348–9151* 🌐 *www.audubon.org* *$10* ⏲ *Oct.–Apr. 10, daily 7–5:30; Apr. 11–Sept., daily 7* AM*–7:30* PM*.*

SPORTS AND THE OUTDOORS

BEACHES

★ The 342-acre **Barefoot Beach Preserve** (✉ *Lely Barefoot Blvd. off Bonita Beach Rd.* ☎ *239/591–8596* *$8*) is a quiet, out-of-the-way place, accessible via a private neighborhood road around the corner from the buzzing public beach. It has picnic tables, a nature trail and learning

9

center, a butterfly garden, a canoe trail, and refreshment stands. Gopher tortoises often cross the road right in front of your car, so drive slowly. Park rangers lead nature walks and canoe trips.

Bonita Beach Park (✉ *Hickory Blvd. at Bonita Beach Rd.* ☎ *239/461–7400* *Parking $1 per hr*), at the south end of Bonita Beach, has picnic tables, beach concessions, volleyball, and a restaurant next door. As far as local beaches go, it's the easiest to access and the most popular south of Fort Myers Beach. It's also great for shell fans.

BIRDING

The last leg of the Great Florida Birding Trail has more than 20 stops in the Lower Gulf Coast. Go to 🌐 *www.floridabirdingtrail.com/sites_south.htm* for a complete listing.

CANOEING

The meandering Estero River is pleasant for canoeing as it passes through Koreshan State Historic Site to the bay. **Estero River Outfitters** (✉ *20991 Tamiami Trail S, Estero* ☎ *239/992–4050* 🌐 *www.esteroriveroutfitters.com*) provides rental canoes, kayaks, and equipment.

SHOPPING

★ **Miromar Outlets** (✉ *Corkscrew Rd. at I–75 Exit 123 in Estero, near Germain Arena* ☎ *239/948–3766* 🌐 *www.miromaroutlets.com*) complex includes Adidas, Nike, Nautica, and more than 140 other stores and eateries, plus a free Playland for kids. **Gulf Coast Town Center** (✉ *9903 Gulf Coast Main St.* 🌐 *www.gulfcoasttowncenter.com*) is a megamall of stores and chain restaurants including a 123,000-square-foot Bass Pro Shops, Borders, Best Buy, Costco, and movie theaters. **Coconut Point** (✉ *23106 Fashion Dr., Estero* ☎ *239/992–9966* 🌐 *www.simon.com/mall/?id=1202*), a 500-acre planned community, tops Gulf Coast with even more upscale stores and restaurants. There's a boardwalk for a breather between impulse purchases, and a castle-themed kids' play area.

WHERE TO EAT

$$$ SEAFOOD ✕ **Blue Water Bistro.** For the convenience of shoppers at the new Coconut Point, several excellent restaurants cluster in the midst of the shopping center. Most are hooked to a chain. This one, although part of a Naples–Bonita Springs dining dynasty, has a personality all its own with a suave indoor–outdoor bar scene and seafood that's anything but timid. Its specialty is grilled fish from around the globe that you can mix and match with a choice of sauces and sides. For instance, try swordfish with a sweet-and-sour mango sauce and onion rings with chipotle barbecue sauce. Other specialties include a classic burger, chipotle baby back ribs, and grouper kung pao. ✉ *23151 Village Shops Way, Coconut Point, Estero* ☎ *239/949–2583* 🌐 *www.bluewaterbistro.net* 💳 *AE, MC, V* ⏲ *No lunch.*

¢ AMERICAN ✕ **Doc's Beach House.** Right next door to the public beach access, Doc's has fed hungry beachgoers for decades. Come barefoot and grab a quick libation or meal downstairs, outside on the beach, or in the courtyard. When the thermometer reaches "searing" take refuge on the air-conditioned 2nd floor, with its great view of beach action. Basic fare on the breakfast and all-day menu includes a popular Angus burger, Chicago-style pizza, and seafood plates. ✉ *27908 Hickory Blvd., Bonita*

Springs ☎ *239/992–6444* 🌐 *www.docsbeachhouse.com* *Reservations not accepted* *No credit cards.*

WHERE TO STAY

$$$$ Fodor's Choice ★ **Hyatt Coconut Point Resort & Spa.** This secluded luxury resort, with its marble-and-mahogany lobby, makes a lovely sanctuary for families. Man-made water features include a slide pool, lap pool, lazy river pool, and fountain waterfall pool. For something more natural catch a ferry to the hotel's private island beach. Handsomely appointed rooms overlook the water or the golf course. Its spa is known for its rare Watsu (water shiatsu) pool, and an interpretive center showcases natural and prehistoric history. **Pros:** top-notch amenities; pampering spa; great ceviche bar. **Cons:** need shuttle to reach the beach; expensive restaurants. ✉ *5001 Coconut Rd., Bonita Springs* ☎ *239/444–1234 or 800/554–9288* 🌐 *www.coconutpoint.hyatt.com* *426 rooms, 30 suites* *In-room: a/c, safe, refrigerator, Internet, Wi-Fi. In-hotel: 5 restaurants, room service, bars, golf course, tennis courts, pools, gym, spa, beachfront, water sports, children's programs (ages 3–12), Internet terminal, Wi-Fi hotspots* *AE, D, DC, MC, V.*

$$–$$$ **Trianon Bonita Bay.** Convenient to Bonita Springs' best shopping and dining, this branch of a downtown Naples favorite has a peaceful, sophisticated feel, and a poolside–lakeside alfresco bar and grill. Rooms are generously sized, and the lobby has a vaulted, coved ceiling and marble columns. Cocktails and complimentary breakfast are served in the library, where a fireplace dominates. **Pros:** shops and restaurants within walking distance; intimate atmosphere; refined amenities. **Cons:** sometimes less-than-friendly staff; far from beach; slightly stuffy. ✉ *3401 Bay Commons Dr., Bonita Springs* ☎ *239/948–4400 or 800/859–3939* 🌐 *www.trianon.com* *100 rooms* *In-room: safe, refrigerator (some), Internet, Wi-Fi. In-hotel: pool, Internet terminal, Wi-Fi hotspot* *AE, D, DC, MC, V* *CP.*

NAPLES

21 mi south of Bonita Springs, on U.S. 41.

Poised between the Gulf of Mexico and the Everglades, Naples belies its wild setting and Indian post past with the trappings of wealth—neo-Mediterranean-style mansions, neatly manicured golfing developments, revitalized downtown streets lined with galleries and one-of-a-kind shops, and a reputation for lively and eclectic dining. Visitors come for its luxury hotels—including two Ritz-Carltons—its fabulous white-sand beaches, fishing, shopping, theater and arts, and a lofty reputation for golf. Yet with all the highfalutin living, Naples still appeals to families, especially with a new water park and the Children's Museum of Naples slated to open here in spring 2010.

GETTING HERE AND AROUND

The Naples Municipal Airport is a small facility east of downtown principally serving Delta Airlines, private planes, commuter flights, and charters. An on-demand taxi for up to three passengers is about $70 to Naples. Extra people are charged $10 each. Once you have arrived, call Naples Taxi. Other transportation options include Aaron Airport

Transportation and Naples Airport Shuttle. Greyhound Lines has service to Naples. In Naples and Marco Island, Collier Area Transit runs regular routes.

If you want someone to be your guide as you go about town, Naples Trolley Tours offers eight narrated tours daily, covering more than 25 points of interest in town. You can board at 24 places around town, including the Coastland Mall. The tour ($25) lasts about two hours, but you can get off and on at no extra cost.

Naples is 21 mi south of Bonita Springs, on U.S. 41. If you're driving here, consider Alligator Alley, a toll section of Interstate 75 that runs from Fort Lauderdale to Naples. In Naples, east–west trunks exiting off Interstate 75 include, from north to south, Immokalee Road (Route 846) at the north edge of town, Pine Ridge Road (Route 896), and Route 951, which takes you also to Marco Island.

ESSENTIALS

Transportation Contacts Aaron Airport Transportation (☎ *239/768–1898 or 800/998–1898*) **Collier Area Transit** (☎ *239/435–0000* 🌐 *www.colliergov.net*). **Greyhound Lines** (✉ *2669 Davis Blvd., Naples* ☎ *239/774–5660 or 800/231–2222* 🌐 *www.greyhound.com*). **Naples Airport Shuttle** (☎ *239/430–4747 or 888/569–2227* 🌐 *www.naplesairportshuttle.com*). **Naples Taxi** (☎ *239/435-0000*). **Naples Trolley Tours** (☎ *239/262–7300 or 800/592–0848* 🌐 *www.naplestrolleytours.com*).

Visitor Information. Naples, Marco Island, Everglades Convention and Visitors Bureau (✉ *2800 Horseshoe Dr. Naples* ☎ *239/252–2384 or 800/688–3600* 🌐 *www.paradisecoast.com*).

EXPLORING

TOP ATTRACTIONS

8 ★ **Collier County Museum.** To get a feel for local history, stroll the indoor and outdoor parklike exhibits at this museum, where a Seminole chickee village, native plant garden, swamp buggy, reconstructed 19th-century fort, steam logging locomotive, and other historical exhibits capture important Naples-area developments from prehistoric times to the World War II era. ✉ *3301 Tamiami Trail E* ☎ *239/252–8476* 🌐 *www.colliermuseums.com* *Free* *Weekdays 9–5, Sat. 9–4.*

10 **Naples Botanical Garden.** This has grown gradually into one of Naples's most exciting attractions. Self-guided tours take in a lovely Date Palm Allée backdropped by an artistic mosaic wall, a fruit and spice garden, a fragrance garden, and the Pollination Pavilion filled with butterflies, bees, geckos, hummingbirds, and lories. In November 2009, the gardens reopened with the addition of a Children's, Brazilian, and Caribbean Garden plus 90 acres of preserved Everglades habitat, and plans to add Florida and Asian gardens. ✉ *4820 Bayshore Dr.* ☎ *239/643–7275* 🌐 *www.naplesgarden.org* *$9.95* *Daily 9–5.*

5 **Naples Nature Center.** On 14 acres bordering a tidal lagoon teeming with wildlife, the Naples Nature Center includes an aviary, a wildlife-rehabilitation clinic, a serpentarium, and a 3,000-gallon sea turtle aquarium. Short trails are marked with interpretive signs, and there are guided walks and boat tours on the mangrove-bordered Gordon River

Clam Pass Beach Park **3**
Collier County Museum **8**
Delnor-Wiggins Pass State Park **1**
Lowdermilk Park **6**
Naples Botanical Garden **10**
Naples Nature Center **5**
Naples Zoo **4**
Palm Cottage **7**
Patty & Jay Baker Naples Museum of Art **2**
Sun-N-Fun Lagoon **9**

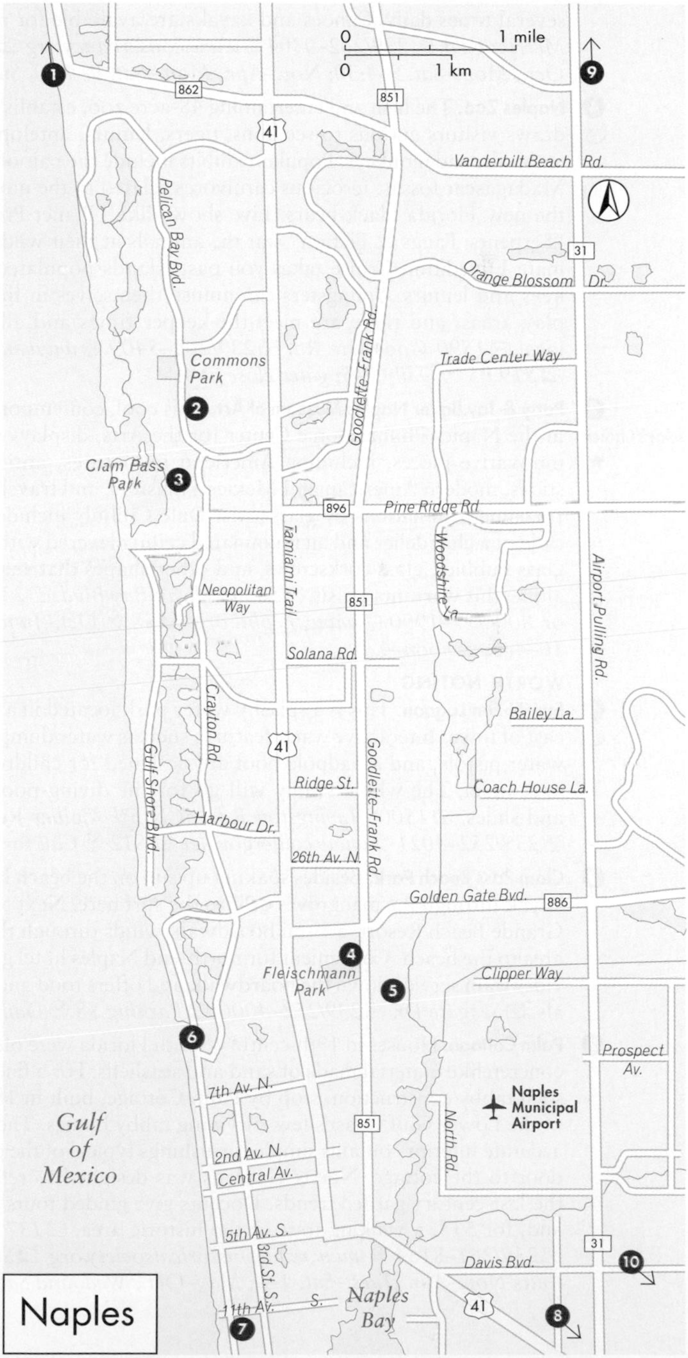

several times daily. Canoes and kayaks are available for rent. *1450 Merrihue Dr. 239/262–0304 www.conservancy.org $9 May–Oct., Mon.–Sat. 9–4:30; Nov.–Apr., Mon.–Sat. 9–4:30, Sun. noon–4.*

4 **Naples Zoo.** The lush and entertaining 48-acre zoo, established in 1919, draws visitors curious to see lions, tigers, lemurs, antelope, panthers, leopards, and monkeys. Popular exhibits include the pair of endangered Madagascar fossas, ferocious carnivores related to the mongoose, and the new Florida black bears. Live shows like "Planet Predator" and "Serpents: Fangs & Fiction" star the animals at their wildest. The Primate Expedition Cruise takes you past islands populated with monkeys and lemurs. Youngsters can amuse themselves in three separate play areas, and there are meet-the-keeper times and alligator feedings. *1590 Goodlette Rd. 239/262–5409 www.napleszoo.org $19.95 Daily 9–5; gates close at 4.*

2 **Patty & Jay Baker Naples Museum of Art.** This cool, contemporary museum in the Naples Philharmonic Center for the Arts, displays provocative, innovative pieces, including American miniatures, antique walking sticks, modern American and Mexican masters, and traveling exhibits. Dazzling installations by glass artist Dale Chihuly include a fiery cascade of a chandelier and an illuminated ceiling layered with many-hued glass bubbles, glass corkscrews, and other shapes that suggest the sea; alone, this warrants a visit. *5833 Pelican Bay Blvd. 239/597–1900 or 800/597–1900 www.thephil.org $8 Oct.–June, Tues.–Sat. 10–4, Sun. noon–4.*

Fodor's Choice ★

WORTH NOTING

9 **Sun-N-Fun Lagoon.** This is a splashy water park located in a county park east of town. Interactive water features such as water dumping buckets, water pistols, and a Tadpole pool are designed for children age seven and under. The whole family will go for the diving pool, lazy river, and slides. *15000 Livingston Rd., at North Collier Regional Park 239/252–4021 www.colliergov.net $12 Call for hrs.*

3 **Clam Pass Beach Park.** Besides soaking up sun on the beach here, you can kayak through the mangroves or into the surf here. Next to the Naples Grande Beach Resort, a ¾-mi boardwalk winds through the mangrove area to the beach. Convenient for north-end Naples hotel guests, it provides tram service down the boardwalk and offers food and beach rentals. *Seagate Dr. 239/252–4000 Parking $8 Daily 8–sunset.*

7 **Palm Cottage.** Houses in 19th-century South Florida were often built of a concretelike material made of sand and seashells. For a fine example of such tabby construction, stop by Palm Cottage, built in 1895 and one of the Lower Gulf Coast's few surviving tabby homes. The historically accurate interior contains simple furnishings typical of the period. Next door to the cottage, Norris Gardens was designed to reflect turn-of-the-last-century garden trends. Docents give guided tours of the home and, for $15, a walking tour of the historic area. *137 12th Ave. S 239/261–8164 www.napleshistoricalsociety.org $8 Guided tours Nov.–Apr., Tues.–Sat. 1–4; May–Oct., Wed. and Sat. 1–4.*

SPORTS AND THE OUTDOORS

BEACHES

1 Fodor's Choice ★ The well-maintained 166-acre **Delnor-Wiggins Pass State Park** has one of Naples's best beaches—all-natural with unobstructed views—plus barbecue grills, picnic tables, a boat ramp, an observation tower, restrooms with wheelchair access, bathhouses, showers, and lots of parking. Fishing is best in Wiggins Pass, at the north end of the park. Rangers conduct sea turtle programs in summer, and birding and other programs year-round. ✉ *11100 Gulf Shore Dr. N, at Rte. 846* ☎ *239/597–6196* 🌐 *www.floridastateparks.org/delnorwiggins* 💵 *$6 per vehicle with up to 8 people, $4 for single drivers, $2 for pedestrians and bicyclists* ⏲ *Daily 8–sunset.*

6 Stretching along Gulf Shore Boulevard, **Lowdermilk Park** is great for families. It has more than 1,000 feet of beach as well as volleyball courts, a playground, restrooms, showers, a snack bar, and picnic tables. ✉ *Gulf Shore Blvd. at Banyan Blvd.* ☎ *239/213–3029* 💵 *Parking 25¢ per 10 min* ⏲ *Daily 7–sunset.*

BIKING

For daily rentals, try **Naples Cyclery** (✉ *813 Vanderbilt Beach Rd. at Pavilion Shopping Center* ☎ *239/566–0600* 🌐 *www.naplescyclery.com*), where rates range from $6 to $40 for two hours and selections include two- and four-passenger surreys, tandems, and more.

BOATING

Naples Watersports at Port-O-Call Marina (✉ *550 Port-O-Call Way* ☎ *239/774–0479*) rents 19-foot pontoon boats and 21-foot deck boats starting at $75 for one hour.

FISHING

The **Lady Brett** (✉ *Tin City, 1200 5th Ave. S* ☎ *239/263–4949* 🌐 *www.tincityboats.com*) makes half-day fishing trips twice daily at $69 each. Take a guided boat and learn to cast and tie flies at **Mangrove Outfitters** (✉ *4111 E. Tamiami Trail* ☎ *239/793–3370 or 888/319–9848* 🌐 *www.mangrove-outfitters.com*).

GOLF

At **Lely Flamingo Island Club** (✉ *8004 Lely Resort Blvd.* ☎ *239/793–2600* 🌐 *www.lely-resort.net*) there are three 18-hole courses—the Classics, Flamingo Island, and the Mustang—plus a golf school. Mustang is the easiest and most wide open; greens fee $165/$39. **Naples Beach Hotel & Golf Club** (✉ *851 Gulf Shore Blvd. N* ☎ *239/435–2475* 🌐 *www.naplesbeachhotel.com*) has 18 holes, a golf school, and a putting green. The region's oldest course, a par 72, it was built in 1929 and last renovated in 1998; greens fee (includes cart) $145 (balls included)/$50. At affordable **Riviera Golf Club** (✉ *48 Marseille Dr.* ☎ *239/774–1081*) ★ there are 18 holes; greens fee $58/$23 (includes cart). **Tiburón Golf Club** (✉ *Ritz-Carlton Golf Resort, 2600 Tiburón Dr.* ☎ *239/593–2000*) has two 18-hole Greg Norman–designed courses, the Black and the Gold, and a golf academy. Challenging and environmentally pristine, the links include narrow fairways, stacked sod wall bunkers, coquina sand, and no roughs; greens fee $190/$115.

DID YOU KNOW?

Beaches are for so much more than sunning and sandcastle building. Many are used for fishing, weddings, and horseback riding. And come July 4th, some, like Naples Beach (shown here), draw people at night for viewing fireworks over the water.

SHOPPING

Old Naples encompasses two distinct shopping areas marked by historic buildings and flowery landscaping: 5th Avenue South and 3rd Street South. Both are known for their abundance of fine-art galleries and monthly musical entertainment. Near 5th Avenue South, **Tin City** (✉ *1200 5th Ave. S* 🌐 *www.tin-city.com*), in a collection of tin-roof former boat docks along Naples Bay, has more than 30 boutiques, eateries, and souvenir shops, with everything from jewelry to T-shirts and seafood. At the classy **Village on Venetian Bay** (✉ *4200 Gulf Shore Blvd.* 🌐 *www.venetianvillage.com*), nearly 60 shops and restaurants line the water's edge.

★ Downtown, **Gattle's** (✉ *1250 3rd St. S* ☎ *239/262–4791 or 800/344–4552*) stocks pricey-but-pretty linens. **Marissa Collections** (✉ *1167 3rd St. S* ☎ *239/263–4333*) showcases designer women's wear. Only in South Florida can you find something like **Waterside Shops** (✉ *Seagate Dr. and U.S. 41* 🌐 *www.watersideshops.net*), four dozen stores plus eateries wrapped around a series of waterfalls, waterways, and shaded open-air promenades. Saks Fifth Avenue and Nordstrom are two of the anchors.

★ The most upscale clothes sometimes go to consignment shops such as **New to You** (✉ *933 Creech Rd.* ☎ *239/262–6869*). Naples's ladies who lunch often donate their year-old Armani castoffs and fine collectibles to a spate of terrific thrift shops such as **Options** (✉ *968 2nd Ave. N* ☎ *239/434–7115*). Among 5th Avenue South's upscale selection, **Regatta** (✉ *750 5th Ave. S* ☎ *239/262–3929*) sells personal and home accessories with a sense of humor and style.

NIGHTLIFE AND THE ARTS

THE ARTS

★ Naples is the cultural capital of this stretch of coast. The **Naples Philharmonic Center for the Arts** (✉ *5833 Pelican Bay Blvd.* ☎ *239/597–1900 or 800/597–1900* 🌐 *www.thephil.org*) has a 1,473-seat performance center with plays, concerts, and exhibits year-round. It's home to the 85-piece Naples Philharmonic, which presents both classical and pop concerts. The Miami Ballet Company performs here during its winter season. The **Naples Players** (✉ *Sugden Community Theatre, 701 5th Ave. S* ☎ *239/263–7990* 🌐 *www.naplesplayers.org*) performs musicals and dramas year-round; winter shows often sell out well in advance.

NIGHTLIFE

Downtown's 5th Avenue South is the scene of lively nightclubs and sidewalk cafés. **McCabe's Irish Pub** (✉ *699 5th Ave. S* ☎ *239/403–7170*) hosts Irish bands most weekends and some weeknights. Audiences often join in on the lusty lyrics. Hit **Ultra Naples** (✉ *15495 U.S. 41 N* ☎ *239/514–3790*) for DJ music and dancing Thursday through Saturday.

WHERE TO EAT

$$$ CARIBBEAN ✕ **Aura**. At the Naples Grande Beach Resort, Aura breaks all the rules with a chic wall-less lobby setting and a short menu of artistically plated creations in a style it calls New American Bistro. Diners can order appetizers and smaller dishes for lunch and dinner. After 6 PM a handful of entrées satisfies hardier appetites. The grilled ahi tuna Niçoise salad or

grilled cheese sandwich with avocado and bacon served with tomato soup are good choices for lunch. Main courses ($17–$24) include well-prepared stars such as seared day-boat scallops with succotash, and pork tenderloin with apple and cranberry chutney. Save room for the delightfully innovative dessert shooters. Breakfast is also served. ✉ *475 Seagate Dr., Naples Grande Resort* ☎ *239/597–3232* ▭ *AE, D, DC, MC, V.*

¢ PIZZA ✕ **Aurelio's Is Pizza.** Transplanted from Chicago, the pizza here is steeped in tradition and flavor. The selections are typical, with a few show-offs such as shrimp barbecue, BLT, and the low-cholesterol spinach Calabrese. There's also pasta with homemade sauces and chicken Parmesan or Alfredo. Black-and-white checkered tablecloths and old Illinois license plates accent this neighborhood-style strip mall café. ✉ *590 N. Tamiami Trail* ☎ *239/403–8882* 🌐 *aureliosofnaples.com* ▭ *AE, MC, V* ⊙ *Closed Mon. No lunch weekends.*

$$$ MIDDLE EASTERN ★ ✕ **Bha! Bha!** Classic and fusion Middle Eastern cooking—some of Naples's finest ethnic food—fill the menu with wonderful, adventurous taste treats. Specialties include plum lamb with tomato-pomegranate sauce, garlic-eggplant chicken, mango-ginger shrimp, and spicy beef in saffron sauce with cucumber yogurt. Ocher walls, a stone fountain, and exotic tapestries confirm the PERSIAN BISTRO on the restaurant's sign. The service lags at times, but intrepid palates still declare it worth heading to the strip mall location. A belly dancer entertains Saturday nights. ✉ *847 Vanderbilt Rd.* ☎ *239/594–5557* 🌐 *www.bhabhapersianbistro.com* ▭ *AE, MC, V* ⊙ *Closed Mon. May–Dec.*

$$$ ECLECTIC Fodor's Choice ★ ✕ **Chops City Grill.** Count on high-quality cuisine that fuses, as its name suggests, chopstick cuisine and fine cuts of meat. Sophisticated yet resort-wear casual, it draws everyone from young businesspeople to local retirees. Sushi and Pacific Rim inspirations such as beef satay and teriyaki-glazed sea bass represent its Asian persuasion; dry-aged T-bone, fillets, and prime rib, its meaty side. They come together in the panko-crusted pork porterhouse. Dine alfresco or inside with a view of the kitchen. ✉ *837 5th Ave. S* ☎ *239/262–4677* ✉ *U.S. 41 at Brooks Grand Plaza, Bonita Springs* ☎ *239/992–4677* 🌐 *www.chopsbonita.com* ✍ *Reservations essential* ▭ *AE, DC, MC, V* ⊙ *No lunch.*

$ MEXICAN ✕ **Cilantro Tamales.** The warm, crispy, and authentic-tasting salsa and chips alone are worth a visit to this bright and lively little spot, with slabs of clay tile for placemats. The signature dish, smoked Gouda–stuffed tamales, reveals freshness, authenticity, and flair. Imaginative touches are also added to other Tex-Mex standards, including enchiladas, fajitas, chiles rellenos, and a Mexican rice bowl. ✉ *10823 N. Tamiami Trail* ☎ *239/597–5855* 🌐 *www.cilantrotamales.com* ▭ *AE, D, MC, V* ⊙ *Closed Mon. July–Sept.*

$$$$ FRENCH ✕ **Côte d'Azur.** Capturing the essence of the French Riviera, Côte d'Azur offers a blend of country fare, exotic ingredients, and slow-cooked goodness with a menu that executes French technique with perfection and joie de vivre. The narrow dining room, with yellow-striped awnings and windows inset with mirrors and decorated with flower boxes, suggests a French provincial sidewalk café. The whole fish of the day is flown in directly from Europe. The regular menu is intriguing, too, with dishes including Maine lobster roasted in a clay pot with artichoke

hearts, porcini mushrooms, and caviar champagne sauce; and roasted duck with sun-dried currants and cherries, green peppercorn port sauce, and roasted pear. ✉ *11224 Tamiami Trail N* ☎ *239/597–8867* 🌐 *www.cotedazurrestaurant.com* ▭ *AE, D, MC, V* ⏲ *No lunch. Closed Mon.*

¢ ECLECTIC ✕ **Old Naples Pub**. Local blue- and white-collar workers gather for affordable sandwiches and seafood in the courtyard of this 20-year-old traditional pub, tucked away from shopping traffic at 3rd Street Plaza. It strikes one as an everybody-knows-your-name kind of place, with jars of pickles on the tables and friendly bartenders. Taste some 27 kinds of beer and order fried "ungrouper sandwiches" (made with "mild flaky white filet" as grouper becomes rarer), burgers, crispy chicken salad, and nachos, as well as such not-so-traditional pub snacks as sesame seared ahi tuna and fried gator tail. There's musical entertainment nightly between Thanksgiving and Easter. ✉ *255 13th Ave. S* ☎ *239/649–8200* 🌐 *www.naplespubs.com* ▭ *AE, D, MC, V.*

$$$ ITALIAN ✕ **Olio on Naples Bay**. Its self-described Napa Valley–style Italian cuisine gives fresh interpretation to both labels with dishes such as limoncello-cured salmon tartare with horseradish mascarpone, prosciutto and truffled ricotta pizzette, shrimp and cavatelli puttanesca, and fall-off-the-bone braised short ribs with roasted vegetable ravioli. For dessert, look for dishes like sweet polenta strawberry shortcake. Opened in 2008 at the Naples Bay Resort, Olio has water views on both sides with indoor and outdoor seating. Locals and hotel guests both gather here for dinner. ✉ *1490 5th Ave. S* ☎ *239/530–5110* 🌐 *www.olioonthebay.com* ▭ *AE, D, MC, V* ⏲ *No lunch.*

$$$ CARIBBEAN ✕ **Tommy Bahama's Tropical Café**. Here Naples takes a youthful curve. Island music sounds on the umbrella-shaded courtyard at this eatery, the prototype for the chain. It has that trademark rattan look that identifies the Tommy Bahama label in clothing and furniture stores across the nation. Indoors and out, everybody's munching sandwiches, salads, and grilled seafood and meats with a tropical flair, like shrimp and scallops in curry-coconut sauce and blackberry-brandy barbecued ribs. Make sure to sample Tommy's Bungalow Brew beer. ✉ *1220 3rd St. S* ☎ *239/643–6889* 🌐 *www.tommybahama.com* ▭ *AE, D, MC, V.*

WHERE TO STAY

$$$$ ★ **Bellasera**. This place is just far enough "off 5th" to be away from the shopping and dining foot traffic and noise but close enough for convenience. Right off a Tuscany postcard, it feels quite villalike with its red tile roofs and burnt-ochre stucco. The privately owned studios and suites, with earthy hues and terra-cotta tiles, huddle three-stories high around a beautifully tiled pool, fountain, and courtyard. Private cabanas line the pool on two sides, and Zizi restaurant spills out onto the patio on another. The studios have in-room whirlpool tubs with plantation shutters opening onto the master bedroom so you can watch TV from your bubble bath. A spa takes the resort's new Green Lodging designation seriously with all-organic products and linens. **Pros:** near shops and restaurants; spacious rooms; screened patio or balcony. **Cons:** must take shuttle to beach; on a busy highway; average restaurant. ✉ *221 9th St. S* ☎ *239/649–7333 or 888/612–1115* 🌐 *www.bellaseranaples.com* *10 studios, 30 1-bedroom suites, 48 2-bedroom*

suites, 12 3-bedroom suites In-room: a/c, safe, kitchen (some), refrigerator, Internet, Wi-Fi. In-hotel: restaurant, room service, bar, pool, gym, Internet terminal, Wi-Fi hotspots ▭ *AE, D, DC, MC, V.*

$$$ ★ **Edgewater Beach Hotel.** This waterfront resort anchors the north end of fashionable Gulf Shore Boulevard. The one- and two-bedroom suites are decorated in a relaxed, contemporary style and have nice touches like fully equipped kitchens with full-sized refrigerators, gingerbread-trimmed patios or balconies, and exquisite gulf views. Have meals by the beachfront pool or in the elegant restaurant in the lobby. You'll also find the small fitness center and business facilities on the same floor. Guests have certain dining and recreational privileges (including golfing) at the Naples Grande Beach Resort, a sister property. **Pros:** beautiful beach; spacious accommodations; fabulous restaurant. **Cons:** far from shopping; surrounded closely by high-rises; no tubs in some rooms. ✉ *1901 Gulf Shore Blvd. N* ☎ *239/403–2000 or 800/821–0196* 🌐 *www.edgewaternaples.com* *97 1-bedroom suites, 28 2-bedroom suites In-room: a/c, safe, kitchen, Wi-Fi. In-hotel: 2 restaurants, bars, pool, gym, beachfront, water sports, bicycles, laundry facilities, Internet terminal, Wi-Fi hotspot* ▭ *AE, D, DC, MC, V.*

$$$$ **Inn on Fifth.** You can't beat this swank property if you want to plant yourself in the heart of Naples nightlife and shopping. Rooms are soundproofed to shut out the activity when you're ready to wrap yourself in the provided robe and sequester yourself in comfort. When you're not, slide open the French doors and tune in to 5th Avenue from the balcony. A spa completes a list of urban amenities that also includes a lively Irish pub, a popular crab restaurant, a rooftop pool, and a columned marble lobby with crystal chandeliers and a dramatic sweeping staircase. A theater is next door, and the beach is six blocks away. The pub is very friendly, but the front-desk staff can be less than helpful at times. **Pros:** near shopping and restaurants; metro vibe; very comfortable rooms. **Cons:** among 5th Street's bustle; pool is eye-level with power lines; not on the beach. ✉ *699 5th Ave. S* ☎ *239/403–8777 or 888/403–8778* 🌐 *www.innonfifth.com* *76 rooms, 11 suites In-room: a/c, safe, Internet, Wi-Fi. In-hotel: restaurant, bar, pool, gym, spa, laundry service, Internet terminal* ▭ *AE, D, DC, MC, V* 🍽 *CP.*

$$$$ Fodor's Choice ★ **LaPlaya Beach & Golf Resort.** LaPlaya bespeaks posh and panache down to the smallest detail—note the custom-designed duvet covers, marble bathrooms, and a palm-tree-patterned teddy bear on your pillow. The boutique resort features a Thai-style spa, rock-waterfall pools, a tony Miami-style beachfront restaurant, and a casual tiki bar that serves food. Of its 189 units, 141 are beachfront with private balconies. Some have jetted soak tubs with a view of the gulf. **Pros:** right on the beach; high-end amenities; beautiful rooms. **Cons:** golf course is off property; no locker rooms in spa. ✉ *9891 Gulf Shore Dr.* ☎ *239/597–3123 or 800/237–6883* 🌐 *www.laplayaresort.com* *180 rooms, 9 suites In-room: a/c, Internet, Wi-Fi. In-hotel: restaurant, bars, golf course, pools, gym, spa* ▭ *AE, D, MC, V.*

$$$$ ★ **Naples Bay Resort.** This place opened in 2008 with all the posh, polish, and incredible dining it takes to steal the hearts and custom of those who thought the Ritz and Naples Grande were the only top-of-

the-line options. Combining yachting and recreational activities with an Italian-motif boutique hotel, Naples Bay Resort offers incredible amenities, including a wide range of pools (one just for adults), an intimate spa, a fitness center, and a friendly pool bar and grill. A free shuttle makes the short trip to the nearest beaches. Accommodations range from standard rooms to one- and two-bedroom suites to cottages. **Pros:** full range of amenities; walking distance to downtown; great dining options. **Cons:** no beach; some highway noise. ✉ *1500 5th Ave. S* ☎ *239/530–1199 or 866/605–1199* 🌐 *www.naplesbayresort.com* *20 rooms, 29 1-bedroom suites, 36 2-bedroom suites, 108 cottages (minimum 6-night stay in cottages)* *In-room: a/c, safe, kitchen (some), refrigerator, Wi-Fi (some). In-hotel: 3 restaurants, room service, bars, tennis courts, pools, gym, spa, water sports, laundry facilities, Internet terminal* *AE, D, MC, V.*

$$$$ **Naples Beach Hotel & Golf Club.** Family-owned and -managed for more than 50 years, this beach resort is a piece of Naples history. On a prime stretch of powdery sand, it stands out for its par-72, 18-hole championship golf course, the first resort course in the state, with a pro shop and golf school. The hotel's lobby has skylights, a coral-rock fireplace, an aquarium, and a coffee shop. Rooms are decorated in light colors and were renovated in 2009 to include flat-screen TVs. Packages make an extended stay affordable. **Pros:** terrific beach; good recreational amenities; complimentary kids' program. **Cons:** expensive nightly rates; showing its age; have to cross street to reach spa and golf facilities. ✉ *851 Gulf Shore Blvd. N* ☎ *239/261–2222 or 800/237–7600* 🌐 *www.naplesbeachhotel.com* *264 rooms, 42 suites, 12 efficiencies* *In-room: a/c, safe, kitchen (some), refrigerator, Wi-Fi. In-hotel: 3 restaurants, bars, golf course, tennis courts, pool, gym, spa, beachfront, children's programs (ages 5–12), laundry service, Internet terminal* *AE, D, DC, MC, V.*

$$$–$$$$ Fodor's Choice ★ **Naples Grande Beach Resort.** Beach access, golf nearby, and top-shelf luxury are all yours at the Naples Grande. If the links aren't your thing, the Golden Door Spa just might be. Accommodations are spacious and comfortable at this high-rise hotel. One of the glories of the property—at least for families—is the immense free-form family pool and 100-foot waterslide. The hotel sits behind dusky, twisted mangrove forests; to get to the 3 mi of powdery white sand, it's a short walk or tram ride. Besides its signature Aura restaurant, its Strip House—a Vegas transplant—serves fine steaks in a bordello setting. Indigenous cypress and pines frame the Naples Grande Golf Club, the hotel's 18-hole Rees Jones–designed course. **Pros:** great tennis and golf; attentive service; top-notch dining. **Cons:** not directly on the beach; high room rates. ✉ *475 Seagate Dr.* ☎ *239/597–3232 or 800/247–9810* 🌐 *www.naplesgrande.com* *395 rooms, 79 suites* *In-room: a/c, Internet, Wi-Fi. In-hotel: 5 restaurants, room service, bars, golf course, tennis courts, pools, gym, spa, beachfront, water sports, bicycles, children's programs (ages 4–12), laundry service, Internet terminal* *AE, DC, MC, V.*

$$$$ ★ **Ritz-Carlton Golf Resort.** Ardent golfers with a yen for luxury will find their dream vacation at Naples's most elegant golf resort. Ritz style prevails, but in a more contemporary vein than at its sister resort, the

Ritz-Carlton, Naples. The lobby is decorated in rich upholstery, with floor-to-ceiling views of manicured greens. Rooms are regal, with marble bathrooms and color schemes in shades of greens and burgundies; half of them have balconies with links views. The golf academy can help you polish your skills, and you have access to the spa, kids' program, and other amenities of the nearby beachside Ritz-Carlton. Dining at Tuscan-style Lemonia is refined but casual, especially popular for Sunday brunch. The cigar bar next door is inviting, with its billiards and fireplace. **Pros:** great golfing; fine dining; very elegant. **Cons:** must take shuttle bus to beach; expensive rates; valets not as careful with cars as they should be. ✉ *2600 Tiburón Dr.* ☎ *239/593–2000 or 800/241–3333* 🌐 *www.ritzcarlton.com* *255 rooms, 40 suites* *In-room: a/c, safe, Wi-Fi. In-hotel: 4 restaurants, room service, bars, golf course, tennis courts, pool, children's programs (ages 5–12), laundry service, Internet terminal, Wi-Fi hotspot, parking (paid), some pets allowed* 💳 *AE, D, DC, MC, V.*

$$$$ Fodor's Choice ★ **Ritz-Carlton, Naples.** This is a classic Ritz-Carlton, with marble statues, antique furnishings, and 19th-century European oil paintings. In the rooms, the comforts of home prevail—assuming your home is a palace. Outside, steps away, the beach is soft, white, and dense with seashells. Given the graciousness of the staff, you quickly get over the incongruity of traipsing through the regal lobby in flip-flops, clutching a plastic bag of beach finds. The elegant spa is one of the Ritz-Carlton brand's first and largest, offering a complete (and divine) menu of indulgences including its new eco-room. **Pros:** very luxurious; flawless service; great beach. **Cons:** valet parking only; short walk to the beach. ✉ *280 Vanderbilt Beach Rd.* ☎ *239/598–3300 or 800/241–3333* 🌐 *www.ritzcarlton.com* *415 rooms, 35 suites* *In-room: a/c, safe, Wi-Fi. In-hotel: 6 restaurants, room service, bars, tennis courts, pools, gym, spa, beachfront, children's programs (ages 5–12), laundry service, Internet terminal, Wi-Fi hotspot, parking (paid)* 💳 *AE, D, DC, MC, V.*

$$$ **Trianon Old Naples.** Oh-so-European in feel, this boutique hotel is just enough removed from 5th Avenue's traffic to feel private, but close enough to be convenient. Wrought-iron balconies and shade trees set the stage outside; inside, the elegant lobby has high ceilings, a working granite fireplace, plush furnishings, and a library that doubles as a wine-and-beer bar and breakfast room. Rooms are large and lavishly furnished, with heavy draperies. **Pros:** close to shops and restaurants; elegant setting; spacious rooms. **Cons:** limited facilities; must drive to beach. ✉ *955 7th Ave. S* ☎ *239/435–9600 or 877/482–5228* 🌐 *www.trianon.com* *55 rooms, 3 suites* *In-room: a/c, safe, Internet, Wi-Fi. In-hotel: bar, pool, Internet terminal, Wi-Fi hotspot* 💳 *AE, D, DC, MC, V* 🍽 *CP.*

MARCO ISLAND

20 mi south of Naples via Rte. 951.

High-rises line part of the shore of Marco Island, which is connected to the mainland by two bridges. Yet it retains an isolated feeling much appreciated by those who love this corner of the world. Some natural areas have been preserved, and the down-home fishing village of Goodland is resisting change. Fishing, boating, sunning, swimming, and tennis are the primary activities.

GETTING HERE AND AROUND

From Naples, Route 951 takes you to Marco Island, about 20 mi to the south. Collier Area Transit runs regular buses through the area. Key West Express operates a ferry from Marco Island (from Christmas through May) and Fort Myers Beach (year-round) to Key West. The cost for the round-trip (four hours each way) from Fort Myers Beach is $145, from Marco Island $119.

ESSENTIALS

Transportation Contacts **Collier Area Transit** (☎ *239/596–7777* 🌐 *www.colliergov.net*). **Key West Express** (☎ *239/394–9700 or 888/539–2628* 🌐 *www.keywestshuttle.com*).

Visitor Information **Marco Island Area Chamber of Commerce** (✉ *1102 N. Collier Blvd., Marco Island* ☎ *239/394–7549 or 800/788–6272* 🌐 *www.marcoislandchamber.org*). **Naples, Marco Island, Everglades Convention and Visitors Bureau** (✉ *2800 Horseshoe Dr., No. 218, Naples* ☎ *239/403–2384* 🌐 *www.paradisecoast.com*).

EXPLORING

Marco Island was once part of the ancient Calusa kingdom. The Marco Cat, a statue found in 1896 excavations, has become symbolic of the island's prehistoric significance. The original is part of the Smithsonian Institution's collection, but a replica of the Marco Cat is among displays illuminating the ancient past at the **Marco Island Historical Museum**, slated to move to a brand-new facility across from the public library in fall 2010. Three rooms examine the island's history with dioramas, artifacts, and signage: the Calusa Room, Pioneer Room, and Modern Marco Room. ✉ *180 Heathwood Dr.* ☎ *239/642–7468* 🌐 *www.themihs.org* 🎫 *Free* 🕙 *Weekdays 9–4.*

★ In the midst of 110,000-acre Rookery Bay National Estuarine Reserve, **Rookery Bay Environmental Learning Center** dramatically interprets the Everglades environment and local history with interactive models, aquariums, original art, a film, tours, and classes. It's on the edge of the estuary, about five minutes east of Marco's north bridge on Collier Boulevard. In 2009 the center debuted a $1 million, 250-foot pedestrian bridge that spans the reserve's creek from the center's 2nd floor, and connects with nature trails by guided or self-guided tour. Kayak tours are also available. Other new exhibits include an interactive research boat with bird sounds and glass-bottom-boat video, and exhibits about the Gulf of Mexico and global climate change. ✉ *300 Tower Rd.* ☎ *239/417–6310* 🌐 *www.rookerybay.org* 🎫 *$5* 🕙 *Dec.–Apr., Mon.–Sat. 9–4. Closed Sat. May–Oct. weekdays 9–4.*

SPORTS AND THE OUTDOORS

BEACH

Tigertail Beach (✉ *490 Hernando Ct.* ☎ *239/353–0404, 239/353–0404 for ranger programs* 🎫 *Parking $8* 🕙 *Daily 8–sunset*) is on the southwest side of the island, 2,500 feet along both developed and undeveloped

9

areas. Once gulf front, in recent years a sand spit known as Sanddollar Island has formed, which means the beach, especially at the north end, has become mud flats—great for birding. There's still plenty of sand on the south end and across the lagoon on the sand spit. Facilities include playgrounds, volleyball, a butterfly garden, free use of a beach wheelchair, a concession stand, restrooms, and showers. Sailboat and kayak rentals are available, and rangers conduct nature programs. ■ **TIP→ The Conservancy of Southwest Florida conducts free educational beach walks at Tigertail Beach every weekday from 8:30 to 9:30 AM January to mid-April.**

FISHING

Sunshine Tours (✉ *Rose Marco River Marina, 951 Bald Eagle Dr.* ☎ *239/642–5415* 🌐 *www.sunshinetoursmarcoisland.com*) operates deep-sea ($99 per person for half day) and backcountry ($60 per person for three hours) fishing charters.

WHERE TO EAT

$$ SOUTHERN **Almost Famous Mel's South Beach Smokehouse BBQ.** After it opened for business in 2008, this barbecue haven became a local favorite for pigging out, drinking, dancing, and watching the game. If you're looking for something "lite," keep driving. The sandwiches, ribs, and seafood specialties are gargantuan and come with a choice of two Southern-style side dishes and four sauces. Smoked to tenderness, the meats tour this nation's finest barbecue styles: Texas, Memphis, and St. Louis. Breakfast is buffet style for $6.99. ✉ *657 S. Collier Blvd.* ☎ *239/394–7111* 🌐 *www.almostfamousmels.com* ▭ *AE, D, MC, V.*

$$$ ITALIAN Fodor's Choice ★ **Arturo's.** This place is huge, with expansive Romanesque dining rooms and more seating on the patio. Still, it fills up year-round with a strong following that appreciates a fun attitude and serious Italian cuisine done comprehensively and traditionally. Start with the plump mussels marinara, then choose from three pages of classic Italian entrées. The stuffed pork chop, a nightly special, is a winner, as is the New York–style cheesecake. ✉ *844 Bald Eagle Dr.* ☎ *239/642–0550* *Reservations essential* 🌐 *www.arturosmarcoisland.com* ▭ *MC, V.*

$ AMERICAN **Crazy Flamingo.** Burgers, conch fritters, and chicken wings draw mostly locals to this neighborhood bar, where there's counter service only and seating indoors and outdoors on the sidewalk. Try the peel-and-eat shrimp, sushi, mussels marinara, chicken bistro salad, or fried grouper basket. ✉ *Marco Island Town Center, 1035 N. Collier Blvd.* ☎ *239/642–9600* 🌐 *www.thecrazyflamingo.com* ▭ *AE, MC, V.*

$$$ SEAFOOD **Old Marco Lodge Crab House.** Built in 1869, this waterfront restaurant is Marco's oldest landmark, and boaters often cruise in and tie up dockside to sit on the veranda and dine on local seafood and pasta entrées. The crab-cake sandwich is a popular lunch option; add a trip to the salad bar and it's a whole meal. For dinner, start with a wholesome bowl of vegetable crab soup. Crab entrées come in four varieties—stone (in season), snow, soft-shell blue, and king—but the menu includes all manner of shellfish, fish, and steak dishes. Save room for the authentic key lime pie. ✉ *401 Papaya St., Goodland* ☎ *239/642–7227* 🌐 *www.oldmarcolodge.com* ▭ *AE, D, MC, V* ⊗ *Closed Sept.; Mon. and Tues., May–Aug.; and Mon., Oct.–mid-Dec.*

> **WORD OF MOUTH**
>
> "You could try Marco Island in the Gulf . . . beautiful, pristine beaches with powder-like sand. There are plenty of condos to rent. You could rent a boat and 'cruise' around the island, stopping at small uninhabited islands to look for shells, etc."—gtravelbugs

$$$ ITALIAN ★ **Sale e Pepe.** Marco's best dining view comes also with some of its finest cuisine. The name means "salt and pepper," an indication that this palatial restaurant with terrace seating overlooking the beach adheres to the basics of home-style Italian cuisine. Pastas, sausages, and ice cream are made right here in the kitchen. Simple dishes—veal ravioli, risotto, yellow pepper–and-shrimp soup, baked salmon with lobster sauce, roasted grouper with saffron sauce, and grilled marinated strip steak—explode with home-cooked, long-simmered flavors. *Marco Beach Ocean Resort, 480 S. Collier Blvd.* *239/393–1600* *www.sale-e-pepe.com* *AE, D, DC, MC, V.*

$$$ ECLECTIC **Verdi's.** There's a Zen feel to this American bistro built on creative American-Italian-Asian fusion cuisine. You might start with steamed littleneck clams in garlic butter or duck potstickers, then move on to entrées such as grilled swordfish with pumpkin seeds, crispy duck, or the New Zealand rack of lamb. Cuban coffee crème brûlée and deep-dish apple strudel are among the tempting desserts. *Sand Dollar Plaza, 241 N. Collier Blvd.* *www.verdisbistro.com* *239/394–5533* *D, DC, MC, V* *No lunch. Closed Aug. and Sept.*

WHERE TO STAY

$$–$$$ **Boat House Motel.** For a great location at a good price, check into this two-story motel. Modest but appealing with its white facade and turquoise trim, it's at the north end of Marco Island, on a canal close to the gulf. Units are light and bright and furnished with blond woods, rattan, and tropical-print fabrics. King-size rooms have a balcony or walled-in terrace, and some have great water views. You can fish from the motel's dock. **Pros:** away from busy beach traffic; affordable; boating docks and access. **Cons:** no beach; hard to find; tight parking area. *1180 Edington Pl.* *239/642–2400 or 800/528–6345* *www.theboathousemotel.com* *20 rooms, 3 condominiums, 1 2-bedroom house* *In-room: a/c, kitchen (some), refrigerator, Wi-Fi. In-hotel: pool, some pets allowed, Wi-Fi hotspot* *MC, V.*

$$$–$$$$ **Hilton Marco Island Beach Resort.** This 11-story beachfront hotel is smaller and more conservative than the Marriott, and it seems less busy and crowded. All rooms are spacious and have private balconies with full or partial gulf views, a sitting area, a dry bar, bathrobes, and a mini-refrigerator. The recently opened spa has 10 treatment rooms and a full range of pampering services. **Pros:** gorgeous wide beach; complete business services; exclusive feel. **Cons:** a little stuffy; charge for Wi-Fi; business focus. *560 S. Collier Blvd.* *239/394–5000 or 800/394–5000* *www.hiltonmarcoisland.com* *271 rooms, 26 suites* *In-room: a/c, safe, refrigerator, Wi-Fi. In-hotel: 3 restaurants, bar, tennis courts, pool, gym, spa, beachfront, water sports, children's programs (ages 5–12), Internet terminal, Wi-Fi hotspots, parking (paid)* *AE, D, DC, MC, V.*

$$$$ Fodor's Choice ★ **Marco Beach Ocean Resort.** One of the island's first condo hotels, this 12-story class act has one- and two-bedroom suites decorated in tasteful neutral tones. All rooms face the gulf and the property's crescent-shaped rooftop pool (on the 5th floor). The bathrooms have marble floors and vanities. The Sale e Pepe Tuscan-style restaurant wins raves and awards. Golf and tennis are nearby. **Pros:** top-rate dining; beach location; boutique hotel feel. **Cons:** high prices; a rather squeezed feel because of neighboring condo buildings; near busy resort. *480 S. Collier Blvd. 239/393–1400 or 800/260–5089 www.marcoresort.com 87 1-bedroom and 16 2-bedroom suites In-room: a/c, kitchen, Wi-Fi (some). In-hotel: 3 restaurants, bars, tennis courts, pool, gym, spa, beachfront, Internet terminal AE, D, DC, MC, V.*

$$$$ ★ **Marco Island Marriott Resort, Golf Club & Spa.** A circular drive and manicured grounds front this beachfront resort made up of twin 11-story towers. It's delightfully beachy outside, where Marco's crescent of sand reaches its widest, yet the interior is elegant, with many shops and restaurants, a polished marble lobby, and large, plush rooms with good-to-exceptional water views. The stand-alone spa is massive and with ultrapampering services. Kids love the zero-entry rock waterfalls pool with slides. The hotel's golf course is 10 minutes away by tram. **Pros:** terrific beach; top-notch amenities; great spa. **Cons:** huge size; lots of convention business; paid parking across the street in uncovered lot. *400 S. Collier Blvd. 239/394–2511 or 800/438–4373 www.marcoislandmarriott.com 664 rooms, 63 suites In-room: a/c, safe, refrigerator, Internet. In-hotel: 6 restaurants, bars, golf course, tennis courts, pools, gym, spa, beachfront, water sports, bicycles, children's programs (ages 5–12), laundry service, Internet terminal, Wi-Fi hotspot, parking (paid) AE, DC, MC, V.*

$$$$ **Olde Marco Island Inn & Suites.** This Victorian with tin roofs and royal-blue shutters and awnings used to be the only place to stay on the island. Lodging back then was in the circa-1883 historic building that now holds the restaurant; today guests stay in a much newer, more modern section. It's in the heart of Old Marco and part of a shopping complex that struggled for a while but seems to be picking up again. The large one- and two-bedroom tiled suites with screened lanais are ideal for families. The number of available rooms changes according to owners placing or removing their units from the rental program. **Pros:** quiet part of the island; modern and upscale facilities; fine restaurants. **Cons:** not on the beach; part of a shopping center. *100 Palm St., 239/394–3131 or 877/475–3466 www.oldemarcoinn.com 51 suites, 6 penthouses In-room: a/c, kitchen (some), Internet. In-hotel: 3 restaurants, bar, pool, Internet terminal, Wi-Fi hotspot AE, D, DC, MC, V.*

Palm Beach and the Treasure Coast

10

WORD OF MOUTH

"If you really want to be close to restaurants and shops in the Palm Beach area, check out the Marriott in Delray Beach or even the adjacent Residence Inn by Marriott . . . about 30 minutes south of Palm beach."

—rattravlers

WELCOME TO PALM BEACH AND THE TREASURE COAST

TOP REASONS TO GO

★ **Beautiful Beaches:** From Jupiter's sandy shoreline, where leashed dogs are welcome, to the broad stretches of sand in Delray Beach and Boca Raton, swimmers, sunbathers, and surfers—and sea turtles looking for a place to hatch their eggs—all find happiness.

★ **Exquisite Resorts:** The Ritz-Carlton and the Four Seasons continue to sparkle with service fit for royalty. Two historic gems—the Breakers in Palm Beach and the Boca Raton Resort—perpetually draw the rich, the famous, and anyone else who can afford the luxury.

★ **Horse Around:** Wellington, with its jumping events and its popular polo season, is often called the winter equestrian capital of the world.

★ **Have a Reel Good Time:** From Lake Okeechobee, a great place to catch bass and perch, to the Atlantic Ocean, teeming with kingfish, sailfish, dolphinfish, and wahoos, anglers will find the waters here a treasure chest.

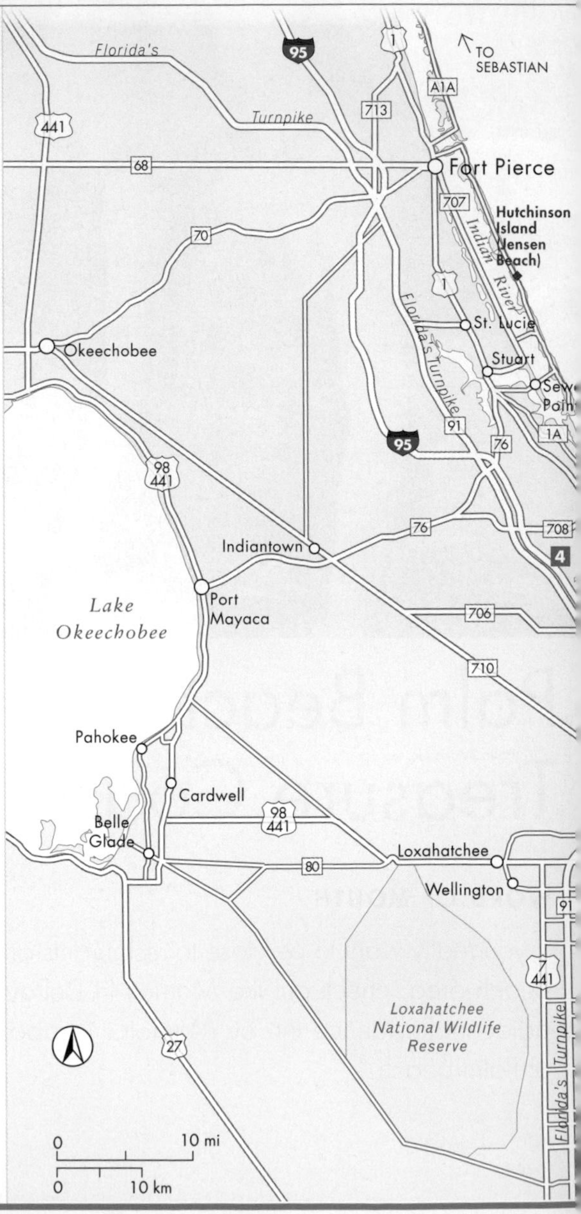

Wellington.

GETTING ORIENTED

This South Florida region extends 120 mi from Sebastian to Boca Raton. The golden stretch of the Atlantic from Palm Beach southward defines old-world glamour and new age sophistication. North of Palm Beach, you'll uncover the comparatively undeveloped Treasure Coast, where towns and wide-open spaces along the road await your discovery. Altogether, there's a delightful disparity, from Palm Beach, pulsing fast with old-money wealth, to low-key Hutchinson Island and Manalapan. The burgeoning equestrian community of Wellington lies 10 mi west of Palm Beach. It is the site of much of the county's new development.

1 Palm Beach. With Gatsby-era architecture, stone-and-stucco estates, extravagant landscaping, and highbrow shops, Palm Beach is a must-see for travelers to the area. Plan to spend some time on Worth Avenue, also called the Mink Mile, a collection of more than 200 chic shops, and Whitehall, once the winter retreat for Henry Flagler, Palm Beach's founder.

2 West Palm Beach. Bustling with its own affluent identity, West Palm Beach has much to offer. Palm Beach–style homes line lovely Flagler Drive, and golf courses are abundant. Culture fans have plenty to cheer about, from the Kravis Center for the Performing Arts, to the Norton Museum of Art and the Armory Arts Center. Kids will love the Palm Beach Zoo.

3 South to Boca Raton. The territory from Palm Beach south to Boca Raton defines old-world glamour and new age sophistication. Delray Beach boasts a lively downtown, with galleries, shops, and restaurants. To the west are the Morikami Japanese Gardens and the headquarters of the American Orchid Society. Boca Raton's Mizner Park has tony boutiques, restaurants, and the Boca Raton Museum of Art.

4 Treasure Coast. Much of the shoreline north of Palm Beach remains blissfully undeveloped. Along the coast, the broad tidal lagoon separates barrier islands from the mainland.

ATLANTIC OCEAN
Jupiter Island
Hobe Sound
Tequesta
Jupiter
1A
Juno Beach
Singer Island
Palm Beach Gardens
Palm Beach Shores
Riviera Beach
1
West Palm Beach
1
Palm Beach
2
1A
Lake Worth
South Palm Beach
Manalapan
Boynton Beach
95
3
Gulf Stream
Delray Beach
Highland Beach
1A
Boca Raton
1

Worth Avenue.

PALM BEACH AND THE TREASURE COAST PLANNER

When to Go

The weather is optimal from November through May, but the trade-off is that roadways and facilities are more crowded and prices higher. In summer it helps to have a tolerance for heat, humidity, and afternoon downpours. Hurricane season runs from June through November, not necessarily a bad time for a trip here as there's always plenty of warning before the big storms. For the best lodging rates consider summer months or the early weeks of December. Make sure to bring insect repellent for outdoor activities.

Specialty Tours

DivaDuck Tours (✉ *Rosemary Ave. and Hibiscus St.* ☎ *561/844–4186* 🌐 *www.divaduck.com*) runs 75-minute amphibious tours of West Palm Beach/Palm Beach in and out of the water. Cruises run two or three times a day for $25.

Alligator.

Getting Here

The best place to fly into is **Palm Beach International Airport** (*PBI* ☎ *561/471–7420*). For a cab, call **Palm Beach Transportation** (☎ *561/689–4222*), the hotline for the Yellow cab company. **Tri-Rail Commuter Bus Service** (☎ *800/874–7245*), the commuter rail system, provides taxi and limousine service. For either, the lowest fares are $2.50 per mile, with the meter starting at $2.50. Tri-Rail has 18 stops altogether between West Palm Beach and Miami, where tickets can be purchased. The one-way fare is $5.50. The city's bus service, **Palm Tran** (☎ *561/841–4200*), runs routes 44 and 40 from the airport to Tri-Rail's nearby Palm Beach airport station daily. **Amtrak** (☎ *800/872–7245* 🌐 *www.amtrak.com*) connects West Palm Beach with cities along Florida's east coast and the northeast daily.

Getting Around

Interstate 95 runs north–south, linking West Palm Beach with Fort Lauderdale and Miami to the south and with Daytona, Jacksonville, and the rest of the Atlantic Coast to the north. Florida's turnpike runs from Miami north through West Palm Beach before angling northwest to reach Orlando. U.S. 1 threads north–south along the coast, connecting most coastal communities, whereas the more scenic Route A1A ventures out onto the barrier islands. Interstate 95 runs parallel to U.S. 1 but a few miles inland.

About the Restaurants

Numerous elegant establishments offer upscale Continental and contemporary fare, but the area also teems with casual waterfront spots serving affordable burgers and fresh seafood feasts. Grouper, fried or blackened, is especially popular here, along with the ubiquitous shrimp. An hour's drive west of the coast, around Lake Okeechobee, dine on catfish panfried to perfection and so fresh it seems barely out of the water. Early-bird menus, a Florida hallmark, typically entice the budget-minded with several dinner entrées at reduced prices offered during certain hours, usually before 5 or 6.

About the Hotels

Palm Beach has a number of smaller hotels in addition to the famous Breakers. Lower-priced hotels and motels can be found in West Palm Beach and Lake Worth. To the south, the coastal town of Manalapan has the Ritz-Carlton, Palm Beach; and the posh Boca Raton Resort & Club is near the beach in Boca Raton. To the north in suburban Palm Beach Gardens is the PGA National Resort & Spa. To the west, small towns near Lake Okeechobee offer country-inn accommodations.

Assume that hotels operate on the European Plan (EP, no meals), unless we specify that they use the Breakfast Plan (BP, with full breakfast), Continental Plan (CP, Continental breakfast), Full American Plan (FAP, all meals), or Modified American Plan (MAP, breakfast and dinner), or are all-inclusive (AI, all meals and most activities).

WHAT IT COSTS

	¢	$	$$	$$$	$$$$
Restaurants	under $10	$10–$15	$15–$20	$20–$30	over $30
Hotels	under $80	$80–$100	$100–$140	$140–$220	over $220

Restaurant prices are per person for a main course at dinner. Hotel prices are for a standard double room, excluding 6½% sales tax (more in some counties) and 1%–4% tourist tax.

Inland Sights

Want to get away from the water? Head 40 mi west of West Palm Beach on to Lake Okeechobee for some wildlife viewing, bird-watching, and fishing.

You are likely to see alligators in the tall grass along the shore, as well as birds, including herons, ibises, and bald eagles, which have made a comeback in the area. A 110-mi trail encircles Lake Okeechobee atop the 34-foot Herbert Hoover Dike. On the lake you'll spot happy anglers hooked on some of the best bass fishing in North America. There are 40 species of fish in "Lake O," including largemouth bass, bluegill, Okeechobee catfish, and speckled perch.

Since the **Okee-Tantie Recreation Area** (✉ *10430 Rte. 78 W., Okeechobee* ☎ *863/763–2622*) has direct lake access, it's a popular fishing outpost, with two public boat ramps, fish-cleaning stations, and a bait shop that stocks groceries. There are also picnic areas and a restaurant.

Getting Here: The best way to drive here from West Palm is to go west on Southern Boulevard from Interstate 95 past the cut-off road to Lion Country Safari. From there, the boulevard is designated U.S. 98/441.

10

PALM BEACH AND TREASURE COAST BEACHES

While not as white and fine as the shores on Florida's west coast, the beaches here provide good stomping grounds for hikers, well-guarded waters for swimmers, decent waves for surfers, and plenty of opportunities for sand-castle building and shell collecting.

Miles of sandy shoreline can be found here beside gorgeous blue-green waters you won't find farther north. The average year-round water temperature is 74°F, much warmer than Southern California beaches that average a comparatively chilly 62°F.

Humans aren't alone in finding the shores inviting. Migratory birds flock to the beaches, too, as do sea turtles, who come between May and August to lay their eggs in the sand. Locally organized watches take small groups out at night to observe mother turtles as they waddle onto shore, dig holes with their flippers and deposit their golf-ball-sized eggs into the sand. Hatchlings emerge about 45 days later.

WHEN TO GO

Palm Beach and Treasure Coast beaches are warm, clear, and sparkling all year long, but the best time to get in the water is between December and March. The shorelines are often more crowded then, but you don't have to worry about jellyfish or sea lice when you take a dip. Sea lice can cause welts, blisters, and rashes. The crowds thin out during summer and fall months, which is inviting, but jellyfish and sea lice can be a problem then.

PALM BEACH AND TREASURE COAST'S BEST BEACHES

DELRAY

If you're looking for a place to see and be seen, head for Delray's wide expanse of sand, which stretches 2 mi, half of it supervised by lifeguards. Reefs off the coast are popular with divers, as is a sunken Spanish galleon less than ½ mi offshore from the Seagate Club on the south end of the beach. **Pros:** good for swimmers and sunbathers; bars and restaurants across the street; cabanas and catamarans available for rent. **Cons:** often a long walk to the public restrooms.

JOHN D. MACARTHUR STATE PARK

If getting far from the madding crowd is your goal, John D. MacArthur State Park on the north end of Singer Island is a good choice. You will find a great place for snorkeling, kayaking, bird-watching, and fishing. Part of the beach was once dedicated to topless bathers, but that is no longer the case. **Pros:** guides to local flora and fauna are available; a good place to spot sea turtles. **Cons:** beach is a long walk from the parking lot.

JUNO BEACH

Juno Beach sports a 990-foot pier and a bait shop for those who like to spend their morning fishing. But the shoreline itself is a favorite for families with kids who drag along sand toys, build castles, and hunt for shells. **Pros:** concession stand and a bait shop. **Cons:** beach isn't as wide as others.

RED REEF PARK

Looking for a great place to snorkel? This Boca Raton beach is just the ticket, and it doesn't matter if you're a beginner or a pro. The reef is only about 50 feet off shore. Expect to see tropical fish and maybe even a manatee or two. **Pros:** the park's showers and bathrooms are kept clean and there's a playground for kids. **Cons:** if you go at low tide, you're not going to see as many tropical fish.

STUART BEACH

When the waves robustly roll in at Stuart Beach, the surfers are rolling in, too. Beginning surfers are especially keen on Stuart Beach because of its ever-vigilant lifeguards, while pros to the sport like the challenges the choppy waters here bring. Beachgoers with kids like the snack bar known for its chicken fingers, and for those who like a side of museum musing with their day in the sun, there's an impressive collection of antique cars at a museum just steps from the beach. **Pros:** parking is easy to find, and there are three boardwalks for easy access to the beach. **Cons:** sand and surf can be rocky.

Updated by Mary Thurwachter

This golden stretch of Atlantic coast resists categorization, and for good reason. The territory from Palm Beach south to Boca Raton defines old-world glamour and new age sophistication.

North of Palm Beach you'll uncover the comparatively undeveloped Treasure Coast—liberally sprinkled with coastal gems—where towns and wide-open spaces along the road await your discovery. Altogether, there's a delightful disparity, from Palm Beach, pulsing fast with plenty of old-money wealth, to low-key Hutchinson Island and Manalapan. Seductive as the beach scene interspersed with eclectic dining options can be, you should also take advantage of flourishing commitments to historic preservation and the arts, as town after town yields intriguing museums, galleries, theaters, and gardens.

Palm Beach, with Gatsby-era architecture, stone-and-stucco estates, extravagant landscaping, and highbrow shops, can reign as the focal point for your sojourn any time of year. From Palm Beach, head off in any of three directions: south via the Gold Coast toward Boca Raton along an especially scenic route known as A1A, back to the mainland and north to the barrier-island treasures of the Treasure Coast, or west for more rustic inland activities such as bass fishing and biking on the dikes around Lake Okeechobee.

PALM BEACH

Long reigning as the place where the crème de la crème go to shake off winter's chill, Palm Beach continues to be a seasonal hotbed of platinum-grade consumption. Other towns like Jupiter Island may rank higher on the per-capita-wealth meter, but there's no competing with the historic social supremacy of Palm Beach. It has been the winter address for heirs of the iconic Rockefeller, Vanderbilt, Colgate, Post, Kellogg, and Kennedy families. Even newer power brokers, with names like Kravis, Peltz, and Trump, are made to understand that strict laws govern everything from building to landscaping, and not so much as a pool awning gets added without a town council nod. If Palm Beach were to fly a flag, it's been observed, there might be three interlocking Cs, standing not only for Cartier, Chanel, and Christian Dior but also for clean, civil, and capricious. Only three bridges allow access to the island, and huge tour buses are a no-no.

To learn who's who in Palm Beach, it helps to pick up a copy of the *Palm Beach Daily News*—locals call it the Shiny Sheet because its high-quality paper avoids smudging society hands or Pratesi linens—for, as it is said, to be mentioned in the Shiny Sheet is to be Palm Beach. All this fabled ambience started with Henry Morrison Flagler, Florida's premier developer, and cofounder, along with John D. Rockefeller, of Standard Oil. No sooner did Flagler bring the railroad to Florida in the 1890s than he erected the famed Royal Poinciana and Breakers hotels. Rail access sent real-estate prices soaring, and ever since, princely sums have been forked over for personal stationery engraved with 33480, the ZIP code of Palm Beach. To provide Palm Beach with servants and other workers, Flagler also developed an off-island community a mile or so west. West Palm Beach now bustles with its own affluent identity.

Setting the tone in this town of unparalleled Florida opulence is the ornate architectural work of Addison Mizner, who began designing homes and public buildings here in the 1920s and whose Moorish-Gothic style has influenced virtually all community landmarks. Thanks to Mizner and his lasting influence, Palm Beach remains a playground of the rich, famous, and discerning.

GETTING HERE AND AROUND

Palm Beach is 78 mi north of Miami. To access Palm Beach off Interstate 95, exit east at Southern Boulevard, Belvedere Road, or Okeechobee Boulevard. The city's Palm Tran buses run between Worth Avenue and Royal Palm Way in Palm Beach and major areas of West Palm Beach and require exact change. Regular fares are $1.50.

For a taste of what it's like to jockey for position in this status-conscious town, stake out a parking place on Worth Avenue or parallel residential streets, and squeeze in among the Mercedeses, Rolls-Royces, and Bentleys. Between admiring your excellent parking skills and feeling car-struck at the surrounding fine specimens of automobile, be sure to note the PARKING BY PERMIT ONLY and TWO-HOUR parking signs, as a $25 parking ticket might take the shine off your spot. **■ TIP→ The best course for a half-day visit is to valet-park at the parking deck next to Saks Fifth Avenue.** Away from downtown, along County Road and Ocean Boulevard (the shore road, also designated as Route A1A), are Palm Beach's other defining landmarks: Mediterranean-style residences, some built of coral rock, that are nothing short of palatial, topped by barrel-tile roofs and often fronted by 10-foot ficus and sea grape hedges. The low wall that separates the dune-top shore road from the sea hides shoreline that varies in many places from expansive to eroded. Here and there, where the strand deepens, homes are built directly on the beach.

ESSENTIALS

Transportation Contact Palm Tran (☎ *561/841–4287*).

Visitor Information Town of Palm Beach Chamber of Commerce (✉ *400 Royal Palm Way, Suite 106, Palm Beach* ☎ *561/655–3282*).

10

A GOOD TOUR: PALM BEACH

Start at the **Henry Morrison Flagler Museum**—a 55-room villa Flagler built for his third wife—to get your first look at the eye-popping opulence of the Gilded Age, which defined Palm Beach. From here, turn left on Cocoanut Row, and right onto Royal Poinciana Way—outdoor cafés on the left and the Breakers golf course to your right—then right onto North County Road. Head south and look for the long, stately driveway on the left that leads to the **Breakers**, built by Flagler in the style of an Italian Renaissance palace. Parking costs $20, and there are many valets under the porte cochere. Have your parking ticket validated while lunching at the Breakers and the parking fee is waived.

Continue south on South County Road to **Bethesda-by-the-Sea**, a Spanish Gothic Episcopal church. Keep driving south on South County Road until you reach Royal Palm Way; turn right, and drive a few blocks until you see the **Society of the Four Arts**. Turn left back onto Royal Palm Way and drive until it ends at the ocean, and turn right onto Ocean Boulevard until you reach famed **Worth Avenue** on the right, which is a one-way street running east to west. Park, stroll, and ogle designer goods. Then drive south back on Ocean Boulevard to peek at magnificent estates, including **El Solano**, designed by Addison Mizner, and the fabled **Mar-a-Lago**, a Mediterranean-revival palace with a distinctive 75-foot tower, now owned by Donald Trump and operating as a private club. At this point, if you want some sun and fresh air, continue south on South County Road until you reach **Phipps Ocean Park** and its stretch of beach, or head back toward town along South Ocean Boulevard to the popular Mid-Town Beach at the east end of Worth Avenue.

TIMING

You'll need half a day, minimum, for these sights. A few shops and attractions are closed Sunday and May through October. From November through April, often heavy traffic gets worse as the day wears on, so plan to explore in the morning.

EXPLORING

Numbers in the margin correspond to the Palm Beach and West Palm Beach map.

TOP ATTRACTIONS

3 **Bethesda-by-the-Sea.** Donald Trump and his wife Melania were married here in 2005, but this Spanish Gothic Episcopal church had a claim to fame upon its creation in 1925: it was built by the first Protestant congregation in southeast Florida. Guided tours follow 11 AM services on the second and fourth Sunday of the month. Adjacent are the formal, ornamental **Cluett Memorial Gardens.** ✉ *141 S. County Rd.* ☎ *561/655–4554* 🌐 *www.bbts.org* 🎫 *Free* ⏲ *Church and gardens daily 8–5.*

2 **The Breakers.** Built by Henry Flagler in 1896 and rebuilt by his descendants after a 1925 fire, this magnificent Italian Renaissance–style resort helped launch Florida tourism with its Gilded Age opulence, attracting influential, wealthy Northerners to the state. The hotel, still owned

Fodor's Choice ★

Draped in European elegance, The Breakers in Palm Beach sits on 140 acres along the oceanfront.

by Flagler's heirs, is a must-see even if you aren't staying here. Walk through the 200-foot-long lobby, which has soaring arched ceilings painted by 72 Italian artisans and hung with crystal chandeliers, and the ornate Florentine Dining Room is decorated with 15th-century Flemish tapestries. ✉ *1 S. County Rd.* ☎ *561/655–6611* 🌐 *www.thebreakers.com.*

❶ Fodor's Choice ★ **Henry Morrison Flagler Museum.** The opulence of Florida's Gilded Age lives on at Whitehall, the palatial 55-room "marble palace" Henry Flagler commissioned in 1901 for his third wife, Mary Lily Kenan. Architects John Carrère and Thomas Hastings were instructed to create the finest home imaginable—and they outdid themselves. Whitehall rivals the grandeur of European palaces and has an entrance hall with a baroque ceiling similar to Louis XIV's Versailles. Here you'll see original furnishings; a hidden staircase Flagler used to sneak from his bedroom to the billiards room; an art collection; a 1,200-pipe organ; and Florida East Coast Railway exhibits, along with Flagler's personal railcar, the *Rambler,* showcased in an 8,000-square-foot beaux arts–style pavilion behind the mansion. Tours take about an hour and are offered at frequent intervals. The café, open after Thanksgiving through mid-April, offers snacks and afternoon tea. ✉ *1 Whitehall Way* ☎ *561/655–2833* 🌐 *www.flagler.org* 🎟 *$18* ⏲ *Tues.–Sat. 10–5, Sun. noon–5.*

❺ ★ **Worth Avenue.** Called the Avenue by Palm Beachers, this ¼-mi-long street is synonymous with exclusive shopping. Nostalgia lovers recall an era when faces or names served as charge cards, purchases were delivered home before customers returned from lunch, and bills were sent directly to private accountants. Times have changed, but a stroll

Ann Norton Sculpture Gardens **10**
Armory Art Center **12**
Bethesda-by-the-Sea **3**
The Breakers **2**
Currie Park **11**
El Solano **6**
Henry Morrison Flagler Museum **1**
Lion Country Safari **18**
Mar-a-Lago **7**
Mounts Botanical Gardens **19**
National Croquet Center **15**
Norton Museum of Art **9**
Okeeheelee Nature Center . **17**
Palm Beach Zoo **13**
Phipps Ocean Park **8**
Pine Jog Environmental Education Center **16**
Society of the Four Arts **4**
South Florida Science Museum **14**
Worth Avenue ... **5**

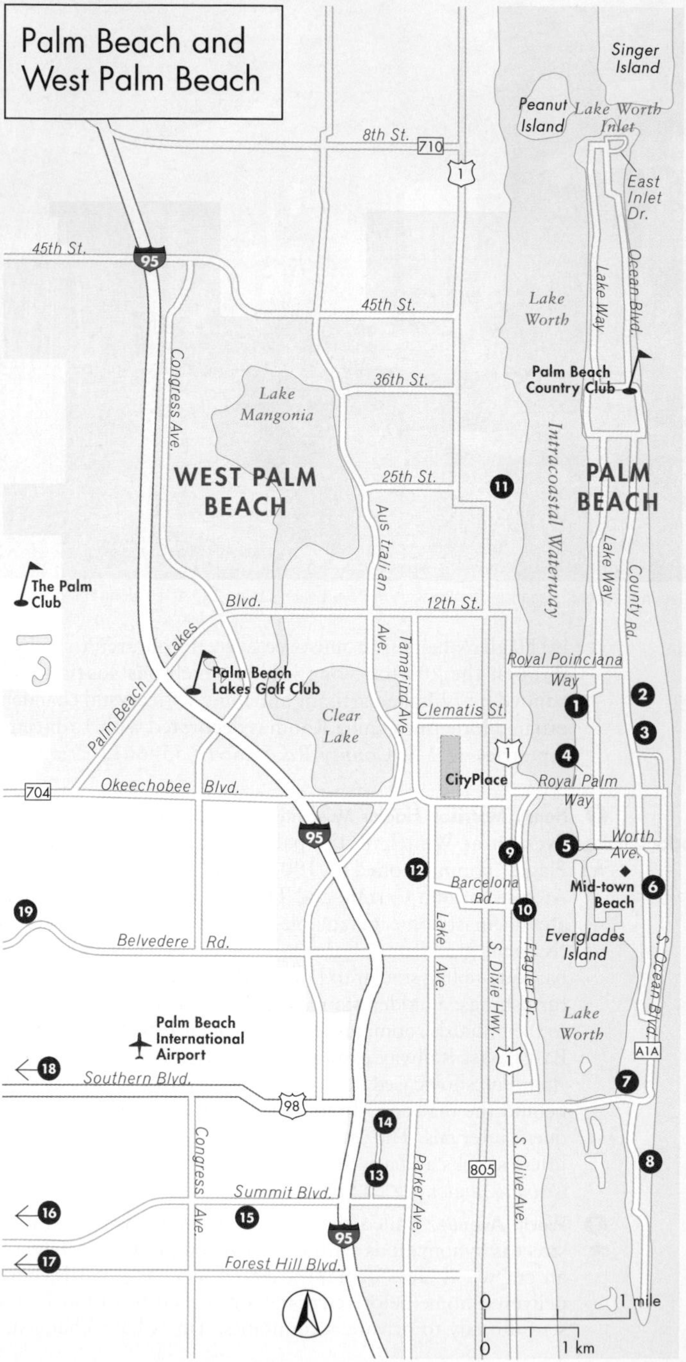

amid the Moorish architecture of its shops offers a tantalizing taste of the island's ongoing commitment to elegant consumerism. Explore the labyrinth of eight pedestrian vias, on both sides of Worth Avenue, that wind past boutiques, tiny plazas, bubbling fountains, and the bougainvillea-festooned wrought-iron balconies of 2nd-floor apartments. ✉ *Between Cocoanut Row and S. Ocean Blvd.*

WORTH NOTING

6 **El Solano.** No Palm Beach mansion better represents the town's luminous legacy than the Spanish-style home built by Addison Mizner as his own residence in 1925. Mizner later sold El Solano to Harold Vanderbilt, and the property was long a favorite among socialites for parties and photo shoots. Vanderbilt held many a gala fund-raiser here. Beatle John Lennon and his wife, Yoko Ono, bought it less than a year before Lennon's death. It's still privately owned and not open to the public. ✉ *721 S. County Rd.*

7 **Mar-a-Lago.** Breakfast-food heiress Marjorie Merriweather Post commissioned a Hollywood set designer to create Ocean Boulevard's famed Mar-a-Lago, a 118-room, 110,000-square-foot Mediterranean-revival palace. Its 75-foot Italianate tower is visible from most areas of Palm Beach and from across the Intracoastal Waterway in West Palm Beach. Owner Donald Trump has turned it into a private membership club. ✉ *1100 S. Ocean Blvd.* ☎ *561/832–2600* 🌐 *www.maralagoclub.com.*

8 **Phipps Ocean Park.** In addition to the shoreline, tennis courts, picnic tables, and grills, this park has a Palm Beach County landmark in the **Little Red Schoolhouse.** Dating from 1886, it served as the first schoolhouse in what was then Dade County. No alcoholic beverages are permitted in the park. ✉ *2185 S. Ocean Blvd.* ☎ *561/838–5400* 🎟 *Free* ⏲ *Daily dawn–dusk.*

4 **Society of the Four Arts.** Despite widespread misconceptions of members-only exclusivity, this privately endowed institution—founded in 1936 to encourage appreciation of art, music, drama, and literature—is funded for public enjoyment. A gallery building—designed by Addison Mizner, of course—artfully melds an exhibition hall, library, and the Philip Hulitar Sculpture Garden, which underwent a major renovation in 2006. Open from about Thanksgiving to Easter, the museum's programs are extensive, and there's ample free parking. In addition to showcasing traveling art exhibitions, the museum offers films, lectures, workshops, and concerts. ✉ 2 *Four Arts Plaza* ☎ *561/655–7226* 🌐 *www.fourarts.org* 🎟 *Program admission varies* ⏲ *Galleries Dec.–mid-Apr., Mon.–Sat. 10–5, Sun. 2–5; library, weekdays 10–5, Sat. 10–1; gardens 10–5 daily.*

SPORTS AND THE OUTDOORS

BIKING

Bicycling is a great way to get a closer look at Palm Beach. Only 14 mi long, ½ mi wide, flat as the top of a billiard table, and just as green, it's a perfect biking place. The palm-fringed **Lake Trail** (✉ *Parallel to Lake Way*) skirts the backyards of many palatial mansions and the edge of Lake Worth. The trail starts at the Society of the Four Arts,

Worth Avenue is the place in Palm Beach for high-end shopping, from international boutiques to art galleries.

heading north 8 mi to the end and back—just follow the signs. A block from the bike trail, the **Palm Beach Bicycle Trail Shop** (✉ *223 Sunrise Ave.* ☎ *561/659–4583* 🌐 *www.palmbeachbicycle.com*) rents by the hour or day. It's open daily.

GOLF

Breakers Hotel Golf Club (✉ *1 S. County Rd.* ☎ *561/659–8407*) has the historic Ocean Course and the Todd Anderson Golf Academy and is open to members and hotel guests only. A $210 greens fee includes range balls, cart, and bag storage at Breakers West or at the redesigned Ocean Course. The **Town of Palm Beach Golf Club** (✉ *2345 S. Ocean Blvd.* ☎ *561/547–0598*) has 18 holes, including six on the Atlantic and three on the inland waterway; greens fee $45 riding, $32 to walk. The course was recently redesigned by Raymond Floyd and is a gem of a short-game course.

SHOPPING

★ One of the world's premier showcases for high-quality shopping, **Worth Avenue** runs ¼ mi east–west across Palm Beach, from the beach to Lake Worth. The street has more than 250 shops (more than 40 of them sell jewelry), and many upscale chain stores (Gucci, Hermès, Pucci, Saks Fifth Avenue, Neiman Marcus, Louis Vuitton, Emanuel Ungaro, Chanel, Dior, Cartier, Tiffany, and Tourneau) are represented—their merchandise appealing to the discerning tastes of the Palm Beach clientele. The six blocks of **South County Road** north of Worth Avenue have interesting (and somewhat less expensive) stores. For specialty items (out-of-town newspapers, health foods, and books), try the shops along the north side of **Royal Poinciana Way.** Most stores are closed on Sunday, and many go on hiatus in summer.

The thrift store **Church Mouse** (✉ *374 S. County Rd.* ☎ *561/659–2154*) is where many high-end resale boutique owners grab their merchandise. **Déjà Vu** (✉ *Via Testa, 219 Royal Poinciana Way* ☎ *561/833–6624*) could be the resale house of Chanel, as it has so many gently used, top-quality pieces. There's no digging through piles here; clothes are in impeccable condition and are well organized.

Giorgio's (✉ *230 Worth Ave.* ☎ *561/655–2446*) is over-the-top indulgence, with 50 colors of silk and cashmere sweaters and 22 colors of ostrich and alligator adorning everything from bags to bicycles.

Jewelry is very important in Palm Beach, and for more than 100 years **Greenleaf & Crosby** (✉ *236 Worth Ave.* ☎ *561/655–5850*) has had a diverse selection that includes investment pieces. **Spring Flowers** (✉ *337 Worth Ave.* ☎ *561/832–0131*) has beautiful children's clothing. Little ones start with a newborn gown set by Kissy Kissy or Petit Bateau and grow into fashions by Cacharel and Lili Gaufrette.

Holding court for more than 60 years, **Van Cleef & Arpels** (✉ *202 Worth Ave.* ☎ *561/655–6767*) is where legendary members of Palm Beach society shop for tiaras and formal jewels.

NIGHTLIFE AND THE ARTS

NIGHTLIFE

Palm Beach is teeming with restaurants that turn into late-night hot spots, plus hotel lobby bars perfect for tête-à-têtes. Popular for lunch and dinner, **Cucina Dell'Arte** (✉ *257 Royal Poinciana Way* ☎ *561/655–0770*) later becomes the in place for the younger and trendy set. The old guard gathers at the **Leopard Lounge** (✉ *Chesterfield Hotel, 363 Cocoanut Row* ☎ *561/659–5800*) for live music during cocktail hour and later to dance until the wee hours every night of the year. Thursday night happy hours spiked by creatively named cocktails and live jazz draw a local crowd to the lobby lounge and outdoor patio of the **Brazilian Court** (✉ *301 Australian Ave.* ☎ *561/655–7740*).

THE ARTS

Society of the Four Arts (✉ *2 Four Arts Plaza* ☎ *561/655–7226*) has concerts, lectures, and films November through March.

WHERE TO EAT

$$$ ITALIAN ✕ **Amici.** The town's premier celebrity-magnet bistro is still a crowd pleaser. When it moved across the street and down the block from its original location, the Palm Beach crowd followed. The northern Italian menu highlights house specialties such as rigatoni with spicy tomato sauce and roasted eggplant, potato gnocchi, grilled veal chops, risottos, and pizzas from a wood-burning oven. There are nightly pasta and fresh fish specials as well. To avoid the crowds, stop by for a late lunch or early dinner. ✉ *375 S. County Rd.* ☎ *561/832–0201* 🌐 *www.amicipalmbeach.com* *Reservations essential* 💳 *AE, DC, MC, V.*

$$$$ ITALIAN **Bice Ristorante**. The bougainvillea-laden trellises set the scene at the main entrance on Peruvian Way. Weather permitting, many patrons prefer to dine on the outdoor terrace on the narrow pedestrian walkway. A favorite of Palm Beach society and Hollywood celebs, both the restaurant and the bar become packed and noisy during high season. The aroma of basil, chives, and oregano fills the air as waiters carry out home-baked focaccia to accompany delectable dishes such as seafood risotto, veal chops, and duck breast sautéed in mushroom sauce with venison-truffle ravioli. ✉ *313½ Worth Ave.* ☎ *561/835–1600* *Reservations essential* ▭ *AE, D, DC, MC, V.*

$$$$ FRENCH Fodor's Choice ★ **Café Boulud**. Celebrated chef Daniel Boulud opened his outpost of New York's Café Boulud in the Brazilian Court hotel. The warm and welcoming French-American venue is casual yet elegant, with a palette of honey, gold, and citron. Plenty of natural light spills through arched glass doors opening to a lush courtyard. Lunch and dinner entrées on Boulud's signature four-muse menu include classic French, seasonal, vegetarian, and a rotating selection of international dishes. The lounge, with its illuminated amber glass bar, is the perfect perch to take in the jet-set crowd that comes for a hint of the south of France in South Florida. A DJ plays on Saturday nights. ✉ *Brazilian Court, 301 Australian Ave.* ☎ *561/655–6060* *www.cafeboulud.com* *Reservations essential* ▭ *AE, DC, MC, V.*

$$$$ ECLECTIC **Café L'Europe**. Even after 25 years, the favorite lunch spot of society's movers and shakers remains a regular stop on foodie itineraries. The management pays close attention to service and consistency, a big reason for its longevity. Best sellers include rack of lamb, Dover sole, and Wiener schnitzel, along with such inspired creations as crispy sweetbreads with poached pears and mustard sauce. Depending on your mood, the champagne-caviar bar can serve up appetizers or desserts. The place has an extensive wine list. A pianist plays nightly from 7 to 11 and a quartet plays dance music Friday and Saturday nights until 1 AM. ✉ *331 S. County Rd.* ☎ *561/655–4020* *www.cafeleurope.com* ▭ *AE, DC, MC, V* *No lunch May–Oct. Closed Mon.*

$$$$ FRENCH Fodor's Choice ★ **Chez Jean-Pierre**. With walls adorned with Dalí- and Picasso-like art, this is where the Palm Beach old guard likes to let down its guard, all the while partaking of sumptuous French cuisine and an impressive wine list. Forget calorie or cholesterol concerns and indulge in scrambled eggs with caviar or homemade duck foie gras, along with desserts like hazelnut soufflé or profiteroles au chocolat. Waiters are friendly and very attentive. Jackets are not required, although many men wear them. ✉ *132 N. County Rd.* ☎ *561/833–1171* *Reservations essential* ▭ *AE, DC, MC, V* *Closed Sun. No lunch.*

$ AMERICAN **Hamburger Heaven**. A favorite with locals since 1945, the quintessential diner with horseshoe-shaped counter as well as booths and tables is loud and casual and has some of the best burgers on the island. Fresh salads, homemade pastries, and daily soup and hot-plate specials featuring comfort foods like meat loaf and chicken potpie are also available. During the week, it's a popular lunch stop for working stiffs. The staff is friendly and efficient. ✉ *314 S. County Rd.* ☎ *561/655–5277* ▭ *MC, V* *Closed Sun.*

$$ PIZZA ✕ **Pizza Al Fresco.** The secret-garden setting is the secret to the success of this popular European-style pizzeria, where you can dine under a canopy of century-old banyans in a charming courtyard. Specialties are 12-inch hand-tossed brick-oven pizzas with such interesting toppings as prosciutto, arugula, and caviar. There's even a dessert pizza topped with Nutella. Piping-hot calzones, salads, and sandwiches round out the selection. Look for the grave markers of Addison Mizner's beloved pet monkey, Johnnie Brown, and Rose Sachs's dog Laddie (she and husband Morton bought Mizner's villa and lived there 47 years) next to the patio. Delivery is available—by limo, of course. This bistro is dog-friendly. ✉ *14 Via Mizner, at Worth Ave.* ☎ *561/832–0032* 🌐 *www.pizzaalfresco.com* ▭ *AE, MC, V.*

$$$ AMERICAN ★ ✕ **Ta-boó.** This 60-year-old landmark with peach stucco walls and green shutters attracts Worth Avenue shoppers looking for a two-hour lunch and a dinner crowd ranging from tuxed and sequined theatergoers to polo-shirted vacationers. Entrées include Black Angus dry-aged beef or roast duck. Don't miss Coconut Lust, a signature dessert. Drop in late night during the winter season when the nightly music is playing and you'll probably spot a celebrity or two. ✉ *221 Worth Ave.* ☎ *561/835–3500* 🌐 *www.taboorestaurant.com* ▭ *AE, DC, MC, V.*

$$$ CAFÉ ✕ **Testa's Palm Beach.** Attracting a loyal clientele since 1921, this restaurant is still owned by the Testa family. Lunches range from burgers to crab salad, and dinner specialties include snapper Florentine and jumbo lump-crab cakes. You can dine inside in an intimate pine-paneled room with cozy bar, out back in a gazebo-style room for large groups, or outside at tables with pink tablecloths next to planters of pink hibiscus, with a view of the Breakers in the distance. Don't miss the signature strawberry pie made with fresh Florida berries. ✉ *221 Royal Poinciana Way* ☎ *561/832–0992* 🌐 *www.testasrestaurants.com* ▭ *AE, D, MC, V.*

WHERE TO STAY

$$$$ ★ **Brazilian Court.** A short stroll from Worth Avenue, the yellow-stucco Spanish-style facade and red tile roof, and lobby with cypress ceilings and stone floors, underscore this boutique hotel's Roaring '20s origins. All of the studio and one- and two-bedroom suites have rich limestone baths and showers, wine refrigerators, and personal butler service. Bay windows look out into the impeccably maintained gardens and enchanting flower-filled courtyards. Amenities include a state-of-the-art business center, a hair salon and spa, and Café Boulud, a local outpost from famed restaurateur Daniel Boulud; hotel guests reportedly have a better shot than outsiders at procuring a table. Don't feel like dressing up for a table? There's 24-hour in-room dining by Café Boulud. **Pros:** one of the best restaurants in town; attracts a hip crowd; gorgeous courtyard; close to shopping and not far from the beach; free shuttle to the hotel's sister property on the beach, The Omphoy. **Cons:** fitness center is tiny; small pool. ✉ *301 Australian Ave.* ☎ *561/655–7740* 🌐 *www.thebraziliancourt.com* *80 rooms* *In-room: a/c, refrigerator, Internet, Wi-Fi. In-hotel: restaurant, room service, bar, pool, gym, spa, bicycles, laundry facilities, some pets allowed* ▭ *AE, D, DC, MC, V.*

$$$$ Fodor's Choice ★ **The Breakers**. Dating from 1896 and on the National Register of Historic Places, this Italian Renaissance–style resort, owned by Henry Flagler's heirs, sprawls over 140 oceanfront acres. Cupids frolic at the main Florentine fountain, and majestic frescoes grace hallways leading to restaurants. For added luxury, cabanas come with personal concierge. More than an opulent hotel, the Breakers is a modern resort packed with amenities, from a 20,000-square-foot luxury spa and beach club to clubhouses for the 10 tennis courts and two 18-hole golf courses. One of the most extensive wine collections in the world is housed here, keeping the hotel's three sommeliers busy. **Pros:** fine attention to detail throughout; beautiful room views; top-rate golf and tennis facilities. **Cons:** big price tag. ✉ *1 S. County Rd.* ☎ *561/655–6611 or 888/273–2537* 🌐 *www.thebreakers.com* *540 rooms, 68 suites* *In-room: a/c, Internet, safe, refrigerator (some), Wi-Fi. In-hotel: 9 restaurants, room service, bars, golf courses, tennis courts, pools, gym, spa, beachfront, water sports, children's programs (ages 3–12), Internet terminal, parking (paid)* *AE, D, DC, MC, V.*

$$$$ **The Chesterfield**. Two blocks north of Worth Avenue, the distinctive white-stucco hotel with coral-colored stucco walls and red-and-white-striped awnings offers 54 inviting rooms ranging from small to spacious. All have plush upholstered chairs, paintings, and marble baths. Settle on a leather couch near the cozy library's fireplace and peruse an international newspaper or classic book, or have a cigar in Churchill's, the only public smoking room on the island. Room keys here are brass and maid service is twice a day. A quiet area surrounds a large pool where you can relax, and the Leopard Lounge draws a convivial crowd. **Pros:** turndown service; complimentary beverages in king rooms and suites; elegant rooms; you can open guest-room windows, which is a treat for those who hate air-conditioning **Cons:** small elevator; narrow steps leading to presidential suite. ✉ *363 Cocoanut Row* ☎ *561/659–5800 or 800/243–7871* 🌐 *www.chesterfieldpb.com* *44 rooms, 11 suites* *In-room: a/c, refrigerator (some), safe Internet. In-hotel: restaurant, room service, bar, pool, Internet terminal, parking (free), some pets allowed* *AE, D, DC, MC, V.*

$$$$ **The Colony**. What distinguishes this legendary British colonial–style hotel is that it's only one block from Worth Avenue and one block from a beautiful beach on the Atlantic Ocean. The hotel's lobby and pool area has ornamental plants, fountains, wicker furniture, and billowing white panels reminiscent of South Beach's luxurious hotels. An attentive staff, youthful yet experienced, is buzzing with competence and a desire to please. Guest rooms are decorated in Caribbean-colonial, with sunny yellow walls and dark mahogany desks, and pineapple-carved poster beds grace some rooms. Roomy suites and luxurious two-bedroom villas have laundry facilities and full kitchens. The pool is shaped like the state of Florida, although the panhandle is severely reduced in size. Reserve early for the dinner cabaret shows, which have featured entertainers such as Faith Prince and Andrea Marcovicci. **Pros:** close to shopping; rich history; lots of luxury. **Cons:** elevators are small; price tag is high. ✉ *155 Hammon Ave.* ☎ *561/655–5430 or 800/521–5525* 🌐 *www.thecolonypalmbeach.com* *64 rooms, 16 suites, 3 penthouse suites, 7*

2-bedroom villas with Jacuzzis ☝ *In-room: a/c, safe, refrigerator upon request, Wi-Fi. In-hotel: restaurant, bar, pools, spa, bicycles, Internet terminal, parking (paid) some pets allowed* ▭ *AE, DC, MC, V.*

$$$$ ★ **Four Seasons Resort Palm Beach.** Relaxed elegance is the watchword at this four-story resort, which sits on 6 acres with a delightful beach at the south end of town. Fanlight windows, marble columns, chintz curtains, and swaying palms are serene and inviting. A fabulous new spa opened in 2008, and guest-room bathrooms were remodeled in 2009. Rooms are spacious, with separate seating areas and private balconies; many have ocean views. On weekends, live music accompanies cocktails in the Living Room lounge. Jazz groups perform on some weekends in season. The restaurants are worth sampling, and all three have children's menus. Children eat free (except for room service). **Pros:** outstanding restaurants; all rooms have balconies and ocean views; kids eat free; well-established spa. **Cons:** far from nightlife; pricey. ✉ *2800 S. Ocean Blvd.* ☎ *561/582–2800 or 800/432–2335* 🌐 *www.fourseasons.com* *210 rooms, 13 suites* ☝ *In-room: a/c, safe, Internet. In-hotel: 3 restaurants, room service, bars, tennis courts, pool, gym, spa, beachfront, bicycles, children's programs (ages 3–12), laundry service, some pets allowed, parking (paid)* ▭ *AE, D, DC, MC, V.*

$$$$ **The Omphoy Ocean Resort.** This Zenlike boutique hotel on 3 acres opened in 2009 and is a hit with young and hip travelers. From exotic ebony pillars in the lobby to bronze-infused porcelain tile floors and a lounge area with a row of gongs guests are welcome to bang on, the hotel has a sexy, sophisticated look. Asian-style guest rooms come with private balconies, flat-screen TVs and sleek four-poster beds that are nothing like your grandmother's. **Pros:** Michelle Bernstein restaurant; rooms have ocean views and most have balconies. **Cons:** the infinity pool is surrounded by a parking lot and you have to walk through or around the hotel to get to the beach from it. ✉ *2842 S. Ocean Blvd.* ☎ *561/540–6440 or 888/344–4321* 🌐 *www.omphoy.com* *134 rooms, 10 suites* ☝ *In-room: a/c, safe, Wi-Fi. In-hotel: 2 restaurants, room service, bars, pool, gym, spa, beachfront, laundry service, Internet terminal, parking (paid),* some pets allowed ▭ *AE, D, DC, MC, V.*

WEST PALM BEACH

Across the Intracoastal Waterway from Palm Beach.

Long considered Palm Beach's less-privileged stepsister, sprawling West Palm has evolved into an economically vibrant destination of its own, ranking as the cultural, entertainment, and business center of the entire county and territory to the north. High-rise buildings like the mammoth Palm Beach County Judicial Center and Courthouse and the State Administrative Building underscore the breadth of the city's governmental and corporate activity. The glittering Kravis Center for the Performing Arts is Palm Beach County's principal entertainment venue.

GETTING HERE AND AROUND

West Palm Beach is across the Intracoastal Waterway from Palm Beach. The city's Palm Tran buses run between Worth Avenue and Royal Palm Way in Palm Beach and major areas of West Palm Beach and require

The Armory Art Center in West Palm Beach helps students of all ages create works or art in various media.

exact change. Regular fares are $1.50. Alternatively, share space with local lawyers and shoppers on the free and frequent Molly's Trolleys, which makes continuous loops down Clematis Street, the city's main street, and through CityPlace, a shopping-restaurant-theater district. Hop on and off at any of the seven stops. The trolleys run Sunday to Wednesday 11–9 and Thursday to Saturday 11–11.

ESSENTIALS

Transportation Contacts Molly's Trolleys (☎ *561/838–9511*). **Palm Tran** (☎ *561/841–4200*).

Visitor Information Chamber of Commerce of the Palm Beaches (✉ *401 N. Flagler Dr.* ☎ *561/833–3711*). **Palm Beach County Convention & Visitors Bureau** (✉ *1555 Palm Beach Lakes Blvd., Suite 800* ☎ *561/233–3000*).

EXPLORING

The heart of revived West Palm Beach is a small, attractive, easy-to-walk downtown area, spurred on by active historic preservation. Along five blocks of beautifully landscaped Clematis Street, which ends at the Intracoastal Waterway, are boutiques and outdoor cafés, plus the 400-seat Cuillo Centre for the Arts, which features shows and concerts; and Palm Beach Dramaworks, an intimate theater that often shows new plays. An exuberant nightlife has taken hold of the area. In fact, downtown rocks every Thursday from 6 PM on with Clematis by Night, a celebration of music, dance, art, and food at Centennial Square. Even on downtown's fringes there are sights of cultural interest.

A GOOD TOUR: WEST PALM BEACH

Head south from downtown and turn right on Southern Boulevard, left onto Parker Avenue, and right onto Summit Boulevard to reach the **Palm Beach.** In the same area (turn right onto Dreher Trail) and also appealing to kids, the **South Florida Science Museum,** with its Aldrin Planetarium and McGinty Aquarium, is full of hands-on exhibits. If a quick game of croquet intrigues you, head to the **National Croquet Center,** less than 2 mi from the museum, by turning onto Summit Boulevard from Dreher Trail north and proceeding to Florida Mango Road, where you will turn left. Backtrack to Summit Boulevard and go west to the 150-acre **Pine Jog Environmental Education Center.** For more natural adventures, head farther west on Summit until you reach Forest Hill Boulevard, where you turn right to reach the **Okeeheelee Nature Center** and its miles of wooded trails. Now retrace your route to Summit Boulevard, drive east until you reach Military Trail, and take a left. Drive north to Southern Boulevard and turn west to reach **Lion Country Safari,** a 500-acre cageless zoo. For the last stop on this tour, backtrack to Military Trail and travel north to the **Mounts Botanical Gardens.**

TIMING

Tailor your time based on specific interests, because you could easily spend most of a day at any of these attractions. Prepare yourself for heavy rush-hour traffic, and remember that sightseeing in the morning (not *too* early, to avoid rush hour) will be less congested.

West Palm Beach's outskirts, flat stretches lined with fast-food outlets and car dealerships, may not inspire, but are worth driving through to reach attractions scattered around the city's southern and western reaches. Several sites are especially rewarding for children and other animal and nature lovers.

DOWNTOWN

10 **Ann Norton Sculpture Gardens.** This monument to the late American sculptor Ann Weaver Norton, second wife of Norton Museum founder Ralph H. Norton, includes a complex of art galleries in the main house and studio, plus 2½ acres of gardens, where you'll find 300 varieties of palm trees, seven granite figures, and six brick megaliths. The plantings were designed to attract native birds. Call ahead—hours sometimes vary. ✉ *253 Barcelona Rd.* ☎ *561/832–5328* 🌐 *www.ansg.org* 🎟 *$5* ⏲ *Wed.–Sun. 10–4.*

10

12 **Armory Art Center.** Built by the WPA in 1939, the facility is now a visual-arts center hosting rotating exhibitions and art classes throughout the year. ✉ *1703 Lake Ave.* ☎ *561/832–1776* 🌐 *www.armoryart.org* 🎟 *Free* ⏲ *Weekdays 10–4, weekends 10–2.*

11 **Currie Park.** Frequent weekend festivals, including an annual celebration of seafood, take place at the scenic city park next to the Intracoastal Waterway. Sit on one of the piers and watch the yachts and fishing boats pass by. Put on your jogging shoes—the park is at the north end of a 6.3-mi biking-jogging-skating path. ✉ *N. Flagler Dr. at 23rd St.*

9 **Norton Museum of Art.** Constructed in 1941 by steel magnate Ralph H. and Elizabeth Norton, the museum has an extensive collection of 19th- and 20th-century American and European paintings—including works by Picasso, Monet, Matisse, Pollock, and O'Keeffe—and Chinese, contemporary, and photographic art. There are a sublime outdoor covered loggia, Chinese bronze and jade sculptures, and a library. Galleries, including the Great Hall, also showcase traveling exhibits. There's a good museum store, and lectures, programs and concerts for children and adults. ■ **TIP→** One of the city's best-kept secrets is this museum's Café 1451, with its artfully presented dishes that taste as good as they look. ✉ *1451 S. Olive Ave.* ☎ *561/832–5196* 🌐 *www.norton.org* 🎫 *$12* ⏲ *Tues.–Sat. 10–5, Sun. 1–5.*

Fodor's Choice ★

AWAY FROM DOWNTOWN

TOP ATTRACTIONS

18 **Lion Country Safari.** Drive your own vehicle along 8 mi of paved roads through a 500-acre cageless zoo with a thousand free-roaming animals. Lions, elephants, white rhinos, giraffes, zebras, antelopes, chimpanzees, and ostriches are among the wild things in residence. Lions are fenced away from roads, but there's a good chance you'll have a giraffe or two nudging at your window. Exhibits include the Kalahari, designed after a South African bush plateau and containing water buffalo and nilgai (the largest type of Asian antelope), and the Gir Forest, modeled after a game forest in India and showcasing a pride of lions. (For obvious reasons, no convertibles or pets are allowed.) A walk-through area has bird feeding and a petting zoo. You can also take a pontoon-boat tour, go paddleboating, play miniature golf, or send the kids off to the play area with rides and sports fields. There's also a restaurant and a snack shop. ✉ *2003 Lion Country Safari Rd., at Southern Blvd. W, Loxahatchee* ☎ *561/793–1084* 🌐 *www.lioncountrysafari.com* 🎫 *$26; $5 parking fee* ⏲ *Daily 9:30–5:30; last entrance 4:30.*

19 ★ **Mounts Botanical Gardens.** Take advantage of balmy weather by walking among the tropical and subtropical plants here. Join a free tour or explore the 14 acres of exotic trees, rain-forest area, and butterfly and water gardens on your own. Many plants were significantly damaged during the 2004 and 2005 hurricanes, and new plantings will take years to reach maturity. There are lots of free brochures about tropical trees, flowers, and fruits in the main building. If you're feeling inspired, be sure to check out the gift shop's wide range of gardening books. ✉ *531 N. Military Trail* ☎ *561/233–1757* 🌐 *www.mounts.org* 🎫 *Gardens: $5 suggested donation; tours $5* ⏲ *Mon.–Sat. 8–4, Sun. noon–4.*

15 ★ **National Croquet Center.** The world's largest croquet complex, the 10-acre center is also the headquarters for the U.S. Croquet Association. Vast expanses of manicured lawn are the stage for fierce competitions—in no way resembling the casual backyard games where kids play with wide wire wickets. There's also a clubhouse with a pro shop and Café Croquet, with verandas for dining and viewing, and a museum hall. You have to be a member, or a guest of a member, to reserve a lawn every day but Saturday, when lessons are free and lawns are open to all. ✉ *700 Florida Mango Rd., at Summit Blvd.* ☎ *561/478–2300*

www.croquetnational.com Free admission. Full day of play $25. June–Sept., Tues.–Sat. 9–5; Oct.–May, daily 9–5.

13 **Palm Beach Zoo.** At this 23-acre wild kingdom there are more than 125 species of animals, from Florida panthers to the giant Aldabra tortoise. Here you'll find the country's first outdoor exhibit of Goeldi's monkeys. The Tropics of America exhibit has 6 acres of rain forest plus an aviary, Maya ruins, and an Amazon River village. Also notable are a nature trail, the otter exhibit, a children's petting zoo, merry-go-round, interactive fountain and a restaurant overlooking the river. *1301 Summit Blvd. 561/533–0887 www.palmbeachzoo.org $14.95 Daily 9–5.*

WORTH NOTING

17 **Okeeheelee Nature Center.** Explore 5 mi of trails through 90 acres of western Palm Beach County's native pine flatwoods and wetlands. A visitor center gift shop has hands-on exhibits and offers guided walks by the center's volunteers. *7715 Forest Hill Blvd. 33413 561/233–1400 Free Visitor center Tues.–Fri. 1–4:35, Sat. 8:15–4:30; trails daily dawn–dusk.*

16 **Pine Jog Environmental Education Center.** The draw here is 135 acres of mostly undisturbed Florida pine flatwoods with 2½-mi of self-guided trails. Formal landscaping around five one-story buildings includes native plants; dioramas and displays illustrate ecosystems. School groups use the trails during the week; special events include camping and campfires. The gift shop is closed on Saturday. Call for an event schedule. *6301 Summit Blvd. 561/686–6600 www.pinejog.org Free Weekdays 9–4, Sat. 9–2.*

14 **South Florida Science Museum.** Here at the museum, which includes the Aldrin Planetarium and McGinty Aquarium, there are hands-on exhibits with touch tanks and laser shows with music by the likes of Dave Matthews. Galaxy Golf is a 9-hole science challenge. Weather permitting you can observe the heavens Friday night through the most powerful telescope in South Florida. *4801 Dreher Trail N 561/832–1988 www.sfsm.org $9, planetarium $4, laser show $5, galaxy golf $2 Weekdays 10–5, Sat. 10–6, Sun. noon–6.*

10

OFF THE BEATEN PATH

Forty miles west of West Palm Beach, rimming the western edges of Palm Beach and Martin counties, **Lake Okeechobee,** the second-largest freshwater lake completely within the United States, is girdled by 120 mi of road yet remains shielded from sight for almost its entire circumference. Lake Okeechobee—the Seminole's Big Water and the gateway of the great Everglades watershed—measures 730 square mi, roughly 33 mi north–south, and 30 mi east–west, with an average natural depth of only 10 feet (flood control brings the figure up to 12 feet and deeper). Six major lock systems and 32 separate water-control structures manage the water. Encircling the lake is a 34-foot-high grassy levee—locals call it "the wall"—and the Lake Okeechobee Scenic Trail, a segment of the Florida National Scenic Trail, an easy, flat ride for bikers. **TIP→** There's no shade, so wear a hat, sunscreen, and bug repellent. Be sure to bring lots of bottled water, too, because restaurants and stores are few and far between.

SPORTS AND THE OUTDOORS

GOLF

The **Palm Beach National Golf & Country Club** (✉ *7500 St. Andrews Rd., Lake Worth* ☎ *561/965–3381* 🌐 *www.palmbeachnational.com*) has an 18-hole classic course with a Joe Lee championship layout; greens fees $49/$75. The Joanne Carner Golf Academy is based here.

SHOPPING

★ West Palm's **Antique Row**, aka South Dixie Highway, is the destination for those who are interested in interesting home decor. From thrift shops to the most exclusive stores, it is all here—furniture, lighting, art, junk, fabric, frames, tile, and rugs. So if you're looking for an art deco, French-provincial, or Mizner pièce de résistance, big or small, schedule a few hours for an Antique Row stroll. You'll find bargains during the off-season (May to November). Antique Row runs north–south from Okeechobee Road to Forest Hill Boulevard, although most stores are bunched between Belvedere Road and Southern Boulevard.

If you're looking for a mix of food, art, performance, landscaping, and retailing, then head to renewed downtown West Palm around **Clematis Street**, which runs east–west from Dixie Highway to Flagler Drive. Water-view parks with attractive gardens—and fountains where kids can cool off—add to the pleasure of browsing, window-shopping, and resting at an outdoor café. Hip national retailers such as Design Within Reach, Ann Taylor Loft, and Z Gallerie blend in with restaurants, pubs, and nightclubs.

The 55-acre **CityPlace** (✉ *700 S. Rosemary Ave.* ☎ *561/366–1000* 🌐 *www.cityplace.com*), a four-block-by-four-block commercial and residential complex centered on Rosemary Avenue, attracts people of all ages to enjoy restaurants, cafés, outdoor bars, a 20-screen Muvico, the Harriet Himmel Theater, and a 36,000-gallon dance, water, and light show. This family-friendly dining, shopping, and entertainment complex has plenty to see and do. Among CityPlace's stores are popular national retailers Macy's, Armani Exchange, Pottery Barn, Lucky Brand Jeans, Nine West, Sephora, and Restoration Hardware; designer boutiques include Betsey Johnson, Kenneth Cole, and Nicole Miller, and several shops unique to Florida. Behind the punchy, brightly colored clothing in the front window of **C. Orrico** (☎ *561/832–9203*) are family fashions and accessories by Lily Pulitzer and girlie casual gear by Three Dots and Trina Turk. **Rhythm Clothiers** (☎ *561/833–7677*) attracts fashion-forward types with a stock of men's and women's clothing by Dolce & Gabbana, Catherine Malandrino, Diesel, Miss Sixty, and J. Lindeberg.

The free downtown trolley runs a continuous loop linking Clematis Street and CityPlace, so you won't miss a shop.

NIGHTLIFE AND THE ARTS

NIGHTLIFE

CityPlace comes alive at **Blue Martini** (✉ *550 S. Rosemary Ave.* ☎ *561/835–8601*), a bar with eclectic music that attracts a diverse crowd. There are guitars hanging above the bar and a DJ booth made from a 1957 Chevy at **Dr. Feelgood's Rock Bar & Grill** (✉ *219 Clematis St.* ☎ *561/833–6500*). Vince Neil, Mötley Crüe's lead singer, is the owner. **ER Bradley's Saloon** (✉ *104 Clematis St.* ☎ *561/833–3520*) is an open-air restaurant and bar where people of all ages congregate to hang out and socialize while overlooking the Intracoastal Waterway.

THE ARTS

★ Starring amid the treasury of local arts attractions is the **Raymond F. Kravis Center for the Performing Arts** (✉ *701 Okeechobee Blvd.* ☎ *561/832–7469* 🌐 *www.kravis.org*), which includes the 2,200-seat Dreyfoos Hall, a glass, copper, and marble showcase just steps from the restaurants and shops of CityPlace. The center also boasts the 300-seat Rinker Playhouse and the Gosman Amphitheatre, which holds 1,400 in seats and on the lawn. A packed year-round schedule unfolds here with drama, dance, and music, including Kravis on Broadway, which features a blockbuster lineup of Broadway's biggest touring productions; and Florida Stage, a theater company that presents new and emerging plays.

Palm Beach Opera (✉ *415 S. Olive Ave.* ☎ *561/833–7888* 🌐 *www.pbopera.org*) stages five productions, including the Vocal Competition Grand Finals, from December to April at the Kravis Center with English translations projected above the stage. The family opera series includes matinee performances such as *Hansel & Gretel*; tickets are $20 to $165.

WHERE TO EAT

$$$ ITALIAN ✕ **Forte.** Its style says "South Beach," but this Italian eatery makes its home in West Palm Beach. And Clematis Street is happy to host the energy. Stephen Asprino, the city's answer to Emeril Lagasse, put together a great wine list and serves up Italian dishes with French, American, and Japanese influences. Be sure to try the spring garlic soup. Also good is buccatini alla carbonara—a tasty pasta with cheese, eggs, and bacon. Honey-ricotta gelato is a good choice for dessert. ✉ *225 Clematis St.* ☎ *561/833–3330* 🌐 *www.fortepalmbeach.com* 💳 *AE, D, DC, MC, V.*

$ CUBAN ✕ **Havana.** Decorated with vintage travel posters of its namesake city, this two-level restaurant serves such authentic Cuban specialties as roast-pork sandwiches and chicken slowly cooked in Spanish sauce. Lunch and dinner dishes are enhanced by the requisite black beans and rice. Open until 1 AM Friday and Saturday, this friendly place attracts a late-night crowd. The popular walk-up window serves strong Cuban coffee, sugary fried churros, and fruit juices in exotic flavors like mamey, mango, papaya, guava, and guanabana. ✉ *6801 S. Dixie Hwy.* ☎ *561/547–9799* 🌐 *www.havanacubanfood.com* 💳 *AE, MC, V.*

$ SEAFOOD ✕ **Howley's.** Since 1950 this diner's eat-in counter and "cooked in sight, it must be right" motto has made a congenial setting for meeting old friends and making new ones. Forgo the counter for the 1950s-style tables or sit out on the patio. The café attracts a loyal clientele for breakfast, lunch, and dinner with such specialties as turkey and dressing, burgers, and chicken salad. ✉ *4700 S. Dixie Hwy.* ☎ *561/833–5691* ▭ *AE, D, MC, V.*

$$ ITALIAN ✕ **Il Bellagio.** In the center of CityPlace, this European-style bistro offers Italian specialties and a wide variety of fine wines. The menu includes classics like chicken parmigiana, risotto, and fettuccine Alfredo. Pizzas from the wood-burning oven are especially tasty. Service is friendly and efficient, but the overall noise level tends to be high. Sit at the outdoor tables next to the main plaza's dancing fountains. ✉ *CityPlace, 600 S. Rosemary Ave.* ☎ *561/659–6160* 🌐 *www.ilbellagiocityplace.com* ▭ *AE, D, MC, V.*

¢ MEDITERRANEAN ✕ **Middle East Bakery.** This hole-in-the-wall Middle Eastern bakery, deli, and market is packed at lunchtime with regulars who are on a first-name basis with the gang behind the counter. From the nondescript parking lot the place doesn't look like much, but inside, delicious hot and cold Mediterranean treats await. Choose from traditional gyro sandwiches and lamb salads with sides of grape leaves, tabbouleh, and couscous. ✉ *327 5th St., at Olive Ave.* ☎ *561/659–7322* ▭ *AE, MC, V* ⏲ *Closed Sun.*

WHERE TO STAY

$$$ ★ **Grandview Gardens Bed & Breakfast.** This 1923 Spanish-style inn is the new kid on the B&B block in West Palm Beach. The cheery yellow building is conveniently located next to Howard Park, across from the Armory Art Center, and a short walk from the Convention Center, CityPlace, and the Kravis Center. It is warmly decorated with terracotta floors, a coral-stone fireplace, and terraces overlooking a swimming pool and gardens. Each spacious room has Mediterranean flair, as well as French doors opening to private terraces overlooking the pool. **Pros:** private entrances; pool; multilingual owners. **Cons:** not close to the beach; steps to climb. ✉ *1608 Lake Ave.* ☎ *561/833–9023* 🌐 *www.grandview-gardens.net* *5 rooms, 1 cottage* *In-room: a/c, Internet. In-hotel: pool, parking (free)* ▭ *AE, DC, MC, V* *BP.*

$$$$ **Hampton Inn & Suites in Wellington.** Taking its cues from the polo fields and the equestrian center nearby, the Hampton sports a handsome look and an equestrian theme. The four-story hotel, about 10 mi west of downtown West Palm Beach, has the feeling of a ritzy clubhouse, with rich wood paneling, hunt prints, and elegant chandeliers. One-bedroom suites have sleeper sofas, refrigerators, and microwaves. All rooms have coffeemakers. Some rooms have a lake view. **Pros:** complimentary hot breakfast; free high-speed Internet access; near shopping. **Cons:** no restaurant. ✉ *2155 Wellington Green Dr.* ☎ *561/472–9696* 🌐 *www.hamptoninn.com* *122 rooms, 32 suites* *In-room: a/c, refrigerator (some), Wi-Fi. In-hotel: pool, gym* ▭ *AE, D, MC, V* *BP.*

$$$ **Hotel Biba.** In the El Cid historic district, this 1940s-era motel has gotten a fun, stylish revamp from designer Barbara Hulanicki. Each of

The posh Palm Beach area has its share of luxury villas on the water; many are Mediterranean in style.

the 43 rooms has a vibrant mélange of colors, along with handcrafted mirrors, mosaic bathroom floors, and custom mahogany furnishings. Luxury touches include Egyptian-cotton sheets, down pillows and duvets, and lavender-scented closets. The hotel is one block from the Intracoastal Waterway and about a mile from Clematis Street nightlife, and the lobby bar attracts a hip happy-hour crowd. **Pros:** cool design; popular wine bar. **Cons:** water pressure is weak; bathrooms are tiny; noisy when the bar is open late. ✉ *320 Belvedere Rd.* ☎ *561/832–0094* 🌐 *www.hotelbiba.com* *43 rooms* *In-room: a/c, Wi-Fi. In-hotel: bar, pool* 💳 *AE, DC, MC, V.*

SOUTH TO BOCA RATON

Strung together by Route A1A, the towns between Palm Beach and Boca Raton are notable for their variety, from high-rise condominiums to small-town public beaches. In one town you'll find a cluster of art galleries and fancy dining, and the very next town will yield mostly hamburger joints and mom-and-pop stores.

LAKE WORTH

2 mi south of West Palm Beach, off I–95 or Federal Hwy.

For years, tourists looked here mainly for inexpensive lodging and easy access to Palm Beach, since a bridge leads from the mainland to a barrier island with Lake Worth's beach. Now Lake Worth has several blocks of restaurants and art galleries, making this a worthy destination on its own.

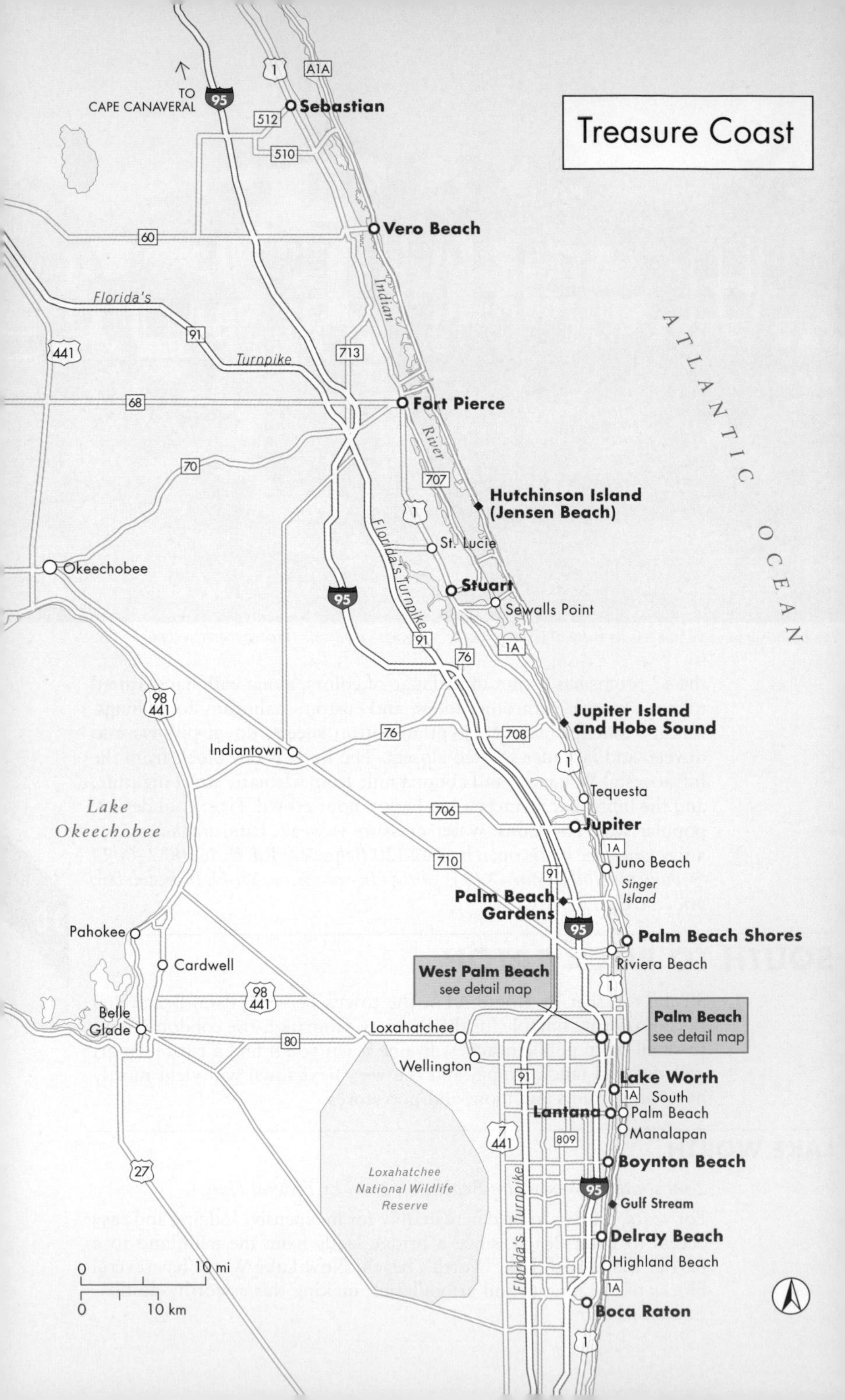

Treasure Coast
TO CAPE CANAVERAL
Sebastian
Vero Beach
Florida's Turnpike
Indian River
Fort Pierce
ATLANTIC OCEAN
Hutchinson Island (Jensen Beach)
St. Lucie
Okeechobee
Stuart
Sewalls Point
Jupiter Island and Hobe Sound
Indiantown
Lake Okeechobee
Tequesta
Jupiter
Juno Beach
Singer Island
Palm Beach Gardens
Palm Beach Shores
Riviera Beach
Pahokee
Cardwell
West Palm Beach see detail map
Palm Beach see detail map
Belle Glade
Loxahatchee
Wellington
Lake Worth
South Palm Beach
Lantana
Manalapan
Boynton Beach
Loxahatchee National Wildlife Reserve
Gulf Stream
Delray Beach
Highland Beach
Boca Raton
0 10 mi
0 10 km

ESSENTIALS

Visitor Information Lake Worth Chamber of Commerce (✉ *501 Lake Ave.* ☎ *561/582–4401*).

EXPLORING

The **Museum of Polo & Hall of Fame** is a good place to start if you're looking for an introduction to polo. See polo memorabilia, art, and a film on the history of the sport. ✉ *9011 Lake Worth Rd.* ☎ *561/969–3210* 🌐 *www.polomuseum.com* *Free* *May–Dec., weekdays 10–4; Jan.–Apr., weekdays 10–4, Sat. 10–2.*

WHERE TO EAT

¢ AMERICAN ✕ **Benny's on the Beach.** Perched on the Lake Worth Pier, Benny's has diner-style food that's cheap and filling, but the spectacular view of the sun glistening on the water and the waves crashing directly below is what dining here is all about. Get here early—it doesn't serve dinner. ✉ *10 Ocean Ave.* ☎ *561/582–9001* *MC, V* *No dinner.*

$ ECLECTIC ✕ **Bizaare Avenue Café.** Decorated with a mix of artwork and antiques, this cozy bistro fits right into downtown Lake Worth's groovy, eclectic scene. Artwork and furnishings can be purchased. Daily specials are available on both the lunch and dinner menus, where crepes, pizzas, pastas, and salads are the staples. ✉ *921 Lake Ave. 33460* ☎ *561/588–4488* *www.bizaareavecafe.com* *AE, D, DC, MC, V.*

$$$ ITALIAN ✕ **Paradiso.** Arguably downtown Lake Worth's finest Italian restaurant, this is the place to go for a romantic evening. Veal chops, seafood, cheese ravioli, and risotto are all good choices. Don't miss the chocolate Grand Marnier soufflé for dessert. As the name implies, the food is heavenly. ✉ *625 Lucerne Ave.* ☎ *561/547–2500* 🌐 *www.paradisolakeworth.com* *AE, MC, V.*

WHERE TO STAY

$$$–$$$$ ★ **Mango Inn.** It's only a 15-minute walk to the beach from this B&B dating from 1915. The two ground-floor rooms have French doors opening onto a patio. A poolside cottage has two bedrooms and two bathrooms. Have your complimentary breakfast of homemade raspberry buttermilk pancakes on the veranda overlooking the heated pool or in the courtyard next to the fountain. **Pros:** close to shops and restaurants; breakfasts served poolside; some suites have whirlpool tubs. **Cons:** some rooms are quite small. ✉ *128 N. Lakeside Dr.* ☎ *561/533–6900 or 888/626–4619* 🌐 *www.mangoinn.com* *7 rooms, 3 suites, 1 cottage* *In-room: a/c, kitchen, refrigerator (some), Internet. In-hotel: pool, no kids under 16* *AE, D, MC, V* *BP.*

$$$–$$$$ ★ **Sabal Palm House.** Built in 1936, this two-story B&B is a short walk from the Intracoastal Waterway. Three rooms and a suite are in the main house, and three others are across a brick courtyard in the carriage house. Each room is inspired by a different artist—including Renoir, Dalí, Norman Rockwell, and Chagall—and all have oak floors, antique furnishings, and private balconies. There's an inviting parlor where afternoon tea and weekend wine and appetizers are served. A full breakfast is offered indoors or in the courtyard, under the palms. **Pros:** fresh flowers in guest rooms; extra pillows; close to shops and restaurants. **Cons:** no pool. ✉ *109 N. Golfview Rd.* ☎ *561/582–1090 or*

888/722–2572 🌐 *www.sabalpalmhouse.com* *5 rooms, 2 suites* *In-hotel: some pets allowed, no kids under 14* *AE, MC, V* *BP.*

LANTANA

2 mi south of Lake Worth, off I–95 or Federal Hwy.

Lantana—just a bit farther south from Palm Beach than Lake Worth—has inexpensive lodging and a bridge connecting the town to its own beach on a barrier island. Tucked between Lantana and Boynton Beach is **Manalapan,** a tiny but posh residential community.

ESSENTIALS

Visitor Information **Lantana Chamber of Commerce** (✉ *212 Iris Ave.* ☎ *561/585–8664*).

SPORTS AND THE OUTDOORS

BEACH

Lantana Public Beach. Ideal for sprawling, beachcombing, or power-walking, Lantana is also worthy for its proximity to one of the most popular food concessions in town, the **Dune Deck Café.** Here the choices are standard, but the food is particularly fresh and the portions are hearty. Try an omelet with a side of fries and melon wedges, Greek salad, homemade yogurt with seasonal fruit topped with honey, or a side of banana-nut bread. There are daily breakfast and lunch specials; dining is outdoors under yellow canopies perched over the beach. ✉ *100 N. Ocean Ave.* ☎ *561/582–0472* *Parking 25¢ for 15 mins* *Daily 9–4:45.*

FISHING

B-Love Fleet (✉ *314 E. Ocean Ave.* ☎ *561/588–7612*) offers three deep-sea fishing excursions daily: 8–noon, 1–5, and 6:30–10:30. No reservations are needed; just show up 30 minutes before the boat is scheduled to leave. The cost is $37 per person and includes fishing license, bait, and tackle.

WHERE TO EAT AND STAY

$$$ SEAFOOD ✕ **Old Key Lime House.** Overlooking the Intracoastal Waterway, the 1889 Lyman family house has grown in spurts over the years and its latest addition is the Manatee Observation Deck. This is an informal seafood house covered by a chiki hut built by the Seminole Indians after the restaurant was damaged by Hurricane Wilma. It's also the largest viewing home for Gator Football. The panoramic water views are the main appeal here for adults—kids love to feed the fish and rock in the glider seats on the dock. Don't miss key lime pie—the house specialty was featured in *Bon Appetite* magazine. ✉ *300 E. Ocean Ave.* ☎ *561/533–5220* 🌐 *www.oldkeylimehouse.com* *AE, MC, V.*

$$$ SEAFOOD ✕ **Station House.** The best Maine lobster in South Florida might well reside at this delicious dive, where all the seafood is cooked to perfection. Sticky seats and tablecloths are an accepted part of the scene, so don't wear your best duds. Although it's casual and family-friendly, reservations are recommended since it's a local favorite. Station Grill, across the street, is less seafood oriented but every "bite" as good.

✉ *233 Lantana Rd.* ☎ *561/547–9487* 🌐 *www.stationhouserestaurants.com* ▭ *AE, D, DC, MC, V* ⊗ *No lunch.*

$$$ JAPANESE ★ ✕ **Suite 225.** On a quaint street lined with shops and boutiques is this historic house that's been transformed into a sleek sushi bar. Glass doors open up to outdoor dining areas, and a bar is nestled under large banyan trees. Start with a sampler platter from the extensive list of eclectic "suite rolls," which includes nearly 40 choices, including the spicy tuna roll and the fantasy roll with salmon and cream cheese. Among the other choices are grilled sake-skirt steak with ginger-barbecue sauce and pork chops with Asian-pear chutney. ✉ *225 E. Ocean Ave.* ☎ *561/582–2255* ▭ *AE, D, MC, V* ⊗ *No lunch.*

$$$$ ★ **Ritz-Carlton, Palm Beach.** Despite its name, this triple-tower landmark is actually in Manalapan, halfway between Palm Beach and Delray Beach. A huge double-sided marble fireplace dominates the elegant lobby and foreshadows the luxury of the guest rooms, which have richly upholstered furnishings and marble tubs. Most rooms have ocean views, and all have balconies. A 2006 expansion added a 3,000-square-foot oceanfront terrace, a second pool, two restaurants, and a grand spa. Coconut palms shade the pools and courtyard—all of which are served by attendants who can fulfill whims from iced drinks to cool face towels. **Pros:** gorgeous rooms; magnificent ocean views; shops across the street. **Cons:** not close to golf course; 15-minute drive to Palm Beach. ✉ *100 S. Ocean Blvd., Manalapan* ☎ *561/533–6000 or 800/241–3333* 🌐 *www.ritz-carlton.com* *310 rooms* *In-room: a/c, safe, refrigerator, Internet, Wi-Fi. In-hotel: 3 restaurants, room service, bars, tennis courts, pools, spa, beachfront, water sports, bicycles, children's programs (ages 5–17), laundry service, Internet terminal, parking (paid)* ▭ *AE, D, DC, MC, V.*

BOYNTON BEACH

3 mi south of Lantana, off I–95 or Federal Highway.

In 1884, when fewer than 50 settlers lived in the area, Nathan Boynton, a Civil War veteran from Michigan, paid $25 for 500 acres with a mile-long stretch of beachfront thrown in. How things have changed, with today's population at about 118,000 and property values still on an upswing. Far enough from Palm Beach to remain low-key, Boynton Beach has two parts, the mainland and the barrier island—the town of Ocean Ridge—connected by two bridges.

10

ESSENTIALS

Visitor Information **Boynton Beach Chamber of Commerce** (✉ *1880 N. Congress Ave., Suite 106* ☎ *561/732–9501*).

EXPLORING

Arthur R. Marshall–Loxahatchee National Wildlife Refuge. The most robust part of the Everglades, this 221-square-mi refuge is one of three huge water-retention areas accounting for much of the Everglades outside the national park. These areas are managed less to protect natural resources, however, than to prevent flooding to the south. Start from the visitor center, where there is a marsh trail to a 20-foot-high observation tower overlooking a pond. The boardwalk takes you through a dense cypress swamp. There's also a 5½-mi canoe trail, best for experienced canoeists since it's overgrown. Wildlife viewing is good year-round, and you can fish for bass and panfish. ✉ *10216 Lee Rd., off U.S. 441 between Rte. 804 and Rte. 806* ☎ *561/734–8303* 🎟 *$5 per vehicle, pedestrians $1* ⏲ *Daily sunrise to sunset; visitor center, weekdays 9–4, weekends 9–4:30.*

★ **Schoolhouse Children's Museum.** Boynton Beach's history is highlighted through interactive exhibits that make the museum a kid and parent pleaser. In this 1913 schoolhouse children can milk a mock cow or pick and wash plastic vegetables at the Pepper Patch Farm. Kids can buy tickets and dress up for a "time travel" train ride that immerses them in Boynton's history. A great outdoor playground castle is adjacent to the museum. ✉ *129 E. Ocean Ave.* ☎ *561/742–6780* 🌐 *www.schoolhousemuseum.org* 🎟 *$5* ⏲ *Tues.–Sat. 10–5.*

SPORTS AND THE OUTDOORS

BEACH

An inviting beach, boardwalk, concessions, grills, and playground await at **Boynton Beach Oceanfront Park** (✉ *6415 Ocean Blvd.* ☎ *No phone* 🎟 *Parking $10 per day* ⏲ *Daily 7:30 AM–11 PM*).

FISHING

West of Boynton Beach, fish the canal at the **Arthur R. Marshall–Loxahatchee National Wildlife Refuge** (✉ *10119 Lee Rd., off U.S. 441 between Rte. 804 and Rte. 806* ☎ *561/734–8303*). There's a boat ramp, and the waters are decently productive, but bring your own equipment. On the other side of town, catch fish swimming between the Atlantic and Intracoastal Waterway at the **Boynton Beach Inlet Pier** (✉ *6990 N. Ocean Blvd.* ☎ *No phone*).

GOLF

Links at Boynton Beach (✉ *8020 Jog Rd.* ☎ *561/742–6500*) has 18-hole and 9-hole executive courses; greens fees $27–$59 champion course, $39–$49 family course (rates vary with time of day; it's busier and costs more in the morning).

WHERE TO EAT

$ AMERICAN ✕ **Banana Boat.** A mainstay for local boaters who cruise up and down the Intracoastal Waterway, Banana Boat is easily recognizable by the lighthouse on its roof. On weekends, casual crowds clad in tank tops, flip-flops, and bikinis dance to live island music while downing frozen drinks. The kitchen serves fish-and-chips, burgers, and ribs. ✉ *739 E. Ocean Ave.* ☎ *561/732–9400* 🌐 *www.bananaboatboynton.com* 💳 *AE, MC, V.*

DELRAY BEACH

2 mi south of Gulf Stream via I–95 or Federal Hwy.

A onetime artists' retreat with a small settlement of Japanese farmers, Delray has grown into a sophisticated beach town. Atlantic Avenue, the once dilapidated main drag, has evolved into a more-than-a-mile-long stretch of palm-dotted sidewalks, lined with stores, art galleries, and

Morikami Museum and Japanese Gardens gives a taste of the Orient through its exhibits and tea ceremonies.

dining establishments. Running east–west and ending at the beach, it's a pleasant place for a stroll, day or night. Another active pedestrian way begins at the eastern edge of Atlantic Avenue and runs along the big, broad swimming beach that extends north to George Bush Boulevard and south to Casuarina Road.

ESSENTIALS

Visitor Information **Delray Beach Chamber of Commerce** (✉ *64-A SE 5th Ave.* ☎ *561/278–0424*).

EXPLORING

Colony Hotel. The chief landmark along Atlantic Avenue since 1926 is this Mediterranean revival–style hotel, which is a member of the National Trust for Historic Preservation. Walk through the lobby to the parking lot of the hotel where original stable "garages" still stand—relics of the days when hotel guests would arrive via horse and carriage. ✉ *525 E. Atlantic Ave.* ☎ *561/276–4123.*

Old School Square Cultural Arts Center. Just off Atlantic Avenue is this cluster of several museums set in restored school buildings dating from 1913 and 1926. The **Cornell Museum of Art & History** offers ever-changing art exhibits. During its season, the **Crest Theatre** showcases performances by local and touring troupes in the restored 1925 Delray High School building. ✉ *51 N. Swinton Ave.* ☎ *561/243–7922* 🌐 *www.oldschool.org* *$6* ⏲ *Tues.–Sat. 10:30–4:30, Sun. 1–4:30.*

Fodor's Choice ★ **Morikami Museum and Japanese Gardens.** Out in the boonies west of Delray Beach seems an odd place to encounter the East, but this is exactly where you can find a cultural and recreational facility heralding the

Yamato Colony of Japanese farmers. The on-site Cornell Café serves light Asian fare. If you don't get your fill of orchids, the American Orchid Society's 20,000-square-foot headquarters is across the street. ✉ *4000 Morikami Park Rd.* ☎ *561/495–0233* 🌐 *www.morikami.org* *$12* ⏲ *Tues.–Sun. 10–5.*

SPORTS AND THE OUTDOORS

BEACHES

★ Enjoy many types of water-sports rentals—sailing, kayaking, windsurfing, Boogie boarding, surfing, snorkeling—or scuba diving at a sunken Spanish galleon less than ½ mi offshore at **Seagate Beach** (✉ *½ mi south of Atlantic Ave. at Rte. A1A*. A scenic walking path follows the main stretch of the public **Delray Beach Municipal Beach** (✉ *Atlantic Ave. at Rte. A1A*), which stretches 2 mi, half of it supervised by lifeguards. Reefs off the coast are popular with divers.

BIKING

There's a bicycle path in Barwick Park and a special oceanfront lane along Route A1A. **Richwagen's Bike & Sport** (✉ *298 NE 6th Ave.* ☎ *561/276–4234*) rents bikes by the hour or day and provides lock, basket, helmet, and maps.

WATERSKIING

At **Lake Ida Park** (✉ *2929 Lake Ida Rd.*) you can water-ski whether you're a beginner or a veteran. The park has a boat ramp, a slalom course, and a trick ski course.

SHOPPING

Atlantic Avenue is a showcase for art galleries, shops, and restaurants. This charming area, from Swinton Avenue east to the ocean, has maintained much of its small-town integrity.

In the historic Colony Hotel, **Escentials Apothecaries** (✉ *533 Atlantic Ave.* ☎ *561/276–7070*) is packed with all things good smelling for your bath, body, and home. **Snappy Turtle** (✉ *1100 Atlantic Ave.* ☎ *561/276–8088*) is where Mackenzie-Childs and Lilly Pulitzer mingle with other fun fashions for the home and family.

NIGHTLIFE

Boston's on the Beach (✉ *40 S. Ocean Blvd.* ☎ *561/278–3364*) grooves to reggae on Monday night and live music from jazz to country to rock most other nights. At **Dada** (✉ *52 N. Swinton Ave.* ☎ *561/330–3232*), bands play in the living room of a historic house. It's a place where those who don't drink will also feel comfortable. **Delux** (✉ *16 E. Atlantic Ave.* ☎ *561/279–4792*) is where a young, hip crowd goes to dance all night long.

WHERE TO EAT

$$$ AMERICAN ★ ✕ **32 East.** Although restaurants come and go on a trendy street like Atlantic Avenue, 32 East remains one of the best restaurants in Delray Beach. A daily menu of wood-oven pizzas, salads, soups, seafood, and meat is all based on what is fresh and plentiful. Dark-wood accents and dim lighting make this large restaurant seem cozy. There's a packed bar in front and an open kitchen in back. ✉ *32 E. Atlantic Ave.* ☎ *561/276–7868* 🌐 *www.32east.com* 💳 *AE, D, MC, V* ⏲ *No lunch.*

$$ BRITISH **Blue Anchor.** Yes, this pub was actually shipped from England, where it stood for 150 years in London's historic Chancery Lane. There it was a watering hole for famed Englishmen, including Winston Churchill. The Delray Beach incarnation has stuck to authentic British pub fare. Chow down on a ploughman's lunch (a chunk of Stilton cheese, a hunk of bread, and pickled onions), shepherd's pie, fish-and-chips, and bangers and mash (sausages with mashed potatoes). Don't be surprised to find a rugby game on TV. English beers and ales are on tap and by the bottle. It's a late-night place open until at least 2. *804 E. Atlantic Ave.* *561/272–7272* *www.theblueanchor.com* *AE, D, MC, V.*

$$$ JAPANESE **Kyoto.** An energetic crew keeps this bustling Japanese eatery running into the wee hours all week long. Sushi and sake are the main draws here, but there are also less traditional dishes on offer. The dining room is stylish and contemporary, with a sleek black sushi bar. You can dine among a bar crowd and watch your sushi being assembled, or take a table in the front courtyard and watch the crowds meander along happening Pineapple Grove. *25 NE 2nd Ave.* *561/330–2404* *AE, DC, MC, V.*

¢ AMERICAN ★ **Old School Bakery.** This place concentrates on sandwich making at its best. Particularly worthy is the cherry chicken salad sandwich with Brie on multigrain. Apart from sandwiches and soups served for lunch every day, order from a diverse baked-goods menu with artisan breads, pastries, several kinds of cookies, and even biscotti. The bakery is primarily takeout, but there are a few small tables in an adjacent open-air courtyard. *814 E. Atlantic Ave.* *561/243–8059* *No credit cards* *AE, MC, V.*

WHERE TO STAY

$$$$ **Colony Hotel & Cabana Club.** In the heart of downtown Delray, this charming building dates back to 1926. Today it's listed on Delray's local Register of Historic Places and maintains an air of the 1920s with its Mediterranean-revival architecture. The Cabana Club is a separate property on the ocean about a mile away, with a private beach, club, and heated saltwater pool. A convivial bar and live music on weekend nights make the lobby area a great place to wind down. In fact, yoga classes are held there daily (except Monday). Fine shops selling leather goods, body products, and stationery fill the lower-level storefronts. **Pros:** great location; close to restaurants; shuttle to the beach. **Cons:** air-conditioning units can be loud; breakfast buffet servings are repetitious. *525 E. Atlantic Ave.* *561/276–4123 or 800/552–2363* *www.thecolonyhotel.com* *69 rooms* *In-room: a/c, Internet, Wi-Fi. In-hotel: bar, pool, beachfront, parking (free)* *AE, DC, MC, V* *CP.*

$$$$ **Delray Beach Marriott.** By far the largest property in Delray Beach, this five-story hotel has a stellar location at the east end of Atlantic Avenue. It sits across the road from the beach and is within walking distance of restaurants, shops, and galleries. Rooms and suites are spacious, and many have stunning ocean views. If you want a bit of pampering, there's also a spa. The free-form pool is surrounded by a comfortable deck. **Pros:** great location; near nightlife; luxurious spa. **Cons:** sprawling resort; chain-hotel feel; service can be impersonal. *10 N. Ocean Blvd.* *561/274–3200* *www.delraybeachmarriott.com* *268 rooms, 88*

10

suites ♿ *In-room: a/c, safe, Internet. In-hotel: 3 restaurants, room service, bars, pool, gym, spa, beachfront, laundry facilities, parking (free)* ▭ *AE, DC, MC, V.*

$$$$ ★ **Sundy House.** Just about everything in this bungalow-style B&B is executed to perfection. Guest rooms are luxuriously decorated, and apartments offer full kitchens and laundry facilities. Situated a few blocks south of Atlantic Avenue, this lodging's only real downside is a long walk to the beach (although the complimentary beach shuttle lessens the inconvenience). Even if you do not stay here, come see the extraordinary tropical gardens. Dine at the exceptional restaurant De la Tierra under an expansive indoor canopy, or on the patios set among koi ponds. **Pros:** beautiful property; excellent restaurant; quiet area. **Cons:** not on the beach. ✉ *106 Swinton Ave.* ☎ *561/272–5678 or 877/434–9601* 🌐 *www.sundyhouse.com* *10 rooms, 1 apartment* ♿ *In-room: Wi-Fi. In-hotel: restaurant, bar, pool, Internet terminal* ▭ *AE, DC, MC, V.*

BOCA RATON

6 mi south of Delray Beach, off I–95.

Less than an hour south of Palm Beach and anchoring the county's south end, upscale Boca Raton has much in common with its fabled cousin. Both reflect the unmistakable architectural influence of Addison Mizner, their principal developer in the mid-1920s. The meaning of the name Boca Raton (pronounced boca rah-*tone*) often arouses curiosity, with many folks mistakenly assuming it means "rat's mouth." Historians say the probable origin is Boca Ratones, an ancient Spanish geographical term for an inlet filled with jagged rocks or coral. Miami's Biscayne Bay had such an inlet, and in 1823 a mapmaker copying Miami terrain confused the more northern inlet, thus mistakenly labeling this area Boca Ratones. No matter what, you'll know you've arrived in the heart of downtown when you spot the town hall's gold dome on the main street, Federal Highway.

TOURS The **Boca Raton Historical Society** (✉ *71 N. Federal Hwy.* ☎ *561/395–6766* 🌐 *www.bocahistory.org*) offers trolley tours of city sites during season on Thursday. **Old Northwood Historic District Tours** (☎ *No phone* 🌐 *www.oldnorthwood.org*) leads two-hour walking tours that include visits to historic home interiors. During season they typically start Sunday at 2; a $5 donation is suggested. Tours for groups of six or more can be scheduled almost any day.

ESSENTIALS

Visitor Information Boca Raton Chamber of Commerce (✉ *1800 N. Dixie Hwy.* ☎ *561/395–4433*).

EXPLORING

2 East El Camino Real. Built in 1925 as the headquarters of the Mizner Development Corporation, this is an example of Mizner's characteristic Spanish-revival architectural style, with its wrought-iron grilles and handmade tiles. As for Mizner's grandiose vision of El Camino Real, the architect-promoter once prepared brochures promising a sweeping wide boulevard with Venetian canals and arching bridges. Camino Real is attractive, heading east to the Boca Raton Resort & Club, but don't count on feeling like you're in Venice. ✉ *2 E. Camino Real.*

★ **Boca Raton Museum of Art.** An interactive children's gallery and changing exhibition galleries showcase internationally known artists at this museum in a spectacular building in the Mizner Park shopping center. The permanent collection upstairs includes works by Picasso, Degas, Matisse, Klee, and Modigliani, as well as notable pre-Columbian art. ✉ *501 Plaza Real* ☎ *561/392–2500* 🌐 *www.bocamuseum.org* *$8* *Tues., Thurs., and Fri. 10–5, Wed. 10–9, weekends noon–5.*

Children's Science Explorium. This hands-on science center offers interactive exhibits, programs and camps designed to enhance 5- to 12-year-old explorers' understanding of everyday physical sciences. The Explorium is in Sugar Sand Community Center. ✉ *300 S. Military Trail* ☎ *561/347–3913* 🌐 *www.scienceexplorium.org* *Suggested donaton: $2* *Weekdays 9–6, weekends 10–5.*

Gumbo Limbo Nature Center. A big draw for kids, this nifty nature center has four huge saltwater tanks brimming with sea life—from coral to stingrays—and a boardwalk through dense forest with a 40-foot tower you can climb to overlook the tree canopy. In spring and early summer, staffers lead nocturnal turtle walks: you can watch nesting females come ashore and lay eggs. (Purchase tickets in advance; see Web site for details.) A great hiking spot, the park has a sturdy boardwalk and a 40-foot observation tower. Spend a little time there and you're likely to see brown pelicans and osprey. Kids love the aquariums, insect tanks, and the butterfly garden. ✉ *1801 N. Ocean Blvd.* ☎ *561/338–1473* 🌐 *www.gumbolimbo.org* *Free but $3 donation suggested; turtle walks $5* *Mon.–Sat. 9–4, Sun. noon–4; turtle walks May–July, Mon.–Thurs. 9 PM–midnight.*

Old Floresta. This residential area was developed by Addison Mizner starting in 1925 and landscaped with palms and cycads. It includes houses that are mainly Mediterranean in style, many with balconies supported by exposed wood columns. Home tours are held twice a year. ✉ *Behind the Boca Raton Art School on Palmetto Park Rd.*

10

SPORTS AND THE OUTDOORS

BEACHES

Red Reef Park (✉ *1400 N. Rte. A1A*) has a beach and playground plus picnic tables and grills, and the beach is a good spot for snorkeling. The reef is only about 50 feet offshore. **South Beach Park** (✉ *400 N. Rte. A1A*) is a pretty stretch of sand popular with sunbathers. In addition to its beach, **Spanish River Park** (✉ *3001 N. Rte. A1A*) has picnic tables, grills, and a large playground.

BOATING

For the thrill of blasting across the water at up to 80 mph, **Palm Breeze Charters** (✉ *107 E. Palmetto Park Rd., Suite 330* ☎ *561/368–3566*) offers a variety weekly cruises and boat charters.

GOLF

Two championship courses are at **Boca Raton Resort & Club** (✉ *501 E. Camino Real* ☎ *561/447–3078*); greens fees $180/$210, includes cart with GPS. The Dave Pelz Golf School is at the country club course.

SHOPPING

★ **Mizner Park** (✉ *Federal Hwy., 1 block north of Palmetto Park Rd.*) is a distinctive 30-acre shopping center with apartments and town houses among its gardenlike retail and restaurant spaces. Some three dozen stores, including national and local retailers, mingle with fine restaurants, sidewalk cafés, galleries, a movie theater, museum, and amphitheater.

NIGHTLIFE

Drop by **Gatsby's Boca** (✉ *5970 SW 18th St., Shoppes at Village Point* ☎ *561/393–3900*) any night of the week to mingle with a lively crowd. Shoot pool at one of 18 tables or watch sporting events on several giant screens. **Pranzo** (✉ *402 Plaza Real* ☎ *561/750–7442*) has a happening weekend bar scene.

WHERE TO EAT

$$ VIETNAMESE ★ ✕ **La Tre.** An adventuresome menu distinguishes this simple Vietnamese eatery. Try the crispy eggplant or the crepe stuffed with pork, shrimp, and vegetables. Tamarind-flavored squid is another winner. The restaurant's black-lacquer furniture seems to date from the 1980s. Don't anticipate a romantic dinner experience, as there's an odd purple hue cast from fluorescent lighting. The food makes it worth the trip, however. ✉ *249 E. Palmetto Park Rd.* ☎ *561/392–4568* ▭ *AE, DC, MC, V* ⊙ *No lunch.*

$$$ ITALIAN ✕ **Tiramisu.** The food is an extravaganza of taste treats; veal chops, tuna, and anything with mushrooms draw raves, but count on hearty fare rather than a light touch. Start with the portobello mushroom with garlic or the Corsican baby sardines in olive oil. For a main course, try ricotta ravioli; scaloppine of veal stuffed with crabmeat, lobster, and Gorgonzola; or Tuscan fish stew. Enjoy it all in an intimate setting as Andrea Bocelli music plays in the background. ✉ *170 W. Camino Real.* ☎ *561/338–9692* ▭ *AE, DC, MC, V* ⊙ *No lunch Sun.*

$$$$ SEAFOOD ✕ **Truluck's.** This popular chain is so serious about seafood that it boasts its own fleet of 16 boats. Stone crabs are the signature dish, and you can have all you can eat on Monday night from December to May. Other recommended dishes include jalapeño salmon topped with blue crabmeat, hot and crunchy trout, crab cakes, and bacon-wrapped shrimp. Portions are huge, so you might want to make a meal of appetizers. The place comes alive each night with its popular piano bar. ✉ *Mizner Park, 351 Plaza Real* ☎ *561/391–0755* 🌐 *www.trulucks.com* ▭ *AE, D, MC, V.*

$$$ CHINESE ✕ **Uncle Tai's.** The draw at this upscale eatery is some of the best Szechuan food on Florida's east coast. Specialties include sliced duck with snow peas and water chestnuts in a tangy plum sauce, and orange beef delight—flank steak stir-fried until crispy and then sautéed with pepper sauce, garlic, and orange peel. They'll go easy on the heat on request. The service is quietly efficient. ✉ *5250 Town Center Circle* ☎ *561/368–8806* 🌐 *www.uncle-tais.com* ▭ *AE, MC, V* ⊙ *No lunch Sun.*

WHERE TO STAY

$$$$ ★ **Boca Raton Resort & Club.** Addison Mizner built this Mediterranean-style hotel in 1926, and additions over time have created this sparkling, sprawling resort. There are many lodging options: traditional rooms are small but warmly decorated; beachfront rooms are light and airy; yacht-club rooms are the most luxurious, with custom-designed Venetian-style canopy beds and carved gold-leaf lamps. The beach is accessible by shuttle. In addition to a redesigned golf course with a two-story clubhouse, there's an expansive tennis and fitness center and the largest spa in Florida. It has 44 treatment rooms reserved for guests and offers treatments that take advantage of local flora. Chef Angela Hartnett opened a restaurant here, immediately drawing locals. **Pros:** historical property; loaded with luxury; plenty of activities. **Cons:** all this luxury is costly; conventions crowd common areas. ✉ *501 E. Camino Real* ☎ *561/447–3000 or 800/327–0101* 🌐 *www.bocaresort.com* *1,047 rooms, 134 suites, 60 1-bedroom bungalows* *In-room: a/c, safe, kitchen (some), Wi-Fi. In-hotel: 12 restaurants, room service, bars, golf course, tennis courts, pools, gym, water sports, children's programs (ages 2–17), laundry service, parking (paid)* *AE, DC, MC, V.*

$$ **Ocean Breeze Inn.** If golf is your game, this smaller resort is an excellent choice. Guests can play the outstanding course at the adjoining Ocean Breeze Golf & Country Club, otherwise available only to club members. Rooms are in a three-story building, and most have a patio or balcony. **Pros:** great spot for golfers; bargain rates. **Cons:** rooms are dated. ✉ *5800 NW 2nd Ave.* ☎ *561/994–0400 or 800/344–6995* 🌐 *www.oceanbreezegolf.com* *46 rooms* *In-room: a/c, refrigerator. In-hotel: restaurant, golf course, tennis courts, pool, laundry facilities, parking (free)* *AE, DC, MC, V.*

$$$$ **Radisson Bridge Resort of Boca Raton.** This resort on the Intracoastal Waterway has views of the ocean that can't be beat, especially from the top-floor restaurant. The ground-floor restaurant, Water Color, offers great views of passing boats. The beach is a five-minute walk away, as are restaurants, galleries, and boutiques. Comfortable accommodations and an ideal location are the main draws. Rooms are decorated in typical Boca style, with pale woods and rattan and a watercolor palette—nothing spectacular, yet quite presentable. **Pros:** great location; affordable rates. **Cons:** can be noisy if you're near the bridge. ✉ *999 E. Camino Real* ☎ *561/368–9500 or 800/333–3333* 🌐 *www.bocaratonbridgehotel.com* *110 rooms, 11 suites* *In-room: a/c, refrigerator (some), Internet. In-hotel: 2 restaurants, room service, bars, pool, gym, beachfront, laundry facilities, parking (free)* *AE, DC, MC, V.*

10

THE TREASURE COAST

In contrast to the Gold Coast—as the Palm Beach/West Palm Beach area is known—is the more rural Treasure Coast, covering northernmost Palm Beach County, plus Martin, St. Lucie, and Indian River counties. Along the coast are barrier islands all the way to Sebastian and beyond. Inland there's cattle ranching in tracts of pine and palmetto scrub, along with sugar and citrus production. Shrimp farming uses techniques for acclimatizing shrimp from saltwater—land near seawater is costly—to freshwater, all the better to serve demand from restaurants popping up all over the region. Despite, a growing number of malls and beachfront condominium, much of the Treasure Coast remains largely blissfully undeveloped.

PALM BEACH SHORES

7 mi north of Palm Beach, on Singer Island.

Rimmed by mom-and-pop motels, this residential town is at the southern tip of Singer Island, across Lake Worth Inlet from Palm Beach. To travel between the two, however, you must cross over to the mainland before returning to the beach.

GETTING HERE AND AROUND

The best way to drive to Palm Beach Shores from West Palm Beach is to head 7 mi north on Interstate 95. Head east on Blue Heron Boulevard/ Route 708 across the Intracoastal Waterway to Atlantic Avenue. Head south and you'll be in Palm Beach Shores.

ESSENTIALS

Visitor Information **Northern Palm Beach County Chamber of Commerce** (*⌧ 800 N. U.S. 1, Jupiter ☎ 561/694–2300*).

SPORTS AND THE OUTDOORS

In the Intracoastal Waterway between Palm Beach Shores and Riviera Beach, 79-acre **Peanut Island** was opened in 1999 as a recreational park. There's a 20-foot-wide walking path surrounding the island, a 19-slip boat dock, a 170-foot T-shape fishing pier, six picnic pavilions, a visitor center, and 20 overnight campsites. The small **Palm Beach Maritime Museum** (☎ *561/832–7428*) is open daily except Friday and showcases the "Kennedy Bunker," a bomb shelter prepared for President John F. Kennedy. Call for tour hours.To get to the island, you can take a water taxi. ☎ *561/339–2504* 🌐 *www.pbmm.org* *$2 donation* ⏲ *Daily dawn–dusk for noncampers.*

FISHING

The **Sailfish Marina and Resort** (⌧ *98 Lake Dr.* ☎ *561/844–1724* 🌐 *www.sailfishmarina.com*) has seasoned captains and a large fleet of 28- to 60-foot boats. Book a full or half day of deep-sea fishing for up to six people.

WHERE TO EAT AND STAY

$$ SEAFOOD ✕ **Sailfish Marina Restaurant.** This waterfront restaurant overlooking Peanut Island is a great place to chill out after a long day of mansion-gawking, boating, or beach-bumming. Choose a table in the dining room or under an umbrella on the terrace and enjoy mainstays like conch chowder or grilled swordfish. More upscale entrées—this, after all, is still Palm Beach County—include lobster tail and baby sea scallops sautéed in garlic and lemon butter. Breakfast is a winner here, too. Sportfishing charters are available at Sailfish's store. ⌧ *98 Lake Dr.* ☎ *561/842–8449* 🌐 *www.sailfishmarina.com* ⏲ *AE, MC, V.*

DID YOU KNOW?

According to the United States Department of Agriculture, 75% of all of the citrus fruits (including oranges, grapefruit, tangerines, lemons, and limes) grown in the United States are grown in Florida.

CLOSE UP

Floridas Sea Turtles: The Nesting Season

From May to October it's turtle-nesting season all along the Florida coast. Female loggerhead, Kemp's ridley, and other species living in the Atlantic Ocean or Gulf of Mexico swim up to 2,000 mi to the Florida shore. By night they drag their 100- to 400-pound bodies onto the beach to the dune line. Then each digs a hole with her flippers, drops in 100 or so eggs, covers them up, and returns to sea.

The babies hatch about 60 days later. Once they burst out of the sand, the hatchlings must get to sea rapidly or risk becoming dehydrated from the sun or being caught by crabs, birds, or other predators.

Instinctively, baby turtles head toward bright light, probably because for millions of years starlight or moonlight reflected on the waves was the brightest light around, serving to guide hatchlings to water. But now light from beach development can lead the babies in the wrong direction, towards the street rather than the water. To help, many coastal towns enforce light restrictions during nesting months. Florida home owners are requested to dim their lights on behalf of baby sea turtles.

At night, volunteers walk the beaches, searching for signs of turtle nests. Upon finding telltale scratches in the sand, they cordon off the sites, so beachgoers will leave the spots undisturbed. Volunteers also keep watch over nests when babies are about to hatch and assist if the hatchlings get disoriented.

It's a hazardous world for baby turtles. They can die after eating tar balls or plastic debris, or they can be gobbled by sharks or circling birds. Only about one in a thousand survives to adulthood. After reaching the water, the babies make their way to warm currents. East Coast hatchlings drift into the Gulf Stream, spending years floating around the Atlantic.

Males never return to land, but when females attain maturity, in 15–20 years, they return to shore to lay eggs. Remarkably, even after migrating hundreds and even thousands of miles out at sea, most return to the very beach where they were born to deposit their eggs. Each time they nest, they come back to the same stretch of beach. In fact, the more they nest, the more accurate they get, until eventually they return time and again to within a few feet of where they last laid their eggs. These incredible navigation skills remain for the most part a mystery despite intense scientific study. To learn more, check out the Sea Turtle Survival League's and Caribbean Conservation Corporation's Web site at 🌐 *www.cccturtle.org.*

—Pam Acheson

$$ **Sailfish Marina Resort.** This waterfront lodging has a marina with deepwater slips and accommodations that include motel-style rooms, efficiencies, and even a three-bedroom house. All rooms open to landscaped grounds, although five rooms are directly on the water. Rooms have peaked ceilings, carpeting, flat-screen TVs and stall showers; all have ceiling fans. From the seawall, you'll see fish through the clear inlet water. **Pros:** inexpensive rates; on the Intracoastal Waterway; water taxi stops here. **Cons:** can be noisy; area attracts a party crowd; dated rooms. ✉ *98 Lake Dr.* ☎ *561/844–1724 or 800/446–4577* 🌐 *www.sailfishmarina.com* *30 units* *In-room: a/c, kitchen (some), Internet. In-hotel: restaurant, bar, pool* *AE, MC, V.*

WORD OF MOUTH

"Palm Beach Gardens is quiet and undiscovered. Lots of local golf. Very low key. It is convenient to Juno Beach—the most gorgeous Florida Beach with free beachside parking." —LindaBrinck

PALM BEACH GARDENS

5 mi north of West Palm Beach, off I-95.

About 15 minutes northwest of Palm Beach is this relaxed, upscale residential community known for its high-profile golf complex, the PGA National Resort & Spa. Although not on the beach, the town is less than a 15 minute drive from the ocean.

ESSENTIALS

Visitor Information **Northern Palm Beach County Chamber of Commerce** (✉ *800 N. U.S. 1, Jupiter* ☎ *561/694–2300*).

SPORTS AND THE OUTDOORS

GOLF

If you're the kind of traveler who takes along a set of clubs, the **PGA National Resort & Spa** (✉ *1000 Ave. of the Champions* ☎ *561/627–1800*) is for you. The resort has five championship courses that are challenging enough for the pros. Among them are the Champion Course, designed by Tom Fazio and Jack Nicklaus (greens fee $350); the General Course, designed by Arnold Palmer ($250); the Haig Course, the first course opened at the resort ($210); the Estate Course, with a practice range and putting green ($210); and the Tom Fazio–designed Squire Course ($210). Lessons are available at the Golf Digest Academy.

EN ROUTE

John D. MacArthur Beach State Park & Nature Center. Almost 2 mi of beach, good fishing and shelling, and one of the finest examples of subtropical coastal habitat remaining in southeast Florida are among the treasures here. To learn about what you see, take an interpretive walk to a mangrove estuary along the upper reaches of Lake Worth. The nature center, open daily 9–5, has exhibits on the coastal environment. ✉ *10900 Rte. A1A, North Palm Beach* ☎ *561/624–6950* 🌐 *www.macarthurbeach.org* *$5 per vehicle, up to 8 people* *Daily 8–sundown.*

10

WHERE TO EAT

$$$ AMERICAN ★ **Café Chardonnay.** At the end of a strip mall, Café Chardonnay is surprisingly elegant. Soft lighting, warm woods, and cozy banquettes set the scene for a quiet lunch or romantic dinner. The place consistently receives praise for its innovative menu and outstanding wine list. Starters include wild-mushroom strudel and truffle-stuffed diver sea scallops. Entrées might include Gorgonzola-crusted filet mignon or pan-seared veal scaloppine with rock shrimp. *4533 PGA Blvd. 561/627–2662 www.cafechardonnay.com AE, D, MC, V No lunch weekends.*

$$$ AMERICAN **Ironwood Grille.** Opened in 2008, this new kid on the block is part of the PGA National Resort & Spa. The contemporary eatery specializes in beef and seafood dishes made with locally grown organic produce. Other good choices include she-crab soup with sherry and grilled filet mignon. The chic lobby restaurant and the adjoining bar share an extensive wine cellar and a room for private wine tastings. On Thursday nights, a DJ plays music from 6 until 9. *400 Ave. of the Champions 561/627–2000 www.ironwoodgrille.com AE, D, MC, V.*

$$ SEAFOOD **Spoto's.** If you like oysters, head to this place where black-and-white photographs of oyster fisherman adorn the walls. The polished tables give the eatery a country club look. A local chain, Spoto's serves up a delightful bowl of New England clam chowder and an impressive variety of oysters and clams. The prime rib Caesar salad with crispy croutons never disappoints. Sit outside on the patio to take advantage of the area's perfect weather. There's a popular brunch on Sunday. *4560 PGA Blvd. 561/776–9448 www.spotosoysterbar.com AE, DC, MC, V.*

WHERE TO STAY

$$$$ ★ **PGA National Resort & Spa.** With five championship courses, this resort has hosted more championship tournaments than any other golf destination in the country. A top-to-bottom renovation has made the facilities even more attractive, as is clear once you step into the massive clubhouse. But while golf is a big draw, only 40% of guests are golfers. The rest come for the other amenities, such as the extensive sports facilities, the excellent dining, and the 240-acre nature preserve. At the pool, simply raise a flag and a server rushes over to take your drink order. The spa is in a building styled after a Mediterranean fishing village, and six outdoor therapy pools are joined by a collection of imported mineral saltwater pools. Guest rooms have luxurious maple furnishings, flat-screen TVs, and private balconies. **Pros:** a golfer's paradise; short drive to shopping; large rooms. **Cons:** not on the beach. *400 Ave. of the Champions 561/627–2000 or 800/633–9150 www.pgaresort.com 280 rooms, 59 suites In-room: a/c, safe, kitchen (some), refrigerator (some), Internet, In-hotel: 7 restaurants, room service, bars, golf courses, tennis courts, pools, gym, spa, Wi-Fi hotspot, parking (free) AE, D, DC, MC, V.*

Away from developed shorelines, Blowing Rocks Preserve on Jupiter Island lets you wander the dunes.

JUPITER

12 mi north of Palm Beach Shores via I–95 and Rte. 706.

Jupiter is one of the few little towns in the region not fronted by an island. Beaches here are part of the mainland, and Route A1A runs for almost 4 mi along the beachfront dunes and beautiful estates.

ESSENTIALS

Visitor Information **Northern Palm Beach County Chamber of Commerce** (*✉ 800 N. U.S. 1, Jupiter ☎ 561/694–2300*).

EXPLORING

Dubois Home. Take a look at how life once was at this modest pioneer outpost dating from 1898. Sitting atop an ancient Jeaga Indian mound 20 feet high and looking onto Jupiter Inlet, it has Cape Cod as well as Cracker (Old Florida) design. It's in Dubois Park, worth a visit for its lovely beaches and swimming lagoons. The park is open dawn to dusk. *✉ 19075 Dubois Rd. ☎ 561/747–8380 ⊕ www.lrhs.org $2 ⊙ Tues. and Wed. 1–4.*

★ **Jupiter Inlet Lighthouse.** Designed by Civil War hero General George Meade, this brick lighthouse has been operated by the Coast Guard since 1860. Tours of the 105-foot-tall landmark unfold every half hour. (Children must be at least 4 feet tall to go to the top.) There's a small museum that tells about efforts to restore this graceful spire to the way it looked from 1860 to 1918. *✉ 500 Capt. Armour's Way, U.S. 1 and Beach Rd. ☎ 561/747–8380 ⊕ www.jupiterlighthouse.org Tour $7 ⊙ Tues.–Sun. 10–5; last tour at 4.*

SPORTS AND THE OUTDOORS

BASEBALL

Both the **St. Louis Cardinals** and **Florida Marlins** (✉ *4751 Main St.* ☎ *561/775–1818*) train at the 7,000-seat Roger Dean Stadium.

BEACHES

Carlin Park. A beach is just one of the draws here. The park also has picnic pavilions, hiking trails, a baseball diamond, a playground, six tennis courts, and fishing sites. The Lazy Loggerhead Café, serving snacks and burgers, is open daily 9–5. ✉ *A1A at Juno Beach* ☎ *561/799–0185* ⊙ *Daily dawn–dusk.* **Juno Beach.** A 990-foot pier and a bait shop are the big draws here, but a section is available for surfing, and there's a snack bar, too. ✉ *14775 S. Rte. A1A* ☎ *561/624–0065* ⊙ *Daily dawn–dusk.*

CANOEING

Canoe Outfitters of Florida (✉ *9060 W. Indiantown Rd.* ☎ *561/746–7053*) leads trips along 8 mi of the Loxahatchee River, where you can see animals in the wild, from otters to eagles. Canoe or kayak rental for two to three hours is $25, including drop-off and pickup.

GOLF

The 18-hole **Abacoa Golf Club** (✉ *105 Barbados Dr.* ☎ *561/622–0036*) is a good alternative to nearby private courses; greens fee $60/$119. The **Golf Club of Jupiter** (✉ *1800 Central Blvd.* ☎ *561/747–6262*) has 18 holes of varying difficulty; greens fee $49/$69. **Jupiter Dunes Golf Club** (✉ *401 Rte. A1A* ☎ *561/746–6654*) has an 18-hole golf course named Little Monster and a putting green near the Jupiter River estuary; greens fee $36/$65.

WHERE TO EAT AND STAY

$$ SEAFOOD ✕ **Food Shack.** This local favorite is a bit tricky to find, but worth the search. The fried-food standards you might expect at such a casual place are not found on the menu; instead there are fried-tuna rolls with basil and fried grouper cheeks with a fruity slaw. A variety of beers are fun to pair with the creatively prepared seafood dishes that include wahoo, mahimahi, and snapper. ✉ *103 South U.S. 1* ☎ *561/741–3626* 🌐 *www.littlemoirsfoodshack.com* ▭ *DC, MC, V* ⊙ *Closed Sun.*

$$$ SEAFOOD ✕ **Sinclair's Ocean Grill.** This popular spot in the Jupiter Beach Resort has sunlight streaming through the glass doors overlooking the pool. The menu has a daily selection of fresh fish, such as cashew-encrusted grouper, Cajun-spice tuna, and mahimahi with pistachio sauce. There are also thick, juicy steaks—filet mignon is the house specialty—and chicken and veal dishes. The Sunday buffet is a big draw. ✉ *5 N. Rte. A1A* ☎ *561/745–7120* 🌐 *www.jupiterbeachresort.com* ▭ *AE, D, MC, V.*

$$$$ **Jupiter Beach Resort.** This time-share resort looks great after a complete renovation that added a 7,500-square-foot spa. Caribbean-style rooms with mahogany sleigh beds and armoires fill the nine-story tower. Most rooms have balconies, and those on higher floors have great ocean views. Some overlook Jupiter Lighthouse, and others face Juno Pier. Families love the casual approach and the plentiful activities, such as turtle-watches from May to October. Snorkeling equipment and bicycles are available for rent. **Pros:** fabulous views; good location. **Cons:**

very high beds; pricey rates. ✉ *5 N. Rte. A1A* ☎ *561/746–2511 or 800/228–8810* 🌐 *www.jupiterbeachresort.com* *133 rooms, 44 suites* *In-room: a/c, safe, Wi-Fi. In-hotel: 3 restaurants, bars, tennis court, pool, gym, spa, beachfront, water sports, bicycles, laundry facilities, parking (free)* 💳 *AE, D, MC, V.*

JUPITER ISLAND AND HOBE SOUND

5 mi north of Jupiter, off Rte. A1A.

Northeast across the Jupiter Inlet from Jupiter is the southern tip of Jupiter Island. Here expansive and expensive estates often retreat from the road behind screens of vegetation, and at the north end of the island turtles come to nest in a wildlife refuge. To the west, on the mainland, is the little community of Hobe Sound.

GETTING HERE AND AROUND

The best way to get to Jupiter Island and Hobe Sound from Jupiter is to drive north 5 mi on Interstate 95 to Indiantown Road. From there, head east to Federal Highway (U.S. 1), then north on U.S. 1.

EXPLORING

Blowing Rocks Preserve. Protected within this 73-acre preserve are plants native to beachfront dune, coastal strand (the landward side of the dunes), mangrove forests, and tropical hardwood forests. The best time to visit is when high tides and strong offshore winds coincide, causing the sea to blow spectacularly through holes in the eroded outcropping. Park in the lot; police ticket cars parked along the road. ✉ *574 South Beach Rd., Rte. 707, Jupiter Island* ☎ *561/744–6668* *$2* ⏲ *Daily 9–4:30.*

Hobe Sound National Wildlife Refuge. Two tracts make up this refuge: 232 acres of sand-pine and scrub-oak forest in Hobe Sound, and 735 acres of coastal sand dune and mangrove swamp on Jupiter Island. Trails are open to the public in both places. Turtles nest and shells wash ashore on the 3½-mi-long beach, which has been severely eroded by high tides and strong winds. ✉ *13640 SE Federal Hwy., Hobe Sound* ☎ *772/546–6141* *$5 per vehicle* ⏲ *Daily dawn–dusk.*

Hobe Sound Nature Center. It's located in the Hobe Sound National Wildlife Refuge, but this nature center is an independent organization. Its museum, which has baby alligators and crocodiles and a scary-looking tarantula, is a child's delight. A ½-mi trail winds through a forest of sand pine and scrub oak—one of Florida's most unusual and endangered plant communities. It lost its original building in 2004 due to hurricanes and moved into a new building in 2007. A new visitor center opened in 2009. ✉ *13640 SE Federal Hwy., Hobe Sound* ☎ *772/546–2067* 🌐 *www.hobesoundnaturecenter.com* *Donation suggested* ⏲ *Trail daily dawn–dusk; nature center weekdays 9–3.*

Jonathan Dickinson State Park. From Hobe Mountain, an ancient dune topped with a tower, you are treated to a panoramic view of this park's 10,285 acres of varied terrain and the Intracoastal Waterway. The Loxahatchee River, which cuts through the park, is home to manatees in winter and alligators all year. Two-hour boat tours of the river depart daily at 9, 11, 1, and 3 and cost $14.50 per person. Among amenities are a dozen cabins for rent, tent sites, bicycle and hiking trails, a campground, and a snack bar. ✉ *16450 SE Federal Hwy., Hobe Sound* ☎ *772/546–2771* 🎫 *$6 per vehicle* ⏲ *Daily 8–dusk.*

SPORTS AND THE OUTDOORS

OUTFITTER

Jonathan Dickinson's River Tours (✉ *Jonathan Dickinson State Park, 16450 SE Federal Hwy., Hobe Sound* ☎ *561/746–1466*) offers boat tours of the Loxahatchee River and canoe, kayak, and boat rentals from 9 to 5 daily.

STUART

7 mi north of Hobe Sound.

This compact little town on a peninsula that juts out into the St. Lucie River has a remarkable amount of shoreline for its size and also has a charming historic district. The ocean is about 5 mi east.

GETTING HERE AND AROUND

To get to Stuart from Jupiter and Hobe Sound, drive north on Federal Highway (U.S. 1).

ESSENTIALS

Visitor Information Stuart Main Street (✉ *201 SW Flagler Ave.* ☎ *772/286–2848*). **Stuart/Martin County Chamber of Commerce** (✉ *1650 S. Kanner Hwy.* ☎ *772/287–1088*).

EXPLORING

Strict architectural and zoning standards guide civic-renewal projects. Stuart has antiques shops, restaurants, and more than 50 specialty shops within a two-block area. A self-guided walking-tour pamphlet is available at assorted locations downtown to clue you in on this once-small fishing village's early days.

★ **Maritime & Yachting Museum.** Linking the watery past with a permanent record of maritime and yachting events contributing to Treasure Coast lore, this museum near a marina has many old ships as well as historic exhibits to explore. Among those leading Saturday tours is a retired ship captain who has many interesting stories to share. ✉ *1707 NE Indian River Dr.* ☎ *772/692–1234* 🌐 *www.mymflorida.com* 🎫 *$5* ⏲ *Mon.–Sat. 10–5, Sun. 1–4.*

SPORTS AND THE OUTDOORS

BEACHES

Stuart Beach. With its ever-vigilant lifeguards, this is a good spot for beginning surfers. More experienced wave riders enjoy the challenges of the choppy waters. Fishing and shelling are also draws. ✉ *801 NE Ocean Blvd.* ☎ *772/221–1418.*

FISHING

Deep-sea charters are available at the **Sailfish Marina** (✉ *3565 SE St. Lucie Blvd.* ☎ *772/221–9456*).

SHOPPING

More than 60 restaurants and shops with antiques, art, and fashion have opened downtown along Osceola Street.

Operating for more than two decades, the **B&A Flea Market**, the oldest and largest such enterprise on the Treasure Coast, has a street-bazaar feel, with shoppers happily scouting for the practical and unusual. *2885 SE Federal Hwy. 772/288–4915 Free Weekends 8–3.*

THE ARTS

On the National Register of Historic Places, the **Lyric Theatre** (*59 SW Flagler Ave. 772/286–7827 www.lyrictheatre.com*) has been revived for live performances. A gazebo has free music performances..

WHERE TO EAT AND STAY

$$ FRENCH **Courtine's.** A husband-and-wife team oversees this quiet and hospitable restaurant under the Roosevelt Bridge. French and American influences are clear in the Swiss chef's dishes, from rack of lamb with Dijon mustard to grilled filet mignon stuffed with Roquefort and fresh spinach. The formal dining room has subtly elegant touches, such as fresh flowers on each table. A more casual menu is available at the bar. *514 N. Dixie Hwy. 772/692–3662 www.courtines.com AE, MC, V Closed Sun. and Mon. No lunch.*

$$ SEAFOOD **Finz Waterfront Grille.** Located on the southern end of the Manatee Pocket in Port Salerno, the popular island-style restaurant is surrounded by boatyards and a lively gallery scene. Sit on the covered dock and take in the breeze while eating the tastiest crab cakes south of Chesapeake Bay. The kitchen also serves up savory teriyaki-marinated steak tips, Maryland crab soup, peel-and-eat shrimp, and maple-glazed salmon. There's live island music on Sunday afternoons from 2–5 and entertainment every Saturday and Sunday night. *4290 SE Salerno Rd. 772/283–1929 www.finzwaterfrontgrille.com AE, D, MC, V.*

$$$ **Pirate's Cove Resort & Marina.** On the banks of the St. Lucie River, this cozy enclave is the perfect place to recoup after a day at sea. The resort is relaxing and casual but packed with plenty of recreational activities. The tropically furnished rooms are spacious and have balconies to enjoy the waterfront views. The few suites include microwaves and refrigerators. A Continental breakfast is included. **Pros:** pretty location; great for boaters. **Cons:** lounge gets noisy at night. *4307 SE Bayview St., Port Salerno 772/287–2500 or 800/332–1414 www.piratescoveresort.net 48 rooms, 2 suites In-room: a/c, refrigerator, Wi-Fi. In-hotel: restaurant, room service, pool, bar, parking (free) BP AE, D, DC, MC, V.*

HUTCHINSON ISLAND (JENSEN BEACH)

5 mi northeast of Stuart.

The down-to-earth town of Jensen Beach, occupying the core of the island, stretches across both sides of the Indian River. Between late April and August more than 600 turtles come here to nest along the town's Atlantic beach. Area residents have taken pains to curb the runaway development that has created the commercial crowding found to the north and south, although some high-rises have popped up along the shore.

GETTING HERE AND AROUND

The best way to reach Jensen Beach from Stuart is to drive north on Federal Highway (U.S. 1) to Northwest Jensen Boulevard, then east on Jensen Beach Boulevard.

ESSENTIALS

Visitor Information Jensen Beach Chamber of Commerce (✉ *1900 NE Ricou Terr., Jensen Beach* ☎ *772/334–3444*).

EXPLORING

Elliott Museum. This pastel-pink museum was erected in 1961 in honor of Sterling Elliott, inventor of an early automated-addressing machine and a four-wheel cycle. The museum, with its antique cars, dolls, toys, and vintage baseball cards, is a nice stop for anyone fond of nostalgic goods. There are also antique fixtures from an early general store, blacksmith shop, and apothecary shop. ✉ *825 NE Ocean Blvd., Jensen Beach* ☎ *772/225–1961* ⊕ *www.elliottmuseumfl.org* *$8* ⏲ *Mon.–Sat. 10–4, Sun. 1–4.*

★ **Florida Oceanographic Coastal Center.** Explore a ½-mi interpretive boardwalk through coastal hardwood and mangrove forest. Guided nature walks through trails and stingray feedings are offered at various times during the day. Boat tours, which include a 20-minute stop at a bird sanctuary, cost $23 per person. Dolphins, manatees, and turtles are often seen on the boat tour, for which reservations are required. ✉ *890 NE Ocean Blvd., Jensen Beach* ☎ *772/225–0505* ⊕ *www.floridaoceanographic.org* *$8* ⏲ *Mon.–Sat. 10–5, Sun. noon–4; guided nature walks Mon.–Sat. 11 and 3, Sun. at 2; boat tours Tues., Fri., and Sat. at 11, Thurs. at 11 and 4.*

Gilbert's House of Refuge Museum. Built in 1875 on Hutchinson Island, the museum is the only remaining building of nine such structures built by the U.S. Life-Saving Service (a predecessor of the Coast Guard) to aid stranded sailors. Exhibits include antique lifesaving equipment, maps, artifacts from nearby wrecks, and boatbuilding tools. ✉ *301 SE MacArthur Blvd., Jensen Beach* ☎ *772/225–1875* *$6* ⏲ *Mon.–Sat. 10–4, Sun. 1–4.*

SPORTS AND THE OUTDOORS

BASEBALL

The **New York Mets** (✉ *525 NW Peacock Blvd., Port St. Lucie* ☎ *772/871–2115*) train at Tradition Field. It's also the home of the St. Lucie Mets Minor League Team.

BEACHES

At the north end of the Indian River Plantation, **Bathtub Reef Park** (✉ *MacArthur Blvd., off Rte. A1A, Jensen Beach*) is ideal for children because the waters are shallow and usually calm. At low tide you can walk to the reef. Facilities include restrooms and showers.

GOLF

Hutchinson Island Marriott Golf Club (✉ *555 NE Ocean Blvd., Jensen Beach* ☎ *772/225–6819*) has 18 holes for members and hotel guests; greens fee $60 for 18 holes. With three separate courses, the PGA–operated **PGA Golf Club at the PGA Villages** (✉ *1916 Perfect Dr., Port St. Lucie* ☎ *772/467–1300 or 800/800–4653*) is a public facility designed by Pete Dye and Tom Fazio; greens fee $55/$99.

WHERE TO EAT AND STAY

$$$ CONTINENTAL ★ ✕ **11 Maple Street.** This cozy spot is as good as it gets on the Treasure Coast. Soft music and a friendly staff set the mood in the antiques-filled dining room, which holds only 16 tables. Appetizers run from panfried conch to crispy calamari, and entrées include seared rainbow trout, wood-grilled venison with onion-potato hash, and beef tenderloin with white-truffle-and-chive butter. Desserts like white-chocolate custard with blackberry sauce are seductive, too. ✉ *3224 Maple Ave., Jensen Beach* ☎ *772/334–7714* 🌐 *www.11maplestreet.net* *Reservations essential* ▭ *MC, V* ⏲ *Closed Mon. and Tues. No lunch.*

$ SEAFOOD ✕ **Conchy Joe's.** Like a hermit crab sliding into a new shell, Conchy Joe's moved up from West Palm Beach in 1983. Built in the 1920s, this rustic stilt house is full of antique fish mounts, gator hides, and snakeskins. It's a popular tourist spot, but the waterfront location, casual vibe, and delicious seafood attract locals, too. Staples include grouper marsala, broiled sea scallops, and fried cracked conch. There's live reggae Thursday through Sunday. ✉ *3945 NE Indian River Dr., Jensen Beach* ☎ *772/334–1130* 🌐 *www.conchyjoes.com* ▭ *AE, D, MC, V.*

$$$–$$$$ **Hutchinson Island Marriott Beach Resort & Marina.** With a 77-slip marina, a full water-sports program, a golf course and tennis courts, and a wide range of restaurants, this self-contained resort is excellent for families. Many of the rooms are in a trio of four-story buildings that form an open courtyard with a large pool. Additional rooms and apartments are scattered throughout the 200-acre property; some overlook the Intracoastal Waterway, others gaze at the ocean or tropical gardens. **Pros:** attentive staff; challenging golf course. **Cons:** no children's program. ✉ *555 NE Ocean Blvd., Hutchinson Island* ☎ *772/225–3700 or 800/775–5936* 🌐 *www.marriott.com* *213 rooms, 70 suites* *In-room: a/c, kitchen (some), Internet. In-hotel: 3 restaurants, room service, bars, golf course, tennis courts, pools, gym, spa, beachfront, laundry facilities, Wi-Fi hotspot, parking (free) , some pets allowed* ▭ *AE, D, DC, MC, V.*

FORT PIERCE

11 mi north of Stuart, off Federal Hwy. (U.S. 1).

About an hour north of Palm Beach, this community has a distinctive rural feel, focusing on ranching and citrus farming. There are several worthwhile stops, including those easily seen while following Route 707.

ESSENTIALS

Visitor Information St. Lucie County Tourist Development Council (✉ *2300 Virginia Ave.* ☎ *800/344–8443*).

EXPLORING

Heathcote Botanical Gardens. Take a self-guided tour of this 3½-acre park, which includes a palm walk, a Japanese garden, and an orchid house. There is also a gift shop with whimsical and botanical knickknacks. Guided tours are available Tuesday through Saturday by appointment. ✉ *210 Savannah Rd.* ☎ *772/464–4672* 🌐 *www.heathcotebotanicalgardens.org* 🎟 *$6* ⏲ *May–Oct., Tues.–Sat. 9–5; Nov.–Apr., Tues.–Sat. 9–5, Sun. 1–5.*

★ **Navy SEAL Museum.** Commemorating more than 3,000 troops who trained here during World War II, the museum has weapons and equipment on view and exhibits depicting the history of the Underwater Demolition Teams. Patrol boats and vehicles are displayed outdoors. ✉ *3300 N. Rte. A1A* ☎ *772/595–5845* 🌐 *www.navysealmuseum.com* 🎟 *$6* ⏲ *Tues.–Sat. 10–4, Sun. noon–4.*

Savannas Recreation Area. Once a reservoir, the 550 acres have been returned to a natural state. Today the wilderness area has campsites, boat ramps, and trails. ✉ *1400 E. Midway Rd.* ☎ *772/464–7855* ⏲ *Daily 8–6.*

Smithsonian Marine Ecosystems Exhibit. Run by the Smithsonian Institute and housed in the St. Lucie County Marine Center, this is where scientists come to study local ecosystems. A highlight is the 3,000-gallon coral-reef tank, originally shown in the Smithsonian's National Museum of Natural History in Washington, D.C. The parklike setting, where children love to play, makes it an ideal picnic destination. ✉ *420 Seaway Dr.* ☎ *772/462–3474* 🎟 *$3, free the first Tues. of the month* ⏲ *Tues.–Sat. 10–4.*

SPORTS AND THE OUTDOORS

Fort Pierce Inlet State Recreation Area. Sand dunes and coastal forests cover this 340-acre reserve. The park has swimming, surfing, picnic facilities, and a self-guided nature trail. ✉ *905 Shorewinds Dr.* ☎ *772/468–3985* 🎟 *$6 per vehicle* ⏲ *Daily 8–dusk.*

Fort Pierce State Park. Accessible only by footbridge, the reserve has 4 mi of trails around Jack Island. The 1½-mi Marsh Rabbit Trail across the island traverses a mangrove swamp to a 30-foot-tall observation tower overlooking the Indian River. ✉ *Rte. A1A* ☎ *772/468–3985* 🎟 *$4 for one, $6 for a vehicle* ⏲ *Daily 8–5:30.*

FISHING

For charter boats and fishing guides, contact the dockmaster at the **Dockside Harborlight Resort** (✉ *1160 Seaway Dr.* ☎ *772/461–4824*).

SCUBA DIVING

On North Hutchinson Island, the **Urca de Lima Underwater Archaeological Preserve,** 200 yards from shore and under 10–15 feet of water, contains remains of a flat-bottom, round-bellied store ship. Once part of a treasure fleet bound for Spain, it was destroyed by a hurricane. ✉ *3375 N. A1A.*

THE ARTS

Home of the Treasure Coast Art Association, the **A. E. "Bean" Backus Museum & Gallery** displays works of one of Florida's foremost landscape artists. It also mounts changing exhibits and offers exceptional buys on work by local artists. *500 N. Indian River Dr. 772/465–0630 www.backusgallery.com Free but $2 donation suggested Wed.–Sun. 11–4.*

WHERE TO EAT AND STAY

$$$ SEAFOOD **Mangrove Mattie's.** This upscale spot on Fort Pierce Inlet provides dazzling waterfront views and delicious seafood. Dine on the terrace or in the dining room, and don't forget to try the coconut-fried shrimp or the chicken and scampi. Go during happy hour (weekdays 5–8) for a free buffet. Many locals come by for Sunday brunch. *1640 Seaway Dr. 772/466–1044 www.mangrovematties.com AE, D, DC, MC, V.*

$–$$ **Dockside Harborlight Resort Inn.** Formerly two adjacent motels, this resort is the best of the lodgings lining the Fort Pierce Inlet along Seaway Drive. Spacious, nicely decorated units on two floors have kitchens or wet bars. Some have a waterfront porch or balcony. A cluster of apartments is across the street, away from the water. Overnight boat docking is available for an additional $25 per night. **Pros:** good value; reasonable rates at marina. **Cons:** basic decor; some steps to climb. *1160 Seaway Dr. 772/468–3555 or 800/286–1745 www.docksideinn.com 72 rooms, 4 apartments In-room: a/c, refrigerator (some). In-hotel: pools, laundry facilities, parking (free) AE, D, DC, MC, V.*

VERO BEACH

12 mi north of Fort Pierce.

Tranquil and charming, this Indian River County town has a strong commitment to the environment and the arts. There are plenty of outdoor activities here, even though many visitors gravitating to the training camp of the Los Angeles Dodgers opt to do little at all. In the town's exclusive Riomar Bay area, roads are shaded by massive live oaks, and a popular cluster of restaurants and shops is just off the beach.

10

GETTING HERE AND AROUND

To get here, you have two options—Route A1A, along the coast, or Route 605 (also called Old Dixie Highway), on the mainland. As you approach Vero on the latter, you pass through an ungussied landscape of small farms and residential areas. On the beach route, part of the drive is through an unusually undeveloped section of the Florida coast.

ESSENTIALS

Visitor Information Indian River Chamber of Commerce (*1216 21st St. 772/567–3491*).

EXPLORING

Environmental Learning Center. In addition to aquariums filled with Indian River creatures, the 51 acres here have a 600-foot boardwalk through the mangrove shoreline and a 1-mi canoe trail. The center is on the northern edge of Vero Beach, and the pretty drive is worth the trip.

✉ 255 Live Oak Dr. ☎ 772/589–5050 🌐 www.elcweb.org 🎟 Donation suggested ⏲ Tues.–Fri. 10–4, Sat. 9–noon, Sun. 1–4.

Heritage Center and Indian River Citrus Museum. You'll learn that more grapefruit is shipped from the Indian River area than anywhere else in the world at this museum. The memorabilia harks back to when families washed and wrapped the luscious fruit to sell at roadside stands, and oxen hauled citrus-filled crates with distinctive Indian River labels to the rail station. *✉ 2140 14th Ave. 🌐 www.veroheritage.org ☎ 772/770–2263 🎟 Free ⏲ Tues.–Fri. 10–4.*

Fodor's Choice ★ **McKee Botanical Garden.** On the National Register of Historic Places, the 18 acres here are both a tropical garden and a horticulture museum. The historic Hall of Giants, a rustic structure built from cedar and hearts of pine, features a beautiful stained glass, bronze bells, and the world's largest single-plank mahogany table. There's a 529-square-foot bamboo pavilion, a gift shop, and the Garden Café, which serves tasty snacks and sandwiches and locally grown tea. This is the place to see spectacular water lilies. *✉ 350 U.S. 1 ☎ 772/794–0601 🌐 www.mckeegarden.org 🎟 $9 ⏲ Tues.–Sat. 10–5, Sun. noon–5.*

Vero Beach Museum of Art. Part of a 26-acre campus dedicated to the arts, the museum is where a full schedule of exhibitions, art movies, lectures, workshops, and classes are hosted. The museum's five galleries and sculpture garden make it the largest art facility in the Treasure Coast. *✉ 3001 Riverside Park Dr. ☎ 772/231–0707 🌐 www.vbmuseum.org ⏲ Mon.–Sat. 10–4:30, Sun. 1–4:30.*

SPORTS AND THE OUTDOORS

BEACHES

Humiston Park (*✉ Ocean Dr. below Beachland Blvd. Vero Beach ☎ 772/231–5790 🎟 Free*) is one of the beach-access parks along the east edge of town that have lifeguards, boardwalks, and steps bridging the dunes, plus there are picnic tables and a children's play area. There are picnic tables, restrooms, and a nice playground for kids at **Treasure Shores Park** (*✉ 11300 A1A, 3 mi north of County Rd. 510 ☎ 772/581–4997*). **Wabasso Beach Park** (*✉ County Rd. 510, east of A1A ☎ 772/581–4998*) has lifeguards, restrooms, a boardwalk, and showers.

GOLF

Sandridge Golf Club (*✉ 5300 73rd St. ☎ 772/770–5000*) has two public 18-hole courses designed by Ron Garl; greens fee $49.

SHOPPING

Along Ocean Drive near Beachland Boulevard, a shopping area includes art galleries, antiques shops, and upscale clothing stores. The eight-block area of Oceanside has an interesting mix of boutiques, specialty shops, and eateries.

Just west of Interstate 95, **Outlets at Vero Beach** (*✉ 1824 94th Dr. ☎ 772/770–6171*) is a discount shopping destination with 70 brand-name stores, including Ann Taylor, Ralph Lauren Polo, and Jones New York.

DID YOU KNOW?

Vero Beach is known for its arts. But like many of Florida's coastal towns, some of the top attractions here are the natural offerings, from Vero Beach's citrus trees to its beautiful sunrises.

THE ARTS

Riverside Children's Theatre (✉ *Agnes Wahlstrom Youth Playhouse, 3280 Riverside Park Dr.* ☎ *772/234–8052* 🌐 *www.riversidetheatre.com*) offers a series of professional touring and local productions. The **Riverside Theatre** (✉ *3250 Riverside Park Dr.* ☎ *772/231–6990* 🌐 *www.riversidetheatre.com*) stages five productions each season in its 650-seat Mainstage and three in its 200-seat Second Stage.

WHERE TO EAT AND STAY

$$$ SEAFOOD **Ocean Grill.** Opened as a hamburger shack in 1938, the Ocean Grill combines its ocean view with Tiffany-style lamps, wrought-iron chandeliers, and paintings of pirates. Count on at least three kinds of seafood any day on the menu, along with steaks, pork chops, soups, and salads. The house drink, "Pusser's Painkiller"—a curious blend first mixed by British sailors in the Virgin Islands and rationed in a tin cup. It commemorates the 1894 wreck of the *Breconshire,* which occurred offshore and from which 34 British sailors escaped. ✉ *Sexton Plaza, 1050 Ocean Dr.* ☎ *772/231–5409* 🌐 *www.ocean-grill.com* ▭ *AE, D, DC, MC, V* ⏲ *Closed 2 wks after Labor Day. No lunch weekends.*

$–$$ **Aquarius Oceanfront Resort.** Right on beautiful South Beach, this small, unpretentious resort has loyal guests who book a year in advance. Ask for Rooms 125 and 126, which have balconies overlooking the beach. Others, most with kitchens, face the parking lot. Walk across the street to the excellent Italian restaurant Monte's and to South Beach Pizza. **Pros:** relaxed vibe; great location; faces the beach. **Cons:** steps to climb; nothing too fancy. ✉ *1526 Ocean Dr.* ☎ *772/231–5218 or 877/767–1526* 🌐 *www.aquariusverobeach.com* *28 rooms* *In-room: a/c, kitchen (some). In-hotel: pool, beachfront, laundry facilities, parking (free)* ▭ *AE, DC, MC, V.*

$$$–$$$$ **Costa d'Este.** Many people know this hotel because of its famous owners, singer Gloria Estefan and producer Emilio Estefan. They bought the property in 2004, just before hurricanes ripped the former Palm Court apart. They brought in a new design and a lively ambience. The architecture features geometrical designs, something you will notice as soon as you arrive at the porte-cochere entrance. Rooms are sleek and filled with custom-made furnishings. You get the feel of being in a modern yacht with broad ocean views. Oriente, the resort's restaurant, has become a favorite of locals who come for the Cuban cuisine. **Pros:** great location; huge showers; faces the beach. **Cons:** marble floors can be cold. ✉ *3244 Ocean Dr.* ☎ *772/562–9919* 🌐 *www.costadeste.com* *90 rooms, 4 suites* *In-room: a/c, safe, refrigerator, Wi-Fi. In-hotel: restaurant, room service, pool, gym, spa, laundry service, parking (free)* ▭ *AE, MC, V.*

$$$$ **Disney's Vero Beach Resort.** This oceanfront, family-oriented retreat operates as a hotel and a Disney Vacation Club. The artfully themed four-story main building, freestanding villas, and six beach cottages are reminiscent of 19th-century Florida. Guests will find hidden treasurers related to sea turtles and Florida's rich history. Many rooms have full kitchens and balconies, and all have bright interiors and tile floors. Shutters serves American food and has character breakfasts on Saturday mornings. Wood-fired steaks and creative seafood are served up at

Sonya's. **Pros:** fun for families; lots to do for kids. **Cons:** not the best place if you don't have children; a bit kitschy. ✉ *9250 Island Grove Terr.* ☎ *772/234–2000 or 800/359–8000* 🌐 *www.disneybeachresorts.com* *161 rooms, 14 suites, 6 cottages* *In-room: a/c, safe, kitchen (some), refrigerator (some), Internet. In-hotel: 3 restaurants, room service, bar, tennis courts, pool, gym, beachfront, bicycles, children's programs (ages 4–12), laundry facilities, parking (free)* *AE, MC, V.*

$–$$ **Driftwood Resort.** On the National Register of Historic Places, this 1935 inn was built entirely from ocean-washed timbers and decorated with such artifacts as ship bells, Spanish tiles, and a cannon from a 16th-century Spanish galleon. The time-share complex includes nine buildings on the beach with both modern and historic rooms. The inn attracts guests from around the world, who sit in wooden rockers facing the beach. **Pros:** great seaside location; near restaurants and shops. **Cons:** older property; rooms can be musty. ✉ *3150 Ocean Dr.* ☎ *772/231–0550* 🌐 *www.thedriftwood.com* *96 1- and 2-bedroom suites, 4 hotel rooms* *In-room: a/c, kitchen refrigerator. In-hotel: restaurant, bar, pools, beachfront, parking (free)* *AE, DC, MC, V.*

SEBASTIAN

14 mi north of Vero Beach, off Federal Hwy. (U.S. 1).

One of the few sparsely populated areas on Florida's east coast, this fishing village has as remote a feeling as you're likely to find between Jacksonville and Miami Beach. That adds to the appeal of the recreation area around Sebastian Inlet, where you can walk for miles along quiet beaches and catch some of Florida's best waves for surfing.

ESSENTIALS

Visitor Information **Sebastian Chamber of Commerce** (✉ *700 Main St.* ☎ *772/589–5969*).

EXPLORING

McLarty Treasure Museum. A National Historical Landmark, this museum underscores this credo: "Wherever gold glitters or silver beckons, man will move mountains." It has displays of coins, weapons, and tools salvaged from a fleet of Spanish treasure ships that sank in the 1715 storm, leaving some 1,500 survivors struggling to shore between Sebastian and Fort Pierce. The museum's last video showing begins at 3. ✉ *13180 N. Rte. A1A* ☎ *772/589–2147* *$2* *Daily 10–4.*

Mel Fisher's Treasures. You'll really come upon hidden loot when you enter this museum operated by the late Mel Fisher's family. See some of what was recovered in 1985 from the Spanish treasure ship *Atocha* and its sister ships of the 1715 fleet. The museum certainly piques one's curiosity about what is still buried at sea: treasures continue to be discovered each year. ✉ *1322 U.S. 1* ☎ *772/589–9875* 🌐 *www.melfisher.com* *$6.50* *Mon.–Sat. 10–5, Sun. noon–5.*

Pelican Island National Wildlife Refuge. Within the Indian River Lagoon and on the barrier island across from Sebastian, Pelican Island was founded in 1903 by President Theodore Roosevelt as the nation's first national wildlife refuge. The island is a closed wilderness area. The

10

historic Pelican Island rockery is viewable from a distance by commercial boat and kayak tours and from a public observation tower on the adjacent barrier island. The Refuge has more than 6 mi of foot trails through the barrier island habitats. A boardwalk and observation tower enable visitors to see birds, endangered species, and habitats. ✉ *1339 20th St.* ☎ *772/562–3909 Ext. 275* 🎟 *Free* ⏲ *Daily 7:30–sunset.*

Sebastian Inlet State Recreation Area. Because of the highly productive fishing waters of Sebastian Inlet, this 578-acre property at the north end of Orchid Island is one of the Florida park system's biggest draws. Both sides of the high bridge spanning the inlet—views are spectacular—attract anglers as well as those eager to enjoy the fine sandy shores, known for having some of the best waves in the state. A concession stand on the inlet's north side sells short-order food, rents various craft, and has a small apparel and surf shop. There's a boat ramp, and not far away is a dune area that's part of the **Archie Carr National Wildlife Refuge.** ✉ *9700 S. Rte. A1A, Melbourne Beach* ☎ *321/984–4852* 🌐 *www.floridastateparks.org* 🎟 *$5 per vehicle* ⏲ *Daily 7–sunset.*

SPORTS AND THE OUTDOORS

FISHING

For sportfishing, try **Big Easy Fishing Charters** (✉ *Capt. Hiram's Restaurant, 1606 N. Indian River Dr.* ☎ *772/664–4068*). For bottom fishing, try **Incentive Charter Fishing** (✉ *Capt. Hiram's Restaurant, 1606 N. Indian River Dr.* ☎ *321/676–1948*).

Fort Lauderdale and Broward County

WORD OF MOUTH

"I think you'll enjoy Fort Lauderdale. The Riverwalk/Las Olas area has lots of good restaurants—you can take a water taxi there from just about anywhere on the Intracoastal waterway."

—321go

WELCOME TO FT. LAUDERDALE AND BROWARD COUNTY

TOP REASONS TO GO

★ **Blue Waves:** Sparkling Lauderdale beaches—from Deerfield Beach and Pompano Beach through Dania Beach and Hollywood—are Florida's first to capture Blue Wave Beach status from the Clean Beaches Council.

★ **Inland Waterways:** More than 300 mi of inland waterways including downtown Fort Lauderdale's historic New River create what's known as the Venice of America.

★ **Everglades Access:** Just minutes from luxury hotels and golf courses, the rugged Everglades tantalize with alligators, colorful birds, and other wildlife.

★ **Vegas-Style Gaming:** In 2008, Vegas-style slots came to Hollywood's glittering Seminole Hard Rock Hotel & Casino, adding to video slots already in play there and at other Broward "racinos."

★ **Cruise Gateway:** Port Everglades—homeport for Royal Caribbean's new *Oasis of the Seas,* the world's largest cruise vessel—hosts cruise ships from major lines.

1 Fort Lauderdale. Anchored by historic New River and its attractive Riverwalk, Fort Lauderdale embraces high-rise condos along with single-family homes, museums, parks, and attractions. Las Olas Boulevard, lined with boutiques, sidewalk cafés, and restaurants, links downtown and the beaches.

2 North on Scenic A1A. Stretching north on Route A1A, seaside attractions range from high-rise Galt Ocean Mile to low-rise resort communities—and a glimpse of a lighthouse, inspiration for the community of Lighthouse Point.

3 South Broward. From Hollywood's beachside Broadwalk and historic Young Circle (the latter transformed into an Arts Park) to Seminole gaming, South Broward provides grit, glitter, and diversity in attractions.

Fort Lauderdale Beach.

rt Lauderdale Beach.

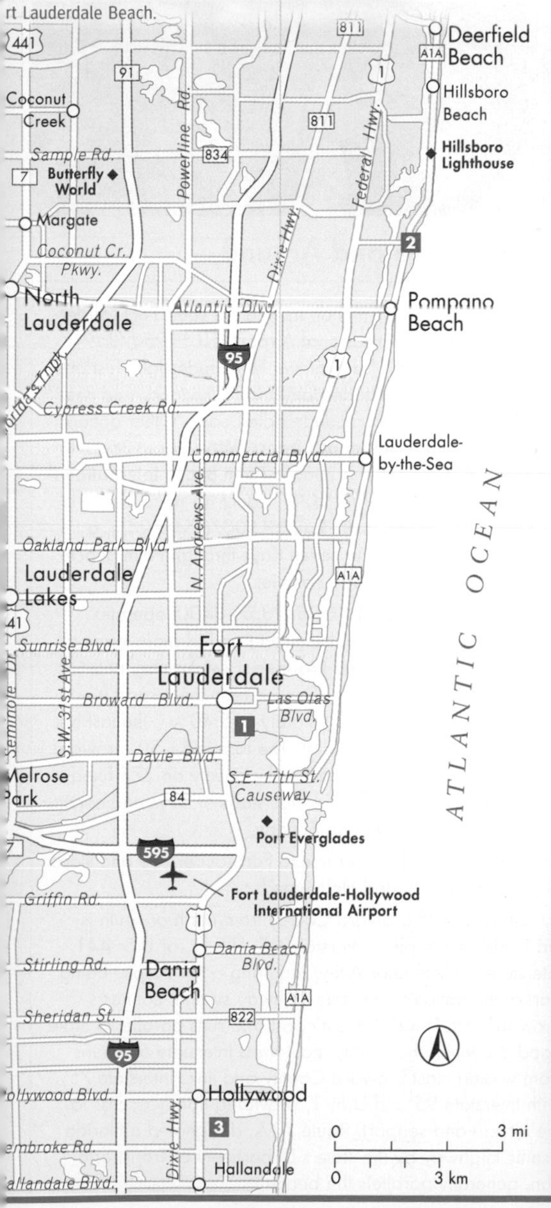
441
91
811
Deerfield Beach
A1A
1
Coconut Creek
Hillsboro Beach
811
Sample Rd.
834
Hillsboro Lighthouse
7
Butterfly World
Powerline Rd.
Federal Hwy.
Margate
Dixie Hwy.
2
Coconut Cr. Pkwy.
North Lauderdale
Atlantic Blvd.
Pompano Beach
95
1
Cypress Creek Rd.
Commercial Blvd.
Lauderdale-by-the-Sea
N. Andrews Ave.
Oakland Park Blvd.
Lauderdale Lakes
A1A
ATLANTIC OCEAN
Sunrise Blvd.
Fort Lauderdale
S.W. 31st Ave.
Broward Blvd.
Las Olas Blvd.
1
Davie Blvd.
Melrose Park
S.E. 17th St. Causeway
84
Port Everglades
595
Griffin Rd.
Fort Lauderdale-Hollywood International Airport
1
Dania Beach Blvd.
Stirling Rd.
Dania Beach
A1A
Sheridan St.
822
95
Hollywood Blvd.
Hollywood
Dixie Hwy.
3
Pembroke Rd.
0
3 mi
Hallandale
Hallandale Blvd.
0
3 km

GETTING ORIENTED

Along the southeast's Gold Coast, Fort Lauderdale and Broward County anchor a delightfully chic middle ground between the historically elite Palm Beaches and the international hubbub of Miami. From downtown Fort Lauderdale, it's about a four-hour drive to either Orlando or Key West, but there's plenty to keep you in Broward. All told, Broward boasts 31 communities from Deerfield Beach to Hallandale Beach along the coast, and from Coral Springs to Southwest Ranches closer to the Everglades. Big—in fact, huge—shopping options await in Sunrise, home of Sawgrass Mills, the upscale Colonnade Outlets at Sawgrass, and IKEA Sunrise.

Las Olas Labor Day Art fair.

FT. LAUDERDALE AND BROWARD COUNTY PLANNER

When to Go

Peak season runs Thanksgiving through March, when concert, art, and entertainment seasons go full throttle. Expect rain, heat, and humidity in summer. Hurricane winds come most notably in August and September, sometimes as late as November. Golfing tee-time waits are longer on weekends year-round. Fort Lauderdale sunshine can burn even in cloudy weather.

TOP FESTIVALS

Fort Lauderdale International Film Festival. Beginning in late October, this event showcases over 200 feature, documentary, and short films from around the world. In addition to 23 days of screenings, you can expect seminars and Hollywood-style parties. Directors and actors in attendence add star power. ☎ *954/760–9898* 🌐 *www.fliff.com.*

Seminole Hard Rock Winterfest Boat Parade. In mid-December, 100-plus vessels decked out with festive decorations light up the Intracoastal Waterway in Fort Lauderdale. Over the years, celebrity grand marshals have included Regis Philbin, Joan Rivers, and Kim Kardashian. ☎ *954/767–0686* 🌐 *www.winterfestparade.com.*

Getting Here and Around

Serving more than 21 million travelers a year, **Fort Lauderdale–Hollywood International Airport** (*FLL* ☎ *954/359–6100*) is 4 mi south of downtown Fort Lauderdale, just off U.S. 1 between Fort Lauderdale and Hollywood, and near Port Everglades and Fort Lauderdale Beach. Other options include **Miami International Airport (MIA),** about 35 mi to the south, and the far less chaotic **Palm Beach International Airport** (*PBI* ☎ *561/471–7420*), about 45 mi to the north. All three airports link to **Tri-Rail** (☎ *800/874–7245*), a commuter train operating seven days through Palm Beach, Broward, and Miami-Dade counties.

Broward County Transit (☎ *954/357–8400*) operates bus route No. 1 between the airport and its main terminal at Broward Boulevard and Northwest 1st Avenue, near downtown Fort Lauderdale. Service from the airport is every 20 minutes and begins daily at 5:40 AM; the last bus leaves the airport at 11:15 PM. The fare is $1.50. Broward County Transit (BCT) also covers the county on 275 fixed routes. The fare is $1.50. Service starts at 5 AM and continues to 11:30 PM, except on Sunday.

Amtrak provides daily service to Fort Lauderdale and stops at Deerfield Beach and Hollywood.

By car, access to Broward County from north or south is via Florida's Turnpike, Interstate 95, U.S. 1, or U.S. 441. Interstate 75 (Alligator Alley, requiring a toll despite being part of the nation's interstate-highway system) connects Broward with Florida's west coast and runs parallel to State Road 84 within the county. East–west Interstate 595 runs from westernmost Broward County and links Interstate 75 with Interstate 95 and U.S. 1, providing handy access to the airport and seaport. Route A1A, designated a Florida Scenic Highway by the state's Department of Transportation, generally parallels the beach.

About the Restaurants

References to "Fort Liquordale" from spring-break days of old have given way to au courant allusions for the decidedly cuisine-oriented "Fork Lauderdale." Greater Fort Lauderdale offers some of the finest, most varied dining of any U.S. city its size, spawned in part by the advent of new luxury hotels and upgrades all around. From among more than 4,000 wining-and-dining establishments in Broward, choose from basic Americana or cuisines of Asia, Europe, or Central and South America, and enjoy more than just food in an atmosphere with subtropical twists.

About the Hotels

Not as posh as Palm Beach or as deco-trendy as Miami Beach, Fort Lauderdale has a growing roster of more-than-respectable lodging choices, from beachfront luxury suites to intimate bed-and-breakfasts to chain hotels along the Intracoastal Waterway. Relatively new on the luxury beachfront are the Atlantic, the Hilton Fort Lauderdale Beach Resort, the Ritz-Carlton, Fort Lauderdale, and Florida's first W resort, and more upscale places to hang your hat are on the horizon while smaller family-run lodging spots disappear. If you want to be *on* the beach, be sure to ask specifically when booking your room, since many hotels advertise "waterfront" accommodations that are along inland waterways or overlooking the beach from across Route A1A. Opened just in time for Superbowl 2010, the iconic Yankee Clipper (shaped like a ship's prow) has regained luster with a major revamp as the Sheraton Fort Lauderdale Beach Hotel, and it's *definitely* smack on the beach.

Assume that hotels operate on the European Plan (EP, no meals), unless we specify that they use the Breakfast Plan (BP, with full breakfast), Continental Plan (CP, Continental breakfast), Full American Plan (FAP, all meals), or Modified American Plan (MAP, breakfast and dinner), or are all-inclusive (AI, all meals and most activities).

WHAT IT COSTS

	¢	$	$$	$$$	$$$$
Restaurants	under $10	$10–$15	$15–$20	$20–$30	Over $30
Hotels	under $80	$80–$100	$100–$140	$140–$220	over $220

Restaurant prices are per person for a main course at dinner. Hotel prices are for a standard double room, excluding 6% sales tax (more in some counties) and 1%–5% tourist tax.

Boat Tours

Carrie B (✉ *Riverwalk at SE 5th Ave., Fort Lauderdale* ☎ *954/768–9920* 🌐 *www.carriebcruises.com*), a 300-passenger day cruiser, gives 90-minute tours on the New River and Intracoastal Waterway. Cruises depart at 11, 1, and 3 each day and cost $19.95.

Fort Lauderdale Duck Tours (✉ *17 S. Fort Lauderdale Beach Blvd., Fort Lauderdale* ☎ *954/761–4002* 🌐 *www.fortlauderdaleducktours.com*), provides 90 minutes of land/water family fun aboard a 45-passenger amphibious hydra terra, cruising Venice of America neighborhoods, historic areas, and the Intracoastal Waterway. Tours depart daily (schedule varies) and cost $30.

Jungle Queen (✉ *Bahia Mar Beach Resort, 801 Seabreeze Blvd., Fort Lauderdale* ☎ *954/462–5596* 🌐 *www.junglequeen.com*) operates *Jungle Queen III* and *Jungle Queen IV*, tour boats seating more than 500 for cruises up New River through the heart of Fort Lauderdale. Sightseeing cruises at 9:30 and 1:30 cost $17.50, and the 6 PM BBQ dinner cruise costs $39.95.

Pro Dive International (✉ *515 Seabreeze Blvd., Fort Lauderdale* ☎ *954/761–3413* 🌐 *www.prodiveusa.com*) operates the 60-foot glass-bottom boat *Pro Diver II* for taking in offshore reefs. Daily two-hour trips cost $28 or $35 to snorkel, equipment provided.

FORT LAUDERDALE AND BROWARD COUNTY BEACHES

A wave-capped, 20-mi shoreline with wide ribbons of golden sand for beachcombing and sunbathing remains the anchor draw for Fort Lauderdale and Broward County.

Fort Lauderdale isn't just for spring breakers. In fact, ever since investors started pouring money into the waterfront scene, beginning in the '90s, the beach has lured a more upscale clientele. That said, it still has great people-watching and opportunities for partying.

Beyond the city, Broward County's beachfront extends for miles without interruption, although character of communities along the shoreline varies. To the south in Hallandale, the beach is backed by towering condominiums, while tee times and nightlife beckon in Hollywood. Deerfield Beach and Lauderdale-by-the-Sea to the north are magnets for active families, and nearby Pompano Beach attracts anglers. Many places along Broward shorelines—blessedly, for purists—are uncluttered with nothing but sand and turquoise waters.

SAFETY TIPS

⚠ **Avoid unguarded waters, and be aware of color codes.** In Fort Lauderdale, double red flags mean water is closed to the public, often because of lightning or sharks; a lone red flag signals strong currents; purple signals presence of marine pests like men-of-war, jellyfish, or sea lice; green means calm conditions. In Hollywood, orange signals rip currents with easterly onshore winds; blue warns of marine life like jellyfish; red means hazardous; green signals good conditions.

FORT LAUDERDALE'S BEST BEACHES

FORT LAUDERDALE BEACH

Alone among Florida's major beachfront communities, Fort Lauderdale's beach remains gloriously open and uncluttered. A wave theme unifies the Fort Lauderdale Beachfront setting—from the low, white, wave-shaped wall between the beach and beachfront promenade to the widened and bricked inner promenade in front of shops, restaurants, and hotels. Walkways line both sides of the beach roadway, and traffic has been trimmed to two gently curving northbound lanes, where in-line skaters skim past slow-moving cars. On the beach side, a low masonry wall doubles as an extended bench, separating sand from the promenade. At night the wall is accented with pretty ribbons of fiber-optic color, often on the blink despite an ongoing search for a permanent fix. The beach is most crowded between Las Olas and Sunrise boulevards.

HOLLYWOOD'S BROADWALK

The name might be Hollywood, but there's nothing hip or chic about Hollywood North Beach Park, which sits at the north end of Hollywood (Route A1A and Sheridan Street). And that's a good thing. It's just a laid-back, old-fashioned place to enjoy the sun, sand, and sea. No high-rises overpower the scene here. Parking is $5. The main part of the Broadwalk is quite a bit more fashionable. Thanks to a $14 million makeover, this popular beach has spiffy new features like a pedestrian walkway, a concrete bike path, a crushed-shell jogging path, an 18-inch decorative wall separating the Broadwalk from the sand, and places to shower off after a dip. Fido fans take note: the 2008 film *Marley & Me,* starring Jennifer Aniston and Owen Wilson and filmed in Greater Fort Lauderdale, spurred a comeback for dog beaches in South Florida, including the year-round Dog Beach of Hollywood.

LAUDERDALE-BY-THE-SEA

For a small village with a pier, Lauderdale-by-the-Sea packs a big punch for beach pleasure. Especially popular with divers and snorkelers, this laid-back stretch of sand provides great access to lovely coral reefs. When you're not down in the waters, look up and you'll likely see a pelican flying by. Gentle trade winds make this an utterly relaxing retreat from the hubbub of the Fort Lauderdale party scene. Things do liven up with nightly entertainment at a couple of local watering holes, but L-B-T-S, as it's known, still provides a small-town, easygoing, family-friendly feel.

Updated by Lynne Helm

Collegians of the 1960s returning to Fort Lauderdale would be hard-pressed to recognize the onetime "Sun and Suds Spring Break Capital of the Universe." Back then, Fort Lauderdale's beachfront was lined with T-shirt shops, and downtown consisted of a lone office tower and dilapidated buildings waiting to be razed.

The beach and downtown have since exploded with upscale shops, restaurants, and luxury resort hotels equipped with enough high-octane amenities to light up skies all the way to western Broward's Alligator Alley. At risk of losing small-town 45-rpm magic in iPod times—when hotel parking fees alone eclipse room rates of old—Greater Fort Lauderdale somehow seems to meld disparate eras into nouveau nirvana, seasoned with a little Gold Coast sand.

The city was named for Major William Lauderdale, who built a fort at the river's mouth in 1838 during the Seminole Indian wars. It wasn't until 1911 that the city was incorporated, with only 175 residents, but it grew quickly during the Florida boom of the 1920s. Today's population hovers around 150,000, and suburbs keep growing—1.6 million live in Broward County's 31 municipalities and unincorporated areas. As elsewhere, many speculators busily flipping property here got caught when the sun-drenched real-estate bubble burst, leaving Broward's foreclosure rate to skyrocket.

Despite economic downturns, gaming options have expanded. South Florida's Indian tribes have long offered bingo, poker, and machines resembling slots. In 2005, Broward became Florida's first county to offer gambling with true slot machines at four wagering facilities referred to as racinos: Gulfstream Park Racing & Casino, the Mardi Gras Racetrack & Gaming, Dania Jai Alai Casino, and the Isle Casino & Racing of Pompano Park. In 2008, Hollywood's Seminole Hard Rock Hotel & Casino, which ranks as the most glittering example of Vegas-style gaming with a tropical twist cut a deal with the state to replace bingo-style machines with genuine Vegas-style slots.

GREAT ITINERARIES

Since many Broward County attractions are close, you can pack a lot into a day—if you have wheels. Catch the history, museums, and shops and bistros in Fort Lauderdale's downtown and along Las Olas Boulevard. Then if you feel like hitting the beach, head east to the intersection of Las Olas and Route A1A and you're there. Neighboring communities like Lauderdale-by-the-Sea and Pompano Beach (to the north) or Dania Beach and Hollywood (to the south) have attractions of their own, and you may not realize when you've crossed municipal lines. As a result, you'll be able to cover most high points in three days, and with 7 to 10 days you can experience virtually all of Broward's mainstream charms.

3 DAYS

With a bigger concentration of hotels, restaurants, and attractions than its suburbs, Fort Lauderdale makes a logical base for any visit. On your first day, see downtown, especially Las Olas Boulevard between Southeast 3rd and Southeast 15th avenues. After lunch at a sidewalk café, head for the nearby Arts and Science District and the downtown **Riverwalk**, which you can enjoy at a leisurely pace in half a day or less. On your second day, spend time at the **Fort Lauderdale Beachfront**, shopping or having a cooling libation at an oceanfront lounge if heat drives you off the sand. Tour the waterways on the third day, either on a rented boat from one of the marinas along Route A1A, or via a sightseeing vessel. Reachable by boat are attractions such as Gallery at Beach Place, Broward Center for the Performing Arts, Galleria Mall, Las Olas Boulevard shops, Las Olas Riverfront, and the **Museum of Art** and **Museum of Discovery & Science/AutoNation IMAX Theater**; restaurants such as 15th Street Fisheries, Grill Room at Riverside Hotel, Shula's on the Beach; and hotels such as the Hyatt Regency Pier Sixty-Six and Bahia Mar Beach Resort.

FORT LAUDERDALE

Like many southeast Florida neighbors, Fort Lauderdale has long been revitalizing. In a state where gaudy tourist zones often stand aloof from workaday downtowns, Fort Lauderdale exhibits consistency at both ends of the 2-mi Las Olas corridor. The sparkling look results from upgrades both downtown and on the beachfront. Matching the downtown's innovative arts district, cafés, and boutiques is an equally inventive beach area, with hotels, cafés, and shops facing an undeveloped shoreline, and new resort-style hotels replacing faded icons of yesteryear. Despite wariness of pretentious overdevelopment, city leaders have allowed a striking number of glittering high-rises. Some nostalgia buffs fret over the diminishing vision of sailboats bobbing in waters near downtown, now that a boxy high-rise has erased one of the area's oldest marinas. Sharp demographic changes are also altering the faces of Greater Fort Lauderdale communities, increasingly cosmopolitan with more minorities, including Hispanics and people of Caribbean descent,

This couple tours Fort Lauderdale via a three-wheeled scooter; photo by rockindom, Fodors.com member.

as well as gays and lesbians. In Fort Lauderdale, especially, a younger populace is growing, whereas longtime residents are dying off or heading north, to a point where one former city commissioner likens the change to that of historic New River—moving with the tide and sometimes appearing at a standstill. "The river of our population is at still point, old and new in equipoise, one pushing against the other."

GETTING HERE AND AROUND

The Fort Lauderdale metro area is laid out in a grid system, and only myriad canals and waterways interrupt the mostly straight-line path of streets and roads. Nomenclature is important here. Streets, roads, courts, and drives run east–west. Avenues, terraces, and ways run north–south. Boulevards can (and do) run any which way. For visitors, trendy Las Olas Boulevard is one of the most important east–west thoroughfares from the beach to downtown, whereas Route A1A—referred to as Atlantic Boulevard, Ocean Boulevard, and Fort Lauderdale Beach along some stretches—runs along the north–south oceanfront. These names can confuse visitors, since there are separate streets called Atlantic and Ocean in Hollywood and Pompano Beach. Boulevards, composed of either pavement or water, give Fort Lauderdale its distinct "Venice of America" character.

The city's transportation system, though less congested than elsewhere in South Florida, suffers from traffic overload. Interstate 595 connects the city and suburbs and provides a direct route to the Fort Lauderdale–Hollywood International Airport and Port Everglades, but lanes slow to a crawl during rush hours. The Intracoastal Waterway, paralleling Route A1A, is the nautical equivalent of an interstate highway. It runs north–south between downtown Fort Lauderdale and the beach and provides easy boating access to neighboring beach communities.

The major taxi company serving the area is Yellow Cab, with vehicles equipped for major credit cards.

TOURS Honeycombed with some 300 mi of navigable waterways, Fort Lauderdale is home port for about 44,000 privately owned vessels, but you don't need to be a boat owner to ply the waters. For a scenic way to really see this canal-laced city, simply hop on a Water Taxi, sometimes called a Water Bus, part of Fort Lauderdale's water-transportation system, made up of a fleet of vessels carrying up to 70 passengers each. Providing transport and quick, narrated tours, a water taxi is a good way to bar-hop or access many waterfront hotels and restaurants. Larger, multiple-deck touring vessels and motorboat rentals for self-guided adventure are other sightseeing options.

Boats won't get you everywhere; you may need to call for taxi service when getting to and from the airport, seaport, or major hotels. Meters run at rates of $4.50 for the first mile and $2.40 for each additional mile; waiting time is 40¢ per minute. There's a $10-fare minimum (at press time reportedly rising to $15) from seaport or airport, and an additional $2 service charge when you are collected from the airport.

Catch an orange-bottomed, yellow-topped Sun Trolley, running every 15 minutes, either free or for $1 or so, depending on routes. Sun Trolley's *Convention Connection*, 50¢ per person, runs round-trip from Cordova Road's Harbor Shops near Port Everglades (where you can park free) to past the Convention Center, over the 17th Street Causeway, and north along Route A1A to Beach Place. Wave at trolley drivers—yes, they will stop—for pickups anywhere along the route.

ESSENTIALS

Transportation Contacts Sun Trolley (☎ *954/761-3543* 🌐 *www.suntrolley.com*). **Water Taxi** (☎ *954/467-0008* 🌐 *www.watertaxi.com*). **Yellow Cab** (☎ *954/565-5400*).

Visitor Information Greater Fort Lauderdale Convention and Visitors Bureau (☎ *954/765-4466* 🌐 *www.sunny.org*).

EXPLORING

Numbers in the margin correspond to the Fort Lauderdale map.

DOWNTOWN

The jewel of downtown along New River is the Arts and Entertainment District, with Broadway shows, ballet, and theater at the riverfront Broward Center for the Performing Arts. Clustered within a five-minute walk are the Museum of Discovery & Science, the expanding Fort Lauderdale Historical Museum, and the Museum of Art, home to stellar touring exhibits. Restaurants, sidewalk cafés, bars, and blues, folk, jazz, reggae, and rock clubs flourish. Tying this district together is the Riverwalk, extending 2 mi along the New River's north and south banks. Tropical gardens with benches and interpretive displays fringe the walk on the north, boat landings on the south.

CLOSE UP

A Black Heritage Gem

West of downtown Fort Lauderdale's Arts and Sciences District, in the heart of the African-American community along Sistrunk Boulevard, lies a gem once discounted as a grand idea unlikely to get off the ground.

Yet in 2002, Fort Lauderdale's **African-American Research Library and Cultural Center** soared into reality as a $14 million repository of history and heritage of African, African-American, and Caribbean cultures, with historic books, papers, and art, much of it pertaining to the African diaspora. There's a 300-seat auditorium, a story-time area, and 5,000 square feet of gallery space for exhibits. African symbols appear as part of the decor.

For Samuel F. Morrison, now-retired Broward County Library director, the center is the culmination of his dream, a vision to create a worthy showcase reflecting African-American heritage. Broward County anted up $5 million for the 60,000-square-foot center, and Morrison raised the rest.

Of the nation's major African-American public research facilities, Fort Lauderdale's also has a Caribbean focus. Offerings include the Alex Haley Collection, with eight unfinished manuscripts. Other components range from Fisk University research of slave narratives to books on Jamaica. You'll also find the Kitty Oliver Oral Histories Collection on Broward and Okeechobee and the Niara Sudarkasa Collection of papers, artwork, and other materials of the former president of Lincoln University.

And there's the collection of Dorothy Porter Wesley—in some eyes the greatest of the black bibliophiles. Her collection includes about 500 inscribed and autographed books—some date to 1836—with personal narratives, histories, fiction, and reference works, which Wesley's daughter, Constance Porter Uzelac, refers to as "Mama's stuff." Wesley was known for going to homes of the recently deceased to make sure nothing of value got tossed. "She'd get to the house before the body was cold," her daughter recalls, heading straight to attics and basements to retrieve bits and scraps of history.

Passionate about his dream, Morrison also remains adamant about the library's widespread appeal, noting that "these pieces provide glimpses [into] the hearts and minds of people who have made a difference in the lives of not only people of color and African culture, but people of many colors and cultures."

✉ *2650 Sistrunk Blvd.* ☎ *954/625–2800* 🌐 *www.broward.org/library/aarlcc.htm* 🎟 *Free* 🕒 *Mon.–Thurs. 10–9, Fri. and Sat. 10–6, Sun. 1–5.*

TOP ATTRACTIONS

5 **Fort Lauderdale History Center.** Surveying city history from the Seminole era to more recent times, the Fort Lauderdale Historical Society's museum has expanded into several adjacent buildings, including the historic King-Cromartie House, New River Inn, and the Hoch Heritage Center, a public research facility archiving original manuscripts, maps, and more than 250,000 photos. ✉ *231 SW 2nd Ave.* ☎ *954/463–4431* 🌐 *www.oldfortlauderdale.org* 🎟 *$10* 🕒 *Tues.–Sun. noon–4.*

- Bonnet House 12
- Broward County Main Library 4
- Fort Lauderdale Antique Car Museum 2
- Fort Lauderdale Beachfront 11
- Fort Lauderdale Fire Museum 8
- Fort Lauderdale History Center ... 5
- Hugh Taylor Birch State Recreation Area 13
- International Swimming Hall of Fame Museum & Aquatic Complex 10
- Museum of Art Fort Lauderdale .. 3
- Museum of Discovery & Science/ AutoNation IMAX Theater 7
- Riverwalk 6
- Sailboat Bend ... 9
- Stranahan House 1

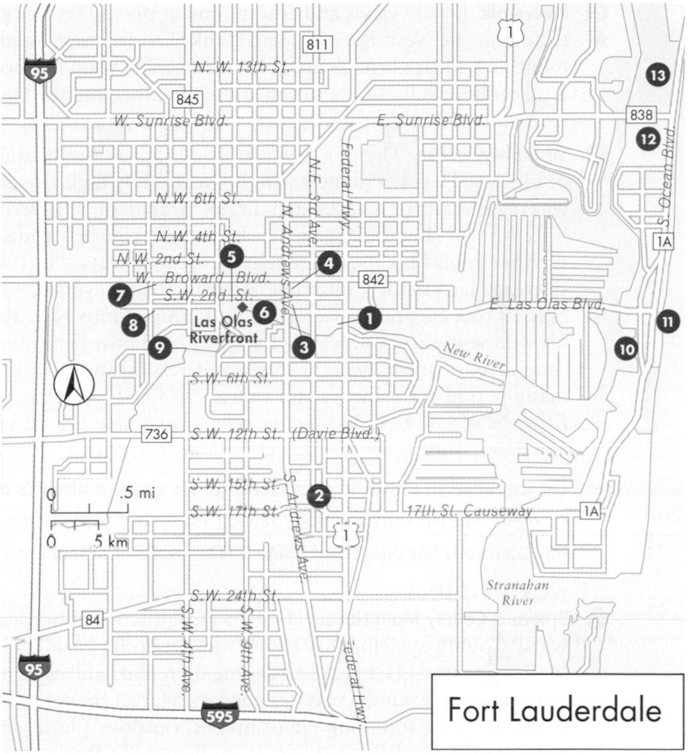

3 ★ **Museum of Art Fort Lauderdale.** Currently in an Edward Larrabee Barnes–designed building that's considered an architectural masterpiece, activists started this museum in a nearby storefront about 50 years ago. MOAFL now coordinates with Nova Southeastern University to host world-class touring exhibits and has an impressive permanent collection of 20th-century European and American art, including works by Picasso, Calder, Dalí, Mapplethorpe, Warhol, and Stella, as well as works by celebrated Ashcan School artist William Glackens. ⊠ *1 E. Las Olas Blvd.* ☎ *954/763–6464* ⊕ *www.moafl.org* *$10* *Tues.–Sat. 11–5, Sun. noon–5.*

7 ★ **Museum of Discovery & Science/AutoNation IMAX Theater.** Open 365 days barring weather-related events, the aim here is to entertain children—*and* adults—with wonders of science. The courtyard's 52-foot-tall Great Gravity Clock lets arrivals know cool experiences await. Exhibits include Kidscience, encouraging youngsters to explore the world; and Gizmo City, a look at how gadgets work. Florida Ecoscapes has a living coral reef, plus sharks, rays, and eels. The AutoNation IMAX theater, part of the complex, shows films, some in 3-D. A Subway sandwich shop is on premises. ⊠ *401 SW 2nd St.* ☎ *954/467–6637 museum, 954/463–4629 IMAX* ⊕ *www.mods.org* *Museum $11, $16 with one IMAX show* *Mon.–Sat. 10–5, Sun. noon–6.*

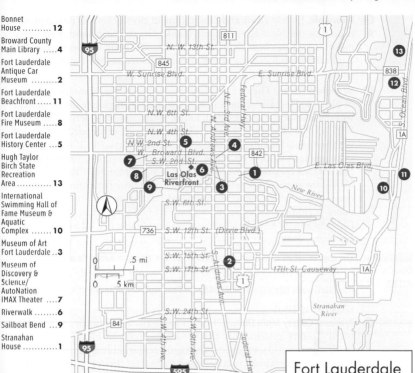

6 ★ **Riverwalk.** Lovely views and entertainment prevail on this paved promenade on the New River's north bank. On the first Sunday of every month a free jazz brunch attracts visitors. The walk has been extended 2 mi on both sides of the urban stream, connecting the facilities of the Arts and Science District.

1 **Stranahan House.** The city's oldest residence, on the National Register of Historic Places, and increasingly dwarfed by high-rise development, was once home for businessman Frank Stranahan, who arrived in 1892. With his wife, Ivy, the city's first schoolteacher, he befriended and traded with Seminole Indians, and taught them "new ways." In 1901 he built a store and later made it his home. After financial reverses, Stranahan tied himself to a concrete sewer grate and jumped into New River, leaving his widow to carry on. Ivy died in 1971, and now her home (at various times a post office, general store, and restaurant) is a museum, with many period furnishings, and tours. ✉ *335 SE 6th Ave., at Las Olas Blvd.* ☎ *954/524–4736* 🌐 *www.stranahanhouse.org* 🎟 *$12* 🕓 *Wed.–Sat. 10–3, Sun. 1–3.*

QUICK BITES

The sweet smell of waffle cones lures pedestrians to Kilwin's of Las Olas (✉ *809 E. Las Olas Blvd.* ☎ *954/523-8338*), an old-fashioned confectionery that also sells hand-paddled fudge and scoops of homemade ice cream.

WORTH NOTING

4 **Broward County Main Library.** One of more than 30 libraries in the Broward County system, this eight-story building of Florida limestone (with a terraced glass facade standing up remarkably well to occasional hurricane-force winds) was designed by Marcel Breuer to showcase the green, leafy surrounding environment, outdoor plaza, and reflecting pool. Works are displayed here from Broward's Public Art and Design Program, including paintings, sculpture, and photographs by nationally renowned and Florida artists. A technology center has personal computers for public use and devices for patrons with disabilities. A 300-seat theater hosts productions from theater to poetry readings. ✉ *100 S. Andrews Ave.* ☎ *954/357–7444* 🌐 *www.broward.org/library* 🎟 *Free* 🕓 *Mon.–Thurs. 9–9, Fri. and Sat. 9–5, Sun. noon–5:30.*

QUICK BITES

Don't miss Charcuterie Too (✉ *100 S. Andrews Ave.* ☎ *954/463-9578*), a cozy cafeteria on Broward County Main Library's 2nd floor. The lunch menu has quiche, soups, salads, and homemade cakes. Open weekdays 10-2:30, it draws library bookworms and downtown worker bees.

2 **Fort Lauderdale Antique Car Museum.** Retired floral company owner Arthur O. Stone set up a foundation to preserve these eye-poppers. Nostalgia includes around two dozen Packards (all in running condition) from 1900 to the 1940s, along with a gallery saluting Franklin Delano Roosevelt. This sparkling museum sports everything from grease caps, spark plugs, and gearshift knobs to Texaco Oil signage, plus a newer wing and an enlarged library. ✉ *1527 SW 11th Ave. (Packard Ave.)* ☎ *954/779–7300* 🌐 *www.antiquecarmuseum.net* 🎟 *$8* 🕓 *Weekdays 10–4, Sat. 10–3.*

DID YOU KNOW?

Sculptor Peter Wolf Toth fashioned this totem pole for Fort Lauderdale's DC Alexander Park on Seabreeze Boulevard near the New River Sound. Toth, who has sculpted works throughout the country, often creates art that represents the lives of early natives.

8 **Fort Lauderdale Fire Museum.** Following its harrowing fire of 1912, Fort Lauderdale residents pushed for more protection, finally opening what became known as Fire Station No. 3 (later No. 8) in 1927. This landmark, designed by architect Francis Abreu and retired from active duty in 2004, now functions as a historical, cultural, and educational facility with an expanding array of Roaring '20s era equipment including a 1928 Ahrens-Fox piston pumper, as well as a 1942 parade engine. There's also a vintage police car. ✉ *1022 W. Las Olas Blvd.* ☎ *954/763–1005* 🌐 *www.fortlauderdalefiremuseum.com* 🎟 *Free, donations appreciated* ⏲ *Sat. 9–1, Sun. noon–5.*

9 **Sailboat Bend.** Between Las Olas and the river lies a neighborhood with a character reminiscent of Key West's Old Town and Miami's Coconut Grove. Although without shops or much in the way of services, it's still worth a visit to be reminded of days gone by. The circa 1927 Fire Station No. 3, designed by local architect Francis Abreu and now housing the Fort Lauderdale Fire Museum, is at the corner of West Las Olas Boulevard and Southwest 11th Avenue. Across the river lies the tree-lined Tarpon River neighborhood, alluding to the canal-like river looping off New River from the southeast quadrant and running to the southwest section, returning to New River near Sailboat Bend.

ALONG THE BEACH

12 ★ **Bonnet House.** A 35-acre oasis in the heart of the beach area, this subtropical estate on the National Register of Historic Places stands as a tribute to the history of Old South Florida. The charming home was the winter residence of the late Frederic and Evelyn Bartlett, artists whose personal touches and small surprises are evident throughout. For architecture, artwork, or the natural environment, this place is special. Be on the lookout for playful monkeys swinging from trees, a source of amusement at even some of the most solemn weddings on the grounds. Hours can vary, so call first. ✉ *900 N. Birch Rd.* ☎ *954/563–5393* 🌐 *www.bonnethouse.org* 🎟 *$20 for house tours, $10 for grounds only* ⏲ *Tues.–Sat. 10–4, Sun. noon–4.*

11 Fodor's Choice ★ **Fort Lauderdale Beachfront.** Fort Lauderdale's increasingly stylish beachfront offers easy access not only to a wide band of beige sand but also to restaurants and shops. Heading north for 2 mi, beginning at the Bahia Mar yacht basin along Route A1A, you'll have clear ocean views (typically across rows of colorful beach umbrellas) to ships passing in and out of nearby Port Everglades. If you're on the beach, gaze back on an exceptionally graceful promenade.

13 **Hugh Taylor Birch State Recreation Area.** Amid the tropical greenery of this 180-acre park, stroll along a nature trail, visit the Birch House Museum, picnic, play volleyball, or paddle a rented canoe. Since parking is limited on Route A1A, park here and take a walkway underpass to the beach (which can be accessed 9–5, daily). ✉ *3109 E. Sunrise Blvd.* ☎ *954/564–4521* 🌐 *www.floridastateparks.org* 🎟 *$6 per vehicle, $2 per pedestrian* ⏲ *Daily 8–sunset.*

10 **International Swimming Hall of Fame Museum & Aquatic Complex.** This monument to underwater accomplishments has two 50-meter pools plus a dive pool open daily to the public. The exhibition building has photos,

CLOSE UP

Cruising for a Taxi

Shout "Taxi! Taxi!" in Fort Lauderdale, and look for your ship to come in.

Actually, you'll be catching what's also called a water bus, as the original fleet of tiny water taxis has been replaced by vessels accommodating up to 70 passengers. Either way, they're floating cabs, and a great way to get around.

For sightseeing, the water-taxi-cum-bus can pick you up at any of several docks along the Intracoastal Waterway or New River, and you can stop off at attractions like the Performing Arts Center, the Museum of Discovery & Science, Stranahan House, or the Gallery at Beach Place. For lunch, sail away to restaurants on Las Olas Boulevard or Las Olas Riverfront. As the sun disappears, water taxis are a superb way to head out for dinner or bar-hop, letting your pilot play the sober role of designated driver.

The water-transport venture was started by Bob Bekoff, a longtime Broward resident and outspoken tourism promoter, who decided to combine the need for transportation with one of the area's most captivating features: waterways that make Fort Lauderdale the Venice of America.

Ride all you want with a day pass, purchased onboard or at a kiosk at the Gallery at Beach Place, 10:30 AM–12:30 AM, for $13. Family all-day passes for two adults and up to four youths are $48, and after 7 PM passes are $7. Annual passes are $180. A dozen or so scheduled stops include Bahia Mar, Gallery at Beach Place, Galleria Mall, Seville Street, Pier 66, Convention Center, and Downtowner Saloon. The winter season South Beach Express, a socko day-trip to the Art Deco District of Miami Beach ($35), leaves Fort Lauderdale around 9 AM, returning to Fort Lauderdale about four hours after arrival in the Miami area at around noon, with the length of the boat ride each way depending on weather conditions, tides, and other variables. For family reunions and such, group tours like the Sunset Cruise, or Mansions and Marinas are on tap. To get around town by boat, contact **Water Bus** (☎ *954/467–6677* 🌐 *www.watertaxi.com*).

medals, and other souvenirs from major swim events, and the Huizenga Theater provides an automated video experience where you can select vintage-Olympic coverage or old films such as Esther Williams' *Million Dollar Mermaid.* ✉ *1 Hall of Fame Dr., 1 block south of Las Olas at Rte. A1A* ☎ *954/462–6536* 🌐 *www.ishof.org* 🎫 *Museum $8, pool $4* 🕒 *Museum mid-Jan.–late Dec., weekdays 9–7, weekends 9–5; pool mid-Jan.–late Dec., weekdays 8–4, weekends 9–5.*

NEED A BREAK?

For respite from the sun, duck into Undergrounds Coffeehaus (✉ *2743 E. Oakland Park Blvd.* ☎ *954/630–1900*), a few blocks west of the beach. It's cozy and one-of-a-kind, with consignment art, new and used books, teas, desserts, and a swoon-worthy PB&J latte. Owner Aileen Liptak promises coffee "so good, we drink it ourselves" along with free Wi-Fi with a beverage purchase. Closed Mon. and Fri., no lunch weekends.

OFF THE BEATEN PATH

A stretch from Fort Lauderdale's beaches, but worth the hour-plus drive, is the **Big Cypress Seminole Reservation** and its two very different attractions. **At the Billie Swamp Safari,** experience the majesty of the Everglades firsthand. Daily tours of wildlife-filled wetlands and hammocks yield sightings of deer, water buffalo, bison, wild hogs, hawks, eagles, alligators, and, if you're really lucky, the rare Florida panther. Animal and reptile shows ($8) are entertaining. Ecotours ($25) are conducted aboard motorized swamp buggies, and airboat rides ($15) are available, too. The on-site Swamp Water Café serves gator nuggets, frogs' legs, catfish, and Indian fry bread with honey. Overnight in a chickee ($35 for 2) or a dorm ($65 for up to 8). ✉ *19 mi north of I–75 Exit 49* ☎ *863/983–6101 or 800/949–6101* 🌐 *www.seminoletribe.com* 🎫 *Free; combined ecotour, reptile or critter show, and airboat ride, $43* 🕒 *Daily 8–5.*

A couple of miles or so from Billie Swamp Safari is **Ah-Tah-Thi-Ki Museum,** whose name means "a place to learn, a place to remember." This museum documents the traditions and culture of the Seminole Tribe of Florida through artifacts, exhibits, and reenactments of rituals and ceremonies. The 60-acre site includes a living-history Seminole village, nature trails, and a wheelchair-accessible boardwalk through a cypress swamp. ✉ *17 mi north of I–75 Exit 49* ☎ *863/902–1113* 🌐 *www.seminoletribe.com* 🎫 *$9* 🕒 *Tues.–Sun. 9–5.*

SPORTS AND THE OUTDOORS

BIKING

Among the most popular routes are Route A1A and Bayview Drive, especially in early morning before traffic builds, and a 7-mi bike path that parallels State Road 84 and New River and leads to Markham Park, which has mountain bike trails. **■ TIP→ Alligator alert: do not dangle your legs from seawalls.**

BIRD-WATCHING

North of Fort Lauderdale's 17th Street Causeway, within the Gothic intrigue of **Evergreen Historic Cemetery** (✉ *1300 SE 10th St.* ☎ *954/745–2140* 🌐 *www.browardcemeteries.com*), lies a bird-watchers' haven.

Sand can sometimes be forgiving if you fall, and bicyclists also appreciate the ocean views.

The circa 1879 graveyard, shaded by gumbo limbo and strangler figs, doubles as a place of fleeting repose for Bahama mockingbirds and other species winging through urban Broward. Warblers are big here, and there are occasional sightings of red-eyed vireos, northern waterthrushes, and scarlet tanagers.

FISHING

If you're interested in a saltwater charter, check out the **Bahia Mar Beach Resort** (✉ *801 Seabreeze Blvd.* ☎ *954/627–6357*). Sportfishing and drift-fishing bookings can be arranged.

SCUBA DIVING AND SNORKELING

Lauderdale Diver (✉ *1334 SE 17th St. Causeway* ☎ *954/467–2822*), which is PADI–affiliated, arranges dive charters up and down Broward's shoreline. Dive trips typically last four hours. Nonpackage reef trips are open to divers for around $50; scuba gear is extra. **Pro Dive** (✉ *429 Seabreeze Blvd.* ☎ *954/761–3413*), a five-star PADI facility, is the area's oldest diving operation. Snorkelers can go out for $35 on a two-hour snorkeling trip, including equipment. Scuba divers pay $55 using their own gear or $115 with full scuba- and snorkel-rental gear included.

SHOPPING

MALLS

Just north of Las Olas Boulevard on Route A1A is **The Gallery at Beach Place** (✉ *17 S. Fort Lauderdale Beach Blvd.*). Browse shops, enjoy lunch or dinner, or carouse at assorted nightspots. Lower-level eateries tend toward the more upscale, whereas upper-level prices are lower (go figure), with superior ocean views. ■ **TIP→** **Beach Place has covered parking, but you can pinch pennies by using a nearby municipal lot that's metered.** Just west of the Intracoastal Waterway, the split-level **Galleria Mall** (✉ *2414 E. Sunrise Blvd.*) entices with Neiman Marcus, Dillard's, and Macy's, plus 150 specialty shops for anything from cookware to exquisite jewelry. Chow down at Capital Grille, Blue Martini, Mama Sbarro's, and Seasons 52, or head for the food court, a decided cut above at this upscale mall open 10–9 Monday through Saturday, noon–5:30 Sunday. The **Swap Shop** (✉ *3291 W. Sunrise Blvd.*) is the South's largest flea market, with 2,000 vendors open daily. While exploring this indoor–outdoor entertainment and shopping complex, hop on the carousel or stick around for movies at the 14-screen Swap Shop drive-in.

Sawgrass Mills (✉ *12801 W. Sunrise Blvd., at Flamingo Rd., Sunrise*), 10 mi west of downtown Fort Lauderdale, has 26 million visitors a year, ranking it Florida's second-biggest tourist attraction (after the one with the mouse). The ever-growing complex has a basic alligator shape, and walking it all amounts to about a 2-mi jaunt. Count on 11,000 self-parking spaces (note your location, or you'll be working those soles), valet parking, and two information centers. More than 400 shops—many manufacturer's outlets, retail outlets, and name-brand discounters—include Abercrombie & Fitch Outlet, Chico's Outlet, Super Target, and Ron Jon Surf Shop. Restaurants such as Cajun Grill, the Cheesecake Factory, Mangia La Pasta, and Rainforest Café are on-site. Wannado City, an "interactive-empowerment environment" is geared toward ages four and up. The adjacent Shops at Colonnade cater to well-heeled patrons with a David Yurman jewelry outlet and other shops including Valentino, Burberry, Kate Spade, and Barneys New York.

SHOPPING DISTRICTS

When you're downtown, check out **Las Olas Riverfront** (✉ *1 block west of Andrews Ave. along New River*), a shopping, dining, and entertainment complex with constantly evolving shops for everything from meals and threads to cigars and tattoos. If only for a stroll and some high-end window-shopping, don't miss **Las Olas Boulevard** (✉ *1 block off New River east of Andrews Ave.*). The city's best boutiques plus top restaurants and art galleries line a beautifully landscaped street.

NIGHTLIFE AND THE ARTS

For the most complete weekly listing of events, check "Showtime!" the *South Florida Sun-Sentinel*'s tabloid-sized entertainment section and events calendar published on Friday. "Weekend," in the Friday Broward edition of *The Herald,* also lists area happenings. The weekly *City Link* is principally an entertainment and dining paper with an "underground" look. *New Times* is a free alternative weekly circulating a Broward–Palm Beach County edition. *East Sider* is another free weekly entertainment guide.

THE ARTS

Broward Center for the Performing Arts (✉ *201 SW 5th Ave.* ☎ *954/462–0222*) is the waterfront centerpiece of Fort Lauderdale's arts district. More than 500 events unfold annually at the 2,700-seat architectural gem, including Broadway-style musicals, plays, dance, symphony, opera, rock, film, lectures, comedy, and children's theater. An enclosed elevated walkway links to a parking garage across the street. **Cinema Paradiso** (✉ *503 SE 6th St.* ☎ *954/525–3456* 🌐 *www.cinemaparadiso.org*) operates as an art-house movie theater from a former church, south of New River near the county courthouse. The space doubles as headquarters for FLIFF, the Fort Lauderdale International Film Festival. Screenings stretch from extreme sports to anime.

★ At **Chef Jean-Pierre Cooking School** (✉ *1436 N. Federal Hwy.* ☎ *954/563–2700* 🌐 *www.chefjp.com* 🎫 *$65 per demonstration class, $120 hands-on class* ⏲ *Store Mon.–Sat. 10–7, class schedules vary*), catering to locals, seasonal snowbirds, and folks winging in for even shorter stays, Jean-Pierre Brehier (former owner of the much missed Left Bank Restaurant on Las Olas) teaches the basics, from boiling water onward. The enthusiastic Gallic transplant has appeared on NBC's *Today* and CNN's *Larry King Live*. For souvenir hunters, this fun cooking facility also sells nifty pots, pastas, oils, and other irresistibles.

NIGHTLIFE

BARS AND LOUNGES

Coyote Ugly (✉ *214 SW 2nd St.* ☎ *954/764–8459*) continues a tradition of being one of the hottest spots in Broward. **Hooters of Beach Place** (✉ *The Gallery at Beach Place, 17 S. Fort Lauderdale Beach Blvd.* ☎ *954/767–0014*) extends its reputation for tacky and unrefined fun to this seaside setting with a fabulous view.

Around since 1948, **Kim's Alley Bar** (✉ *1920 E. Sunrise Blvd.* ☎ *954/763–2143*) has two bar areas, a jukebox, and pool tables that provide endless entertainment. **Maguire's Hill 16** (✉ *535 N. Andrews Ave.* ☎ *954/764–4453*) hosts live music in classic Irish-pub surroundings. **Parrot Lounge** (✉ *911 Sunrise La.* ☎ *954/563–1493*) favored by Philadelphia Eagles fans, backs up libations and revelry with wings, fingers, poppers, and skins.

WHERE TO EAT

$$$ SEAFOOD ✕ **15th Street Fisheries & Dockside Cafe**. A prime Intracoastal Waterway view is a big part of the allure at this two-story seafood landmark alternately drawing praise and pans from patrons, some complaining about lackluster service during financial seminars—also known as plate lickers—booked upstairs. Despite fluctuating tides in quality, the old 15th carries on solidly with spicy conch chowder, cold seafood salads, and homemade breads. Grilled mahimahi and fried alligator are among the more than 50 entrées, and there's key lime pie. You can feed giant tarpon at the dock with shrimp from the dock store around 5 PM. Valet parking costs $2 at dinner, but it's free at lunch. ✉ *1900 SE 15th St.* ☎ *954/763–2777* 🌐 *www.15streetfisheries.com* 💳 *AE, D, DC, MC, V.*

$$ AMERICAN ✕ **Alligator Alley**. At this taproom and music hall big on nightly music from rockabilly to funk rock, chefs ladle up memorable gumbo, and alligator ribs so good they once were featured on the Food Network. Wash down your beer with Gator Bites or Buffalo Fingers, or for delicacy, go

for an appetizer of scallopini of gator with Szechuan sauce. Vegetarians can bulk up on cheese fries, or keep trim with a garden salad. ✉ *1321 E. Commercial Blvd.* ☎ *954/771–2220* 🌐 *www.alligatoralleyflorida.com* ▭ *AE, D, MC, V.*

$$$$ SEAFOOD ★ ✕ **Blue Moon (EAST) Fish Company.** Most tables have stellar views of the Intracoastal Waterway, but Blue Moon East's true magic comes from the kitchen, where chefs Baron Skorish and Bryce Statham create moon-and-stars-worthy seafood dishes. Start with the raw bar, a sushi sampler, or pan-seared fresh-shucked oysters. Salads include hydroponic lettuce with candied walnuts, and among the entrée favorites are lump crab and corn-roasted grouper with asparagus risotto and peppercorn-crusted big-eye tuna with sticky rice. Carnivores might opt for prosciutto-stuffed veal tenderloin. Wrap up an evening with the tartelette of bananas Foster. For Sunday champagne brunches book early, even in the off-season. For the record, a Blue Moon West has risen in Coral Springs. ✉ *4405 W. Tradewinds Ave.* ☎ *954/267–9888* ▭ *AE, D, DC, MC, V.*

$$$$ AMERICAN ★ ✕ **By Word of Mouth.** Unassuming but outstanding, this restaurant never advertises, hence its name. Mere word has sufficed for nearly a quarter century because locals consistently put this dining spot along the railroad tracks just off Oakland Park Boulevard at the top of "reader's choice" polls. Although bare at lunch, a dozen interior tables are dressed in champagne-colored cloths at dinner, but what's magnetic here is the food, not the vaguely Tuscan decor. There's no menu per se, but you'll be shown the day's specials on display to make your choice. Count on a solid gourmet lineup of fish, fowl, beef, pasta, and vegetarian entrées to be enjoyed inside or out on the patio, perhaps with a glass of wine. ✉ *3200 NE 12th Ave.* ☎ *954/564–3663* 🌐 *www.bywordofmouthfoods.com* ▭ *AE, D, MC, V.*

$$$$ SOUTHWESTERN ✕ **Canyon Southwest Cafe.** Southwestern fusion fare helps you escape the ordinary at this small, stylish enclave. It's been run for the past dozen years by owner and executive chef Chris Wilber. Order, for example, bison medallions with scotch bonnets, a tequila-jalapeño smoked salmon tostada, coriander-crusted tuna, or blue-corn fried oysters. Chipotle, wasabi, mango, and red chilies accent fresh seafood and wild game. Start off with a prickly pear margarita or choose from a well-rounded wine list or beer selection. ✉ *1818 E. Sunrise Blvd.* ☎ *954/765–1950* 🌐 *www.canyonfl.com* ▭ *AE, MC, V* ⏲ *No lunch.*

$ MEXICAN ✕ **Carlos & Pepe's.** In a strip shopping center west of the 17th Causeway, this local favorite has long been known for icy margaritas, crunchy chips and salsa, and tasty fare from omelets to pizza. On the downside, its iconic margaritas for the past few years have been served in beer-style tumblers rather than stemmed margarita ware of old. (Management mumbles about breakage.) On the upside, the tuna dip that goes so well with libations retains its luster. ✉ *1302 SE 17th St., Harbor Beach* ☎ *954/467–7192* ▭ *AE, D, MC, V* ⏲ *No lunch weekdays.*

$$$ ITALIAN ✕ **Casa D'Angelo.** Owner-chef Angelo Elia has created a gem of a Tuscan-style white-tablecloth restaurant, tucked in the Sunrise Square shopping center. Casa D'Angelo's oak oven turns out marvelous seafood and beef dishes. The pappardelle with porcini mushrooms takes pasta to pleasant heights. Another favorite is the calamari and scungilli salad with garlic

and lemon. Ask about the oven-roasted fish of the day or the snapper oreganta at market price. ✉ *1201 N. Federal Hwy.* ☎ *954/564–1234* 🌐 *www.casa-d-angelo.com* ▭ *AE, D, DC, MC, V* ⊙ *No lunch.*

$$$ AMERICAN Fodor's Choice ★ ✕ **Casablanca Cafe.** You'll get a fabulous ocean view and a good meal to boot at this historic two-story Moroccan-style villa, built in the 1920s by local architect Francis Abreu. This piano bar's menu is a potpourri with both tropical and Asian influence (try the Korean-style roasted duck) along with North African specialties like lamb shank and couscous. There's a deck for outside dining. It's a lively spot with friendly service. ✉ *Rte. A1A and Alhambra St.* ☎ *954/764–3500* 🌐 *www.casablancacafeonline.com* ▭ *AE, D, MC, V.*

$ AMERICAN ✕ **Elbo Room.** You can't go wrong wallowing in the past, lifting a drink, and exercising your elbow at the Elbo, a noisy, suds-drenched hot spot since 1938. This watering hole phased out food (except for light nibbles) ages ago, but kept a hokey sense of humor: upstairs a sign proclaims WE DON'T SERVE WOMEN HERE. YOU HAVE TO BRING YOUR OWN. ✉ *241 S. Fort Lauderdale Beach Blvd.* ☎ *954/463–4615* 🌐 *www.elboroom.com* ▭ *AE, D, MC, V.*

$ SOUTHERN ✕ **Ernie's Barbecue.** Walls once plastered with philosophical quotes from a former owner have been scrubbed clean at Ernie's, where the menu proclaims CONCH IS KING, BARBECUE IS A WAY OF LIFE, AND THE BAR IS OPEN LATE. Fortunately for patrons, barbecue platters of pork or beef and conch chowder are as lip-smacking as ever. Bimini bread, thick-sliced for sandwiches, is also sold by the loaf to go, along with racks of ribs and conch chowder by the quart. Seafood, salads, and burgers pass muster here, and there's a children's menu. Eat downstairs, or, if you don't mind the Federal Highway traffic buzz, take the stairs to 2nd-floor open-air patio tables near a pool table. ✉ *1843 S. Federal Hwy.* ☎ *954/523–8636* ▭ *AE, D, MC, V.*

$$ AMERICAN ✕ **Floridian.** This Las Olas landmark is plastered with photos of Monroe, Nixon, and local notables past and present in a succession of brightly painted rooms with funky chandeliers. The kitchen dishes up some of the best breakfasts around (no matter the hour), with oversize omelets that come with biscuits, toast, or English muffins, plus a choice of grits or tomato. With sausage or bacon on the side, you'll forget about eating again soon. Count on savory sandwiches and hot platters for lunch, tempting meat-loaf plates for dinner, and friendly, efficient service. It's open 24 hours—even during hurricanes, as long as the power holds out. Feeling flush? Try the Fat Cat Breakfast (New York strip steak, hash browns or grits, toast, and worthy champagne) or the Not-So-Fat-Cat, with the same grub and a lesser-quality vintage. ✉ *1410 E. Las Olas Blvd.* ☎ *954/463–4041* ▭ *No credit cards.*

$$$ FRENCH ✕ **Le Café de Paris.** Serving the classics for lunch and dinner under ownership of Swiss-born (and jeans-clad) Louis Flematti since 1962, Le Café seats upward of 150 in several rooms but keeps everything cozy with comfort foods like crusty bread, onion soup, and savory crepes, as well as duck, lamb, and beef dishes. A celebration dinner (under $90 for two) includes a bottle of wine and baked Alaska. There's also a mouthwatering pastry wagon. ✉ *715 Las Olas Blvd.* ☎ *954/467–2900* 🌐 *www.cafedeparislasolas.com* ▭ *AE, D, DC, MC, V* ⊙ *Closed Sun. No lunch Sat.*

$ AMERICAN **Lester's Diner**. Home to steaming coffee and a tempting skip-your-dinner dessert display, Lester's has stood as a 24-hour haven for the hungry along State Road 84 since 1967. Truckers stop here on their way to Port Everglades, as do workers from the area's thriving marine industry, suits from downtown toting briefcases, along with sunburned visitors. A stick-to-the-ribs menu includes breakfast anytime, homemade soups, sandwiches (try the Monte Cristo), salads, and dinners of generous portions. If your cholesterol count can take the hit, try the country-fried steak or the chicken-liver omelet. Two other Lester's—in western Broward's Margate and Sunrise—close at midnight on weeknights. *250 State Rd. 84* *954/525–5641* *4701 Coconut Creek Pkwy., Margate* *954/979–4722* *1399 NW 136th Ave., Sunrise* *954/838–7473* *D, MC, V.*

$ IRISH **Maguire's Hill 16**. With the requisite lineup of libations and sandwiches, this long-popular Irish pub also has a very tasty potato soup, shepherd's pie, bangers and mash, fish-and-chips, corned beef and cabbage, and Irish stew, daily specials, and nightly live music. *535 N. Andrews Ave.* *954/764–4453* *www.maguireshill16.com* *AE, D, DC, MC, V.*

$$$ AMERICAN **Oasis Cafe**. On a spit of land near Route A1A, this outdoor-only spot has swing-glide tables covered by green-striped awnings affording plenty of shade. Friendly staffers serve up libations and casual fare from burgers and wraps to salads and steak. Try the club sandwich for lunch. Be aware that a 15% gratuity is tacked on no matter what your party size. A free valet assists with cramped parking. *600 Seabreeze Blvd.* *954/463–3130* *AE, D, MC, V.*

$$ GERMAN **Old Heidelberg Restaurant & Deli**. Likened to a Bavarian mirage plucked from the Alps and plopped along State Road 84 near the airport and seaport, the Old Heidelberg's beer stein–cowbell–cuckoo-clock decor accents the Bavarian lamb shanks, various schnitzels, sauerkraut, and other specialties, from apple strudel to Black Forest cake. For better or wurst in takeout, Old Heidelberg Deli next door (open Tuesday through Saturday 9–6) stocks kielbasa, liver dumplings, Bitburger beer, breads, and nearly a dozen mustards. *900 State Rd. 84* *954/463–6747* *www.oldheidelbergdeli.com* *AE, D, MC, V* *Closed Mon. No lunch Sat.*

$$$ ITALIAN **Primavera**. You could drive past this unremarkable-looking spot tucked into an unremarkable shopping plaza, but you'd be missing out on a remarkable dining experience. Among chef-owner Giacomo Dresseno's favorites is a double-cut veal chop, but there's also fresh pasta with rich sauces and risotto entrées, and creative fish, poultry, and beef dinners. If you're in town for a while, check out the chef's two-hour cooking classes ($40), accompanied by a light meal. Ticket holders appreciate the reasonably priced pre-theater menu. *830 E. Oakland Park Blvd.* *954/564–6363* *www.trueitalian.com* *AE, D, DC, MC, V* *Closed Mon. No lunch.*

$$$$ STEAK Fodor's Choice ★ **Shula's on the Beach**. For anyone getting positively misty-eyed at mere mention of Don Shula's Miami Dolphins 17–0 Perfect Season of '72, the good news for steak—and sports—fans is that this beachfront spot also turns out culinary winners. Certified Angus beef is grilled over a

super-hot fire for quick charring. Steak Mary Anne, named for Shula's wife, consists of two sliced fillets in a savory sauce, and for hearty appetites there's the humongous Shula-cut porterhouse that just might qualify you for the famed 48-ounce Club, for folks who can tuck all that away in one sitting. Seafood is excellent, too, as is the apple cobbler à la mode. Patio tables provide views of sand and ocean, and inside seating gives you access to sports memorabilia and large-screen TVs. ✉ *Westin Beach Resort, 321 N. Fort Lauderdale Beach Blvd.* ☎ *954/355–4000* 🌐 *www.shulas.com* ▭ *AE, D, DC, MC, V.*

$ THAI ✕ **Siam Cuisine.** Some locals claim that this eatery, tucked away in a small storefront in Wilton Manors, serves the best Thai in the Fort Lauderdale area, and they may be right. The family-run kitchen turns out appealing, flavorful delights including sushi and crispy whole fish, usually red snapper. Curry dishes with chicken, beef, pork, or shrimp are favorites, along with steamed dumplings and roast duck. Wines are by the bottle or glass. ✉ *2010 Wilton Dr.* ☎ *954/564–3411* 🌐 *www.siamcuisineflorida.com* ▭ *AE, MC, V.*

$ SEAFOOD ✕ **Southport Raw Bar.** You can't go wrong at this unpretentious spot where the motto, on bumper stickers for miles around, proclaims EAT FISH, LIVE LONGER, EAT OYSTERS, LOVE LONGER, EAT CLAMS, LAST LONGER. Raw or steamed clams, raw oysters, and peel-and-eat shrimp are market priced. Sides range from Bimini bread to key lime pie, with conch fritters, beer-battered onion rings, and corn on the cob in between. Order wine by the bottle or glass, and beer by the pitcher, bottle, or can. Eat outside overlooking a canal, or inside at booths, tables, or in the front or back bars. Limited parking is free, and a grocery-store parking lot is across the street. ✉ *1536 Cordova Rd.* ☎ *954/525–2526* 🌐 *www.southportrawbar.com* ▭ *MC, V.*

$ SOUTHERN ✕ **Tom Jenkins.** Big portions of deliciously dripping barbecue are dispensed at this handy spot for eat-in or takeout, south of the New River Tunnel and north of the 17th Street Causeway. Think you don't have time to stop? Roll down your window and inhale on the way by, and you're likely to change your mind. Furnishings include an old Singer sewing machine and a wringer washer, and diners partake at picnic-style tables. Side dishes with dinners for around $10 include baked beans, collards, and mighty tasty macaroni and cheese. For lunch, Tom's pork, beef, and catfish sandwiches are a shortcut to satisfaction. Leave room for sweet-potato pie or peach cobbler. Heading to a park or the beach? Family samplers ($49.95) with pork spare ribs, chicken, beef, and sides feed four to six. ✉ *1236 S. Federal Hwy.* ☎ *954/522–5046* 🌐 *www.tomjenkinsbbq.com* ▭ *MC, V* ⏲ *Closed Sun. and Mon.*

¢ MEXICAN ✕ **Tortillería Mexicana.** With a machine cranking out 1,000 pounds of cornmeal tortillas daily (double that on weekends), this hole-in-the-wall Tortillería Mexicana, near Oakland Park City Hall, has authentic fare attracting Broward's growing Mexican population and plenty of gringos to boot. Staples include tacos, tamales, chicken with rice and beans, enchiladas, quesadillas, and flautas with chicken, salad, and hot pepper slices. Owner Eliseo Martinez opened a second tortilla haven, in Pompano Beach, this one with a bakery and butcher shop. ✉ *4115 N.*

Dixie Hwy., Oakland Park ☎ *954/563–2503* ✉ *1614 E. Sample Rd., Pompano Beach* ☎ *954/943–0057* ▭ *MC, V.*

$$$ STEAK ✕ **Tropical Acres.** The Studiale family's sprawling restaurant has served up sizzling steaks from a fireplace grill since 1949—a millennium by South Florida standards. Juicy prime rib is big at this bastion of yesteryear ambience. Choose from more than 35 entrées, including sautéed frogs' legs, rack of lamb, and boneless New York strip for two, or ask friendly servers for recommendations. You'll find some of the best early-bird specials around, including prime rib for well under $20. A wine list of some 60 labels ranges from $20 to $70, with a dozen or so poured by the glass. ✉ *2500 Griffin Rd.* ☎ *954/989–2500* 🌐 *www.tropical-acres.com* ▭ *AE, DC, MC, V.*

WHERE TO STAY

DOWNTOWN AND BEACH CAUSEWAYS

$$$–$$$$ Fodor's Choice ★ **Hyatt Regency Pier Sixty-Six Resort & Spa.** Unfortunately, the trademark of this high-rise resort—the rooftop Pier Top Lounge—has closed. Happily, that space with the most eye-popping views around is open to the public for a pricey Sunday brunch with unlimited champagne ($65 per head). The iconic 17-story tower dominates a lovely 22-acre spread that includes the full-service Spa 66. Each room has a balcony with views of the 142-slip marina, pool, ocean, or the Intracoastal Waterway. Some guests prefer the ground-level lanai rooms. Lush landscaping and convenience to beach and causeway, shopping, and restaurants add to overall allure, plus each room has complimentary Wi-Fi. Hail the Water Taxi at the resort's dock for access to downtown or the beach. **Pros:** great views; plenty of activities; ideal location. **Cons:** not on the beach; spa's location seems like an afterthought. ✉ *2301 SE 17th St. Causeway* ☎ *954/525–6666 or 800/327–3796* 🌐 *www.pier66.com* *380 rooms, 8 suites* *In-room: safe, refrigerator, Wi-Fi. In-hotel: 6 restaurants, bars, tennis courts, pools, gym, spa, water sports, Wi-Fi hotspot* ▭ *AE, D, DC, MC, V.*

$$$–$$$$ **Riverside Hotel.** On Las Olas Boulevard, just steps from boutiques, restaurants, and art galleries, Fort Lauderdale's oldest hotel debuted in 1936. Frequent renovations have kept it looking great. Penthouse suites in the newer 12-story executive tower have balconies with sweeping views of Las Olas, New River, and the downtown skyline. Historic photos grace hallways, and rooms are outfitted with antique oak furnishings and framed prints. Enjoy afternoon tea in the spruced-up lobby with free Wi-Fi, and dine at Indigo, where American favorites include steaks and seafood. For private dining, the hotel's Wine Room has a 4,000-bottle cellar; a reservations-only English afternoon-tea program (choose from Classic, Full, or Royal) unfolds in the lobby. **Pros:** historic appeal; in the thick of Las Olas action; nice views. **Cons:** no quick access to beach. ✉ *620 E. Las Olas Blvd.* ☎ *954/467–0671 or 800/325–3280* 🌐 *www.riversidehotel.com* *203 rooms, 10 suites* *In-room: Internet, safe, refrigerator. In-hotel: 2 restaurants, bars, pool* ▭ *AE, DC, MC, V.*

Lago Mar Resort & Club in Fort Lauderdale has its own private beach on the Atlantic Ocean.

$$$–$$$$ **Schubert Resort.** This restored 1950s art-deco hotel is an all-male, clothing-optional boutique resort tucked into tropical landscaping within the Victoria Park neighborhood. Suites are oversize and have marble-and-granite baths; most have either a king-size bed or two double beds. Continental breakfast is served overlooking the pool. The pet-friendly property feels secluded yet is a short walk from shopping and restaurants. **Pros:** friendly staff; well-managed property; clean and tidy. **Cons:** somewhat dated decor. ✉ *855 NE 20th Ave.* ☎ *954/763–7434 or 866/338–7666* 🌐 *www.schubertresort.com* *31 rooms* *In-room: kitchen (some). In-hotel: pool* *AE, D, MC, V* *CP.*

ALONG THE BEACH

$–$$$ **The Alcazar Resort.** Once a family-oriented Sea Chateau, this two-story enclave is now a clothing-optional resort for gay men. A heated pool and shaded courtyard are within the now-fenced property, and corner efficiencies with kitchenettes have been renamed junior suites. Most beds are kings, although some rooms have pairs of queen-size beds. All rooms have complimentary Wi-Fi. **Pros:** interesting architecture; nice pool area. **Cons:** not on the beach; no view. ✉ *555 N. Birch Rd.* ☎ *954/567–2525* 🌐 *www.alcazarresort.com* *15 rooms, 5 suites* *In-room: kitchen (some), refrigerator. In-hotel: pool* *AE, D, DC, MC, V.*

$$$$ ★ **The Atlantic Hotel.** Functional but elegant, this luxury condo hotel is steps from Las Olas Boulevard and the Atlantic. A British-colonial scheme is picked up throughout, from the marble and wood and beiges and browns of the lobby to the spacious, unfussy rooms, decorated with simple, dark-wood furniture, ample marble kitchen areas, creamy

fabrics, and plush carpeting. The decor chooses to frame, rather than compete with, balcony views of city or ocean (choose the latter if available). Among on-premises amenities are a European-style spa offering treatments and massages within the spa or in-room, the tony lobby-level Trina lounge and restaurant, and the 5th-floor Ocean Terrace, for light fare with a pool view. **Pros:** sophisticated lodging option; rooms have high-tech touches. **Cons:** across highway from beach; some traffic noise. ✉ *601 N. Fort Lauderdale Beach Blvd.* ☎ *954/567–8020* 🌐 *www.atlantichotelfl* *61 rooms, 58 suites, 4 penthouses* *In-room: kitchen, refrigerator (some), Internet, Wi-Fi. In-hotel: 2 restaurants, bar, pool, gym, spa, laundry service, parking (paid), Wi-Fi hotspot* ▭ *AE, D, DC, MC, V.*

> **WORD OF MOUTH**
>
> "Loved Lago Mar. The rooms are spacious and clean, nice pools and nice beach. Restaurant is very good. You would need a car to get to other places in Fort Lauderdale but I think it is worth it."
>
> —lindafromNJ

$$–$$$ ★ **Lago Mar Resort and Club**. The sprawling Lago Mar, owned by the Banks family since the early 1950s, has retained its sparkle thanks to frequent renovations. Most accommodations are spacious suites with pullout sofas and kitchens, making then ideal for families. Brilliantly colored bougainvilleas edge the swimming lagoon, and you have direct access to a large private beach in an exclusive neighborhood. Acquario serves northern Italian cuisine nightly and a divine filet mignon; kids and kids-at-heart gravitate toward the Soda Shop, a bakery and ice-cream parlor. **Pros:** secluded setting; plenty of activities; on the beach. **Cons:** not the easiest to find. ✉ *1700 S. Ocean La.* ☎ *954/523–6511 or 800/524–6627* 🌐 *www.lagomar.com* *52 rooms, 160 suites* *In-room: kitchen, Wi-Fi. In-hotel: 3 restaurants, tennis court, pools, Wi-Fi hotspot* ▭ *AE, DC, MC, V.*

$$$–$$$$ ★ **Pelican Grand Beach Resort**. Smack on the beach, this already lovely property has been transformed with a new tower, restaurant and lounge, an old-fashioned ice-cream parlor, and a circulating lazy-river pool that allows guests to float 'round and 'round. Most rooms and one-bedroom suites have ocean views. (Pelican fans of old may care to know that the original Sun Tower has gotten a makeover but now operates separately from the resort). Free Wi-Fi is available in public spaces and by the pool. **Pros:** you can't get any closer to the beach in Fort Lauderdale. **Cons:** you'll need wheels to access Las Olas beach-area action. ✉ *2000 N. Atlantic Blvd.* ☎ *954/568–9431 or 800/525–6232* 🌐 *www.pelicanbeach.com* *121 rooms (remainder of 155 total are condominiums)* *In-room: safe, refrigerator, Internet. In-hotel: restaurant, bar, pool, Wi-Fi hotspot* ▭ *AE, DC, MC, V.*

$$$–$$$$ **The Pillars Hotel at New River Sound**. A "small secret" kept by locals in the know, this gem is one block from the beach and on the Intracoastal Waterway. Its design recalls the colorful architecture of 18th-century British colonial Caribbean plantations. Most rooms have views of the waterway or pool, with French doors opening to individual patios or balconies. Rooms have rattan-and-mahogany headboards and antique-reproduction desks and nightstands; suites include wet bars with

refrigerators and microwaves. The Secret Garden is a tiny restaurant for hotel guests. **Pros:** attentive staff; lovely decor; idyllic pool area. **Cons:** small rooms; not for families with young kids given proximity to dock and water with no lifeguard on duty. ✉ *111 N. Birch Rd.* ☎ *954/467–9639* 🌐 *www.pillarshotel.com* *17 rooms, 5 suites* *In-room: refrigerator (some), Internet, Wi-Fi. In-hotel: restaurant, room service, pool, no kids under 12* *AE, D, DC, MC, V.*

$$$–$$$$ **Ritz-Carlton, Fort Lauderdale.** After a short-lived debut as the St. Regis, this shimmering luxury tower became a Ritz-Carlton in 2008. It's an eye-popper, with 24 dramatically tiered, glass-walled stories rising behind a tropical sundeck and a pool looking out toward the ocean. A sun-filled lobby and public areas sparkle with white-and-charcoal marble floors, crystal chandeliers, leather banquettes, and murals inspired by work of French artist Jean Cocteau. Cero, serving breakfast, lunch, and dinner, and the Lobby Bar, with a King Neptune mural, provide ocean views. The Wine Room, separated by glass from the bar, beckons with fine vintages from a 5,000-bottle collection. Guest rooms, overlooking the Atlantic or the Intracoastal Waterway, are intended to evoke the golden era of luxury travel with vintage photographs of the city. Luxury also awaits at the spa, with exotic therapies and a treatment suite for couples. **Pros:** golfers have privileges at the private Grande Oaks Golf Course, where *Caddyshack* was filmed. **Cons:** golf facilities off site; no complimentary Wi-Fi in public spaces. ✉ *1 N. Fort Lauderdale Beach Blvd.* ☎ *954/465–2300* 🌐 *www.ritzcarlton.com* *138 rooms, 54 suites* *In-room: safe, Wi-Fi. In-hotel: 2 restaurants, bar, pool, gym, spa* *AE, D, MC, V.*

NORTH ON SCENIC A1A

North of Fort Lauderdale's Birch Recreation Area, Route A1A edges away from the beach through a stretch known as Galt Ocean Mile, and a succession of oceanside communities line up against the sea. Traffic can line up, too, as it passes through a changing pattern of beach-blocking high-rises and modest family vacation towns and back again. Here and there a scenic lighthouse or park dots the landscape, and other attractions and recreational activities are found inland.

Towns are shown on the Broward County map.

LAUDERDALE-BY-THE-SEA

5 mi north of Fort Lauderdale.

Just north of Fort Lauderdale's northern boundary, this low-rise family resort town traditionally digs in its heels at mere mention of high-rises. The result is choice shoreline access that's rapidly disappearing in nearby communities, and Lauderdale-by-the-Sea takes delight in enhancing the beachgoing experience, adding such amenities as showers and bike racks.

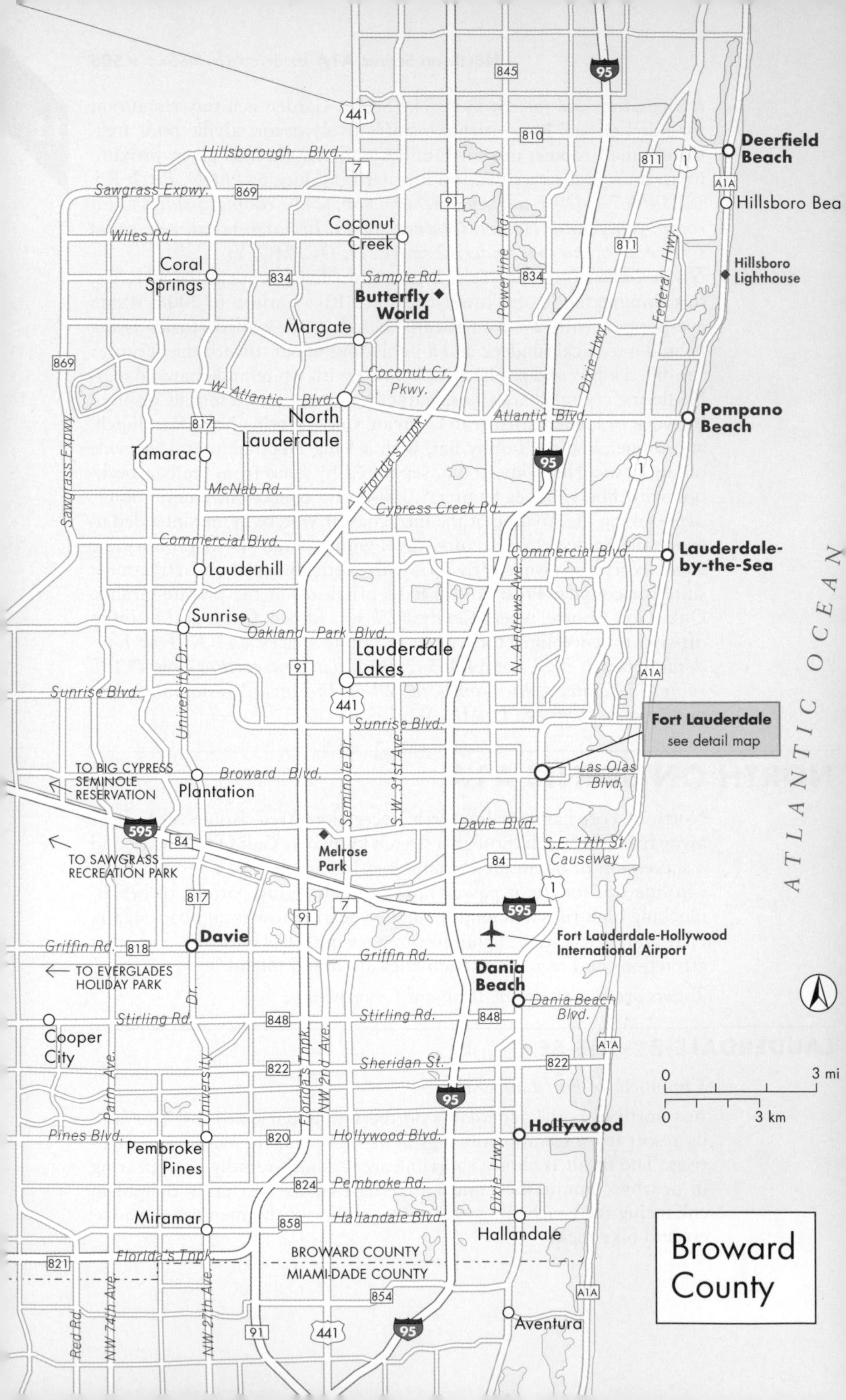

Broward County
845
95
441
810
Hillsborough Blvd.
7
811
1
Deerfield Beach
A1A
Sawgrass Expwy.
869
91
Hillsboro Bea
Coconut Creek
Wiles Rd.
811
Federal Hwy.
Powerline Rd.
Hillsboro Lighthouse
Coral Springs
834
Sample Rd.
834
Butterfly World
Margate
Dixie Hwy.
869
Coconut Cr. Pkwy.
W. Atlantic Blvd.
North Lauderdale
Atlantic Blvd.
Pompano Beach
817
Sawgrass Expwy.
Tamarac
95
1
McNab Rd.
Florida's Tnpk.
Cypress Creek Rd.
Commercial Blvd.
Commercial Blvd.
Lauderdale-by-the-Sea
Lauderhill
N. Andrews Ave.
Sunrise
Oakland Park Blvd.
ATLANTIC OCEAN
Lauderdale Lakes
91
A1A
Sunrise Blvd.
University Dr.
441
Sunrise Blvd.
Fort Lauderdale
see detail map
S.W. 31st Ave.
Seminole Dr.
TO BIG CYPRESS SEMINOLE RESERVATION
Broward Blvd.
Plantation
Las Olas Blvd.
595
Davie Blvd.
84
TO SAWGRASS RECREATION PARK
Melrose Park
S.E. 17th St. Causeway
84
817
1
7
595
91
Fort Lauderdale-Hollywood International Airport
Griffin Rd.
818
Davie
Griffin Rd.
TO EVERGLADES HOLIDAY PARK
Dania Beach
Dania Beach Blvd.
Cooper City
Stirling Rd.
848
Stirling Rd.
848
A1A
Palm Ave.
University Dr.
Florida's Tnpk.
NW 2nd Ave.
822
Sheridan St.
822
0
3 mi
0
3 km
95
Pines Blvd.
820
Hollywood Blvd.
Hollywood
Pembroke Pines
824
Pembroke Rd.
Dixie Hwy.
Miramar
858
Hallandale Blvd.
Hallandale
821
Florida's Tnpk.
BROWARD COUNTY
MIAMI-DADE COUNTY
A1A
854
Aventura
Red Rd.
NW 74th Ave.
NW 27th Ave.
91
441
95

GETTING HERE AND AROUND

Lauderdale-by-the-Sea is just north of Fort Lauderdale. If you're driving from Interstate 95, exit east onto Commercial Boulevard and head over the Intracoastal Waterway. From U.S. 1 (aka Federal Highway), turn east on Commercial Boulevard.

Catch free rides on the Pelican Hopper, a pelican-white, air-conditioned bus running south to the top of the Galt Ocean Mile and north to Terra Mar Drive. Lauderdale-by-the-Sea's 25-seat shuttle operates seven days with various stops, including the Publix Supermarket at the Village Shopping Center in Sea Ranch Lakes.

ESSENTIALS

Transportation Contact **Pelican Hopper** (☎ *954/776–0576*).

Visitor Information **Lauderdale-by-the-Sea Chamber of Commerce** (✉ *4201 N. Ocean Dr., Lauderdale-by-the-Sea* ☎ *954/776–1000* 🌐 *www.lbts.com*).

SPORTS AND THE OUTDOORS

★ **Anglin's Fishing Pier** (☎ *954/491–9403*), a longtime favorite for 24-hour fishing, has a fresh, renovated appearance after shaking off repeated storm damage that closed the pier at intervals during the past decade. What's more, Anglin's Café (☎ *954/491–6007*) has reopened, 7 AM to 4 PM.

WHERE TO EAT

$$ CAFÉ Fodor's Choice ★ ✕ **Aruba Beach Café**. A big beachside barn of a place—very casual, always crowded, always fun—Aruba Beach serves Caribbean conch chowder and a Key West soup loaded with shrimp, calamari, and oysters. There are also fresh tropical salads, sandwiches, and seafood. For around $10, Aruba serves a mighty juicy burger with custom toppings. A band performs day and night, so head for the back corner with eye-popping views of the beach if you want conversation while you eat and drink. A Sunday breakfast buffet starts at 9 AM. ✉ *1 E. Commercial Blvd.* ☎ *954/776–0001* 🌐 *www.arubabeachcafe.com* 💳 *AE, D, DC, MC, V.*

$ AMERICAN ✕ **LaSpada's Original Hoagies**. The crew at this seaside hole-in-the-wall puts on quite a show of ingredient-tossing flair while assembling take-out hoagies, subs, and deli sandwiches. Locals rave that they are the best around. Fill up on the Monster (ham, cheese, roast beef, and turkey, $10.95), Hot Meatballs Marinara ($8.50), or an assortment of salads. ✉ *4346 Seagrape Dr.* ☎ *954/776–7893* 🌐 *www.laspadashoagies.com* 💳 *AE, D, DC, MC, V.*

$$$ SEAFOOD ✕ **Sea Watch**. Since 1974, this nautical-themed restaurant with a prime beach location has catered to crowds for lunch and dinner. Among appetizers are oysters Rockefeller, gulf shrimp, clams casino, and Bahamian conch fritters. Main courses might include oat-crusted yellowtail snapper, charbroiled swordfish, grilled orange roughy, or paella. Early-bird dinners (May through December) are $19.95, and 6-pound Maine lobsters are around $100. ✉ *6002 N. Ocean Blvd. (Rte. A1A), Fort Lauderdale* ☎ *954/781–2200* 🌐 *www.seawatchontheocean.com* 💳 *AE, D, DC, MC, V.*

WHERE TO STAY

$$–$$$ **A Little Inn by the Sea.** Subtropical charm flourishes at this two-story inn, which caters to an international clientele. Bamboo and rattan pieces are gradually being replaced by more traditional hotel furnishings, but this Little Inn still retains its tropical feel, especially when you are planted on the private balconies, many facing the beach. Count on a complimentary Continental-breakfast buffet, plus free Wi-Fi in lobby and some rooms. **Pros:** smack on the beach; shaded by pretty palms. **Cons:** casual housekeeping standards; towels can be in short supply. ✉ *4546 El Mar Dr.* ☎ *954/772–2450 or 800/492–0311* 🌐 *www.alittleinnhotel.com* *10 rooms, 7 suites, 12 efficiencies* *In-room: Wi-Fi (some). In-hotel: pool, beachfront, Wi-Fi hotspot* *AE, D, DC, MC, V* *CP.*

$$–$$$ **Blue Seas Courtyard.** Innkeeper Cristie Furth, with her husband, Marc, runs this small motel in a quiet resort area across from the beach. Lattice fences, gurgling fountains, and gardens of cactus and impatiens provide privacy around the brick patio and heated pool. A palm-fringed Mexican-hacienda look predominates, and guest quarters have free Wi-Fi, hand-painted and stenciled furnishings, and terra-cotta tiles. **Pros:** south-of-the-border vibe; friendly owners. **Cons:** lower rooms lack ocean views. ✉ *4525 El Mar Dr.* ☎ *954/772–3336* 🌐 *www.blueseascourtyard.com* *12 rooms* *In-room: kitchen, Wi-Fi. In-hotel: pool, laundry facilities* *MC, V.*

$–$$ **Great Escape Hotel.** For comfortable accommodations amid palms and other tropical plants, this two-story property could be your great—and economical—escape. Guests tend to congregate around the pretty pool (despite free Wi-Fi in rooms!). **Pros:** walk to the beach; bargain rates. **Cons:** no ocean view. ✉ *4620 N. Ocean Dr.* ☎ *954/772–1002* 🌐 *www.greatescapehotel.com* *11 units* *In-room: Wi-Fi. In-hotel: pool, laundry facilities* *AE, MC, V.*

$$–$$$ ★ **High Noon Beach Resort.** Flanked by the Nautilus Resort to the north and the Sea Foam Resort to the south, High Noon—family-run since 1961—plays the central role for this resort trio on the beach, where you'll find a comfortable place to relax morning, noon, or night. Accommodations, poolside or oceanfront, range from standard rooms to efficiencies with kitchens to apartments with separate bedrooms and one or two baths. Nine rooms have private balconies. There's also a two-bedroom beach house. Wicker furnishings prevail at all three properties, and there's free Wi-Fi in common areas and most rooms. **Pros:** smack on the beach; friendly vibe. **Cons:** early booking required. ✉ *4424 El Mar Dr.* ☎ *954/776–1121 or 800/382–1265* 🌐 *www.highnoonresort.com* *40 rooms* *In-room: kitchen (some), refrigerator (some), Wi-Fi. In-hotel: pool, beachfront, Wi-Fi hotspot* *AE, D, DC, MC, V.*

$$ **Tides Inn Oceanfront Resort.** Set on the beach, you'll find this small lodging oasis convenient to pier and surrounding activity yet with a private courtyard and a well-located (if not overly landscaped) rectangular pool. Units, from rooms to oceanview and oceanfront efficiencies, plus a 2nd-floor "penthouse," are well-appointed, and the phone system allows for private voice-mail. **Pros:** on the beach. **Cons:** older property. ✉ *4628 El Mar Dr.,* ☎ *954/772–2933* 🌐 *www.tidesinnresort.com* *5*

DID YOU KNOW?

Seagulls can drink both fresh and saltwater, and they can make short order of your lunch, since they eat everything from crabs and fish to bread, cookies, and potato chips. They announce their presence by squawking.

rooms, 4 efficiencies, 1 one-bedroom unit. *In-room: Wi-Fi in rooms. In-hotel: pool* *AE, D, MC, V* *CP.*

$$–$$$ **Tropic Seas Resort Motel.** This two-story property has an unbeatable location—directly on the beach and two blocks from municipal tennis courts. Built in the 1950s and renovated in 2007, tiled units are clean and comfortable, with tropical rattan furniture and ceiling fans. Coffee and Danish pastry are served daily. **Pros:** family-owned friendliness; great location. **Cons:** must reserve far ahead; basic decor. *4616 El Mar Dr.* *954/772–2555 or 800/952–9581* *www.tropicseasresort.com* *3 rooms, 6 efficiencies, 7 apartments* *In-hotel: pool, beachfront* *AE, D, DC, MC, V* *CP.*

POMPANO BEACH AND DEERFIELD BEACH

Pompano Beach and Deerfield Beach are 3 mi and 6½ mi north of Lauderdale-by-the-Sea, respectively.

As Route A1A enters this town directly north of Lauderdale-by-the-Sea the high-rise scene resumes. Sportfishing is big in Pompano Beach, as its name implies, but there's more to beachside attractions than the popular Fisherman's Wharf. Behind a low coral-rock wall, Alsdorf Park (also called the 14th Street boat ramp) extends north and south of the wharf along the road and beach. Farther north is Deerfield Beach.

GETTING HERE AND AROUND

From Interstate 95, Pompano Beach exits include Sample Road, Copans Road, or Atlantic Boulevard. For Deerfield Beach, take the Hillsboro Boulevard exit east.

ESSENTIALS

Visitor Information Greater Pompano Beach Chamber of Commerce (*954/941–2940* *www.pompanobeachchamber.com*). **Greater Deerfield Beach Chamber of Commerce** (*954/427–1050* *www.deerfieldchamber.com*).

EXPLORING

Quiet Waters Park. Its name belies what's in store for kids here. Splash Adventure is a high-tech water-play system with slides and tunnels, among other activities. A Rent-A-Tent program ($35 per night for up to four campers) provides already set-up tents or teepees. There's also cable water-skiing and boat rental on this county park's lake, and a skate park. *401 S. Powerline Rd., Deerfield Beach* *954/360–1315* *wwww.broward.org/parks/qw.htm* *Park $1 weekends, free weekdays* *Apr.–Sept., daily 8–6; Oct.–Mar., daily 8–5:30.*

OFF THE BEATEN PATH

Deerfield Island Park. Reached only by boat (and with a new dock for vessels longer than 25 feet in the works), this officially designated Urban Wilderness Area showcases coastal hammock island and contains a mangrove swamp that provides a critical habitat for gopher tortoises, gray foxes, raccoons, and armadillos. County-operated boat shuttles run 9–5 on weekends. Amenities include a boardwalk, walking trails, and an observation tower. *1720 Deerfield Island Park* *954/360–1320* *Free.*

SPORTS AND THE OUTDOORS

FISHING

Pompano Pier. The 24-hour pier extends more than 1,000 feet into the Atlantic. Upscale seafood and steak restaurants, part of a planned renovation, have been delayed by the economic downtown. Meanwhile, the pier tackle shop sells beer and snacks. Admission is $4 to fish, $1 to sightsee; rod-and-reel rental is $16.50 (including admission, plus a $20 deposit) for the day. Anglers brag about catching barracuda, jack, and snapper here in the same sitting, along with bluefish, cobia, and, yes, even pompano. ☎ 954/226–6411.

OUTFITTERS The **Cove Marina** (✉ *Hillsboro Blvd. and the Intracoastal Waterway, Deerfield Beach* ☎ *954/427–9747*) has a deep-sea charter fleet. In winter there are excellent runs of sailfish, kingfish, dolphin, and tuna. A half-day charter for six costs about $600, or $1,000 for a full day. For drift-fishing, try **Fish City Pride** (✉ *Fish City Marina, 2621 N. Riverside Dr., Pompano Beach* ☎ *954/781–1211*). Morning, afternoon, and evening trips cost $37 and include fishing gear and bait. Arrange for a saltwater-charter boat through the **Hillsboro Inlet Marina** (✉ *2705 N. Riverside Dr., Pompano Beach* ☎ *954/943–8222*). The eight-boat fleet offers half-day charters for $550, six hours for $750, or a full day for $950, including gear for up to six anglers.

SCUBA DIVING

As namesake of the **SS Copenhagen State Underwater Archaeological Preserve**, the wreck of the SS*Copenhagen* lies in 15- to 30-foot depths just outside the second reef on the Pompano Ledge, 3.6 miles south of Hillsboro Inlet. The 325-foot-long steamer's final voyage, from Philadelphia bound for Havana, began May 20, 1900, ending six days later when the captain—attempting to avoid gulf currents—crashed onto a reef off what's now Pompano Beach. In 2000, the missing bow section was identified a half mile to the south. The wreck, a haven for colorful fish and corals and a magnet for skin and scuba divers, became Florida's fifth Underwater Archaeological Preserve in 1994, listed on the National Register of Historic Places in 2001.

Among the area's most popular dive operators, **Dixie Divers** (✉ *Cove Marina, Hillsboro Blvd. and the Intracoastal Waterway, Deerfield Beach* ☎ *954/420–0009* 🌐 *www.dixiedivers.com*) has morning and afternoon dives aboard the 48-foot *Lady-Go-Diver,* plus evening dives on weekends. Snorkelers and certified divers can explore the marine life of nearby reefs and shipwrecks. The cost is $60; ride-alongs are welcome for $35.

SHOPPING

Bargain hunters head to the **Festival Flea Market Mall** (✉ *2900 W. Sample Rd., Pompano Beach* ☎ *954/979–4555* 🌐 *www.festival.com*), where more than 800 vendors sell new, brand-name merchandise at discounts. The Hillsboro Antiques Mall relocated here (you'll find it at the southeast corner), adding classy antiquity to good, old-fashioned, shopping fun. For diversion, there's also a food court.

WHERE TO EAT

DEERFIELD BEACH

$$$ FRENCH ★ ✕ **Brooks.** This is one of Broward's more elegant dining spots, thanks to French perfectionist Bernard Perron. Brooks is now run by Perron's son-in-law John Howe. Updated Continental fare is served in a series of rooms filled with old-master replicas, cut glass, antiques, and floral wallpaper. Fresh ingredients go into distinctly Floridian dishes, including sautéed Key Largo yellowtail snapper. Roast rack of lamb is also popular. Put your order in early for the chocolate or Grand Marnier soufflé. ✉ *500 S. Federal Hwy.* ☎ *954/427–9302* ▭ *AE, D, MC, V.*

$ SEAFOOD ★ ✕ **Olympia Flame Diner.** The family-owned Flame burned white-hot in 2009 when finance guru Suze Orman did a star turn as a waitress here for an Oprah TV segment. Orman has a condo nearby, and her fitness trainer—who dines here regularly—suggested the blue-awning diner as an illuminated best bet for a hot, home-style meal accompanied by megawatt chatter. Greek specialties from spinach pie to baklava dominate the menu, but you can order seafood, deli-style sandwiches, and burgers along with beer or wine. And no, Oprah and Ormon mega-exposure hasn't changed the homey mood here at all. ✉ *80 S. Federal Hwy.* ☎ *954/480–8402* 🌐 *www.olympiaflamediner.com* ▭ *MC, V.*

$$ SEAFOOD ★ ✕ **Whale's Rib.** For a casual, almost funky, nautical experience near the beach, look no farther. If you want to blend in, order a fish special with whale fries—thinly sliced potatoes that look like hot potato chips. Those with smaller appetites can choose from salads and fish sandwiches, or raw-bar favorites like Ipswich clams. ✉ *2031 NE 2nd St.* ☎ *954/421–8880* ▭ *AE, MC, V.*

POMPANO BEACH

$$$$ ECLECTIC ★ ✕ **Cafe Maxx.** New-wave epicurean dining had its South Florida start here in the early 1980s, and Cafe Maxx remains fresh. The menu changes nightly but showcases tropical appeal with jerk-spiced sea scallops or jumbo stone crab claws with honey-lime mustard sauce and black-bean-and-banana-pepper chili with Florida avocado. Appetizers include caviar pie and crispy sweetbreads. Desserts such as Trio of Sorbet (or ice cream) with a flurry of fruit sauces including mango stay the tropical course. Select from 300 wines by the bottle, and many by the glass. ✉ *2601 E. Atlantic Blvd.* ☎ *954/782–0606* 🌐 *www.cafemaxx.com* ▭ *AE, D, DC, MC, V* ⏲ *No lunch.*

WHERE TO STAY

DEERFIELD BEACH

$$$–$$$$ 🏨 **Royal Flamingo Villas.** This cluster of villas sits near the Intracoastal Waterway on more than 7 acres of manicured grounds. Roomy one- and two-bedroom villas are decorated in sunny pastels, rattan, and wicker, all keeping with the tropical theme. If you don't need lavish public facilities, this is your upscale choice at a reasonable price with complimentary Wi-Fi. **Pros:** serene atmosphere; attractive landscaping. **Cons:** don't look for vibrant decor. ✉ *1225 Hillsboro Mile (Rte. A1A), Hillsboro Beach* ☎ *954/427–0660 or 800/241–2477* 🌐 *www.royalflamingovillas.com* 🛏 *40 villas* 👍 *In-hotel: pool, beachfront, laundry facilities* ▭ *D, MC, V.*

POMPANO BEACH

$$–$$$ **Beachcomber Resort & Villas.** This property's beachfront location is close to most local attractions and a mile from the Pompano Pier. Ocean views are everywhere, from the oversize guest-room balconies to dining rooms. Although there are also villas and penthouse suites atop the eight-story structure, the standard rooms are spacious, and all units have free Wi-Fi. The multilingual staff is attentive to guest requests. **Pros:** Old Florida feel; lots of laid-back charm. **Cons:** worn around the edges. ✉ *1200 S. Ocean Blvd.* ☎ *954/941–7830 or 800/231–2423* 🌐 *www.beachcomberresort.com* *143 rooms, 9 villas, 4 suites* *In-room: Internet. In-hotel: restaurant, bar, pools, beachfront* *AE, D, DC, MC, V.*

$$–$$$ **Wyndham Palm-Aire.** In its heyday (and hey, that's many a day ago), stars like Elizabeth Taylor checked in here to slim down and chill out. Now a time-share, this resort has studios and one-, two-, and four-bedroom apartments that are individually owned but share similar decor. Some units have whirlpool tubs and washers and dryers; kitchens range from partial to full. Housekeeping is provided weekly, and more frequently for a charge. The spa and fitness complex has a sauna, steam room, and fitness equipment. Five championship golf courses at the Palm-Aire Country Club are just a chip shot away. The Palms Café serves lunch and dinner, and drinks are on tap at the Tiki Hut. **Pros:** roll out of bed onto the golf course; home-away-from-home feel. **Cons:** a bit past its prime. ✉ *2601 Palm-Aire Dr. N* ☎ *954/972–3300* 🌐 *www.wyndhampalmaire.com* *298 units* *In-room: safe, refrigerator, Wi-Fi. In-hotel: restaurant, bar, golf courses, tennis courts, pools, gym, spa* *AE, D, DC, MC, V.*

EN ROUTE

About 2 mi north of Pompano Beach you are afforded a beautiful view across Hillsboro Inlet to **Hillsboro Lighthouse**, often called the brightest lighthouse in the southeast and used by mariners as a landmark for decades. When at sea you can see its light from almost halfway to the Bahamas. Although the octagonal-pyramid, iron-skeletal tower lighthouse is on private property inaccessible to the public, it's well worth a peek, even from afar. The Hillsboro Lighthouse Preservation Society (🌐 *www.hillsborolighthouse.org*) offers tours about four times a year; call ☎ *954/942–2102* for schedule and tips on viewing vantage points.

SOUTH BROWARD

South Broward's roots are in early Florida settlements. Thus far it has avoided some of the glitz and glamour of neighbors to the north and south, and folks here like it that way. Still, there's plenty to see and do—excellent restaurants in every price range, world-class pari-mutuels, and a new focus on the arts.

DANIA BEACH

Dania Beach is 4 mi south of Fort Lauderdale.

This town at the south edge of Fort Lauderdale is probably best known for its antiques dealers, but there are other attractions as well.

Early-bird anglers at Dania Beach get not only a jump-start on fishing, but can watch the sunrise.

GETTING HERE

From Interstate 95, exit east on Griffin Road or Stirling Road.

ESSENTIALS

Visitor Information **Greater Dania Beach Chamber of Commerce** (*102 W. Dania Beach Blvd., Dania Beach* *954/926–2323* *www.greaterdania.org*).

EXPLORING

Dania Beach Hurricane. Accessed via Boomers! fun park, and visible from Interstate 95, this isn't the world's highest, fastest, or longest roller coaster, but it's near the top in all those categories, and ranks as the tallest wooden coaster south of Atlanta. This retro-feel ride creaks like an old staircase while you race along 3,200 feet of track and plummet from 100 feet at speeds up to 55 mph. Access to the park is free, but the Hurricane will cost you $6 per ride, or $13 for an all-day wristband. *1760 NW 1st St.* *954/921–7433* *www.boomersparks.com* *$6* *Sun.–Thurs. 11–11, Fri. and Sat. 10 AM–1 AM.*

★ **IGFA Fishing Hall of Fame and Museum.** This creation of the International Game Fishing Association is a shrine to the sport. It has an extensive museum and research library where seven galleries feature fantasy fishing and other interactive displays. At the Catch Gallery, you can cast off virtually to reel in a marlin, sailfish, trout, tarpon, or bass. (If you suddenly get an urge to gear up for your own adventures, a Bass Pro Shops Outdoor World is next door.) *300 Gulfstream Way* *954/922–4212* *www.igfa.org* *$8* *Daily 10–6.*

SPORTS AND THE OUTDOORS

FISHING

The 920-foot, 24-hour **Dania Pier** (☎ *954/367–4423*) has gussied up with chickee huts, restrooms, and a concessionaire restaurant of sorts, offering peel-and-eat shrimp and other dishes, doled out with a take-it-or-leave it attitude. If you leave it, you can get hot dogs with much friendlier service at the bait shop. Fishing is $3 (with parking another $5 for the day), tackle rental $6, bait about $3, and spectators pay $2.

MINIATURE GOLF

Boomers! (✉ *1801 NW 1st St.* ☎ *954/921–1411* 🌐 *www.boomersparks.com* 🎫 *Free* ⏲ *Mon.–Thurs. noon–11, Fri. noon–1* AM, *Sat. 10* AM*–1* AM, *Sun. 10* AM*–11* PM) has action games for kids of all ages—go-karts, miniature golf, batting cages, bumper boats, and a skycoaster.

WHERE TO EAT

$ AMERICAN ✕ **Jaxson's Ice Cream Parlour & Restaurant.** This local landmark whips up malts, shakes, and jumbo sundaes from ice creams prepared daily on premises, plus sandwiches and salads, amid an antique-license-plate decor. Owner Monroe Udell's trademarked Kitchen Sink—a small sink full of ice cream, topped by sparklers—for parties of four or more goes for $12.95 per person. Less ambitious appetites lean toward Jaxson's Sampler (Junior or Senior). ✉ *128 S. Federal Hwy.* ☎ *954/923–4445* 🌐 *www.jaxsonsicecream.com* 💳 *AE, D, MC, V.*

HOLLYWOOD

Hollywood is 3 mi south of Dania Beach.

Hollywood has had a face-lift, with more nips and tucks to come. Young Circle, once down-at-heel, has become Broward's first Arts Park. On Hollywood's western outskirts, the flamboyant Seminole Hard Rock Hotel & Casino has permanently etched the previously downtrodden section of State Road 7/U.S. 441 corridor on the map of trendy excitement, drawing local weekenders, architecture buffs, and gamblers. But Hollywood's redevelopment effort doesn't end there: new shops, restaurants, and art galleries open at a persistent clip, and the city has spiffed up its Broadwalk—a wide pedestrian walkway along the beach—where rollerbladers are as commonplace as snowbirds from the north.

GETTING HERE AND AROUND

From Interstate 95, exit east on Sheridan Street or Hollywood Boulevard.

ESSENTIALS

Visitor Information **Hollywood Chamber of Commerce** (✉ *330 N. Federal Hwy., Hollywood* ☎ *954/923–4000* 🌐 *www.hollywoodchamber.org*).

EXPLORING

Art and Culture Center of Hollywood. This is a visual- and performing-arts facility with an art reference library, outdoor sculpture garden, and arts school. It's southeast of Young Circle, melding urban open space with a fountain, a 2,000-plus-seat amphitheater, and an indoor theater. Nearby, on trendy Harrison Street and Hollywood Boulevard, are chic lunch places, bluesy entertainment spots, and shops. ✉ *1650 Harrison*

St. ☎ *954/921–3274* 🌐 *artandculturecenter.org* 🎫 *$7* ⏲ *Mon.–Sat. 10–5, Sun. noon–4.*

SPORTS AND THE OUTDOORS

West Lake Park. Rent a canoe, kayak, or take the 40-minute boat tour at this park bordering the Intracoastal Waterway. At 1,500 acres, it is one of Florida's largest urban nature facilities. Extensive boardwalks traverse mangrove forests that shelter endangered and threatened species. A 65-foot observation tower showcases the entire park. At the free **Anne Kolb Nature Center,** named after Broward's late environmental advocate, there's a 3,500-gallon aquarium. The center's exhibit hall has 27 interactive displays. ✉ *1200 Sheridan St.* ☎ *954/926–2410* 🎫 *Weekends $1.50, weekdays free* ⏲ *Daily 9–5.*

BEACH

Fodor's Choice ★

Broadwalk. With the Intracoastal Waterway to the west and the beach and ocean immediately east, this spiffed-up 2-mi paved promenade has lured pedestrians and cyclists since 1924. With a recent $14 million makeover, this stretch has taken on added luster for the buff, the laid-back, and the retired. Kids also thrive here: there are play areas, rental bikes, trikes, and other pedal-powered gizmos. Expect to hear French spoken here, since Hollywood Beach has long been a favorite getaway for Quebecois. Conversations in Spanish and Portuguese are also frequently overheard on this path. ✉ *Rte. A1A and Sheridan St.* 🎫 *Parking $7* ⏲ *Wed.–Mon. 8–6.*

FISHING

Sea Leg's III (✉ *5398 N. Ocean Dr.* ☎ *954/923–2109*) runs drift-fishing trips during the day and bottom-fishing trips at night. Trips cost $35–$38, including rod rental.

GOLF

The **Diplomat Country Club & Spa** (✉ *501 Diplomat Pkwy., Hallandale* ☎ *954/883–4000*) has 18 holes and a spa; greens fee $69/$209. The course at **Emerald Hills** (✉ *4100 N. Hills Dr.* ☎ *954/961–4000*) has 18 holes; greens fee $55/$190.

HORSE RACING

Gulfstream Park Racing & Casino is the winter home of top thoroughbreds, as well as the year-round home of slot-machine and bingo action. The season is capped by the $1 million Florida Derby, with Kentucky Derby hopefuls. Racing unfolds January through April. After 37 years on Miami Beach, **Christine Lee's,** known for Asian specialties and prime steaks, has opened shop here. ✉ *901 S. Federal Hwy., Hallandale* ☎ *954/454–7000 or 800/771–8873* 🌐 *www.gulfstreampark.com* 🎫 *Grandstand free, clubhouse $5* ⏲ *Racing Wed.–Mon. at 1 PM.*

NIGHTLIFE AND THE ARTS

THE ARTS

Harrison Street Art and Design District in downtown Hollywood has galleries featuring original artwork (eclectic paintings, sculpture, photography, and mixed media). Friday night the artists' studios, galleries, and shops stay open later while crowds meander along Hollywood Boulevard and Harrison Street. **The Shade Post** (✉ *2028 Harrison St.* ☎ *954/920–0029* 🌐 *www.artofshade.com*) features Kayce Armstrong's

Art of Shade creations, fashioned from recycled garments, old shower curtains, etc., showcased in a boutique outfitted with racks made of old masts and rigging. Hours are also offbeat, Tuesday through Saturday, 4–10. **Mosaica** (✉ *2020 Hollywood Blvd.* ☎ *954/923–7006*) is a design studio with handcrafted, one-of-a-kind mosaic-tile tables, mirrors, and art.

WHERE TO EAT

$$$ SEAFOOD ✕ **Giorgio's Grill.** Good food and service are hallmarks of this expansive 400-seat restaurant overlooking the Intracoastal Waterway. Seafood is a specialty, but you'll also find pasta and meat dishes, and a solid Sunday brunch for around $20. A great watery view especially around sunset and friendly staff add to the experience, and there's a surprisingly extensive, reasonably priced wine list. ✉ *606 N. Ocean Dr.* ☎ *954/929–7030* 🌐 *www.giorgiosgrill.com* ▭ *AE, D, DC, MC, V.*

$$$ ARGENTINE ✕ **Las Brisas.** Next to the beach, this cozy bistro offers seating inside or out, and the food is Argentine with Italian flair. A small pot, filled with *chimichurri*—a paste of oregano, parsley, olive oil, salt, garlic, and crushed pepper—for spreading on steaks, sits on each table. Grilled fish is a favorite, as are pork chops, chicken, and pasta entrées. Desserts include a flan like *mamacita* used to make. ✉ *600 N. Surf Rd.* ☎ *954/923–1500* ▭ *AE, D, DC, MC, V* ⊙ *No lunch.*

$$ AMERICAN ✕ **LeTub.** Formerly a Sunoco gas station, this quirky waterside saloon has an enduring affection for claw-foot bathtubs. Hand-painted porcelain is everywhere—under ficus, sea grape, and palm trees. If a potty doesn't appeal, there's a secluded swing facing the water north of the main dining area. Despite molasses-slow service and an abundance of flies at sundown, this eatery is favored by locals, and management seemed genuinely appalled when hordes of trend-seeking city slickers started jamming bar stools and tables after Oprah declared its thick, juicy Angus burgers the best around. A plain burger and small fries will run you around $15. ✉ *1100 N. Ocean Dr.* ☎ *954/921–9425* 🌐 *www.theletub.com* ▭ *No credit cards.*

$$ JAPANESE ✕ **Sushi Blues Café.** Run by husband-and-wife-team Kenny Millions and Junko Maslak, this place proves that sushi has gone global. Japanese chefs prepare conventional and macrobiotic-influenced dishes, including lobster teriyaki and steamed snapper with miso sauce. Poached pears steamed in cabernet sauce and cappuccino custard are popular desserts. Music is a big part of the appeal of this place, especially when the Sushi Blues Band performs on weekends. ✉ *2009 Harrison St.* ☎ *954/929–9560* 🌐 *www.sushiblues.com* ▭ *AE, MC, V.*

WHERE TO STAY

$$–$$$ 🏨 **Driftwood on the Ocean.** Facing the beach at Surf Road's secluded south end, this sprawling motel has been around since the 1950s. The setting is what draws guests, but attention to maintenance and refurbishing in recent seasons makes it an improved value. Accommodations range from a studio to a deluxe two-bedroom, two-bath suite. Most units have a kitchen; all have balconies or terraces and free wireless Internet access. **Pros:** wide ribbon of beachfront; bargain rates. **Cons:** not all rooms face ocean; no restaurant or bar. ✉ *2101 S. Surf Rd.* ☎ *954/923–9528 or 800/944–3148* 🌐 *www.driftwoodontheocean.com* ⇨ *7 rooms,*

9 2-bedroom apartments, 13 1-bedroom apartments, 20 efficiencies In-room: kitchen (some), Wi-Fi. In-hotel: pool, beachfront, bicycles, laundry facilities AE, D, MC, V.

$$–$$$ ★ **Manta Ray Inn.** Canadians Donna and Dwayne Boucher run this immaculate, affordable, two-story inn on the beach. Dating from the 1940s, the inn, with new pale-pink tile in downstairs rooms and moss-green carpet in upstairs rooms, offers casual, comfortable beachfront accommodations with wicker or rattan furnishings, and cable TV, free Wi-Fi, and off-street parking. Kitchens are equipped with microwaves, pots, pans, and serving utensils. One-bedroom apartments have marble shower stalls, and two-bedroom units also have tubs. Manta Ray guests also have access to the pool next door at the Enchanted Isle time-share. **Pros:** on the beach; low-key atmosphere. **Cons:** no restaurant. *1715 S. Surf Rd. 954/921–9666 or 800/255–0595 www.mantarayinn.com 12 units In-room: Wi-Fi. In-hotel: beachfront AE, D, MC, V.*

$$–$$$ **Sea Downs.** Facing the Broadwalk and ocean, this three-story lodging is a good choice for families, as one-bedroom units can be joined to create two-bedroom apartments. All but two units have ocean views, and all have been upgraded with new appliances, furnishings, and free high-speed internet. Outside of rooms, there's free Wi-Fi, to go with free parking—an increasing value in Hollywood. Kitchens are fully equipped, and most units have tub-showers and closets. Housekeeping is provided once a week, with fresh towels provided daily, and a coin washer and dryer are on-site. **Pros:** facing ocean; reasonable rates. **Cons:** minimum stay often required. *2900 N. Surf Rd. 954/923–4968 www.seadowns.com 4 efficiencies, 8 1-bedroom apartments In-room: Internet, Wi-Fi. In-hotel: pool, laundry facilities No credit cards.*

$$$–$$$$ ★ **The Westin Diplomat Resort & Spa.** This 39-story property had its 15 minutes recently as host to Senator John Edwards's mistress, Reille Hunter, but the central atrium with ceilings soaring to 60 feet are worth talking about, too. A signature of the resort is its 120-foot, bridged infinity pool, extending from lobby to oceanfront. Rooms are light and spacious, and patio furnishings are recyclable. A Mediterranean-inspired spa offers more than a dozen pampering treatments, including a caviar facial. The hotel's country club, across the Intracoastal Waterway, has golf and tennis facilities. Shuttle service takes you across in no time. Enjoy sushi and other Asian specialties at Aizia, or head across to the Links Restaurant and Lounge for American fare. **Pros:** Heavenly beds for adults and kids now, too; in-room workouts and great spa; eye-popping architecture. **Cons:** beach is eroding. *1995 E. Hallandale Beach Blvd. 954/602–6000 or 800/327–1212 www.starwoodhotels.com 900 rooms, 100 suites In-room: refrigerator, Internet, Wi-Fi. In-hotel: 5 restaurants, bars, golf course, tennis courts, pools, gym, spa AE, DC, MC, V.*

12

Miami and Miami Beach

WORD OF MOUTH

"South beach is perfect . . . plenty of shopping, beautiful beach . . . great restaurants, lots of fun."

—flep

WELCOME TO MIAMI AND MIAMI BEACH

South beach.

TOP REASONS TO GO

★ **The Beach:** Miami Beach has been rated as one of the 10 best in the world. White sand, warm water, and bronzed bodies everywhere provide just the right mix of relaxation and people-gazing.

★ **Dining Delights:** Miami's eclectic residents have transformed the city into a museum of epicurean wonders, ranging from Cuban and Argentine fare to fusion haute cuisine.

★ **Wee-Hour Parties:** A 24-hour liquor license means clubs stay open until 5 AM, and after-parties go until noon the following day.

★ **Picture-Perfect People:** Miami is a watering hole for the vain and beautiful of South America, Europe, and the Northeast. Watch them—or join them—as they strut their stuff on Lincoln Road, chow down in style at the Forge, and flaunt their tans on the white beds of the Shore Club hotel.

★ **Art Deco District:** Candy colors and neon as far as the eye can see will put a lift in your step.

1 Downtown Miami. Weave through the glass-and-steel labyrinth of new condo construction to catch a Miami Heat game at the American Airlines Arena or a ballet at the spaceship-like Adrienne Arsht Center for the Performing Arts. To the far north is Little Haiti. To the southwest is Little Havana.

2 South Beach. People-watch from sidewalk cafés along Ocean Drive, lounge poolside at posh Collins Avenue hotels, and party 'til dawn at the nation's hottest clubs.

3 Coral Gables. Dine and shop on family-friendly Miracle Mile, and take a driving tour of the Mediterranean-style mansions in the surrounding neighborhoods.

4 Coconut Grove. Catch dinner and a movie and listen to live music at CocoWalk, or cruise the bohemian shops and locals' bars in this hip neighborhood.

5 Key Biscayne. Pristine parks and tranquility make this upscale enclave a total antithesis to the South Beach party.

outh beach.

LITTLE HAITI
95
N.W. 79th St.
JFK Causeway
9
441
N.W. 62nd St.
N.W. 54th St.
944
N. Miami Ave.
N.E. 2nd Ave.
Biscayne Blvd.
1
MIAMI BEACH
Robert Frost Expwy.
N.W. 36th St.
Julia Tuttle Causeway
195
2
27
N.W. 17th Ave.
N.W. 20th St.
SOUTH BEACH
Art Center
Venetian Causeway
A1A
395
Watson Island
DOWNTOWN MIAMI
95
American Airlines Arena
MacArthur Causeway
Art Deco District
W. Flagler St.
1
41
N.W. 27th Ave.
S.W. 8th St.
S.W. 12th Ave.
41
LITTLE HAVANA
S.W. 3rd.
Fisher Island
S.W. 22nd St.
Marine Stadium
S. Dixie Hwy.
Rickenbacker Causeway
COCONUT GROVE
4
Virginia Key
Grove Isle
Coco Walk
Biscayne Bay
ATLANTIC OCEAN
5 KEY BISCAYNE
Cape Florida Lighthouse

GETTING ORIENTED

Long considered the gateway to Latin America, Miami is as close to Cuba and the Caribbean as you can get within the United States. The 36 square-mi city is located at the southern tip of the Florida peninsula, bordered on the east by Biscayne Bay. Over the bay lies a series of barrier islands, the largest being a thin 18-square-mi strip called Miami Beach. To the east of Miami Beach is the Atlantic Ocean. To the south are the Florida Keys.

Miami beach.

MIAMI AND MIAMI BEACH PLANNER

When to Go

Miami and Miami Beach are year-round destinations. Most visitors come October through April, when the weather is close to perfect; hotels, restaurants, and attractions are busiest; and each weekend holds a festival or event. "Season" kicks off in December with Art Basel Miami Beach, and hotel rates don't come down until after the college kids have left from spring break.

It's hot and steamy from May through September, but nighttime temperatures are usually pleasant. Also, summer is a good time for the budget traveler. Many hotels lower their rates considerably, and many restaurants offer discounts—especially during **Miami Spice** in August, when slews of top restaurants offer special tasting menus at a steep discount (sometimes Spice runs for two months, check *www.iLoveMiamiSpice.com* for details).

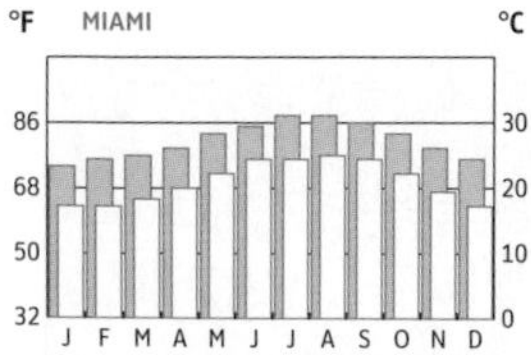

Getting Here

By Air: Miami is serviced by Miami International Airport (MIA) near downtown and Fort Lauderdale-Hollywood International Airport (FLL) 18 mi north. Many discount carriers, like Spirit Airlines, Southwest Airlines, and AirTran fly into FLL, making it a smart bargain if you are renting a car. Otherwise, look for flights to MIA on American Airlines, Delta, and Continental. MIA is undergoing extensive renovations that are expected to conclude in the summer of 2011; delays and long walks to gates are a common occurrence.

By Car: Interstate 95 is the major expressway connecting South Florida with points north; State Road 836 is the major east–west expressway and connects to Florida's Turnpike, State Road 826, and Interstate 95. Seven causeways link Miami and Miami Beach, Interstate 195 and Interstate 395 offering the most convenient routes; the Rickenbacker Causeway extends to Key Biscayne from Interstate 95 and U.S. 1. **Remember U.S. 1** (*aka* **Biscayne Boulevard**)—you'll hear it often in directions. It starts in Key West, hugs South Florida's coastline, and heads north straight through to Maine.

By Train: Amtrak provides service from 500 destinations to the Greater Miami area. The trains make several stops along the way; north–south service stops in the major Florida cities of Jacksonville, Orlando, Tampa, West Palm Beach, and Fort Lauderdale. For extended trips, or if you want to visit other areas in Florida, you can come via Auto Train (where you bring your car along) from Lorton, Virginia, just outside Washington, D.C., to Sanford, Florida, just outside Orlando. From there it's less than a four-hour drive to Miami. Fares vary, but expect to pay between $269 and $346 for a basic sleeper seat and car passage each way. **■ TIP→ You must be traveling with an automobile to purchase a ticket on the Auto Train.**

Getting Around

Greater Miami resembles Los Angeles in its urban sprawl and traffic. You'll need a car to visit many attractions and points of interest. If possible, avoid driving during the rush hours of 7–9 AM and 5–7 PM—the hour just after and right before the peak times also can be slow going. During rainy weather, be especially cautious of flooding in South Beach and Key Biscayne.

Some sights are accessible via the public transportation system, run by the **Metro-Dade Transit Agency** (☎ *305/770–3131* 🌐 *www.miamidade.gov/transit*), which maintains 650 Metrobuses on 70 routes; the 21-mi Metrorail elevated rapid-transit system; and the Metromover, an elevated light-rail system. The bus stops for the **Metrobus** are marked with blue-and-green signs with a bus logo and route information. The fare is $1.50 (exact change only). Transfers cost 50¢. Some express routes carry surcharges of $1.85. Elevated **Metrorail** trains run from downtown Miami north to Hialeah and south along U.S. 1 to Dadeland. The system operates daily 5 AM–midnight. The fare is $2; 50¢ transfers to Metrobus must be purchased at the station where you originally board the system. **Metromover** resembles an airport shuttle and runs on two loops around downtown Miami, linking major hotels, office buildings, and shopping areas. The system spans 4 mi, including the 1-mi Omni Loop and the 1-mi Brickell Loop. There is no fee to ride; transfers to Metrorail are $2.

Tri-Rail (☎ *800/874–7245* 🌐 *www.tri-rail.com*), South Florida's commuter-train system, offers shuttle service to and from MIA from 3797 NW 21st Street. Tri-Rail stops at 18 stations along a 71-mi route. Prices range from $3.50 to $9.25 for a round-trip ticket.

Cab It

Except in South Beach, it's difficult to hail a cab on the street; in most cases you'll need to call a cab company or have a hotel doorman hail one for you. Fares run $4.50 for the first mile and $2.40 every mile thereafter; flat-rate fares are also available from the airport to a variety of zones. Many cabs now accept credit cards; inquire before you get in the car.

Taxi Companies: Central Cabs (☎ *305/532–5555*). **Diamond Cab Company** (☎ *305/545–5555*). **Flamingo Taxi** (☎ *305/599–9999*). **Metro Taxi** (☎ *305/888–8888*). **Society Cab Company** (☎ *305/757–5523*). **Super Yellow Cab Company** (☎ *305/888–7777*). **Tropical Taxi** (☎ *305/945–1025*). **Yellow Cab Company** (☎ *305/633–0503*).

Visitor Information

For additional information about Miami and Miami Beach, contact the city's visitors bureaus:

Greater Miami Convention & Visitors Bureau (✉ *701 Brickell Ave., Suite 2700, Miami* ☎ *305/539–3000, 800/933–8448 in U.S.* 🌐 *www.miamiandbeaches.com*).
Miami Beach Chamber of Commerce & Visitors Center (✉ *1920 Meridian Ave., Miami Beach* ☎ *305/674–1300 or 800/666–4519* 🌐 *www.miamibeachchamber.com*).

MIAMI BEACHES

Almost every side street in Miami Beach dead-ends at the ocean. Sandy shores also stretch along the southern side of the Rickenbacker Causeway to Key Biscayne, where you'll find more popular beaches.

Beaches tend to have golden, light brown, or gray-tinted sand with coarser grains than the fine white stuff on Florida's Gulf Coast beaches. Although pure white-sand beaches are many peoples' idea of picture-perfect, darker beach sand is much easier on the eyes on a sunny day and—bonus!—your holiday photos (and the people in them) will have a subtle warm glow rather than harsh highlights.

Expect gentle waves, which can occasionally turn rough, complete with riptides, depending on what weather systems are lurking out in the ocean—always check and abide by the warnings posted on the lifeguard's station. One thing that isn't perfect here is shelling, but for casual shell collectors Bal Harbour Beach is the best bet; enter at 96th Street and Collins Avenue.

SOUTH BEACH PARKING TIPS

Several things are plentiful in South Beach. Besides the plethora of cell phones and surgically enhanced bodies, there are a lot of cars for a small area, and plenty of seriously attentive meter maids. On-street parking is scarce, tickets are given freely, and towing charges are high. Check your meter to see when you must pay to park; times vary. It's \$1 for meters north and \$1.25 for meters south of 23rd Street. There are also public parking lots that accept cash and credit cards. Or, buy a Parking Meter Card at Miami Beach Visitors Center and Publix supermarkets for \$25.

MIAMI'S BEST BEACHES

LUMMUS PARK BEACH

Want glitz and glamour? On South Beach's Ocean Drive from 6th to 14th streets, this beach is crowded with beautiful people working hard on their tans, muscle tone, and social lives. It's also the place for golden sands, blue water, and gentle waves. However, as this place is all about seeing and being seen, the less perfect among us may feel intimidated or bored.

MATHESON HAMMOCK PARK BEACH

Kids will thrill to the tender waves and warm water of the beach at 4000 Crandon Boulevard in Key Biscayne. The golden sands of this 3-mi beach are only part of the attraction: the park includes children's rides and a playground, picnic areas—even a golf course. The manmade lagoon is perfect for inexperienced swimmers, and it's the best place in Miami for a picnic. But the water can be a bit murky, and with the emphasis on families, it's not the best place for singles.

BILL BAGGS CAPE FLORIDA STATE PARK

All the way at the end of Key Biscayne, at 1200 S. Crandon Boulevard, is a wide peachy-brown beach with usually gentle waves. The picnic area is popular with local families on the weekends, but the beach itself never feels crowded. The

park also includes miles of nature trails; bike, boat, beach chair, and umbrella rentals; and casual dining at the Lighthouse Café. You can fish off the piers by the marina, too. Come here for an escape from city madness.

HOLLYWOOD BEACH

Halfway between Miami and Fort Lauderdale, Hollywood Beach is a perfect retreat. Sun yourself on the pristine golden-white sands, join a volleyball game, take a tai chi or yoga lesson, then walk along the 2-mi boardwalk and visit its small shops, cafés, and restaurants. Head north on the boardwalk and you'll find North Beach Park's sea turtle hatchery, part of the Endangered Sea Turtle Protection Program (kids love it); it's open Thursday through Monday. Meander south and you end up at the Ocean Walk Mall.

HAULOVER BEACH

Want to bare it all? Just north of Bal Harbour, at 10800 Collins Avenue in Sunny Isles, sits the only legal clothing-optional beach in the area. Haulover has more claims to fame than its casual attitude toward swimwear—it's also the best beach in the area for body-boarding and surfing as it gets what passes for impressive swells in these parts. Plus the sand here is fine-grain white, unusual for the Atlantic coast.

Updated by
Teri Evans

Think of Miami as a teenager: a young beauty with growing pains, cocky yet confused, quick to embrace the latest fads, exasperating yet lovable. This analogy may help you understand how best to tackle this imperfect paradise.

As cities go, Miami and Miami Beach really are young. Just a little more than 100 years ago, Miami was mosquito-infested swampland, with an Indian trading post on the Miami River. Then hotel builder Henry Flagler brought his railroad to the outpost known as Fort Dallas. Other visionaries—Carl Fisher, Julia Tuttle, William Brickell, and John Sewell, among others—set out to tame the unruly wilderness. Hotels were erected, bridges were built, the port was dredged, and electricity arrived. The narrow strip of mangrove coast was transformed into Miami Beach—and the tourists started to come.

Greater Miami is many destinations in one. At its best it offers an unparalleled multicultural experience: melodic Latin and Caribbean tongues, international cuisines and cultural events, and an unmistakable joie de vivre—all against a beautiful beach backdrop. In Little Havana the air is tantalizing with the perfume of strong Cuban coffee. In Coconut Grove, Caribbean steel drums ring out during the Miami/Bahamas Goombay Festival. Anytime in colorful Miami Beach restless crowds wait for entry to the hottest new clubs.

Many visitors don't know that Miami and Miami Beach are really separate cities. Miami, on the mainland, is South Florida's commercial hub. Miami Beach, on 17 islands in Biscayne Bay, is sometimes considered America's Riviera, luring refugees from winter with its warm sunshine; sandy beaches; graceful, shady palms; and tireless nightlife. The natives know well that there's more to Greater Miami than the bustle of South Beach and its Art Deco district. In addition to well-known places such as Coconut Grove and Bayside, the less reported spots—like the Museum of Contemporary Art in North Miami, the burgeoning Design District in Miami, and the mangrove swamps of Matheson Hammock Park in Coral Gables—are great insider destinations.

EXPLORING MIAMI AND MIAMI BEACH

If you had arrived here 40 years ago with a guidebook in hand, chances are you'd be thumbing through listings looking for alligator wrestlers and you-pick strawberry fields or citrus groves. Things have changed. While Disney sidetracked families in Orlando, Miami was developing a unique culture and attitude that's equal parts beach town/big business, Latino/Caribbean meets European/American—all of which fuels a great art and food scene, as well as an exuberant nightlife and myriad festivals.

To find your way around Greater Miami, learn how the numbering system works. Miami is laid out on a grid with four quadrants—northeast, northwest, southeast, and southwest—which meet at Miami Avenue and Flagler Street. Miami Avenue separates east from west and Flagler Street separates north from south. Avenues and courts run north–south; streets, terraces, and ways run east–west. Roads run diagonally, northwest–southeast. But other districts—Miami Beach, Coral Gables, and Hialeah—may or may not follow this system, and along the curve of Biscayne Bay the symmetrical grid may shift diagonally. It's best to buy a detailed map, stick to the major roads, and ask directions early and often. However, make sure you're in a safe neighborhood or public place when you seek guidance; cabdrivers and cops are good resources.

DOWNTOWN MIAMI, LITTLE HAVANA, AND LITTLE HAITI

Downtown Miami dazzles from a distance. The skyline is fluid, thanks to the sheer number of sparkling glass high-rises between Biscayne Boulevard and the Miami River. Business is the key to downtown Miami's daytime bustle. Traffic congestion from the high-rise offices and expensive parking tend to keep the locals away, unless they're bringing out-of-town guests to touristy Bayside Marketplace. But change is in the air—the influx of condos and offices is bringing in shops and restaurants, most notably Mary Brickell Village, which serves as a culinary oasis for the starved business district. Thanks to the free Metromover, which runs inner and outer loops through downtown and to nearby neighborhoods to the south and north, this is an excellent tour to take by rail. Attractions are conveniently located within about two blocks of the nearest station. If you're coming from north or east of downtown, leave your car near a Metromover stop and take the Omni Loop downtown. If you're coming from south or west, park your car at a Metrorail station and take a leg of the 21-mi elevated commuter system downtown.

Little Havana is southwest of downtown Miami. See our "Caribbean Infusion" spotlight for a map of this neighborhood as well as one of Little Haiti in north Miami.

EXPLORING

Numbers correspond to the Downtown Miami map.

DOWNTOWN MIAMI

1 **Adrienne Arsht Center for the Performing Arts.** Lovers of culture and other artsy types are drawn to this stunning home of the Florida Grand Opera, Miami City Ballet, New World Symphony, Concert Association

of Florida, and other local and touring groups, which have included Broadway hits like *Wicked* and *Mamma Mia!* Think of it as a sliver of savoir faire to temper Miami's often-over-the-top vibe. Designed by architect César Pelli, the massive development contains a 2,400-seat opera house, 2,200-seat concert hall, a black-box theater, and an outdoor Plaza for the Arts. ✉ *1300 Biscayne Blvd., at NE 13th St., Downtown* ☎ *305/949–6722* 🌐 *www.arshtcenter.org.*

2 **Freedom Tower**. In the 1960s this ornate Spanish-baroque structure was the Cuban Refugee Center, processing more than 500,000 Cubans who entered the United States after fleeing Fidel Castro's regime. Built in 1925 for the *Miami Daily News,* it was inspired by the Giralda, an 800-year-old bell tower in Seville, Spain. Preservationists were pleased to see the tower's exterior restored in 1988. Today, it is owned by Miami-Dade College, and continues to maintain the tower as a cultural and educational center, which includes a museum depicting Cuban history, the experiences of refugees, and the achievements of Cuban-Americans. ✉ *600 Biscayne Blvd., at NE 6th St., Downtown* ☎ *No phone* ⏲ *Tues.–Sun. noon–7.*

3 ★ **Miami-Dade Cultural Center**. Containing three cultural resources, this fortress-like 3-acre complex is a downtown focal point. **The Miami Art Museum** (☎ *305/375–3000* 🌐 *www.miamiartmuseum.org* 🎟 *$8 [free for families every second Sat.]* ⏲ *Tues.–Fri. 10–5 [until 9 the third Thurs. of month], weekends noon–5*) is waiting to move into its new 120,000-square-foot home in Museum Park, which is to be completed in 2012. Meanwhile, the museum presents major touring exhibitions of work by international artists, with an emphasis on art since 1945. Every second Saturday entrance is free for families. Discover a treasure trove of colorful stories about the region's history at **HistoryMiami** (☎ *305/375–1492* 🌐 *www.hmsf.org* 🎟 *$8 museum, $10 combo ticket art and history museums* ⏲ *Tues.–Fri. 10–5, weekends noon–5*), formerly known as the Historical Museum of Southern Florida. Exhibits celebrate Miami's multicultural heritage, including an old Miami streetcar, and unique items chronicling the migration of Cubans to Miami. The **Main Public Library** (☎ *305/375–2665* 🌐 *www.mdpls.org* ⏲ *Aug.–May, Mon.–Wed., Fri., and Sat. 9–6, Thurs. 9–9, Sun. 1–5*) contains nearly 4 million holdings and a Florida Department that includes rare books, documents, and photographs recording Miami history. It also has art exhibits in the auditorium and in the 2nd-floor lobby. ✉ *101 W. Flagler St., between NW 1st and 2nd Aves., Downtown.*

4 ★ **Wynwood Art District**. Just north of downtown Miami, the up-and-coming Wynwood Art District is peppered with galleries, art studios, and private collections accessible to the public. Visit during Wynwood's monthly gallery walk on the second Saturday evening of each month when studios and galleries are all open at the same time. Make sure a visit includes a stop at the **Margulies Collection at the Warehouse** (✉ *591 NW 27th St., between NW 5th and 6th Aves., Downtown* ☎ *305/576–1051* 🌐 *www.margulieswarehouse.com*). Martin Margulies's collection of vintage and contemporary photography, videos, and installation art in a 45,000-square-foot space makes for eye-popping viewing. Entrance fee is a $10 donation, which goes to a local homeless

Continued on page 537

Downtown Miami
TO AIRPORT
TO LITTLE HAITI
TO SOUTH BEACH/ MIAMI BEACH
TO PORT OF MIAMI
395
95
41
MacArthur Causeway
Dolphin Expressway
South American Way
SCHOOL BOARD
OMNI
BICENTENNIAL PARK
ELEVENTH STREET
OMNI EXTENSION
PARK WEST
FREEDOM TOWER
COLLEGE NORTH
COLLEGE BAYSIDE
FIRST STREET
BAYFRONT PARK
KNIGHT CENTER
THIRD STREET
MIAMI AVE.
GOVERNMENT CENTER
OVERTOWN/ ARENA
STATE PLAZA/ ARENA
METROMOVER
CULMER
BRICKELL EXTENSION
FIFTH STREET
EIGHTH STREET
METRORAIL
Bicentennial Park
AmericanAirlines Arena
Bayside Marketplace
Bayfront Park
Gusman Center for the Performing Arts
Mary Brickell Village
Brickell Park
Brickell Key
Miami River
Biscayne Blvd.
Biscayne Blvd. Way
N. Miami Ave.
S. Miami Ave.
N. E. 2nd Ave.
N. E. 1st Ave.
N. W. 1st Ave.
N. W. 2nd Ave.
N. W. 3rd Ave.
N. W. 4th Ave.
N. W. 5th Ave.
S. W. 2nd Ave.
S. W. 3rd Ave.
S. W. 4th Ave.
S. W. 5th Ave.
N. E. 15th St.
N. E. 14th St.
N. W. 14th St.
N. W. 13th St.
N. E. 13th St.
N. W. 12th St.
N. W. 11th St.
N. E. 11th St.
N. W. 10th St.
N. E. 10th St.
N. W. 9th St.
N. E. 9th St.
N. W. 8th St.
N. E. 8th St.
N. W. 7th St.
N. E. 7th St.
N. W. 6th St.
N. E. 6th St.
N. W. 5th St.
N. W. 4th St.
N. E. 4th St.
N. E. 3rd St.
N. E. 2nd St.
N. W. 1st St.
N. E. 1st St.
W. Flagler St.
E. Flagler St.
S. W. 1st St.
S. E. 1st St.
S. W. 2nd St.
S. E. 2nd St.
S. W. 3rd St.
S. W. 4th St.
S. E. 4th St.
S. W. 5th St.
S. E. 5th St.
S. W. 6th St.
S. E. 6th St.
S. W. 7th St.
S. E. 7th St.
S. W. 8th St.
S. E. 8th St.
0 1/4 mile
0 1/4 km
KEY
Metro stops
Metromover

CARIBBEAN INFUSION

by Michelle Delio

Miami has sun, sand, and sea, but unlike some of Florida's other prime beach destinations, it also has a wave of cultural traditions that spice up the city.

It's with good reason that people in Miami fondly say that the city is an easy way for Americans to visit another country without ever leaving the United States. According to the U.S. Census Bureau, more than half of Miami's population is foreign born and more than 70% speak a language other than English at home (in comparison, only 36.7% of New York City residents were born in another country). The city's Latin/Caribbean immigrants and exiles make up the largest segments of the population.

Locals merrily merge cultural traditions, speaking "Spanglish" (a mix of Spanish and English), sipping Cuban coffee with Sicilian pastries, eating Nuevo Latino fusion food, and dancing to the beat of other countries' music. That said, people here are just as interested in keeping to their own distinct ways—think of the city as a colorful mosaic composed of separate elements rather than a melting pot.

Miami's diverse population creates a city that feels alive in a way that few other American cities do. Nothing is set in stone here, for better or worse, and there's always a new flavor to explore, a new holiday to celebrate, a new accent to puzzle over.

No visit to Miami would be complete without a stop at one of the two neighborhoods famed for their celebrations of cultural traditions— Little Haiti and Little Havana—places that have a wonderful foreign feel even amid cosmopolitan Miami.

Playing dominoes is a favorite pastime at Maximo Gomez Park in Little Havana (left).

LA PETITE HAÏTI—LITTLE HAITI

Little Haiti is a study in contrasts. At first glance you see the small buildings painted in bright oranges, pinks, reds, yellows, and turquoises, with signs, some handwritten, touting immigration services, lunch specials with *tassot* (fried cubed goat), and voodoo supplies.

But as you adjust to this dazzle of color, you become aware of the curious juxtapositions of poverty and wealth in this evolving neighborhood. Streets dip with potholes in front of trendy art galleries, and dilapidated houses struggle to survive near newly renovated soccer fields and arts centers.

Miami's Little Haiti is the largest Haitian community outside of Haiti itself, and while people of different ethnic backgrounds have begun to move to the neighborhood, people here tend to expect to primarily see other Haitians on these streets. Obvious outsiders may be greeted with a few frozen stares on the streets, but owners of shops and restaurants tend to be welcoming. Creole is commonly spoken, although some people—especially younger folks—also speak English.

WHEN TO GO

The neighborhood is best visited during the daytime, combined with a visit to the nearby Miami Design District, an 18-block section of art galleries, interior design showrooms, and restaurants between N.E. 41st Street and N.E. 36th Street, Miami Avenue, and Biscayne Boulevard.

CREOLE EXPRESSIONS

Creole, one of Haiti's two languages (the other is French), is infused with French, African, Arabic, Spanish, and Portuguese words.

Komon ou ye? How are you? *(also spelled Kouman)
N'ap boule! Great!
Kisa ou ta vla? What would you like?
Mesi. Thanks.
Souple. Please.

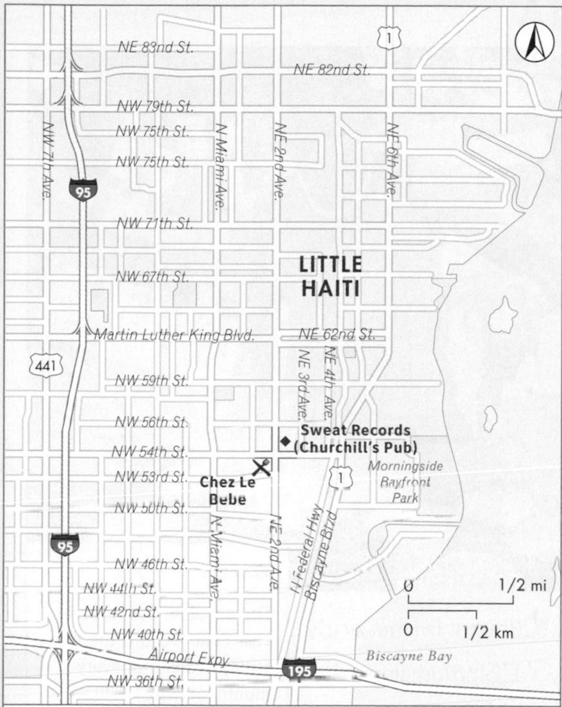

MANGÉ KRÉYOL (HAITIAN FOOD)

Traditional Caribbean cuisines tend to combine European and African culinary techniques. Haitian can be a bit spicier—though never mouth-scorching hot—than many other island cuisines. Rice and beans are the staple food, enlivened with a little of whatever people might have: fish, goat, chicken, pork, usually stewed or deep-fried, along with peppers, plantains, and tomatoes.

Chez Le Bebe (✉ *114 N.E. 54th St.* ☎ *305/751–7639* 🌐 *www.chezlebebe.com*) offers Haitian home cooking—if you want to try stewed goat, this is the place to do it. Chicken, fish, oxtail, and fried pork are also on the menu; each plate comes with rice, beans, plantains, and salad for less than $12.

Tap Tap restaurant (✉ *819 Fifth St.* ☎ *305/672–2898*) is outside of Little Haiti, but this Miami institution will immerse you in the island's culture with an extensive collection of Haitian folk art displayed everywhere in the restaurant. On the menu is pumpkin soup, *spageti kreyol* (pasta, shrimp, and a Creole tomato sauce), goat stewed in Creole sauce (a mildly spicy tomato-based sauce), conch, and "grilled goat dinner." You can eat well here for $15 or less.

GETTING ORIENTED

Little Haiti, once a small farming community outside of Miami proper, is slowly becoming one of the city's most vibrant neighborhoods. Its northern and southern boundaries are 85th Street and 36th Street, respectively, with Interstate–95 to the west and Biscayne Boulevard to the east. The best section to visit is along North Miami Avenue from 54th to 59th streets. Driving is the best way to get here; parking is easy to find on North Miami Avenue. Public transit (☎ *305/891–3131*) is limited.

SHOPPING

The cluster of botanicas at N.E. 54th Street and N.E. 2nd Avenue offer items intended to sway the fates, from candles to plastic and plaster statues of Catholic saints that, in the voodoo tradition, represent African deities. While exploring, don't miss **Sweat Records** (✉ *5505 N.E. 2nd Ave.* ☎ *305/342–0953* 🌐 *www.sweatrecordsmiami.com*). Sweat sells a wide range of music—rock, pop, punk, electronic, hip-hop, and Latino. Check out the vegan-friendly organic coffee bar at the store, which is open from noon to 10 PM every day but Sunday.

LITTLE HAVANA

First settled en masse by Cubans in the early 1960s, after that country's Communist revolution, Little Havana is a predominantly working-class area and the core of Miami's Hispanic community. Spanish is the main language, but don't be surprised if the cadence is less Cuban than Salvadoran or Nicaraguan: the neighborhood is now home to people from all Latin American countries.

If you come to Little Havana expecting the Latino version of New Orleans's French Quarter, you're apt to be disappointed—it's not yet that picturesque. But if great, inexpensive food (not just Cuban; there's Vietnamese, Mexican, and Argentinean here as well), distinctive, affordable art, cigars, and coffee interest you, you'll enjoy your time in Little Havana. It's not a prefab tourist destination, so don't expect Disneyland with a little Latino flair—this is real life in Miami.

WHEN TO GO

The absolute best time to visit Calle Ocho is the last Friday evening of every month, between 6:30 and 11 PM on 8th Street from 14th to 17th avenues. Known as **Viernes Culturales** (🌐 *www.viernesculturales.com*), it's a big block party that everyone is welcome to attend. Art galleries, restaurants, and stores stay open late, and music, mojitos, and avant-garde street performances bring a young, hip crowd to the neighborhood where they mingle with locals.

If you come in mid-March, your visit may coincide with the annual **Calle Ocho festival** (🌐 *www.carnavalmiami.com*), which draws more than a million visitors in search of Latin music, food, and shopping.

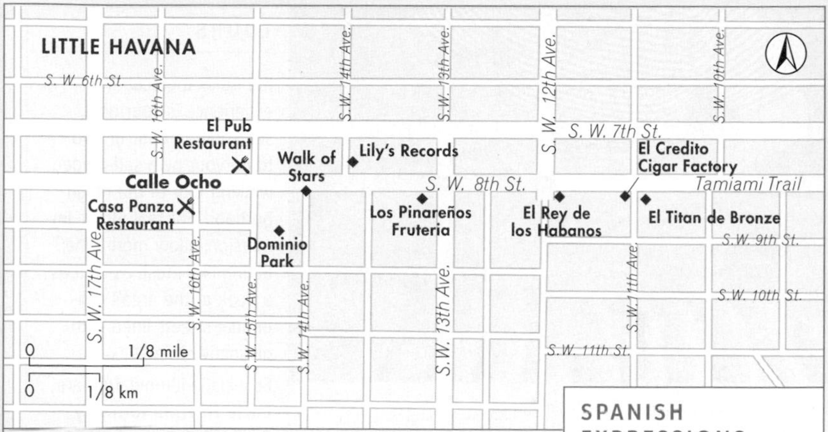

SPANISH EXPRESSIONS

Qué deseaba? Can I help you?

Algo más? Anything else?

Muchas gracias! Thank you very much!

No hay de qué. / De nada. You're welcome.

No entiendo. I don't understand.

Oye! All-purpose word used to get attention or express interest, admiration, and appreciation.

GETTING ORIENTED

Little Havana's semi-official boundaries are 27th Avenue to 4th Avenue on the west, Miami River to the north, and S.W. 11th Street to the south. Much of the neighborhood is residential, but its heart and tourist hub is Calle Ocho (8th Street), between 14th and 18th avenues.

The best way to get here is by car. Park on the side streets off **Calle Ocho** (some spots have meters; most don't). Other options include the free **Metromover** (☎ *305/891–3131*) and a cab ride. From Miami Beach the 15-minute ride should cost just under $30 each way.

THE SIGHTS

Stroll down Calle Oche from 12th to 17th avenues and look around you: cafés are selling guava pastries and rose petal flan, a botanica brims with candles and herbs to heal whatever ails you. Over there at a tropical fruit stand someone is hacking off the top of a coconut with a machete, while nearby, thimble-size cups of liquid energy (aka *café cubano*) are passed through the open windows of coffee shops. Small galleries showcasing modern art jostle up next to mom-and-pop food shops and high-end Cuban clothes and crafts. At Dominio Park (officially Maximo Gomez Park), guayabera-clad seniors bask in the sun and play dominoes, while at corner bodegas and coffee shops (particularly Versailles) regulars share neighborhood gossip and political opinions. A few steps away is the "Paseo de las Estrellas" (Walk of Stars). The Latin version of its Hollywood namesake, the strip of sidewalk embedded with stars honors many of the world's top Hispanic celebrities, among them the late salsa queen Celia Cruz, crooner Julio Iglesias, and superstar Gloria Estefan.

Calle Ocho Carnaval

Rolling cigars by hand in a Little Havana factory.

THE SOUNDS

Salsa and merengue pour out of storefronts and restaurants, while other businesses cater to the snap and shuffles of flamenco performances and Sevillaña *tablaos* (dances performed on a wood-plank stage, using castanets). If you want to join in the merriment along Calle Ocho, dance with locals on the patio of **El Pub Restaurant** (near 15th Avenue), or snack on tapas at **Casa Panza Restaurant** (near 16th), where the background music is the restaurant owner's enthusiastic singing. Any time of day, you can hear the constant backbeat of people speaking Spanish and the occasional crowing of a stray, time-confused rooster. To take these sounds home with you, wander over to **Lily's Records** (✉ *1419 S.W. 8th St, near 14th* ☎ *305/856–0536*), for its huge selection of Latin music.

THE SCENTS

Bottled, the essence of Little Havana would be tobacco, café cubano, and a whiff of tropical fruit. To indulge your senses in two of these things, head to **Los Pinareños Fruteria** on Calle Ocho just west of 13th Avenue. Here you can sip a sweet, hot *cortadito* (coffee with milk), a *cafecito* (no milk), or a cool *coco frio* (coconut water). For more subsistence, dig into a Cuban-style tamale. There are stools out front of the shop, or take your drink to go and wander over to S.W. 13th Avenue, which has monuments to Cuban heroes, and sit under the ceiba trees. For cigars, head to Calle Ocho near 11th Avenue and visit any of these three stores: **El Credito Cigar Factory**, **El Rey de los Habanos**, and **El Titan de Bronze**. At these family-owned businesses employees deftly hand-roll millions of stogies a year.

TOURS

If a quick multicultural experience is your goal, set aside an hour or two to do your own self-guided walking tour of the neighborhood. For real ethnic immersion, allow more time; eating is a must, as well as a peek at the area's residential streets lined with distinctive homes.

Especially illuminating are **Little Havana tours by Dr. Paul George** (✉ *101 W. Flagler St.* ☎ *305/375–1621* ✉ *historictours@hmsf.org*). A history professor at Miami Dade College and historian for the Historical Museum of Southern Florida, George covers architecture and community history on his tours. These take place only a few times a year. Private three-hour tours are available for groups of up to 20 people for $400 ($20 per person above 20 people).

For customized offerings, try **Miami Cultural Tours** (✉ *305/416-6868* 🌐 *www.miamiculturaltours.com*), interactive tours that introduce people to Little Havana and Little Haiti. Group and private tours are available, with prices ranging from $39 to $79 a person.

GREAT ITINERARIES

3 DAYS

Grab your lotion and head to the ocean, more specifically **Ocean Drive** on **South Beach**, and catch some rays while relaxing on the warm sands. Afterward, take a guided or self-guided tour of the **Art Deco district** to see what all the fuss is about, drop in at the News Café for breakfast anytime (or a snack), great coffee, and an outstanding selection of international magazines. Keep the evening free to socialize at Ocean Drive cafés or have a special dinner at one of the many Latin-European fusion restaurants. The following day drive through **Little Havana** to witness the heartbeat of Miami's Cuban culture (stop for a high-octane Cuban coffee at Versaille's outside-counter window) on your way south to Coconut Grove's Vizcaya. Wrap up the evening a few blocks away in downtown **Coconut Grove**, enjoying its laid-back party mood and many nightspots. On the last day head over to **Coral Gables** to take in the eye-popping display of 1920s Mediterranean-revival architecture in the neighborhoods surrounding the city center and the majestic **Biltmore Hotel**; then take a dip in the fantastic thematic **Venetian Pool.** Early evening, stroll and shop Coral Gable's Miracle Mile—contrary to its name it's just a half mile, but every bit is packed with upscale shops, art galleries, and interesting restaurants.

5 DAYS

Follow the suggested three-day itinerary, and on Day 4 visit the beaches of **Virginia Key** and **Key Biscayne.** Take a diving trip or fishing excursion, learn to windsurf, or just watch the water. On Day 5, tour the 18-block design district and browse its 130-plus art galleries, home-decor shops, and interesting restaurants, or explore the Fairchild Tropical Botanic Garden. Then return to **South Beach** for an evening of shopping, drinking, and outdoor dining at **Lincoln Road Mall.**

shelter for women and children. It's open October to April, Wednesday to Saturday 11–4. Fans of edgy art will appreciate the **Rubell Family Collection** (✉ *95 NW 29th St., between N. Miami Ave. and NW 1st Ave., Downtown* ☎ *305/573–6090* 🌐 *www.rfc.museum).* Mera and Don Rubell have accumulated work by artists from the 1970s to the present, including Jeff Koons, Cindy Sherman, Damien Hirst, and Keith Haring. Admission is $10, and the gallery is open Wednesday to Saturday 10–6.

LITTLE HAVANA

❺ **Cuban Memorial Boulevard.** Two blocks in the heart of Little Havana are filled with monuments to Cuba's freedom fighters. Among the memorials are the *Eternal Torch of the Brigade 2506,* commemorating those who were killed in the failed Bay of Pigs invasion of 1961; a bust of 19th-century hero Antonio Maceo; and a bas-relief map of Cuba depicting each of its *municipios.* There's also a bronze statue in honor of Tony Izquierdo, who participated in the Bay of Pigs invasion, served in Nicaragua's Somozan forces, and was also on the CIA payroll. ✉ *SW 13th Ave., south of SW 8th St., Little Havana.*

6 **El Credito Cigar Factory**. A peek at the intently focused cigar rollers through the giant windows doesn't prepare you for the rich, pungent scent that jolts your senses as you step inside the store. Many of the workers at this once family-owned business date back three generations, as they learned their trade in prerevolutionary Cuba. Today the tobacco leaf they use comes from Cuban seeds grown in the Dominican Republic, Ecuador, and Nicaragua. A walk-in humidor has many brands of full-bodied cigars with varying blends of tobacco favored by customers such as Arnold Schwarzenegger, Bill Clinton, Robert De Niro, and Bill Cosby. Informational tours are available weekdays. ⊠ *1106 SW 8th St., near SW 11th Ave., Little Havana* ☎ *305/858–4162* 🌐 *www.elcreditocigars.com* ⊙ *Weekdays 8–5, Sat. 9–4. Factory closed Sat. but store is open.*

MIAMI BEACH

The hub of Miami Beach is South Beach (SoBe, but you'll never hear locals calling it that), with its energetic Ocean Drive. Here, life unfolds 24 hours a day. Beautiful people pose in hotel lounges and sidewalk cafés, tanned cyclists zoom past palm trees, and visitors flock to see the action. On Lincoln Road, café crowds spill onto the sidewalks, weekend markets draw all kinds of visitors and their dogs, and thanks to a few late-night lounges the scene is just as alive at night.

Quieter areas to the north on Collins Avenue are Surfside (from 88th to 96th streets), fashionable Bal Harbour (beginning at 96th Street), and Sunny Isles (between 157th and 197th streets). If you're interested in these areas and you're flying in, the Fort Lauderdale airport might be a better choice.

EXPLORING

Numbers correspond to the Miami Beach and South Beach map.

SOUTH BEACH

TOP ATTRACTIONS

5 ★ **Española Way**. There's a bohemian feel to this street lined with Mediterranean-revival buildings constructed in 1925. Al Capone's gambling syndicate ran its operations upstairs at what is now the Clay Hotel, a youth hostel. At a nightclub here in the 1930s, future bandleader Desi Arnaz strapped on a conga drum and started beating out a rumba rhythm. Visit this quaint avenue on a weekend afternoon, when merchants and craftspeople set up shop to sell everything from handcrafted bongo drums to fresh flowers. Between Washington and Drexel avenues the road has been narrowed to a single lane and Miami Beach's trademark pink sidewalks have been widened to accommodate sidewalk cafés and shops selling imaginative clothing, jewelry, and art. ⊠ *Española Way, between 14th and 15th Sts. from Washington to Jefferson Aves.*

7 ★ **Holocaust Memorial**. A bronze sculpture depicts refugees clinging to a giant bronze arm that reaches out of the ground and 42 feet into the air. Enter the surrounding courtyard to see a memorial wall and hear the music that seems to give voice to the 6 million Jews who died at the hands of the Nazis. It's easy to understand why Kenneth Treister's dramatic memorial is in Miami Beach: the city's community of Holocaust survivors was once the second-largest in the country. ⊠ *1933–1945*

- Art Deco District Welcome Center 2
- Bass Museum of Art 8
- Española Way 5
- Holocaust Memorial 7
- Lincoln Road Mall 6
- Miami Children's Museum 9
- Jungle Island .. 10
- Sanford L. Ziff Jewish Museum of Florida 1
- Wolfsonian–Florida International University 3
- World Erotic Art Museum 4

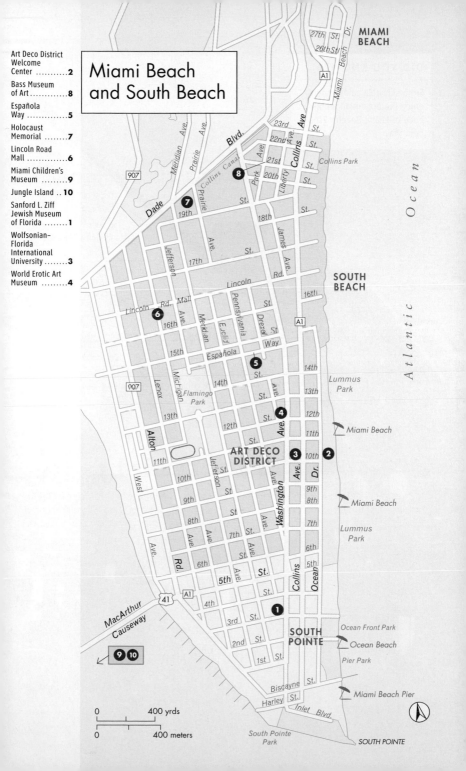

DID YOU KNOW?

From sidewalk cafés, diners enjoy the bohemian ambience of Miami Beach's Española Way.

Meridian Ave., at Dade Blvd. ☎ *305/538–1663* 🌐 *www.holocaustmmb.org* 💵 *Free (donations welcome)* ⏲ *Daily 9–9.*

6 **Lincoln Road Mall.** A playful 1990s redesign spruced up this open-air pedestrian mall, adding a grove of 20 towering date palms, five linear pools, and colorful broken-tile mosaics to the once-futuristic 1950s vision of Fontainebleau designer Morris Lapidus. Some of the shops are owner-operated boutiques with a delightful variety of clothing, furnishings, jewelry, and decorative design. Others are the typical chain stores of American malls. Remnants of tired old Lincoln Road—beauty supply and discount electronics stores on the Collins end of the strip—somehow fit nicely into the mix. The new Lincoln Road is fun, lively, and friendly for people old, young, gay, and straight—and their dogs. Folks skate, scoot, bike, or jog here. The best times to hit the road are during Sunday morning farmers' markets and on weekend evenings, when cafés bustle, art galleries open shows, street performers make the sidewalk their stage, and stores stay open late.

Fodor's Choice ★

12

Two of the landmarks worth checking out at the eastern end of Lincoln Road are the massive 1940s keystone building at 420 Lincoln Road, which has a 1945 Leo Birchanky mural in the lobby, and the 1921 mission-style Miami Beach Community Church, at Drexel Avenue. The Lincoln Theatre (No. 541–545), at Pennsylvania Avenue, is a classical four-story art deco gem with friezes. The New World Symphony, a national advanced-training orchestra led by Michael Tilson Thomas, rehearses and performs here, and concerts are often broadcast via loudspeakers, to the delight of visitors. Just west, facing Pennsylvania, a fabulous Cadillac dealership sign was discovered underneath the facade of the Lincoln Road Millennium Building, on the south side of the mall. At Euclid Avenue there's a monument to Lapidus, who in his 90s watched the renaissance of his whimsical creation. At Lenox Avenue, a black-and-white art deco movie house with a Mediterranean barrel-tile roof is now the Colony Theater (No. 1040), where live theater and experimental films are presented. ✉ *Lincoln Rd., between Collins Ave. and Alton Rd.*

QUICK BITES

Lincoln Road is a great place to cool down with an icy treat while touring South Beach. Try homemade ice cream and sorbets—including Indian mango, key lime, and litchi—from the Frieze Ice Cream Factory (✉ *1626 Michigan Ave., south of Lincoln Rd.* ☎ *305/538–2028*). Or try an authentic Italian gelato (or the Spanish-inspired delicious *dulce de leche* gelato) at the sleek glass-and-stainless-steel Gelateria Parmalat (✉ *670 Lincoln Rd., between Euclid and Pennsylvania Aves.* ☎ *786/276–9475*). If you visit on a Sunday, stop at one of the many juice vendors, who will whip up made-to-order smoothies from mangoes, oranges, and other fresh local fruits.

WORTH NOTING

2 **Art Deco District Welcome Center.** Run by the Miami Design Preservation League, the center provides information about the buildings in the district. A gift shop sells 1930s–50s art deco memorabilia, posters, and books on Miami's history. Several tours—covering Lincoln Road,

Española Way, North Beach, and the entire Art Deco district, among others—start here. You can rent audiotapes for a self-guided tour, join one of the regular morning (Friday through Wednesday) or Thursday-evening walking tours. All of the options provide detailed histories of the art deco hotels. Don't miss the special boat tours during Art Deco Weekend, in early January. ✉ *1001 Ocean Dr., at Barbara Capitman Way (10th St.)* ☎ *305/531–3484* 🎫 *Tours $20* ⏲ *Sun.–Thurs. 10–7, Fri. and Sat. 10–6.*

■ **TIP→ For a map of the Art Deco district and info on some of the sites there, see our "A Stroll Down Deco Lane" in-focus feature.**

❽ **Bass Museum of Art.** The Bass, in historic Collins Park, is part of the Miami Beach Cultural Park, which includes the Miami City Ballet's Arquitectonica-designed facility and the Miami Beach Regional Library. The original building, constructed of keystone, has unique Maya-inspired carvings. The expansion designed by Japanese architect Arata Isozaki houses another wing and an outdoor sculpture garden. Special exhibitions join a diverse collection of European art. Works on permanent display include *The Holy Family,* a painting by Peter Paul Rubens; *The Tournament,* one of several 16th-century Flemish tapestries; and works by Albrecht Dürer and Henri de Toulouse-Lautrec. Special exhibits often cost a little extra. ✉ *2121 Park Ave., at 21st St.* ☎ *305/673–7530* 🌐 *www.bassmuseum.org* 🎫 *$8* ⏲ *Wed.–Sun. noon–5.*

❶ **Sanford L. Ziff Jewish Museum of Florida.** Listed on the National Register of Historic Places, this former synagogue, built in 1936, contains art deco chandeliers, 80 impressive stained-glass windows, and a permanent exhibit, MOSAIC: Jewish Life in Florida, which depicts more than 235 years of the Florida Jewish experience. The museum, which includes a store filled with books, jewelry, and other souvenirs, also hosts traveling exhibits and special events. ✉ *301 Washington Ave., at 3rd St.* ☎ *305/672–5044* 🌐 *www.jewishmuseum.com* 🎫 *$6, free on Sat.* ⏲ *Tues.–Sun. 10–5. Museum store closed Sat.*

❸ ★ **Wolfsonian–Florida International University.** An elegantly renovated 1926 storage facility is now a research center and museum showcasing a 120,000-item collection of modern design and "propaganda arts" amassed by Miami native Mitchell ("Micky") Wolfson Jr., a world traveler and connoisseur. Broad themes of the 19th and 20th centuries—nationalism, political persuasion, industrialization—are addressed in permanent and traveling shows. Included in the museum's eclectic holdings, which represent art deco, art moderne, art nouveau, Arts and Crafts, and other aesthetic movements, are 8,000 matchbooks collected by Egypt's King Farouk. ✉ *1001 Washington Ave., at 10th St.* ☎ *305/531–1001* 🌐 *www.wolfsonian.org* 🎫 *$7, free after 6* PM *Fri.* ⏲ *Mon., Tues., and weekends noon–6, Thurs. and Fri. noon–9.*

❹ **World Erotic Art Museum (WEAM).** The sexy collection of more than 4,000 erotic items, all owned by millionaire Naomi Wilzig, unfolds with unique art of varying quality—fertility statues from around the globe and historic Chinese shunga books (erotic art offered as gifts to new brides on the wedding night) share the space with some kitschy knickknacks. If this is your thing, an original phallic prop from Stanley Kubrick's

A Clockwork Orange and an over-the-top Kama Sutra bed is worth the price of admission, but the real standout is "Miss Naomi," who is usually on hand to answer questions and provide behind-the-scenes anecdotes. Kids 17 and under are not admitted. ✉ *1205 Washington Ave., at 12th St.* ☎ *305/532–9336* 🌐 *www.weam.com* 🎟 *$15* ⏲ *Daily 11* AM*–midnight.*

WORD OF MOUTH

"The best people-watching spots are News Cafe on Ocean Drive and Van Dyke Cafe or Segafredo on Lincoln Road. Go in the evening when its cooler and the beautiful people are out."

— SoBchBud1

12

WATSON ISLAND

10 **Jungle Island.** South Florida's original tourist attraction, the park is home to just about every unusual and endangered species you would want to see, including a rare albino alligator, a liger (lion and tiger mix), a 28-foot-long "crocosaur," and a myriad of exotic birds. The most intriguing offerings are the interactive animal tours, including the Lemur Experience ($45 for 45 minutes), in which the highly social primates make themselves at home on your lap or shoulders, and the Penguin Encounter ($30 for 30 minutes), where you can pet and feed warm-weather South African penguins. ✉ *1111 Parrot Jungle Trail, off MacArthur Causeway (I–395)* ☎ *305/400–7000* 🌐 *www.jungleisland.com* 🎟 *$29.95, $23.95 for kids, plus $7 parking* ⏲ *Daily 10–6.*

9 **Miami Children's Museum.** This Arquitectonica-designed museum, both imaginative and geometric in appearance, is directly across the MacArthur Causeway from Jungle Island. Twelve galleries house hundreds of interactive, bilingual exhibits. Children can scan plastic groceries in the supermarket, scramble through a giant sand castle, climb a rock wall, learn about the Everglades, and combine rhythms in the world-music studio. ✉ *980 MacArthur Causeway* ☎ *305/373–5437* 🌐 *www.miamichildrensmuseum.org* 🎟 *$12, parking $1 per hr* ⏲ *Daily 10–6.*

CORAL GABLES

You can easily spot Coral Gables from the window of a Miami-bound jetliner—just look for the massive orange tower of the Biltmore Hotel rising from a lush green carpet of trees concealing the city's gracious homes. The canopy is as much a part of this planned city as its distinctive architecture, all attributed to the vision of George E. Merrick nearly 100 years ago.

The story of this city began in 1911, when Merrick inherited 1,600 acres of citrus and avocado groves from his father. Through judicious investment he nearly doubled the tract to 3,000 acres by 1921. Merrick dreamed of building an American Venice here, complete with canals and homes. Working from this vision, he began designing a city based on centuries-old prototypes from Mediterranean countries. Unfortunately for Merrick, the devastating no-name hurricane of 1926, followed by the Great Depression, prevented him from fulfilling many of his plans. He died at 54, an employee of the post office. Today Coral Gables has a population of about 43,000. In its bustling downtown, more than 150 multinational companies maintain headquarters or regional offices, and the University of Miami campus in the southern part of the Gables brings a youthful vibrancy to the area. A southern branch of the city extends down the shore of Biscayne Bay through neighborhoods threaded with canals. The gorgeous Fairchild Tropical Botanic Garden and beachfront Matheson Hammock Park dominate this part of the Gables.

ESSENTIALS

Visitor Information Coral Gables Chamber of Commerce (✉ *224 Catalonia Ave., Coral Gables* ☎ *305/446–1657* 🌐 *www.gableschamber.org*).

EXPLORING

Numbers correspond to the Coral Gables, Coconut Grove, and Key Biscayne map.

TOP ATTRACTIONS

❶ ★ **Biltmore Hotel.** Bouncing back stunningly from its dark days as an Army hospital, this hotel has become the jewel of Coral Gables—a dazzling architectural gem with a colorful past. First opened in 1926, it was a hot spot for the rich and glamorous of the Jazz Age until it was converted to an Army–Air Force regional hospital in 1942. Until 1968, the Veterans Administration continued to operate the hospital after World War II. The Biltmore then lay vacant for nearly 20 years before it underwent extensive renovations and reopened as a luxury hotel in 1987. Its 16-story tower, like the Freedom Tower in downtown Miami, is a replica of Seville's Giralda Tower. The magnificent pool, reportedly the largest hotel pool in the continental United States, is steeped in history—Johnny Weissmuller of Tarzan fame was a lifeguard here, and in the 1930s grand aquatic galas featuring alligator wrestling, synchronized swimming, and bathing beauties drew thousands. More recently it was President Clinton's preferred place to stay and golf. To the west is the Biltmore Country Club, a richly ornamented beaux arts–style structure with a superb colonnade and courtyard; it was reincorporated into the hotel in 1989. Sunday champagne brunch is a local legend; try to get a table in the courtyard. Afterward join one of the free tours offered at 1:30, 2:30, and 3:30. ✉ *1200 Anastasia Ave., near De Soto Blvd., Coral Gables* ☎ *305/445–1926* 🌐 *www.biltmorehotel.com.*

❻ Fodor's Choice ★ **Fairchild Tropical Botanic Garden.** With 83 acres of lakes, sunken gardens, a 560-foot vine pergola, orchids, bellflowers, coral trees, bougainvillea, rare palms, and flowering trees, Fairchild is the largest tropical botanical garden in the continental United States. The tram tour highlights the best of South Florida's flora; then you can set off exploring on your own. A 2-acre rain-forest exhibit showcases tropical plants from around the world complete with a waterfall and stream. The conservatory, Windows to the Tropics, is home to rare tropical plants, including the Titan Arum (*Amorphophallus titanum*), a fast-growing variety that attracted thousands of visitors when it bloomed in 1998. (It was only the sixth documented bloom in this country in the 20th century.) The Keys Coastal Habitat, created in a marsh and mangrove area in 1995 with assistance from the Tropical Audubon Society, provides food and shelter to resident and migratory birds. Check out the Montgomery

Botanical Center, a research facility devoted to palms and cycads. Spicing up Fairchild's calendar are plant sales, afternoon teas, and genuinely special events year-round, such as the International Mango Festival the second weekend in July. The excellent bookstore–gift shop carries books on gardening and horticulture, and the Garden Café serves sandwiches and, seasonally, smoothies made from the garden's own crop of tropical fruits. ✉ *10901 Old Cutler Rd., Coral Gables* ☎ *305/667–1651* 🌐 *www.fairchildgarden.org* 🎫 *$20* ⏲ *Daily 9:30–5.*

Fodor's Choice ★

❸ **Venetian Pool.** Sculpted from a rock quarry in 1923 and fed by artesian wells, this 825,000-gallon municipal pool completed a major face-lift in 2010. It remains quite popular because of its themed architecture—a fantasy version of a waterfront Italian village—created by Denman Fink. The pool has earned a place on the National Register of Historic Places and showcases a nice collection of vintage photos depicting 1920s beauty pageants and swank soirees held long ago. Paul Whiteman played here, Johnny Weissmuller and Esther Williams swam here, and you should, too (but no kids under 3). A snack bar, lockers, and showers make this must-see user-friendly as well. ✉ *2701 De Soto Blvd., at Toledo St., Coral Gables* ☎ *305/460–5356* 🌐 *www.gablesrecreation.com* 🎫 *$11 adults, free parking across De Soto Blvd.* ⏲ *June–Aug., weekdays 11–7:30, weekends 10–4:30; Sept., Oct., Apr., and May, Tues.–Fri. 11–5:30, weekends 10–4:30; Nov.–Mar., Tues.–Fri. 10–4:30, weekends 10–4:30.*

WORTH NOTING

❷ **Coral Gables Congregational Church.** With George Merrick as a charter member (he donated the land on which it stands) this parish was organized in 1923. Rumor has it that Merrick built this small church, the first in the Gables, in honor of his father, a congregational minister. The original interior is still in magnificent condition, and a popular concert series is held here every other Thursday evening in the summer. ✉ *3010 De Soto Blvd., at Anastasia Ave., Coral Gables* ☎ *305/448–7421* 🌐 *www.coralgablescongregational.org* ⏲ *Weekdays 8:30–5, Sun. services at 9 and 11.*

❹ **Coral Gables Merrick House and Gardens.** In 1976 the city of Coral Gables acquired Merrick's boyhood home. Restored to its 1920s appearance, it contains Merrick family furnishings and artwork. The breezy veranda and coral-rock construction are details you'll see repeated on many of the grand homes along Coral Way. ✉ *907 Coral Way, at Toledo St., Coral Gables* ☎ *305/460–5361* 🎫 *House $5, grounds free* ⏲ *House tours Wed. and Sun. at 1, 2, and 3; grounds daily 8–sunset.*

❺ **Miracle Mile.** Even with competition from some impressive malls, this half-mile stretch of retail stores continues to thrive because of its intriguing mixture of unique boutiques, bridal shops, art galleries, charming restaurants, and upscale nightlife venues. ✉ *Coral Way between SW 37th and SW 42nd Aves., Coral Gables.*

OFF THE BEATEN PATH

Metrozoo. Don't miss a visit to this top-notch zoo, 14 mi south of Miami. The only subtropical zoo in the continental United States, it has 340 acres that are home to more than 2,000 animals, including 40 endangered species, which roam on islands surrounded by moats. Take the monorail ($3 for an all-day pass) for a cool overview, then walk around for a closer look, including the latest attraction Amazon & Beyond, which encompasses 27 acres of simulated tropical rain forests showcasing 600 animals indigenous to the region, such as giant river otters, harpy eagles, anacondas, and jaguars. Other exhibits include Tiger Temple, where white tigers roam, and the African Plains exhibit, where giraffes, ostriches, and zebras graze in a simulated natural habitat. You can even feed veggies to the giraffes at Samburu Station. The Wings of Asia aviary has about 300 exotic birds representing 70 species flying free within the junglelike enclosure. There's also a petting zoo with a meerkat exhibit and interactive opportunities, such as those at Dr. Wilde's World and the Ecology Theater, where kids can touch Florida animals like alligators and opossums. An educational and entertaining wildlife show is given three times daily. ✉ *12400 Coral Reef Dr. (SW 152nd St.), Richmond Heights, Miami* ☎ *305/251–0400* 🌐 *www.miamimetrozoo.com* *$15.95, $11.95 children ages 3 to 12; 45-min tram tour $4.95* ⏲ *Daily 9:30–5:30, last admission 4.*

OFF THE BEATEN PATH

Everglades Alligator Farm. Here's your chance to see gators, gators, gators—2,000 or so—and other wildlife such as blue herons, snowy egrets, and perhaps a rare roseate spoonbill. You can also take in alligator wrestling, reptile shows, and other animal exhibits as well as an airboat ride (they're not allowed inside Everglades National Park). This place is a little more than 30 mi south of Miami, just south of the former pioneer town of Homestead. ✉ *40351 SW 192nd Ave., Florida City* ☎ *305/247–2628* 🌐 *www.everglades.com* *$15.50, $23 with airboat tour* ⏲ *Daily 9–6.*

COCONUT GROVE

Eclectic and intriguing, Miami's Coconut Grove can be considered the tropical equivalent of New York's Greenwich Village. A haven for writers and artists, the neighborhood has never quite outgrown its image as a small village. During the day it's business as usual in Coconut Grove, much as in any other Miami neighborhood. But in the evening, especially on weekends, it seems as if someone flips a switch and the streets come alive. Locals and tourists jam into small boutiques, sidewalk cafés, and stores lodged in two massive retail-entertainment complexes. For blocks in every direction, students, honeymooning couples, families, and prosperous retirees flow in and out of a mix of galleries, restaurants, bars, bookstores, comedy clubs, and theaters. With this weekly influx of traffic, parking can pose a problem. There's a well-lighted city garage at 3315 Rice Street, or look for police to direct you to parking lots where you'll pay $5–$10 for an evening's slot. If you're staying in the Grove, leave the car behind, and your night will get off to an easier start.

Nighttime is the right time to see Coconut Grove, but in the day you can take a casual drive around the neighborhood to see its diverse architecture. Posh estates mingle with rustic cottages, modest frame homes, and stark modern dwellings, often on the same block. If you're into horticulture, you'll be impressed by the Garden of Eden–like foliage that seems to grow everywhere without care. In truth, residents are determined to keep up the Grove's village-in-a-jungle look, so they lavish attention on exotic plantings even as they battle to protect any remaining native vegetation.

ESSENTIALS

Visitor Information Coconut Grove Chamber of Commerce (✉ *2820 McFarlane Rd., Coconut Grove, Miami* ☎ *305/444–7270* 🌐 *www.coconutgrovechamber.com*).

EXPLORING

Numbers correspond to the Coral Gables, Coconut Grove, and Key Biscayne map.

7 **Barnacle Historic State Park.** A pristine bay-front manse sandwiched between cramped luxury developments, Barnacle is Miami's oldest house still standing on its original foundation. To get here, you'll hike along an old buggy trail through a tropical hardwood hammock and landscaped lawn leading to Biscayne Bay. Built in 1891 by Florida's first snowbird—New Yorker Commodore Ralph Munroe—the large home, built of timber that Munroe salvaged from wrecked ships, has many original furnishings, a broad sloping roof, and deeply recessed verandas that channel sea breezes into the house. If your timing is right, you may catch one of the monthly Moonlight Concerts, and the old-fashioned picnic on the Fourth of July is popular. ✉ *3485 Main Hwy.* ☎ *305/442–6866* 🌐 *www.floridastateparks.org/thebarnacle* 🎟 *$1, concerts $5* ⏲ *Fri.–Mon. 9–5; tours at 10, 11:30, 1, and 2:30; group tours for 10 or more Weds. and Thurs. by reservation; concerts Sept.–May on evenings near the full moon 6–9, call for dates.*

8 **CocoWalk.** This indoor-outdoor mall has three floors of nearly 40 name-brand (Victoria's Secret, Gap, Banana Republic, etc.) and independent shops that stay open almost as late as its popular restaurants and clubs. Kiosks with beads, incense, herbs, and other small items are scattered around the ground level; street entertainers hold court on weekends; and the movie theaters and nightspots are upstairs. If you're ready for an evening of touristy people-watching, this is the place. ✉ *3015 Grand Ave.* ☎ *305/444–0777* 🌐 *www.cocowalk.net* ⏲ *Sun.–Thurs. 10–10, Fri. and Sat. 10 AM–11 PM.*

9 **Miami Museum of Science and Planetarium.** This small, fun museum is chock-full of hands-on sound, gravity, and electricity displays for children and adults alike. For animal lovers, its wildlife center houses native Florida snakes, turtles, tortoises, and birds of prey. Check the museum's schedule for traveling exhibits that appear throughout the year. If you're here the first Friday of the month, stick around for a laser-light rock-and-roll show, presented in the planetarium at 9, 10, and 11 PM, or gaze at the planets through two powerful Meade telescopes at the Weintraub Observatory for free. ✉ *3280 S. Miami Ave.* ☎ *305/646–4200* 🌐 *www.miamisci.org* 🎟 *Museum exhibits, planetarium shows, and wildlife center $14.95, laser show $7* ⏲ *Museum daily 10–6.*

10 **Vizcaya Museum and Gardens.** Of the 10,000 people living in Miami between 1912 and 1916, about 1,000 of them were gainfully employed by Chicago industrialist James Deering to build this European-inspired residence. Once comprising 180 acres, this national historic landmark

Fodor's Choice ★

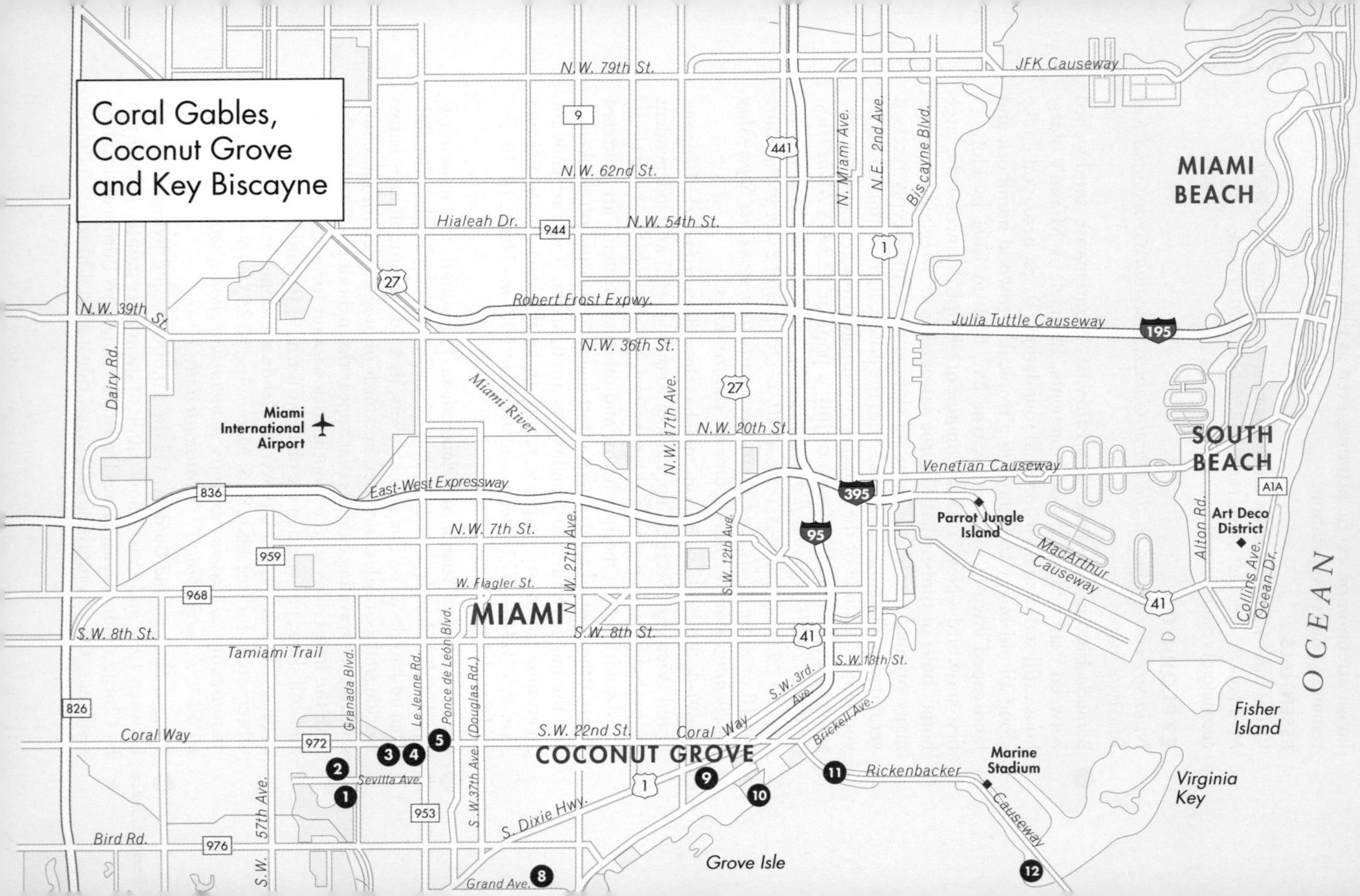
Coral Gables, Coconut Grove and Key Biscayne
N.W. 79th St.
JFK Causeway
9
441
N.W. 62nd St.
N. Miami Ave.
N.E. 2nd Ave.
Biscayne Blvd.
MIAMI BEACH
Hialeah Dr.
944
N.W. 54th St.
1
27
Robert Frost Expwy.
N.W. 39th St.
Julia Tuttle Causeway
195
N.W. 36th St.
Dairy Rd.
Miami River
27
N.W. 17th Ave.
Miami International Airport
N.W. 20th St.
SOUTH BEACH
Venetian Causeway
836
East-West Expressway
395
A1A
Parrot Jungle Island
Alton Rd.
Art Deco District
N.W. 7th St.
N.W. 27th Ave.
95
959
S.W. 12th Ave.
MacArthur Causeway
Collins Ave.
Ocean Dr.
W. Flagler St.
968
MIAMI
41
OCEAN
S.W. 8th St.
S.W. 8th St.
41
Tamiami Trail
Granada Blvd.
Le Jeune Rd.
Ponce de León Blvd.
S.W. 37th Ave. (Douglas Rd.)
S.W. 13th St.
S.W. 3rd. Ave.
826
Brickell Ave.
Fisher Island
Coral Way
972
S.W. 22nd St.
Coral Way
5
3
4
COCONUT GROVE
Marine Stadium
2
Sevilla Ave.
9
11
Rickenbacker
1
1
10
Virginia Key
953
Causeway
S. Dixie Hwy.
Bird Rd.
976
S.W. 57th Ave.
Grove Isle
12
8
Grand Ave.

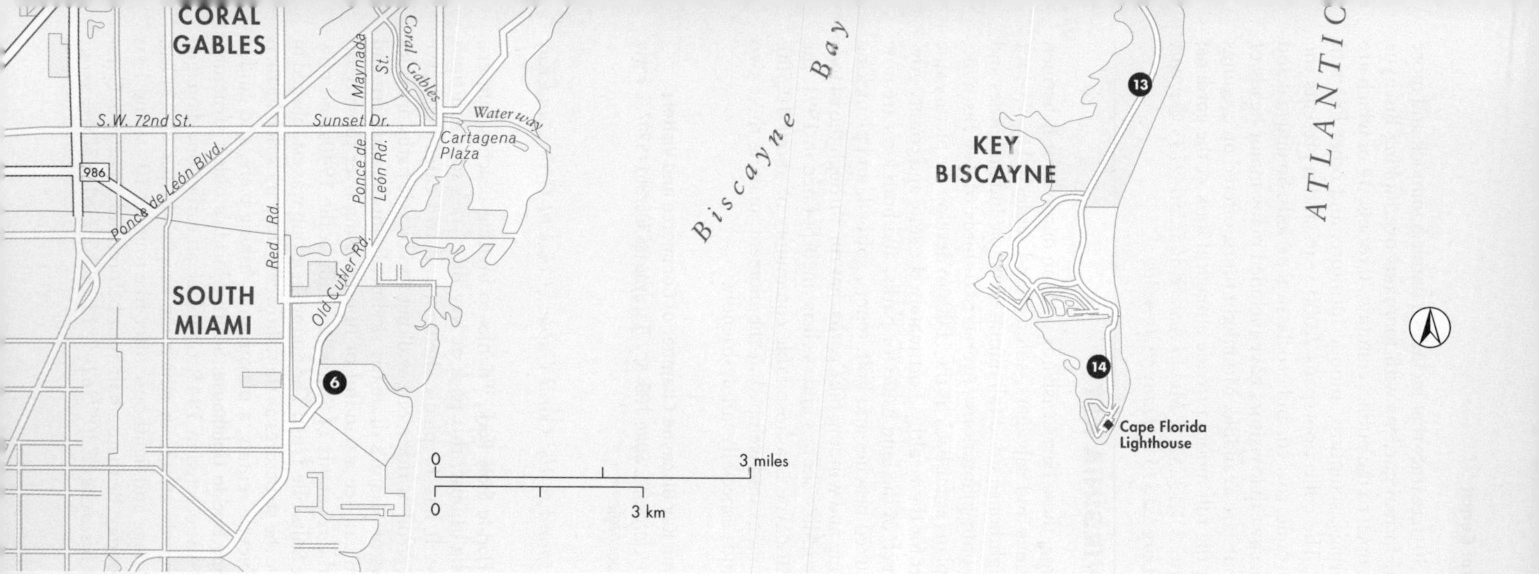
CORAL GABLES
SOUTH MIAMI
KEY BISCAYNE
ATLANTIC
Biscayne Bay
S.W. 72nd St.
Sunset Dr.
Ponce de León Blvd.
986
Red Rd.
Old Cutler Rd.
Maynada St.
Ponce de León Rd.
Coral Gables Waterway
Cartagena Plaza
Cape Florida Lighthouse
13
14
6
0
3 miles
0
3 km

Barnacle Historic State Park ... 7
Bill Baggs Cape Florida State Park ... 14
Biltmore Hotel ... 1
CocoWalk ... 8
Coral Gables Congregational Church ... 2
Coral Gables Merrick House and Gardens ... 4
Crandon Park ... 13
Fairchild Tropical Botanic Garden ... 6
Miami Museum of Science and Planetarium ... 9
Miami Seaquarium ... 12
Miracle Mile ... 5
Old Rickenbacker Causeway Bridge ... 11
Venetian Pool ... 3
Vizcaya Museum and Gardens ... 10

now occupies a 30-acre tract that includes a native hammock and more than 10 acres of formal gardens with fountains overlooking Biscayne Bay. The house, open to the public, contains 70 rooms, 34 of which are filled with paintings, sculpture, antique furniture, and other fine and decorative arts. The collection spans 2,000 years and represents the Renaissance, baroque, rococo, and neoclassical periods. So unusual and impressive is Vizcaya that visitors have included many major heads of state. Guided tours are available. Moonlight tours, offered on evenings that are nearest the full moon, provide a magical look at the gardens; call for reservations. ✉ *3251 S. Miami Ave.* ☎ *305/250–9133* 🌐 *www.vizcayamuseum.org* 🎫 *$15* ⏲ *Daily 9:30–4:30.*

KEY BISCAYNE AND VIRGINIA KEY

Once upon a time, these barrier islands were an outpost for fishermen and sailors, pirates and salvagers, soldiers and settlers. The 95-foot Cape Florida Lighthouse stood tall during Seminole Indian battles and hurricanes. Coconut plantations covered two-thirds of Key Biscayne, and there were plans as far back as the 1800s to develop the picturesque island as a resort for the wealthy. Fortunately, the state and county governments set much of the land aside for parks, and both keys are now home to top-ranked beaches and golf, tennis, softball, and picnicking facilities. The long and winding bike paths that run through the islands are favorites for in-line skaters and cyclists. Incorporated in 1991, the village of Key Biscayne is a hospitable community of about 10,500; Virginia Key remains undeveloped at the moment, making these two playground islands especially family-friendly.

ESSENTIALS

Visitor Information **Key Biscayne Chamber of Commerce and Visitors Center** (✉ *88 W. McIntyre St., Suite 100, Key Biscayne* ☎ *305/361–5207* 🌐 *www.keybiscaynechamber.org*).

EXPLORING

Numbers correspond to the Coral Gables, Coconut Grove, and Key Biscayne map.

14 **Bill Baggs Cape Florida State Park.** Thanks to inviting beaches, sunsets, and a tranquil lighthouse, this park at Key Biscayne's southern tip is worth the drive. It has 19 picnic shelters, and two cafés that serve light lunches. A stroll or ride along walking and bicycle paths provides wonderful views of Miami's dramatic skyline. From the southern end of the park you can see a handful of houses rising over the bay on wooden stilts, the remnants of Stiltsville, built in the 1940s and now protected by the Stiltsville Trust. The nonprofit group was established in 2003 to preserve the structures as they showcase the park's rich history. Bill Baggs has bicycle rentals, a playground, fishing piers, and guided tours of the **Cape Florida Lighthouse,** South Florida's oldest structure. The lighthouse was erected in 1845 to replace an earlier one damaged in an 1836 Seminole attack, in which the keeper's helper was killed. The restored cottage and lighthouse offer free tours at 10 AM and 1 PM Thursday to Monday. Be there a half hour beforehand. ✉ *1200 S. Crandon Blvd., Key Biscayne* ☎ *305/361–5811 or 305/361–8779* 🌐 *www.*

Fodor's Choice ★

Not all the fun is for grown-ups. With sandy shores great for kite flying, Miami beaches appeal to kids, too.

floridastateparks.org/capeflorida *$4 per single-occupant vehicle, $8 per vehicle with 2–8 people; $2 per person on bicycle, bus, motorcycle, or foot* *Daily 8–dusk, tours Thurs.–Mon. at 10 and 1; sign up 1 hr beforehand (on weekdays you can almost always simply show up shortly before tour time).*

13 **Crandon Park North Beach.** This relaxing oasis in northern Key Biscayne is popular with families, and many educated beach enthusiasts rate the 3-mi beach here among the top 10 beaches in North America. The sand is soft, there are no riptides, there's a great view of the Atlantic, and parking is both inexpensive and plentiful. The park is dotted with picnic tables and grills, so it's a weekend favorite of locals often showcasing Miami's a multicultural flavor with salsa and hip-hop, jerk chicken and barbecue ribs. **Crandon Gardens** at Crandon Park was once the site of a zoo. There are swans, waterfowl, and dozens of huge iguanas running loose. Nearby are a restored carousel (open weekends and major holidays), outdoor roller rink, and playground. At the north end of the beach is the free **Marjory Stoneman Douglas Biscayne Nature Center** (*305/361–6767* *www.biscaynenaturecenter.org* *Daily 10–4*), where you can explore sea-grass beds on a tour with a naturalist; see red, black, and white mangroves; and hike along the beach and hammock in the Bear Cut Preserve. The park also sponsors hikes and tours. (⇨ *Crandon Park in Beaches section, under Sports and the Outdoors.*) *4000 Crandon Blvd., Key Biscayne* *305/361–5421* *www.biscaynenaturecenter.org* *$5 per vehicle* *Daily 8–sunset.*

12 **Miami Seaquarium.** This classic family attraction stages shows with sea lions, dolphins, and Lolita the killer whale. The Crocodile Flats exhibit

has 26 Nile crocodiles. Discovery Bay, an endangered mangrove habitat, is home to sea turtles, alligators, herons, egrets, and ibis. You can also visit a shark pool, a tropical reef aquarium, and West Indian and Florida manatees. But the newest interactive attraction is the Stingray Touch Tank, where you can touch and feed cownose rays and southern stingrays. Another big draw is the Swim with Our Dolphins program. For $199, a two-hour session allows you to touch, kiss, and swim with the gentle marine mammals on the Dolphin Odyssey, $139 ($99 for kids) to participate in the shallow water Dolphin Encounter. It may seem pricey but it does include park admission, towel, and a wet suit. Reservations required. Children 9 and younger pay $10 less. ✉ *4400 Rickenbacker Causeway, Virginia Key* ☎ *305/361–5705* 🌐 *www.miamiseaquarium.com* 🎟 *$37.95, dolphin swim program $199, parking $8* ⏲ *Daily 9–6, last admission 4:30; dolphin swim daily at 9:30 10,11:30, 1, and 2:30; dolphin encounter daily at 12:15 and 3:15.*

> **WORD OF MOUTH**
>
> "Stay in South Beach and take a drive out to Key Biscayne—you'll love it!! Nice place to ride bikes."
>
> —JerseySue

11 **Old Rickenbacker Causeway Bridge.** Here you can watch boat traffic pass through the channel, pelicans and other seabirds soar and dive, and dolphins cavort in the bay. Park at the bridge entrance, about a mile from the tollgate, and walk past anglers tending their lines to the gap where the center draw span across the Intracoastal Waterway was removed. On the right, on cool, clear winter evenings, the water sparkles with dots of light from hundreds of shrimp boats. ✉ *Rickenbacker Causeway south of Powell Bridge, east of Coconut Grove.*

SPORTS AND THE OUTDOORS

Sun, sand, and crystal-clear water mixed with an almost nonexistent winter and a cosmopolitan clientele make Miami and Miami Beach ideal for year-round sunbathing and outdoor activities. Whether the priority is showing off a toned body, jumping on a Jet Ski, or relaxing in a tranquil natural environment, there's a beach tailor-made to please. But tanning and water sports are only part of this sun-drenched picture. Greater Miami has championship golf courses and tennis courts, miles of bike trails along placid canals and through subtropical forests, and skater-friendly concrete paths amidst the urban jungle. For those who like their sports of the spectator variety, the city offers up a bonanza of pro teams for every season. The Miami Dolphins remain the only NFL team to have ever played a perfect season, the scrappy Florida Marlins took the World Series title in 2003, and the Miami Heat were the 2006 NBA champions. There's even a crazy ball-flinging game called jai alai that's billed as the fastest sport on earth.

In addition to contacting the venues *below* directly, get tickets to major events from **Ticketmaster** (☎ *800/745–3000* 🌐 *www.ticketmaster.com*).

12

MIAMI TOURS

BOAT TOURS

Duck Tours Miami (✉ *1665 Washington Ave., Miami Beach* ☎ *877/382–5849 or 786/276–8300* 🌐 *www.ducktoursmiami.com* 🎟 *$32*) uses amphibious vehicles to offer daily 90-minute tours of Miami that combine land and sea views. Comedy and music are part of the mix. Tickets are $18 for children 4–12.

Island Queen, Island Lady, **and** ***Miami Lady*** (✉ *401 Biscayne Blvd., Miami* ☎ *305/379–5119* 🌐 *www.islandqueencruises.com* 🎟 *$25*) are 140-passenger double-decker tour boats docked at Bayside Marketplace. Daily 90-minute narrated tours of the Port of Miami and Millionaires' Row cost of $17 for those 11 and under.

For something a little more private and luxe, **RA Charters** (☎ *305/666–7979 or 305/989–3959* 🌐 *www.racharters.com* 🎟 *Call for prices*) sails out of the Dinner Key Marina in Coconut Grove. Full- and half-day charters include sailing lessons, with occasional extended trips to the Florida Keys. For a romantic night, have Captain Masoud pack some gourmet fare and sail sunset to moonlight while you enjoy Biscayne Bay's spectacular skyline view of Miami.

WALKING TOURS

Operated by the Miami Design Preservation League, the **Art Deco District Tour** (✉ *1001 Ocean Dr., South Beach, Miami Beach* ☎ *305/531–3484* 🌐 *www.mdpl.org* 🎟 *$20 guided tour, $15 audio tour*) is a 90-minute guided walking tour that departs from the league's welcome center at Ocean Drive and 10th Street. It starts at 10:30 AM Friday through Wednesday, and at 6:30 PM Thursday. Alternatively, you can go at your own pace with the league's self-guided audio tour, which takes roughly an hour and a half.

AUTO RACING

★ **Homestead–Miami Speedway.** For NASCAR Nextel Cup events, head south to this famous speedway, which hosts the Ford 400 Nextel Cup Series season finale. The highlight of the speedway schedule, it's held the third Sunday in November in conjunction with the NASCAR Craftsman Truck Series season finale and other races. The speedway, built in 1995 and improved with steeper banking in 2003, is also home to the Toyota Indy 300 IRL season opener each February and other Indy-car racing. ✉ *1 Speedway Blvd., Exit 6 of Florida's Tpke. (Rte. 821) at SW 137th Ave., Homestead* ☎ *866/409–7223* 🌐 *www.homesteadmiamispeedway.com* ⏲ *Weekdays 9–5* 🎟 *Prices vary according to event.*

BASEBALL

Florida Marlins. Miami's baseball team won't be playing at Dolphin Stadium much longer. In 2012 it will move into a brand-new stadium on the grounds of Miami's famous Orange Bowl. Go see the team that came out of nowhere to beat the New York Yankees and win the 2003 World Series before they move. Home games are April through early

October. ✉ *Land Shark Stadium, 2267 NW 199th St., 16 mi northwest of Downtown, between I–95 and Florida's Tpke.* ☎ *305/626–7400 or 877/627–5467* 🌐 *www.marlins.com* 🎟 *$9–$315, parking $10.*

BASKETBALL

Miami Heat. The 2006 NBA champs play at the 19,600-seat, waterfront AmericanAirlines Arena. The state-of-the-art venue features restaurants, a wide patio overlooking Biscayne Bay, and a silver sun-shape special-effects scoreboard with rays holding wide-screen TVs. During Heat games, when the 1,100 underground parking spaces are reserved for season-ticket holders, you can park across the street at Miami's Bayside Marketplace ($20), at metered spaces along Biscayne Boulevard, or in lots on side streets, where prices range from $5 to $25, depending on the distance from the arena (a limited number of spaces for people with disabilities are available on-site for non-season-ticket holders). Better yet, take the Metromover to the Park West or Freedom Tower station. Home games are held November through April. ✉ *AmericanAirlines Arena, 601 Biscayne Blvd., Downtown* ☎ *786/777–4328, 800/462–2849 ticket hotline* 🌐 *www.nba.com/heat* 🎟 *$10–$425.*

BEACHES

MIAMI BEACH

NORTH MIAMI BEACH

Haulover Beach Park. This popular clothing-optional beach is embraced by naturists of all ages, shapes, and sizes. Once you park in the North Lot, you'll walk through a short tunnel covered with trees and natural habitat until you emerge on the unpretentious beach, where nudity is rarely met by gawkers. There are volleyball nets, and plenty of beach chair and umbrella rentals to protect your birthday suit from too much exposure—to the sun, that is. The sections of beach requiring swimwear are popular, too, given the park's ample parking and relaxed atmosphere. Lifeguards stand watch. More active types might want to check out the kite rentals, charter-fishing excursions, and a par-3, nine-hole golf course. ✉ *10800 Collins Ave., north of Bal Harbour in Sunny Isles* ☎ *305/947–3525* 🎟 *$6 per vehicle* ⏲ *Daily sunrise–sunset.*

★ **Oleta River State Park.** Tucked away in North Miami Beach is a ready-made family getaway. Nature lovers will find it easy to embrace the 1,128 acres of subtropical beauty along Biscayne Bay. Swim in the calm bay waters and bicycle, canoe, kayak, and bask among egrets, manatees, bald eagles, and fiddler crabs. Dozens of picnic tables, along with 10 covered pavilions, dot the stunning natural habitat, which has recently been restored with red mangroves to revitalize the ecosystem and draw endangered birds, like the roseate spoonbill. There's a playground for tots, a mangrove island accessible only by boat, 15 mi of mountain-bike trails, a half-mile exercise track, concessions, and outdoor showers. If you want to continue the nature adventure into the evening, then reserve an overnight stay in minimalist (but still air-conditioned) cabins, which run $62.15 per night. ✉ *3400 NE 163rd St., North Miami Beach* ☎ *305/919–1844* 🌐 *www.floridastateparks.*

org/oletariver 🎫 *$1 per person on foot or bike; $3 for single-occupant vehicle; $5 per vehicle up to 8 people; $1 each additional. Free entrance if renting a cabin.* ⏲ *Daily 8–sunset.*

Surfside Beach. *Parlez-vous français?* If the answer is "*Oui,*" you'll feel quite comfortable at this serene stretch of beach, which draws many French Canadian snowbird tourists who come to thaw out from the winter here. ✉ *Collins Ave. between 88th and 96th Sts., Surfside.*

SOUTH BEACH
Fodor's Choice ★

The 10-block stretch of white sandy beach hugging the turquoise waters along **Ocean Drive**—from 5th to 15th streets—is one of the most popular in America, known for drawing unabashedly modelesque sunbathers and posers. The beaches crowd quickly on the weekends with a blend of European tourists, young hipsters, and sun-drenched locals offering Latin flavor. Separating the sand from the traffic of Ocean Drive is palm-fringed Lummus Park, with its volleyball nets and chickee huts (huts made of palmetto thatch over a cypress frame) for shade. The beach at 12th Street is popular with gays, a section often marked with rainbow flags. Locals hang out on 3rd Street beach, where they watch fit Brazilians play foot volley, a variation of volleyball that uses everything but the hands. Because much of South Beach leans toward skimpy sunning—women are often in G-strings and casually topless—many families prefer the tamer sections of Mid- and North Beach. Metered parking spots next to the ocean are a rare find. Instead, opt for a public garage a few blocks away and enjoy the people-watching as you walk to find your perfect spot on the sand. ✉ *Ocean Dr., between 1st and 22nd Sts., Miami Beach* ☎ *305/673–7714.*

KEY BISCAYNE AND VIRGINIA KEY

Fodor's Choice ★

Bill Baggs Cape Florida State Park. The picturesque drive down to the southern tip of Key Biscayne is only a hint of the natural beauty you will find when exploring this 410-acre park. For swimmers, the beach here is frequently ranked among the top 10 in North America by the University of Maryland's esteemed sandman, Dr. Beach. Families often picnic here, choosing the shade under any of the 19 shelters. For active wanderers, explore the nature trails, try your hand at the fishing piers, or take a breezy bike ride along paths that offer breathtaking views of the bay and Miami's skyline. History buffs can enjoy guided tours of the Cape Florida Lighthouse, South Florida's oldest structure. ✉ *1200 S. Crandon Blvd., Key Biscayne* ☎ *305/361–5811 or 305/361–8779* 🎫 *$2 per person on foot, bike, motorbike, or bus; $8 per vehicle with 2 to 8 people* ⏲ *Daily 8–sunset, lighthouse tours Thurs.–Mon. 10 and 1.*

★ **Crandon Park North Beach.** The 3-mi sliver of beach paradise is dotted with palm trees to provide a respite from the steamy sun, until it's time to take a dip in the clear-blue waters. On weekends, be prepared for a long hike from your car to the beach. There are bathrooms, outdoor showers, plenty of picnic tables, and concession stands. The family-friendly park offers abundant options for kids who find it challenging to simply sit and build sand castles. There are marine-theme play sculptures, a dolphin-shaped spray fountain, an old-fashioned outdoor roller rink, and a restored carousel (it's open weekends and major holidays 10–5, until 6 in summer, and you get three rides for $1). (⇨ *Crandon Park in*

Exploring section for more on the park.) ✉ *4000 Crandon Blvd., Key Biscayne* ☎ *305/361–5421* *$5 per vehicle* ⏲ *Daily 8–sunset.*

BICYCLING

Perfect weather and flat terrain make Miami-Dade County a popular place for cyclists; however, biking here can also be quite dangerous. Be very vigilant when biking on Miami Beach, or better yet, steer clear and bike the beautiful paths of Key Biscayne.

Key Cycling (✉ *328 Crandon Blvd., Key Biscayne* ☎ *305/361–0061* 🌐 *www.keycycling.com*) rents bikes for $15 for two hours, $24 for the day, and $80 for the week.

BOATING AND SAILING

Boating, whether on sailboats, powerboats, luxury yachts, Wave Runners, or Windsurfers, is a passion in greater Miami. The Intracoastal Waterway, wide and sheltered Biscayne Bay, and the Atlantic Ocean provide ample opportunities for fun aboard all types of watercraft.

The best windsurfing spots are on the north side of the Rickenbacker Causeway at Virginia Key Beach or to the south at, go figure, Windsurfer Beach. Kitesurfing adds another level to the water-sports craze. The shallow waters off the parking lot in Matheson Hammock Park are like catnip for local kiteboarders. They also blast off from 87th Street in Miami Beach at North Shore Open Space Park.

MARINAS

Haulover Marine Center (✉ *15000 Collins Ave., north of Bal Harbour, Miami Beach* ☎ *305/945–3934* 🌐 *www.haulovermarinecenter.net*), which has a bait-and-tackle shop and a 24-hour marine gas station, is low on glamour but high on service.

Near the Art Deco district, **Miami Beach Marina** (✉ *MacArthur Causeway, 300 Alton Rd., Miami Beach* ☎ *305/673–6000* 🌐 *www.miamibeachmarina.com*) has plenty to entice sailors and landlubbers alike: restaurants, charters, boat rentals, a complete marine-hardware store, a dive shop, excursion vendors, a large grocery store, a fuel dock, concierge services, and 400 slips accommodating vessels of up to 250 feet. There's also a U.S. Customs clearing station and a charter service, Florida Yacht Charters. Picnic tables along the docks make this marina especially visitor-friendly.

Busy **Bayshore Landing Marina** (✉ *2560 S. Bayshore Dr., Coconut Grove* ☎ *305/854–7997*) is home to a lively seafood restaurant that's good for viewing the nautical eye candy.

OUTFITTERS AND EXPEDITIONS

You can rent 18- to 68-foot powerboats through **Club Nautico** (✉ *Miami Beach Marina, 300 Alton Road, #112, Miami Beach* ☎ *305/673–2502* 🌐 *www.clubnauticousa.com* ✉ *Crandon Park Marina, 5400 Crandon Blvd., Key Biscayne* ☎ *305/361–9217*), a national powerboat-rental company. You can also get a 100-foot powerboat, but make sure to call a week in advance. Half- to full-day rentals range from $200 to

$699. You may want to consider buying a club membership; it'll cost a bundle at first, but you'll save about 50% on all your future rentals. **Playtime Watersports** (✉ *Collins Ave., Miami Beach* ☎ *786/234–0184* 🌐 *www.playtimewatersport.com* ✉ *Eden Roc, 4525 Collins Ave.* ✉ *Miami Beach Resort and Spa, 4833 Collins Ave.* ✉ *Ritz-Carlton, 455 Grand Bay Dr.* ✉ *Alexander Hotel, 5225 Collins Ave.*) sells and rents high-end water-sports equipment, including Wave Runners and wind-driven devices. n addition to renting equipment, the friendly folks at **Sailboards Miami** (✉ *Site E1 Rickenbacker Causeway, Key Biscayne* ☎ *305/361–7245* 🌐 *www.sailboardsmiami.com*) say they teach more windsurfers each year than anyone in the United States, and promise to teach you to windsurf within two hours—for $69. Rentals average $30 for the first hour and $25 for each additional hour.

FOOTBALL

Fodor's Choice ★ The **Miami Dolphins** have one of the largest average attendance figures in the league. September through January, on home-game days the Metro Miami-Dade Transit Agency runs buses to the stadium. ✉ *Dolphin Stadium, 2267 NW 199th St., 16 mi northwest of Downtown, between I–95 and Florida's Tpke.* ☎ *305/620–2578* 🌐 *www.miamidolphins.com.*

GOLF

Greater Miami has more than 30 private and public courses. Costs at most courses are higher on weekends and in season, but you can save by playing on weekdays and after 1 or 3 PM, depending on the course—call ahead to find out when afternoon-twilight rates go into effect. For information on most courses in Miami and throughout Florida, you can visit 🌐 *www.floridagolferguide.com*. The 18-hole, par-71 championship **Biltmore Golf Course** (✉ *1210 Anastasia Ave., Coral Gables* ☎ *305/460–5364*), known for its scenic layout, has been restored to its original Donald Ross design, circa 1925. Greens fees in season range from $145 to $165 for nonresidents. The optional cart is $27. Overlooking the bay, the **Crandon Golf Course** (✉ *6700 Crandon Blvd., Key Biscayne* ☎ *305/361–9129* 🌐 *www.crandongolfclub.com*) is a top-rated 18-hole, par-72 public course in a beautiful tropical setting. Expect to pay $160 for a round in winter, $63.50 in summer, cart included. Twilight rates from $40 apply after 3 PM. **Don Shula's Hotel & Golf Club** (✉ *7601 Miami Lakes Dr., 154th St. Exit off Rte. 826, Miami Lakes* ☎ *305/820–8106* 🌐 *www.donshulahotel.com*), in northern Miami, has one of the longest championship courses in the area (7,055 yards, par 72), a lighted par-3 course, and a golf school. Greens fees are $134–$175, depending on the season. Hotel guests get discounted rates. You'll pay in the lower range on weekdays, more on weekends, and $45 after 3 PM. Golf carts are included. The par-3 course is $12 weekdays, $15 weekends. The club hosts more than 75 tournaments a year.

Among its five courses and many annual tournaments, the **Doral Golf Resort and Spa** (✉ *4400 NW 87th Ave., 36th St. Exit off Rte. 826, Doral, Miami* ☎ *305/592–2000 or 800/713–6725* 🌐 *www.doralresort.com*), just west of Miami proper, is best known for the par-72 Blue Monster course and the PGA's annual World Golf Championship. (The week of festivities planned around this tournament, which offers $8 million in prize money, brings hordes of pro-golf aficionados in late March.) Greens fees range from $95 to $325. Carts are not required. it the links in the heart of South Beach at the lovely 18-hole, par-72 **Miami Beach Golf Club** (⊠ *2301 Alton Rd., Miami Beach* ☎ *305/532–3350* 🌐 *www.miamibeachgolfclub.com*). Greens fees are $125 in summer, $200 in winter, including mandatory cart.

IN-LINE SKATING

Miami Beach's ocean vistas, wide sidewalks, and flat terrain make it a perfect locale for in-line skating—and don't the locals know it. Very popular is the **Lincoln Road Mall** from Washington Avenue to Alton Road; many of the restaurants along this pedestrian mall have outdoor seating where you can eat without shedding your skates. For a great view of the Art Deco district and action on South Beach, skate along the sidewalk on the east side of **Ocean Drive** from 5th to 14th streets. In South Miami an often-traversed concrete path winds **under the elevated Metrorail** from Vizcaya Station (across U.S. 1 from the Miami Museum of Science) to Red Road at U.S. 1 (across from the Shops at Sunset Place). You don't have to bring your own; a number of in-line skate shops offer rentals that include protective gear.

OUTFITTER

Fritz's Bike, Skate and Surf (⊠ *1620 Washington Ave., Miami Beach* ☎ *305/532–1954* 🌐 *www.fritzsmiamibeach.com* ⏲ *Daily 10–10*) charges $10 an hour or $24 for 24 hours, which includes a helmet. A deposit of $100 is required.

SCUBA DIVING AND SNORKELING

Diving and snorkeling on the offshore coral wrecks and reefs on a calm day can be comparable to the Caribbean. Chances are excellent you'll come face-to-face with a flood of tropical fish. One option is to find Fowey, Triumph, Long, and Emerald reefs in 10- to 15-foot dives that are perfect for snorkelers and beginning divers. On the edge of the continental shelf a little more than 3 mi out, these reefs are just ¼ mi away from depths greater than 100 feet. Another option is to paddle around the tangled prop roots of the mangrove trees that line the coast, peering at the fish, crabs, and other creatures hiding there.

It's a bit of a drive, but the best diving and definitely the best snorkeling to be had in Miami-Dade is on the incredible living coral reefs in **Biscayne Underwater Park** (⊠ *9710 SW 328th St., Exit 6 of Florida's Tpke., Homestead* ☎ *305/230–1100* 🌐 *www.nps.gov/bisc*), in the rural southeast corner of the county. With 95% of its 173,000 acres underwater, this is the national-park system's largest marine park. The huge park includes the northernmost islands of the Florida Keys and the beginning of the world's third-longest coral reef. Guided snorkeling and scuba trips, offered from the concession near the visitor center, cost $35.95

Continued on page 564

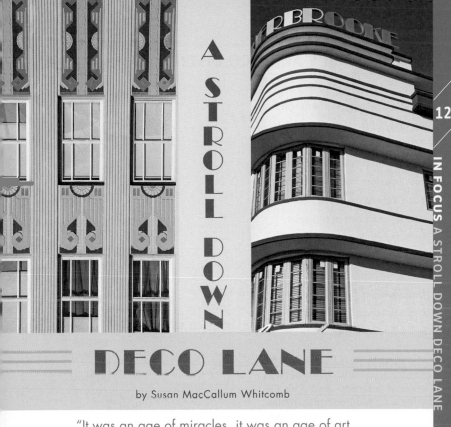

A STROLL DOWN DECO LANE

by Susan MacCallum Whitcomb

"It was an age of miracles, it was an age of art,
it was an age of excess, and it was an age of satire."

—F. Scott Fitzgerald, *Echoes of the Jazz Age*

The 1920s and '30s brought us flappers and gangsters, plunging stock prices and soaring skyscrapers, and plenty of headline-worthy news from the arts scene, from talking pictures and the jazz craze to fashions where pearls piled on and sequins dazzled. These decades between the two world wars also gave us an art style reflective of the changing times: art deco.

Distinguished by geometrical shapes and the use of industrial motifs that fused the decorative arts with modern technology, art deco became the architectural style of choice for train stations and big buildings across the country (think New york's Radio City Music Hall and Empire State Building).

Using a steel-and-concrete box as the foundation, architects dipped into art deco's grab bag of accessories, initially decorating facades with spheres, cylinders, and cubes. They later borrowed increasingly from industrial design, stripping elements used in ocean liners and automobiles to their streamlined essentials.

The style was also used in jewelry, furniture, textiles, and advertising. The fact that it employed inexpensive materials, such as stucco or terrazzo, helped art deco thrive during the Great Depression.

MIAMI BEACH'S ART DECO DISTRICT

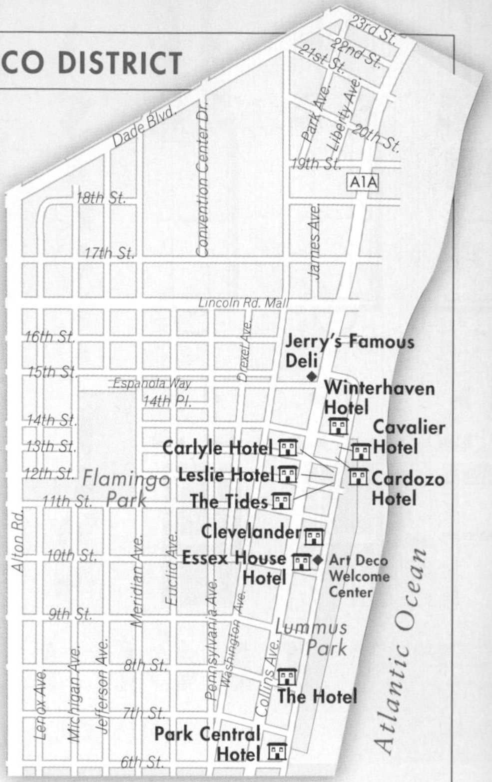

With its warm beaches and tropical surroundings, Miami Beach in the early 20th century was establishing itself as America's winter playground. During the roaring '20s luxurious hostelries resembling Venetian palaces, Spanish villages, and French châteaux sprouted up. In the 1930s, middle-class tourists started coming, and more hotels had to be built. Designers like Henry Hohauser chose art deco for its affordable yet distinctive design.

An antidote to the gloom of the Great Depression, the look was cheerful and tidy. And with the whimsical additions of portholes, colorful racing bands, and images of rolling ocean waves painted or etched on the walls, these South Beach properties created an oceanfront fantasy world for travelers.

Many of the candy-colored hotels have survived and been restored. They are among the more than 800 buildings of historical significance in South Beach's art deco district. Composing much of South Beach, the 1-square-mi district is bounded by Dade Boulevard on the north, the Atlantic Ocean on the east, 6th Street on the south, and Alton Road on the west.

Because the district as a whole was developed so rapidly and designed by like-minded architects—**Henry Hohauser, L. Murray Dixon, Albert Anis,** and their colleagues—it has amazing stylistic unity. Nevertheless, on this single street you can trace the evolution of period form from angular, vertically emphatic early deco to aerodynamically rounded Streamline Moderne. The relatively severe Cavalier and more curvaceous Cardozo are fine examples of the former and latter, respectively.

To explore the district, begin by loading up on literature in the **Art Deco Welcome Center** (✉ *1001 Ocean Dr.* ☎ *305/531–3484* 🌐 *www.mdpl.org*). If you want to view these historic properties on your own, just start walking. A four-block stroll north on Ocean Drive gets you up close to camera-ready classics: the **Clevelander** (1020), the **Tides** (1220), the **Leslie** (1244), the **Carlyle** (1250), the **Cardozo** (1300), the **Cavalier** (1320), and the **Winterhaven** (1400).

ART DECO TOURS

See the bold looks of classic Art Deco architecture along Ocean Drive.

SELF-GUIDED AUDIO TOURS

Expert insight on the architecture and the area's history is yours on the Miami Design Preservation League's (MDPL) 90-minute self-guided walks that use an iPod or cell phone and include a companion map. You can pick up the iPod version and companion map at the Art Deco Welcome Center from 9:30 AM to 5 PM daily; the cost is $15. The cell-phone option ($10) is available anytime by calling 786/312–1229 and charging the amount to your credit card; your payment allows you access to audio commentary for up to 24 hours after purchase.

WALKING TOURS

The MDPL's 90-minute "Ocean Drive and Beyond" group walking tour gives you a guided look at area icons, inside and out. (A number of interiors are on the itinerary, so it's a good chance to peek inside spots that might otherwise seem off-limits.) Morning tours depart at 10:30 AM from the Art Deco Welcome Center Gift Shop on Tuesday, Wednesday, Friday, Saturday, and Sunday. An evening tour departs at 6:30 PM on Thursdays. Reservations can't be made in advance, so arrive 15–20 minutes early to buy tickets ($20).

BIKE TOURS

Rather ride than walk? Three-hour cycling tours of the city's art deco history are organized daily for groups (5 or more) by **South Beach Bike Tours** (☎ *305/673–2002* 🌐 *www.southbeachbiketours.com*). The $59 cost includes equipment, snacks, and water.

ART DECO WEEKEND

Tours, lectures, film screenings, and dozens of other '30s-themed events are on tap every January, during the annual **Art Deco Weekend** (☎ *305/672–2014*, 🌐 *www.ArtDecoWeekend.com*). Festivities—many of them free—kick off with a Saturday morning parade and culminate in a street fair. More than a quarter of a million people join in the action, which centers on Ocean Drive between 5th and 15th streets. The 2011 dates are Jan. 14–16.

Celebrate the 1930s during Art Deco Weekend.

ARCHITECTURAL HIGHLIGHTS

FRIEZE DETAIL, CAVALIER HOTEL

The decorative stucco friezes outside the Cavalier Hotel at 1320 Ocean Drive are significant for more than aesthetic reasons. Roy France used them to add symmetry (adhering to the "Rule of Three") and accentuate the hotel's verticality by drawing the eye upward. The pattern he chose also reflected a fascination with ancient civilizations engendered by the recent rediscovery of King Tut's tomb and the Chichén Itzá temples.

Cavalier Hotel

LOBBY FLOOR, PARK CENTRAL HOTEL

Terrazzo—a compound of cement and stone chips that could be poured, then polished—is a hallmark of deco design. Terrazzo floors typically had a geometric pattern, like this one in the Park Central Hotel, a 1937 building by Henry Hohauser at 640 Ocean Drive.

Park Central Hotel

CORNER FACADE, ESSEX HOUSE HOTEL

Essex House Hotel, a 1938 gem that appears permanently anchored at 1001 Collins Avenue, is a stunning example of Maritime deco (also known as Nautical Moderne). Designed by Henry Hohauser to evoke an ocean liner, the hotel is rife with marine elements, from the rows of porthole-style windows and natty racing stripes to the towering smokestack-like sign. With a prow angled proudly into the street corner, it seems ready to steam out to sea.

Essex House Hotel

NEON SPIRE, THE HOTEL

The name spelled vertically in eye-popping neon on the venue's iconic aluminum spire—Tiffany—bears evidence of the hotel's earlier incarnation. When the L. Murray Dixon–designed Tiffany Hotel was erected at 801 Collins Avenue in 1939, neon was still a novelty. Its use, coupled with the spire's rocket-like shape, combined to create a futuristic look influenced by the sci-fi themes then pervasive in popular culture.

The Hotel

ENTRANCE, JERRY'S FAMOUS DELI

Inspired by everything from car fenders to airplane noses, proponents of art deco's Streamline Moderne look began to soften buildings' hitherto boxy edges. But when Henry Hohauser designed Hoffman's Cafeteria in 1940 he took moderne to the max. The landmark at 1450 Collins Avenue (now Jerry's Famous Deli) has a sleek, splendidly curved facade. The restored interior echoes it through semicircular booths and rounded chair backs.

Jerry's Famous Deli

ARCHITECTURAL TERMS

The Rule of Three: Early deco designers often used architectural elements in multiples of three, creating tripartite facades with triple sets of windows, eyebrows, or banding.

Eyebrows: Small shelf-like ledges that protruded over exterior windows were used to simultaneously provide much-needed shade and serve as a counterpoint to a building's strong vertical lines.

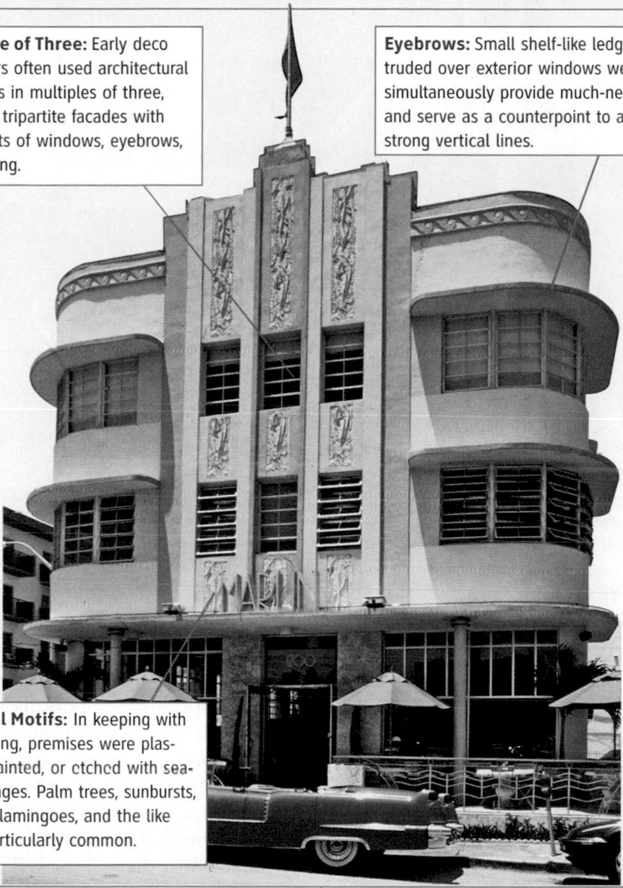

Tropical Motifs: In keeping with the setting, premises were plastered, painted, or etched with seaside images. Palm trees, sunbursts, waves, flamingoes, and the like were particularly common.

Banding: Enhancing the illusion that these immobile structures were rapidly speeding objects, colorful horizontal bands (also called "racing stripes") were painted on exteriors or applied with tile.

Stripped Classic: The most austere version of art deco (sometimes dubbed Depression Moderne) was used for buildings commissioned by the Public Works Administration.

(top) Hotel Marlin; (left) Sherbrooke Hotel; (right) U.S. Post Office in Miami Beach.

For locals, the beach scene is often incorporated into daily life, from getting exercise to walking the dog.

for a three-hour snorkel trip (daily 1:30–4:30), including equipment, and $54 for a four-hour, two-tank dive trip (weekends 8:30–1). Scuba equipment is available for rent. ⇨ *See the Everglades chapter for more on Homestead.*

Perhaps the area's most unusual diving options are its **artificial reefs** (✉ *1920 Meridian Ave., Miami Beach* ☎ *305/672–1270*). Since 1981, Miami-Dade County's Department of Environmental Resources Management has sunk tons of limestone boulders and a water tower, army tanks, and almost 200 boats of all descriptions to create a "wreck-reational" habitat where divers can swim with yellow tang, barracudas, nurse sharks, snapper, eels, and grouper. Most dive shops sell a book listing the locations of these wrecks. Information on wreck diving can be obtained from the Miami Beach Chamber of Commerce.

Divers Paradise of Key Biscayne (✉ *5400 Crandon Blvd., Key Biscayne* ☎ *305/361–3483* 🌐 *www.keydivers.com*) has a complete dive shop and diving-charter service next to the Crandon Park Marina, including equipment rental and scuba instruction with PADI and NAUI affiliation. Dive trips are offered Tuesday through Friday at 10 and 1, weekends 8:30 and 1:30. The trip is $60. **South Beach Dive and Surf Center** (✉ *850 Washington Ave., Miami Beach* ☎ *305/531–6110* 🌐 *www.southbeachdivers.com*), an all-purpose dive shop with PADI affiliation, runs dives with instructors on Tuesday, Thursday, and Saturday at 10 AM, night dives on Wednesday at 5 PM, and wreck and reef dives on Sunday at 11:45 AM. The center also runs dives in Key Largo's Spiegel Grove, the second-largest wreck ever to be sunk for the intention of recreational diving, and in the Neptune Memorial Reef, inspired by the city of Atlantis and created in part using the ashes of cremated bodies. Boats depart from marinas in Miami Beach and Key Largo, in the Florida Keys.

SHOPPING

Miami teems with sophisticated shopping malls and the bustling avenues of commercial neighborhoods. But this is also a city of tiny boutiques tucked away on side streets—such as South Miami's Red, Bird, and Sunset roads intersection—and outdoor markets touting unusual and delicious wares. Stroll through Spanish-speaking neighborhoods where shops sell clothing, cigars, and other goods from all over Latin America. At an open-air flea-market stall, score an antique glass shaped like a palm tree and fill it with some fresh Jamaican ginger beer from the table next door. Or stop by your hotel gift shop and snap up an alligator magnet for your refrigerator, an ashtray made of seashells, or a bag of gumballs shaped like Florida oranges. Who can resist?

MALLS

People fly to Miami from all over the world just to shop, and the malls are high on their list of spending spots. Stop off at one or two of these climate-controlled temples to consumerism, many of which double as mega-entertainment centers, and you'll understand what makes Miami such a vibrant shopping destination.

Fodor's Choice ★ **Bal Harbour Shops.** Local and international shoppers flock to this swank collection of 100 high-end shops, boutiques, and department stores, which include such names as Christian Dior, Gucci, Hermès, Salvatore Ferragamo, Tiffany & Co., and Valentino. Many European designers open their first North American signature store at this outdoor, pedestrian-friendly mall, and many American designers open their first boutique outside of New York here. Restaurants and cafés, in tropical garden settings, overflow with style-conscious diners. People-watching at outdoor café Carpaccio is the best in town. ✉ *9700 Collins Ave., Bal Harbour* ☎ *305/866–0311* 🌐 *www.balharbourshops.com.*

CocoWalk. This popular three-story outdoor mall is busier than ever after a beautiful renovation. Chain stores like Victoria's Secret and Gap blend with specialty shops like Koko & Palenki and Edward Beiner, blending the bustle of a mall with the breathability of an open-air venue. Kiosks with cigars, beads, incense, herbs, and other small items are scattered around the ground level, and restaurants and nightlife (Cheesecake Factory, Fat Tuesday, and a 16-screen AMC theater, to name a few) line the upstairs perimeter. Hanging out and people-watching is something of a pastime here. The stores stay open almost as late as the popular restaurants and clubs. ✉ *3015 Grand Ave., Coconut Grove, Miami* ☎ *305/444–0777* 🌐 *www.cocowalk.net.*

Fodor's Choice ★ **Village of Merrick Park.** At this Mediterranean-style shopping and dining venue Neiman Marcus and Nordstrom anchor 115 specialty shops. Designers such as Etro, Tiffany & Co., Burberry, Carolina Herrera, and Gucci fulfill most high-fashion needs, and Brazilian contemporary-furniture designer Artefacto provides a taste of the haute-decor shopping options. International food venues like C'est Bon and a day spa, Elemis, offer further indulgences. ✉ *358 San Lorenzo Ave., Coral Gables* ☎ *305/529–0200* 🌐 *www.villageofmerrickpark.com.*

SHOPPING DISTRICTS

If you're over the climate-controlled slickness of shopping malls and can't face one more food-court "meal," you've got choices in Miami. Head out into the sunshine and shop the city streets, where you'll find big-name retailers and local boutiques alike. Take a break at a sidewalk café to power up on some Cuban coffee or fresh-squeezed OJ and enjoy the tropical breezes.

DOWNTOWN MIAMI

★ Miami is synonymous with good design, and this visitor-friendly shopping district is an unprecedented melding of public space and the exclusive world of design. Covering a few city blocks around NE 2nd Avenue and NE 40th Street, the **Miami Design District** (🌐 *www.miamidesigndistrict.net*) contains more than 200 showrooms and galleries, including Kartell, Ann Sacks, Poliform, and Luminaire. Recent openings of Michael's Genuine Food & Drink and Domo Japones sushi also make this trendy neighborhood a hip place to dine. Unlike most showrooms, which are typically the beat of decorators alone, the Miami Design District's showrooms are open to the public and occupy windowed, street-level spaces. Bring your quarters, as all of the parking is on the street and metered. The neighborhood even has its own high school (of art and design, of course) and hosts street parties and gallery walks. Although in many cases you'll need a decorator to secure your purchases, browsers are encouraged to consider for themselves the array of rather exclusive furnishings, decorative objects, antiques, and art.

MIAMI BEACH

★ Give your plastic a workout in South Beach shopping at the many high-profile tenants on this densely packed two-block stretch of **Collins Avenue between 5th and 10th streets.** Think Club Monaco, M.A.C, Kenneth Cole, Barney's Co-Op, and A/X Armani Exchange. Sprinkled among the upscale vendors are hair salons, spas, cafés, and such familiar stores as the Gap, Urban Outfitters, and Banana Republic. Be sure to head over one street east and west to catch the shopping on Ocean Drive and Washington Avenue.

Fodor's Choice ★ The eight-block-long pedestrian **Lincoln Road Mall** is the trendiest place on Miami Beach. Home to more than 150 shops, 20-plus art galleries and nightclubs, about 50 restaurants and cafés, and the renovated Colony Theatre, Lincoln Road, between Alton Road and Washington Avenue, is like the larger, more sophisticated cousin of Ocean Drive. The see-and-be-seen theme is furthered by outdoor seating at every restaurant, where well-heeled patrons lounge and discuss the people (and pet) parade passing by. An 18-screen movie theater anchors the west end of the street, which is where most of the worthwhile shops are; the far east end is mostly discount and electronics shops. Sure, there's a Pottery Barn, a Gap, and a Williams-Sonoma, but the emphasis is on emporiums with unique personalities, like En Avance, Chroma, Base, and Jonathan Adler.

WORD OF MOUTH

"South Beach is filled with cutting-edge, hip clothing shops for young women, and in addition has great nightlife and a lively street scene."

—montereybob

DOWNTOWN CORAL GABLES

Lined with trees and busy with strolling shoppers, **Miracle Mile** is the centerpiece of the downtown Coral Gables shopping district (*www.shopcoralgables.com*), which is home to men's and women's boutiques, jewelry and home-furnishings stores, and a host of exclusive couturiers and bridal shops. Running from Douglas Road to LeJeune Road and Aragon Avenue to Andalusia Avenue, more than 30 first-rate restaurants offer everything from French to Indian cuisine, and art galleries and the Actors' Playhouse give the area a cultural flair.

SPECIALTY STORES

Beyond the shopping malls and the big-name retailers, Greater Miami has all manner of merchandise to tempt even the casual browser. For consumers on a mission to find certain items—art deco antiques or cigars, for instance—the city streets burst with a rewarding collection of specialty shops.

ANTIQUES

★ **Architectural Antiques** (✉ *2520 SW 28th La., Coconut Grove* ☎ *305/285–1330* *www.miamiantique.com*) carries an enormous selection of antique lighting, as well as large and eclectic items—railroad crossing signs, statues, English roadsters. There's also antique furniture, paintings, and silverware, all in a cluttered setting that makes shopping an adventure.

Artisan Antiques Art Deco (✉ *110 NE 40th St., Miami Design District* ☎ *305/573–5619*) purveys china, crystal, mirrors, and armoires from the French–art deco period, but an assortment of 1930s radiator covers, which can double as funky sideboards, is what's really neat here. The shop is open Monday through Friday.

★ **Senzatempo** (✉ *1680 Michigan Ave., Suite 1015, South Beach, Miami Beach* ☎ *305/534–5588* *www.senzatempo.com*), once a popular showroom, is now a warehouse, but buyers can stop in its Lincoln Road area offices to place orders for great vintage home accessories by European and American designers of the 1930s through the 1970s, including electric fans, klieg lights, and chrome furniture.

Valerio Antiques (✉ *250 Valencia Ave., Coral Gables* ☎ *305/448–6779*) carries fine French art deco furniture, bronze sculptures, shagreen boxes, and original art glass by Gallé and Loetz, among others.

BEAUTY

Fodor's Choice ★ **Brownes & Co.** (✉ *841 Lincoln Rd., Miami Beach* ☎ *305/532–8703* *www.brownesbeauty.com*) provides luxurious products to those who appreciate them the most. Cosmetics include Molton Brown, Nars, Le Clerc, and others. It also sells herbal remedies and upscale hair and body products from Bumble and bumble. Just try to resist something from the collection of French, Portuguese, and Italian soaps in various scents and sizes. A popular in-house salon, **Some Like It Hot** (☎ *305/538–7544*), offers some of the best waxing in town.

BOOKS

Fodor's Choice ★ **Books & Books, Inc.** (✉ *265 Aragon Ave., Coral Gables* ☎ *305/442–4408* ✉ *927 Lincoln Rd., Miami Beach* ☎ *305/532–3222* ✉ *9700 Collins Ave., Bal Harbour* ☎ *305/864–4241*), Greater Miami's only independent English-language bookshops, specialize in contemporary and classical literature as well as in books on the arts, architecture, Florida, and Cuba. At any of its three locations you can lounge at a café or, at the Coral Gables store, browse the photography gallery. All stores host regular poetry and other readings.

CIGARS

El Credito Cigars (✉ *1106 SW 8th St., Little Havana* ☎ *305/858–4162*), in the heart of Little Havana, employs rows of workers at wooden benches. They rip, cut, and wrap giant tobacco leaves, and press the cigars in vises. El Credito cigars are known for their good quality and relatively low price. Dedicated smokers find their way here to pick up a $90 bundle or to peruse the *gigantes, supremos, panatelas*, and Churchills available in natural or *maduro* wrappers. **Sabor Havana Cigars** (✉ *2309 Ponce de León Blvd, Coral Gables* ☎ *305/444–1764* 🌐 *www.saborhavanacigar.com*) offers rare cigars and Spanish wine to help you relax. **Sosa Family Cigars** (✉ *3475 SW 8th St., Little Havana* ☎ *305/446–2606*), once known as Macabi, carries a wide selection of premium and house cigars in a humidified shop. There's a selection of wines for purchase. Humidors and other accessories are also available.

CLOTHING FOR MEN AND WOMEN

★ **Base** (✉ *939 Lincoln Rd., Miami Beach* ☎ *305/531–4982* 🌐 *www.baseworld.com*) is a constantly evolving shop with an intriguing magazine section, an international CD station with DJ, and groovy home accessories. Stop here for men's and women's eclectic clothing, shoes, and accessories that mix Japanese design with Caribbean-inspired materials. The often-present house-label designer may help select your wardrobe's newest addition.

Intermix (✉ *634 Collins Ave., Miami Beach* ☎ *305/531–5950* 🌐 *www.intermixonline.com*) is a modern New York–based boutique with the variety of a department store. You'll find fancy dresses, stylish shoes, slinky accessories, and trendy looks by sassy and somewhat pricey designers like Chloé, Stella McCartney, Marc Jacobs, Moschino, and Diane von Furstenberg.

Kristine Michael (✉ *7271 SW 57th Ave., South Miami* ☎ *305/665–7717*) is a local fashion institution for suburban moms and University of Miami students. The store's hip and up-to-the-minute selection of pieces from Theory, Alice & Olivia, Kors, and C & C California stands out from the national retailers across the street at the Shops at Sunset Place.

★ **Silvia Tcherassi** (✉ *350 San Lorenzo Ave., Coral Gables* ☎ *305/461–0009* 🌐 *www.silviatcherassi.com*), the Colombian designer's signature boutique in the Village of Merrick Park, features feminine and frilly dresses and separates accented with chiffon, tulle, and sequins.

SWIMWEAR

South Beach Surf & Dive Shop (✉ *850 Washington Ave., Miami Beach* ☎ *305/531–6110* 🌐 *www.southbeachdivers.com*) is a one-stop shop for beach gear—from clothing and swimwear for guys and gals to wake-, surf-, and skateboards. The shop also offers multilingual surfing, scuba, snorkeling, and dive lessons and trips.

JEWELRY

Fodor's Choice ★ **Beverlee Kagan** (✉ *5831 Sunset Dr., South Miami* ☎ *305/663–1937* 🌐 *kaganjewelry.com*) deals in a wide selection of vintage and antique jewelry, including art deco–era bangles, bracelets, and cuff links.

Jose Roca Fine Jewelry Designs (✉ *297 Miracle Mile, Coral Gables* ☎ *305/448–2808*) designs fine jewelry from precious metals and stones. If you have a particular piece that you would like to create, this is the place to have it meticulously executed.

Me & Ro (✉ *Shore Club hotel, 1901 Collins Ave., Miami Beach* ☎ *305/672–3566* 🌐 *www.meandrojewelry.com*) is a trendy New York–based jewelry shop run by Michele Quan and Robin Renzi, with a celebrity clientele that reads like a who's who. Designs are crafted from silver, gold, and semiprecious stones.

★ **MIA Jewels** (✉ *1439 Alton Rd., Miami Beach* ☎ *305/532–6064* 🌐 *www.miajewels.com*) is an Alton Road jewelry and accessories boutique known for its colorful, gem- and bead-laden, gold and silver earrings, necklaces, bracelets, and brooches by lines such as Cousin Claudine, Amrita, and Alexis Bittar. This is a shoo-in store for everyone: you'll find things for trend lovers (gold-studded chunky Lucite bangles), classicists (long, colorful, wraparound beaded necklaces), and ice lovers (long Swarovski crystal cabin necklaces) alike.

ONLY IN MIAMI

★ **Dog Bar** (✉ *1684 Jefferson Ave., Miami Beach* ☎ *305/532–5654*), just north of Lincoln Road's main drag, caters to enthusiastic animal owners with a variety of unique items for the pampered pet, including a luxurious, over-the-top pet sofa imported from Italy and offered in cowhide, leather, or vinyl fitted into a chrome frame.

La Casa de las Guayaberas (✉ *5840 SW 8th St., Little Havana* ☎ *305/266–9683*) sells custom-made guayaberas, the natty four-pocket dress shirts favored by Latin men. Hundreds are also available off the rack.

SHOES

★ Design your own couture stiletto or stylish sandal in just a half hour (cobblers are fast at work while you wait) at **Morgan Miller Shoes** (✉ *618 Lincoln Rd., Miami Beach* ☎ *305/672–8700* 🌐 *www.morganmillershoes.com*). The selection of materials is seemingly endless: wood, resin, or cork heels or sandals; leather, alligator, snake, or ostrich straps in a myriad of vibrant colors; and more than 100 crystals and jewels to choose from. Prices range from a basic sandal with a denim strap for about $70 to an over-the-top pair of strappy lime-green, snakeskin stilettos laced with Swarovski crystals, colored tacks, and hanging jewels, topping $500. This is a great store for footwear fashionistas, but you don't have to be a shoe addict to enjoy finding the right fit here.

OUTDOOR MARKETS

Pass the mangoes! Greater Miami's farmers' markets and flea markets take advantage of the region's balmy weather and tropical delights to lure shoppers to open-air stalls filled with produce and collectibles.

★ **Coconut Grove Farmers Market.** The most organic of Miami's outdoor markets specializes in a mouthwatering array of local produce as well as such ready-to-eat goodies as cashew butter, homemade salad dressings, and fruit pies (some of the offerings can taste stodgy to the non-organic eater). If you are looking for a downright granola crowd and experience, pack your Birkenstocks because this is it. ✉ *Grand Ave. and Margaret St., Coconut Grove* ☎ *305/238–7747.*

Coral Gables Farmers Market. Some 25 local produce growers and plant vendors sell herbs, fruits, fresh-squeezed juices, chutneys, cakes, and muffins at this market between Coral Gables' City Hall and Merrick Park. Artists also join in. Regular events include gardening workshops, children's activities, and cooking demonstrations offered by Coral Gables' master chefs. Mid-January through late March only. ✉ *405 Biltmore Way, Coral Gables* ☎ *305/460–5311.*

★ **Lincoln Road Antique and Collectibles Market.** Interested in picking up samples of Miami's ever-present modern and moderne furniture and accessories? This outdoor show offers eclectic goods that should satisfy post impressionists, deco-holics, Edwardians, Bauhausers, Goths, and '50s junkies. ✉ *Lincoln and Alton Rds., Miami Beach* ☎ *305/673–4991.*

Lincoln Road Farmers Market. With all the familiar trappings of a farmers' market (except for farmers—most of the people selling veggies appear to be resellers), this is quickly becoming a must-see event before or after visiting the Antique and Collectibles Market. It brings local produce and bakery vendors to the Lincoln Road Mall and often features plant workshops, art sales, and children's activities. This is a good place to pick up live orchids, too. ✉ *Lincoln Rd. between Meridian and Euclid Aves., Miami Beach* ☎ *305/673–4166.*

NIGHTLIFE

Miami's pulse pounds with nonstop nightlife that reflects the area's potent cultural mix. On sultry, humid nights with the huge full moon rising out of the ocean and fragrant night-blooming jasmine intoxicating the senses, who can resist Cuban salsa, Jamaican reggae, and Dominican merengue, with some disco and hip-hop thrown in for good measure? When this place throws a party, hips shake, fingers snap, bodies touch. It's no wonder many clubs are still rocking at 5 AM.

FIND OUT WHAT'S GOING ON

The *Miami Herald* (🌐 *www.miamiherald.com*) is a good source for information on what to do in town. The Weekend section of the newspaper, included in the Friday edition, has an annotated guide to

From salsa and merengue to disco and hip-hop, Miami's dance clubs cater to diverse styles of music.

everything from plays and galleries to concerts and nightclubs. The "Ticket" column of this section details the week's entertainment highlights. Or, you can pick up the free weekly tabloid *Miami New Times* (🌐 *www.miaminewtimes.com*), the city's largest free alternative newspaper, published each Thursday. It lists nightclubs, concerts, and special events; reviews plays and movies; and provides in-depth coverage of the local music scene. "Night & Day" is a rundown of the week's cultural highlights. *Ocean Drive* (🌐 *www.oceandrive.com*), Miami Beach's model-strewn, upscale fashion and lifestyle magazine, squeezes club, bar, restaurant, and events listings in with fashion spreads, reviews, and personality profiles. Paparazzi photos of local party people and celebrities give you a taste of Greater Miami nightlife before you even dress up to paint the town.

The Spanish-language *El Nuevo Herald* (🌐 *www.elnuevoherald.com*), published by the *Miami Herald,* has extensive information on Spanish-language arts and entertainment, including dining reviews, concert previews, and nightclub highlights. Spanish-language radio, primarily on the AM dial, is also a good source of information about arts events. Tune in to WXDJ (95.7 FM), Amor (107.5 FM), or Radio Mambi (710 AM).

BARS AND LOUNGES

One of Greater Miami's most popular pursuits is barhopping. Bars range from intimate enclaves to showy see-and-be-seen lounges to loud, raucous frat parties. There's a New York–style flair to some of the newer lounges, which are increasingly catering to the Manhattan party crowd

THE VELVET ROPES

How to get past the velvet ropes at the hottest South Beach nightspots? First, if you're staying at a hotel, use the concierge. Decide which clubs you want to check out (consult *Ocean Drive* magazine celebrity pages if you want to be among the glitterati), and the concierge will e-mail, fax, or call in your names to the clubs so you'll be on the guest list when you arrive. This means much easier access and usually no cover charge (which can be upward of $20) if you arrive before midnight. Guest list or no guest list, follow these pointers: make sure there are more women than men in your group. Dress up—casual chic is the dress code. For men this means no sneakers, no shorts, no sleeveless vests, and no shirts unbuttoned past the top button. For women, provocative and seductive is fine; overly revealing is not. Black is always right. At the door: don't name-drop—no one takes it seriously. Don't be pushy while trying to get the doorman's attention. Wait until you make eye contact, then be cool and easygoing. If you decide to tip him (which most bouncers don't expect), be discreet and pleasant, not big-bucks obnoxious—a $10 or $20 bill quietly passed will be appreciated, however. With the right dress and the right attitude, you'll be on the dance floor rubbing shoulders with South Beach's finest clubbers in no time.

who escape to South Beach for long weekends. If you're looking for a relatively non-frenetic evening, your best bet is one of the chic hotel bars on Collins Avenue.

COCONUT GROVE

Monty's in the Grove. The outdoor bar here has Caribbean flair, thanks especially to live calypso and island music. It's very kid-friendly on weekends, when Mom and Dad can kick back and enjoy a beer and the raw bar while the youngsters dance to live music. Evenings bring a DJ and reggae music. ✉ *2550 S. Bayshore Dr., at Aviation Ave.* ☎ *305/856–3992* 🌐 *www.montysbayshore.com.*

CORAL GABLES

Bar at Ponce and Giralda. One of the oldest bars in South Florida, the old Hofbrau has been reincarnated and now serves vibrant, live reggae music on Saturday nights and a non-touristy vibe. ✉ *172 Giralda Ave., at Ponce de León Blvd., Coral Gables* ☎ *305/442–2730.*

Globe. The centerpiece of Coral Gables's emphasis on nightlife draws crowds of twentysomethings who spill into the street for live jazz on Saturday evenings and a bistro-style menu nightly. Free appetizers and drink specials every weekday attract a strong happy-hour following. Outdoor tables and an art-heavy, upscale interior are comfortable, if you can find space to squeeze in. ✉ *377 Alhambra Circle, at Le Jeune Rd.* ☎ *305/445–3555* 🌐 *www.theglobecafe.com.*

John Martin's Restaurant and Irish Pub. The cozy upscale Irish pub hosts an Irish cabaret on Saturday night with live contemporary and traditional music—sometimes by an Irish band—storytelling, and dancers.

✉ *253 Miracle Mile, at Ponce de León Blvd.* ☎ *305/445–3777* 🌐 *www.johnmartins.com.*

DOWNTOWN MIAMI

Fodor's Choice ★ **Tobacco Road.** Opened in 1912, this classic holds Miami's oldest liquor license: No. 0001! Upstairs, in a space that was occupied by a speakeasy during Prohibition, local and national blues bands perform nightly. There is excellent bar food, a dinner menu, and a selection of single-malt scotches, bourbons, and cigars. This is the hangout of grizzled journalists, bohemians en route to or from nowhere, and club kids seeking a way station before the real parties begin. ✉ *626 S. Miami Ave., Downtown Miami* ☎ *305/374–1198* 🌐 *www.tobacco-road.com.*

SOUTH BEACH

★ **Buck 15.** This hidden lounge above popular Lincoln Road eatery Miss Yip Café is one of Miami's best-kept secrets. The tiny club manages to play amazing music—a rock-heavy mix of songs you loved but haven't heard in ages—and maintain a low-key, unpretentious attitude. The drinks are reasonable, and the well-worn couches are great to dance on. The club attracts local hipsters and some gay couples. ✉ *707 Lincoln Rd., Miami Beach* ☎ *305/538–3815* 🌐 *www.buck15.com.*

Club Deuce. Although it's completely unglam, this pool hall attracts a colorful crowd of clubbers, locals, celebs—and just about anyone else. Locals consider it the best spot for a cheap drink. ✉ *222 14th St., at Collins Ave., Miami Beach* ☎ *305/531–6200.*

Lost Weekend. Players at this pool hall are serious about their pastime, so it's hard to get a table on weekends. The full bar, which has 150 kinds of beers, draws an eclectic crowd, from yuppies to drag queens to slumming celebs like Lenny Kravitz and the guys in Hootie and the Blowfish. ✉ *218 Española Way, at Collins Ave., Miami Beach* ☎ *305/672–1707.*

Mynt Ultra Lounge. The name of this upscale nightclub, which opens its doors at midnight, is meant to be taken literally—not only are the walls bathed in soft green shades, but an aromatherapy system pumps out different fresh scents, including mint. Celebs like Enrique Iglesias, Angie Everhart, and Queen Latifah have cooled down here. ✉ *1921 Collins Ave., Miami Beach* ☎ *786/276–6132* 🌐 *www.myntlounge.com.*

★ **The National.** Don't miss a drink at the hotel's nifty wooden bar, one of many elements original to the 1939 building, which give it such a sense of its era that you'd expect to see Ginger Rogers and Fred Astaire hoofing it along the polished lobby floor. The adjoining Martini Room has a great collection of cigar and old airline stickers and vintage Bacardi ads on the walls. Don't forget to take a peek at the long, sexy pool. ✉ *1677 Collins Ave., Miami Beach* ☎ *305/532–2311* 🌐 *www.nationalhotel.com.*

Fodor's Choice ★ **Rose Bar at the Delano.** The airy lobby lounge at South Beach's trendiest hotel manages to look dramatic but not cold, with long, snow-white, gauzy curtains and huge white pillars separating conversation nooks (this is where Ricky Martin shot the video for "La Vida Loca"). A pool table brings the austerity down to earth. There's also an expansive poolside

12

bar, dotted with intimate poolside beds (bottle service required) and private cabanas to reserve for the evening—for a not-so-nominal fee, of course. ✉ *1685 Collins Ave., South Beach, Miami* ☎ *305/672–2000.*

Santo Restaurant. This Lincoln Road lounge is where Miami's Latin crowd (and anyone who loves Latin music) comes to party. During the day, Santo serves eclectic fare with a Latin twist. On Thursday through Saturday evenings, the back half of the venue turns into a stage for nightly live and DJ performances, ranging from salsa to reggaeton. ✉ *430 Lincoln Rd., Miami Beach* ☎ *305/532–2882 or 305/531–0900.*

Fodor's Choice ★ **SkyBar at the Shore Club.** Splendor-in-the-garden is the theme at this haute spot by the sea, where multiple lounging areas are joined together. Daybeds, glowing Moroccan lanterns, and maximum atmosphere make a visit to this chic outdoor lounge worthwhile. Groove to dance music in the Red Room, or enjoy an aperitif and Japanese bar bites at Nobu Lounge. The Red Room, Nobu Restaurant and Lounge, Italian restaurant Ago, and SkyBar all connect around the Shore Club's pool area. ✉ *1901 Collins Ave., Miami Beach* ☎ *305/695–3100.*

CABARET, COMEDY, AND SUPPER CLUBS

You can still find the kind of song-and-dance extravaganzas that were produced by every major Miami Beach hotel in the 1950s (think scantily clad showgirls and feathered headdresses). But also on tap are modern-day affairs like flamenco shows, salsa dancing, and comedy clubs.

COCONUT GROVE

Improv Comedy Club. This long-standing comedy club hosts nationally touring comics nightly. Comedy-club regulars will recognize Margaret Cho and George Wallace, and everyone knows Damon Wayans and Chris Rock, both of whom have taken the stage here. Urban Comedy Showcase is held Tuesday and Wednesday, with an open-mike part of the evening on Wednesday. A full menu is available. ✉ *Streets of Mayfair, 3390 Mary St., at Grand Ave.* ☎ *305/441–8200* 🌐 *www.miamiimprov.com.*

LITTLE HAVANA

Casa Panza. The visionary Madrileñan owners of this Little Havana restaurant have energized the neighborhood with a twice-weekly tribute to *La Virgen del Rocío* (the patron saint of a province in Andalusia), in which the room is darkened and diners are handed lighted candles and sheet music. Everyone readily joins in the singing, making for a truly enjoyable evening. There is flamenco dancing on Friday and Saturday. ✉ *1620 SW 8th St.* ☎ *305/643–5343.*

12

DANCE CLUBS

DOWNTOWN MIAMI

Lombardi's. You can shake it salsa- or merengue-style until midnight to live bands that perk up diners on Friday, Saturday, and Sunday nights at this downtown restaurant and bar. ✉ *Bayside Marketplace, 401 Biscayne Blvd.* ☎ *305/381–9580* 🌐 *www.lombardisbayside.com.*

Space. Want 24-hour partying? Here's the place. Created from four downtown warehouses, Space has two levels (one blasts house music; the other reverberates with hip-hop), an outdoor patio, a New York–style industrial look, and a 24-hour liquor license. It's open on weekends only, and you'll need to look good to be allowed past the velvet ropes. ✉ *34 NE 11th St.* ☎ *305/375–0001* 🌐 *www.clubspace.com.*

SOUTH BEACH

Greater Miami's gay action centers on the night clubs in South Beach. That tiny strip of sand rivals New York and San Francisco as a hub of gay nightlife—if not in the number of clubs then in the intensity of the partying. The neighborhood's large gay population and the laissez-faire attitudes of the hip straights that live and visit here encourage gay-friendliness at most South Beach venues that are not specifically gay.

Fodor's Choice ★ **Cameo.** One of Miami's ultimate dance clubs, Cameo, formerly known as Crobar, has gotten a welcome face-lift. Gone is the industrial feel, but all-star DJs and plentiful dance space remain, and plush VIP lounges have been added. If you can brave the velvet rope, Saturday-night parties are the best. ✉ *1445 Washington Ave.* ☎ *305/532–2667.*

Nikki Beach Club. With its swell on-the-beach location, the full-service Nikki Beach Club has become a favorite pretty-people and celeb hangout. Tepees and hammocks on the sand, dance floors both under the stars and inside, and beach parties make this a true South Beach experience. ✉ *1 Ocean Dr.* ☎ *305/538–1111.*

Score. This popular bar is the see-and-be-seen central of Miami's gay community. DJs spin every night of the week except Sunday, a popular karaoke night where everything goes. ✉ *727 Lincoln Rd.* ☎ *305/535–1111* 🌐 *www.scorebar.net.*

LIVE MUSIC

DOWNTOWN MIAMI

Fodor's Choice ★ **Tobacco Road.** Live blues, R&B, and jazz bands are on tap seven days a week along with food and drink at this Miami institution. ✉ *626 S. Miami Ave.* ☎ *305/374–1198* 🌐 *www.tobacco-road.com.*

SOUTH BEACH

★ **Jazid.** If you're looking for an unpretentious alternative to the velvet-rope nightclubs, this unassuming, live-music hot spot is a standout on the strip. Eight-piece bands play danceable Latin rhythms, as well as reggae, hip-hop, and fusion sounds. Get ready for a late night though, as bands are just getting started at midnight. They play every night of the week. Call ahead to reserve a table. ✉ *1342 Washington Ave.* ☎ *305/673–9372* 🌐 *www.jazid.net.*

WHERE TO EAT

Updated by Michael de Zayas

Miami's restaurant scene has exploded in the last few years, with dozens of great new restaurants springing up left and right. The melting pot of residents and visitors has brought an array of sophisticated, tasty cuisine. Little Havana is still king for Cuban fare, while Miami Beach is swept up in a trend of fusion cuisine, which combines Asian, French, American, and Latin cuisine with sumptuous—and pricy—results. Downtown Miami and the Design District especially are home to some of the city's best spots, and they're all new. Since Miami dining is a part of the trendy nightlife scene, most dinners don't start until 8 or 9 PM, and may go well into the night. Hot spots fill up quickly, so come before 7 or make reservations. Attire is usually casual-chic, but patrons like to dress to impress. Prices tend to stay high in hot spots like Lincoln Road; but if you venture off the beaten path, you can find delicious food for reasonable prices. When you get your bill, check whether a gratuity is already included; most restaurants add between 15% and 18% (ostensibly for the convenience of, and protection from, the many Latin American and European tourists who are used to this practice in their homelands), but supplement it depending on your opinion of the service.

WHAT IT COSTS

	¢	$	$$	$$$	$$$$
AT DINNER	under $10	$10–$15	$15–$20	$20–$30	over $30

Price per person for a median main course or equivalent combination of smaller dishes.

COCONUT GROVE, CORAL GABLES, AND KEY BISCAYNE

COCONUT GROVE

$–$$ FRENCH

✕ **Le Bouchon du Grove.** This French bistro with a supercharged atmosphere is a great spot in the heart of the Grove. Waiters tend to lean on chairs while taking orders, and managers and owners freely mix with the clientele, making Le Bouchon perhaps the last remaining vestige of the Grove's bohemian days. The result is one big happy family, all enjoying traditional French pâtés, gratins, quiches, chicken fricassee, mussels, duck-leg confit, and steak frites. The lively mood inside is matched by the throngs that parade outside the French doors. Breakfast is served daily. ✉ *3430 Main Hwy.* ☎ *305/448–6060* 🌐 *www.lebouchondugrove.com* 💳 *AE, MC, V* ✣ *5C.*

CORAL GABLES

$ CUBAN

Fodor's Choice ★

✕ **Havana Harry's.** When Cuban families want a home-cooked meal but don't want to cook it themselves, they come to this big, unassuming restaurant. In fact, you're likely to see whole families here, from babes in arms to grandmothers. The fare is traditional Cuban: the long thin steaks known as *bistec palomilla* (a panfried steak), roast chicken with citrus marinade, and fried pork chunks; contemporary flourishes—mango sauce and guava-painted pork roast—are kept to a minimum.

BEST BETS FOR MIAMI DINING

Fodor's writers and editors have selected their favorite restaurants by price, cuisine, and experience in the Best Bets lists *below*. In the first column, Fodor's Choice designations represent the "best of the best" in every price category. Find specific details about a restaurant in the full reviews, listed alphabetically by neighborhood.

Fodor's Choice ★

Azul, Downtown Miami, p. 581
Big Pink, South Beach, p. 585
The Forge, Mid-Beach, p. 584
Havana Harry's, Coral Gables, p. 576
Joey's, Wynwood, p. 579
Michael's Genuine Food & Drink, Design District, p. 579
Michy's, Design District, p. 581
Palacio de los Jugos, Coral Gables, p. 578
Pascal's on Ponce, Coral Gables, p. 578
Sra. Martinez, Design District, p. 581
Timó, Sunny Isles, p. 585

By Price

¢

Palacio de los Jugos, Coral Gables, p. 578

$

Big Pink, South Beach, p. 585
Las Culebrinas, Coral Gables, p. 578
Tobacco Road, Downtown Miami, p. 582
Tutto Pasta, Little Havana, p. 583
Versailles, Little Havana, p. 583

$$

Hy-Vong Vietnamese Cuisine, Little Havana, p. 583
Joey's, Wynwood, p. 579
Novecento, Downtown Miami, p. 582
Sra. Martinez, Design District, p. 581

$$$

Michael's Genuine Food & Drink, Downtown Miami, p. 579

$$$$

Azul, Downtown Miami, p. 581
The Forge, Mid-Beach, p. 584
Pascal's on Ponce, Coral Gables, p. 578

By Cuisine

AMERICAN

Big Pink, South Beach, p. 585
Michael's Genuine Food & Drink, Downtown Miami, p. 579
News Café, South Beach, p. 592

ASIAN

Hy-Vong Vietnamese Cuisine, Little Havana, p. 583
SushiSamba Dromo, South Beach, p. 593

ITALIAN

Café Prima Pasta, North Beach, p. 584
Osteria del Teatro, South Beach, p. 593
Timó, Sunny Isles, p. 585

SEAFOOD

Joe's Stone Crab, South Beach, p. 589
La Marea, South Beach, p. 589
Nemo, South Beach, p. 592
Prime One Twelve, South Beach, p. 593
Tuscan Steak, South Beach, p. 594

By Experience

CHILD-FRIENDLY

Tutto Pasta, Little Havana, p. 583
Versailles, Little Havana, p. 583

HOT SPOTS

Blue Door at the Delano, South Beach, p. 588
Meat Market, South Beach, p. 589
Michael's Genuine Food & Drink, Downtown Miami, p. 579

Most dishes come with white rice, black beans, and a choice of ripe or green plantains. The sweet ripe ones offer a good contrast to the savory dishes. This is an excellent value. Start with the $5.95 *mariquitas* (plantain chips) with guacamole. ✉ *4612 Le Jeune Rd.* ☎ *305/661–2622* ▭ *AE, D, MC, V* ✥ *5C.*

$ SPANISH ✕ **Las Culebrinas.** Each of Las Culebrinas' five locations in Miami tends to draw throngs of adoring diners for Spanish tapas and Cuban steaks. Tapas here are not small; some are entrée size like the Frisbee-size Spanish *tortilla* (omelet). Our suggestion: indulge in a tender fillet of crocodile, fresh fish, or the grilled pork stuffed with mashed bananas, followed by a dessert of *crema Catalana,* caramelized at your table with a blowtorch—this is a good time to remind your kids not to touch. ✉ *4700 W. Flagler St., at NW 47th Ave.* ☎ *305/445–2337* ⊕ *www.culebrinas.com* ▭ *AE, MC, V* ✥ *4C.*

$$$$ CARIBBEAN ✕ **Ortanique on the Mile.** Cascading ortaniques, a Jamaican hybrid orange, are hand-painted on columns in this warm, welcoming yellow dining room. Food is vibrant in taste and color, as delicious as it is beautiful. Though there is no denying that the strong, full flavors are imbued with island breezes, chef-partner Cindy Hutson's personal cuisine goes beyond Caribbean refinements. The menu centers on fish, since Hutson has a special way with it, and the Caribbean bouillabaisse is not to be missed. On Sunday there is live jazz. ✉ *278 Miracle Mile* ☎ *305/446–7710* ⊕ *www.cindyhutsoncuisine.com* ▭ *AE, DC, MC, V* ⊗ *No lunch weekends* ✥ *5C.*

¢ CUBAN Fodor's Choice ★ ✕ **Palacio de los Jugos.** This joint is one of the easiest and truest ways to see Miami's local Latin life in action. It's also one of the best fruit-shake shacks you'll ever come across (ask for a juice of—"*jugo de*"—mamey, melón, or guanabana, a sweet-tart equatorial fruit, and you can't go wrong). Besides the rows and rows of fresh tropical fruits and vegetables, and the shakes you can make with any of them, this boisterous indoor-outdoor market has numerous food counters where you can get just about any Cuban food—tamales, rice and beans, a *pan con lechón* (roast pork on Cuban bread), fried pork rinds, or a coconut split before you and served with a straw. Order your food at a counter and eat it along with local families at rows of outdoor picnic-style tables next to the parking lot. It's disorganized, chaotic, and not for those cutting calories, but it's delicious and undeniably the real thing. ✉ *5721 W. Flagler St.* ☎ *305/264–4557* ⊕ *www.elpalaciodelosjugosonline.com* ▭ *No credit cards* ✥ *4B.*

$$$$ FRENCH Fodor's Choice ★ ✕ **Pascal's on Ponce.** This French gem amid the Coral Gables restaurant district is always full, thanks to chef-proprietor Pascal Oudin's assured and consistent cuisine. Oudin forgoes the glitz and fussiness often associated with French cuisine, and instead opts for a simple, small, refined dining room that won't overwhelm patrons. The equally sensible menu includes a superb gnocchi appetizer (ask for mushrooms on top). The main course is a tough choice between oven-roasted duck with poached pears, milk-fed veal loin, and diver sea scallops with beef short rib. It opened in 2000. Ask your expert waiter to pair dishes with a selection from Pascal's impressive wine list, and, for dessert, order the bittersweet chocolate soufflé. ✉ *2611 Ponce de León Blvd.* ☎ *305/444–2024*

www.pascalmiami.com AE, D, DC, MC, V *Closed Sun. No lunch Sat.* *5C.*

KEY BISCAYNE

$$$$ ITALIAN **Cioppino.** Few visitors think to venture out to the far end of Key Biscayne for dinner, but making the journey to the soothing grounds of this quiet Ritz-Carlton property on the beach is worth it. Choose your view: the ornate dining room near the exhibition kitchen or the alfresco area with views of landscaped gardens or breeze-brushed beaches. Choosing your dishes may be more difficult, given the many rich, luscious Italian options, including imported cheeses, olive oils, risottos and fresh fish flown in daily. Items range from the creamy burrata mozzarella and authentic pasta dishes to tantalizing risotto with organic spinach and roasted quail, all expertly matched with fine, vintage, rare, and boutique wines. An after-dinner drink and live music at the old-Havana-style RUMBAR inside the hotel is another treat. *Ritz-Carlton, 455 Grand Bay Dr.* *305/365–4286* AE, D, DC, MC, V *6E.*

12

MIAMI

DESIGN DISTRICT

$$ ITALIAN Fodor's Choice ★ **Joey's.** This joyfully good and merrily buzzing new place is literally the only restaurant in Wynwood, an emerging neighborhood to the south of the Design District. But this new restaurant already has that rarest of blessings—the sizzling vibe of a thriving neighborhood restaurant that everyone seems to adore. Its contagious charm begins with the service: informal, but focused, very professional, and attentive. Then comes the food: Veneto native chef Ivo Mazzon does homage to fresh ingredients prepared simply and perfectly. A full line of original flatbread pizzas contend for tops in Miami. The *dolce e piccante* has figs, Gorgonzola, honey, and hot pepper; it's unexpectedly sweet at first bite, and at bite 10 you'll be swearing it's the best you've ever had. The wine list is small but the product of much discernment. Because it's little and in a weird spot, Joey's makes you feel that you're the first to discover it; and that you've made a new friend in Miami—one you'll need to visit again very soon. *2506 NW 2 Ave., Design District* *305/438–0488* *www.joeyswynwood.com* AE, D, MC, V *4D.*

$$$ AMERICAN Fodor's Choice ★ **Michael's Genuine Food & Drink.** Though it's new, Michael's is already frequently cited as Miami's top restaurant. This indoor-outdoor bistro in Miami's Design District relies on fresh ingredients and a hip but unpretentious vibe to lure diners. Beautifully arranged combinations like crispy beef cheek with whipped celeriac, and sweet-and-spicy pork belly with kimchi explode with unlikely but satisfying flavor. Owner and chef Michael Schwartz, famous for South Beach's popular Nemo restaurant, aims for sophisticated American cuisine with an emphasis on local and organic ingredients. He gets it right. Portions are divided into small, medium, and large plates, and the smaller plates are more inventive, so you can order several and explore. Reserve two weeks in advance for weekend tables; also, consider brunch. *130 NE 40th St., Design District* *305/573–5550* *www.michaelsgenuine.com* AE, MC, V *No lunch weekends* *3D.*

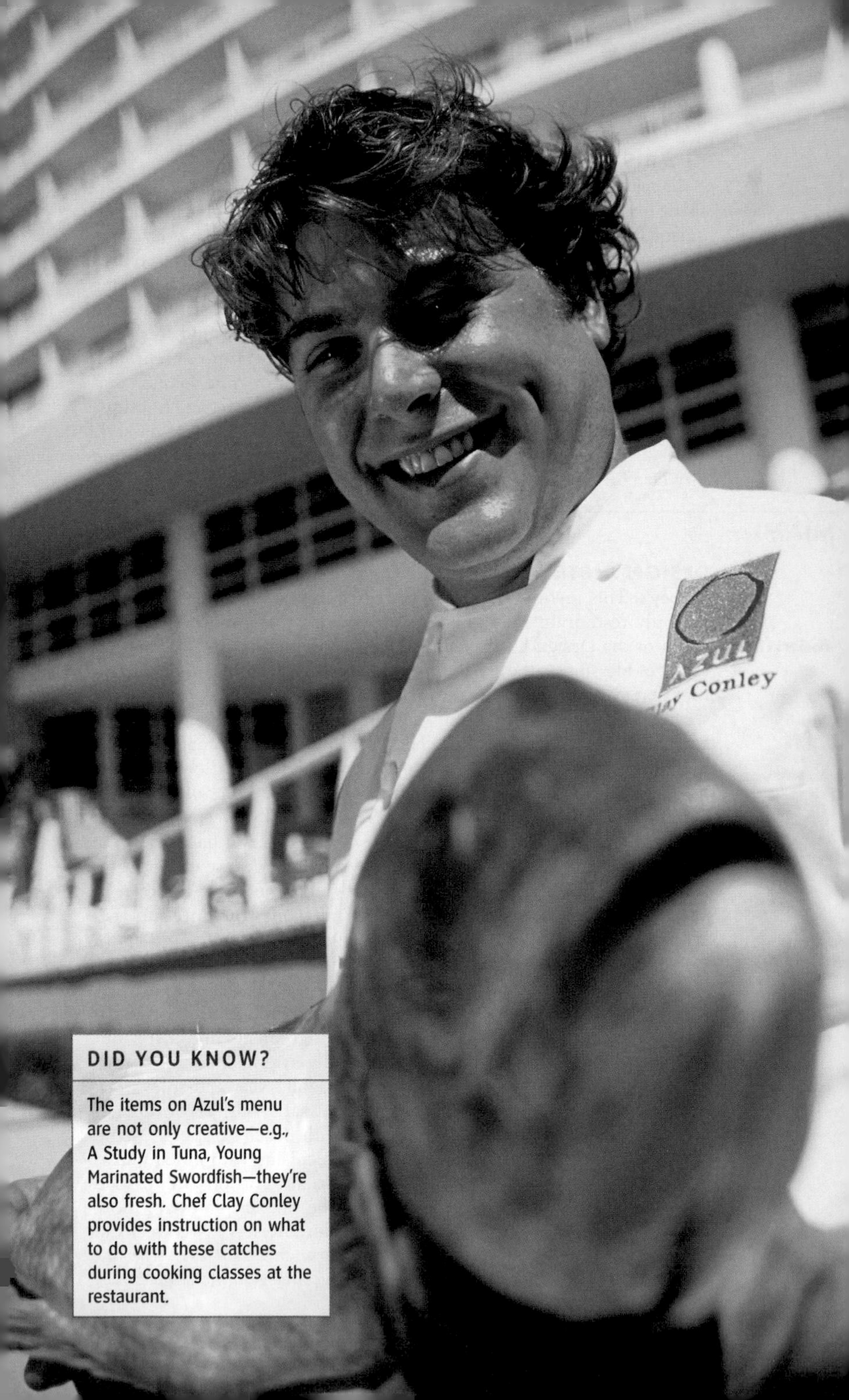

DID YOU KNOW?

The items on Azul's menu are not only creative—e.g., A Study in Tuna, Young Marinated Swordfish—they're also fresh. Chef Clay Conley provides instruction on what to do with these catches during cooking classes at the restaurant.

12

$$$ MEDITERRANEAN Fodor's Choice ★ ✕ **Michy's.** Miami's homegrown star chef Michelle Bernstein made a huge splash with the shabby-chic decor and self-named restaurant on the north end of Miami's Design District. Bernstein serves exquisite French- and Mediterranean-influenced seafood dishes at over-the-causeway (read: non-tourist-trap) prices. Plates come in half portions and full portions, which makes the restaurant even more of a deal. Can't-miss entrées include the blue cheese and *jamón serrano* (serrano ham) *croquetas*, the beef short rib, and the steak frites au poivre. ✉ *6927 Biscayne Blvd., Design District* ☎ *305/759–2001* ⊕ *www.chefmichellebernstein.com* ▭ *AE, D, DC, MC, V* ⊗ *Closed Mon. No lunch* ✣ *3E.*

$$$ SEAFOOD ✕ **Pacific Time.** Veteran travelers to Miami Beach will remember Pacific Time from Lincoln Road, where it was a favorite for nearly 15 years. The restaurant has reopened in an airy setting in the Design District that is hip and airy and unpretentious. The food is as fresh as ever, and the drinks are superb. The dinner menu has 20 inexpensive small plates, including local black grouper with red curry. Entrées include a pan-seared salt-and-pepper skate wing served over a bed of celery root with lemon butter and green apple. Try sitting in the courtyard, a pleasing lunch spot for blue-cheese burgers or tasty shrimp po' boys served on focaccia. (Note: Pacific Time is a convenient backup if you can't get a reservation at Michael's Genuine, one of the city's most popular restaurants; it's a short block away.) Finally, something amazing at PT: a truly sophisticated kids tasting menu; if you're a foodie with young kids, bring 'em here. ✉ *35 NE 40th St., Design District* ☎ *305/722–7369* ⊕ *www.pacifictimerestaurant.com* ▭ *AE, D, MC, V* ✣ *3D.*

$$ SPANISH Fodor's Choice ★ ✕ **Sra. Martinez.** For a good time with food, dial up Sra. Martinez. Michelle Bernstein's second restaurant (her, first, Michy's, is a must-visit for Miami foodies) opened in November 2008; the name is a sly take on her name—her husband is David Martinez—which is good, because something as artful as this new restaurant deserves a signature. Bernstein anchors her menu at Sra. Martinez in traditional Spanish cuisine, a brilliant jumping-off point for her wildly successful experiments in flavor, texture, and plate composition. Order several dishes from the Cold & Crisp ($5–$18) and Warm & Lush ($8–$23) sections, which feature small plates of takes on traditional tapas. The cuisine is modern, colorful and, above all, fun. Cocktail lovers will be delighted by the inventive, high-quality selections like the Jalisco Mule, a sly (and spicy) take on the traditional Moscow Mule, made with tequila and ginger beer, and laced with chili syrup. It's no wonder this restaurant has already become one of the best and most exciting in the city. ✉ *4000 NE 2 Ave., Design District* ☎ *305/573–5474* ⊕ *www.chefmichellebernstein.com* ▭ *AE, D, DC, MC, V* ⊗ *Closed Sun. No Lunch Sat.* ✣ *3D.*

DOWNTOWN MIAMI

$$$$ ECLECTIC Fodor's Choice ★ ✕ **Azul.** From chef Clay Conley's exotically rendered Asian-Mediterranean cuisine to the thoughtful service staff who graciously anticipate your broader dining needs, Azul has sumptuously conquered the devil in the details. Does your sleeveless blouse leave you too cold to properly appreciate the Moroccan lamb and seared red snapper? Forgot your reading glasses and can't decipher the hanger steak with foie-gras sauce? Request a pair from the host. A risotto with Alba white truffles

is typical of the way Azul will reach across the globe for the finest ingredients. The Moroccan-inspired Colorado lamb with eggplant and harissa is a perennial favorite. There is a lot of new competition for dining attention in town, but Azul is still at the pinnacle of its game. ✉ *Mandarin Oriental Hotel, 500 Brickell Key Dr., Downtown Miami* ☎ *305/913–8358* ✍ *Reservations essential* ▭ *AE, MC, V* ⊗ *Closed Sun. No lunch weekends* ✣ *5D.*

$$ MEDITERRANEAN ✕ **Eos.** This new restaurant at the snazzy Viceroy Hotel on Brickell is definitely worth a visit if you're downtown. Chef Michael Psilakis and restaurateur Donatella Arpaia are culinary superstars whose involvement gives this restaurant a lot of attention. The sophisticated, bold design is by Kelly Wearstler, who was also responsible for La Marea at the Tides in South Beach. The large menu of inexpensive light dishes is divided by ingredients—cheese and crostini; vegetable and potato; pasta; fish; and meats, poultry, and game. The influences are vast, with Greek, Italian, French, and Spanish flavors all evident. There's also a sushi and sashimi selection. ✉ *485 Brickell Ave., Downtown* ☎ *305/503–4400 or 866/781–9923* ⊕ *www.viceroymiami.com* ▭ *AE, D, DC, MC, V* ✣ *4D.*

$$ ARGENTINE ✕ **Novecento.** This Argentine eatery is the Financial District's answer to Ocean Drive: the people are still beautiful, but now they're wearing suits. Known for its empanadas (tender chicken or spinach and cheese), simple grilled meats (luscious grilled skirt steak with chimichurri sauce), and the innovative Ensalada Novecento (grilled skirt steak, french fries, and baby mixed greens), it's no wonder Novecento is Brickell Avenue's best power-lunch and happy-hour spot. Come for Sunday brunch and enjoy the signature *parillada*, a small grill with an assortment of steaks, sausages, and sweetbreads (not sweet bread, but rather the sweet pancreas of a lamb or calf). ✉ *1414 Brickell Ave., Downtown Miami* ☎ *305/403–0900* ⊕ *www.bistronovecento.com* ▭ *AE, D, DC, MC, V* ✣ *5D.*

$$ ITALIAN ✕ **Perricone's Marketplace and Café.** Brickell Avenue south of the Miami River is burgeoning with Italian restaurants, and this lunch place for local bigwigs is the biggest and most popular among them. It's housed partially outdoors and partially indoors in a 125-year-old Vermont barn. Recipes were handed down from generation to generation, and the cooking is simple and good. Buy your wine from the on-premises deli, and enjoy it (for a small corking fee) with homemade minestrone; a generous antipasto; linguine with a sauté of jumbo shrimp, scallops, and calamari; or gnocchi with four cheeses (which won the *Miami New Times'* Best Gnocchi category in 2008). The homemade tiramisu and cannoli are top-notch. ✉ *Brickell Village, 15 SE 10th St., Downtown Miami* ☎ *305/374–9449* ⊕ *www.perricones.com* ▭ *AE, MC, V* ✣ *5D.*

$ AMERICAN ✕ **Tobacco Road.** If you like your food (or your drink) the way you like your blues—gritty, honest, and unassuming—then this almost-100-year-old joint will earn your respect. This is Miami's oldest bar and restaurant, and it manages to stay up the latest, too: 5 AM. A live band plays daily, making this hangout one of Miami's low-key gems. The road burger is a popular choice, as are appetizers like nachos and chicken wings; the chili may induce a call for a fire hose. Fine single-malt scotches are stocked behind the bar. ✉ *626 S. Miami Ave., Downtown Miami* ☎ *305/374–1198* 🌐 *www.tobacco-road.com* 💳 *AE, D, DC, MC, V* ✥ *4D.*

LITTLE HAVANA

$$$$ SPANISH ✕ **Casa Juancho.** This meeting place for the movers and shakers of the Cuban *exilio* community is also a haven for lovers of fine Spanish regional cuisine. Strolling balladeers serenade amid brown brick, rough-hewn dark timbers, hanging smoked meats, ceramic plates, and oil still lifes: a bit of old España dropped on Calle Ocho. Try the hake prepared in a fish stock with garlic, onions, and Spanish white wine or the *carabineros a la plancha* (jumbo red shrimp with head and shell on, split and grilled). For dessert, *crema Catalana* is a rich pastry custard with a delectable crust of burnt caramel. The house features one of the largest lists of reserve Spanish wines in the United States. Jackets are recommended for men at dinner. ✉ *2436 SW 8th St., Little Havana* ☎ *305/642–2452* 🌐 *www.casajuancho.com* 💳 *AE, D, DC, MC, V* ✥ *5C.*

$$ VIETNAMESE ✕ **Hy-Vong Vietnamese Cuisine.** Spring springs forth in spring rolls of ground pork, cellophane noodles, and black mushrooms wrapped in homemade rice paper. People are willing to wait on the sidewalk for hours—come before 7 PM to avoid a wait—to sample the fish panfried with mango or with *nuoc man* (a garlic-lime fish sauce), not to mention the thinly sliced pork barbecued with sesame seeds, almonds, and peanuts. Beer-savvy proprietor Kathy Manning serves a half-dozen top brews (Double Grimbergen, Peroni, and Spaten, among them) to further inoculate the experience from the ordinary—well, as ordinary as a Vietnamese restaurant on Calle Ocho can be. ✉ *3458 SW 8th St., Little Havana* ☎ *305/446–3674* 🌐 *www.hyvong.com* 💳 *AE, D, MC, V* ⏲ *Closed Mon. and Tues. No lunch* ✥ *5C.*

$ ITALIAN ✕ **Tutto Pasta.** Tourists might pay $30 for linguine elsewhere, but locals are more likely to frequent Tutto Pasta, where they feast on the delicious homemade pasta for less than $15. Start with fresh-baked goat-cheese foccacia with truffle oil. Then try the famous lobster ravioli garnished with plantain chips, or the tilapia sautéed with shrimp, calamari, scallops, and tomato sauce. Hop over to Tutto Pizza next door to enjoy innovative Brazilian-inspired thin pizzas like the Portuguesa, topped with ham, mozzarella, black olives, eggs, and onions. Finish with Tutto chocolate cake or creamy Brazilian Pave. ✉ *1751 SW 3rd Ave. at SW 18th Rd., Little Havana* ☎ *305/857–0709* 🌐 *www.tuttopasta.com* 💳 *MC, V* ✥ *5D.*

$ CUBAN ✕ **Versailles.** *¡Bienvenido a Miami!* To the area's Cuban population, Miami without Versailles is like rice without black beans. The storied eatery, where old émigrés opine daily about all things Cuban, is a stop on every political candidate's campaign trail, and it should be a stop for you as well. Order a heaping platter of *lechon asado* (roasted pork loin), *ropa vieja* (shredded beef), or *picadillo* (spicy ground beef), all served with rice, beans, and fried plantains. Battle the oncoming food coma with a cup of the city's strongest cafecito, which comes in the tiniest of cups but packs a lot of punch. Versailles operates a bakery next door as well—take some pastelitos home. ✉ *3555 SW 8th St., between*

SW 35th and SW 36th Aves., Little Havana ☎ *305/444–0240* 🌐 *www.versaillescuban.com* 💳 *AE, D, DC, MC, V* ⊕ *5C.*

MIAMI BEACH

MID-BEACH AND NORTH

$$$ ITALIAN ✕ **Café Prima Pasta.** If Tony Soprano lived in Miami, this is where you'd find him. This famous, bustling Italian eatery is infused with the energy of the Argentine Cea family, whose clan cooks, serves, and operates this place, while somehow finding the time to pose for photos with the hundreds of celebrities who have eaten here over the years (see them in the photos on the walls). It's on a busy street, yet the low light, soothing music, and intimate seating on this restaurant's outdoor veranda can make Café Prima Pasta a romantic spot. Everything is made in-house—from the fragrant rosemary butter to the pasta, which tastes best as crab-stuffed ravioli or as linguine dyed in squid ink and served with seafood in a lobster sauce. ✉ *414 71st St., North Beach* ☎ *305/867–0106* 🌐 *www.primapasta.com* 💳 *MC, V* ⊗ *No lunch.* ⊕ *3F.*

$$$ CONTINENTAL ✕ **Chef Allen's.** Chef Allen Susser has long been a figure of Miami's culinary scene, a member of the original, self-designated "Mango Gang," who created contemporary American masterpieces from a global menu. Over the past couple of years, though, his namesake restaurant been renovated with a new look and jolt of fresh energy as a "modern seafood bistro," focusing on sustainable fish. The restaurant is still the best in northern Miami. After trying the famous Devil's on a Horseback (manchego- and mango-stuffed dates wrapped in bacon), order a salad of baby greens and warm wild mushrooms or a rock-shrimp hash with roasted corn. Allen serves only locally caught seafood, so you may want to consider the swordfish with conch-citrus couscous, macadamia nuts, and lemon. It's hard to resist the dessert soufflé; order it when you order your appetizer to eliminate a mouthwatering wait at the end of your meal. ✉ *19088 NE 29th Ave., Aventura* ☎ *305/935–2900* 🌐 *www.chefallens.com* 💳 *AE, D, MC, V* ⊕ *1F.*

$$$–$$$$ STEAKHOUSE Fodor's Choice ★ ✕ **The Forge.** Legendary for its opulence, this restaurant has been wowing patrons in its present form since 1968. The Forge is a steak house, but a steak house the likes of which you haven't seen before. Antiques, gilt-framed paintings, a chandelier from the Paris Opera House, and Tiffany stained-glass windows from New York's Trinity Church are the fitting background for some of Miami's best steaks. The tried-and-true menu also includes prime rib, bone-in fillet, lobster thermidor, chocolate soufflé, and decadent side dishes like creamed spinach and roasted-garlic mashed potatoes. The focaccia bread is to die for. For its walk-in humidor alone, the over-the-top Forge is worth visiting. ✉ *432 Arthur Godfrey Rd., Miami Beach* ☎ *305/538–8533* ✍ *Reservations essential* 🌐 *www.theforge.com* 💳 *AE, MC, V* ⊗ *No lunch.* ⊕ *4F.*

$$$ CANTONESE ★ ✕ **Hakkasan.** This stateside sibling of the Michelin-starred London restaurant is one of the best-looking restaurants on Miami Beach. Intricately carved, lacquered-black-wood Chinois panels divide seating sections, creating a deceptively cozy dining experience. The music is clubby, the waitresses' matching outfits are slinky, and the shadowy

lighting is thoughtfully designed to make everyone look about as good as they can. Chef Alan Yau, a pioneer of the haute-Chinese-food movement, has collected mostly simple and authentic Cantonese recipes, many featuring fresh seafood. Don't overlook the tofu dishes in lieu of other proteins: this isn't supermarket soy. The braised tofu and aubergine claypot in black bean pairs glorious little pillows of silken tofu with expertly cooked eggplant in a perfectly seasoned, thick, funky sauce. Unfortunately, not all dishes are as successful. ✉ *4441 Collins Ave., Miami Beach* ☎ *305/538–2000* ▭ *AE, D, DC, MC, V* ⊙ *No lunch* ⊕ *2F.*

$ DELICATESSENS ✕ **Roasters 'N Toasters.** This small Jewish delicatessen chain took over from Arnie and Richie's, a longtime family establishment, in 2008. Gone are the baskets of plastic silverware. The prices are slightly higher, but the faithful still come for the onion rolls, smoked whitefish salad, as well as the new "Corky's Famous Zaftig Sandwich," a deliciously juicy skirt steak served on twin challah rolls with a side of apple sauce. Service can be brusque, but it sure is quick. ✉ *525 41st St., Miami Beach* ☎ *305/531–7691* 🌐 *www.roastersntoasters.com* ▭ *AE, MC, V* ⊕ *3F.*

$$$ ITALIAN Fodor's Choice ★ ✕ **Timó.** Located in a glorified strip mall 5 mi north of South Beach, Timo (Italian for "thyme") is worth the trip from anywhere in South Florida. It's a kind of locals' secret that it's the best food in South Florida. The handsome bistro, co-owned by chef Tim Andriola and Rodrigo Martinez (former general manager and wine director at Norman's), has dark-wood walls, Chicago brick, and a stone-encased wood-burning stove. Andriola has an affinity for robust Mediterranean flavors: sweetbreads with bacon, honey, and aged balsamic vinegar; inexpensive, artisanal pizzas; and homemade pastas. Wood roasted meats and Parmesan dumplings in a truffled broth are not to be missed. Every bite of every dish attests to the care given, and the service is terrific. ✉ *17624 Collins Ave., Sunny Isles* ☎ *305/936–1008* 🌐 *www.timorestaurant.com* ▭ *AE, DC, MC, V* ⊙ *No lunch weekends* ⊕ *1F.*

SOUTH BEACH

$ AMERICAN Fodor's Choice ★ ✕ **Big Pink.** The decor in this innovative, super-popular diner may remind you of a roller-skating rink—everything is pink Lucite, stainless steel, and campy (think sports lockers as decorative touches)—and the menu is 3 feet tall, complete with a table of contents. Food is solidly all-American, with dozens of tasty sandwiches, pizzas, turkey or beef burgers, and side dishes, each and every one composed with gourmet flair. Big Pink also makes a great spot for brunch. ✉ *157 Collins Ave., South Beach* 🌐 *www.mylesrestaurantgroup.com* ☎ *305/532–4700* ▭ *AE, MC, V* ⊕ *5H.*

$$$$ STEAK ✕ **BLT Steak.** Miami suddenly has a plethora of good steak houses. This 2009 newbie is in the light-filled, open lobby of the snazzy Betsy Hotel at the very northern end of Ocean Drive and has the distinction of being open for breakfast daily—get the sensational steak and eggs. The clever name stands for Bistro Laurent Tourondel, Mr. T being the highly regarded chef who created the chain of BLTs. You can count on the highest quality cuts of USDA prime, certified Black Angus, and American Wagyu beef, in addition to blackboard specials and raw-bar selections. The grilled Kobe beef–skirt salad is juicy and delicious. ✉ *1440*

CUBAN FOOD

If the tropical vibe has you hankering for Cuban food, you've come to the right place. Miami is the top spot in the country to enjoy authentic Cuban cooking.

The flavors and preparations of Cuban cuisine are influenced by the island nation's natural bounty (yucca, sugarcane, guava), as well as its rich immigrant history, from near (Caribbean countries) and far (Spanish and African traditions). Chefs in Miami tend to stick with the classic versions of beloved dishes, though you'll find some variation from restaurant to restaurant as recipes have often been passed down through generations of home cooks. Try the popular **Versailles** (✉ *3555 SW 8th St.* ☎ *305/444–0240*) in Little Havana or Coral Gables' **Havana Harry's** (✉ *4612 Le Jeune Rd.* ☎ *305/661–2622*), appealing to families seeking a home-cooked, Cuban-style meal. In North Miami, **Little Havana Restaurant** (✉ *12727 Biscayne Blvd.* ☎ *305/899–9069*) serves traditional Cuban fare, and in South Beach, **David's Café** (✉ *1058 Collins Ave.* ☎ *305/534–8736*) is a hole-in-the-wall with excellent eats.

THE CUBAN SANDWICH

A great *cubano* (Cuban sandwich) requires pillowy Cuban bread layered with ham, garlic-citrus-marinated slow-roasted pork, Swiss cheese, and pickles (plus salami, if you're eating in Tampa; lettuce and tomatoes if you're in Key West), butter and/or mustard. The sandwich is grilled in a sandwich press until the cheese melts and all the elements are fused together. Try one, usually about $6, at **Enriqueta's Sandwich Shop** (✉ *2830 NE 2nd Ave.* ☎ *305/573–4681* ⏲ *weekdays 6 AM–4 PM, Sat. 6 AM–2 PM*) in the Design District, or **Exquisito Restaurant** (✉ *1510 SW 8 St.* ☎ *305/643–0227* ⏲ *Open daily, 7 AM–midnight*) in Little Havana.

KEY CUBAN DISHES

ARROZ CON POLLO

This chicken-and-rice dish is Cuban comfort food. Found throughout Latin America, the Cuban version is typically seasoned with garlic, paprika, and onions, then colored golden or reddish with saffron or achiote (a seed paste), and enlivened with a sizable splash of beer near the end of cooking. Green peas and sliced, roasted red peppers are a standard topping.

BISTEC DE PALOMILLA

This thinly sliced sirloin steak is marinated with lime juice and garlic, and fried with onions. The steak is often served with chimichurri sauce, an olive oil, garlic, and cilantro sauce that is sometimes served with bread as a dip (slather bread with butter and dab on the chimichurri). Also try *Ropa Vieja*, a slow-cooked, shredded flank steak in a garlic-tomato sauce.

LECHON ASADO

Fresh ham or an entire suckling pig marinated in *Mojo Criollo* (parsley, garlic, sour orange, and olive oil) and roasted until fork tender. Served with white rice, black beans, and *tostones* (fried plantains) or yucca (pronounced YU-kah), a starchy tuber with a mild nut taste that's often sliced into fat sticks and deep-fried like fries.

(below) Cuban sandwich; (top) *tres leches*

FRITAS

If you're in the mood for an inexpensive, casual Cuban meal, have a *frita*—a hamburger with distinctive Cuban flair. It's made with ground beef that's mixed with ground or finely chopped chorizo, spiced with pepper, paprika, and salt, topped with sautéed onions and shoestring potatoes fries, and then served on a bun slathered with a special tomato-based ketchup-like sauce.

DRINKS

Sip *guarapo* (gwa-RA-poh), a fresh sugarcane juice that isn't really as sweet as you might think, or grab a straw and enjoy a frothy *batido* (bah-TEE-doe), a Cuban-style milk shake made with tropical fruits like mango, *piña* (pineapple), or *mamey* (mah-MAY, a tropical fruit with a melon-cherry taste). For a real twist, try the *batido de trigo*—a wheat shake that will remind you of sugar-glazed breakfast cereal.

DESSERTS

Treat yourself to a slice of *tres leches* cake. The "three milks" come from the sweetened condensed milk, evaporated milk, and heavy cream that are poured over the cake until it's an utterly irresistible gooey mess. Also, don't miss the *pastelitos*, Cuban fruit-filled turnovers. Traditional flavors include plain guava, guava with cream cheese, and cream cheese with coconut. Yum!

Pink as cotton candy and bubble gum, the Big Pink diner fits right in with its art deco surroundings.

Ocean Dr., South Beach ☎ *305/673–0044* 🌐 *www.bltrestaurants.com* ▭ *AE, D, DC, MC, V* ✣ *2H.*

$$$$ FRENCH ✕ **Blue Door at the Delano.** In a hotel where style reigns supreme, this high-profile restaurant provides both glamour and solid cuisine. The four white-curtained, high-ceilinged walls make it the most theatrically focused dining room in the city. Acclaimed consulting chef Claude Troisgros combines the flavors of classic French cuisine with South American influences to create a seasonal menu that might include foie gras with berries or lobster with caramelized banana. Equally pleasing is dining with the crème de la crème of Miami (and New York and Paris) society. Don't recognize the apparent bigwig next to you? If you hear bits of his cell-phone conversation, you'll be filled in pronto. ✉ *1685 Collins Ave., South Beach* ☎ *305/674–6400* ✍ *Reservations essential* ▭ *AE, D, DC, MC, V* ✣ *2H.*

$$ SOUTHERN ✕ **Emeril's.** "It's getting happy in here" is one of Emeril Lagasse's stock phrases, and now he has brought his brand of happy to Miami Beach. You can expect a different gumbo each day and other New Orleans specialties at Lagasse's chain, which appears to have the winning formula down. The seafood naturally shines in these parts (an andouille-crusted redfish signals the imported Lagasse touch), and the chef has his own take on mango pie and banana-cream pie. As a bonus, the restaurant delivers without even a hint of South Beach attitude—though a view of the pool at its Loews hotel location is a perk. ✉ *1601 Collins Ave., at Loews Miami Beach Hotel, South Beach* ☎ *305/695–4550* ▭ *AE, D, DC, MC, V* ✣ *2H.*

$$$ AMERICAN ✕ **Joe Allen.** Crave a good martini along with a terrific burger? Locals head to this hidden hangout in an exploding neighborhood of condos, town houses, and stores. The eclectic crowd includes kids and grandparents, and the menu has everything from pizzas to calves' liver to steaks. Start with an innovative salad, such as arugula with pear, prosciutto, and a Gorgonzola dressing, or roast-duck salad with blue cheese and pears. Home-style desserts include banana-cream pie and ice-cream-and-cookie sandwiches. Comfortable and homey, this is the perfect place to go when you don't feel like going to a restaurant. ✉ *1787 Purdy Ave., South Beach* ☎ *305/531–7007* 🌐 *www.joeallenrestaurant.com* 💳 *MC, V* ✥ *4E.*

$$$ SEAFOOD ✕ **Joe's Stone Crab Restaurant.** In South Beach's decidedly new-money scene, the stately Joe's Stone Crab is an old-school testament to good food and good service. South Beach's most storied restaurant started as a turn-of-the-century eating house when Joseph Weiss discovered succulent stone crabs off the Florida coast. Almost a century later, the restaurant stretches a city block and serves 2,000 dinners a day to local politicians and moneyed patriarchs. Stone crabs, served with legendary mustard sauce, crispy hash browns, and creamed spinach, remain the staple. But don't think you need a trust fund to eat here: Joe's serves sensational fried chicken for $5.95. Finish your meal with tart key lime pie, baked fresh daily. ■ **TIP→** Joe's famously refuses reservations, and weekend waits can be three hours long—yes, you read that correctly—so come early or order from Joe's Take Away next door. ✉ *11 Washington Ave., South Beach* ☎ *305/673–0365, 305/673–4611 for takeout, 800/780–2722 for overnight shipping* ⚠ *Reservations not accepted* 🌐 *www.joesstonecrab.com* 💳 *AE, D, DC, MC, V* ⏲ *Closed May–mid-Oct. No lunch Sun. and Mon.* ✥ *5G.*

$$$$ SEAFOOD ✕ **La Marea.** Come here if you're looking for a sophisticated, intimate dining experience in Miami Beach. Choose one of two dining areas—on the hedge-edged terrace that leads to the entrance of The Tides hotel or inside the coolly surreal dining room, where dramatic faux tortoise shells line the walls and hooded wood chairs line the outer tables. Everything on the menu is tasty, but chef Gonzalo Rivera, a Michael Mina protégé, shines most in dishes inspired by his Mexican heritage. Try the Colorado Rack of Lamb with cinnamon and dark mole sauce complemented by dried bing cherry–quinoa salad and stuffed zucchini blossom with goat cheese. The tiny little bar in the back, the gorgeous Coral Room, is a Miami secret. ✉ *1220 Ocean Dr., at The Tides hotel, South Beach* ☎ *305/604–5070* 💳 *AE, D, DC, MC, V* ✥ *3H.*

$$$ STEAK ★ ✕ **Meat Market.** Yes, it's a great name for a steak-inspired restaurant, and a name seemingly destined for a place like this on Lincoln Road, where sexy people amble by in skimpy clothes year-round. But here's the great news: this is a sophisticated place with a large non-steakhouse menu. When this reviewer was there recently with friends, it was a thrilling night of drinks, plus appetizers that were just sitting at the bar—cedar-scented hamachi (yellowtail sashimi) topped with mango caviar, white truffle, fresh lime, and rice-paper tuna tacos with guajillo chili, cabbage, grilled watermelon, micro watercress, and roasted garlic. The seafood selection, like the seared Florida grouper in browned goat

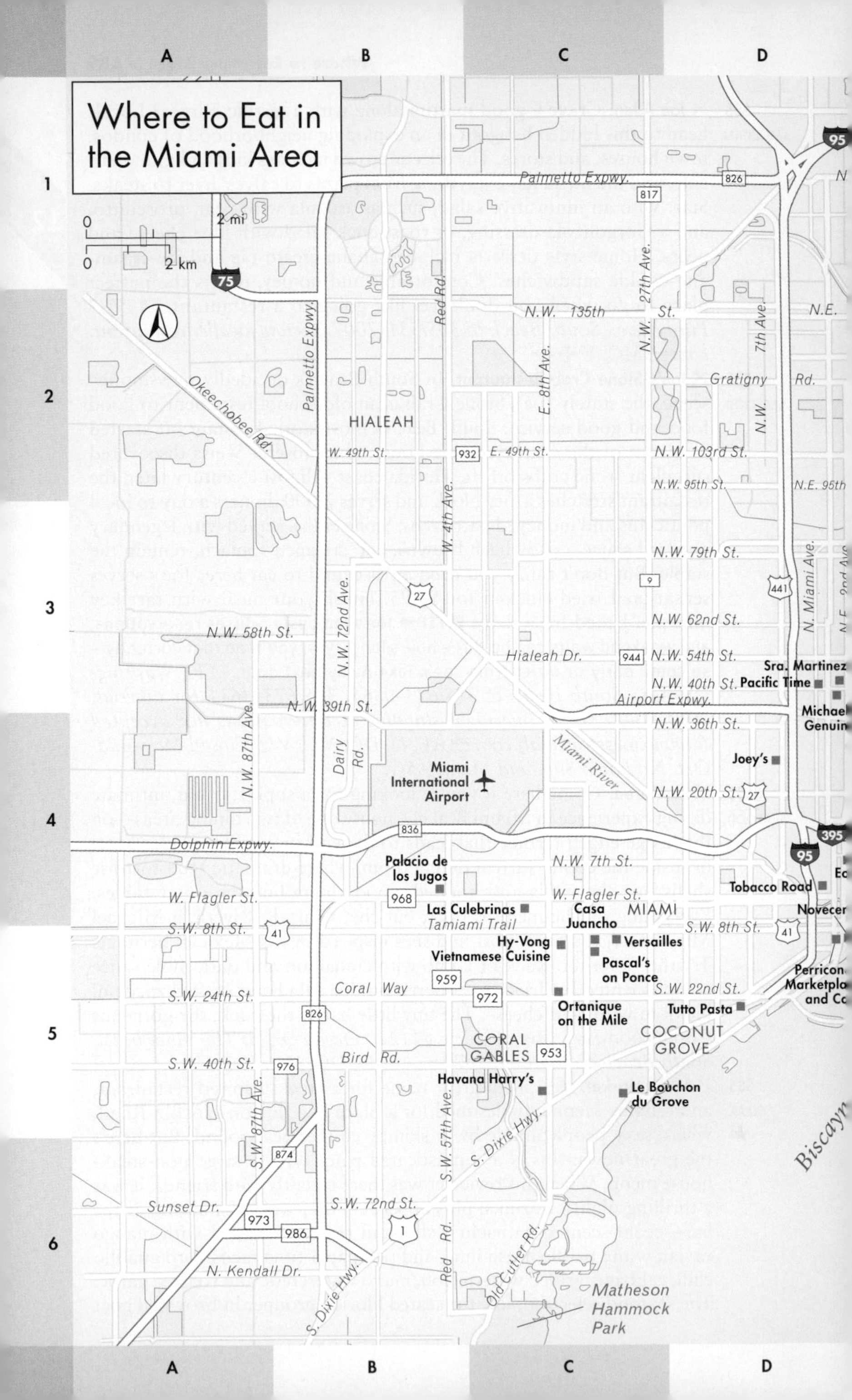
Where to Eat in the Miami Area
A
B
C
D
1
2
3
4
5
6
0
2 mi
0
2 km
75
95
826
817
Palmetto Expwy.
Palmetto Expwy.
Red Rd.
N.W. 27th Ave.
N.W. 135th St.
N.E.
7th Ave.
E. 8th Ave.
Gratigny Rd.
N.W.
Okeechobee Rd.
HIALEAH
W. 49th St.
932
E. 49th St.
N.W. 103rd St.
N.W. 95th St.
N.E. 95th
W. 4th Ave.
N.W. 79th St.
9
441
N. Miami Ave.
N.E. 2nd Ave.
27
N.W. 72nd Ave.
N.W. 62nd St.
N.W. 58th St.
Hialeah Dr.
944
N.W. 54th St.
Sra. Martinez
N.W. 40th St.
Pacific Time
Airport Expwy.
N.W. 87th Ave.
N.W. 39th St.
Michael's Genuine
N.W. 36th St.
Miami River
Joey's
Dairy Rd.
Miami International Airport
N.W. 20th St.
27
836
395
Dolphin Expwy.
95
Palacio de los Jugos
N.W. 7th St.
Tobacco Road
W. Flagler St.
968
W. Flagler St.
Las Culebrinas
Casa Juancho
MIAMI
Novecento
S.W. 8th St.
41
Tamiami Trail
S.W. 8th St.
41
Hy-Vong Vietnamese Cuisine
Versailles
Pascal's on Ponce
Perricone's Marketplace and Cafe
959
Coral Way
S.W. 24th St.
972
S.W. 22nd St.
Ortanique on the Mile
Tutto Pasta
826
CORAL GABLES
953
COCONUT GROVE
S.W. 40th St.
976
Bird Rd.
Havana Harry's
Le Bouchon du Grove
S.W. 87th Ave.
S.W. 57th Ave.
S. Dixie Hwy.
Biscayne
874
Sunset Dr.
S.W. 72nd St.
973
986
1
Red Rd.
Old Cutler Rd.
N. Kendall Dr.
S. Dixie Hwy.
Matheson Hammock Park

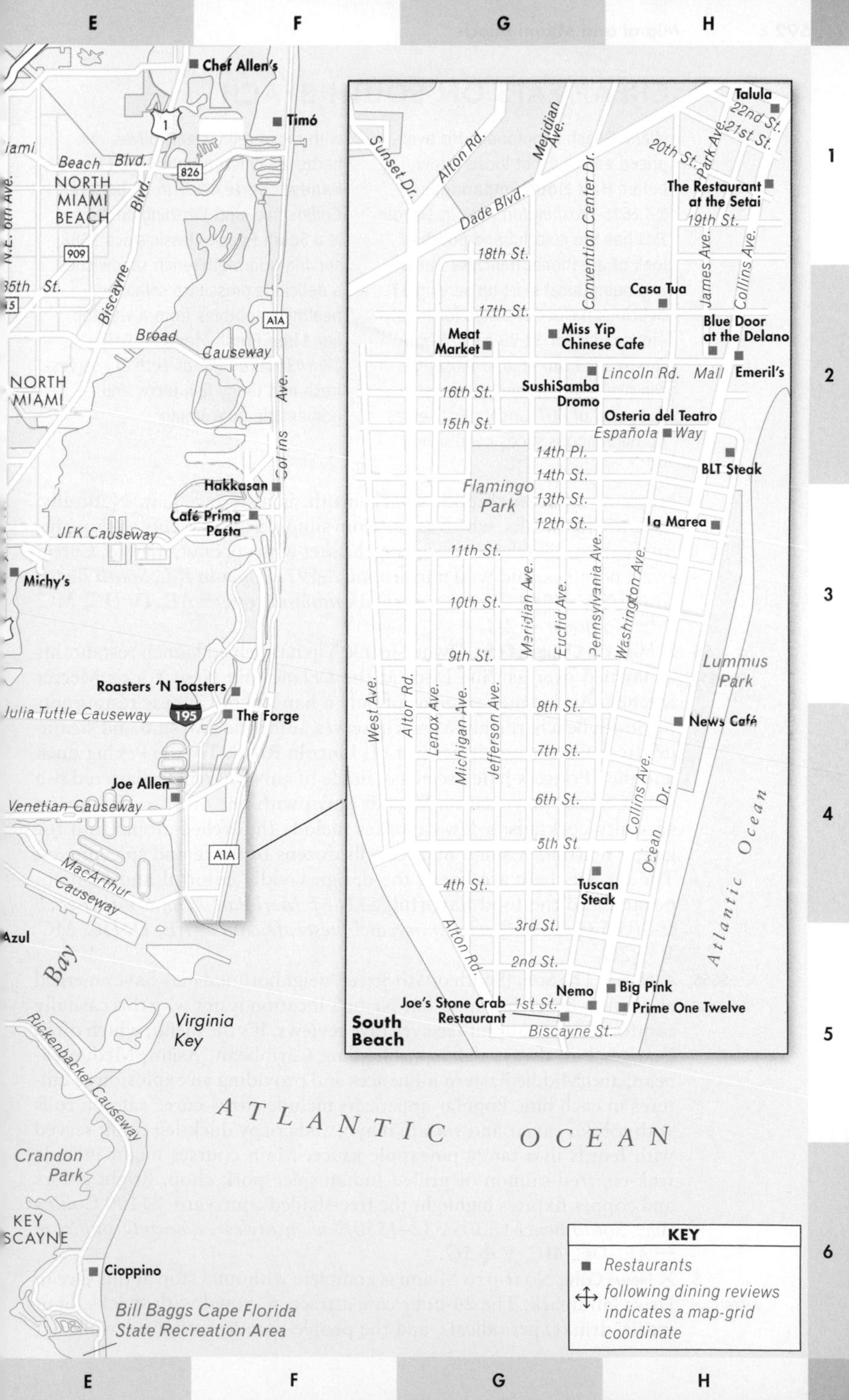
E
F
G
H
1
2
3
4
5
6
Chef Allen's
Timó
NORTH
MIAMI
BEACH
Beach Blvd.
Biscayne Blvd.
826
909
1
35th St.
A1A
Broad Causeway
NORTH
MIAMI
Collins Ave.
Hakkasan
Café Prima Pasta
JFK Causeway
Michy's
Roasters 'N Toasters
195
The Forge
Julia Tuttle Causeway
Joe Allen
Venetian Causeway
A1A
MacArthur Causeway
Azul
Bay
Virginia Key
Rickenbacker Causeway
Crandon Park
KEY
SCAYNE
Cioppino
Bill Baggs Cape Florida
State Recreation Area
ATLANTIC OCEAN
Sunset Dr.
Alton Rd.
Meridian Ave.
Dade Blvd.
Convention Center Dr.
Talula
22nd St.
21st St.
20th St.
Park Ave.
The Restaurant at the Setai
19th St.
18th St.
James Ave.
Collins Ave.
Casa Tua
17th St.
Meat Market
Miss Yip Chinese Cafe
Blue Door at the Delano
Lincoln Rd. Mall
Emeril's
16th St.
SushiSamba Dromo
15th St.
Osteria del Teatro
Española Way
14th Pl.
14th St.
BLT Steak
Flamingo Park
13th St.
12th St.
La Marea
11th St.
Pennsylvania Ave.
Washington Ave.
10th St.
Meridian Ave.
Euclid Ave.
9th St.
Lummus Park
West Ave.
Alton Rd.
Lenox Ave.
Michigan Ave.
Jefferson Ave.
8th St.
News Café
7th St.
Collins Ave.
6th St.
Ocean Dr.
Atlantic Ocean
5th St.
Tuscan Steak
4th St.
3rd St.
Alton Rd.
2nd St.
Big Pink
Nemo
Joe's Stone Crab Restaurant
1st St.
Prime One Twelve
Biscayne St.
South Beach
KEY
Restaurants
following dining reviews indicates a map-grid coordinate

CHEAP EATS ON SOUTH BEACH

Miami Beach is notorious for overpriced eateries, but locals know better. **Half Moon Empanadas** (✉ *1616 Washington Ave., at Lincoln Rd.*) has the colorful and polished look of a national franchise but is a genuine local start-up serving 17 delicious flavors of baked (or fried) empanadas for $1.99 each. **Pizza Rustica** (✉ *8th St. and Washington Ave., 14th St. and Washington Ave., and at 667 Lincoln Rd.*) serves up humungous slices overflowing with mozzarella, steak, olives, and barbecue chicken until 4 AM. **La Sandwicherie** (✉ *14th St. between Collins Ave. and Washington Ave.*) is a South Beach classic since 1988, serving gourmet French sandwiches, a delicious prosciutto salad, and healthy smoothies from a walk-up bar. **Lime Fresh Mexican Grill** (✉ *1439 Alton Rd. at 14th St.*) serves fresh and tangy fish tacos and homemade guacamole.

butter and bacon-chipotle conch broth, is also excellent. Naturally, there are the steaks, which range from simple à la carte cuts to thoughtful creations like the braised prime brisket with coconut, mango, Cuban sweet potatoes, and wild mushrooms. ✉ *915 Lincoln Rd., South Beach* ☎ *305/532–0088* 🌐 *www.meatmarketmiami.com* 💳 *AE, D, DC, MC, V* ⏲ *No lunch* ✣ *2G.*

$$ CHINESE ✕ **Miss Yip Chinese Cafe.** Owner Jennie Yip has helped launch restaurants as fawned over as Blue Door at the Delano and New York's Mercer Kitchen. At the most popular of only a handful of Chinese restaurants on South Beach, the hip Miss Yip serves authentic dim sum and steaming fresh Cantonese dishes just off Lincoln Road. Try the Peking duck and the "Princess Jade" sea bass, made of cubes of tender battered fish with Chinese mayo sauce. Wash it down with one of Miss Yip's many specialty cocktails: a few favorites include the lychee mojito and the ginger martini. A small market sells dozens of sauce and spice mixes. The crowds here are lively, the design vividly colorful and contemporary, and the food flavorful. ✉ *1661 Meridian Ave., South Beach* ☎ *305/534–5488* 🌐 *www.missyipchinesecafe.com* 💳 *AE, D, DC, MC, V* ✣ *2G.*

$$$$ SEAFOOD ✕ **Nemo.** The SoFi (South of 5th Street) neighborhood may have emerged as a South Beach hot spot, but Nemo's location is not why this casually comfortable restaurant receives rave reviews. It's the menu, which often changes but always delivers, blending Caribbean, Asian, Mediterranean, and Middle Eastern influences and providing an explosion of cultures in each bite. Popular appetizers include citrus-cured salmon rolls with tobiko caviar and wasabi mayo, and crispy duck-leg confit served with lentils in a tangy pineapple sauce. Main courses might include wok-charred salmon or grilled Indian-spice pork chop. Bright colors and copper fixtures highlight the tree-shaded courtyard. ✉ *100 Collins Ave., South Beach* ☎ *305/532–4550* 🌐 *www.mylesrestaurantgroup.com* 💳 *AE, DC, MC, V* ✣ *5G.*

$ AMERICAN ✕ **News Café.** No trip to Miami is complete without a stop at this Ocean Drive landmark. The 24-hour café attracts a crowd with snacks, light meals, drinks, periodicals, and the people-parade on the sidewalk out front. Most prefer sitting outside, where they can feel the salt breeze and gawk at the human scenery. Sea-grape trees shade a patio where you can watch from a quiet distance. Offering a little of this and a little of that—bagels, pâtés, chocolate fondue, sandwiches, and a terrific wine list—this joint has something for everyone. Although service can be indifferent to the point of laissez-faire, the café remains a must. ✉ *800 Ocean Dr., South Beach* ☎ *305/538–6397* ✍ *Reservations not accepted* 🌐 *www.newscafe.com* ▭ *AE, DC, MC, V* ✥ *4H.*

$$$ ITALIAN ✕ **Osteria del Teatro.** Thanks to word of mouth, this northern Italian restaurant is constantly full of the most refined clink and clatter along sometimes-seedy Washington Avenue. Because of inventive and fresh dishes you might stray from the printed menu, and order one of the many daily specials. A representative appetizer is poached asparagus served over polenta triangles with a Gorgonzola sauce. Stuffed pastas, including spinach crepes overflowing with ricotta, can seem heavy but taste light; fish dishes yield a rosemary-marinated tuna or salmon in a rosemary-shiitake-lemon sauce. ✉ *1443 Washington Ave., South Beach* ☎ *305/538–7850* ✍ *Reservations essential* 🌐 *www.osteriadelteatromiami.com* ▭ *AE, DC, MC, V* ⊗ *Closed Sun. No lunch* ✥ *2H.*

$$$$ STEAK ✕ **Prime One Twelve.** This wildly busy steak house is particularly renowned for its highly marbleized prime beef (try the 30-ounce bone-in rib eye for two, $68), creamed corn, truffle macaroni and cheese, and buzzing scene: while you stand at the bar awaiting your table (everyone has to wait—at least a little bit), you'll clamor for a drink with all facets of Miami's high society, from the city's top real-estate developers and philanthropists to striking models and celebrities (Lenny Kravitz, Jay-Z, and Matt Damon are among a big list of celebrity regulars). ✉ *112 Ocean Dr., South Beach* ☎ *305/532–8112* 🌐 *www.mylesrestaurantgroup.com* ▭ *AE, D, DC, MC, V* ✥ *5H.*

$$$$ ECLECTIC ★ ✕ **The Restaurant at The Setai.** With its harmonious courtyard reflecting pool and polished-stone interiors, the setting of the Setai is so dramatically beautiful that a less-than-heavenly dining experience would be a blow. Even so, The Restaurant, as it's called, exceeds expectations. It has foreign chefs dedicated to producing delicious dishes from their native homelands—Thailand, India, China, Singapore, Malaysia, and Indonesia. Dining here is a culinary tour of Asia. Dishes, such as steamed whole yellowtail with ginger soy and green onions, perfectly cooked dim sum, and curries, come family-style in native crockery. The leather-bound wine list is 45 pages long. ✉ *2001 Collins Ave., South Beach* ☎ *305/520–6400* 🌐 *www.setai.com/dining* ▭ *AE, D, DC, MC, V* ⊗ *No lunch* ✥ *1H.*

$$$ JAPANESE ✕ **SushiSamba Dromo.** This sibling to the New York City SushiSamba makes an eclectic pairing of Japanese, Peruvian, and Brazilian cuisines. The results are fabulous if a bit mystifying: miso-marinated sea bass, hamachi taquitos (basically a yellowtail tartare), *mocqueca mista* (Brazilian seafood stew), and caramel–passion fruit sponge cake. Loaded with customers in the heart of pedestrian Lincoln Road, SushiSamba has a vibe that hurts the ears but warms the trendy heart. ✉ *600 Lincoln Rd., South Beach* ☎ *305/673–5337* ✍ *Reservations essential* 🌐 *www.sushisamba.com* ▭ *AE, MC, V* ✥ *2G.*

$$$$ AMERICAN ✕ **Talula.** Husband-and-wife Frank Randazzo and Andrea Curto share the kitchen while keeping their own cooking styles. The cuisine Curto developed at Wish joins Asian and tropical influences. Randazzo, from the Gaucho Room, grills with a Latin influence. Together they call their style "American creative." Florida wahoo ceviche, barbecued quail, steamed mussels in a saffron broth, grouper with lime and chili, and a tender and moist barbecued pork tenderloin stand out. The key lime pie alone is worth a visit. ✉ *210 23rd St., South Beach* ☎ *305/672–0778* 🌐 *www.talulaonline.com* ▭ *AE, D, MC, V* ⏲ *No lunch. Sat. Closed Mon.* ✣ *1H.*

$$$$ ITALIAN ✕ **Tuscan Steak.** Dark wood, mirrors, and green upholstery define this chic, masculine place, where big platters of meats and fish are served family-style, assuming yours is a royal family. Tuscan can be as busy as a subway stop, and still the staff is gracious and giving. The chefs take their cues from the Tuscan countryside, where pasta is rich with truffles and main plates are simply but deliciously grilled. Sip red wine with a house specialty: three-mushroom risotto with white-truffle oil, gnocchi with Gorgonzola cream, Florentine T-bone with roasted garlic puree, or filet mignon with a Gorgonzola crust in a red-wine sauce. Portions are enormous. Bring your friends and share, share, share. ✉ *433 Washington Ave., South Beach* ☎ *305/534–2233* 🌐 *www.chinagrillmgt.com* ▭ *AE, DC, MC, V* ✣ *4G.*

WHERE TO STAY

Updated by Michael de Zayas

Room rates in Miami tend to swing wildly. In high season, which is January through May, expect to pay at least $150 per night. In summer, however, prices can be as much as 50% lower than the dizzying winter rates. You can also find great values between Easter and Memorial Day, which is actually a delightful time in Miami.

Business travelers tend to stay in downtown Miami, while most tourists stay on Miami Beach, as close as possible to the water. If money isn't an object, stay in one of the glamorous hotels lining Collins Avenue between 15th and 21st streets. Otherwise, stay on the quiet beaches farther north, or in one of the small boutique hotels on Ocean Drive, Collins, or Washington avenues between 10th and 15th streets. Two important considerations that affect price are balcony and view. If you're willing to have a room without an ocean view, you can sometimes get a price much lower than the standard rate. Many hotels are aggressive with specials and change their rates hour to hour, so it's worth calling around.

WHAT IT COSTS

	¢	$	$$	$$$	$$$$
FOR TWO PEOPLE	under $150	$150–$200	$200–$300	$300–$400	over $400

Prices for hotels are for two people in a standard double room in high season, excluding 12.5% city and resort taxes.

12

BEST BETS FOR MIAMI LODGING

Fodor's offers a selective listing of quality lodging experiences in every price range, from the city's best budget beds to its most sophisticated luxury hotels. Here, we've compiled our top recommendations by price and experience. The very best properties are designated in the listings with the Fodor's Choice logo. Find specific details about a hotel in the full reviews, listed alphabetically by neighborhood.

Fodor's Choice ★

Acqualina Resort & Spa on the Beach, p. 605
Biltmore Hotel, p. 596
Circa 39 Hotel, p. 602
Delano Hotel, p. 609
Fisher Island Hotel & Resort, p. 601
Fontainebleau, p. 603
Four Seasons Hotel Miami, p. 600
Mandarin Oriental Miami, p. 600
National Hotel, p. 611
Ritz-Carlton Key Biscayne, p. 596
The Tides, p. 613
Travelodge Monaco Beach Resort, p. 605

By Price

¢

Circa 39 Hotel, p. 602
Travelodge Monaco Beach Resort, p. 605
Villa Paradiso, p. 614

$

Century Hotel, p. 609
Essex House Hotel, p. 609

$$

Cadet Hotel, p. 608
Catalina Hotel & Beach Club, p. 608
The Hotel, p. 610
National Hotel, p. 611
Pelican, p. 611
Townhouse, p. 613

$$$

Biltmore Hotel, p. 596
Fontainebleau, p. 603

$$$$

Acqualina Resort, p. 605
Delano Hotel, p. 609
Fisher Island Hotel, p. 601
Four Seasons Hotel Miami, p. 600
Mandarin Oriental Miami, p. 600
Ritz-Carlton Key Biscayne, p. 596
Setai, p. 612
The Tides, p. 613

By Experience

BEST POOL

Biltmore Hotel, p. 596
National Hotel, p. 611
Ritz-Carlton South Beach, p. 612
The Standard, p. 601
Viceroy, p. 600

BEST HOTEL BAR

The Hotel, p. 610
Mandarin Oriental Miami, p. 600
National Hotel, p. 611
The Standard, p. 601
Viceroy (rooftop bar), p. 600

BEST SERVICE

Acqualina Resort, p. 605
Four Seasons Hotel Miami, p. 600
Ritz-Carlton Key Biscayne, p. 596

BEST VIEWS

Mandarin Oriental Miami, p. 600
The Regent Bal Harbour, p. 604
The Tides, p. 613

HIPSTER HOTELS

Catalina Hotel & Beach Club, p. 608
Gansevoort South, p. 610
Shore Club, p. 612

BEST LOCATION

National Hotel, p. 611
Pelican, p. 611

BEST-KEPT SECRET

Acqualina Resort, p. 605
National Hotel, p. 611
Ocean Surf Hotel, p. 603
Travelodge Monaco Beach Resort, p. 605

COCONUT GROVE, CORAL GABLES, AND KEY BISCAYNE

COCONUT GROVE

$$$ **Ritz-Carlton, Coconut Grove.** Although it's the smallest and least exciting of the three Ritz-Carlton properties in the Miami area, it provides the best service experience in Coconut Grove. Overlooking Biscayne Bay, the hotel has rooms that are appointed with marble baths, a choice of down or nonallergenic foam pillows, and private balconies. A 5,000-square-foot spa is on hand to soothe away stress, and the open-air Bizcaya is among Coconut Grove's loveliest dining spots. **Pros:** best service in Coconut Grove; high-quality spa. **Cons:** of the three Miami Ritz-Carltons this one has the least interesting location and the fewest amenities. ✉ *3300 SW 27th Ave.* ☎ *305/644–4680 or 800/241–3333* 🌐 *www.ritzcarlton.com* *88 rooms, 27 suites* *In-room: a/c, safe, refrigerator, Internet, Wi-Fi. In-hotel: 2 restaurants, room service, bar, pool, gym, spa, laundry service, Internet terminal, Wi-Fi hotspot, parking (paid), some pets allowed* *AE, D, DC, MC, V* ✣ *5D.*

CORAL GABLES

$$$ Fodor's Choice ★ **Biltmore Hotel.** Built in 1926, this landmark hotel has had several incarnations over the years—including a stint as a hospital during World War II—and has changed hands more than a few times. Through it all, this grandest of grandes dames remains an opulent reminder of yesteryear, with its palatial lobby and grounds, enormous pool, and distinctive 315-foot tower, which rises above the canopy of trees shading Coral Gables. Fully updated, the Biltmore has on-site golf and tennis, a spa and fitness center, extensive meeting facilities, and the celebrated Palme d'Or restaurant. The $65 Sunday brunch is a must. **Pros:** historic property; possibly best pool in the Miami area; great tennis and golf. **Cons:** far from Miami Beach. ✉ *1200 Anastasia Ave.* ☎ *305/445–1926 or 800/727–1926* 🌐 *www.biltmorehotel.com* *241 rooms, 39 suites* *In-room: a/c, Wi-Fi. In-hotel: 4 restaurants, room service, bars, golf course, tennis courts, pool, gym, spa, Wi-Fi hotspot, parking (paid)* *AE, D, DC, MC, V* ✣ *5C.*

KEY BISCAYNE

$$$$ Fodor's Choice ★ **Ritz-Carlton, Key Biscayne.** There is probably no other place in Miami where slowness is lifted to a fine art. On Key Biscayne there are no pressures, there's no nightlife (outside of the hotel's great live Latin music weekends), and the dining choices are essentially limited to the hotel (which has four dining options, including the languorous, Havana-style RUMBAR). In this kind of setting, it's natural to appreciate the Ritz brand of pampering. Need something to do? The "tequilier" at the seaside Cantina Beach can educate you on the finer points of his native region's drink. Hitting the spa? In one of 21 treatment rooms, try signature Coco-Luscious body treatments, a nod to the island's history as the country's largest coconut plantation. An 11-court tennis "garden" with daily clinics, a private beach, and beachside water sports are other options. Recently renovated guestrooms have custom-made touches like mother-of pearl wall coverings. Updated technology includes plasma televisions and jack packs. In-room luxuries like robes,

slippers, fine linens and toiletries, are par for the course. The Club Level offers five food presentations throughout the day, and the Ritz Kids club has expanded its full- and half-day and Saturday-night programs to include island history, fishing, beach treasure hunts and a kid-friendly blue and gold macaw. Borrow bikes here to explore Billy Baggs park and its lighthouse. **Pros:** private beach; quiet, luxurious family retreat. **Cons:** it will be too quiet if you're looking for a party—so you have to drive to Miami for nightlife. ✉ *455 Grand Bay Dr.* ☎ *305/365–4500 or 800/241–3333* 🌐 *www.ritzcarlton.com/resorts/key_biscayne* *365 rooms, 37 suites* *In-room: a/c, safe, DVD (some), Internet, Wi-Fi. In-hotel: 2 restaurants, room service, bars, tennis courts, pools, gym, spa, beachfront, water sports, bicycles, laundry service, Internet terminal, Wi-Fi hotspot, parking (paid), some pets allowed* ▭ *AE, D, DC, MC, V* ✣ *6E.*

DOWNTOWN MIAMI

$$ **Doubletree Grand Hotel Biscayne Bay.** Like the Biscayne Bay Marriott, this elegant waterfront option is at the north end of downtown off a scenic marina, and near many of Miami's headline attractions: the Port of Miami, Bayside, the Arena, and the Carnival Center. Rooms are spacious, and most have a view of Biscayne Bay and the port. Some suites have full kitchens. You can rent Jet Skis or take deep-sea-fishing trips from the marina. **Pros:** great bay views; deli and market on-site. **Cons:** need a cab to get around. ✉ *1717 N. Bayshore Dr., Downtown Miami* ☎ *305/372–0313 or 800/222–8733* 🌐 *www.doubletree.com* *152 suites* *In-room: a/c, safe, kitchen (some), Wi-Fi. In-hotel: restaurant, room service, bar, pool, gym, spa, Wi-Fi hotspot, parking (paid)* ▭ *AE, D, DC, MC, V* ✣ *4E.*

$$$$ **Epic Hotel.** Located in an area mostly known for its gritty office buildings and glittery high-rise condominiums, the Epic Hotel is a real gem in downtown Miami. Even the most basic rooms are plushly outfitted with Frette linens, iPod docking stations, 37-inch flat-screen TVs, balconies, and Acqua Di Parma bath amenities. Although it's the kind of place you'll likely choose if you have business in the area, you should consider staying through the weekend with your family. Ask for a table outside or by the window at Area 31, an elegant, delicious seafood restaurant on the 16th floor. **Pros:** sprawling pool deck with a view of the water; complimentary wine in the lobby every day from 5 to 6 PM; complimentary in-room yoga mats and yoga television programming; tennis courts and golf courts available through partnerships with nearby tennis clubs and golf courses. **Cons:** not located directly near the beach; some rooms overlook tall condominiums and office buildings. ✉ *270 Biscayne Blvd. Way, Downtown Miami* ☎ *305/424–5226* 🌐 *www.epichotel.com* *411 rooms* *In-room: a/c, safe, Wi-Fi. In-hotel: restaurant, room service, bar, pool, gym, spa, water sports, bicycles, children's programs (ages 2–12), laundry service, Wi-Fi hotspot, parking (paid)* ▭ *AE, D, MC, V* ✣ *5D.*

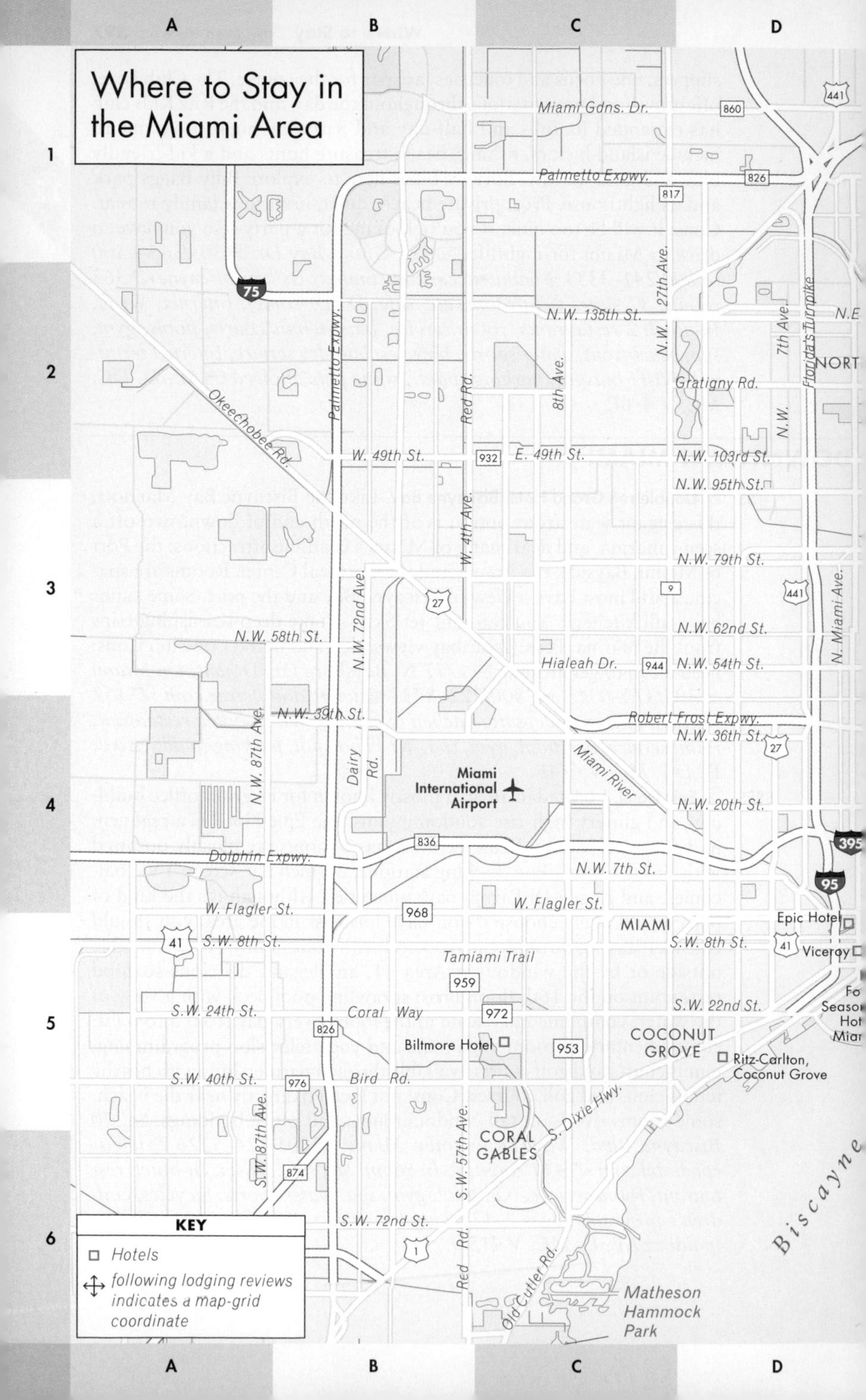

Where to Stay in the Miami Area

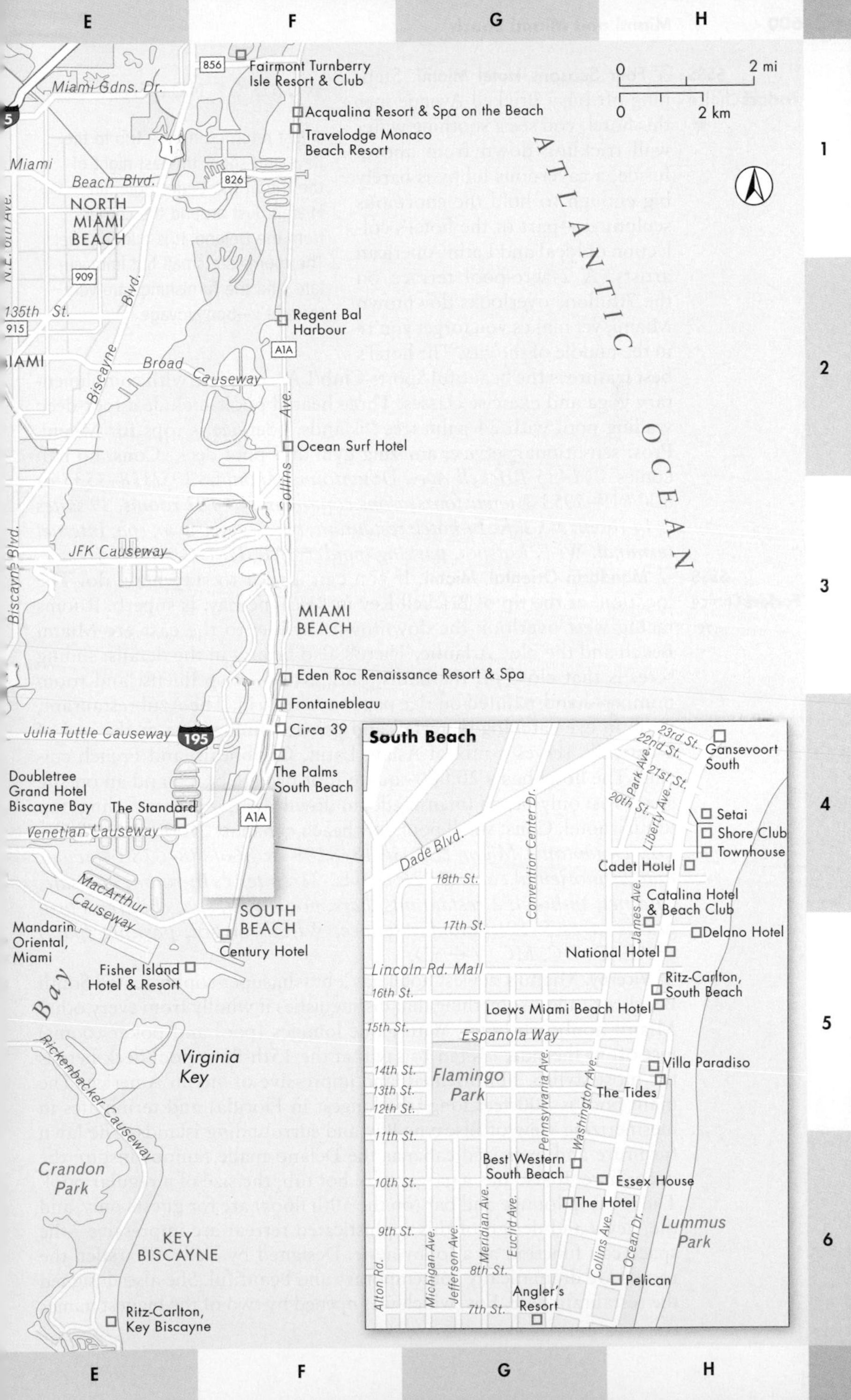

E
F
G
H
1
2
3
4
5
6
0
2 mi
0
2 km
ATLANTIC OCEAN
Fairmont Turnberry Isle Resort & Club
Acqualina Resort & Spa on the Beach
Travelodge Monaco Beach Resort
Miami Gdns. Dr.
B56
Miami
Beach Blvd.
1
826
NORTH MIAMI BEACH
909
135th St.
915
Biscayne Blvd.
Regent Bal Harbour
A1A
Broad Causeway
Collins Ave.
Ocean Surf Hotel
JFK Causeway
Biscayne Blvd.
MIAMI BEACH
Eden Roc Renaissance Resort & Spa
Fontainebleau
Circa 39
Julia Tuttle Causeway
195
The Palms South Beach
Doubletree Grand Hotel Biscayne Bay
The Standard
A1A
Venetian Causeway
MacArthur Causeway
SOUTH BEACH
Century Hotel
Mandarin Oriental, Miami
Fisher Island Hotel & Resort
Bay
Rickenbacker Causeway
Virginia Key
Crandon Park
KEY BISCAYNE
Ritz-Carlton, Key Biscayne
South Beach
23rd St.
22nd St.
21st St.
20th St.
Park Ave.
Liberty Ave.
Gansevoort South
Setai
Shore Club
Townhouse
Dade Blvd.
Convention Center Dr.
18th St.
Cadet Hotel
James Ave.
Catalina Hotel & Beach Club
17th St.
Delano Hotel
National Hotel
Lincoln Rd. Mall
Ritz-Carlton, South Beach
16th St.
Loews Miami Beach Hotel
15th St.
Espanola Way
14th St.
13th St.
12th St.
Flamingo Park
Villa Paradiso
The Tides
Pennsylvania Ave.
Washington Ave.
11th St.
Best Western South Beach
10th St.
Essex House
The Hotel
9th St.
Lummus Park
Alton Rd.
Michigan Ave.
Jefferson Ave.
Meridian Ave.
Euclid Ave.
Collins Ave.
Ocean Dr.
8th St.
Pelican
7th St.
Angler's Resort

> **WORD OF MOUTH**
>
> "I just returned from a trip to the Keys and spent the last night of the trip at the Cadet Hotel (in Miami). Just around the corner from the Delano, it is a little jewel. The rooms are small but immaculate, and the furnishings are very tasteful." —bon_voyage

$$$$ Fodor's Choice ★ **Four Seasons Hotel Miami.** Stepping off busy Brickell Avenue into this hotel, you see a soothing water wall trickling down from above. Inside, a cavernous lobby is barely big enough to hold the enormous sculptures—part of the hotel's collection of local and Latin American artists. A 2-acre-pool terrace on the 7th floor overlooks downtown Miami, yet makes you forget you're in the middle of the city. The hotel's best feature is the beautiful Sports Club/LA, complete with complimentary yoga and exercise classes. Three heated pools include a foot-deep wading pool with 24 palm tree "islands." Service is tops for Miami. **Pros:** sensational service; amazing gym and pool deck. **Cons:** no balconies. ✉ *1435 Brickell Ave., Downtown Miami* ☎ *305/358–3535 or 800/819–5053* 🌐 *www.fourseasons.com/miami* *182 rooms, 39 suites* *In-room: a/c, safe. In-hotel: restaurant, bars, pools, gym, spa, Internet terminal, Wi-Fi hotspot, parking (paid)* *AE, D, DC, MC* ✥ *5D.*

$$$$ Fodor's Choice ★ **Mandarin Oriental, Miami.** If you can afford to stay here, do. The location, at the tip of Brickell Key in Biscayne Bay, is superb. Rooms facing west overlook the downtown skyline; to the east are Miami Beach and the blue Atlantic. There's also beauty in the details: sliding screens that close off the baths, dark wood, crisp linens, and room numbers hand-painted on rice paper at check-in. The Azul restaurant, with an eye-catching waterfall and private dining area at the end of a catwalk, serves a mix of Asian, Latin, Caribbean, and French cuisine. The hotel has a 20,000-square-foot private beach and an on-site spa. **Pros:** only beach (man-made) in downtown; intimate feeling; top luxury hotel. **Cons:** small pool; few beach cabanas. ✉ *500 Brickell Key Dr., Downtown Miami* ☎ *305/913–8288 or 866/888–6780* 🌐 *www.mandarinoriental.com* *326 rooms, 31 suites* *In-room: a/c, safe, Internet. In-hotel: 2 restaurants, bars, pool, gym, spa, children's programs (ages 5–12), laundry service, Wi-Fi hotspot, parking (paid)* *AE, D, DC, MC, V* ✥ *5D.*

$ **Viceroy.** Miami's newest hotel has a brash, super-sophisticated South Beach attitude—something that distinguishes it wholly from every other Miami nonbeach hotel. With game lounges (pool and poker rooms) just off to the side, it's fair to say that the 15th-floor pool deck here is the most stylish, fun-oriented, and impressive of any in America. The main pool is 300 feet long (the longest in Florida) and terminates in mesmerizing view of Biscayne Bay and surrounding islands. The lawn furniture and oversized cabanas the Delano made famous inspire the decor here. It also has a gargantuan hot tub, the size of a regular pool. The rooftop lounge and bar (on the 50th floor) are for guests only, and the views and design of this sophisticated retreat are impressive—the space can function as a lobby aerie. Designed by Kelly Wearstler, the rooms are dramatically contemporary and beautiful. She also designed the restaurant here, Eos, which was opened by two of the biggest names in American gastronomy: chef Michael Psilakis and restaurateur Donatella Arpaia. **Pros:** sensationally designed spa area; fantastic game room and pool deck; sleek rooms. **Cons:** downtown location rather than the beach; tiny lobby. ✉ *485 Brickell Ave., Downtown Miami* ☎ *305/503–4400 or 866/781–9923* 🌐 *www.viceroymiami.com* *150 rooms, 18 suites* *In-room: a/c, safe, kitchen (some), refrigerator (some), DVD (some), Wi-Fi. In-hotel: restaurant, room service, bars, pools, gym, spa, laundry service, Internet terminal, Wi-Fi hotspot, parking (paid), some pets allowed* ▭ *AE, D, DC, MC, V* *BP* ✥ *5D.*

FISHER AND BELLE ISLANDS

$$$$ **Fisher Island Hotel & Resort.** Want to explore Fisher Island? Assuming you don't have a private yacht, there are three ways to gain access to the island just off South Beach: you can either become a club member (initiation fee alone: $25,000), be one of the 750 equity members who have vacation places here (starting price: $8 million), or book a night at the club hotel (basic villa: $900 a night). Once you've made it, you'll be welcomed at reception with champagne. Considering you get a private house, a golf cart, and a fenced-in backyard with a hot tub, villas are a value for a memorable honeymoon or other lifetime event, if not a casual weekend. Families should stay in one of three former guest cottages of the former Italianate mansion of William K. Vanderbilt (in 1925 he swapped Carl Fisher *his* yacht for the island), which forms the centerpiece of this resort. A 9-hole golf course, the surprisingly affordable Spa Internazionale, and 18 lighted tennis courts (hard, grass, and clay), kids' programs, and 1 mi of very private (and very quiet) white-sand beach imported from the Bahamas means there's plenty of sweet nothing to do here. Oh, and there are eight restaurants and a fun sunset tiki bar to choose from—Porto Cervo is the best Italian restaurant nobody knows about. The Garwood Lounge features nightly piano and seats just 16. Remarkably, this true exclusivity and seclusion is minutes from South Beach. **Pros:** great private beaches; exclusive surroundings; varied dining choices. **Cons:** expensive ferry rides take time. ✉ *1 Fisher Island Dr., Fisher Island* ☎ *305/535–6000 or 800/537–3708* 🌐 *www.fisherisland.com* *5 junior suites, 50 condo units, 6 villas, 3 cottages* *In-room: a/c, safe, refrigerator, DVD, Wi-Fi. In-hotel: 8 restaurants, golf course, tennis courts, pools, gym, spa, beachfront, water sports, children's programs (ages 4–12), laundry service, Internet terminal, Wi-Fi hotspot, parking (free), some pets allowed* ▭ *AE, D, DC, MC, V* ✥ *5E.*

Fodor's Choice ★

$$ **The Standard.** An extension of André Balazs's trendy, budget hotel chain, the Standard is a Hollywood newcomer that set up shop a few minutes from South Beach on an island just over the Venetian Causeway. The message: we'll do what we please, and the cool kids will follow. The scene is trendy 30- and 40-year-olds interested in the hotel's many "do-it-yourself" spa activities, including mud bathing, scrubbing with sea salts, soaking in hot or arctic-cold waters, and yoga. An 8-foot, 103-degree cascade into a Roman hot tub is typical of the handful of adult pleasures spread around the pool deck. An informal restaurant overlooks the bay's Mediterranean-style mansions and the cigarette boats that float past. If you choose, you can go kayaking around the

island. On the hotel facade you'll see the monumental signage of a bygone occupant, the Lido Spa Hotel, and the much smaller sign of its current occupant, hung, with a wink, upside down. The rooms are small and simple, though they have thoughtful touches like a picnic basket and embroidered fabric covers for the small flat-screen TVs. First-floor rooms have outdoor soaking tubs but very limited privacy, so few take that plunge. **Pros:** interesting island location; free bike and kayak rentals; swank pool scene; great spa; inexpensive. **Cons:** removed from South Beach nightlife; small rooms with no views; outdoor tubs are gimmicks; mediocre service. ✉ *40 Island Ave., Belle Isle* ☎ *305/673–1717* 🌐 *www.standardhotel.com* *104 rooms, 1 suite* *In-room: a/c, safe, refrigerator, DVD, Internet, Wi-Fi. In-hotel: restaurant, room service, bars, pool, gym, spa, water sports, bicycles, laundry service, Wi-Fi hotspot, parking (paid), some pets allowed, no kids under 14* *AE, D, DC, MC, V* ✢ *4E.*

MID-BEACH

¢–$ Fodor's Choice ★ **Circa 39 Hotel.** This stylish budget boutique hotel pays attention to every detail and gets them all right. In its lobby, inspired in miniature by the Delano hotel, tall candles burn all night. The pool has cabanas and umbrella-shaded chaises that invite all-day lounging. Beyond the pool is a cute bar with board games. Rooms have wood floors and a cool, crisp look with white furnishings dotted with pale-blue pillows. The name Circa 39? It was built in 1939 and is on 39th Street. **Pros:** affordable; chic; intimate; beach chairs provided. **Cons:** not on the beach side of Collins Avenue; no Wi-Fi in rooms (however, there is Wi-Fi in the hotel, for a fee). ✉ *3900 Collins Ave., Mid-Beach* ☎ *305/538–4900 or 877/824–7223* 🌐 *www.circa39.com* *96 rooms* *In-room: a/c, safe, kitchen, refrigerator, Internet. In-hotel: restaurant, bar, pool, gym, Wi-Fi hotspot, parking (paid), some pets allowed* *AE, D, DC, MC, V* *CP* ✢ *4F.*

$$$$ **Eden Roc Renaissance Resort & Spa.** Like its next-door neighbor, the Fontainebleau, this grand 1950s hotel designed by Morris Lapidus just completed a head-to-toe renovation, with the addition of a new 21-story tower and huge pool complex. In the process, the Eden Roc doubled its room count and is now one of the biggest and sleekest hotels in the city. The landmark public areas have retained their grand elegance, including the monumental rosewood columns that surround the social lobby space, centered by an upscale bar. The room renovations have renewed the allure and perhaps returned the swagger of a stay at the Eden Roc to the heights it had reached after opening in the 1950s. For a glimpse of the old glamour, visit Harry's Grille, which has murals of former guests, a veritable roll call of '50s and '60s stars. **Pros:** all-new rooms and facilities; great pools. **Cons:** not on South Beach. ✉ *4525 Collins Ave., Mid-Beach* ☎ *305/531–0000 or 800/327–8337* 🌐 *www.edenrocresort.com* *631 rooms* *In-room: a/c, safe, kitchen (some), refrigerator, Wi-Fi. In-hotel: 3 restaurants, room service, bars, pools, gym, spa, beachfront, Wi-Fi hotspot, parking (paid)* *AE, D, DC, MC, V* ✢ *3F.*

$$$ Fodor's Choice ★ **Fontainebleau**. Look out, South Beach—Mid-Beach is back. When this classic property reopened in late 2008 it became Miami's biggest hotel—twice the size of the Loews, with more than 1,500 rooms; it became, indeed, the fruit of the most ambitious and expensive hotel-renovation project in the history of Greater Miami. So what does a $1 billion renovation get you? Eleven restaurants and lounges, a huge nightclub, sumptuous pools with cabana islands, a state-of-the-art fitness center and a 40,000-square-foot spa, and more than 100,000 square feet of meeting and ballroom space—all of it built from scratch. Also, two all-suites lavish towers come with full kitchens including dishwashers. In possibly a first for a big hotel anywhere, all rooms on the property have Apple desktop computers. But not everything is brand-new: two Morris Lapidus–designed, landmarked exteriors and lobbies were restored to their original state. To make way, though, all original rooms were completely gutted, down to the beams, to create new, contemporary rooms. This is a complex of historic proportions. **Pros:** historic design mixed with all-new facilities; fabulous pools. **Cons:** away from the South Beach pedestrian scene; too big to be intimate. ✉ *4441 Collins Ave., Mid-Beach* ☎ *305/538–2000 or 800/548–8886* 🌐 *www.fontainebleau.com* *1,504 rooms* *In-room: a/c, safe, kitchen (some), refrigerator, DVD (some), Wi-Fi. In-hotel: 11 restaurants, bars, pools, gym, spa, water sports, laundry service, Internet terminal, Wi-Fi hotspot, parking (paid)* *AE, D, DC, MC, V* ✥ *4F.*

¢–$ **Ocean Surf Hotel**. Don't expect luxury in this colorful art deco lodge, but if you want a cheap stay away from everybody and ideal beach access, you can't beat the tiny Ocean Surf Hotel. The hotel is on a cute one block stretch called Ocean Terrace that's directly across the street from the beach. The area will feel like your secret. There's also a small Days Inn here, but the Ocean Surf has more art deco charm. Sure the beds are squishy and look like they're 20 years old, and frankly the hallways are small and humid, but where else will you stay across from the beach for $80 a night? The location off 74th Street puts this quiet hotel well out of the reach of boisterous South Beach. Add in free Continental breakfast, and you've got a great crash pad for a low-key vacation. **Pros:** adorable art deco hotel; cheap; free Continental breakfast. **Cons:** basic rooms; no Internet; spotty service. ✉ *7436 Ocean Terr., Mid-Beach* ☎ *305/866–1648 or 800/555–0411* 🌐 *www.theoceansurfhotel.com* *49 rooms* *In-room: a/c, safe, refrigerator. In-hotel: beachfront, parking (paid)* *AE, MC, V* *CP* ✥ *2F.*

$$ **The Palms South Beach**. Stay here if you're seeking an elegant, relaxed property away from the noise but still near South Beach. The Palms has an exceptional beach, an easy pace, and beautiful gardens with soaring palm trees and inviting hammocks. A 2008 renovation has left the rooms looking as fabulous as the grounds, and a 5,000-square-foot Aveda spa was in the works. There are more large palms inside the Great Room lounge just off the lobby and designer Patrick Kennedy used subtle, natural hues of ivory, green, and blue for the homey, well-lighted rooms. **Pros:** tropical garden; relaxed and quiet. **Cons:** no balconies; away from South Beach. ✉ *3025 Collins Ave., Mid-Beach* ☎ *305/534–0505 or 800/550–0505* 🌐 *www.thepalmshotel.com* *220*

rooms, 22 suites ♁ *In-room: a/c, safe, refrigerator, Wi-Fi. In-hotel: restaurant, room service, bars, pool, beachfront, laundry service, Wi-Fi hotspot, parking (paid)* ▭ *AE, D, DC, MC, V* ✥ *4F.*

NORTH MIAMI BEACH

AVENTURA

$$$$ **Fairmont Turnberry Isle Resort & Club.** Golfers and families will enjoy this upscale resort with one of the best service staffs in the city. The lush resort doesn't just feel like a country club: the LPGA Tour hosts an annual tournament here every April. The sprawling 300-acre resort has a tremendous lagoon pool with a winding waterslide and a lazy river, a wonderful three-story spa, and a delicious new steak house from Michael Mina called Bourbon. The rooms are also jumbo-sized, decorated in calming tan hues and equipped with every amenity you could need. Add two Robert Trent Jones–designed golf courses, four clay tennis courts, and a 117-boat marina, and you've got a corporate vacationer's dream. South Beach may seem a world away—and it's about a 10-minute drive to any beach—but anyone who wants to delve into Ocean Drive madness can access the resort's private Ocean Club at Collins Avenue and 17th Street. **Pros:** great golf, pools, and restaurants; free shuttle to Aventura Mall. **Cons:** far from the beach; no nightlife. ✉ *19999 W. Country Club Dr., Aventura* ☎ *305/932–6200 or 800/327–7028* 🌐 *www.turnberryisle.com* ⇨ *392 rooms, 41 suites* ♁ *In-room: a/c, safe, kitchen (some), refrigerator, DVD (some), Wi-Fi. In-hotel: 2 restaurants, bars, golf courses, tennis courts, pools, gym, spa, water sports, bicycles, laundry service, Internet terminal, Wi-Fi hotspot, parking (paid), some pets allowed* ▭ *AE, D, DC, MC, V* ✥ *1F.*

BAL HARBOUR

$$$$ **The Regent Bal Harbour.** The tiny, tony town of Bal Harbour finally has a hotel worthy of its ultra-high-end mall. The new Regent is the latest word in contemporary luxury design. Rooms are outfitted with mahogany floors; large terraces offering panoramic views of the water and city (the northwest corner suites have the best views in Miami); bathrooms with 10-foot, floor-to-ceiling windows; and 42-inch flat-screen TVs (plus a small TV incorporated into the bathroom mirror—the latest technological interior-design trick). Suites are furnished with fully equipped kitchens with cooktops, microwaves, convection ovens, dishwashers, and refrigerators. Split your afternoons between the outdoors—enjoying the pool and 750 feet of pristine beachfront—and the hotel's lavish, on-site Guerlain Spa and fitness center, as well as a nice bar and fancy restaurant. **Pros:** great views; beachfront; great contemporary-art collection. **Cons:** pricey; limited lobby socializing. ✉ *10295 Collins Ave., Bal Harbour* ☎ *305/455–5400* 🌐 *www.regenthotels.com* ⇨ *124 rooms, 63 suites* ♁ *In-room: a/c, safe, kitchen, refrigerator, DVD, Wi-Fi. In-hotel: restaurant, room service, bar, tennis courts, pools, gym, spa, beachfront, water sports, bicycles, laundry service, parking (paid)* ▭ *AE, D, MC, V* ✥ *2F.*

12

SUNNY ISLES

$$$$ **Fodor's Choice** ★ **Acqualina Resort & Spa on the Beach.** When it opened in 2006, this hotel raised the bar for luxury in Miami, and it stands as one of the city's best hotels. You'll pay for it, too: Acqualina promises a lavish Mediterranean lifestyle with lawns and pool set below terraces that evoke Vizcaya, and Ferraris and Lamborghinis lining the driveway. There is much to love about the amenities here, including three gorgeous pools, the colossal ESPA spa, and the trendiest of restaurants, including one of only a handful in Miami to offer unobstructed beach views. And, upon arrival, you're escorted to your room for a personal in-room check-in. Rooms are sinfully comfortable, with every conceivable frill. Even standard rooms facing away from the ocean seem grand; they have huge flat-screens that rise out of the foot of the bed, making recumbent TV watching seem like a theater experience. If you're planning to pop the big question on your vacation, a Proposal Concierge will help set the scene. **Pros:** in-room check-in; luxury amenities; huge spa. **Cons:** guests have to pay an extra $40 to use the steam room or sauna. ✉ *17875 Collins Ave., Sunny Isles* ☎ *305/918–8000* 🌐 *www.acqualinaresort.com* *54 rooms, 43 suites* *In-room: a/c, safe, refrigerator, Wi-Fi. In-hotel: 3 restaurants, room service, bars, pools, gym, spa, beachfront, water sports, children's programs (ages 5–12), laundry service, Internet terminal, Wi-Fi hotspot, parking (paid)* *AE, D, DC, MC, V* ✢ *1F.*

¢ **Fodor's Choice** ★ **Travelodge Monaco Beach Resort.** The last of a dying breed, the Travelodge Monaco is a true find. Peek inside the courtyard and you'll see older men and women playing shuffleboard. Some have been coming here for 50 years, and it seems almost out of charity that the Monaco stays open for them today. In high season, rooms peak at only $130, and are nearly half that much of the year. Want a kitchen? Ten dollars more. Naturally the furnishings are simple, but they're clean, and the oceanfront wing literally extends out onto the sand. So there's no wireless Internet in the rooms—who needs it? Read a book under one of the tiki huts on the beach. You don't need to reserve them, and you don't pay extra. This is easily the best value of any hotel in Miami. **Pros:** steps to great beach; wholly unpretentious; bottom-dollar cost. **Cons:** older rooms; not service-oriented; no Wi-Fi in room, and public Wi-Fi in hotel has a fee. ✉ *17501 Collins Ave., Sunny Isles* ☎ *305/932–2100 or 800/227–9006* 🌐 *www.monacomiamibeachresort.com* *110 rooms* *In-room: a/c, safe, kitchen (some), refrigerator. In-hotel: restaurant, bar, pool, beachfront, Wi-Fi hotspot, parking (paid)* *AE, D, DC, MC, V* ✢ *1F.*

SOUTH BEACH

$ **Angler's Boutique Resort.** Angler's has the feel of a sophisticated private Mediterranean villa community. Duplex apartments here are like wonderful contemporary apartments, complete with private sunning gardens or private rooftop terraces with hot tubs. Single-floor studio options are set around a wonderful pool. This property has a pervasive air of serenity and privacy, largely created by the spotless cleanliness and the wonderful gardens—all of which make you completely forget

Fodor's Choice ★

Acqualina Resort & Spa on the Beach

Biltmore Hotel

Circa 39 Hotel

Delano Hotel

Fodor's Choice ★

Ritz-Carlton, Key Biscayne

Four Seasons Hotel Miami

The Tides South Beach

Mandarin Oriental

that the hotel is off busy Washington Avenue, two blocks from the beach. Instead it's a private little oasis. The hotel was originally built in 1930 by architect Henry Maloney. Hemingway was a guest. The property was completely redone and opened again in 2008. There's a good restaurant in the lobby. **Pros:** gardened private retreat. **Cons:** on busy Washington Ave. ✉ *660 Washington Av., South Beach* ☎ *305/534–9600* 🌐 *www.theanglersresort.com* *24 rooms, 20 suites* *In-room: a/c, safe, kitchen (some), refrigerator (some), DVD (some), Internet (some), Wi-Fi. In-hotel: restaurant, room service, bar, pool, laundry service, Internet terminal, Wi-Fi hotspot, parking (paid), some pets allowed* ▭ *AE, D, DC, MC, V* *BP* ✣ *G6*

¢ **Cadet Hotel.** You can trace the fact that this is one of the sweetest, quietest hotels in South Beach to the ways of its independent female owner, a local doctor named Vilma Biaggi. (There are very few privately owned hotels here anymore.) The placid patio-garden is the perfect spot to enjoy a full breakfast. Little touches, like candles in the lobby, fresh flowers all around, high-thread-count sheets, and small pouches that contain fresh lavender or seashells, depending on the season, show care and sophistication. The boutique hotel is two blocks from Lincoln Road, two blocks from the beach, across the street from Casa Tua. Clark Gable stayed in Room 225 when he came to Miami for Army Air Corps training in the 1940s; he'd been enrolled at West Point, and thus the hotel's name. A new spa pool and restaurant, Pied-a-Terre, opened in the back in 2010. **Pros:** well run with friendly service; lovely garden; great value. **Cons:** no pool. ✉ *1701 James Ave., South Beach* ☎ *305/672–6688 or 800/432–2338* 🌐 *www.cadethotel.com* *32 rooms, 3 suites* *In-room: a/c, safe, Wi-Fi. In-hotel: bar, laundry service, Wi-Fi hotspot* ▭ *AE, D, DC, MC, V* *CP* ✣ *4H.*

$–$$ **Catalina Hotel & Beach Club.** The Catalina is the budget party spot in the heart of South Beach's hottest block. It's across the street from the beach, but makes up for it with free drinks nightly, airport shuttles, bike rentals, two fun pools, and beach chairs, all for south of $300 a night. Each of the Catalina's three buildings has a distinct feel: The original Catalina (with the smallest, most inexpensive rooms) is an exercise in camp, with red-shag carpets, two-story glass windows, and monumental sheer drapes. The midrange rooms are in the old Maxine Hotel, decorated in rock baroque and featuring a karaoke machine in the lobby. Room 400 here is one of the beach's best values, with a private sundeck overlooking the strip. The newest, and most luxurious, addition is the Dorset Hotel, which now houses Catalina's biggest rooms as well as its new sushi restaurant, Kung Fu Chus. Another outdoor restaurant overlooking the passersby on this very sexy strip of Collins Avenue makes the Catalina an entertainment complex in its own right. **Pros:** free drinks; free bikes; free airport shuttle; good people-watching. **Cons:** $15 wireless fee; service not a high priority; loud. ✉ *1732 Collins Ave., South Beach* ☎ *305/674–1160* 🌐 *www.catalinahotel.com* *200 rooms* *In-room: a/c, safe, refrigerator, Wi-Fi. In-hotel: restaurant, bars, pool, bicycles, laundry service, Wi-Fi hotspot, parking (paid), some pets allowed* ▭ *AE, D, DC, MC, V* ✣ *5H.*

$ **Century Hotel.** If this is your second time staying in South Beach, consider this cheap but tidy hotel at the southern end of the island. It's a dozen blocks south of the big scene but offers the same amazing (though quieter) beach, and it gives you a chance to discover some of the city's best restaurants, which happen to be steps away: Big Pink, Joe's, Prime One Twelve, and Nemo's. Designed in 1939 by art deco master Henry Hohauser, the Century is a cute two-story art deco masterpiece, impeccably maintained down to the terrazzo floors. Rooms are wonderful values for their wood floors, and clean, new furniture. A rarity anywhere in Miami: this is a pet-friendly hotel. Off-season weekend rooms are $199; weekday rooms off-season are $89. The owner, West Tucker, works at the front desk. **Pros:** quiet South Beach location; clean; across from beach; classic art deco building; personal attention. **Cons:** not in the heart of South Beach; no pool; simple rooms. ✉ *140 Ocean Dr., South Beach* ☎ *305/674–8855 or 888/982–3688* 🌐 *www.centurysouthbeach.com* *26 rooms* *In-room: a/c, safe, Wi-Fi. In-hotel: Internet terminal, parking (paid), some pets allowed* ▭ *AE, DC, MC, V* *CP* ✣ *F5.*

$$$$ Fodor's Choice ★ **Delano Hotel.** The decor of this grand hotel is inspired by Lewis Carroll's Alice in Wonderland, and as you make your way from the sparse, busy, spacious lobby past cascading white curtains and through rooms dotted with strange, whimsical furniture pieces, you will feel like you are indeed falling down a rabbit hole. Brush by celebrities and expatriates as you make your way to the vast oceanfront gardens and enormous pool outside, where the rich and famous lounge in white cabanas. Like most hotels on South Beach's hottest strip, the Delano boasts glamour and wealth. Unlike some of the other hotels, the Delano's smartly designed rooms and helpful staff make the illusion a reality. Make sure to visit the hotel's brand-new "Florida Room," an über-exclusive lounge designed by Lenny Kravitz with a glass baby grand piano that he plays whenever he's in town. **Pros:** electrifying design; lounging among the beautiful and famous. **Cons:** crowded; scene-y; small rooms; expensive. ✉ *1685 Collins Ave., South Beach* ☎ *305/672–2000 or 800/555–5001* 🌐 *www.delano-hotel.com* *184 rooms, 24 suites* *In-room: a/c, safe, refrigerator, Wi-Fi. In-hotel: 3 restaurants, room service, bars, pool, gym, spa, beachfront, laundry service, Wi-Fi hotspot, parking (paid)* ▭ *AE, D, DC, MC, V* ✣ *5H.*

$ **Essex House.** You'll get your own South Beach people-watching perch on the outdoor patio at this wonderfully restored art deco gem. A favorite with Europeans, especially the British, Essex House has average-size rooms with midcentury-style red furniture and marble tubs. The suites, reached by crossing a courtyard, are well worth the price: each has a wet bar, king-size bed, pull-out sofa, 100-square-foot bathroom, refrigerator, and hot tub. The lobby mural was created in 1938 by artist Earl Le Pan, and touched up by him 50 years later. Ask for a discount when you're booking; off-season rates are under $100. **Pros:** a social, heated pool; great art deco patio; good service. **Cons:** small pool; not on the beach. ✉ *1001 Collins Ave., South Beach* ☎ *305/534–2700 or 800/815–829* 🌐 *www.essexhotel.com* *61 rooms, 15 suites* *In-*

room: a/c, Wi-Fi. In-hotel: bar, pool, laundry service, Wi-Fi hotspot, parking (paid) ▭ *AE, D, DC, MC, V* ✥ *6H.*

$$$$ **Gansevoort South**. For the well-heeled, party-seeking, jet-setting crowd, there's a new South Beach hotel to toy with: this southern cousin of New York's trendsetting Meatpacking District hotel is better than the original, starting with a fantastic beachfront setting. Want to swim or lounge around with a drink? The huge rooftop pool and bar is the best use of a rooftop in Miami; and the 50,000-square-foot plaza level has a big pool and an informal open-air restaurant. The contemporary aesthetic starts in the big, sleek lobby, awash in funky lights and a massive aquarium stocked with small sharks. Not in the thick of South Beach, the hotel has privacy and is relatively quiet. Rooms are quite large, and highly comfortable, though views are disappointing. The hotel has a David Barton Gym and Spa, and fabulous restaurants STK and Phillipe. **Pros:** spacious rooms (averaging 700 square feet); big, fun setting with huge pool deck and rooftop; fancy on-site restaurants. **Cons:** room views aren't amazing; a few blocks too far from most SoBe foot traffic. ✉ *2377 Collins Ave., South Beach* ☎ *305/604–1000* 🌐 *www.gansevoortsouth.com* *334 rooms* *In-room: a/c, safe, kitchen (some), refrigerator, Internet, Wi-Fi. In-hotel: 2 restaurants, room service, bar, pool, gym, spa, beachfront, water sports, laundry service, Wi-Fi hotspot, parking (paid)* ▭ *AE, D, MC, V* ✥ *4H.*

$$ **The Hotel**. Fashion designer Todd Oldham wanted to preserve the art deco roots of the Hotel, which inhabits the historic Tiffany building, while making it modern. So, he made it tie-dye. Everything in this quirky, romantic boutique hotel, from the decor of four-star restaurant, Wish, to the bathrobes hanging in the small but cute bathrooms, is stained blue and green. Somehow the décor, paired with soft browns and whites and accented with the knowing eye of a mega-designer, works. Add soft lighting and two-person bathtubs, and you have all the makings of a romantic retreat. The hotel's most exquisite treat is a rooftop bar, a low-key hangout where locals and hotel guests lounge under the neon light of the Tiffany sign on Thursday, Friday, and Saturday nights. **Pros:** great service; coolest roof-deck bar in town; good for couples. **Cons:** pool is tiny; rooms have no view. ✉ *801 Collins Ave., South Beach* ☎ *305/531–2222 or 877/843–4683* 🌐 *www.thehotelofsouthbeach.com* *48 rooms, 4 suites* *In-room: a/c, safe, Wi-Fi. In-hotel: restaurant, room service, bar, pool, laundry service, Internet terminal, Wi-Fi hotspot, parking (paid)* ▭ *AE, D, DC, MC, V* ✥ *6H.*

$$$$ **Loews Miami Beach Hotel**. The oldest of South Beach's "new hotels," Loews Miami Beach is marvelous for families, businesspeople, and groups. The 800-room megahotel combines top-tier amenities, a massive new spa, a great pool, and a direct beachfront setting in its pair of enormous 12- and 18-story towers. When it was built in 1998, Loews managed not only to snag 99 feet of beach, but also to take over the vacant St. Moritz next door and restore it to its original 1939 art deco beauty. The entire complex combines boutique charm with updated opulence. How big is it? The Loews has 85,000 square feet of meeting space and an enormous ocean-view grand ballroom. Emeril Lagasse

opened a restaurant here, and a three-story spa has 15 treatment rooms and a state-of-the-art fitness center. In the grand lobby you'll find a dozen black-suited staffers behind the counter, and a half dozen other bellboys and valets. Rooms are great: contemporary and very comfortable, with flat-screen TVs and high-end amenities. If you like big hotels with all the services, this is your choice in South Beach. **Pros:** top-notch amenities include a beautiful oceanfront pool and immense spa. **Cons:** intimacy is lost due to its large size. ✉ *1601 Collins Ave., South Beach* ☎ *305/604–1601 or 800/235–6397* 🌐 *www.loewshotels.com/miamibeach* *733 rooms, 57 suites* *In-room: a/c, Internet, Wi-Fi. In-hotel: 3 restaurants, room service, bars, pool, gym, spa, beachfront, laundry service, Internet terminal, Wi-Fi hotspot, parking (paid), some pets allowed* ▭ *AE, D, DC, MC, V* ✣ *5H.*

WORD OF MOUTH

"If you can get a hotel room at a good price than you should come to Miami during Art Basel week (first weekend in Dec.). It's a very, very cosmopolitan atmosphere. It will be busy but if you like being in a city then you'll enjoy the energy with all sorts of interesting people, art lovers, artists, celebrities, and art everywhere. It's the best week to feel alive in Miami."
—SoBchBud1

12

$$ **National Hotel.** This luxurious, beautiful hotel serves as a bastion of calm in the sea of white-on-white mod decor and raucous reveling usually reserved for the beachfront masterpieces lining Collins Avenue between 15th and 20th streets. Unlike its neighbors, the National hasn't parted with its art deco past. Most of the chocolate- and ebony-hued pieces in the lobby date back to the 1930s, and the baby grand piano beckons toward a throwback D-Bar Lounge. The most spectacular feature is Miami Beach's longest and most beautiful pool, which stretches from the tower to a duo of tropical tiki bars, a series of comfy black-and-white-striped cabanas and poolside tables, and then the beach. Note, however, that rooms in the main tower are disappointing and far from the pool; stay in the cabana wing if you can. **Pros:** stunning pool; perfect location. **Cons:** tower rooms aren't impressive; neighboring hotels can be noisy on the weekends. ✉ *1677 Collins Ave., South Beach* ☎ *305/532–2311 or 800/327–8370* 🌐 *www.nationalhotel.com* *143 rooms, 9 suites* *In-room: a/c, safe, DVD, Internet, Wi-Fi. In-hotel: 2 restaurants, room service, bars, pools, gym, beachfront, laundry service, Internet terminal, Wi-Fi hotspot, parking (paid), some pets allowed* ▭ *AE, DC, MC, V* ✣ *5H.*

Fodor's Choice ★

$$ **Pelican.** The spirit of Diesel clothing company, which owns this Ocean Drive boutique, permeates the hotel. Each room is completely different, fashioned from a mix of antique and garage-sale furnishings selected by the designer of Diesel's clothing-display windows. Each room has its own name, and repeat guests either try to stay in a different one each time, or else fall in love with one room and request it for every stay. For example, the "Me Tarzan, You Vain" room has a jungle theme, with African wood sculptures and a stick lamp; "Up, Up in the Sky" has a space theme, with a model rocket and off-kilter furniture. The best bet is to head down to the Pelican's porch-front restaurant, which

offers one of the most extensive wine lists in town and a bar-none view of Ocean Drive's people parade. **Pros:** unique, over-the-top design; central Ocean Drive location. **Cons:** rooms are so tiny that the quirky charm wears off quickly; no no-smoking rooms. ✉ *826 Ocean Dr., South Beach* ☎ *305/673–3373 or 800/773–5422* 🌐 *www.pelicanhotel.com* *28 rooms, 4 suites* *In-room: a/c, safe, refrigerator, Wi-Fi. In-hotel: restaurant, room service, bar, beachfront, laundry service, Wi-Fi hotspot, parking (paid)* *AE, D, DC, MC, V* ✣ *6H.*

$$$$ **Ritz-Carlton, South Beach.** A sumptuous affair, the Ritz-Carlton is the only truly luxurious property on the beach that *feels* like it's on the beach, because its long pool deck leads you right out to the water. There are all the usual high-level draws the Ritz is known for, that is, attentive service, a kids' club, a club level with five food presentations a day, and high-end restaurants. The spa has exclusive brands of scrubs and creams, and dynamite staff, including a "tanning butler" who will make sure you're not burning, and will apply lotion in the hard-to-reach places. Thursday through Saturday, enjoy Grammy-nominated percussionist Sammy Figueroa, who plays Latin Jazz by the pool. The wonderful diLido Beach club restaurant is, believe it or not, one of the very few places in Miami where you can get a beachside meal. (You may recognize the handsome chef Jeff McInnis from a successful stint on TV's "Top Chef.") The ocean is on one side and the pedestrian Lincoln Road begins on the other: the locale is tops. Overall, this landmarked 1954 art moderne hotel, designed by Melvin Grossman and Morris Lapidus, has never been hotter. **Pros:** luxury rooms; great service; great location. **Cons:** too big to be intimate. ✉ *1 Lincoln Rd., South Beach* ☎ *786/276–4000 or 800/241–3333* 🌐 *www.ritzcarlton.com* *375 rooms* *In-room: a/c, safe, refrigerator, Wi-Fi. In-hotel: 4 restaurants, room service, bars, pools, gym, spa, beachfront, children's programs (ages 5–12), laundry service, Wi-Fi hotspot, parking (paid), some pets allowed* *AE, D, DC, MC, V* ✣ *5H.*

$$$$ **Setai.** Even if you can't afford a stay at Miami's priciest hotel, take time to visit the city's most beautifully designed space. The place feels like an Asian museum, serene and beautiful, with heavy granite furniture lifted by orange accents, warm candlelight, and the soft bubble of seemingly endless pools and ponds. The oceanfront gardens are expansive, lush, and painstakingly manicured. Three infinity pools, heated to 75°F, 85°F, and 95°F lead to an oceanfront terrace and then, white sand. The rooms are as expansive as the premises and furnished in an Asian style that is at once minimalist and cozy. **Pros:** quiet and classy; beautiful grounds. **Cons:** somewhat cold aura; TVs are far from the beds. ✉ *101 20th St., South Beach* ☎ *305/520–6000 or 888/625–7500* 🌐 *www.setai.com* *110 rooms* *In-room: a/c, safe, refrigerator, DVD, Wi-Fi. In-hotel: restaurant, room service, bars, pools, gym, spa, beachfront, laundry service, Wi-Fi hotspot, parking (paid), some pets allowed* *AE, D, DC, MC, V* ✣ *4H.*

$$$$ **Shore Club.** Unquestionably the destination for the young, the rich, and the ready to party, Shore Club is the perfect adult playground. Don't spend your time in the rooms—they're nothing special, and the white-on-white decor feels more cold than cool. Instead, venture down to the lobby, where a peek behind the cascading white curtains can yield a celebrity, a scandal, or a make-out session. More debauchery awaits at Sky Bar, the glitziest outdoor bar on the strip. Step into Tuscan restaurant Ago, or Nobu (if you can afford it), and watch Hollywood royalty graze on Japanese-Peruvian delicacies. In terms of lounging, people-watching, and poolside glitz, this is the best of South Beach. **Pros:** good restaurants and bars; nightlife in your backyard. **Cons:** uninviting rooms; snooty service. ✉ *1901 Collins Ave., South Beach* ☎ *305/695–3100 or 877/640–9500* 🌐 *www.shoreclub.com* *309 rooms, 79 suites* *In-room: a/c, safe, refrigerator, Wi-Fi. In-hotel: 2 restaurants, room service, bars, pools, gym, spa, beachfront, laundry service, Wi-Fi hotspot, parking (paid), some pets allowed* ▭ *AE, D, DC, MC, V* ✥ *4H.*

$$$$ Fodor's Choice ★ **The Tides.** The Tides is the best boutique hotel in Miami, and the classiest of the Ocean Drive art deco hotels. The exceptionally tactful personalized service makes every guest feel like a celebrity, and the hotel looks like no other in the city. A head-to-toe renovation modeled the interior after a jewelry box: gone is the stark white-on-white minimalism that made it famous, replaced with soft pinks and corals, gilded accents, and marine-inspired decor. The new Coral Bar—a tiny space irresistibly ensconced in the back of the lobby—boasts rums from around the world, and La Marea restaurant offers delectable seafood. The Tides' main competition is its neighbor, Hotel Victor, but the Tides' rooms are large and all have direct ocean views. The pool here is private as can be. Seeking taste and discretion? *Voilà.* **Pros:** superior service; great beach location; ocean views from all suites plus the terrace restaurant. **Cons:** tiny elevators. ✉ *1220 Ocean Dr., South Beach* ☎ *305/604–5070 or 866/438–4337* 🌐 *www.thetideshotel.com* *45 suites* *In-room: a/c, safe, Internet, Wi-Fi. In-hotel: restaurant, pool, gym, beachfront, laundry service, Wi-Fi hotspot, parking (paid)* ▭ *AE, D, DC, MC, V* ✥ *5H.*

$ ★ **Townhouse.** Though sandwiched between the Setai and the Shore Club—two of the coolest hotels on the planet—the Townhouse doesn't try to act all dolled up: it's comfortable being the shabby-chic, lighthearted, relaxed, no-frills, fun hotel on South Beach. Rooms aren't luxurious, and you won't find many amenities (no gym, no spa, no pool), but if you want to stay in the middle of the action for under $200, in simple, clean digs with a good sense of simple style, this may be a good choice. Enter through a brightly lit, spacious white lobby; after check-in, head to a small but freshly adorned white-and-red room that comes with a beach ball you can keep. The hotel has a rooftop terrace with plush red lounge chairs and a DJ on weekends. A hip sushi restaurant, Bond St. Lounge, is downstairs, and delivers to rooms during restaurant hours. With its clean white backdrops and discounts for crew members, there's always a good chance a TV production or magazine shoot is happening. **Pros:** a great budget buy for the style-hungry. **Cons:** no pool; small rooms not designed for long stays. ✉ *150 20th St., east of Collins Ave., South Beach* ☎ *305/534–3800 or 877/534–3800* 🌐 *www.townhousehotel.com* *69 rooms, 2 suites* *In-room: a/c, safe, Internet, Wi-Fi. In-hotel: restaurant, room service, bar, bicycles, laundry* *facilities, laundry service, Wi-Fi hotspot, parking (paid)* ▭ *AE, D, DC, MC, V* 🍽 *CP* ✣ *4H.*

¢ 🏨 **Villa Paradiso.** One of South Beach's best deals, Paradiso has huge rooms with kitchens and a charming tropical courtyard with benches for hanging out at all hours. There's even another smaller courtyard on the other side of the rooms. Peeking out from a sea of tropical foliage, the hotel seems at first to be a rather unassuming piece of art deco architecture. But for all its simplicity, value shines bright. Rooms have polished hardwood floors, French doors, and quirky wrought-iron furniture. They are well suited for extended visits—discounts begin at 10% for a week's stay. **Pros:** great hangout spot in courtyard; good value; great location. **Cons:** no Wi-Fi; no pool; no restaurant. ✉ *1415 Collins Ave., South Beach* ☎ *305/532–0616* 🌐 *www.villaparadisohotel.com* ⇨ *17 studios* ⌂ *In-room: a/c, kitchen, refrigerator, Internet. In-hotel: some pets allowed* ▭ *AE, D, DC, MC, V* ✣ *5H.*

The Everglades

WORD OF MOUTH

"Sign up at the Ernest Coe Visitor Center or call ahead to Flamingo Visitor Center for the free ranger-led canoe tour. Fantastic experience. The group met at the Nine-Mile Pond at 8 a.m. and paddled for 4 hours on the pond and through mangroves. Only 4 other couples and 1 family with a 10 year-old on the trip. No experience necessary—maneuvering the long canoe through the twists and turns of the mangroves was a bit of a challenge, but very fun."

—JC98

WELCOME TO THE EVERGLADES

Airboat.

TOP REASONS TO GO

★ **Fun Fishing:** Cast for some of the world's fightingest game fish—600 species of fish in all—in the Everglades' backwaters.

★ **Abundant Birdlife:** Check hundreds of birds off your life list, including—if you're lucky—the rare Everglades snail kite.

★ **Cool Kayaking:** Do a half-day trip in Big Cypress National Preserve or reach for the ultimate—the 99-mi Wilderness Trail.

★ **Swamp Cuisine:** Been hankering for alligator tail and frogs' legs? Or how about swamp cabbage, made from hearts of palm? Better yet, try stone crab claws fresh from the traps.

★ **Great Gator-Spotting:** This is ground zero for alligator viewing in the United States, and you won't leave without spotting your quota.

1 Everglades National Park. Alligators, Florida panthers, black bears, manatees, dolphins, bald eagles, and roseate spoonbills call this vast habitat home.

2 Biscayne National Park. Mostly underwater, here's where the string of coral reefs and islands that form the Florida Keys begin.

Nature tour boat.

Great White Egret.

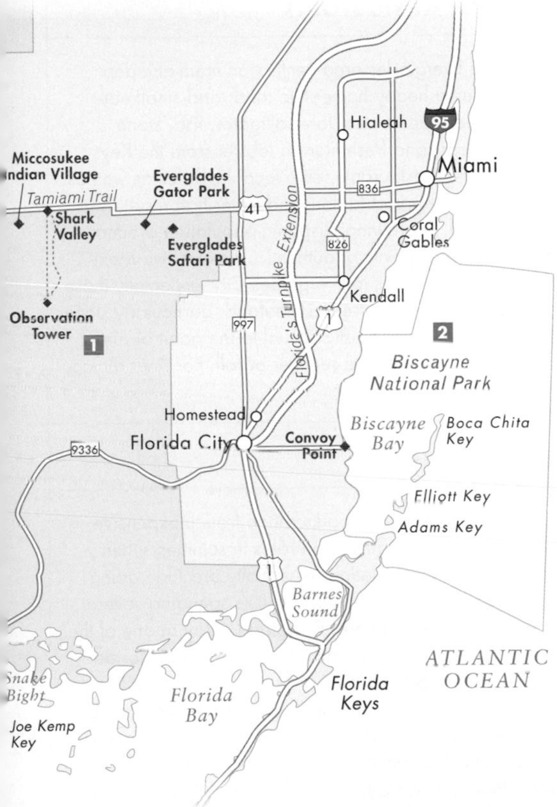

3 Big Cypress National Preserve. Neighbor to Everglades National Park, it's an outdoor-lover's paradise.

Shark Valley.

13

GETTING ORIENTED

The southern third of the Florida peninsula is largely taken up by protected government land that includes Everglades National Park, Big Cypress National Preserve, and Biscayne National Park. Miami lies to the northeast, while Naples and Marco Island are northwest. Land access to Everglades National Park is primarily by two roads. The park's main road traverses the southern Everglades from the gateway towns of Homestead and Florida City to the outpost of Flamingo, on Florida Bay. In the northern Everglades, Tamiami Trail (U.S. 41) runs from the Greater Miami area on the east coast or from Naples on the west coast to the western park entrance in Everglades City at Route 29.

THE EVERGLADES PLANNER

When to Go

Winter is the best time to visit the Everglades, and the busiest. Temperatures and mosquito activity are more tolerable, low water levels concentrate the resident wildlife, and migratory birds swell the avian population. In late spring the weather turns hot and rainy, and tours and facilities are less crowded. Migratory birds depart, and you must look harder to see wildlife. Summer brings intense sun and afternoon rainstorms. Water levels rise and mosquitoes descend, making outdoor activity virtually unbearable, unless you swath yourself in netting. Mosquito repellent is a necessity any time of year.

Flying In

Miami International Airport (MIA) is 34 mi from Homestead and 47 mi from the eastern access to Everglades National Park. *For MIA airline carrier information, refer to the Miami chapter.* Shuttles run between MIA and Homestead. Southwest Florida International Airport (RSW) in Fort Myers, a little over an hour's drive from Everglades City, is the closest major airport to the Everglades' western access. On-demand taxi transportation from the airport to Everglades City is available.

About the Restaurants

Dining in the Everglades area centers on mom-and-pop places that serve hearty home-style food, and small eateries that specialize in local fare: alligator, fish, stone crab, frogs' legs, and fresh Florida lobster from the Keys. American Indian restaurants serve local favorites as well as catfish, Indian fry bread (a flour-and-water flatbread), and pumpkin bread. A growing Hispanic population around Homestead means plenty of authentic, inexpensive Mexican cuisine. Restaurants in Everglades City, especially those along the river, have the freshest seafood, particularly stone crab. These places are mostly casual to the point of rustic, and are often closed in late summer or fall. For finer dining, go to Marco Island or Naples.

About the Hotels

Accommodations near the parks range from inexpensive to moderate and offer off-season rates in summer, when rampant mosquito populations essentially preclude going outdoors for any length of time. If you're spending several days exploring the east coast Everglades, stay in one of the park's campgrounds; 11 mi away in Homestead–Florida City, where there are reasonably priced motels and RV parks; or in the Florida Keys or the Greater Miami–Fort Lauderdale area. Lodgings and campgrounds are also available on the Gulf Coast in Everglades City, Naples, and Marco Island. Florida City's selection is mostly of the chain variety and geared toward business travelers.

WHAT IT COSTS

	¢	$	$$	$$$	$$$$
Restaurants	Under $10	$10–$15	$15–$20	$20–$30	over $30
Hotels	Under $80	$80–$100	$100–$140	$140–$220	over $220

Restaurant prices are per person for a main course at dinner. Hotel prices are for a standard double room, excluding 6% sales tax (more in some counties) and 1%–5% tourist tax.

Everglades National Park

More than 1.5 million acres of South Florida's 4.3 million acres of subtropical, watery wilderness were given national-park status and protection in 1947 with the creation of Everglades National Park. It is one of the country's largest national parks and is recognized by the world community as a Wetland of International Importance, an International Biosphere Reserve, and a World Heritage Site. Come here if you want to spend the day biking, hiking, or boating in deep, raw wilderness with lots of wildlife.

Biscayne National Park

To the east of Everglades National Park, Biscayne National Park brings forth a pristine, magical, subtropical Florida. It is the nation's largest marine park and the largest national park within the continental United States boasting living coral reefs. A small portion of the park's 172,000 acres consists of mainland coast and outlying islands, but 95% is under water. Of particular interest are the mangroves and their tangled masses of stiltlike roots that thicken the shorelines. These "walking trees," as locals call them, have curved prop roots, which arch down from the trunk, and aerial roots drop from branches. The trees draw freshwater from saltwater and create a coastal nursery that sustains myriad types of marine life. You can see Miami's high-rise buildings from many of Biscayne's 44 islands, but the park is virtually undeveloped and large enough for escaping everything that Miami and the Upper Keys have become. To truly escape, don scuba diving or snorkeling gear, and lose yourself in the wonders of the coral reefs.

Big Cypress National Preserve

On the northern edge of Everglades National Park is Big Cypress National Preserve, one of South Florida's least-developed watersheds. Established by Congress in 1974 to protect the Everglades, it comprises extensive tracts of prairie, marsh, pinelands, forested swamps, and sloughs. Hunting is allowed, as is off-road-vehicle use. Come here if you like alligators. Stop at the Oasis Visitor Center to walk the boardwalk with alligators lounging underneath and then drive Loop Road for a backwoods experience. If time permits, kayak the Turner River. **■TIP→ Many activities in the parks and preserve are based on water, so be prepared to get a bit damp on the marshy trails.**

Nearby Towns

Surrounding the parks and preserve are several small communities: Everglades City, Florida City, and Homestead, home to many area outfitters.

⇨ *While outfitters are listed with the parks and preserve, see our What's Nearby section later in this chapter for information about each town.*

Camping in the Everglades

For an intense stay in the "real" Florida, consider one of some four dozen backcountry campsites deep in Everglades National Park, many inland, some on the beach. You'll have to carry in your food, water, and supplies, and carry out all your trash. You'll also need a site-specific permit, available on a first-come, first-served basis from the Flamingo or Gulf Coast visitors centers. Permits cost $10, plus $2 per night for sites, with a 14-night limit, and are only issued up to 24 hours in advance. Front-country camping fees at park campgrounds are $16 per night.

THE FLORIDA
EVERGLADES

by Lynne Helm

Alternately described as elixir of life or swampland muck, the Florida Everglades is one of a kind—a 50-mi-wide "river of grass" that spreads across hundreds of thousands of acres. It moves at varying speeds depending on rainfall and other variables, sloping south from the Kissimmee River and Lake Okeechobee to estuaries of Biscayne Bay, Florida Bay, and the Ten Thousand Islands.

Today, apart from sheltering some 70 species on America's endangered list, the Everglades also embraces more than 7 million residents, 50 million annual tourists, 400,000 acres of sugarcane, and the world's largest concentration of golf courses.

Demands on the land threaten the Everglades' finely balanced ecosystem. Irrigation canals for agriculture and roadways disrupt natural water flow. Drainage for development leaves wildlife scurrying for new territory. Water runoff, laced with fertilizers, promotes unnatural growth of swamp vegetation. What remains is a miracle of sorts, given decades of these destructive forces.

Creation of the Everglades required unique conditions. South Florida's geology, linked with its warm, wet subtropical climate, is the perfect mix for a marshland ecosystem. Layers of porous, permeable limestone create water-bearing rock, soil, and aquifers, which in turn affects climate, weather, and hydrology.

This rock beneath the Everglades reflects Florida's geologic history—its crust was once part of the African region. Some scientists theorize that continental shifting merged North America with Africa, and then continental rifting later pulled North America away from the African continent but took part of northwest Africa with it—the part that is today's Florida. The Earth's tectonic plates continued to migrate, eventually placing Florida at its current location as a land mass jutting out into the ocean, with the Everglades at its tip.

EXPERIENCING THE ECOSYSTEMS

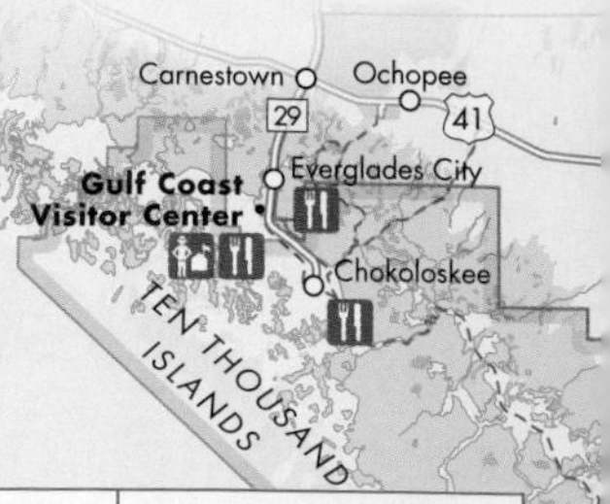

Eight distinct habitats exist within Everglades National Park, Big Cypress National Preserve, and Biscayne National Park.

ECOSYSTEMS	EASY WAY	MORE ACTIVE WAY
COASTAL PRAIRIE: An arid region of salt-tolerant vegetation lies between the tidal mud flats of Florida Bay and dry land. **Best place to see it: The Coastal Prairie Trail**	Take a guided boat tour of Florida Bay, leaving from Flamingo Marina.	Hike the Coastal Prairie Trail from Eco Pond to Clubhouse Beach.
CYPRESS: Capable of surviving in standing water, cypress trees often form dense clusters called "cypress domes" in natural water-filled depressions. **Best place to see it: Big Cypress National Preserve**	Drive U.S. 41 (also known as Tamiami Trail—pronounced Tammy-Amee), which cuts across Southern Florida, from Naples to Miami.	Hike (or drive) the scenic Loop Road, which begins off Tamiami Trail, running from the Loop Road Education Center to Monroe Station.
FRESH WATER MARL PRAIRIE: Bordering deeper sloughs are large prairies with marl (clay and calcium carbonate) sediments on limestone. Gators like to use their toothy snouts to dig holes in prairie mud. **Best place to see it: Pahayokee Overlook**	Drive there from the Ernest F. Coe Visitor Center.	Take a guided tour, either through the park service or from permitted, licensed guides. You also can set up camp at Long Pine Key.
FRESH WATER SLOUGH AND HARDWOOD HAMMOCK: Shark River Slough and Taylor Slough are the Everglades' two sloughs, or marshy rivers. Due to slight elevation amid sloughs, dense stands of hardwood trees appear as teardrop-shaped islands. **Best place to see it: The Observation Tower**	Take a two-hour guided tram tour from the Shark Valley Visitor Center to the tower and back.	Walk or bike (rentals available) the route to the tower via the tram road and (walkers only) Bobcat Boardwalk trail and Otter Cave Hammock Trail.
MANGROVE: Spread over South Florida's coastal channels and waterways, mangrove thrives where Everglades fresh water mixes with salt water. **Best place to see it: The Wilderness Waterway**	Picnic at the area near Long Pine Key, which is surrounded by mangrove, or take a water tour at Biscayne National Park.	Boat your way along the 99-mi Wilderness Waterway. It's six hours by motorized boat, seven days by canoe.
MARINE AND ESTUARINE: Corals, sponges, mollusks, seagrass, and algae thrive in the Florida Bay, where the fresh waters of the Everglades meet the salty seas. **Best place to see it: Florida Bay**	Take a boat tour from the Flamingo Visitor Center marina.	Canoe or kayak on White Water Bay along the Wilderness Waterway Canoe Trail.
PINELAND: A dominant plant in dry, rugged terrain, the Everglades' diverse pinelands consist of slash pine forest, saw palmettos, and more than 200 tropical plant varieties. **Best place to see it: Long Pine Key trails**	Drive to Long Pine Key, about 6 mi off the main road from Ernest F. Coe Visitor Center.	Hike or bike the 28 mi of Long Pine Key trails.

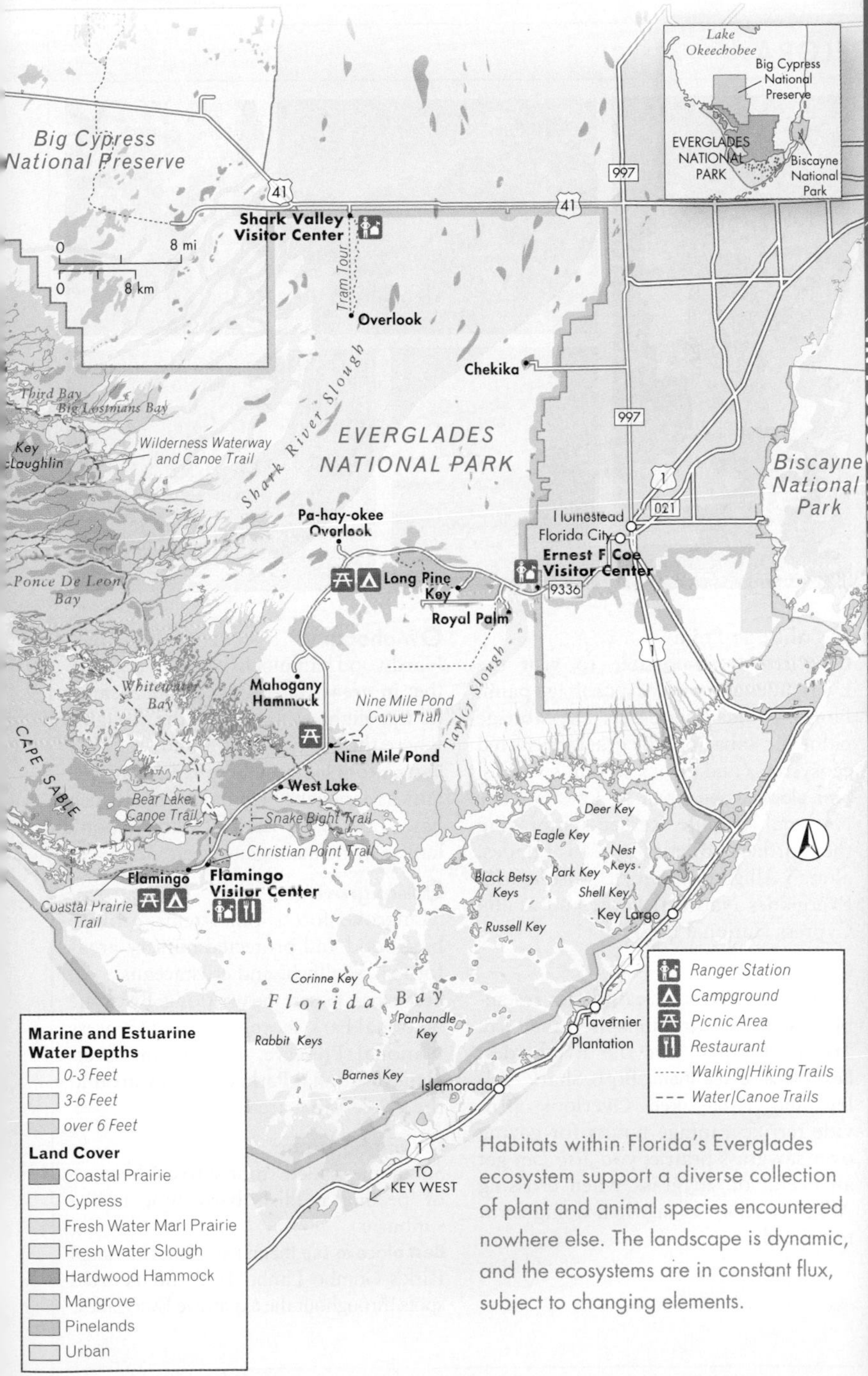
Lake Okeechobee
Big Cypress National Preserve
EVERGLADES NATIONAL PARK
Biscayne National Park
Big Cypress National Preserve
41
997
Shark Valley Visitor Center
Tram Tour
Overlook
0 8 mi
0 8 km
Chekika
Third Bay
Big Lostmans Bay
Key McLaughlin
Wilderness Waterway and Canoe Trail
Shark River Slough
EVERGLADES NATIONAL PARK
Biscayne National Park
1
021
Homestead
Florida City
Ernest F Coe Visitor Center
9336
Pa-hay-okee Overlook
Long Pine Key
Royal Palm
Ponce De Leon Bay
Whitewater Bay
Mahogany Hammock
Nine Mile Pond Canoe Trail
Taylor Slough
Nine Mile Pond
CAPE SABLE
West Lake
Bear Lake Canoe Trail
Snake Bight Trail
Christian Point Trail
Deer Key
Eagle Key
Nest Keys
Black Betsy Keys
Park Key
Shell Key
Flamingo
Flamingo Visitor Center
Coastal Prairie Trail
Key Largo
Russell Key
Corinne Key
Florida Bay
Panhandle Key
Rabbit Keys
Tavernier
Plantation
Barnes Key
Islamorada
TO KEY WEST
Ranger Station
Campground
Picnic Area
Restaurant
Walking/Hiking Trails
Water/Canoe Trails
Marine and Estuarine Water Depths
0-3 Feet
3-6 Feet
over 6 Feet
Land Cover
Coastal Prairie
Cypress
Fresh Water Marl Prairie
Fresh Water Slough
Hardwood Hammock
Mangrove
Pinelands
Urban

Habitats within Florida's Everglades ecosystem support a diverse collection of plant and animal species encountered nowhere else. The landscape is dynamic, and the ecosystems are in constant flux, subject to changing elements.

FLORA

❶ Cabbage Palm

It's virtually impossible to visit the Everglades and not see a cabbage palm, Florida's official state tree. The cabbage palm (or sabal palm), graces assorted ecosystems and grows well in swamps. **Best place to see them:** At Loxahatchee National Wildlife Refuge (embracing the northern part of the Everglades, along Alligator Alley), throughout Everglades National Park, and at Big Cypress National Preserve.

❷ Sawgrass

With spiny, serrated leaf blades resembling saws, sawgrass inspired the term "river of grass" for the Everglades. **Best place to see them:** Both Shark Valley and Pahayokee Overlook provide terrific vantage points for gazing over sawgrass prairie; you also can get an eyeful of sawgrass when crossing Alligator Alley, even when doing so at top speeds.

❸ Mahogany

Hardwood hammocks of the Everglades live in areas that rarely flood because of the slight elevation of the sloughs, where they're typically found.

Best place to see them: Everglades National Park's Mahogany Hammock Trail (which has a boardwalk leading to the nation's largest living mahogany tree).

❹ Mangrove

Mangrove forest ecosystems provide both food and protected nursery areas for fish, shellfish, and crustaceans.

Best place to see them: Along Biscayne National Park shoreline, at Big Cypress National Preserve, and within Everglades National Park, especially around the Caple Sable area.

❺ Gumbo Limbo

Sometimes called "tourist trees" because of peeling reddish bark (not unlike sunburns).

Best place to see them: Everglades National Park's Gumbo Limbo Trail and assorted spots throughout the expansive Everglades.

FAUNA

❶ American Alligator

In all likelihood, on your visit to the Everglades you'll see at least a gator or two. These carnivorous creatures can be found throughout the Everglades swampy wetlands.

Best place to see them: Loxahatchee National Wildlife Refuge (also sheltering the endangered Everglades snail kite) and within Everglades National Park at Shark Valley or Anhinga Trail. Sometimes (logically enough) gators hang out along Alligator Alley, basking in early morning or late-afternoon sun along four-lane I–75.

❷ American Crocodile

Crocs gravitate to fresh or brackish water, subsisting on birds, fish, snails, frogs, and small mammals.

Best place to see them: Within Everglades National Park, Big Cypress National Preserve, and protected grounds in or around Billie Swamp Safari.

❸ Eastern Coral Snake

This venomous snake burrows in underbrush, preying on lizards, frogs, and smaller snakes.

Best place to see them: Snakes typically shy away from people, but try Snake Bight or Eco Pond near Flamingo, where birds are also prevalent.

❹ Florida Panther

Struggling for survival amid loss of habitat, these shy, tan-colored cats now number around 100, up from lows of near 30.

Best place to see them: Protected grounds of Billie Swamp Safari sometimes provide sightings during tours. Signage on roadway linking Tamiami Trail and Alligator Alley warns of panther crossings, but sightings are rare.

❺ Green Tree Frog

Typically bright green with white or yellow stripes, these nocturnal creatures thrive in swamps and brackish water.

Best place to see them: Within Everglades National Park, especially in or near water.

BIRDS

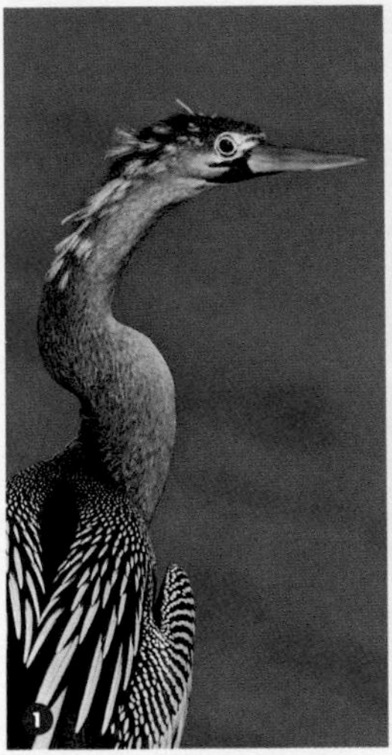

❶ Anhinga

The lack of oil glands for waterproofing feathers helps this bird to dive as well as chase and spear fish with its pointed beak. The Anhinga is also often called a "water turkey" because of its long tail, or a "snake bird" because of its long neck.

Best place to see them: The Anhinga Trail, which also is known for attracting other wildlife to drink during especially dry winters.

❷ Blue-Winged Teal

Although it's predominantly brown and gray, this bird's powder-blue wing patch becomes visible in flight. Next to the mallard, the blue-winged teal is North America's second most abundant duck, and thrives particularly well in the Everglades.

Best place to see them: Near ponds and marshy areas of Everglades National Park or Big Cypress National Preserve.

❸ Great Blue Heron

This bird has a varied palate and enjoys feasting on everything from frogs, snakes, and mice to shrimp, aquatic insects, and sometimes even other birds! The all-white version, which at one time was considered a separate species, is quite common to the Everglades.

Best place to see them: Loxahatchee National Wildlife Refuge or Shark Valley in Everglades National Park.

❹ Great Egret

Once decimated by plume hunters, these monogamous, long-legged white birds with S-shaped necks feed in wetlands, nest in trees, and hang out in colonies that often include heron or other egret species.

Best place to see them: Throughout Everglades National Park, along Alligator Alley, and sometimes even on the fringes of Greater Fort Lauderdale.

6

5

8

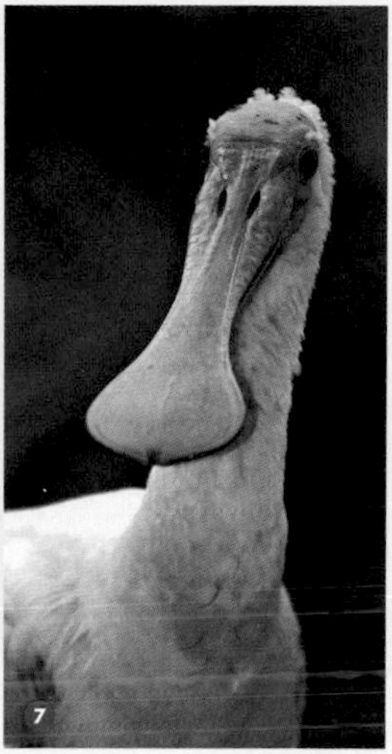
7

❺ Greater Flamingo

Flocking together and using long legs and webbed feet to stir shallow waters and mud flats, color comes a couple of years after hatching from ingesting shrimplike crustaceans along with fish, fly larvae, and plankton.

Best place to see them: Try Snake Bight or Eco Pond, near Flamingo Marina.

❻ Osprey

Making a big comeback from chemical pollutant endangerment, ospreys (sometimes confused with bald eagles) are distinguished by black eyestripes down their faces. Gripping pads on feet with curved claws help them pluck fish from water.

Best place to see them: Look near water, where they're fishing for lunch in the shallow areas. Try the coasts, bays, and ponds of Everglades National Park. They also gravitate to trees. You can usually spot them from the Gulf Coast Visitor Center, or you can observe them via boating in the Ten Thousand Islands.

❼ Roseate Spoonbill

These gregarious pink-and-white birds gravitate toward mangroves, feeding on fish, insects, amphibians, and some plants. They have long, spoon-like bills, and their feathers can have a touch of red and yellow. These birds appear in the Everglades year-round.

Best place to see them: Sandy Key, southwest of Flamingo, is a spoonbill nocturnal roosting spot, but at sunrise these colorful birds head out over Eco Pond to favored day hangouts throughout Everglades National Park.

❽ Wood Stork

Recognizable by featherless heads and prominent bills, these birds submerge in water to scoop up hapless fish. They are most common in the early spring and often easiest to spot in the morning.

Best place to see them: Amid the Ten Thousand Island areas, Nine Mile Pond, Mrazek Pond, and in the mangroves at Paurotis Pond.

● =Extremely Common ● =Very Common ● =Somewhat Common ● =Rare

THE BEST EVERGLADES ACTIVITIES

HIKING

Top experiences: At Big Cypress National Preserve, you can hike along designated trails or push through unmarked acreage. (Conditions vary seasonally, which means you could be tramping through waist-deep waters.) Trailheads for the Florida National Scenic Trail are at Loop Road off U.S. 41 and Alligator Alley at mile marker 63.

What will I see? Dwarf cypress, hardwood hammocks, prairies, birds, and other wildlife.

For a short visit: A 6.5-mi section from Loop Road to U.S. 41 crosses Robert's Lake Strand, providing a satisfying sense of being out in the middle nowhere.

With more time: A 28-mi stretch from U.S. 41 to I–75 (Alligator Alley) reveals assorted habitats, including hardwood hammocks, pinelands, prairie, and cypress.

Want a tour? Big Cypress ranger-led exploration starts from the Oasis Visitor Center, late November through mid-April.

WALKING

Top experiences: Everglades National Park magnets: wheelchair accessible walkways at Anhinga Trail, Gumbo Limbo Trail, Pahayokee Overlook, Mahogany Hammock, and West Lake Trail.

What will I see? Birds and alligators at Anhinga; tropical hardwood hammock at Gumbo Limbo; an overlook of the River of Grass from Pahayokee's tower; a subtropical tree island with massive mahogany growth along Mahogany Hammock; and a forest of mangrove trees on West Lake Trail.

For a short visit: Flamingo's Eco Pond provides for waterside wildlife viewing.

With more time: Shark Valley lets you combine the quarter-mile Bobcat Boardwalk (looping through sawgrass prairie and a bayhead) with the 1-mi-long round-trip Otter Cave, allowing you to steep in subtropical hardwood hammock.

Want a tour? Pahayokee and Flamingo feature informative ranger-led walks.

The Anhinga Trail near the Royal Palm Visitor Center at Everglades National Park

BOATING

Top experiences: Launch a boat from the Gulf Coast Visitors Center or Flamingo Marina. Bring your own watercraft or rent canoes or skiffs at either location.

What will I see? Birds from bald eagles to roseate spoonbills, plus plenty of mangrove and wildlife—and maybe even some baby alligators with yellow stripes.

For a short visit: Canoe adventurers often head for Hells Bay, a 3-mi stretch about 9 mi north of Flamingo. Or put in at the Turner River alongside the Tamiami Trail in the Big Cypress National Preserve and paddle all the way (about eight hours) to Chocoloskee Bay at Everglades City.

With more time: Head out amid the Ten Thousand Islands and lose yourself in territory once exclusively the domain of only the hardiest pioneers and American Indians. If you've got a week or more for paddling, the 99-mi Wilderness Waterway stretches from Flamingo to Everglades City.

Want a tour? Sign on for narrated boat tours at the Gulf Coast or Flamingo visitor center.

BIRD WATCHING

Top experiences: Anhinga Trail, passing over Taylor Slough.

What will I see? Anhinga and heron sightings are a nearly sure thing, especially in early morning or late afternoon. Also, alligators can be seen from the boardwalk.

For a short visit: Even if you're traveling coast to coast at higher speeds via Alligator Alley, chances are you'll spot winged wonders like egrets, osprey, and heron.

With more time: Since bird-watching at Flamingo can be a special treat early in the morning or late in the afternoon, try camping overnight even if you're not one for roughing it. Reservations are recommended. (Flamingo Lodge remains under reconstruction from 2005 hurricane damage.)

Want a tour? Ranger-led walks at Pahayokee and from Everglades National Park visitor centers provide solid birding background for novices.

(top left) Tourists cruise the Everglades by airboat; (bottom left) Green Heron; (right) Eastern Meadowlark

THE BEST EVERGLADES ACTIVITIES

BIKING

Top experiences: Shark Valley (where bicycling is allowed on the tram road) is great for taking in the quiet beauty of the Everglades. Near Ernest F. Coe Visitor Center, Long Pine Key's 14-mi nature trail also can be a way to bike happily away from folks on foot.

What will I see? At Shark Valley, wading birds, turtles, and, probably alligators. At Long Pine Key, shady pinewood with subtropical plants and exposed limestone bedrock.

For a short visit: Bike on Shark Valley tram road but turn around to fit time schedule.

With more time: Go the entire 15-mi tram road route, which has no shortcuts. Or try the 22-mi route of Old Ingraham Highway near the Royal Palm Visitor Center, featuring mangrove, sawgrass, and birds (including hawks).

Want a tour? In Big Cypress National Preserve, Bear Island Bike Rides (8 mi round-trip over four to five hours) happen on certain Saturdays.

SNORKELING

Top experiences: Biscayne National Park, where clear waters incorporate the northernmost islands of the Florida Keys.

What will I see? Dense mangrove swamp covering the park shoreline, and, in shallow waters, a living coral reef and tropical fish in assorted colors.

For a short visit: Pick a sunny day to optimize your snorkeling fun, and be sure to use sunscreen.

With more time: Advanced snorkel tours head out from the park on weekends to the bay, finger channels, and around shorelines of the barrier islands. Biscayne National Park also has canoe and kayak rentals, picnic facilities, walking trails, fishing, and camping.

Want a tour? You can swim and snorkel or stay dry and picnic aboard tour boats that depart from Biscayne National Park's visitor center.

(top left) Biking near the Shark Valley Visitor Area. (top right) Snorkeling on the surface in the Atlantic Ocean.

DID YOU KNOW?

You can tell you're looking at a crocodile if you can see its lower teeth protruding when its jaws are shut, whereas an alligator shows no teeth when his mouth is closed. Gators are much darker in color—a grayish black—compared with the lighter tan color of crocodiles. Alligators' snouts are also much broader than their long, thin crocodilian counterparts.

THE STORY OF THE EVERGLADES

Dreams of draining southern Florida took hold in the early 1800s, expanding in the early 1900s to convert large tracts from wetlands to agricultural acreage. By the 1920s, towns like Fort Lauderdale and Miami boomed, and the sugar industry—which came to be known as "Big Sugar"—established its first sugar mills. In 1947 Everglades National Park opened as a refuge for wildlife.

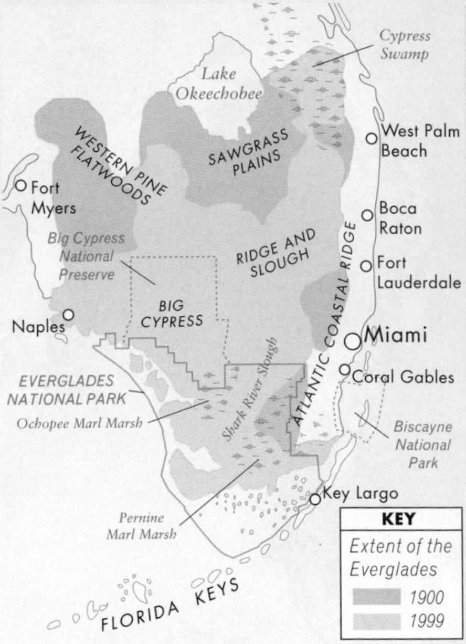

Meanwhile, the sugar industry grew. In its infancy, about 175,000 tons of raw sugar per year was produced from fields totaling about 50,000 acres. But once the U.S. embargo stopped sugar imports from Cuba in 1960 and laws restricting acreage were lifted, Big Sugar took off. Less than five years later, the industry produced 572,000 tons of sugar and occupied nearly a quarter of a million acres.

Fast-forward to 2008, to what was hailed as the biggest conservation deal in U.S. history since the creation of the national parks. A trailblazing restoration strategy hinged on creating a water flow-way between Lake Okeechobee and the Everglades by buying up and flooding 187,000 acres of land. The country's largest producers of cane sugar agreed to sell the necessary 187,000 acres to the state of Florida for $1.75 billion. Environmentalists cheered.

But within months, news broke of a scaled-back land acquisition plan: $1.34 billion to buy 180,000 acres. By spring 2009, the restoration plan had shrunk to $536,000 to buy 73,000 acres. With the purchase still in limbo, critics claim the state might overpay for acreage appraised at pre-recession values and proponents fear dwindling revenues may derail the plan altogether.

The Big Sugar land deal is part of a larger effort to preserve the Everglades. In 2010, two separate lawsuits charged the state, along with the United States Environmental Protection Agency, with stalling Everglades cleanup that was supposed to begin in 2006. "Glacial delay" is how one judge put it. The state must reduce phosphorus levels in water that flows to the Everglades or face fines and sanctions for violating the federal Clean Water Act. The fate of the Everglades remains in the balance.

EVERGLADES NATIONAL PARK

45 mi southwest of Miami International Airport.

Updated by Lynne Holm

If you're heading across South Florida on U.S. 41 from Miami to Naples, you'll breeze right through the Everglades. Also known as Tamiami Trail, this mostly two-lane road along much of the route skirts the edge of Everglades National Park and cuts across the Big Cypress National Preserve. You'll also be near the park if you're en route from Miami to the Florida Keys on U.S. 1, which travels through Homestead and Florida City, two communities east of the main park entrance. Basically, if you're in South Florida you can't get away from at least fringes of the Everglades. With tourist strongholds like Miami, Naples, and the Florida Keys so close by, travelers from all over the world typically make day trips to the park.

Everglades National Park has three main entry points: the park headquarters at Ernest F. Coe Visitor Center, southwest of Homestead and Florida City; the Shark Valley area, in the northern reaches and accessed by Tamiami Trail (U.S. 41); and the Gulf Coast Visitor Center, just south of Everglades City to the west and closest to Naples.

You can explore on your own or participate in free ranger-led hikes, bicycle tours, bird-watching tours, and canoe trips; the number and variety of these excursions are greatest from mid-December through Easter, and some (canoe trips, for instance) typically aren't offered in the sweltering summer. Among the more popular are the Anhinga Amble, a 50-minute walk around the Taylor Slough (departs from the Royal Palm Visitor Center), and the Early Bird Special, a 90-minute walk centered on birdlife (departs from Flamingo Visitor Center at 7:30 AM). Ask at the visitor centers for details.

PARK ESSENTIALS

Admission Fees $10 per vehicle, $5 per pedestrian, bicycle, or motorcycle. Admission, payable at gates, is good for seven days. Annual passes are $25.

Admission Hours The park is open daily, year-round, and both the main entrance near Florida City and Homestead, and the Gulf Coast entrance are open 24 hours. The Shark Valley entrance is open 8:30 AM to 6 PM.

COE VISITOR CENTER TO FLAMINGO

About 30 mi from Miami.

The most popular access to Everglades National Park is via the park headquarters entrance just southwest of Homestead and Florida City. If you're coming to the Everglades from Miami, the highway you'll take is Route 836 west to Route 826/874 south to the Homestead Extension of Florida's Turnpike, U.S. 1, and Krome Avenue (Route 997/ old U.S. 27). To reach the Ernest F. Coe Visitor Center from Homestead, go right (west) from U.S. 1 or Krome Avenue onto Route 9336 (Florida's only four-digit route) in Florida City and follow signs to the park entrance.

EXPLORING

To explore this section of the park, follow Route 9336 from the park entrance to Flamingo; there are many opportunities to stop along the way, and an assortment of activities to pursue in the Flamingo area. The following is arranged in geographic order.

Ernest F. Coe Visitor Center. Don't just grab your park map and go; this visitor center has numerous interactive exhibits and films that are well worth your time. The 15-minute film *River of Life,* updated frequently, provides a succinct park overview with emphasis on the river of grass. There is also a movie on hurricanes and a 35-minute wildlife film for children available upon request. A bank of telephones offers differing viewpoints on the Great Water Debate, detailing how last century's gung-ho draining of swampland for residential and agricultural development also cut off water-supply routes for precious wetlands in the Everglades ecosystem. A schedule of daily ranger-led activities parkwide, mainly walks and talks, and information on canoe rentals and boat tours at Flamingo is maintained. The Everglades Discovery Shop stocks books and jewelry including bird-oriented earrings, and you can browse through cool nature, science, and kids' stuff or pick up extra insect repellent. Coe Visitor Center is outside park gates, so you can stop in without paying park admission. ✉ *11 mi southwest of Homestead on Rte. 9336* ☎ *305/242–7700* ⏲ *Daily 8–5; hrs sometimes shortened in off-season.*

Main road to Flamingo. Route 9336 travels 38 mi from the Ernest F. Coe Visitor Center southwest to the Florida Bay at Flamingo. It crosses a section of the park's eight distinct ecosystems: hardwood hammock, freshwater prairie, pinelands, freshwater slough, cypress, coastal prairie, mangrove, and marine-estuarine. Route highlights include a dwarf cypress forest, the transition zone between sawgrass and mangrove forest, and a wealth of wading birds at Mrazek and Coot Bay ponds—where in early morning or late afternoon you can observe the hundreds of birds feeding. Boardwalks, looped trails, several short spurs, and observation platforms help you stay dry. You also may want to stop along the way to walk several short trails (each takes about 30 minutes): the popular, wheelchair-accessible **Anhinga Trail,** which cuts through sawgrass marsh and allows you to see lots of wildlife (be on the lookout for alligators and the trail's namesake, water birds known as anhingas); and junglelike—yet, also wheelchair-accessible—**Gumbo-Limbo Trail;** the **Pinelands Trail,** where you can see the limestone bedrock that underlies the park; the **Pahayokee Overlook Trail,** which ends at an observation tower; and the **Mahogany Hammock Trail** with its dense growth.

■ **TIP→** Before you head out on the trails, inquire about insect and weather conditions and plan accordingly, stocking up on bug repellent, sunscreen, and water as necessary. Also, even on seemingly nice days, it's probably smart to bring along a rain jacket.

13

★ **Royal Palm Visitor Center.** A must for anyone wanting to experience the real Everglades, and ideal for when there's limited time, this small center with a bookstore and vending machines permits access to the **Anhinga Trail boardwalk,** where in winter catching sight of alligators congregating in watering holes is almost guaranteed. Or follow the neighboring **Gumbo Limbo Trail** through a hardwood hammock. Both strolls are short (½ mi) and expose you to two Everglades ecosystems. Rangers conduct daily Anhinga Ambles in season (check for dates by calling ahead) starting at 10:30. At 1:30 the Glades Glimpse program takes place daily in season. Ask also about starlight walks and bike tours in season. ✉ *4 mi west of Ernest F. Coe Visitor Center on Rte. 9336* ☎ *305/242–7700* ⏲ *Daily 8–4:15.*

NEED A BREAK?

Good spots to pull over for a picnic lunch are Paurotis Pond, about 10 mi north of Florida Bay, or Nine Mile Pond, less than 30 mi from the main visitor center. Another option is along Bear Lake, 2 mi north of the Flamingo Visitor Center.

Flamingo. At the far end of the main road to Flamingo lies this community along Florida Bay, where you'll find a marina, visitor center, and campground, with nearby hiking and nature trails. Before hurricanes Katrina and Wilma washed them away in 2005, a lodge, cabins, and restaurants in Flamingo provided Everglades National Park's only accommodations. At press time, rebuilding of Flamingo Lodge was projected to materialize sometime after 2012, but for now, you can still pitch a tent or bring an RV to the campground, where improvements include solar-hot-water showers and electricity for RV sites. A long-popular houseboat rental concession may return in 2011.

Flamingo Visitor Center. Check the schedule here for ranger-led activities, such as naturalist discussions, hikes along area trails, and evening programs in the 100-seat campground amphitheater, opened in winter 2009–10 to replace the old gathering spot destroyed by 2005 hurricanes. Also, find natural history exhibits and pamphlets on canoe, hiking, and biking trails in the small Florida Bay Flamingo Museum on the 2nd floor of the visitor center. ✉ *1 Flamingo Lodge Hwy., Flamingo* ☎ *239/695–2945, 239/695–3101 marina* ⏲ *Exhibits are always open, staffed mid-Nov.–mid-Apr., daily 8–4:30.*

SPORTS AND THE OUTDOORS

BIRDING

Some of the park's best birding is in the Flamingo area.

BOATING

The 99-mi inland **Wilderness Trail** between Flamingo and Everglades City is open to motorboats as well as canoes, although powerboats may have trouble navigating the route above Whitewater Bay. Flatwater canoeing and kayaking are best in winter, when temperatures moderate, rainfall diminishes, and mosquitoes back off—a little, anyway. You don't need a permit for day trips, although there is a $5, 7-day launch fee for all boats brought into the park. The Flamingo area has well-marked canoe trails, but be sure to tell someone where you're going and when you expect to return. Getting lost is easy, and spending the night without proper gear can be unpleasant, if not dangerous.

> **GOOD READS**
>
> ■ *The Everglades: River of Grass.* This circa-1947 classic by pioneering conservationist Marjory Stoneman Douglas (1890–1998) is a must-read.
>
> ■ *Everglades Wildguide.* Jean Craighead George gives an informative account of the park's natural history in this official National Park Service handbook.
>
> ■ *Everglades: The Park Story.* Wildlife biologist William B. Robertson Jr. presents the park's flora, fauna, and history.

OUTFITTER **Flamingo Lodge, Marina, and Everglades National Park Tours** (✉ *1 Flamingo Lodge Hwy., on Buttonwood Canal, Flamingo* ☎ *239/695–3101*) is the official Everglades National Park concessionaire. The long-popular Flamingo Lodge, a victim of massive hurricane damage in 2005, remains closed pending funding for a new start, but Flamingo's marina and tours are back in action, going strong. The almost two-hour backcountry *Pelican* cruise ($26.50) is the most popular of its tours, winding under a heavy canopy of mangroves, and revealing abundant wildlife—from alligators, crocodiles, and turtles to herons, hawks, and egrets. The marina has charter boats, and rents 17-foot power skiffs from 7 AM for $195 per day (eight hours, if returned by 4 PM) $155 per half day, $80 for two hours. Small (up to two paddlers) and family-size (up to four) canoes rent from $16 per two-hour minimum, $22 for four hours, and $40 for overnight. Two-person charter fishing trips can be arranged for weekends ($350 for a half day or $450 a day; each additional person pays $25). Cost includes tackle, ice, and license. The concessionaire rents rods, reels, and other equipment by the half and full day.

WHERE TO CAMP

■ **TIP→ In the dry winter season, be careful with campfires and matches; this is when the wildfire-prone sawgrass prairies and pinelands are most vulnerable.**

★ **Flamingo.** This campground has 234 drive-in sites; most overlook the bay, and nine of 64 walk-in sites are along water. Ninety sites are available through a reservation system from mid-November through March and on a first-come, first-served basis the rest of the year. In low season, be prepared to pay with cash in case a park employee is not at the campground kiosk when you arrive. If this is the case, just deposit cash into yellow envelopes at what's called the kiosk's "iron ranger." Park personnel cross-check paid envelopes with sites on a regular basis. < *Flush toilets, dump station, drinking water, showers (cold), general store* *234 drive-up sites, 64 walk-in sites* *877/444–6777 campsite reservations, 305/242–7700 park information, 239/695–0124 camping information* *www.recreation.gov* *D, MC, V.*

¢ **Long Pine Key.** About 6 mi west of the park's main entrance, Long Pine Key has drive-up sites for tents and RVs, several area hiking trails, and a pond for fishing (permit required). Sites are available on a first-come, first-served basis. Be prepared to pay cash via park-supplied yellow envelope on arrival if a park employee is not at the campground kiosk between December and April. Camping is free the rest of the year. *Flush toilets, dump station, drinking water, picnic tables* *108 drive-up sites* *305/242–7700* *www.nps.gov/ever* *D, MC, V.*

13

GULF COAST ENTRANCE

To reach the park's western gateway, take U.S. 41 west from Miami for 77 mi, turn left (south) onto Route 29, and travel another 3 mi through Everglades City to the Gulf Coast Ranger Station. From Naples on the Gulf Coast, take U.S. 41 east for 35 mi, then turn right onto Route 29.

Gulf Coast Visitor Center. The best place to bone up on Everglades National Park's watery western side is at this visitor center just south of Everglades City, where rangers are on hand to answer any of your questions. In winter, canoeists check in here for trips to the Ten Thousand Islands and 99-mi Wilderness Waterway Trail, nature lovers view interpretive exhibits on local flora and fauna while waiting for naturalist-led boat trip departures, and backcountry campers purchase permits. In season (Christmas through Easter), rangers lead bike tours and canoe trips. No direct roads run from here to other sections of the park, and admission is free only to this section of the park. *Rte. 29, Everglades City* *239/695–3311* *Mid-Nov.–mid-Apr., daily 8–4:30; mid-Apr.–mid-Nov., daily 9–4:30.*

OUTFITTERS On the west side, **Everglades National Park Boat Tours** (*Gulf Coast Visitor Center, Everglades City* *239/695–2591 or 866/628–7275* *www.nps.gov/ever*), operating in conjunction with boat tours at Flamingo, runs 1½-hour trips ($26.50) through the Ten Thousand Islands National Wildlife Refuge, where passengers often see dolphins, manatees, bald eagles, and roseate spoonbills. In the height of the season, 49-passenger boats run every 30 to 45 minutes daily. Mangrove wilderness tours are also conducted on smaller boats for up to six passengers. These one-hour, 45-minute trips ($35) are the best option to see alligators. The outfitter also rents 16-foot aluminum canoes. Reservations are not accepted.

Fodor's Choice ★ **Everglades Rentals & Eco Adventures** (*Ivey House, 107 Camellia St., Everglades City* *Box 5038, Everglades City 34139* *877/567–0679 or 239/695–3299* *www.evergladesadventures.com*) is an established source for canoes, sea kayaks, and guided Everglades paddling tours

Much skill is required to navigate boats through the shallow, muddy waters of the Everglades.

year-round, and a Swamp Stomp walking tour ($104, October–April) includes a box lunch. Canoe rentals cost from $35 the first day, $27 for each day thereafter. Day-long kayak rentals are from $45. All half-day rentals are from 1 to 5 PM. Shuttles deliver you to major launching areas such as Turner River ($30 for up to two people) and Collier-Seminole State Park ($60). Tour highlights include bird and gator sightings, mangrove forests, no-man's-land beaches, relics of hideouts for infamous and just-plain-reclusive characters, and spectacular sunsets. Longer adventures ($800 for two nights to $1,300 for six nights, with a two-person minimum) include canoe/kayak and equipment rental, all necessary camping equipment, a guide, and meals.

SHARK VALLEY

23½ mi west of Florida's Turnpike, off Tamiami Trail. Approximately 45 minutes west of Miami.

One thing you won't see at Shark Valley is sharks. The name comes from the Shark River, also called the River of Grass, which flows through the area. Several species of shark swim up this river from the coast (about 45 mi south of Shark Valley) to give birth. Young sharks (called pups), vulnerable to being eaten by adult sharks and other predators, gain strength in waters of the slough before heading out to sea to fend for themselves.

EXPLORING

Though Shark Valley is the national park's north entrance, no roads here lead directly to other parts of the park. However, it's still worth stopping here to take a tram tour and climb the observation tower halfway through the ride.

Prefer to do the trail on foot? It takes a bit of nerve to walk the paved 15-mi loop in Shark Valley because in the winter months alligators lie on and alongside the road, basking in the sun—most, however, do move quickly out of the way.

> **WORD OF MOUTH**
>
> "We drove from Ft. Lauderdale to the Everglades and rented bikes to do the loop at Shark Valley. Lots of wildlife to see! It took us the morning. I think you get better views of the wildlife on the bikes than the tram and of course since you can stop anytime you want, better pics. It's a very easy ride since it's flat and paved."
>
> — klam_chowder

You can also ride a bicycle (the outfitter here rents one-speed, well-used bikes daily 8:30–4 for $7 per hour) or take a two-hour guided tram tour (reservations recommended in winter). Just behind the bike-rental area a short boardwalk trail meanders through the sawgrass, and another one passes through a tropical hardwood hammock. An underwater live camera in the canal behind the center (viewed from the gift shop) lets visitors sporadically see the alligators and otters.

Shark Valley Visitor Center. The small center has rotating exhibits, a bookstore, and park rangers ready for your questions. ✉ *23½ mi west of Florida's Turnpike, off Tamiami Trail* ☎ *305/221–8776* ⏲ *Late Mar.–late Dec., daily 9:15–5:15; late Dec.–late Mar., daily 8:45–5:15; gate daily 8:30–6.*

Observation Tower. At the Shark Valley trail's end (really, the halfway point of the 15-mi loop), you can pause to navigate the now wheelchair-accessible ramp of this tower, first built in 1984, spiraling 50 feet upward. Once on top, the River of Grass gloriously spreads out as far as your eye can see. Observe water birds as well as alligators and, perhaps even river otters crossing the road.

TOUR ★ **Shark Valley Tram Tours**. Starting at the Shark Valley visitor center, two-hour, narrated tours ($16.25) follow a 15-mi loop road—especially good for viewing gators—into the interior, stopping at a 50-foot observation tower. Reservations are recommended December through April. ✉ *Valley Visitor Center* ☎ *305/221–8455* 🌐 *www.sharkvalleytramtours.com* 🎫 *$16.25 per person* ⏲ *Tours Dec.–Apr., hourly 9–4; May–Nov., hourly 9–3.*

SPORTS AND THE OUTDOORS

BOATING

Many Everglades-area tours operate only in season, roughly November through April.

From the Shark Valley area, **Buffalo Tiger's Airboat Tours** (✉ *5 mi east of Shark Valley* ☎ *305/559–5250* 🌐 *www.buffalotigersairboattours.com*) is operated by a former chief of Florida's Miccosukee tribe, who, at 90 (or so) years old doesn't skipper the boat anymore, but still gets out to meet and greet when he can. Guides narrate the 45-minute trip from the

American Indian perspective. Trips run on the north side of Tamiami Trail and include a stop at an old American Indian camp. Tours go from 10–5 Saturday through Thursday and cost $25 per person for two, $20 per person for more than two, up to 12 people. Reservations are not required.

BIG CYPRESS NATIONAL PRESERVE

Through the 1950s and early 1960s the world's largest cypress-logging industry prospered in Big Cypress Swamp. As the industry died out, the government began buying parcels. Today, 729,000 acres, or nearly half of the swamp, form this national preserve. The word "big" refers not to the size of the trees but to the swamp, which juts into the north edge of Everglades National Park like a jigsaw-puzzle piece. Size and strategic location make Big Cypress an important link in the region's hydrological system, where rainwater first flows through the preserve, then south into the park, and eventually into Florida Bay. Its variegated pattern of wet prairies, ponds, marshes, sloughs, and strands provides a wildlife sanctuary, and thanks to a policy of balanced land use—"use without abuse"—the watery wilderness is devoted to recreation as well as research and preservation.

The preserve allows—in limited areas—hiking, hunting, and off-road-vehicle (airboat, swamp buggy, four-wheel-drive vehicles) use by permit. Compared with Everglades National Park, the preserve is less developed and hosts fewer visitors. That makes it ideal for naturalists, birders, and hikers who prefer to see more wildlife than humans.

Several scenic drives link off Tamiami Trail; some require four-wheel-drive vehicles, especially in wet summer months. A few lead to camping areas, and roadside picnic areas.

PARK ESSENTIALS

Admission Fees: There is no admission fee to visit the preserve.

Admission Hours: The park is open daily, year-round. Accessible only by boat, Adams Key is for day use only.

Contact Information:Big Cypress National Preserve (✉ *HCR 61, Box 11, Ochopee 34141* ☎ *239/695–1201* 🌐 *www.nps.gov/bicy*).

EXPLORING

Ochopee Post Office. This former irrigation pipe shed is North America's smallest post office. Buy a postcard of the one-room shack and mail it to a friend, to help keep this picturesque outpost in business during times of governmental cutbacks and layoffs. ✉ *4 mi east of Rte. 29, at 38000 E. Tamiami Trail, Ochopee* ☎ *239/695–2099* ⏲ *Weekdays 10–noon and 1–4:30, Sat. 10–11:30.*

Oasis Visitor Center. The biggest attraction here is the observation deck where you can view huge gators as well as fish, birds, and other wildlife. There's also a small butterfly garden where native plants seasonally attract winged wonders. Inside the information center you'll find a small exhibit area, a bookshop, and a theater that shows a dated but informative 15-minute film on the Big Cypress Preserve swamplands. ✉ *24 mi east of Everglades City, 50 mi west of Miami, 20 mi west of Shark Valley* ☎ *239/695–1201* *Free* ⏲ *Daily 9–4:30.*

RANGER PROGRAMS

From the Oasis Visitor Center you can get in on one of the seasonal ranger-led or self-guided activities, such as campfire and wildlife talks, hikes, slough slogs, and canoe excursions. The 8-mi Turner River Canoe Trail begins nearby and crosses through Everglades National Park before ending in Chokoloskee Bay, near Everglades City. Rangers lead four-hour canoe trips and two-hour swamp walks in season; call for days and times. Bring shoes and long pants for the swamp walks and be prepared to wade at least knee-deep in water. Ranger program reservations are accepted up to 14 days in advance.

SPORTS AND THE OUTDOORS

There are three types of trails—walking (including part of the extensive Florida National Scenic Trail), canoeing, and bicycling. All three trail types are easily accessed from the Tamiami Trail near the preserve visitor center, and one boardwalk trail departs from the center. Canoe and bike equipment can be rented from outfitters in Everglades City, 24 mi west, and Naples, 40 mi west.

Hikers can tackle the Florida National Scenic Trail, which begins in the preserve and is divided into segments 6.5 to 28 mi each. Two 5-mi trails, Concho Billy and Fire Prairie, can be accessed off Turner River Road, a few miles east. Turner River Road and Birdon Road form a 17-mi gravel loop drive that's excellent for birding. Bear Island has about 32 mi of scenic, flat, looped trails that are ideal for bicycling. Most trails are hard-packed lime rock, but a few miles are gravel. Cyclists share the road with off-road vehicles, most plentiful from mid-November through December.

To see the best variety of wildlife from your car, follow 26-mi Loop Road, south of U.S. 41 and west of Shark Valley, where alligators, raccoons, and soft-shell turtles crawl around beside the gravel road, often swooped upon by swallowtail kites and brown-shouldered hawks. Stop at H.P. Williams Roadside Park, west of the Oasis, and walk along the boardwalk to spy gators, turtles, and garfish in the river waters.

WHERE TO CAMP

For lodging options in the area, see the Where to Stay sections under each town in What's Nearby, later in this chapter.

¢ **Big Cypress National Preserve.** There are four no-fee primitive campgrounds within the preserve along Tamiami Trail and Loop Road, including Burns Lake, Bear Island, Pinecrest, and Mitchell's Landing. Some are open year-round, others seasonally (September to early January); all are subject to closure from flooding or for repairs, so check

DID YOU KNOW?

The Everglades shelter four types of mangroves: white, black, red, and buttonwood. The red mangrove plant (rhizophora mangle), shown here in Key Biscayne National Park, has tall, arching roots and a high tolerance for salt.

ahead. A fifth site for both RVs and tents, Monument Lake, has restrooms, a cold shower, an amphitheater, and activities and seasonal programs (mid-December through March). Campers can use the dump station on Dona Drive in Ochopee. The sixth, Midway, is the only campground with RV electrical hookups and an on-site dump station, free to campers. It is tidily maintained and an improvement upon private campgrounds in the area. All campgrounds are first-come, first-served, and stays are limited to 10 nights. *Flush toilets, dump station, showers (cold), running water 40 sites at Burns Lake; 40 sites at Bear Island; 10 sites at Pinecrest; 15 sites at Mitchell's Landing; 10 tent, 26 RV sites at Monument Lake; 10 tent, 26 RV sites at Midway ✉ Tamiami Trail (Hwy. 41), between Miami and Naples HCR 61, Box 110, Ochopee 34141 ☎ 239/695–1201 No credit cards.*

¢ **Trail Lakes Campground.** Close to Everglades City and Big Cypress National Preserve, Trail Lakes spreads out over 30 acres, is near a canoe launch, and has the added attraction of a nature park and wildlife exhibits. Complex owner David Shealy is the self-proclaimed expert on the Skunk Ape, the Everglades version of Big Foot, and has appeared on national television. RV and tent campsites circle a small lake and front the River of Grass. *Flush toilets, drinking water, electricity, public telephone, general store 80 RV sites, 25 tent sites ✉ 40904 Tamiami Trail E (Hwy. 41), Ochopee ☎ 239/695–2275 www.skunkape.info AE, MC, V.*

BISCAYNE NATIONAL PARK

Occupying 172,000 acres along the southern portion of Biscayne Bay, south of Miami and north of the Florida Keys, this national park is 95% submerged, and its altitude ranges from 4 feet above sea level to 60 feet below. Contained within from shore to sea are four distinct zones: mangrove forest along the coast, Biscayne Bay, the undeveloped upper Florida Keys, and coral reefs. Mangroves line the mainland shore much as they do elsewhere along South Florida's protected bay waters. Biscayne Bay functions as a lobster sanctuary and a nursery for fish, sponges, and crabs. Manatees and sea turtles frequent its warm, shallow waters.

GETTING HERE

To reach Biscayne National Park from Homestead, take Krome Avenue to Route 9336 (Palm Drive) and turn east. Follow Palm Drive for about 8 mi until it becomes South West 344th Street and follow signs to park headquarters in Convoy Point. The entry is 9 mi east of Homestead and 9 mi south and east of Exit 6 (Speedway Boulevard/Southwest 137th Avenue) off Florida's Turnpike.

PARK ESSENTIALS

Admission Fees There is no fee to enter Biscayne National Park, and you don't have to pay a fee to access the islands, but there is a $20 overnight camping fee that includes a $5 dock fee to berth vessels at some island docks. The park concessionaire charges for trips to the coral reefs and the islands (⇨ *see Outfitters and Expeditions*).

Admission Hours The park is open daily, year-round.

Contact Information Biscayne National Park (*Dante Fascell Visitor Center* ✉ *9700 SW 328th St., Homestead* ☎ *305/230–7275* 🌐 *www.nps.gov/bisc*).

WHAT TO SEE

Biscayne is a great place if you want to dive, snorkel, canoe, camp, birdwatch, or learn about marine ecology. The best place to hike is Elliott Key *(see Islands, below)*.

THE CORAL REEF

Biscayne's corals range from the soft, flagellant fans, plumes, and whips found chiefly in the shallower patch reefs to the hard brain corals, elkhorn, and staghorn forms that can withstand the heavier wave action and depths along the ocean's edge.

THE ISLANDS

To the east, about 8 mi off the coast, lie 44 tiny keys, stretching 18 nautical mi north–south and accessible only by boat. There's no commercial transportation between the mainland and the islands, and only a handful can be visited: Elliott, Boca Chita, Adams, and Sands keys. The rest are wildlife refuges, are too small, or have rocky shores or waters too shallow for boats. It's best to explore the Keys between December and April, when the mosquito population is less aggressive. Repellent is a must.

★ **Boca Chita Key,** 10 mi northeast of Convoy Point, was once owned by the late Mark C. Honeywell, former president of Honeywell Company. A ½-mi hiking trail curves around the south side of the island. Climb the 65-foot-high ornamental lighthouse (by ranger tour only) for a panoramic view of Miami or check out the cannon from the HMS *Fowey*. There's no fresh water, access is by private boat only, and no pets are allowed. Pending restroom upgrades, only portable toilets are on-site. A $20 fee for overnight docking between 6 PM and 6 AM covers a campsite; pay at the automated kiosk near the harbor. Boca Chita Key is listed on the National Register of Historic Places for its 10 historic structures.

The largest of the islands, **Elliott Key,** 9 mi east of Convoy Point, has a mile-long loop trail on the bay side of the island at the north end of the campground. Boaters may dock at any of 36 slips, and a $20 fee for stays between 6 PM and 6 AM covers a campsite. Take an informal, ranger-led nature walk or head out on your own to hike the 6-mi trail along so-called Spite Highway, a 225-foot-wide swath of green that developers mowed down in hopes of linking this key to the mainland. Luckily the federal government stepped in, and now it's a hiking trail through tropical hardwood hammock. Facilities include restrooms, picnic tables, fresh drinking water, showers (cold), grills, and a campground. Leashed pets are allowed in developed areas only, not on trails. A 30-foot-wide sandy beach about a mile north of the harbor on the west (bay) side of the key is the only one in the national park. Boaters like to anchor off it to swim. The beach is for day use only; it has picnic areas and a short trail that follows the shore and cuts through the hammock.

A stone's throw from the western tip of Elliott Key and 9 mi southeast of Convoy Point, **Adams Key, onetime site of the Cocolobo Club, a yacht club famous for once hosting presidents Harding, Hoover, Johnson, Nixon and other luminaries,** is open for day use and has picnic areas, restrooms, dockage, and a short trail that runs along the shore and through a hardwood hammock. Rangers live on-island. Access is by private boat.

BISCAYNE IN ONE DAY

Most visitors come to snorkel or dive. Divers should plan to spend the morning on the water and the afternoon exploring the Convoy Point Visitor Center. The opposite is true for snorkelers, as snorkel trips (and one-tank shallow-dive trips) depart in the afternoon. If you want to hike as well, turn to the trails at Elliott Key—just be sure to apply insect repellent (and sunscreen, too, no matter what time of year).

13

VISITOR CENTER

★ **Dante Fascell Visitor Center.** Go out on the wide veranda here to take in views across mangroves and Biscayne Bay. Inside the museum, artistic vignettes and on-request videos including the 11-minute *Spectrum of Life* explore the park's four ecosystems, while the Touch Table gives both kids and adults a feel for bones, feathers, and coral. Facilities include the park's canoe and tour concessionaire, restrooms with showers, a ranger information area, gift shop with books, and vending machines. Various ranger programs take place daily during busy fall and winter seasons. On the second Sunday of each month from January through May, the Family Fun Fest program offers three hours of hands-on activities for kids and families. Rangers also give informal tours of Elliott and Boca Chita keys; arrange in advance. Outside are picnic tables and grills. A short trail and boardwalk lead to a jetty. This is the only area of the park accessible without a boat. *9700 SW 328th St., Homestead/Convoy Point 305/230–7275 www.nps.gov/bisc Free Daily 9–4:30.*

SPORTS AND THE OUTDOORS

BIRD-WATCHING

More than 170 species of birds have been identified around the park. Expect to see flocks of brown pelicans patrolling the bay—suddenly rising, then plunging beak first to capture prey in their baggy pouches. White ibis probe exposed mud flats for small fish and crustaceans. Although all the Keys are excellent for birding, Jones Lagoon (south of Adams Key, between Old Rhodes Key and Totten Key) is outstanding. It's approachable only by nonmotorized craft.

DIVING AND SNORKELING

Diving is great year-around, but best in summer, when calmer winds and smaller seas result in clearer waters. Ocean waters, another 3 mi east of the Keys, showcase the park's main attraction—the northernmost section of Florida's living tropical coral reefs. Some are the size of an office desk, others as large as a football field. You can take a glass-bottom-boat ride to see this underwater wonderland, but you really should snorkel or scuba dive to fully appreciate it.

Native plants along the Turner River Canoe Trail hem paddlers in on both sides, and alligators lurk nearby.

A diverse population of colorful fish—angelfish, gobies, grunts, parrot fish, pork fish, wrasses, and many more—flits through the reefs. Shipwrecks from the 18th century are evidence of the area's international maritime heritage, and a Maritime Heritage Trail is being developed to link six of the major shipwreck and underwater cultural sites. Thus far, three sites, including a 19th-century wooden sailing vessel, have been plotted with GPS coordinates and marked with mooring buoys. Plastic dive cards are being developed that will contain navigational and background information.

WHERE TO CAMP

For lodging options in the area, see the Where to Stay sections under each town in What's Nearby, later in this chapter.

- ¢ **Boca Chita Campground.** This small, flat island has a grassy, waterside campground shaded by palms whispering in the breeze. Views are awesome, and a nature trail circles the island, accessible only by private boat. Campsites are first-come, first-served (if there's an open boat slip, a campsite is available) and cost $20 per night for up to six campers (that includes a boat dockage fee of $5). There's no running fresh water. Campers must carry out all trash. *Flush toilets, picnic tables 39 sites Visitor center: 9700 SW 328th St., Homestead 305/230–7275 No credit cards.*
- ¢ **Elliott Key Campground.** You'll need a private boat to get here, but grassy, beachfront tent sites with awesome views and populated with plenty of native hardwood trees make it worth the inconvenience. Spend the day swimming, snorkeling, hiking trails, and fishing, and spend the

night gazing into the brilliant star-strewn, light-pollution-free skies. Parties of up to 25 campers and six tents can reserve one of the three group sites for $30 a night; all other campsites are available on a first-come, first-served basis (if there's an open boat slip, a site is available) and cost $20 per night for up to six (including boat dockage). Bring plenty of insect repellent and drinking water (pumps go out on occasion), and try to pick a breezy spot to pitch your tent. Keep in mind you must carry out all trash. Leashed pets are welcome. *Flush toilets, drinking water, showers (cold), picnic tables, swimming (bay) 40 sites Visitor center: 9700 SW 328th St., Homestead 305/230–7275, 305/230–1100 transportation, 305/230–1144 Ext. 3074 for group campsite www.nps.gov/bisc No credit cards.*

WHAT'S NEARBY

EVERGLADES CITY

35 mi southeast of Naples and 83 mi west of Miami.

Aside from a chain gas station or two, Everglades City is perfect Old Florida. No high-rises (other than an observation tower) mar the landscape at this western gateway to Everglades National Park, just off the Tamiami Trail. It was developed in the late 19th century by Barron Collier, a wealthy advertising entrepreneur, who built it as a company town to house workers for his numerous projects including construction of the Tamiami Trail. It grew and prospered until the Depression and World War II. Today it draws adventure-seekers heading to the park for canoeing, fishing, and bird-watching excursions. Airboat tours, though popular, are banned within the preserve and park because of the environmental damage they cause to the mangroves. The Everglades Seafood Festival, going strong for nearly 40 years and held the first full weekend of February, draws crowds of up to 75,000 for delights from the sea, music, and craft displays. At quieter times, dining choices are limited to a handful of basic eateries. The town is small, fishing-oriented, and unhurried, making it excellent for boating and bicycling. Pedal along the waterfront on a 2-mi ride along the strand out to Chokoloskee Island.

Visitor Information Everglades Area Chamber of Commerce (*Rte. 29 and Tamiami Trail 239/695–3172 www.evergladeschamber.com*).

EXPLORING

★ **Fakahatchee Strand Preserve State Park.** The ½-mi boardwalk through this linear swamp forest gives you an opportunity to see rare plants, bald cypress, nesting eagles, and North America's largest stand of native royal palms and largest concentration and variety of epiphytic orchids, including more than 30 varieties of threatened and endangered species blooming most extravagantly in hotter months. It's particularly famous for its ghost orchids (as featured in the novel *The Orchid Thief* by Susan Orlean), visible only on guided hikes. In your quest for ghost orchids, also keep a hopeful eye out for white-tailed deer, black bears, bobcats, and the Florida panther. For park nature on parade, take the

12-mi-long (one way) W.J. Janes Memorial Scenic Drive, and, if you have the time, hike the spur trails leading off it. Rangers lead swamp walks and canoe trips November through April. ✉ *Boardwalk on north side of Tamiami Trail, 7 mi west of Rte. 29; W.J. Janes Scenic Dr., ¾ mi north of Tamiami Trail on Rte. 29; ranger station on W.J. Janes Scenic Dr.* ☎ *239/695–4593* 🌐 *www.floridastateparks.org/fakahatcheestrand* 🎫 *Free* 🕒 *Daily 8 AM–sunset.*

OFF THE BEATEN PATH

★ **Collier-Seminole State Park.** Nature trails, biking, hiking, camping, and canoeing into Everglades territory make this park a prime introduction to this often forbidding land. Of historical interest, a Seminole War blockhouse has been re-created to hold the interpretative center, and one of the "walking dredges"—a towering black machine invented to carve the Tamiami Trail out of the muck—stands silent on the grounds amid tropical hardwood forest. Campsites ($22 per night) include electricity, water, and picnic table. Restrooms have hot water, and one has a laundry. ✉ *20200 E. Tamiami Trail, Naples* ☎ *239/394–3397* 🌐 *www.floridastateparks.org/collier-seminole* 🎫 *$5 per car, $4 with lone driver* 🕒 *Daily 8–sunset.*

Museum of the Everglades. Through artifacts and photographs you can meet the American Indians, pioneers, entrepreneurs, and fishermen who played a role in the development of southwest Florida. Exhibits and a short film chronicle the tremendous feat of building the Tamiami Trail through the mosquito-ridden and gator-infested Everglades wetlands. In addition to the permanent displays, monthly exhibits rotate the work of local artists. ✉ *105 W. Broadway* ☎ *239/695–0008* 🎫 *Free* 🕒 *Tues.–Sat. 10–4.*

SPORTS AND THE OUTDOORS

BOATING AND CANOEING

On the Gulf Coast explore the nooks, crannies, and mangrove islands of Chokoloskee Bay and Ten Thousand Islands National Wildlife Refuge, as well as the many rivers near Everglades City. The Turner River Canoe Trail, a pleasant day trip with a guarantee of bird and alligator sightings, passes through mangrove, dwarf cypress, coastal prairie, and freshwater slough ecosystems of Everglades National Park and Big Cypress National Preserve.

OUTFITTER **Glades Haven Marina** (✉ *801 Copeland Ave. S, Everglades City* ☎ *239/695–2628* 🌐 *www.gladeshaven.com*) can put you on the water to explore the Ten Thousand Islands in 16-foot Carolina skiffs and 24-foot pontoon boats. Rates start at $150 a day, with half-day and hourly options. The outfitter also rents kayaks and canoes and has a 24-hour boat ramp and dockage for vessels up to 24 feet long.

WHERE TO EAT

$$–$$$ SEAFOOD

✕ **Everglades Seafood Depot.** Count on an affordable, scenic breakfast, lunch, or dinner at this storied 1928 Spanish-style stucco structure fronting Lake Placid. It began its life as the original Everglades train depot, was later deeded to the University of Miami for marine research, and appeared in scenes from the film *Winds across the Everglades,* before becoming a haven for assorted restaurants through the years. Well-prepared seafood including shrimp, frogs' legs, and alligator—much from local boats—dominates today's menu. For big appetites, there are generously portioned entrées of steak and fish specials and combination platters that include warm, fresh-baked biscuits. All-you-can-eat specials, such as fried chicken, a taco bar, or a seafood buffet are available on selected nights. Ask for a table on the back porch or for a window seat overlooking the lake. Bargain hunters arrive early for the 99¢ breakfast menu, served Friday and Saturday from 5:30 AM–10:30 AM. ✉ *102 Collier Ave.* ☎ *239/695–0075* 🌐 *www.evergladesseafooddepot.com* 💳 *AE, D, MC, V.*

¢ CUBAN ✕ **Havana Cafe**. Cuban specialties are a tasty change from the shanty seafood houses of Everglades City; brightly painted walls and floral tablecloths make this little eatery with 10 indoor tables and four porch tables a cheerful spot. Service is order-at-the-counter for breakfast and lunch (8 AM–3 PM; with dinner on Friday and Saturday nights in season). Jump-start your day with café con leche and a pressed-egg sandwich; For lunch, you'll find the ubiquitous Cuban sandwich, burgers, shrimp, grouper, steak, and pork plates with rice and beans and yucca. ✉ *191 Smallwood Drive, Chocoloskee* ☎ *239/695–2214* 💳 *No credit cards* ⏲ *No dinner Apr.–Oct. No dinner Sun.–Thurs. Nov.–Mar.*

$$–$$$ SEAFOOD ✕ **Oyster House Restaurant**. One of the town's oldest and most old-fashioned fish houses, Oyster serves all the local staples—shrimp, gator tail, frogs' legs, oysters, stone crab, and grouper—in a lodgelike setting where mounted wild game decorates walls and rafters. Shrimp and grouper smothered in tomatoes are among the few exceptions to fried preparation. Deep-frying remains an art in these parts, so if you're going to indulge, do it here. Consider the stone crab soup, in season, and try to dine at sunset for golden rays with your watery view. ✉ *Hwy. 29 S* ☎ *239/695–2073* 🌐 *www.oysterhouserestaurant.com* 💳 *AE, D, MC, V.*

$$$ SEAFOOD ✕ **Rod and Gun Club**. The striking, polished pecky-cypress woodwork in this historic building dates from the 1920s when wealthy hunters, anglers, and yachting parties from around the world arrived for the winter season. The main dining room holds the overflow from the popular, enormous screened porch overlooking the river. Like life in general here, servers move slowly and upkeep is minimal. Fresh seafood dominates, from stone crab claws in season to a surf-and-turf combo of steak and grouper, a swamp-and-turf combo of frogs' legs and steak, seafood and pasta pairings, and you can have your catch cooked for $14.95. Pie offerings include key lime and chocolate–peanut butter. The main lobby is worth a look—even if you plan to eat elsewhere. Arrive by boat or land. ✉ *200 Riverside Dr.* ☎ *239/695–2101* 🌐 *www.evergladesrodandgun.com* 💳 *No credit cards.*

$ SEAFOOD ✕ **Triad Seafood**. Along the Barron River, seafood houses, fishing boats, and crab traps populate one shoreline; mangroves the other. Some of the seafood houses, selling fresh off the boat, added picnic tables and eventually grew into restaurants. Family-owned Triad is one, with a screened dining area seating 44, and additional outdoor seating under a breezeway and on a deck overhanging the scenic river where you can savor fresh seafood during stone crab season, October 15 to May 15. Nothing fancy (although smoked salmon and blue crab salad have been added to the lineup), but you won't find a better grouper sandwich. An all-you-can-eat fresh stone crab jumbo feast will set you back around $80; or $50 for large, $35, medium. Hours vary but it's usually open from 6 AM to 3 PM Monday through Thursday and from 6 AM to 5 PM Friday through Sunday. Lunch starts at 10:30 AM with fried shrimp, oyster, crab cake, and soft-shell blue crab baskets, plus Reubens, hamburgers, Philly cheesesteak sandwiches, and, on Friday, smoked ribs. ✉ *401 School Dr.* ☎ *239/695–0722* 🌐 *www.triadseafood.com* 💳 *AE, D, MC, V* ⏲ *Closed May 16–Oct. 15.*

WHERE TO STAY

$–$$ **Glades Haven Cozy Cabins.** Bob Miller wanted to build a Holiday Inn next to his Oyster House Restaurant on marina-channel shores. When that didn't fly, he sent for cabin kits and set up mobile-home-size units around a pool on his property. Guests renting the cabins get free boat docking. A full cabin, done up in wood, tin roof, and polished floor, has a full kitchen and separate bedroom with screened porch. Duplex cabins—among the best deals in town—have a small fridge and microwave, with or without a screened porch. **Pros:** good food options; convenient to ENP boating; free docking; marina. **Cons:** crowded trailer-park feel; no phones. ✉ *801 Copeland Ave.* ☎ *239/695–2746 or 888/956–6251* 🌐 *www.gladeshaven.com* *24 cabins, 4 3-bedroom houses* *In-room: no phone, kitchen (some). In-hotel: 2 restaurants, pool, laundry facilities* 💳 *AE, D, MC, V.*

$–$$ Fodor's Choice ★ **Ivey House.** A remodeled 1928 boardinghouse originally for workers building the Tamiami Trail, Ivey House today fits many budgets. One part is a friendly B&B bargain with shared baths and a cottage. The newer inn, connected to the B&B, has rooms with private baths—some of Everglades City's plushest accommodations. Most inn rooms surround the screen-enclosed pool and courtyard. Display cases of local flora and fauna decorate the inn, along with Everglades and Ten Thousand Islands photography. The layout is designed to promote camaraderie, but there are secluded patios with chairs and tables for private moments. Rates include breakfast (hot breakfast in season). The owners of 30-year-old NACT-Everglades Rentals & Eco Adventures run Ivey House, so you'll save 20% on their canoe and kayak rentals and tours if you stay here. In 2007, the property became the first Collier County hotel to achieve state "Green Lodging" certification. **Pros:** canoe and kayak rentals and tours; pleasant; affordable. **Cons:** not on water; some small rooms. ✉ *107 Camellia St.* ☎ *877/567–0679 or 239/695–3299* 🌐 *www.iveyhouse.com* *31 rooms, 18 with bath; 1 2-bedroom cottage* *In-room: refrigerator (some), Internet, Wi-Fi (some). In-hotel: restaurant, pool, laundry facilities, Wi-Fi hotspot* 💳 *MC, V* *BP.*

FLORIDA CITY

3 mi southwest of Homestead on U.S. 1.

Florida's Turnpike ends in Florida City, the southernmost town on the peninsula, spilling thousands onto U.S. 1 and eventually west to Everglades National Park, east to Biscayne National Park, or south to the Florida Keys. Florida City and Homestead run into each other, but the

SHUTTLES FROM MIAMI

Airporter (☎ *800/830–3413*) runs shuttle buses three times daily that stop at the Ramada Inn in Florida City on the way between MIA and the Florida Keys. Shuttle service, which takes about an hour, runs 6:10 AM–5:20 PM from Florida City, 7:30 AM–6 PM from the airport. Reserve at least 48 hours in advance. Pickups can be arranged for all baggage-claim areas. The cost is $30 one way. **Super Shuttle** (☎ *305/871–2000* 🌐 *www.supershuttle.com*) runs 11-passenger air-conditioned vans 24 hours a day between MIA and the Homestead–Florida City area; pickup is outside baggage claim and costs $53 per person. For the return to MIA, reserve 24 hours in advance and know your pickup zip code for a price quote. Taxi fare from the airport to Everglades City runs about $100.

difference couldn't be more noticeable. As the last outpost before 18 mi of mangroves and water, this stretch of U.S. 1 is lined with fast-food eateries, service stations, hotels, bars, dive shops, and restaurants. Hotel rates increase significantly during NASCAR races at the nearby Homestead Miami Speedway. Like Homestead, Florida City is rooted in agriculture, with hundreds of acres of farmland west of Krome Avenue and a huge farmers' market that processes produce shipped nationwide.

VISITOR INFORMATION

Tropical Everglades Visitor Center (✉ *160 U.S. 1* ☎ *305/245–9180 or 800/388–9669* 🌐 *www.tropicaleverglades.com*).

SHOPPING

★ **Robert Is Here** (✉ *19200 SW 344th St.* ☎ *305/246–1592*), a remarkable fruit stand, sells vegetables, fresh-fruit milk shakes (try the key lime shake), 10 flavors of honey, more than 100 types of jams and jellies, fresh juices, salad dressings, and some 30 kinds of tropical fruits, including (in season) carambola, lychee, egg fruit, monstera, sapodilla, dragonfruit, genipa, sugar apple, and tamarind. The stand started in 1960, when seven-year-old Robert sat at this spot selling his father's bumper crop of cucumbers. Today, Robert (still on the scene daily with his wife and kids), ships all over the United States, donating seconds to needy area families. An odd assortment of animals out back—from goats to emus—adds entertainment value. The stand opens at 8 AM and stays open until at least 7 PM. It shuts down, however, during September and October.

WHERE TO EAT

$$ ITALIAN ✕ **Capri Restaurant.** Locals have been coming to this family-owned enterprise for affordable, traditional Italian-American fare since 1958. Outside it's a rock-walled building with a big parking lot filling up nightly. Interior dining areas have redbrick accent walls with plenty of round tables; a sunny courtyard with umbrellaed tables affords outdoor dining. Tasty options range from pizza with a light, crunchy crust and ample toppings to broiled steaks and seafood-pasta classics, plus spaghetti 16 ways. Bargain hunters have two choices: the daily early-

bird entrées, 4:30–6:30 for $12–$14, which include soup or salad and potato or spaghetti, and the Tuesday family night (after 4 PM), with all-you-can-eat pasta with salad or soup for $6.95. Specialty martinis and fruity cocktails supplement the international wine list. ✉ *935 N. Krome Ave.* ☎ *305/247–1542* 🌐 *www.dinecapri.com* ▭ *AE, D, MC, V* ⊙ *No lunch Sun.*

$$ SEAFOOD ✕ **Captain's Restaurant and Seafood Market.** A comfortable place where the chef knows how to do seafood with flair, this is among the town's best bets. Locals and visitors alike gather in the cozy dining room or outdoors on the patio. Blackboards describe a varied menu of sandwiches, pasta, seafood, steak, and nightly specials running up to $23.95. Inventive offerings include lobster Reuben sandwich, crawfish pasta, and pan-seared tuna topped with balsamic onions and shallots. ✉ *404 SE 1st Ave.* ☎ *305/247–9456* ▭ *AE, MC, V.*

$ AMERICAN ★ ✕ **Farmers' Market Restaurant.** Although it's in the farmers' market on the edge of town and serves fresh vegetables, seafood figures prominently on the menu of home-cooked specialties. A family of fishermen runs the place, so fish and shellfish are only hours from the sea, and there's a fish fry on Friday nights. Catering to anglers and farmers, it opens at 5:30 AM, serving pancakes, jumbo eggs, and fluffy omelets with home fries or grits in a pleasant dining room with checkered tablecloths. Lunch and dinner menus have fried shrimp, seafood pasta, country-fried steak, roast turkey, and fried conch, as well as burgers, salads, and sandwiches. ✉ *300 N. Krome Ave.* ☎ *305/242–0008* ▭ *MC, V.*

$$$ SEAFOOD ✕ **Mutineer Restaurant.** Families and older couples flock to the quirky yet well-dressed setting of this roadside steak-and-seafood outpost with a fish-and-duck pond and a petting zoo for kids. It was built in 1980 to look like a ship, back when Florida City was barely on the map. Etched glass divides the bi-level dining rooms, with velvet-upholstered chairs, an aquarium, and nautical antiques. The menu has 12 seafood entrées, including stuffed grouper (a favorite), Florida lobster tails, and snapper Oscar, plus another half-dozen daily seafood specials, as well as poultry, ribs, and steaks. Burgers and seafood sandwiches are popular for lunch, as is a happy-hour buffet all day until 7 PM in the lounge for $2.25 and the purchase of a drink. You also can dine in the restaurant's Wharf Lounge. Friday and Saturday are dance nights with live entertainment. ✉ *11 SE 1st Ave. (U.S. 1), at Palm Dr.* ☎ *305/245–3377* 🌐 *www.mutineer.biz* ▭ *AE, D, DC, MC, V.*

¢ MEXICAN ★ ✕ **Rosita's Restaurante.** With its big Mexican population this area can boast the authentic flavors that you just don't get in the Tex-Mex chains. Order à la carte specialties or dinners and combos with beans and rice, and salad. Forty-three breakfast, lunch, and dinner entrées are served all day and range from Mexican eggs, enchiladas, and taco salad to stewed beef, shrimp ranchero-style, and fried pork chop. Food is on the spicy side, and if you like more fire, each table is equipped with fresh-tasting salsa, pickled jalapeños, and bottled habanero sauce. Clean (with lingering faint whiffs of bleach to prove it) and pleasant, with an open kitchen, take-out counter, and Formica tables, it's a favorite with locals and budget-minded guests at the Everglades International Hostel across the street. ✉ *199 W. Palm Dr.* ☎ *305/246–3114* ▭ *AE, MC, V.*

WHERE TO STAY

$$–$$$ **Best Western Gateway to the Keys.** If you want easy access to Everglades and Biscayne national parks as well as the Florida Keys, you'll be well placed at this modern, two-story motel two blocks off Florida's Turnpike. Standard rooms, done in tropical colors, have two queen-size beds or one king-size bed. Rooms around the lushly landscaped pool cost the most. There's high-speed Internet access available in rooms, plus Wi-Fi in the lobby. **Pros:** convenient to national parks and Keys; business services; pretty pool area. **Cons:** traffic noise; generic rooms; fills up fast during high season. *411 S. Krome Ave. 305/246–5100 or 888/981–5100 www.bestwestern.com/gatewaytothekeys 114 rooms In-room: refrigerator, Internet. In-hotel: pool, laundry facilities, Wi-Fi hotspot AE, D, DC, MC, V CP.*

$–$$ **Econo Lodge.** Close to Florida's Turnpike and with access to the Keys, this is a good overnight pullover spot. Rooms are uncramped, with attractive bedspreads, coffeemakers, and in-room Wi-Fi. The pool sits in the parking lot, but tall ficus hedges separate it from busy U.S. 1. **Pros:** convenient location; business services; microwaves and refrigerators in rooms. **Cons:** urban-ugly location; noisy; lacks character. *553 NE 1st Ave. 305/248–9300 or 800/553–2666 www.econolodge.com 42 rooms In-room: refrigerator, Internet, Wi-Fi. In-hotel: pool, laundry facilities, Internet terminal AE, D, DC, MC, V CP.*

¢ **Everglades International Hostel.** Stay in clean and spacious private or dorm-style rooms (generally six to a room), relax in indoor or outdoor quiet areas, watch videos or TV on a big screen, and take affordable airboat, hiking, biking, and sightseeing tours (the all-day Everglades Tour is one of the most complete and affordable tours in the area and includes canoeing and a wet-walk). This privately owned facility is in a minimally restored art deco building on a lush, secluded acre between Everglades and Biscayne national parks, 20 mi north of Key Largo. Enjoy a free all-you-can-make pancake breakfast in the communal kitchen, and pitch in for occasional communal dinners ($5 each if one of the on-site volunteers is cooking), or walk to a nearby restaurant. Pets are welcome in private rooms with a $20 refundable deposit. You can make free domestic long-distance calls from the phone in a common room off the lobby. **Pros:** affordable; Everglades tours; free services. **Cons:** communal living; no elevator; old structure. *20 SW 2nd Ave. 305/248–1122 or 800/372–3874 www.evergladeshostel.com 46 beds in dorm-style rooms with shared bath, 2 private rooms with shared bath In-room: no phone, no TV. In-hotel: water sports, bicycles, laundry facilities, Internet terminal, Wi-Fi hotspot, some pets allowed D, MC, V.*

$–$$ **Fairway Inn.** Two stories high with a waterfall pool, this motel has some of the area's lowest chain rates, and it's next to the chamber of commerce visitor center so you'll never be short of reading and planning material. Rooms, with either one king-size bed or two doubles, have tiled bathrooms and closet areas. No-pet policy. **Pros:** affordable; convenient to restaurants, parks, and raceway; free in-room Wi-Fi. **Cons:** no character; plain, small rooms. *100 SE 1st Ave. 305/248–4202 or*

888/340–4734 160 *rooms* *In-room: refrigerator, Internet, Wi-Fi. In-hotel: pool, laundry facilities* *AE, D, MC, V* *CP.*

$$ ★ **Ramada Inn.** Racing fans can hear the engines roar from this two-story motel next to an outlet mall and within 15 minutes of the raceway and Everglades and Biscayne national parks. If you're looking for an upgrade from the other chains, this one offers more amenities and comfort, such as 32-inch flat-screen TVs, closed closets, and stylish furnishings. Carpeted rooms are bright and clean and have upholstered chairs, a coffeemaker, and an iron and ironing board. Included are a Continental breakfast with some hot items and local calls. **Pros:** extra room amenities; business clientele perks; convenient location. **Cons:** chain anonymity. *124 E. Palm Dr.* *305/247–8833* *www.hotelfloridacity.com* *123 rooms* *In-room: refrigerator, Internet, Wi-Fi. In-hotel: pool, laundry service* *AE, D, DC, MC, V* *CP.*

$–$$ **Travelodge.** This bargain motor lodge is close to Florida's Turnpike, Everglades and Biscayne national parks, the Florida Keys, and the Homestead Miami Speedway. In fact, many racers stay here, which makes it difficult to get a room when track events are scheduled. Clean, colorful rooms are small, but have more amenities than typical in this price range, including complimentary breakfast and newspaper, coffeemaker, hair dryer, iron with ironing board, and high-speed Internet access (there's free Wi-Fi in rooms, and two computers in the lobby for guest use). Fast-food and chain eateries, gas stations, and a visitor's bureau are within walking distance. **Pros:** in-room refrigerator and microwave; convenience to U.S. 1; complimentary breakfast. **Cons:** lacks character; small rooms; busy location. *409 SE 1st Ave.* *305/248–9777 or 800/758–0618* *www.tlflcity.com* *88 rooms* *In-room: safe, refrigerator, Internet, Wi-Fi. In-hotel: pool, laundry facilities, Internet terminal* *AE, D, MC, V* *CP.*

HOMESTEAD

30 mi southwest of Miami.

In recent years Homestead has redefined itself as a destination for tropical agro- and ecotourism. Seated at the juncture between Miami and the Keys as well as Everglades National Park and Biscayne National Park, the area has the added dimension of shopping centers, residential development, hotel chains, and the Homestead Miami Speedway—when car races are scheduled, hotels hike up their rates and require minimum stays. The historic downtown has become a preservation-driven Main Street. Krome Avenue, where it cuts through the city's heart, is lined with restaurants, an arts complex, antiques shops, and low-budget, sometimes undesirable accommodations. West of north–south Krome Avenue, miles of fields grow fresh fruits and vegetables. Some are harvested commercially, and others beckon with U-PICK signs. Stands selling farm-fresh produce and nurseries that grow and sell orchids and tropical plants abound. In addition to its agricultural legacy, the town has an eclectic flavor, attributable to its population mix: descendants of pioneer Crackers, Hispanic growers and farm workers, professionals escaping Miami hubbub, and latter-day Northern retirees.

Are baby alligators more to your liking than their daddies? You can pet one at Everglades Gator Park.

WHAT TO SEE

Coral Castle. Driven by unrequited love, 100-pound immigrant Ed Leedskalnin built this castle in the early 1900s out of massive slabs of coral rock, a feat likened to the building of the pyramids. Visitors can learn how he peopled his fantasy world with his imaginary wife and three children, studied astronomy, and created his simple home and elaborate courtyard with no engineering education and tools he mostly fashioned himself. Highlights of this National Register of Historic Places site include the Polaris telescope built to spot the North Star, a working sundial, a 5,000-pound heart-shaped table featured in Ripley's *Believe It or Not*, a banquet table in the shape of Florida, and a playground Ed named "Grotto of the Three Bears." ✉ *28655 S. Dixie Hwy.* ☎ *305/248–6345* 🌐 *www.coralcastle.com* 💵 *$9.75* ⏲ *Sun.–Thurs. 8–6, Fri. and Sat. 8–8.*

SPORTS AND THE OUTDOORS

AUTO RACING

Homestead-Miami Speedway. This state-of-the-art facility with 65,000 grandstand seats, club seating eight stories above racing action, and two tracks has a 2.21-mi continuous road course and a 1.5-mi oval. There's a schedule of year-round manufacturer and race-team testing, club racing, and other national events. ✉ *1 Speedway Blvd.* ☎ *866/409–7223* 🌐 *www.homesteadmiamispeedway.com.*

WATER SPORTS

Homestead Bayfront Park. Boaters, anglers, and beach-goers give high ratings to the facilities at this recreational area adjacent to Biscayne National Park. The 174-slip marina has a ramp, dock, bait-and-tackle shop, fuel station, ice, dry storage, and boat hoist, which can handle vessels up to 50 feet long. The park also has a tidal swimming area, a beach with lifeguards, a playground, ramps for people with disabilities (including a ramp that leads into the swimming area), and a picnic pavilion with grills, showers, and restrooms. ✉ *9698 SW 328th St.* ☎ *305/230–3033* *$6 per passenger vehicle; $12 per vehicle with boat Mon.–Thurs., $15 Fri.–Sun.; $15 per RV; $10 hoist* ⏲ *Daily sunrise–sunset.*

WHERE TO EAT

¢ MEXICAN ✕ **NicaMex**. Among the local Latin population this 68-seat eatery is a low-budget favorite. It helps if you speak Spanish, but usually some staffers on hand speak English, and the menu is bilingual. Although they term it *comidas rapidas* (fast food), the cuisine is not Americanized. You can get authentic huevos rancheros or *chilaquiles* (corn tortillas cooked in red-pepper sauce) for breakfast, and specialties such as *chicharron en salsa verde* (fried pork skin in hot-green-tomato sauce) and shrimp in garlic all day. Hearty seafood and beef soups are best-sellers. Choose a domestic or imported beer, pop a coin into the Wurlitzer jukebox, select a Latin tune, and escape south of the border. ✉ *32 NW 1st St., across from the Krome Ave. bandstand* ☎ *305/247–0727* ▭ *AE, D, MC, V.*

¢ SOUTHERN ✕ **Sam's Country Kitchen**. For good, old, Southern-style home cooking, locals come to Sam's. Burgers, sandwiches, and dinners—including chicken livers, chicken and dumplings, and fried clams—come with fresh-baked corn bread and a daily selection of sides such as okra with tomatoes, turnip greens, pickled beets, or onion rings. Don't miss out on the changing selection of homemade soups and desserts. All this goodness comes cheap, but at the expense of anything-but-glamorous dining environs and often slow service. ✉ *1320 N. Krome Ave.* ☎ *305/246–2990* ▭ *MC, V* ⏲ *No dinner Sun.*

WHERE TO STAY

$ ★ **Grove Inn Country Guesthouse**. Away from downtown but close to Homestead's agricultural attractions, Grove Inn derives much of its personality from co-owners Craig, an artist, and Paul, a former showman. The lush garden is awash in organic, tropical fruit trees and native plants (in addition to a guest book, there's a live signature tree for signing leaves in the courtyard), and rooms named after tropical fruits like Carambola and Mango are decorated with antique furnishings and table settings. The owners go out of their way to pamper you, starting with a country breakfast using local produce, served family-style in a dining room done in Victorian florals. They offer behind-the-scenes tours of orchid nurseries and farms not otherwise open to the public. A vending machine dispenses complimentary cold drinks. **Pros:** fresh fruit; privacy; delicious breakfast; rural location. **Cons:** far from downtown and national parks; no restaurants nearby; not suited to families. ✉ *22540 SW Krome Ave., 6 mi north of downtown* ☎ *305/247–6572 or 877/247–6572* 🌐 *www.groveinn.com* *13 rooms, 1 2-bedroom suite, 1 cottage* *In-room: kitchen (some), refrigerator, Wi-Fi. In-hotel: pool, laundry facilities, some pets allowed* ▭ *AE, D, MC, V* *BP.*

$–$$ ★ **Redland Hotel**. Of downtown Homestead's smattering of mom-and-pop lodging options, this historic inn is the most desirable and has the most character. When it opened in 1904, the inn was the town's first hotel, later becoming the first mercantile store, first post office, first library, and first boardinghouse. Each room has a different layout and furnishings, and some have access to a shared balcony. The style is Victorian, with lots of pastels and reproduction antique furniture. The pub is popular with locals, and there are good restaurants and antiques shops nearby. A coffee shop–Internet café serving burgers, wings and such, with free Wi-Fi in rooms and public spaces was added in 2006. **Pros:** historic character; convenient to downtown; well maintained. **Cons:** traffic noise; small rooms; ugly street location. ✉ *5 S. Flagler Ave.* ☎ *305/246–1904 or 800/595–1904* 🌐 *www.redlandhotel.com* *13 rooms* *In-room: Internet, Wi-Fi. In-hotel: restaurant, room service, bar* ▭ *AE, D, MC, V.*

TAMIAMI TRAIL

An 80-mi stretch of U.S. 41 (known as the Tamiami Trail) traverses the Everglades, Big Cypress National Preserve, and Fakahatchee Strand Preserve State Park. The road was conceived in 1915 to link Miami to Fort Myers and Tampa. When it finally became a reality in 1928, it cut through the Everglades and altered natural flow of water and lives of the Miccosukee Indians, who were trying to eke out a living fishing, hunting, farming, and frogging here. The landscape is surprisingly varied, changing from hardwood hammocks to pinelands, then abruptly to tall cypress trees dripping with Spanish moss and back to sawgrass marsh. Slow down to take in the scenery and you'll likely be rewarded with glimpses of alligators sunning themselves along the banks of roadside canals or in the shallow waters, and hundreds of waterbirds, especially in the dry winter season. The man-made landscape has American Indian villages, chickee huts, and airboats parked at roadside enterprises. Between Miami and Naples the road goes by several names, including Tamiami Trail, U.S. 41, 9th Street in Naples, and, at the Miami end, Southwest 8th Street. ■ **TIP→ Businesses along the trail give their addresses either based on their distance from Krome Avenue, Florida's Turnpike, and Miami on the east coast or Naples on the west coast.**

WHAT TO SEE

Everglades Gator Park. Here you can get face-to-face with and even touch an alligator—albeit a baby one—during the park's exciting Wildlife Show. You also can squirm in a "reptilium" of venomous and nonpoisonous native snakes or learn about American Indians of the Everglades through a reproduction of a Miccosukee village. The park also has 35-minute airboat tours and RV campsites ($30 per night) , as well as a gift shop and restaurant serving burgers to gator tail. ✉ *24050 Tamiami Trail, 12 mi west of Florida's Turnpike, Miami* ☎ *305/559–2255 or 800/559–2205* 🌐 *www.gatorpark.com* *Tours, wildlife show, and park $21* ⏲ *Daily 9–5.*

Everglades Safari Park. A perennial favorite with tour-bus operators, the park has an arena seating up to 300 for an alligator show and wrestling demonstration. Before and after the show, get a closer look at both alligators and crocodiles on Gator Island; walk through a small wildlife museum, follow the jungle trail, or climb aboard an airboat for a 40-minute ride on the River of Grass (included in admission). There's also a restaurant, gift shop, and an observation platform looking out over the Glades. Small, private airboats are available for an extra charge for tours lasting 40 minutes to 2½ hours. ✉ *26700 Tamiami Trail, 15 mi west of Florida's Turnpike, Miami* ☎ *305/226–6923 or 305/223–3804* 🌐 *www.evsafaripark.com* 🎫 *$23* 🕑 *Daily 9–5, last tour departs 3:30.*

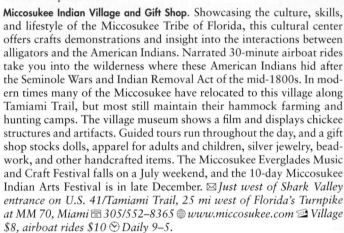

CROCS OR GATORS?

You can tell you're looking at a crocodile, not an alligator, if you can see its lower teeth protruding when its jaws are shut. Gators are much darker in color—a grayish black—compared with the lighter tan color of crocodiles. Alligator snouts are also much broader than their long, thin crocodilian counterparts.

★ **Miccosukee Indian Village and Gift Shop**. Showcasing the culture, skills, and lifestyle of the Miccosukee Tribe of Florida, this cultural center offers crafts demonstrations and insight into the interactions between alligators and the American Indians. Narrated 30-minute airboat rides take you into the wilderness where these American Indians hid after the Seminole Wars and Indian Removal Act of the mid-1800s. In modern times many of the Miccosukee have relocated to this village along Tamiami Trail, but most still maintain their hammock farming and hunting camps. The village museum shows a film and displays chickee structures and artifacts. Guided tours run throughout the day, and a gift shop stocks dolls, apparel for adults and children, silver jewelry, beadwork, and other handcrafted items. The Miccosukee Everglades Music and Craft Festival falls on a July weekend, and the 10-day Miccosukee Indian Arts Festival is in late December. ✉ *Just west of Shark Valley entrance on U.S. 41/Tamiami Trail, 25 mi west of Florida's Turnpike at MM 70, Miami* ☎ *305/552–8365* 🌐 *www.miccosukee.com* 🎫 *Village $8, airboat rides $10* 🕑 *Daily 9–5.*

SPORTS AND THE OUTDOORS

BOAT TOURS

Many Everglades-area tours operate only in season, roughly November through April.

Running since 1945, **Coopertown Airboats** (✉ *11 mi west of Florida's Turnpike, on Tamiami Trail* ☎ *305/226–6048* 🌐 *www.coopertownairboats.com*) operates the oldest airboat rides in the Everglades. The 35- to 40-minute tour ($21) takes you 9 mi to hammocks and alligator holes. Private charters are also available. Southwest of Florida City near the entrance to Everglades National Park, **Everglades Alligator Farm** (✉ *40351 SW 192nd Ave.* ☎ *305/247–2628* 🌐 *www.everglades.com*) runs a 4-mi, 30-minute airboat tour of the River of Grass with departures 20 minutes after the hour. The tour ($23) includes free hourly alligator, snake, and wildlife shows, or take in shows only ($15.50). **Everglades Safari Park** (✉ *26700 SW 8th St., 15 mi west of Florida's Turnpike, on Tamiami Trail* ☎ *305/226–6923 or 305/223–3804* 🌐 *www.evsafaripark.com*) runs 40-minute eco-adventure airboat rides for $23 and small, private airboat tours for an extra charge; they last from 40 minutes to 2½ hours. The price includes alligator show, natural-museum admission, and walking-trail access. **Gator Park Airboat Tours** (✉ *12 mi west of Florida's Turnpike, on Tamiami Trail* ☎ *305/559–2255 or 800/559–2205* 🌐 *www.gatorpark.com*) offers 45-minute narrated airboat tours ($21, including park tour and wildlife show).

A classic Florida roadside attraction, **Wooten's Everglades Airboat Tour** (✉ *Wooten's Alligator Farm, 1½ mi east of Rte. 29 on Tamiami Trail, Ochopee* ☎ *239/695–2781 or 800/282–2781* 🌐 *www.wootensairboats.com* *$25 for half-hour tour, $8 for animal exhibits* ⏲ *Daily 8:30–5; last ride departs at 4:30*) runs airboat tours through the Everglades and swamp-buggy tours through the Big Cypress Swamp lasting approximately 30 minutes each (swamp buggies are giant tractorlike vehicles with oversize rubber wheels). More personalized airboat tours on smaller boats (seating six to eight) are also available for 45 minutes to one hour and start at $37.10. The on-site animal sanctuary offers the typical Everglades array of alligators, snakes, panthers, and other creatures. Discounts are available online.

13

SHOPPING

Shopping alone might lure you to the **Miccosukee Indian Village** (✉ *Just west of Shark Valley entrance, 25 mi west of Florida's Turnpike at MM 70* ☎ *305/223–8380*). Wares include American Indian crafts such as beadwork, moccasins, dolls, pottery, baskets, and patchwork fabric and clothing.

WHERE TO EAT

$ ECLECTIC ✕ **Coopertown Restaurant.** Make this a pit stop for local color and cuisine fished straight from the swamp. Starting a half century ago as a sandwich stand, this small, casual eatery inside an airboat concession storefront has attracted the famous and the humbly hungry. House specialties are frogs' legs and alligator tail breaded in cornmeal and deep-fried, casually served on paper ware with a lemon wedge and Tabasco. More conventional options include catfish, shrimp, burgers, hot dogs, or grilled cheese sandwiches. ✉ *22700 SW 8th St., 11 mi west of Florida's Turnpike, on Tamiami Trail, Miami* ☎ *305/226–6048* 🌐 *www.coopertownairboats.com* ▭ *AE, MC, V.*

$–$$ SOUTHWESTERN ★ ✕ **Miccosukee Restaurant.** For a taste of local culture at a reasonable price, this roadside cafeteria a quarter mile from the Miccosukee Indian Village and overlooking the River of Grass, provides the best variety of food along Tamiami Trail in Everglades territory. The River of Grass view, servers wearing traditional Miccosukee patchwork vests, and mural depicting American Indian women cooking and men engaged in a powwow, all provide atmosphere. Favorites are catfish and frogs' legs breaded and deep-fried, Indian fry bread, and pumpkin bread, but you'll also find more common fare, such as huge burgers, sandwiches, salads, and dishes from south of the border. Try the Miccosukee Platter ($24.95) for a sampling of local favorites, including gator bites. Gator Nuggets (slightly larger than gator bites) are $2.25 each. Breakfast and lunch are served daily. ✉ *U.S. 41 (Tamiami Trail), 18 mi west of Miccosukee Resort and Gaming; 25 mi west of Florida's Turnpike* ☎ *305/894–2374* ▭ *AE, D, MC, V.*

¢–$ SOUTHERN ✕ **Pit Bar-B-Q.** At the edge of Miami, this old-fashioned roadside eatery along Tamiami Trail near Krome Avenue was launched in 1965 by the late Tommy Little, who wanted anyone heading into or out of the Everglades to have access to cold drinks and rib-sticking fare. His vision remains a holdout from the Everglades' backwoods heritage and a popular, affordable option for families. Order at the counter, pick up your food, and eat at one of the picnic tables on the screened porch or outdoors. Specialties include barbecued chicken and ribs with a tangy sauce, fries, coleslaw, and a fried biscuit, plus burgers and fish sandwiches. The whopping double-decker beef or pork sandwich with slaw requires at least five napkins. Latin specialties include corn tamales in the husk and fried green plantains. Beer is by the bottle or pitcher, wine by the bottle or glass. Locals flock here with kids on weekends for pony rides. ✉ *16400 Tamiami Trail, 5 mi west of Florida's Turnpike, Miami* ☎ *305/226–2272* 🌐 *www.thepitbarbq.com* ▭ *AE, D, MC, V.*

WHERE TO STAY

$$$ **Miccosukee Resort & Gaming.** Like an oasis on the horizon of endless sawgrass, this nine-story resort at the southeastern edge of the Everglades can't help but attract your eye, even if you're not on the lookout for 24-hour gaming action. The casino occupies the lobby (making for a cigarette-smoky welcome at check-in), and features over 1,800 video machines, 58 poker tables, a 1,200-seat Bingo Hall, and nonsmoking gaming areas. If you ever leave the lobby, you'll find that most rooms and suites have a view of Everglades sawgrass and wildlife. On-site there's a well-maintained indoor pool, Jacuzzi, sauna, spa, fitness center, indoor play area for children, and a game arcade for teens and tweens, plus Club Egret child care for kids under age 12. There are tours to the Miccosukee Indian Village, shuttles to area malls, and a 27-hole golf club and tennis courts just 15 mi away. **Pros:** casino; most modern resort in these parts; golf. **Cons:** cigarette odor in lobby; parking lot fills with gamblers; feels incompatible with the Everglades. ✉ *500 SW 177th Ave., 6 mi west of Florida's Turnpike, Miami* ☎ *305/925–2555 or 877/242–6464* 🌐 *www.miccosukee.com* *256 rooms, 46 suites* *In-room: safe, Wi-Fi. In-hotel: 5 restaurants, room service, bars, golf course, pool, gym, spa, children's programs (up to 12 years old), laundry service, Internet terminal, Wi-Fi hotspot, parking (free)* ▭ *AE, D, DC, MC, V.*

The Florida Keys

WORD OF MOUTH

"The keys are definitely a get out on the water type place instead of a driving up and down US 1 kind of place. Bars and restaurants open early and close early. Get out over the water. That is where the most amazing things in the keys are."

—GoTravel

WELCOME TO THE FLORIDA KEYS

TOP REASONS TO GO

★ **John Pennekamp Coral Reef State Park:** A perfect introduction to the Florida Keys, this nature reserve offers snorkeling, diving, camping, and kayaking. An underwater highlight is the massive Christ of the Deep statue.

★ **Under the Sea:** Whether you scuba, snorkel, or ride a glass-bottom boat, don't miss gazing at the coral reef and its colorful denizens.

★ **Sunset at Mallory Square:** Sure it's touristy, but just once while you're here you've got to witness the circus-like atmosphere of this nightly event.

★ **Duval Crawl:** Shop, eat, drink, repeat. Key West's Duval Street and the nearby streets make a good day's worth of window-shopping and people-watching.

★ **Get on the Water:** From angling for trophy-size fish to zipping out to the Dry Tortugas, a boat trip is in your future. It's really the whole point of the Keys.

1 The Upper Keys. As the doorstep to the islands' coral reefs and blithe spirit, the Upper Keys introduce all that is sporting and sea-oriented about the Keys. They stretch from Key Largo to the Long Key Channel (MM 106–65).

2 The Middle Keys. Centered around the town of Marathon, the Middle Keys hold most of the chain's historic and natural attractions outside of Key West. They go from Conch (pronounced *konk*) Key through Marathon to the south side of the Seven Mile Bridge, including Pigeon Key (MM 65–40).

Key West.

3 The Lower Keys. Pressure drops another notch in this laid-back part of the region, where wildlife and the fishing lifestyle peak. The Lower Keys go from Little Duck Key south through Big Coppitt Key (MM 40–9).

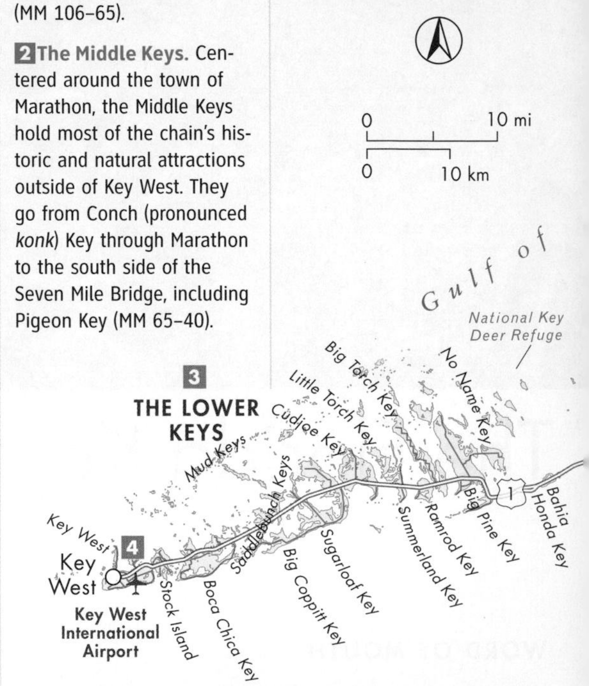
0
10 mi
0
10 km
Gulf of
National Key Deer Refuge
3
THE LOWER KEYS
Big Torch Key
Little Torch Key
No Name Key
Cudjoe Key
Mud Keys
Saddlebunch Keys
1
Bahia Honda Key
Big Pine Key
Ramrod Key
Summerland Key
Sugarloaf Key
Big Coppitt Key
Boca Chica Key
Stock Island
Key West
4
Key West
Key West International Airport

4 Key West. The ultimate in Florida Keys craziness, the party town Key West isn't the place for those seeking a quiet retreat. The Key West area encompasses MM 9-0.

Key West.

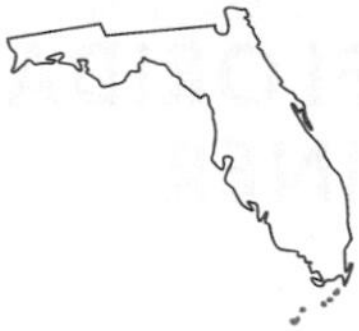

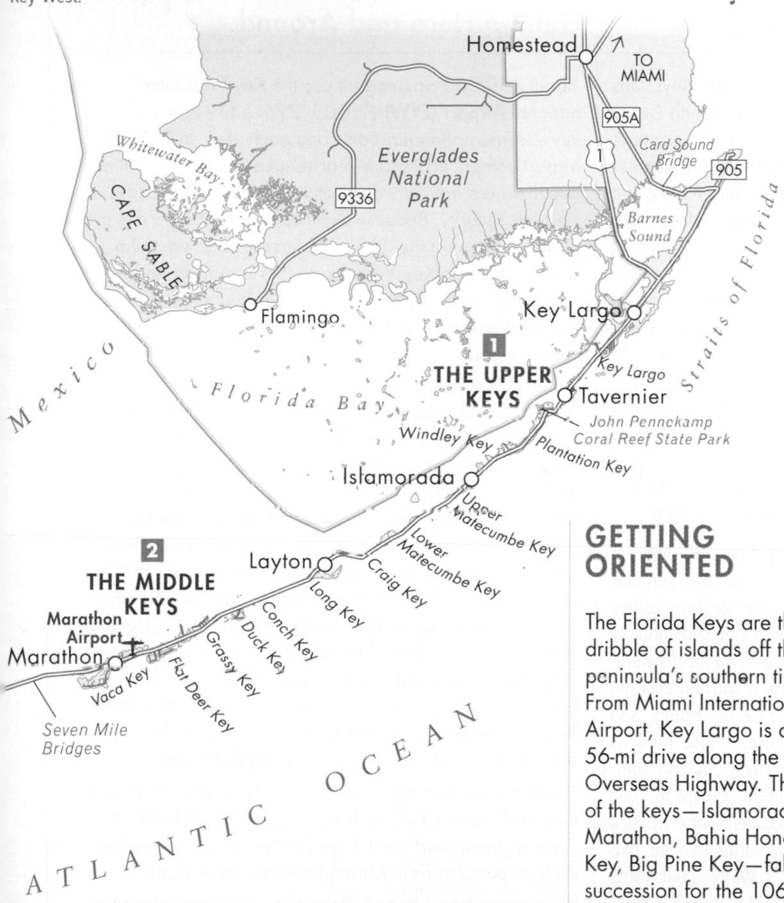
Homestead
TO MIAMI
905A
1
Card Sound Bridge
905
Everglades National Park
9336
Whitewater Bay
CAPE SABLE
Barnes Sound
Straits of Florida
Flamingo
Key Largo
1
THE UPPER KEYS
Key Largo
Tavernier
John Pennekamp Coral Reef State Park
Mexico
Florida Bay
Windley Key
Plantation Key
Islamorada
Upper Matecumbe Key
Lower Matecumbe Key
Layton
Craig Key
2
THE MIDDLE KEYS
Marathon Airport
Marathon
Long Key
Conch Key
Duck Key
Grassy Key
Flat Deer Key
Vaca Key
Seven Mile Bridges
ATLANTIC OCEAN

GETTING ORIENTED

The Florida Keys are the dribble of islands off the peninsula's southern tip. From Miami International Airport, Key Largo is a 56-mi drive along the Overseas Highway. The rest of the keys—Islamorada, Marathon, Bahia Honda Key, Big Pine Key—fall in succession for the 106 mi between Key Largo and Key West. At their north end, the Florida Keys front Florida Bay, which separates it from Everglades National Park. The Middle and Lower Keys front the Gulf of Mexico; the Atlantic Ocean borders the length of the chain on its eastern shores.

THE FLORIDA KEYS PLANNER

When to Go

High season in the Keys falls between Christmas and Easter. November to mid-December crowds are thinner, the weather is wonderful, and hotels and shops drastically reduce their prices. Summer, which is hot and humid, is becoming a second high season, especially among Floridians, families, and European travelers. If you plan to attend the wild Fantasy Fest in October, book your room at least six months in advance. Accommodations are also scarce during the first weekend in August, the start of lobster season.

Winter is typically 10°F warmer than on the mainland; summer is usually a few degrees cooler. The Keys also get substantially less rain, around 40 inches annually, compared with an average 55–60 inches in Miami and the Everglades. Most rainfalls are quick downpours on summer afternoons, except in June through October, when tropical storms can dump rain for two to four days. Winter cold fronts occasionally stall over the Keys, dragging overnight temperatures down to the low 50s.

Getting Here and Around

About 450,000 passengers use the **Key West International Airport (EYW)** (☎ *305/296–5439* 🌐 *www.keywestinternationalairport.com*) each year. In 2009, the airport completed its four-year renovation, which includes a beach where travelers can catch their last blast of rays after clearing security. Because flight schedules can be iffy, many prefer driving via the 110-mi Overseas Highway (aka U.S. 1). Besides Key West International Airport, many visitors to the region fly into Miami International Airport, Fort Lauderdale–Hollywood International Airport, and others on the mainland.

By car, from Miami International Airport (MIA), follow signs to Coral Gables and Key West, which puts you on LeJeune Road, then Route 836 west. Take the Homestead Extension of Florida's Turnpike south (toll road), which ends at Florida City and connects to the Overseas Highway (U.S. 1, currently under construction so expect delays). Tolls from the airport run approximately $3. The alternative from Florida City is Card Sound Road (Route 905A), which has a bridge toll of $1. Continue to the only stop sign and turn right on Route 905, which rejoins Overseas Highway 31 mi south of Florida City. The best Keys road map, published by the Homestead–Florida City Chamber of Commerce, can be obtained for $5.50 from the **Tropical Everglades Visitor Center** (☎ *305/245–9180 or 800/388–9669* 🌐 *www.tropicaleverglades.com*).

Those unwilling to tackle the route's 43 bridges and peak-time traffic can take Greyhound's (☎ *800/231–2222* 🌐 *www.greyhound.com*) Keys Shuttle, which has multiple daily departures from Miami International Airport.

Boaters can travel to and along the Keys either along the Intracoastal Waterway through Card, Barnes, and Blackwater sounds and into Florida Bay or along the deeper Atlantic Ocean route through Hawk Channel. The Keys are full of marinas that welcome transient visitors, but there aren't enough slips for all the boats heading to these waters. Make reservations far in advance and ask about channel and dockage depth—many marinas are quite shallow.

About the Restaurants

Seafood rules on the Keys, which is full of chef-owned restaurants with not-too-fancy food. Things get more exotic once you reach Key West. Restaurants serve cuisine that reflects the proximity of the Bahamas and Caribbean. Tropical fruits figure prominently—especially on the beverage side of the menu. Florida spiny lobster should be local and fresh from August to March, and stone crabs from mid-October to mid-May. And don't dare leave the islands without sampling conch, be it in a fritter or in ceviche. Keep an eye out for authentic key lime pie—yellow custard in a graham-cracker crust. If it's green, just say "no." **Note:** Particularly in Key West and particularly during spring break, the more affordable and casual restaurants can get loud and downright rowdy, with young visitors often more interested in drinking than eating. Live music contributes to the decibel levels. If you're more the quiet, intimate dining type, avoid such overly exuberant scenes by eating early or choosing a restaurant where the bar is not the main focus.

About the Hotels

Throughout the Keys, the types of accommodations are remarkably varied, from '50s style motels to cozy inns to luxurious lodges. Most are on or near the ocean, so water sports reign supreme. Key West's lodging portfolio includes historic cottages, restored Conch houses, and large resorts. Some larger properties throughout the Keys charge a mandatory daily resort fee of $15 or more, which can cover equipment rental, fitness-center use, and other services, plus expect another 12.5% (or more) sales/resort tax. Some guesthouses and inns do not welcome children, and many do not permit smoking.

WHAT IT COSTS

	¢	$	$$	$$$	$$$$
Restaurants	under $10	$10–$15	$15–$20	$20–$30	over $30
Hotels	under $80	$80–$100	$100–$140	$140–$220	over $220

Restaurant prices are per person for a main course at dinner. Hotel prices are for a standard double room, excluding 12.5% sales tax (or more) in sales and resort taxes.

The Milemarker System

Getting lost in the Keys is almost impossible once you understand the unique address system. **Many addresses are simply given as a mile marker (MM) number.** The markers are small, green, rectangular signs along the side of the Overseas Highway (U.S. 1). They begin with MM 126, 1 mi south of Florida City, and end with MM 0, in Key West. **Keys residents use the abbreviation BS for the bay side of Overseas Highway and OS for the ocean side.** From Marathon to Key West, residents may refer to the bay side as the gulf side.

Key Biscayne.

THE FLORIDA KEYS BEACHES

Because the Bahama Islands steal the Keys' offshore sand, the region has fewer natural beaches than one might expect. But the ones it does have are award-winning, specifically those at Bahia Honda State Park.

Also, just because a beach is not natural, doesn't mean it should be overlooked. Some of the Keys' public man-made beaches provide solid recreation and sunning options for visitors looking to work on their tan. Many resorts additionally provide their own private beachfronts.

The Keys may not have a surplus of beaches, but one nice perk is the availability of camping on some of them. It's one of many ways to enjoy nature while on the beach. Another is keeping an eye out for sea turtles. April through October female sea turtles lay their eggs into the sand for a nearly two-month period of nesting.

■ TIP→ Don't let pests ruin your day at the beach. To avoid the stings of sea lice, remove your swimsuit and shower thoroughly upon exiting the water. Sand fleas, (aka no-see-ums) are tiny insects with big teeth that are most likely to attack in the morning and around sunset.

BIRD-WATCHING ON THE BEACH

The Florida Keys beaches can be great places to look to the skies and waters for all varieties of birds. Permanent residents include shorebirds—plovers, ruddy turnstones, willets, and short-billed dowitchers; wading birds—great blue herons, great white herons, snowy egrets, tri-colored herons, and white ibis; brown pelicans; osprey; and turkey vultures. In the autumn, hawks migrate through the region, while in winter ducks make their debut. In the summer, white-crowned pigeons are commonly seen.

FLORIDA KEYS' BEST BEACHES

LONG KEY STATE PARK

The beach at Long Key State Park at MM 67.5 is typical of Middle Key's beaches, which are more like sand flats where low tide reveals the coral bedrock of the ecosystem. Here you can snorkel or fish (bonefishing is quite popular) during the day and then be lulled to sleep by the sound of gentle sea waves if you spend the night camping. (The beach is accessible only to campers.)

SOMBRERO BEACH

Something of a local hangout—especially on weekends, when it can get crowded—Sombrero Beach in Marathon is worth getting off the beaten Overseas Highway path for (exit at MM 50 onto Sombrero Beach Road). Families will find much to do on the man-made coved beach and its grassy green, manicured lawn, playground area, and clear, calm waters. Separate sections also accommodate boaters and windsurfers.

BAHIA HONDA STATE PARK

This state park at MM 37 holds three beaches, all of different character. Sandspur Beach is the most removed from crowds with long stretches of powdery sands and a campground. Loggerhead Beach is closer to the park's concession area, where you can rent snorkel equipment and kayaks. Like Sandspur, it faces the Atlantic Ocean, but waves are typically wimpy. Near Loggerhead, Calusa Beach on the Gulf side near the marina is popular with families, offering a small and safe swimming venue and picnic facilities, as well as camping.

HIGGS BEACH, KEY WEST

Situated on Atlantic Boulevard, this is as urban as beaches in the Keys get, with lots of amenities, activities, and distractions. Visitors can check out a historic site, eat at a popular beachfront Italian restaurant, rent a kayak, play volleyball, tennis, or at the playground—and all within walking distance of the long sweep of man-made beach and sparkling clear, shallow, and calm water.

ZACHARY TAYLOR HISTORIC STATE PARK

This man-made beach is part of a Civil War–era fort complex at the end of Southard Street and is arguably the best beach in Key West with its typically small waves, swaying Australian pines, water-sports rentals, and shaded picnic grounds. It also hosts, from mid-January through mid-April, an alfresco collection of oversized art called Sculpture Key West, which changes annually and showcases artists from across the country.

Updated by Chelle Koster Walton

Being a Conch is a condition of the heart, and foreclosure on the soul. Many throughout the Florida Keys wear that label proudly, yet there's anything but a shared lifestyle here.

To the south, Key West has a Mardi Gras mood with Fantasy Festivals, Hemingway look-alike contests, and the occasional threat to secede from the Union. It's an island whose melting-pot character allows crusty natives to mingle (more or less peacefully) with eccentrics and escape artists who lovingly call this 4-mi sandbar "Paradise." Although life elsewhere in the island chain isn't quite as offbeat, it's nearly as diverse. Flowering jungles, shimmering seas, and mangrove-lined islands are also, conversely, overburdened. Key Largo, nearest the mainland, is becoming more congested as it evolves into a bedroom community and weekend hideaway for residents of Miami and Fort Lauderdale.

A river of tourist traffic gushes along Overseas Highway, the 110-mi artery linking the inhabited islands. The expansion of U.S. 1 to the mainland to four lanes by 2012 will open the floodgates to increased traffic, population, and tourism. Observers wonder if making Overseas Highway four lanes throughout the Keys can be far away. For now, however, take pleasure as you cruise down Overseas Highway along the islands. Gaze over the silvery blue-and-green Atlantic and its still-living reef, with Florida Bay, the Gulf of Mexico, and the backcountry on your right (the Keys extend southwest from the mainland). At a few points the ocean and gulf are as much as 10 mi apart; in most places, however, they are from 1 to 4 mi apart, and on the narrowest landfill islands they are separated only by the road. Try to get off the highway. Once you do, rent a boat, anchor, and then fish, swim, or marvel at the sun, sea, and sky. In the Atlantic, dive spectacular coral reefs or pursue grouper, blue marlin, dolphinfish, and other deepwater game fish. Along Florida Bay's coastline, kayak and canoe to secluded islands and bays or seek out the bonefish, snapper, snook, and tarpon that lurk in the grass flats and in the shallow, winding channels of the backcountry.

14

GREAT ITINERARIES

3 DAYS

Spend your first morning diving or snorkeling at John Pennekamp Coral Reef State Park in **Key Largo.** If you aren't certified, sign up for a resort course and you'll be exploring the reefs by the afternoon. Dinner at a bay-side restaurant will give you your first look at a fabulous Keys sunset. On Day 2 get an early start to savor the breathtaking views on the two-hour drive to Key West. Along the way make a stop at the natural-history museum that's part of Crane Point Museum, Nature Center and Historic Site in **Marathon.** Another worthwhile detour is Bahia Honda Key State Park on **Bahia Honda Key,** where you can stretch your legs on a forest trail or snorkel on an offshore reef. Once you arrive in **Key West,** watch the sunset at one of the island's restaurants. The next morning, stroll Duval Street, visit a museum or two, or take a trolley tour of Old Town.

4 DAYS

Spend the first day as you would above, staying overnight in **Key Largo.** Start Day 2 by renting a kayak and exploring the mangroves of Florida Bay, or taking an ecotour of the sandy islands in Everglades National Park. In the afternoon, head down to **Islamorada** and visit Windley Key Fossil Reef Geological State Park. Before day's end, make plans for the next day's fishing. Spend the night in Islamorada. After a morning spent with a rod and reel, stop at one of the many restaurants that happily prepare your catch for you. In the afternoon, set off for **Key West.** Enjoy the sunset celebration at Mallory Square.

THE UPPER KEYS

Diving and snorkeling rule in the Upper Keys, thanks to the tropical coral reef that runs a few miles off the seaward coast. Divers of all skill levels benefit from accessible dive sites and an established tourism infrastructure. Fishing is another huge draw, especially around Islamorada, known for its sportfishing in both deep offshore waters and in the backcountry. Offshore islands accessible only by boat are popular destinations for kayakers. In short, if you don't like the water you might get bored here.

Other nature lovers won't feel shortchanged. Within 1½ mi of the bay coast lie the mangrove trees and sandy shores of Everglades National Park, where naturalists lead tours of one of the world's few saltwater forests. Here you'll see endangered manatees, curious dolphins, and other underwater creatures. Although the number of birds has dwindled since John James Audubon captured their beauty on canvas, the rare Everglades snail kite, bald eagles, ospreys, and a colorful array of egrets and herons delight bird-watchers. At sunset flocks take to the skies as they gather to find their night's roost, adding a swirl of activity to an otherwise quiet time of day.

The Upper Keys are full of low-key eateries where the owner is also the chef and the food is tasty and never too fussy. The one exception is Islamorada, where you'll find the more upscale restaurants. Restaurants may close for a two- to four-week vacation during the slow season between mid-September and late October.

In the Upper Keys, the accommodations are as varied as they are plentiful. The majority of lodgings are in small waterfront complexes with efficiencies and one- or two-bedroom units. These places offer dockage and often arrange boating, diving, and fishing excursions. There are also larger resorts with every type of activity imaginable and smaller boutique hotels where the attraction is personalized service.

Depending on which way the wind blows and how close the property is to the highway, there may be some noise from Overseas Highway. If this is an annoyance for you, ask for a room as far from the traffic as possible. Some properties require two- or three-day minimum stays during holiday and high-season weekends. Conversely, discounts apply for midweek, weekly, and monthly stays.

GETTING HERE AND AROUND

Airporter operates scheduled van and bus pick-up service from all Miami International Airport (MIA) baggage areas to wherever you want to go in Key Largo ($50) and Islamorada ($55). Groups of three or more passengers receive discounts. There are three departures daily; reservations are preferred 48 hours in advance. The SuperShuttle charges $102 per passenger for trips from Miami International Airport to the Upper Keys. For trip to the airport, place your request 24 hours in advance.

ESSENTIALS

Transportation Contacts Airporter (☎ *305/852–3413 or 800/830–3413*). **SuperShuttle** (☎ *305/871–2000* 🌐 *www.supershuttle.com*).

KEY LARGO

The first of the Upper Keys reachable by car, 30-mi-long Key Largo is also the largest island in the chain. Key Largo—named Cayo Largo ("Long Key") by the Spanish—makes a great introduction to the region.

The history of Largo is similar to that of the rest of the Keys, with its succession of native people, pirates, wreckers, and developers. The first settlement on Key Largo was named Planter, back in the days of pineapple and later key lime plantations. For a time it was a convenient shipping port, but when the railroad arrived Planter died on the vine. Today three communities—North Key Largo, Key Largo, and Tavernier—make up the whole of Key Largo.

If you've never tried diving, Key Largo is the perfect place to learn. Dozens of companies will be more than happy to show you the ropes. Nobody comes to Key Largo without visiting John Pennekamp Coral Reef State Park, one of the jewels of the state-park system. Also popular is the adjacent Key Largo National Marine Sanctuary, which encompasses about 190 square mi of coral reefs, sea-grass beds, and mangrove estuaries. Both are good for underwater exploration.

Fishing is the other big draw, and world records are broken regularly. There are plenty of charter operations to help you find the big ones and teach you how to hook the elusive bonefish, sometimes known as the ghost fish. On land, restaurants will cook your catch or dish up their own offerings with inimitable style.

Key Largo offers all the conveniences of a major resort town, with most businesses lined up along Overseas Highway (U.S. 1), the four-lane highway that runs down the middle of the island. Cars whiz past at all hours—something to remember when you're booking a room. Most lodgings are on the highway, so you'll want to be as far back as possible.

GETTING HERE AND AROUND

Key Largo is 56 mi south of Miami International Airport, with the mile markers going from 106 to 91. The island runs northeast–southwest, with Overseas Highway running down the center. If the highway is your only glimpse of the island, you're likely to feel barraged by its tacky commercial side. Make a point of driving Route 905 in North Key Largo to get a better feel for it.

ESSENTIALS

Visitor Information Key Largo Chamber of Commerce (✉ *MM 106 BS, Key Largo* ☎ *305/451–4747 or 800/822–1088* 🌐 *www.keylargochamber.org*).

EXPLORING

Dagny Johnson Key Largo Hammock Botanical State Park. American crocodiles, mangrove cuckoos, Schaus swallowtail butterflies, mahogany mistletoe, wild cotton, and 100 other rare critters and plants call these 2,400 acres home. The park is also a user-friendly place to explore the largest remaining stand of the vast West Indian tropical hardwood hammock and mangrove wetland that once covered most of the Keys' upland areas. Interpretive signs describe many of the tropical tree species along a 1-mi paved road (2-mi round-trip) that invites walking and biking. There are also more than 6 mi of nature trails accessible to bikes and wheelchairs. Pets are welcome if on a leash no longer than 6 feet. You'll also find restrooms, information kiosks, and picnic tables. ✉ *1 mi north of Overseas Hwy. on Rte. 905 OS, North Key Largo* ☎ *305/451–1202* 🌐 *www.floridastateparks.org/keylargohammock* 🎫 *$2.50* ⏲ *Daily 8–sundown.*

Jacobs Aquatic Center. Take the plunge at one of three swimming pools: an 8-lane, 25-meter lap pool with a diving well; a 3- to 4-foot-deep pool accessible to people with mobility problems; and an interactive play pool with a waterslide, pirate ship, waterfall, and sloping zero entry instead of steps. ✉ *320 Laguna Ave. (MM 99.6 OS)* ☎ *305/453–7946* 🌐 *www.jacobsaquaticcenter.org* 🎫 *$8* ⏲ *Daily 10–7.*

Fodor's Choice ★

John Pennekamp Coral Reef State Park. This state park is on everyone's list for the best diving and snorkeling sites in the Sunshine State. The underwater treasure encompasses 78 square mi of coral reefs, sea-grass beds, and mangrove swamps. Its reefs contain 40 of the 52 species of coral in the Atlantic Reef System and nearly 600 varieties of fish, from the colorful stoplight parrot fish to the demure cocoa damselfish. The park's visitor center has a 30-gallon floor-to-ceiling fish tank surrounded by smaller ones, so you can get a closer look at many of the underwater creatures. When you want to head out to sea, a concessionaire rents kayaks and powerboats, as well as snorkeling and diving equipment. You can also sign up for snorkeling and diving trips ($30 and $60, respectively) and glass-bottom-boat rides to the reef ($24). One of the most popular excursions is the snorkeling trip to see Christ of the Deep, the 2-ton underwater statue of Jesus at Key Largo National Marine Sanctuary. The park also has short nature trails, two man-made beaches, picnic shelters, a snack bar, and a campground. ✉ *102601 Overseas Hwy. (MM 102.5 OS)* ☎ *305/451–1202 for park, 305/451–6300 for excursions* 🌐 *www.pennekamppark.com* 💵 *$4.50 for 1 person, $9 for 2 people, 50¢ each additional person* 🕒 *Daily 8–sunset.*

> **WORD OF MOUTH**
>
> "Went on the snorkeling trip out of John Pennekamp State Park. The total was $44 for snorkel trip, full rental including wet suit. Really enjoyed the trip, but wished I had driven down for the 9 AM trip—there were fewer snorkelers and the Web site offered a discount coupon for the morning tour." —starrsville

SPORTS AND THE OUTDOORS

BOATING

Captain Sterling's **Everglades Eco-Tours** (✉ *Dolphin's Cove, 101900 Overseas Hwy. [MM 102 BS], Key Largo* ☎ *305/853–5161 or 888/224–6044* 🌐 *www.captainsterling.com*) operates Everglades and Florida Bay ecology tours ($49 per person) and sunset cruises ($79 per person). **M.V. Key Largo Princess** (✉ *99701 Overseas Hwy. [MM 100 OS], Key Largo* ☎ *305/451–4655 or 877/648–8129* 🌐 *www.keylargoprincess.com*) offers two-hour glass-bottom-boat trips ($30) and sunset cruises on a luxury 75-foot motor yacht with a 280-square-foot glass viewing area, departing from the Holiday Inn docks three times a day.

CANOEING AND KAYAKING

Sea kayaking continues to gain popularity in the Keys. You can paddle for a few hours or the whole day, on your own or with a guide. Some outfitters even offer overnight trips. The **Florida Keys Overseas Paddling Trail,** part of a statewide system, runs from Key Largo to Key West. You can paddle the entire distance, 110 mi on the Atlantic side, which takes 9–10 days. The trail also runs the chain's length on the bay side, which is a longer route.

At John Pennekamp Coral Reef State Park, **Coral Reef Park Co.** (✉ *102601 Overseas Hwy. [MM 102.5 OS]* ☎ *305/451–6300* 🌐 *www.pennekamppark.com*) has a fleet of canoes and kayaks for gliding around the 2½-mi mangrove trail or along the coast. It also rents powerboats. Rent canoes or sea kayaks from **Florida Bay Outfitters** (✉ *104050 Overseas Hwy. [MM 104 BS]* ☎ *305/451–3018* 🌐 *www.kayakfloridakeys.com*). The company, which helps with trip planning and matches equipment to your skill level, sets up self-guided trips on the Florida Keys Overseas Paddling Trail. It also runs myriad guided tours around Key Largo. Take a full-moon paddle, or a one- to seven-day canoe or kayak tour to the Everglades, Lignumvitae Key, or Indian Key. Trips run $60–$795.

FISHING

Private charters and big head boats (so named because they charge "by the head") are great for anglers who don't have their own vessel.

DID YOU KNOW?

The bronze Christ of the Deep (also called Christ of the Abyss) statue of Jesus Christ underwater near John Pennekamp Coral Reef State Park is modeled after one in the Mediterranean Sea near where Italian Dario Gonzatti died while scuba diving.

Sailors Choice (✉ *Holiday Inn Resort & Marina, 99701 Overseas Hwy. [MM 100 OS]* ☎ *305/451–1802 or 305/451–0041* 🌐 *www.sailorschoicefishingboat.com*) has fishing excursions departing twice daily ($40 for half-day trips). The 65-foot boat leaves from the Holiday Inn docks. Rods, bait, and license are included.

SCUBA DIVING AND SNORKELING

Much of what makes the Upper Keys a singular dive destination is variety. Places like Molasses Reef, which begins 3 feet below the surface and descends to 55 feet, have something for everyone from novice snorkelers to experienced divers. The *Spiegel Grove,* a 510-foot vessel, lies in 130 feet of water, but its upper regions are only 60 feet below the surface. On rough days, Key Largo Undersea Park's Emerald Lagoon is a popular spot. Expect to pay about $80 for a two-tank, two-site-dive trip with tanks and weights, or $35–$40 for a two-site-snorkel outing. Get big discounts by booking multiple trips.

Amy Slate's Amoray Dive Resort (✉ *104250 Overseas Hwy. [MM 104.2 BS]* ☎ *305/451–3595 or 800/426–6729* 🌐 *www.amoray.com*) makes diving easy. Stroll down to the full-service dive shop (NAUI, PADI, TDI, and BSAC certified), then onto a 45-foot catamaran. The rate for a two-dive trip is $80.

★ **Conch Republic Divers** (✉ *90800 Overseas Hwy. [MM 90.8 BS]* ☎ *305/852–1655 or 800/274–3483* 🌐 *www.conchrepublicdivers.com*) offers instruction as well as scuba and snorkeling tours of all the wrecks and reefs of the Upper Keys. Two-location dives are $80 with tank and weights. **Coral Reef Park Co.** (✉ *102601 Overseas Hwy. [MM 102.5 OS]* ☎ *305/451–6300* 🌐 *www.pennekamppark.com*), at John Pennekamp Coral Reef State Park, gives 3½-hour scuba ($60) and 2½-hour snorkeling ($30) tours of the park. Besides the great location and the dependability of this operation, it's suited for water adventurers of all levels. **Ocean Divers** (✉ *522 Caribbean Dr. [MM 105.5 BS]* ✉ *105800 Overseas Hwy. [MM 100 OS]* ☎ *305/451–0037 or 800/451–1113* 🌐 *www.oceandivers.com*) operates two shops in Key Largo. The PADI five-star Caribbean Drive facility offers day and night dives, a range of courses, and dive-lodging packages. The cost is $80 for a two-tank reef dive with tank and weight rental. Snorkel trips from the other shop cost $5 with snorkel, mask, and fins provided. **Quiescence Diving Services** (✉ *103680 U.S. 1/Overseas Hwy. [MM 103.5 BS]* ☎ *305/451–2440* 🌐 *www.quiescence.com*) sets itself apart in two ways: it limits groups to six to ensure personal attention and offers day and night dives, as well as twilight dives when sea creatures are most active. Two-dive trips start at $66 without equipment.

SHOPPING

For the most part, shopping is sporadic in Key Largo, with a couple of shopping centers and fewer galleries than you find on the other big islands. If you're looking to buy scuba or snorkel equipment, you'll have plenty of places from which to choose.

You can find lots of shops in the Keys that sell cheesy souvenirs—snow globes, alligator hats, and shell-encrusted anything. **Shellworld** (✉ *97600 Overseas Hwy. [MM 97.5]* ☎ *305/852–8245*) is the granddaddy of them all. This sprawling building in the median of Overseas Highway has clothing, jewelry, and, delightfully tacky souvenirs, too.

NIGHTLIFE

The semiweekly *Keynoter* (Wednesday and Saturday), weekly *Reporter* (Thursday), and Friday through Sunday editions of the *Miami Herald* are the best sources of information on entertainment and nightlife. Daiquiri bars, tiki huts, and seaside shacks pretty well summarize Key Largo's bar scene.

Mingle with locals over cocktails and sunsets at **Breezers Tiki Bar & Grille** (✉ *103800 Overseas Hwy. [MM 103.8 BS]* ☎ *305/453–0000*), in Marriott's Key Largo Bay Beach Resort. Walls plastered with Bogart memorabilia remind customers that the classic 1948 Bogart-Bacall flick *Key Largo* has a connection with the **Caribbean Club** (✉ *MM 104 BS* ☎ *305/451–4466*). It draws boaters, curious visitors, and local barfly types, happiest while they're shooting the breeze or shooting pool. Postcard-perfect sunsets and live music draw revelers on weekends. **Coconuts** (✉ *528 Caribbean Dr. [MM 100 OS]* ☎ *305/453–9794*) has live music Tuesday to Sunday. The crowd is primarily thirty- and fortysomething, sprinkled with a few more-seasoned townies.

14

WHERE TO EAT

$ SEAFOOD ✕ **Alabama Jack's**. Calories be damned—the conch fritters here are heaven on a plate. The crab cakes, made from local blue crabs, earn hallelujahs, too. The conch salad is as good as any you'll find in the Bahamas and a third of the price in trendy Keys restaurants. This weathered, circa-1950 restaurant floats on two roadside barges in an old fishing community. Regulars include weekend cyclists, Miamians on the lam, and boaters, who come to admire tropical birds in the nearby mangroves, the occasional crocodile in the canal, or the bands that play on weekend afternoons. ■ **TIP→ It's about a half-hour drive from Key Largo, so you may want to plan a visit for your drive in or out.** Jack's closes by 7, when the mosquitoes start biting. ✉ *58000 Card Sound Rd., Key Largo* ☎ *305/248–8741* ▭ *MC, V.*

$$$ SEAFOOD ★ ✕ **The Fish House**. Restaurants not on the water have to produce the highest quality food to survive in the Keys. That's how the Fish House has succeeded since the 1980s—so much so that it built The Fish House Encore next door to accommodate fans. The pan-sautéed black grouper will make you moan with pleasure, but it's just one of many headliners in this nautical eatery. On the fin side, the choices include mahimahi, swordfish, tuna, and yellowtail snapper that can be broiled, blackened, baked, or fried. The Matecumbe Catch prepares the day's fresh fish so simply flavorful it should be patented—baked with tomatoes, capers, olive oil, and lemon juice. Prefer shellfish? Choose from shrimp, lobster, and (mid-October to mid-May) stone crab. For a sweet ending, try the homemade key lime pie. ✉ *102341 Overseas Hwy. (MM 102.4 OS)* ☎ *305/451–4665 or 305/451–0650* 🌐 *www.fishhouse.com* ▭ *AE, D, MC, V* ⊗ *Closed Sept.*

¢ AMERICAN ✕ **Harriette's Restaurant**. If you're looking for comfort food—like melt-in-your-mouth buttermilk biscuits—try this refreshing throwback. The kitchen makes fresh muffins daily, in flavors like mango, chocolate, and key lime. Little has changed over the years in this yellow-and-turquoise eatery. Owner Harriette Mattson often personally greets guests who come for steak and eggs with hash browns or old-fashioned hotcakes with sausage or bacon. Stick to simple dishes; the eggs Benedict are a disappointment. At lunch and dinner time, Harriette's shines in the burger department, but there are also hot meals such as chicken-fried steak and steak-and-shrimp combo. ✉ *95710 Overseas Hwy. (MM 95.7 BS)* ☎ *305/852–8689* ▭ *MC, V* ⊙ *No dinner Fri.–Sun.*

$ SEAFOOD ✕ **Mrs. Mac's Kitchen.** Townies pack the counters and booths at this tiny eatery, where license plates are stuck on the walls and made into chandeliers. Got a hankering for meatloaf or crab cakes? You'll find them here, along with specials like grilled yellowfin tuna. Bring your appetite for the all-you-can-eat fish specials on Tuesday and Thursday. There's also champagne breakfast, an assortment of tasty burgers and sandwiches, and its famous chili and key lime freeze. Ask about the hogfish special du jour. ✉ *99336 Overseas Hwy. (MM 99.4 BS)* ☎ *305/451–3722* ⊕ *www.mrsmacskitchen.com* ▭ *AE, D, MC, V* ⊙ *Closed Sun.*

$$ SEAFOOD ✕ **Rib Daddy's Chop House.** You'll swoon after tasting the Memphis-style mesquite-smoked prime rib, beef ribs, and pork baby back ribs flavored with specially formulated rubs and sauces. The menu extends beyond barbecue standards to include steak and seafood such as crab cakes and all-you-can-eat lobster and stone crab specials. Try the biscuits and gravy for breakfast or barbecue sandwiches for lunch. Save room for the key lime pie, creamy mango pie, or coconut cake. Kids love staring at the reef aquarium, the highlight of this rather plain, open dining room. ✉ *102570 Overseas Hwy. (MM 102.2 BS)* ☎ *305/451–0900* ⊕ *www.ribdaddysrestaurant.com* *Reservations not accepted* ▭ *MC, V.*

$$$ SEAFOOD ★ ✕ **Snapper's.** "You hook 'em, we cook 'em" is the motto here. Alas, "cleanin' 'em" is not part of the bargain. If you bring in your ready-for-the-grill fish, dinner here is $13.95 per person. Otherwise, they'll catch and cook you a plank-roasted yellowtail snapper, a grilled tuna steak, fish of the day baked with 36 herbs and spices, or a little something from the raw bar. The ceviche of yellowtail, shrimp, and conch (merrily spiced) wins raves, too. Lunch's seafood burrito is a keeper. All this is served up in a lively, mangrove-ringed waterfront setting with live music, an aquarium bar, Sunday brunch, killer rum drinks, and seating alongside the fishing dock. Three-course early-bird specials are available 5–6 PM for $18.50. ✉ *139 Seaside Ave. (MM 94.5 OS)* ☎ *305/852–5956* ⊕ *www.snapperskeylargo.com* ▭ *AE, D, MC, V.*

$$$ AMERICAN ✕ **Sundowners.** The name doesn't lie. If it's a clear night and you can snag a reservation, this restaurant will treat you to a sherbet-hued sunset over Florida Bay. If you're here in mild weather—anytime other than the dog days of summer or the rare winter cold snap—the best seats are on the patio. The food is excellent: try the key lime seafood, a happy combo of sautéed shrimp, lobster, and lump crabmeat swimming in a tangy sauce spiked with Tabasco served over penne or rice. Wednesday and Saturday are all about prime rib, and Friday draws the crowds with an all-you-can-eat fish fry ($16). Sunday brunch features beignets and Bloody Marys. ✉ *103900 Overseas Hwy. (MM 104 BS)* ☎ *305/451–4502* ⊕ *sundownerskeylargo.com* ▭ *AE, D, MC, V.*

WHERE TO STAY

$$$$ ★ **Azul del Mar.** The dock points the way to many beautiful sunsets at this adults-only boutique hotel. Advertising executive Karol Marsden and her husband, Dominic, a commercial travel photographer, transformed a run-down mom-and-pop place into this waterfront gem. As you'd expect from innkeepers with a background in the image business, the property offers great visuals, from marble floors and granite countertops to yellow-leather sofas and ice-blue bathroom tiles. Kayaks, barbecue grills, and a movie library are available for guest use, and two chickee huts on the beach are equipped with DVD players and comfortable seating. **Pros:** great garden; good location; sophisticated design. **Cons:** small beach; close to highway; high-priced. ✉ *104300 Overseas Hwy. (MM 104.3 BS),* ☎ *305/451–0337 or 888/253–2985* 🌐 *www.azulhotels.us* *2 studios, 3 1-bedroom suites, 1 2-bedroom suite* *In-room: no phone, kitchen, DVD, Wi-Fi. In-hotel: beachfront, water sports, no kids under 16, Wi-Fi hotspot* *AE, D, MC, V.*

$–$$ **Coconut Bay Resort & Bay Harbor Lodge.** Some 200 feet of waterfront is the main attraction at this property, a combination of two lodging options. Coconut palms whisper in the breeze, and gumbo-limbo trees shade the 2½-acre grounds. Nice features abound, like well-placed lounge chairs for gazing out over the water, and kayaks and paddleboats (for when you want to get closer). Everybody shows up on the sundeck or the 16-foot dock to watch the sun slip into Davy Jones's Locker. Rooms are a bit tight but not without island character. Pale-yellow cottages are simply furnished. Ask for Unit 25 and 26, a two-bedroom villa that will give you extra space and a water view. **Pros:** bay front; neatly kept gardens; walking distance to restaurants; complimentary kayak and paddleboat use. **Cons:** a bit dated; small sea-walled sand beach. ✉ *97702 Overseas Hwy.2 Overseas Hwy. (MM 97.7 BS)* ☎ *305/852–1625 or 800/385–0986* 🌐 *www.coconutbaykeylargo.com* *8 rooms, 5 efficiencies, 1 suite, 1 2-bedroom villa, 6 1-bedroom cottages* *In-room: kitchen (some), refrigerator, Wi-Fi (some). In-hotel: pool, beachfront, Wi-Fi hotspot, some pets allowed* *AE, D, MC, V.*

$$$–$$$$ **Dove Creek Lodge.** Old-school anglers will likely be scandalized by this 2004 fishing camp's sherbet-hued paint and plantation-style furnishings. But when they get a load of the massive flat-screen TV, the comfy leather couch, and the stack of fishing magazines in the lobby, they might never want to leave. You can head out on a boat from the marina, chase billfish offshore or bonefish on the flats, and come to brag to your buddies about the one that got away. The surprisingly plush rooms range in size from simple lodge rooms to luxury suites, all with private screened porch or balcony. Avoid rooms 201 and 202, and you'll avoid the "lively" noise from the seafood restaurant next door. **Pros:** great for fishing enthusiasts; luxurious rooms; close to Snapper's restaurant with charging privileges. **Cons:** Formica countertops in suites; loud music next door. ✉ *147 Seaside Ave. (MM94.5 OS)* ☎ *305/852–6200 or 800/401–0057* 🌐 *www.dovecreeklodge.com* *14 rooms* *In-room: safe, kitchen (some), refrigerator, Internet, Wi-Fi. In-hotel: pool, Wi-Fi hotspot* *AE, D, MC, V* *CP.*

14

$$$$ Fodor's Choice ★ **Kona Kai Resort & Gallery**. Brilliantly colored bougainvilleas, coconut palms, guava trees, and a new botanical garden make this 2-acre hideaway one of the prettiest places to stay in the Keys. Each of the intimate cottages has furnishings that add to the tropical feel. Spacious studios and one- and two-bedroom suites—with full kitchens and original art—are filled with natural light. Outside, kick back in a lounge chair or hammock, soak in the hot tub, or contemplate sunset from the deck. The resort also has an art gallery and an orchid house with more than 225 plants. Maid service is every third day to prolong your privacy; however, fresh linens and towels are available at any time. At the pool, help yourself to complimentary bottled water and fruit. **Pros:** lush landscaping; free use of sports equipment; knowledgeable staff. **Cons:** expensive rates; some rooms are very close together. *✉ 97802 Overseas Hwy. (MM 97.8 BS) ☎ 305/852–7200 or 800/365–7829 🌐 www.konakairesort.com ⇨ 8 suites, 3 rooms ⚐ In-room: no phone, kitchen (some), refrigerator, DVD. In-hotel: tennis court, pool, beachfront, Wi-Fi hotspot, no kids under 16 ▭ AE, D, MC, V ⊗ Closed Sept.*

$$$ ★ **Largo Lodge**. When you drive under the dense canopy of foliage at the entrance of Largo Lodge you'll feel like you've gone back in time. Vintage 1950s cottages are tucked amid 3 acres of palm trees, sea grapes, and orchids. Baby-boomer couples seem right at home here in rooms that might call to mind places they stayed as kids (though their own kids are not allowed here now!). Cottage accommodations—surprisingly spacious—feature small kitchen and dining areas and large screened porches. A lavish swath of bay frontage is perfect for communing with the friendly squirrels, iguanas, and ibises. For swimming, you'll need to drive about 1 mi to John Pennekamp Coral Reef State Park, but kayak use is complimentary here. **Pros:** lush grounds; great sunset views; affordable rates; boat docking. **Cons:** no pool; some traffic noise outdoors. *✉ 101740 Overseas Hwy. (MM 101.7 BS) ☎ 305/451–0424 or 800/468–4378 🌐 www.largolodge.com ⇨ 2 rooms, 6 cottages ⚐ In-room: no phone, kitchen (some), refrigerator, Wi-Fi. In-hotel: beachfront, Wi-Fi hotspot, no kids under 16 ▭ MC, V.*

$$$$ ★ **Marriott's Key Largo Bay Beach Resort**. Park the car and toss the keys in the bottom of your bag; there's no need to go anywhere else (except maybe John Pennekamp Coral Reef State Park, just a half mile north). This 17-acre bay-side resort has plenty of diversions, from diving to parasailing to a day spa. Given all that, the pool still rules, so a stroll to the tiki bar could well be your most vigorous activity of the day. The resort's lemon-yellow facade exudes an air of warm, indolent days. This isn't the poshest chain hotel you've ever encountered, but it's fresh looking and suitably tropical in style. Some of the best rooms and suites offer sunset views. **Pros:** lots of activities; free covered parking; lovely pool. **Cons:** rooms facing highway can be noisy. *✉ 103800 Overseas Hwy. (MM 103.8 BS) ☎ 305/453–0000 or 866/849–3753 🌐 www.marriottkeylargo.com ⇨ 132 rooms, 20 2-bedroom suites, 1 penthouse suite ⚐ In-room: safe, kitchen (some), Wi-Fi. In-hotel: 3 restaurants, room service, bars, pool, gym, spa, beachfront, diving, water sports, bicycles, children's programs (ages 5–13), laundry facilities, laundry service, Wi-Fi hotspot, some pets allowed ▭ AE, D, DC, MC, V.*

¢–$ **The Pelican.** This 1950s throwback is reminiscent of the days when parents packed the kids into the station wagon and headed to no-frills seaside motels, complete with an old-timer fishing off the dock. The owners have spiffed things up with cute, artsy touches and added a small sunning beach, but basically it's just a motel, not fancy but comfortable. Guests here don't mind skimping on space and a few frills in favor of homey digs, socializing under the chickee, and a low price tag. **Pros:** free use of kayaks and paddleboats; well-maintained dock; reasonable rates. **Cons:** some small rooms; basic accommodations and amenities. ✉ *99340 Overseas Hwy. (MM 99.3)* ☎ *305/451–3576 or 877/451–3576* 🌐 *www.thepelicankeylargo.com* *13 rooms, 4 efficiencies, 4 suites* *In-room: no phone, kitchen (some), refrigerator, DVD (some), Wi-Fi. In-hotel: beachfront, water sports, Wi-Fi hotspot* *AE, D, DC, MC, V.*

14

$–$$ **Seafarer Resort.** It's budget lodging, but the Seafarer Resort is not without its charms. There's a pond and hammocks, and most rooms have water views, and some have private patios. Rooms 3 and 4 are spacious and best for families. Unit 6, a one-bedroom cottage called the "beach house," has a large picture window with an awesome view of the bay. Guests gather at the beachfront picnic table for alfresco dining and on the dock and lounge chairs for sunset-watching. **Pros:** sandy beach; complimentary kayak use. **Cons:** some rooms close to road noise; basic accommodations. ✉ *97684 Overseas Hwy. (MM 97.6 BS)* ☎ *305/852–5349* 🌐 *www.seafarerresort.com* *8 rooms, 3 studios, 3 1-bedroom cottages, 1 2-bedroom cottage, 2 apartments* *In-room: no phone, kitchen (some), refrigerator, Wi-Fi. In-hotel: beachfront, water sports, laundry facilities, Wi-Fi hotspot* *MC, V.*

CAMPING

★ **John Pennekamp Coral Reef State Park.** Divers and snorkelers won't find a better location in the Upper Keys. Pennekamp's campsites are carved out of hardwood hammock, providing shade and privacy away from the heavy day-use areas. Activities include boating, fishing, scuba diving, snorkeling, and hiking. There's no restaurant, but there are vending machines for late-night snack attacks. *Flush toilets, partial hookups (electric and water), dump station, drinking water, showers, fire pits, picnic tables, electricity, public telephone, general store, ranger station, swimming (ocean)* *47 partial hookups for RVs and tents* ✉ *102601 Overseas Hwy. (MM 102.5 OS)* ☎ *305/451–1202 park, 800/326–3521 reservations* 🌐 *www.reserveamerica.com* *AE, D, MC, V.*

Kings Kamp. Florida Bay breezes keep things cool at this campground, and the neighboring waterway gives boaters direct access to John Pennekamp Coral Reef State Park. The campground has a marina for storing boats ($10 per day). The park can accommodate RVs up to 40 feet long, and if you don't want to bring your own, you can rent one ($110–$125). This property also has a cottage ($195–$220), motel-style units ($55–$75), and tent sites ($50). *Partial hookups (electric and water), dump station, drinking water, picnic tables, electricity, public telephone, swimming (ocean), Wi-Fi hotspot* *60 hookups for RVs and tents* ✉ *103620 Overseas Hwy. (MM 103.5 BS)* ☎ *305/451–0010* 🌐 *www.kingskamp.com* *MC, V.*

ISLAMORADA

Islamorada is between mile markers 90.5 and 70.

Early settlers named this key after their schooner, *Island Home,* but to make it sound more romantic they translated it into Spanish: *Isla Morada.* The chamber of commerce prefers to use its literal translation "Purple Island," which refers either to a purple-shelled snail that once inhabited these shores or to the brilliantly colored orchids and bougainvilleas.

Early maps show Islamorada as encompassing only Upper Matecumbe Key. But the incorporated "Village of Islands" is made up of a string of islands that the Overseas Highway crosses, including Plantation Key, Windley Key, Upper Matecumbe Key, Lower Matecumbe Key, Craig Key, and Fiesta Key. In addition, two state-park islands accessible only by boat—Indian Key and Lignumvitae Key—belong to the group.

Islamorada (locals pronounce it "*eye*-la-mor-*ah*-da") is one of the world's top fishing destinations. For nearly 100 years, seasoned anglers have fished these clear, warm waters teeming with trophy-worthy fish. There are numerous options for those in search of the big ones, including chartering a boat with its own crew or heading out on a vessel rented from one of the plethora of marinas along this 20-mi stretch of the Overseas Highway. More than 150 backcountry guides and 400 offshore captains are at your service.

Islamorada is one of the more affluent resort areas of the Keys. Sophisticated resorts and restaurants meet the needs of those in search of luxury, but there's also plenty for those looking for something more casual and affordable. Art galleries and boutiques make Islamorada's shopping scene the best in the Upper Keys, but if you're shopping for groceries, head to Marathon or Key Largo.

ESSENTIALS

Visitor Information Islamorada Chamber of Commerce (✉ *MM 83.2 BS, Upper Matecumbe Key, Islamorada* ☎ *305/664–4503 or 800/322–5397* 🌐 *www.islamoradachamber.com*).

EXPLORING

History of Diving Museum. Adding to the region's reputation for world-class diving, this museum plunges into the history of man's thirst for undersea exploration. Among its 13 galleries of interactive and other interesting displays are a submarine and helmet from the film *20,000 Leagues Under the Sea.* Historic equipment, sunken treasures, and photographs are part of the extensive collection donated by a local couple. ✉ *82990 Overseas Hwy. (MM 83 BS), Upper Matecumbe Key* ☎ *305/664–9737* 🌐 *www.divingmuseum.org* 💵 *$12* ⏲ *Daily 10–5.*

The fossilized-coral reef at **Windley Key Fossil Reef Geological State Park,** dating back about 125,000 years, shows that the Florida Keys were once beneath the ocean. Excavation of Windley Key's limestone bed by the Florida East Coast Railway exposed the petrified reef, full of beautifully fossilized brain coral and sea ferns. The park contains the **Alison Fahrer Environmental Education Center,** with historic, biological, and geological displays about the area. There also are guided and self-guided tours

Islamorada's warm waters attract large fish and the anglers, including charters, who want to catch them.

along trails that lead to the railway's old quarrying equipment and cutting pits, where you can make rubbings of the interesting quarry walls. The first Saturday in March is Windley Key Day, when the park sells native plants and hosts environmental exhibits. ✉ *MM 85.5 BS, Windley Key* ☎ *305/664–2540* 🌐 *www.floridastateparks.org/windleykey* 🎫 *Education center free, $2.50 for park, $1 for ranger-guided tours* ⏲ *Education center Thurs.–Mon. 8–5; tours at 10 and 2.*

The second-oldest marine-mammal center in the world, **Theater of the Sea** doesn't attempt to compete with more modern, more expensive parks. Even so, it's among the better attractions north of Key West, especially if you have kids in tow. Like the pricier parks, there are dolphin, sea lion, and stingray encounters ($55–$175, including general admission) where you can get up close and personal with underwater creatures. These are popular, so reserve in advance. Ride a "bottomless" boat to see what's below the waves and take a guided tour of the marine-life exhibits. Entertaining educational shows highlight conservation issues. You can stop for lunch at the grill, shop in the boutique, or sunbathe at a lagoon-side beach. This easily could be an all-day attraction. ✉ *84721 Overseas Hwy. (MM 84.5 OS), Windley Key* ☎ *305/664–2431* 🌐 *www.theaterofthesea.com* 🎫 *$26* ⏲ *Daily 9:30–5 (last ticket sold at 3:30).*

Upper Matecumbe Key was one of the first of the Upper Keys to be permanently settled. Early homesteaders were so successful at growing pineapples in the rocky soil that at one time the island yielded the country's largest annual crop. However, foreign competition and the hurricane of 1935 killed the industry. Today, life centers on fishing and tourism, and the island is filled with bait shops, marinas, and charter-fishing boats. ✉ *MM 84–79.*

OFF THE BEATEN PATH

Indian Key Historic State Park. Mystery surrounds 10-acre Indian Key, on the ocean side of the Matecumbe islands. Before it became one of the first European settlements outside of Key West, it was inhabited by American Indians for several thousand years. The islet served as a base for 19th-century shipwreck salvagers until an Indian attack wiped out the settlement in 1840. Dr. Henry Perrine, a noted botanist, was killed in the raid. Today his plants grow in the town's ruins. Most people kayak or canoe here from Indian Key Fill to explore the nature trails and the town ruins or snorkel. Florida Keys Kayak has an office at Robbie's Marina. There are no restrooms or picnic facilities on the island. *Box 1052 ☎ 305/664–2540 www.floridastateparks.org/indiankey Free Daily sunrise–sunset.*

OFF THE BEATEN PATH

Lignumvitae Key Botanical State Park. On the National Register of Historic Places, this 280-acre bay-side island is the site of a virgin hardwood forest and the 1919 home of chemical magnate William Matheson. His caretaker's cottage serves as the park's visitor center. Access is by boat—your own, a rented vessel, or a ferry operated by Robbie's Marina at 10 AM and 2 PM Thursday to Monday. (Paddling here from Indian Key Fill, at MM 78.5, is a popular pastime.) The only way to do the trails is by a guided ranger walk, offered Thursday through Monday for ferry passengers on the 10 and 2 excursions. Wear long sleeves and pants, and bring mosquito repellent. On the first weekend in December is the Lignumvitae Christmas Celebration. *Box 1052 ☎ 305/664–2540* park, 305/664–9814 ferry *www.floridastateparks.org/lignumvitaekey Free; ferry and tour $20 Park open Thurs.–Mon. 9–5; house tours Fri.–Sun 10 and 2.*

★ Huge, prehistoric-looking denizens of the not-so-deep, silver-sided tarpon congregate around the docks at **Robbie's Marina** on Lower Matecumbe Key. Children—and lots of adults—pay $4 to feed them sardines or $1 just to watch. Spend some time hanging out at this authentic Keys community, where you can grab a bite to eat, do a little shopping, or charter a boat. ✉ *77522 Overseas Hwy. (MM 77.5 BS), Lower Matecumbe Key ☎ 305/664–9814 or 877/664–8498 www.robbies.com Dock access $1 Daily 8–5.*

On Lower Matecumbe Key, **Anne's Beach Park** is a popular village park whose "beach" (really a typical Keys-style sand flat) is best enjoyed at low tide. The nicest feature here is a ½-mi, elevated, wooden boardwalk that meanders through a natural wetland hammock. Covered picnic areas along the way give you places to linger and enjoy the view. Restrooms are at the north end. Weekends are packed with Miami day-trippers as it's the only public beach until you reach Marathon. ✉ *MM 73.5 OS, Lower Matecumbe Key ☎ 305/853–1685.*

SPORTS AND THE OUTDOORS

BOATING

Marinas pop up every mile or so in the Islamorada area, so finding a rental or tour is no problem. Robbie's Marina is a prime example of a salty spot where you can find it all—from fishing charters and kayaking rentals to lunch and tarpon feeding.

Bump & Jump (✉ *81197 Overseas Hwy. [MM 81.2 OS], Upper Matecumbe Key* ☎ *305/664–9404 or 877/453–9463* 🌐 *www.keysboatrental.com*) is a one-stop shop for windsurfing, sailboat and powerboat rentals, sales, and lessons. This company delivers to your hotel or house, or drops it off right at the beach.

See the islands from the comfort of your own boat (captain's cap optional) when you rent from **Houseboat Vacations of the Florida Keys** (✉ *85944 Overseas Hwy. [MM 85.9 BS], Plantation Key* ☎ *305/664–4009* 🌐 *www.floridakeys.com/houseboats*). The company maintains a fleet of 42- to 55-foot boats that accommodate up to 10 people and come outfitted with everything you need besides food. (You may provision yourself at a nearby grocery store.) The three-day minimum starts at $1,112; one week costs $1,950 and up. Kayaks, canoes, and skiffs suitable for the ocean are also available.

Robbie's Boat Rentals & Charters (✉ *77522 Overseas Hwy. [MM 77.5 BS], Lower Matecumbe Key* ☎ *305/664–9814 or 877/664–8498* 🌐 *www.robbies.com*) does it all. The company will give you a crash course on how not to crash your boat. The rental fleet includes an 18-foot skiff with a 60-horsepower outboard for $150 for four hours and $200 for the day to a 23-foot deck boat with a 130-horsepower engine for $185 for a half day and $235 for eight hours. Robbie's also rents fishing and snorkeling gear (there's good snorkeling nearby) and sells bait, drinks and snacks, and gas. Want to hire a guide who knows the local waters and where the fish lurk? Robbie's offers offshore-fishing trips, patch-reef trips, and party-boat fishing. Backcountry flats trips are a specialty. Captains Pam and Pete Anderson of **Treasure Harbor Marine** (✉ *200 Treasure Harbor Dr. [MM 86.5 OS], Plantation Key* ☎ *305/852–2458 or 800/352–2628* 🌐 *www.treasureharbor.com*) provide everything you'll need for a vacation at sea. Best of all, they give excellent advice on where to find the best anchorages, snorkeling spots, or lobstering sites. Vessels range from a 23.5-foot Hunter to a 41-foot Morgan Out Island. Rates start at $160 a day; $700 a week. Hire a captain for $175–$200 a day. Marina facilities are basic—water, electric, ice machine, laundry, picnic tables, and restrooms with showers. A store sells snacks, beverages, and sundries.

FISHING

Here in the self-proclaimed "Sportfishing Capital of the World," sailfish is the prime catch in the winter and dolphinfish in the summer. Buchanan Bank just south of Islamorada is a good spot to try for tarpon in the spring. Blackfin tuna and amberjack are generally plentiful in the area, too. ■ **TIP→ The Hump at Islamorada ranks highest among anglers' favorite fishing spots in Florida (declared *Florida Monthly* magazine's best for seven years in a row) due to the incredible offshore marine life.**

14

Renting wave runners is a fun way to catch some surf and sun in Florida Keys. Each fits one to three people.

Captain Ted Wilson (✉ *79851 Overseas Hwy. [MM 79.9 OS], Upper Matecumbe Key* ☎ *305/942–5224 or 305/664–9463* 🌐 *www.captaintedwilson.com*) takes you into the backcountry for bonefish, tarpon, redfish, snook, and shark aboard a 17-foot boat that accommodates up to three anglers. For two people, half-day trips run $350, full-day trips $525, and evening excursions $375. There's a $100 charge for an extra person.

Long before fly-fishing became popular, Sandy Moret was fishing the Keys for bonefish, tarpon, and redfish. Now he attracts anglers from around the world with the **Florida Keys Outfitters** (✉ *Green Turtle, 81219 Overseas Hwy. [MM 81.2], Upper Matecumbe Key* ☎ *305/664–5423* 🌐 *www.floridakeysoutfitters.com*). Weekend fly-fishing classes, which include classroom instruction, equipment, and daily lunch, cost $985. Add $1,070 for two additional days of fishing. Guided fishing trips cost $395 for a half day, $535 for a full day. Packages combining fishing and accommodations at Islander Resort are available. The 65-foot party boat ***Miss Islamorada*** (✉ *Bud n' Mary's Marina, 79851 Overseas Hwy. [MM 79.8 OS], Upper Matecumbe Key* ☎ *305/664–2461 or 800/742–7945*) has full-day trips for $60. Bring your lunch or buy one from the dockside deli.

★ Captain Ken Knudsen of the **Hubba Hubba Charters** (✉ *MM 79.8 OS, Upper Matecumbe Key* ☎ *305/664–9281* 🌐 *www.capthubbahubba.com*) quietly poles his flatboat through the shallow water, barely making a ripple. Then he points and his clients cast. Five seconds later there's a zing, and the excitement of bringing in a snook, redfish, trout, or tarpon begins. Knudsen has fished Keys waters for more than 40 years. Now a licensed backcountry guide, he's ranked among Florida's top 10 by national fishing magazines. He offers four-hour sunset trips for tarpon ($400–$425) and two-hour sunset trips for bonefish ($200), as well as half- ($375) and full-day ($550) outings. Prices are for one or two anglers, and tackle and bait are included.

Like other top fly-fishing and light-tackle guides, Captain Geoff Colmes of **Florida Keys Fly Fish** (✉ *105 Palm La., Upper Matecumbe Key* ☎ *305/853–0741* 🌐 *www.floridakeysflyfish.com*) helps his clients land trophy fish in the waters around the Keys ($500–$550).

SCUBA DIVING AND SNORKELING

About 1¼ nautical mi south of Indian Key is the **San Pedro Underwater Archaeological Preserve State Park,** which includes the wreck of a Spanish treasure-fleet ship that sank in 1733. The state of Florida protects the site for divers; no spearfishing or souvenir collecting is allowed. Resting in only 18 feet of water, its ruins are visible to snorkelers as well as divers and attract a colorful array of fish.

14

Florida Keys Dive Center (✉ *90451 Overseas Hwy. [MM 90.5 OS], Plantation Key* ☎ *305/852–4599 or 800/433–8946* 🌐 *www.floridakeysdivectr.com*) organizes dives from John Pennekamp Coral Reef State Park to Alligator Light. The center has two 46-foot Coast Guard–approved dive boats, offers scuba training, and is one of the few Keys dive centers to offer nitrox and trimix (mixed gas) diving. With a resort, pool, restaurant, lessons, and twice-daily dive and snorkel trips, **Holiday Isle Dive Shop** (✉ *84001 Overseas Hwy. [MM 84 OS], Windley Key* ☎ *305/664–3483 or 800/327–7070* 🌐 *www.diveholidayisle.com*) is a one-stop dive shop. Rates start at $75 for a two-tank dive without equipment.

WATER SPORTS

Florida Keys Kayak (✉ *Robbie's Marina, 77522 Overseas Hwy. [MM 77.5 BS], Lower Matecumbe Key* ☎ *305/664–4878*) rents kayaks for trips to Indian and Lignumvitae keys, two favorite destinations for paddlers. Kayak rental rates are $20 per hour for a single, and $27.50 for a double. Half-day rates (and you'll need plenty of time to explore those mangrove canopies) are $40 for a single kayak and $55 for a double. The company also offers guided two- and three-hour tours ($39 and $49 per person).

SHOPPING

Art galleries, upscale gift shops, and the mammoth World Wide Sportsman (if you want to look the part of a local fisherman, you must wear a shirt from here) make up the variety and superior style of Islamorada shopping.

At the **Banyan Tree** (✉ *81197 Overseas Hwy. [MM 81.2 OS], Upper Matecumbe Key* ☎ *305/664–3433 or 877/453–9463* 🌐 *www.banyantreegarden.com*), a sharp-eyed husband-and-wife team successfully combines antiques and contemporary gifts for the home and garden with plants, pots, and trellises in a stylishly sophisticated indoor–outdoor setting. The go-to destination for one-of-a-kind gifts is **Gallery Morada** (✉ *81611 Old Hwy. [MM 81.6 OS], Upper Matecumbe Key* ☎ *305/664–3650* 🌐 *www.gallerymorada.com*), where blown-glass objects are beautifully displayed, as are the original sculptures, paintings, lithographs,

Continued on page 695

DID YOU KNOW?

The coral making up the Barrier Reef is living and provides an ecosystem for small marine creatures. Bumping against or touching the coral can kill these creatures as well as damage the reef itself.

UNDER THE SEA
SNORKELING AND DIVING IN THE FLORIDA KEYS

by Lynne Helm

Up on the shore they work all day…

While we devotin',

Full time to floatin',

Under the sea…

–"Under the Sea,"

from Disney's *Little Mermaid*

All Floridians—even those long-accustomed to balmy breezes and swaying palms—turn ecstatic at the mere thought of tripping off to the Florida Keys. Add the prospect of underwater adventure, and hot diggity, it's unparalleled bliss.

Perennially laid back, the Keys annually attract nearly 800,000 snorkeling and scuba diving aficionados, and why not? There's arguably no better destination to learn these sports that put you up close to the wonders of life under the sea.

THE BARRIER REEF

The continental United States' only living coral barrier reef stretches 5 mi offshore of the Keys and is a teeming backbone of marine life, ranging from brilliant corals to neon-colored fish from blue-striped grunts to green moray eels. This is the prime reason why the Keys are where you descend upon intricate natural coral formations and encrusted shipwrecks, some historic, others sunk by design to create artificial reefs that attract divers and provide protection for marine life. Most diving sites have mooring buoys (nautical floats away from shore, sometimes marking specific sites); these let you tie up your boat so you don't need to drop anchor, which could damage the reef. Most of these sites also are near individual keys, where dozens of dive operators can cater to your needs.

Reef areas thrive in waters as shallow as 5 feet and as deep as 50 feet. Shallow reefs attract snorkelers, while deeper reefs suit divers of varying experience levels. The Keys' shallow diving offers two benefits: longer time safely spent on the bottom exploring, and more vibrant colors because of sunlight penetration. Most divers log maximum depths of 20 to 30 feet.

(left) Shallow-water coral reef, (top) Nine Foot Stake is a popular site for underwater photography.

WHERE TO SNORKEL AND DIVE

KEY WEST

Nine Foot Stake

Mile Marker 0–4

You can soak up a mesmerizing overview of submerged watery wonders at the **Florida Keys Eco-Discovery Center**, opened in 2007 on Key West's Truman Annex waterfront. Both admission and parking are free at the 6,000 square-foot center (*9–4 Tues.–Sat. 305/809-4750*); interactive exhibits here focus on Keys marine life and habitats. Key West's offshore reefs are best accessed via professional charters, but it's easy to snorkel from shore at **Key West Marine Park.** Marked by a lighthouse, **Sand Key Reef** attracts snorkelers and scuba divers. **Joe's Tug**, at 65-foot depths, sets up encounters with Goliath grouper. **Ten-Fathom Ledge**, with coral caves and dramatic overhangs, shelters lobster. The **Cayman Salvor**, a buoy tender sunk as an artificial reef in 1985, shelters baitfish. Patch reef **Nine Foot Stake**, submerged 10 to 25 feet, has soft corals and juvenile marine life. **Kedge Ledge** features a pair of coral-encrusted anchors from 18th-century sailing vessels. *Florida Keys main visitor line at 800/FLA-KEYS (352-5397).*

BIG PINE KEY/LOWER KEYS

Mile Marker 4–47

Many devotees feel a Florida dive adventure would not be complete without heading 5 mi from Big Pine Key to **Looe Key National Marine Sanctuary**, an underwater preserve named for the HMS Looe running aground in 1744. If you time your visit for July, you might hit the one-day free underwater music festival for snorkelers and divers. Go under here and you'll likely encounter more tropical marine species than perhaps anywhere in the hemisphere. Looe Key's reef ecosystem extends from fossilized corals to a reef flat of turtle grass and large star and brain corals, from 20 to 40 feet. A deeper reef showcases eagle rays, turtles, and sometimes the rare whale shark. About 3 mi west of Looe Key, the 210-foot island freighter **Adolphus Busch** rests on the ocean floor at 110-foot depths, sheltering a 350-pound Goliath grouper near the wheelhouse. Sunk in 1988, it acts as an artificial reef providing additional habitat for marine species. *Big Pine Key and Lower Keys Tourist information line, at MM 31, 800/872-3722.*

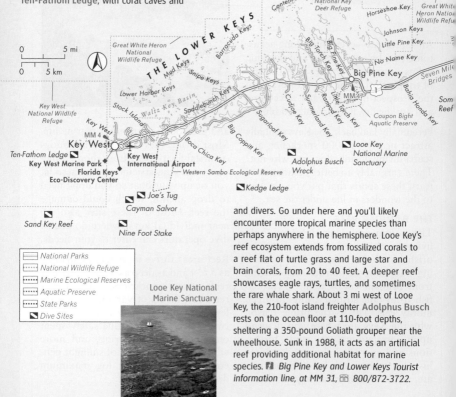

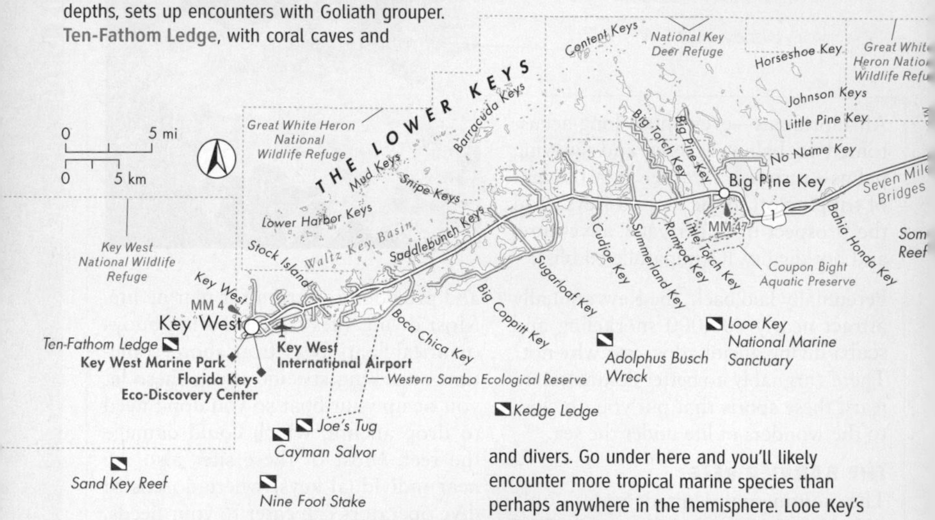

Looe Key National Marine Sanctuary

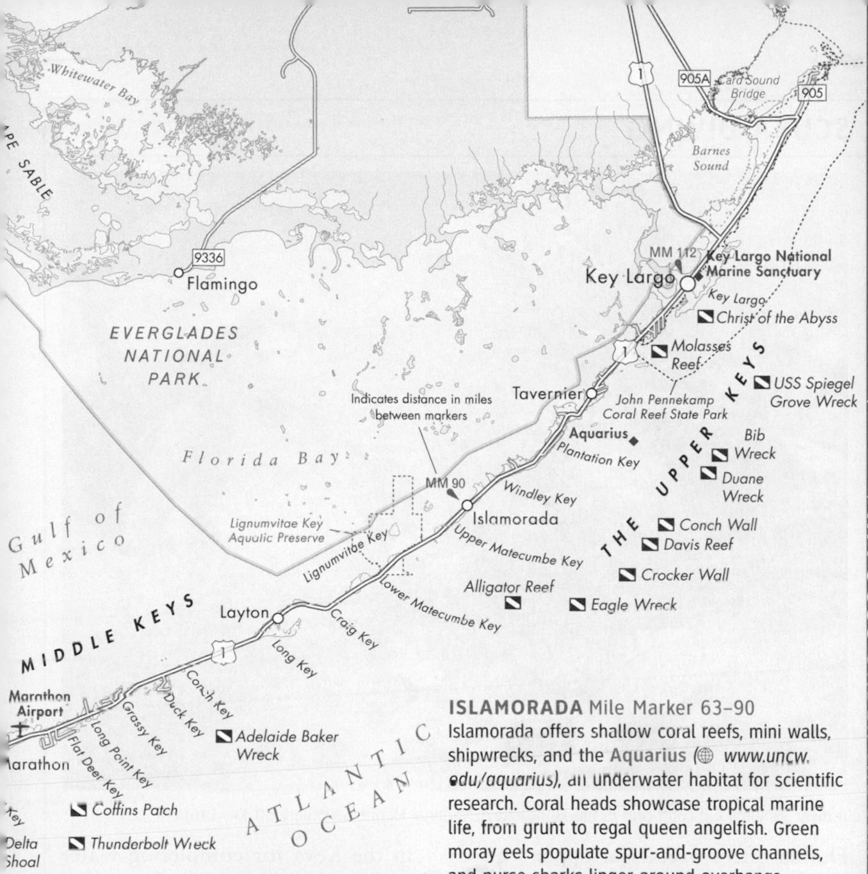

Whitewater Bay
CAPE SABLE
9336
Flamingo
EVERGLADES NATIONAL PARK
Florida Bay
Gulf of Mexico
905A
Card Sound Bridge
905
1
Barnes Sound
MM 112
Key Largo
Key Largo National Marine Sanctuary
Key Largo
Christ of the Abyss
Molasses Reef
USS Spiegel Grove Wreck
Tavernier
John Pennekamp Coral Reef State Park
Indicates distance in miles between markers
Aquarius
Plantation Key
Bib Wreck
Duane Wreck
THE UPPER KEYS
MM 90
Windley Key
Islamorada
Lignumvitae Key Aquatic Preserve
Lignumvitae Key
Upper Matecumbe Key
Conch Wall
Davis Reef
Crocker Wall
Alligator Reef
Eagle Wreck
Lower Matecumbe Key
Layton
Craig Key
MIDDLE KEYS
Long Key
Marathon Airport
Conch Key
Duck Key
Grassy Key
Adelaide Baker Wreck
Long Point Key
Flat Deer Key
Marathon
Coffins Patch
Delta Shoal
Thunderbolt Wreck
ATLANTIC OCEAN

MARATHON/MIDDLE KEYS

Mile Marker 47–63

Sombrero Reef

The Middle Keys yield a marine wilderness of a spur-and-groove coral and patch reefs. The **Adelaide Baker** historic shipwreck has a pair of stacks in 25 feet of water. Popular **Sombrero Reef**, with coral canyons and archways, is marked by a 140-foot lighted tower. Six distinct patch reefs known as **Coffin's Patch** have shallow elkhorn forests. **Delta Shoals**, a network of coral canyons fanning seaward from a sandy shoal, attracts divers to its elkhorn, brain, and star coral heads. Marathon's **Thunderbolt**, a 188-foot ship sunk in 1986, sits upright at 115-foot depths, coated with sponge, coral, and hydroid, and attracting angelfish, jacks, and deep-water pelagic creatures. *Greater Marathon Chamber and visitors center at MM 53.5, 800/262–7284.*

ISLAMORADA Mile Marker 63–90

Islamorada offers shallow coral reefs, mini walls, shipwrecks, and the **Aquarius** (*www.uncw.edu/aquarius*), an underwater habitat for scientific research. Coral heads showcase tropical marine life, from grunt to regal queen angelfish. Green moray eels populate spur-and-groove channels, and nurse sharks linger around overhangs. Submerged attractions include the **Eagle**, a 287-foot ship in 110 feet of water; **Davis Reef**, with gorgonian coral; **Alligator Reef**, where the *USS Alligator* sank while fighting pirates; the sloping **Conch Wall**, with barrel sponges and gorgonian; and **Crocker Wall**, featuring spur-and-groove and block corals. *Islamorada Chamber and visitor center at MM 83.2, 800/322–5397.*

KEY LARGO Mile Marker 90–112

Key Largo marine conservation got a big leg up with creation of **John Pennekamp Coral Reef State Park** in 1960, the nation's first undersea preserve, followed by 1975's designation of the **Key Largo National Marine Sanctuary**. A popular underwater attraction is the bronze statue of **Christ of the Abyss** between coral formations. Explorers with a "lust for rust" can dive down to 60 to 90 feet and farther to see the murky cemetery for two twin 327-foot U.S. Coast Guard cutters, ***Duane*** and ***Bibb***, used during World War II; ***USS Spiegel Grove***, a 510-foot Navy transport ship sunk in 2002 to create an artificial reef; and **Molasses Reef**, showcasing coral heads. *Key Largo Chamber at MM 106, 800/822–1088.*

SCUBA DIVING

A diver explores the coral reef in the Florida Keys National Marine Sanctuary off Key Largo.

Florida offers wonderful opportunities to spend your vacation in the sun and become a certified diver at the same time. In the Keys, count on setting aside three to five days for entry-level or so-called "Open Water" certification offered by many dive shops. Basic certification (covering depths to about 60 feet) involves classroom work and pool training, followed by one or more open-water dives at the reef. After passing a knowledge test and completing the required water training (often starting in a pool), you become a certified recreational scuba diver, eligible to rent dive gear and book dive trips with most operations worldwide. Learning through video or online computer programs can enable you to complete classroom work at home, so you can more efficiently schedule time in the Keys for completing water skills and getting out to the reef for exploration.

Many would-be divers opt to take the classroom instruction and pool training at home at a local dive shop and then spend only two days in the Keys completing four dives. It's not necessarily cheaper, but it can be far more relaxing to commit to only two days of diving.

Questions you should ask: Not all dive shops are created equal, and it may be worthwhile to spend extra money for a better diving experience. Some of the larger dive shops take out large catamarans that can carry as many as 24 to 40 people. Many people prefer the intimacy of a smaller boat.

Good to know: Divers can become certified through PADI *(www.padi.com)*, NAUI *(www.naui.org)*, or SSI *(www.divessi.com)*. The requirements for all three are similar, and if you do the classroom instruction and pool training with a dive shop associated with one organization, the referral for the open water dives will be honored by most dive shops. Note that you are not allowed to fly for at least 24 hours after a dive, because residual nitrogen in the body can pose health risks upon decompression. While there are no rigid rules on diving after flying, make sure you're well-hydrated before hitting the water.

Cost: The four-day cost can range from $300 to $475, but be sure to ask if equipment, instruction manuals, and log books are extra. Some dive shops have relationships with hotels, so check for dive/stay packages. Referral dives (a collaborative effort among training agencies) run from $285 to $300 and discover scuba runs around $175 to $200.

SNUBA

Beyond snorkeling or the requirements of scuba, you also have the option of "Snuba." The word is a trademarked portmanteau or combo of snorkel and scuba. Marketed as easy-to-learn family fun, Snuba lets you breathe underwater via tubes from an air-supplied vessel above, with no prior diving or snorkel experience required.

NOT CERTIFIED?

Not sure if you want to commit the time and money to become certified? Not a problem. Most dive shops and many resorts will offer a discover scuba day-long course. In the morning, the instructor will teach you the basics of scuba diving: how to clear your mask, how to come to the surface in the unlikely event you lose your air supply, etc. In the afternoon, instructors will take you out for a dive in relatively shallow water—less than 30 feet. Be sure to ask where the dive will take place. Jumping into the water off a shallow beach may not be as fun as actually going out to the coral. If you decide that diving is something you want to pursue, the open dive may count toward your certification.

■ TIP→ You can often book the discover dives at the last minute. It may not be worth it to go out on a windy day when the currents are stronger. Also the underwater world looks a whole lot brighter on sunny days.

(top) Scuba divers; (bottom) Diver ascending line.

SNORKELING

Snorklng lets you see the wonders of the sea from a new perspective.

The basics: Sure, you can take a deep breath, hold your nose, squint your eyes, and stick your face in the water in an attempt to view submerged habitats . . . but why not protect your eyes, retain your ability to breathe, and keep your hands free to paddle about when exploring underwater? That's what snorkeling is all about.

Equipment needed: A mask, snorkel (the tube attached to the mask), and fins. In deeper waters (any depth over your head), life jackets are advised.

Steps to success: If you've never snorkeled before, it's natural to feel a bit awkward at first, so don't sweat it. Breathing through a mask and tube, and wearing a pair of fins take getting used to. Like any activity, you build confidence and comfort through practice.

If you're new to snorkeling, begin by submerging your face in shallow water or a swimming pool and breathing calmly through the snorkel while gazing through the mask.

Next you need to learn how to clear water out of your mask and snorkel, an essential skill since splashes can send water into tube openings and masks can leak. Some snorkels have built-in drainage valves, but if a tube clogs, you can force water up and out by exhaling through your mouth. Clearing a mask is similar: lift your head from water while pulling forward on mask to drain. Some masks have built-in purge valves, but those without can be cleared underwater by pressing the top to the forehead and blowing out your nose (charming, isn't it?), allowing air to bubble into the mask, pushing water out the bottom. If it sounds hard, it really isn't. Just try it a few times and you'll soon feel like a pro.

Now your goal is to get friendly with fins—you want them to be snug but not too tight—and learn how to propel yourself with them. Fins won't help you float, but they will give you a leg up, so to speak, on smoothly moving through the water or treading water (even when upright) with less effort.

Flutter stroking is the most efficient underwater kick, and the farther your foot bends forward the more leg power you'll be able to transfer to the water and the farther you'll travel with each stroke. Flutter kicking movements involve alternately separating the legs and then drawing them back together. When your legs separate, the leg surface encounters drag from the water, slowing you down. When your legs are drawn back together, they produce a force pushing you forward. If your kick creates more forward force than it causes drag, you'll move ahead.

Submerge your fins to avoid fatigue rather than having them flailing above the water when you kick, and keep your arms at your side to reduce drag. You are in the water—stretched out, face down, and snorkeling happily away—but that doesn't mean you can't hold your breath and go deeper in the water for a closer look at some fish or whatever catches your attention. Just remember that when you do this, your snorkel will be submerged, too, so you won't be breathing (you'll be holding your breath). You can dive head-first, but going feet-first is easier and less scary for most folks, taking less momentum. Before full immersion, take several long, deep breaths to clear carbon dioxide from your lungs.

If your legs tire, flip onto your back and tread water with inverted fin motions while resting. If your mask fogs, wash condensation from lens and clear water from mask.

TIPS FOR SAFE SNORKELING

- Snorkel with a buddy and stay together.
- Plan your entry and exit points prior to getting in the water.
- Swim into the current on entering and then ride the current back to your exit point.
- Carry your flippers into the water and then put them on, as it's difficult to walk in them.
- Make sure your mask fits properly and is not too loose.
- Pop your head above the water periodically to ensure you aren't drifting too far out, or too close to rocks.
- Think of the water as someone else's home—don't take anything that doesn't belong to you, or leave any trash behind.
- Don't touch any sea creatures; they may sting.
- Wear a T-shirt over your swimsuit to help protect you from being fried by the sun.
- When in doubt, don't go without a snorkeling professional; try a guided tour.

Cayman Salvor

TOP OUTFITTERS

COMPANY	ADDRESS & PHONE	COST	DESCRIPTION
AMY SLATE'S AMORAY DIVE CENTER www.amoray.com	104250 Overseas Hwy. (MM 104.2), Key Largo 305/451-3595	Daily Scuba classes for kids ages 8 and up and adults $100-$200.	Sign up for dive/snorkel trips, scuba instruction and kid programs.
DIVE KEY WEST www.divekeywest.com	3128 N. Roosevelt Blvd., Key West 305/296-3823	Snorkel from $49, dive from $69	Operating nearly 40 years. Has charters, instruction, and gear.
ECO SCUBA KEY WEST www.ecoscuba.com	5930 Peninsular Ave. (MM 5), Key West 305/851-1899	Daily Snorkel from $35, scuba from $99.	Debuted in 2009. Offers eco-tours, lobstering, snorkeling, and scuba.
FLORIDA KEYS DIVE CENTER www.floridakeys-divectr.com	90451 Old Hwy. (MM 90.5), Tavernier 305/852-4599	Daily Classes from $175.	Charters for snorkerlers and divers go to Pennekamp, Key Largo, and Islamorada.
HORIZON DIVERS www.horizondivers.com	100 Ocean Dr. #1, Key Largo 305/453-3535	Daily Snorkel from $50, scuba from $80.	Take customized dive/snorkel trips on a 45-foot catamaran.
ISLAND VENTURES www.islandventure.com	103900 Overseas Hwy. (MM 103.9), Key Largo 305/451-4957	Two trips daily Snorkel $45, scuba from $80.	Go on snorkeling and scuba explorations to the Key Largo reef and shipwrecks.
KEYS DIVER SNORKEL TOURS www.keysdiver.com	99696 Overseas Hwy. (MM 99.6), Key Largo 305/451-1177	Three daily snorkel tours from $28. Includes gear.	Family-oriented snorkel-only tours head to coral reefs such as Pennekamp.
LOOE KEY REEF RESORT & DIVE CENTER www.diveflakeys.com	27340 Overseas Hwy. (MM 27.5), Ramrod Key 305/872-2215	Daily Snorkel from $44, scuba from $85.	Beginner and advanced scuba instruction, a photographer course, and snorkel gear rental.
RON JON SURF SHOP www.ronjons.com	503 Front St., Key West 305/293-8880	Daily Sells snorkel gear.	Several locations in Florida; its HQ is in Cocoa Beach.
SNUBA OF KEY WEST www.snubakeywest.com	600 Palm Ave., Key West 305/292-4616	Daily $99 per person, $44 for ride-alongs.	Swimmers ages 8 and up can try Snuba.
TILDENS SCUBA CENTER www.tildensscuba-center.com	4650 Overseas Hwy. (MM 49.5), Marathon 305/743-7255	Daily Snorkel from $35.99, scuba from $60.99.	Operating for 25 years. Has lessons, tours, snorkeling, scuba, snuba, gear, and a kids club.

and jewelry, of top South Florida artists. Among the best buys in town are the used best-sellers at **Hooked on Books** (✉ *82681 Overseas Hwy. [MM 82.6 OS], Upper Matecumbe Key* ☎ *305/517–2602* 🌐 *www.hookedonbooksfloridakeys.com*), which also sells new titles, audiobooks, and CDs. **Island Silver & Spice** (✉ *81981 Overseas Hwy. [MM 82 OS], Upper Matecumbe Key* ☎ *305/664–2714*) has tropical-style furnishings, rugs, and home accessories. The shop also stocks women's and men's resort wear and a large jewelry selection with high-end watches and marine-theme pieces. The **Rain Barrel** (✉ *86700 Overseas Hwy. [MM 86.7 BS], Plantation Key* ☎ *305/852–3084*) is a natural and unhurried shopping showplace. Set in a tropical garden of shady trees, native shrubs, and orchids, the crafts village has shops with works by local and national artists and resident artists in studios, including John Hawver, noted for Florida landscapes and seascapes. The **Redbone Gallery** (✉ *200 Industrial Dr. [MM 81.5 OS), Upper Matecumbe Key* ☎ *305/664–2002* 🌐 *www.redbone.org*), one of the largest sportfishing–art galleries in Florida, stocks hand-stitched clothing and giftware, in addition to work by wood and bronze sculptors such as Kendall van Sant; watercolorists Chet Reneson, Jeanne Dobie, and Kathleen Denis; and painters C.D. Clarke and Tim Borski. Proceeds benefit cystic fibrosis research.

Former U.S. presidents, celebrities, and record holders beam alongside their catches in black-and-white photos on the walls at **World Wide Sportsman** (✉ *81576 Overseas Hwy. [MM 81.5 BS], Upper Matecumbe Key* ☎ *305/664–4615 or 800/327–2880*), a two-level retail center that sells upscale fishing equipment, resort clothing, sportfishing art, and other gifts. When you're tired of shopping, relax at the Zane Grey Long Key Lounge just above World Wide Sportsman.

NIGHTLIFE

Islamorada is not known for its raging nightlife, but for local fun Lorelei's is legendary. Others cater to the town's sophisticated clientele and fishing fervor.

★ Behind a larger-than-life mermaid, the **Lorelei Restaurant & Cabana Bar** (✉ *81924 Overseas Hwy. [MM 82 BS], Upper Matecumbe Key* ☎ *305/664–2692* 🌐 *www.loreleifloridakeys.com*) is the kind of place you fantasize about during those long, cold winters up north. It's all about good drinks, tasty pub grub, and beautiful sunsets set to live bands playing island tunes and light rock.

WHERE TO EAT

$$$ SEAFOOD ✕ **Green Turtle Inn.** This circa-1928 landmark inn and its vintage neon sign is a slice of Florida Keys history. Period photographs decorate the wood-paneled walls. Breakfast and lunch options include surprises like coconut French toast and yellowfin tuna tartare. Award-winning chef Andy Niedenthal relies heavily on Continental classics tossed with a few Latin touches for his dinner menu; think turtle chowder (don't gasp; it's made from farm-raised freshwater turtles), churrasco steak with yucca hash, and rum-glazed duck with sweet plantain mash. Naturally, there's a Turtle Sundae on the dessert menu. The chef uses organic produce wherever possible. ✉ *81219 Overseas Hwy. (MM 81.2 OS), Upper Matecumbe Key* ☎ *305/664–2006* 🌐 *www.greenturtlekeys.com* ✍ *Reservations essential* 💳 *AE, MC, V* ⊗ *Closed Mon.*

$$ SEAFOOD ★ **Island Grill**. Don't be fooled by appearances; this shack on the waterfront takes island breakfast, lunch, and dinner cuisine up a notch. The eclectic menu tempts you with such dishes as guava-barbecue shrimp wrapped in bacon, and lobster rolls. Southern-style shrimp and andouille sausage with grits join island-style specialties such as grilled mahi-mahi with black bean and corn salsa on the list of entrées. There's an air-conditioned dining room and bar as well as outdoor seating under the trees. The outdoor bar hosts live entertainment Wednesday to Sunday. ✉ *85501 Overseas Hwy. (MM 85.5 OS), Windley Key* ☎ *305/664–8400* 🌐 *www.keysislandgrill.com* ▭ *AE, D, MC, V.*

$$ JAPANESE ★ **Kaiyó**. Kaiyó's decor—an inviting setting that includes colorful abstract mosaics, polished wood floors, and upholstered banquettes—almost steals the show here, but the food is equally interesting. The menu, a fusion of East and West, offers sushi and sashimi and rolls that combine local ingredients with traditional Japanese tastes. The key lime lobster roll is a blend of Florida lobster with hearts of palm and essence of key lime ($18). The baby conch roll surrounds tempura conch, ponzu mayo, and kimchi with sushi rice for an inside-out effect. Entrees in the $19-and-up range include a noodle seafood bowl, teriyaki chicken, and a grilled-fillet-and-lobster-tail combo. ✉ *81701 Overseas Hwy. (MM 81.5 OS), Upper Matecumbe Key* ☎ *305/664–5556* 🌐 *www.kaiyokeys.com* ▭ *AE, MC, V* ⊙ *Closed Sun.*

$$ SEAFOOD ★ **Marker 88**. A few yards from Florida Bay, this seafood restaurant has been popular for more than 40 years. Large picture windows offer great sunset views, but the bay is lovely no matter what time of day you visit. Chef Sal Barrios serves such irresistible entrées as grilled yellowfin tuna and yellowtail snapper in a tomato-basil sauce. Landlubbers find dishes like Parmesan-crusted filet mignon. If you're not that hungry, there's also a long list of sandwiches. The extensive wine list is an oenophile's delight. ✉ *88000 Overseas Hwy. (MM 88 BS), Plantation Key* ☎ *305/852–9315* 🌐 *www.marker88.info* ⌂ *Reservations essential* ▭ *AE, D, MC, V.*

$$$ ECLECTIC ★ **Morada Bay Beach Café**. This bay-front restaurant wins high marks for its surprisingly stellar cuisine, tables planted in the sand, and tiki torches that bathe the evening in romance. Entrées feature alluring combinations like broiled lobster with tropical fruit salsa and caramelized jumbo sea scallops with wild mushroom risotto. Seafood takes center stage, but you can always get roasted organic chicken (flavored with lemon) or a steak. Nightly specials like triple tail fish and lobster with green curry sauce strut the kitchen's stuff. Sit in a dining room outfitted with surfboards or outdoors on a beach, where the sunset puts on a mighty show and kids (and your feet) play in the sand. There's nightly live music and a monthly full-moon party. ✉ *81600 Overseas Hwy. (MM 81 BS), Upper Matecumbe Key* ☎ *305/664–0604* 🌐 *www.moradabay-restaurant.com* ▭ *AE, MC, V.*

$$$$ FRENCH Fodor's Choice ★ **Pierre's**. One of the Keys' most elegant restaurants, Pierre's marries colonial style with modern food trends. Full of interesting architectural artifacts, the place oozes style, especially the wicker chair–strewn veranda overlooking the bay. Save your best "tropical chic" duds for dinner here, so you don't stand out from your surroundings. The food,

drawn from French and Floridian influences, is multilayered and beautifully presented. Among the appetizer choices, few can resist the lamb ravioli or shrimp bisque. A changing list of entrées might include hogfish meunière and pan-seared duck breast with caramelized sweet potatoes. The downstairs bar is a perfect spot for catching sunsets, sipping martinis, and enjoying light eats. ✉ *81600 Overseas Hwy. (MM 81.5 BS), Upper Matecumbe Key* ☎ *305/664–3225* 🌐 *www.pierres-restaurant.com* *Reservations essential* *AE, MC, V.*

$$$ ITALIAN ✕ **Uncle's Restaurant.** Former fishing guide Joe LePree adds flair to standard seafood dishes by expanding the usual grilled, broiled, or blackened options. Here you can also have your seafood almandine, Milanese (breaded and fried), or LePree (with artichokes, mushrooms, and lemon-butter wine sauce). You also can feast on mussels or littleneck clams in a marinara or garlic sauce. Specials sometimes combine game (bison, caribou, or elk) with seafood. Portions are huge, so share dishes or take home a doggie bag, or order off the $13.95 light menu. Weather permitting, sit outdoors in the garden; poor acoustics make dining indoors unusually noisy. ✉ *80900 Overseas Hwy. (MM 81 OS), Upper Matecumbe Key* ☎ *305/664–4402* *AE, D, DC, MC, V* ⊗ *Closed Mon.*

WHERE TO STAY

$$$$ Fodor's Choice ★ **Casa Morada.** This relic from the 1950s was rescued and restyled into a suave, design-forward, all-suites property in 2000. Subsequent renovations have added outdoor showers and Jacuzzis to some of the suites, each of which claims its own design personality, many with an Asian feel. Lush landscaping, a pool surrounded by a sandy "beach" on its own island accessible by a bridge, and lounge chairs at the water's edge lend a spalike vibe; complimentary yoga classes, a Zen garden, and a rock waterfall complete the scene. Cool tile-and-terrazzo floors invite you to kick off your shoes and step out onto your private patio overlooking the gardens and the bay. Breakfast and lunch are served on the waterside terrace. **Pros:** cool design; complimentary snacks and bottled water; complimentary use of bikes, kayaks, and snorkel gear. **Cons:** trailer park across the street; beach is small and inconsequential. ✉ *136 Madeira Rd. (MM 82 BS), Upper Matecumbe Key* ☎ *305/664–0044 or 888/881–3030* 🌐 *www.casamorada.com* *16 suites* *In-room: safe, DVD, Wi-Fi. In-hotel: restaurant, room service, bar, pool, water sports, bicycles, laundry service, no kids under 16* *AE, MC, V* *CP.*

$$$$ ★ **Cheeca Lodge & Spa.** Newly renovated after a fire closed it down for a year, Cheeca came back better than ever in December 2009. The fire demolished its historic main lodge, but in its place are West Indian–style rooms boasting luxurious touches like elegant balcony tubs that fill from the ceiling. If soaking in the tub is not your thing, soak in the great views from the updated showers. The renovation includes a newly formatted main dining room plus a sushi bar and an upgraded swimming pool with underwater speakers and new tiki bar. The resort's other buildings have remained much as they were, but the spa got a face-lift with the addition of mud baths, an adults-only lap pool, and a fitness center. For families, there's the 1,200-foot private beach, a nature trail, and Camp Cheeca—a fun and educational program that makes use of

a playground. Golf (nine holes), tennis, and all manner of water sports cater to sports enthusiasts. **Pros:** beautifully landscaped grounds; new designer rooms; plenty of activities. **Cons:** expensive rates; $39 resort fee for activities; busy. ✉ *MM 82 OS, Box 527, Upper Matecumbe Key* ☎ *305/664–4651 or 800/327–2888* 🌐 *www.cheeca.com* *214 rooms, 44 1-bedroom suites, 4 2-bedroom suites* *In-room: safe, kitchen (some) refrigerator, DVD, Wi-Fi. In-hotel: 2 restaurants, room service, bar, golf course, tennis courts, pools, gym, spa, beachfront, diving, water sports, bicycles, children's programs (ages 5–12), laundry service, Wi-Fi hotspot* *AE, D, DC, MC, V.*

$$–$$$ ★ **Drop Anchor Resort and Marina.** It's easy to find your cottage here, as they are painted in an array of Crayola colors. Immaculately maintained, this place has the feel of an old friend's beach house. Inside you'll find soothing West Indies–type furnishings and kitschy-cool, 1950s-era tile in the bathrooms. Welcoming as the rooms may be, you didn't come to the Keys to sit indoors: there's a luscious expanse of white sand awaiting, and you can catch ocean breezes from either your balcony, a comfy Adirondack chair, or a picnic table perched in the sand. There's a boat ramp to accommodate anglers. **Pros:** bright and colorful; attention to detail; laid-back charm. **Cons:** noise from the highway; beach is better for fishing than swimming. ✉ *84959 Overseas Hwy. (MM 85 OS), Windley Key* ☎ *305/664–4863 or 888/664–4863* 🌐 *www.dropanchorresort.com* *18 rooms and suites* *In-room: kitchen (some), refrigerator. In-hotel: pool, beachfront, laundry facilities* *AE, D, DC, MC, V.*

$$$$ **The Islander Resort.** Although the vintage sign is straight out of a *Happy Days* rerun, this property has undergone a top-to-bottom transformation while the general layout retained a 1950s feel. The decor is modern yet comfortable, with white cottage-style furnishings, elegant fabrics, and sunny yellow bedrooms. Private screened porches lead to a coral-shell oceanfront beach with palm trees bending in the sea breeze. Families snap up suites in the oceanfront Beach House; couples looking for more privacy head to rooms set back from the beach. The pools—one saltwater, one freshwater—win raves, as do the full kitchens. A 200-foot dock, lighted at night, plus shuffleboard, basketball, and volleyball add to the resort feel. **Pros:** spacious rooms; nice kitchens; eye-popping views. **Cons:** pricey for what you get; beach has rough sand; no a/c in the screened gym. ✉ *82200 Overseas Hwy. (MM 82.1 OS), Upper Matecumbe Key* ☎ *305/664–2031 or 800/753–6002* 🌐 *www.islanderfloridakeys.com* *114 rooms* *In-room: safe, kitchen, Wi-Fi. In-hotel: restaurant, bar, pools, gym, beachfront, water sports, bicycles, laundry facilities, Wi-Fi hotspot, some pets allowed* *AE, D, DC, MC, V* *CP.*

$$$$ Fodor's Choice ★ **The Moorings Village.** This tropical retreat is everything you imagine when you think of the Keys—from hammocks swaying between towering trees to sugar-white sand (arguably the Keys' best resort beach) lapped by aqua-green waves. West Indies–style cottages with cypress and Dade County pine accents, colorful shutters, private verandas, and wicker furniture sit in a canopy of coconut palms and old forest landscaping on a residential street off the highway. This is a high-end slice of

Old Florida, so don't expect tacky tiki bars. The one-, two-, and three-bedroom cottages all have modern kitchens with modern appliances. A palm-lined walkway leads to the beach, where a swimming dock awaits. The spa offers massages (in the beach chickee, if you desire) and beauty treatments. During busy season, there may be a two-night minimum-stay requirement for one-bedroom cottages, and a one-week minimum on other lodgings. Neighboring Cheeca Lodge, the Moorings has the same high standards but is less cramped, more private and exclusive, and possibly the most beautiful property in the Keys. **Pros:** romantic setting; good dining options with room-charging privileges; beautiful beach. **Cons:** no room service; extra fee for housekeeping; daily resort fee for activities. ✉ *123 Beach Rd. (MM 81.6 OS), Upper Matecumbe Key* ☎ *305/664–4708* 🌐 *www.themooringsvillage.com* *4 cottages, 14 houses* *In-room: kitchen, Wi-Fi. In-hotel: tennis court, pool, gym, spa, beachfront, water sports, laundry facilities, Wi-Fi hotspot* 💳 *AE, D, MC, V.*

14

$ **Ragged Edge Resort.** Tucked away in a residential area at the ocean's edge, this hotel is big on value but short on style. Ragged Edge draws returning guests who would rather fish off the dock and hoist a brew than loll around in Egyptian cotton sheets. Even those who turn their noses up at the cheap plastic deck furniture and pine paneling admit that the place has a million-dollar setting, with fabulous ocean views all around. There's no beach to speak of, but you can ride a bike across the street to Islamorada Founder's Park, where you'll find a nice little beach and water toys for rent. If a bit of partying puts you off, look elsewhere. Although the rooms are plain-Jane, they are clean and fairly spacious. Ground-floor units have screened porches; upper units have large decks, more windows, and beam ceilings. **Pros:** oceanfront location; boat docks and ramp; cheap rates. **Cons:** dated decor; guests can be noisy. ✉ *243 Treasure Harbor Rd. (MM 86.5 OS), Plantation Key* ☎ *305/852–5389 or 800/436–2023* 🌐 *www.ragged-edge.com* *10 units* *In-room: kitchen (some), refrigerator, Wi-Fi. In-hotel: pool, bicycles, Wi-Fi hotspot* 💳 *AE, MC, V.*

LONG KEY

Long Key isn't a tourist hot spot, making it a favorite destination for those looking to avoid the masses and enjoy some cultural and ecological history in the process.

GETTING HERE AND AROUND

Long Key runs from mile markers 70 to 65.5, with the tiny town of Layton at its heart. Many people get around by bike.

EXPLORING

Long Key State Park. Come here for solitude, hiking, fishing, and camping. On the ocean side, the Golden Orb Trail leads to a boardwalk that cuts through the mangroves (may require some wading) and alongside a lagoon where waterfowl congregate (as do mosquitoes, so be prepared). A 1¼-mi canoe trail leads through a tidal lagoon, and a broad expanse of shallow grass flats is perfect for bonefishing. Bring a mask and snorkel to observe the marine life in the shallow water. The park is particularly popular with campers who long to stake their tent at the campground on a beach. In summer, no-see-ums (local reference for biting sand flies) also love the beach, so again—be prepared. The picnic area is on the water, too, but lacking beach. Canoes rent for $5 per hour, and single kayak rentals start at $17 for two hours, $21.50 for a double. ✉ *67400 Overseas Hwy. (MM 67.5 OS)* ☎ *305/664–4815* 🌐 *www.floridastateparks.org/longkey* 🎫 *$4.50 for 1 person, $5.50 for 2 people, and 50¢ for each additional person in the group* ⏲ *Daily 8–sunset.*

SPORTS AND THE OUTDOORS

BEACH

Long Key State Park. Camping, snorkeling, and bonefishing are the favored activities along this narrow strip of natural, rocky beach. It lines the park's campground, which is open only to registered campers. ✉ *67400 Overseas Hwy. (MM 67.5 OS)* ☎ *305/664–4815* 🌐 *www.floridastateparks.org/longkey* 🎫 *$4.50 for 1 person, $5.50 for 2 people, and 50¢ for each additional person in the group* ⏲ *Daily 8–sunset.*

WHERE TO EAT AND STAY

$ ITALIAN ✕ **Little Italy.** It's your basic Italian joint that looks like it's been around forever. In 2009, the chef who once made the place locally famous returned with a standard-issue Italian menu but with a few surprises like conch parmigiana and mahimahi with sherry and mushroom sauce. The lunch and dinner menus offer plenty of variety—dishes include lobster po'boy, steaks, and a fisherman's platter—but few can resist the pull of the pasta. (Maybe it's the garlicky aroma that permeates the place.) ✉ *68500 Overseas Hwy. (MM 68.5 BS)* ☎ *305/664–4472* 💳 *AE, MC, V* ⏲ *Closed Wed.*

$$ **Lime Tree Bay Resort.** Easy on the eye and the wallet, this 2½-acre resort on Florida Bay is far from the hustle and bustle of the larger islands. Walls are painted in faux finishes and display tropical art. The five apartments offer stunning gulf views, while four deluxe rooms have cathedral ceilings and skylights. The best bet for two couples traveling together is the upstairs Tree House. Most units have a shared balcony or porch. Hammocks and chickee huts dot the gravelly beach. Water sports and bicycle rentals are close by. **Pros:** great views; friendly staff; close to Long Key State Park. **Cons:** only one restaurant nearby, shared balconies. ✉ *68500 Overseas Hwy. (MM 68.5 BS), Layton* ☎ *305/664–4740 or 800/723–4519* 🌐 *www.limetreebayresort.com* *10 rooms, 10 studios, 8 suites, 5 apartments* *In-room: kitchen (some), refrigerator. In-hotel: tennis court, pool, beachfront, Wi-Fi hotspot* 💳 *AE, D, DC, MC, V.*

EN ROUTE

As you cross Long Key Channel, look beside you at the old **Long Key Viaduct.** The second-longest bridge on the former rail line, this 2-mi-long structure has 222 reinforced-concrete arches. The old bridge is popular with anglers who fish off the sides day and night.

THE MIDDLE KEYS

Most of the activity in this part of the Florida Keys centers around the town of Marathon—the region's third-largest metropolitan area. On either end of it, smaller keys hold resorts, wildlife research and rehab facilities, a historic village, and a state park. The Middle Keys make a fitting transition from the Upper Keys to the Lower Keys not only geographically but mentally. Crossing Seven Mile Bridge prepares you for the slow pace and don't-give-a-damn attitude you'll find a little farther down the highway. Fishing is one of the main attractions—in fact, the region's commercial-fishing industry was founded here in the early 1800s. Diving is another popular pastime. There are many beaches and natural areas to enjoy in the Middle Keys, where mainland stress becomes an ever more distant memory.

If you get bridge fever—the heebie-jeebies when driving over long stretches of water—you may need a pair of blinders (or a couple of tranquilizers) before tackling the Middle Keys. Stretching from Conch Key to the far side of the Seven Mile Bridge, this zone is home to the region's two longest bridges: Long Key Viaduct and Seven Mile Bridge, both historic landmarks.

Overseas Highway takes you from one end of the region to the other in a direct line that takes in most of the sights, but you'll find some interesting resorts and restaurants off the main drag.

GRASSY KEY

Grassy Key is between mile markers 60 and 57.

Local lore has it that this sleepy little key was named not for its vegetation—mostly native trees and shrubs—but for an early settler by the name of Grassy. There's no marked definition between it and Marathon, so it feels sort of like a suburb of its much larger neighbor to the south. Grassy Key's sights-to-see tend toward the natural, including a worthwhile dolphin attraction and a small state park.

EXPLORING

★ **Dolphin Research Center.** The 1963 movie *Flipper* popularized the notion of humans interacting with dolphins, and Milton Santini, the film's creator, also opened this center, which is home to a colony of dolphins and sea lions. The nonprofit center has tours, narrated programs, and programs that allow you to greet the dolphins from dry land or play with them in their watery habitat. You can even paint a T-shirt with a dolphin—you pick the paint, the dolphin "designs" your shirt ($55). The center also offers five-day programs for children and adults with disabilities. ✉ *58901 Overseas Hwy. (MM 59 BS)* ☎ *305/289–1121 or 305/289–0002* 🌐 *www.dolphins.org* 🎟 *$19.50* ⏲ *Daily 9–4:30.*

OFF THE BEATEN PATH

Looking for a slice of the Keys that's far removed from tiki bars? On the ocean and bay sides of Overseas Highway, **Curry Hammock State Park** (✉ *56200 Overseas Hwy. [MM 57 OS], Crawl Key* ☎ *305/289–2690* 🌐 *www.floridastateparks.org/curryhammock* 🎟 *$4.50 for 1 person, $6 for 2, 50¢ per additional person* ⏲ *Daily 8–sunset*) covers 260 acres of

CLOSE UP

Swimming with Dolphins

Here in the Florida Keys, where the 1963 movie *Flipper* was filmed, close encounters of the mammalian kind are an everyday occurrence. There are a handful of facilities that allow you to commune with trained dolphins. In-water programs, where you actually swim with these intelligent creatures, are extremely popular and require advance reservations. All programs begin with a course on dolphin physiology and behavior. Afterward you learn a few important dos and don'ts. Finally, you take the plunge, quite literally.

The best time to swim with dolphins is when it's warm, from March through December. You spend a lot of time in and out of the water, and you can feel your teeth chattering on a chilly day. Waterside programs let you feed, shake hands, and do tricks with dolphins from a submerged platform. These are great for people who aren't strong swimmers or for youngsters who don't meet a facility's minimum age requirements for in-water programs.

Dolphin Connection. Hawk's Cay Resort's Dolphin Connection offers three programs, including Dockside Dolphins, a 30-minute encounter from the dry training docks ($60); Dolphin Discovery, an in-water program that lasts about 45 minutes and lets you kiss, touch, and feed the dolphins ($155); and Trainer for a Day, a three-hour session with the animal training team ($295). ✉ *61 Hawks Cay Blvd. (MM 61 OS), Duck Key* ☎ *305/743-7000* 🌐 *www.dolphinconnection.com.*

Dolphin Cove. This educational program begins during a 30-minute boat ride on adjoining Florida Bay. Afterward, you slip into the water for some frolicking with your new dolphin pals. The cost is $125–$185 for the interactive Wade Program, Natural Swim (no interaction), and hands-on Structured Swim. ✉ *101900 Overseas Hwy. (MM 101.9 BS), Key Largo* ☎ *305/451-4060 or 877/365-2683* 🌐 *www.dolphinscove.com.*

Dolphin Research Center. This nonprofit organization has a colony of bottlenose dolphins and California sea lions. Programs range from a stay-dry Meet the Dolphin program for $50 to get-wet Dolphin Dip ($104), Dolphin Encounter ($189), and Trainer for a Day ($650) programs. You can even paint with a dolphin. ✉ *58901 Overseas Hwy. (MM 59 BS), Marathon Shores* ☎ *305/289-1121 or 305/289-0002* 🌐 *www.dolphins.org.*

Dolphins Plus. A sister property to Dolphin Cove, Dolphin Plus offers some of the same programs. Costing $135, the Natural Swim program begins with a one-hour briefing; then you enter the water to become totally immersed in the dolphins' world. In this visual orientation, participants snorkel and are not allowed to touch or interact with the dolphins. For tactile interaction (kissing, fin tows, etc.), sign up for the Structured Swim program ($165–$185 depending on time of year). Other interactions include the sea lion swim ($120) and Cuddle with Castaway shallow-water experience ($150). ✉ *31 Corrine Pl. (MM 99), Key Largo* ☎ *305/451-1993 or 866/860-7946* 🌐 *www.dolphinsplus.com.*

DID YOU KNOW?

Dolphins come in various forms, from the Atlantic bottlenose dolphin to the killer whale. These playful and smart creatures love to leap out of the water and synchronize their movements with others. By swimming next to ships, dolphins can conserve energy.

upland hammock, wetlands, and mangroves. On the bay side, there's a trail through thick hardwoods to a rocky shoreline. The oceanside is more developed, with a sandy beach, a clean bathhouse, picnic tables, a playground, grills, and a 28-site campground open November to May. Locals consider the paddling trails under canopies of arching mangroves one of the best kayaking spots in the Keys. Manatees frequent the area, and it's a great spot for bird-watching. Herons, egrets, ibis, plovers, and sanderlings are commonly spotted. Raptors are often seen in the park, especially during migration periods.

WHERE TO EAT AND STAY

$$$ AMERICAN ✕ **Hideaway Café**. The name says it all. Tucked between Grassy Key and Marathon, it's easy to miss if you're barnstorming through the middle islands. When you find it (upstairs at Rainbow Bend Resort), you'll discover a favorite of locals who appreciate a well-planned menu, lovely ocean view, and quiet evening away from the crowds. For starters, dig into escargots à la Edison (sautéed with vegetables, pepper, cognac, and cream). Then feast on several specialties, such as a rarely found chateaubriand for one, a whole roasted duck, or the seafood medley combining the catch of the day with scallops and shrimp in a savory sauce. ✉ *Rainbow Bend Resort, 57570 Overseas Hwy. (MM 58 OS), Grassy Key* ☎ *305/289–1554* 🌐 *www.hideawaycafe.com* ▭ *AE, MC, V* ⏲ *No lunch.*

$–$$ **Bonefish Resort**. Set on a skinny lot bedecked with palm trees, banana trees, and hibiscus plantings, this motel-style hideaway is the best choice among the island's back-to-basics properties. It's not fancy, but it's cheap, clean, and a good base for paddling a kayak, wading for bonefish, and watching the waves roll in from a lounge chair. Rooms are decorated with tropical motifs like the colorful metal lizards on the doors. A narrow gravel courtyard lined with umbrella-shaded tables leads to a small beach and a waterfront pool. The kayaks and paddleboats encourage exploration of the waterfront. The communal deck is scattered with hammocks and chaises. Check-in is at next-door sister property Yellowtail Inn, which has cottages and efficiencies. **Pros:** decent price for the location; oceanside setting. **Cons:** decks are small; simple decor. ✉ *58070 Overseas Hwy. (MM 58 OS)* ☎ *305/743–7107 or 800/274–9949* 🌐 *www.bonefishresort.com* *3 rooms, 11 efficiencies* *In-room: kitchen (some), refrigerator, Wi-Fi. In-hotel: beachfront, pool, bicycles, laundry facilities, Wi-Fi hotspot, some pets allowed* ▭ *D, MC, V.*

MARATHON

Marathon runs from mile markers 53 to 47.5. Most of what there is to see lies right off the Overseas Highway, with the exception of a couple of hidden restaurants.

Marathon is a bustling town, at least compared to other communities in the Keys. As it leaves something to be desired in the charm department, Marathon will probably not be your first choice of places to stay. But there are a number of good dining options, so you'll definitely want to stop for a bite even if you're just passing through on the way to Key West.

Outside of Key West, Marathon has the most historic attractions, which merit a visit. Fishing, diving, and boating are the main events here. It throws tarpon tournaments in April and May, more fishing tournaments in June and September, a birding festival in September, and lighted boat parades around the holidays.

GETTING HERE AND AROUND

The SuperShuttle charges $102 per passenger for trips from Miami International Airport to the Upper Keys. To go farther into the Keys, you must book an entire 11-person van, which costs about $250 to Marathon. For a trip to the airport, place your request 24 hours in advance.

Miami Dade Transit provides daily bus service from MM 50 in Marathon to the Florida City Walmart Supercenter on the mainland. The bus stops at major shopping centers as well as on-demand anywhere along the route during daily round trips on the hour from 6 AM to 10 PM. The cost is $1.85 one way, exact change required. The Lower Keys Shuttle bus runs from Marathon to Key West ($2 one way), with scheduled stops along the way.

ESSENTIALS

Transportation Contacts **Lower Keys Shuttle** (☎ *305/809–3910* 🌐 *www.kwtransit.com*). **Miami Dade Transit** (*formerly the Dade–Monroe Express* ☎ *305/770–3131*). **SuperShuttle** (☎ *305/871–2000* 🌐 *www.supershuttle.com*).

Visitor Information **Greater Marathon Chamber of Commerce and Visitor Center** (✉ *12222 Overseas Hwy. [MM 53.5 BS], Marathon* ☎ *305/743–5417 or 800/262–7284* 🌐 *www.floridakeysmarathon.com*).

EXPLORING

★ **Crane Point Museum, Nature Center, and Historic Site.** Tucked away from the highway behind a stand of trees, Crane Point—part of a 63-acre tract that contains the last-known undisturbed thatch-palm hammock—is delightfully undeveloped. This multiuse facility includes the **Museum of Natural History of the Florida Keys,** which has displays about local wildlife, a seashell exhibit, and a marine-life display that makes you feel you're at the bottom of the sea. Also here is the **Children's Activity Center,** with a replica of a 17th-century galleon and pirate dress-up room where youngsters can play swashbuckler. On the 1-mi indigenous loop trail, visit the **Wild Bird Center** and the remnants of a Bahamian village, site of the restored **George Adderly House.** It is the oldest surviving example of Bahamian tabby (a concrete-like material created from sand and seashells) construction outside of Key West. A re-created Cracker house demonstrates the vernacular housing of the early 1900s. A boardwalk crosses wetlands, rivers, and mangroves before ending at Adderly Village. From November to Easter docent-led tours, are available; bring good walking shoes and bug repellent during warm weather. Events include a Bahamian Heritage Festival in January. ✉ *5550 Overseas Hwy. (MM 50.5 BS)* ☎ *305/743–9100* 🌐 *www.cranepoint.net* 🎫 *$11* ⏲ *Mon.–Sat. 9–5, Sun. noon–5; call to arrange trail tours.*

QUICK BITES

If you don't get a buzz from breathing in the robust aroma at Leigh Ann's (More Than Just A) Coffee House (✉ *7537 Overseas Hwy. [MM 50 OS]* ☎ *305/743–2001* 🌐 *www.leighannscoffeehouse.com*), **order an espresso**

shot, Cuban or Italian, for a satisfying jolt. Pastries are baked fresh daily, but the biscuits with sausage gravy and the Italian frittata cooked without added fat are among the big movers. Leigh Ann's also serves lunch—quiche, chicken potpie, and hot and cold sandwiches. It's open weekdays 7–5, Saturday 7–3, and Sunday 8–noon.

Seven Mile Bridge. This is one of the most photographed images in the Keys. Actually measuring slightly less than 7 mi, it connects the Middle and Lower Keys and is believed to be the world's longest segmental bridge. It has 39 expansion joints separating its various concrete sections. Each April runners gather in Marathon for the annual Seven Mile Bridge Run. The expanse running parallel to Seven Mile Bridge is what remains of the **Old Seven Mile Bridge,** an engineering and architectural marvel in its day that's now on the National Register of Historic Places. Once proclaimed the Eighth Wonder of the World, it rested on a record 546 concrete piers. No cars are allowed on the old bridge today, but a 2-mi segment is open for biking, walking, and fishing.

OFF THE BEATEN PATH

Pigeon Key. There's much to like about this 5-acre island under the Old Seven Mile Bridge. You can reach it by walking across a 2-mi section of the bridge or by ferry. Once there, tour the island on your own or join a guided tour to explore the buildings that formed the early-20th-century work camp for the Overseas Railroad that linked the mainland to Key West. Later the island became a fish camp, a state park, and then government-administration headquarters. Exhibits in a small museum recall the history of the Keys, the railroad, and railroad baron Henry M. Flagler. Pick up the ferry outside the gift shop, which occupies an old railroad car on Knight's Key (MM 47 OS), for a two-hour excursion. ✉ *1 Knights Key Blvd. (MM 45 OS), Pigeon Key* ☎ *305/289–0025 general information, 305/743–5999 tickets* 🌐 *www.pigeonkey.net* 🎫 *$11* ⏲ *Daily 9:30–4; ferryboat departures at 10, 11:30, 1, 2:30.*

The Turtle Hospital. More than 70 injured sea turtles check in here every year. The guided tours take you into recovery and surgical areas at the world's only state-certified veterinary hospital for sea turtles. If you're lucky, you can visit hatchlings. Call ahead—tours are sometime cancelled due to medical emergencies. ✉ *2396 Overseas Hwy. (MM 48.5 BS)* ☎ *305/743–2552* 🌐 *www.turtlehospital.org* 🎫 *$15* ⏲ *Daily 9–5; tours at 10, 1, and 4.*

SPORTS AND THE OUTDOORS

BEACH

Sombrero Beach. Here, pleasant, shaded picnic areas overlook a coconut palm–lined grassy stretch and the Atlantic Ocean. Separate areas allow swimmers, boaters, and windsurfers to share the narrow cove. Facilities include barbecue grills, showers, and restrooms, as well as a large playground, a pier, and a volleyball court. Sunday afternoons draw lots of local families toting coolers. The park is accessible for those with disabilities and allows leashed pets. Turn east at the traffic light in Marathon and follow signs to the end. ✉ *Sombrero Beach Rd. (MM 50 OS)* ☎ *305/743–0033* 🎫 *Free* ⏲ *Daily 8–sunset.*

BIKING

Tooling around on two wheels is a good way to see Marathon. There's easy cycling on a 1-mi off-road path that connects to the 2 mi of the Old Seven Mile Bridge leading to Pigeon Key.

"Have bikes, will deliver" could be the motto of **Bike Marathon Bike Rentals** (☎ *305/743–3204*), which gets beach cruisers to your hotel door for $45 per week, including a helmet. It's open Monday through Saturday 9–4 and Sunday 9–2. **Overseas Outfitters** (✉ *1700 Overseas Hwy. [MM 48 BS]* ☎ *305/289–1670*) rents aluminum cruisers and hybrid bikes for $10 to $12 per day. The company also rents tandem bikes and children's bikes. It's open weekdays 9–6, and Saturday 9–5.

BOATING

Sail, motor, or paddle—whatever your choice of modes, boating is what the Keys is all about. Brave the Atlantic waves and reefs or explore the backcountry islands on the gulf side. If you don't have a lot of boating and chart-reading experience, it's a good idea to tap into local knowledge on a charter.

Captain Pip's (✉ *1410 Overseas Hwy. [MM 47.5 OS]* ☎ *305/743–4403 or 800/707–1692* 🌐 *www.captainpips.com*) rents 19- to 24-foot outboards, $175–$330 per day, as well as tackle and snorkeling gear. You also can charter a small boat with a guide, $500–$685 for a half day and $750–$925 for a full day. **Fish 'n Fun** (✉ *4590 Overseas Hwy. [MM 49.5 OS] at Banana Bay Resort & Marina* ☎ *305/743–2275 or 800/471–3440* 🌐 *www.fishnfunrentals.com*) lets you get out on the water on 19- to 26-foot powerboats starting at $140 for a half day, $190 for a full day. The company offers free delivery in the Middle Keys. You also can rent Jet Skis and kayaks.

FISHING

For recreational anglers, the deepwater fishing is superb in both bay and ocean. Marathon West Hump, one good spot, has depths ranging from 500 to more than 1,000 feet. Locals fish from a half-dozen bridges, including Long Key Bridge, the Old Seven Mile Bridge, and both ends of Tom's Harbor. Barracuda, bonefish, and tarpon all frequent local waters. Party boats and private charters are available.

★ Morning, afternoon, and night, fish for mahimahi, grouper, and other tasty catch aboard the 73-foot ***Marathon Lady*** (✉ *MM 53 OS, at 117th St.* ☎ *305/743–5580* 🌐 *fishfloridakeys.com/marathonlady*), which departs on half-day ($45) excursions from the Vaca Cut Bridge, north of Marathon. Join the crew for night fishing ($50) from 6:30 to midnight from Memorial Day to Labor Day; it's especially beautiful on a full-moon night. Captain Jim Purcell, a deep-sea specialist for ESPN's *The American Outdoorsman,* provides one of the best values in Keys fishing. **Sea Dog Charters** (✉ *1248 Overseas Hwy. [MM 47.5 BS]* ☎ *305/743–8255* 🌐 *www.seadogcharters.net*), next to the Seven Mile Grill, has half- and full-day offshore, reef and wreck, and backcountry fishing trips, as well as fishing and snorkeling trips aboard 30- to 37-foot boats. The cost is $60 per person for a half day, regardless of whether your group fills the boat, and includes bait, light tackle, ice, coolers, and fishing licenses. If you prefer an all-day private charter on a 37-foot boat, he offers those, too, for $600 for up to six people. A fuel surcharge may apply.

SCUBA DIVING AND SNORKELING

Local dive operations take you to Sombrero Reef and Lighthouse, the most popular down-under destination in these parts. For a shallow dive and some lobster-nabbing, Coffins Patch, off Key Colony Beach, is a good choice. A number of wrecks such as *Thunderbolt* serve as artificial reefs. Many operations out of this area will also take you to Looe Key Reef.

Hall's Diving Center & Career Institute (✉ *1994 Overseas Hwy. [MM 48.5 BS]* ☎ *305/743–5929 or 800/331–4255* 🌐 *www.hallsdiving.com*) has been training divers for more than 40 years. Along with conventional twice-a-day snorkel and two-tank dive trips ($40–$55) to the reefs at Sombrero Lighthouse and wrecks like the *Thunderbolt,* the company has more unusual offerings like digital and video photography.

Twice daily, **Spirit Snorkeling** (✉ *1410 Overseas Hwy., Slip No. 1 [MM 47.5 BS]* ☎ *305/289–0614* 🌐 *www.spiritsnorkeling.net*) departs on snorkeling excursions to Sombrero Reef and Lighthouse Reef for $30 a head.

WHERE TO EAT

$$$ ECLECTIC ✕ **Barracuda Grill.** Sparsely decorated with fish and bird art and filled with tables covered with butcher paper, this restaurant is not much to look at. But when it comes to the food, Barracuda Grill delivers. The sophisticated, eclectic menu capitalizes on local seafood (take a test drive with the mangrove snapper), but gives equal treatment to aged Angus beef, rack of lamb, and braised pork shank. Smaller entrées such as mini-mahi and baby steak appeal to light appetites. Favorite main courses include Francesca's spicy voodoo stew with scallops, shrimp, and vegetables in a tomato-saffron stock; a 22-ounce cowboy rib eye; and sashimi of yellowfin tuna accompanied by wasabi and tamari. For dessert, slices of oh-so-rich key lime cheesecake fly out of the kitchen. The well thought out wine list is heavily Californian. Call ahead, as the owners often close during the off-season. ✉ *4290 Overseas Hwy. (MM 49.5 BS)* ☎ *305/743–3314* ✍ *Reservations not accepted* ▭ *AE, MC, V* ⊙ *No lunch. Closed Sun.–Tues.*

¢ SEAFOOD ✕ **Fish Tales Market and Eatery.** This roadside eatery with its own seafood market serves signature dishes such as oysters on a roll and snapper on grilled rye with coleslaw and melted Muenster cheese. You also can slurp lobster bisque or red-conch chowder. There are burgers, chicken, and dogs for those who don't do seafood. Plan to dine early; it's only open until 6:30 PM. This is a no-frills kind of place with a loyal local following, a couple of picnic tables, and friendly service. ✉ *11711 Overseas Hwy. (MM 52.5 OS)* ☎ *305/743–9196 or 888/662–4822* 🌐 *www.floridalobster.com* ▭ *AE, MC, V* ⊙ *Closed Sun.*

$$ ITALIAN ✕ **Key Colony Inn.** The inviting aroma of an Italian kitchen pervades this family-owned favorite with a supper club atmosphere. As you'd expect, the service is friendly and attentive. For lunch there are fish and steak entrées served with fries, salad, and bread in addition to Italian specialties. At dinner you can't miss with traditional dishes like veal

Oscar and New York strip, or such specialties as seafood Italiano, a dish of scallops and shrimp sautéed in garlic butter and served with marinara sauce over a bed of linguine. The place is renowned for its Sunday brunch, served from November to April. ✉ *700 W. Ocean Dr. (MM 54 OS), Key Colony Beach* ☎ *305/743–0100* 🌐 *www.kcinn.com* 💳 *AE, MC, V.*

$$ SEAFOOD ★ ✕ **Keys Fisheries Market & Marina.** From the parking lot, this commercial warehouse flanked by fishing boats and lobster traps barely hints at the restaurant inside. Order at the window outside, pick up your food, then dine at one of the waterfront picnic tables outfitted with rolls of paper towels. Fresh seafood (and a token hamburger) are the only things on the menu. A huge lobster Reuben ($14.95) served on thick slices of toasted bread is the signature dish. Other delights include the shrimpburger, very rich whiskey-peppercorn snapper, and the Keys Kombo (broiled or grilled lobster, shrimp, scallops, and mahimahi for $29). There's also an eight-flavor ice-cream station and a bar serving beer and wine. ✉ *3390 Gulfview Ave. (turn west on 35th St.), end of 35th St. (MM 49 BS)* ☎ *305/743–4353 or 866/743–4353* 🌐 *www.keysfisheries.com* 💳 *MC, V.*

¢ AMERICAN ✕ **The Stuffed Pig.** With only eight tables and a counter inside, this breakfast-and-lunch place is always hopping. When the weather's right, grab a table out back. The kitchen whips up daily lunch specials like burgers, seafood platters, or pulled pork with hand-cut fries, but a quick glance around the room reveals that the all-day breakfast is the main draw. You can get the usual breakfast plates, but most newcomers opt for oddities like the lobster omelet, alligator tail and eggs, or "grits and grunts" (that's fish, to the rest of us). ✉ *3520 Overseas Hwy. (MM 49 BS)* ☎ *305/743–4059* 🌐 *www.thestuffedpig.com* 💳 *No credit cards* ⏲ *No dinner.*

WHERE TO STAY

$$$$ ★ 🏨 **Tranquility Bay.** Ralph Lauren might have designed the rooms at this luxurious beach resort. The 87 two- and three-bedroom town houses have gingerbread trim, white-picket fences, and open-floor-plan interiors decorated in trendy cottage style. The picture-perfect theme continues with the palm-fringed pool and the sandy beach edged with a ribbon of blue bay (and echoed in the blue-and-white stripes of the poolside umbrellas). Guests look like models on a photo shoot: attractive young families enjoying themselves at the sunny decks, casual outdoor bar, or elegant restaurant. **Pros:** secluded setting; gorgeous design; lovely crescent beach. **Cons:** a bit sterile; no real Keys atmosphere; cramped building layout. ✉ *2600 Overseas Hwy. (MM 48.5 BS)* ☎ *305/289–0888 or 866/643–5397* 🌐 *www.tranquilitybay.com* 🛏 *45 2-bedroom suites, 41 3-bedroom suites* 🛎 *In-room: kitchen, refrigerator, DVD, Wi-Fi. In-hotel: 2 restaurants, bars, pools, gym, beachfront, diving, water sports, Wi-Fi hotspot* 💳 *AE, D, MC, V.*

THE LOWER KEYS

Beginning at Bahia Honda Key, the islands of the Florida Keys become smaller, more clustered, and more numerous—a result of ancient tidal water flowing between the Florida Straits and the gulf. Here you're likely to see more birds and mangroves than other tourists, and more refuges, beaches, and campgrounds than museums, restaurants, and hotels. The islands are made up of two types of limestone, both denser than the highly permeable Key Largo limestone of the Upper Keys. As a result, freshwater forms in pools rather than percolating through the rock, creating watering holes that support alligators, snakes, deer, rabbits, raccoons, and migratory ducks. (Many of these animals can be seen in the National Key Deer Refuge on Big Pine Key.) Nature was generous with her beauty in the Lower Keys, which have both Looe Key Reef, arguably the Keys' most beautiful tract of coral, and Bahia Honda State Park, considered one of the best beaches in the world for its fine-sand dunes, clear warm waters, and panoramic vista of bridge, hammocks, and azure sky and sea. Big Pine Key is fishing headquarters for a laid-back community that swells with retirees in the winter. South of it, the dribble of islands can flash by in a blink of an eye if you don't take the time to stop at a roadside eatery or check out tours and charters at the little marinas.

EXPLORING THE LOWER KEYS

In truth, the Lower Keys include Key West, but since it is as different from the rest of the Lower Keys as peanut butter is from jelly, it is covered in its own section.

GETTING HERE AND AROUND

The Lower Keys in this section include the keys between MM 37 and MM 9. The Seven Mile Bridge drops you into the lap of this homey, quiet part of the Keys.

Heed speed limits in these parts. They may seem incredibly strict given the traffic is lightest of anywhere in the Keys, but the purpose is to protect the resident Key deer population, and officers of the law pay strict attention and will readily issue speeding tickets.

BAHIA HONDA KEY

Bahia Honda Key is between mile markers 38 and 36.

All of Bahia Honda Key is devoted to its eponymous state park, which keeps it in a pristine state. Besides the park's outdoor activities, it offers an up-close look at the original railroad bridge.

EXPLORING

Fodor's Choice ★ **Bahia Honda State Park.** Most first-time visitors to the region are dismayed by the lack of beaches—but then they discover sun-soaked Bahia Honda Key. The 524-acre park here sprawls across both sides of the highway, giving it 2½ mi of fabulous sandy coastline. The snorkeling isn't bad, either; there's underwater life (soft coral, queen conchs, random little fish) just a few hundred feet offshore. Although swimming,

DID YOU KNOW?

An old railroad bridge used to connect Bahia Honda Key with Key West until a hurricane destroyed it in 1935. While it is no longer in operation, the bridge is used by visitors as a place for viewing the island.

kayaking, fishing, and boating are the main reasons to visit, you shouldn't miss biking along the 2½ mi of flat roads or hiking the Silver Palm Trail, with rare West Indian plants and several species found nowhere else in the nation. Along the way you'll be treated to a variety of butterflies. Seasonal ranger-led nature programs take place or depart from the Sand and Sea Nature Center. There are rental cabins, a campground, snack bar, gift shop, 19-slip marina, nature center, and facilities for renting kayaks and arranging snorkeling tours. Get a panoramic view of the island from what's left of the railroad—the Bahia Honda Bridge. ✉ *36850 Overseas Hwy. (MM 37 OS)* ☎ *305/872–2353* 🌐 *www.floridastateparks.org/bahiahonda* 🎫 *$4.50 for 1 person, $9 for 2 people, 50¢ per additional person* ⏲ *Daily 8–sunset.*

SPORTS AND THE OUTDOORS

BEACH

Bahia Honda State Park contains three beaches in all—on both the Atlantic Ocean and the Gulf of Mexico. Sandspur Beach, the largest, is regularly declared the best beach in Florida, and you'll be hard pressed to argue. The sand is baby-powder soft, and the aqua water is warm, clear, and shallow. With their mild currents, the beaches are great for swimming, even with small fry. ✉ *36850 Overseas Hwy. (MM 37 OS)* ☎ *305/872–2353* 🌐 *www.floridastateparks.org/bahiahonda* 🎫 *$4.50 for 1 person, $9 for 2 people, 50¢ per additional person* ⏲ *Daily 8–sunset.*

SCUBA DIVING AND SNORKELING

Bahia Honda Dive Shop (✉ *36850 Overseas Hwy. [MM 37 OS]* ☎ *305/872–3210* 🌐 *www.bahiahondapark.com*), the concessionaire at Bahia Honda State Park, manages a 19-slip marina; rents wet suits, snorkel equipment, and corrective masks; and operates twice-a-day offshore-reef snorkel trips ($30 plus $9 for equipment). Park visitors looking for other fun can rent kayaks ($10 per hour for a single, $18 for a double) and beach chairs.

WHERE TO STAY

$$$ ★ 🏨 **Bahia Honda State Park.** Elsewhere you'd pay big bucks for the wonderful water views available at these cabins on Florida Bay. Each of three cabins have two, two-bedroom units with a full kitchen and bath and air-conditioning (but no television, radio, or phone). The park also has popular campsites ($43 per night) suitable for either tents or motor homes. Some are directly on the beach—talk about a room with a view! Cabins and campsites book up early, so reserve up to 11 months before your planned visit. **Pros:** great bay-front views; beachfront camping; affordable rates. **Cons:** books up fast; area can be buggy. ✉ *36850 Overseas Hwy. (MM 37 OS)* ☎ *305/872–2353 or 800/326–3521* 🌐 *www.reserveamerica.com* *80 partial hookup campsites, 6 cabin units* *In-room: no phone, kitchen, no TV. In-hotel: beachfront, water sports, bicycles, dump station* 💳 *AE, D, MC, V.*

BIG PINE KEY

Big Pine Key runs from mile marker 32 to 30.

Welcome to the Keys' most natural holdout, where wildlife refuges protect rare and endangered animals. Here you have left behind the commercialism of the Upper Keys for an authentic backcountry atmosphere.

ESSENTIALS

Visitor Information **Big Pine and the Lower Keys Chamber of Commerce** (✉ *31020 Overseas Hwy. [MM 31 OS], Big Pine Key* ☎ *305/872-2411 or 800/ 872-3722* 🌐 *www.lowerkeyschamber.com*).

EXPLORING

★ **National Key Deer Refuge.** This 84,351-acre refuge was established in 1957 to protect the dwindling population of the Key deer, one of more than 20 animals and plants classified as endangered or threatened in the Florida Keys. The Key deer, which stands about 30 inches at the shoulders and is a subspecies of the Virginia white-tailed deer, once roamed throughout the Lower and Middle Keys, but hunting, destruction of their habitat, and a growing human population caused their numbers to decline to 27 by 1957. The deer have made a comeback, increasing their numbers to approximately 750. The best place to see Key deer in the refuge is at the end of Key Deer Boulevard and on No Name Key, a sparsely populated island just east of Big Pine Key. Mornings and evenings are the best time to spot them. Deer may turn up along the road at any time of day, so drive slowly. They wander into nearby yards to nibble tender grass and bougainvillea blossom, but locals do not appreciate tourists driving into their neighborhoods after them. Feeding them is against the law and puts them in danger. The refuge also has 21 other listed endangered and threatened species of plants and animals, including five that are found nowhere else.

Blue Hole. A quarry left over from railroad days, the Blue Hole is the largest body of freshwater in the Keys. From the observation platform and nearby walking trail, you might see the resident alligator (its mate died recently from ingesting a plastic toy), turtles, and other wildlife. There are two well-marked trails: the Jack Watson Nature Trail (.6 mi), named after an environmentalist and the refuge's first warden; and the Fred Mannillo Nature Trail, one of the most wheelchair-accessible places to see an unspoiled pine-rockland forest and wetlands. The visitor center has exhibits on Keys biology and ecology. The refuge also provides information on the Key West National Wildlife Refuge and the Great White Heron National Wildlife Refuge. Accessible only by water, both are popular with kayak outfitters. ✉ *Visitor Center–Headquarters, Big Pine Shopping Center, MM 30.5 BS, 28950 Watson Blvd.* ☎ *305/872-2239* 🌐 *www.fws.gov/nationalkeydeer* 🎫 *Free* ⏲ *Daily sunrise–sunset; headquarters weekdays 8–5.*

SPORTS AND THE OUTDOORS

BIKING

A good 10 mi of paved roads run from MM 30.3 BS, along Wilder Road, across the bridge to No Name Key, and along Key Deer Boulevard into the National Key Deer Refuge. Along the way you might see some Key deer. Stay off the trails that lead into wetlands, where fat tires can do damage to the environment.

Marty Baird, owner of **Big Pine Bicycle Center** (✉ *31 County Rd. [MM 30.9 BS]* ☎ *305/872–0130*), is an avid cyclist and enjoys sharing his knowledge of great places to ride. He's also skilled at selecting the right bike for the journey, and he knows his repairs, too. His old-fashioned single-speed, fat-tire cruisers rent for $8 per half day and $10 for a full day. Helmets, baskets, and locks are included. Although the shop is officially closed on Sunday, join Marty there most Sunday mornings at 8 from December to Easter for a free off-road fun ride.

BOATING

Strike Zone Charters (✉ *29675 Overseas Hwy. [MM 29.6 BS], Big Pine Key* ☎ *305/872–9863 or 800/654–9560* 🌐 *www.strikezonecharter.com*) has glass-bottom-boat excursions into the backcountry and Atlantic Ocean. The five-hour Island Excursion ($55 plus fuel surcharge) emphasizes nature and Keys history; besides close encounters with birds, sea life, and vegetation, there's a fish cookout on an island. Snorkel and fishing equipment, food, and drinks are included. This is one of the few nature outings in the Keys with wheelchair access.

KAYAKING

★ **Big Pine Kayak Adventures** (✉ *Old Wooden Bridge Fishing Camp, MM 30 BS, turn right at traffic light, continue on Wilder Rd. toward No Name Key* ☎ *305/872–7474* 🌐 *www.keyskayaktours.com*) makes it very convenient to rent kayaks by delivering them to your lodging or anywhere between Seven Mile Bridge and Stock Island. The company, headed by *The Florida Keys Paddling Guide* author Bill Keogh, will rent you a kayak and then ferry you—called taxi-yakking—to remote islands with clear instructions on how to paddle back on your own. Rentals are by the half day or full day. Group kayak tours ($50 for three hours) explore the mangrove forests of Great White Heron and Key Deer National Wildlife Refuges. Custom tours ($125 and up, four hours) transport you to exquisite backcountry areas teeming with wildlife. Kayak fishing charters are also popular.

SCUBA DIVING AND SNORKELING

Strike Zone Charters (✉ *29675 Overseas Hwy. [MM 29.5 BS]* ☎ *305/872–9863 or 800/654–9560*) leads dive excursions to the wreck of the 110-foot *Adolphus Busch* ($55), and scuba ($45) and snorkel ($35) trips to Looe Key Reef aboard glass-bottom boats. Strike Zone also offers a five-hour island excursion that combines snorkeling, fishing, and an island cookout for $55 per person. A large dive shop is on-site.

WHERE TO EAT

¢ VEGETARIAN ✕ **Good Food Conspiracy.** Like good wine, this small natural-foods eatery and market surrenders its pleasures a little at a time. Step inside to the aroma of brewing coffee, and then pick up the scent of fresh strawberries or carrots blending into a smoothie, the green aroma of wheatgrass juice, followed by the earthy odor of hummus. Order raw or cooked vegetarian and vegan dishes, organic soups and salads, and organic coffees and teas. Bountiful sandwiches (available halved) include the popular tuna melt or hummus and avocado. If you can't sit down for a bite, stock up on healthful snacks like dried fruits, raw nuts, and carob-covered almonds. Dine early: the shop closes at 7 PM Monday to Saturday, and at 5 PM on Sunday. ⊠ *30150 Overseas Hwy. (MM 30.2 OS)* ☎ *305/872–3945* ▭ *AE, D, MC, V.*

$ AMERICAN ✕ **No Name Pub.** This no-frills honky-tonk has been around since 1936, delighting inveterate locals and intrepid vacationers who come for the excellent pizza, cold beer, and *interesting* companionship. The decor, such as it is, amounts to the autographed dollar bills that cover every inch of the place. The full menu printed on place mats includes a tasty conch chowder, a half-pound fried-grouper sandwich, spaghetti and meatballs, and seafood baskets. The lighting is poor, the furnishings are rough, and the music is oldies. This former brothel and bait shop is just before the No Name Key Bridge. It's a bit hard to find, but worth the trouble if you want a singular Keys experience. ⊠ *MM 30 BS, turn west on Wilder Rd., left on South St., right on Avenue B, right on Watson Blvd.* ☎ *305/872–9115* 🌐 *www.nonamepub.com* ▭ *D, MC, V.*

14

WHERE TO STAY

$ ★ **Big Pine Key Fishing Lodge.** There's a congenial atmosphere at this lively family-owned lodge-campground-marina. It's a happy mix of tent campers (who have the fabulous waterfront real estate), RVers (who look pretty permanent), and motel-dwellers who like to mingle at the rooftop pool and challenge each other to a game of poker. Rooms have tile floors, wicker furniture, and doors that allow sea breezes to waft through. A skywalk joins the upper story rooms with the pool and deck. Campsites range from rustic to full hookups. Everything is spotless—even the campground's bathhouse—and the service is good-natured and efficient. The staff will book you a room, sell you bait, or hook you up with a fishing charter. There are plenty of family-oriented activities, so the youngsters will never complain about being bored. Discounts are available for weeklong or longer stays. **Pros:** local fishing crowd; nice pool; great price. **Cons:** RV park is too close to motel; deer will eat your food if you're camping. ⊠ *33000 Overseas Hwy. (MM 33 OS)* ☎ *305/872–2351* *16 rooms; 158 campsites, 97 with full hookups, 61 without hookups* *In-room: no phone, kitchen (some), refrigerator. In-hotel: pool, laundry facilities, Internet terminal, Wi-Fi hotspot* ▭ *D, MC, V.*

$$$$ **Deer Run Bed & Breakfast.** Key deer wander the grounds of this beachfront B&B, set on a quiet street lined with buttonwoods and mangroves. Innkeepers Jen DeMaria and Harry Appel were way ahead of the green-lodging game when they opened in 2004. They continue to make strides in environmental- and guest-friendliness, and were recognized as one of the most sustainable inns in the United States by *Islands* magazine in 2009. Two large oceanfront rooms are decorated in soothing earth tones and furnished with mahogany and pecan-wood furnishings. The beach-level unit is decorated in key lime and flamingo-pink, with wicker

furnishings, and the garden-view room is an eclectic mix that includes Victorian farmhouse doors serving as the headboard of the queen-size bed. Guests share a living room and a veranda. The mostly organic breakfast menu is suitable for vegans. Guest rooms are stocked with organic cotton towels and cruelty-free toiletries. **Pros:** quiet location; healthy breakfasts; complimentary bike and kayak use. **Cons:** price is a bit high; hard to find. ✉ *1997 Long Beach Dr. (MM 33 OS)* ☎ *305/872–2015* 🌐 *www.deerrunfloridabb.com* *4 rooms* *In-room: no phone, refrigerator, Wi-Fi. In-hotel: pool, beachfront, water sports, bicycles, no kids under 18* 💳 *D, MC, V* 🍽 *BP.*

LITTLE TORCH KEY

Little Torch Key is between mile markers 29 and 10.

Little Torch Key and its neighbor islands, Ramrod Key and Summerland Key, are good jumping-off points for divers headed for Looe Key Reef. The islands also serve as a refuge for those who want to make forays into Key West but not stay in the thick of things.

The undeveloped backcountry at your door makes Little Torch Key an ideal location for fishing and kayaking. Nearby **Ramrod Key,** which also caters to divers bound for Looe Key, derives its name from a ship that wrecked on nearby reefs in the early 1800s.

NEED A BREAK?

The aroma of rich roasting coffee beans at Baby's Coffee (✉ *3178 Overseas Hwy. [MM 15 OS], Saddlebunch Keys* ☎ *305/744–9866 or 800/523–2326* 🌐 *www.babyscoffee.com*) arrests you at the door of "the Southernmost Coffee Roaster." Buy it by the pound or by the cup along with fresh baked goods.

SPORTS AND THE OUTDOORS

For something with more of an adrenaline boost, book with **White Knuckle Thrill Boat Ride** (✉ *Sunset Marina, Overseas Hwy., 5555 College Rd., Key West* ☎ *305/797–0459* 🌐 *www.whiteknucklethrillboatride.com*). The speedboat holds up to 12 people and does 360s, fishtails, and other water stunts in the gulf. Cost is $59 each, and includes pickup shuttle.

SCUBA DIVING AND SNORKELING

★ In 1744 the HMS *Looe,* a British warship, ran aground and sank on one of the most beautiful coral reefs in the Keys. Today **Looe Key Reef** (✉ *216 Ann St. [MM 27.5 OS], Key West* ☎ *305/292–0311*) owes its name to the ill-fated ship. The 5.3-square-nautical-mi reef, part of the **Florida Keys National Marine Sanctuary,** has strands of elkhorn coral on its eastern margin, purple sea fans, and abundant sponges and sea urchins. On its seaward side, it drops almost vertically 50 to 90 feet. In its midst, **Shipwreck Trail** plots the location of nine historic wreck sites in 14 to 120 feet of water. Buoys mark the sites, and underwater signs tell the history of each site and what marine life to expect. Snorkelers and divers will find the sanctuary a quiet place to observe reef life—except in July, when the annual Underwater Music Festival pays homage to Looe Key's beauty and promotes reef awareness with six hours of music broadcast via underwater speakers. Dive shops, charters, and private boats transport about 500 divers and snorkelers to hear the spectacle, which includes classical, jazz, and new age, Caribbean music, as well as a little Jimmy Buffett. There are even underwater Elvis impersonators. Rather than the customary morning and afternoon two-tank, two-location trips offered by most dive shops, **Looe Key Reef Resort & Dive Center** (✉ *Looe Key Reef Resort, 27340 Overseas Hwy. [MM 27.5 OS], Ramrod Key* ☎ *305/872–221 or 800/942–5397* 🌐 *www.diveflakeys.com*), the closest dive shop to Looe Key Reef, runs a single three-tank, three-location dive ($80 for divers, $40 for snorkelers). The maximum depth is 30 feet, so snorkelers and divers go on the same boat. On Wednesday it runs a dive-only trip that visits the wreck and reefs in the area ($80). The dive boat, a 45-foot catamaran, is docked at the full-service Looe Key Reef Resort.

WATER SPORTS

Rent a paddle-propelled vehicle for exploring local gulf waters at **Sugarloaf Marina** (✉ *17015 Overseas Hwy. [MM 17 BS], Sugarloaf Key* ☎ *305/745–3135*); rates for one- or two-person kayak, and canoes start at $15 for one hour to $35 for a full day. Extra days are $25. Delivery is free for multiple-day rentals.

WHERE TO EAT

$ AMERICAN ✕ **Geiger Key Marina Smokehouse.** There's a strong hint of the Old Keys at this oceanside marina restaurant, on the backside of paradise, as the sign says. Locals usually outnumber tourists; they come for the daily dinner specials: meat loaf on Monday, pasta on Tuesday, and so on. For lunch, try the fresh catch or lobster BLT. Weekends are the most popular; the place is packed on Saturday for steak-on-the-grill night and on Sunday for the chicken and ribs barbecue. In season, local fishermen stop here for breakfast before heading out in search of the big ones. ✉ *Geiger Key at 5 Geiger Key Rd., off Boca Chica Rd. (MM 10)* ☎ *305/296–3553 or 305/294–1230* 🌐 *www.geigerkeymarina.com* ▭ *MC, V* ⊗ *Closed for breakfast Apr.–Dec.*

$$$$ ECLECTIC ★ ✕ **Little Palm Island Restaurant.** The oceanfront setting calls to mind St. Barts and the other high-end destinations of the Caribbean. Keep that in mind as you reach for the bill, which can also make you swoon. The restaurant at the exclusive Little Palm Island Resort—its dining room and adjacent outdoor terrace lit by candles and warmed by live music—is one of the most romantic spots in the Keys. The seasonal menu is a melding of French and Caribbean flavors, with exotic little touches. Think shrimp and yellowtail ceviche or coconut lobster bisque as a starter, followed by mahimahi with cilantro and creamy polenta. The Saturday and Sunday brunch buffet, the full-moon dinners with live entertainment, and Chef's Table Dinner are very popular. The dining room is open to nonguests on a reservations-only basis. ✉ *28500 Overseas Hwy. (MM 28.5 OS)* ☎ *305/872–2551* 🌐 *www.littlepalmisland.com* ✍ *Reservations essential* ▭ *AE, D, DC, MC, V.*

WHERE TO STAY

$$$$ Fodor's Choice ★ **Little Palm Island Resort & Spa.** *Haute tropicale* best describes this luxury retreat, and "second mortgage" might explain how some can afford the extravagant prices. But for those who can, it's worth the price. This property sits on a 5-acre palm-fringed island 3 mi offshore from Little Torch Key. The 28 oceanfront thatch-roof bungalow suites have slate-tile baths, mosquito-netting-draped king-size beds, and British colonial–style furnishings. Other comforts include an indoor and outdoor shower, private veranda, separate living room, and comfy robes and slippers. Two Island Grand Suites are twice the size of the others and offer his-and-hers bathrooms, an outdoor hot tub, and uncompromising ocean views. To preserve the quiet atmosphere, cell phones are highly discouraged in public areas. **Pros:** secluded setting; heavenly spa; easy wildlife viewing. **Cons:** expensive; might be too quiet for some. ✉ *28500 Overseas Hwy. (MM 28.5 OS)* ☎ *305/872–2524 or 800/343–8567* 🌐 *www.littlepalmisland.com* *30 suites* *In-room: no phone, safe, refrigerator, no TV, Internet. In-hotel: restaurant, room service, bars, pool, gym, spa, beachfront, diving, water sports, Wi-Fi hotspot, parking (free), no kids under 16* *AE, D, DC, MC, V* *MAP.*

$–$$ **Looe Key Reef Resort & Center.** If your Keys vacation is all about diving, you'll be well served at this scuba-obsessed operation. The closest place to stay to the stellar reef and affordable to boot, it's popular with the bottom-time crowd. Rooms are basic but perfect for sleeping between dives and hanging out at the tiki bar. The one suite is equipped with a fridge and microwave. Single rooms are available. **Pros:** guests get discounts on dive and snorkel trips; fun bar. **Cons:** small rooms; unheated pool; close to road. ✉ *27340 Overseas Hwy. (MM 27.5 OS), Ramrod Key* ☎ *305/872–2215 Ext. 2 or 800/942–5397* 🌐 *www.diveflakeys.com* *23 rooms, 1 suite* *In-room: Wi-Fi. In-hotel: bar, pool, Wi-Fi hotspot* *D, MC, V.*

$$–$$$ **Parmer's Resort.** Almost every room at this budget-friendly option has a view of South Pine Channel, with the lovely curl of Big Pine Key in the foreground. Waterfront cottages, with decks or balconies, are spread out on 6 landscaped acres, with a heated swimming pool and a five-hole putting green. There are water sports galore, and the staff will book you a kayak tour, a fishing trip, or a bike excursion, or tell you which local restaurants will deliver dinner to your room. So what if the decor feels a little like Grandma's house and you have to pay extra ($10) if you want your room cleaned daily? **Pros:** bright rooms; pretty setting; good value. **Cons:** a bit out of the way; housekeeping costs extra; little shade around the pool. ✉ *565 Barry Ave. (MM 28.7 BS)* ☎ *305/872–2157* 🌐 *www.parmersresort.com* *18 rooms, 12 efficiencies, 15 apartments, 1 penthouse* *In-room: no phone, kitchen (some). In-hotel: pool, laundry facilities, Wi-Fi hotspot* *AE, D, MC, V* *CP.*

EN ROUTE

The huge object that looks like a white whale floating over Cudjoe Key (MM 23–21) is not a figment of your imagination. It's Fat Albert, a radar balloon that monitors local air and water traffic.

KEY WEST

Situated 150 mi from Miami, 90 mi from Havana, and an immeasurable distance from sanity, this end-of-the-line community has never been like anywhere else. Even after it was connected to the rest of the country—by the railroad in 1912 and by the highway in 1938—it maintained a strong sense of detachment.

Key West reflects a diverse population: Conchs (natives, many of whom trace their ancestry to the Bahamas), freshwater Conchs (longtime residents who migrated from somewhere else years ago), Hispanics (primarily Cuban immigrants), recent refugees from the urban sprawl of mainland Florida, military personnel, and an assortment of vagabonds, drifters, and dropouts in search of refuge. The island was once a gay vacation hot spot, and it remains a decidedly gay-friendly destination. Some of the most renowned gay guesthouses, however, no longer cater to an exclusively gay clientele. Key Westers pride themselves on their tolerance of all peoples, all sexual orientations, and even all animals. Most restaurants allow pets, and it's not surprising to see stray cats, dogs, and even chickens roaming freely through the dining rooms. The chicken issue is one that government officials periodically try to bring to an end, but the colorful fowl continue to strut and crow, particularly in the vicinity of Old Town's Bahamian Village.

Although the rest of the Keys are known for outdoor activities, Key West has something of a city feel. Few open spaces remain, as promoters continue to churn out restaurants, galleries, shops, and museums to interpret the city's intriguing past. As a tourist destination, Key West has a lot to sell—an average temperature of 79°F, 19th-century architecture, and a laid-back lifestyle. Yet much has been lost to those eager for a buck. Duval Street looks like a miniature Las Vegas lined with garish signs for T-shirt shops and tour company offices. Cruise ships dwarf the town's skyline and fill the streets with day-trippers gawking at the hippies with dogs in their bike baskets, gay couples walking down the street holding hands, and the oddball lot of locals, some of whom bark louder than the dogs.

GETTING HERE AND AROUND

Between mile markers 4 and 0, Key West is the one place in the Keys where you could conceivably do without a car, especially if you plan on staying around Old Town. If you've driven the 106 mi down the chain, you're probably ready to abandon your car in the hotel parking lot anyway. Trolleys, buses, bikes, scooters, and feet are more suitable alternatives. To explore the beaches, New Town, and Stock Island, you'll probably need a car.

Greyhound Lines runs a special Keys shuttle two times a day (depending on the day of the week) from Miami International Airport (departing from Concourse E, lower level) and stops throughout the Keys. Fares run about $39 for Key West (3535 S. Roosevelt, Key West International Airport). Keys Shuttle runs scheduled service six times a day in 15-passenger vans between Miami Airport and Key West with stops throughout the Keys for $70 to $90 per person. Key West Express operates air-conditioned ferries between the Key West Terminal (Caroline

KEY WEST'S COLORFUL HISTORY

The United States acquired Key West from Spain in 1821, along with the rest of Florida. The Spanish had named the island Cayo Hueso, or Bone Key, after the American Indians' skeletons they found on its shores. In 1823, President James Monroe sent Commodore David S. Porter to chase pirates away. For three decades the primary industry in Key West was wrecking—rescuing people and salvaging cargo from ships that foundered on the nearby reefs. According to some reports, when pickings were lean the wreckers hung out lights to lure ships aground. Their business declined after 1849 when the federal government began building lighthouses.

In 1845 the army began construction on Fort Taylor, which kept Key West on the Union side during the Civil War even though most of Florida seceded. After the fighting ended, an influx of Cubans unhappy with Spain's rule brought the cigar industry here. Fishing, shrimping, and sponge-gathering became important industries, as did pineapple canning. Through much of the 19th century and into the 20th, Key West was Florida's wealthiest city in per-capita terms. But in 1929 the local economy began to unravel. Cigar-making moved to Tampa, Hawaii dominated the pineapple industry, and the sponges succumbed to blight. Then the Depression hit, and within a few years half the population was on relief.

Tourism began to revive Key West, but that came to a halt when a hurricane knocked out the railroad bridge in 1935. To help the tourism industry recover from that crushing blow, the government offered incentives for islanders to turn their charming homes—many of them built by shipwrights—into guesthouses and inns. The wise foresight has left the town with more than 100 such lodgings, a hallmark of Key West vacationing today. In the 1950s the discovery of "pink gold" in the Dry Tortugas boosted the economy of the entire region. Harvesting Key West shrimp required a fleet of up to 500 boats and flooded local restaurants with sweet, luscious shrimp. The town's artistic community found inspiration in the colorful fishing boats.

and Grinnell streets) and Miami, Marco Island, and Fort Myers Beach. The trip from Fort Myers Beach takes at least four hours each way and costs $85.50 one way, $145 round-trip. Ferries depart from Fort Myers Beach at 8:30 AM and from Key West at 6 PM. The Miami and Marco Island ferry costs $85.50 one way and $119 round-trip, and departs at 8:30 am. A photo ID is required for each passenger. Advance reservations are recommended. The SuperShuttle charges $102 per passenger for trips from Miami International Airport to the Upper Keys. To go farther into the Keys, you must book an entire 11-person van, which costs about $350 to Key West. You need to place your request for transportation back to the airport 24 hours in advance.

The City of Key West Department of Transportation has six color-coded bus routes traversing the island from 6:30 AM to 11:30 PM. Stops have signs with the international bus symbol. Schedules are available on buses and at hotels, visitor centers, and shops. The fare is $2 one way.

The Lower Keys Shuttle bus runs from Marathon to Key West ($3 one way), with scheduled stops along the way.

Old Town Key West is the only place in the Keys where parking is a problem. There are public parking lots that charge by the hour or day (some hotels and B&Bs provide parking or discounts at municipal lots). If you arrive early, you can sometimes find a spot on side streets off Duval and Whitehead, where you can park for free—just be sure it's not marked for residential parking only. Your best bet is to bike or take the trolley around town if you don't want to walk. You can disembark and reboard at will.

ESSENTIALS

Transportation Contacts City of Key West Department of Transportation (☎ *305/809–3910*). **Greyhound Lines** (☎ *800/410–5397 or 800/231–2222*). **Keys Shuttle** (☎ *305/289–9997 or 888/765–9997* 🌐 *www.floridakeysshuttle.com*). **Key West Express** (✉ *100 Grinnell St.* ☎ *888/539–2628* 🌐 *www.seakeywestexpress.com*). **Lower Keys Shuttle** (☎ *305/809–3910* 🌐 *www.monroecounty-fl.gov*). **SuperShuttle** (☎ *305/871–2000* 🌐 *www.supershuttle.com*).

Visitor Information Greater Key West Chamber of Commerce (✉ *402 Wall St.* ☎ *305/294–2587 or 800/527–8539* 🌐 *www.keywestchamber.org*).

EXPLORING

Numbers in the margin correspond to the Key West map.

OLD TOWN

TOP ATTRACTIONS

The heart of Key West, this historic Old Town area runs from White Street to the waterfront. Beginning in 1822, wharves, warehouses, chandleries, ship-repair facilities, and eventually in 1891 the U.S. Custom House sprang up around the deep harbor to accommodate the navy's large ships and other sailing vessels. Wreckers, merchants, and sea captains built lavish houses near the bustling waterfront. A remarkable number of these fine Victorian and pre-Victorian structures have been restored to their original grandeur and now serve as homes, guesthouses, shops, restaurants, and museums. These, along with the dwellings of famous writers, artists, and politicians who've come to Key West over the past 175 years, are among the area's approximately 3,000 historic structures. Old Town also has the city's finest restaurants and hotels, lively street life, and popular nightspots.

5 **Audubon House and Tropical Gardens.** If you've ever seen an engraving by ornithologist John James Audubon, you'll understand why his name is synonymous with birds. See his works in this three-story house, which was built in the 1840s for Captain John Geiger and filled with period furniture. It now commemorates Audubon's 1832 stop in Key West while he was traveling through Florida to study birds. A children's room makes his work accessible to youngsters. Docents lead a guided tour that points out the rare indigenous plants and trees in the garden. An art gallery sells lithographs of the artist's famed portraits. ✉ *205 Whitehead St.* ☎ *305/294–2116 or 877/294–2470* 🌐 *www.audubonhouse.com* 🎟 *$11* 🕒 *Daily 9:30–5, last tour starts at 4:30.*

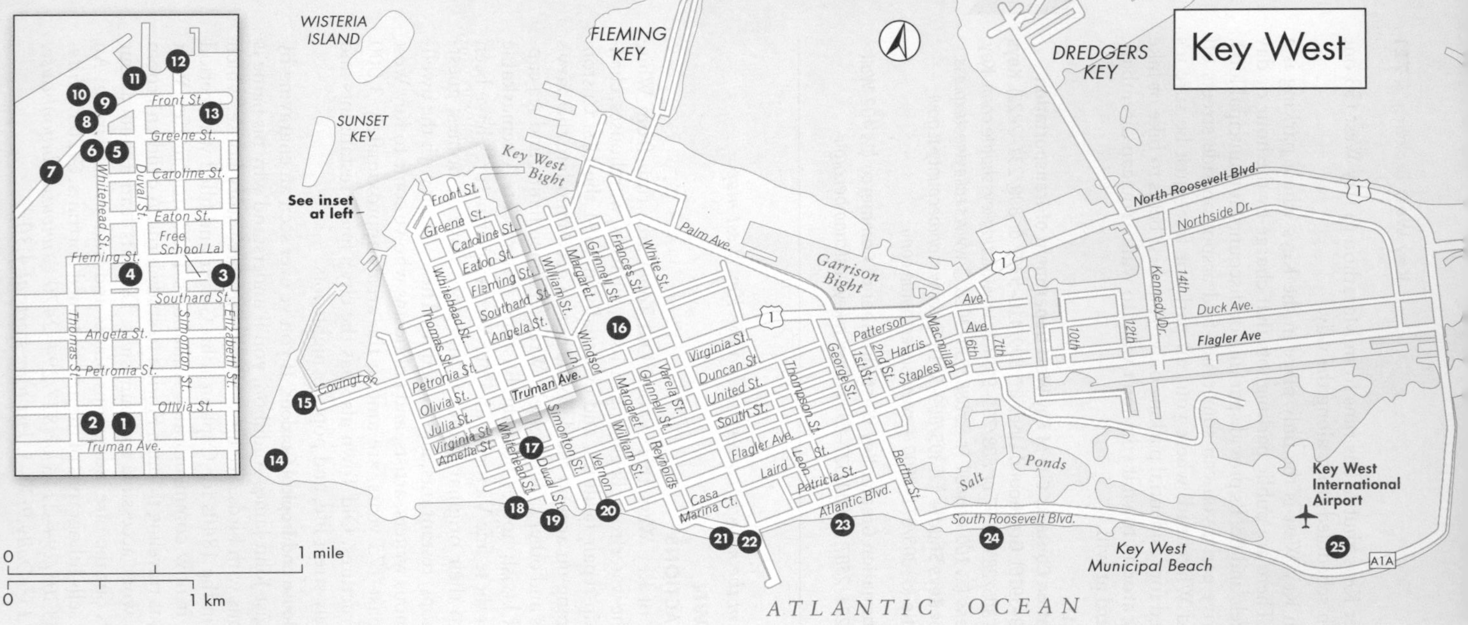

Audubon House and Tropical Gardens **5**
C.B. Harvey Rest Beach **23**
City Cemetery **16**
Dog Beach **20**
Eco-Discovery Center **15**
Ernest Hemingway Home and Museum **1**
Fort East Martello Museum & Gardens **25**
Fort Zachary Taylor Historic State Park **14**
Harry S. Truman Little White House Museum **7**
Higgs Beach—Astro City Playground **21**
Historic Seaport at Key West Bight **12**
Key West Aquarium **9**
Key West Butterfly & Nature Conservatory **17**
Key West Museum of Art & History in the Custom House **8**
Key West Lighthouse Museum and Keeper's Quarters Museum **2**
Key West Shipwreck Treasures Museum **10**
Mallory Square and Pier .. **11**
Mel Fisher Maritime Museum **6**
Nancy Forrester's Secret Garden **3**
Pirate Soul Museum **13**
San Carlos Institute **4**
Smathers Beach **24**
South Beach **19**
Southernmost Point **18**
West Martello Tower **22**

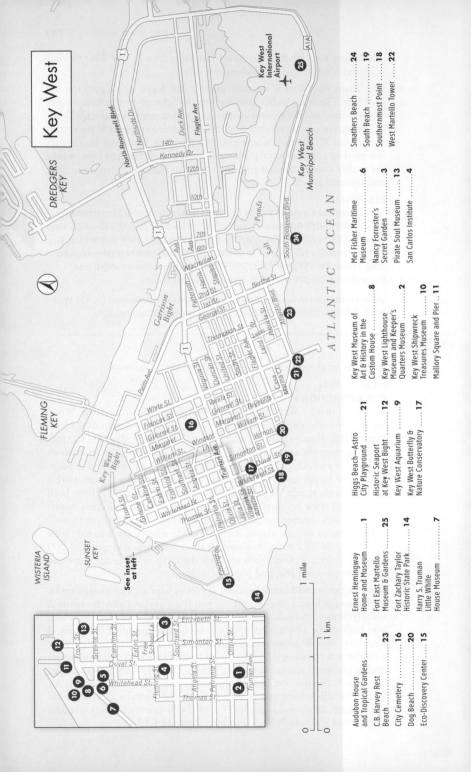

KEY WEST: A GOOD TOUR

To cover many sights, take the **Old Town Trolley,** which lets you get off and reboard a later trolley. Old Town is also manageable on foot, bicycle, moped, or electric cars. The area is expansive, so you'll want either to pick and choose from the stops on this tour or break it into two or more days. Start on Whitehead Street at the ❶ **Ernest Hemingway Home and Museum,** and then cross the street and climb to the top of the ❷ **Key West Lighthouse Museum & Keeper's Quarters Museum** for a spectacular view. Return to Whitehead Street and follow it north to Angela Street, where you'll turn right. At Margaret Street, the ⓰ **City Cemetery** is worth a look for its aboveground vaults and unusual headstone inscriptions. Head north on Margaret Street, turn left onto Southard Street, then right onto Simonton Street. Halfway up the block, ❸ **Nancy Forrester's Secret Garden** occupies Free School Lane. Follow Southard Street south through Truman Annex to ⓮ **Fort Zachary Taylor Historic State Park.**

Walk west into Truman Annex to see the ❼ **Harry S. Truman Little White House Museum,** President Truman's vacation residence. Return east on Caroline and turn left on Whitehead to visit the ❺ **Audubon House and Tropical Gardens,** honoring the famed artist and naturalist. Follow Whitehead north to Greene Street and turn left to see the salvaged sea treasures of the ❻ **Mel Fisher Maritime Museum.** At Whitehead's northern end are the ❾ **Key West Aquarium** and the ❽ **Key West Museum of Art & History,** the historic former U.S. Custom House. By late afternoon you should be ready to cool off with a dip or catch a few rays at the beach. From the aquarium, head east about a mile, where you'll find ⓳ **South Beach,** located at Southernmost Hotel at the Beach and named for its location at the southern end of Duval Street. If you've brought your pet, stroll a few blocks east to ⓴ **Dog Beach,** at the corner of Vernon and Waddell streets. A little farther east is ㉑ **Higgs Beach–Astro City Playground,** on Atlantic Boulevard between White and Reynolds streets. As the sun starts to sink, return to the west side of Old Town and follow the crowds to Mallory Square, behind the aquarium, to watch Key West's nightly sunset spectacle. (Those lucky enough may see a green flash—the brilliant splash of green or blue that sometimes appears as the sun sinks into the ocean on a clear night.) For dinner, head east on Caroline Street to ⓬ **Historic Seaport at Key West Bight,** a renovated area where there are numerous restaurants and bars.

TIMING

Allow two full days to see all the Old Town museums and homes, especially with a little shopping thrown in. For a narrated trip on the tour train or trolley, budget 1½ hours to ride the loop without getting off, or an entire day if you plan to get off and on the trolley at sights and restaurants.

Sailboats big and small make their way into Key West Harbor; photo by John Franzis, Fodors.com member.

1 ★ **Ernest Hemingway Home and Museum**. Amusing anecdotes spice up the guided tours of Ernest Hemingway's home, built in 1801 by the town's most successful wrecker. While living here between 1931 and 1942, Hemingway wrote about 70% of his life's work, including classics like *For Whom the Bell Tolls*. Few of his belongings remain aside from some books, and there's little about his actual work, but photographs help you visualize his day-to-day life. The supposed six-toed descendants of Hemingway's cats—many named for actors, artists, authors, and even a hurricane—have free rein of the property. Tours begin every 10 minutes and take 25–30 minutes; then you're free to explore on your own. ✉ *907 Whitehead St.* ☎ *305/294–1136* 🌐 *www.hemingwayhome.com* 🎟 *$12* 🕓 *Daily 9–5.*

14 ★ **Fort Zachary Taylor Historic State Park**. Construction of the fort began in 1845 but was halted during the Civil War. Even though Florida seceded from the Union, Yankee forces used the fort as a base to block Confederate shipping. More than 1,500 Confederate vessels were detained in Key West's harbor. The fort, finally completed in 1866, was also used in the Spanish-American War. Take a 30-minute guided walking tour of the fort, a National Historic Landmark, at noon and 2. In February a celebration called Civil War Heritage Days includes costumed reenactments and demonstrations. From mid-January to mid-April the park serves as an open-air gallery for pieces created for Sculpture Key West. One of its most popular features is its man-made beach. ✉ *Box 6565; end of Southard St., through Truman Annex* ☎ *305/292–6713* 🌐 *www.floridastateparks.org/forttaylor* 🎟 *$4.50 for 1 person, $7 for 2 people, 50¢ per additional person* 🕓 *Daily 8–sunset, tours noon and 2.*

NEED A BREAK?

Check out the pretty palm garden next to the Key West Library at 700 Fleming Street, just off Duval. This leafy, outdoor reading area, with shaded benches, is the perfect place to escape the frenzy and crowds of downtown Key West. There's free Internet access in the library, too.

7 **Harry S. Truman Little White House Museum.** Recent renovations to this circa-1890 landmark have restored the home and gardens to the Truman era, down to the wallpaper pattern. A free photographic review of visiting dignitaries and presidents—John F. Kennedy, Jimmy Carter, and Bill Clinton are among the chief executives who passed through here—is on display in the back of the gift shop. Engaging 45-minute tours begin every 15 minutes until 4:30. They start with an excellent 10-minute video on the history of the property and Truman's visits. On the grounds of **Truman Annex,** a 103-acre former military parade grounds and barracks, the home served as a winter White House for presidents Truman, Eisenhower, and Kennedy. Note: the tour does require climbing steps. ✉ *111 Front St.* ☎ *305/294–9911* 🌐 *www.trumanlittlewhitehouse.com* *$12* ⏲ *Daily 9–5, grounds sunrise–6; last tour at 4:30.*

14

21 **Higgs Beach–Astro City Playground.** This Monroe County park with its groomed pebbly sand is a popular sunbathing spot. A nearby grove of Australian pines provides shade, and the West Martello Tower provides shelter should a storm suddenly sweep in. Kayak and beach-chair rentals are available, as is a volleyball net. The beach also has a marker and cultural exhibit commemorating the gravesite of 295 enslaved Africans who died after being rescued from three South America–bound slave ships in 1860. Across the street, **Astro City Playground** is popular with young children. ✉ *Atlantic Blvd. between White and Reynolds Sts.* ☎ *No phone* *Free* ⏲ *Daily 6 AM–11 PM.*

12 **Historic Seaport at Key West Bight.** What used to be a funky—in some places even seedy—part of town is now an 8½-acre historic restoration project of 100 businesses, including waterfront restaurants, open-air bars, museums, clothing stores, bait shops, dive shops, docks, a marina, water-sports concessions, and the Waterfront Market. It's all linked by the 2-mi waterfront **Harborwalk,** which runs between Front and Grinnell streets, passing big ships, schooners, sunset cruises, fishing charters, and glass-bottom boats. ✉ *100 Grinnell St.* ☎ *305/293–8309.*

NEED A BREAK?

Get your morning (or afternoon) buzz at Coffee Plantation (✉ *713 Caroline St.* ☎ *305/295–9808* 🌐 *www.coffeeplantationkeywest.com*), where you can also hook up to the Internet in the comfort of a homelike setting in a circa-1890 Conch house. Poets, writers, and minstrels sometimes show up to perform while you munch pastries or luncheon sandwiches and wraps and sip your hot or cold espresso beverage.

17 **Key West Butterfly & Nature Conservatory.** This air-conditioned refuge for butterflies, birds, and the human spirit gladdens the soul with hundreds of colorful wings—more than 45 species of butterflies alone—in a lovely glass-encased bubble. Waterfalls, artistic benches, paved pathways, birds, and lush, flowering vegetation elevate this above most butterfly attractions. The gift shop and gallery are worth a visit on their

See the typewriter Hemingway used at his home-office in Key West. He lived here from 1931 to 1942.

own. ✉ *1316 Duval St.* ☎ *305/296–2988 or 800/939–4647* 🌐 *www.keywestbutterfly.com* 🎟 *$12* 🕒 *Daily 9–5 (last admission 4:30); gallery and shop open until 5:30.*

8 **Key West Museum of Art & History in the Custom House.** When Key West was designated a U.S. port of entry in the early 1820s, a custom house was established. Salvaged cargoes from ships wrecked on the reefs were brought here, setting the stage for Key West to become for a time the richest city in Florida. The imposing redbrick-and-terra-cotta Richardsonian Romanesque–style building reopened as a museum and art gallery in 1999. Smaller galleries have long-term and changing exhibits about the history of Key West, including a Hemingway room and a fine collection of folk artist Mario Sanchez's wood paintings. ✉ *281 Front St.* ☎ *305/295–6616* 🌐 *www.kwahs.com* 🎟 *$10* 🕒 *Daily 9:30–4:30.*

Fodor's Choice ★

2 **Key West Lighthouse Museum & Keeper's Quarters Museum.** For the best view in town, climb the 88 steps to the top of this 1847 lighthouse. The 92-foot structure has a Fresnel lens, which was installed in the 1860s at a cost of $1 million. The keeper lived in the adjacent 1887 clapboard house, which now exhibits vintage photographs, ship models, nautical charts, and lighthouse artifacts from all along the Key reefs. ✉ *938 Whitehead St.* ☎ *305/295–6616* 🌐 *www.kwahs.com* 🎟 *$10* 🕒 *Daily 9:30–5; last admission at 4:30.*

11 **Mallory Square and Pier.** For cruise-ship passengers, this is the disembarkation point for an attack on Key West. For practically every visitor, it's the requisite venue for a nightly sunset celebration that includes street performers—human statues, sword swallowers, tightrope walkers, musicians, and more—plus craft vendors, conch fritter fryers, and

CLOSE UP

Hemingway Was Here

In a town where Pulitzer Prize–winning writers are almost as common as coconuts, Ernest Hemingway stands out. Bars and restaurants around the island claim that he ate or drank there (except Bagatelle, where the sign reads "Hemingway never liked this place").

Hemingway came to Key West in 1928 at the urging of writer John dos Passos and rented a house with wife number two, Pauline Pfeiffer. They spent winters in the Keys and summers in Europe and Wyoming, occasionally taking African safaris. Along the way they had two sons, Patrick and Gregory. In 1931, Pauline's wealthy uncle Gus gave the couple the house at 907 Whitehead Street. Now known as the Ernest Hemingway Home & Museum, it's Key West's number-one tourist attraction. Renovations included the addition of a pool and a tropical garden.

In 1935, when the visitor bureau included the house in a tourist brochure, Hemingway promptly built the brick wall that surrounds it today. He wrote of the visitor bureau's offense in a 1935 essay for *Esquire*, saying, "The house at present occupied by your correspondent is listed as number eighteen in a compilation of the forty-eight things for a tourist to see in Key West. So there will be no difficulty in a tourist finding it or any other of the sights of the city, a map has been prepared by the local F.E.R.A. authorities to be presented to each arriving visitor. This is all very flattering to the easily bloated ego of your correspondent but very hard on production."

During his time in Key West, Hemingway penned some of his most important works, including *A Farewell to Arms, To Have and Have Not, Green Hills of Africa,* and *Death in the Afternoon.* His rigorous schedule consisted of writing almost every morning in his 2nd-story studio above the pool, then promptly descending the stairs at midday. By afternoon and evening he was ready for drinking, fishing, swimming, boxing, and hanging around with the boys.

One close friend was Joe Russell, a craggy fisherman and owner of the rugged bar Sloppy Joe's, originally at 428 Greene Street but now at 201 Duval Street. Russell was the only one in town who would cash Hemingway's $1,000 royalty check. Russell and Charles Thompson introduced Hemingway to deep sea fishing, which became fodder for his writing. Another of Hemingway's loves was boxing. He set up a ring in his yard and paid local fighters to box with him, and he refereed matches at Blue Heaven, then a saloon at 729 Thomas Street.

Hemingway honed his macho image dressed in cutoffs and old shirts and took on the name Papa. In turn, he gave his friends new names and used them as characters in his stories. Joe Russell became Freddy, captain of the *Queen Conch* charter boat in *To Have and Have Not.*

Hemingway stayed in Key West for 11 years before leaving Pauline for wife number three. Pauline and the boys stayed on in the house, which sold in 1951 for $80,000, 10 times its original cost.

—Jim and Cynthia Tunstall

14

other regulars who defy classification. (Wanna picture with my pet iguana?) With all the activity, don't forget to watch the main show: a dazzling tropical sunset. ✉ *Mallory Sq.* ☎ *No phone.*

18 **The Southernmost Point.** Possibly the most photographed site in Key West, this is a must-see for many visitors. Who wouldn't want his picture taken next to the big striped buoy that marks the southernmost point in the continental United States? A plaque next to it honors Cubans who lost their lives trying to escape to America and other signs tell Key West history. ✉ *Whitehead and South Sts.* ☎ *No phone.*

WORTH NOTING

16 **City Cemetery.** You can learn almost as much about a town's history through its cemetery as through its historic houses. Key West's celebrated 20-acre burial place may leave you wanting more, with headstone epitaphs such as "I told you I was sick," and, for a wayward husband, "Now I know where he's sleeping at night." Among the interesting plots are a memorial to the sailors killed in the sinking of the battleship USS *Maine,* carved angels and lambs marking graves of children, and grand aboveground crypts that put to shame many of the town's dwellings for the living. There are separate plots for Catholics, Jews, and refugees from Cuba. You're free to walk around the cemetery on your own, but the best way to see it is on a 60-minute tour given by the staff and volunteers of the Historic Florida Keys Foundation. Tours leave from the main gate, and reservations are required. ✉ *Margaret and Angela Sts.* ☎ *305/292–6718* *Tours $15* ⏲ *Daily sunrise–6* PM, *tours Tues. and Thurs. at 9:30 year-round; call for additional times.*

20 **Dog Beach.** Next to Louie's Backyard, this tiny beach—the only one in Key West where dogs are allowed unleashed—has a shore that's a mix of sand and rocks. ✉ *Vernon and Waddell Sts.* ☎ *No phone* *Free* ⏲ *Daily sunrise–sunset.*

15 **Eco-Discovery Center.** While visiting Fort Zachary Taylor Historic State Park, stop in at this 6,400-square-foot interactive attraction, which encourages visitors to venture through a variety of Florida Keys habitats from pinelands, beach dunes, and mangroves to the deep sea. Walk through a model of NOAA's (National Oceanic and Atmospheric Administration) Aquarius, a unique underwater ocean laboratory 9 mi off Key Largo, to virtually discover what lurks beneath the sea. Touchscreen computer displays, a dramatic movie, a 2,450-gallon aquarium, and live underwater cameras show off North America's only contiguous barrier coral reef. ✉ *35 E. Quay Rd., at end of Southard St. in Truman Annex* ☎ *305/809–4750* 🌐 *floridakeys.noaa.gov* *Free, donations accepted* ⏲ *Tues.–Sat. 9–4.*

9 **Key West Aquarium.** Pet a nurse shark and explore the fascinating underwater realm of the Keys without getting wet at this historic aquarium. Hundreds of tropical fish and enormous sea creatures live here. A touch tank enables you to handle starfish, sea cucumbers, horseshoe and hermit crabs, even horse and queen conchs—living totems of the Conch Republic. Built in 1934 by the Works Progress Administration as the world's first open-air aquarium, most of the building has been enclosed for all-weather viewing. Guided tours, included in the admission price,

feature shark feedings. ✉ *1 Whitehead St.* ☎ *305/296–2051* 🌐 *www.keywestaquarium.com* 🎫 *$12* ⏲ *Daily 10–6; tours at 11, 1, 3, and 4:30.*

PELICAN PATH

Pelican Path is a free walking guide to Key West published by the **Old Island Restoration Foundation.** The guide discusses the history and architecture of 43 structures along 25 blocks of 12 Old Town streets. Pick up a copy at the Chamber of Commerce.

10 **Key West Shipwreck Treasures Museum** (✉ *1 Whitehead St.,* ☎ *305/292–8990* 🌐 *www.shipwreckhistoreum.com* 🎫 *$12* ⏲ *Daily 9:40–5*). Much of Key West's history, early prosperity, and interesting architecture come from ships that ran aground on its coral reef. Artifacts from the circa-1856 *Isaac Allerton,* which yielded $150,000 worth of wreckage, comprises the museum portion of this multifaceted attraction. Actors and films add a bit of Disneyesque drama. The final highlight is climbing to the top the 65-foot lookout tower, a reproduction of the 20 or so towers used by Key West wreckers during the town's salvaging heydays.

6 **Mel Fisher Maritime Museum.** In 1622 two Spanish galleons laden with riches from South America foundered in a hurricane 40 mi west of the Keys. In 1985 diver Mel Fisher recovered the treasures from the lost ships, the *Nuestra Señora de Atocha* and the *Santa Margarita.* Fisher's incredible adventure tracking these fabled hoards and battling the state of Florida for rights is as amazing as the loot you'll see, touch, and learn about in this museum. Artifacts include a gold bar (that you can lift to get an idea what $15,000 feels like) and a 77.76-carat natural emerald crystal worth almost $250,000. Exhibits on the 2nd floor rotate and might cover slave ships, including the excavated 17th-century *Henrietta Marie,* or the evolution of Florida maritime history. ✉ *200 Greene St.* ☎ *305/294–2633* 🌐 *www.melfisher.org* 🎫 *$12* ⏲ *Weekdays 8:30–5, weekends 9:30–5.*

3 **Nancy Forrester's Secret Garden.** It's hard to believe that this green escape still exists in the middle of Old Town Key West. Despite damage by hurricanes and pressures from developers, Nancy Forrester has maintained her naturalized garden for more than 40 years. Growing in harmony are rare palms and cycads, ferns, bromeliads, bright gingers and heliconias, gumbo-limbo trees strewn with orchids and vines, and a colorful crew of birds, reptiles, cats, and a few surprises. An art gallery has botanical prints and environmental art. One-hour private tours cost $15 per person, four-person minimum. ✉ *1 Free School La.* ☎ *305/294–0015* 🌐 *www.nancyforrester.com* 🎫 *$10* ⏲ *Daily 10–5.*

13 **Pirate Soul Museum.** Enter if you dare! This swashbuckling attraction combines an animatronic Blackbeard's head, hands-on exhibits about buccaneers, and a collection of nearly 500 artifacts, including the only authentic surviving pirate chest in America, dating back to the 1600s. Don't miss the Disney-produced, three-dimensional sound program that takes you below decks into a completely dark mock prison cell. ✉ *524 Front St.* ☎ *305/292–1113* 🌐 *www.piratesoul.com* 🎫 *$14* ⏲ *Weekdays 9–5, weekends 10–5.*

4 **San Carlos Institute.** South Florida's Cuban connection began long before Fidel Castro was born. The institute was founded in 1871 by Cuban immigrants. Now it contains a research library and museum rich with the history of Key West and 19th- and 20th-century Cuban exiles. Cuban patriot Jose Martí delivered speeches from the balcony of the auditorium, and opera star Enrico Caruso sang in the opera house, which has exceptional acoustics. It's frequently used for concerts, lectures, films, and exhibits. ✉ *516 Duval St.* ☎ *305/294–3887* 🌐 *www.institutosancarlos.org* 🎟 *Free* ⏲ *Fri.–Sun. noon–6.*

19 **South Beach.** On the Atlantic, this stretch of sand, also known as City Beach, is popular with travelers staying at nearby motels. It is now part of the new Southernmost Hotel on the Beach resort, but is open to the public with a fun beach bar and grill. There's no parking however, so visitors must walk or bike to the beach. ✉ *Foot of Duval St.* ☎ *No phone* 🎟 *Free* ⏲ *Daily 7* AM–*11* PM.

NEW TOWN

The Overseas Highway splits as it enters Key West, the two forks rejoining to encircle New Town, the area east of White Street to Cow Key Channel. The southern fork runs along the shore as South Roosevelt Boulevard (Route A1A) skirting Key West International Airport. Along the north shore, North Roosevelt Boulevard (U.S. 1) passes the Key West Welcome Center. Part of New Town was created with dredged fill. The island would have continued growing this way had the Army Corps of Engineers not determined in the early 1970s that it was detrimental to the nearby reef.

23 **C. B. Harvey Rest Beach.** This beach and park were named after Cornelius Bradford Harvey, former Key West mayor and commissioner. It has half a dozen picnic areas, dunes, and a wheelchair and bike path. ✉ *Atlantic Blvd., east side of White St. Pier* ☎ *No phone* 🎟 *Free* ⏲ *Daily 7* AM–*11* PM.

25 ★ **Fort East Martello Museum & Gardens.** This Civil War citadel was *semper paratus,* or "always ready" as the U.S. Coast Guard motto says, but, like most of Florida during the war, it never saw a lick of action. Today it serves as a museum, with historical exhibits about the 19th and 20th centuries. Among the latter are relics of the USS *Maine,* a Cuban refugee raft, and books by famous writers—including seven Pulitzer Prize winners—who have lived in Key West. The tower, operated by the Key West Art and Historical Society, also has a collection of Stanley Papio's "junk art" sculptures and Cuban folk artist Mario Sanchez's chiseled and painted wooden carvings of historic Key West street scenes. ✉ *3501 S. Roosevelt Blvd.* ☎ *305/296–3913* 🌐 *www.kwahs.com* 🎟 *$6* ⏲ *Weekdays 10–4, weekends 9:30–4:30.*

24 **Smathers Beach.** This wide beach has nearly 2 mi of sand, plus restrooms, picnic areas, and volleyball courts, all of which make it popular with the spring-break crowd. Trucks along the road rent rafts, windsurfers, and other beach "toys." Metered parking is on the street. ✉ *S. Roosevelt Blvd.* ☎ *No phone* 🎟 *Free* ⏲ *Daily 7* AM–*11* PM.

22 **West Martello Tower.** Among the arches and ruins of this redbrick Civil War–era fort the Key West Garden Club maintains lovely gardens of

WORD OF MOUTH

"The historic Key West Garrison Bight Marina is crowded with pleasure and commercial boats. We always skip the 'short cut' around the harbor and take the long walk by the boats. We never tire of seeing the variety and arrangement of boats." —photo by John Franzis, Fodors.com member.

KEY WEST TOURS

BICYCLE TOURS

Lloyd's Original Tropical Bike Tour (✉ *Truman Ave. and Simonton St., Key West* ☎ *305/304–4700* 🌐 *www.lloydstropicalbiketour.com*), led by a 30-year Key West veteran, explores the natural, noncommercial side of Key West at a leisurely pace, stopping on backstreets and in backyards of private homes to sample native fruits and view indigenous plants and trees; at City Cemetery; and at the Medicine Garden, a private meditation garden. The behind-the-scenes tours run two hours and cost $35, including bike rental.

Victoria Impallomeni, a 34-year wilderness guide and marine scientist, invites up to six nature lovers—especially children—aboard the *Imp II*, a 25-foot Aquasport, for four-hour ($500) and seven-hour ($700) **Dancing Dolphin Spirit Charters** (✉ *MM 5 OS at Murray's Marina, 5710 Overseas Hwy., Key West* ☎ *305/304–7562 or 888/822–7366* 🌐 *www.captainvictoria.com*) ecotours that frequently include encounters with wild dolphins. While island-hopping, you visit underwater gardens, natural shoreline, and mangrove habitats. For her Dolphin Day for Humans tour, Impallomeni pulls you through the water, equipped with mask and snorkel, on a specially designed "dolphin water massage board" that simulates dolphin swimming motions. Sometimes dolphins follow the boat and swim among participants. All equipment is supplied. Tours leave from Murray's Marina (☎ *305/296–0364* 🌐 *www.murraymarine.com*).

KAYAK TOURS

Lazy Dog Kayak Guides (✉ *5114 Overseas Hwy., Key West* ☎ *305/295–9898* 🌐 *www.lazydog.com*) runs four-hour guided sea kayak–snorkel tours around the mangrove islands just east of Key West. The $60 charge covers transportation, bottled water, a snack, and supplies, including snorkeling gear. A $35 two-hour guided kayak tour is also available.

WALKING TOURS

In addition to publishing several good guides on Key West, the **Historic Florida Keys Foundation** (✉ *510 Greene St., Old City Hall, Key West* ☎ *305/292–6718*) conducts tours of the City Cemetery Tuesday and Thursday at 9:30.

native and tropical plants, fountains, and sculptures. It also holds art, orchid, and flower shows February through April and leads private garden tours one weekend in March. ✉ *Atlantic Blvd. and White St.* ☎ *305/294–3210* 🌐 *www.keywestgardenclub.com* 🎫 *Donation welcome* ⏲ *Tues.–Sat. 9:30–3:15.*

OFF THE BEATEN PATH

History buffs might remember long-deactivated Fort Jefferson as the prison that held Dr. Samuel Mudd for his role in the Lincoln assassination. But today's "guests" are much more captivated by this sanctuary's thousands of birds and marine life. **Dry Tortugas National Park** (📫 *Box 6208, Key West 33040* ☎ *305/242–7700* 🌐 *www.nps.gov/drto* 🎫 *$5*) is 70 mi off the shores of Key West and consists of seven small islands. Tour the fort; then lay out your blanket on the sunny beach for a picnic before you head out to snorkel on the protected reef. Many people like to camp here ($3 per person per night, eight sites plus group site and

THE CONCH REPUBLIC

Beginning in the 1970s, pot smuggling became a source of income for islanders who knew how to dodge detection in the maze of waterways in the Keys. In 1982, the U.S. Border Patrol threw a roadblock across the Overseas Highway just south of Florida City to catch drug runners and undocumented aliens. Traffic backed up for miles as Border Patrol agents searched vehicles and demanded that the occupants prove U.S. citizenship. Officials in Key West, outraged at being treated like foreigners by the federal government, staged a protest and formed their own "nation," the so-called Conch Republic. They hoisted a flag and distributed mock border passes, visas, and Conch currency. The embarrassed Border Patrol dismantled its roadblock, and now an annual festival recalls the city's victory.

overflow area; first come, first served), but note that there's no freshwater supply and you must carry off whatever you bring onto the island. The fast, sleek, 100-foot catamaran *Yankee Freedom II,* of the **Dry Tortugas National Park Ferry** (✉ *Lands End Marina, 240 Margaret St., Key West* ☎ *305/294–7009 or 800/634–0939* 🌐 *www.yankeefreedom.com* 🎟 *$160, plus $5 park fee* ⏲ *Trips daily at 8* AM), cuts the travel time to the Dry Tortugas to 2¼ hours. The time passes quickly on the roomy vessel equipped with three restrooms, two freshwater showers, and two bars. Stretch out on two decks: one an air-conditioned salon with cushioned seating, the other an open sundeck with sunny and shaded seating. Continental breakfast and lunch are included. On arrival, a naturalist leads a 40-minute guided tour, which is followed by lunch and a free afternoon for swimming, snorkeling (gear included), and exploring. The vessel is ADA–certified for visitors using wheelchairs.

■ **TIP→ The Dry Tortugas lies in the central time zone.**

SPORTS AND THE OUTDOORS

Unlike the rest of the region, Key West isn't known for outdoor pursuits. But everyone should devote at least half a day to relaxing on a boat tour, heading out on a fishing expedition, or pursuing some other adventure at sea. The ultimate excursion is a boat trip to Dry Tortugas National Park for snorkeling and exploring Fort Jefferson. Other excursions cater to nature lovers, scuba divers and snorkelers, and those who would just like to get out in the water and enjoy the scenery and sunset. For those who prefer their recreation land based, biking is the way to go. Hiking is limited, but walking the streets of Old Town provides plenty of exercise.

BEACH

⑬ ★ **Fort Zachary Taylor Historic State Park.** The park's beach is the best and safest to swim in Key West. There's an adjoining picnic area with barbecue grills and shade trees, a snack bar, and rental equipment, including snorkeling gear. A café serves sandwiches and other munchies.

✉ Box 6565; end of Southard St., through Truman Annex ☎ 305/292–6713 🌐 www.floridastateparks.org/forttaylor 🎟 $4.50 for 1 person, $7 for 2 people, 50¢ per additional person ⏲ Daily 8–sunset, tours noon and 2.

THE FISH GUIDE

Chambers of commerce, marinas, and dive shops offer free **Teall's Guides** (*📫 Box 522409, Marathon Shores 33052 ☎ 305/872–3123*) with land and nautical charts pinpointing popular fishing and diving areas throughout the Keys.

BIKING

Key West was practically made for bicycles, but don't let that lull you into a false sense of security. Narrow and one-way streets along with car traffic result in several bike accidents a year. Some hotels rent or lend bikes to guests; others will refer you to a nearby shop and reserve a bike for you. Rentals usually start at about $12 a day, but some places also rent by the half-day. ■ **TIP→ Lock up; bikes—and porch chairs!—are favorite targets for local thieves.**

Eaton Bikes (*✉ 830 Eaton St. ☎ 305/295-0057 🌐 www.eatonbikes.com*) has tandem, three-wheel, and children's bikes in addition to the standard beach cruisers ($18 for first day) and seven-speed cruisers ($18). It delivers free to all Key West rentals. **Keys Moped & Scooter** (*✉ 523 Truman Ave. ☎ 305/294–0399*) rents beach cruisers with large baskets for $10 a day. Rates for scooters start at $35. Look for the huge American flag on the roof. **Moped Hospital** (*✉ 601 Truman Ave. ☎ 305/296–3344 or 866/296–1625 🌐 www.mopedhospital.com*) supplies balloon-tire bikes with yellow safety baskets for adults and kids ($12 per day), as well as mopeds ($40) and double-seater scooters ($65). **Paradise Scooter Rentals** (*✉ 112 Fitzpatrick St. ☎ 305/923–6063 🌐 www.paradisescooterrentals.com*) rents bikes starting at $8 for two hours and scooters for $60–$70 a day.

FISHING

Key West Bait & Tackle (*✉ 241 Margaret St. ☎ 305/292–1961 🌐 www.keywestbaitandtackle.com*) carries live bait, frozen bait, and fishing equipment. It also has the Live Bait Lounge, where you can sip ice-cold beer while telling fish tales.

Key West Pro Guides (*✉ G-31 Miriam St. ☎ 866/259–4205 🌐 www.keywestproguides.com*) has several different trips, including flats and backcountry fishing ($400 for a half day) and reef and offshore fishing ($600 for half day).

GOLF

Key West Resort Golf Course (*✉ 6450 E. College Rd. ☎ 305/294–5232 🌐 www.keywestgolf.com*) is an 18-hole, par 70 course on the bay side of Stock Island; greens fees are $70–$95.

KAYAKING

Key West is surrounded by marinas, so it's easy to find what you're looking for, whether it's sailing with dolphins or paddling in the mangroves. At **Key West Eco-Tours** (*✉ Historic Seaport, 100 Grinnell St. ☎ 305/294–7245 🌐 keywestecotours.co*), the sail-kayak-snorkel excursions take you into backcountry flats and mangrove forests. The 4½-hour trip costs $95 per person and includes lunch. Sunset sails and private charters are also available.

SCUBA DIVING AND SNORKELING

Captain's Corner (✉ *125 Ann St.* ☎ *305/296–8865* 🌐 *www.captainscorner.com*), a PADI–certified dive shop, has classes in several languages and twice-daily snorkel and dive trips ($40–$45) to reefs and wrecks aboard the 60-foot dive boat *Sea Eagle*. Equipment rental is extra. Safely dive the coral reefs without getting a scuba certification with **Snuba of Key West** (✉ *Garrison Bight Marina, Palm Ave. between Eaton St. and N. Roosevelt Blvd.* ☎ *305/292–4616* 🌐 *www.snubakeywest.com*). Ride out to the reef on a catamaran, then follow your guide underwater for a one-hour tour of the coral reefs. You wear a regulator with a breathing hose that is attached to a floating air tank on the surface. No prior diving or snorkeling experience is necessary, but you must know how to swim. The $99 price includes beverages.

SHOPPING

On these streets you'll find colorful local art of widely varying quality, key limes made into everything imaginable, and the raunchiest T-shirts in the civilized world. Browsing the boutiques—with frequent pub stops along the way—makes for an entertaining stroll down Duval Street.

Where to start? **Bahama Village** is an enclave of spruced-up shops, restaurants, and vendors responsible for the restoration of the colorful historic district where Bahamians settled in the 19th century. The village lies roughly between Whitehead and Fort streets and Angela and Catherine streets. Hemingway frequented the bars, restaurants, and boxing rings in this part of town.

ARTS AND CRAFTS

Key West is filled with art galleries, and the variety is truly amazing. Much is locally produced by the town's large artist community, but many galleries carry international artists from as close as Haiti and as far away as France. Local artists do a great job of preserving the island's architecture and spirit.

Cuba, Cuba! (✉ *814 Duval St.* ☎ *305/295–9442* 🌐 *cubacubastore.com*) stocks paintings, sculptures, and photos by Cuban artists. The **Gallery on Greene** (✉ *606 Greene St.* ☎ *305/294–1669* 🌐 *www.galleryongreene.com*) showcases politically incorrect art by Jeff MacNelly and three-dimensional paintings by Mario Sanchez. This is the largest gallery-exhibition space in Key West. The oldest private art gallery in Key West, **Gingerbread Square Gallery** (✉ *1207 Duval St.* ☎ *305/296–8900* 🌐 *www.gingerbreadsquaregallery.com*), represents local and internationally acclaimed artists, including Sal Salinero and Michael Palmer, in media ranging from graphics to art glass. **Glass Reunions** (✉ *825 Duval St.* ☎ *305/294–1720* 🌐 *www.glassreunions.com*) showcases a collection of wild and impressive fine-art glass. It's worth a stop in just to see the imaginative and over-the-top glass chandeliers, jewelry, dishes, and platters.

Nightlife, shops, and some interesting street art can all be found on Key West's Duval Street.

Historian, photographer, and painter Sharon Wells opened **KW Light Gallery** (✉ *1203 Duval St.* ☎ *305/294–0566* 🌐 *www.kwlightgallery.com*) to showcase her own fine-art photography and painted tiles and canvases, as well as the works of other national artists. You can find historic photos here as well. **Lucky Street Gallery** (✉ *1130 Duval St.* ☎ *305/294–3973*) sells high-end contemporary paintings. There are also a few pieces of jewelry by internationally recognized Key West–based artists. Changing exhibits, artist receptions, and special events make this a lively venue. **Pelican Poop Shoppe** (✉ *314 Simonton St.* ☎ *305/296–3887* 🌐 *www.pelicanpoopshoppe.com*) sells Caribbean art in a tropical courtyard garden. The owners buy directly from the artisans every year, so the prices are very attractive. Potters Charles Pearson and Timothy Roeder can be found at **Whitehead St. Pottery** (✉ *322 Julia St.* ☎ *305/294–5067* 🌐 *www.whiteheadstreetpottery.com*, where they display their porcelain stoneware and raku-fired vessels. The setting, around two koi ponds with a burbling fountain, is as sublime as the art.

BOOKS

The **Key West Island Bookstore** (✉ *513 Fleming St.* ☎ *305/294–2904*) is a home away from home for the large Key West writers' community. It carries new, used, and rare titles. It specializes in Hemingway, Tennessee Williams, and South Florida mystery writers.

CLOTHING AND FABRICS

Don't leave town without a browse through the legendary **Fairvilla Megastore** (✉ *520 Front St.* ☎ *305/292–0448* 🌐 *www.fairvilla.com*), where you'll find an astonishing array of fantasy wear, outlandish costumes (check out the pirate section), and other interesting souvenirs.

Take home a shopping bag full of scarlet hibiscus, fuchsia heliconias, blue parrot fish, and even pink flamingo fabric from the **Seam Shoppe** (✉ *1114 Truman Ave.* ☎ *305/296–9830* 🌐 *www.tropicalfabricsonline.com*), which has the city's widest selection of tropical-print fabrics.

FOOD AND DRINK

★ The **Blond Giraffe** (✉ *802 Duval St.* ☎ *305/293–7874* ✉ *614 Front St.* ☎ *305/296–2020* ✉ *1209 Truman Ave.* ☎ *305/295–6776* 🌐 *www.blondgiraffe.com*) turned an old family recipe for key lime pie into one of the island's success stories. You'll often encounter a line out the door waiting for a pie with delicate pastry, sweet-tart custard filling, and thick meringue topping. The key lime rum cake is the best-selling product for shipping home. For a snack on the run, try the pie on a stick. **Fausto's Food Palace** (✉ *522 Fleming St.* ☎ *305/296–5663* ✉ *1105 White St.* ☎ *305/294–5221*) is a market in the traditional town-square sense. Since 1926 Fausto's has been the spot to catch up on the week's gossip and to chill out in summer—it has groceries, organic foods, marvelous wines, a sushi chef on duty from 8 AM–6 PM, and box lunches to go. You'll be pleasantly surprised with the fruit wines sold at the **Key West Winery** (✉ *103 Simonton St.* ☎ *305/292–1717 or 866/880–1717* 🌐 *www.thekeywestwinery.com*). Display crates hold bottles of wines made from blueberries, blackberries, pineapples, cherries, mangoes, watermelons, tomatoes, and, of course, key limes. Stop in for a free tasting. If you like it hot, you'll love **Peppers of Key West** (✉ *602 Greene St.* ☎ *305/295–9333 or 800/597–2823* 🌐 *www.peppersofkeywest.com*). The shop has hundreds of sauces, salsas, and sweets guaranteed to light ★ your fire. A sea-life mural cleverly hides the fact that **Waterfront Market** (✉ *201 William St.* ☎ *305/296–0778*) occupies a big and ugly concrete building. The family-owned, upscale market sells items from around the world, including health food, organic produce, fresh salads, gourmet coffees, imported cheeses, baked goods, and more. Don't miss the fish market, arguably the best in town; there's also a juice bar, sushi, and vegan dishes.

GIFTS AND SOUVENIRS

Part museum, part shopping center, **Cayo Hueso y Habana** (✉ *410 Wall St., Mallory Sq.* ☎ *305/293–7260*) occupies a circa-1879 warehouse with a hand-rolled cigar shop, one-of-a-kind souvenirs, a Cuban restaurant, and exhibits that tell of the island's Cuban heritage. Outside, a memorial garden pays homage to the island's Cuban ancestors. **Fast Buck Freddie's** (✉ *500 Duval St.* ☎ *305/294–2007* 🌐 *www.fastbuckfreddies.com*) sells a classy, hip selection of gifts, including every flamingo item imaginable. It has a whole department called "Tropical Trash," and carries such imaginative items as an electric fan in the shape of a rooster. **Half Buck Freddie's** (✉ *920 Caroline St.* ☎ *305/294–2007* is the discount-outlet store for Fast Buck Freddie's.

★ For that unique (but slightly overpriced) souvenir of your trip to Key West head to **Montage** (✉ *512 Duval St.* ☎ *305/395–9101 or 877/396–4278* 🌐 *montagekeywest.com*), where you'll discover hundreds of handcrafted signs of popular Key West guesthouses, inns, hotels, restaurants, bars, and streets. If you can't find what you're looking for, they'll make it for you.

NIGHTLIFE

Rest up: much of what happens in Key West does so after dark. Open your mind and have a stroll. Scruffy street performers strum next to dogs in sunglasses. Brawls tumble out the doors of Sloppy Joe's. Drag queens strut across stages in Joan Rivers garb. Tattooed men lick whipped cream off of women's body parts. And margaritas flow like a Jimmy Buffett tune.

BARS AND LOUNGES

Capt. Tony's Saloon (✉ *428 Greene St.* ☎ *305/294–1838* 🌐 *www.capttonyssaloon.com*) was the original Sloppy Joe's in the mid-1930s, when Hemingway was a regular. Later, a young Jimmy Buffett sang here and made this watering hole famous in his song "Last Mango in Paris." Bands play nightly. No matter your mood, **Durty Harry's** (✉ *208 Duval St.* ☎ *305/296–5513* 🌐 *www.ricksanddurtyharrys.com*) can fill the bill. The megasize entertainment complex has live music in a variety of indoor-outdoor bars including Rick's Dance Club Wine & Martini Bar and the tiny Red Garter strip club. Pause for a libation at the open-air **Green Parrot Bar** (✉ *601 Whitehead St., at Southard St.* ☎ *305/294–6133* 🌐 *www.greenparrot.com*). Built in 1890, the bar is said to be Key West's oldest. The sometimes-rowdy saloon has locals outnumbering out-of-towners, especially on weekends when bands play. Belly up to the bar for a cold mug of the signature Hog's Breath Lager at the infamous **Hog's Breath Saloon** (✉ *400 Front St.* ☎ *305/296–4222* 🌐 *www.hogsbreath.com*), a must-stop on the Key West bar crawl. Live bands play daily 1 PM–2 AM. A youngish, touristy crowd, sprinkled with aging Parrot Heads, frequents **Margaritaville Café** (✉ *500 Duval St.* ☎ *305/292–1435* 🌐 *www.margaritaville.com*), owned by former Key West resident and recording star Jimmy Buffett, who has been known to perform here. The drink of choice is, of course, a margarita. There's live music nightly, as well as lunch and dinner. Nightlife at the **Pier House** (✉ *1 Duval St.* ☎ *305/296–4600 or 800/327–8340* 🌐 *www.pierhouse.com*) begins with a steel-drum band to celebrate the sunset on the beach (on select Thursdays and Fridays), then moves indoors to the Wine Galley piano bar for live jazz. The **Schooner Wharf Bar** (✉ *202 William St.* ☎ *305/292–3302* 🌐 *www.schoonerwharf.com*), an open-air waterfront bar and grill in the historic seaport district, retains its funky Key West charm and hosts live entertainment daily. Its margarita ranks among Key West's best. There's history and good times at **Sloppy Joe's** (✉ *201 Duval St.* ☎ *305/294–5717* 🌐 *www.sloppyjoes.com*), the successor to a famous 1937 speakeasy named for its founder, Captain Joe Russell. Decorated with Hemingway memorabilia and marine flags, the bar is popular with travelers and is full and noisy all the time. A Sloppy Joe's T-shirt is a de rigueur Key West souvenir, and the gift shop sells them like crazy. **The Top** (✉ *430 Duval St.* ☎ *305/296–2991* 🌐 *www.laconchakeywest.com/thetop.htm*) is on the 7th floor of the La Concha

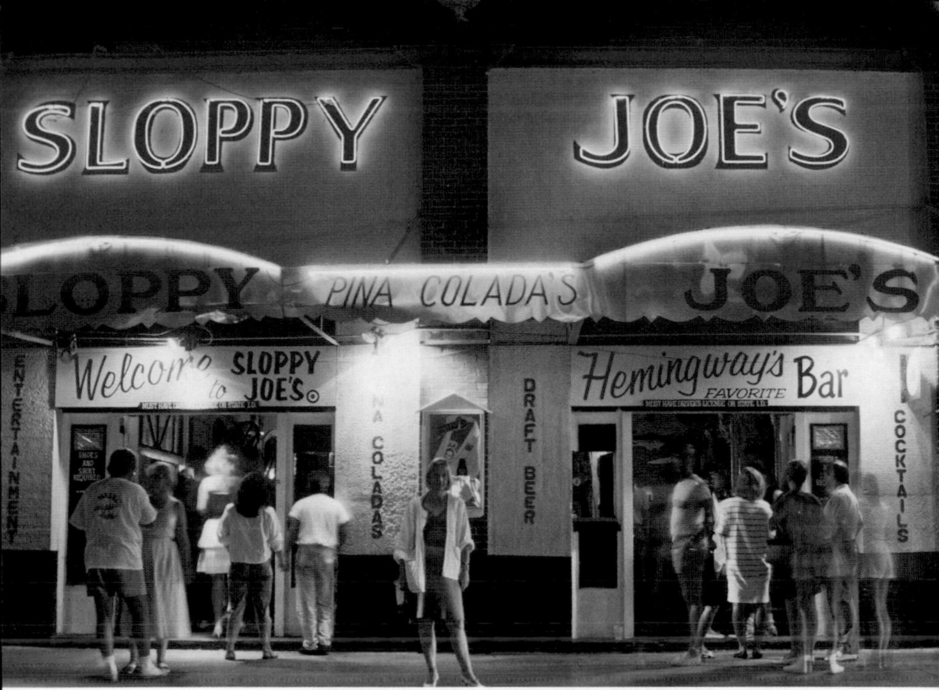

Sloppy Joe's is one stop on most Key West visitors' bar-hop stroll, also known as the Duval Crawl.

Crowne Plaza and is one of the best places in town to view the sunset and enjoy live entertainment.

In the best traditions of a 1950s cocktail lounge, **Virgilio's** (✉ *524 Duval St.* ☎ *305/296-8118* 🌐 *www.virgilioskeywest.com*) serves chilled martinis to the soothing tempo of live jazz and blues nightly.

WHERE TO EAT

$$–$$$
JAPANESE

✕ **Ambrosia.** Ask any savvy local where to get the best sushi on the island and you'll undoubtedly be pointed to this tiny wood-and-tatami-paneled dining room with indoor waterfall tucked away into a resort near the beach. Grab a seat at the sushi bar and watch owner and head sushi chef Masa prepare an impressive array of superfresh sashimi delicacies. Sushi lovers can't go wrong with the Ambrosia special ($35), a sampler of five kinds of sashimi, seven pieces of sushi and sushi rolls. There's an assortment of lightly fried tempura and teriyaki dishes and a killer bento box at lunch. Enjoy it all with a glass of premium sake or a cold glass of Sapporo beer. ✉ *Santa Maria Resort, 1401 Simonton St.* ☎ *305/293–0304* ▭ *AE, MC, V* ⊙ *No lunch weekends. Closed 2 weeks after Labor Day.*

$$$
CARIBBEAN
★

✕ **Blue Heaven.** The outdoor dining area here is often referred to as "the quintessential Keys experience," and it's hard to argue. There's much to like about this historic restaurant where Hemingway refereed boxing matches and customers cheered for cockfights. Although these events are no more, the free-roaming chickens and cats add that "what-a-hoot" factor. Nightly specials include black bean soup, Provençal sea scallops, jerk chicken, and sautéed yellowtail snapper in citrus

EVERYTHING'S FISHY IN THE KEYS

Fish. It's what's for dinner in the Florida Keys. The Keys' runway between the Gulf of Mexico or Florida Bay and Atlantic warm waters means fish of many fin. Restaurants take full advantage by serving it fresh, whether you caught it or a local fisherman did.

Menus at a number of colorful waterfront shacks such as **Snapper's** (✉ *139 Seaside Ave., Key Largo* ☎ *305/852–5956*) in Key Largo and **Half Shell Raw Bar** (✉ *231 Margaret St., Key West* ☎ *305/294–7496*) range from basic raw, steamed, broiled, grilled, or blackened fish to some Bahamian and New Orleans–style interpretations. Other seafood houses dress up their tables in linens and their fish in creative haute-cuisine styles, such as **Pierre's** (✉ *MM 81.5 BS, Islamorada* ☎ *305/664–3225*) hogfish *meunière* or sashimi of yellowfin tuna at **Barracuda Grill** (✉ *4290 Overseas Hwy., Marathon* ☎ *305/743–3314*). And if you're looking for that seafood breakfast Keys-style, try the "grits and grunts"—fried fish and grits—at **The Stuffed Pig** (✉ *3520 Overseas Hwy., Marathon* ☎ *305/743–4059*).

BUILT-IN FISH

You know it's fresh when you see a fish market as soon as you open the door to the restaurant where you're dining. It happens all the time in the Keys. You can even peruse the seafood showcases and pick the fish fillet or lobster tail you want.

Many of the Keys' best restaurants are found in marina complexes, where the commercial fishermen bring their catches straight from the sea. Some, however, such as the seafood restaurants in **Stock Island** (one island north of Key West) and at **Keys Fisheries Market & Marina** (✉ *End of 35th St., Marathon, MM 49 BS* ☎ *305/743–4353 or 866/743–4353*), take some finding.

FLORIDA LOBSTER
What happened to the claws? Stop looking for them: Florida spiny lobsters don't have 'em, never did. The sweet tail meat, however, makes up for the loss. Commercial and sports divers harvest these glorious crustaceans from late July through March. Check with local dive shops on restrictions, then get ready for a fresh feast. Restaurants serve them broiled with drawn butter or in creative dishes such as lobster Benedict, lobster sushi rolls, lobster Reuben, and lobster tacos.

CONCH
One of the tastiest legacies of the Keys' Bahamian heritage, conch shows up on nearly every restaurant menu. It's so prevalent in local diets, that natives refer to themselves as Conchs. Conch fritter is the most popular culinary manifestation, followed by cracked (pounded, breaded, and fried) conch, and conch salad, a ceviche-style refresher. Since the harvesting of queen conch is now illegal, most of the islands' conch come from the Bahamas.

STONE CRAB
In season October 15 through May 15, it gets its name from its rock-hard shell. Most fishermen take only one of its claws, which it can regenerate in a sustainable manner. Connoisseurs prefer it chilled with tangy mustard sauce. Some restaurants give you a choice of hot claws and drawn butter, but this means the meat will be cooked twice, because it's usually boiled or steamed quickly after taken from its crab trap.

YELLOWTAIL SNAPPER
The preferred species of snappers, it is more plentiful in the Keys than any other Florida waters. As pretty as it is tasty, it's a favorite of divers and snorkelers. Mild, sweet, and delicate, its meat lends itself to any number of preparations. It is available pretty much year-round, and many restaurants will give you a choice of broiled, baked, fried, or blackened. Chefs top it with everything from key lime beurre blanc to mango chutney. **Ballyhoo's** in Key Largo (✉ *MM 97.8, In the median* ☎ *305/852–0822*) serves it seven different ways.

GROUPER
Once central to Florida's trademark seafood dish—fried grouper sandwich—its populations have been overfished in recent years, meaning that the state has exerted more control over bag regulations and occasionally closes grouper fishing on a temporary basis. Some restaurants have gone anti-grouper to try to bring back the abundance, but most grab it when they can. Black grouper is the most highly prized of the several varieties.

(left) conch fritters; (above) stone crabs

beurre blanc sauce. Desserts and breads are baked on the premises; the banana bread and lobster Benedict with key lime hollandaise are hits during "breakfast with the roosters." Breakfast is the signature meal here. ✉ *729 Thomas St.* ☎ *305/296–8666* 🌐 *www.blueheavenkw.com* *Reservations not accepted* 💳 *AE, D, MC, V* ⊗ *Closed after Labor Day for 6 weeks.*

¢–$ SEAFOOD ✕ **B.O.'s Fish Wagon.** What started out as a fish house on wheels appears to have broken down on the corner of Caroline and William Streets and is today the cornerstone for one of Key West's junkyard-chic dining institutions. Step up to the wood-plank counter window and order the specialty: a grouper sandwich fried or grilled and topped with key lime sauce. Other choices include fish nuts (don't be scared, they're just fried nuggets), hot dogs, and shrimp or soft-shell-crab sandwich. Talk sass with your host and find a picnic table or take a seat at the plank. Grab some paper towels off one of the rolls hanging around and busy yourself reading graffiti, license plates, and irreverent signs. It's a must-do Key West experience. ✉ *801 Caroline St.* ☎ *305/294–9272* 💳 *No credit cards.*

$ VEGETARIAN ✕ **The Café, A Mostly Vegetarian Place.** You don't have to be a vegetarian to love this new-age café decorated with bright artwork and a corrugated tin–fronted counter. Local favorites include homemade soup, veggie burgers (order them with a side of sweet potato fries), grilled portobello mushroom salad, seafood, vegan specialties, and grilled Gorgonzola pizza. For bigger appetites there are offerings like the Szechuan-style vegetable stir-fry. ✉ *509 Southard St.* ☎ *305/296–5515* 💳 *MC, V.*

$$$ CONTINENTAL Fodor's Choice ★ ✕ **Café Marquesa.** Chef Susan Ferry presents seven or more inspired entrées on her changing menu each night; delicious dishes can include yellowtail snapper with pear, ricotta pasta purses with caponata, and red pepper coulis; and Australian rack of lamb crusted with goat cheese and a port-cranberry sauce. End your meal on a sweet note with key lime napoleon with tropical fruits and berries. There's also a fine selection of wines and custom martinis such as the key limetini and the Irish martini. Adjoining the intimate Marquesa Hotel, the dining room is equally relaxed and elegant. ✉ *600 Fleming St.* ☎ *305/292–1244* 🌐 *www.marquesa.com* 💳 *AE, DC, MC, V* ⊗ *No lunch.*

$$$ FRENCH ★ ✕ **Café Solé.** Welcome to the "home of the hog snapper," a deliciously roasted local fish seasoned with a red-pepper-custard sauce. This little piece of France is concealed behind a high wall and a gate in a residential neighborhood. Inside, chef John Correa marries his French training with local ingredients, creating delicious takes on classics, including portobello mushroom soup, snapper with mango salsa, and some of the best bouillabaisse that you'll find outside of Marseilles. From the land, there is filet mignon with a wild-mushroom demi-glace. If you can't decide, a three-course tasting dinner costs $27. Creative salads, carpaccios, and sandwiches star on the lunch menu. ✉ *1029 Southard St.* ☎ *305/294–0230* 🌐 *www.cafesole.com* 💳 *AE, D, DC, MC, V.*

$$ CARIBBEAN ✕ **El Meson de Pepe.** If you want to get a taste of the island's Cuban heritage, this is the place. Perfect for after Mallory Square sunset, you can dine alfresco or in the dining room on refined versions of Cuban classics. Begin with a megasized mojito while you enjoy the basket of

bread and savory sauces. The expansive menu offers *tostones rellenos* (green plantains with different traditional fillings), ceviche (raw fish "cooked" in lemon juice), and more. Choose from Cuban specialties such as roasted pork in a cumin mojo sauce and *ropa vieja* (shredded beef stew). At lunch, the local Cuban population and cruise-ship passengers enjoy Cuban sandwiches and smaller versions of dinner's most popular entrées. A salsa band performs outside at the bar during sunset celebration. ✉ *Mallory Sq., 410 Wall St.* ☎ *305/295–2620* 🌐 *www.elmesondepepe.com* ▭ *AE, D, MC, V.*

$ CARIBBEAN ✕ **El Siboney.** Dining at this family-style restaurant is like going to Mom's for Sunday dinner—if your mother is Cuban. The dining room is noisy, and the food is traditional *cubano*. There are well-seasoned black beans, a memorable paella, traditional ropa vieja (shredded beef and roast pork), and local seafood served grilled, stuffed, and breaded. Dishes come with Cuban bread, salad or plantains, and rice or fries. To make a good thing even better, the prices are very reasonable. ✉ *900 Catherine St.* ☎ *305/296–4184* 🌐 *www.elsiboneyrestaurant.com* ▭ *AE, DC, MC, V.*

$ IRISH ✕ **Finnegan's Wake Irish Pub and Eatery.** "Come for the beer. Stay for the food. Leave with the staff," is the slogan of this popular pub. The pictures of Beckett, Shaw, Yeats, and Wilde on the walls and the creaky wood floors underfoot exude Irish country warmth. The certified Angus beef is a bit pricey ($30 for an 18-ounce rib eye), but most of the other dishes are bargains. Traditional fare includes bangers and mash, chicken potpie, and colcannon—rich mashed potatoes with scallions, sauerkraut, and melted white cheddar cheese. Bread pudding soaked with a honey-whiskey sauce is a true treat. Live music on weekends and daily happy hours from 4 to 7 and midnight to 2 featuring nearly 30 beers on tap make it popular with the spring break and sometimes noisy drinking crowd. ✉ *320 Grinnell St.* ☎ *305/293–0222* 🌐 *www.keywestirish.com* ▭ *AE, D, MC, V.*

$–$$ SEAFOOD ✕ **Half Shell Raw Bar.** Smack-dab on the docks, this legendary institution gets its name from the oysters, clams, and peel-and-eat shrimp that are a departure point for its seafood-based diet. It's not clever recipes or fine dining (or even air-conditioning) that packs 'em in; it's fried fish, po'boy sandwiches, and seafood combos. For a break from the deep fryer, try the fresh and light conch ceviche "cooked" with lime juice. The potato salad is flavored with dill, and the "Pama Rita" is a new twist in Margaritaville. ✉ *Lands End Village at Historic Seaport, 231 Margaret St.* ☎ *305/294–7496* 🌐 *www.halfshellrawbar.com* ▭ *AE, MC, V.*

¢ AMERICAN ✕ **Lobo's Mixed Grill.** White Castle attained national cult status with its burgers; the equivalent among Key West denizens is Lobo's belly buster. The 8-ounce, charcoal-grilled chunk of ground chuck is thick and juicy and served with lettuce, tomato, and pickle on a toasted bun. The 30 wraps (rib eye, oyster, grouper, and others) are equally popular. The menu includes salads and quesadillas, as well as a fried shrimp and oyster combo. Beer and wine are served. This courtyard food stand closes at 6, so eat early. Most of Lobo's business is takeout (it has a half-dozen outdoor picnic tables), and it offers free delivery within Old Town. ✉ *5 Key Lime Sq., east of intersection of Southard and Duval Sts.* ☎ *305/296–5303* 🌐 *www.loboskeywest.com* ▭ *No credit cards* ⏲ *Closed Sun. Apr.–early Dec.*

> **WORD OF MOUTH**
>
> "My favorite fine dining restaurant is Louie's Backyard, though we always go for lunch rather than dinner. The food is just as good, the view is wonderful during the day, and the prices are reasonable." —SusanCS

$$$$ ECLECTIC ★ ✕ **Louie's Backyard.** Feast your eyes on a steal-your-breath-away view and beautifully presented dishes prepared by executive chef Doug Shook. Once you get over sticker shock on the seasonally changing menu (appetizers cost around $9–$18; entrées hover around the $35 mark), settle in on the outside deck and enjoy dishes like shrimp with bacon and stone-ground grits, pistachio-crusted king salmon and potato cake with horseradish cream, and chicken breast with sour-orange mustard and farro. Louie's key lime pie has a gingersnap crust and is served with a berry sauce. If you come for lunch, the menu is less expensive but the view is just as fantastic. For night owls, the tin-roofed Afterdeck Bar serves cocktails on the water until the wee hours. ✉ *700 Waddell Ave.* ☎ *305/294–1061* 🌐 *www.louiesbackyard.com* ✍ *Reservations essential* ▭ *MC, V* ⏲ *Closed Labor Day to mid-Sept.*

$–$$ ITALIAN ★ ✕ **Mangia Mangia.** This longtime favorite serves large portions of homemade pastas that can be matched with any of the homemade sauces. Tables are arranged in a brick garden hung with twinkling lights and in a nicely dressed-up dining room in an old house. Everything out of the open kitchen is outstanding, including the *bollito misto di mare* (fresh seafood sautéed with garlic, shallots, white wine, and pasta) or the memorable spaghettini "schmappellini," homemade pasta with asparagus, tomatoes, pine nuts, and Parmesan. The wine list—with more than 350 offerings—includes old and rare vintages, and also has a good by-the-glass selection. ✉ *900 Southard St.* ☎ *305/294–2469* 🌐 *www.mangia-mangia.com* ▭ *AE, D, MC, V* ⏲ *No lunch.*

$$$ AMERICAN ✕ **Michaels Restaurant.** White tablecloths, subdued lighting, and romantic music give Michaels the feel of an urban eatery. Garden seating reminds you that you are in the Keys. Chef-owner Michael Wilson flies in prime rib, cowboy steaks, and rib eyes from Allen Brothers in Chicago, which has supplied top-ranked steak houses for more than a century. Also on the menu is a melt-in-your-mouth grouper stuffed with jumbo lump crab, veal saltimbocca, and a variety of made-to-order fondue dishes (try the pesto pot, spiked with hot pepper and basil). The Hemingway (mojito-style) and the Third Degree (raspberry vodka and white crème de cacao) top the cocktail menu. ✉ *532 Margaret St.* ☎ *305/295–1300* 🌐 *www.michaelskeywest.com* ▭ *AE, MC, V* ⏲ *No lunch.*

$$$ ECLECTIC ✕ **Nine One Five.** Twinkling lights draped along the lower- and upper-level outdoor porches of a 100-year-old Victorian mansion set an elegant—though unstuffy—stage at this very cool tapas-style eatery. If you like to sample and sip, you'll appreciate the variety of smaller plate selections and wines by the glass. Taster-portioned tapas include olives, cheese, shrimp, and pâté, or try a combination with the tapas platter or the signature "tuna dome" with fresh crab, lemon-miso dressing, and an ahi tuna–sashimi wrapping. There are also larger plates if you're craving something like seafood soup or steak au poivre frites.

Dine outdoors and people-watch along upper Duval, or sit at a table inside while listening to light jazz. ✉ *915 Duval St.* ☎ *305/296–0669* 🌐 *www.915duval.com* 💳 *AE, MC, V* ⊙ *No lunch.*

$$$$ CONTINENTAL ★ ✕ **Pisces.** In a circa-1892 former store and home, chef William Arnel and staff create a contemporary setting with a stylish granite bar, Andy Warhol originals, and glass oil lamps. On the menu of this reinvented restaurant, once known as Café des Artistes, favorites include "lobster tango mango," flambéed in cognac and served with saffron butter sauce and sliced mangoes. Other dishes include Pisces Aphrodite (seafood in puff pastry), veal chops with wild mushrooms, and champagne-braised black grouper. ✉ *1007 Simonton St.* ☎ *305/294–7100* 🌐 *www.pisceskeywest.com* 💳 *AE, MC, V* ⊙ *No lunch.*

$$ ITALIAN ★ ✕ **Salute Ristorante at the Beach.** This colorful restaurant sits on Higgs Beach, giving it one of the island's best lunch views—and a bit of sand and salt spray on a windy day. Owners of the popular Blue Heaven restaurant recently took it over and have designed an intriguing dinner menu that includes linguine with mussels, vegetable or three-meat lasagna, and white bean soup with grilled bread. At lunch there are calamari marinara, antipasti sandwich, and pasta primavera, as well as a fresh-fish sandwich. New this year, breakfast is also served. ✉ *1000 Atlantic Blvd., Higgs Beach* ☎ *305/292–1117* 💳 *AE, D, MC, V.*

$$ SEAFOOD ★ ✕ **Seven Fish.** A local hot spot, this off-the-beaten track eatery is good for an eclectic mix of dishes like tropical shrimp salsa, wild-mushroom quesadilla, seafood marinara, and sometimes even an old-fashioned meat loaf with real mashed potatoes. Those in the know arrive for dinner early to snag one of the 12 or so tables clustered in the bare-bones dining room. ✉ *632 Olivia St.* ☎ *305/296–2777* 🌐 *www.7fish.com* 💳 *AE, D, MC, V* ⊙ *Closed Tues. No lunch.*

$$ SEAFOOD ✕ **Turtle Kraals.** Named for the kraals, or corrals, where sea turtles were once kept until they went to the cannery, this place calls to mind the island's history. The menu offers an assortment of marine cuisine that includes seafood enchiladas, mesquite grilled lobster and oyster combo, and mango crab cakes. The newest addition, a slow-cook wood smoker, results in wonderfully tender ribs, brisket, and North Carolina–style pork with peppered vinegar sauce topped with coleslaw. Breakfast offers some interesting and quite tasty options like barbecued hash and eggs or huevos rancheros. The open restaurant overlooks the marina at the Historic Seaport. ✉ *231 Margaret St.* ☎ *305/294–2640* 🌐 *www.turtlekraals.com* 💳 *AE, MC, V.*

WHERE TO STAY

Historic cottages, restored century-old Conch houses, and large resorts are among the offerings in Key West, the majority charging from $100 to $300 a night. In high season, December through March, you'll be hard pressed to find a decent room for less than $200, and most places raise prices considerably during holidays. Many guesthouses and inns do not welcome children under 16, and most do not permit smoking indoors; rates often include an expanded Continental breakfast and afternoon wine or snack.

$$$$ ★ **Ambrosia Key West.** If you desire personal attention, a casual atmosphere, and a dollop of style, stay at these twin inns spread out on nearly 2 acres. Ambrosia is more intimate, with themed rooms such as the Treetop, Sailfish Suites, and Havana Cabana. Ambrosia Too is a delightful art-filled hideaway. Rooms and suites have original work by local artists, wicker or wood furniture, and spacious bathrooms. Each has a private entrance and deck, patio, or porch. Poolside Continental breakfast is included, and children are welcome. **Pros:** spacious rooms; poolside breakfast; friendly staff. **Cons:** on-street parking can be tough to come by; a little too spread out. ✉ *615, 618, 622 Fleming St.* ☎ *305/296–9838 or 800/535–9838* 🌐 *www.ambrosiakeywest.com* *22 rooms, 3 town houses, 1 cottage, 6 suites* *In-room: kitchen (some), refrigerator, Wi-Fi. In-hotel: pools, bicycles, Wi-Fi hotspot, parking (free), some pets allowed* *AE, D, MC, V* *BP.*

$$–$$$ **Angelina Guest House.** The high rollers and ladies of the night were chased away long ago, but this charming guesthouse revels in its past as a gambling hall and bordello. In the heart of Old Town Key West, it's a home away from home that offers simple, clean, attractively priced accommodations. Accommodations range from small rooms sharing a bath to spacious rooms with king beds and sleeper sofas. Built in the 1920s, this yellow-and-white clapboard building has 2nd-floor porches, gabled roofs, and a white picket fence. The current owners prettied the rooms with flower-print curtains and linens and added homemade cinnamon rolls, which receive rave reviews in the guest book, to the breakfast bar. A lagoon-style pool, fountain, and old-brick walkways accent a lovely garden. **Pros:** good value; nice garden; friendly staff. **Cons:** thin walls; basic rooms; shared balcony. ✉ *302 Angela St.* ☎ *305/294–4480 or 888/303–4480* 🌐 *www.angelinaguesthouse.com* *13 rooms* *In-room: no phone, refrigerator (some), no TV, Wi-Fi. In-hotel: pool, no kids under 18, Wi-Fi hotspot* *D, MC, V* *CP.*

$$$ **Azul Key West.** The ultramodern—nearly minimalistic—redo of this classic circa-1903 Queen Anne mansion is a break from the sensory overload of Key West's other abundant Victorian guesthouses. The adults-only boutique hotel, 3½ blocks from Duval Street, combines original trim, high ceilings, and shiny wood floors with sleek furnishings, including a curved frosted-glass-and-chrome check-in desk, leather loungers, and a state-of-the-art sound system. Spacious, serene rooms, some with private verandas, have leather headboards, flat-screen TVs, and remote-controlled fans and lights. **Pros:** lovely building; marble-floored baths; luxurious linens. **Cons:** on a busy street. ✉ *907 Truman Ave.* ☎ *305/296–5152 or 888/253–2985* 🌐 *www.azulhotels.us* *10 rooms, 1 suite* *In-room: Wi-Fi. In-hotel: pool, Wi-Fi hotspot, no kids under 21* *AE, D, MC, V* *CP.*

$$$$ ★ **Casa Marina Resort & Beach Club.** At any moment, you expect the landed gentry to walk across the oceanfront lawn, just as they did when this 13-acre resort was built back in the 1920s. Set on a private, 1,100-foot rocky beach, it has the same richly appointed lobby with beamed ceilings, polished pine floor, and original art. Guest rooms are stylishly decorated with Italian tiled floors, sleeper sofas, and teak captain's chairs that add a lot of warmth. Fluffy bathrobes, espresso

machines, iHome clock radios, and luxurious designer toiletries make it feel like a boutique hotel. Two-bedroom loft suites with balconies face the ocean. The main building's rooms open onto large outdoor living rooms, and the pools have a nice view of the Atlantic. Guests also have privileges at its nearby sister property, the Reach Resort. **Pros:** nice beach; historic setting; away from the crowds. **Cons:** long walk to Old Town. ✉ *1500 Reynolds St.* ☎ *305/296–3535 or 866/203–6392* 🌐 *www.casamarinaresort.com* *239 rooms, 72 suites* *In-room: safe, refrigerator, Internet, Wi-Fi. In-hotel: restaurant, room service, bars, tennis courts, pools, gym, spa, beachfront, diving, water sports, bicycles, children's programs (ages 4–12), laundry service, some pets allowed* *AE, D, DC, MC, V.*

14

$$$ **Courtney's Place.** If you like kids, cats, and dogs, you'll feel right at home in this collection of accommodations ranging from cigar-maker cottages to shotgun houses. The interiors are equally varied in coloring and furnishings, but all rooms have at least a refrigerator, microwave, and coffeepot, if not a full kitchen. The family-owned property is tucked into a residential neighborhood, though within easy walking distance of Duval Street. All rooms are not created equal here; tiny loft rooms are tucked into attic space. **Pros:** near Duval Street; fairly priced. **Cons:** small parking lot; small pool. ✉ *720 Whitemarsh La., off Petronia St.* ☎ *305/294–3480 or 800/869–4639* 🌐 *www.courtneysplacekeywest.com* *6 rooms, 2 suites, 2 efficiencies, 8 cottages* *In-room: kitchen (some), refrigerator. In-hotel: pool, bicycles, parking (free), some pets allowed.* *AE, D, MC, V* *CP.*

$$$–$$$$ ★ **Eden House.** From the vintage metal rockers on the street-side porch to the old neon hotel sign in the lobby, this 1920s rambling Key West mainstay hotel is high on character, low on gloss. You'll get a taste of authentic Old Key West, without sacrificing convenience or comfort. Rooms come in all shapes and sizes, from shared-bath basic to large apartments with full kitchens and private decks or porches. The spacious outdoor area is shaded by towering palms. Grab a book and plop in a hammock in the outdoor library, tucked into a sun-dappled corner with a gurgling waterfall and potted bonsai. **Pros:** sunny garden; hot tub is actually hot; daily happy hour around the pool. **Cons:** cutesy signage is overdone; pricey. ✉ *1015 Fleming St.* ☎ *305/296–6868 or 800/533–5397* 🌐 *www.edenhouse.com* *36 rooms, 8 suites.* *In-room: kitchen (some), refrigerator (some), Wi-Fi. In-hotel: restaurant, pool, bicycles, Internet terminal, parking (free), Wi-Fi hotspot* *MC, V.*

$$$$ **Fodor's Choice** ★ **The Gardens Hotel.** Built in 1875, this gloriously shaded property covers a third of a city block in Old Town. Peggy Mills, who bought it as a private estate in 1931, coiffed it with orchids, ponytail palms, and black bamboo. She added walks, fountains, and earthen pots imported from Cuba. After her death in 1971, the property was turned into a romantic inn that offers several types of accommodations, from standard rooms with garden and courtyard views to a two-bedroom carriage house suite. Decorated with Bahamian plantation-style furnishings, the quiet and elegant rooms are a luxurious tropical retreat. Most have private verandas. **Pros:** luxurious bathrooms; secluded garden seating; free phone calls. **Cons:** hard to get reservations; expensive. ✉ *526 Angela*

St. ☎ *305/294–2661 or 800/526–2664* 🌐 *www.gardenshotel.com* ➪ *17 rooms* 🛎 *In-room: safe, refrigerator, Wi-Fi. In-hotel: bar, pool, parking (free), no kids under 16, Wi-Fi hotspot* ▭ *AE, D, MC, V* 🍴 *CP.*

$$$$ **Hyatt Key West Resort and Spa.** With its own man-made beach, the Hyatt Key West is one of few resorts where you can dig your toes in the sand, then walk a short distance away to the streets of Old Town. A top-to-bottom renovation in 2007 transformed this hotel into a tropical escape with plenty of panache. It offers a wide range of water sports, two good restaurants, and fitness amenities—all with an eye toward keeping green. Rooms are bright and airy, with walk-in showers with rain showerheads, and balconies that overlook the gulf. It pampers you with little extras such as down comforters and fluffy robes. **Pros:** a little bit away from the bustle of Old Town; plenty of activities. **Cons:** beach is small; cramped-feeling property; chain-hotel feel. ✉ *601 Front St.* ☎ *305/809–1234* 🌐 *www.keywest.hyatt.com* ➪ *118 rooms* 🛎 *In-room: safe, Internet, Wi-Fi. In-hotel: 2 restaurants, room service, bars, pool, gym, spa, beachfront, diving, water sports, laundry service, parking (paid), no-smoking rooms* ▭ *AE, D, DC, MC, V.*

$$$–$$$$ **Key Lime Inn.** This 1854 Grand Bahama–style house on the National Register of Historic Places succeeds by offering amiable service, a great location, and simple rooms with natural-wood furnishings. The cluster of pastel-painted cottages, surrounded by white picket fences, has a residential feel, a bit like a beach colony without the beach, or the backlot of a movie set. The Garden Cottages have one room; a few include a porch or balcony. Some rooms in the historic Maloney House have a porch or patio. **Pros:** free parking; some rooms have private outdoor spaces. **Cons:** standard rooms are pricey; pool faces a busy street; mulch-covered paths. ✉ *725 Truman Ave.* ☎ *305/294–5229 or 800/549–4430* 🌐 *www.keylimeinn.com* ➪ *37 rooms* 🛎 *In-room: safe, refrigerator (some), Internet, Wi-Fi. In-hotel: pool, Wi-Fi hotspot, parking (free)* ▭ *AE, D, MC, V* 🍴 *CP.*

$$–$$$ ★ **Key West Bed and Breakfast/The Popular House.** Local art—large, splashy canvases and a Gauguinesque mural—decorates the walls, while handmade textiles (owner Jody Carlson is a talented weaver) drape chairs, couches, and beds at this historic home. There are accommodations for every budget, but the owners reason that budget travelers deserve as pleasant an experience (and lavish a tropical Continental breakfast) as their well-heeled counterparts. Less expensive rooms burst with bright colors (hand-painted dressers add a whimsical flourish) and balconies on the 2nd-floor rooms overlook the gardens. Spacious, and more expensive, 3rd-floor rooms are decorated with a paler palette and original furniture. **Pros:** lots of art; tiled outdoor shower; hot tub and sauna area is a welcome hangout. **Cons:** some rooms are small. ✉ *415 William St.* ☎ *305/296–7274 or 800/438–6155* 🌐 *www.keywestbandb.com* ➪ *8 rooms, 6 with bath* 🛎 *In-room: no phone, no TV, Wi-Fi (some). In-hotel: pool, bicycles, Wi-Fi hotspot, no kids under 18, no-smoking rooms* ▭ *AE, D, DC, MC, V* 🍴 *CP.*

$$$$ Fodor's Choice ★ **Marquesa Hotel.** In a town that prides itself on its laid-back luxury, this complex of four restored 1884 houses stands out. Guests—typically shoeless in Marquesa robes—relax among two richly landscaped

pools, rock waterfalls, and peaceful gardens. Elegant rooms surround a courtyard and have antique and reproduction furnishings, earthy tones with black-and-white accents, marble baths, and outdoor sitting areas. Six off-site cottages are also for rent. The lobby resembles a Victorian parlor, with Audubon prints, vases overflowing with flowers, and photos of early Key West. The clientele is mature, well traveled, and affluent, mostly straight, but the hotel is gay-friendly. **Pros:** elegant setting; romantic atmosphere; turndown service. **Cons:** street-facing rooms can be noisy; expensive rates. ✉ *600 Fleming St.* ☎ *305/292–1919 or 800/869–4631* 🌐 *www.marquesa.com* *27 rooms* *In-room: safe, refrigerator, DVD, Wi-Fi. In-hotel: restaurant, room service, pools, laundry service, Internet terminal, Wi-Fi hotspot, parking (free), no kids under 14* ▭ *AE, DC, MC, V.*

$$$–$$$$ **Marriott Key West Beachside Hotel.** This new hotel, branded a Marriott in 2008, vies for convention business with the biggest ballroom in Key West. It also appeals to families with its spacious condo units decorated with impeccable good taste. Designer furnishings reflect the resort's waterfront location. Frette linens on the beds, real china in the kitchens, and marble hot tubs add touches of luxury. Rooms have spiral staircases down to the gardens and up to the rooftop sundecks. Families enjoy the beach and pool area. Complimentary shuttles take guests to Old Town and the airport. **Pros:** private beach; poolside cabanas. **Cons:** small beach; can't walk to Old Town; cookie-cutter facade. ✉ *3841 N. Roosevelt Blvd., New Town* ☎ *305/296–8100 or 800/546–0885* 🌐 *www.beachsidekeywest.com* *93 rooms, 80 1-bedroom suites, 15 2-bedroom suites, 21 3-bedroom suites* *In-room: kitchen (some), Internet. In-hotel: 2 restaurants, room service, bars, pool, gym, Wi-Fi hotspot, parking (paid)* ▭ *AE, D, DC, MC, V.*

$$$ ★ **Merlin Guesthouse.** Key West guesthouses don't usually welcome families, but this laid-back jumble of rooms and suites is an exception. If you can live with a few flaws, you'll grab a bargain. Accommodations in the 1930s Simonton House, with four-poster beds, are most suitable for couples. The one- and two-bedroom suites are popular with families. Bright, roomy cottages are perfect if you want a bit more privacy. Get a room in the back if you are bothered by noise. The leafy courtyard and pool area are where guests hang out day and night. **Pros:** good location near Duval Street; good rates. **Cons:** neighbor noise; common areas are dated; street parking. ✉ *811 Simonton St.* ☎ *305/296–3336 or 800/642–4753* 🌐 *www.merlinguesthouse.com* *10 rooms, 6 suites, 4 cottages* *In-room: no phone, safe, kitchen (some), refrigerator (some). In-hotel: pool, Internet terminal, Wi-Fi hotspot* ▭ *AE, D, MC, V* *CP.*

$$$–$$$$ ★ **Mermaid & the Alligator.** An enchanting combination of flora and fauna makes this 1904 Victorian house a welcoming retreat. The property is bathed in palms, banyans, birds of paradise, and poincianas, with cages of colorful, live parrots and swarms of butterflies adding tropical punch. Rooms are Caribbean colonial–inspired, with wood-slat floors, elegant trim, and French doors. The color scheme—key lime, cantaloupe, and other rich colors—couldn't be more evocative of the Keys. Some downstairs rooms open onto the deck, pool, and gardens

designed by one of the resident owners, a landscape designer. Upstairs rooms overlook the gardens. A full breakfast is served poolside, and guests can take advantage of complimentary bottled waters, soda, and evening wine. **Pros:** hot plunge pool; massage pavilion; island-getaway feel. **Cons:** minimum stay required (length depends on season); dark public areas; plastic lawn chairs. ✉ *729 Truman Ave.* ☎ *305/294–1894 or 800/773–1894* 🌐 *www.kwmermaid.com* *9 rooms* *In-room: no phone, no TV, Wi-Fi. In-hotel: pool, Internet terminal, no kids under 16* *AE, D, MC, V* *BP.*

$$$$ ★ **Ocean Key Resort & Spa.** A pool and lively open-air bar and restaurant sit on Sunset Pier, a popular place to watch the sun sink into the horizon. Toast the day's end from private balconies that extend from spacious rooms that are both stylish and homey. High ceilings, hand-painted furnishings, sleigh beds, wooden chests, and lavish whirlpool tubs create a personally designed look. This is a full-service resort, with excellent amenities such as a Thai-inspired spa—small and without locker rooms, but each treatment room comes with a Japanese-style tub on the balcony—and a (new in 2009) pool bar. Its 2nd-floor elegant restaurant is cleverly named Hot Tin Roof, a reference to its construction as well as to Tennessee Williams' Key West connection. **Pros:** well-trained staff; lively pool scene; best spa on the island. **Cons:** confusing layout; too bustling for some. ✉ *Zero Duval St.* ☎ *305/296–7701 or 800/328–9815* 🌐 *www.oceankey.com* *64 rooms, 36 suites* *In-room: kitchen (some), refrigerator, Wi-Fi In-hotel: 2 restaurants, room service, bars, pool, spa, diving, water sports, bicycles, laundry service, parking (paid), Wi-Fi hotspot* *AE, D, DC, MC, V.*

$$$$ ★ **Pier House Resort and Caribbean Spa.** The location—on a quiet stretch of beach at the foot of Duval—is ideal as a buffer from and gateway to the action. Its sprawling complex of weathered gray buildings includes an original Conch house. The courtyard is riotous with tall coconut palms and hibiscus blossoms, and rooms are cozy and colorful, with a water, pool, or garden view. Six top-of-the-line suites extend over the water with sunset views. Rooms nearest the public areas can be noisy. **Pros:** beautiful beach; good location; nice spa. **Cons:** lots of conventions; cookie-cutter feel; poolside rooms are small. ✉ *1 Duval St.* ☎ *305/296–4600 or 800/327–8340* 🌐 *www.pierhouse.com* *113 rooms, 29 suites* *In-room: refrigerator, Wi-Fi. In-hotel: 2 restaurants, room service, bars, pool, gym, spa, beachfront, bicycles, laundry service, Wi-Fi hotspot* *AE, D, DC, MC, V.*

$$$$ ★ **The Reach Resort.** Embracing Key West's only natural beach, this recently reinvented and reopened full-service resort has its roots in the 1980s when locals rallied against the loss of the topless beach it displaced. As a tip of the hat to the city's bohemian spirit, the resort devotes a portion to topless sunbathing. And then there's the Strip House, its naughty little steak house with nude images and a bordello feel. Top luxury prevails these days from turndown service and plushly lined seersucker robes in the room to life-sized chess and boccie in the courtyard and a pool concierge delivering popsicles and drinks du jour. In addition to its own facilities, guests are privy to the spa, tennis, and other amenities at sister resort Casa Marina nearby. Sleek

Sunset Key cottages are right on the water's edge, far away from the action of Old Town.

rooms with various layouts contain all the conveniences, including iPod docks, espresso machines, and wet bars. The private pier-gazebo makes a perfect spot for weddings and watching the sun rise. **Pros:** removed from Duval hubbub; great sunrise views; pullout sofas in most rooms. **Cons:** $20 per day per room resort fee; expensive. ✉ *1435 Simonton St.* ☎ *305/296–5000 or 888/318–4316* 🌐 *www.reachresort.com* *150 rooms, 76 suites* *In-room: safe, refrigerator, Wi-Fi. In-hotel: restaurant, room service, bars, pools, gym, beachfront, water sports, laundry service, Internet terminal, Wi-Fi hotspot, parking (paid), some pets allowed* *AE, D, DC, MC, V.*

$$$$ ★ **Simonton Court.** A small world all of its own, this lodging makes you feel deliciously sequestered from Key West's crasser side, but close enough to get there on foot. The "basic" rooms are in an old cigar factory, each with its own unique decor. There's also a restored shotgun house and cottages. But top-of-the-line units occupy a Victorian home and the town house facing the property's pool and brick-paved breakfast courtyard. **Pros:** lots of privacy; well-appointed accommodations; friendly staff. **Cons:** minimum stays required in high season. ✉ *320 Simonton St.* ☎ *305/294–6386 or 800/944–2687* 🌐 *www.simontoncourt.com* *17 rooms, 6 suites, 6 cottages* *In-room: safe, kitchen (some), refrigerator, Wi-Fi. In-hotel: pools, no kids under 18, Wi-Fi hotspot* *D, DC, MC, V* *CP.*

$$$–$$$$ **Southernmost Hotel.** This hotel's location on the quiet end of Duval means you don't have to deal with the hustle and bustle of downtown unless you want to—it's within a 20-minute walk (but around sunset, this end of town gets its share of car and foot traffic). Cookie-cutter rooms are spacious, bright, and airy, and have cottage-style furnishings

and the required tropical color schemes. Grab a cold drink from the Tiki Hut bar and join the crowd around the pool, or venture across the street to the beach, where there's a restaurant and a beach resort. **Pros:** pool attracts a lively crowd; access to nearby properties; free parking. **Cons:** public beach is small; can get crowded around the pool and public areas. ✉ *1319 Duval St.* ☎ *305/296–6577 or 800/354–4455* 🌐 *www.southernmostresorts.com* *127 rooms* *In-room: safe, refrigerator, Internet, Wi-Fi. In-hotel:, pool, laundry facilities, Wi-Fi hotspot* ▭ *AE, D, DC, MC, V.*

$$$ **Speakeasy Inn.** During Prohibition, Raul Vasquez made this place popular by smuggling in liquor from Cuba. Today the booze is legal, and there's a daily happy hour so you can fully appreciate it. The Speakeasy Inn is still well known, only now its reputation is for having reasonably priced rooms within walking distance of the beach. Accommodations have bright-white walls offset by bursts of color in rugs, pillows, and seat cushions. Queen-size beds and tables are fashioned from salvaged pine. The rooms are basic, but some have nice touches like claw-foot tubs. Room 1A has a deck that's good for people-watching. **Pros:** good location; reasonable rates; high-quality cigar store attached. **Cons:** no pool; basic decor. ✉ *1117 Duval St.* ☎ *305/296–2680 or 800/217–4884* 🌐 *www.speakeasyinn.com* *2 suites, 4 studios* *In-room: refrigerator, Wi-Fi. In-hotel: Internet terminal Wi-Fi hotspot* ▭ *AE, D, MC, V* *CP.*

$$$$ Fodor's Choice ★ **Sunset Key.** This private island retreat feels completely cut off from the world, yet you're just minutes away from the action. Board a 10-minute launch to 27-acre Sunset Key, where you'll find sandy beaches, swaying palms, flowering gardens, and a delicious sense of privacy. A favorite of yacht owners, the hotel has a 40-slip marina. The comforts are first-class at the cluster of one-, two-, and three-bedroom cottages at the water's edge. Baked goods, freshly squeezed juice, and a newspaper are delivered each morning. Each of the accommodations has a kitchen, but you can use the grocery shopping service or hire a private chef (both for a fee, of course). You can use all the facilities at the Westin Key West Resort in Old Town, but be warned: you may never want to leave Sunset Key and its great restaurants, pretty pool, and very civilized beach complete with attendants and cabanas. **Pros:** peace and quiet; roomy verandas; free 24-hour shuttle. **Cons:** luxury doesn't come cheap. ✉ *245 Front St.* ☎ *305/292–5300 or 888/477–7786* 🌐 *www.sunsetkeyisland.com* *37 cottages* *In-room: safe, kitchen, DVD, Internet, Wi-Fi. In-hotel: restaurant, room service, bars, tennis courts, pool, gym, beachfront, laundry facilities, laundry service, Internet terminal, parking (paid), no-smoking rooms* ▭ *AE, D, DC, MC, V* *CP.*

Travel Smart Florida

WORD OF MOUTH

"[T]he trip to the car rental aroas [from Miami International Airport] is somewhat hellish. That will change in the next year as the Miami Intermodal Rental Car Center (http://www.micdot.com/) opens. All the car rental agencies will be housed in one building on the main road with a people mover to and from the airport terminal. By 2012 the Intermodal Center will be a "Grand Central" for all ground transportation with connections to Metrorail, buses, and trains. That is good news for travelers who find it a pain to get in and out of Miami International."

—SoBchBud1

www.fodors.com/community

GETTING HERE AND AROUND

AIR TRAVEL

Flying times to Florida vary based on the city you're flying to, but typical times are 3 hours from New York, 4 hours from Chicago, 2¾ hours from Dallas, 4½–5½ hours from Los Angeles, and 8–8½ hours from London.

AIRPORTS

Both major and regional airports are plentiful in Florida so you can usually pick one quite close to your destination and often choose from a couple of nearby options. If you're destined for the north side of Miami-Dade County (metro Miami), or are renting a car at the airport, consider flying into Fort Lauderdale–Hollywood International; it's much easier to use than Miami International, and often—if not always—cheaper. The airports are only 40 minutes apart by car.

Airport Information **Daytona Beach International Airport (DAB)** (☎ *386/248–8069* 🌐 *www.volusia.org/airport*). **Fort Lauderdale–Hollywood International (FLL)** (☎ *954/359–6100 or 866/435–9355* 🌐 *www.broward.org/airport*). **Jacksonville International Airport (JAI)** (☎ *904/741–4902* 🌐 *www.jaa.aero*). **Miami International Airport (MIA)** (☎ *305/876–7000* 🌐 *www.miami-airport.com*). **Orlando International (MCO)** (☎ *407/825–2001* 🌐 *www.orlandoairports.net*). **Palm Beach International (PBI)** (☎ *561/471–7420* 🌐 *www.pbia.org*). **Northwest Florida Beaches International Airport (ECP)** (☎ *850/763–6751* 🌐 *www.newpcairport.com*). **Sarasota-Bradenton International Airport (SRQ)** (☎ *941/359–5200* 🌐 *www.srq-airport.com*). **Southwest Florida International Airport (FMY)** (☎ *239/590–4800* 🌐 *www.flylcpa.com*). **St. Petersburg–Clearwater International Airport (PIE)** (☎ *727/453–7800* 🌐 *www.fly2pie.com*). **Tampa International (TPA)** (☎ *813/870–8700* 🌐 *www.tampaairport.com*).

GROUND TRANSPORTATION

SuperShuttle has service to and from Miami International and Tampa International airports. Downtown St. Pete to Tampa International Airport is approximately $25; the shuttle will pick you up 2½ hours before your scheduled departure. There is one shared-shuttle service from downtown Tampa to Tampa International Airport, but SuperShuttle also can book you with its car-service operators: Exclusive, which costs $120 from downtown to the airport; or ExecuCar, which runs approximately $65 from downtown to the airport. SuperShuttle will pick you up from a hotel, office, or residence; it's best to make reservations at least 24 hours in advance. Inside the airports there are hubs where you can obtain SuperShuttle tickets to go from the airport to your desired local destination.

Taxis are available at Miami International's arrival zone; flat rates vary by the zone you will be traveling to but run between $22 and $52 in the immediate Miami area—the flat rate to Miami Beach is $32. Yellow Cab taxis from Orlando International to downtown Orlando run approximately $35. Yellow Cab and United Cab have service to and from downtown Tampa and have a flat rate of $25.

FLIGHTS

Major Airlines **American Airlines** (☎ *800/433–7300* 🌐 *www.aa.com*). **Delta Airlines** (☎ *800/221–1212 for U.S. reservations, 800/241–4141 for international reservations* 🌐 *www.delta.com*). **jetBlue** (☎ *800/538–2583* 🌐 *www.jetblue.com*). **Southwest Airlines** (☎ *800/435–9792* 🌐 *www.southwest.com*). **United Airlines** (☎ *800/864–8331 for U.S. reservations, 800/538–2929 for international reservations* 🌐 *www.united.com*). **US Airways** (☎ *800/428–4322 for U.S. and Canada reservations, 800/622–1015 for international reservations* 🌐 *www.usairways.com*).

Car Rental Resources

LOCAL AGENCIES		
Continental Florida Auto Rental	800/327-3791 or 954/764-1125 in Fort Lauderdale	
Sunshine Rent-A-Car	888/786-7446 or 954/467-8100 in Fort Lauderdale	
U-Save Auto Rental/ Specialty Van Rental	888/440-8744 in Clearwater, Orlando, Palm Harbor, Sanford, and Tampa–St. Petersburg	
MAJOR AGENCIES		
Alamo	800/462-5266	www.alamo.com
Avis	800/230-4898	www.avis.com
Budget	800/527-0700	www.budget.com
Hertz	800/654-3131	www.hertz.com
National Car Rental	800/227-7368	www.nationalcar.com

Smaller Airlines AirTran (☎ *800/247-8726* 🌐 *www.airtran.com*) to Miami, Fort Lauderdale, Fort Myers, Jacksonville, Orlando, Sarasota, Tampa, and West Palm Beach. **jetBlue** (☎ *800/538-2583* 🌐 *www.jetblue.com*) to Tampa, Fort Lauderdale, Sarasota, Fort Myers, West Palm Beach, and Orlando. **Midwest Airlines** (☎ *800/452-2022* 🌐 *www.midwestairlines.com*) to Fort Lauderdale, Fort Myers, Orlando, and Tampa. **Southwest Airlines** (☎ *800/435-9792* 🌐 *www.southwest.com*) to Fort Lauderdale, Fort Myers, Jacksonville, Orlando, Tampa, and West Palm Beach.

BUS TRAVEL

Greyhound passes through practically every major city in Florida. For schedules and fares, contact your local Greyhound Information Center.

Using a major credit card, you can purchase Greyhound tickets online or by using the carrier's toll-free phone numbers. You can also purchase tickets—using cash, traveler's checks, or major credit cards—at any Greyhound terminal where tickets are sold or through one of the many independent agents representing Greyhound. A complete state-by-state list of agents is available at the Greyhound Web site.

Bus Information Greyhound Lines (☎ *800/231-2222* 🌐 *www.greyhound.com*).

CAR TRAVEL

Three major interstates lead to Florida. Interstate 95 begins in Maine, runs south through the Mid-Atlantic states, and enters Florida just north of Jacksonville. It continues south past Daytona Beach, the Space Coast, Vero Beach, Palm Beach, and Fort Lauderdale, ending in Miami.

Interstate 75 begins in Michigan at the Canadian border and runs south through Ohio, Kentucky, Tennessee, and Georgia, then moves south through the center of the state before veering west into Tampa. It follows the west coast south to Naples, then crosses the state through the northern section of the Everglades, and ends in Fort Lauderdale.

California and most Southern and Southwestern states are connected to Florida by Interstate 10, which moves east from Los Angeles through Arizona, New Mexico, Texas, Louisiana, Mississippi, and Alabama; it enters Florida at Pensacola and runs straight across the northern part of the state ending in Jacksonville.

RENTAL CARS

Car rental is highly recommended for travelers in Florida, since public transportation is limited and restrictive. In-season rates in Miami begin at $36 a day and $170 a week for an economy car with air-conditioning, automatic transmission, and unlimited mileage. Rates in Orlando begin at $35 a day and $149 a week. Rates in Fort Lauderdale begin at $36 a day and $159 a week. Rates in Tampa begin at $34 a day and $149 a week. This does not include tax on car rentals, which varies from county to county. Bear in mind that rates fluctuate tremendously—both above and below these quoted figures—depending on demand and the season.

In the past major rental agencies were at the airport, whereas cheaper firms weren't. Now, however, all over Florida, even the majors might be off airport property. Speedy check-in and frequent shuttle buses make off-airport rentals almost as convenient as on-site service. However, it's wise to allow a little extra time for bus travel between the rental agency and the airport.

In Florida you must be 21 to rent a car, and rates are higher if you're under 25.

ROAD CONDITIONS

Florida has its share of traffic problems. Downtown areas of such major cities as Miami, Orlando, and Tampa can be extremely congested during rush hours, usually 7–9 AM and 3:30–6 PM on weekdays. When you drive the interstate system in Florida, try to plan your trip so that you are not entering, leaving, or passing through a large city during rush hour when traffic can slow to 10 mph for 10 mi or more. In addition, snowbirds usually rent in Florida for a month at a time, which means they all arrive on the first of the month and leave on the 31st. Believe it or not, from November to March, when the end and beginning of a month occur on a weekend, north–south routes like Interstate 75 and Interstate 95 almost come to a standstill during daylight hours. It's best to avoid traveling on these days if possible.

ROADSIDE EMERGENCIES

If you need emergency assistance while traveling on roads in Florida, dial 911 or *FHP (*347) from your cell phone.

Emergency Services Florida Highway Patrol (☎ *911 or *FHP [*347]* 🌐 *www.dot.state.fl.us*); its Web site provides real-time traffic information—including areas congested with construction or accidents.

RULES OF THE ROAD

Speed limits are 60 mph on state highways, 30 mph within city limits and residential areas, and 70 mph on interstates and Florida's Turnpike. Be alert for signs announcing exceptions.

In Florida you must strap a child six or younger into a child-restraint device: children up to three years old must be in a separate carrier or child seat; children four through six can be secured in a separate carrier, integrated child seat, or by a seat belt. The driver will be held responsible for passengers 15 and younger who are not wearing seat belts. All front-seat passengers are required to wear seat belts.

Florida's Alcohol/Controlled Substance DUI Law is one of the toughest in the United States. A blood-alcohol level of .08 or higher can have serious repercussions even for the first-time offender.

ESSENTIALS

ACCOMMODATIONS

Florida has every conceivable type of lodging—from tree houses to penthouses, from mansions for hire to hostels. Even with occupancy rates inching above 70%, there are almost always rooms available, except maybe at Christmas and other holidays.

Children are welcome generally everywhere in Florida. Pets are another matter, so inquire ahead of time if you're bringing an animal with you.

In the busy seasons—over Christmas and from late January through Easter in the southern half of the state, during the summer along the Panhandle and around Jacksonville, and all over Florida during holiday weekends in summer—always reserve ahead for the top properties. Fall is the slowest season; rates are low and availability is high, but this is also the prime time for hurricanes. St. Augustine stays busy all summer because of its historic flavor. Key West is jam-packed for Fantasy Fest at Halloween.

TIP→ Assume that hotels operate on the European Plan (**EP**, no meals) unless we specify that they use the Breakfast Plan (**BP**, with full breakfast), Continental Plan (**CP**, continental breakfast), Full American Plan (**FAP**, all meals), or Modified American Plan (**MAP**, breakfast and dinner), or are **all-inclusive** (**AI**, all meals and most activities).

APARTMENT AND HOUSE RENTALS

Contacts **American Realty** (*Box 1133, Captiva33924 ☎ 800/547-0127 ⊕ www.captiva-island.com*). **Florida Keys Rental Store/Marr Properties** (*✉ 99980 Overseas Hwy., Key Largo 33037 ☎ 800/585-0584 or 305/451-3879 ⊕ www.floridakeysrentalstore.com*). **Freewheeler Vacations** (*✉ 85992 Overseas Hwy., MM 86, Islamorada 33036 ☎ 866/664-2075 or 305/664-2075 ⊕ www.freewheeler-realty.com*). **Interhome** (*☎ 954/791-8282 or 800/882-6864 ⊕ www.interhome.us*). **ResortQuest International** (*✉ 546 Mary Esther Cut-off, Suite 3, Fort Walton Beach 32548 ☎ 800/336-4853 ⊕ www.resortquest.com*). **Sand Key Realty** (*✉ 2701 Gulf Blvd., Indian Rocks Beach 33785 ☎ 800/377-4971 or 727/595-5441 ⊕ www.sandkey.com*). **Suncoast Vacations Rentals** (*✉ 224 Franklin Blvd., St. George Island 32328 ☎ 800/341-2021 ⊕ www.uncommonflorida.com*). **Villas International** (*☎ 415/499-9490 or 800/221-2260 ⊕ www.villasintl.com*). **Wyndham Vacation Resorts** (*✉ 5259 Coconut Creek Pkwy., Margate 33063 ☎ 800/251-8736 ⊕ www.wyndhamvacationresorts.com*).

BED-AND-BREAKFASTS

Small inns and guesthouses are increasingly numerous in Florida, but they vary tremendously, ranging from economical places that are plain but serve a good home-style breakfast to elegantly furnished Victorian houses with four-course breakfasts and rates to match. Many offer a homelike setting. In fact, many are in private homes with owners who treat you almost like family; others are more businesslike. The associations listed below offer descriptions and suggestions for B&Bs throughout Florida.

Reservation Services **Bed & Breakfast.com** (*☎ 512/322-2710 or 800/462-2632 ⊕ www.bedandbreakfast.com*) also sends out an online newsletter. **Bed & Breakfast Inns Online** (*☎ 800/215-7365 ⊕ www.bbonline.com*). **BnB Finder.com** (*☎ 888/547-8226 ⊕ www.bnbfinder.com*). **Daytona Beach Convention and Visitors Bureau** (*✉ 126 E. Orange Ave., Daytona Beach ☎ 800/854-1234 or 386/255-0415*). **Florida Bed & Breakfast Inns** (*☎ 877/303-3224 ⊕ www.florida-inns.com*).

HOTELS

Wherever you look in Florida you'll find lots of plain, inexpensive motels and luxurious resorts, independents alongside national chains, and an ever-growing number of modern properties as well as quite a few timeless classics. In fact, since

Florida has been a favored travel destination for some time, vintage hotels are everywhere: there are grand edifices like the Breakers in Palm Beach, Boca Raton Resort & Club in Boca Raton, the Biltmore in Coral Gables, and Casa Marina in Key West.

All hotels listed have private bath unless otherwise noted.

■ TIP→ You know you can save a bundle on trips to warm-weather destinations by traveling in rainy season. But there's also a chance that a severe storm will disrupt your plans. The solution? Look for hotels and resorts that offer storm/hurricane guarantees. Although they rarely allow refunds, most guarantees do let you rebook later if a storm strikes.

> **WORD OF MOUTH**
>
> Was the service stellar or not up to snuff? Did the food give you shivers of delight or leave you cold? Did the prices and portions make you happy or sad? Rate restaurants and write your own reviews in "Travel Ratings" or start a discussion about your favorite places in "Travel Talk" on www.fodors.com. Your comments might even appear in our books. Yes, you, too, can be a correspondent!

EATING OUT

An antismoking amendment endorsed in 2002 by Florida voters bans smoking statewide in most enclosed indoor workplaces, including restaurants. Exemptions are permitted for stand-alone bars where food takes a backseat to the libations.

A cautionary word: raw oysters have been identified as a potential problem for people with chronic illness of the liver, stomach, or blood, or who have immune disorders. All Florida restaurants that serve raw oysters are required to post a notice in plain view of all patrons, warning of the risks associated with consuming them.

MEALS AND MEALTIMES

Unless otherwise noted, the restaurants listed in this guide are open daily for lunch and dinner.

RESERVATIONS AND DRESS

Regardless of where you are, it's a good idea to make a reservation if you can. We mention them specifically only when reservations are essential (there's no other way you'll ever get a table) or when they are not accepted. For popular restaurants, book as far ahead as you can (often 30 days), and reconfirm as soon as you arrive. (Large parties should always call ahead to check the reservations policy.) We mention dress only when men are required to wear a jacket or a jacket and tie.

Contacts OpenTable (🌐 *www.opentable.com*). **DinnerBroker** (🌐 *www.dinnerbroker.com*).

WINES, BEER, AND SPIRITS

Beer and wine are usually available in Florida's restaurants, whether you're dining first class or at a beachside bistro. A few chain restaurants in the major cities are also microbreweries and have a variety of premise-made beers that change with the season. Liquor is generally available at fine-dining establishments only.

HEALTH

If you are unaccustomed to strong subtropical sun, you run a risk of sunburn and heat prostration, even in winter. So hit the beach or play tennis, golf, or another outdoor sport before 10 AM or after 3 PM. If you must be out at midday, limit strenuous exercise, drink plenty of liquids, and wear a hat. If you begin to feel faint, get out of the sun immediately and sip water slowly. Even on overcast days, ultraviolet rays shine through the haze, so use a sunscreen with an SPF of at least 15, and have children wear a waterproof SPF 30 or higher.

While you're frolicking on the beach, steer clear of what look like blue bubbles on the sand. These are Portuguese men-of-war, and their tentacles can cause an allergic reaction. Also be careful of other large jellyfish, some of which can sting.

If you walk across a grassy area on the way to the beach, you'll probably encounter sand spurs. They are quite tiny, light brown, and remarkably prickly. You'll feel them before you see them; if you get stuck with one, just pull it out.

HOURS OF OPERATION

Many museums in Florida are closed Monday, but offer extended hours on another weekday and are usually open on weekends. Some museums reserve a day of the week for free admission. Popular visitor attractions are usually open daily, with the exception of Thanksgiving and Christmas Day.

MONEY

Prices throughout this guide are given for adults. Substantially reduced fees are almost always available for children, students, and senior citizens.

CREDIT CARDS

Throughout this guide, the following abbreviations are used: **AE,** American Express; **D,** Discover; **DC,** Diners Club; **MC,** MasterCard; and **V,** Visa.

It's a good idea to inform your credit-card company before you travel. Otherwise, the credit-card company might put a hold on your card owing to unusual activity—not a good thing halfway through your trip. Record all your credit-card numbers—as well as the phone numbers to call if your cards are lost or stolen—in a safe place, so you're prepared should something go wrong. Both MasterCard and Visa have general numbers you can call if your card is lost, but you're better off calling the number of your issuing bank, since MasterCard and Visa usually just transfer you to your bank; your bank's number is usually printed on your card.

Reporting Lost Cards American Express (☎ *800/992-3404* 🌐 *www.americanexpress.com*). **Diners Club** (☎ *800/234-6377* 🌐 *www.dinersclub.com*). **Discover** (☎ *800/347-2683* 🌐 *www.discovercard.com*). **MasterCard** (☎ *800/622-7747* 🌐 *www.mastercard.com*). **Visa** (☎ *800/847-2911 in U.S., 410/581-9994 collect from abroad* 🌐 *www.visa.com*).

PACKING

The northern part of the state is much cooler in winter than the southern part, and you'll want to take a heavy sweater if you plan on traveling north in winter months. Even in summer, ocean breezes can be cool, so always take a sweater or jacket just in case.

Miami and the Naples–Fort Myers areas are warm year-round and often extremely humid in summer months. Be prepared for sudden storms all over Florida in summer, but keep in mind that plastic raincoats are uncomfortable in the high humidity. Often storms are quick and the sun comes back in no time.

Dress is casual throughout the state—sundresses, jeans, or walking shorts are appropriate during the day; bring comfortable walking shoes or sneakers for theme parks. A few restaurants request that men wear jackets and ties, but most do not. Be prepared for air-conditioning working in overdrive.

You can generally swim year-round in peninsular Florida from about New Smyrna Beach south on the Atlantic coast and from Tarpon Springs south on the Gulf coast. Be sure to take a sun hat and sunscreen—the sun can be fierce even in winter and even if it's chilly or overcast. Don't leave valuables on your beach blanket while you walk the beach or go for a dip.

SAFETY

Stepped-up policing of thieves who prey on tourists in rental cars has helped address what was a serious issue in the early 1990s. Still, visitors should be especially wary when driving in strange neighborhoods and leaving the airport, especially

FOR INTERNATIONAL TRAVELERS

CURRENCY

The dollar is the basic unit of U.S. currency. A dollar has 100 cents. Coins are the penny (1¢); the nickel (5¢), dime (10¢), quarter (25¢), half-dollar (50¢), and the very rare golden $1 coin and even rarer silver $1. Bills are denominated $1, $5, $10, $20, $50, and $100, all mostly green and identical in size; designs and background tints vary. You may come across a $2 bill, but the chances are slim.

CUSTOMS

Information **U.S. Customs and Border Protection** (*www.cbp.gov*).

DRIVING

Driving in the United States is on the right. Speed limits are posted in miles per hour (usually between 55 mph and 70 mph). Watch for lower limits in small towns and on back roads (usually 30 mph to 40 mph). Most states require front-seat passengers to wear seat belts; many states require children to sit in the back seat and to wear seat belts. In major cities rush hour is 7–10 AM; afternoon rush hour is 4–7 PM. To encourage carpooling, some freeways have special lanes, ordinarily marked with a diamond, for high-occupancy vehicles (HOV)—cars carrying two people or more.

Highways are well paved. Interstates—limited-access, multilane highways designated with an "I–" before the number—are fastest. Interstates with three-digit numbers circle urban areas, which may also have other limited-access expressways, freeways, and parkways. Tolls may be levied on limited-access highways. U.S. and state highways aren't necessarily limited access, but may have several lanes.

ELECTRICITY

The U.S. standard is AC, 110 volts/60 cycles. Plugs have two flat pins set parallel to each other.

EMBASSIES

Contacts **Australia** (202/797–3000 *www.austemb.org*).

Canada (202/682–1740 *www.canadianembassy.org*).

United Kingdom (202/588–7800 *ukinusa.fco.gov.uklen*).

EMERGENCIES

For police, fire, or ambulance, dial 911 (0 in rural areas).

HOLIDAYS

New Year's Day (Jan. 1); Martin Luther King Jr. Day (3rd Mon. in Jan.); Presidents' Day (3rd Mon. in Feb.); Memorial Day (last Mon. in May); Independence Day (July 4); Labor Day (1st Mon. in Sept.); Columbus Day (2nd Mon. in Oct.); Thanksgiving Day (4th Thurs. in Nov.); Christmas Eve and Christmas Day (Dec. 24 and 25); and New Year's Eve (Dec. 31).

MAIL

You can buy stamps and aerograms and send letters and parcels in post offices. Stamp-dispensing machines can occasionally be found in airports, bus and train stations, and convenience stores. U.S. mailboxes are dark blue steel bins; pickup schedules are posted on the bin. Parcels weighing more than 13 ounces must be mailed from a post office or from a private mailing center.

Within the United States a first-class letter weighing 1 ounce or less costs 44¢; each additional ounce costs 17¢. Postcards cost 28¢. A 1-ounce airmail letter or a postcard to most countries costs 98¢; a 1-ounce letter or a postcard to Canada or Mexico costs 75¢ or 79¢, respectively.

To receive mail on the road, have it sent c/o GENERAL DELIVERY at your destination's main post office (use the correct five-digit ZIP code). You must pick up mail in person within 30 days, with a driver's license or passport for identification.

Contacts DHL (☎ *800/225–5345* 🌐 *www.dhl.com*).

Federal Express (☎ *800/463–3339* 🌐 *www.fedex.com*).

Mail Boxes, Etc./The UPS Store (☎ *800/789–4623* 🌐 *www.mbe.com*).

United States Postal Service (🌐 *www.usps.com*).

PASSPORTS AND VISAS

Visitor visas aren't necessary for citizens of Australia, Canada, the United Kingdom, and most citizens of European Union countries coming for tourism and staying for fewer than 90 days. If you require a visa, the cost is $100—waiting time can be substantial depending on where you live. Apply for a visa at the U.S. consulate in your place of residence; check the U.S. State Department's special visa Web site for further information.

VISA INFORMATION

Destination USA (🌐 *www.travel.state.gov/visa/visa_1750.html*).

PHONES

Phone numbers consist of a three-digit area code and a seven-digit local number. Within many local calling areas you dial only the seven digits; in others you dial "1" first and all 10 digits—just as you would for calls between area-code regions. The same is true for calls to numbers prefixed by "800," "888," "866," and "877"—all toll-free. For calls to numbers prefixed by "900" you must pay—usually dearly.

For international calls, dial "011" followed by the country code and the local number. For help, dial "0" and ask for an overseas operator. Most phone books list country codes and U.S. area codes. The country code for Australia is 61, New Zealand 64, and the United Kingdom 44. Calling Canada is the same as calling within the United States, whose country code, by the way, is 1.

For operator assistance, dial "0." For directory assistance, call 555–1212 or occasionally 411 (free at many public phones). You can reverse long-distance charges by calling "collect"; dial "0" instead of "1" before the 10-digit number.

Instructions are generally posted on pay phones. Usually you insert coins in a slot (usually 25¢–50¢ for local calls) and wait for a steady tone before dialing. On long-distance calls the operator tells you how much to insert; prepaid phone cards, widely available in various denominations, can be used from any phone. Follow the directions to activate the card (there's usually an access number, then an activation code), then dial your number.

CELL PHONES

The United States has several GSM (Global System for Mobile Communications) networks, so multiband mobiles from most countries (except for Japan) work here. Unfortunately, it's almost impossible to buy a pay-as-you-go mobile SIM card in the United States—which allows you to avoid roaming charges—without also buying a phone. However, cell phones with pay-as-you-go plans are available for well under $100. The cheapest ones with decent national coverage are the GoPhone from AT&T and Virgin Mobile, which only offers pay-as-you-go service.

Contacts AT&T (☎ *888/333–6651* 🌐 *www.att.com*).

Virgin Mobile (☎ *888/322–1122* 🌐 *www.virginmobileusa.com*).

in the Miami area. Don't assume that valuables are safe in your hotel room; use in-room safes or the hotel's safety-deposit boxes. Try to use ATMs only during the day or in brightly lighted, well-traveled locales.

GOVERNMENT ADVISORIES

If you are visiting Florida during the June through November hurricane season and a hurricane is imminent, be sure to follow directions from local authorities.

Safety Transportation Security Administration (*TSA; www.tsa.gov*).

TAXES

Florida's sales tax is 6% or higher depending on the county, and local sales and tourist taxes can raise what you pay considerably, especially for certain items, such as lodging. Miami Beach hoteliers, for example, collect 14% for city and resort taxes. It's best to ask about additional costs up front, to avoid a rude awakening.

TIME

The western portion of the Panhandle is in the central, while the rest of mainland Florida is in the Eastern time zone.

TIPPING

Whether they carry bags, open doors, deliver food, or clean rooms, hospitality employees work to receive a portion of your travel budget. In deciding how much to give, base your tip on what the service is and how well it's performed.

In transit, tip airport valets $1–$3 per bag and taxi drivers 15%–20% of the fare.

For hotel staff, recommended amounts are $1–$3 per bag for bellhops, $1–$2 per night per guest for chambermaids, $5–$10 for special concierge service, $1–$3 for a doorman who hails a cab or parks a car, 15% of the greens fee for caddies, 15%–20% of the bill for a massage, and 15% of a room-service bill (bear in mind that sometimes 15%–18% is automatically added to room-service bills, so don't add it twice).

In a restaurant, give 15%–20% of your bill before tax to the server, 5%–10% to the maître d', 15% to bartenders, and 15% of the wine bill for a wine steward who makes a special effort in selecting and serving wine.

VISITOR INFORMATION

Welcome centers are on Interstate 10, Interstate 75, Interstate 95, and U.S. 231 (near Campbellton), and in the lobby of the New Capitol in Tallahassee. *For regional tourist bureaus and chambers of commerce, see individual chapters.*

Contacts Visit Florida (*✉ 2540 W. Executive Center Circle, Suite 200, Tallahassee ☎ 850/488–5607 www.visitflorida.com*).

INDEX

D

N

O

PHOTO CREDITS

1, Visit Florida. 2-3, Tim Souter, Fodors.com member. 5, PhotoStockFile/Alamy. Chapter 1: Experience Florida: 8-9, Steven Widoff/Alamy. 10, Fritz Poelking/age fotostock. 11 (left), Stuart Pearce/World Pictures/age fotostock. 11 (right), J.D. Heaton/Picture Finders/age fotostock. 12, ACE STOCK LIMITED/Alamy. 13 (left), Richard Cummins/viestiphoto.com. 13 (right), Jeff Greenberg/age fotostock. 14, borabora98, Fodors.com member. 15, GlyndaK, Fodors.com member. 16, Jeff Greenberg/age fotostock. 17, Visit Florida. 18, Jeff Greenberg/Alamy. 19 (left), St. Petersburg/Clearwater Area CVB. 19 (right), Regina Stancel/iStockphoto. 20 (left), Kirk Peart Professional Imaging/Shutterstock. 20 (right), PhotoStockFile/Alamy. 21 (left), Stephen Frink Collection/Alamy. 21 (right), Dennis MacDonald/Alamy. 22 and 23, Jeff Greenberg/age fotostock. 24 (left), Cogoli Franco/SIME/eStock Photo. 24 (right) and 25 (left), Visit Florida. 25 (top right), John Henshall/Alamy. 25 (bottom right), Jeremy Edwards/iStockphoto. 26 (left) Visit Florida. 26 (right), Rob Keaton/wikipedia.org. 27 (left), Martin Sasse/Laif/Aurora Photos. 27 (top right), RIEGER Bertrand/age fotostock. 27 (bottom right), Danita Delimont/Alamy. 28 (left), Jeff Greenberg/Alamy. 28 (top right), the SuperStar/Flickr. 28 (bottom right), Ken Canning/Shutterstock. 29 (left), Cogoli Franco/SIME/eStock Photo. 29 (right), Robert Harding Picture Library Ltd/Alamy. 30, Joe Viesti/viestiphoto.com. 31 (left), culliganphoto/Alamy. 31 (right), Orlando CVB. 32, Visit Florida. 34, J Loveland/Shutterstock. Chapter 2: Panhandle: 35 and 36 (top and bottom), Cheryl Casey/Shutterstock. 37 (top), Todd Taulman/Shutterstock. 37 (bottom), Visit Florida. 38, rj lerich/Shutterstock. 40, Cheryl Casey/Shutterstock. 41 (top), Jeff Kinsey/Shutterstock. 41 (bottom), Cheryl Casey/Shutterstock. 42, divemasterking2000/Flickr. 50, Kathy Hicks/iStockphoto. 58, Brandon Cole Marine Photography/Alamy. 61, Visit Florida. 62 (top), Ernest Hemingway Photograph Collection, John F. Kennedy Presidential Library and Museum, Boston. 62 (bottom), Visit Florida. 63 (top), Linda Brinck, Fodors.com member. 63 (bottom), George Peters/iStockphoto. 64, Michael Zegers/imagebroker.net/photolibrary.com. 67, Andrew Woodley/Alamy. 70, geishaboy500/Flickr. 75, Gorilla/Shutterstock. 79, nate steiner/Flickr. 90-91, imagebroker/Alamy. 93, Dennis MacDonald/age fotostock. Chapter 3: Northeast Florida: 95, FRILET Patrick/age fotostock. 96 (top), The Freewheeling Daredevil/Flickr. 96 (bottom), Henryk Sadura/Shutterstock. 97 (top and bottom), Cogoli Franco/SIME/eStock-photo. 98, David S. Baker/Shutterstock. 100, Visit Florida. 101 (top), Tom Hirtreiter/Shutterstock. 101 (bottom), Deborah Wolfe/Shutterstock. 102, Visit Florida. 106, Karel Gallas/Shutterstock. 110, Jeff Greenberg/age fotostock. 119, Therese McKeon/iStockphoto. 124, funinthetub, Fodors.com member. 129, Roberto A Sanchez/iStockphoto. 135, Visit Florida. 143, Visit Florida. 146-47, Visit Florida. 148 (top), U.S. Air Force photo by Larry McTighe/wikipedia.org. 148 (bottom left), David Allio/Icon SMI. 148 (bottom 2nd from left), JACK BRADEN/wikipedia.org. 148 (bottom 3rd from left), Arni Katz/Alamy. 148 (bottom right), Bryan Eastham/Shutterstock. 149 (left), Jeff Greenberg/Alamy. 149 (right), brianc/Flickr. 153, greg pelt/iStockphoto. 166-67, jurvetson/Flickr. 168, thelastminute/Flickr. 169, yeowatzup/Flickr. 170 (top left), hyku/Flickr. 170 (top right and bottom) and 171 (left), thelastminute/Flickr. 171 (center), yeowatzup/Flickr. 171 (right), divemasterking2000/Flickr. 172, by jonworth/Flickr. 173, bnhsu/Flickr. 174-75, jurvetson/Flickr. 178, breezy421/Flickr. Chapter 4: Orlando & Environs: 181, Visit Florida. 182, SeaWorld Orlando. 183 (top), Nick Hotel. 183 (bottom), Universal Orlando. 188, © Disney. 190, Universal Orlando. 194, Gary Bogdon/Visit Florida. 228 (top left), Universal Orlando Resort. 228 (top right), erin MC hammer/Flickr. 228 (center left), The Ritz-Carlton. 228 (center right), Daniels & Roberts INC/The Waldorf Astoria Orlando. 228 (bottom left), Nick Hotel.

228 (bottom right), Greencolander/Flickr. Chapter 5: Walt Disney World: 233, © Disney. 234, d4rr3ll/Flickr. 235, vanguardist/Flickr. 236, Universal Orlando. 238 and 239, Orlando CVB. 240, © Disney. 241 (top), vanguardist/Flickr. 241 (bottom), FAN travelstock/Alamy. 246, Orlando CVB. 247 (top), Joe Shlabotnik/Flickr. 247 (bottom), Orlando CVB. 249, © Disney. 252, Universal Orlando. 253 (top), wikipedia.org. 253 (bottom), Universal Orlando Resort. 255, dawnzy58/Flickr. 258, Joe Shlabotnik/Flickr. 259 (top and bottom), Allie_Caulfield/Flickr. 260, dawnzy58/Flickr. 264-65 (all) and 267, © Disney. Chapter 6: Universal Orlando: 273 and 274 (both), Universal Orlando Resort. 275, bea&txm/Flickr. 276, SkierGirl77/wikipedia.org. 278, divemasterking/Flickr. 279, Visit Florida. 280-89, Universal Orlando Resort. 292-93, Wet 'n Wild. Chapter 7: SeaWorld Orlando: 299-304 and 305 (top), SeaWorld Parks & Entertainment. 305 (bottom), Visit Florida. 307, Orlando CVB. 310-11, Jason Collier/SeaWorld Parks & Entertainment. 314, SeaWorld Parks & Entertainment. Chapter 8: The Tampa Bay Area: 315, Joe Stone/Shutterstock. 316 (top), gppilot, Fodors.com member. 316 (bottom), Visit Florida. 317 (top), Marje Cannon/iStockphoto. 317 (bottom), William Hamilton/SuperStock. 319, iStockphoto. 320, St. Petersburg/Clearwater Area CVB. 321 (top), Visit Florida. 321 (bottom), Graca Victoria/Shutterstock. 322, iStockphoto. 326-27, Busch Entertainment Corporation. 332, Martin Bennett/Alamy. 340, Seymour Levy, Fodors.com member. 345, Ed Wolfstein/Icon SMI. 346 (top), Palm Beach Post/ZUMA Press/Icon SMI. 346 (bottom), Cliff Welch/Icon SMI. 347 (top), Evan Meyer/Shutterstock. 347 (bottom) and 348 (top), GARY I ROTHSTEIN/Icon SMI. 348 (bottom background photo), Ed Wolfstein/Icon SMI. 349 (background photo), Ed Wolfstein Photo/Icon SMI. 348-49 (logos), wikipedia.org. 352, watland, Fodors.com member. 356, Richard T. Nowitz/age fotostock. 360, TIPTON DONALD/age fotostock. 365, Elizabeth Shevloff, Fodors.com member. Chapter 9: The Lower Gulf Coast: 367, Dan Leffel/age fotostock. 369 (top), Cogoli Franco/SIME/eStock Photo. 369 (center), Visit Florida. 369 (bottom), Heeb Photos/eStock Photo. 370 (top), Mitch Aunger/Shutterstock. 370 (bottom), Visit Florida. 371, Denise Kappa/Shutterstock. 372, Travelshots.com/Alamy. 373 (top), jeff gynane/iStockphoto. 373 (bottom), Visit Florida. 374, Alan Briere/SuperStock. 377 and 383, Visit Florida. 386, Walter Bibikow/age fotostock. 389, blewisphotography/Shutterstock. 390, Mitch Aunger/Shutterstock. 408, Dennis Guyitt/iStockphoto. Chapter 10: Palm Beach and the Treasure Coast: 419, RIEGER Bertrand/age fotostock. 421 (top), Perry Correll/Shutterstock. 421 (bottom), Bill Bachmann/Alamy. 422 (top), Brian Dunne/Shutterstock. 422 (bottom), Todd S. Holder/Shutterstock. 424, Masa Ushioda/Alamy. 425 (top), Stephen Frink Collection/Alamy. 425 (bottom), Denny Medley/Random Photography/iStockphoto. 426, FloridaStock/Shutterstock. 429, Jon Arnold Images Ltd/Alamy. 432, Andre Jenny/Alamy. 438, mrk_photo/Flickr. 445, FloridaStock/Shutterstock. 451, wikipedia.org. 459, Paddy Eckersley/age fotostock. 460, Tap10/Shutterstock. 463 and 473, Visit Florida. Chapter 11: Fort Lauderdale and Broward County: 477, Jeff Greenberg/age fotostock. 478, Rick Gomez/age fotostock. 479 (top), Dean Bergmann/iStockphoto. 479 (bottom), Jeff Greenberg/Alamy. 480, jirijura/Shutterstock.

482, Nicholas Pitt/Alamy. 483 (top), Christina Dearaujo/Flickr. 483 (bottom), Claudette, Fodors.com member. 484, Qole Pejorian/Flickr. 486, rockindom, Fodors.com member. 491, Nicholas Pitt/Alamy. 493, AchimH/Flickr. 495, Eric Gevaert/Shutterstock. 503, Lago Mar Resort & Club - Fort Lauderdale. 509, Pat Cahill/iStockphoto. 514, FloridaStock/Shutterstock. Chapter 11: Miami and Miami Beach: 519, iStockphoto. 520, Stuart Westmorland/age fotostock. 521 (top), Jeff Greenberg/age fotostock. 521 (bottom), VISUM Foto GmbH/Alamy. 523, Jonathan G/Shutterstock. 524, Jeff Greenberg/age fotostock. 525 (top), Picasa 2.7/Flickr. 525 (bottom), murray cohen/iStockphoto. 526, Ivan Cholakov/Shutterstock. 530, Chuck Mason/Alamy. 531 (top), Jeff Greenberg/Alamy. 531 (bottom), David R. Frazier Photolibrary, Inc./Alamy. 532 and 534, Jeff Greenberg/Alamy. 535, Jeff Greenberg/age fotostock. 536, Gregory Wrona/Alamy. 540, Robert Harding Picture Library Ltd/Alamy. 551, Visit Florida. 559 (left), dk/Alamy. 559 (right), Nicholas Pitt/Alamy. 561 (top), M. Timothy O'Keefe/Alamy. 561 (bottom), Miami Design Preservation League. 562 (top), Nicholas Pitt/Alamy. 562 (2nd from top), Park Central Hotel. 562 (3rd from top), Ian Patrick Alamy. 562 (4th from top), Laura Paresky. 562 (bottom), ICIMAGE/Alamy. 563 (top), INTERFOTO Pressebildagentur/Alamy. 563 (bottom left), Ian Patrick/Alamy. 563 (bottom right), culliganphoto/Alamy. 564, iStockphoto. 571, alexdecarvalho/Flickr. 580, LOOK Die Bildagentur der Fotografen GmbH/Alamy. 586, Roxana Gonzalez/Shutterstock. 587 (top), JUPITERIMAGES/Brand X/Alamy. 587 (bottom), iStockphoto. 588, Jeff Greenberg/Alamy. 606 (top), Acqualina Resort & Spa on the Beach. 606 (bottom left), Nile Young. 606 (center right), Circa 39. 606 (bottom right), Morgans Hotel Group. 607 (top), Mark Wieland. 607 (center left), Kevin Syms/Four Seasons Hotels and Resorts. 607 (bottom left), Kor Hotel Group. 607 (bottom right), Mandarin Oriental Hotel Group. Chapter 13: The Everglades: 615, David Lyons/Alamy. 616 (top), Visit Florida. 616 (bottom), Jeff Greenberg/age fotostock. 617 (top), FloridaStock/Shutterstock. 617 (bottom), Walter Bibikow/age fotostock. 619, Pamela McCreight/Flickr. 620-21, tbkmedia.de/Alamy. 624 (left), inga spence/Alamy. 624 (top center), FloridaStock/Shutterstock. 624 (bottom center), Andrewtappert/

wikipedia.org. 624 (top right), wikipedia.org. 624 (bottom), David R. Frazier Photolibrary, Inc./Alamy. 625 (top left), Larsek/Shutterstock. 625 (bottom left), Caleb Foster/Shutterstock. 625 (bottom center), mlorenz/Shutterstock. 625 (top right), umar faruq/Shutterstock. 625 (bottom right), Peter Arnold, Inc./ Alamy. 626 (left), John A. Anderson/Shutterstock. 626 (top right), FloridaStock/Shutterstock. 626 (bottom center), Norman Bateman/Shutterstock. 626 (bottom right), FloridaStock/Shutterstock. 627 (top left), David Drake & Deborah Jaffe. 627 (bottom left), Krzysztof Slusarczyk/Shutterstock. 627 (bottom center), Norman Bateman/Shutterstock. 627 (right), Jerry Zitterman/Shutterstock. 628, Patricia Schmidt/iStockphoto. 629 (top left), Brett Charlton/iStockphoto. 629 (bottom left, bottom center, and right), David Drake & Deborah Jaffe. 630 (left), Walter Bibikow/age fotostock. 630 (right), Stephen Frink Collection/Alamy. 631, Leatha J. Robinson/Shutterstock. 633, Larsek/Shutterstock. 638, Steven Widoff/Alamy. 642, Marc Muench/Alamy. 646, Sarah and Jason/Flickr. 655, Visit Florida. Chapter 14: The Florida Keys: 661, Stephen Frink/Aurora Photos. 662 (top), Pawel Lipiec/iStockphoto. 662 (bottom), David L Amsler/iStockphoto. 663 (top), Pacific Stock/SuperStock. 663 (bottom), Visit Florida. 665, Laurin Johnson/iStockphoto. 666, Nick Greaves/Alamy. 667 (top), Ingolf Pompe 77/Alamy. 667 (bottom), Visit Florida. 668, iStockphoto. 673, Stephen Frink/ Florida Keys News Bureau. 681, flasporty/Flickr. 684, Visit Florida. 686, PBorowka/Shutterstock. 687 and 688 (top), Douglas Rudolph. 688 (bottom), ANDY NEWMAN/Visit Florida. 689, M. Timothy O'Keefe/Alamy. 690 (top), Bob Care/ Florida Keys News Bureau. 690 (bottom), Julie de Leseleuc/iStockphoto. 691 (left), Visit Florida. 691 (right), Charles Stirling (Diving)/Alamy. 692 (top), Visit Florida. 692 (bottom), Gert Vrey/iStockphoto. 693, Scott Wilson, FKCC Student. 703, Melissa Schalke/iStockphoto. 711, Henryk Sadura/Alamy. 724, John P Franzis. 726, CedarBendDrive/Flickr. 731, John P Franzis. 736, Laure Neish/iStockphoto. 739, Harold Smith/Alamy. 740, Gregory Wrona/Alamy. 741 (top), Claudio Lovo/Shutterstock. 741 (bottom), Michael Ventura/Alamy. 751, Starwood Hotels & Resorts.

NOTES

NOTES

ABOUT OUR WRITERS

Miami native **Michael de Zayas** spent nights in 50 hotels and had dozens more meals to bring you the lodging and dining coverage for Miami and Miami Beach. When not on assignment for Fodor's (he's contributed to titles on Bermuda, Mexico, Argentina, Chile, Spain, New York City, New England, the Caribbean, among many others), he now lives in Brooklyn and Vermont and runs the clothing website Neighborhoodies.com. He's also at work on a novel about a travel writer in Cuba.

Jennifer Edwards is an Associated Press Award–winning journalist who grew up on the shores of Northeast Florida. Her work has appeared in dozens of newspapers, including the *International Herald Tribune, Dallas Morning News,* and *Atlanta Journal-Constitution,* among others. She is currently the environmental reporter for her hometown newspaper, *The St. Augustine Record.*

Native Floridian and freelance writer **Teri Evans** updated the beaches, shopping, nightlife and exploring sections of the Miami and Miami Beach chapter.

After being hired sight unseen by a South Florida newspaper, Fort Lauderdale–based freelance travel writer and editor **Lynne Helm** arrived from the Midwest anticipating a few years of palm-fringed fun. More than a quarter century later (after covering the state for several newspapers, consumer magazines, and trade publications), she's still enamored of Florida's sun-drenched charms. Lynne updated the Greater Fort Lauderdale and the Everglades chapters.

Snowbird **Susan MacCallum-Whitcomb** spends as much time as possible in the Sunshine State. Little wonder: winters in her Nova Scotian hometown can be *looong*. Having already contributed to Fodors.com and more than two dozen Fodor's guide books, she jumped at the chance to write the Experience chapter for this edition.

Gary McKechnie, who reported on the Panhandle and parts of the Orlando chapter, knows a lot about his native Florida, having worked as a Walt Disney World ferryboat pilot, Jungle Cruise skipper, steam-train conductor and double-decker bus driver. A two-time Lowell Thomas Travel Journalism Award winner, he writes for Harley-Davidson and is the author of *Great American Motorcycle Tours* and *National Geographic's USA 101.* He lectures on American history and icons aboard the Cunard Line's Queen Mary 2.

Palm Beach and the Treasure Coast writer **Mary Thurwachter,** a Florida resident since 1979, writes travel stories for *The Palm Beach Post, Miami Herald* and INNside-Florida.com, a travel site she launched in 2008.

Christina Tourigny is a Florida native who has written about her home state for dozens of publications including Fodor's, Berlitz, Insight Guides, and USAToday.com. She lives on six acres of paradise in Lecanto, a radar blip 55 miles north of Tampa.

From her home of more than 25 years on Sanibel Island, **Chelle Koster Walton**—author of the Keys and Lower Gulf Coast chapters—has written and contributed to a dozen guidebooks, two of which have won Lowell Thomas Awards. She has penned thousands of articles about Florida and the Caribbean for *Miami Herald, USA Today,* Concierge.com, FoxNews.com, and other print and electronic media, including an iTunes guidebook application for Sanibel and Captiva islands.

Orlando, Walt Disney World, Universal, and SeaWorld were updated by a full and very talented team of freelance writers, including **Elise Allen** (Orlando Planner), **Nathan and Sam Benjamin** (the Disney water parks), **Rona Gindin** (Where to Eat), **Jennifer Greenhill-Taylor** (Where to Stay), **Jennie Hess** (all of Disney but the water parks), **Gary McKechnie** (all of Universal and SeaWorld), and **Joseph Reed Hayes** (Orlando and its environs).